Historical Dictionary of Russian and Soviet Cinema

Peter Rollberg

Historical Dictionaries of
Literature and the Arts, No. 30

The Scarecrow Press, Inc.
Lanham, Maryland • Toronto • Plymouth, UK
2009

SCARECROW PRESS, INC.

Published in the United States of America
by Scarecrow Press, Inc.
A wholly owned subsidiary of
The Rowman & Littlefield Publishing Group, Inc.
4501 Forbes Boulevard, Suite 200, Lanham, Maryland 20706
www.scarecrowpress.com

Estover Road
Plymouth PL6 7PY
United Kingdom

British Library Cataloguing in Publication Information Available

Library of Congress Cataloging-in-Publication Data

Rollberg, P.
  Historical dictionary of Russian and Soviet cinema / Peter Rollberg.
     p. cm. — (Historical dictionaries of literature and the arts ; no. 30)
  Includes bibliographical references.
  ISBN-13: 978-0-8108-6072-8 (cloth : alk. paper)
  ISBN-10: 0-8108-6072-4 (cloth : alk. paper)
  eISBN-13: 978-0-8108-6268-5
  eISBN-10: 0-8108-6268-9
1. Motion pictures–Soviet Union–Biography–Dictionaries. 2. Motion pictures–
Russia–Biography–Dictionaries. 3. Motion pictures–Soviet Union–Dictionaries.
4. Motion pictures–Russia–Dictionaries. I. Title.
  PN1998.2.R578 2008
  791.430947'03–dc22   2008022529

♾ ™ The paper used in this publication meets the minimum requirements of
American National Standard for Information Sciences—Permanence of Paper
for Printed Library Materials, ANSI/NISO Z39.48-1992.
Manufactured in the United States of America.

Historical Dictionaries of Literature and the Arts
Jon Woronoff, Series Editor

To Vladimir Borisovich Berenshtein,
filmmaker and mentor,
and to Anastasia Platonovna Zueva,
actress and friend

Contents

Editor's Foreword

This is a rather special volume in the cinema subseries because it deals, partly, with the same place under different names and regimes: namely, Russia both before and after Communism, as well as with the broader realm of the Union of Soviet Socialist Republics (USSR) during the Communist era, which means it also includes a large circle of other national cinemas. There is a notable lack of continuity regarding the geographical spread, but that is nothing compared to the lack of continuity regarding the regimes under which the cinema industry evolved: tsarism, Communism, and the present state, however it may be defined. These three regimes have precious little in common, aside from one thing—namely, adversity. There was initially scant interest and support in tsarist Russia for cinema to flourish, and then far too much interference in the Soviet Union, which is hardly compensated by the present lack of concern. Yet, amazingly enough, despite all the constraints and hardships, Russian/Soviet/Russian cinema has produced some remarkable actors, directors, cameramen, and composers. And it has given the world some utterly unforgettable films.

The unique challenge of this *Historical Dictionary of Russian and Soviet Cinema* is thus to present a comprehensible overview of more than a century of cinema and yet to show the specifics of each period and place, and how they affected the work of sometimes the very same filmmakers who knew how to adapt as well as the work of some who could not have emerged in any other context. This is done most easily in the chronology, which traces the frequently chaotic and often stultifying events. The introduction helps us to understand any similarities and differences and to make sense of the whole thing. But it is the dictionary section with its many telling details that allows us to develop a better feel for the many directors, performers, and cinematographers—those favored by the regime and those discarded (or worse), the production companies and distributors, the themes that enjoyed official patronage, and especially the films (greater and considerably less so). The bibliography then directs readers to many other useful sources, in various languages and on various subjects, but all helpful in fathoming a very intriguing, if often hard to understand, cinema.

This volume was written by Peter Rollberg, whose career has also undergone distinct phases, although all contributing to the same end. He grew up in East Germany, where his access to Soviet cinema was doubtlessly greater than on the other side of the Berlin Wall, and also in Russia, where he was cast as the lead in a children's film. His stays in Russia covered both the Communist and post-Communist periods. He received his doctorate at the University of Leipzig, where he also taught Russian literature, before he moved to the United States, where he taught at George Washington University, eventually becoming the director of the Film Studies Program and at present the chair of the Department of Romance, German, and Slavic Languages and Literatures. During much of this time, Dr. Rollberg has lectured and written on Russian and Soviet cinema, including many articles and papers, and has also served as editor of *The Modern Encyclopedia of East Slavic, Baltic, and Eurasian Literatures*. This volume therefore benefits from its author's long and varied exposure to the topic and offers the reader an exceptional insight into one of the world's great cinemas.

Jon Woronoff
Series Editor

Preface

In the past, the terms *Russian cinema* and *Soviet cinema* were often used interchangeably. They commonly denoted the state-run, ideologically dominated, Communist film culture of the USSR that emerged in the 1920s and existed until the late 1980s. Great filmmakers such as Sergei Eizenshtein and Andrei Tarkovskii were known as prominent representatives of Russian—and Soviet—cinema, and as its martyrs too. The art of Dziga Vertov, Vsevolod Pudovkin, and Mikhail Kalatozov, among others, has won Soviet cinema many admirers among cinephiles worldwide. Yet, with the disappearance of the Soviet Union, the term *Soviet* is less frequently applied to film artists of the past. Indeed, how should one call a filmmaker such as Sergei Paradjanov, who was born to Armenian parents in Georgia, studied in Moscow, and became a household name with a film made in Ukraine? By citizenship, he was Soviet; by worldview, anything but. To call him "a Russian director" would be incorrect too, unless one sloppily identifies Russia with the Soviet Union and the director with his passport. Despite my awareness of the painful complexity of these issues, this dictionary's subject is still called "Russian and Soviet cinema" because the Soviet Union was a multiethnic, multinational state, with Russia as its central component.

It must be remembered that the history of Russian cinema began 20 years before its Soviet period, in the Russian Empire, as did the history of Georgian and Ukrainian and other national cinemas. Indeed, imprecise notions associated with the terms *Russian* and *Soviet*, understandable though they may be, can obliterate the fact that Soviet cinema during the 70 years of its existence referred not just to Russian but also to Ukrainian, Belarusian, Georgian, Armenian, Azerbaijani, Kazakh, Uzbek, Kyrgyz, Tadjik, Turkmen, and, for some 40 years, Lithuanian, Latvian, Estonian, and Moldovan cinema. In this dictionary I have tried my best to shed light on the richness and diversity of the phenomenon called "Russian and Soviet cinema." Therefore, the book includes numerous important directors and other film artists from all former Soviet republics as well as assessments of their specific cinematic contributions.

The chronology lists events such as the first film screenings and the first feature film productions for each nation, whether before or after the establishment of Soviet power. The histories of the non-Russian national cinemas are provided in entries on their major studios; for example, essential facts on the history of Belarusian cinema can be found under "Belarusfilm Studio," whereas a survey of Armenian cinema is contained in the entry on "Armenfilm Studio." All entries on the respective national cinemas are listed in cross-reference entries such as "Georgian cinema," "Kazakh cinema," and so forth.

The multinational nature of Soviet cinema, enforced as a matter of political principle, was used as a propaganda tool first and foremost. Yet for some of the indoctrinated cultures, the establishment of studios and administrative structures proved to be a blessing in disguise, creating film industries in regions that otherwise would likely have remained without a national film culture for a long time. Thus, although the Soviet political system has been delegitimized for some time now, its cultural legacy is somewhat more ambivalent, particularly in the field of cinema where generous state funding and centralized distribution are remembered fondly by many film professionals and viewers. On the one hand, the centralized structure of Soviet cinema can be viewed as a curse, stifling independent national cinematic developments and forcing individual artistic creativity into the Procrustean bed of Communist conformity. But the dissolution of the USSR in 1991, which brought independence to the former Soviet republics and democratic rights to some of them, caused not only the disintegration of what was known as Soviet cinema—with its comparatively efficient distribution networks, nomenclatures, and censors—but also the disappearance of an audience in the tens of millions and secure funding for some worthy artistic achievements.

The present *Historical Dictionary of Russian and Soviet Cinema* is an attempt to do justice to all abovementioned aspects: Russian cinema and the cinema of the various national cultures within the former Soviet Union, popular and elitist cinema, propaganda and art, and the creative individuals and the industry of which they were part. Moreover, I have tried to pay tribute not just to the directors and performers but have also included a number of cinematographers, screenwriters, composers, art designers, and inventors so that the broad spectrum of cinema-related arts and technologies is represented as well.

Although encyclopedic dictionaries belong to the more impersonal academic genres, the motivation to devote six years of my life to this endeavor is rooted in my personal background. I have been fortunate enough to meet some of this book's protagonists in person. Living with my family in Moscow as a boy, I watched countless Soviet movies and even kept a diary in which I gave each film a numerical grade, from "1" for the worst to "5" for the best. My Russian high school was located not far from the Gor'kii Studio for Children's and Youth Films, and talent scouts showed up regularly, picking kids for screen tests. Much to my chagrin, whenever these scouts learned that I was a foreigner, their interest waned. Until one day, in the summer of 1970, an assistant director chose me for the role of Johann (*Iogann* in Russian) in a film about an international pioneer camp. The film's title was *Hurray! We Have Holidays!* (Ura! U nas kanikuly!). Months of location shooting in Artek at the Black Sea, in Moscow, Dresden, and Vilnius convinced me that I had found my vocation: cinema. Alas, the film's destiny was a sad one. Taken to task for its "abstract humanism" in dealing with issues of détente, the director, Vladimir Berenshtein, was forced to resign and was replaced by a hack who finished the job in a lackluster manner. Although the butchered end product was finally released in 1972 and also repeatedly shown on Soviet television, it had lost its teeth and became the last in Berenshtein's filmography; after the fiasco of *Hurray! We Have Holidays!* he was only allowed to dub foreign movies and remaster old Soviet classics.

But for me, a young foreign boy, the immersion in the world of Russian and Soviet film was nothing short of miraculous. Walking along the hallways of Gor'kii Studio that were graced with stills from famous pictures of decades past, I could literally breathe the intense air of collective creativity that characterizes cinema. One of the "living classics," Mark Donskoi—short, stocky, with vivacious, warm eyes—came along, surrounded by his respectful entourage; the master of the fairy-tale film, Aleksandr Rou, worked on his final picture; Uzbek filmmaker Ali Khamraev was surprised that I, an 11-year-old schoolboy, could name his films. Years later, in 1987, while working on my dissertation in Moscow, I was asked to testify before the conflict commission of the Union of Soviet Filmmakers about the mistreatment of *Hurray! We Have Holidays!* and its makers by dogmatic authorities. That was a unique opportunity to witness the complicated process of Russian filmmakers coming to terms with their past. During the deliberations, I met the elegant and perceptive Gleb Panfilov, as well as another star, Mikhail Gluzskii—stern and unwilling to understand why such a "propaganda film" needed any rehabilitation in the first place. I wrote a letter to Elem Klimov, explaining in detail what had happened to "my film," until finally *Hurray! We Have Holidays!* was rehabilitated both symbolically and financially.

My scholarly interest in Russian cinema and theater brought me countless opportunities to meet film artists and to indulge in their splendor privately or on stage: from director Grigorii Aleksandrov to animator Iurii Norshtein; from Lev Kuleshov's sound engineer Nikolai Ozornov to cinematographer Tat'iana Lobova, who worked with Sergei Eizenshtein and Vsevolod Pudovkin in the 1930s and 1940s; and from screenwriter Iurii Lukin to actress Anastasiia Zueva—the latter became a friend and a living connection to the age of Stanislavskii, whose theory of acting gave cinema so many vital impulses.

I harbor few illusions about the political nature of the Soviet system, yet the culture that I experienced and fell in love with as a child had deep roots in the beauty of Russia's Golden Age and in the moralism of the great masters of 19th-century Russian literature. The same holds true for my attitude toward the film cultures of other nations: the gripping analytical drama of Lithuanian director Vytautas Žalakevičius; the inimitable, sad irony of Georgian masters Giorgi Shengelaia and Tengiz Abuladze; and the mystical perception of nature in the pictures of Kyrgyz directors Bolotbek Shamshiev and Tolomush Okeev. In their oeuvres, there is still so much to discover for Western viewers. This dictionary was written with the intention to promote interest in Russian, Soviet, and post-Soviet cinema, blending and balancing critical distance, honesty about the facts, and grateful affection.

I am indebted to a number of friends, colleagues, and assistants for their practical help and encouragement, including Bernard Portier, who provided some rare sources; Vladimir Matlin, who shared many stories about the film milieu of the 1950s and 1960s; Barney Mergen, who interviewed Bolotbek Shamshiev in Bishkek; members of the Research Institute for Film Studies in Moscow (Tat'iana Simacheva,

Dmitrii Karavaev, Evgenii Margolit, and others); and Daniel McFadden, who patiently and thoroughly proofread numerous drafts. My sincere thanks go to the George Washington University's Columbian College of Arts and Sciences for granting me a sabbatical leave and to the Institute for European, Russian, and Eurasian Studies for funding research assistants.

Peter Rollberg
The George Washington University

Reader's Note

For the transliteration of Russian, Ukrainian, and Belarusian names and titles, the Library of Congress system is used, including soft and hard signs (' and "). This may sometimes yield curious spellings—for example, Sergei Eisenstein appears as "Eizenshtein," or Vsevolod Meyerhold as "Meierkhol'd"—but the purpose of consistency in a reference work outweighed considerations of common usage. For all other languages, the original Latin spellings are used, with diacritics added, or the respective countries' official transliteration systems.

Each personal entry starts with the last and first name of its subject; for Russian, Ukrainian, and Belarusian individuals, the traditional patronymic (or "father's name") is also added. Since Russian was the lingua franca of Soviet cinema, deviating Russian spellings of non-Russian subjects are listed in brackets, too. At the end, the personal entries list important titles awarded to the artists. To some, this may seem a Soviet-style formality. Yet for the careers of the artists, titles were of vital importance. Beginning with the lowest, "Merited Artist of the Russian Soviet Federative Socialist Republic" (RSFSR)—or the similar "of the Ukrainian SSR," "of the Lithuanian SSR," and so forth—each step on the title ladder came with salary raises, access to special health facilities and spas, food distributors, apartment buildings, and the likelihood of being included in a delegation to the West. Holders of the title "People's Artist of the RSFSR" (or "Kyrgyz SSR," "Belarusian SSR," etc.) were entitled to one wing of a summer country house (dacha), a genuine status symbol, while a "People's Artist of the USSR" was given an entire dacha by the Soviet government. The fact that avant-gardist Dziga Vertov never received an honorary title speaks for itself and had serious consequences for his quality of life.

Another fact listed in personal entries is the membership in the Communist Party of the Soviet Union (CPSU). In general, the CPSU was interested in absorbing as many representatives of what was called "the creative intelligentsia" as possible. After all, fundamental questions of political and artistic relevance were discussed in Party meetings (*part-sobraniia*), to which nonmembers were usually not admitted. Resisting Party membership on political grounds was unthinkable, but self-deprecation ("I'm not yet worthy of being a member . . .") could be accepted, just as religious reasons could; a number of famous artists kept their church allegiance, and the Communist watchdogs quietly accepted this. Listing a person's membership in the Communist Party, therefore, can be an important indicator of political loyalty.

All film titles are first listed in English, then in parentheses in the original language, followed by the production and/or release year. For non-Russian films, whenever possible the Russian distribution title is added to the original title in parentheses, since the Russian usually was the basis for the international distribution title.

In the multinational, multiethnic Soviet Union, questions of nationality and ethnicity have always been ticklish. The policy of the Communist establishment was to downplay the national background of individuals; in many reference works, the nationality of the artist was not mentioned at all. Actors, directors, or cameramen were simply called "Soviet," but their titles could be a giveaway ("People's Artist of the Turkmen SSR," "Merited Artist of the Armenian SSR," etc.), although this was not foolproof either. A blatant example is the title "People's Artist of the RSFSR" (i.e., the Russian Federation) awarded in 1950 to Ukrainian filmmaker Aleksandr Dovzhenko, a man for whom his national roots were a matter of vital importance. The approach in this dictionary is neither ethnocentric nor exclusively geographic; rather, various aspects were taken into account, including ethnic origins and the place where an artist was creative for the most part of his life. Thus, Sergei Bondarchuk, ethnically Ukrainian, worked all of his life in Moscow and considered himself a Russian artist.

For the Soviet Union, World War II held a distinct, identity-shaping meaning. Therefore, in many cases the official Soviet term "Great Patriotic War" is used when referring to this event. It should be noted, though, that not only did the Great Patriotic War begin later than World War II (on 22 June 1941, i.e., almost two years after 1 September 1939), it also ended earlier, on 9 May 1945, with the capitulation of Nazi Germany, not Japan. For understandable reasons, in the context of the Baltic republics, the neutral term "World War II" is used.

Abbreviations and Acronyms

AKFU	Azerbaijani Photo and Film Administration
ANS	Aleksandr Nikolaevich Skriabin (electronic music device)
ARK	Association of Revolutionary Cinematography
ASSR	Autonomous Soviet Socialist Republic
b/w	black and white
BDT	Grand Dramatic Theater (St. Petersburg)
ChK	Soviet secret police (Chrezvychainaia Komissiia—Extraordinary Committee, 1917–1922)
codir.	codirected
CP	Communist Party
CPSU	Communist Party of the Soviet Union
doc.	documentary
EKKIu	Iutkevich's Experimental Film Collective
FEKS	Factory of the Eccentric Actor
GEKTEMAS	State Experimental Theater Workshops
GITIS	State Institute for Stage Arts, State Theater Institute
GPU	Soviet secret service (Gosudarstvennoe politicheskoe upravlenie—State Political Administration, 1922–1934)
GTK	State Film College (Gosudarstvennyi tekhnikum kinematografii)
GUFK	Main Administration of the Film and Photo Industry of the USSR
GULAG	Glavnoe Upravlenie Ispravitel'no-trudovykh Lagerei (Chief directorate of prison camps in former Soviet Union)

GVyRM	Supreme Directing Workshops aka Workshop of Communist Dramaturgy (Masterskaia kommunisticheskoi dramaturgii)
KEM	Film Experimental Workshop (kinoeksperimental'naia masterskaia)
KGB	Committee for State Security (Komitet Gosudarstvennoi Bezopasnosti, 1954–1991)
KShE	Komsomol Shef Elektrofikatsii
LEF	Left Front of the Arts (Levyi Front Iskusstv)
LIKI	Leningrad Institute of Film Engineering
MISI	Moscow Institute for Construction and Engineering
MKhAT	Moscow Art Theater
MOS	Moscow Office of Advertising
MUZhVZ	Moscow School for Painting, Sculpture and Architecture
NEP	New Economic Policy
NKVD	Narodny Komissariat Vnutrennikh Del (People's Commissariat for Internal Affairs, former Soviet Union, 1934–1954)
OGPU	Soviet secret police (Ob"edinennoe Glavnoe politicheskoe upravlenie—United Main Political Administration)
OPOIAZ	Society for the Study of Poetic Language
POW	prisoner of war
ROSTA	Russian Telegraphic Agency
RSFSR	Russian Soviet Federative Socialist Republic
SNK	Council of People's Commissars
SSR	Soviet Socialist Republic
TIuZ	Theater of the Young Viewer
TRAM	Theater of the Workers' Youth
TsOKS	Central United Film Studio for Feature Films (Tsentral'naia ob"edinennaia kinostudiia khudozhestvennykh fil'mov)
UFA	Universum Film Ag (German film studio)
USSR	Union of Soviet Socialist Republics
VFKO	All-Russian Department of Photography and Cinema (Vserossiiskii fotokinootdel)
VGIK	All-Soviet State Film School

VKhUTEIN	Supreme Institute for Art and Technology, Moscow (Vysshii khudozhestvenno-tekhnicheskii institut, Moscow)
VKhUTEMAS	Supreme State Workshops for Art and Technology (Vysshie khudozhestvenno-tekhnicheskie masterskie)
VKSR	Supreme Courses for Screenwriters and Directors (Vysshie kursy stsenaristov i rezhisserov)
VUFKU	All-Ukrainian Photo-Cinema Administration

Chronology

1896 **4 May:** First film screening in Russia, in the summer garden Aquarium in St. Petersburg. **26 May:** First screening in Moscow, in the Hermitage pleasure garden. **May:** First film shot in Russia by cinematographers of the Lumière brothers company, filming the coronation of Tsar Nikolai II in Moscow.

1897 Opening of the first Russian Electrical Theater (i.e., movie theater) in a Moscow warehouse, GUM.

1898 **2 August:** First film screening in Azerbaijan, in a Baku theater, by French engineer Henri Michon; the shorts included *Caucasus Folk Dance* and *Oil Gush Fire in Bibi-Heibat*.

1906 Founding of Aleksandr Khanzhonkov's company, initially a commission agency selling foreign equipment and films.

1907 **January:** First film studio founded in St. Petersburg by professional photographer Aleksandr Drankov. Also, first event shot in Armenia—the burial of the country's Katolikos, Mkrtych Hrimyan. In Kiev (Kyiv), the first Ukrainian feature was shot, *Kochubei in the Dungeon* (Kochubei v temnitse).

1908 **15 October:** Premiere of *Sten'ka Razin* (Ponizovaia vol'nitsa), the first feature film with Russian subject matter, directed by Vladimir Romashkov from a screenplay by Vasilii Goncharov, with Nikolai Kozlovskii behind the camera and music by Mikhail Ippolitov-Ivanov, director of the Moscow Conservatory.

1909 First Georgian feature film, *Berikaoba Keenoba*, released, directed by Aleksandre Tsutsunava. American-Lithuanian cameraman

Antanas Račiūnas began his yearly tours filming events and customs in Lithuania that he then screened to expatriates in the United States.

1911   15 October: Premiere of the world's first full-length feature film, *The Defense of Sevastopol* (Oborona Sevastopolia), directed by Vasilii Goncharov and produced by Aleksandr Khanzhonkov, a reconstruction of episodes of the 1854–1855 Crimean War.

1912   First full-length documentary released in Georgia, *The Journey of Georgian Poet Akaki Tsereteli to Racha-Lechkhumi* (Akakis Mogzauroba), directed by Vasili Amashukeli.

1914   First Estonian film, *A Bear's Hunt in Pärnu District* (Karujaht Pärnumaal), shot by Johannes Pääsuke (1892–1918).

1915   First Armenian feature film, *Under the Rule of the Kurds* (Pod vlast'iu kurdov), released, directed by A. Minervin.

1916   14 May: Premiere of the first Azerbaijani feature film, *In the Realm of Oil and Millions* (V tsarstve nefti i millionov), directed by Boris Svetlov. The Georgian film *Christinė*—sometimes credited as the country's first feature—released, directed by Aleksandre Tsutsunava. Georgii Shavel'skii, responsible for the Russian Army and Navy, develops a project to nationalize the Russian film industry with the approval of Tsar Nikolai II.

1917   February: Abolition of censorship in the Russian Empire. The Skobelev Committee put in charge of producing and distributing the newsreel *Free Russia* (Svobodnaia Rossiia).

1918   4 March: Film committees (*kinokomitety*) formed as part of the city councils in Moscow and St. Petersburg; the committees monitored the private film industry, censored new films, and collected taxes from movie theaters (50 percent of the profits). **17 July:** Decree "On Censoring the Cinemas" (O tsenzure nad kinematografami) approved by Moscow City Council. First Soviet feature film, the *agitka* short *The Condensation* (Uplotnenie), released, written by Anatolii Lunacharskii and directed by Aleksandr Panteleev.

1919   Spring: All-Russian Department of Photography and Cinema (Vserossiiskii fotokinootdel, VFKO) established, with Bolshevik leader Dmitrii Leshchenko as head. **April:** First agit-train (*agit-poezd*), equipped with film projectors, left Moscow for the Russian provinces. **27 August:** Decree issued on the nationalization of the film industry in Soviet Russia, signed by Vladimir Lenin. The "photographic and cinematographic industry and trade" were transferred to the People's Commissariat of Education. **11 September:** Censorship Committee established as part of the Moscow City Council.

1920   15 February: The Moscow studios of Aleksandr Khanzhonkov, Iosif Ermol'ev, and other entrepreneurs transferred to the care of the All-Russian Department of Photography and Cinema. **July:** Nariman Narimanov, chairman of the Revolutionary Committee of Azerbaijan, signed decree on the nationalization of cinema.

1921   Nationalization of the Georgian film industry. Foundation of State Film Production organization (Goskinprom), the first Georgian film studio. *Arsena Jiorjashvili* (aka *The Murder of General Griaznov*, 1921), the first full-length Soviet Georgian feature film, directed by Ivan Perestiani.

1922   The government of Azerbaijan founded the country's first film studio in Baku, located in close proximity to the government building. **December:** In Soviet Russia, the All-Russian Department of Photography and Cinema (Vserossiiskii fotokinootdel, VFKO) renamed State Cinema Agency (Goskino).

1923   Hayfilm (Armenkino), the first Armenian film studio, founded. **28 April:** AKFU (Azerbaijani Photo and Film Administration/ Azerbaidzhanskoe fotokinoupravlenie), founded. The film office of the International Workers' Aid organization (Mezhrabpom) formed joint venture with the private film company Rus', becoming the German-Soviet stockholding film company Mezhrabpom-Rus' (since 1928, Mezhrabpom-fil'm).

1924   *The Legend of the Girl's Tower* (Legenda o devich'ei bashne), the first Azerbaijani feature film, released, directed by Vladimir

Balliuzek. The 13th Congress of the Bolshevik Party decided to not centralize the Soviet film industry and to leave the control of film production and distribution with each national republic. The Communist Parties of the national republics formed special film committees. Goskino transformed into Sovkino, defined as an all-Russian stockholding company. First large-scale Soviet production *Aelita* released, directed by Iakov Protazanov.

1925 Film journal *Sovetskii ekran* (Soviet Screen) founded (in the 1930s, its name changed a number of times; after the breakdown of the USSR, it became *Ekran*). **December:** Decree of the Communist Party "On the Question of Unifying Film Censorship" published.

1926 Hamo Bek-Nazaryan directed first Armenian full-length feature, *Honor* (Namus). **7 February:** The Council of People's Commissars of the Turkmen SSR issued decree on the foundation of the Turkmen film factory, later renamed Turkmenfilm Studio.

1927 **24 January:** The Department of Agitation and Propaganda (Agitprop) of the Communist Party held meeting devoted to the production of children's films under the leadership of Lenin's widow, Nadezhda Krupskaia. The entrepreneur Ismailov established the first cinema in Dushanbe, Tadjikistan. First Estonian studio, Theodor Lutsu Filmiproduktsioon, established by the entrepreneur Theodor Luts (1896–1980).

1928 Vostokkino studio founded in Leningrad, with a branch in Almaty (Alma-Ata), Kazakhstan. **15–21 March:** First All-Union Conference of the Communist Party devoted to problems of cinema. The sound film system "Tagephone" (*Tagefon SGK-7*) by Pavel Tager demonstrated for the first time on a number of shorts. **June:** The Council of People's Commissars of the RSFSR adopted resolution on the transformation of the Soviet film industry, planning to achieve its complete independence of foreign companies by 1932. **17 December:** The Council of People's Commissars of the USSR (Sovnarkom) decided to establish a Film Committee.

1929 Aleksandr Shorin's "Shorinophone" (*shorinofon*), a sound film system developed in close cooperation with Sovkino (later: Lenfilm Studio) in Leningrad, first publicly demonstrated.

1930   December: Establishment of Soiuzkino, the central Soviet State Cinema organization; Boris Shumiatskii named head. The "Tagephone" used for the first Soviet sound documentary, Abram Room's feature-length *The Plan of the Great Works* (Plan velikikh rabot, aka *Five-Year Plan*/Piatiletka, 1930). The "Shorinophone" used in Dziga Vertov's feature-length documentary *Enthusiasm* (Entuziazm, aka *Symphony of Donbass*/Simfoniia Donbassa, 1930).

1931   1 June: First Soviet sound feature film *A Start in Life* (aka *Road to Life*/Putevka v zhizn') released, directed by Nikolai Ekk. First full-length Lithuanian feature film, *Onyte and Jonelis* (Onyte ir Jonelis), calling upon young people to stay in the country, released. The Eesti Kultuurfilm foundation, an Estonian film company that became a state institution in 1936, established.

1932   Summer: At the world's first film festival in Venice, Nikolai Ekk received the Best Director award for *A Start in Life*; the film was sold to 26 countries. In the Soviet Union, 27 foreign feature films were released: 21 from the United States, 3 from Germany, 2 from France, and 1 from Italy. For the first time, the Soviet film industry yielded a profit (92,000 rubles), after years of financial losses.

1933   11 February: The Council of People's Commissars issued decree establishing the Main Administration of the Film and Photo Industry of the USSR (GUFK), centralizing film production, distribution, and import and export for the first time; Boris Shumiatskii appointed head. *The Torn Shoes* (aka *Broken Shoes*/Rvanye bashmaki, 1933), directed by Margarita Barskaia, the first Soviet sound film for children, released.

1934   16 May: Resolution of the Council of People's Commissars "On the Necessity to Transform the Teaching of National History in Soviet Schools and Universities." In Kazakhstan, the Alma-Ata (Almaty) Documentary Film Studio was founded.

1935   8–13 January: The All-Soviet Congress of Soviet Film Workers in Moscow confirmed Socialist Realism as the guiding dogma of cinema. **10–18 January:** Celebration of the 15th anniversary of the Soviet film industry. **Summer:** The first International Moscow Film

Festival took place; 19 countries participated with 47 films in the competition. **17 November:** The weekly newspaper *Kino* published letter of Stakhanovite worker activists to Soviet filmmakers with the demand "to depict the new Soviet life in the movies." **13–15 December:** Party meeting devoted to administrative and thematic problems of cinema during which Boris Shumiatskii laid out plans for a gigantic, Hollywood-type Soviet film studio near the Black Sea.

1936   22 February: The Soviet State Film Archive (Gosfil'mofond) founded. **8 June:** Closing of Mezhrabpomfilm Studio; its assets were transferred to the newly founded Soviet Children's Film studio (Soiuzdetfil'm), later Gor'kii Film Studio for Children's and Youth Films.

1937   *Baltic Deputy* (Deputat Baltiki) by Iosif Kheifits and Aleksandr Zarkhi received medal at Venice Film Festival.

1938   9 January: Boris Shumiatskii, head of the Soviet film industry, fired. **23 March:** The Committee on Cinema Affairs (Komitet po delam kinematografii), a body reporting directly to the Council of Ministers, established; Semen Dukel'skii put in charge. **28 March:** The decree "On the Improvement of the Organization of Film Production" issued by the Council of People's Commissars. **June:** The Council of People's Commissars of the Kyrgyz SSR established a branch of the Tashkent Newsreel Studio in Frunze; it later became Kyrgyzfilm Studio. In the United States, 57 Soviet films were released in 1938, attracting a total of 1.6 million viewers.

1939   4 June: Ivan Bol'shakov appointed head of the Committee on Cinema Affairs. According to Soviet statistics, there were 900 million moviegoers per annum in the USSR. On average, every Soviet citizen went to the movies five times a year.

1940   4 February: The first stereoscopic movie theater opened in Moscow. **15 March:** The Committee on Cinema Affairs announced the organization of artistic councils (*khudsovety*) assisting the executive artistic directors of Soviet film studios.

1941   The USSR had 31,000 film projectors in movie theaters, clubs, and schools: 20,000 in the countryside, 11,000 in cities. After Nazi Germany's attack on the USSR, hundreds of cinematographers were drafted as front cameramen. **7 August:** The artistic council of Mosfilm Studio began the production of *War Film Almanacs* (Voennye kinoal'manakhy), consisting of short features and documentaries. **September/October:** The Central United Film Studio (Tsentral'naia ob"edinennaia kinostudiia) established in Almaty, Kazakhstan, consisting of the evacuated studios Mosfilm and Lenfilm; Fridrikh Ermler appointed head. **November:** The Moscow Children's Film Studio (Soiuzdetfil'm) under the leadership of its executive director Sergei Iutkevich evacuated to Stalinabad (Dushanbe), using the facilities of Tadjikfilm Studio. The animation studio Soiuzmul'tfil'm was evacuated from Moscow to Samarkand.

1942   21–22 August: Soviet conference on U.S. cinema took place in Moscow, with Sergei Eizenshtein, Vsevolod Pudovkin, and Roman Karmen among its speakers.

1943   February: Return of evacuated film studios from Central Asia to their home cities began. *The Defeat of the German Troops near Moscow* (Razgrom nemetskikh voisk pod Moskvoi, 1942), a feature-length documentary directed by Il'ia Kopalin and Leonid Varlamov, won Academy Award for Best Documentary under the title *Moscow Strikes Back.*

1946   25 January: The Alma-Ata (Almaty) Documentary Film Studio was transformed into a studio for feature and newsreel production. **20 March:** Establishment of the Ministry of Cinema (Ministerstvo kinematografii), headed by Ivan Bol'shakov. **4 September:** Decree of the Central Committee of the Communist Party "About the Film *A Great Life*, Part 2." **31 September:** Decree of the Council of Ministers of the USSR demanding increase in production of feature films. At the Venice Film Festival, Mikheil Chiaureli's *The Vow* (Pitsi/Kliatva, 1946) and Mark Donskoi's *The Undefeated* (Nepokorennye, 1945) received gold medals (of a total of seven awarded at the festival). At the Cannes Film Festival, Fridrikh Ermler's *The Great Turning Point* (Velikii perelom,

1945) received a Grand Prize and Iulii Raizman's *Berlin* a prize for Best Documentary. Sergei Gerasimov represented the USSR in the jury.

1947 At the Locarno Film Festival, Anatolii Golovnia and Tamara Lobova received the prize for Best Camera Work for *Admiral Nakhimov*, directed by Vsevolod Pudovkin.

1948 24–28 February: An executive meeting of the Soviet movie industry leadership criticized the "Kowtowing toward the West" (*Nizkopoklonstvo pered Zapadom*), initiating a campaign "against cosmopolitanism," implicating predominantly Jewish film artists. **16 June:** Cinema minister Bol'shakov declared Soviet studios will produce fewer but better films, beginning the period of "film shortage" (*malokartin'e*). **October:** The Turkmen film studio in Ashgabad was completely destroyed by a major earthquake; among the dead are numerous film artists.

1949 January: Cinema minister Bol'shakov declared there was "a group of antipatriotic, cosmopolitan filmmakers," in particular Leonid Trauberg, then head of the Leningrad House of Cinema.

1952 October: The 19th Congress of the Communist Party passed a resolution demanding an increase in the number of films.

1953 March: The Main Cinema Administration (Glavnoe upravlenie kinematografii), one of the branches of the USSR Ministry of Culture, established, replacing the former Ministry of Cinema; Vladimir Surin appointed first head. Aleksandr Ptushko's *Sadko* won Silver Prize at the Venice Film Festival.

1954 November: The Main Administration of Film Production (Glavnoe upravlenie po proizvodstvu fil'mov) replaced the Main Cinema Administration; Konstantin Kuzakov appointed first head.

1955 Spring: At the Cannes Film Festival, Sergei Iutkevich was a member of the international jury. *The Big Family* (Bol'shaia sem'ia, 1954) by Iosif Kheifits won prize for the best ensemble performance, while Sergei Vasil'ev received Best Director award for *Heroes of*

Shipka (Geroi Shipki). **Fall:** At the Venice Film Festival, Samson Samsonov's *The Grasshopper* (Poprygun'ia) won a Silver Lion.

1956 **Spring:** Sergei Vasil'ev appointed member of the international jury of the Cannes Film Festival. Sergei Iutkevich won Best Director award for *Othello*. Tengiz Abuladze and Revaz Chkheidze's *Magdana's Donkey* (Magdanas Lurja/Lurdzha Magdany) won the prize for Best Short film.

1957 After years of struggle, the blue-ribbon committee for the creation of a Union of Soviet Filmmakers, headed by Ivan Pyr'ev, was established. **Spring:** Grigorii Chukhrai won Special Jury Prize of the Cannes Film Festival for *The Forty-first* (Sorok pervyi, 1956). **Fall:** Dzidra Ritenbergs won Best Actress award at the Venice Film Festival for her performance in Vladimir Braun's *Mal'va*.

1958 Release of the second part of Sergei Eizenshtein's *Ivan the Terrible* (Ivan Groznyi, 1946), the second part of Leonid Lukov's *A Great Life* (Bol'shaia zhizn', 1946), and other formerly prohibited films. **18 May:** Mikhail Kalatozov's *The Cranes Are Flying* (Letiat zhuravli) won Golden Palm award of the Cannes Film Festival.

1959 After a hiatus of almost 25 years, the Second International Moscow Film Festival took place. **15 September:** Office for the Propaganda of Soviet Cinema established as part of the planned Union of Soviet Filmmakers.

1961 **Spring:** Iuliia Solntseva won Best Director award at the Cannes Film Festival for *Chronicle of the Flaming Years* (Istoriia plamennykh let, 1960)—the first Soviet 70mm film with stereo sound. **Fall:** Aleksandr Alov and Vladimir Naumov won Special Jury Prize for *Peace to Him Who Enters* (Mir vkhodiashchemu) at the Venice Film Festival.

1962 **Fall:** Andrei Tarkovskii won the Golden Lion of the Venice Film Festival for *Ivan's Childhood* (aka *My Name Is Ivan*/Ivanovo detstvo).

1963 **23 March:** Committee of Cinema (Komitet po kinematografii) of the USSR Council of Ministers established; Aleksei Romanov appointed chairman. **Spring:** Samson Samsonov won Special Jury Prize at Cannes Film Festival for *An Optimistic Tragedy* (Optimisticheskaia tragediia).

1964   Fall: Grigorii Kozintsev won Special Jury Prize at the Venice Film Festival for *Hamlet*.

1965   November: The Union of Soviet Filmmakers founded in Moscow; Lev Kulidzhanov elected first chairman. The 14 national Soviet republics—the Armenian SSR, Azerbaijani SSR, Belorussian (Belarusian) SSR, Estonian SSR, Georgian SSR, Kazakh SSR, Kirgiz (Kyrgyz) SSR, Latvian SSR, Lithuanian SSR, Moldavian (Moldovan) SSR, Tadjik SSR, Turkmen SSR, Ukrainian SSR, and Uzbek SSR—established their own filmmakers' unions, with a limited degree of independence. **Fall:** Marlen Khutsiev won Special Jury Prize at the Venice Film Festival for *I Am Twenty* (Mne dvadtsat' let). Arūnas Žebriūnas won Special Jury Prize at the Locarno Film Festival for *The Girl and the Echo* (Paskutinė atostogų diena/Devochka i ekho).

1966   Sergei Iutkevich won Special Jury Prize for *Lenin in Poland* (Lenin v Pol'she) at the Cannes Film Festival. **Fall:** Natal'ia Arinbasarova won Volpi Cup for Best Actress at the Venice Film Festival for her performance in Andrei Mikhalkov-Konchalovskii's *The First Teacher* (Pervyi uchitel').

1969   Spring: Sergei Bondarchuk's adaptation of Lev Tolstoi's *War and Peace* (Voina i mir, 1962–1967) won Academy Award for Best Foreign Picture. **Fall:** Gleb Panfilov won Grand Prize of the Locarno Film Festival for *There's No Ford through Fire* (V ogne broda net).

1972   Spring: Andrei Tarkovskii won Special Jury Prize of the Cannes Film Festival for *Solaris*. **4 August:** Filipp Ermash appointed head of Goskino, the State Committee of Cinema of the Council of Ministers.

1975   Akira Kurosawa's *Dersu Uzala*, adapted from Vladimir Arsen'ev's book and produced by the Soviet Union, with Maksim Munzuk and Iurii Solomin in the lead roles, won Academy Award for

Best Foreign Picture. Sergei Solov'ev's *One Hundred Days after Childhood* (Sto dnei posle detstva, 1975) won Special Jury Prize at the Berlin Film Festival.

1977 Larisa Shepit'ko won Golden Bear at the Berlin Film Festival for *The Ascension* (Voskhozhdenie).

1978 **5 July:** Goskino became an independent committee, ranked like a ministry and renamed Goskino SSSR, with Filipp Ermash as chairman.

1980 Vladimir Men'shov's comedy *Moscow Does Not Believe in Tears* (Moskva slezam ne verit, 1979) won Academy Award for Best Foreign Picture.

1981 Anatolii Solonitsyn won Silver Bear for Best Actor in Aleksandr Zarkhi's *Twenty-six Days from the Life of Dostoevskii* (26 dnei iz zhizni Dostoevskogo) at the Berlin Film Festival.

1984 Inna Churikova won Silver Lion for Best Actress in Petr Todorovskii's *Wartime Romance* (Voenno-polevoi roman, 1984).

1986 **February:** Georgian director Giorgi Shengelaia won Silver Bear for *Sojourn of a Young Composer* (Akhalgarzda kompozitoris mogzauroba/Puteshestvie molodogo kompozitora) at Berlin Film Festival. **13–15 May:** Fifth Congress of Soviet Filmmakers' Union took place in Moscow; after fiery debates and demands for the abolition of censorship, the organization's previous leadership with First Secretary Lev Kulidzhanov was completely replaced. Elem Klimov elected new first secretary. Aleksandr Kamshalov appointed new chairman of the USSR State Committee of Cinema (Goskino SSSR).

1987 **January:** Tengis Abuladze's *Repentance* (Monanieba/Pokaianie, 1984) released, the first radical anti-Stalinist picture made in the Soviet Union; it won the Grand Special Jury Prize at the Cannes Film Festival. Gleb Panfilov's formerly shelved *The Theme* (Tema, 1979) won the Golden Bear at the Berlin Film Festival.

1988 **April:** The last all-Soviet Film Festival took place in Baku. The entire Soviet film industry transferred to self-financing mode (*khozraschet*). Private studios and distribution companies for film and video legalized. Aleksandr Askol'dov's *The Commissar* (Komissar, 1968), an iconoclastic depiction of the revolution, won Special Jury Prize at the Berlin Film Festival, 20 years after it had been ordered destroyed.

1989 **October:** At the Festival of Silent Cinema in Pordenone, Italy, representatives of the Russian State Film Archive (Gosfil'mofond) showed retrospective of early Russian silents never before seen abroad; the audience's reaction was enthusiastic.

1990 Official abolition of censorship: henceforth, the state may not interfere in the production and distribution of films, except in cases of war propaganda, disclosure of state secrets, and pornography. **28 February:** Union of Filmmakers of Russia (Soiuz kinematografistov Rossii) founded. **5–7 June:** Sixth Congress of Soviet Filmmakers took place in Moscow; Davlat Khudonazarov elected new first secretary.

1991 **14 November:** As part of the abolition of all central Soviet administrative units, the Cinema Committee of the USSR was dissolved. Nikita Mikhalkov won the Golden Lion at the Venice Film Festival for *Close to Eden* (*Urga*).

1992 **5 February:** The Cinema Committee of the Russian Federation (Roskomkino) was established as independent government unit, with Armen Medvedev as chairman. **April:** The Central State Museum of Cinema founded in Moscow.

1993 *The Sun of the Sleepless* (Solntse nespiashchikh) by Teimuraz Babluani won Special Jury Prize of the Berlin Film Festival. **December:** Fedor Khitruk, Iurii Norshtein, Andrei Khrzhanovskii, and Eduard Nazarov founded independent studio school for animation directors, Shar (Shkola-studiia animatorov-rezhisserov). Among its graduates were Aleksei Demin, Aleksandr Petrov, and Oksana Cherkasova, whose films later won multiple prestigious national and international prizes.

1994 16–17 April: Second Congress of the Union of Filmmakers of Russia took place; Sergei Solov'ev elected first secretary. **Spring:** Nikita Mikhalkov's *Burnt by the Sun* (Utomlennye solntsem) won Grand Special Jury Prize of the Cannes Film Festival. Semen Aranovich's *The Year of the Dog* (God sobaki) won Special Jury Prize of the Berlin Film Festival.

1995 March: Nikita Mikhalkov's *Burnt by the Sun* (Utomlennye solntsem) won Academy Award for Best Foreign Picture.

1996 16 January: The government of Russia issued a decree to preserve the memory of filmmaker Andrei Tarkovskii. **19 March:** The Directors' Guild of Russia (Gil'diia kinorezhisserov Rossii) officially registered by Ministry of Justice. **17 July:** Russia's parliament, the State Duma, adopted law on the support of cinema by the Russian state; law signed by President Boris El'tsin on 22 August. **14 August:** The State Cinema Committee of the Russian Federation (Goskino Rossii) established, with Armen Medvedev as chairman.

1997 May: The government of Estonia established the *Estonian Film Foundation*, providing financial aid to film producers and spreading information about Estonian cinema. **21–23 December:** The Third Congress of the Union of Filmmakers of Russia took place in Moscow; Nikita Mikhalkov elected chairman of the Union of Russian Filmmakers. Pavel Chukhrai's *The Thief* (Vor) short-listed for the Academy Award for Best Foreign Picture.

1998 May: The Fourth Congress of Russian Filmmakers took place in Moscow. **22 May:** Aleksei German's *Khrustalev, the Car!* (Khrustalev, mashinu! 1998), the first Russian film invited to the Cannes Film Festival after four years, encounters a critical fiasco.

1999 November: The Union of Russian Filmmakers left the Confederation of Filmmakers' Unions (of the former Soviet republics). Aleksandr Golutva appointed chairman of the State Cinema Committee of the Russian Federation (Goskino Rossii).

2000 *The Old Man and the Sea* (Starik i more) by Aleksandr Petrov won Academy Award for Best Animated Film. **28 March:** The Shaken Aimanov Kazakhfilm Studio was merged with other film organizations into the state-run Shaken Aimanov Kazakhfilm National Company.

2001 **4 April:** Decree of the president of Russia "On the Reorganization of the Federal State Film Studios" and "On the Creation of the Stock Holding Russian Film Distribution" issued.

2002 **March:** Founding meeting of the National Academy of Film Arts and Research (Natsional'naia akademiia kinematograficheskikh iskusstv i nauk) in Moscow; Vladimir Naumov elected president. The academy decided to award annual prizes named "Golden Eagle" for the first time in January 2003.

2003 Ukraine's parliament, the Rada, adopted law, "On a Development Program for the National Film Industry in 2003–2007." **Fall:** *The Return* (Vozvrashchenie), Andrei Zviagintsev's directorial debut, won the Golden Lion of the Venice Film Festival. **December:** Turkmenfilm Studio merged with Turkmen television.

2007 **April:** Actor Vasilii Livanov who portrayed Sherlock Holmes in Igor' Maslennikov's popular miniseries (1979–1986) based on Arthur Conan Doyle's novels, awarded the Order of the British Empire; a monument to Sherlock Holmes and Dr. Watson, rendered by sculptor Aleksandr Orlov and bearing the likeness of Livanov and Vitalii Solomin (1941–2002), unveiled in front of the British embassy in Moscow. **August:** Nikita Mikhalkov won Special Jury Prize of the Venice Film Festival for *Twelve* (Dvenadtsat').

2008 **August:** "Film Train 2008" (*Kinopoezd-2008*) with Russian and foreign cinematographers went from Moscow to Vladivostok, celebrating Aleksandr Medvedkin's famous mobile newsreel studio (1932). **September:** Aleksei German Jr. won the Silver Lion for Best Director at the Venice Film Festival for *The Paper Soldier* (Bumazhnyi soldat); Alisher Khamidkhodiaev and Maksim Drozdov won prize for Best Camera Work.

Introduction

For Western viewers, Soviet cinema often presents an aesthetic challenge, and to fully enjoy it, one may need an "acquired taste." Highly politicized, propagandistic, or hopelessly sentimental, Soviet films can easily put off those accustomed to Hollywood or Western European films with their clearly distinguished genres and target audiences. *Kino*—as Jay Leyda, the American pioneer in researching the phenomenon of Soviet cinema, called his groundbreaking book—was originally based on a different, noncommercial vision of what moving pictures should be: they were meant to educate politically *and* entertain, or, from a negative viewpoint, brainwash and distract from the unsightly Soviet reality. As a result, the majority of Soviet films today may seem stale and preposterous in their pathos, boring for their lack of action, and disingenuous because of the primacy given to simplified political frameworks over human complexity.

However, there were times when Soviet films enthused and enamored millions all over the world: *Polikushka*, a 1919 Lev Tolstoi adaptation with a heartbreaking performance by Ivan Moskvin; the revolutionary rhapsodies of Sergei Eizenshtein and Vsevolod Pudovkin in the 1920s; the harshly realistic documentaries about common Soviet heroism in World War II; Mikhail Kalatozov's *The Cranes Are Flying*, which brought tears to Pablo Picasso's eyes; Iosif Kheifits's delicate adaptation of Anton Chekhov's *The Lady with a Lapdog* (1959) that baffled Ingmar Bergman and George Cukor; and Sergei Bondarchuk's monumental epic *War and Peace* (1962–1967), whose mere dimensions proved astounding to international professionals and laymen alike. In later years, Vladimir Men'shov's *Moscow Does Not Believe in Tears* (1979) united East and West in peaceful sentimentality, while Tengiz Abuladze's *Repentance* (1984–1987) and Vasilii Pichul's *Little Vera* (1988) demonstrated even to the last believer that

1

the "Soviet experiment" had morally exhausted itself. In the first post-Soviet decade, it seemed as if only the savvy Nikita Mikhalkov could stay in touch with Western tastes, but then came Andrei Zviagintsev's *The Return* (2003) and literally signaled a return of Russian cinema to world screens, albeit in art houses, while Timur Bekmambetov's *Night Watch* (2005) attracted flabbergasted Western crowds with its peculiar blend of common horror conventions and Russian mysticism.

Today, each of the national cultures that have emancipated themselves from the Soviet paradigm is facing the question of how to deal with the legacy of films made with the imprimatur of USSR. How much of that legacy can be a source of pride, how much is a source of embarrassment that better remains hidden in archives? The answer to this question is very different depending on whether one turns to Ukraine or Kazakhstan, Georgia or Belarus, Russia or Armenia. The supreme task of this historical dictionary is to help understand the achievements and shortcomings of Soviet cinema, its roots, and its offspring.

The periodization of film history is one of the most challenging and risky scholarly tasks. In the case of Russia and the Soviet Union, the political paradigm is, unsurprisingly, generally seen as dominant for the history of cinema. Thus, the period from 1896 to 1917 has often been termed "prerevolutionary," the first Soviet decade has been associated with the New Economic Policy (NEP, 1921–1928), followed by the "Stalin period" (1929–1953), the "Thaw," or "Khrushchev period" (1954–1964), the "Brezhnev years," or "stagnation period" (1965–mid-1980s), and the perestroika period (1985–1991). Given the film industry's fundamental dependence on political factors, such a periodization certainly makes sense. Still, it may also reduce artists and art to mere objects determined by political circumstances, postulating a mechanical causality that is refuted, or at least complicated, by countless facts. With this inevitable dilemma in mind, the following brief survey of Russian and Soviet film history is an attempt to outline major trends in the development of the art and the industry while pointing out individual achievements too.

BEGINNINGS (1896–1918)

What was to become *Soviet* cinema in the early 1920s started out at the very end of the 19th century in many ways similar to cinema in the

West: a commercially oriented, market-regulated, moderately censored form of entertainment with enormous mass appeal, shaped by egotistical directors, competitive producers, and narcissistic stars. Four months after the Lumière brothers' first film screening in Paris on 28 December 1895, the new attraction was shown in St. Petersburg, Moscow, and later in Nizhnii Novgorod at the national trade fair. These screenings entertained thousands, including the country's autocratic ruler, Tsar Nikolai II, as well as some of the leading critical minds such as Lev Tolstoi and Maksim Gor'kii. Russia's vast market was of interest to foreign companies whose branches and commission agencies distributed both projection equipment and films. For more than a decade, Russian viewers were served exclusively foreign fare. Newsreel cameramen working for Pathé Frères, Gaumont, and other companies traveled through Russia in search of exotic sites and sensational events—fires and famines, floods and festivities. The everyday life of Russian citizens was shown in *Picturesque Russia*, a series of five-minute documentaries. At the same time, in Georgia and Azerbaijan, Pathé and other companies established their branches as well.

In Russia, cinema became the subject of a cultural debate. While Nikolai II characterized it as "an empty, useless, and even pernicious distraction," writers such as Tolstoi and Leonid Andreev recognized its educational and cultural potential. After a decade of exposure to mostly non-Russian subject matter, a noticeable fatigue occurred, followed by increasing demands for native themes that conspicuously coincided with modest democratic beginnings in the political sphere after the tumultuous events of 1905–1906. The earliest Russian producers were genuine pioneers: Aleksandr Drankov and Aleksandr Khanzhonkov. The first Russian feature, the short *Sten'ka Razin* (Ponizovaia vol'nitsa) by Vladimir Romashkov, was produced by Drankov in 1908. A former photographer and inventive entrepreneur, never choosy in his methods of outsmarting competitors, Drankov in later years became a scapegoat for Russian film historians, who accused him of promoting shameless commercialism in cinema. The public image of Khanzhonkov, however, was that of a gentleman-producer whose ultimate goal it was to turn cinema into a respectable modern art. Indeed, by the early 1910s, Khanzhonkov's Moscow studio had become the heart of the national film industry. Moving pictures produced and distributed in the large Russian cities, and increasingly in the provinces as well, eventually became serious competitors for the established foreign companies.

Cinema's power of spreading political, especially patriotic values was demonstrated not just in the endless footage of royal life but also in feature films, beginning with Vasilii Goncharov and Khanzhonkov's *The Defense of Sevastopol* (Oborona Sevastopolia, 1911)—the world's first full-length moving picture. However, genuine quality pictures had to compete in movie theaters against low-brow thriller serials, often about bold criminals such as "Little Sonia, the Golden Hand" or "Anton Krechet," whose stars survived from sequel to sequel. The overall production output of Russian feature films grew exponentially, from 30 in 1910, to over 100 in 1912 and 330 in 1914.

A unique quality of early Russian cinema was its reliance on 19th-century classical literature. From the earliest days, Russian filmmakers adapted the works of Aleksandr Pushkin, Nikolai Gogol', Lev Tolstoi, Fedor Dostoevskii, Ivan Turgenev, and Anton Chekhov for the screen. At first, these were primitive illustrations made as quickly and as cheaply as possible, but already by 1915 and 1916 a number of artistically serious adaptations were released, including Vladimir Gardin's *Anna Karenina* and Iakov Protazanov's *Queen of Spades* (Pikovaia dama, 1916). They won the new, initially despised art of cinema respectability among bourgeois audiences and intellectual circles and to some extent contributed to mass education in the predominantly illiterate country. Three filmmakers of bourgeois Russian cinema developed their own distinct style. Evgenii Bauer is remembered as the master of psychologically refined melodramas such as *Tears* (Slezy, 1914) and *Silent Witnesses* (Nemye svideteli, 1914), set in elegantly designed and inventively lit decorations. Iakov Protazanov acquired a reputation as a careful interpreter of Russian and foreign literary masterpieces. Wladyslaw Starewicz amazed his viewers with stop-motion shorts such as *The Revenge of a Cinematographer* (Mest' kinematograficheskogo operatora, 1912), combining technical prowess and exceptional wit. Among the less original yet no less productive filmmakers were Petr Chardynin, Viacheslav Viskovskii, and Boris Chaikovskii.

Initially, Russian thespians treated cinema with contempt—the imperial theaters even prohibited their performers from working in motion pictures. The exception were the so-called People's Houses (*narodnye doma*), popular theaters in St. Petersburg and Moscow whose troupes were cast in countless films. Typical of the acting style in the mid-1910s was its almost somnambulistic slowness and often theatrical and bombastic hyperbole. The leading stars of bourgeois Russian cinema were Vera Kholodnaia, Ivan Mozzhukhin, Natal'ia Lisenko, Vladimir Maksimov, Vera Karalli, Vitol'd Polonskii, Ol'ga Preobrazhenskaia, Ivan Perestiani, Vera Orlova, Mikhail Chekhov, Ol'ga Baklanova, and Hamo Bek-Nazaryan (then known as Amo Bek-Nazarov). The non-Russian provinces of the tsarist empire were mostly supplied with Russian and Western European films and were rarely able to muster a film production of their own, despite some promising initiatives in Georgia and Azerbaijan. And yet, according to some sources, the first feature film made in the Russian Empire was not Russian but Ukrainian: *Kochubei in the Dungeon* (1907).

Between 1908 and 1919, about 2,000 feature films were produced in the Russian Empire, with the largest number appearing during World War I when the import of foreign films was restricted. About 280 of those films have survived. Soviet scholars who devoted monographs to "prerevolutionary Russian cinema," particularly Nikolai Lebedev and Semen Ginzburg, usually downplayed its artistic value. For decades, that legacy was so completely overshadowed and aesthetically negated by the Soviet avant-garde of the 1920s that it took half a century before scholars such as Yuri Tsivian and Rashit Iangirov rehabilitated it.

THE BIRTH OF SOVIET CINEMA (1918–1930)

As the Russian Empire was economically and psychologically exhausted by World War I and its ruling class delegitimized, the country's societal structures were shaken in February 1917 and completely shattered in the fall of that year. Initially, under the provisional government of Aleksandr Kerenskii, film censorship was abolished, enabling filmmakers to address formerly taboo subjects such as the immoral lifestyle of the Romanov court and its darling, Grigorii Rasputin. When on 7 November 1917 (15 October, old style), the Bolshevik wing of the Social Democratic Workers' Party removed the provisional government and usurped power in Petrograd and Moscow, most members of the film community fled from the ensuing unrest to the Crimean peninsula at the Black Sea, which was in the hands of the White Army, taking equipment and film stock with them. After a brief interlude, producers, directors, stars, and their entourages emigrated to France and Germany, where producer Iosif Ermol'ev and director Iakov Protazanov, among others, were able to achieve considerable commercial success. In Russia, the industrial basis of motion picture production and distribution lay in shambles. Studios in Moscow and Petrograd were deserted and looted, and only a few professionals decided to stay. Even when funds were available, film stock could not be imported because of a trade embargo imposed on the Bolshevik rulers by a Western alliance that also supported the White Army in the horrific 1918–1921 Civil War.

This period, named War Communism (*voennyi kommunizm*) in order to justify the Bolsheviks' drastic measures, displayed an utterly utilitarian approach to culture, assessing it solely by its political usefulness. In a huge country with more than 85 percent of the population illiterate, cinema seemed the medium best suited to spread the teachings of Marxism-Leninism. Vladimir Lenin formulated—recorded from a conversation with Commissar Anatolii Lunacharskii—his later canonized statement that "cinema is the most important of all arts for us Bolsheviks." The People's Commissariat of Education of the Russian Federation (Narkompros) was put in charge of a film department (*kinootdel*) and later of the so-called cinema committees in Petrograd (May 1918) and Moscow that nationalized movie theaters and studios and also produced newsreels. Lenin's signature under the decree "On the Transfer of the Photo and Film Trade and Industry under the Authority of the People's Commissariat of Education," issued on 27 August 1919, made the nationalization of what was left of the Russian film industry an indisputable fact.

Roughly a thousand film projectors had survived the unrest, far too small a number to service Russia's large regions. One solution was "film trains" equipped with projectors that screened newsreels and educational shorts for rural and provincial audiences, providing evidence of the beginning Communist construction. Also under the auspices of Narkompros, on 1 September 1919, a state film school (*goskinoshkola*) was founded in Moscow, the nucleus of what would become the All-Soviet State Film School, VGIK. Its director, Vladimir Gardin, managed to attract some of the remaining specialists, among them production designer Lev Kuleshov, who got a chance to practice his ideas about film-specific acting with a group of disciples that included Aleksandra Khokhlova, Vsevolod Pudovkin, Boris Barnet, Vladimir Fogel', Sergei Komarov, and Leonid Obolenskii. Other professionals who continued their careers under the Communist regime included director Boris Chaikovskii who opened his own film school, movie star and director Ol'ga Preobrazhenskaia, cameraman Iurii Zheliabuzhskii, and erstwhile decorator turned director Aleksandr Razumnyi. The predominant genre, apart from weekly newsreels, was the so-called *agitka*, a short with a simple plot that illustrated a political point in the most direct and effective way. Indeed, the first Soviet feature was an *agitka*, *The Condensation* (Uplotnenie, 1918), supported by Commissar Lunacharskii, who also wrote the screenplay (the director was Aleksandr Panteleev). Produced on a shoestring budget by the Petrograd film committee, it initiated a stream of a total of about 50 *agitki*. But the continuing lack of celluloid and funding kept the number of films low; among the few artistically worthy exceptions was Aleksandr Sanin's Tolstoi adaptation *Polikushka* (1919), which eventually became a worldwide hit.

On 19 December 1922, the State Film Organization (Goskino), which initially had the monopoly over the distribution of all films within the Russian Federation, was founded; it was renamed Sovkino in 1924. However, the era of the New Economic Policy (NEP, 1921–1928) also allowed for semicommercial forms of production such as the Mezhrabpomfilm Studio, a joint venture with the German company Prometheus. The number of feature films produced in the Russian Federation rose from 7 in 1921 to 52 in 1924. Most foreign films were reedited so as to conform to Soviet ideological norms; future directors such as Sergei Eizenshtein, Esfir' Shub, Grigorii Aleksandrov, and the Vasil'ev brothers learned the basics of editing from rearranging the films of D. W. Griffith, Abel Gance, and Fritz Lang.

Based on Lenin's suggestions, Soviet moviegoers were subjected to newsreels, propaganda films, and educational shorts (so-called culture films, *kul'turfil'my*), before being allowed to enjoy an entertaining feature. During those years, an increasingly intense struggle for the supremacy in Soviet cinema unfolded. The innovative—albeit theoretically diverse and sometimes mutually exclusive—artistic efforts of Eizenshtein (*Battleship Potemkin*/Bronenosets Potemkin, 1925), Dziga Vertov (*Forward, Soviet!*/Shagai, Soviet! 1926), Kuleshov (*By the Law*/Po zakonu, 1926), Pudovkin (*The Mother*/Mat', 1926), and Abram Room (*Bay of Death*/Bukhta smerti, 1926) were accompanied by debates of Communist critics fighting the perceived remnants of "degenerate" bourgeois cinema. Original theoretical concepts of the motion picture were developed by Kuleshov, who early on proclaimed montage to be the most film-specific element in cinema; Dziga Vertov, whose antifictional dogma was realized by his Cine-Eyes group (*kinoki*); and Eizenshtein, who coined the term "montage of attractions." In Petrograd, Grigorii Kozintsev and Leonid Trauberg's group FEKS (Factory of the Eccentric Actor), which counted Sergei Gerasimov, Ianina Zheimo, Sergei Iutkevich, and Elena Kuz'mina among its members, practiced a provocatively clownish, iconoclastic approach to theater and cinema, while the Film Experimental Workshop (KEM, kinoeksperimental'naia masterskaia) founded by Fridrikh Ermler, Eduard Ioganson, and Fedor Nikitin, followed a more realistic path.

The best silent pictures of the Soviet avant-garde astounded film audiences in Western Europe and the United States, making stars of Eizenshtein, Pudovkin, Vertov, and Room, enthusing both workers' audiences and leftist intellectuals, and often turning out more success-ful at international box offices than in their homeland. For a limited period in the 1920s, Bolshevik cultural priorities and avant-garde aesthetics coincided: for the latter, the traditional hierarchy of arts was reversed, so that the lowest ranking arts of circus and motion-pictures were proclaimed to be supreme—democratic, iconoclastic, antiemo-tional, and nonpsychological.

In 1924, the first Soviet workshop for drawn animation was founded; among its young masters were Mikhail Tsekhanovskii, Ivan Ivanov-Vano, and Aleksandr Ptushko. Esfir' Shub demonstrated the power of pure montage with her compilation film *The Fall of the Romanov Dynasty* (Padenie dinastii Romanovykh, 1927). Various principles of montage, formulated in the early 1920s, influenced filmmakers in the new Soviet republics. In Georgia, where Bolshevik power was established in 1921, Ivan Perestiani directed a hugely popular movie that mixed adventure, action, and Civil War lore, *The Little Red Devils* (Tsiteli eshmakunebi/ Krasnye d"iavoliata, 1923). Hamo Bek-Nazaryan, whose shared activi-ties in Georgia, Azerbaijan, and his native Armenia were typical of the multinational trend in Soviet cinema, made *Honor* (Namus/Chest', 1926) as a Georgian-Armenian coproduction. In Ukraine, Aleksandr Dovzhenko integrated national elements in montage-dominated cinema; his silent masterpieces, beginning with *Zvenigora* (Zvenyhora, 1928), were powerful proof that the form of revolutionary cinema did not have to be "internationalist"—that is, neutral in regards to national traditions and motifs. Indeed, the late 1920s were a period during which a number of artists made attempts to formulate a national identity with the help of the new art, among them the Georgians Nikoloz Shengelaia and Mikheil Chiaureli and the Ukrainians Dovzhenko and Ivan Kavaleridze.

While the New Economic Policy had tolerated a temporary coexistence of avant-garde cinema and commercially oriented films, the Communist Party conference on cinema in March 1928 ordered a reorientation. Directors such as Gardin and Viskovskii (the latter had tried his luck for some years in Central Asia), who had learned their craft in the 1910s and who after the 1917 revolution had given their exploitative melodramas a superficial pro-Bolshevik coating, were ousted from cinema altogether. Others, including Protazanov, who had returned from emigration in 1924, and Preobrazhenskaia, who scored a huge international hit with *Peasant Women of Riazan'* (Baby riazanskie, 1927), were able to better adjust to the circumstances and survived the first purging of Soviet cinema.

THE TRANSITION TO SOUND AND IMPLEMENTATION OF STALINIST VALUES (1931–1953)

By the late 1920s, it had become obvious that the days of silent cinema were numbered and that the USSR was not willing to buy the expensive U.S. or German sound film patents. Aleksandr Shorin in Leningrad, simultaneously with his Moscow-based competitor Pavel Tager, developed a system to record and reproduce sound on film. The "Shorinophone" (*shorinofon*) was used by Dziga Vertov for the feature-length documentary *Enthusiasm* (Entuziazm, aka *Symphony of Donbass*/Simfoniia Donbassa, 1930), which includes live recordings. Tager named his device "Tagephone" (Tagefon SGK-7); its first application was on a documentary, Abram Room's feature-length *The Plan of the Great Works* (Plan velikikh rabot, aka *Five-Year Plan*/Piatiletka, 1930), and the first Soviet sound feature film, Nikolai Ekk's *A Start in Life* (aka *Road to Life*/Putevka v zhizn'), released on 1 June 1931. But the implementation of sound film in the USSR proved a costly and slow process that was not completed until the end of the 1930s.

With the official endorsement of sound pictures such as *The Counterplan* (Vstrechnyi, 1932) by Sergei Iutkevich and Fridrikh Ermler in which dialogues are dominant and the camera work is kept deliberately static, the leading avant-garde filmmakers of the 1920s faced the need to determine how the artistic achievements of silent cinema could be upheld. After passionate debates that had started already in 1928, Eizenshtein now defined the silent montage cinema as "poetry" and the new trend in sound film as "prose"—a temporary compromise at best. The avant-garde also had to come to terms with a new cultural-political phenomenon: Socialist Realism. The primary purpose of the doctrine of Socialist Realism (*sotsrealizm*), developed and proclaimed in 1932–1934, was cultural unification, homogenization, and consolidation under Communist Party control. Neither entertainment for entertainment's sake nor avant-garde experimentation was tolerated any longer. Now, any novel, symphony, painting, and film had to comply with the strict standards of ideological commitment (*ideinost'*), Communist Party spirit (*partiinost'*), popular accessibility (*narodnost'*), and the prominent presence of at least one positive hero (*polozhitel'nyi geroi*). If any one of these criteria was missing, this could have grave consequences for the artist; indeed, numerous control mechanisms ensured that no writer, painter, composer, or filmmaker would ever forget them. The first film to comply with all criteria and thus be declared a template of Socialist Realism in cinema was *Chapaev* (1934), directed by Georgii and Sergei Vasil'ev (although unrelated, they henceforth were credited as "the Vasil'ev brothers"). Other Socialist-Realist template pictures of the 1930s were Ermler's *The Great Citizen* (Velikii grazhdanin, 1937–1939), Kozintsev and Trauberg's *Maxim Trilogy* (1934–1938), and Mikhail Romm's dilogy about Lenin (1937–1939).

In the 1930s, most capitals of the Soviet republics were supplied with their own film studio, from Ashgabat to Yerevan. With enormous investments, several of them managed to produce their first sound films: Dovzhenko's *Ivan* (1932) made at Ukrainfilm Studio (i.e., the predecessor to Dovzhenko Film Studio); Chiaureli's *The Last Masquerade* (Ukanaskneli maskaradi/Poslednii maskarad, 1934) at Gruziya-Film Studio; Bek-Nazaryan's *Pepo* (1935) at Armenfilm Studio; Aleksandr Usol'tsev's *The Oath* (Kliatva, 1936) at Uzbekfilm Studio; Viktor Turin's *The People of Baku* (Bakintsy, 1938) at Azerfilm (i.e., Azerbaijanfilm) Studio; and Nikolai Dostal''s *The Garden* (Sad, 1938) at Tadjikfilm Studio. However, with the exception of Georgia and Ukraine, these projects remained singular efforts; the main task of the national film studios was the production of newsreels and propaganda documentaries. Moreover, the Stalinist *nomenklatura* demanded an emphasis on "all-Soviet" values and an effective neutralization of national elements, which were always viewed with some degree of suspicion.

By the mid-1930s, Soviet citizens were prepared for war, not just by regular exercises on the use of gas masks but also by films illustrating the official doctrine on how the coming war would be conducted. Whether in Romm's *The Thirteen* (Trinadtsat', 1937), Efim Dzigan's *If Tomorrow Is War* (Esli zavtra voina, 1938), or Room's *Squadron No. 5* (Eskadril'ia No 5, 1939), the expected clashes were naïvely depicted as an adventure that could easily be won by Soviet troops. Other films infused viewers with a cozy, protected feeling. The peculiar charm of "lyrical comedies"—among them Aleksandrov's musicals *Jolly Fellows* (Veselye rebiata, 1934), *Circus* (Tsirk, 1936), and *Volga-Volga* (1938), Tat'iana Lukashevich's sensational hit *The Foundling* (Podkidysh, 1939), Konstantin Iudin's *A Girl with Personality* (Devushka s kharakterom, 1939), and Aleksandr Ivanovskii and Gerbert Rappaport's *Musical Story* (Muzykal'naia istoriia, 1940)—garnered immense popularity and contributed to an unobtrusive patriotism that made the Soviet homeland seem worth fighting for, despite the gruesome repressions against millions of Soviet citizens happening at the same time.

Still, when Nazi Germany attacked the Soviet Union at 4:00 A.M. on 22 June 1941, the country was ill prepared for the massive onslaught. Adolf Hitler's armies made fast headway, encircling Kiev, advancing toward Moscow within months, paralyzing Iosif Stalin's administration, and causing widespread confusion among the Soviet population. Film professionals were organized in special units and put under the command of army chiefs of staff, documenting the planning and carrying out of operations and battles. Documentary filmmakers such as Roman Karmen, Il'ia Kopalin, and Leonid Varlamov assembled full-length pictures describing large-scale operations, significant battles, and even the underground partisan struggle in the occupied territories. The newsreel production was centralized in Moscow, where the footage was edited. *The Destruction of the German Troops near Moscow* (Razgrom nemetskikh voisk pod Moskvoi, 1942) was released in the United States under the title *Moscow Strikes Back* and won an Academy Award for Best Documentary in 1943. Other important documentaries were *Leningrad in Struggle* (Leningrad v bor'be, 1942) by

Karmen and Efim Uchitel', and *Fascism Will Be Destroyed* (Fashizm budet razbit) by Esfir' Shub.

Immediately after the outbreak of the war, the production of short features began; from July to December 1941, they were put together in seven *War Film Almanacs* (Boevye kinosborniki)—temporary substitutes for full-length features whose production was logistically impossible (between February and August 1942, five more almanacs were produced). Mosfilm and Lenfilm, the largest Soviet studios, were evacuated to Alma-Ata (Almaty) in Kazakhstan and set up in a House of Culture under the name Central United Film Studio (Tsentral'naia ob"edinennaia kinostudiia). The Moscow Children's Film Studio (Soiuzdetfilm) was evacuated to Stalinabad in Tadjikistan, while the Kiev Film Studio settled in Ashgabat; other units worked in Tashkent, Tbilisi, Baku, and Yerevan. The evacuation was completed by the end of 1941. Under immense difficulties, the production of feature films began. Some of the leading Soviet directors—such as Ivan Pyr'ev (*Secretary of the District Party Committee*/Sekretar' raikoma, 1942), Iulii Raizman (*Mashen'ka*, 1942), Fridrikh Ermler (*She Defends the Motherland*/Ona zashchishchaet rodinu, 1943), Leonid Lukov (*Two Fighters*/Dva boitsa, 1943), Mark Donskoi (*The Rainbow*/Raduga, 1943), and Abram Room (*The Invasion*/Nashestvie, 1944)—managed to create masterpieces. However, a number of films were shelved by order of military censors, including Pudovkin's *Murderers Are on Their Way* (Ubiitsy vykhodiat na dorogu, 1942) and Sergei Iutkevich's *Schwejk Is Preparing for Battle* (Shveik gotovitsia k boiu, 1942).

Large-scale historical epics were intended as analogies to current events, predicting the victory of the Russian people and allied nations. Chiaureli made *Georgii Zaakadze* (1942–1943), about a 17th-century Georgian leader who defeated both the Turks and the Persians, while Bek-Nazaryan praised the strategic genius of 18th-century leader *David Bek* in his 1944 biopic. But in general, the feature films produced during the war emphasized the heroism of rank-and-file citizens, as well as the harmony within Soviet society, which was depicted like a family, protecting, trusting, and worth making sacrifices for.

The major studios returned to their respective hometowns in 1943–1944, after the Battle of Stalingrad had turned the tide of the war, and an end to the Nazi aggression was in sight. Major filmmakers—Raizman, Iutkevich, and Iosif Kheifits—were assigned to oversee the production of feature-length war documentaries. At the end of what became known as the Great Patriotic War (*Velikaia Otechestvennaia voina*), Stalin ordered a cinematic reconstruction of some major battles. Fridrikh Ermler was entrusted with *The Great Turning Point* (Velikii perelom, 1945), Ihor' Savchenko with *The Third Blow* (Tretii udar, 1948), Vladimir Petrov with *The Battle of Stalingrad* (Stalingradskaia bitva, 1949), while Chiaureli made *The Fall of Berlin* (aka *Battle of Berlin*/Padenie Berlina, 1949)—all of them lengthy, elephantine, and impersonal exercises in monumentalism in which the horrific suffering of the people received scarce attention. An exceptional achievement of the war years is Sergei Eizenshtein's *Ivan the Terrible* (Ivan Groznyi, 1943–1945). While its first part was conceived as the typical, Stalin cult-inspired secular hagiography, the second part shows the consequences of ruthless statism with a Shakespearean power unprecedented not just in Soviet but in world cinema.

The victory over Nazi Germany and the subsequent Cold War harshened the cultural atmosphere in the Soviet Union. A decree issued by the Central Committee of the Communist Party against the second part of Leonid Lukov's *A Great Life* (Bol'shaia zhizn') on 4 September 1946 was followed by aggressive attacks on Pudovkin's *Admiral Nakhimov*, Kozintsev and Trauberg's *Simple People* (Prostye liudi), and Eizenshtein's *Ivan the Terrible II*, all of which were shelved. In 1949, Ivan Bol'shakov, the USSR minister of cinema, publicly criticized filmmaker Leonid Trauberg as an example of "antipatriotic" and "cosmopolitan" attitudes in the Soviet film world; the underlying anti-Semitic nature of this campaign became clear from the list of names of those who were targeted. The number of films produced fell drastically; each new project had to pass through endless controls and supervisory boards consisting of scared dogmatics who found it safer to prohibit than to release. As a result, Dovzhenko needed years to complete *Michurin* (1949) and Kozintsev struggled with countless demands of minor and major changes on his *Belinskii* (1949); both were, sadly, rather stale biopics whose never-ending censorial problems brought their makers to the verge of nervous breakdowns and almost drove them out of cinema. Strangely, instead of new domestic films, the movie theaters were flooded with so-called lute films (*trofeinye fil'my*), for the most part apolitical musicals populated by Nazi stars such as Heinz Rühmann and Marika Rökk. Combined with Stalin cult pictures such as Chiaureli's

The Oath (Kliatva, 1946) and ultraparanoid Cold War propaganda like Romm's *Secret Mission* (Sekretnaia missiia, 1950), this made for a peculiar repertoire indeed. Gerasimov's partisan tragedy *The Young Guard* (Molodaia gvardiia, 1948), although first taken to task for its unflattering depiction of Soviet retreat at the beginning of the war, became one of the few films of lasting value.

In the studios of Georgia and Armenia, Belarus and Ukraine, Uzbekistan and Azerbaijan, film production was reduced to one or two films per year, mostly musicals in the spirit of Pyr'ev but with some national coloration or bombastic biopics about national leaders of the past with a blatant pro-Russian mission. The Baltic states, now transformed into "Soviet republics," were particular objects of cinematic indoctrination: experienced directors such as Raizman, Rappaport, Aleksandr Faintsimmer, and Vera Stroeva were assigned to the production of pro-Soviet features based on Lithuanian, Latvian, or Estonian subject matter.

All Soviet studios competed in producing films that concealed the harsh reality of the postwar years and praised Soviet life as prosperous and happy—Aleksandrov's *Spring* (Vesna, 1947), Pyr'ev's *The Tale of the Siberian Land* (aka *Symphony of Life*/Skazanie o zemle sibirskoi, 1946) and *Cossacks of the Kuban* (Kubanskie kazaki, 1950), Aleksandr Stolper's *Far from Moscow* (Daleko ot Moskvy, 1950), and Raizman's *Cavalier of the Golden Star* (aka *Dream of a Cossack*/Kavaler zolotoi zvezdy, 1950) are among the most infamous examples. By 1950, Soviet cinema had entered its most severe quantitative and qualitative crisis, with no end in sight.

THAW, STAGNATION, AND FINAL CRISIS (1954–1985)

The order to start the systematic "remaking" of Soviet film classics, only this time in color, is symptomatic of the absurdity of Soviet cultural politics during the late Stalin era that seemed no longer sustainable. Eventually, the Communist Party officially (and hypocritically) "demanded" the production of more films. Experienced directors such as Iosif Kheifits were allowed to provide their stories with recognizable fragments of social reality. Thus, *The Big Family* (Bol'shaia sem'ia, 1954) initiated a string of "private films" in which Soviet citizens act as individuals whose personal lives are no less important than their labor accomplishments, who fall unhappily in love and are taken advantage of by two-faced crooks—indeed, homegrown crooks, no longer the infamous "foreign saboteurs" of the 1930s. Marlen Khutsiev's *Springtime on Zarechnaia Street* (Vesna na Zarechnoi ulitse, 1956, codirected with Feliks Mironer) and *The Two Fedors* (Dva Fedora, 1958) conveyed as much harsh realism as warmth in human relations. A new pathos permeated the best Thaw pictures, as they came to be known, bringing back genuine drama and tragedy to screens from which they had been banned under the late 1940s slogan of "conflictlessness." Film acting regained emotional depth, replacing hollow rhetoric and grand gestures. The careers of the superstars of Stalinist cinema such as Marina Ladynina, Liubov' Orlova, Boris Andreev, Boris Chirkov, Nikolai Bogoliubov, Boris Livanov, Mikhail Zharov, and Mikheil Gelovani had passed their zenith. They were replaced by more authentic, down-to-earth performers: Aleksei Batalov, Nikolai Rybnikov, Mikhail Ul'ianov, Nonna Mordiukova, Vasilii Shukshin, and Viacheslav Tikhonov.

Finally, the Great Patriotic War could be shown as the gigantic trauma that it was; Lev Kulidzhanov and Iakov Segel''s *The House I Live In* (Dom, v kotorom ia zhivu, 1956), Mikhail Kalatozov's *The Cranes Are Flying* (Letiat zhuravli, 1957), Sergei Bondarchuk's *The Fate of a Man* (Sud'ba cheloveka, 1959), and Grigorii Chukhrai's *Ballad of a Soldier* (Ballada o soldate, 1959) moved audiences worldwide, revealing the human dimension of a nation's hardships that had been hidden behind the Iron Curtain for too long. Biting satire and carefree entertainment made a comeback, famously in El'dar Riazanov's *Carnival Night* (Karnaval'naia noch', 1956), although comedies remained the most suspiciously watched genre, as Leonid Gaidai and Leonid Bykov had to learn the hard way from their butchered debuts. High-caliber literary adaptations such as Samson Samsonov's *The Grasshopper* (Poprygun'ia, 1955), Iutkevich's *Othello* (1956), Pyr'ev's *The Idiot* (Idiot, 1956), Kozintsev's *Don Quijote* (1957), and Kheifits's *The Lady with a Lapdog* (Dama s sobachkoi, 1959) signaled a return of the Russian humanistic heritage, which had been ignored or falsified by Stalinist cinema.

In the Baltic republics, following a string of pseudonational implants, the late 1950s saw the emergence of a group of highly gifted native directors: in Lithuania, Vytautas Žalakevičius, Marijonas Giedrys, and Arūnas Žebriūnas; in Latvia, Leonids Leimanis and Aleksandrs

Leimanis; and in Estonia, Kaljo Kiisk and Arvo Kruusement. In Kazakhstan, the accomplished actor and theater director Shaken Aimanov laid the foundations for a national cinema, as did Bension Kimyagarov in Tadjikistan. These were modest, often timid, beginnings, but they marked an awakening of a national self-consciousness in cinema that had been suppressed for decades. The search for truth and for means of expressing it in new cinematic ways led to a heightened significance of the documentary. A number of shorts, no longer than 10 or 15 minutes and often devoted to subjects of national culture, brought fame to Kyrgyz filmmakers Bolotbek Shamshiev (*Manaschi*, 1965; *The Shepherd*/Chaban, 1967), and Tolomush Okeev (*These Are Horses*/Eto—loshadi, 1965), proving to be eye-openers not just at international festivals where they won prestigious prizes but to native audiences as well. In Georgia, Otar Ioseliani (*Molten Iron*/Tudzhi/Chugun, 1964) and Giorgi Shengelaia used keen observations of the documentary camera without verbal commentary in a similar fashion, shaping a new cultural self-consciousness and preparing a wave of innovative feature films in the late 1960s and early 1970s. In Lithuania and Estonia, too, feature film directors regularly switched to documentary filmmaking, which allowed a greater flexibility and a more immediate contact with everyday life. Russian veterans such as Ermler and Romm, who looked back at long careers marked both by artistic achievement and political opportunism, used the documentary genre as a way to take stock of the cause to which they had dedicated their lives. Thus, Romm's *Ordinary Fascism* (aka *Triumph over Violence*/Obyknovennyi fashizm, 1965) was in part an apt analysis of totalitarian brainwashing techniques.

The thematization and visualization of national traditions emerged in the 1960s on an unprecedented scale. Many films made in the studios of Georgia, Armenia, Kyrgyzstan, and Lithuania made headlines throughout the Soviet Union and internationally. Žalakevičius triumphed with the grim postwar drama *Nobody Wanted to Die* (Nekas nenorejo mirti/Nikto ne khotel umirat', 1965), while Žebriūnas impressed audiences with a poetic study of a child's psyche, *The Girl and the Echo* (Paskutinė atostogų diena/Devochka i ekho, 1964). Turkmen director Bulat Mansurov developed a daring visual style in *Quenching of Thirst* (Utolenie zhazhdy, 1966); Armenian-born Sergei Paradjanov initiated the rebirth of Ukrainian national cinema with *Shadows of Forgotten Ancestors* (Tini zabutykh predkiv/Teni zabytykh predkov,

1964), encouraging young colleagues such as Yury Il'enko, Leonid Osyka, and Ivan Mykolaichuk to follow along this path. In Moldova, Vadim Derbenev, Mikhail Kalik, Vasile Pascaru, and especially Emil Loteanu turned to tragic aspects of recent history, creating passionate pictures whose rhapsodic imagery was as important as their often gypsy-inspired music.

A prominent theme of the 1960s was the artist and the moral duty to pursue his mission. Such was the focus of Andrei Tarkovskii's *Andrei Rublev* (1966/1969), Giorgi Shengelaia's *Pirosmani* (1969), and Paradjanov's *The Color of Pomegranate* (Hran guyne/Tsvet granata, 1967), to name the most prominent. The individualism and metaphysical view of art in these pictures were perceived as challenges by ruling Communist doctrinaires who resisted their release. But the establishment of an elitist, art-house cinema—which the Socialist-Realist paradigm was supposed to prevent—had become an irreversible fact. Films that appealed to a relatively small audience of connoisseurs had acquired legitimacy, as had crowd-pleasing comedies and musicals such as Gaidai's *Prisoner of the Caucasus* (aka *Kidnapping Caucasian Style*/ Kavkazskaia plennitsa, 1966), Latvian director Aleksandrs Leimanis's *The Devil's Servants* (Vella kalpi/Slugi d"iavola), or Estonian Grigorii Kromanov's *The Last Relic* (Viimne relikviia/Posledniaia relikviia, 1969). Other newly emerged genres included thrillers (directed by Gerbert Rappaport, among others), fictionalized nature films (by Aleksandr Zguridi, Boris Dolin, and Vladimir Shneiderov), Civil War adventures (by Edmond Keosayan, Vladimir Motyl'), and war and postwar melodramas (by Evgenii Matveev, Aleksei Saltykov, Georgii Natanson, and numerous others). For all of these genres, the ideological framework was well known and enforced by a variety of control mechanisms but, first and foremost, by internalized censorship. Attempts to push the envelope were made by Aleksandr Askol'dov, Andrei Mikhalkov-Konchalovskii, and Gennadii Poloka; they all ended with the shelving or outright destruction of the films.

Two epics of unheard-of proportions were devoted to Russia's Great Patriotic wars, implicitly promoting the USSR's status as a superpower: the first, of 1812, in Bondarchuk's *War and Peace* (Voina i mir, 1962–1967), and the second, of 1941–1945, in Iurii Ozerov's *Liberation* (Osvobozhdenie, 1970–1972). Although Bondarchuk's Tolstoi adaptation is doubtless artistically superior to Ozerov's quasi-documentary reconstruction, both pictures share magnitude (seven and eight hours duration, respectively), indulgence in the large-scale re-creation of historical battles, and alternation between the "trench" (i.e., rank-and-file) and the "command hill" points of view.

The 1970s were characterized by voluntary adjustment to the societal status quo. The melancholic comedies of Riazanov, Georgii Daneliia, and Vladimir Men'shov signaled resignation and acceptance, while still professing to believe in ideal "Soviet values" of state justice, communal trust, and neighborly support. Some idealists were unwilling to buy into the system of convenient corruption; most prominently, screenwriter and director Gennadii Shpalikov eventually committed suicide, while Otar Ioseliani and Andrei Tarkovskii left the USSR. Ongoing harassment poisoned the careers of Sergei Paradjanov and, in a different yet no less pernicious fashion, actor and singer Vladimir Vysotskii. Conspicuously, the post-Thaw era, symbolized by its Communist leader Leonid Brezhnev and later called "stagnation," brought a reasonable number of imports to Soviet screens, exposing viewers to the delights of Robert Wise's *The Sound of Music* (1965) and the grim reality of Sydney Pollack's *They Shoot Horses, Don't They?* (1969), burlesque comedies starring Louis de Funès, and the lavish decadence of Luchino Visconti's *Conversation Piece* (1974). Missing from Soviet screens were Robert Bresson and Ingmar Bergman, Luis Buñuel and Francis Ford Coppola, Michelangelo Antonioni and Rainer Werner Fassbinder, and so many others of whom Soviet cinephiles knew but were never allowed to watch.

THE END OF SOVIET CINEMA AND BEYOND (1986–2008)

Among the arts, cinema in the Soviet Union was no less rigorously controlled than music or literature, and yet phenomena such as the provocatively apolitical, spiritual films of Andrei Tarkovskii and Sergei Paradjanov are hard to imagine in any other branch of Soviet culture. Although the release of these films was slowed down by political scheming and demagoguery, the Soviet Union, paradoxically, gained international recognition through these masterpieces, a factor that carried particular weight during the détente of the 1970s and 1980s. The cultural liberalization that followed the perestroika initiated by Mikhail Gorbachev and a team of like-minded reformers in the mid-1980s allowed Soviet film artists a greater degree of creative freedom while continuing the generous state funding of the country's three dozen studios. The Fifth Congress of Soviet Filmmakers in May 1986 exposed and largely removed the corrupt film elite—especially long-term "leaders" such as Kulidzhanov, Bondarchuk, and Stanislav Rostotskii—and established a model that was open to artistic experiments and individual approaches. However, the healthy political reform impulses soon generated a systemic destabilization that at some point in the late 1980s proved irreversible. In cinema, the straightjacket of Goskino control was taken off, but with it went the centralized distribution, the organized export and import of films, and finally state funding itself, which was cut to a fraction. At first, though, the weakening and ultimate removal of censorial oversight allowed for an unprecedented productivity, with 300 to 500 full-length feature films churned out annually between 1988 and 1991.

But with the privatization of film production and distribution, and the enormous waves of American movies flooding the film and video market, this productivity soon came to an end. In Russia, the number of feature films produced annually dropped to about 40 by the mid-1990s; sadly, none of them regained their costs at the box office. The majority of Russian feature films were still state funded, especially quality products intended for prestigious festivals, but in much smaller numbers than before. Among the few survivors of this crisis were the entrepreneurial Nikita Mikhalkov and his protégés, Vladimir Khotinenko and Sergei Solov'ev, as well as Karen Shakhnazarov and Vladimir Men'shov. Of the established Soviet masters, Riazanov and Daneliia still managed to direct a film every few years, whereas other influential directors such as Ozerov, Rostotskii, and Kulidzhanov withdrew completely from filmmaking. At the same time, the great individualist of Russian cinema Aleksandr Sokurov, harassed throughout the 1980s, saw an astounding raise to world fame in the 1990s, albeit limited to art-house cinemas.

The newly independent republics surely had other problems on their mind than the maintenance of a steady film production. As a result of political turmoil and economic crises, the once blooming studios of Minsk and Kiev, Tbilisi and Yerevan, Almaty and Baku stood empty for most of the year, with catastrophically aging equipment and unemployed, impoverished film professionals. Of course, some differentiation is still necessary: while Moldova did not release one feature film in the mid-1990s, Kazakhstan saw the emergence of a New Wave, in part funded by French producers, that raised eyebrows at international festivals. Idiosyncratic Ukrainian filmmaker Kira Muratova has enjoyed continuous funding and international festival success throughout the post-Soviet years. Apparently, the cinemas of the former Soviet republics fare best when dealing in coproductions with Western and/or Russian partners.

The revival of Russian cinema began, paradoxically, with television miniseries. As if their appetite for Western fare had been overindulged, in the late 1990s, post-Soviet viewers were craving domestic films featuring both new stars such as Vladimir Mashkov and Evgenii Mironov and some familiar faces of Soviet cinema such as Inna Churikova, Armen Dzhigarkhanyan, and Oleg Basilashvili. A phenomenon such as Vladimir Bortko's masterful adaptation of Fedor Dostoevskii's *The Idiot* (2003), a critically acclaimed miniseries, demonstrates how close television and cinema had become: Bortko himself started his career as a film director, and most of his stars are accomplished film actors as well. Russia's economic rebirth in the new millennium led to a further strengthening of the film industry, an increasing professionalization, and a successful specialization in genres that in the early 1990s had just yielded embarrassing imitations of Western models: thrillers and horror films with a touch of Russian mysticism. The spirit of nationalist self-consciousness and self-confidence infused into many movies reflects the Russian elite's new sense of legitimacy, although one should not neglect the unmistakable irony that subverts the patriotic messages in the pictures of Aleksei Balabanov and others of his generation. The varying degrees of continuity and discontinuity between pre-Soviet, Soviet, and post-Soviet cinema remain to be analyzed by the ever-increasing numbers of scholars in this field.

The Dictionary

– A –

ABASHIDZE, DAVID (DODO) [Russian sources list the patronymic Ivanovich] (b. 1 May 1924, Tbilisi–d. 26 January 1990, Tbilisi). Georgian actor and director. Abashidze studied at the Shota Rustaveli Theater Institute in Tbilisi, graduating in 1949. He then joined the troupe of the Rustaveli Theater but after a few years dedicated himself fully to cinema.

Abashidze's film debut was the role of Bichiko in **Siko Dolidze**'s touching **comedy** *The Dragonfly* (Chrichina/Strekoza, 1954, from Nikoloz Baratashvili's *Marine*), which became a box-office hit throughout the USSR. Over the following three decades, the actor worked with all leading directors of **Georgian cinema** and excelled in a variety of genres ranging from historical adventure to contemporary drama and musical comedy. **Tengiz Abuladze** and **Revaz Chkheidze** cast him in their successful joint debut *Magdana's Donkey* (Magdanas Lurja/Lurdzha Magdany, 1955), **Otar Ioseliani** in *Fall of the Leaves* (Giorgobistve/Listopad, 1966), **Eldar Shengelaia** in *An Unusual Exhibition* (Arakhveulebrivi gamopena/Neobyknovennaia vystavka, 1968), and **Georgii Daneliia** in *Don't Grieve* (Ar daidardo/Ne goriui! 1969). Another remarkable achievement was the part of the likeable shepherd Sosana who stubbornly resists the assault of urban modernization in *The Grand Green Valley* (Didi mtsvane veli/Bol'shaia zelenaia dolina, 1968). The many facets of Abashidze's talent enabled him to equally succeed in quality pictures such as **Giorgi Shengelaia**'s masterpiece *Pirosmani* (1969) where he played the painter's friend, Shavua, as well as in solid entertainment, for example, the popular soccer comedy *The First Swallow* (Pirveli mertskhali/Pervaia lastochka, 1975).

The crowning achievement of Abashidze's career was the codirection of two outstanding pictures with **Sergei Paradjanov**: *Legend of the Surami Fortress* (Ambavi suramis tsikhitsa/Legenda o Suramskoi kreposti, 1984) and *Ashik Kerib* (Ashugi Quaribi, 1988), artfully blending mythological motifs with astounding visual inventiveness. In these pictures Abashidze also played important parts, adding an element of enigmatic impenetrability to his usual aura of melancholic manliness, generosity, and elegance.

Abashidze, who joined the Communist Party in 1960, was named People's Artist of Georgia in 1967. After his passing, a Tbilisi street was named in his honor.

Other films: *Matsi Kvitia* (aka *He Did Not Mean to Kill*/On ubivat' ne khotel, 1966); *Light in Our Windows* (Sinatle chvens panjrebshi/Svet v nashikh oknakh, 1969); *The Siberian Grandfather* (Tsimbireli papa/Sibirskii dedushka, 1973); *The Top* (Mtservali/Vershina, 1976); *Roots* (Pesvebi/Korni, 1987).

ABBASOV, SHUKHRAT [Russian sources list the patronymic Salikhovich] (b. 16 January 1931, Kokanda, Ferghana). Uzbek director and screenwriter. Abbasov initially studied medicine at the Tashkent Medical College, graduating in 1949. He then enrolled in the Department of Directing of the Aleksandr Ostrovskii Theater Institute in Tashkent, graduating in 1954, and in **Mosfilm Studio**'s Supreme Directors Courses, which he completed in 1958.

Abbasov's diploma film was the short *The Filipino and the Drunkard* (Filippinets i p'ianyi, 1958), adapted from a story by William Saroyan. His first full-length feature, the **comedy** *The Entire Makhalia Is Talking about This* (Ob etom govorit vsia makhallia, 1961), was shot at **Uzbekfilm Studio**. It describes the tensions between the younger and older generations in a realistic, recognizable manner and became a hit with viewers and critics, who praised its wit and authentic everyday life details. *You Are Not an Orphan* (Ty ne sirota, 1963) was hailed as a new page in the history of **Uzbek cinema**. Avoiding sentimentality, the film tells the true story of a couple who adopted and raised fourteen orphaned children of different nationalities during the Great Patriotic War.

Abbasov's deliberately **documentary**-like style had an impact on other Uzbek directors of the 1960s. *Tashkent Is a City of Bread* (Tashkent—gorod khlebnyi, 1968), from a semifictional novel by Aleksandr Neverov (1886–1923) that **Andrei Mikhalkov-Konchalovskii** adapted for the screen, gave a believable picture of the hardships of War Communism (*voennyi kommunizm*). Set in 1921, it tells about two peasant boys who are escaping the starved Russian countryside, hoping to find food in Central Asia. Abbasov then helmed the large-scale, two part biopic *Abu-Raikhan Beruni* (1975), produced on the occasion of the 1,000th anniversary of the medieval thinker, and *Fiery Paths* (Ognennye dorogi, 1977–1985), a prestige television miniseries about the life of Uzbek author Hamza Hakim-zada (1889–1929).

Abbasov was named People's Artist of the USSR in 1981.

Other films: *The Sun within You* (Solntse v tebe, aka Prozrenie (1966); *Love Drama* (Drama liubvi, 1972); *The Little Man in the Great War* (Malen'kii chelovek v bol'shoi voine, 1989).

ABDRASHITOV, VADIM IUSUPOVICH (b. 19 January 1945, Khar'kiv [Khar'kov]). Russian director and screenwriter. Born into the family of an officer, Abdrashitov's childhood was marked by numerous relocations across the Soviet Union. An early interest in technology and the hard sciences determined his educational choices: in Alma-Ata he enrolled in a professional school for railway mechanics, and in Moscow in the Institute for Physics and Technology, from which he graduated in 1967. Later, at the Mendeleev Institute of Chemistry and Technology, Abdrashitov discovered his passion for cinema in the institute's amateur film studio. While working as an engineer, he made several failed attempts to enroll in the Soviet State Film School **VGIK**. He finally was admitted in 1970, first studying with **Mikhail Romm** and, after Romm's passing, with **Lev Kulidzhanov**, graduating in 1974.

Abdrashitov's diploma film, the satirical short feature *Stop Potapov* (Ostanovite Potapova, 1974), defined the general direction of his work: analytical explorations of contemporary morals, with increasingly complex, subversive conclusions. *A Statement for the Defense* (Slovo dlia zashchity, 1977), Abdrashitov's first full-length feature, is a court drama about an attorney and her female defendant who, although of similar age, fail to comprehend each other. To a large extent, the film's considerable box-office success was due to Aleksandr Mindadze's antistereotypical script that marked the beginning of a fruitful collaboration with Abdrashitov for years to come. In *The Turn* (Povorot, 1978), the stability of a family is threatened by an accident; in *Fox Hunt* (Okhota na lis, 1980), an attack of juvenile criminals on a worker makes him conscious of his responsibility for others (Abdrashitov was suspended from completing the controversial picture; its planned ending, in which the erstwhile victim beats up his former attacker, was deleted). *The Train Stopped* (Ostanovilsia poezd, 1982), on the surface a critique of negligence and incompetence in the Soviet railway system, sheds doubts on the drastic methods employed by an authoritarian investigator.

The central characters in Abdrashitov's films often undergo a process of intense self-exploration that forces them to challenge the societal status quo. Thus, in *Parade of Planets* (Parad planet, 1985), a group of men in their 40s are drafted for a military exercise that gives them a week to revise their lives, with devastating results. All of Abdrashitov's and Mindadze's stories feature disquieting plots with mysterious elements and were particularly valued by intellectual viewers. *Plumbum, or a Dangerous Game* (Pliumbum, ili opasnaia igra, 1986), loosely based on the 1930s Pavlik Morozov case in which a brainwashed boy informed authorities on his own family, became part of the perestroika revision—and ultimate rejection—of fundamental Soviet values. Focusing on an intelligent 16-year-old who offers the Soviet militia his services as an undercover agent, the film demonstrates the danger of self-righteousness and moral dogmatism.

Abdrashitov, who never made a secret of his skeptical attitude toward the naïve pathos dominating perestroika and glasnost discourses, transcended simplistic ideological patterns in *The Servant* (Sluga, 1989), showcasing the persistence of internalized slavedom. *Armavir* (1991), a thoughtful parable about rescue efforts after the drowning of a vessel, warns of blind enthusiasm for the vanishing of the old ways of life. Along similar parabolic lines, *Piece for a Passenger* (P'esa dlia passazhira, 1995) develops the theme of guilt and conscience in a father-daughter relationship, while *The Dancer's Time* (Vremia tantsora, 1997) is a witty, sarcastic reflection on Russia's troubles in the Caucasus. *Magnet Storms* (Magnitnye buri, 2003) makes an impressive attempt to historicize the reforms of the late 1980s and their disastrous effects on a Ural industrial city. As in all his films, Abdrashitov deliberately avoids graphic violence, instead opting for stylized choreography while disclosing the misery of provincial life with its gangs, prostitution, and pseudodemocratization in an often surrealist fashion.

Typical of Abdrashitov's films of the Soviet period is their persistent moral ambiguity and psychological penetration, reflecting society's growing unease about itself (albeit largely unadmitted and unconscious). In post-Soviet years, the atmosphere in Abdrashitov's pictures turned even darker, slowly luring the viewer into a disturbing, nightmarish maze, with all orientation being lost at the end. Abdrashitov is a paradoxicalist who has carved out a unique position for himself in Russian cinema, avoiding commercial entrapment as much as political opportunism of whatever coloration. The enigmatic atmosphere of his films, with their unexpected and sometimes logic-defying plot turns, can prove both funny and engaging but also irritating. Abdrashitov is at his best when plot and cinematic means generate subversiveness, offering unexpected insights in an otherwise opaque reality.

Although Abdrashitov has served as secretary of the Soviet (later Russian) Filmmakers' Union since 1986 and as a member of its board from 1989 to 1997, he was able to maintain an enviable artistic productivity throughout the political turbulences that deeply affected Russia's film industry. Several of his films won prizes at national and international festivals; he has a particularly strong following in Italy. In 1987, Abdrashitov was named Merited Artist of the RSFSR, and in 1992, People's Artist of Russia. Since 1991, Abdrashitov has been the artistic director of Ark-Film company, which coproduces his films.

ABRAMYAN [Abrahamyan], **KHOREN** [Russian sources also list the patronymic Babkenovich] (b. 1 April 1930, Yerevan–d. 9 December 2004, Yerevan). Armenian actor and director. Abramyan studied at the Yerevan Institute of Theater and Fine Arts, graduating in 1951. Upon graduation he joined the troupe of the Sundukyan Academic Theater in Yerevan; in 1980, he was appointed its executive director.

As a student, Abramyan played several small parts in movies, including **Hamo Bek-Nazaryan**'s kolkhoz musical *The Girl from Ararat Valley* (Araratyan dashti aghchike/Devushka s Araratskoi doliny, 1949), as well as in Russian productions such as **Aleksandr Rou**'s **children's film** *The Secret of the Mountain Lake* (Taina gornogo ozera, 1954), **Mikhail Kalatozov**'s drama about the cultivation of untilled ("virgin") soil in the steppes of Kazakhstan *The First Echelon* (Pervyi eshelon, 1956), and **Aleksandr Zarkhi**'s industrial construction tale *The Height* (Vysota, 1957). More significant roles included Arsen in *Song of the First Love* (Arajin siro yerge/Pesnia pervoi liubvi, 1958) and Armen in Grigory Melik-Avakyan's psychological drama *The Heart of a Mother* (Mor sirte/Serdtse materi, 1958).

Abramyan rose to stardom with his performance as Gevork in the Civil War drama *The Brothers Saroyan* (Saroyan yeghbayrnere/Brat'ia Saroiany, 1968), which he also codirected, and as the shepherd Pavle in **Henrik Malyan**'s *We and Our Mountains* (Menq enq, mer sarere/My i nashi gory, 1970) from Hrant Matevosyan's well-known novel. He played the lead, the compassionate archivist Armen Abramyan, in **Frunze Dovlatyan**'s *A Chronicle of Yerevan Days* (Yerevanyan oreri khronikan/Khronika erevanskih dnei, 1974). A leading actor of **Armenian cinema** in the 1970s, Abramyan also portrayed historical characters, among them the Bolshevik administrator Aleksandr Miasnikyan in Dovlatyan's *The Birth* (Yerkunq/Rozhdenie, 1978) and Ter-Avetis in **Edmond Keosayan**'s 18th-century epic *The Star of Hope* (Huso astgh/Zvezda nadezhdy, 1979). A psychologically complex character study is the role of Sisakyan in the drama of terminal illness *Live Long* (Apretseq yerkar/Zhivite dolgo, 1980). Abramyan's artistic profile comprised roles in adventures as well as contemporary social drama, **comedy**, and thriller.

Abramyan was honored with the title People's Artist of the USSR in 1980.

Other films: *The Bride-Show* (Pesates/Smotriny, 1954); *Rings of Glory* (Parqi oghakner/Kol'tsa slavy, 1962); *Echoes of the Past* (Antsyali ardzaganqnere/Otzvuki proshlogo, 1971); *As Long as We Are Alive* (Kani der aprum enk/Poka zhivem, 1986); *The Breath* (Dykhanie, 1989).

ABULADZE, TENGIZ [Russian sources list the patronymic Evgen'evich] (b. 31 January 1924, Kutaisi–d. 6 March 1994, Tbilisi). Georgian director and screenwriter. Abuladze studied at the Shota Rustaveli Theater Institute in Tbilisi in 1943–1946 and at the Soviet State Film School **VGIK** with **Lev Kuleshov, Aleksandra**

Khokhlova, **Sergei Iutkevich**, and **Mikhail Romm**, graduating in 1953. At **Gruziya-Film Studio** he began his career with **documentaries** on cultural subjects.

Abuladze's feature debut, the short *Magdana's Donkey* (Magdanas Lurja/Lurdzha Magdany, 1955, codirected with **Revaz Chkheidze**), a 19th-century melodrama depicting grave social injustice, won immediate international recognition. His first full-length feature, the contemporary family melodrama *Somebody Else's Children* (Skhvisi shvilebi/Chuzhie deti, 1958), shot in a neorealist style, juxtaposes the indifference of a biological father toward his children to their stepmother's affection. The successful **comedy** *Me, Grandmother, Iliko, and Illarion* (Me, bebia, Iliko da Ilarioni/Ia, babushka, Iliko i Illarion, 1963, from Nodar Dumbadze's novella) about a rural community in the Great Patriotic War, made a lasting impression on viewers throughout the Soviet Union and, with its unmistakable national flavor and blending of popular humor with sudden tragic turns, put the director's name on the country's cultural map.

Abuladze moved to a new level of virtuosity in *The Plea* (Vedreba/Mol'ba, 1967), a complex black-and-white drama about two mountain villages whose century-old animosity proves beyond reconciliation. Georgia as a historical-cultural space appears not in exotic bloom but mysterious and tragically opaque; the ascetic imagery conveys an air of mourning and hopelessness. The film's majestic, gloomy vision, the medieval poetic text read off camera, and the slow narrative pace revealed a degree of uncompromising artistry and deliberate inaccessibility that astonished intellectuals both in Georgia and Russia and is comparable to **Andrei Tarkovskii**'s and **Sergei Paradjanov**'s aesthetic and philosophical searches during that period.

The carefree contemporary comedy *A Necklace for My Beloved* (Samkauli satrposatris/Ozherel'e dlia moei liubimoi, 1971), once again set in a rural milieu and intended perhaps as a light counterpoint to *The Plea*, neither fully justified the high expectations of Abuladze's cinephile admirers nor pleased popular tastes. However, the director's following picture, *The Wishing Tree* (Natris khe/Drevo zhelanii, 1977), turned into a veritable cinematic sensation. This historical romance of a love destroyed by societal interference is arguably the most serene in Abuladze's entire oeuvre. Despite its tragic content, *The Wishing Tree* is dominated by visual harmony, beauty, and a subtle, quasi-metaphysical optimism. It became a sleeper hit, especially among Moscow cinephiles.

The crowning achievement of Abuladze's career was the anti-Stalinist parable **Repentance** (Monanieba/Pokaianie, 1984). Released three years after its completion, and the subject of a political battle among Communist Party officials, the film's title itself became a code word for the attempted self-liberation of Soviet society from Stalinist patriarchy. Openly allegorical and intentionally vague in its political concept, *Repentance* aims to reveal the very essence of totalitarianism. Thus its main character, Varlam Avaridze, mayor of a small Georgian town, resembles Lavrentii Beriia, Adolf Hitler, and Benito Mussolini alike. But the film, although touted as *the* cinematic testimonial of perestroika and released to great acclaim worldwide, frustrated unprepared viewers with its enigmatic form and complex symbolism. The surrealist elements proved an interpretive challenge, and the alternation between the grotesque and the lofty made it unfit for simplistic didactic usage.

Ultimately, Abuladze stood for the humanistic cleansing and reformation of Soviet society, not its destruction. As a result, the outbreak of nationalism and extremism in post-Soviet Georgia could only shock this intellectual aristocrat; it is certainly telling that he did not complete another project in the decade before his passing. (According to some accounts, he worked for years on an adaptation of Lev Tolstoi's *Hadzhi Murat*.) In the course of his career, Abuladze experimented with a multitude of styles; his films betray a variety of powerful national and international influences. This sometimes baffling stylistic heterogeneity corresponds to the unusually long intervals between Abuladze's films that were not always caused by censorship quarrels but by the filmmaker's own high standards for inspiration and exploration of uncharted territory. The one element common to Abuladze's entire oeuvre is his consistently harsh criticism of patriarchal structures that destroy love, human decency, and the provincial idylls where most of his stories take place.

Abuladze's self-confident individualism was protected by the predominantly benevolent cultural atmosphere in his native Georgia, indeed, by the country's age-old respect for the arts and cultural traditions—one of the vital factors that made the emergence of a "poetic film miracle" in **Georgian cinema** possible in the first place. Abuladze's pictures were milestones in the development of a self-conscious Georgian national cinema, demonstratively independent in their narrative principles albeit filled with symbols and subtle allusions that are at times hard to grasp for non-Georgians.

Abuladze joined the Communist Party in 1978; he was named People's Artist of the Georgian SSR in 1968 and People's Artist of the USSR in 1980. He taught at the Shota Rustaveli Theater Institute in Tbilisi from 1974. His daughter-in-law, Nana Janelidze, author of the script for *Repentance*, is also a filmmaker.

Other films: *Our Palace* (Chveni sasakhle/Nash dvorets, 1953, doc., codirected with Chkheidze); *The Svansky Sketches* (Svanur-Tushuri chanakhatebi, 1965, doc.).

ADOMAITIS, REGIMANTAS (b. 31 January 1937, Šiauliai). Lithuanian actor. Adomaitis initially studied physics (1954–1959), then switched to acting, graduating from Vilnius Conservatory in 1962. He belonged to the troupe of Kapsukas Theater in 1962–1963, of Kaunas Drama Theater in 1963–1967, and, since 1967, has worked at the National Academic Theater of Lithuania in Vilnius.

With the role of Donatas in **Vytautas Žalakevičius**'s postwar drama **Nobody Wanted to Die** (Niekas nenorejo mirti/Nikto ne khotel umirat', 1965), Adomaitis demonstrated an extraordinary psychological intensity that soon made him one of the best-known and continually employed Lithuanian film actors who has worked successfully both at home and abroad to this day. Predominantly cast in historical films and political thrillers, Adomaitis has portrayed virile, complex, impulsive, and strong yet also torn characters whose emotions take them to extremes. Conspicuously, Žalakevičius cast him in roles of Latin American revolutionaries in his propagandistic—and visually effective—thrillers *That Sweet Word: Liberty!* (Eto sladkoe slovo—svoboda, 1973) and *Centaurs* (Kentaurai/Kentavry, 1978). Among Adomaitis's most memorable performances are Edmund in **Grigorii Kozintsev**'s Shakespeare adaptation *King Lear* (Korol' Lir, 1971), the young lover Girdvainis in **Arūnas Žebriūnas**'s musical *The Devil's Bride* (Velnio nuotaka/Chertova nevesta, 1972), and the title role in East German Günter Reisch's controversial *Wolz—Life and Illusions of a German Anarchist* (Wolz—Leben und Verklärung eines deutschen Anarchisten, 1974). Adomaitis, one of the all-time stars of **Lithuanian cinema**, has also many television roles to his credit, among them in Žebriūnas's successful adaptation of Irwin Shaw's *Rich Man, Poor Man* (Turtuolis vargšas/Bogach, bedniak, 1982).

Adomaitis was awarded the title People's Artist of the USSR in 1985.

Other films: *The Fiancée* (Die Verlobte, 1980, East Germany); *It's Hard to Be a God* (Trudno byt' bogom/Es ist nicht leicht, ein Gott zu sein, 1987); *A Man for a Young Girl* (Muzhchina dlia molodoi devushki, 1996); *The Amphibian Man* (Chelovek-amfibiia, 2005); *Iskyss* (2008, Norway).

AGADZHANOVA-SHUTKO, NINA (NUNE) FERDINANDO-VNA (b. 8 November 1889, Ekaterinodar–d. 14 December 1974, Moscow). Russian screenwriter. Born into the family of a merchant, Agadzhanva, who joined the Bolshevik Party in 1907, studied history and philology at the Pedagogical College in Ekaterinodar. She then started a career as a revolutionary activist in Voronezh, Moscow, and St. Petersburg, often operating illegally. Agadzhanova was sentenced to jail terms five times and was exiled twice. She played a leading role in the 1917 February and October Revolutions. In 1921–1922, she was on the staff of the Soviet embassy in Prague.

In the early 1920s, Agadzhanova developed an interest in cinema, perhaps stimulated by her husband, Communist cultural functionary Kirill (Mikhail) Shutko (1884–1941), who promoted her career. The first picture made from her script was *In the Whites' Rear* (V tylu u belykh, 1925), directed by **Boris Chaikovskii** and Ol'ga Rakhmanova; it reflects the author's own experiences of 1918–1919 when she was on a propaganda mission among White Army troops in Novorossiisk. *The Year 1905*, written for the 20th anniversary of the 1905 revolutionary unrest, was entrusted to budding director **Sergei Eizenshtein** who, primarily due to time constraints, turned a relatively brief episode about the battleship *Kniaz' Potemkin Tavricheskii* (*Prince Potemkin of Tauris*) into the groundbreaking **Battleship Potemkin** (1925). Agadzhanova-Shutko's fame mainly rests on this one work, although she disagreed with certain liberties taken by Eizenshtein. In hindsight, despite Eizenshtein's continued praise for the screenwriter, it is obvious that Agadzhanova-Shutko primarily provided the raw material that inspired the filmmaker's unique vision. Another piece of the initially extensive *1905* script was turned into the short *Krasnaia presnia* (1926), shot in record time by four directors—among them **Abram Room**—but far from the originality of Eizenshtein's picture.

Agadzhanova-Shutko cowrote and codirected with **Lev Kuleshov** *Two-Buldi-Two* (Dva-Bul'di-dva, 1929), a Civil War adventure about a clown and his son who participate in the revolutionary struggle. Her best-remembered effort in sound cinema is the screenplay for **Vsevolod Pudovkin**'s innovative yet ultimately hapless drama *The Deserter* (Dezertir, 1933) about a German docker who dreams of staying in the Soviet Union where Communism is already becoming reality. Another project with Pudovkin, *The Intervention* (Interventsiia), did not make it beyond the planning stage.

For a number of years, Agadzhanova-Shutko was on the staff of **Mezhrabpomfilm Studio** as a scriptwriting consultant. From 1945 to 1952, she taught screenwriting at the Soviet State Film School **VGIK** in Moscow.

Other films: *The Sailor Ivan Gallai* (Matros Ivan Gallai, 1929).

AGITKA [plural *agitki*] or *agitfil'm* (agit-film). A genre of political shorts with a fictitious or semifictitious plot; a related variety are "film-posters" (*fil'm-plakaty*), shorter in duration and even more reduced in their message.

Agitki are characterized by their openly didactic approach and brevity, consisting only of a few scenes, simplified argumentation, and direct appeals to the audience. Often their titles were slogans or calls to action: *Red Army Soldier, Who Is Your Enemy?* (Krasnoarmeets, kto tvoi vrag?), *To the Front!* (Na front!), *For the Red Banner* (Za krasnoe znamia), or *Toward the Bright Kingdom of the Third International* (K svetlomu tsarstvu III Internatsionala).

The simplicity of *agitki* allowed for extremely short production times, illustrating and explaining urgent political and economic problems and tasks through a linear plot. The first shorts that can be defined as *agitki* were made during the brief period of bourgeois rule following the revolution in February 1917 when films such as *Long Live Free Russia* (Da zdravstvuet svobodnaia Rus'!) and *The Motherland Is in Danger* (Rodina v opasnosti) conveyed messages in accordance with the political line of Aleksandr Kerenskii's provisional government. Soviet *agitki* were produced on a massive scale during the Civil War (1918–1921) when the term was coined and altogether about 50 films were released, sometimes only in one copy because the raw material was so hard to obtain. Targeted subjects of Soviet *agitki* included the White Army, the Orthodox Church, foreign interventionist forces, illiteracy, starvation, and laziness. The production of *agitki* was administered through the Commissariat of Enlightenment; their main target audience was illiterate or semiliterate peasants and soldiers. The White Army, too, produced some propaganda shorts, such as Aleksandr Volkov's *My Life—for the Motherland, My Honor—for Nobody* (Zhizn'—Rodine, chest'—nikomu, 1919), the aesthetics of which was similar to that of pro-Bolshevik films.

When Lenin formulated his famous statement about cinema being "the most important of all arts for us Bolsheviks," he likely had *agitki* in mind; they were a high priority for the Communist administration. Of the scriptwriters penning *agitki*, a number were well established, for example, Aleksandr Serafimovich (1863–1949), **Anatolii Lunacharskii**, and Dem'ian Bednyi (1883–1945); among the directors shooting *agitki* were **Vladimir Gardin, Lev Kuleshov, Ivan Perestiani, Aleksandr Ivanovskii, Iurii Zheliabuzhskii, Aleksandr Panteleev**, and **Aleksandr Razumnyi**. Lunacharskii, the influential commissar of enlightenment in 1917–1929, functioned as a governmental enabler of *agitka* production who helped organize free-of-charge screenings of these films in many cities.

Under the leadership of **Aleksandr Medvedkin**, the genre was revived in the early 1930s when a specially equipped "film train" (*kinopoezd*) traveled the country in search of industrial hot spots, and filmmakers reported about achievements and problems. The related *agitpropfil'm*s of the 1930s were longer (sometimes feature length), usually nonfictional, artistically more sophisticated, and used sound, for example, **Abram Room**'s *Manometer No. 1* (1930) and *Manometer No. 2* (1932).

AGONY (aka *Rasputin*/Agoniia, 1975–1981). **Mosfilm Studio**. 152 min., color and b/w. Directed by **Elem Klimov**. Script: Semen Lungin, Il'ia Nusinov. Cinematography: Leonid Kalashnikov. Music: **Al'fred Shnitke**. Cast: **Aleksei Petrenko**, Anatolii Romashin, Velta Line, **Alisa Freindlikh**, Aleksandr Romantsov, Iurii Katin-Iartsev.

In 1916, Grigorii Rasputin (Petrenko), a Siberian priest and faith healer, returns to the court of Tsar Nikolai II (Romashin). His outrageous behavior, hypnotizing gaze, and aura of a prophet who emerged from the depths of the people regain him the protection of the tsarina (Line) and her close aide, Anna Vyrubova (Freindlikh). But Rasputin has numerous foes, including the right-wing politician Vladimir Purishkevich (Katin-Iartsev) and Prince Iusupov (Romantsov). With the military success of the Russian Army waning, the opposition to the tsar and his unholy protégé increases; plotters finally manage to lure Rasputin into a trap where he is murdered. The event points to the agony of Russian autocracy.

AIMANOV, SHAKEN [some sources list the patronymic Kenzhetae-vich] (b. 15 February 1914, Bayanaul, Kazakhstan–d. 23 December 1970, Moscow). Kazakh actor, director, and screenwriter. Aimanov was born in a village near the Irtysh River, in the Pavlodar district of eastern Kazakhstan. He studied at the Kazakh Institute of Education in Semipalatinsk in 1931–1933, where he was also active in a theater club. Upon graduation, he was invited to join the Kazakh Drama Theater both as an actor and director; he was the theater's executive artistic director in 1947–1951.

Aimanov made his movie debut in Efim Aron's lyrical triangle **comedy** *White Rose* (Belaia roza, 1942), which was not released (other sources list the 1940 *Raikhan* as his first acting credit). Aimanov's national reputation was established by two major biopics: **Grigorii Roshal**'s *The Songs of Abai* (Pesni Abaia, 1945, codirected with Aron), in which the actor plays Abai's treasonous student Aship, and the title role in **Efim Dzigan**'s *Djambul* (1952) about the Kazakh national poet; however, Aimanov in later years spoke rather skeptically about the artistic merits of these two pictures.

In 1953, Aimanov became a film director and decided to abandon theater altogether. His first efforts were harmless stories in which conflicts are smoothed over rather than developed, for example, in *Poem about Love* (Poema o liubvi, 1954)—the first independently produced Kazakh feature ever and, in essence, a filmed theater production based on the national legend of Kozy-Korpesh and Baian-Sulu. Despite various shortcomings, Aimanov gained real popularity with the light musical comedy *Our Dear Doctor* (Nash milyi doktor, 1957) in which the patients of a spa surprise their physician with a concert-revue. The comedy *Beardless Swindler* (Bezborodyi obman-shchik, 1965) is a portrait of one of the most popular characters of Kazakh folklore, Aldar-Kose (played by Aimanov himself), a pica-resque, Robin Hood–like helper of the poor.

Aimanov impressed critics with the solemn *Land of the Fathers* (Zemlia ottsov, 1966) from a script by poet Olzhas Suleimenov (b. 1936). In accordance with tradition, the remains of a Kazakh sol-dier must be brought to his native land, yet the soldier's aged father and his son ultimately decide to leave them in the grave near Lenin-grad with fighters from other Soviet republics. Much to the director's chagrin, this elegy—arguably his supreme artistic achievement—was largely ignored by viewers. Aimanov's greatest popular success was the Civil War thriller *The End of the Ataman* (Konets atamana, 1970), an adventurous yarn based on the true story of the anti-Bolshevik chieftain Ataman Dutov who was killed with the help of Kazakh members of Cheka, the Soviet secret police.

Without ever attending a film school, Aimanov made more than a dozen pictures that marked the birth of **Kazakh cinema**. The director died in a traffic accident shortly after the completion of *The End of the Ataman*. In 1984, **Kazakhfilm Studio** was named after him.

Aimanov joined the Communist Party in 1940. He received a Sta-lin Prize in 1952 for his stage work and was named People's Artist of the USSR in 1959. On Aimanov's 90th anniversary, large-scale celebrations were held in his native Pavlodar region.

Other films: *Daughter of the Steppe* (Doch' stepei, 1955); *The Crossroad* (Perekrestok, 1961); *Angel in a Cap* (Angel v tiubeteike, 1969).

AIMEDOVA, MAIA-GOZEL (b. 28 May 1941, Ashgabat [formerly Ashkhabad]). Turkmen actress and screenwriter. Aimedova studied at the Lunacharskii State Theater Institute, graduating in 1964. That same year she joined the troupe of the Turkmen Theater of the Young Viewer (TIuZ) in Ashgabat.

As a film actress, Aimedova debuted in the drama *Incident in Dash-Kala* (Sluchai v Dash-Kale, 1961) about a teacher who wit-nesses medieval marriage practices and fights them. Aimedova's most famous role is that of a woman who refuses to believe that her husband, a pilot in the Great Patriotic War, has been killed, in *The*

Daughter-in-Law (Nevestka, 1972) by **Khodjakuli Narliev**. This powerful performance earned her a USSR State Prize and has remained one of the most memorable in all of **Turkmen cinema**. Quiet intensity, beauty, and inner strength became Aimedova's trademarks, which she continued to use to great effect in melodramas such as *When a Woman Saddles a Horse* (Kogda zhenshchina osedlaet konia, 1975), for which she also coauthored the script. *Djamal's Tree* (Derevo Dzhamal, 1980, also screenplay) tells about the tribulations of a woman whose husband returns from the Great Patriotic War as an invalid, only to face rumors about his wife's infidelity. *Karakumy, 45 Degrees in the Shadow* (Karakumy, 45 gradusov v teni, 1982) describes the difficult construction of a gas pipeline.

After the Soviet Union disintegrated and Turkmenistan gained its independence (1991), the state-ordered shutdown of the country's film industry effectively ended Aimedova's career; her last film role was in Narliev's **Chingiz Aitmatov** adaptation *Mankurt* (1990), a grim parable about the enslavement of the human mind.

Aimedova joined the Communist Party in 1971. She was named People's Artist of Turkmen SSR in 1982 and People's Artist of the USSR in 1987. She is married to director Khodjakuli Narliev.

Other films: *You Must Be Able to Say No* (Umei skazat' net, 1976); *Fragi—Separated from Happiness* (Fragi—razluchennyi so schast'em, 1984); *Good-bye, My Parthian* (Do svidaniia, moi parfinianin, 1987); *The Mad Woman* (Beshenaia, 1988).

AITMATOV, CHINGIZ [some sources list the patronymic Torekulovich] (b. 12 December 1928, Sheker, Kyrgyzstan–d. 10 June 2008, Nuremberg, Germany). Kyrgyz writer, screenwriter, and politician. Aitmatov's father was a Communist activist who perished in the purges in 1937. Aitmatov grew up with his grandmother, who led a nomadic life and was a major source for the writer's intimate knowledge of Kyrgyz folklore and ancient beliefs. After studying veterinary medicine and agriculture, Aitmatov was sent to Moscow, where he enrolled in the Supreme Literary Courses in 1956, graduating in 1958.

The publication of the novella "Djamilia" in 1958 brought Aitmatov national and international fame. Almost from the beginning, Aitmatov's literary career was paralleled by an active interest in cinema. He wrote his first screenplay, *The Pass* (Pereval, adapted from the story "My Little Poplar in a Red Headscarf"/Topolek moi v krasnoi kosynke), in 1961. Directed by Aleksei Sakharov, this film about the disloyalty of a truck driver was a critical failure. More successful was **Larisa Shepit'ko**, who made her diploma film *Torrid Heat* (Znoi, 1963) from Aitmatov's short story "Camel Eye" (Verbliuzhii glaz), about a young man participating in the "virgin soil" campaign for the cultivation of untilled soil in the Kyrgyz steppe. Aitmatov subsequently adapted many of his own stories for the screen. Thus, *The First Teacher* (Pervyi uchitel', 1965), about a 1920s Bolshevik who overcomes the ignorance and backwardness of a barren, patriarchal village, was turned by **Andrei Mikhalkov-Konchalovskii** into a visually superb picture. Still, some of Aitmatov's most accomplished narratives failed to make an equal impression on the screen, despite fine casts and excellent camera work. Such is the case with *Djamilia* (1969), directed by Irina Poplavskaia, as well as **Sergei Urusevskii**'s rendition of *Farewell, Gul'sary!* (Proshchai, gul'sary, aka Beg inokhodtsa, 1968), which neutralized the original's powerful anti-Stalinist motifs.

In the hands of Kyrgyz directors, Aitmatov's screenplays became masterpieces whose psychological and social maturity as well as innovative aesthetic approach amazed Soviet and international audiences. Particularly successful were **Tolomush Okeev**'s story of unattainable love, *The Red Apple* (Krasnoe iabloko, 1975), and **Bolotbek Shamshiev**'s myth-saturated allegory *The White Steamship* (Belyi parakhod, 1976). More consistently than other directors, Shamshiev associated his career with Aitmatov's, beginning with the made-for-television drama *Echo of Love* (Ekho liubvi, 1974), to the gritty story of a wartime childhood, *Early Cranes* (Rannie zhuravli, 1979), and the polemical anti-Stalinist parable *The Climb to Fujiyama* (Voskhozhdenie na Fudziiamu, 1988).

Aitmatov's morally rigorous rejection of Stalinism shaped the cultural-political discourses during perestroika. Moreover, the writer's genuine—if at times simplistic—respect for religion, spirituality, and myths opened the way for a rediscovery of national identity in several Soviet republics and their increasing sense of cultural independence. Thus, Turkmen director **Khodjakuli Narliev** turned a chapter from Aitmatov's novel *The Day Lasts Longer than a Century* (I dol'she veka dlitsia den', 1980) into the historical parable *Mankurt* (1990) about the enslavement of man's memory by totalitarian forces. Aitmatov's yearning for a new ethical and ecological universalism found a positive reflection in Karen Gevorkian's *Spotted Dog Running on the Edge of the Sea* (Pegii pes begushchii kraem moria, 1989). Using the milieu of the small tribe of Nivkhs in the far north for fine visual effects, the ethical message is conveyed without preaching, in a stringent, stylistically persuasive manner.

Both Aitmatov's artistic ingenuity and political and cultural influence made a decisive impact on **Kyrgyz cinema** and other Central Asian cinemas, helping them to thematically and aesthetically emancipate themselves and find cinematic approaches in tune with their national traditions.

Throughout his career, Aitmatov managed to combine artistic ambition with countless administrative positions and responsibilities. In 1961, he was charged with organizing a Kyrgyz Filmmakers' Union and became its first secretary in 1964, a position he held until 1989. Aitmatov, who joined the Communist Party in 1959, won a Lenin Prize in 1963, USSR State Prizes in 1968, 1977, and 1983, and the title Hero of Socialist Labor in 1978. In 1990, he embarked on a diplomatic career as Kyrgyzstan's ambassador that took him to Luxemburg, Belgium, and the Netherlands.

ALEINIKOV BROTHERS. Gleb Olegovich (b. 12 March 1966, Groznyi) and Igor' Olegovich (b. 15 March 1962, Groznyi–d. 23 March 1994). Russian directors, screenwriters, and film theorists. Igor' Aleinikov studied at the Moscow Institute of Engineering and Physics, graduating in 1984, while Gleb Aleinikov received his degree from the Moscow Institute of Construction Engineering in 1988.

In their spare time, the brothers founded and promoted an underground film movement, Parallel Cinema (*parallel'noe kino*), which they had conceived in the mid-1980s. In close communication with the Leningrad group Necrorealists, they produced cheap 8mm and 16mm shorts, deliberately violating the most basic standards of cinematic narration. Their films were implicit attacks on the state-run Soviet mainstream, delightfully subversive to the connoisseur and brutally provocative to an uninitiated viewer. *The Cruel Disease of Males* (Zhestokaia bolezn' muzhchin, 1987), *Awaiting de Bil* (Ozhidanie de Bila, 1990), and numerous others alluded to stylistic—but not political—clichés of Soviet cinema without explicitly satirizing them—that is, without offering an alternative system of signification. The roots of the movement can be traced to Russian literary absurdism (Daniil Kharms, Aleksandr Vvedenskii); specific cinematic impulses came from masters of minimalism such as Jean-Marie Straub. Parallel Cinema challenged the Soviet official cultural establishment through its absence of logic and perceived anti-aesthetics, indulging in nonsensical violence and primitively imitated sexual acts.

From 1985 to 1990, the Aleinikov brothers edited a photocopied journal, *Cine Phantom* (Sine fantom), which published theoretical articles and film scripts. In 1990, they were awarded the main prize at the Oberhausen Short Film Festival for *Awaiting de Bil*. In the late 1980s, due to their growing reputation and the willingness of agonizing Soviet studios to integrate alternative approaches, **Mosfilm Studio** produced their short *Someone Was Here* (Zdes' kto-to byl, 1989) and the full-length *Tractor Drivers II* (Traktoristy II, 1992), a strangely cold and incoherent "remake" of **Ivan Pyr'ev**'s 1939 Stalinist **comedy**. After Igor' Aleinikov's death in a plane crash, Gleb continues to make short and medium-length features, predominantly on video. At the 2000 Oberhausen Festival, he presented *Ameriga*, a spoof on conspiracy obsession, consisting of footage filmed on a trip to the United States in 1990. In 1999, Gleb published his late brother's diaries.

Other films: *M.E.* (1986); *Tractors* (Traktora, 1987); *Boris and Gleb* (Boris i Gleb, 1988); *We Are Your Children, Moscow* (My deti tvoi, Moskva, 1997).

ALEINIKOV, PETR MARTYNOVICH (b. 12 July 1914, village Krivel', Belarus–d. 9 June 1965, Moscow). Belarusian and Russian actor. Aleinikov was an orphan and raised in a children's commune in Mogilev. He studied with **Sergei Gerasimov** at the Leningrad Institute of Stage Arts, graduating in 1935.

Aleinikov made his film debut as a factory worker in **Fridrikh Ermler** and **Sergei Iutkevich**'s seminal *The Counterplan* (Vstrechnyi, 1932). He gained wide popularity with the role of the cook Pet'ka Moliboga in Gerasimov's contemporary Arctic adventure *The Bold Seven* (Semero smelykh, 1936) and, appearing under his own name, in the industrial utopia *Komsomol'sk* (aka *City of Youth*, aka *The*

Frozen North, 1938). Aleinikov's fame was solidified with **Leonid Lukov**'s *A Great Life* (Bol'shaia zhizn', 1940; second part released in 1958); the role of Vania Kurskii became synonymous with the actor's unbridled joy of life and sly, easygoing manner, cultivating an image of the "guy next door" who seamlessly fits into a working-class milieu. Fairy-tale specialist **Aleksandr Rou** made good use of this image in his *The Little Humpbacked Horse* (Konek-Gorbunok, 1941), in which Aleinikov played the lead, the good-natured and street-smart Little Ivan (Ivanushka). During the Great Patriotic War, Aleinikov's ability to believably convey patriotism in rank-and-file characters was featured in pictures such as **Vsevolod Pudovkin**'s *In the Name of the Motherland* (Vo imia rodiny, 1943), Gerasimov's *The Invincible* (Nepobedimye, 1943, codirected with **Mikhail Kala-tozov**), and especially **Iulii Raizman**'s *Moscow Sky* (Nebo Moskvy, 1944), in which Aleinikov portrays a pilot.

Eventually, Aleinikov's charmingly roguish—and hugely popular—screen persona became a cage from which he tried to escape. Yet when **Leo Arnshtam** cast the comedian as poet Aleksandr Pushkin in his biopic *Glinka* (aka *The Great Glinka*, 1947), audiences' roaring laughter at the actor's screen appearances caused a scandal. In the following years, despite some memorable parts—for example, in **Lev Kulidzhanov**'s *Our Father's House* (aka *A Home for Tanya*/Otchii dom, 1959)—Aleinikov no longer was given the same artistic opportunities as in the 1930s. Only his last role of an aging worker in **Bulat Mansurov**'s controversial *Quenching of Thirst* (Utolenie zhazhdy, 1966) became a belated triumph for the actor. Aleinikov, who died as a result of his severe alcoholism, was the subject of a **documentary**, *Petr Martynovich and the Years of Great Life* (Petr Martynovich i gody bol'shoi zhizni, 1974).

Other films: *Aleksandr Parkhomenko* (1942); *The Miners of Donetsk* (Donetskie shakhtery, 1950).

ALEKSANDR NEVSKII (1938). **Mosfilm Studio**. 111 min., b/w. Directed by **Sergei Eizenshtein**; codirector Dmitrii Vasil'ev. Script: Petr Pavlenko, Sergei Eizenshtein. Cinematography: **Eduard Tissé**. Music: **Sergei Prokof'ev**. Cast: **Nikolai Cherkasov**, **Nikolai Okhlo-pkov**, Andrei Abrikosov, Dmitrii Orlov, Valentina Ivasheva, Vladi-mir Ershov, Varvara Massalitinova. Premiere: 1 December 1938.

In the 13th century, German crusaders, driven by religious fanaticism and greed, attack Russian principalities that are deeply divided among themselves. The Teutonic knights occupy the city of Pskov, burning women and children. After internal debates, the citizens of Novgorod decide to ask Prince Aleksandr Nevskii (Cherkasov) to lead them into battle. Two young Novgorodian men, Gavrilo Oleksich (Abrikosov) and Vasilii Buslai (Okhlopkov) both love Ol'ga Danilovna (Ivasheva) who promises to marry the one who proves more courageous. During the decisive battle on Lake Chudskoe (Peipus) on 5 April 1242, Aleksandr defeats the crusaders, many of whom drown when the ice on the lake cracks. The citizens of Novgorod celebrate Aleksandr and his troops and punish the traitors.

ALEKSANDROV, GRIGORII VASIL'EVICH [real name: Mormonenko] (b. 23 January 1903, Ekaterinburg–d. 16 December 1983, Moscow). Russian director, scriptwriter, and actor. Aleksandrov's early love for the theater took him to Ekaterinburg Opera House, where he worked in minor jobs in 1912–1917. In 1917, he also finished the violin class at the local school of music and joined the Bolshevik armed forces as the head of a front theater. In 1920, Aleksandrov began to study directing at the Ekaterinburg Workers and Peasants' Theater, which was administered by the local office of the Commissariat of Enlightenment. Subsequently, he was assigned to oversee the cinema repertoire in his hometown, including the reediting of old films according to new political standards.

In 1921, after joining the Proletarian Culture (Proletkul't) movement as an actor in the First Workers' Theater in Moscow, he met **Sergei Eizenshtein** and became his close associate on theatrical productions and later on his first full-length feature, *Strike* (Stachka, 1924). Apart from being Eizenshtein's right hand in all of his silent pictures, Aleksandrov also played the title role in *Glumov's Diary* (Dnevnik Glumova, 1923); an episodic role in *Strike*; and, quite authentically, the sadistic lieutenant Giliarovskii in **Battleship Potemkin** (Bronenosets Potemkin, 1925).

In 1929–1932, assigned to study sound film production, Aleksandrov traveled with Eizenshtein and cameraman **Eduard Tissé** to Western Europe and the United States. In Switzerland, he contributed to Tissé's abortion drama *Women's Misery—Women's Happiness*

(Frauennot—Frauenglück, 1929), and in France, to *Romance sentimentale*, a sound film experiment, both of which were supervised by Eizenshtein. Aleksandrov was also involved in the ill-fated *¡Que Viva Mexico!* (1932), which he restored and released 35 years later—truly an act of reverence to his great teacher and friend with whom he had a never-explained fallout shortly before returning to the Soviet Union.

Back in the USSR, Aleksandrov decided to start a directing career of his own. His debut was the short *Internationale* (1932), an official contribution to the celebrations of the 15th anniversary of the October Revolution. In 1933, Maksim Gor'kii introduced Aleksandrov to Iosif Stalin, who spoke of the need to create genuinely Soviet, popular film **comedies**. Aleksandrov delivered the hilarious musical *Jolly Fellows* (Veselye rebiata, 1934), featuring **Isaak Dunaevskii**'s unforgettable tunes and Vasilii Lebedev-Kumach's simple yet memorable lyrics. The film's unbeatable optimism and radiant atmosphere earned Stalin's appreciation. Although jazz music—otherwise maligned by the Communist establishment—plays a crucial role in it, the dictator gave the film the green light against the objections of cultural hacks. Aleksandrov was entrusted with *The Report of Comrade Stalin on the Project of the USSR Constitution at the VIII Extraordinary Congress of Soviets* (Doklad tov. Stalina o proekte konstitutsii SSSR na VIII chrezvychainom s"ezde sovetov, 1936). He and his wife, actress **Liubov' Orlova**, became the first glitzy star couple of the Soviet Union whose luxurious lifestyle was the object of admiration, envy, and countless legends.

Aleksandrov's next feature, *Circus* (Tsirk, 1936), is an antiracist comedy-melodrama about an American artist who flees the United States because of her black child and eventually finds a new home in the Soviet Union. The movie's leitmotiv tune, "Broad Is My Homeland" (Shiroka strana moia rodnaia), quickly turned into a veritable folksong, as did other songs from Aleksandrov's films, in spite of their ludicrous lyrics. *Volga-Volga* (1938), another superhit, shows the victory of grassroots over elite culture, or folk music over the classical canon. Its attacks on bureaucratic self-importance reveal the true spirit of Aleksandrov's movies—a sometimes witty, sometimes crude populism. This spirit also carries the weaker and less funny *Radiant Path* (aka *Tanya*/Svetlyi put', 1940), a modern fairy tale (originally titled *Cinderella*) about a textile worker, as well as *Spring* (Vesna, 1947), where the humor appears rather forced and the overall tone is restrained. *Meeting at the Elbe* (Vstrecha na El'be, 1949), a Cold War propaganda flick with a few comedic sprinkles, vilifies the United States and its troops in divided post-Nazi Germany. That picture and *The Composer Glinka* (aka *Man of Music*/Kompozitor Glinka, 1952), a biopic as stale and bombastic as its title, shows Aleksandrov's talent in steep decline, although no critic was yet free to say so.

Critical vengeance hit only after Stalin's passing, when the détente farce *Russian Souvenir* (Russkii suvenir, 1960) proved that the old populist formula had become an anachronism. The story of a group of Western tourists who accidentally land in Siberia and gradually overcome their anti-Soviet prejudice is merely ridiculous, not amusing. Aleksandrov's last major directorial attempt, the spy drama *Woodpecker and Lyre* (Skvorets i lira, 1975), turned out so embarrassing that even the director's high-ranking supporters found it unfit for audiences' consumption; it was shelved and had a limited release in the mid-1990s. Thus, in the last two decades of his life, Aleksandrov, member of countless boards and committees, was mostly occupied with hackwork and representation.

Aleksandrov's films of the 1930s are rendered with professional perfection and inventiveness and appear visually smooth, rhythmically precise, and to this day immensely watchable. This filmmaker's historical significance lies in the fact that he shaped an important segment of Soviet cinematic mainstream in the 1930s and 1940s. His trademark blend of lavish, Hollywood-style musicals, witty satire, and sentimental love stories—all placed within an unequivocal propaganda framework—helped define the internal cultural norms and values of Soviet society and thus exclusively targeted the domestic market. On the other hand, it cannot be denied that Aleksandrov's best pictures appeal to basic human desires and are clever and genuinely entertaining in their praise of art, community, and love. Precisely because their political ingredients may seem naïve and even negligible, it is still hard for many contemporary Russian viewers to resent these films, despite their erstwhile demagogical function. Thus, even after countless revelations about the GULAG concentration camp system, the murderous collectivization campaign, show trials, and purges, many post-Soviet viewers remain loyal to Stalinist entertainment, a paradox that few pictures reflect better than Aleksandrov's.

Aleksandrov, who joined the Communist Party in 1954, taught at the Soviet State Film School **VGIK** in 1950–1957, holding the rank of a full professor. The honors bestowed upon him were legion: two Stalin Prizes (1941, 1950), the titles People's Artist of the USSR (1948) and Hero of Socialist Labor (1973), as well as innumerable medals and prizes. He is buried at Novodevich'e cemetery. The house where he and Orlova lived in 1965–1983 (Bol'shaia Bronnaia street 29) carries a memorial plaque.

Other films: *One Family* (Odna sem'ia, 1943); *Human to Human* (Chelovek cheloveku, 1958, a concert compilation film of the Moscow World Youth Festival).

ALOV [real name: Lapsker], **ALEKSANDR ALEKSANDROVICH** (b. 26 September 1923, Khar'kov [Khar'kiv]–d. 12 June 1983, Moscow). Ukrainian and Russian director and scriptwriter. After military service in the Great Patriotic War, Alov studied with **Ihor' Savchenko** at the Soviet State Film School **VGIK**, graduating in 1951. He worked as an assistant to Savchenko on the monumental war picture *The Third Blow* (Tretii udar, 1948). After his teacher's untimely death, he and fellow student **Vladimir Naumov** were entrusted with the completion of Savchenko's last picture, the biopic *Taras Shevchenko* (1949). Following the success of that debut, Alov and Naumov began to make films at the Kiev film studio (later **Dovzhenko Film Studio**) as a team; the label "Alov and Naumov," unlike other such pairings, never disintegrated.

Restless Youth (Trevozhnaia molodost', 1954), their first film, praises the idealism of Ukrainian Komsomol members who successfully defeat an incompetent and subversive administrator. *Pavel Korchagin* (1956), adapted from Nikolai Ostrovskii's inspirational novel *How the Steel Was Tempered* (1932), continues along similar lines, responding to a widespread need for uncorrupted Communist faith as a counterweight to the shocking revelations about the Stalinist system. The third installment of this loose trilogy about Soviet youth, *Wind* (Veter, 1958), was made after Alov and Naumov's 1957 move to **Mosfilm Studio**. It tells the story of four friends' sojourn to the first Komsomol Congress in Moscow; tragically, only one of them survives. Alov and Naumov demonstratively focus on the enormous hindrances that had to be overcome in the name of the revolution and the frantic efforts that were necessary in order to achieve victory.

Their subsequent pictures showed them as an ambitious, serious, creative team always good for surprises. *Peace to Him Who Enters* (Mir vkhodiashchemu, 1961) explores anew the experience of the Great Patriotic War. Dark and largely skeptical of humankind's ability to improve, it was criticized for its gloomy atmosphere and pessimism. After a short television interlude with the Albert Maltz adaptation *The Coin* (Moneta, 1964), Alov and Naumov directed *A Nasty Anecdote* (Skvernyi anekdot, 1966), adapted from a Fedor Dostoevskii story. The film, featuring partly surreal images of stuffy 19th-century Russian life, reveals its makers' bitter disillusionment with the Russian intelligentsia and the nation's democratic potential; it became one of the first victims of the post-Thaw cultural rollback strategy and remained shelved for two decades.

Despite numerous setbacks, Alov and Naumov were able to realize what would become their finest achievement, *The Flight* (Beg, 1970), a masterful adaptation of Mikhail Bulgakov's tragedy about the 1918–1921 Civil War and subsequent mass emigration, visually stunning in its alternation of nightmarish sequences and realistic drama. Soviet viewers also loved *The Legend of Till* (Legenda o Tile, 1977), a six-hour Ulenspiegel adventure in which Charles de Coster's characters were brought to life with picturesque stylishness, if not narrative dynamics. Indeed, Alov and Naumov's trend toward epic breadth, in obvious contrast to their early pictures' over-the-top vigor and pace, became obsessive in their films of the 1980s. The sensationalist Soviet-Swiss-French blockbuster *Teheran-43* (aka *Spy Ring*, aka *Assassination Attempt*, 1980), starring Alain Delon and Curd Jürgens, is a long-winded, ahistorical secret service yarn. The underlying message sought to corroborate the need for peaceful coexistence and cooperation between the Soviet Union and the West, the Leninist-Brezhnevist formula to avoid major military clashes while maintaining minimal civility. The Soviet-German coproduction *The Shore* (Bereg, 1984, adapted from a novel by Iurii Bondarev) attempts to visualize the Cold War and its consequences, including a looming nuclear conflict. Yet the romance between a Soviet writer and a German woman shortly after World War II, rehashing elements of *Peace to Him Who Enters*, appears philosophically overburdenend and insufferably grandiose in style.

Alov was awarded the title People's Artist of the USSR in 1983.

AMAL'RIK, LEONID ALEKSEEVICH (b. 8 July 1905, Moscow–d. 22 October 1997, Moscow). Russian animation director, scriptwriter, and animator. Amal'rik, who was born into an aristocratic family that stayed in Russia after the 1917 revolution, began to work at the Mezhrabpom-Rus' (**Mezhrabpomfilm Studio**) in 1926 while studying at the Soviet State Film School (Goskinoshkola, later named **VGIK**). As an artist, he contributed to one of the earliest Soviet **animation** films, *China in Flames* (Kitai v ogne, 1925). Upon graduation in 1928, he joined Mezhrabpomfilm as an animator and switched to Soiuzmultfilm studio upon its foundation in 1936.

Amal'rik's directorial debut was the anticolonial short *Black and White* (Blek end Uait, 1932, from Vladimir Maiakovskii's poem), made with **Ivan Ivanov-Vano**. He then turned to **children's films**, creating all of his drawn animation films over the next two decades in partnership with Vladimir Polkovnikov (1906–1982). Amal'rik's first independently directed picture was *The Arrow Flies into the Fairy Tale* (Strela uletaet v skazku, 1952) in which the world of contemporary children and the realm of fantasy are smoothly blended.

One of the leading masters of Russian drawn animation, Amal'rik developed a style both accessible to children and allowing for subtle stylization. Among his most notable achievements are *The Magic Store* (Volshebnyi magazin, 1953), *The Behemoth Who Was Afraid of Injections* (Pro begemota, kotoryi boialsia privivok, 1966), *The Cat's House* (Koshkin dom, 1958), and the very popular *Thumbelina* (Diuimovochka, 1966). Some of his pictures were made for adult viewers, such as the social satires *The Abstinent Sparrow* (Nep'iushchii vorobei, 1961, based on a Sergei Mikhalkov script) and *Grandma's Little Goat* (Babushkin kozlik, 1963). Other films were adaptations of classical stories, for example, *Grey Neck* (Seraia sheika, 1948) from Dmitrii Mamin-Sibiriak (1852–1912), and *The Girl and the Elephant* (Devochka i slon, 1970) from a story by Aleksandr Kuprin (1870–1938).

Amal'rik was named Merited Artist of the Russian Federation in 1965.

Other films: *Limpopo* (1939); *Barmalei* (1941); *The Cuckoo and the Woodpecker* (Kukushka i skvorets, 1950); *The Little Tower Chamber* (Terem-teremok, 1970).

ANDJAPARIDZE, VERIKO [Vera] (b. 6 October 1900, Kutaisi–d. 30 January 1987, Tbilisi). Georgian actress. Andjaparidze studied at the Aidarov Drama Studio in Moscow in 1916–1917 and at the Aleksandre Djabadari studio in Tbilisi in 1918–1921. From 1920 to 1926, she belonged to the troupe of the Shota Rustaveli Theater in Tbilisi. The great theater innovator Kote Mardjanishvili, whose troupe she joined in 1928, shaped Andjaparidze's intensely psychological approach to acting, which later allowed her to transcend simplistic typecasting patterns in cinema. However, her acting style also included grand gestures and unabashed pathos, especially in historical dramas.

Andjaparidze's film debut was the lead role of a peasant wife in Vladimir Barskii's *Horrors of the Past* (Tsarsulis sashinelebani, 1925). She then played supporting parts in **Iurii Zheliabuzhskii**'s *Dina Dza-Dzu* (1926) and **Nikoloz Shengelaia**'s *Twenty-six Commissars* (Dvadtsat' shest' komissarov, 1932). In 1929, Andjaparidze was successful in her husband **Mikheil Chiaureli**'s antialcoholism drama *Saba*. She soon achieved a unique status as one of the leading female actresses of **Georgian cinema**, a living legend who was honored under all Soviet political leaders, from Iosif Stalin to Mikhail Gorbachev. Although predominantly a stage actress, Andjaparidze's appearances on screen always became noted events even in superficially designed stock roles. Among her achievements are the part of Rusudan in Chiaureli's monumental epic *Georgii Zaakadze* (1942–1946), the kolkhoz director Nino in Nikoloz Sanishvili's **comedy** *Happy Encounter* (Bednieri shekhvedra/Schastlivaia vstrecha, 1949), and the lead in **Siko Dolidze**'s popular rural drama *Encounter with the Past* (Shekhvedra tsarsultan/Vstrecha s proshlym, 1966). **Tengiz Abuladze** gave Andjaparidze a minute yet essential role in his antitotalitarian testament *Repentance* (Monanieba/Pokaianie, 1984), in which the actress utters the rhetorical question, "Who needs a road if it does not lead to a temple?"

Andjaparidze was awarded the title People's Artist of the USSR in 1950 and Hero of Socialist Labor in 1979. She received Stalin Prizes in 1943, 1946, and 1952. Her daughter was actress **Sofiko Chiaureli**, her nephew film director **Georgii Daneliia**.

Other films: *You Cannot See What I Have Seen* (Rats ghinakhavs, vegar nakhav/Inye nynche vremena, 1965); *Don't Grieve* (Ardaidardo/ Ne goriui! 1969); *The Legend of Surami Fortress* (Ambari Suramis tsikhitsa/Legenda o Suramskoi kreposti, 1985).

ANDREEV, BORIS FEDOROVICH (b. 9 February 1915, Saratov– d. 25 April 1982, Moscow). Russian actor. Andreev studied at the theater college (*tekhnikum*) in Saratov, graduating in 1937. In 1938, **Ivan Pyr'ev** cast him in the musical **comedy** *Tractor Drivers* (Traktoristy, 1939) as Nazar Duma, a role that made the portly and likeable actor an overnight star. In later Pyr'ev films, especially *Cossacks of the Kuban* (Kubanskie kazaki, 1950), Andreev revived the cliché of the "kind yet able-bodied bear" created in *Tractor Drivers*.

Andreev's screen image was that of a strong, sometimes naïve and awkward, yet invariably positive "man of the people," usually a collective farmer or worker, for example, as the miner Balun in **Leonid Lukov**'s *A Great Life* (Bol'shaia zhizn', 1940). In the 1940s and early 1950s the actor embodied the loyal fighter for Iosif Stalin and the Soviet homeland, most memorably as "Sasha from Uralmash factory" (*Sasha s Uralmasha*) in Lukov's popular *Two Fighters* (Dva boitsa, 1943) and in **Mikheil Chiaureli**'s elephantine *Fall of Berlin* (Padenie Berlina, 1950). During the Thaw, while continuing with parts of senior, class-conscious workers such as Il'ia Zhurbin in **Iosif Kheifits**'s *Grand Family* (Bol'shaia sem'ia, 1954), Andreev also played legendary patriotic heroes in fairy tales, including the title role in **Aleksandr Ptushko**'s *Il'ia Muromets* (aka *The Sword and the Dragon*, 1956). While the actor's typical monumentality was artistically justified in that genre, it looked increasingly anachronistic and false in more realistic films.

Andreev won Stalin Prizes for Pyr'ev's *The Tale of the Siberian Land* (aka *Symphony of Life*/Skazanie o zemle sibirskoi, 1946) and *Fall of Berlin*. He joined the Communist Party in 1948 and was named People's Artist of the USSR in 1962.

Other films: *Malakhov Hill* (Malakhov kurgan, 1944); *Maksimka* (1952); *Cruelty* (Zhestokost', 1959); *Optimistic Tragedy* (Optimisticheskaia tragediia, 1963); *Sergei Ivanovich Is Retiring* (Sergei Ivanovich ukhodit na pensiiu, 1981).

ANDREI RUBLEV (aka *The Passion According to Andrei*/Strasti po Andreiu, 1966). **Mosfilm Studio.** 2 parts, 185 min. (originally 209 min.), b/w and color. Directed by **Andrei Tarkovskii**. Script: **Andrei Mikhalkov-Konchalovskii**, Andrei Tarkovskii. Cinematography: **Vadim Iusov**. Music: **Viacheslav Ovchinnikov**. Cast: **Anatolii Solonitsyn**, **Ivan Lapikov**, **Nikolai Grin'ko**, **Nikolai Burliaev**, Nikolai Sergeev, Irma Raush, Iurii Nazarov, **Rolan Bykov**, **Iurii Nikulin**, Mikhail Kononov, **Bolot Beishenaliev**. Premiere: 17 February 1969.

Part I. Prologue: A peasant has invented a hot air balloon, but the euphoria of his first flight ends in a crash. 1. In 1400, monks Andrei Rublev (Solonitsyn), Kirill (Lapikov), and Daniil Chernyi (Grin'ko) wander through Russia as icon painters. In a hut, they meet a buffoon (Bykov) who is arrested for cracking subversive jokes. 2. In 1405, Kirill asks the famous Feofan Grek (Sergeev) for the assignment to paint the Annunciation Cathedral in Moscow; when Rublev is chosen instead, Kirill leaves in bitterness. 3. In 1406, Rublev travels with his teacher, Feofan Grek, and his own young disciple, Foma (Kononov), debating to whom their art should be addressed. Rublev has a vision of a crucifixion. 4. In 1408, Rublev encounters a community of pagans. After an orgiastic feast, he spends the night with a pagan woman named Marfa. When the pagans are arrested the next morning, Marfa swims to safety. 5. In 1408, while Rublev is working on the murals at Uspenskii Cathedral, the grand prince (Nazarov) pays a visit. Shortly thereafter, his soldiers blind the errant stone masons.

Part II. 6. The ambitious brother of the grand prince has formed an alliance with a Tatar khan (Beishenaliev). Together they attack the city of Vladimir, murdering, burning, and torturing; among their victims is the monk Patrikei (Nikulin) who refuses to tell where the church's treasures are hidden. Rublev kills a soldier who rapes a mentally disabled girl (Raush), after which he makes a vow of silence. 7. 1412. The repentant Kirill returns to the monastery, while marauding Tatars invite the disabled girl who had accompanied Rublev to come with them. 8. In 1423, soldiers of the grand prince are looking for a bell maker. The teenager Boriska (Burliaev) claims to have inherited the secret of the craft from his father and is put in charge of the complex casting process. Impressed by Boriska's inspired artistry and dedication, Rublev breaks his silence and resumes painting. The film concludes with a montage of Rublev's icon *Holy Trinity*.

ANIMATION. One of the world's pioneers of animation was the Polish-born **Wladyslaw Starewicz** whose stop-motion shorts *The Beautiful Leukanida, or, The War between the Stag Beetles and the Capricorn Beetles* (Prekrasnaia Liukanida, ili Voina rogachei i usachei, 1912) and *The Revenge of a Cinematographer* (Mest' kinematograficheskogo operatora, 1912), produced for **Aleksandr Khanzhonkov**, are among the earliest examples of the genre. In the following years, Starewicz made shorts based on fables such as *The Grasshopper and the Ant* (Strekoza i muravei, 1913), as well as World War I propaganda films.

Following Starewicz's immigration to France in 1918, animation in Russia came to a halt. It took several years before a new start was attempted. The 1920s were characterized by the use of animation clips both as animated political cartoons such as "Soviet Toys" and "Humoresques" in the *Kino-Truth* series by **Dziga Vertov**, and as industrial commercials. The first major successes in drawn animation were the propagandistic *The Interplanetary Revolution* (Mezhplanetnaia revoliutsiia) and *China on Fire* (Kitai v ogne, 1925). The production of the medium-length film on China's past and present under the patronage of the State Film College (the later **VGIK**) attracted a number of artists, including Iurii Merkulov, Zenon Kommissarenko, Nikolai Khodataev, **Ivan Ivanov-Vano**, Vladimir Suteev, and Valentina and Zinaida Brumberg, who subsequently devoted their careers to animation. Stylistically, the propaganda shorts were influenced by the 1920s avant-garde, in particular Vladimir Maiakovskii's Russian Telegraphic Agency (ROSTA) windows, the graphic works of Dmitrii Moor and Vladimir Favorskii, and children's books illustrations.

Children's films such as *The Skating Rink* (Katok, 1927) by Ivanov-Vano and Daniil Cherkes, and *The Huge Cockroach* (Tarakanishche, 1927) by Aleksandr Ivanov demonstrated the aesthetic variety of which drawn animation was capable. One of the most inventive Russian animation directors was **Mikhail Tsekhanovskii**, whose debut, *Mail* (aka *Post*/Pochta, 1928), about a letter that travels around the world, became an instant hit. However, Tsekhanovskii's *Tale of the Priest and His Worker, Blockhead* (Skazka o pope i rabotnike ego Balde, 1932), adapted from Aleksandr Pushkin, was never completed due to censorship interference. **Leonid Amal'rik**'s *Black and White* (Blek end Uait, 1932), a diatribe against colonial exploitation, and **Lev Atamanov**'s *The Tale of the Little White Bull* (Skazka pro belogo bychka, 1933, with Vladimir Suteev), which lampooned the League of Nations, treaded on safer ground. *The Little Organ* (Organchik, 1934) adapted by Khodataev from a chapter of Mikhail Saltykov-Shchedrin's novel *History of a City* (Istoriia odnogo goroda), deliberately embraced Favorskii's style, while Russian folklore traditions inspired *The Fairy Tale of Tsar Durondai* (Skazka o tsare Durondae, 1934) by Ivanov-Vano and the Brumberg sisters.

Aleksandr Ptushko, who had begun to experiment with stop-motion techniques in the late 1920s, made headlines releasing the world's first feature-length stop-motion tale, *The New Gulliver* (Novyi Gulliver, 1935), the mere scale of which is still astonishing, despite its obvious political naiveté. However, Soviet filmmakers' struggle to create their own unique form of animation was cut off by the leading Soviet film administrator, **Boris Shumiatskii**, who ordered the acquisition of Walt Disney's technology—and, implicitly, his smooth, deindividualized style—and stifled any other stylistic approaches. If before 1935, animated films were produced in various studios, including **Mezhrabpomfilm**, **Mosfilm**, and **Lenfilm**, the creation of Soiuzmultfilm studio in Moscow was intended to unite these efforts. However, one of the regrettable outcomes was the exclusion of stop-motion production and concentration on drawn animation. The more efficient technology and institutionalized division of labor helped increase the number of animated films yet neutralized the stylistic heterogeneity that had emerged in the 1920s and early 1930s. The only method now allowed was the so-called éclair, which implies the filming of live action in a conventional manner, after which animators use these frames as the basis of their drawings. Any deviation from such naturalistic emulation of nonanimation film was

prohibited. By the end of the 1930s, artists such as Merkulov, Khodataev, and Kommisarenko left Soviet animation in disappointment.

In Georgia, Vladimir Mudjiri (1907–1953) began the production
of animated films in 1929; his *Argonauts* (Argonavty, 1937) was
the first major animated picture of **Georgian cinema**. In Russia, the
theme of military watchfulness and preparation for the impending
war was raised in Babichenko's *Military Pages* (Boevye stranitsy,
1939), an animated history of the Red Army. In 1941, after the beginning of the Great Patriotic War, Soiuzmultfilm studio was evacuated
to Samarkand, yet the technical conditions were so inadequate that
the animated shorts intended for the War Film Almanac series were
completed at a time when the events to which they referred were no
longer relevant. Some of the work done during evacuation became
the basis for large-scale projects after the studio's return to Moscow,
among them *The Tale of Tsar' Saltan* (Skazka o tsare Saltane, 1943)
by the Brumberg sisters. Arguably the greatest achievement of Soviet animators in the postwar years was the feature-length *The Little
Humpbacked Horse* (Konek-Gorbunok, 1947) by Ivanov-Vano, a
picture whose wit and stylistic peculiarity are derived from Russian folklore. Subsequently, the fairy tale became the most popular
source for Soviet drawn animation, loved by millions of children
around the world who flocked to box-office hits such as *Grey Neck*
(Seraia sheika, 1948) by Amal'rik and Vladimir Polkovnikov, Tsekhanovskii's *The Tale of the Fisherman and the Little Fish* (Skazka o
rybake i rybke, 1949), Atamanov's *The Golden Antelope* (Zolotaia
antilopa, 1954) and *The Snow Queen* (Snezhnaia koroleva, 1957),
and *The Bewitched Boy* (Zakoldovannyi mal'chik, 1956) by Aleksandra Snezhko-Blotskaia and Polkovnikov. Fantastic elements became
such a mainstay of animation that they even entered contemporary
subject matter, for example, in *Fedia Zaitsev* (1948) by the Brumberg
sisters, a didactic story of an unruly boy who must learn a lesson from
toys and drawn figures.

In 1953, the production of stop-motion pictures was resumed, first
through a specialized department at Soiuzmultfilm, then at **Tallinfilm Studio** where **Elbert Tuganov** began Estonian animation with
children's puppet films such as *Little Peter's Dream* (Peetrikese Un-
enägu/Son Petrika, 1958) and *Ott in Outer Space* (Ott kosmoses/Ott"

v kosmose, 1961), and found worthy successors in **Heino Pars, Priit Pärn**, and other filmmakers.

The 1960s witnessed the appearance of a new generation of animation artists who made films both for adult audiences and for children; such artists included the former animator **Fedor Khitruk**, whose witty, surprising pictures betray the enjoyment of stylistic experimentation and the ability to express an idea with a minimum of means; **Andrei Khrzhanovskii**, a master of complex allegories and historical fantasies inspired by classical Russian literature and motifs of world culture; and **Iurii Norshtein**, perhaps Russia's internationally best-known animation filmmaker, whose masterpiece *Tale of Tales* (Skazka skazok, 1979) gained worldwide critical recognition.

In the years following the breakup of the Soviet Union, a number of private animation studios were founded in Russia and some of the former Soviet republics. Inventive animation shorts by **Garri Bardin**, as well as masterful literary adaptations by Aleksandr Petrov (*Dream of a Ridiculous Man*/Son smeshnogo cheloveka, 1992; *The Old Man and the Sea*/Starik i more, 1999), and others have won international recognition. *The Old Man and the Sea* won the 2000 Academy Award for Best Animated Picture. In August 2004, the Russian Film Committee (Roskomkino) decided to develop a federal plan to strengthen the Russian animation industry.

ANNENSKII, ISIDOR MARKOVICH (b. 13 March 1906, Ol'viopol' [Pervomaisk, Ukraine]–d. 2 May 1977, Moscow). Russian director and screenwriter. Annenskii studied at a music school in Odessa and graduated from the Odessa Theater School in 1922. He then worked as a stage actor and director in Odessa, Arkhangel'sk, Baku, and Moscow, before enrolling in the State Theater Institute in Moscow, where he stayed until 1934, and in the Soviet State Film School **VGIK**, graduating in 1936.

Annenskii debuted at Belgoskino (**Belarusfilm Studio**) with the medium-length Anton Chekhov adaptation *The Bear* (Medved', 1938), which immediately brought him fame as a knowledgeable, cultivated, and lively interpreter of classical literature. Another Chekhov adaptation, *The Man in the Shell* (Chelovek v futliare, 1939), featured—like the majority of Annenskii's films—an all-star cast. One of the director's greatest box-office successes was a brilliant screen version of Chekhov's early **comedy** *The Wedding* (Svad'ba, 1944). In part social satire, in part a comedy of manners, *The Wedding* on the surface reveals the hypocrisy of Russia's 19th-century petit-bourgeois milieu, yet its inspired depiction of philistinism ultimately exposes human weakness in general. The film has been appreciated by generations of grateful audiences on television.

Annenskii was a reliable, versatile, albeit critically underappreciated professional who succeeded in a variety of genres: adventure movies such as the patriotic pilot drama *The Fifth Ocean* (Piatyi okean, 1940), melodrama (*Ekaterina Voronina*, 1957), musical (*A Sailor from the Comet*/Matros s Komety, 1958), harmless youth comedy (*The First Trolley Bus*/Pervyi trolleibus, 1964), and revolutionary chronicle (*Tatyana's Day*/Tat'ianin den', 1967). But his true love was Russian classical literature, which he regularly adapted and popularized into the 1970s, ending his career with Aleksandr Ostrovskii's comedy *Talents and Admirers* (Talanty i poklonniki, 1973). All of Annenskii's adaptations are distinguished by precise timing and intonation, as well as a keen sense of the Russian mentality.

Annenskii was named Merited Artist of the RSFSR in 1971.

Other films: *The Anna Cross* (Anna na shee, 1954); *The Three* (Troe, 1969).

ANTONOV, ALEKSANDR PAVLOVICH (b. 13 February 1898, Moscow–d. 26 November 1962, Moscow). Russian actor. Antonov was a member of the Moscow Proletarian Culture (Proletkul't) Theater in 1920–1924 when he met **Sergei Eizenshtein**, who cast him in an episode of his first full-length feature *Strike* (Stachka, 1924). Eizenshtein then gave Antonov the part of Vakulinchuk, the politically conscious Bolshevik leader—and first martyr—of the mutiny on *Battleship Potemkin* (Bronenosets Potemkin, 1925), a role that inscribed the actor's name in world film history, despite its clichéd nature.

Unlike many Soviet actors of the early silent period, Antonov was able to continue his career into both the late silent and the sound period where he usually was employed in episodic roles of wise proletarians or sailors boasting physical prowess and political instinct. He worked with leading directors, including **Ivan Pyr'ev** on *A Rich Bride* (aka *The Country Bride*/Bogataia nevesta, 1938), **Vsevolod**

Pudovkin on *Suvorov* (1941), **Mikhail Romm** on *Secret Mission* (Sekretnaia missiia, 1950), and **Iulii Raizman** on *Cavalier of the Golden Star* (aka *Dream of a Cossack*/Kavaler zolotoi zvezdy, 1950). In supporting roles in **comedies** such as **Konstantin Iudin**'s *A Girl with Personality* (Devushka s kharakterom, 1939), Antonov managed to transcend his earlier screen image, adding a humorous and even mildly satirical flavor to his characterizations.

Antonov was named Merited Artist of the Russian Federation in 1950.

Other films: *Murderers Are on Their Way* (Ubiitsy vykhodiat na dorogu, 1942); *Hearts of Four* (aka *Four Hearts*/Serdtsa chetyrekh, 1941, released 1945); *Twelfth Night* (aka *As You Like It*/Dvenadtstataia noch', 1955).

ARANOVICH, SEMEN DAVIDOVICH (b. 23 July 1934, Derazhnia Station, Khmel'nitskii District, Ukraine–d. 8 September 1996, St. Petersburg). Russian director and screenwriter. Aranovich attended the Supreme Naval Aviation School in Nikolaev, graduating in 1955, and served for two years in the Soviet naval aviation troops. In 1965, he graduated from the Soviet State Film School **VGIK**, where he studied under **Roman Karmen**.

While on the staff of the Leningrad Documentary Studio in 1965–1970, Aranovich directed the biographical *Time That Is Always with Us* (Vremia, kotoroe vsegda s nami, 1965) and *The Friend of Gor'kii's—Andreeva* (Drug Gor'kogo—Andreeva, 1966), among others. Two of his **documentaries**—one about Maksim Gor'kii's last years, made in 1967, and one codirected with **Aleksandr Sokurov** on **Dmitrii Shostakovich** (1980)—were shelved and only released during the perestroika years.

The director's documentary origins made a stylistic impact on his feature films, all of which share an air of harsh realism. Two films about the Great Patriotic War betray Aranovich's firsthand knowledge of military life: *A Summer Trip to the Sea* (Letniaia poezdka k moriu, 1978) and *Torpedo Bombers* (Torpedonostsy, 1983); the latter became the filmmaker's greatest critical and box-office success. Despite their unquestionable patriotism, the depiction of war in these films is shockingly sober and antiromantic.

Until the late 1980s, Aranovich gave little indication of dissident views. His international business drama, *" . . . and Other Officials"* (" . . . i drugie offitsial'nye litsa," 1976), as well as the five-part television miniseries *Resistance* (Protivostoianie, 1985) and its six-part successor *The Great Game* (Bol'shaia igra, 1988), both based on Iulian Semenov's peculiar, self-aggrandizing secret service yarns, display a solid pro-Soviet and anti-Western foundation and won the director much official acclaim. However, during the deepening crisis and ultimate disintegration of the Soviet state, Aranovich revealed his profound skepticism about the Communist system and its past. His feature-length documentaries *The Anna Akhmatova File* (Lichnoe delo Anny Akhmatovoi, 1989), *I Was Stalin's Bodyguard* (Ia sluzhil v okhrane Stalina, 1989, defined as "an exercise in documentary mythology"), and *Peoples' Grand Concert* (Bol'shoi kontsert narodov, 1991) denounce common opportunism, everyday cruelty, cowardice, anti-Semitism, and other aspects of Soviet history. Aranovich's last film, the feature *Year of the Dog* (God sobaki, 1994), a Russian-French coproduction, is a gritty drama about an ex-convict in post-Communist Russia.

Beginning in 1992, Aranovich taught filmmaking at St. Petersburg University. In 1994, he was awarded the title People's Artist of Russia.

Other films: *The Red Diplomat* (Krasnyi diplomat, 1970, TV); *Rafferty* (1980, TV); *Islands* (Ostrova, 1993).

ARINBASAROVA, NATAL'IA [Russian sources list the patronymic Utelevna] (b. 24 September 1946, Frunze [now: Bishkek]). Kazakh actress. Arinbasarova studied at the Bolshoi Theater ballet school in Moscow until 1964 and joined the dance troupe of Almaty Opera Theater upon graduation. In 1965, director **Andrei Mikhalkov-Konchalovskii** cast her in the role of Altynai, a peasant girl who supports and ultimately loves the Communist teacher in her village and discovers her own destiny along the way, in *The First Teacher* (Pervyi uchitel'). For her performance, Arinbasarova won the prize for Best Female Lead at the Venice Film Festival in 1966. This sensational debut launched a career consistently successful over the following three decades, but without another highlight that could match her debut.

Arinbasarova, who was married to Mikhalkov-Konchalovskii and is the mother of director Egor Konchalovskii (b. 1966), subsequently enrolled in the Soviet State Film School **VGIK**, where she studied in **Sergei Gerasimov** and **Tamara Makarova**'s workshop, graduating in 1971. Gerasimov gave her the role of a young Kyrgyz ballet dancer in his contemporary epic *At the Lake* (U ozera, 1970). Important leads include the title role in the **Chingiz Aitmatov** adaptation *Djamila* (1969) and the World War II heroine Manshuk Mamedova in *The Song of Manshuk* (Pesn' o Manshuk, 1970) by Kazakh director Magit Begalin (1922–1978). Arinbasarova was cast by **Tolomush Okeev** in the social drama *The Ulan* (Ulan, 1977), by Polish filmmaker Jerzy Hoffman in the adventurous *Beautiful Stranger* (Piekna nieznajoma, 1992), and by **Ermek Shinarbaev** in the Kazakh-French coproduction *A Tender Heart* (Alciz Shurek/Coeur fragile, 1994).

By the mid-1990s Arinbasarova's career seemed to falter; however, she had a worthy comeback in a supporting role in the prize-winning Kazakh picture *Leila's Prayer* (Molitva Leily, 2002), a humanistic account of a young girl living near the Semipalatinsk nuclear testing site.

In 1979 Arinbasarova was named Merited Artist of the Russian Federation. In 1979, the actress won a USSR State Prize for the role of Kamshat Sataeva in Aleksei Sakharov's four-part epic *The Taste of Bread* (Vkus khleba, 1978).

Other films: *Tashkent, City of Bread* (Tashkent—gorod khlebnyi, 1968); *The Ship of Aliens* (Korabl' prishel'tsev, 1986); *Mika and Alfred* (Mika i Al'fred, 2008).

ARMENFILM STUDIO [Hayfilm]. Almost immediately after seizing power in Armenia in December 1920, the Communist administration put the country's meager cinema resources under the control of "revolutionary councils." Moscow-based cameraman **Aleksandr Lemberg** regularly traveled to Armenia and filmed historical events for Soviet newsreels. In 1922, the Armenian Council of People's Commissars (Sovnarkom) issued a decree to nationalize all privately owned movie theaters. On 16 April 1923, Sovnarkom announced the foundation of a State Cinema Organization (Goskino) as part of the Commissariat of Political Education, under the leadership of Daniel Dznuni. Moreover, the stockholding company State Photo and Film

Factory (Gosfotokino) was established in the country's capital, Yerevan. Over the next two years, it acquired more than 100 films from Russian and foreign companies. It also created a film laboratory that in 1924 released the feature-length **documentary** *Soviet Armenia* (Sovetskaia Armenia), made under Lemberg's supervision. In 1928, the film factory was renamed Armenkino.

The first Armenian feature film, the realistic melodrama *Honor* (Namus/Chest', 1926), adapted from Aleksandr Shirvanadze's novel, put its director, **Hamo Bek-Nazaryan**, who had begun his film career as an actor in Russian salon dramas and as a director in Georgia, at the helm of Armenian silent cinema. He solidified his reputation as a formally innovative film artist with *Zare* (1927) about the plight of the Kurdish people, the slapstick **comedy** *Shor and Shorshor* (Shor u Shorshore, 1928), and the somber *Khaspush* (1928), all of which were hailed for their authentic, nonexotic depiction of everyday life and enjoyed success with viewers and critics. *House on the Volcano* (Tune Hrabkhi Vra/Dom na vulkane, 1928), an impressive reconstruction of the struggle of oil workers in 1907–1908, was an Armenian-Azerbaijani coproduction with **Aleksandr Gal'perin** as cinematographer. Other leading directors were Patvakan Barkhurdyan (1898–1948; *Evil Spirit*/Zloi dukh, 1928), who had learned his craft from **Ivan Perestiani** in Georgia, and Amasi Martirosyan (1897–1971), whose *Gikor* (1934), about a sensitive boy crushed by the cruelty of rural life, was the last Armenian silent. It is noteworthy that **Armenian cinema** from its inception was closely connected with the country's theaters, whose stars provided it with high-quality performances.

In 1938, the studio was renamed Yerevan Film Studio. Prior to this, Bek-Nazaryan had created the first Armenian sound film, the social drama *Pepo* (1935), which became an international success. World-renowned composer **Aram Khachaturyan** wrote its score, as well as for the Civil War tale *Zangezur* (1938). However, the subsequent two decades were marked by an ever-decreasing number of films and narrowing genre diversity, with an emphasis on revolutionary themes and historical grandiosity, as evidenced by Bek-Nazaryan's *David-Bek* (1944). Even in the 1950s and early 1960s, when the studio was able to produce about four feature films annually, the preferred genre remained the revolutionary potboiler, of which **Erazm Karamyan** and **Stepan Kevorkov**'s *Personally Known* (Andzamb tchanachum em/Lichno izvesten, aka Kamo, 1958) and its sequels about the Communist activist Ter-Petrosyan (1882–1922)—aka "Kamo"—found particular official praise. In 1957, Yerevan Film Studio was renamed Armenfilm Studio.

By the mid-1960s, Armenian cinema began to blossom again. Two filmmakers defined new stylistic directions that were both specifically national in tone and rooted in a Soviet multinational framework. **Frunze Dovlatyan**'s *Hello, It's Me* (Barev, yes em/Zdravstvui, eto ia, 1966) conveyed genuine humanity and warmth in a war story blending tragic and nostalgic elements. **Henrik Malyan**'s *The Triangle* (Yerankyuni/Treugol'nik, 1967), which also thematizes the Great Patriotic War, features memorable performances by actors who soon became all-Soviet stars: **Armen Dzhigarkhanyan** and **Frunze Mher Mkrtchyan**. Malyan's forte remained dramas with a very limited number of characters whose experiences reflect large-scale historical processes, including *We and Our Mountains* (Menq enq, mer sarere/My i nashi gory, 1970) from Hrant Matevosyan's novel and *Nahapet* (aka *Life Triumphs*, 1977) about the 1915 genocide against the Armenian people. Dovlatyan took considerable risks with *The Brothers Saroyan* (Saroyan yeghbayrnere/Brat'ia Saroiany, 1968, codirected with **Khoren Abramyan**), in which the 1920s Civil War is depicted as a national tragedy.

While Malyan's and Dovlatyan's oeuvres were thematically essential for the renaissance of Armenian national cinema, the films of **Sergei Paradjanov** and **Artavazd Peleshyan** made a huge international impact due to their radical aesthetic innovations. Although Paradjanov worked less in his homeland than in Ukraine and Georgia, his *Sayat-Nova* (aka *The Color of Pomegranate*/Nran guyne/Tsvet granata, 1967), about medieval poet Arution Sayadian, had a groundbreaking effect. Peleshyan's extreme minimalism explored unexpected paths for cinematic language. Both directors' uncompromising vision made them classics of world cinema.

In 1976, Armenfilm was relocated to a newly built studio area in a Yerevan suburb. One of its most popular directors was **Edmond Keosayan**, who shared his activities between Moscow and Yerevan. His large-scale epic *The Star of Hope* (Huso astgh/Zvezda nadezhdy, 1979) about Armenia's 18th-century conflicts with the Ottoman Empire features Russia as a rescuer from annihilation. In the mid-1980s, a more self-conscious, explicit cinematic discourse on Stalinism and its influence on Armenian society began. The country's independence, declared in 1992, brought freedom of censorship but also isolation from international markets and increasing economic hardships. After a brief upsurge in production numbers in the early 1990s, Armenian cinema underwent a crisis similar to that in most former Soviet republics. The $600,000–$800,000 allocated every year by the government for the needs of cinema were barely sufficient to pay salaries and maintain the rapidly aging, underused equipment. Coproductions with France and other Western countries, however, helped to counter this trend so that filmmakers such as Edgar Baghdasaryan, Albert Mkrtchyan, Armen Dovlatyan, and Suren Babayan could develop a reputation at international festivals.

In 2005, Bagrat Sargsyan, president of the CS Media City holding, acquired Armenfilm Studio for 350 million drams (about $750,000)—against the protest of the country's filmmakers—and promised to bring its infrastructure up to date, retain its staff, and fund four full-length feature films per year.

ARMENIAN CINEMA. *See* ABRAMYAN, KHOREN; ARMEN-FILM STUDIO; ATAMANOV, LEV; BEK-NAZARYAN, HAMO; DOVLATYAN, FRUNZE; DZHIGARKHANYAN, ARMEN; GAL'PERIN, ALEKSANDR; KARAMYAN, ERAZM; KEO-SAYAN, EDMOND; KEVORKOV, STEPAN; KHACHATU-RYAN, ARAM; LEMBERG, ALEKSANDR; MALYAN, HENRIK; MKRTCHYAN, MHER FRUNZE; PELESHYAN, ARTAVAZD.

ARNSHTAM, LEO [in some sources: Lev] **OSKAROVICH** (b. 15 January 1905, Ekaterinoslavl' [Dnepropetrovsk]–d. 27 December 1979, Moscow). Russian director and screenwriter. Arnshtam studied piano at Petrograd Conservatory, graduating in 1923, and began a career as a professional pianist. He worked as the chief musical consultant for Vsevolod Meierkhol'd's theater in 1924–1927, before turning to cinema, where he became an expert in sound engineering.

From 1929 to 1931, Arnshtam helped develop a sound track for **Sergei Iutkevich**'s *Golden Mountains* (Zlatye gory), which originally had been conceived as a silent; he also contributed to its screenplay.

On Iutkevich's and **Fridrikh Ermler**'s groundbreaking *The Counterplan* (Vstrechnyi, 1932), Arnshtam was one of the screenwriters; according to some sources, he also worked as codirector.

Arnshtam's first independently directed picture was *Girlfriends* (Podrugi, 1936), a romanticized view of the events in Petrograd following the 1917 revolution. The film's three heroines grow from poor orphans to conscious Bolshevik fighters who actively participate in the historical turmoil and defend Petrograd against the attacking White Army. Due to its authentic atmosphere and the combination of melodrama and chronicle, the film achieved considerable popularity. *Friends* (Druz'ia, 1938) marked the beginning of what would become Arnshtam's favorite genre—the biopic, in this case re-creating episodes from the life of Communist hack Sergei Kirov and his political struggle in the Northern Caucasus. The harrowing drama *Zoia* (1944) about partisan martyr Zoia Kosmodemianskaia won Arnshtam a Stalin Prize in 1946 and a prize for Best Screenplay at the 1946 Cannes Film Festival. The score for *Zoia*, as for almost all of Arnshtam's films, was written by **Dmitrii Shostakovich**, his former fellow student at the conservatory.

With *Glinka* (aka *The Great Glinka*, 1947), Arnshtam turned to the founder of Russian opera. The film had to be reedited because of a portrayal of poet Aleksandr Pushkin by the popular comedic actor **Petr Aleinikov**, but ultimately won its maker another Stalin Prize. The Soviet-Bulgarian coproduction *A Lesson in History* (Urok istorii, 1957) is an attempt to reconstruct the events surrounding the burning of the German Reichstag in 1933 and the subsequent Leipzig trial against Bulgarian Communist leader Georgi Dimitrov. *Five Days, Five Nights* (Piat' dnei, piat' nochei, 1960), coproduced with East Germany, tells about the dramatic rescue of artwork from the Dresden Gallery by Soviet soldiers in 1945. Arnshtam's final picture was the biopic *Sof'ia Perovskaia* (1968), devoted to the famous terrorist (1853–1881) who organized the murder of Tsar Aleksandr II.

Arnshtam was named People's Artist of the RSFSR in 1969.

ARSENAL (aka *The January Upheaval in Kiev in 1918*/Ianvarskoe vosstanie v Kieve v 1918 godu, 1929). VUFKU studio, Odessa. 93 min., b/w. Directed by **Aleksandr Dovzhenko**. Script: Aleksandr Dovzhenko. Cinematography: **Danylo Demutskii**. Cast: Semen

Svashenko, **Amvrosii Buchma**, N. Kuchinskii, D. Erdman, Mykola Nademskii. Premiere: 26 July (other sources: 25 February) 1929.

At the end of World War I, a mother is waiting for her three sons. One of them returns without legs, so she—now aged and frail—must do the hard field work. Another mother cannot feed her crying children and beats them, while a furious soldier hits his weakened horse. The legendary Timosh (Svashenko) works at the arms factory Arsenal, where everybody is tired of the Ukrainian bourgeois government. The rank-and-file people distrust nationalist politicians under their leader Petliura (Kuchinskii). When the armed forces of the Central Rada break up a strike at Arsenal, the workers defend themselves. No bullet can kill Timosh, who confronts Petliura's reactionary forces with his bare chest.

ARTEM'EV, EDUARD NIKOLAEVICH (b. 30 November 1937, Novosibirsk). Russian composer. Artem'ev enrolled in the Moscow Choral School in 1945. After completing the program in 1955, he entered Moscow Conservatory, where he studied with Iurii Shaporin (1887–1966) until 1960. Upon graduation, Artem'ev joined the laboratory of Evgenii Murzin (d. 1970), creator of the first Soviet electronic musical device called ANS (Aleksandr Nikolaevich Skriabin).

As a composer, Artem'ev has been equally fascinated by Russian folklore and the musical avant-garde. Although he has written a number of symphonic pieces, including a concerto for piano and orchestra (1994), as well as operas (among them *Raskol'nikov*, 1987, from Fedor Dostoevskii's *Crime and Punishment*), Artem'ev's main creative interest is film music. His debut with the score for Otar Koberidze's *Toward a Dream* (Mechte navstrechu, 1963, jointly with Vano Muradeli) marked the first time ever that electronic music was used in Soviet cinema. Artem'ev's greatest achievements are associated with the films of **Andrei Tarkovskii** (*Solaris*, 1971; *The Mirror*/Zerkalo, 1975; *Stalker*, 1980), **Andrei Mikhalkov-Konchalovskii** (*Sibiriade*/Sibiriada, 1979; *The Inner Circle*, 1992; *The Odyssey*, 1994; *House of Fools*/Dom durakov, 2002; *Gloss*/Glianets, 2007), **Nikita Mikhalkov** (*Urga*, 1993; *Burnt by the Sun*/Utomlennye solntsem, 1995; *Barber of Siberia*/Sibirskii tsiriul'nik, 1999), and **Vadim Abdrashitov**. All in all, Artem'ev has written scores for over 100 films, some of them produced in the United States. His stylistic versatility and sense of contemporary atmosphere helped modernize Soviet cinema in the 1960s; conspicuously, Artem'ev has often been imitated by less original composers.

Artem'ev was named Merited Artist of the RSFSR in 1985 and People's Artist of Russia in 1999. His son, Artemii Artem'ev (b. 1966), studied music and foreign languages in Moscow and Los Angeles and also works as a film composer.

Other films: *A Driver for Vera* (Voditel' dlia Very, 2004); *Doktor Zhivago* (2005, TV); *Twelve* (Dvenadtsat', 2007).

ARTMANE, VIJA [real first name: Alida; Russian sources also list the patronymic Fritsevna] (b. 12 July [other sources: August] 1929, Tukuma, Latvia). Latvian actress. Artmane, daughter of a Polish mother and a German father, began her distinguished screen and stage career after studying in the drama studio of Rainis Academic Art Theater in Riga, which hired her upon graduation in 1949.

Artmane's debut in **Latvian cinema** was the female lead in the historical epic *Following the Swan Flock of Clouds* (Kā gulbji balti padebeši iet/Za lebedinoi staei oblakov, 1956), directed by Pavel Armand. However, it was the role of Sonia in Mikhail Ershov's blockbuster melodrama *Kindred Blood* (Rodnaia krov', 1963) that made a lasting impression on tens of millions of Soviet viewers. Artmane's delicate features contrasted strangely with her character's physical job on a ferry, yet the actress conveyed the death of a mother of three with such emotional depth that critical objections to the film seemed petty. For the next 25 years, Artmane's warm femininity, dignity, and natural elegance made her the Baltic darling of Russian directors, who featured her in numerous pictures, albeit of uneven quality.

Artmane joined the Communist Party in 1968 and was a candidate to the Central Committee of the Latvian CP from 1971 to 1976. In 1965, she was named People's Artist of the Latvian SSR and in 1969, People's Artist of the USSR; in 1980, a documentary about the actress, *Conversation with a Queen* (Razgovor s korolevoi), was released.

After Latvia's newly won independence, Artmane was publicly accused of political opportunism during the Soviet period, evicted from her apartment, and virtually left without roles, forcing her to switch theaters in the late 1990s. Only in 2000 did Russian television producers remember the still popular actress and cast her in several successful miniseries, one of which, **Vladimir Khotinenko**'s *The Golden Age* (Zolotoi vek, 2003), features Artmane as Catherine the Great.

Other films: ***Nobody Wanted to Die*** (Nekas nenorejo mirti/Nikto ne khotel umirat', 1965); *Edgar and Christina* (1967); *Theater* (Teātris/Teatr, 1978); *Only for the Crazy* (Ai hult hulludele/Tol'ko dlia sumasshedshikh, 1989); *Kamenskaia* (2000, TV).

ASANOVA, DINARA KULDASHEVNA (b. 24 October 1942, Frunze [now: Bishkek]–d. 4 April 1985, Murmansk). Kyrgyz and Russian director and screenwriter. After finishing high school in 1959, Asanova began to work at **Kyrgyzfilm Studio** as an assistant cutter, assistant director—among others, on **Larisa Shepit'ko**'s *Heat* (Znoi, 1963)—and an actress in episodic roles. She then studied at the Soviet State Film School **VGIK** with **Mikhail Romm** and **Aleksandr Stolper**, graduating in 1969.

In 1974, Asanova was hired by **Lenfilm Studio** and immediately made a name for herself with her first feature, *The Woodpecker Doesn't Get Headaches* (Ne bolit golova u diatla, 1975). Both this film and *Private Key* (Kliuch bez prava peredachi, 1977) deal with Asanova's preferred theme: the emotional turmoils and moral choices of youngsters. *The Teenagers* (aka *Tough Kids*/Patsany, 1983), the story of a selfless pedagogue who founds a camp for juvenile delinquents, became Asanova's greatest box-office success and also won her a USSR State Prize. Her last completed film, *"My Sweet, Dear, Beloved, Only One . . ."* ("Milyi, dorogoi, liubimyi, edinstvennyi . . . ," 1984), tells of an 18-year-old who steals a baby to test her lover's loyalty.

In her pictures, Asanova neither idealizes young people nor depicts them in overly harsh tones. Often, she confronts youthful naïveté and lack of stable principles with older people's aggressiveness, materialism, and petty-mindedness. In order to achieve natural, authentic performances from her nonprofessional actors, Asanova used improvisation in dialogues and sometimes even in plot development. Visually, her films resemble **documentaries**.

Asanova died of heart ailment during the shooting of *The Unknown Woman* (Neznakomka), which remains unfinished. Three documentaries that were made after her passing testify to the enormous respect and love that she enjoyed: In 1987, Igor' Alimpiev directed *I Love You All Very Much* (Ochen' vas vsekh liubliu), in 1988 Viktor Titov made *Dinara*, and in 2003, Marina Chudina released *Dinara Asanova* (the first two films are feature-length).

Asanova was named Merited Artist of the Russian Federation in 1980. In Asanova's hometown Bishkek in Kyrgyzstan, a street has been named after her.

Other films: *Rudol'fio* (1969, short); *Disaster* (Beda, 1978); *My Wife Left Me* (Zhena ushla, 1980, TV); *What Would You Choose?* (Chto by ty vybral? 1981, TV).

ASCENSION, THE (Voskhozhdenie, 1976). **Mosfilm Studio.** 111 min., b/w. Directed by **Larisa Shepit'ko.** Script: Iurii Klepikov, Larisa Shepit'ko from Vasil' Bykau's 1970 novella "Sotnikau." Cinematography: Vladimir Chukhnov. Music: **Al'fred Shnitke.** Cast: Boris Plotnikov, Vladimir Gostiukhin, **Anatolii Solonitsyn,** Sergei Iakovlev, Liudmila Poliakova, Viktoriia Gol'dentul'. Premiere: 2 April 1978.

In Belarus in 1942, the Red Army officer Sotnikau (Plotnikov) and the partisan Rybak (Gostiukhin) are arrested in a village, following a raid by Nazi police. Together with the peasant woman Demchikha (Poliakova) and the Jewish girl Basia, they are sentenced to death by hanging. The Nazi collaborator Portnov (Solonitsyn) interrogates the partisans, trying to break them with threats and cold, cynical logic. While Rybak gives in and becomes a traitor, Sotnikau resists to the end, displaying exemplary dignity even when facing execution.

ASHIMOV, ASANALI (b. 8 May 1939 [other sources: 1937], Baikadam, Kazakhstan). Kazakh actor, director, and scriptwriter. Ashimov studied at the Kurmangazy State Conservatory of Kazakhstan and graduated from the Almaty Institute of Theater and Art in 1961. Since 1963, he has been an actor and director at the Mukhtar Auezov Kazakh State Academic Theater in Almaty.

Preeminent director **Shaken Aimanov** gave Ashimov his first major role in **Kazakh cinema** in the drama *In One District* (V odnom raione, 1961). The actor gained national renown in Aimanov's revolutionary thriller *The End of the Ataman* (Konets atamana, 1970), portraying the Cheka (secret police) Captain Chad"iarov, a former prince who works undercover as a White Army officer. Ashimov was later cast in similar parts in the historical spy drama *Trans-Siberian Express* (Transsibirskii ekspress, 1977) and its sequel, *The Manchurian Variant* (Manchzhurskii variant, aka *Hotel Hokuman*, 1989). In 1998, he impressed critics with a paradoxical reversal of his Soviet heroic image, playing a former Cheka/NKVD agent who is responsible for the deaths of many innocent people and must suddenly confront his Stalinist past, in Damir Manabaev's *Uncle, I Will Kill You!* (aka *A Purely Kazakh Affair*, released 2002). This role brought Ashimov the award for Best Male Lead at the first national Kazakh film festival, Shaken's Stars, in 2003.

Ashimov debuted as a director with *The Year of the Dragon* (God drakona, 1981), the adaptation of Uighur author Ziya Samadi's historical novel *Mayimkan* about a failed 19th-century popular uprising. In 1985, he made a biographical miniseries about scholar and explorer Chokan Valikhanov (1835–1865). In *Kozi Korpesh and Bayan Sulu* (1992), Ashimov adapted the popular Romeo and Juliet legend of Kazakh folklore for the screen (incidentally, his teacher Aimanov had started his filmmaking career 40 years earlier with the same tale, in *Poem about Love*/Poema o liubvi, 1954). In 2004, Ashimov directed *The House at the Salt Lake* (Dom u solenogo ozera), a moving if stylistically uneven account of the war years in Kazakhstan, conveying a message of forgiveness and hope for peaceful togetherness among nations.

Ashimov, a member of the Communist Party since 1973, was named People's Artist of the USSR in 1980. He is the chairman of Kazakhstan's Union of Filmmakers. His son Sagi Ashimov (1961–1999) also worked as an actor.

Other films: (as actor) *The Choice* (Vybor, 1976); *Turksib* (1987); *Abulkhair Khan* (1993); *Ermak* (1996).

ASKOL'DOV, ALEKSANDR IAKOVLEVICH (b. 17 June 1932, Moscow). Russian director. Upon graduation from Moscow Lomonosov University in 1955 and the Gor'kii Institute of World Literature in 1958, Askol'dov worked as an administrator for the USSR Ministry of Culture and for Goskino's Main Department of Feature Film Production, where he was the supervisor for the **Gor'kii Studio for Children's and Youth Films**. Askol'dov then studied film direction with **Leonid Trauberg** at the Supreme Courses for Screenwriters and Directors (VKSR), graduating in 1966.

Perhaps Askol'dov's previous high-ranking administrative position and his familiarity with the cultural bureaucracy helped him outwit censors when launching his own first feature project, a black-and-white Civil War drama about a female commissar who gives birth to an unwanted child and leaves it with the family of a Jewish artisan in the town of Berdichev. Daringly original in its visual style and handling of sound, *The Commissar* (Komissar, 1968), adapted from a short story by Vasilii Grossman (1905–1964), challenged virtually every written and unwritten law of Soviet cinema by sharply juxtaposing family values and revolutionary principles, religious humanism and the inhumane Bolshevik dogma, rank-and-file naiveté and the ruthlessness of Communist military commanders. Only upon the film's completion did officials realize that this was not another example of Aesopian language allowing for partial corrections; *The Commissar* as a whole and in each of its parts was beyond ideological repair, and thus ordered destroyed. Askol'dov was never given a chance to redeem himself. Ostracized by his colleagues, excluded from the Communist Party, and fired from the staff of Gor'kii Studio, he was forced out of cinema altogether. Only his unexpected appeal to international media at a press conference during the 1987 Moscow Film Festival brought *The Commissar*, of which one negative had been rescued, finally to the attention of audiences worldwide.

For Askol'dov, however, prizes and fame came too late. Having held jobs such as concert hall director, he never found his way back into the film industry. Since the early 1990s, Askol'dov has lived in Germany, lecturing in film schools. The dramatic story of his one and only completed work has itself become part of Soviet film history.

ATAMANOV, LEV KONSTANTINOVICH (b. 21 February 1905, Moscow–d. 11 February 1981, Moscow). Russian animation director, scriptwriter, and animator. Born into the family of russified Armenians, Atamanov studied acting and directing with **Lev Kuleshov** at the First State Film School, graduating in 1926. He devoted himself to drawn **animation** and subsequently became one of the pioneers of that genre in the Soviet Union. Atamanov first worked as an assistant to the famous painter and animator Iurii Merkulov (1901–1979) and later joined **Mezhrabpomfilm Studio**.

Atamanov's debut was the didactic short *Across the Street* (Ulitsa poperek, 1931, with Vladimir Suteev), explaining traffic rules in a humorous, entertaining manner. He then made one of the first animated sound pictures, *The Tale of the Little White Bull* (Skazka pro belogo bychka, 1933), an allegorical anti-Western pamphlet directed against the League of Nations.

In 1936 Atamanov moved to Yerevan where at **Armenfilm Studio** he directed the first animated pictures of **Armenian cinema**, *Dog and Cat* (Shun u katun/Pes i kot, 1938), from a fairy tale by Hovanes Tumanian, and *The Priest and the Goat* (Tertern u aytze/Pop i koza, 1941). During the Great Patriotic War, Atamanov served in the Red Army. After his discharge, he completed one more animated film in Armenia—where he sometimes is credited as Lev Atamanyan—*The Magic Carpet* (Kakhardakan gorg/Volshebnyi kover, 1948). He then returned to Moscow and joined Soiuzmultfilm studio. Atamanov's full-length animated pictures—*The Golden Antelope* (Zolotaia antilopa, 1954) from Indian fairy tales and *The Snow Queen* (Snezhnaia koroleva, 1957) from Hans Christian Andersen's tale—proved huge national and international hits with children and adults alike. He later tried out a variety of styles and topics, among them political satire, for example, in *That's in Our Power* (Eto v nashikh silakh, 1970), from caricatures of Danish Communist cartoonist Herlup Bidstrup (1912–1988), who was very popular in the Soviet Union.

Atamanov was named People's Artist of the Russian Federation in 1978.

Other films: *Blot in the Arctic* (Kliaksa v Arktike, 1934); *The Scarlet Flower* (Alen'kii tsvetochek, 1952); *Ballerina on the Ship* (Balerina na korable, 1969); *A Kitten Named Bow-Wow* (Kotenok po imeni Gav, 1977–1980, four parts).

AVERBAKH, IL'IA ALEKSANDROVICH (b. 28 July 1934, Leningrad–d. 11 January 1986, Leningrad [other sources: Moscow]). Russian director and screenwriter. Averbakh graduated from Leningrad Medical Institute in 1958 and practiced as a doctor before enrolling in Goskino's Advanced Screenwriting Courses, where he studied with **Evgenii Gabrilovich** until 1964. He joined the Supreme Courses for Screenwriters and Directors (affiliated with **Lenfilm Studio**), which he completed in 1967; one of his teachers was **Grigorii Kozintsev**.

In his first full-length feature, *Degree of Risk* (Stepen' riska, 1968), Averbakh describes the intense interaction between an old surgeon and a young patient whose life is saved against all odds. Based on a book by legendary cardiologist Nikolai Amosov (1913–2002), its unabashed focus on purely intellectual approaches to life and death came as a surprise to discriminating viewers and made this debut a remarkable success. Generational tensions also define Averbakh's best-known film, *Monologue* (Monolog, 1972), about a reclusive scientist who has to confront changing realities and his own illusions when living with his daughter and granddaughter. *Other People's Letters* (Chuzhie pis'ma, 1975) depicts the difficult relations between an idealistic provincial teacher and her cynical students with painful accuracy; Russian critics have interpreted this film as Averbakh's testament to the ideals of the 1960s generation, the so-called *shestidesiatniki*. Averbakh's last film, the beautiful yet underrated *The Voice* (Golos, 1982), was eerily prophetic for the director's own life: a young actress suffering from a terminal illness desperately tries to define the meaning of her creative efforts.

Often described as the leader of intellectual cinema within the Leningrad School of filmmaking in the 1970s, Averbakh consistently devoted his films to the Soviet intelligentsia and its social and ethical problems. The majority of conflicts in Averbakh's pictures arise from intergenerational miscommunication; the alienation between individuals is depicted as a common aspect of urban rather than specifically Soviet life. Averbakh points to communication as a value per se—indeed, only by communicating do his characters gain fulfillment, despite temporary doubts and ethical confusion. At the same time, Averbakh's films reflected the ever-increasing and irreversible disenchantment of Soviet intellectuals with their mission; thematically, his oeuvre corresponds with Iurii Trifonov's urban novellas. Averbakh's cinematic style is not as cerebral as might be expected from his preferred themes; rather, it betrays taste and a fine sense of rhythm. Nonetheless, the lack of action and clear plot structure prevented his films—with the exception of *Degree of Risk*—from achieving mass popularity.

In 1976, Averbakh was awarded the title Merited Artist of the RSFSR. His wife, screenwriter Natal'ia Riazantseva (b. 1938), wrote the scripts for several of his pictures. In 2003, Andrei Kravchuk made a **documentary** about the director.

Other films: *The Personal Life of Kuziaev Valentin* (Lichnaia zhizn' Kuziaeva Valentina, 1967; Averbakh contributed the episode "Papania" to this omnibus project); *Drama from the Old Life* (Drama iz starinnoi zhizni, 1971); *Fariatiev's Fantasies* (Fantazii Fariat'eva, 1979, TV).

AZERBAIJANFILM STUDIO. Founded in 1922 in Baku, the capital of Soviet Azerbaijan, the studio was established as a "film factory" by the government of Azerbaijan. It was integrated into the People's Commissariat of Education (Narkompros) as part of the Azerbaijani Photo and Film Administration (AKFU), which oversaw the existing film theaters and production facilities that had been nationalized by decree in 1920. (The first Azerbaijani feature film, *In the Realm of Oil and Millions* [V tsarstve nefti i millionov] was created by Boris Svetlov from a novel by Ibrahim Musabeyov in 1916; it deals with the oil boom and the sudden riches that it brought to entrepreneurs.)

The new film factory initially focused on the production of newsreels and **documentaries**. The first Azerbaijani feature film made under Soviet rule, *The Legend of the Maiden Tower* (Legenda o devich'ei bashne), was directed by prominent set designer Vladimir Balliuzek (1881–1957) in 1924. Early on, the studio established educational facilities in which future native film specialists received professional training. Among non-Azeri directors and cameramen who taught or worked at the film factory were **Hamo Bek-Nazaryan**, **Vsevolod Pudovkin**, **Nikoloz Shengelaia**, **Boris Barnet**, and **Leonid Kosmatov**. From 1926 to 1930, when the studio was called Azerbaijani State Cinema (Azgoskino), several of its productions delivered antireligious messages. Thus, Islamic traditions are the focus of *In the Name of God* (Bismillah/Vo imia boga, 1925) by Abbas Mirza Sharif-Zade (1893–1937), an actor and one of the first native Azerbaijani directors, and in Bek-Nazaryan's *Sevil* (1929), which called upon women to take off their veils. Bek-Nazaryan helmed a visually original re-creation of a strike of oil workers at the turn of the century in *House on the Volcano* (Tune Hrabkhi Vra/Dom na vulkane, 1928).

From 1930 to 1933, the studio was called Azkino, and in 1933–1934 Azfilm. A number of its pictures dealt with contemporary developments, especially the country's forced industrialization, for example, *The First Komsomol Brigade* (Pervaia komsomol'skaia, 1931). One of the most famous films, *Twenty-six Commissars* (Dvadtsat' shest' komissarov, 1933), directed by **Nikoloz Shengelaia** and **Stepan Kevorkov**), commemorated events in 1918 when the Bolsheviks in Baku were temporarily defeated.

In 1934–1935, the studio was renamed Azgoskinprom, and from 1935 to 1940 was called Azerfilm. Barnet shot *By the Bluest of Seas* (U samogo sinego moria, 1936) in Baku, with Samed Ashum ogly Nardanov (1911–1939) as his codirector; Nardanov is the first professional artist of **Azerbaijani cinema** who had received his education at the Soviet State Film School **VGIK** and later completed one film of his own, *Kendlidliar* (1940). **Viktor Turin** of *Turksib* fame made the first Azerbaijani sound film, *The People of Baku* (Bakintsy, 1938), which is distinguished by an exceptional choreography.

From 1941 to 1959, the studio was called Baku Film Studio. One of its greatest successes was *The Cloth-Peddler* (Arshin Mal Alan, 1945), from a 1910 operetta by Uzeyir Hajibeyov; this film won its director, Rza Takhmazib (1894–1980), a Stalin Prize in 1946, the first Azerbaijani feature film to receive such recognition. The large-scale *Fatali Khan* (1947), directed by **Efim Dzigan**, tells about the 18th-century struggles to unify the existing khanates into one Azerbaijan. Among the filmmakers whose careers span several decades was actor and director Aga Rza Kuliev (1898–1976).

In the 1960s, several early films were remade, among them *The Twenty-six Commissars* (1965), *The Cloth-Peddler* (1966), and *Sevil* (1970). The 1970s were characterized by a turn to contemporary problems, for example, in the films of Eldar Tofil ogly Kuliev (b. 1941) and Tofik Tagi-zade (b. 1929). In 1979, the studio raised eyebrows with the radical anticorruption drama *Interrogation* (Istintag/Dopros) by **Rasim Ojagov**. The internationally best-known Azerbaijani film-maker is **Rustam Ibrahimbekov**, who successfully continued his career after the breakup of the Soviet Union. In 1997, he organized an annual East-West Film Festival in Baku that presents Azerbaijani, Russian, and Georgian films. Among Azerbaijani filmmakers who came to prominence in the 1980s and 1990s are Vaghif Mustafayev (b. 1954) and Ayaz Salayev (b. 1960).

From 1992 to 2005, numerous small businesses found a home at the studio's premises, while film production came to a halt. In 2005, Azerbaijanfilm Studio was put under the auspices of the country's Ministry of Culture, which assigned $20 million to its renovation. Each year, between two and four full-length feature films are produced. The studio facilities are also leased to other companies.

AZERBAIJANI CINEMA. *See* AZERBAIJANFILM STUDIO; BEK-NAZARYAN, HAMO; IBRAHIMBEKOV, RUSTAM; OJA-GOV, RASIM MIRKASUM-OGLY; SAYIDBEYLI, HASAN MEHDI-OGLY.

– B –

BABKAUSKAS, BRONIUS (b. 9 April 1921, Pilviskiai–d. 21 October 1975). Lithuanian actor. Babkauskas studied at the Workhouse acting studio in Kaunas and with renowned theater innovator Juozas Miltinis in the studio of Panevėžys, graduating in 1940. He then became a member of the Panevėžys theater.

In **Lithuanian cinema**, Babkauskas was valued for his strong, natural screen presence, which allowed him to succeed in both lead and supporting roles and gained him considerable popularity. He began his career in **Aleksandr Faintsimmer**'s opportunistic *Dawn over the Neman* (Aušra prie Nemuno/Nad Nemanom rassvet, 1953) and later appeared in **Vytautas Žalakevičius**'s *Adam Wants to Be a Man* (Adomas nori buti zmogumi/Adam khochet byt' chelovekom, 1959). Žalakevičius made Babkauskas a mainstay in other films as well—as the old Communist Rimša in the dramatic postwar *Chronicle of One Day* (Vienos dienos kronika/Khronika odnogo dnia, 1963), as

Marcinkus in *Nobody Wanted to Die* (Nekas nenorejo mirti/Nikto ne khotel umirat', 1965), and in his stylish propaganda flick about contemporary Latin America, *That Sweet Word: Liberty!* (Eto sladkoe slovo—svoboda, 1973).

Babkauskas also was a preferred actor in the films of **Arūnas Žebriūnas**, including *The Last Shot* (Paskutinis šūvis/Poslednii vystrel), part of the prize-winning omnibus project *Living Heroes* (Gyvieji didvyriai/Zhivye geroi, 1960), and the poetic *The Girl and the Echo* (Paskutinė atostogų diena/Devochka i ekho, 1964) in which he played the father. He worked with **Marijonas Giedrys** (*Alien People*/Svetimi/Chuzhie, 1961) and **Raimondas Vabalas** (*The Cannonade*/Kanonada, 1961, codirected with Žebriūnas), and appeared in the remarkable humanist parable *Insanity* (Hullumeelsus/Bezumie, 1968) by Estonian filmmaker **Kaljo Kiisk**. Apart from such artistically challenging performances, the actor was also cast in espionage and war films, as well as fairy tales.

Babkauskas, who joined the Communist Party in 1955, was named People's Artist of the Lithuanian SSR in 1965.

Other films: *The Agent's Fate* (Sud'ba rezidenta, 1970); *May There Be Life* (Ave vita/Da budet zhizn', 1970); *The Chairman's Son* (Syn predsedatelia, 1976).

BABOCHKIN, BORIS ANDREEVICH (b. 18 January 1904, Saratov–d. 17 July 1975, Moscow). Russian actor and director. Babochkin briefly studied with **Mikhail Chekhov** and, in 1920–1921, in Illarion Pevtsov's studio Young Masters. He began his acting career on the stage of various provincial theaters before joining the troupe of the Leningrad Theater of Satire in 1927. In 1948–1951 and from 1955 until his death, Babochkin worked as an actor and director at the Moscow Malyi Theater.

In cinema, Babochkin debuted with the role of Karavaev in **Semen Timoshenko**'s silent revolutionary drama *The Uproar* (Miatezh, 1929). He gained legendary fame as Red Army commander *Chapaev* (1934) in the **Vasil'ev brothers'** cult hit. Energetic, flamboyant, occasionally stubborn and merciless, sometimes melancholic and humane—all of these facets were impressively blended in Babochkin's interpretation of the semianarchist hothead and endeared both the actor and his character to generations of Soviet viewers. Sadly, audiences identified Babochkin with Chapaev to a degree that became irritating and stifling for this cultured artist. He continued to work for the Vasil'ev brothers in less significant fare, such as *The Defense of Tsaritsyn* (Oborona Tsaritsyna, 1942, interestingly, in the part of a White Army officer), and also played under other leading directors such as **Sergei Gerasimov** and **Mikhail Kalatozov** (*The Invincible*/ Nepobedimye, 1942), **Aleksandr Stolper** (*Story of a Real Man*/ Povest' o nastoiashchem cheloveke, 1948), and **Fridrikh Ermler** (*The Great Force*/Velikaia sila, 1950). Among the actor's later film roles, that of Sam Bolder in **Mikhail Shveitser**'s Leonid Leonov adaptation *The Escape of Mr. MacKinly* (Begstvo mistera Mak-Kinli, 1975) is noteworthy; it was recognized with a posthumous USSR State Prize in 1977.

In 1945, Babochkin directed *Native Fields* (Rodnye polia) about a Soviet village community; he also played the lead. His second feature, the sea adventure *Story of "The Furious"* (Povest' o 'Neistovom,' 1947) was generally seen as a failure.

Babochkin began to teach at the Soviet State Film School **VGIK** in 1944 and was promoted to the rank of full professor in 1966. He joined the Communist Party in 1948 and received Stalin Prizes for *Chapaev* in 1941 and *The Great Force* in 1951. He was named People's Artist of the USSR in 1963 and Hero of Socialist Labor in 1974. Babochkin is buried at Novodevich'e cemetery in Moscow.

Other films: *Vozvrashchenie Neitana Bekkera* (The Return of Nathan Becker, 1933); *Chapaev Is with Us* (Chapaev s nami, 1941); *Summer Folk* (Dachniki, 1967, also codirector); *Carpenters' Tales* (Plotnitskie rasskazy, 1972, TV).

BAKLANOVA, OL'GA VLADIMIROVNA [American spelling: Olga Baclanova] (b. 19 August 1896, Moscow–d. 6 September 1974, Vevey, Switzerland). Russian and American actress. Baklanova started her stage career at the Moscow Art Theater (MKhAT) in 1912 and made her film debut two years later. Fellow MKhAT members Viacheslav Turzhanskii, whose forte was mystical tales, and Boris Sushkevich, who specialized in adaptations of classical literature, who also risked working in cinema, cast Baklanova in their pictures. Baklanova, displaying fragility and hypersensitivity in her performances, appeared in Sushkevich's *When the Strings of the*

Heart Sound (Kogda zvuchat struny serdtsa, 1914), Turzhanskii's *Wanderer beyond the Grave* (Zagrobnaia skitalitsa, 1915) in which she portrays a vampire (and the director of one of her victims), and numerous others. Jay Leyda writes that, when her teacher, Konstantin Stanislavskii, heard of Baklanova's role in the occult drama *The Great Magaraz* (Velikii Magaraz, 1915), he refused to talk to her for six months. Undisturbed by the erstwhile dubious reputation of a movie star, Baklanova continued to work in cinema, being cast in Sushkevich's Anton Chekhov adaptation *Belated Flowers* (Tsvety zapozdalye, 1917) as the female lead. She also participated in the *agitka* Bread (Khleb, 1918).

In 1923 (other sources: 1925), Baklanova toured the United States with the troupe of ballerina Anna Pavlova and decided to not return to the Soviet Union. Initially, she worked in theaters in New York, before moving to Hollywood in the late 1920s. After a few successful roles in silents, including Josef von Sternberg's *The Docks of New York* (1928), she struggled with the transition to sound film. However, one of her appearances became part of film history: she portrayed the trapeze artist Cleopatra in Tod Browning's *Freaks* (1931). In later years, Baklanova returned to the stage and also worked for radio programs.

According to one source, Baklanova received the title Merited Artist of the (Soviet) Republic in 1925.

Other films: *Mozart and Salieri* (Motsart i Sal'eri, 1915); *Love under a Mask* (Liubov' pod maskoi, 1915); *He Who Gets Slapped* (Tot, kto poluchaet poshchechiny, 1916); *Avalanche* (1928); *Downstairs* (1932); *Claudia* (1943).

BALABANOV, ALEKSEI OKTIABRINOVICH (b. 25 February 1959, Sverdlovsk). Russian director and screenwriter. Balabanov studied translation at the Pedagogical Institute in Gor'kii (now: Nizhnii Novgorod), graduating in 1981, and served in the Soviet armed forces until 1983. He worked as an assistant director at Sverdlovsk film studio in 1983–1987 and studied at the Supreme Courses for Screenwriters and Directors (VKSR) in Moscow until 1990.

In his directorial debut, the black-and-white *Happy Days* (Schastlivye dni, 1991), which uses motifs from Samuel Beckett, Balabanov emerged with a fully developed cinematic style—minimalist, sarcastic, and quietly subversive. His adaptation of Franz Kafka's *The Castle* (Zamok, 1994) was filled with dark humor and mystical satire, depicting the absurdity of modern, bureaucratized, creativity-wrecking civilization. Balabanov then contributed the ironic episode "Trofim'" to the omnibus *The Arrival of a Train* (Pribytie poezda, 1995), Russia's peculiar yet worthy homage to the 100th anniversary of cinema.

The director proved that he had his finger on the pulse of contemporary Russian audiences with the melancholic thriller *Brother* (Brat, 1997), which marks the beginning recovery of Russia's moribund film industry and its turn to specific Russian themes and perceptions. The picture's clever use of rock music—played by the group Nautilus Pompilius—and numerous cultural and cinematic allusions made it fascinating for both viewers craving a modern superhero and more sophisticated film buffs. However, to some critics, Balabanov's deliberate moral ambiguity seemed troubling and fraught with potential abuse by nationalist, xenophobic forces.

His next picture, *Of Freaks and Men* (Pro urodov i liudei, 1999), silenced those who had bemoaned Balabanov's increasing commercialization. Shot in gloomy black-and-white, the story of Siamese twins who are exploited by a ruthless impresario conveys a deep pessimism about human nature and the illusions driving idealists and their followers. The complex, multifaceted picture can be interpreted as a cleverly calculated attack on one of the post-Soviet intelligentsia myths—namely, that of the splendor of Silver Age, revealing its inherent morbid voyeurism and lack of morality.

Brother 2 (2000), an openly—and self-mockingly—commercial sequel, shows patriotic superhero Danila Bagrov gloriously beating American crooks on their own turf. This huge video-market success caused considerable controversy due to its provocative challenge to common Western values and beliefs. *War* (Voina, 2002), a more serious and stylistically coherent film, once again took no prisoners. An openly partisan account of the Chechen conflict, it exposes Western attitudes of tolerance and fair play as dangerously naïve and potentially suicidal not just for Russia but for the entire Occidental civilization. Balabanov, who seems to deliberately invite accusations of nationalism and anti-Islamic bias, does not, however, idealize the reality of Russia, depicting its administration as incompetent and corrupt and its provincial youth as hopelessly degenerate and self-destructive. It seems safe to say that Balabanov's stories generally meander between moderate patriotism and bohemian individualism.

Balabanov was mentor to actor **Sergei Bodrov Jr.**, who became a star in the role of Danila Bagrov in the *Brother* dilogy and whose directing efforts he supported.

Other films: *Nastia and Egor* (Nastia i Egor, 1989, doc.); *On Aeronautics in Russia* (O vozdushnom letanii v Rossii, 1990, doc.); *Blind Man's Bluff* (Zhmurki, 2005); *I Feel No Pain* (Mne ne bol'no, 2006); *Freight 200* (Gruz 200, 2007); *Morphium* (Morfii, 2008).

BALAIAN, ROMAN GURGENOVICH (b. 15 April 1941, Nerkin Oratag, Azerbaijan). Ukrainian director and scriptwriter. Balaian, who has Armenian roots, worked as an actor in the theater of Stepanakert (located in the Nagornyi Karabakh region) in 1959–1961. He studied directing at the Yerevan Theater Institute and film directing at the Kiev Institute for the Performing Arts, graduating in 1969. Since 1970, he has been on the staff of **Dovzhenko Film Studio** in Kiev.

Balaian's preferred genre is the literary adaptation, which he approaches in a nontraditional, lively, antitheatrical manner that often proves inconvenient for viewers. Among the authors whose works he has adapted for the screen are Anton Chekhov (*Kashtanka*, 1975; *The Kiss*/Potselui, 1983, TV), Ivan Turgenev (*The Lone Wolf*/Biriuk, 1977; *First Love*/Pervaia liubov', 1995), and Nikolai Leskov (*Lady Macbeth of Mtsensk*/Ledi Makbet mtsenskogo uezda, 1989). Peculiar to Balaian's approach to canonical literary texts is his implied "polemics" not just with the conventional Soviet adaptations of the 1930s–1960s but also with non-Russian directors such as Andrzej Wajda or Maximilian Schell and their idiosyncratic renditions of the same works. However, Balaian is neither an iconoclast nor a traditionalist. He might best be described as a cerebral filmmaker with a strong sense of interpretive independence whose readings of literature can be surprising and frustrating, literal and direct, and conceptually ambiguous.

Ironically, the one film immediately associated with Balaian's name is not an adaptation, although filled with unmistakable Chekhovian spirit: *Flights in Dream and in Reality* (Polety vo sne i naiavu, 1982), a disturbing contemporary drama of hopelessness and depression amid cynical materialism. **Oleg Iankovskii** impressively portrays a creative man in his 40s who finds himself completely out of place in society—a situation for which the film deliberately offers no solution. At the time of its release, *Flights* was perceived as an uncompromising condemnation of Brezhnevian "stagnation." From a post-Soviet viewpoint, though, the main character's dilemma seems existential per se and less dependent on sociopolitical factors.

No less subversive is *The Spy* (Filer, 1987), arguably Balaian's finest artistic achievement so far. Disguised as a turn-of-the-century, pre-Soviet psychological drama, the picture analyzes the temptations offered by the corrupt tsarist system, represented by its officials, informants, and petty guards, to a teacher whose efforts to retain his decency fail because of his inherent lack of principles. *The Spy* is distinguished by exquisite imagery contributing to an almost hypnotic atmosphere of gloom and societal pressure.

In 1997 Balaian was awarded the title People's Artist of Ukraine.

Other films: *Protect Me, My Talisman* (Khrani menia, moi talisman, 1986); *Two Moons, Three Suns* (Dve luny, tri solntsa, 1998); *The Night Is Bright* (Noch' svetla, 2004); *The Chosen One* (Izbrannik, 2007).

BALLAD OF A SOLDIER (Ballada o soldate, 1959). **Mosfilm Studio**. 90 min., b/w. Directed by **Grigorii Chukhrai**. Script: Valentin Ezhov, Grigorii Chukhrai. Cinematography: Vladimir Nikolaev, Era Savel'eva. Music: Mikhail Ziv. Cast: **Vladimir Ivashov**, Zhanna Prokhorenko, **Nikolai Kriuchkov**, **Evgenii Urbanskii**, Antonina Maksimova, Lev Borisov, Ella Lezhdei. Premiere: 1 December 1959.

During an attack by German forces, young Red Army soldier Aleksei Skvortsov (Ivashov) single-handedly destroys two tanks. As a reward, his commander (Kriuchkov) grants him one week of leave to go to his native village and help his mother (Maksimova) repair the roof of her hut. Along the way, he encounters numerous people to whom he provides help and encouragement, among them an invalid soldier (Urbanskii) desperately waiting for his wife. Alesha falls in love with a girl, Shura (Prokhorenko), who accompanies him for a while. After a brief meeting with his mother, he must go back to the front, never to return home again.

BALTIC DEPUTY (Deputat Baltiki, 1937). **Lenfilm Studio**. 96 min., b/w. Directed by **Iosif Kheifits** and **Aleksandr Zarkhi** Script: D. Del' (Leonid Liubashevskii), Aleksandr Zarkhi, Iosif Kheifits, Leonid Rakhmanov. Cinematography: Mikhail Kaplan, L. Shtyrtzkover. Music: Nikolai Timofeev. Cast: **Nikolai Cherkasov, Boris Livanov, Oleg Zhakov**, Aleksandr Mel'nikov, Mariia Domasheva. Premiere: 27 March 1937.

After the October Revolution, world-famous biologist Polezhaev (Cherkasov) declares his solidarity with the Bolshevik administration. The old professor's newspaper article causes outrage among his colleagues and students who reject Communism. However, Polezhaev wins friends among Red Army soldiers and sailors of the Baltic fleet to whom he gives lectures. His assistant, Vorob'ev (Zhakov), turns out to be a counterrevolutionary trying to steal one of Polezhaev's manuscripts and smuggle it abroad. But another former student, Bocharov (Livanov), supports the fragile professor, as does Vladimir Lenin, who calls him personally on the phone. After Vorob'ev's exposure and arrest, the Baltic sailors elect Polezhaev to the Petrograd city council and listen to his passionate speech before departing for the Civil War.

BANIONIS, DONATAS [some sources list the patronymic Iuozovich] (b. 28 April 1924, Kaunas). Lithuanian actor. Banionis learned ceramics before joining the acting studio of famed theater innovator Juozas Miltinis in the town of Panevėžys in 1941. **Vytautas Žalakevičius** gave Banionis his first significant movie role in *Adam Wants to Be a Man* (Adomas nori buti zmogumi/Adam khochet byt' chelovekom, 1959) and later entrusted him with the plum part of farmer Vaitkus in the extraordinary postwar drama *Nobody Wanted to Die* (Nekas nenorejo mirti/Nikto ne khotel umirat', 1965), which brought Banionis national and international fame.

Savva Kulish used the actor's popularity for his Cold War spy thriller *Dead Season* (Mertvyi sezon, 1968), another major hit in which Banionis played the noble, humanistic Soviet undercover agent Ladeinikov operating in some vaguely defined Western country. Subsequently Banionis, an exceptionally cultured and refined artist, accepted dozens of film roles, not all of which were worthy of his talent. However, when faced with artistic challenges, he rose to the occasion in a brilliant manner, for example, when **Grigorii Kozintsev** cast him as the Duke of Albany in the Shakespeare adaptation *King Lear* (Korol' Lir, 1970). Arguably, the actor's most lasting achievement in cinema is psychologist Kris Kelvin in **Andrei Tarkovskii**'s *Solaris* (1972)—Banionis's ability to quietly convey intense intellectual and emotional processes, his willingness to show insecurity and vulnerability when faced with inexplicable phenomena, and his believable deep bond with earthly nature became an integral part of this contemplative masterpiece. In *Goya* (1971), a lavish adaptation of Lion Feuchtwanger's novel by East German director Konrad Wolf (1925–1982), Banionis created an inspired portrait of the Spanish painter who is torn between his calling as an artist and political schemes at the royal court. Also in East Germany, the actor played composer Ludwig van Beethoven in Horst Seemann's atypical 1976 biopic.

Apart from his distinguished career in **Lithuanian cinema** and international film, Banionis remained active for over sixty years at the small Panevėžys town theater both as actor and director, appearing in more than 100 plays. The actor joined the Communist Party in 1960, was named People's Artist of the USSR in 1974, and was a member of the Soviet parliament in 1974–1979. One of his sons, Raimundas Banionis (b. 1957), works as a film director and producer.

Other films: *Marite* (1947); *Mister MacKinley's Escape* (Begstvo mistera Mak-Kinli, 1975); *Nicolo Paganini* (1982); *The Courtyard* (Kiemas, 1999); *Just Once* (Tol'ko raz, 2002); *Leningrad* (2007).

BARANOVSKAIA, VERA VSEVOLODOVNA [other sources list the patronymic Fedorovna] (b. 7 April 1885, Moscow [other sources: St. Petersburg]–d. 7 December 1935, Paris). Russian actress. Baranovskaia studied with Konstantin Stanislavskii and became a member of the Moscow Art Theater (MKhAT) in 1903. Having gained a considerable artistic reputation, she began to freelance in 1915 with theaters in Khar'kiv, Odessa, Tiflis (Tbilisi), Kazan', and other cities. In 1922, the actress founded her own theater studio, the Baranovskaia Workshop (Masterskaia Baranovskoi, or "Mastbar").

Baranovskaia's screen debut was in *The Thief-Benefactor* (Vorblagodetel', 1916), a trivial Anton Chekhov adaptation. Ten years later, **Vsevolod Pudovkin** cast her as Nilovna, the heroine of his revolutionary tragedy *The Mother* (Mat', 1926), an adaptation of

Maksim Gor'kii's 1906 novel. By critical consent, Baranovskaia's performance is one of the great acting achievements in silent cinema and deservedly brought her world fame. Baranovskaia, only 40 at the time of shooting, believably impersonates a much older, repressed, and fragile woman who is guided by the devotion to her son and ultimately accepts the inevitability of class struggle and self-sacrifice. It was the power of Baranovskaia's psychologically nuanced acting that stood out in an environment dominated by **Lev Kuleshov**'s reductionist dogma; it encouraged other Soviet filmmakers to revise their dismissal of a psychological, cathartic approach to film acting. Pudovkin also persuaded Baranovskaia to accept the part of a selfish, harsh worker's wife who undergoes a deep transformation in *The End of St. Petersburg* (Konets Sankt Peterburga, 1927). One of her last roles in Soviet cinema was in **Abram Room**'s social drama *Pits* (Ukhaby, 1928).

In 1928, purportedly for health reasons (or, according to other sources, accompanying her husband, **Valerii Inkizhinov**), Baranovskaia left the USSR for Czechoslovakia, Germany, and later France, where she appeared in films of varying quality. Some of the leads that she played recycled her proletarian screen image, for example, in Mikhail Dubson's *Poisonous Gas* (Giftgas, 1929) and Carl Junghans's *Such Is Life* (So ist das Leben, 1929). Her last part, however, was as a duchess in Max Neufeld's adaptation of a Viennese operetta, *Eternal Waltz* (Valse éternelle, 1935).

Other films: *The Yoke of Fate* (Gnet roka, 1917); *Revolt in the Juvenile Facility* (Revolte im Erziehungshaus, 1930); *The Adventures of King Pausole* (Les aventures du roi Pausole, 1933).

BARDIN, GARRI IAKOVLEVICH (b. 11 September 1941, Orenburg). Russian **animation** director, scriptwriter, and actor. Bardin studied acting at the studio school of the Moscow Art Theater (MKhAT) under Pavel Massal'skii, graduating in 1968, and joined the troupe of the Moscow Gogol' Theater. At the same time, he authored and directed puppet plays at the legendary theater of Sergei Obrastsov (1901–1992)—among others, a version of *Don Juan* (1974)—and performed voice parts in animated pictures. **Ivan Ivanov-Vano** encouraged Bardin to try directing animated films.

Bardin began with traditional drawn animation shorts such as the fairy tale *The Flying Ship* (Letuchii korabl', 1978). He then experimented with other media, revealing an exceptional degree of inventiveness and originality. The "acting" objects in his stop-motion films are usually taken from everyday life, and surprise and enchant viewers with their expressive potential. Thus, *The Conflict* (Konflikt, 1983) deals with the dangers of untamed aggression by using matches as "performers" that end up burning each other; *Marriage* (Brak, 1987) exemplifies the ups and downs of a relationship by two ropes; *Extravaganzas* (Vykrutasy, 1988) demonstrates the consequences of social paranoia using wire, and so forth. Other noteworthy films are *Bang-Bang, Oy-oy-oy!* (Pif-paf, oi-oi-oi!, 1980), a spoof on opera and theater clichés, and *Break!* (Brek! 1985), a critical look at the world of boxing carried out in claymation.

Bardin landed a popular success with *Tchoo-Tchoo* (Chucha, 1997; sequels in 2001 and 2004) in which a boy creates a nannylike companion from a pillow. Other Bardin films are openly intellectual, featuring sudden switches from humor to parabolic significance, most prominently in *Adagio* (2000), an allegory on mass manipulation acted out by a swarm of origami birds. Stylistically, Bardin seems to reinvent himself with each new picture.

In 1991, Bardin founded his own studio, Strayer, where he since has worked. In 1999, the filmmaker was awarded a State Prize of Russia; many of his pictures won prizes at international festivals. Bardin has also played episodic roles in feature films, for example in **Vladimir Men'shov**'s *Moscow Does Not Believe in Tears* (Moskva slezam ne verit, 1979).

Other films: *Khoma's Adventures* (Prikliucheniia Khomy, 1979); *The Banquet* (Banket, 1986).

BARNET, BORIS VASIL'EVICH (b. 18 June 1902, Moscow–d. 8 January 1965, Riga). Russian director, actor, and screenwriter. Barnet, whose English grandfather had moved to Russia in the 19th century, grew up in the family of an entrepreneur and owner of a printing press. He studied at the Moscow School of Art and Architecture but left in his sophomore year to serve in the Red Army on a Red Cross train.

In 1923, Barnet graduated from the Central Military School for Physical Education and worked as a sports teacher while simultaneously studying in **Lev Kuleshov**'s film workshop. The athletic Barnet was an ideal candidate for putting into practice Kuleshov's theory of film acting, which rests on physical expression rather than psychological penetration. Thus, Barnet was cast as Cowboy Jeddy in the slapstick experiment *The Extraordinary Adventures of Mr. West in the Land of the Bolsheviks* (Neobychainye prikliucheniia Mistera Vesta v strane bol'shevikov, 1924); its popular success encouraged him to begin a professional film career. Barnet learned the film crafts from scratch, with colleagues and friends such as **Vsevolod Pudovkin**, **Sergei Komarov**, Porfirii Podobed, **Aleksandra Khokhlova**, Sergei Galadzhev, and **Leonid Obolenskii**.

In his directorial debut, the comedic thriller *Miss Mend* (1926, based on a 1923 novel by Marietta Shaginian, codirected with **Fedor Otsep**), Barnet indulges in car chases and expertly staged stunts, all of which made the film a sensational box-office hit for its company, **Mezhrabpomfilm Studio**. *The Girl with the Hatbox* (Devushka s korobkoi, 1927) was solicited by the Soviet Ministry of Finance and aimed to popularize the state lottery while ridiculing petit-bourgeois greed and hypocrisy. The film truthfully reflects the atmosphere of NEP—the 1920s New Economic Policy—which had culturally mellowed the grim War Communism and created plenty of room for melodramatic and comical situations. That film and Barnet's next, *The House on Trubnaia Square* (Dom na Trubnoi, 1928), were among the most popular Soviet **comedies** of the silent era; they show a remarkable talent for well-timed physical jokes and ran in Soviet movie theaters for years.

With the advent of sound film, Barnet contributed significantly to the development of appropriate narrative strategies. The departure from the highly intellectualized visual principles of classical Soviet silents—in part imposed by the Communist Party's "antiformalist" line, in part caused by the inherent necessities of sound film—proved relatively easy for Barnet who never harbored excessive formal ambitions. His very first sound film, ***The Outskirts*** (aka *Patriots/ Okraina*, 1933), also became the greatest artistic accomplishment of his entire career. Set in tsarist Russia during World War I, it lovingly portrays a group of provincial townsfolk: a shoemaker, his daughter who falls in love with a German POW, and two brothers volunteering for the front. Several episodes of this remarkable picture culminate in expressive image- and sound-montage sequences, proving the director's ability to incorporate achievements of the classical avant-garde to great emotional effect.

As a reward for this critical and popular triumph, Barnet received a two-month trip to France. Sadly, his next project, a triangle romance set among Caspian fishermen who compete for the same woman, failed; for reasons that are difficult to reconstruct, the harmless *By the Bluest of Seas* (U samogo sinego moria, 1936) was harshly criticized and only given a limited release. Perhaps in order to rehabilitate himself, Barnet made *A Night in September* (Noch' v sentiabre, 1939), a simplistic propaganda vehicle based on Aleksei Stakhanov's widely publicized labor record. *The Old Horseman* (Staryi naezdnik, 1940) once again dealt with an inoffensive subject—an aging jockey at a Moscow hippodrome who is forced to retire—yet it was prohibited and released only in 1959. *A Valuable Head* (Beztsennaia golova, 1942), a short, was also criticized because it portrayed heroism as a question of moral choice (a doctor who needs medication for her child is willing to compromise with the Nazi occupants but later corrects her "mistake").

In 1947, Barnet received the highest official recognition for the suspenseful *The Scout's Quest* (aka *Secret Agent*/Podvig razvedchika)—the only Stalin Prize of his career. This clever thriller about a Soviet spy who manages to capture a Nazi general in the occupied territories laid the groundwork for the 1960s–1970s cult movies about Soviet agents spying in the heart of Nazi Germany. Among Barnet's later films, *The Wrestler and the Clown* (Borets i kloun, 1958), begun by **Konstantin Iudin** but completed—after Iudin's sudden death—by Barnet, deserves mention. It tells the touching turn-of-the-century story of the friendship between Ivan Poddubnyi, a legendary wrestler, and the clown Anatolii Durov. Barnet's other comedic melodramas received little critical attention (although some were successful at the box office): *Annushka* (1959) about a widow raising her children in the country; *Alenka* (1962) about a nine-year old who must leave her parents during harvest time because their village, built on "virgin soil"—newly developed steppe lands—has no school; and *The Whistle Stop* (Polustanok, 1963), a contemporary village tale.

→Barnet committed suicide while filming on location in Latvia, purportedly blaming his waning rapport with contemporary viewers. Other sources cite personal problems as the reason for the filmmaker's growing depression.

As a lifelong Soviet loyalist and Communist Party member since 1943, Barnet kept satirical elements in his comedies at an agreeable level and never displayed bitterness toward Soviet society; however, blatant political propaganda, too, is kept to a minimum, while genuine humanism dominates his pictures' atmosphere. For a long time, Barnet's reputation was overshadowed by more theory-minded directors, but in recent years his films have received increasing recognition in Russia and abroad.

Barnet was awarded the title Merited Artist of the Russian Federation in 1935, and Merited Artist of the Ukrainian SSR in 1951. French film historian Georges Sadoul once called him "the best Soviet comedy director." He was married to film and theater actress Alla Kazanskaia (1920–2008).

Other films: *Moscow in October* (Moskva v oktiabre, 1927); *Breaking of the Ice* (Ledolom, aka Anka, 1931); *A Good Lad* (Slavnyi malyi, aka Novgorodtsy, 1941); *Pages of Life* (Stranitsy zhizni, 1948, codirected with **Aleksandr Macheret**); *Bountiful Summer* (Shchedroe leto, 1951); *Liana* (1955).

BARSKAIA (married **CHARDYNINA**), **MARGARITA ALEKSAN-DROVNA** (b. 19 June 1903, Baku–d. 1939 [other sources: 1937], Moscow). Ukrainian and Russian director, screenwriter, and actress. Barskaia studied in the State Dramatic Studio of Azerbaijan, graduating in 1922, and joined the troupe of the Odessa theater Red Torch. In the movies, she began her career with minor roles in silent **Ukrainian cinema**. After marrying filmmaker **Petr Chardynin**, Barskaia worked as an assistant director on a number of his pictures.

Barskaia founded a workshop for **children's films** in 1929. She gained international fame as the author and director of the first Soviet sound film for children, *The Torn Shoes* (aka *Broken Shoes*/ Rvanye bashmaki, 1933), produced for **Mezhrabpomfilm Studio**, about workers' children in pre-Nazi Germany. By refusing to depict infants as "sweet" and "cute," and by taking their daily plights seriously, Barskaia achieved a degree of natural performance unseen in cinema before.

One of the film's consultants was the Communist official Karl Radek, whose subsequent arrest and execution led to suspicions and accusations against Barskaia and to her increasing isolation. Although she enjoyed the support of **Boris Shumiatskii** and was allowed to create an experimental children's film studio in which unrehearsed dialogues between toddlers were recorded, her project *Father and Son* (Otets i syn, 1936), an attempt to realistically show family problems on the backdrop of rather unsightly industrial areas of Moscow, was brought to a halt shortly before completion; the already shot footage was partially destroyed. Barskaia, who refused to make any compromise with the leadership of the Soviet film industry, later committed suicide.

Other films: *Who Is More Important—What Is More Urgent* (Kto vazhnee—chto nuzhnee, 1930, short).

BASILASHVILI, OLEG VALERIANOVICH (b. 16 September 1934, Moscow). Russian actor. Basilashvili, who has Georgian roots on his father's side, studied at the studio school of the Moscow Art Theater (MKhAT) under Pavel Massal'skii (1904–1979), graduating in 1956. In 1959, he joined the troupe of the Grand Dramatic Theater under legendary director Georgii Tovstonogov (1913–1989), who challenged him to superb stage performances.

Basilashvili made his film debut as the groom Andrei Andreevich in the Anton Chekhov adaptation *The Bride* (Nevesta, 1956). Although the 1960s saw the actor cast in interesting roles under leading filmmakers—among them **Abram Room**'s *The Garnet Bracelet* (Granatovyi braslet, 1964, from Kuprin)—it was only in the late 1970s that Basilashvili became a household name through the efforts of three directors: **El'dar Riazanov**, **Georgii Daneliia**, and **Karen Shakhnazarov**. Riazanov cast him as the scheming opportunist Samokhvalov in *Office Romance* (Sluzhebnyi roman, 1978) and the wrongly convicted pianist Platon Gromov in *A Railway Station for Two* (Vokzal dlia dvoikh, 1983), both of them blockbusters that catapulted Basilashvili to national stardom. Daneliia, in his popular *Autumn Marathon* (Osennii marafon, 1979), emphasized the likeable features of this stressed-out intellectual whose indecisiveness results in personal fiasco. Shakhnazarov added a satirical component to Basilashvili's screen persona in the sarcastic comedies *The Messenger Boy* (Kur'er, 1987) and *Zero City* (Gorod Zero, 1989). These three directors also secured the continuation of Basilashvili's career in the 1990s when his roles reflected the catastrophic deconstruction of his former image: in Riazanov's *The Prophecy* (Predskazanie, 1991), in Daneliia's *Heads and Tails* (Orel i reshka, 1995), and in Shkahnazarov's *Dreams* (Sny, 1993), among others.

The early 2000s brought a remarkable revival to Basilashvili's career. He proved his undiminished power of subtle expression as General Epanchin in **Vladimir Bortko**'s Fedor Dostoevskii adaptation *The Idiot* (Idiot, 2003, TV) and portrayed a cold and world-weary Woland, the sarcastic prince of darkness, in Bortko's *The Master and Margarita* (Master i Margarita, 2005, TV) from Mikhail Bulgakov's cult classic.

Basilashvili was named People's Artist of the USSR in 1984. In 1991–1993, the outspoken liberal activist was elected member of the Russian parliament in the Radical Democrats faction.

Other films: *Say a Kind Word about the Poor Hussar* (O bednom gusare zamolvite slovo, 1980, TV); *Resistance* (Protivostoianie, 1985); *Son'ka, the Golden Hand* (Son'ka—zolotaia ruchka, 2007).

BASNER, VENIAMIN EFIMOVICH (b. 1 January 1925, Iaroslavl'–3 September 1996, Komarovo near St. Petersburg). Russian composer. Basner studied violin at Leningrad Conservatory, graduating in 1949, and subsequently worked as an orchestra violinist.

Basner's exceptionally prolific career as a film composer began with the World War II tragedy *The Immortal Garrison* (Bessmertnyi garnizon, 1956), directed by Zakhar Agranenko and **Eduard Tissé**. He worked closely with director **Vladimir Basov** on such hits as the industrial drama *Battle Underway* (Bitva v puti, 1961), the anti-Stalinist *The Silence* (Tishina, 1963), and the spy epic *The Shield and the Sword* (Shchit i mech, 1968). Basner also wrote the scores for such diverse pictures as **Sergei Bondarchuk**'s *The Fate of a Man* (Sud'ba cheloveka, 1959), **Mikhail Shveitser**'s *Warrant Officer Panin* (Michman Panin, 1960), **Evgenii Matveev**'s *The Gypsy* (Tsygan, 1966), **Aleksandrs Leimanis**'s *The "Wagtail" Army Is*

Fighting Again (Armiia "Triasoguzka" snova v boiu, 1968), **Georgii Natanson**'s *Ambassador of the Soviet Union* (Posol Sovetskogo Soiuza, 1969), and **Igor' Gostev**'s scout trilogy *Front without Flanks* (Front bez flangov, 1974–1981). The patriotic power of these and dozens of other films featuring Basner's scores was enhanced by his memorable, quasi-folkloric songs that took on a life of their own; the most famous—and often parodied—among them is "What Does the Homeland Begin With?" (*S chego nachinaetsia rodina?*) from *The Shield and the Sword.*

The composer's name is associated with some of the greatest artistic achievements and popular successes of Soviet cinema, often displaying a strong civic component. However, in the 1980s, the quality of the films for which Basner wrote the music declined noticeably, with the exception of two ironic, nostalgic pictures about the Soviet past by **Gennadii Poloka**, *Was There a Karotin at All?* (A byl li Karotin? 1989) and *Return of the Battleship* (Vozvrashchenie bronenostsa, 1996).

Basner, who also composed chamber music and symphonic pieces, was named Merited Artist of the RSFSR in 1974 and People's Artist of the RSFSR in 1982.

Other films: *Scouts* (Razvedchki, 1969); *Seven Screams in the Ocean* (Sem' krikov v okeane, 1986); *Why Does an Honest Man Need an Alibi?* (Zachem alibi chestnomu cheloveku? 1993).

BASOV, VLADIMIR PAVLOVICH (b. 28 July 1923, Urazov, Kursk province–d. 17 September 1987, Moscow). Russian director, screenwriter, and actor. Basov studied under **Mikhail Romm** and **Sergei Iutkevich** at the Soviet State Film School **VGIK**, graduating in 1952. He made his directorial debut with *The Boarder* (Nakhlebnik, 1953), a filmed stage production of an Ivan Turgenev play. The Civil War adventure *School of Courage* (Shkola muzhestva, 1954) targeted juvenile audiences and became a box-office success; like in many of his later films, Basov also appeared in an episodic role. He scored high reviews from critics and discriminating audiences with the historical dilogy *First Joys* (Pervye radosti, 1957) and *An Unusual Summer* (Neobyknovennoe leto, 1957) from Konstantin Fedin's autobiographical novels; narratively solid and only moderately propagandistic, these films have preserved a degree of atmospheric authenticity.

With the social drama *Life Passed By* (Zhizn' proshla mimo, 1958), Basov for the first time tried himself at contemporary material, telling the story of a criminal and his milieu. Here and in his following projects, the director responded to Thaw debates, tackling controversial questions and addressing issues of democratic decision making, de-Stalinization—however mildly—and self-fulfillment in private life. Basov often used contemporary best-sellers as his literary source. Particularly successful were the industrial drama *Battle Underway* (Bitva v puti, 1961) from Galina Nikolaeva's much-touted novel, and *The Silence* (Tishina, 1963), from Iurii Bondarev's novel about loyalty and betrayal during the Great Patriotic War and in postwar years. With almost 70 million viewers, the four-part, six-hour spy adventure *The Shield and the Sword* (Shchit i Mech, 1968) was one of the superhits of the decade; thematically and stylistically, it is a predecessor to **Tat'iana Lioznova**'s cult series *Seventeen Moments of Spring* (Semnadtsat' mgnovenii vesny, TV).

Basov managed to carve out for himself a parallel career as an actor, gaining popularity with dozens of supporting roles, especially in **comedies**, where he proved a scene-stealer. The long gallery of his "weird types" includes the polisher in **Georgii Daneliia**'s *I Stroll in Moscow* (aka *Meet Me in Moscow*/Ia shagaiu po Moskve, 1963), the militia man in **Leonid Gaidai**'s *Operation "Y" and Other Adventures of Shurik* (Operatsiia 'Y' i drugie prikliucheniia Shurika, 1965), and the guest in **Vladimir Men'shov**'s *Moscow Doesn't Believe in Tears* (Moskva slezam ne verit, 1979). Basov's cameos were also effective in two Mikhail Bulgakov adaptations: **Aleksandr Alov** and **Vladimir Naumov**'s *The Flight* (Beg, 1970) as the owner of the cockroach races, and the TV miniseries *The Days of the Turbins* (Dni Turbinykh, 1976), in which he played the opportunist Myshlaevskii.

As a filmmaker, Basov was somewhat unusual in his nondidactic attitude toward viewers. A critic of society but never a dissident, Basov was a solid, epical storyteller who could keep audiences' attention for three hours and more (most of his films are two-part efforts) and settled for domestic success, displaying little ambition to make films with international festival appeal.

Basov, who joined the Communist Party in 1948, was named People's Artist of the USSR in 1983. Basov's son from his marriage to actress Natal'ia Fateeva, Vladimir Basov Jr. (b. 1959), is a film actor and director.

Other films: (as director) *The Fall of the Emirate* (Krushenie emirata, 1955, codirected with **Latif Faiziev**); *Incident at Mine Eight* (Sluchai na shakhte vosem', 1957); *The Snowstorm* (Metel', 1964); *Nylon—100%* (Neilon—100%, 1974); *The Facts of the Previous Day* (Fakty minuvshego dnia, 1981); (as actor) *Thirty-three* (Tridtsat' tri, 1965); *The Cottage* (Dacha, 1973).

BATALOV, ALEKSEI VLADIMIROVICH (b. 20 November 1928, Vladimir). Russian actor, director, screenwriter, and pedagogue. Batalov, the son of actor and director Vladimir Batalov, graduated in 1950 from the studio school of the Moscow Art Theater (MKhAT), where he had studied with Viktor Stanitsyn (1897–1976).

Although he debuted on screen as a teenager in the supporting role of Alesha in **Leo Arnshtam**'s partisan drama *Zoia* (1943), it was not until the mid-1950s that Batalov became a star by creating the male screen prototype of the Thaw, a period in which Communist morality was proclaimed to be fully compatible with traditional humanist ideals. Veteran director **Iosif Kheifits** exercised the most influence on Batalov's career, making him famous with four seminal roles: the young factory worker Aleksei Zhurbin in *A Great Family* (Bol'shaia sem'ia, 1954), the unfairly suspected driver Sasha Rumiantsev in *The Rumiantsev Case* (Delo Rumiantseva, 1956), Dr. Volodia Ustimenko in *My Beloved Man* (Dorogoi moi chelovek, 1957), and the blasé aristocrat Gurov in the exceptional Anton Chekhov adaptation *Lady with a Dog* (Dama s sobachkoi, 1960). Batalov's popularity in those years was unique: blending uncompromising candor and courage with noble dignity and sensitivity, he embodied the very qualities believed to be essential for overcoming Stalinist hypocrisy and cruelty.

For **Mark Donskoi**, Batalov portrayed worker-activist Pavel Vlasov in an underrated remake of *The Mother* (Mat', 1956), a role in which the actor's uncle, **Nikolai Batalov**, had triumphed three decades earlier. With the part of Boris Borozdin in **Mikhail Kalatozov**'s war drama *The Cranes Are Flying* (Letiat zhuravli, 1957), Batalov earned worldwide recognition. He went on to play parts of modern intellectuals, for example, the physicist Gusev in **Mikhail Romm**'s *Nine Days of a Year* (Deviat' dnei odnogo goda, 1962), as well as roles in historical films and literary adaptations such as Golubkov in **Aleksandr Alov** and **Vladimir Naumov**'s Mikhail Bulgakov adaptation *The Flight* (Beg, 1970).

Batalov has also shown genuine talent as a filmmaker. His debut, the excellent Nikolai Gogol' adaptation *The Overcoat* (Shinel', 1960), was followed by a colorful and dynamic screen version of Iurii Olesha's fairy tale *Three Fat Men* (Tri tolstiaka, 1966). *The Gambler* (Igrok, 1972) is one of the few Fedor Dostoevskii adaptations to authentically capture the atmosphere of the original; unfortunately, it remained the last of Batalov's directorial efforts that held great promise (he did, however, continue directing adaptations of classical literature for the radio).

Batalov made a spectacular appearance as the deus ex machina Georgii Ivanovich, in **Vladimir Men'shov**'s *Moscow Does Not Believe in Tears* (Moskva slezam ne verit, 1979), contributing authentic quality to this charming lightweight. Although regularly employed in Soviet cinema until the late 1980s, the fading of Thaw idealism rendered Batalov's screen persona an anachronism; in the 1990s, the actor was credited more as an off-screen narrator than a performer.

Batalov works as the head of the Department of Acting at the State Film School **VGIK** where he began to teach in 1975. In 1964, he was named Merited Artist of the Russian Federation, in 1969 People's Artist of the RSFSR, and in 1976, People's Artist of the USSR.

Other films: *A Day of Happiness* (Den' schast'ia, 1964); *Star of Captivating Bliss* (Zvezda plenitel'nogo schast'ia, 1975); *An Umbrella for Newlyweds* (Zontik dlia novobrachnykh, 1986).

BATALOV, NIKOLAI PETROVICH (b. 6 December 1899, Moscow–d. 10 November 1937, Moscow). Russian actor. Batalov joined the Second Studio of the Moscow Art Theater (MKhAT) in 1916 and became a member of the theater's main troupe in 1924.

Batalov's film debut was the supporting role of Red Army private Gusev in **Iakov Protazanov**'s science fiction megaproduction *Aelita* (1924), which made fine use of this actor's comedic charm. Batalov gained worldwide fame as the heroic worker Pavel Vlasov in **Vsevolod Pudovkin**'s *The Mother* (Mat', 1926). A counterpoint to this powerful, pathos-filled performance is the selfish, philistine, but also funny mason in **Abram Room**'s controversial social drama *Third Meshchanskaia Street* (aka *Bed and Sofa*/Tret'ia Meshchanskaia, 1927). Batalov became one of the most popular Soviet silent film actors, memorable for his radiating joy of life, warmth, and clever, optimistic energy.

Because of his excellent voice qualities, Batalov effortlessly mastered the transition to sound film and further enhanced his star status with the first Soviet sound feature, **Nikolai Ekk**'s *A Start in Life* (aka *Road to Life*/Putevka v zhizn', 1931), in which he portrayed Communist educator Nikolai Sergeev who wins the trust of homeless juvenile delinquents and converts them to Soviet ideals. **Lev Kuleshov** gave Batalov the title role of Jewish watchmaker Leo Horizon in *Horizon* (aka *Horizon: The Wandering Jew*/Gorizont, 1932), the second Soviet sound movie, released in early 1933. Although Horizon's voyage to his dreamland America and, following his bitter disappointment, back to Russia—now a happy USSR—failed to enthuse Soviet or Western audiences, it inspired Kuleshov to modify his dogma on cinema acting. Batalov also starred in a number of historical and adventure films such as *The Shepherd and the Tsar* (Pastukh i tsar', 1935). **Semen Timoshenko**'s modern **comedy** *Three Comrades* (aka *Three Friends*/Tri tovarishcha, 1935), in which Batalov played an efficient manager—"Communist entrepreneur" Latsis—also proved successful.

Batalov's last years were overshadowed by severe tuberculosis, which cut his career tragically short. He was awarded the title Merited Artist of the Russian Federation in 1933. His nephew is actor and director **Aleksei Batalov**.

Other films: *Soil in Chains* (aka *The Yellow Pass*/Zemlia v plenu, 1927); *Treasures of the Wrecked Vessel* (Sokrovishcha pogibshego korablia, 1935).

BATTLESHIP POTEMKIN (Bronenosets Potemkin, 1925). Goskino. 75 min, b/w. Directed by **Sergei Eizenshtein**. Script: **Nina Agadzhanova-Shutko**, Sergei Eizenshtein. Cinematography: **Eduard Tissé**. Cast: **Aleksandr Antonov**, **Grigorii Aleksandrov**, Vladimir Barskii, Mikhail Gomorov, Aleksandr Levshin, Andrei Fait. Premiere: 25 December 1925 (release: 18 January 1926).

In June 1905, the sailors of the ship *Prince Potemkin of Tauris* (*Kniaz' Potemkin Tavricheskii*) refuse to eat the rotten meat offered to them for lunch. At a roll call, the captain (Barskii) orders the protesters shot. The Bolshevik Vakulinchuk (Antonov) calls for action; during the ensuing riot, First Officer Giliarovskii (Aleksandrov) mortally wounds him. Vakulinchuk's funeral in Odessa turns into a powerful demonstration, unifying citizens from all social strata. Police attempt to break up the demonstration at the Odessa steps, causing carnage. The ship's crew supports the demonstrators by firing their canons. In open sea, a clash with the approaching Black Sea fleet seems inevitable, but the sailors on the other ships refuse to attack, showing their solidarity with the mutineers.

BAUER, EVGENII FRANTSEVICH (b. 1865 [other sources: 1867]–d. 22 June 1917, Yalta, Crimea). Russian director, scriptwriter, art director, and cinematographer. Bauer, whose father was a well-known court musician of Czech origin, studied at the Moscow School of Painting, Sculpture and Architecture from 1882 to 1887, after which he tried various vocations, including cartoonist, actor, and photographer. As a successful stage designer, Bauer worked for a number of operetta and drama companies. He joined the movie industry in 1912 as the art director for **Aleksandr Drankov**'s company on *The Tercentenary of the Romanov Dynasty* (Trekhsotletie tsarstvovania doma Romanovykh, released 1913) and began directing his first pictures in 1913. Later that year, he switched to **Aleksandr Khanzhonkov**'s company, where he soon became one of the leading Russian filmmakers, churning out close to 20 pictures annually and commanding top salaries.

Bauer's career as film director lasted for merely four years. The question whether an artistic evolution can be detected within this time span—considering that only one third of his oeuvre has survived—is still under debate. Some scholars, among them Semen Ginzburg, held that Bauer moved from conventional psychological drama to an original visual approach that eventually dominated all other elements in his films, especially acting, and that other directors, particularly **Iakov Protazanov**, profited from Bauer's discoveries in this area.

Whether treated in a dramatic, tragic, or comedic light, the plot ingredients in Bauer's pictures remained the same: pain brought about by class confines; lack or overabundance of money; male betrayal of female love; cruelty of fate; inconsolability over the death of a lover; and the destructive power of blind chance. The seemingly infinite recombinations of these elements constitute the typical flavor of Bauer's pictures, whose sentimental titles are giveaways: *Bloody Fame* (Krovavaia slava, 1913), *Twilight of a Woman's Soul* (Sumerki zhenskoi dushi, 1913), *Child of the Big City* (Ditia bol'shogo goroda, 1914), *Silent Witnesses* (Nemye svideteli, 1914), and so on. *Life in Death* (Zhizn' v smerti, 1914, from a script by famous symbolist author Valerii Briusov) added mysticism to the formula, as did *Daydreams* (Grezy, 1915). Bauer also tried himself at literary adaptations—for example, in *Song of Triumphant Love* (Pesn' liubvi torzhestvuiushchei, 1915) from a story by Ivan Turgenev—but was less ambitious than his rival Protazanov in trying to preserve the spirit of the original work or transcending the framework of melodrama.

Bauer demonstrated his patriotic loyalty at the beginning of World War I with the propagandistic *Glory to Us, Death to the Enemy* (Slava—nam, smert'—vragam, 1914) and the potboiler *The Secret of the German Embassy* (Taina germanskogo posol'stva, 1914), but returned to his favorite apolitical melodrama as soon as the public's need for more escapist fare became apparent. How adaptable that framework was, is revealed in *The Revolutionary* (Revoliutsioner, 1917), which effortlessly blends love story, father-son conflict, liberal bourgeois reformism, and Russian patriotism.

Bauer, together with Protazanov and **Petr Chardynin**, undoubtedly was a director who raised Russian cinema's respectability by using film-specific, albeit trivial, plots that appealed both to middle- and lower-class audiences. Bauer's films indulged viewers who were craving unabashed emotion and noble deeds amid elegant tableaux that were structured by lavish decorations (columns, flower bouquets, curtains, etc.) and adorned by sophisticated lighting techniques. Bauer's unerring eye for facial expressions and poses that were effective on the screen made superstars of his protagonists—most prominently **Vera Kholodnaia**, **Ivan Mozzhukhin**, **Vera Karalli**, and **Vitol'd Polonskii**. Clearly, Bauer's films abound in many of the stereotypes for which silent cinema is infamous and easily parodied—the rich gentleman who abuses and then drops his tearfully naïve, lower-class girl; the wife who hides her lover in a closet at the husband's arrival;

and similar tropes. Thus, with the triumph of the Soviet revolutionary avant-garde in the mid-1920s, Bauer's films were dismissed as decadent, reactionary trash. Some attempts by sympathetic Soviet scholars to rescue his reputation in the 1960s yielded little result; only when the surviving prints were reexamined by film scholars such as Yuri Tsivian and David Robinson in the 1980s, many characteristics of Bauer's that had previously been dismissed—slow editing, luscious decorations—were now regarded as elements of a stylistic homogeneity that should not be juxtaposed negatively to the 1920s avant-garde but rather respected as a worthy style of its own.

The gradual reevaluation of Bauer's work in the public mind was promoted by **Aleksei Kapler**'s popular television program "Film Panorama" (Kinopanorama), which made a strong case for the merits of early Russian cinema, as well as **Nikita Mikhalkov**'s nostalgic hit, *Slave of Love* (Raba liubvi, 1976), a tribute to the self-indulgent beauty and follies of a film crew in the Crimea clearly modeled after Bauer's story. Whether a radical reassessment—turning Bauer from kitschmeister to great artist—will persist and not eventually be challenged as yet another extreme depends on the further direction that the discourse on Russian silent cinema will take.

According to some accounts, Bauer was married to stage actress Lina Ancharova-Bauer; others list Emma Bauer as his wife. Bauer died from pneumonia after an accident during preproduction of a new film.

Other films: *After Death* (Posle smerti, 1915); *The One Thousand Second Trick* (Tysiacha vtoraia khitrost, 1915); *A Life for a Life* (Zhizn' za zhizn', 1916); *The Dying Swan* (Umiraiushchii lebed', 1917); *Alarm* (Nabat, 1917); *Toward Happiness* (Za schast'em, 1917).

BEISHENALIEV, BOLOT [Bolotbek] (b. 25 June 1937, Toktogul, Kyrgyzstan–d. 17 November 2001, Bishkek). Kyrgyz actor. Beishenaliev studied at the studio of the Kyrgyz State Theater of Opera and Ballet, graduating in 1957, and at the Aleksandr Ostrovskii Institute of Theater Art in Tashkent until 1963. He subsequently worked as an assistant director at **Kyrgyzfilm Studio**.

The young actor's debut as the male lead, Duishen, in **Andrei Mikhalkov-Konchalovskii**'s *The First Teacher* (Pervyi uchitel',

1965) from a novella by **Chingiz Aitmatov**, created a minor sensation. Beishenaliev's ascetic features and his controlled, intensive body language believably conveyed the image of a passionate Bolshevik whose unshakeable convictions border on fanaticism. The international success of *The First Teacher* brought the actor several high-caliber assignments, among them the conceptually important part of a cunning Tatar khan in **Andrei Tarkovskii**'s *Andrei Rublev* (1966) and the Red Army soldier Chingiz in Hungarian director Miklós Jancsó's *Stars and Soldiers* (aka *The Red and the White/ Csillagosok, katonák/Zvezdy i soldaty*, 1967). **Ali Khamraev** cast Beishenaliev in his controversial contemporary drama *White, White Storks* (Belye, belye aisty, 1966). The actor subsequently appeared in dozens of Russian, Kyrgyz, Kazakh, Uzbek, Mongolian, and Czech films of all genres, often playing stoic and violent characters and occasionally the positive hero, for example, in the Ukrainian World War II blockbuster *Where Is 042?* (Gde 042?) as the Yakut survivor Nomokonov.

Among Beishenaliev's later roles are the lead in Ardak Amirkulov's monumental historical fresco *The Fall of Otrar* (Otyrardynknureni Shinvyshkhan, 1991) and the village senior in **Aleksei Balabanov**'s original Kafka adaptation *The Castle* (1994). The last years of the actor's life were overshadowed by a lack of employment caused primarily by the decline of the Central Asian film industries, including **Kyrgyz cinema**. His final performance was in Dalmira Tilepbergenova's medium-length *The Falcon's Hood* (Tomogo, 2001) as an old man selling birds on the market whose bitterness about the present is only matched by his disappointment in the Communist past.

Beishenaliev was named Merited Artist of the Kyrgyz SSR in 1974.

Other films: *The Maternal Field* (Materinskoe pole, 1967); *The Seventh Bullet* (Sed'maia pulia, 1972); *The Asian* (Aziat, 1991); *Abai* (1995).

BEK-NAZARYAN, HAMO [real name Ambartsum Beknazaryan; many sources list him as Amo Ivanovich Bek-Nazarov] (b. 31 May 1892, Yerevan–d. 27 April 1965, Moscow). Armenian actor, director, and screenwriter. Bek-Nazaryan had a brief career as a professional athlete before enrolling in the Moscow Commercial School, where he studied until 1918. In 1914, while a student, he began to play leads and supporting parts in Russian movies, especially romantic lovers, under the pseudonym Amo Bek for the companies of G. I. Libken in Iaroslavl' and **Aleksandr Khanzhonkov** in Moscow. He made his screen debut in **Vladimir Gardin**'s World War I propaganda thriller *Enver-Pasha, the Traitor of Turkey* (Enver-Pasha, predatel' Turtsii, 1914). Bek-Nazaryan soon became a star, appearing in "society dramas" by **Evgenii Bauer**, **Petr Chardynin**, Viacheslav Turzhanskii, **Wladyslaw Starewicz**, **Ivan Perestiani**, and others.

In 1919, Bek-Nazaryan moved to Georgia where he worked in Tbilisi theaters. In 1921, he joined the local People's Commissariat of Enlightenment as head of the cinema section, and directed two films for the Georgian State Film Industry (Goskinprom), *At the Pillory* (U pozornogo stolba) in 1923, and *Lost Treasures* (Propavshchie sokrovishcha) in 1924. Later in 1924, Bek-Nazaryan went to Armenia and became one of the founders of Hayfilm (**Armenfilm Studio**), where in 1926 he helmed Armenia's first full-length feature, the Georgian-Armenian coproduction *Honor* (Namus/Chest'), "a traditional romance of thwarted young lovers and a forced marriage" (Denise Youngblood). Back in Georgia, Bek-Nazaryan made *Natella* (1926), a romantic picture about a noble robber and his love, starring **Nato Vachnadze**. In Armenia, he directed *Zare* (1927) about the hardships endured by the Kurdish people, the slapstick **comedy** *Shor and Shorshor* (Shorn u Shorshore, 1928) about the adventures of two drunkards, and the somber *Khaspush* (1928), a re-creation of the 1891 revolt of Persian workers and peasants against their foreign oppressors. The visually impressive *House on the Volcano* (Tune Hrabkhi Vra/Dom na vulkane, 1928), an Armenian-Azerbaijani coproduction, depicts a strike in 1907–1908 against the capitalist oil industry.

Bek-Nazaryan landed a veritable hit with the first sound film of **Armenian cinema**, the court drama *Pepo* (1935) from a play by Armenia's classic Gabriel Sundukyan. It tells the story of a poor fisherman and his family who suffer great hardship from a wealthy dealer. *Zangezur* (1938), a chronicle of the 1920s Civil War in Armenia, won Bek-Nazaryan a Second-Class Stalin Prize in 1941. The film describes the struggle of Soviet forces in the mountainous Zangezur region against the so-called *dashnaks* who were officially described as "counterrevolutionary gangsters." After helming a dramatic short, *The Daughter* (Dustre/Dochka, 1942), about the rescue of two orphans, Bek-Nazaryan was entrusted with *David-Bek* (1944), a grandiose historical epic about the anti-Persian liberation struggle of Armenians in the 18th century that draws clear parallels to Nazi Germany's assault on the Soviet Union and praises the title hero, a politician who had forged an alliance with Russia.

The Girl from Ararat Valley (Araratyan dashti aghchikr/Devushka s Araratskoi doliny, 1949) is an attempt to transplant **Ivan Pyr'ev**'s kolkhoz comedies on Armenian soil. A thematically intriguing project dealing with the repatriation of Armenians living outside the USSR, *The Second Caravan* (Yerkrord karavan/Vtoroi karavan, 1950), was stopped before completion.

Bek-Nazaryan played an important role as a film industry pioneer in his native Armenia, as well as in **Georgian cinema** and **Azerbaijani cinema**, where he proved both an energetic administrator and a versatile director in a variety of genres. Stylistically, he was a perceptive artist who incorporated avant-gardist innovations into more conventional narrative frameworks.

Bek-Nazaryan was honored with the title People's Artist of the Armenian SSR in 1935. In 1966, the Armenian film studio was named after him. Bek-Nazaryan's brother, Harush Bek-Nazaryan (1894–?, pseudonym "Garosh") was a prominent Armenian cinematographer.

Other films: *Igdenba* (1930); *The Country of Nairi* (Yerkir Nairi/ Strana gol'dov, 1930, doc.); *Anahit* (1947); *Nasreddin in Khodjent, or The Enchanted Prince* (Nasreddin v Khodzhente, ili Ocharovannyi prints, 1959, codirected with **Ezram Karamyan**).

BELARUSFILM STUDIO [*Belarus'fil'm*]. Founded on 17 December 1924 by a decree of the Belarusian Council of People's Commissars and initially named Belgoskino Film Factory, the studio was predominantly occupied with newsreel production. Until 1939, most technical operations were carried out by **Mosfilm** (1925–1928) and **Lenfilm** (1928–1940); since the studio did not have special facilities in Belarus, all indoor scenes from 1924 to 1927 were filmed on the Moscow and Leningrad premises of Sovkino. According to some sources, the first Belarusian feature film was made at the Third Film Factory of Goskino in Moscow by Oleg Frelikh, *The Prostitute* (Prostitutka), about the social implications of prostitution during the New Economic Period (NEP). In 1927, the studio was given a building in Leningrad, where it began the production of feature films on a regular basis; however, the physical distance from Belarus remained problematic.

Among the directors working for Belgoskino were **Iurii Tarich**, who helmed what has been officially declared the first Belarusian feature film, the anti-Polish Civil War drama *Forest Tale* (Liasnaia byl/Lesnaia byl', 1928); **Vladimir Gardin** (*Kastus' Kalinovskii*, 1928), about the 1863 uprising of Belarusian peasants; **Mark Donskoi** (*In the Big City*/V bol'shom gorode, 1928, codirected with Mikhail Averbakh [1904–1980]); **Aleksandr Faintsimmer** (Hotel 'Savoy/Otel' 'Savoi,' 1930); **Vladimir Korsh-Sablin** (*Born in the Fire*/U ahni narodzhanaia/V ogne rozhdennaia, aka *The Giant*/Velikan, 1930); and **Isidor Annenskii** (*The Bear*/Medved', 1938, and *The Man in the Shell*/Chelovek v futliare, 1939, both adapted from Anton Chekhov). Korsh-Sablin's *The First Platoon* (Pershy uzvod/Pervyi vzvod, 1933), a realistic depiction of the horrors of World War I, was the first Belarusian sound film (other sources credit Eduard Arshanskii's *Toward Battles*/Boiam navstrechu, 1932 as having that distinction). Among the studio's critical successes were **Efim Dzigan**'s *A Woman* (Zhanchyna/Zhenshchina, 1932), Faintsimmer's anti-tsarist satire *Lieutenant Kizhe* (aka *The Czar Wants to Sleep*/Poruchik Kizhe, 1934, with outstanding cinematography by **Arkadii Kol'tsatyi** and music by **Sergei Prokof'ev**), and Korsh-Sablin's social transformation tale, *Seekers of Happiness* (aka *Birobidjan*, *A Greater Promise*/Shukal'niki shchascia/Iskateli schast'ia, 1935), featuring a cheerful score by **Isaak Dunaevskii**. Belgoskino celebrated a great popular success with the romantic **comedy** *A Girl Rushes to the Rendezvous* (Devushka speshit na svidanie, 1936) by Mikhail Verner (1881–1941).

In 1938–1944, the studio's name was Savetskaia Belarus'. In 1940, its premises were transferred to Minsk. A year later, with the outbreak of the Great Patriotic War, the production came to a halt; only Tarich and Korsh-Sablin were able to continue their work during evacuation to Central Asia. In 1946, the studio got its present name, Belarusfilm. In the postwar period, Faintsimmer and Korsh-Sablin won a Stalin Prize for *Konstantin Zaslonov* (aka *The Secret Brigade*/Kanstancin Zaslonau, 1949). Among the leading directors of the 1950s–1980s were Nikolai Figurovskii (1923–), Lev Golub (1904–?) who specialized in **children's films**, Sergei Sploshnov (1907–1979), and **Viktor Turov**. In 1950–1955, **Aleksandr Zarkhi** worked at Belarusfilm. Turov's thoughtful, poetic, and profoundly tragic films dealing with the Great Patriotic War and its impact on children (*I Hail from Childhood*/Ia rodam z dziacinstva/Ia rodom iz detstva, 1966) won critical praise. *Alpine Ballad* (Al'piiskaia ballada, 1967), a tragic love story on the backdrop of World War II, was directed by Boris Stepanov (b. 1927) from Vasyl Bykau's novella and became an international success. The war's traumatic effect on Belarusian society caused many filmmakers to repeatedly return to this subject; one of the most impressive variations on the war theme is **Elem Klimov**'s *Come and See* (Idzi i hliadzi/Idi i smotri, 1985).

Of the 58 Belarusian feature films produced between 1924 and 1940, all but four were made in Leningrad. From 1947 to 1955, only seven feature films were made at Belarusfilm. The subsequent moderate reforms brought about a quantitative normalization, enabling both native Belarusian filmmakers and directors from other republics to work regularly. In 1968, Belarusfilm began the production of made-for-TV feature films, and in 1973, the production of **animation**. In 1988, the studio contributed an example of gritty social realism to perestroika cinema, *My Name Is Arlekino* (Menia zavut Arlekino), directed by Valerii Rybarev, dealing with juvenile gangs.

After the disintegration of the USSR and the independence of Belarus (1991), the state maintained the ownership of Belarusfilm Studio. In 2003, the country's authoritarian leader, Aliaksandar Lukashenka, provided it with Dolby stereo equipment worth US$520,000. In 2006, Belarusfilm Studio got a new director, Viacheslav Shen'ko, and received 6.5 billion Belarusian rubles in funding. The studio produces about 5–6 feature films, 10 **documentaries**, and 5 animated pictures per year. Many Russian television miniseries are made on the studio's premises. Among the officially promoted Belarusian films was the box-office success *Anastasia of Slutsk* (Anastasiia Slutskaia, 2003), directed by Iurii Elkhov, about a 16th-century princess entangled in Christian-Muslim warfare. Filmmaker Margarita Kasymova (b. 1938), who in the 1980s moved from Tadjikistan to Belarus, continues her career in children's and youth films. Films critical of the country's political conditions are usually produced independently.

BELARUSIAN [Belorussian] CINEMA. *See* ALEINIKOV, PETR; BELARUSFILM STUDIO; FAINTSIMMER, ALEKSANDR; KLIMOV, ELEM; KORSH-SABLIN, VLADIMIR; TARICH, IURII; TUROV, VIKTOR.

BELORUSSIAN STATION (Belorusskii vokzal, 1970). **Mosfilm Studio.** 101 min., color. Directed by **Andrei Smirnov.** Script: Vadim Trunin. Cinematography: **Pavel Lebeshev.** Music: **Al'fred Shnitke**, Bulat Okudzhava. Cast: Aleksei Glazyrin, **Evgenii Leonov, Anatolii Papanov**, Vsevolod Safonov, Nina Urgant. Premiere: 30 April 1971.

Viktor (Glazyrin), a factory director, Ivan (Leonov), a locksmith, Nikolai (Papanov), a bureaucrat, and Aleksei (Safonov), a journalist, fought together in the Great Patriotic War. Twenty-five years later, they meet at the funeral of one of their former comrades, Valentin, who later had achieved the rank of general. The ongoing attempts of the four to communicate candidly about the past and the present prove difficult. Facing the banality of everyday life, both at work and at home, something seems to stop them from opening up. However, when they visit the nurse Raika (Urgant), another friend from wartime, and she sings a song to the guitar, the emotional blockages melt away.

BERGER, ARTUR SEMENOVICH (b. 27 May 1892, Vienna–d. 1 January 1981, Moscow). Austrian-Russian art director and designer. Berger studied at the Vienna School for Applied Art, graduating in 1915, and was also a student of architect Josef Hoffmann. In 1920, he began to work as an art director for the Vienna company Sascha Films, as well as film studios in Prague and Paris, including on several pictures by Michael Kertesz, later known as Michael Curtiz.

In 1936, Berger immigrated to the USSR. He worked with director **Aleksandr Macheret** on the anti-Nazi film *Moor Soldiers* (Bolotnye soldaty, 1937) and the thriller *Engineer Kochin's Error* (Oshibka inzhenera Kochina, 1939), before specializing in musical **comedies** and other light fare. Berger soon became one of the most valued art directors in Soviet cinema, designing the sets for such leading filmmakers as **Boris Barnet** on *The Old Horseman* (Staryi naezdnik, 1940, released 1959), **Ivan Pyr'ev** on *Beloved Girl* (Liubimaia devushka, 1940) and *Swineherd and Shepherd* (aka *They Met in Moscow*/Svinarka i pastukh, 1941), **Vladimir Korsh-Sablin** on *Belorussian Novellas* (Belorusskie novelly, 1942), and **Aleksandr Stolper** on *Wait for Me* (Zhdi menia, 1943). Pyr'ev's postwar melodrama, *The Tale of the Siberian Land* (aka *Symphony of Life*/Skazanie o zemle sibirskoi, 1946), demonstrates Berger's typical strengths: highly decorative sets that make even a village cafeteria look lavish, and a spectrum of richly saturated colors.

Among Berger's later accomplishments are exotic fairy tales such as **Aleksandr Ptushko**'s *The Tale of Lost Time* (Skazka o poteriannom vremeni, 1964), which features a particularly impressive, weird "underworld," and **Leonid Gaidai**'s superhit *Operation "Y" and Other Adventures of Shurik* (Operatsiia 'Y' i drugie prikliucheniia Shurika, 1965), as well as romanticized Communist propaganda such as **Sergei Iutkevich**'s *Tales about Lenin* (Rasskazy o Lenine, 1957).

Berger was honored with the title Merited Artist of the RSFSR in 1968.

Other films: *The Struggle Goes On* (Bor'ba prodolzhaetsia, 1938); *The Downfall of the Emirate* (Krushenie emirata, 1955); *Annushka* (1959); *The Man in Civilian Clothes* (Chelovek v shtatskom, 1972).

BERNES, MARK NAUMOVICH (b. 8 October 1911, Nizhin, Ukraine–d. 17 [other sources: 25] August 1969, Moscow). Russian actor and singer. Bernes studied acting in Khar'kov (Khar'kiv) until 1929, then worked in theaters in Khar'kov and Moscow. In 1936, he debuted in **Evgenii Cherviakov**'s *The Convicts* (aka *Prisoners*/Zakliuchennye, 1936), a demagogical account of the GULAG concentration camps and their efficiency in "transforming" criminals into useful Soviet citizens.

Bernes played supporting roles in films by **Sergei Iutkevich** and **Leonid Lukov** and leads such as a Soviet Air Force pilot in the sleeper hit *Fighters* (Isstrebiteli, 1939), which revealed his considerable artistic talent. National fame came to Bernes during the Great Patriotic War, when his sincere, loyal, and charming, albeit somewhat wooden personifications of Soviet soldiers won the hearts of millions. Especially his performance as "the man from Odessa," Arkadii Dziubin, in Lukov's *Two Soldiers* (Dva boitsa,

1943), irradiated optimism, wit, and unshakeable faith in the right cause. A number of films profited from the actor's characteristic soft, hoarse voice when he sang to the guitar, a gift that eventually helped him launch a parallel career as a solo singer with concert tours both in the USSR and abroad.

After roles in Stalinist propaganda fare such as **Ihor' Savchenko**'s *The Third Blow* (Tretii udar, 1948) and **Aleksandr Stolper**'s *Far from Moscow* (Daleko ot Moskvy, 1950)—the latter won him a Stalin Prize—Bernes in later years was able to prove his potential as a versatile character actor who was sometimes cast against type, for example, as the thief Ogonek in the hugely successful thriller *Night Guard* (Nochnoi patrul', 1957).

Bernes, who joined the Communist Party in 1953, was awarded the title People's Artist of the Russian Federation in 1965.

Other films: *The Man with the Rifle* (Chelovek s ruzh'em, 1938); *A Great Life* (Bol'shaia zhizn', 1940); *The Great Turning Point* (Velikii perelom, 1945); *Taras Shevchenko* (1951); *It Happened at the Militia Station* (Eto sluchilos' v militsii, 1963).

BIRMAN, SERAFIMA GERMANOVNA (b. 10 August 1890, Kishinev [now: Chisinau, Moldova]–d. 11 May 1976, Moscow). Russian actress. After graduating from A. I. Adashev's Moscow drama school in 1911, Birman began her acting career with small parts at the Moscow Art Theater (MKhAT). Predominantly a theater actress with a strong, concentrated stage presence, Birman was among the founders of the Theater of the Lenin Komsomol (Lenkom). In 1958, she joined the troupe of the Mossovet Theater where she also worked as a director.

Birman made her movie debut in 1918 in *And He, the Restless, Seeks the Storm* (A on, miatezhnyi, ishchet buri). In 1925, **Iakov Protazanov** picked her for the role of Kuma in *The Tailor from Torzhok* (Zakroishchik iz Torzhka); in this **comedy**—as in most of her subsequent films—she carried a highly expressive episode. A great success was her performance as the hysterical petit-bourgeois Madame Irène in **Boris Barnet**'s delightful *Girl with the Hatbox* (Devushka s korobkoi, 1927). In later years, **Andrei Tutyshkin** made use of Birman's rare talent as a comedienne in the turbulent vaudeville *A Crazy Day* (Bezumnyi den', 1956).

Unsurpassed among Birman's relatively few screen performances remains her portrayal of Evrosin'ia Staritskaia, the tsar's power-obsessed antagonist, in **Sergei Eizenshtein**'s *Ivan the Terrible* (Ivan Groznyi, 1943–1945). After delivering the required cliché of pure scheming evil in the film's first part, Birman deepened that image to an unexpected tragic grandeur in part II, displaying genuine motherly care and grief over her murdered son. The role won Birman a Stalin Prize in 1946, the same year she was awarded the title People's Artist of the Russian Federation.

Although Birman appeared in some episodic parts in works of leading filmmakers such as **Sergei Iutkevich** and **Grigorii Kozintsev**, Russian cinema largely neglected her extraordinary talent.

Other films: *Woman's Victory* (Pobeda zhenshchiny, 1927); *The Man with the Rifle* (Chelovek s ruzh'em, 1938); *Friends* (Druz'ia, 1938); *Don Quijote* (1957).

BLEIMAN, MIKHAIL IUR'EVICH (b. 19 May 1904, Rostov-on-the-Don–d. 3 December 1973, Moscow). Russian screenwriter. Bleiman studied history and philology in Rostov in 1920–1923 and at the Valerii Briusov Supreme Institute for Literature and Art in Moscow in 1923–1924. He worked as a journalist before specializing in screenplays.

Bleiman's first two scripts were made into satirical shorts: *History of an Advance* (Istoriia odnogo avansa, 1924), an attack on alcohol abuse, and *The Adventures of Van'ka Gvozd'* (Pokhozhdeniia Van'ki Gvozdia, 1924), a mockery of the Orthodox Church. Both were produced by a Komsomol-based company in Bleiman's hometown Rostov-on-the Don and directed by Manuel' Bol'shintsov (1902–1954).

Bleiman's reputation mainly rests on pictures in the 1930s and 1940s that openly pursue a propagandistic purpose. Their plots convey a sense of officially inspired paranoia, often featuring foreign spies or homegrown saboteurs who conceal their sinister intentions behind fiendishly deceptive masks of civility while pursuing their destructive goals. Bleiman's most significant achievement is the screenplay for **Fridrikh Ermler**'s *The Great Citizen* (Velikii grazhdanin, 1937–1939, coauthored with Bol'shintsov), a reflection of Stalinist strategies within the Bolshevik Party in the 1930s, showing Iosif Stalin's struggle against the "leftist and rightist oppositions."

Bleiman was also successful with war stories, authoring or coauthoring the scripts for **Iulii Raizman**'s *Moscow Sky* (Nebo Moskvy, 1944), **Leonid Lukov**'s *It Happened in the Donbass* (Eto bylo v Donbasse, 1945), and most notably for **Boris Barnet**'s *The Scout's Quest* (aka *Secret Agent*/Podvig razvedchika, with **Konstantin Isaev**), an entertaining spy tale that won both the director and the screenwriters Stalin Prizes.

Bleiman was involved—and attacked—in debates about "formalism" in the early 1930s. In 1948–1949, despite his loyal service to Stalin and the Communist Party, he became one of the major targets of the anti-Semitic campaign "against cosmopolitanism." Among his noteworthy later screenwriting efforts are the Civil War story *Restless Youth* (Trevozhnaia molodost', 1954)—the directing debut of **Aleksandr Alov** and **Vladimir Naumov**—and a hugely popular espionage dilogy, *The Path to Saturn* (Put' v Saturn, 1967) and *The End of Saturn* (Konets Saturna, 1968).

Bleiman participated in discussions about genre specifics of the screenplay and the function of the screenwriter. He was also a prolific film critic who regularly published his views on ideological and aesthetic aspects of Soviet cinema, displaying increasingly liberal views in post-Stalin years when he worked as an official advisor to the minister of cinematography.

Other films: *Happy Kent* (Schastlivyi Kent, 1930); *She Defends Her Motherland* (aka *No Greater Love*/Ona zashchishchaet rodinu, 1943).

BLIUMENTAL'-TAMARINA [born Klimova]**, MARIIA MIK-HAILOVNA** (b. 16 July 1859, St. Petersburg–d. 16 October 1938, Moscow). Russian actress. A teacher by training, Bliumental'-Tamarina began her acting career in 1887 with various troupes in Moscow and later in the Russian provinces. In 1901–1914 and 1921–1932, she belonged to the ensemble of the Korsh Theater in Moscow; in 1933, after the theater's closing, she became a star of Malyi Theater.

Bliumental'-Tamarina was one of the few reputable Russian stage actresses with no prejudice toward cinema. She made her debut in the role of Liza in the scandalous adaptation of Lev Tolstoi's drama *The Living Corpse* (Zhivoi trup), directed by **Boris Chaikovskii** in 1911. After a number of appearances in lighthearted **comedies** such as *The*

Jolly Little Nursery (Veselyi pitomnichek, 1916, as Kozel'skaia), she played a supporting part in **Aleksandr Razumnyi**'s popular pro-Bolshevik comedy *Brigade Commander Ivanov* (Kombrig Ivanov, released in the United States as *The Beauty and the Bolshevik*, 1923). Bliumental'-Tamarina became one of the mainstays in **Iakov Protazanov**'s Soviet pictures, who cast her in episodic roles in *His Call* (Ego prizyv, 1925, as grandma Katia) and the Civil War drama *The Last Shot* (Poslednii vystrel, 1927), and later gave her the female lead in his comedy *Don Diego and Pelageia* (Don Diego i Pelageia, 1928).

In sound film, her most famous roles were Babchenko's wife in **Fridrikh Ermler** and **Sergei Iutkevich**'s *The Counterplan* (Vstrechnyi, 1932) and the wise grandmother Dvoira in **Vladimir Korsh-Sablin**'s didactic comedy *Seekers of Happiness* (aka *Birobidjan, A Greater Promise*/Shukal'niki shchascia/Iskateli schast'ia, 1935) about a Jewish family finding a new homeland and happiness in Birobidzhan in the Far East. The latter role became her best-remembered performance; characterized by dignity, warm humor, and generosity toward human weaknesses, it includes a final monologue expressing astonishment and gratitude about the stroke of luck that brought her and her loved ones to the Soviet Union.

Bliumental'-Tamarina was honored with the title People's Artist of the USSR in 1936.

Other films: *In the Thicket of Everyday Life* (V debriakh byta, 1924); *Bricklayers* (Kirpichiki, 1925); *The Sailor Ivan Galai* (Matros Ivan Galai, 1929); *Daughter of the Motherland* (Doch' rodiny, 1937).

BODROV, SERGEI SERGEEVICH [sometimes credited as Sergei Bodrov Jr.] (b. 27 December 1971, Moscow–d. 20 September 2002, North Ossetia). Russian actor and director. Bodrov was born into the family of filmmaker **Sergei Bodrov**. He studied history at Lomonosov State University in Moscow in 1989–1993 and earned a PhD with a dissertation on Venetian Renaissance painting in 1998.

After an episodic role in his father's Russian-Swiss coproduction *White King, Red Queen* (Belyi korol', krasnaia koroleva, 1992), he came into his own with the male lead in ***Prisoner of the Caucasus*** (aka *Prisoner of the Mountains*/Kavkazskii plennik, 1996), also directed by Bodrov Sr. The amateur performer's ability to authentically portray an unsophisticated, kindhearted Russian prisoner of war who wins the trust of the local Muslim population made headlines and won Bodrov prestigious prizes at national festivals. This success led to his casting as Danila Bagrov in **Aleksei Balabanov**'s *Brother* (Brat, 1997), a clever, gloomy post-Soviet thriller whose oscillation between moral criticism of the neocapitalist malaise and provocative nationalism gains persuasiveness from Bodrov's minimalistic acting. While *Brother* captured the atmosphere of crisis and decay of the late 1990s in an artistically pioneering manner, Balabanov and Bodrov's elevation of Danila to an anti-Western superman in *Brother 2* (2000) merely exploited a cliché, albeit with a modicum of irony, rather than deepening the emblematic character. But the controversies generated by Danila Bagrov—coined "the last hero" in some quarters—also proved how aptly his creators had grasped Russia's fears and hopes for a new idol who could bring orientation, protection, and order.

Bodrov quickly became a national celebrity who anchored his own television show (*The Look/Vzgliad*, 1997–1999). He also appeared in foreign films such as Régis Wargnier's fascinating *East-West* (East-Ouest/Vostok-Zapad, 1999), in which he portrays an athlete who ultimately manages to swim from Communist oppression to freedom. Producer Sergei Sel'ianov gave Bodrov a chance to try his hands at directing. Although the outcome, *Sisters* (Sestry, 2001), betrays Balabanov's mentorship, it shows a remarkably surefooted handling of the youthful cast in this witty, humane thriller.

Bodrov and many members of his crew tragically died when their hotel was crushed by a 300-foot ice glacier that moved into the Caucasus valley during the filming of *The Messenger* (Sviaznoi), Bodrov's second project as director in which he was also to play the title role.

Other films: *Stringer* (1998, TV, Great Britain); *The Quickie* (aka Davai sdelaem eto po-bystromu, 2001); *War* (Voina, 2002); *Bear's Kiss* (2002).

BODROV, SERGEI VLADIMIROVICH [sometimes credited as Sergei Bodrov Sr.] (b. 28 June 1948, Khabarovsk). Russian director, scriptwriter, and producer. Bodrov grew up in the Far East and later studied screenwriting at the Soviet State Film School **VGIK**, graduating in 1974. Of Bodrov's 30-odd scripts, several became successful movies such as the coming-of-age **comedy** *The Trouble-Maker* (Balamut, 1978), directed by **Vladimir Rogovoi**, the wedding drama *Mechanic Gavrilov's Beloved Woman* (Liubimaia zhenshchina mekhanika Gavrilova, 1981), directed by **Petr Todorovskii**, and the seminal Cold War eye-opener *East-West* (1999, coauthored with **Rustam Ibrahimbekov**), directed by Régis Wargnier. In 1984, Bodrov turned to directing, although he continued to author and coauthor screenplays at an enviable pace, including those for his own films.

Bodrov's first pictures focused on generational problems, for example, the juvenile romance *The Sweet Juice inside Grass* (Sladkii sok vnutri travy, 1984, codirected with Amanbek Al'piev), produced at **Kazakhfilm Studio**; *The Nonprofessionals* (Neprofessionaly, 1985), about a rock group trying to make ends meet; and *Freedom Is Paradise* (Svoboda—eto rai, 1989), about a juvenile delinquent who wants to meet his imprisoned father. The latter drama, bold and shocking, won several prizes and brought Bodrov international renown. *Katala* (aka *The Gambler*, 1989, codirected with Aleksandr Buravskii), a thriller about the grim underworld of criminal card players, surprised audiences with its gritty realism and complete disillusionment in Soviet society—a rarity at the time of the film's release when perestroika idealism was still dominating the media.

In the early 1990s, Bodrov moved to the United States with his wife, writer and producer Carolyn Cavallero (their collaboration had begun with the thriller *I Wanted to See Angels*/Ia khotela uvidet' angelov, 1992). Many of his subsequent productions were realized with international, mostly Western European funding. ***Prisoner of the Caucasus*** (aka *Prisoner of the Mountains*/Kavkazskii plennik, 1996) marks the high point of Bodrov's career so far. Based on a short story by Lev Tolstoi and permeated by the writer's pacifism, it won international acclaim and was nominated for a Best Foreign Picture Academy Award. Like all of Bodrov's films, it reveals his fine perception of social milieus, as well as his keen sense of ethnic peculiarities—indeed, the clash of national mentalities is often a plot-driving element. However, as his subsequent work shows, Bodrov's view of human nature, with the possible exception of children, tends to be grim: friends, lovers, colleagues, and relatives betray each other as a matter of course. Interestingly, when approaching their conclusion, Bodrov's films often begin to slip into open pathos, which stands in strong contrast to the previously displayed sobriety and disenchantment.

Bodrov is the father of actor and director **Sergei Bodrov Jr.**

Other films: *I Hate You* (Ia tebia nenavizhu, 1986); *White King, Red Queen* (Belyi korol', krasnaia koroleva, 1992); *Running Free* (1999); *The Quickie* (Davai sdelaem eto po-bystromu, 2001); *Bear's Kiss* (2002); *The Nomad* (Kazakhstan/U.S., 2006); *The Mongol* (Mongol, 2007).

BOGATYREV, IURII GEORGIEVICH (b. 2 March 1947, Riga–d. 2 February 1989, Moscow). Russian actor. Bogatyrev studied at the Shchukin Theater studio, graduating in 1971, and joined the troupe of The Contemporary (Sovremennik) thereafter. In 1977, he switched to the Moscow Art Theater (MKhAT).

Nikita Mikhalkov cast Bogatyrev in his diploma short, *A Quiet Day at the End of the War* (Spokoinyi den' v kontse voiny, 1970), and as the secret agent (*chekist*) Egor Shilov in the Civil War thriller *At Home among Strangers* (Svoi sredi chuzhikh, chuzhoi sredi svoikh, 1974). In Mikhalkov's subsequent pictures, Bogatyrev got excellent opportunities to demonstrate his artistic versatility: as Maksakov in the nostalgic homage to silent cinema *Slave of Love*/Raba liubvi, 1976), as Voinitsev in the Anton Chekhov adaptation *Unfinished Piece for Mechanical Piano* (Neokonchennaia p'esa dlia mekhanicheskogo pianino, 1977), and especially as Andrei Shtol'ts in *Oblomov* (Neskol'ko dnei iz zhizni I. I. Oblomova, 1979) from Ivan Goncharov's novel. In the latter, Bogatyrev's strengths—dynamic body language, visible concentration, rationality, and a hard-to-define, enigmatic presence—were used to utmost effect.

The actor gained critical recognition for his performances as the innovative aviation engineer Zherekhov in Iurii Egorov's *There, behind the Horizon* (Tam, za gorizontom, 1975), as the naïve, idealistic writer Filippok in **Il'ia Averbakh**'s *Declaration of Love* (Ob"iasnenie v liubvi, 1977), as Saiapin in **Vitalii Mel'nikov**'s *Vacation in September* (Otpusk v sentiabre, 1979), as the cynical doctor Petrov in **Vladimir Bortko**'s *My Father Is an Idealist* (Moi papa—idealist, 1980), and as the pompous Manilov in **Mikhail Shveitser**'s *Dead Souls* (Mertvye dushi, 1984) from Nikolai Gogol''s novel.

Bogatyrev's reputation as a stand-alone actor passionately devoted to his artistic calling has survived his early death. He was named Merited Artist of the RSFSR in 1981 and People's Artist of the RSFSR in 1988.

Other films: *Two Lines in Small Print* (Dve strochki melkim shriftom, 1981); *Relatives* (Rodnia, 1982); *Quarantine* (Karantin, 1983); *Presumption of Innocence* (Prezumptsiia nevinovnosti, 1988).

BOGOLIUBOV, NIKOLAI IVANOVICH (b. 22 October 1899, Ivanovskoe, Riazan' province–d. 9 March 1980, Moscow). Russian actor. Bogoliubov attended the studio school of the Riazan' town theater and joined its troupe in 1919. In 1923–1926, he studied at the school of the Theater of the Russian Federation (RSFSR) named after its director, Vsevolod Meierkhol'd. From 1938 to 1958, the actor belonged to the Moscow Art Theater (MKhAT).

Bogoliubov made his film debut in 1931 in **Iakov Protazanov**'s ill-fated first sound picture, *Tommy* (aka *Siberian Patrol*/Tommi). He demonstrated his strong screen presence with a superb performance in **Boris Barnet**'s *The Outskirts* (Okraina, 1933) as the cheerful, courageous Bolshevik Nikolai who is executed for initiating fraternization with the German enemy at the end of World War I.

Bogoliubov created one of the characteristic screen types of the 1930s, the dogmatic Stalinist functionary, in **Fridrikh Ermler**'s *Peasants* (Krest'iane, 1935), where he was cast as Nikolai Mironovich, head of the Political Department, who gives his all to transform the "backward farmer's psychology." In 1937–1939, Ermler entrusted Bogoliubov with the role of Party leader Petr Shakhov in *The Great Citizen* (Velikii grazhdanin), for which the actor received a Stalin Prize in 1941. Bogoliubov soon became one of the prototypical faces of Stalinist cinema, expressing unshakeable class consciousness, mercilessness, and absolute loyalty to Communist principles. He worked with leading Soviet directors, including **Sergei Gerasimov** (*The Bold Seven*/Semero smelykh, 1936), the **Vasil'ev brothers** (*The Defense of Tsaritsyn*/Oborona Tsaritsyna, 1942, Stalin Prize), and **Mikheil Chiaureli** (*The Oath*/Kliatva, 1944; *The Fall of Berlin*/Padenie Berlina, 1949). Because of his likeness to Marshall Kliment Voroshilov (1881–1969), he became his screen double, for example, in **Ihor' Savchenko**'s *The Third Blow* (Tretii udar, 1948).

Following the Thaw, Bogoliubov's fame waned quickly, although directors with whom he had worked in the past occasionally gave him parts, for example, Barnet in *Alenka* (1962) and Chiaureli in *The General and the Daisies* (General i margaritki, 1964).

Bogoliubov, who joined the Communist Party in 1950, received Stalin Prizes for his stage work in 1946, 1947, 1949, and 1950. He was named People's Artist of the Russian Federation in 1945.

Other films: *The Great Force* (Velikaia sila, 1950); *Life Passed By* (Zhizn' proshla mimo, 1959).

BOGOSLOVSKII, NIKITA VLADIMIROVICH (b. 22 May [other sources: 9 September] 1913, St. Petersburg–d. 3 April 2004, Moscow). Russian composer. Bogoslovskii, who was born into an aristocratic family, studied composition with Aleksandr Glazunov (1865–1936) in 1927–1928 and as an audit at Leningrad Conservatory in 1930–1934.

Bogoslovskii's favorite musical genre was the song, intended for professionals and laymen alike; altogether, he composed more than 300 of them. Many of his most popular songs were written for movies. Thus, Bogoslovskii's score for **Vladimir Vainshtok**'s Robert Louis Stevenson adaptation *Treasure Island* (Ostrov sokrovishch, 1936) included "I've Inspired You to a Heroic Deed" (Ia na podvig tebia provozhala), which became an immediate hit. Equally successful were Bogoslovskii's melodies for **Leonid Lukov**'s optimistic miners' drama *A Great Life* (Bol'shaia zhizn', 1940), the **Mark Bernes** vehicle *Fighters* (Isstrebiteli, 1939), and **Boris Barnet**'s *A Good Lad* (Slavnyi malyi, aka Novgorodtsy, 1941). During the Great Patriotic War, Bogoslovskii worked most fruitfully with Lukov, in particular on the Civil War adventure *Aleksandr Parkhomenko* (1942) and the extremely popular war-buddy picture *Two Fighters* (Dva boitsa, 1943) in which Bernes inimitably sings "Dark Night" (Temnaia noch') to the guitar.

In the post-Stalin period, Bogoslovskii was particularly successful with music for **comedies**, including **Andrei Tutyshkin**'s harmlessly entertaining *A Crazy Day* (Bezumnyi den', 1956), **Leonid Gaidai**'s hilarious shorts *Barbos the Dog and an Unusual Cross-Country Race*

(Pes Barbos i neobychainyi kross, 1961) and *Bootleggers* (Samogon-shchiki, 1961), and **Igor' Il'inskii**'s *An Old Acquaintance* (Staryi znakomyi, 1969). But the composer excelled in other genres too, contributing scores to Vainshtok's attempt in the genre of Western, *Horseman without Head* (Vsadnik bez golovy, 1973), and Turkmen filmmaker **Bulat Mansurov**'s exceptional World War II parable *There Is No Death, Pals* (Smerti net, rebiata! 1970). Bogoslovskii's considerable stylistic versatility ranged from pop to folklore and neoclassical symphonic tunes, at times expressing pathos, at times comedic cheerfulness or dramatic thrill.

Noteworthy is Bogoslovskii's work in **animation**, especially his partnership with director **Leonid Amal'rik**, whose social satires *The Abstinent Sparrow* (Nep'iushchii vorobei, 1961) and *Grandma's Little Goat* (Babushkin kozlik, 1963), as well as fairy tales for children such as *The Cat's House* (Koshkin dom, 1958) and the very popular *Thumbelina* (Diuimovochka, 1966), derive their witty and optimistic air in no small part from the composer's melodies.

Bogoslovskii, whose crude practical jokes and lavish lifestyle were legendary, was named Merited Artist of the RSFSR in 1968 and People's Artist of the USSR in 1983.

Other films: *The Mother* (Mat', 1941); *The Fifteen-Year Old Captain* (Piatnadtsatiletnii kapitan, 1945); *It Happened in the Donbass* (Eto bylo v Donbasse, 1946); *Various Destinies* (Raznye sud'by, 1958); *The Unknown Woman* (Neznakomka, 1979).

BOL'SHAKOV, IVAN GRIGOR'EVICH (b. 1902, Tula–d. 20 March 1980, Moscow). Russian film industry executive. Bol'shakov, who hailed from a peasant family, began to work at a Tula arms factory at the age of 14. Following the 1917 Bolshevik takeover, Bol'shakov embarked on a political and administrative career. He studied at a workers' college (*rabfak*) and the Plekhanov Institute of Economics in the 1920s. After graduating in 1931, he joined the Soviet government (Council of People's Commissars, or SNK) as a consultant on economic issues, working his way up to chief of staff for the SNK chairman, Viacheslav Molotov, who also happened to be his uncle.

In June 1939, Iosif Stalin appointed Bol'shakov head of the Committee for Cinema Affairs of the SNK. When the committee was transformed into a full-blown ministry in 1946, Bol'shakov became the first film minister of the USSR, responsible for the entire industry. He organized the required regular film screenings in the Kremlin, taking notes of any remark that Stalin or members of the Politburo made, and avoided stating opinions of his own. As a skillful mediator between the country's political leadership and its cultural elite, Bol'shakov demonstrated perceptiveness, flexibility, and occasional harshness but without open malevolence or autocratic ambition.

Apart from his unconditional loyalty to the Communist Party and its leader, Bol'shakov proved useful to Soviet cinema through his organizational skills, unfailing memory, and a modicum of predictability and even decency, unburdening a number of leading Soviet filmmakers who were traumatized by the arbitrary dictatorial style of his predecessors, **Boris Shumiatskii** and Semen Dukel'skii. Among Bol'shakov's indisputable achievements was the evacuation of the major Soviet studios, **Lenfilm** and **Mosfilm**, to Central Asia in fall 1941 and their relocation to Leningrad and Moscow in 1944. Amid chaos, starvation, and defeatism, he ensured the continuation of film production: at first, shorts for the front, then, beginning in fall 1942, full-length features. But Bol'shakov also helped implement the infamous campaign "against cosmopolitanism," whose implicitly anti-Semitic concepts were propagated in his speeches in 1948–1949.

After Stalin's death, Bol'shakov remained in the government apparatus as the first deputy minister of culture of the USSR responsible for cinema (until January 1954). He then was appointed deputy minister of foreign trade and deputy chairman of the Society for Cultural Ties with Foreign Countries, before being honored as a "distinguished pensioner" (*personal'nyi pensioner soiuznogo znacheniia*).

Bol'shakov joined the Communist Party in 1918. He earned a PhD in art history in 1950 and authored a number of articles and books on Soviet cinema. A highly decorated member of the Soviet *nomenklatura*, Bol'shakov received two Orders of Lenin, among other signs of distinction. He is buried at Novodevich'e cemetery in Moscow.

BONDARCHUK, NATAL'IA SERGEEVNA (b. 10 May 1950, Moscow). Russian actress, director, and screenwriter. The daughter of actress Inna Makarova and actor/director **Sergei Bondarchuk** studied with **Sergei Gerasimov** and **Tamara Makarova** (unrelated) at the Soviet State Film School **VGIK**, graduating in 1971. She continued her education at the same school, receiving a degree from the Directing Department in 1975.

As a student, Bondarchuk already played supporting parts in films by her teacher Gerasimov, as well as **Vera Stroeva**, **Nikolai Gubenko**, and **Larisa Shepit'ko**. She was superb as a suicidal young woman in Shepit'ko's *You and I* (Ty i ia, 1972) before **Andrei Tarkovskii** gave her the plum part of Hari in his science fiction parable *Solaris* (1972). None of Bondarchuk's numerous subsequent roles could recap the quiet intensity and dark sensuality of that interpretation, although some performances certainly attracted attention, for example, as Princess Volkonskaia in **Vladimir Motyl'**'s remarkable Decembrist saga *Star of Captivating Happiness* (Zvezda plenitel'nogo schast'ia, 1975).

As a director, Bondarchuk debuted with the episode "The Hapless Matrenka" ("Besschastnaia Matrenka") in *Old Times in Poshekhonia* (Poshekhonskaia starina, 1975), an original adaptation of a novel by 19th-century satirist Mikhail Saltykov-Shchedrin. She then specialized in films for and about children, including *Living Rainbow* (Zhivaia raduga, 1982), about village kids saving orphaned ducklings, and the dilogy *Bambi's Childhood* (Detstvo Bembi, 1985) and *Bambi's Youth* (Iunost' Bembi, 1986) from Felix Salten's classic about a deer—"the Prince of the Forest"—who has to grasp the existence of evil and acquire the strength to fight it. Perhaps the most ambitious of Bondarchuk's directorial undertakings so far is the Leskov adaptation *Lord, Hear My Prayer* (Gospodi, uslyshi molitvu moiu, 1991), which conveys a strong Orthodox Christian message. Bondarchuk has played parts in all of her films, as have her longtime husband, **Nikolai Burliaev**, and their son, Ivan Burliaev.

Bondarchuk has taught at VGIK since 1979. In 1977 she was awarded the title Merited Artist of the Russian Federation.

Other films: (as director) *The One Love of My Soul* (Odna liubov' dushi moei, 1999); *Pushkin: The Last Duel* (Pushkin. Posledniaia duel', 2006); (as actress) *At the Lake* (U ozera, 1970); *The Heart of Russia* (Serdtse Rossii, 1971); *Came a Soldier from the Front* (Prishel soldat s fronta, 1971); *Lermontov* (1986).

BONDARCHUK, SERGEI FEDOROVICH (b. 25 September 1920, Belozerka, Ukraine–d. 20 October 1994, Moscow). Russian director, actor, and screenwriter. Bondarchuk played on the stage of the Eisk Drama Theater in 1937–1938 and studied acting at the Theater Institute of Rostov-on-the-Don in 1938–1942. During the Great Patriotic War he served in a theater unit of the Red Army and was discharged in 1946. He then studied acting at the Soviet State Film School **VGIK** in the workshop of **Sergei Gerasimov** and **Tamara Makarova**, graduating in 1948.

Bondarchuk's screen debut as partisan Val'ko in Gerasimov's legendary *Young Guard* (Molodaia gvardiia, 1948) immediately catapulted him into the ranks of Soviet movie stars. **Iulii Raizman** cast Bondarchuk in the lead role of engineer-cum-Party activist Sergei Tutarinov in the Stalinist saga *Knight of the Golden Star* (Kavaler zolotoi zvezdy, 1950). Shortly thereafter, Bondarchuk's performance in the title role of **Ihor' Savchenko**'s biopic *Taras Shevchenko* (1951) proved that the young actor's first successes were not accidental. Still, Bondarchuk's most indisputable artistic achievements as an actor were in adaptations of Russian classical literature, starting with the naïve and devoted Dr. Dymov in **Samson Samsonov**'s exemplary Anton Chekhov adaptation *The Grasshopper* (Poprygun'ia, 1955). Bondarchuk also played the title role in **Sergei Iutkevich**'s *Othello* (1956), Dr. Astrov in **Andrei Mikhalkov-Konchalovskii**'s Chekhov adaptation *Uncle Vania* (Diadia Vania, 1971), and Prince Kasatskii/Father Sergius in **Igor' Talankin**'s *Father Sergius* (Otets Sergii, 1978) from Lev Tolstoi's novella.

Bondarchuk delivered a masterpiece with his first attempt as a filmmaker, *The Fate of a Man* (Sud'ba cheloveka, 1959). Based on a novella by Mikhail Sholokhov (1905–1984), it became an instant classic and impressed millions of viewers all over the world. Shot in black and white, the picture's narrative style features Bondarchuk's typical blend of understatement and pathos. In the title role of Andrei Sokolov, a soldier who loses his entire family in the Great Patriotic War and adopts an orphan in the end, Bondarchuk conveys the most intense emotions through close shots, whereas to his environment this character displays impenetrable manly stoicism.

Following this triumphant start, Bondarchuk was entrusted with the most ambitious project of Russian film history—the four-part, seven-hour screen adaptation of Tolstoi's *War and Peace* (Voina i mir, 1962–1967). Carried out with practically unlimited financial and personnel resources and enormous directorial inventiveness, Bondarchuk made maximum use of his home studio **Mosfilm**'s funds. Unfortunately, the statistical records set by this megaproduction blinded many critics to its significant artistic achievements. While there were indeed "tens of thousands of extras," the meticulous reconstruction of several major battles could only succeed because of Bondarchuk's unprecedented visual design and choreographic skill. Although this screen version, unlike its predecessors helmed by **Iakov Protazanov** and King Vidor, kept almost all plot lines of the original text, what truly matters is the preservation of the spirit of the literary original. While the snobbish comments made at the film's release are now safely forgotten, an increasing number of Russian and foreign film historians have realized this picture's unique status.

Dino de Laurentiis hired Bondarchuk to direct *Waterloo* (1971) as an international coproduction, a critically underrated, powerful historical fresco featuring stars such as Rod Steiger, Orson Welles, and Christopher Plummer with outstanding performances. Bondarchuk's own international star status was demonstrated as Red Army soldier Fedor in Roberto Rosselini's *It Was Night in Rome* (Eva notta a Roma, 1960) and in the Yugoslav-Italian coproduction *Battle at the River Neretva* (Bitka na Neretvi, 1969), among others.

Bondarchuk's first two films marked the peak of his directorial career; his subsequent output matched neither of them. The director's second Sholokhov adaptation, the large-scale *They Fought for the Motherland* (Oni srazhalis' za Rodinu, 1975), contains some impressive episodes, yet the film's epic breadth is not controlled by inner narrative coherence—a fundamental problem that began to haunt Bondarchuk's artistry in general. To a certain extent, the shortcomings were predetermined by the literary source, a peculiar torso that Sholokhov never managed to complete. Bondarchuk's decision to adapt Chekhov's *The Steppe* (Step', 1977), a virtually unfilmable text, was an attempt to return to the more intimate style of his debut yet resulted in a strenuously slow and rather shapeless exercise, despite several atmospherically intense episodes.

The gigantic two-part, five-hour *Red Bells* (Krasnye kolokola, 1982), based on the books of American journalist John Reed about the revolutions in Mexico and Russia, failed to attract viewers inside or outside the USSR despite an international star cast. Decorated with a USSR State Prize in 1984, it marked Bondarchuk's artistic fall from grace and his ultimate transformation into a state official who had apparently lost his creative prowess. Faced with the disturbing transformation of Soviet society in the mid-1980s, Bondarchuk turned to Aleksandr Pushkin's 1825 tragedy *Boris Godunov* (1986). This adaptation became the cinematic testament of a perestroika skeptic: the visibly distraught director, who plays the title role, interpreted Godunov as a talented, well-meaning, and intelligent authoritarian ruler who is alienated from the Russian people by his hesitant nature and an unspeakable crime committed to achieve power, and thus loses all legitimacy. The classical material, presented in a rather academic and cold fashion, resonated with Bondarchuk's own experiences when he became the prime target of fierce attacks by the champions of democratization and decentralization in Soviet cinema, in particular during the tempestuous fifth Congress of the Soviet Filmmakers' Union in May of 1986 when he was not even allowed to respond to the accusations directed against him.

However, Bondarchuk remained a bankable star, one of the few Soviet actors with worldwide renown who was offered leads in international productions such as *Battle of the Three Kings* (1990), a monumental Soviet-Spanish-Moroccan-Italian coproduction. Bondarchuk's last role was in a historical epic aptly entitled *Thunder over Russia* (Groza nad Rus'iu, 1992), **Aleksei Saltykov**'s adaptation of Aleksei K. Tolstoi's novel *The Silver Prince* (Kniaz' Serebriannyi). His final years were overshadowed by a struggle with an Italian producer who financed the director's longtime favorite project, a 10-hour, made-for-television version of Sholokhov's *And Quiet Flows the Don* (Tikhii Don, 1989–1992). It was first shown on Russian television in 2006, to mixed reviews.

In hindsight, Bondarchuk's extraordinary talent as actor and filmmaker is beyond doubt; this, and an enormous willpower in carrying out his ambitious projects, caused both admiration and envy in the Soviet film world. What compromised Bondarchuk's public image was his excessive involvement in USSR officialdom. A member of the Communist Party since 1970, Bondarchuk was named People's

Artist of the USSR at the unprecedented young age of 32 (on Stalin's personal order) and Hero of Socialist Labor in 1980. He won a Stalin Prize for *Taras Shevchenko* in 1951, a Lenin Prize for *Fate of a Man* in 1960, and an Academy Award for Best Foreign Picture for *War and Peace* in 1968.

Beginning in 1971, Bondarchuk was in charge of a workshop at VGIK with his wife, actress Irina Skobtseva (b. 1927). His daughter **Natal'ia Bondarchuk** is an actress and director, as is his son, Fedor (b. 1967), who dedicated his Afghanistan war blockbuster, *The Ninth Company* (Deviataia rota, 2005), to his father.

Other films: (as actor) *Admiral Ushakov* (1953); *Serezha* (aka *A Summer to Remember*, 1960); *Choice of a Goal* (Vybor tseli, 1976); *Ovod* (1980, TV).

BONUS, THE (Premiia, 1974). **Lenfilm Studio**. 83 min. (other sources: 90 min.), color. Directed by Sergei Mikaelyan. Script: Aleksandr Gel'man from his 1974 play. Cinematography: Vladimir Chumak. Cast: **Evgenii Leonov**, Vladimir Samoilov, **Oleg Iankovskii**, **Mikhail Gluzskii**, **Armen Dzhigarkhanyan**, Nina Urgant, Svetlana Kriuchkova, Borislav Brondukov. Premiere: 22 September 1975.

A team of construction workers under their leader, Potapov (Leonov), refuses to accept the bonus awarded to them for exceeding the production goals. At a meeting with factory administrators and Communist Party officials headed by the dogmatic Batartsev (Samoilov) and his deputy Solomakhin (Iankovskii), Potapov points to the constant rule violations and the abominable work ethics that had necessitated the adjustment of the production plan figures. His soft-spoken yet passionate argumentation persuades most of the participants at the meeting. They realize that a profound change in workers' and managers' attitudes toward their responsibilities is vital.

BORISOV, ALEKSANDR FEDOROVICH (b. 1 May 1905, St. Petersburg–d. 12 [other sources: 19] May 1982, Leningrad). Russian actor and director. Borisov studied at the studio of the Leningrad Academic Pushkin Theater—the former Aleksandrinskii—joining the troupe of its studio theater upon graduation in 1927 and its main troupe in 1928.

Borisov's fame rests on biopics, a genre that enjoyed supreme official status in Stalinist cinema. Thus, he appeared in the title roles of **Grigorii Roshal'**'s *Academician Ivan Pavlov* (Akademik Ivan Pavlov, 1949) and *Musorgskii* (1950), as Rybkin in **Gerbert Rappaport**'s *Aleksandr Popov* (1950), and as Aleksandr Herzen (Gertsen) in **Grigorii Kozintsev**'s ill-fated *Belinskii* (1953). Despite strict canonical rules that were in place for these quasi-hagiographic films—which implied that Musorgskii's severe alcoholism or Pavlov's unabashed religiousness could not even be hinted at—Borisov was able to avoid the trivializing flatness that was typical of performances in this genre.

Beginning with the Thaw, Borisov was given opportunities to display other facets of his talent, for example, as Professor Lapin in **Mikhail Kalatozov**'s fine **comedy** *Loyal Friends* (Vernye druz'ia, 1954) and as Marko Mukha in the blockbuster *Maksim Perepelitsa* (1956). The actor was also a valued interpreter in adaptations of classical Russian literature such as **Sergei Bondarchuk**'s *War and Peace* (Voina i mir, 1962–1967), in which he portrayed Uncle Rostov, and **Iosif Kheifits**'s *In the Town of S.* (V gorode S., 1967) from Anton Chekhov's story "Ionych." In 1960, he directed an adaptation of Fedor Dostoevskii's short story *The Meek One* (Krotkaia) with **Iia Savvina** in the title role.

Borisov was a member of the Supreme Soviet of the USSR in 1962–1966. He won four Stalin Prizes (in 1947 for his theatrical work, in 1950 for *Pavlov*, and twice in 1951, for *Aleksandr Popov* and *Musorgskii*) and was honored with the title People's Artist of the USSR in 1951 and Hero of Socialist Labor in 1981.

Other films: *Dnepr on Fire* (Dnepr v ogne); *Rimskii-Korsakov* (1952); *Freebooters* (aka *Flames of the Volga*/Vol'nitsa, 1955); *The Station Master* (Stantsionnyi smotritel', 1972); *Personal Scores* (Lichnye schety, 1982).

BORISOV, OLEG [real first name: Al'bert] **IVANOVICH** (b. 8 November 1929, Privolzhsk, Ivanovo district–d. 28 April 1994, Moscow). Russian actor. Borisov studied at the studio school of the Moscow Art Theater (MKhAT) in 1947–1951 and joined the Russian Dramatic Theater Lesia Ukrainka in Kiev. He worked at the State Academic Grand Dramatic Theater in Leningrad in 1964–1989 and at MKhAT in Moscow (1989–1990). In his last years, Borisov ran his own theater (Antrepriza Olega Borisova).

After an unremarkable film debut with an episodic role in **Mark Donskoi**'s *Mother* (aka *1905*/Mat', 1956), Borisov demonstrated his natural versatility—including singing and dancing—in the popular, albeit critically underrated musical *The Girl from the Black Sea* (Chernomorochka, 1959). He displayed joyful energy in other **comedic** leads, for example, **El'dar Riazanov**'s *Hand Me the Complaint Book* (Daite zhalobnuiu knigu, 1964). A fine method actor, Borisov made the deepest impression in adaptations of classical Russian literature, for example, as the unprincipled nihilist Versilov in *The Adolescent* (Podrostok, 1983, TV), a loyal version of Fedor Dostoevskii's novel.

In the 1980s, **Vadim Abdrashitov** gave Borisov some of his most challenging parts, using the actor's ascetic, sometimes pain-ridden features to convey an all-pervasive feeling of crisis: the self-righteous investigator Ermakov in *The Train Halted* (Ostanovilsia poezd, 1982), the alienated astrophysicist Kostin in *Parade of Planets* (Parad planet, 1985), and the Communist hack in *The Servant* (Sluga, 1988). His last significant film roles were in **Pavel Lungin**'s *Luna Park* (1992) about the tribulations of a terminally ill Jewish man who has to come to terms with his radical right-wing son, and in *Thunder over Russia* (Groza nad Rus'iu, 1992), **Aleksei Saltykov**'s adaptation of Aleksei K. Tolstoi's novel *The Silver Prince* (Kniaz' Serebriannyi), in which Borisov portrayed Ivan the Terrible.

Borisov was named People's Artist of the USSR in 1978, the year when his stage work was recognized with a USSR State Prize. His brother, Lev Borisov (b. 1933), is a prolific stage and film actor who gained national fame as a cold-blooded Mafioso in the miniseries *Criminal Petersburg* (Kriminal'nyi Peterburg, 2000, TV).

Other films: *A Living Corpse* (Zhivoi trup, 1968); *The Wedding* (Zhenit'ba, 1978); *The Theft* (Krazha, 1982); *I Am Bored, Devil* (Mne skuchno, bes, 1993).

BORTKO, VLADIMIR VLADIMIROVICH (b. 7 May 1946, Moscow). Russian director, scriptwriter, and producer. Bortko studied geology in Kiev until 1965, then served in the Soviet armed forces and worked as an electrician in military construction (1966–1969).

He majored in film direction at the Karpenko-Karii Institute of Stage Arts in Kiev, graduating in 1974, and became an assistant director at the **Dovzhenko Film Studio**. Bortko moved to Leningrad in 1980, directing his subsequent pictures at **Lenfilm Studio**. His debut film, *The Investigative Commission* (Komissiia po rassledovaniiu, 1978), deals with an incident at a nuclear power station. It was followed by a contemporary melodrama, *My Father Is an Idealist* (Moi papa—idealist, 1980). Bortko scored his first box-office hit with *The Blonde behind the Corner* (Blondinka za uglom, 1984); although heavily censored, this story of an intellectual who is both attracted to and put off by vulgar consumerism reflected growing unease with the state of Soviet society. A similar approach characterized *Once a Liar* (Edinozhdy solgav, 1987), about a ruthless opportunist betraying his artistic mission.

Bortko's name acquired national renown at the height of perestroika when he delivered a poignant adaptation of Mikhail Bulgakov's anti-Soviet satire *Heart of a Dog* (Sobach'e serdtse, 1988, TV). Truthful to the original, although somewhat heavy-handed, it revealed a complete disillusionment in the beliefs of Communism. The spectacular military thriller *The Afghan Breakdown* (Afganskii izlom, 1991), with Italian star Michele Placido portraying a disenchanted Soviet Army major, featured graphic violence unknown in Russian cinema before. The fact that it flopped commercially had more to do with the moribund state of the Soviet distribution system than with the film's inherent narrative qualities.

Bortko returned to more aesthetically ambitious filmmaking with *The Circus Burned Down, and the Clowns Ran Away* (Tsirk sgorel, i klouny razbezhalis', 1998), a visually and psychologically impressive testimony to the dire situation of artists in post-Communist Russia. In the 1990s Bortko agreed to direct a number of episodes in television miniseries such as *The Street of Broken Lanterns* (Ulitsa razbitykh fonarei, 1997) and *Bandits' Petersburg* (Banditskii Peterburg, 2000), using the sarcastic pseudonym "Ian Khudokormov" (Jan Poorly Fed).

The triumphant success of the 10-part television adaptation of Fedor Dostoevskii's 1868 novel *The Idiot* in 2003 came as a surprise to many critics who had underestimated Bortko's artistic potential. Impeccably bridging the gap between popular and highbrow, Bortko managed to turn a complex literary text into an almost flawless screen version without trivializing any of its aspects. *The Master and Margarita* (Master i Margarita, 2005) features similar qualities, although the format of a miniseries proved less suitable for Mikhail Bulgakov's novel, despite a number of brilliant episodes.

Bortko is a versatile professional who has weathered the Russian film industry's troubles with remarkable stoicism and adaptability. Even his weaker movies display keen social alertness and melancholic idealism, never stepping over the line into cynicism and indifference. Such worldview resonates with viewers from the disenfranchised post-Soviet "middle class" that was nourished by 19th-century classics and finds itself at a loss in Russia's new autocratic capitalism.

Bortko was named People's Artist of Russia in 2000.

Other films: *Without Family* (Bez sem'i, 1984, TV); *Good Luck to You, Gentlemen!* (Udachi vam, gospoda!, 1992); *Taras Bul'ba* (2008).

BUCHMA, AMVROSII MAKSIMILIANOVICH (b. 14 March 1891, L'viv–d. 6 January 1957, Kiev). Ukrainian actor, director, and pedagogue. Buchma, born into the family of a railway worker, graduated from the Lysenko Institute in 1905 and worked as an extra in the Rus'ka Besida (Russkaia Beseda) theater in L'viv (L'vov) until 1912. After serving in the Austro-Hungarian army in World War I, he returned to the stage and appeared in leading roles in Khar'kiv and, since 1936, at the Ivan Franko Theater in Kiev where he also worked as a director.

Buchma made his film debut in 1924 in two satirical comedies by Les' Kurbas: *Vendetta*, an attack on the Church, and *Macdonald*, a grotesque caricature of the British politician and his anti-Soviet activities (Buchma played the title role). The actor gained national fame in two films by **Petr Chardynin**: the biopic *Taras Shevchenko* (1926) in which he portrayed the legendary Ukrainian poet, and the historical drama *Taras Triasilo* (1927). In 1929, Buchma made film history as the German soldier going insane during a World War I gas attack in **Aleksandr Dovzhenko**'s *Arsenal*. The actor demonstrated his extraordinary capacity for psychological nuance, capturing an introverted personality on screen in the title role of Gordei Iaroshchuk in *Night Coach* (Nochnoi izvozchik, 1928, directed by Georgii Tasin), which describes the tragedy of an apolitical, rank-and-file man who awakens politically and sacrifices his life to avenge the slaughter of his beloved daughter.

Buchma, one of the leading Ukrainian actors of the silent period, mastered the transition to sound film without difficulty. The most memorable among his many performances is Taras, a proud man who refuses to bow to the Nazi occupants, in **Mark Donskoi**'s holocaust tragedy *The Undefeated* (Nepokorennye, 1945). Buchma's artistic intensity can be witnessed in **Sergei Eizenshtein**'s *Ivan the Terrible* (Ivan Groznyi, 1943–1945) in the role of Aleksei Basmanov.

As director, Buchma helmed the silent *Behind the Wall* (Za stenoi, 1929), and a sound film in 1954, *Earth* (Zemlia, codirected with A. Zhvachko).

Buchma, a member of the Communist Party since 1942, was director of the Kiev Film Studio (**Dovzhenko Film Studio**) from 1945 to 1948. Beginning in 1940, he taught at the Karpenko-Karii Theater Institute in Kiev. Buchma received Stalin Prizes for his theater work in 1941 and 1949 and was named People's Artist of the USSR in 1944.

Other films: *Tolstopuzenko's Dream* (Son Tolstopuzenko, 1924); *Jimmy Higgins* (Dzhimmi Khiggins, 1928); *The Sold Appetite* (Prodannyi appetit, 1928); *Wind from the East* (Veter s vostoka, 1941); *Stolen Happiness* (Ukradennoe schast'e, 1952).

BUDRAITIS, JUOSAS STASIO (b. 6 October 1940, Liepynai, Lithuania). Lithuanian actor. Budraitis was a student of law at Vilnius University when **Vytautas Žalakevičius** cast him as Jonas Lkisov in his post–World War II drama *Nobody Wanted to Die* (Nekas nenorejo mirti/Nikto ne khotel umirat', 1965), a film that launched the successful screen careers of several actors in **Lithuanian cinema**—among them **Donatas Banionis** and **Regimantas Adomaitis**. Cultivating a screen image of virile willpower and determinacy, Budraitis worked both in Russian and Baltic studios, for example, in the Civil War hit *Once Two Comrades Were Serving* (Sluzhili dva tovarishcha, 1968) and **Vladimir Basov**'s espionage superhit *The Shield and the Sword* (Shchit i mech', 1968). Admittedly, most of Budraitis's performances were in mediocre genre fare, especially political espionage and social thrillers, and brought him popularity if not artistic repute.

In the 1970s and 1980s, he was also employed in Czech, Bulgarian, Yugoslav, and East German films. His reputation of a solid craftsman survived the breakdown of the Soviet Union's film industry, enabling Budraitis to continue his career into the new millennium.

Among Budraitis's numerous movie roles, two stand out artistically: in **Grigorii Kozintsev**'s *King Lear* (Korol' Lir, 1971) and **Aleksandr Alov**'s and **Vladimir Naumov**'s *The Legend of Till* (Legenda o Tile, 1977). Budraitis often worked for television as well, for example, in the successful miniseries *Rich Man, Poor Man* (Turtuolis vargšas/Bogach, bedniak, 1982), directed by **Arūnas Žebriūnas** from Irwin Shaw's novel.

Budraitis was named People's Artist of the Lithuanian SSR in 1982. In the late 1990s, he was appointed cultural attaché of the Lithuanian embassy to Russia.

Other films: *When Rivers Flow Together* (Kogda slivaiutsia reki, 1961); *That Sweet Word: Liberty!* (Eto sladkoe slovo—svoboda, 1973); *The Velvety Season* (Barkhatnyi sezon, 1979, USSR/Yugoslavia); *Ar'e* (2004); *The Tanker "Tango"* (Tanker 'Tango,' 2006).

BUKHOVETSKII [spelling in non-Russian sources: Buchowetzki], **DMITRII SAVEL'EVICH** (b. 1885–d. 1932, Los Angeles). Russian director and actor. After studying law, Bukhovetskii starred in a number of silents, mostly playing boorish and treacherous characters, for example, in **Iakov Protazanov**'s melodramas *Giant of the Spirit* (Bogatyr' dukha, 1918) and *Maidservant Jenny* (Gornichnaia Dzhenni, 1918). He was the hussar officer Minskii in **Aleksandr Ivanovskii**'s Pushkin adaptation *The Station Master* (Stantsionnyi smotritel', 1918) and appeared in the title role of **Aleksandr Razumnyi**'s pro-Bolshevik **agitka** *Comrade Abram* (Tovarishch Abram, 1919).

In 1919, Bukhovetskii immigrated to Germany, via Poland, where he directed his most artistically challenging works: the expressionistic Fedor Dostoevskii adaptation *The Brothers Karamazov* (Die Brüder Karamasoff, 1921), the historical drama *Danton* (1921, based on Georg Büchner's classical play), and *Othello* (1922), all starring Emil Jannings. Bukhovetskii also made big-budget period pieces such as *Peter the Great* (Peter der Große, 1922). The Polish-American star Pola Negri (1894–1987), whom Bukhovetskii had directed in the German-made *Sappho* (1924), invited him to Hollywood, where he directed her in a series of erotic melodramas, including *Men* (1924), *Lily of the Dust* (1926), and *The Crown of Lies* (1926). When Negri's success began to fade, so did Bukhovetskii's. In the early 1930s, he was merely in charge of the international versions of American pictures.

Other films: (as actor) *The Boor* (Khamka, 1918); (as director) *The Swan* (1924); *Valencia* (1926); *Television* (1931).

BURGASOV, FEDOR [credited in French films as Fédote Bourgas-soff] (b. 1890, Likhvin–d. 1944, Paris). Russian and French cinematographer. Burgasov began his career as a still photographer and cameraman with **Iosif Ermol'ev**'s company and gained a reputation as a solid craftsman, shooting **Iakov Protazanov**'s masterpieces *Queen of Spades* (Pikovaia dama, 1916) and *Father Sergius* (Otets Sergii, 1918), among others. Burgasov's work is distinguished by inventive lighting techniques that often evoke an atmosphere of gloom and vague threats, resonating with audiences during World War I and the ensuing political catastrophes.

After his immigration to France as a member of Ermol'ev's entourage, Burgasov became the most prolific cinematographer in the newly founded Paris company Les Films Ermolieff, renamed later, after Ermol'ev's departure, Productions Albatros. Thus, he filmed Aleksandr Volkov's serial *The House of Mystery* (La Maison du Mystère, 1923), Viacheslav Turzhanskii's *The Song of Triumphant Love* (Le Chant de l'amour triomphant, 1923), and numerous others. Burgasov successfully worked with French directors whose films also were produced by Ermol'ev, including Jean Epstein (*The Lion of the Moguls*/Le Lion des Mogols, 1924) and Marcel L'Herbier (*The Late Mattia Pascal*/Feu Mathias Pascal, 1925).

With the onset of the sound period, Russian émigré cinema went into decline; however, Burgasov's career continued, albeit on a slower pace. He was the cameraman on several sound versions of silent movie hits such as *Casanova's Loves* (Les amours de Casanova, 1933) and *The Child of Carnival* (L'enfant du carnaval, 1934); among his noteworthy artistic achievements are Jean Renoir's *The Lower Depths* (Les bas-fonds, 1936) from Maksim Gor'kii's play, and Max Ophüls's *Werther* (1938), an adaptation of Goethe's novel. His last film was Sacha Guitry's *La Malibran* (1944), a biopic about a French opera singer.

Other films: *Family Happiness* (Semeinoe schast'e, 1916); *Satan Triumphant* (Satana likuiushchii, 1917); *The Parasite* (Darmoedka, 1918); *The Last Encounter* (Posledniaia vstrecha, 1918); *Kean* (1923); *Oriental Secrets* (Geheimnisse des Orients, 1928).

BURLIAEV, NIKOLAI PETROVICH (b. 3 August 1946, Moscow). Russian actor, director, screenwriter, and cultural activist. Burliaev majored in acting at the Shchukin theater school in Moscow, graduating in 1967. He then studied film direction at the Soviet State Film School **VGIK** with **Mikhail Romm** and **Lev Kulidzhanov**, graduating in 1975.

Burlieaev's movie debut was the lead in **Andrei Mikhalkov-Konchalovskii**'s short *The Boy and the Dove* (Mal'chik i golub', 1960). A phenomenally gifted child actor, Burliaev stunned audiences in **Igor' Talankin**'s postwar drama *Entry* (Vstuplenie, 1962) and particularly in **Andrei Tarkovskii**'s early masterpiece *Ivan's Childhood* (aka *My Name Is Ivan*/Ivanovo detstvo, 1962) with his rare ability to convey passionate juvenile idealism paired with tenderness and vulnerability while never overstepping the boundaries of natural boyishness. In Tarkovskii's *Andrei Rublev* (1966) Burliaev carried a 40-minute key episode, the casting of a huge bell that calls the Russian nation to unity in the face of Mongolian occupation.

In later years, Burliaev's best work as an actor was in literary adaptations that used his pale, tormented features and ascetic nervousness, sometimes bordering on fanatical obsession. Fine examples are the gambling-addict-cum-teacher Aleksei Ivanovich in **Aleksei Batalov**'s screen version of Dostoevskii's *The Gambler* (Igrok, 1972) and Evgenii in **Mikhail Shveitser**'s *Little Tragedies* (Malen'kie tragedii, 1979, TV, from Aleksandr Pushkin). He also played supporting parts in **Petr Todorovskii**'s *Frontline Romance* (Voenno-polevoi roman, 1983) and his one-time wife **Natal'ia Bondarchuk**'s dilogy *Bambi's Childhood* (Detstvo Bembi, 1985) and *Bambi's Youth* (Iunost' Bembi, 1986).

As a filmmaker, Burliaev debuted with the short "Little Vania the Kain" (Van'ka-Kain, 1977) from the omnibus project *Old Times in Poshekhonia* (Poshekhonskaia starina, 1975), the adaptation of a novel by 19th-century satirist Mikhail Saltykov-Shchedrin. He put his artistic reputation at risk with two ideologically charged feature-length efforts: *Lermontov* (1986), a biopic that attributes the poet's lifelong troubles to freemason conspiracies, and *Everything Lies Ahead* (Vse vperedi, 1990), adapted from Vasilii Belov's controversial novel about the destruction of family relations and traditional gender roles in modern urban society. Both films were derided by the majority of Soviet critics and seen by few viewers.

In the 1990s Burliaev became a prominent cultural voice with strong Slavophile leanings. He organized a film school named after **Sergei Bondarchuk** in 1998 and a film festival for Slavic and Orthodox nations, Golden Vitiaz (Zolotoi Vitiaz'), held since 1992. In 2004, the festival's main prize went to Mel Gibson's *The Passion of the Christ*. The wide range of positions and initiatives in which Burliaev has been involved has largely kept him from acting and filmmaking.

Burliaev, who was named Merited Artist of the Russian Federation in 1984 and People's Artist of Russia in 1996, has also published poetry and prose.

Other films: (as actor) *A Hero of Our Time* (Geroi nashego vremeni, 1967); *Check-up on the Roads* (Proverka na dorogakh, 1971); *Lord, Hear My Prayer* (Gospodi, uslyshi molitvu moiu, 1991); *The Master and Margarita* (Master i Margarita, unreleased, 1994); *Admiral Kolchak* (2008).

BYKOV, LEONID FEDOROVICH (b. 12 December 1928, Znamenskoe, Donetsk district–d. 12 April 1979, near Kiev). Ukrainian director and screenwriter. After a failed attempt to become a military pilot, Bykov studied at Khar'kiv Theater Institute from 1946 to 1951 and joined the troupe of the Taras Shevchenko Theater in Khar'kiv, working on stage until 1960.

Bykov's screen image of a fair-haired, somewhat naïve, likeable dreamer-idealist and modest yet principled fighter for justice brought him popularity in Thaw films, beginning with the memorable supporting role of a country bumpkin in *Marina's Fate* (Sud'ba Mariny, 1953). His performance as Petia Mokin in **Aleksandr Ivanovskii**'s and **Nadezhda Kosheverova**'s blockbuster comedy *Tiger Girl* (Ukrotitel'nitsa tigrov, 1955) and in the title role of *Maksim Perepelitsa* (1956) defined the positive framework within which Bykov henceforth would be seen. Bykov also appeared as a hapless, utterly sincere romantic in pathos-filled tales such as Iurii Egorov's

Volunteers (Dobrovol'tsy, 1958), **Stanislav Rostotskii**'s *May Stars* (Maiskie zvezdy, 1961), and **Iosif Kheifits**'s *My Dear Man* (Dorogoi moi chelovek, 1958).

As a director, Bykov debuted at **Lenfilm Studio** in 1962 with the 10-minute satire *However the Rope Is Twisted* (Kak verevochka ni v'etsia, codirected by **Gerbert Rappaport**), which attacked some absurdities of the Soviet economy. The popular yet critically maligned **comedy** *Bunny* (Zaichik, 1965), in which Bykov also played the lead, portrays a quixotic idealist who struggles against bureaucratic routine. After moving back to Ukraine, Bykov addressed the theme of the Great Patriotic War with mournful solemnity and gentle humor. His most famous film is *Only "Seniors" Go to Battle* (V boi idut odni 'stariki,' 1974), a melodrama about human relations in a unit of music-loving pilots, none of them older than 20 yet already boasting huge battleground experience—hence their nickname "seniors." In 1977, Bykov made another successful World War II film, *One-Two, the Soldiers Were Marching* (Aty-baty, shli soldaty), this time contrasting a historical storyline against a contemporary one in which the soldiers' children are trying to come to terms with their memories and feelings of guilt and responsibility. The film enamored millions of viewers with its unpretentiousness and humanity.

Bykov was named Merited Artist of the Ukrainian SSR in 1958, Merited Artist of the Russian Federation in 1965, and People's Artist of the Ukrainian SSR in 1974. Bykov's life and untimely death in a car accident were subject of a documentary by **Leonid Osyka**, . . . *He Who Was Loved by All* (. . . kotorogo liubili vse, 1982).

Other films: (as director) *Where Are You, Knights?* (Gde vy, rytsari? 1971, TV); (as actor) *Watch Out, Grandma!* (Ostorozhno, babushka! 1960); *Scouts* (Razvedchiki, 1968).

BYKOV, ROLAN [Roland] **ANATOL'EVICH** [other sources: Antonovich] (b. 12 November 1929, Kiev–d. 6 October 1998, Moscow). Russian actor, director, screenwriter, and producer. Bykov was born into the family of a Red Army officer. He studied at the Moscow Shchukin Theater School, graduating in 1951. Until 1958, he worked as an actor and director for the Theater of the Young Viewer (TIuZ) in Moscow and in 1958–1960 as chief director of the Theater of Lenin Komsomol in Leningrad. He also founded the Student Theater of Moscow Lomonosov University in 1957 that attracted the attention of intellectual audiences with a number of innovative productions.

Bykov made his debut as a film actor in 1955 with the tiny part of a thief in the popular Anton Makarenko adaptation *Pedagogical Poem* (Pedagogicheskaia poema). In his acting career, with almost 90 roles to his credit, Bykov was equally brilliant as a lead—for example, as Akakii Akakievich Bashmachkin in **Aleksei Batalov**'s fine Gogol' adaptation *The Overcoat* (Shinel', 1960), the Jewish artisan Efim Magazanik in **Aleksandr Askol'dov**'s *The Commissar* (Komissar, 1967), or the nuclear war survivor in **Konstantin Lopushanskii**'s *Letters of a Dead Man* (Pis'ma mertvogo cheloveka, 1986)—and as a supporting actor, for example, as the loudmouth buffoon in **Andrei Tarkovskii**'s *Andrei Rublev* (1966). Of small physical stature, energetic, and mobile, his characters are often pitiful on the outside yet reveal inner strength when challenged.

Bykov also made a name for himself as an original filmmaker who specialized in **children's and youth films**, often with openly didactic purposes. His debut was the successful *Seven Nurses* (Sem' nianek, 1962), the story of a juvenile delinquent and his gradual inner growth. *Aibolit 66* (1966) is a stylish, carnivalesque adaptation of Kornei Chukovskii's fairy tale "Doctor Aibolit"; its experimental components, reminiscent of Russian absurdism and Vsevolod Meierkhol'd's stage practice, alarmed cultural administrators. In *The Cable* (Telegramma, 1971), schoolkids explore the Great Patriotic War and discover that the past is intimately connected to their own generation. *The Car, the Violin, and Stain the Dog* (Avtomobil', skripka i sobaka Kliaksa, 1974), another musical **comedy**, features several of the Soviet Union's most beloved comedians and was very popular.

In the late 1970s, Bykov's films turned noticeably darker. His masterful Gogol' adaptation *The Nose* (Nos, 1977, TV) is a bitter satire, while the drama *Scarecrow* (Chuchelo, 1983) thematized the cruelty of children toward their peers in a graphic openness previously unseen on Soviet screens. *Scarecrow*, arguably Bykov's best picture, was a veritable wake-up call for society and became one of the major cinematic signals preceding perestroika. These last two films made obvious that hidden behind Bykov's mask of a friendly clown and children's entertainer was a pensive mind, sad, caring, and deeply concerned about the future of humanity and culture.

Bykov was named People's Artist of the USSR in 1990. In the decade following the demise of the Soviet Union, he headed a bank that provided him with the financial means to fund the production of children's films. The foundation was named Rolan Bykov Foundation after his passing.

Bykov was married to actress Elena Sanaeva (b. 1943), who appeared in several of his pictures.

Other films: (as director) *The Summer Is Lost* (Propalo leto, 1964); *Attention, a Turtle!* (Vnimanie, cherepakha, 1969); *The Wedding Gift* (Svadebnyi podarok, 1983); (as actor) *When Someone Rings, Open the Door* (Zvoniat, otkroite dver', 1965); *Checkpoint* (Proverka na dorogakh, 1971); *Gray Wolves* (Serye volki, 1993).

BYSTRITSKAIA, ELINA AVRAAMOVNA (b. 4 April 1928, Kiev). Russian actress. Born into the family of a military physician, Bystritskaia first studied medicine. Then, pursuing her passion for acting, she studied at the Karpenko-Karyi Theater Institute in Kiev and was hired by the Russian Drama Theater in Vilnius upon graduation in 1953. In 1958, Bystritskaia joined the troupe of Malyi Theater in Moscow where she soon became one of the leading stars.

In 1955, **Fridrikh Ermler** cast Bystritskaia as a doctor in love with her patient in the melodrama *Unfinished Story* (Neokonchennaia povest'). The plum part of Aksin'ia, a passionate Cossack woman, in **Sergei Gerasimov**'s monumental, three-part *And Quiet Flows the Don* (Tikhii Don, 1957–1958) from Mikhail Sholokhov's epic shot her to international fame. It was Soviet cinema's loss that Bystritskaia's exquisite beauty, sensual femininity, and grace have not been employed more frequently in the years thereafter. One of the few exceptions was a lead in **Georgii Natanson**'s inspirational drama *Everything Remains for the People* (Vse ostaetsia liudiam, 1963).

Bystritskaia, who became a member of the Communist Party in 1970, was named People's Artist of the Russian Federation in 1966 and People's Artist of the USSR in 1978. For many years, she served as the president of the Soviet Federation of Artistic Gymnastics.

Other films: *Volunteers* (Dobrovol'tsy, 1958); *Russian Souvenir* (Russkii suvenir, 1960); *Nikolai Bauman* (1968); *Courageous Guys* (Bravye parni, 1993).

– C –

CARNIVAL NIGHT (Karnaval'naia noch', 1956). **Mosfilm Studio.** 78 min., color. Directed by **El'dar Riazanov.** Script: Boris Laskin, Vladimir Poliakov. Cinematography: **Arkadii Kol'tsatyi** (credited as Kal'tsatyi). Music: Anatolii Lepin. Cast: **Igor' Il'inskii, Liudmila Gurchenko,** Iurii Belov, Georgii Kulikov, Sergei Filippov, **Andrei Tutyshkin,** Tamara Nosova, Vladimir Zel'din. Premiere: January 1957.

A group of students is planning a large-scale, cheerful New Year's Eve ball with jazz music, stand-up comedians, and dance. However, the director of the House of Culture, staunch bureaucrat Ogurtsov (Il'inskii), intends to turn the evening into a sober official event, featuring speeches and lectures. Morose and uncompromising, he censors comedic sketches in advance and rejects all suggestions toward creating a lighthearted atmosphere. In the end, the youthful group led by enthusiastic Lena Krylova (Gurchenko) manages to outwit Ogurtsov, enjoying themselves and their innocent love affairs.

CHAIKOVSKII, BORIS VITAL'EVICH (b. 1888–d. 5 November 1924, Moscow). Russian director, film critic, and pedagogue. Chaikovskii began to work for **Aleksandr Khanzhonkov**'s company in 1909, after 1911 as a director. He helmed the Lev Tolstoi adaptation *A Living Corpse* (Zhivoi trup, 1911), causing a scandal, and in 1912, the first Russian film treating the topic of prostitution, *A Story Like Many* (Istoriia, kakikh mnogo). Most of Chaikovskii's pictures are melodramas: *Romance of a Ballerina* (Roman baleriny, 1916); *Marionets of Fate* (Marionetki roka, 1916, codirected with **Evgenii Bauer**); *Fall Asleep, Worrying Heart* (Usni, bespokoinoe serdtse, 1917); *Miss Mary* (aka *The Man Who Killed*/Chelovek, kotoryi ubil, 1918), and the Émile Zola adaptation *Thérèse Raquin* (1917–1918, unreleased).

In 1918 Chaikovskii—one of the few Russian filmmakers who made a conscious decision to stay in Russia despite the chaos—founded a private film school in Petrograd. Its mission was to help rebuild the ailing Russian film industry using the worthy achievements of early national cinema as point of departure. Chaikovskii, who also was the editor of *Cinema Bulletin* (Vestnik kinematografii), outlined his guiding principles in a number of articles, in particular, about cinema's focus on the actor. He hired famed theater director Evgenii Vakhtangov (1883–1922) to lecture on Stanislavskii's theories of acting.

Chaikovskii also continued to make films, among them *agitka* shorts for the Bolshevik Commissariat of Enlightenment, including *On Peasant Soil* (Na muzhitskoi zemle, 1919) and *It Must Not Be Thus!* (Tak byt' ne dolzhno!), both with **Eduard Tissé** as cameraman. He directed a number of full-length features, blending superficial pro-Communist declarations with adventure and melodrama: *The Diplomatic Secret* (Diplomaticheskaia taina, 1923), *In the Whites' Rear* (V tylu u belykh, 1925, codirected with Ol'ga Rakhmanova), and *Fight to Life and Death* (Na zhizn' i na smert', 1925, codirected with Pavel Petrov-Bytov).

After Chaikovskii's death, his film school was nationalized and named after him. A number of renowned filmmakers and actors such as **Efim Dzigan**, **Aleksandr Rou**, **Boris Dolin**, and **Liudmila Semenova** studied there in the 1920s.

Other films: *Decoration of Happiness* (Dekoratsiia schast'ia, 1918).

CHAIRMAN, THE (Predsedatel', 1964). **Mosfilm Studio**. Two parts, 95 and 71 min., b/w. Directed by **Aleksei Saltykov**. Script: Iurii Nagibin. Cinematography: Vladimir Nikolaev. Music: Aleksandr Kholminov. Cast: **Mikhail Ul'ianov**, **Ivan Lapikov**, **Nonna Mordiukova**, Kira Golovko, Vladimir Etush. Premiere: 28 December 1964.

Part I, "Brothers" (Brat'ia): In 1946, after being discharged from the army, Egor Trubnikov (Ul'ianov) returns to his native village. He is elected chairman of the dilapidated collective farm, applying authoritarian methods in order to reconstruct the kolkhoz, which is largely run by women and children. Semen (Lapikov), Egor's alienated brother, disapproves of the entire direction in which the Russian peasantry was forced, while Communist Party and secret service officials—especially the head of the NKVD department, Kaloev (Etush)—scheme against the forthright, headstrong Egor because he refuses to follow their orders.

Part II, "To Be Human" (Byt' chelovekom): Stalin's death is perceived as a sign of liberation and hope. Egor's efforts to improve the lot of the farmers begin to bear fruit, but Semen and his wife (Mordi-ukova) move to the city. The chairman's relationship with a widow, Nadia (Golovko), suffers a severe blow when their baby dies. But in the family of a young farmer a child is born, symbolizing the future of the village.

CHAPAEV (1934). **Lenfilm Studio**. 95 min., b/w. Directed by the **Vasil'ev brothers**. Script: Vasil'ev brothers from Dmitrii Fur-manov's 1926 novel. Cinematography: Aleksandr Sigaev, Aleksandr Ksenofontov. Music: Gavriil Popov. Cast: **Boris Babochkin**, Boris Blinov, Varvara Miasnikova, Leonid Kmit, Illarion Pevtsov, **Stepan Shkurat**, **Nikolai Simonov**, **Boris Chirkov**, **Georgii Zhzhenov**. Premiere: 7 November 1934.

A Red Army division led by famous commander Vasilii Ivanovich Chapaev (Babochkin) fights White Army troops in a region near the Urals when the Communist Party decides that a political commissar should be sent to their support. The commissar, Furmanov (Blinov), is initially greeted with distrust but soon proves that he is politically savvy and can be useful for the hot-headed commander. Chapaev, assisted by loyal adjutant Pet'ka (Kmit) and his love interest, ma-chine gunner An'ka (Miasnikova), defeats a large White Army unit. However, one night, the unsuspecting Bolshevik troops are attacked by cunning Colonel Borozdin (Pevtsov), and the mortally wounded Chapaev drowns in the Ural River.

CHARDYNIN [real name: Krasavchikov or Krasavtsev]**, PETR IVANOVICH** (b. 10 February 1878, Simbirsk [other sources: 1873, 1877]–d. 14 August 1934, Odessa). Russian-Ukrainian director, scriptwriter, cinematographer, and actor. Chardynin hailed from peasant stock. In 1891, he enrolled in the School of Music and Drama of the Moscow Philharmonic Society where Vladimir Nemirovich-Danchenko was his teacher. After touring the Russian provinces, Chardynin became a member of the Vvedenskii People's House, a stage company in Moscow, working both as an actor and a director. **Aleksandr Khanzhonkov**, searching for an established professional troupe for his movies, developed a close relationship with the Vve-denskii House and continuously hired actors from its troupe, among them Chardynin and his colleague, **Ivan Mozzhukhin**.

Chardynin first experimented with so-called cinema declamations (*kinodeklamatsii*) around 1907. These were short, silent film clips that were projected on the screen while the featured actor lip-synched to them. In 1908 Chardynin played a part in **Vasilii Goncharov**'s *Choice of the Tsar's Bride* (Vybor tsarskoi nevesty), and a year later he directed his first feature. Chardynin's success, based in part on his ability to work well with actors and in part on his highly developed entrepreneurial spirit, was overwhelming, and he soon gave up stage work altogether. Chardynin became the most productive of all Russian filmmakers; estimates of his total output before 1918 vary between 120 and 200 films, of which 34 have survived. While directing at a frantic pace, he remained active as a lead and supporting actor.

Politically, the notoriously adaptable Chardynin was capable of making staunchly pro-tsarist pictures such as *On the Eve of the Proclamation of 19th of February* (Nakanune manifesta 19 fevralia, 1911), war propaganda (*The King, the Law, and Freedom*/Korol', zakon i svoboda, 1914), as well as "progressive" pictures such as *Sof'ia Perovskaia* (1917) about the notorious terrorist. Many of his pictures were literary adaptations; to criticism he responded that one of moving pictures' primary missions was to popularize classical works. Chardynin was able to adapt almost all authors of the Russian canon for the screen: Aleksandr Pushkin (*The Queen of Spades*/Pikovaia dama, 1910), Fedor Dostoevskii (*The Idiot*/Idiot, 1910), Nikolai Gogol' (*Dead Souls*/Mertvye dushi, 1909; he also played the part of Nozdrev in one of the film's two episodes), Lev Tolstoi (*Kreutzer Sonata*/Kreitserova sonata, 1911), and Ivan Goncharov (*The Precipice*/Obryv, 1913). Film historian Semen Ginzburg sympathetically characterized Chardynin's adaptations as "conscientious and cultivated," helping readers already familiar with the literary works "to visualize a novel's characters." Another genre that Chardynin introduced to the screen was the fairy tale. Thus, he made *The Tale of the Fisherman and His Wife* (Skazka o rybake i rybke, 1913) and *The Tale of the Dead Princess and the Seven Heroes* (Skazka o mertvoi tsarevne i semi bogatyriakh, 1914).

In 1916, after a fallout with Khanzhonkov, Chardynin switched to the company of Dmitrii I. Kharitonov, taking many stars with him and becoming one of the company's owners. He helmed the first Russian all-star pictures, whose success was staggering. Among his greatest blockbusters were *By the Fireplace* (U kamina, 1917), starring Chardynin's longtime lead **Vera Kholodnaia**, and its sequel, *Forget the Fireplace—Its Flames Are Dead* (Pozabud' pro kamin, v nem ugasli ogni, 1917). Among Chardynin's last films before the Bolshevik takeover were *Hush, Sadness . . . Hush . . .* (Molchi, grust' . . . molchi . . . , 1918) and *The Death of Vera Kholodnaia* (Smert' Very Kholodnoi, 1918).

In 1919 Chardynin agreed to participate in the production of pro-Bolshevik shorts, so-called *agitki*, of which he made seven. However, in 1920, distressed by Communist administrative intrusion as well as economic misery, he settled in Latvia, where he made four full-length feature films.

The All-Ukrainian Photo-Cinema Administration (VUFKU) invited Chardynin to return to the Russian Federation in 1923 and offered him a leading position in **Ukrainian cinema**. He agreed to settle in Odessa, where he directed about two dozen films of which the two-part biopic *Taras Shevchenko* (1926) enjoyed the greatest success. Chardynin also tried his hand at antireligious satire (*The Owner of the Black Rocks*/Khoziain chernykh skal, 1923) and a thriller about Bolshevik underground struggle (*Ukraziia [7+2]*, 1925), which became a hit. After VUFKU was dissolved in 1930, Chardynin's career was at a dead end. His last film, *An Event in the Steppe* (Sobytie v stepi, aka *The Class Enemy*/Klassovyi vrag), was released in 1932.

Despite lifelong accusations of artistic opportunism, commercial ruthlessness, and lack of originality, Chardynin's work has merit within the framework of early filmmaking in Russia. Critical opinion about Chardynin's legacy remains divided, given the insufferable theatricality and visual monotony of his films. However, many actors and directors who worked with him at different stages of their career—including **Natal'iia Lisenko**, **Vera Karalli**, **Vitol'd Polonskii**, and **Vladimir Maksimov**—proudly called him their teacher, and even **Amvrosii Buchma**, despite critical objections to Chardynin's style and method, mentioned him with respect.

One of Chardynin's several marriages was to director **Margarita Barskaia** (Chardynina), who worked as an assistant director on eleven of his films in the 1920s.

Other films: *Spiritual Invalids* (Invalidy dukha, 1915); *The Seven Who Were Hanged* (Rasskaz o semero poveshennykh, 1920/1924); *Taras Triasilo* (1927).

CHEKHOV, MIKHAIL ALEKSANDROVICH [English spelling Michael Chekhov] (b. 29 August 1891, St. Petersburg–d. 30 September 1955, Beverly Hills, California). Russian-American actor and pedagogue. Chekhov, the nephew of Anton Chekhov, enrolled in the Suvorin acting school in 1907. In 1913, he joined the troupe of the Moscow Art Theater (MKhAT) and soon became one of Konstantin Stanislavskii's preferred stars.

Chekhov's screen debut was the role of Tsar Mikhail Fedorovich Romanov in the chronicle *The Tercentenary of the Accession of the Romanov Dynasty (1613–1913)* (Trekhsotletie tsarstvovaniia doma Romanovykh, 1913), produced by **Aleksandr Drankov** for a ladies' charity organization with the approval of the court. The actor often appeared in literary adaptations such as Aleksandr Ural'skii's *Surgery* (Khirurgiia, 1915), from a Chekhov story, and *The Cricket on the Hearth* (Sverchok na pechi, 1915), based on an MKhAT production of a Charles Dickens story. He earned recognition in two **comedies** directed by **Viacheslav Viskovskii**: *A Closet with a Surprise* (Shkaf s siurprizom, 1915) and *Love's Futile Surprises* (Liubvi siurprizy chetnye, 1916).

In 1918–1921, Chekhov ran his own acting studio in Moscow, was a member of the Hebrew theater Habima, and in charge of the First Studio Theater of the MKhAT in 1922 and of the Second Studio in 1924–1927. After more than a decade-long absence from the screen, Chekhov portrayed a "superfluous man" in **Iakov Protazanov**'s melodrama *The Man from the Restaurant* (Chelovek iz restorana, 1927). In July 1928, he left the Soviet Union.

Chekhov first worked on stage in Max Reinhardt productions in Vienna and Berlin and also appeared in a number of German films, including *Troika* (1930). He moved to Paris in 1931, to Latvia in 1932, and to Italy in 1934. After spending some time in Great Britain and the United States, he returned to Europe and managed to escape with his troupe shortly before German soldiers entered Paris in 1940. Chekhov was cast in supporting roles in pro-Soviet American films such as Gregory Ratoff's *Song of Russia* (1943). For his performance as the psychoanalytic Dr. Alexander Brulov in Alfred Hitchcock's *Spellbound* (1944) he was nominated for an Academy Award. Chekhov was a valued acting teacher at the Tamirov School until 1950 and wrote theoretical books on acting techniques; among his students were Yul Brynner, Jack Palance, Marilyn Monroe, and Ingrid Bergman.

Chekhov was named Merited Artist of the Republic in 1924. He was married to Russian-German actress Olga Tschechowa (1897–1980); their daughter was actress Ada Tschechowa (1916–1966), their granddaughter is actress Vera Tschechowa (b. 1940).

Other films: *When the Strings of the Heart Sound* (Kogda zvuchat struny serdtsa (1914); *The Price of Freedom* (1949).

CHERKASOV, NIKOLAI KONSTANTINOVICH (b. 27 July 1903, St. Petersburg–d. 14 September 1966, Leningrad). Russian actor. Cherkasov was born into the family of a railway clerk; as a boy he was already a regular at St. Petersburg's Mariinskii Theater, where he eventually began to work as an extra (1919–1923). In 1923–1927 Cherkasov studied acting and dancing at the Leningrad Institute for Stage Arts. After touring with various troupes until 1933, he joined the Leningrad Academic Pushkin Theater (the former Aleksandrinskii).

In cinema, Cherkasov debuted with the supporting part of hairdresser Charles in **Vladimir Gardin**'s 1927 Pushkin biopic *The Poet and the Tsar* (Poet i tsar'). Yet only in sound film did his mimic art and voice qualities came to the fore—first as Kol'ka Loshakov in **Iosif Kheifits**'s and **Aleksandr Zarkhi**'s *Goriachie denechki*, then as the cumbersome Jacques Paganel in **Vladimir Vainshtok**'s popular *Children of Captain Grant* (Deti kapitana Granta,1936). The lead role of nonconformist biologist Polezhaev in Kheifits' and Zarkhi's **Baltic Deputy** (Deputat Baltiki, 1937)—an unlikely casting, since the 33-year-old played a frail old man—propelled Cherkasov to national stardom. Cherkasov's impersonation of Tsarevich Aleksei, a religious fanatic and opponent of his father, in **Vladimir Petrov**'s *Peter the First* (Petr Pervyi, 1937), and the title role in **Sergei Eizenshtein**'s patriotic *Aleksandr Nevskii* (1938) were performed with equal persuasiveness. Other directors used Cherkasov's phenomenal ability to transform himself rather mechanically, at times reducing his art to mere imitation. Thus, **Mikhail Romm** cast him as Maksim Gor'kii in *Lenin in 1918* (Lenin v godu, 1938), **Grigorii Roshal'** as Gor'kii in *Academician Ivan Pavlov* (Akademik Ivan Pavlov, 1949), while **Gerbert Rappaport** gave him the rather bland title role of radio inventor Aleksandr Popov in his 1949 ultrapatriotic biopic.

It was Eizenshtein who allowed Cherkasov to transcend the stiff framework of monumental, larger-than-life impersonations in the second part of *Ivan the Terrible* (Ivan Groznyi, 1943–1945), in which the ruler's psychopathology and disintegration become almost physically tangible. In **Grigorii Kozintsev**'s *Don Quijote* (1957), Cherkasov created the definitive image of the immortal knight, emphasizing his humanity and idealism rather than ridiculous unworldliness. Finally, **Georgii Natanson** gave the actor one last opportunity to revive his "activist-hero" image in *Everything Remains with the People* (Vse ostaetsia liudiam, 1963), which won him a 1964 Lenin Prize.

Cherkasov's pathos-filled gestures and often grandiose speechifying were considered the trademarks of great acting in his day and age. Some critical dissent notwithstanding, this actor's international reputation remained unchallenged after his passing and is corroborated by such facts as Luchino Visconti's declaring him his first choice for the role of Prince Salinas in the 1963 epic *The Leopard* (Il gattopardo).

Cherkasov joined the Communist Party in 1940 and held numerous political positions, including member of the Supreme Soviet of the USSR in 1950–1958. He won five Stalin Prizes (1941, 1946, 1950, and twice in 1951), was named Merited Artist of the Russian Federation in 1937, People's Artist of the Russian Federation in 1939, and of the USSR in 1947. In St. Petersburg, a street has been named in Cherkasov's honor. The actor is buried at Aleksandro-Nevskii lavra, where a monument by Mikhail Anikushin adorns his grave.

Other films: *My Son* (Moi syn, 1928); *Spring* (Vesna, 1947); *Pirogov* (1947).

CHERVIAKOV, EVGENII VENIAMINOVICH (b. 9 January 1899, Abdulino, Samara district–d. 17 February 1942, Mga near Leningrad). Russian director, screenwriter, and actor. Cherviakov studied in the acting department of Ufa drama studio in 1917–1918 before starting a career as a stage actor and director in Eisk (1919–1921) and other cities. In 1923–1925, he studied at the State Cinema College (GTK)—the later **VGIK**—and worked as an assistant to **Vladimir Gardin**.

Cherviakov made a name for himself with the role of Aleksandr Pushkin in Gardin's popular but critically maligned *The Poet and the Tsar* (Poet i tsar', 1927), which he also codirected. Together with cameraman Sviatoslav Beliaev (1907–1942), art director Semen Meinkin (1892–1942), actress Roza Sverdlova (1908–2003), and actor Gennadii Michurin (1897–1970), Cherviakov founded a group of like-minded artists who aimed to develop the expressive tools of silent cinema in a psychological, pensive, and lyrical direction. His first independently helmed picture, *The Girl from a Faraway River* (Devushka s dalekoi reki, aka Bumazhnaia lenta [The Paper Tape], 1928), which he called a "film poem" (*kinopoema*), describes the experiences of a provincial girl on her first visit to Moscow. A similar interest in the private sphere and subjective viewpoint is betrayed in *My Son* (Moi syn, 1928), in which a husband has to accept the fact that his newborn was fathered by another man. Cherviakov's historical picture *The Golden Beak* (Zolotoi kliuv, 1929) follows a group of 17th-century serfs who escape and try to build their own free, utopian society in the Altai region.

The German-Soviet coproduction *Cities and Years* (Goroda i gody, 1930) from Konstantin Fedin's novel, was met by critical disapproval. The director then helmed the drama *Convicts* (Zakliuchennye, 1936) from Nikolai Pogodin's script, which was inspired by the infamous 1934 writers' sojourn to the White Sea Canal concentration camp. In a demagogical manner, the film treats the "re-education" of GULAG camp inmates by forced labor as a noble undertaking; it "depicts ordinary criminals with more sympathy than the members of the imprisoned intelligentsia" (Peter Kenez). *Honor* (Chest', 1938) deals with the issue of sabotage in the Soviet railway system, while *Stanitsa Dal'niaia* (1940) is a **comedy** about a group of women whose desire is to participate in Red Army maneuvers.

Throughout his career, Cherviakov appeared in supporting parts in his own films and those of other directors. His last role was Napoleon in **Grigorii Kozintsev**'s satirical short *An Occurrence at the Telegraph* (Sluchai na telegrafe, 1941), part of the second *War Film Almanac*.

Cherviakov's directorial work is characterized by a predilection for prolonged close shots that convey complex psychological processes, static compositions charged with metaphors and symbols, as well as occasional moral ambiguity. His silent films, of which only the last has survived, represent a poetic alternative to the dominating intellectual montage. Cherviakov, whom film historian Evgenii Margolit called "one of the most original and enigmatic directors of Leningrad silent cinema," is remembered for his death at the front in the Great Patriotic War.

Other films: (as actor) *The Gold Reserve* (Zolotoi zapas, 1927); *Blood of the Earth* (Krov' zemli, 1931); (as director) *Musical Olympics* (Muzykal'naia olimpiada, 1932).

CHIAURELI, MIKHEIL [Russian sources list the patronymic Edisherovich] (b. 6 February 1894, Tiflis [Tbilisi]–d. 31 October 1974, Tbilisi). Georgian director, screenwriter, and actor. Chiaureli studied at the School of Painting and Sculpture in Tbilisi from 1912 to 1916 and subsequently worked as a singer, theater actor, director, and sculptor in Tbilisi, Kutaisi, and Batumi. From 1922 to 1924, with funding from the Georgian government, Chiaureli continued to study sculpture in Germany. Upon his return he worked at the Red Theater (Krasnyi teatr) of the Proletarian Culture (Proletkul't) movement, directing experimental plays, and at the Georgian Theater of Musical **Comedy**.

In **Georgian cinema**, Chiaureli began his career as an actor, playing parts in several silents. He was cast in the title role of **Ivan Perestiani**'s *Arsena Jiorjashvili* (aka *The Murder of General Griaznov*, 1921) about a 1905 political assassin, and played a lead in Perestiani's *The Suram Fortress* (Suramis tsikhe/Suramskaia krepost', 1923), based on a medieval Georgian myth about betrayal and self-sacrifice for the sake of the country's integrity. Other notable roles were the lead in Vladimir Barskii's *Horrors of the Past II* (Tsarsulis sashinele bani/Koshmary proshlogo, 1922) and in **Hamo Bek-Nazaryan**'s *Natale* (1926). Yet, despite these achievements, Chiaureli—already an accomplished painter, political cartoonist, and sculptor—was dissatisfied with the state of Georgian cinema and decided to abandon acting altogether.

As a film director, he made his debut with *In the Last Hour* (Ukanaskuel saats/V poslednii chas, 1928), a suspenseful albeit technically incompetent adventure movie about the 1918–1921 Civil War. Chiaureli's next picture, *First Cornet Streshnyov* (Pirveli korneti Streshniovi/Pervyi kornet Streshnev, also 1928, codirected with **Efim Dzigan**), revealed the strong influence of Russian avant-garde directors, in particular **Vsevolod Pudovkin**. Only in his third feature, *Saba* (1929), an attack on alcoholism combining humorous scenes with a scientific lecture about the effects of imbibing, did Chiaureli display an original style. His satire *Get Out of the Way!* (Khabarda/Postoronites', 1931) was intended to show the conflict between petit bourgeois and Communist values, focusing on a church building that is being demolished and replaced by living quarters.

Chiaureli helmed the first Georgian sound film, *The Last Masquerade* (Ukanaskneli maskaradi/Poslednii maskarad, 1934), a satirical family chronicle on the backdrop of the emergence of the Georgian Republic after World War I. *Arsen* (Arsena Jorjashvili, 1937), about the very anti-tsarist rebel whom he had played in 1921, won the director his first Stalin Prize (1941). The picture, filled with Georgian music and dance, emphasizes Arsen's pro-Russian proclivities. Both *The Last Masquerade* and *Arsen*, in Jay Leyda's words, ensure Chiaureli "a place in Soviet film history no matter how low, in our judgements, his later 'big films' about Stalin may sink."

By the late 1930s, when Chiaureli turned to the monumental historical epics that would become his trademark, his transformation from an avant-gardist into a leading representative of pathos-filled cinematic officialdom was complete. In *The Great Glow* (aka *They Wanted Peace*/Diadi gantiadi/Velikoe zarevo, 1938, Stalin Prize 1941) Iosif Stalin—portrayed by **Mikheil Gelovani**—is depicted for the first time. The two-part *Georgii Saakadze* (1942–1943) about a 17th-century prince who fails to unite the divided Georgian principalities, was rewarded with Stalin Prizes in 1943 and 1946. Chiaureli's visual style became increasingly bombastic, indulging in huge, canvaslike compositions; it defined Stalinism in Soviet cinema at its most blatant. *The Vow* (Pitsi/Kliatva, 1946), which won a special prize at the festival in Venice (1946) and a Stalin Prize in 1947, was, according to Polish film historian Jerzy Toeplitz, the most accomplished and coherent of Chiaureli's Stalin films. Shot mostly at original sites, including the Kremlin halls, the film reenacts crucial moments of Stalin's life, beginning with his 1924 vow to continue the cause of Lenin, and ending on the eve of World War II. The two-part *Fall of Berlin* (aka *Battle of Berlin*/Padenie Berlina, 1949) focuses on the contrast between Stalin and Hitler, giving ample room to sensationalist images of the morbid Nazi elite milieu; the leadership perspective is complemented by allegorical characters, most importantly the miner Ivanov (**Boris Andreev**). Hailed for its gigantic battle scenes, grandiose music (composed by **Dmitrii Shostakovich**), and creative use of color, this monumental historical panorama was later characterized as a prime example of shameless falsification of history and withdrawn from distribution after Stalin's death. *The Unforgettable Year 1919* (Nezabyvaemyi 1919 god, 1952) retold crucial events of the Civil War, subjugating the known facts to Stalin's wishful thinking in that he alone saved the capital Petrograd from the onslaught of the White Army and its foreign interventionist allies.

Sharply criticized during the Thaw, Chiaureli was stripped of all administrative positions in the mid-1950s and moved from Moscow, with a short interlude at the Sverdlovsk film studio, back to Tbilisi. At **Gruziya-Film Studio** he was given an opportunity to continue his career. However, *Otar's Widow* (Otaraant qvrivi/Otarova vdova, 1958) based on a story by Ilia Chavchavadze (1837–1907), *Story of a Young Girl* (Ambavi erti kalishvilisa/Povest' ob odnoi devushke, 1960) about the contemporary Georgian countryside, and the drama *The General and the Daisies* (Generali da zizilebi/General i margaritki, 1963) about U.S. militarism received little critical attention. Chiaureli's last feature was the comedy *You Cannot See What I Have Seen* (Rats ghinakhavs, vegar nakhav/Inye nynche vremena, 1965).

Toward the end of his life, Chiaureli turned to animated shorts based on fables and fairy tales, among them *How the Mice Buried the Cat* (Rogor damarkhes tagvebma kata/Kak myshi kota khoronili, 1969)—which is reputed to contain satirical allusions to post-Stalinist hypocrisy—and *The Butter Jug* (Qila erbo/Kuvshin masla, 1973).

Chiaureli, a highly gifted artist, was admired at the outset of his career for his daring innovation and perfectionism, feared and kowtowed to at the peak of his influence, and ridiculed at the end, paying a high price for his unbridled ambition and lust for power. An even-handed and detailed biography of this filmmaker would likely shed light on many fundamental questions about the temptations and pitfalls of artists in totalitarian societies.

Chiaureli joined the Communist Party in 1940; he was named People's Artist of the USSR in 1948. From 1950 to 1960, he was a full professor at the Soviet State Film School **VGIK**. Chiaureli is buried at the Pantheon of Georgian Writers and Artists at the holy mountain Mtatsminda.

Chiaureli's wife, **Veriko Andjaparidze**, played the female leads in her husband's later films; son Otar (1917–1966) was a director of ethnographic and cultural **documentaries**; daughter **Sofiko Chiaureli** was a celebrated actress. Chiaureli's nephew is director **Georgii Daneliia**, his son-in-law is filmmaker **Giorgi Shengelaia**.

Other films: (as director) *The Heroic Deed of the People* (Podvig naroda, 1956, documentary); *Singer of Sunrise* (Pevets zari, 1968, short); *The Rooster-Surgeon* (Petukh-muravei, 1970, short); *The Inventive Hare* (Nakhodchivyi zaiats, 1974).

CHIAURELI, SOFIKO [Russian sources list her name and patronymic as Sof'ia Mikhailovna] (b. 21 May 1937, Tbilisi–2 March 2008, Tbilisi). Georgian actress. Born into the family of famous director **Mikheil Chiaureli** and actress **Veriko Andjaparidze**, Chiaureli studied acting at the Soviet State Film School **VGIK** from 1955 to 1960 and joined the troupes of Moscow Ermolova Theater, the Kote Mardjanishvili Academic Theater (1960–1964 and since 1968), and the Shota Rustaveli Theater (1964–1968) in Tbilisi.

Chiaureli's screen debut was the female lead, Tsitsino, in **Revaz Chkheidze**'s youth romance *Our Court* (Chveni ezo/Nash dvor, 1957). She also appeared in her father's Cold War pamphlet *The General and the Daisies* (Generali da zizilebi/General i margaritki, 1963) and *You Cannot See What I Have Seen* (Rats ginakhvars, vegar nakhav/Inye nynche vremena, 1965), as well as **Georgii Daneliia**'s superb comedy *Don't Grieve* (Ar daidardo/Ne goriui!, 1969). Other memorable performances were Sidoniia in *The Warmth of Your Hands* (aka *Life*/Tsutisopeli/Teplo tvoikh ruk, 1972) by Nodar and Shota Managadze, Vardo in her then-husband **Giorgi Shengelaia**'s musical *Melodies of Veris Quarter* (Veris ubnis melodiebi/Melodii Veriiskogo kvartala, 1973), and Fufal in **Tengiz Abuladze**'s parable *The Wishing Tree* (Natris khe/Drevo zhelaniia, 1977). The breadth of Chiaureli's repertoire is demonstrated by **documentary**-style, social-psychological drama such as **Lana Gogoberidze**'s *Several Interviews on Personal Questions* (Ramodenime interviu pirad sakitkhebze/Neskol'ko interv'iu po lichnym voprosam, 1979)—for which she was awarded a USSR State Prize—and **Sergei Paradjanov**'s imaginative, nonrealistic *The Color of Pomegranate* (Tsvet granata, 1968) in which Chiaureli was cast as the young poet Sayat-Nova, a nun, a pantomime, and an angel. Chiaureli, one of Paradjanov's favorite actresses, also appeared in *Legend of Suram Fortress* (Ambavi suramis tsikhitsa/Legenda o Suramskoi kreposti, 1984) and *Ashik Kerib* (Ashugi Quaribi, 1988). Distinguished by delicate features, an air of pensiveness, and feminine warmth, Chiaureli enjoyed star status among discriminating cineastes and regular viewers alike.

Chiaureli was named People's Artist of the Georgian SSR in 1976 and People's Artist of the Armenian SSR in 1979.

Other films: *Shores* (Data Tutashkhia/Berega, 1977/80, TV); *Averik* (1979, TV); *Repentance* (Monanieba/Pokaianie, 1984); *Wandering Stars* (Bluzhdaiushchie zvezdy, 1991); *Just Once* (Tol'ko raz, 2002); *The Lighthouse* (Maiak, 2007).

CHILDREN'S AND YOUTH FILMS. Films specifically intended for children and youth audiences played a central role in Soviet cultural politics. Films before 1917 did not target young viewers per se, although fairy tales and **Wladislaw Starewicz**'s **animation** shorts held a particularly strong appeal for that group, and special screenings for children were common.

The educational and propaganda value of children's films was understood by the Bolshevik establishment early on. Thus, **Ivan Perestiani**'s 1923 superhit *The Little Red Devils* (Tsiteli eshmakunebi/Krasnye d"iavoliata) was given wide release all across the Soviet Union; its equally successful 1966 remake *The Uncatchable Avengers* (Neulovimye mstiteli, 1966) and two sequels—all directed by **Edmond Keosayan**—proved that the subgenre of "Revolution and Civil War adventure" with its fast-paced action sequences and sensational stunts remained a lasting attraction for Soviet youngsters. On 24 January 1927, under the supervision of Vladimir Lenin's widow, Nadezhda Krupskaia, the Department of Agitation and Propaganda (Agitprop) of the Communist Party held a meeting devoted to the production of children and school films. One of its outcomes was an increased number of screenings for children and youth audiences.

Among the directors who devoted large periods of their careers to children's films were **Ol'ga Preobrazhenskaia** (*Fedka's Truth*/ Fed'kina pravda, 1926; *Kashtanka*, 1927, from Anton Chekhov's story, among others) and **Vladimir Petrov** (*Lenin's Address* aka *Children of the New Day*/Adres Lenina, 1929). The first Soviet sound film for children was **Margarita Barskaia**'s *The Torn Shoes* (aka *Broken Shoes*/Rvanye bashmaki, 1933), a tale about class struggle in Germany in which workers' children are involved. Two years before, **Nikolai Ekk**'s superhit *A Start in Life* (aka *Road to Life*/Putevka v zhizn', 1931), which was inspired by Semen Makarenko's youth communes, made a case for the Communist transformation of juvenile delinquents into Soviet citizens. Its producer, **Mezhrabpomfilm Studio**, in 1936 was transformed into Soiuzdetfilm and later into **Gor'kii Studio for Children's and Youth Films**. This and other steps furthered the enormous upsurge in the production of Soviet children and youth films in the 1930s. Many pictures were adapted from classical literary sources or were devoted to historical events. **Aleksandr Ptushko** created the spectacular *New Gulliver* (Novyi Gulliver, 1935) from Jonathan Swift's novel, **Vladimir Vainshtok** helmed *The Children of Captain Grant* (Deti kapitana Granta, 1936, after Jules Verne) and *Treasure Island* (Ostrov sokrovishch, 1938, after R. L. Stevenson), and **Tat'iana Lukashevich** adapted an episode from Victor Hugo's *Les Misérables* in the immensely successful *Gavroche* (1937). **Mark Donskoi**'s atmospherically rich *Gor'kii's Childhood* and its 1938 and 1940 sequels, from Maksim Gor'kii's autobiography, demonstrated how hard it was to draw an exact line between films for children and those for adults.

The educational purpose of films for children and youth was not always placed at the surface but was wrapped in adventurous, suspenseful plots, rendering Communist ideology easily palatable. Thus, **Aleksandr Razumnyi**'s *Timur and His Gang* (Timur i ego komanda, 1940), from a popular story by Arkadii Gaidar, encouraged youngsters of all ages to play an active role in the efforts of adults and be watchful of "enemies." A subgenre that regained new life in the late 1930s was the fairy tale, with Ptushko and **Aleksandr Rou** (*On the Pike's Order*/Po shchuch'emu veleniiu, 1938, and others) emerging as its supreme masters. The first Soviet child star was **Ianina Zheimo** (*Wake Up Little Lena*/Razbudite Lenochku, 1934, among others), whose juvenile looks enabled her to play such roles far beyond her real age.

During the Great Patriotic War, when the Soiuzdetfilm studio was evacuated to Dushanbe, the number of children's films dwindled dramatically, although various directors tried to adjust to the circumstances. Thus, Rou's *The Immortal Kashchei* (Kashchei bessmertnyi, 1944) uses a traditional fairy-tale monster to predict the victorious outcome of the war. *Once Lived a Girl* (Zhila-byla devochka, 1944) by Viktor Eisymont (1904–1964) shows the hardships endured by children during the siege of Leningrad.

The postwar years with their generally low production numbers saw only a few films for children, including Ptushko's picturesque fairy tale *The Stone Flower* (Kamennyi tsvetok, 1946) and the first efforts of **Il'ia Frez** (*The Elephant and the String*/Slon i verevochka, 1945), who devoted his entire career to films for young viewers. Starting in the mid-1950s, films for children and youths were produced in larger numbers and a greater variety of genres in all major and national studios. Adventurous and humorous movies adapted from Gaidar's stories—including *Chuk and Gek* (Chuk i Gek, 1953), *The Fate of the Drummer* (Sud'ba barabanshchika, 1956), and *On the Count's Ruins* (Na grafskikh razvalinakh, 1958)—treated children's problems in a serious manner and avoided an overtly didactic message. **Rolan Bykov** successfully combined **comedic** and dramatic elements in his colorful children's films such as *The Car, the Violin, and Stain the Dog* (Avtomobil', skripka i sobaka Kliaksa, 1974). He was one of the first directors to alert Soviet society to the catastrophic moral degradation among juveniles in his powerful *Scarecrow* (Chuchelo, 1983) from Vladimir Zheleznikov's novel.

Children's sensitivity and perceptiveness sometimes were used as a natural standard of sincerity and contrast to social adaptation and corruption in adults. Directors such as **Tengiz Abuladze** (*Magdana's Donkey*/Magdanas Lurja/Lurdzha Magdany, 1955, codirected with **Revaz Chkheidze**), **Andrei Tarkovskii** (*The Steamroller and the Violin*/Katok i skripka, 1960), **Georgii Daneliia** (*Serezha*, aka *A Summer to Remember*, 1960, codirected with **Igor' Talankin**), and **Andrei Mikhalkov-Konchalovskii** (*The Boy and the Dove*/Mal'chik i golub', 1960) began their careers with films in which children play a conceptually decisive role.

The breakdown of the Soviet production and distribution system in the early 1990s hit hard on the genre of children's and youth films. However, when the crisis was partially overcome, entertaining, quality productions made specifically for young audiences reappeared, for example, the highly entertaining canine adventure *Spartak and Kalashnikov* (Spartak i Kalashnikov, 2002).

CHIRKOV, BORIS PETROVICH (b. 13 August 1901, Nolinsk [other sources: Lozovaia-Pavlovka, Ukraine]–d. 28 May 1982, Moscow). Russian actor. Chirkov, who hailed from a peasant family, studied at the Leningrad Institute for Stage Arts, graduating in 1926. One of his first film roles was a parody of Patachon in **Evgenii Cherviakov**'s *My Son* (Moi syn, 1928), with **Nikolai Cherkasov** playing Pat.

Grigorii Kozintsev and **Leonid Trauberg** cast Chirkov in a supporting role in their early sound film *Alone* (Odna, 1931) and four years later entrusted him with the title role in their seminal *Maksim Trilogy*, about the evolution of a young Petrograd worker who becomes a professional revolutionary. In this groundbreaking picture, Chirkov developed a screen persona that stayed with him until the end of his career: a "regular guy," witty, cunning, and utterly devoted to the Bolshevik cause. Physically unimposing, with friendly, slightly squinty eyes and a warm, hoarse voice, Chirkov embodied fundamental kindness based on natural strength and unshakeable faith in the future. Singing the leitmotiv song, "The blue globe is whirling and twirling" ("*Krutitsia, vertitsia shar goluboi*") to the guitar, Chirkov's Maksim entered modern-day Soviet folklore.

The near-legendary popularity of the trilogy initiated Maksim's revival in **Fridrikh Ermler**'s *The Great Citizen* (Velikii grazhdanin, 1939), where he is already an influential Party hack, and in **Sergei Gerasimov**'s short *Encounter with Maksim* (Vstrecha s Maksimom, 1941, in *War Almanac* #1) fighting the Nazis. Chirkov's attempts to bring life to assigned official impersonations did not always succeed; for example, he was badly miscast as Glinka in **Leo Arnshtam**'s 1946 biopic of the same title. However, after the onset of the Thaw, the actor was able to reveal his sense of humor and humanity more fully, for example, in **Mikhail Kalatozov**'s **comedy** *Loyal Friends*

(Vernye druz'ia, 1954). Chirkov was continuously employed in Soviet films until the late 1970s, often, ad nauseam, being typecast as a revolutionary worker.

Chirkov, who joined the Communist Party in 1945, won four Stalin Prizes, was named People's Artist of the USSR in 1950 and Hero of Socialist Labor in 1975, and was elected to the USSR Supreme Soviet. He taught at the Soviet State Film School **VGIK** in 1955–1963.

Other films: *There Lived Three Bachelors* (Zhili tri kholostiaka, 1927); *The Teacher* (Uchitel', 1939); *Antosha Rybkin* (1942); *The Living and the Dead* (Zhivye i mertvye, 1963); *The Strogovs* (Strogovy, 1976, TV miniseries).

CHKHEIDZE, REZO [real first name **REVAZ**; Russian sources also list the patronymic Davidovich] (b. 8 December 1926, Kutaisi). Georgian director, screenwriter, actor, and film administrator. Chkheidze studied with famous Russian director Georgii Tovstonogov (1913–1989) at the Shota Rustaveli Theater Institute in Tbilisi in 1943–1946. In 1953, he graduated from the Soviet State Film School **VGIK**, where his teachers were **Mikhail Romm** and **Sergei Iutkevich**. Together with fellow student and director **Tengis Abuladze**, he made the **documentary** *Our Palace* (Chveni sasakhle/ Nash dvorets, 1953) and debuted—also with Abuladze—as a feature film director with the short *Magdana's Donkey* (Magdanas Lurja/ Lurdzha Magdany, 1955), a parable about a poor woman who saves a starving donkey only to have it taken away by its former cruel owner. The film's realism in depicting the social injustice in the 19th century and its minimalist approach garnered critical praise both at home and abroad.

Chkheidze's first independent picture, the neorealist *Our Court* (Chveni ezo/Nash dvor, 1957), depicts contemporary youth in Soviet Georgia. After years of searching, Chkheidze's artistic triumph came with the war tragedy *Father of a Soldier* (Djariskatsis mama/Otets soldata, 1965), one of the greatest achievements of **Georgian cinema**. Contrasting the life-respecting wisdom of an old vintner (who is looking for his son at the front and accompanying the Red Army all the way to Berlin) with the ruthless destructiveness of war, Chkheidze and the performer of the title character, **Sergo Zakariadze**, created a universally relevant story that moved audiences worldwide.

What a Youth! (Gmilis bichebi/Nu i molodezh'! 1969) deals with a high school class graduating in 1941, on the outbreak of the Great Patriotic War. *The Saplings* (Nergebi/Sazhentsy, 1972), filmed in black and white, is a parable about human dignity and respect for age-old traditions, embodied by an old man and his grandson who gather rare young plants representing the future of life. The two-part contemporary epic *Your Son, Earth* (Mshobliuro chemo mitsov/Tvoi syn, zemlia, aka *The Story of a Party District Committee Secretary/* Povest' o sekretare raikoma, 1980) almost destroyed Chkheidze's reputation because of its blatant pro-Brezhnevist opportunism; it was released as a TV-miniseries and Chkheidze purportedly refused to accept the Lenin Prize awarded to him in 1986. The director then helmed the six-hour Soviet-Spanish coproduction *Life of Don Quijote and Sancho Panza* (Tskhovreba Don Kikhotisa da Sancho Panchosi/Zhitie Don Kikhota i Sancho, 1988), an adaptation that took generous creative liberties with the Cervantes text and was seen as an artistic failure at the time of its release.

Chkheidze was appointed executive director of **Gruziya-Film Studio** in 1973, a position he held—with a brief interruption—into the 1990s, struggling to bridge the gap between administrative and political obligations and artistic ambition. His tendency to approve numerous film projects without being able to secure funding for their completion led to stark criticism.

Chkheidze was named People's Artist of the USSR in 1980. He joined the Communist Party in 1958 and was a member of its Georgian Central Committee as well as a member of the Supreme Soviet of the USSR.

Other films: *Maya from Tskhneti* (Maya Tskhneteli/Maia iz Tskhneti, 1958); *The Treasure* (Gandzi/Klad, 1961); *The Seaside Shore* (Zgvis biliki/Morskaia tropa, 1963).

CHKHIKVADZE, RAMAZ [Russian sources list the patronymic Grigor'evich] (b. 28 February 1928, Tbilisi). Georgian actor. Chkhikvadze studied at the Shota Rustaveli State Theater Institute, graduating in 1951, and joined the troupe of the Rustaveli Theater, becoming one of its leading stars who celebrated triumphs in Shakespeare productions (*Richard III, King Lear*) and Bertolt Brecht's *Caucasian Chalk Circle* (for the latter, he was awarded a USSR State Prize in 1979).

Chkhikvadze made his screen debut with the role of Shota in **Siko Dolidze**'s popular musical **comedy** *The Dragonfly* (Chrichina/ Strekoza, 1954). He is a multifaceted performer who has worked with all leading Georgian directors and has played parts in numerous gems of **Georgian cinema**, including Matsil in **Tengiz Abuladze**'s *The Plea* (Vedreba/Mol'ba, 1967), the priest in Abuladze's *The Wishing Tree* (Natris khe/Drevo zhelaniia, 1977), the wise grandfather Luka in **Rezo Chkheidze**'s parable *The Saplings* (Nergebi/Sazhentsy, 1972), and Panke in **Giorgi Shengelaia**'s *Melodies of Veris Quarter* (Veris ubnis melodiebi/Melodii Veriiskogo kvartala, 1973).

In **Aleksandr Sokurov**'s *Mournful Anaesthesia* (Skorbnoe be-schuvstvie, 1983, released 1987), a peculiar adaptation of George Bernard Shaw's *Heartbreak House,* Chkhikvadze played the lead, Captain Shotover. He gave a respectful portrait of Iosif Stalin in **Iurii Ozerov**'s *Victory* (Pobeda, 1984) and a mocking one in Iraklii Kvirikadze's *The Sojourn of Comrade Stalin to Africa* (Puteshestvie tovarishcha Stalina v Afriku, 1991). Chkhikvadze appeared in the philosophical picture *The Wall* (Stena, 1990) from Jean-Paul Sartre's play (transposed to Georgian soil) and was part of the star-studded cast in Nana Jordjadze's international production *A Thousand and One Recipes of a Chef in Love* (1996).

Chkhikvadze was honored with the titles People's Artist of the USSR in 1981 and Hero of Socialist Labor in 1988.

Other films: *The Song of Eteri* (Eteris simgera/Pesn' Eteri, 1956); *Love at First Sight* (Liubov' s pervogo vzgliada, 1977, released 1988); *Life of Don Quijote and Sancho Panza* (Tskhovreba Don Kik-hotisa da Sancho Panchosi/Zhitie Don Kikhota i Sancho, 1988); *The Train Moved On and On* (Midioda matarebeli, 2005).

CHOKMOROV, SUIMENKUL (b. 9 November 1939, Chon-Tan kishlak, Kyrgyzstan–d. 28 September 1992). Kyrgyz actor. Chok-morov was a painter who graduated from the School of Fine Arts in Frunze (now: Bishkek) in 1958 and studied at the Leningrad Repin Institute of Art, Sculpture, and Architecture until 1964. For three years, Chokmorov taught painting and composition at the Frunze Art School. Today, his artwork is displayed in leading Kyrgyz museums.

As an actor in **Kyrgyz cinema**, Chokmorov debuted with the role of Bakhtygul in **Bolotbek Shamshiev**'s turn-of the-century drama *The Shot at Karash Pass* (Vystrel na perevale Karash, 1969), playing a poor man who is fooled by his master and takes violent revenge in the end (Shamshiev had met Chokmorov while shooting his **documentary** *Manaschi* in 1965). Chokmorov's understated acting manner excelled in several adaptations of famed Kyrgyz author **Chingiz Aitmatov**: Irina Poplavskaia's *Djamilia* (1971), **Tolomush Okeev**'s *The Red Apple* (Krasnoe iabloko, 1975) where Chokmorov was cast as the painter Temir, and Shamshiev's *Early Cranes* (Rannie zhuravli, 1979). These films, constituting what has been called the "Kyrgyz film miracle," feature highly poetic reflections about the impact of modernization and Sovietization on rural Kyrgyzstan, its gender relations, and mythical worldview.

Uzbek director **Ali Khamraev** used Chokmorov's quiet, virile intensity to great effect in the historical thriller *The Extraordinary Commissar* (Chrezvychainyi komissar, 1970), as did Shamshiev in the action-filled *Scarlet Poppies of Issyk Kul'* (Alye Maki Issyk-Kulia, 1972). Okeev gave him two more outstanding parts: the poor peasant Akhangul in *The Fierce One* (Liutyi, 1973) about a boy growing up with a wolf, and Azat Bairamov in *The Ulan* (Ulan, 1977), describing the tragic degradation of an alcoholic.

Chokmorov has been called a "red samurai" and compared to Japanese superstar Toshiro Mifune for his extremely restrained mimics concealing inner tension and depth; this assumption was corroborated by the fact that Akira Kurosawa chose him for a supporting role in his 1975 epic *Dersu Uzala*.

The actor was named People's Artist of the USSR in 1981; he joined the Communist Party in 1975. In 1988, a documentary about Chokmorov, *Descendants of Manas* (Potomki Manasa), was released.

Other films: *Worship the Fire* (Poklonis' ogniu, 1971); *Men without Women* (Muzhchiny bez zhenshchin, 1981); *Sunday Strolls* (Voskresnye progulki, 1988).

CHUKHRAI, GRIGORII NAUMOVICH (b. 23 May 1921, Dnepropetrovsk [now: Zaporozhsk] district–d. 29 October 2001, Moscow). Russian director, scriptwriter, and producer. Born into the family of an officer, Chukhrai was raised by his stepfather, a kolkhoz director, after his parents' divorce. He was drafted in 1939, serving in infantry units and later as a paratrooper. In August 1941, Chukhrai volunteered for the front, where he was wounded four times. After his discharge, Chukhrai was admitted into the Soviet State Film School **VGIK** in 1946, studying with **Sergei Iutkevich** and **Mikhail Romm**. In 1953, he joined the staff of the Kiev Film Studio as an assistant director; in 1955, he switched to **Mosfilm Studio**.

Chukhrai's directorial debut caused a sensation and brought him instant name recognition: *The Forty-first* (Sorok pervyi, 1956), a visually stunning and psychologically complex Civil War drama adapted from a story by Boris Lavrenev (1891–1959). The two young actors who carried this politically even-handed drama of love and revolutionary loyalty—Izol'da Izvitskaia (1932–1971) as Red Army sniper Mariutka and **Oleg Strizhenov** as White Army cadet Govorukha-Otrok—gave the film a rare freshness and erotic thrill, while **Sergei Urusevskii**'s stylish camera work graced it with a unique poetic softness.

Chukhrai outdid himself with his next picture, ***Ballad of a Soldier*** (Ballada o soldate, 1959). Telling a seemingly insignificant episode of the Great Patriotic War, the film delivers a powerful statement on universal ethical principles, praising virtues such as trust, mutual support, sincerity, and selflessness; the heartfelt lament for the human losses of the Great Patriotic War is persuasive because it is exemplified through an authentic human being. Indirectly, *Ballad* also reflected problems of Soviet society in the 1950s, especially its unease about growing individualism.

Backed by Nikita Khrushchev, Chukhrai's *Clear Sky* (aka *Clear Heaven*/Chistoe nebo, 1961) was an attempt to come clean on the legacy of Stalinism. The story of a pilot who survives German captivity only to be ostracized by his own as a suspicious POW is not as well structured as *Ballad*, yet the film, one of the biggest box-office attractions of its time, is still breathtaking in its civic fearlessness and directness.

Chukhrai's career then took an inexplicable turn downward. *There Was an Old Couple* (aka *The Couple*/Zhili-byli starik so starukhoi, 1964) again preached altruism but already seemed an anachronism at the time of its release. Even the most well-meaning critics could tell that Chukhrai's message and method had lost its original appeal and that the time for Thaw idealism was over. In 1965, the energetic filmmaker accepted the administrative position of artistic manager of Mosfilm's experimental unit, which he held until 1977. Based on the principle of financial self-support (*khozraschet*), the insights he gained in that phase of his career might well have been useful for the perestroika reforms in the mid-1980s, had Chukhrai not already largely withdrawn from public life by then. He made only four more pictures, two of which were **documentaries**: *Memory* (Pamiat', 1970), an artistically original reflection on the battle of Stalingrad using numerous live interviews, and *I Will Teach You to Dream* (Ia nauchu vas mechtat', 1984) about his fellow idealist and former mentor, **Mark Donskoi**. *Quagmire* (Triasina, 1977), a psychological drama about a woman and her draft-dodger son, did reasonably well at the box office but could hardly match the director's earlier achievements. The Italian-Soviet coproduction *Life Is Beautiful* (La vita è bella/Zhizn' prekrasna, 1980), an attempt to create a humanistic political thriller, was little seen in either country despite its stellar cast—a disappointing conclusion to an otherwise exceptional career.

Chukhrai remains the prototypical filmmaker of the Thaw who fought hard to combine loyalty to the Communist cause with civic duty and humanist values. No other director presented the positive intentions of that era with comparable emotional purity. Chukhrai's best films are realistic parables of good and evil in a world torn apart by physical brutality and moral relativism, and are carried by an unshakeable faith in human dignity. The filmmaker's own uncompromising behavior was legendary; thus, as jury president of the 1963 Moscow Film Festival, he insisted on awarding the Grand Prize to Federico Fellini's *8½*, a film as far as one could imagine from Socialist Realism and never released in the USSR.

Chukhrai joined the Communist Party in 1944 and won numerous medals for his distinguished service in WWII. In 1961, he was awarded a Lenin Prize and in 1981 the title People's Artist of the USSR. Chukhrai taught at VGIK in 1966–1971. His son is director **Pavel Chukhrai**.

CHUKHRAI, PAVEL GRIGOR'EVICH (b. 14 October 1946, Moscow). Russian director, screenwriter, and producer. Chukhrai, the son of director **Grigorii Chukhrai**, studied at the Soviet State Film School **VGIK** in the master class of cinematographer **Boris Volchek**, graduating in 1971. While working as an assistant cameraman, Chukhrai continued his studies at VGIK with **Igor' Talankin**, graduating with a degree in directing in 1974.

Chukhrai's directorial debut, *You Should Remember Occasionally* (Ty inogda vspominai, 1977), boasted screen legend **Nikolai Kriuchkov** as the male lead. The story of a military surgeon who loses his only son in a disaster and retires but is suddenly called for duty combines dramatic action with intense ethical reflection—a trademark of all of Chukrai's pictures. *People in the Ocean* (Liudi v okeane, 1980), about a tsunami at the Soviet Far Eastern border, became a box-office hit, as did *A Cage for Canaries* (Kletka dlia kanareek, 1984), the love story of a juvenile delinquent. Chukhrai's gift for capturing authentic contemporary atmosphere and eliciting natural performances, together with his uncommonly honest approach toward social ills, were further developed in *Zina—Little Zina* (Zina-Zinulia, 1986), a genuine eye-opener about the working-class milieu that is shown with dignity yet without typical Soviet embellishments.

Chukhrai proved his ability to bring historical events to life in the French-Russian coproduction *The Key* (Kliuch/La Clé, 1996, TV) from Mark Aldanov's novel, an interesting attempt to lay open the roots of the Bolshevik victory in 1917. Turning to the early 1950s in *The Thief* (Vor, 1997), he tells the heart-wrenching story of a little boy in search of a father figure. With harsh realism and emotional intensity, the film portrays the Stalin era as a shiny façade that misleads naïve, benevolent people and hides the activities of the most despicable deceivers. Visually stunning and graced with exceptional performances, *The Thief* won national and international kudos and was short-listed for an Academy Award for Best Foreign Film. *A Driver for Vera* (Voditel' dlia Very, 2004) possesses similar qualities: the fascinating, believable re-creation of an era—the early 1960s—populated by gullible, poor, but also dependable people who are ruled by a cruel, ruthless elite engaged in internal power struggles. However, unlike *The Thief*, *A Driver for Vera* failed to convince Russian critics, who accused it of opportunism and catering to foreign tastes.

Chukhrai, who shot some commercials in the 1990s, made **documentaries** as well, among them a critical portrait of maverick politician Vladimir Zhirinovskii, *The Hawk* (Iastreb, 1993). Chukhrai was named Merited Artist of Russia in 1993.

Other films: *Freedom to the Free* (Vol'nomu—voli, 1974, short); *Remember Me Like This* (Zapomnite menia takoi, 1988, TV); *Rakhmaninov* (1994, doc.); *The Russian Game* (Russkaia igra, 2007).

CHURIKOVA, INNA MIKHAILOVNA (b. 5 October 1943, Belibei, Bashkirostan). Russian actress. Churikova, who hails from peasant stock, studied at the Shchepkin Theater School in Moscow, graduating in 1965. From 1965 to 1968, she worked at the Moscow Theater of the Young Spectator (TIuZ) and in 1973 joined the troupe of the prestigious Lenkom Theater, where she since has become one of the most prominent stars.

While still a student, Churikova's debuted as Raika in Vasilii Ordynskii's antireligious film *Clouds over Borsk* (Tuchi nad Borskom, 1960), followed by an episodic part in **Georgii Daneliia**'s *I Stroll in Moscow* (aka *Meet Me in Moscow*/Ia shagaiu po Moskve, 1963). Her performance as the spoiled, lazy Marfushka in **Aleksandr Rou**'s popular fairy tale *Morozko* (aka *Father Frost*, 1965) proved a scene-stealer.

Yet only under the direction of **Gleb Panfilov** could the actress fully realize her artistic potential, depicting lofty idealism and high moral principles beneath a plain, sometimes clownish and awkward appearance. The tragic power of Churikova's performance as aspiring artist Tania Tetkina in *There's No Ford through Fire* (V ogne broda net, 1967), the original title of which was "A Sacred Soul," stunned critics and viewers alike. Her Pasha Stroganova/Joan of Arc in *The Debut* (Nachalo, 1970) became another veritable triumph. Churikova's ability to believably embody spiritual depth that stands in stark contrast to her rather modest societal position resonated with audiences who were tired of sugarcoated cliché revolutionaries.

Among Churikova's major cinematic achievements are the city administrator Uvarova in Panfilov's *I Wish to Speak* (Proshu slova, 1975), Vera in **Valerii Todorovskii**'s melodramatic *Wartime Romance* (Voenno-polevoi roman, 1984), Nina in Viacheslav Krishtofovich's *Adam's Rib* (Rebro Adama, 1990), and Madame Epanchina in **Vladimir Bortko**'s Fedor Dostoevskii adaptation *The Idiot* (Idiot, 2003).

When the Soviet system degenerated and Panfilov, rather unexpectedly, turned to the works of the founder of Socialist Realism,

Maksim Gor'kii (1868–1936), it was Churikova who gave the plum roles of Vassa Zheleznova in *Vassa* (1983) and Pelageia Vlasova in *The Mother* (Mat', 1990) a completely new treatment, reinforcing her reputation as Russia's most powerful antistereotypical actress.

Churikova was named People's Artist of the Russian Federation in 1985 and People's Artist of the USSR in 1991. Her son, Ivan Panfilov (b. 1978), a specialist in international law and former child actor, coauthored with Churikova the script for *The Romanovs—An Imperial Family* (Romanovy—ventsenosnaia sem'ia, 2000).

Other films: *The Theme* (Tema, 1979); *Valentina* (1981); *The Messenger Boy* (Kur'er, 1987); *Bless the Woman* (Blagoslovite zhenshchinu, 2003); *Moscow Saga* (Moskovskaia saga, 2004, TV miniseries); *In the First Circle* (V kruge pervom, 2006).

CILINSKIS, GUNĀRS [some Russian sources spell the last name Tsilinskii and list the patronymic Al'fredovich] (b. 23 [other sources: 25] May 1931, Riga–d. 25 July 1992, Balterezā, Riga district). Latvian actor, screenwriter, and director. Cilinskis studied at the Theater Department of the Latvian Conservatory, graduating in 1955, and joined the troupe of the Latvian Academic Drama Theater.

The actor's screen debut was the role of Janis in Ada Neretniece's *Stranger in the Village* (Chuzhaia v poselke, 1959). **Leonids Leimanis** entrusted him with the role of Imant in his drama about fishermen, *Captain Nulle* (Kapteinis Nulle/Kapitan Nul', 1964). Many directors capitalized on Cilinskis's athletic built and romantic looks, including **Aleksandrs Leimanis** in his pro-Soviet adventure dilogy for children *The 'Wagtail' Army* (Armiia "Triasoguzka," 1964) and *The 'Wagtail' Army Is Fighting Again* (Armiia 'Triasoguzka' snova v boiu, 1968), as well as the historical **comedy** *In the Claws of the Black Crab* (Melna vîza spiles/V kleshniakh chernogo raka, 1975). Cilinskis often portrayed selfless, heroic Communists, for example, in *Nocturne* (Noktirne/Noktiurn, 1966) about Latvians who participated in the Spanish Civil War. The actor gained fame throughout the Soviet Union playing the scout Kuznetsov in Viktor Georgiev's blockbuster *Those Who Are Strong in Spirit* (Sil'nye dukhom, 1968) about a covert operation in World War II. Subsequently, Cilinskis shared his activities between Riga and Moscow but made his most interesting appearances in **Latvian cinema**, including Gunars Piesis's

In the Shadow of Death (Nāves ēnā/V teni smerti, 1971), the story of fishermen on a forlorn ice flow; Rolands Kalnins's popular satire *Ceplis* (Afera Tseplisa, 1972) about a Latvian self-made man in the 1930s; and Jānis Streičs's *Theater* (Teātris/Teatr, 1978) from Somerset Maugham's novel, with Cilinskis as Julia's husband.

In the 1970s, Cilinskis turned to directing, often playing lead roles in his own pictures. His debut was the critically and commercially successful *Sonata at the Lake* (Ezera sonāte/Sonata nad ozerom, 1976, codirected with Varis Brasla) from Regina Ezera's novel. A contemporary melodrama characterized by psychological accuracy and atmospheric intensity, it touched upon questions of responsibility, loyalty, and fulfillment in private life (Cilinskis played the frustrated surgeon Rudolf). His other films, including the love triangle romance *Night without Birds* (Nakts bez putniem/Noch' bez ptits, 1979) and the thriller *When the Brakes Fail* (Kad bremzes netur/Kogda sdaiut tormoza, 1984), address contemporary problems. *Early Rust* (Agrā rūsa/Ranniaia rzhavchina, 1980) is a historical melodrama about a woman in the 1930s and her search for personal happiness and economic security that ends in murder.

Cilinskis was named Merited Artist of the Latvian SSR in 1965, People's Artist of the Latvian SSR in 1969, and People's Artist of the USSR in 1979.

Other films: (as director) *Tarāns* (Taran, 1982); *Fear* (Bailes/Strakh, 1986); *This Strange Moonlight* (Dīvainā mēnessgaisma/Etot strannyi lunnyi svet, 1987); (as actor) *Captain Enrico's Watch* (Kapitano Enriko pulksteinis/Chasy kapitana Enriko, 1968); *Werewolf Tom* (Vilkaitis Tom/Oboroten' Tom, 1984); *Victoria* (1988).

COLOR OF POMEGRANATE, THE (Nran guyne/Tsvet granata, 1967). **Armenfilm Studio**. 74 min., color. Directed by **Sergei Paradjanov**. Script: Sergei Paradjanov. Cinematography: Suren Shakhbazyan. Music: Tigran Mansuryan. Cast: **Sofiko Chiaureli**, Melkop Alekyan, Vilen Galstyan, Georgii Gegechkori, Onik Minasyan, Avet Avetisyan, Spartak Bagashvili. Premiere: 29 August 1970; released in 1973 (edited by **Sergei Iutkevich**).

The life of 18th-century Armenian, Georgian-born poet Arutin Sayadjan (Sayat-Nova) is told in eight chapters, including his childhood and youth, life at the court of a Georgian prince, withdrawal into the Akhpatski monastery, and his death. Rather than attempting a reconstruction of actual events, the film is composed of a series of complex, mostly static images saturated with symbols that refer to history, national culture, and mythology.

COMEDY. The genre of film comedy (*kinokomediia*) has been among the most popular in Russian and Soviet cinema from its very inception. By various accounts, about 350 comedies were produced in pre-Bolshevik Russia, most of them imitations of French and Danish films. Specific Russian characters such as "Antosha," embodied by Polish actor Anton Fertner, country bumpkin "Mitiukha," the clownish "the Bald One" (*Lysyi*), and the muscular "Uncle Pud" (*diadia Pud*, 1913–1917) competed for audience affection against numerous foreign rivals. Thus, about 30 comedies appeared as part of the *Antosha* series in 1915–1917 (*Antosha—Tamer of the Mother-in-Law/ Antosha—ukrotitel' teshchi*, etc.).

Soviet cinema, acknowledging full well audiences' affection for Max Linder, Charlie Chaplin, Harold Lloyd, and other foreign comedians, pursued a twofold strategy: attracting viewers to movie theaters and, if possible, infusing the genre with propaganda elements. Such was **Aleksandr Panteleev**'s anti-Christian pasquinade *The Miracle Worker* (Chudotvorets, 1922), which, according to Vladimir Lenin's wife, the Soviet leader enjoyed. An interesting experiment in transplanting American comedic characters to Soviet soil was **Lev Kuleshov**'s *The Unusual Adventures of Mr. West in the Land of the Bolsheviks* (Neobychainye prikliucheniia mistera Vesta v strane bol'shevikov, 1924), a homage to U.S.-type slapstick humor and an excellent opportunity to unobtrusively apply the director's montage theories. **Iakov Protazanov** regained his pre-1917 reputation of a first-class director with a number of witty, well-timed comedies, some of them blasphemous (*Holiday of St. Iorgen*, aka *St. Jorgen's Day*/Prazdnik sviatogo Iorgena, 1929), others apt social satires (*The Tailor from Torzhok*/Zakroishchik iz Torzhka, 1925). Overall, the moderately open atmosphere of the New Economic Policy (NEP, 1921–1929) allowed for some depoliticized, charming romantic comedies such as **Boris Barnet**'s *The Girl with the Hatbox* (Devushka s korobkoi, 1927), **Iurii Zheliabuzhskii**'s *The Cigarette Girl from Mossel'prom* (Papirosnitsa ot Mossel'proma, 1924), and **Sergei Komarov**'s *The Kiss of Mary Pickford* (Potselui Meri Pikford, 1927).

In Ukraine, Lev Kurbas made innovative comedies, while **Nikolai Okhlopkov** began his directing career with two satires, *Mitia* (1927) and *The Sold Appetite* (Prodannyi appetit, 1928). In Georgia, **Mikheil Chiaureli** became famous with his satirical assaults on alcoholism (*Saba*, 1929) and the Church (*Get Out of the Way!*/Khabarda/ Postoronites', 1931). In Russia, **Aleksandr Medvedkin** demonstrated inventive, sharp wit with satirical shorts released in the early 1930s; he made an attempt to expand his unique brand of comedy with the full-length silent *Happiness* (Schast'e, 1934), a stand-alone feature that was hailed by colleagues, then long forgotten and, after its rediscovery in the 1960s, declared a classic.

Some directors remained at least partially loyal to film comedy in the sound period when it turned into an ideological battlefield. Others, such as Medvedkin, consciously abstained from the genre because their notion of satire and laughter as healing forces was attacked by dogmatic critics who denounced it as anti-Soviet and subversive. Even the harmless jokes about unpleasant contemporaries that are characteristic of **Grigorii Aleksandrov**'s musical comedies such as *Jolly Fellows* (Veselye rebiata, 1934) had to be defended against accusations from Party hacks. It was not by chance that Ukrainian filmmaker **Ihor' Savchenko**, who proved his superb sense of humor with *The Accordion* (Garmon', 1934), stayed clear from comedy for more than a decade following the critical onslaught against his *Month of May* (Mesiats mai, 1936). While even Savchenko's noncomedic works contain a wealth of funny gags, his *Old Vaudeville* (aka *The Lucky Bride*/Starinnyi vodevil', 1946) became a huge box-office success but also the object of malicious attacks. Similarly, **Ivan Pyr'ev**, who proved his natural penchant for satire in *The Civil Servant* (Gosudarstvennyi chinovnik, 1931), had his picture first prohibited and then deformed by censorial intrusion; the experience made him more cautious, and *A Rich Bride* (aka *The Country Bride*/Bogataia nevesta, 1938), *Tractor Drivers* (Traktoristy, 1939), and the infamous *Swineherd and Shepherd* (aka *They Met in Moscow*/Svinarka i pastukh, 1941) follow Communist Party guidelines impeccably, avoiding satirical colors and only poking mild fun at human weaknesses. Thematically exceptional is Belarusian director **Vladimir**

Korsh-Sablin's *Seekers of Happiness* (aka *Birobidjan*, *A Greater Promise*/Shukal'niki shchascia/Iskateli schast'ia, 1935), a comedy about Jewish immigrants to the Soviet Far East, illustrating the claim that the new societal relations are free from greed and exploitation.

Although different from Pyr'ev's musical comedies in pacing and setting, Aleksandrov's hits such as *Circus* (Tsirk, 1936), *Volga-Volga* (1938) and *Radiant Path* (aka *Tanya*/Svetlyi put', 1940) share with Pyr'ev's efforts their loud patriotism whose only saving grace is a naïve devotion to general human values such as love, courage, and honesty. A comedy director with a peculiar style of his own was the critically underrated **Semen Timoshenko**, whose *The Goalkeeper* (Vratar', 1936) enjoyed lasting popularity. Soviet urban everyday life—usually observed in Moscow, the exemplary city where Communist living conditions seemed to be already achieved—was depicted in a civil, kindhearted, and at times funny manner in **Tat'iana Lukashevich**'s charming *The Foundling* (Podkidysh, 1939), **Konstantin Iudin**'s *A Girl with Personality* (Devushka s kharakterom, 1939), and **Aleksandr Ivanovskii**'s *Musical Story* (Muzykal'naia istoriia, 1940, codirected with **Gerbert Rappaport**).

During the Great Patriotic War, some filmmakers tried satirical asides against the Nazi intruders, but the military objected to **Sergei Iutkevich**'s *Schwejk Is Preparing for Battle* (Shveik gotovitsia k boiu, 1942) and **Grigorii Kozintsev**'s *Young Fritz* (Iunyi Frits, 1943), which were both shelved. However, Iudin's *Antosha Rybkin* comedies (1941, 1942) about a witty Red Army cook enjoyed official and popular approval.

The film comedies of post–World War II years, although few in numbers, attracted huge crowds yearning for entertainment and willing to forgive the rather stale humor and the fact that the warm human touch and fast-paced action of the 1930s comedies were replaced by artificial situations and wooden acting, with pathos dominating over wit. **Iulii Raizman**'s *The Train Goes Eastward* (Poezd idet na vostok, 1947), Aleksandrov's *Spring* (Vesna, 1947), and Pyr'ev's *Cossacks of the Kuban* (Kubanskie kazaki, 1950) revealed that the genre finally had been stifled by Stalinist ideological parameters. Conspicuously, the cautious de-Stalinization of the 1950s was marked by waves of liberating laughter in the movie theaters. The Thaw period brought an increasing number of genuinely funny comedies with contemporary subject matter: **Mikhail Kalatozov**'s *Loyal Friends* (Vernye druz'ia, 1954), **Nadezhda Kosheverova**'s *Tiger Girl* (Ukrotitel'nitsa tigrov, 1955, codirected with Ivanovskii), **El'dar Riazanov**'s *Carnival Night* (Karnaval'naia noch', 1956), **Andrei Tutyshkin**'s *A Crazy Day* (Bezumnyi den', 1956), and Iurii Chuliukin's *The Defiant Ones* (Nepoddaiushchiesia, 1959). These films filled the screens with refreshing optimism and joy of life, and also contained some noteworthy satirical elements.

The liberalization of the 1950s and early 1960s enabled filmmakers in the Soviet republics to define a comedic style imbued with national specifics. Thus, Kazakh director **Shaken Aimanov** directed a number of cheerful musical comedies such as *Our Dear Doctor* (Nash milyi doktor, 1957) and *Beardless Swindler* (Bezborodyi obmanshchik, 1965) that in part draw on national myths and were particularly popular in Central Asia. Estonian filmmaker **Kaljo Kiisk** was successful with his action comedy *Naughty Curves* (Vallatud kurvid/Ozornye povoroty, 1959) and its panorama screen version, *Dangerous Turns* (Ohtlikud kurvid/Opasnye povoroty, 1961).

In the 1960s, **Leonid Gaidai** created a peculiar mélange of slapstick and social satire that resulted in some all-time box-office hits of Soviet cinema, including *Operation "Y" and Other Adventures of Shurik* (Operatsiia 'Y' i drugie prikliucheniia Shurika, 1965), *Prisoner of the Caucasus* (aka *Kidnapping Caucasian Style*/Kavkazskaia plennitsa, 1966), and *The Diamond Arm* (Brilliantovaia ruka, 1968). Riazanov emphasized psychological and sometimes even tragic elements in his comedic melodramas, in particular, the antimaterialist *Watch Out for the Automobile* (Beregis' avtomobilia, 1966). **Georgii Daneliia**'s comedies evolved from biting satire (*Thirty-three*/Tridtsat' tri, 1965) to a more mellow approach that was aptly formulated in *Don't Grieve* (Ar daidardo/Ne goriui!, 1969), produced in his native Georgia. Also in Georgia, Mikheil Kobakhidze created remarkable, almost silent shorts: *The Wedding* (1965), *The Umbrella* (1967), and *The Musicians* (1969). Their unique poetic humor emerges from pantomimic acting and an all-pervasive understanding of human desires.

The 1970s were a less funny decade in cinema; among the noteworthy exceptions are literary adaptations such as Gaidai's *The Twelve Chairs* (Dvenadtsat' stul'ev, 1971, from Il'f and Petrov) and *Ivan Vasil'evich Changes His Job* (aka *Ivan Vasilievich: Back to the Future*/Ivan Vasil'evich meniaet professiiu, 1973, from Mikhail Bulgakov's comedy). Contemporary subject matter was treated both in slapstick-like and melodramatic manners, for example, in Riazanov's *The Unbelievable Adventures of Italians in Russia* (Neveroiatnye prikliucheniia italiantsev v Rossii, 1974) and *Office Romance* (Sluzhebnyi roman, 1978), respectively. Conspicuously, social satire in those years was the exception, arguably represented at its most apt in Riazanov's uncompromising *The Garage* (Garazh, 1979). Rather, blockbuster comedies such as Daneliia's *Afonia* (1975) and *Autumn Marathon* (Osennii marafon, 1979), and especially **Vladimir Men'shov**'s amusing *Moscow Does Not Believe in Tears* (Moskva slezam ne verit, 1980) reflected the societal status quo and the resignation accompanying it.

An interesting color to the comedic spectrum was added by the historical musical comedies of Latvian director **Aleksandrs Leimanis**, *The Devil's Servants* (Vella kalpi/Slugi d''iavola), its sequel, *The Devil's Servants at the Devil's Mill* (Vella kalpi vella dzirnavās/Slugi d''iavola na chertovoi mel'nitse, 1972), and *In the Claws of the Black Crab* (Melna vîza spiles/V kleshniakh chernogo raka, 1975), all of which were popular with Soviet audiences everywhere. In Georgia, **Giorgi Shengelaia** created the musical *Melodies of Veris Quarter* (Veris ubnis melodiebi/Melodii Veriiskogo kvartala, 1973), while his brother **El'dar Shengelaia** painted a gently funny portrait of lovable outsiders in *Crackpots* (Sherekilebi/Chudaki, 1974).

Another distinctive subgenre in the 1970s was the lyrical comedy, which often deals with the cultural clash between urban and rural life styles, for example, in **Vasilii Shukshin**'s *Happy Go Lucky* (Pechki-lavochki, 1972), **Vitalii Mel'nikov**'s *The Seven Brides of Corporal Zbruev* (Sem' nevest efreitora Zbrueva, 1971), and **Sergei Nikonenko**'s *Dawn and Dusk Are Kissing* (Tseluiutsia zori, 1978). Their humor is usually soft and melancholic, and driven by a nostalgic longing for the harmonious life of the past.

After the virtual absence of satire in the toothless 1970s, the following decade saw an increasingly sarcastic humor in dark anti-utopias such as Daneliia's *Kin-Dza-Dza* (1986) and **Karen Shakhnazarov**'s *Zero City* (Gorod Zero, 1989), biting social commentary in Eldar Shengelaia's *Blue Mountains, or An Unbelievable Story* (Tsisperi mtebi anu arachveulebrivi ambavi/Golubye gory, ili nepravdopodobnaia istoriia, 1984), and Iurii Mamin's *The Fountain* (Fontan, 1988), all of which reflected the breakdown of the Communist belief system, which is exposed as mere façade.

When the Soviet Union met its disastrous finale in 1991, comedy seemed well suited to bid farewell to its false promises and illusions; yet, since the centralized distribution system had fallen apart too, even the most hilarious films found only a limited number of viewers. Such was the fate of Gaidai's travesty *On Deribasovskaia the Weather Is Fine, or On Brighton Beach It's Raining Again* (Na Deribasovskoi khoroshaia pogoda, ili Na Braiton-Bich opiat' idut dozhdi, 1992), Mel'nikov's bittersweet *Chicha* (1992), and even Men'shov's big-budget *What a Mess* (Shirli-myrli, 1995). Only by the mid-1990s did film comedies regain their once-enjoyed popularity, most significantly in **Aleksandr Rogozhkin**'s *Peculiarities of the National Hunt* (Osobennosti natsional'noi okhoty, 1995) and its sequels, films that initiated the process of overcoming the estrangement between post-Soviet cinema and its audiences.

COMMISSAR, THE (Komissar, 1967). **Gor'kii Studio for Children's and Youth Films**. 110 min., b/w. Directed by **Aleksandr Askol'dov**. Script: Aleksandr Askol'dov from Vasilii Grossman's short story "In the Town of Berdichev" (V gorode Berdicheve, 1934). Cinematography: Valerii Ginzburg. Music: **Al'fred Shnitke**. Cast: **Nonna Mordiukova**, **Rolan Bykov**, Raisa Nedashkovskaia, **Vasilii Shukshin**, Liudmila Volynskaia. Premiere: 11 July 1987.

During the 1918–1920 Civil War, Bolshevik commissar Klavdiia Vavilova (Mordiukova) arrives with her Red Army unit in a small Ukrainian town. She orders that a man who had escaped to his family be executed. After confessing to the commander (Shukshin) that she is pregnant and an abortion is no longer possible, she moves in with the family of Jewish artisan Efim Magazanik (Bykov), his wife Mariia (Nedashkovskaia), their five children, and grandmother (Volynskaia). Vavilova gives birth to a boy and initially enjoys motherhood, but when warfare continues she leaves the baby behind to rejoin the revolutionary struggle.

COMMUNIST, A (Kommunist, 1957). **Mosfilm Studio**. 111 min., color. Directed by **Iulii Raizman**. Script: **Evgenii Gabrilovich**.

Cinematography: Aleksandr Shelenkov, Chen Ju-lan (Iolanda Chen). Music: Rodion Shchedrin. Cast: **Evgenii Urbanskii**, Sof'ia Pavlova, Boris Smirnov, Evgenii Shutov, Sergei Iakovlev, Valentin Zubkov, **Ivan Koval'-Samborskii**. Premiere: 3 February 1958.

In 1918, Vasilii Gubanov (Urbanskii), a young Bolshevik, returns from World War I and settles in a rural area. He falls in love with Aniuta (Pavlova), the wife of his landlord, the patriarchal peasant Fedor Fokin (Shutov). The Communist Party sends Gubanov to a gigantic construction site, the first Soviet hydroelectric power plant. Gubanov's passion energizes his environment, including Aniuta, who has followed him and has given birth to their son. The Communist even travels to Moscow where he talks to Vladimir Lenin (Smirnov) about the urgent need for building materials. One day, Gubanov is killed by anti-Soviet criminals, but his martyrdom will continue to inspire others.

COUNTERPLAN, THE (Vstrechnyi, 1932). Soiuzfilm (**Lenfilm Studio**). 118 min., b/w. Directed by **Fridrikh Ermler** and **Sergei Iutkevich**. Script: **Leo Arnshtam**, Fridrikh Ermler, Sergei Iutkevich, D. Del' (Leonid Liubashevskii). Cinematography: Arkadii Gintsburg, Zhosef Martov, Vladimir Rappoport. Music: **Dmitrii Shostakovich**. Cast: **Vladimir Gardin**, **Mariia Bliumental'-Tamarina**, Tat'iana Guretskaia, Andrei Abrikosov, Boris Tenin, Boris Poslavskii, **Petr Aleinikov**. Premiere: 7 November 1932.

The workers of a factory in Leningrad decide to present an alternative to the industrial plan assigned by the ministry, proposing even higher increases in production quotas. The goal is to deliver a new, very efficient turbine faster than originally planned. Semen Babchenko (Gardin), an experienced metal worker, will render one of the essential details, overcoming anachronistic practices and prejudices. After a saboteur, Skvortsov, is exposed, the factory's staff can finally celebrate the completion of the first Soviet turbine.

CRANES ARE FLYING, THE (Letiat zhuravli, 1957). **Mosfilm Studio**. 97 min., b/w. Directed by **Mikhail Kalatozov**. Script: Viktor Rozov from his play *Eternally Alive* (Vechno zhivye). Cinematography: **Sergei Urusevskii**. Music: Moisei Vainberg. Cast: **Tat'iana Samoilova**, **Aleksei Batalov**, **Vasilii Merkur'ev**, Aleksandr Shvorin,

Svetlana Kharitonova, Konstantin Nikitin, Valentin Zubkov, Antonina Bogdanova. Premiere: 12 October 1957.

In June 1941, lovers Boris (Batalov) and Veronika (Samoilova) frolic in the streets of Moscow when suddenly the radio announces the beginning of war. Despite objections from his father, a doctor (Merkur'ev), Boris volunteers and later is killed in action. Veronika gives in to the advances of Boris's cousin, Mark (Shvorin), a pianist. When Mark's draft exemption turns out a sham, Veronika, plagued by guilt, is close to suicide, but in the last moment she saves an orphaned toddler named Boris. In May 1945, Veronika receives confirmation of Boris's death; however, she overcomes her grief, surrounded by family and other Muscovites celebrating victory and peace.

– D –

DANELIIA [Danelia]**, GEORGII** [Giorgi] **NIKOLAEVICH** (b. 25 August 1930, Tbilisi, Georgia). Georgian-Russian director and screenwriter. Daneliia grew up in Moscow, where his father worked as a transportation engineer and his mother as an assistant film director (Daneliia's uncle was film director **Mikheil Chiaureli**, his aunt actress **Veriko Andjaparidze**). In 1954, he graduated from the Moscow Institute of Architecture; in 1956, he enrolled in **Mosfilm Studio**'s Advanced Directing Courses, studying under **Mikhail Romm**, **Sergei Iutkevich**, and **Mikhail Kalatozov**. His diploma film, the short *People, Too* (Tozhe liudi, 1959), was based on an episode from Lev Tolstoi's *War and Peace*.

Daneliia's first full-length feature, *Serezha* (aka *A Summer to Remember*, 1960, codirected with **Igor' Talankin** from a novella by Vera Panova), brought him immediate renown. In hindsight, the film's kind, slightly ironic view of Soviet reality, shown from the point of view of a perceptive five-year-old boy, proves more characteristic of Daneliia's evolving style than of his codirector's, who has a stronger predilection for dramatic collisions within a clearly marked historical framework.

I Stroll in Moscow (aka *Meet Me in Moscow*/Ia shagaiu po Moskve, 1963) engrained Daneliia's name in audiences' memories. A harmless **comedy**, it nonetheless manages to capture the sparkling youthfulness and cultural vivacity of the Russian capital in a unique way. The hilarious *Thirty-three* (Tridtsat' tri, 1965) marks a deviation from Daneliia's typical kindness; the story of a simple man who has one more tooth than everyone else is a bitter parable of the difficulties to remain an individual.

Arguably, Daneliia's most artistically accomplished picture is *Don't Grieve* (Ar daidardo/Ne goriui! 1969), the title of which could be a credo for the filmmaker's overall oeuvre. Based on Claude Tillier's novel *My Uncle Benjamin*, which screenwriter **Revaz Gabriadze** transposed to 19th-century Georgia, it endeared Daneliia to the Soviet intelligentsia and became the foundation of his status as a cult director; together with **Leonid Gaidai** and **El'dar Riazanov**, he was one of the few filmmakers whose name alone brought millions of people to the movie theaters. However, Daneliia's next project, an adaptation of Lev Tolstoi's masterpiece *Hadji Murat*, was stopped in its tracks—the classic's interpretation of the Caucasus conflict obviously rang too close to home. Daneliia retreated to familiar contemporary territory and directed three major hits in the 1970s: *Afonia* (1975), whose over 60 million viewers made it the greatest box-office success of his career, *Mimino* (1977), and *Autumn Marathon* (Osennii marafon, 1979). The filmmaker's formula, blending a benevolent attitude toward people with a mellow acceptance of life, is applied to middle-class professionals—the plumber Afonia, the pilot Mimino, and the literature professor Buzykin in *Autumn Marathon*—in rather chaotic urban settings.

Little of Daneliia's comforting warmth can be sensed in *Kin-Dza-Dza* (1986), a dark, disturbing anti-utopian farce in which the future is primitive and dirty. With the disintegration of the Soviet Union, Daneliia, who embodied many of the compromises on which the superpower's culture was functioning, seemed to lose his loyal mass audience. *The Passport* (Pasport, 1990), which took up the taboo subject of immigration to Israel, seemed forlorn in the tumult of late perestroika. *Nastia* (1993) and *Heads and Tails* (Orel i reshka, 1995), the latter based on Vladimir Makanin's novella "On the First Breathing," are entertaining and did well on video, but their theatrical releases were far from the national events that Daneliia's earlier films had been. The comedy *Fortuna* (2000) boasts a surprising vitality and believable optimism, so rare in contemporary Russian cinema.

As a director, Daneliia is a perfectionist in conceptualizing and planning each minute detail and its effect on the viewer. Societal factors consistently prove secondary in his world—what counts is a human being's individual decency and common sense, often more present in the young than in the elderly. Most importantly, his films are never grandiose or false—one might call them "antigrandiose," which perhaps best explains their consistent appeal. As his teacher Romm once aptly formulated referring to *Meet Me in Moscow*, "You think of this film, and it makes you smile."

Daneliia was awarded the title People's Artist of the Russian Federation in 1974 and People's Artist of the USSR in 1989. His wife, Galina Daneliia-Iurkova, is a film director whose tragicomedy *The Frenchman* (Frantsuz, 1988) is based on Daneliia's script. His oldest son, Nikolai (1959–1985), was a director and poet.

Other films: *The Road to Berth* (Put' k prichalu, 1962); *Hopelessly Lost* (aka *The Adventures of Huckleberry Finn*/Sovsem propashchii, 1972); *Tears Were Falling* (Slezy kapali, 1982).

DAYS OF ECLIPSE (Dni zatmeniia, 1988). **Lenfilm Studio**. 139 min., color and b/w. Directed by **Aleksandr Sokurov**. Script: Iurii Arabov, Petr Kadochnikov, Arkadii and Boris Strugatskii from their story "Ten Billion Years before the End of the World" (1976). Cinematography: Sergei Iurizditskii. Music: Iurii Khanin. Cast: Aleksei Ananishnov, Eskender Umarov, Irina Sokolova, Vladimir Zamanskii, Kirill Dudkin, Aleksei Ianovskii. Premiere: December 1988.

Dmitrii Malianov (Ananishnov), a young doctor from Moscow, works in a remote settlement in the Turkmen desert where he encounters a peculiar mix of premodern and modern attitudes and a confusing cacophony of languages and cultures. Inexplicable phenomena defy the rational principles that he has been brought up on, and he loses his motivation to practice. An eclipse seems to cover in darkness the town and all of civilization, pointing to the final convulsions of the Soviet system. Only the encounter with a sick boy who needs his help restores the doctor's faith in the importance of his calling.

DEFENSE OF SEVASTOPOL, THE (Oborona Sevastopolia, 1911). Khanzhonkov Company. 100 min., b/w. Directed by **Vasilii Goncharov** (studio scenes) and **Aleksandr Khanzhonkov** (battle scenes).

Script: Vasilii Goncharov and Aleksandr Khanzhonkov. Cinematography: Louis Forestier, Aleksandr Ryllo. Music for the Moscow premiere: Grigorii Kazachenko (other sources: Mikhail Ippolitov-Ivanov). Military consultant: Colonel M. Liakhov. Cast: A. Gromov, N. Semenov, O. Petrova-Zvantseva, **Ivan Mozzhukhin**, **Vladimir Maksimov**. Premiere: 15 October 1911 (Other sources: 9 December 1911). The film was made under special protectorate of Grand Prince Aleksandr Mikhailovich.

A feature-length reconstruction of one of the dramatic events of the Crimean War (1853–1856), the defense of the city of Sevastopol in 1854. Historical figures such as Admiral Nakhimov (Gromov), Admiral Kornilov (Mozzhukhin), and the surgeon Pirogov are portrayed by professional actors, while thousands of extras were provided by the Russian Army. The ending features a group of survivors of the historical events, now old men and women, respectfully bowing toward the audience.

DEMIDOVA, ALLA SERGEEVNA (b. 29 September 1936, Moscow). Russian actress. Demidova studied economics at Moscow Lomonosov University and was active in its prestigious student theater. After graduating in 1960, she enrolled in the Shchukin Theater School, which she finished in 1964. She then joined the troupe of Iurii Liubimov's Taganka Theater, soon becoming one of its major assets.

Demidova made her first appearance on screen in 1957 in the episodic role of a student in Zakhar Agranenko's *Leningrad Symphony* (Leningradskaia simfoniia). **Igor' Talankin** cast her as the female lead in *Daytime Stars* (Dnevnye zvezdy, 1966–1969) about the poet Ol'ga Berggol'ts who survived the Leningrad blockade and Stalinist persecution and was able to save her faith in humanity and culture. Talankin made the most consistent use of Demidova's talent in the following decades, casting her in the biopic *Chaikovskii* (1970) as Julia von Meck, as the humble Pashen'ka in the Lev Tolstoi adaptation *Father Sergius* (Otets Sergii, 1978), and as Mar'ia Lebiadkina in the Fedor Dostoevskii adaptation *The Devils* (Besy, 1992), among others.

Demidova's unique appearance, irradiating nervous intellectualism, a strong spiritual foundation, and a femininity both brittle and irritable, rendered her a preferred choice for leading Russian filmmakers in the 1970s. Thus, she portrayed the previously maligned Social

Revolutionary activist Mariia Spiridonova (1884–1941) with dignity and compassion in Iulii Karasik's chronicle *Sixth of July* (Shestoe iulia, 1968), and was impressive as Liza in one of the key episodes of **Andrei Tarkovskii**'s autobiographical *Mirror* (Zerkalo, 1975). **Mikhail Shveitser** cast her in *The Escape of Mr. MacKinley* (Begstvo mistera Mak-Kinli, 1975), and **Aleksandr Alov** and **Vladimir Naumov** as Katlina in *The Legend of Till* (Legenda o Tile, 1977). The actress's arguably greatest artistic achievement in cinema is the female lead in **Larisa Shepit'ko**'s brilliant contemporary drama about privacy and the frustrations of self-realization, *You and I* (Ty i ia, 1972), a film that has managed to preserve some of its stunning psychological intensity despite brutal censorship intrusions.

Demidova was named People's Artist of the RSFSR in 1984; she received a USSR State Prize in 1977.

Other films: *The Shield and the Sword* (Shchit i mech, 1968); *The Living Corpse* (Zhivoi trup, 1970); *Autumn, Chertanovo* (Osen', Chertanovo, 1988); *The Invisible Traveller* (Nezrimyi puteshestvennik, 1998); *The Tuner* (Nastroishchik, 2004); *Russian Money* (Russkie den'gi, 2006).

DEMUTSKII, DANYLO [Daniil Porfir'evich] (b. 16 July 1893, Okhmatovo, Kiev district–d. 7 May 1954, Kiev). Ukrainian cinematographer. Demutskii was born into the family of a physician and devotee of Ukrainian folk music. As a teenager, he began to pursue his lifelong passion for photography, participating in national and international exhibitions. He graduated from Kiev University in 1917.

Hired as the head of the photo laboratory of the Odessa Film Factory in 1925, Demutskii began to shoot his first moving pictures in 1926. His encounter with **Aleksandr Dovzhenko** proved mutually beneficial: after some early "training" pictures such as *Vasia the Reformer* (Vasia-reformator, 1926), Demutskii turned out to be the ideal camera artist to visualize Dovzhenko's semimythological parable on class struggle, *Arsenal* (1928), gracing it with a distinctly Ukrainian flavor. His preferred image-softening lens gave his portraits and landscapes a warm glow, supporting Dovzhenko's romantic style and its rhapsodic pathos.

Demutskii's supreme cinematographic achievement is his camera work on Dovzhenko's *Earth* (1930). This last great virtuoso act of silent cinema features previously unseen lengthy close-ups of apples in the rain, nightly landscapes with the moon shining softly on somnambulant lovers, and undulating lavish fields extending to the horizon, all forming a vitalist, pro-Communist symphony of great lyrical expressiveness. The cinematographer was able to carry over his poetic mastery into sound film, starting with Dovzhenko's *Ivan* (1932, with Iurii Ekel'chik) about the construction of the Dnieproges dam. It was, sadly, their last joint project. According to historian George Liber, the Ukrainian branch of the secret service (GPU) began to investigate Demutskii for alleged political unreliability as early as 1930; he was arrested and jailed for several months in 1932 and 1934 and finally exiled to Central Asia, where he was again arrested and kept in prison for a year and a half. When not in jail, Demutskii worked for the Tashkent newsreel studio. During World War II, he was the cameraman on films by **Iakov Protazanov**, Vladimir Braun, and **Nabi Ganiev** at Tashkent Film Studio (later: **Uzbekfilm Studio**).

Demutski's last two significant pictures, made after his return from exile, were **Boris Barnet**'s *The Scout's Quest* (aka *Secret Agent/ Podvig razvedchika*, 1947) and **Ihor' Savchenko**'s color biopic *Taras Shevchenko* (1951), for which he received a Stalin Prize.

Demutski's fame as a genuine camera poet rests on his expertly sublime landscapes that convey an agitated vitality, as if the fields, forests, gardens, rivers, and flower beds were able to communicate with their human inhabitants. An outstanding master of lighting, Demutskii was inspired by the chiaroscuro of German expressionism, as well as Soviet constructivism and 19th-century Russian and Ukrainian painting.

Demutskii was named Merited Art Worker of the Uzbek SSR in 1944 and of the Ukrainian SSR in 1954.

Other films: *Love's Little Berry* (Iagodka liubvi, 1926); *Nasreddin in Bukhara* (Nasreddin v Bukhare, 1943); *Takhir and Zukhra* (1945); *The Adventures of Nasreddin* (Pokhozhdeniia Nasreddina, 1947); *In Peaceful Days* (V mirnye dni, 1950). *See also* UKRAINIAN CINEMA.

DENISOV, EDISON VASIL'EVICH (b. 6 April 1929, Tomsk–d. 24 November 1996, Paris). Russian composer and music theorist. Denisov was born into the family of a radio physicist who named his son in honor of Thomas Alva Edison. Denisov initially studied physics and mathematics at Tomsk University in 1946–1951. After sending some of his musical compositions to **Dmitrii Shostakovich**, who responded favorably (and remained a lifelong friend and mentor), he enrolled in Moscow Conservatory where he studied with Vissarion Shebalin from 1951 to 1959. Denisov quickly gained a reputation as one of the most daring innovators in Russian music; he was hailed in the West but often sharply criticized by Soviet officials in the 1960s and 1970s.

While film music was hardly the major focus of Denisov's artistry, his contributions are large enough in number and consistency to merit attention. His first score was for the **children's film** *The Blue Cup* (Golubaia chasha, 1964, TV) from Arkadii Gaidar's story. Denisov's approach proved successful in *Those Who Are Strong in Spirit* (Sil'nye dukhom, 1968), a two-part blockbuster about a secret operation during the Great Patriotic War directed by Viktor Georgiev. For Georgiev, Denisov later also wrote the music for another spy drama, *At the Dangerous Line* (U opasnoi cherty, 1983) and the Oscar Wilde adaptation *An Ideal Husband* (Ideal'nyi muzh, 1980). Among the reputable filmmakers with whom the composer worked are **Iuliia Solntseva** (*The World in Three Dimensions*/Mir v trekh izmereniiakh, 1979, a working-class tale) and **Vitalii Mel'nikov** (the 18th-century drama *The Tsar's Hunt*/Tsarskaia okhota, 1990).

It is hard to tell why this rather elitist composer agreed to write the scores for so many second-rate movies, admittedly in a great variety of genres, from revolutionary adventure (*February Wind*/Fevral'skii veter, 1981), to war drama (*Born Twice*/Dvazhdy rozhdennyi, 1983) and realistic depiction of contemporary schoolchildren's lives (*On the Margin, Somewhere in the City . . .*/Na okraine, gde-to v gorode . . . , 1988), and science fiction in *The Temptation of B.* (Iskushenie B., 1990). Denisov was an uncompromising avant-gardist whose techniques such as seriality may have been less noticeable and heretical to Soviet administrators in cinema than in concert halls. His style betrays the influence of French impressionism, Pierre Boulez, and Anton Webern. Several of Denisov's orchestral and choral works have religious themes, as does one of his films, *The Free Zone* (Svobodnaia zona, 1992).

For many years, Denisov taught musical analysis, instrumentation, and composition at Moscow Conservatory. In 1990, he was honored with the title Merited Artist of the RSFSR and in 1995, People's Artist of Russia. He is buried in Paris.

Other films: *Prishvin's Paper Eyes* (Bumazhnye glaza Prishvina, 1989); *The Body* (Telo, 1990); *The Anomaly* (Anomaliia, 1993).

DERBENEV, VADIM KLAVDIEVICH (b. 18 June 1934, Iaroslavl'). Russian and Moldovan director, screenwriter, and cinematographer. Derbenev studied with **Boris Volchek** at the Soviet State Film School **VGIK**, graduating in 1957. He made a name for himself with the stylish, effective camera work on **Mikhail Kalik**'s Moldovan pictures: the potboiler *Ataman Kodr* (1958), the moving postwar drama *Lullabye* (Kolybel'naia, 1960)—both of them considerable box-office successes—and the childhood ballad *Man Follows the Sun* (aka *Sandu Follows the Sun*/Chelovek idet za solntsem, 1961).

At **Moldova-Film Studio**, Derbenev made his directorial debut with the **comedy** *Voyage into April* (Calatorie in april/Puteshestvie v aprel', 1962) about a young, nonconformist journalist. The elegiac *Last Month of Autumn* (Ultima luna de toamna/Poslednii mesiats oseni, 1965), from Ion Druta's screenplay, about an old peasant who says farewell to life, became a national and international critical success. *Knight of Dream* (Cavalerul viselor/Rytsar' mechty, 1967), a biopic about fantasy writer Aleksandr Grin (1880–1932), skillfully juxtaposes the shabbiness of reality and the loftiness of noble imagination.

After leaving Moldova, Derbenev specialized on effectively visualized ballet pictures (*The Ballerina*/Balerina, 1969; *Spartacus*/Spartak, 1975). Back in Moldova, he directed two suspenseful tales adapted from British novels: *The Woman in White* (Femeia in alb/Zhenshchina v belom, 1982) from Wilkie Collins, and *The Secret of the Black Thrush* (Taina chernykh drozdov, 1984) from Agatha Christie. He landed a hit with the social thriller *The Snake Catcher* (Smeelov, 1985), produced at **Mosfilm Studio**, and made a contribution to the perestroika discourse on tabooed aspects of the past with *The Black Corridor* (Chernyi koridor, 1988) from a Vladimir Tendriakov novella. In the 1990s, Derbenev continued to make thrillers, ballet films, and **documentaries** on cultural subjects but without achieving the visual and psychological intensity and originality of his 1960s pictures.

In 1962–1969, Derbenev headed the Moldovan Filmmakers' Union. He was named Merited Artist of the Moldavian SSR in 1962 and People's Artist of Russia in 1994.

Other films: *On the Ruler's Trace* (Po sledu vlastelina, 1980); *The Queen of Spades* (Pikovaia dama, 1972, TV); *Hunt for a Souteneur* (Okhota na sutenera, 1990); *Coppelia* (1993). *See also* MOLDO-VAN CINEMA.

DOCUMENTARY. The documentary genre dates back to the very beginning of filmmaking in Russia; the first screenings in May 1896 were followed by a rapidly growing production of newsreels documenting current events—the imperial family, military parades, appearances of celebrities, visits of foreign dignitaries, and picturesque views of Russian cities. Among the earliest regular producers of nonfiction films were **Aleksandr Drankov** and **Aleksandr Khanzhonkov**. Initially, the genre was valued both for its sensational footage—such as natural disasters—and educational usefulness. However, documentary films increasingly addressed Russia's multifaceted social reality, including aspects such as the life of the homeless. During World War I, newsreel and documentary production was heavily censored by the so-called Skobelev Committee and played a largely propagandistic role.

Following the 1917 February Revolution, the Moscow Council of Workers and Soldiers Deputies founded a film department charged with documenting the ongoing political changes; a similar decision was made by the Skobelev Committee in Petrograd, authorizing cameramen to film demonstrations and political leaders. On 1 June 1918, the first issue of *Film Week* (Kinonedelia), a regular newsreel almanac, was released under the supervision of the Moscow Film Committee (kinokomitet). Directed by **Dziga Vertov**, its main focus was Vladimir Lenin; the cameramen who had a rare chance to film the Soviet leader—**Aleksandr Lemberg**, Grigorii Giber (1891–1951), **Eduard Tissé**, **Aleksandr Levitskii**—were later recognized by the Communist government, while their footage was elevated to a quasi-hagiographic status. Lenin realized the political potency of the new medium; in a conversation with **Anatolii Lunacharskii** he made his subsequently canonized remark about cinema being "the most important of all arts for the Bolsheviks," specifically referring to documentaries that could reflect reality in a Communist spirit. He also demanded that all feature film screenings be preceded by news-reels and educational documentaries.

Given the scarcity of celluloid material in the first years after the Bolshevik Revolution, working in the newsreel branch presented one of the rare opportunities for filmmakers to learn and practice their craft. Inevitably, the aesthetics of the newsreel documentary with its gritty authenticity and perceived factual irrefutability made an impact on the style of the Soviet avant-garde. **Lev Kuleshov** included docu-mentary footage in his lighthearted **comedy** *The Unusual Adventures of Mr. West in the Land of the Bolsheviks* (Neobychainye prikliuche-niia mistera Vesta v strane bol'shevikov, 1924). **Sergei Eizenshtein** stylized key episodes of his *Strike* (Stachka, 1924), *Battleship Po-temkin* (Bronenosets Potemkin, 1925), and especially *October* (aka *Ten Days That Shook the World*/Oktiabr'/Desiat' dnei, kotorye potri-asli mir, 1927) in documentary-like shot composition and montage, which in later years gave these sequences a quasi-documentary va-lidity for Soviet propaganda. The high esteem in which documentary film production was held resulted in the creation of a "film factory" specializing in newsreels, Soviet Newsreel (Soiuzkinokhronika).

The most influential practitioner and theorist of nonfiction film in the 1920s was Dziga Vertov. Driven by the ambition to define and create genuinely Communist cinema, Vertov and his group (**Elizaveta Svilova**, Mikhail Kaufman, **Il'ia Kopalin**, among others) searched for methods to increase the political effectiveness of the documentary genre, moving beyond a simple chronicling of events. The monthly news almanacs *Cine-Truth* (Kino-Pravda, begun in 1922), which consisted of various "stories," were crafted along the lines of leading Soviet newspapers, especially *Pravda*. Vertov's de-clared ultimate goal was to replace the need for fictional film, which he denounced as reactionary and unbecoming both to the medium and "new" Soviet audiences. His feature-length documentaries such as *Forward, Soviet!* (Shagai, Soviet! 1926), *One Sixth of the World* (Shestaia chast' mira, 1926), and *The Eleventh* (Odinnadtsatyi, 1928) must be understood in this context—as a new form of film experience that put "truth" above entertainment. Indeed, Vertov's silent masterpiece *Man with the Movie Camera* (Chelovek s kinoapparatom, 1929), the most perfect realization of his concepts, graces nonfiction filmmaking with philosophical depth and a visual-rhythmic beauty that goes far beyond newsreel factuality or Communist propaganda.

Vertov's colleague **Esfir' Shub** demonstrated the power of montage by assembling premade documentary footage into a new narrative, working with strong contrasts and within stringent ideological parameters. Her feature-length *The Fall of the Romanov Dynasty* (Padenie dinastii Romanovykh, 1927) and a number of follow-up pictures marked the emergence of a new genre, the compilation documentary. The exceptionally energetic and inventive **Aleksandr Medvedkin** organized a "film train" (*kinopoezd*), a mobile studio on wheels that from 1932 to 1934 undertook 12 trips to major construction sites of the first five-year plan in Ukraine, Kuban', Transcaucasia, and the Urals. The equipment mounted on the train enabled the crew to capture events on site and immediately develop and cut their materials, responding to the accelerated tempo of industrialization with an equal rapidity. Vertov's and Medvedkin's ideas, forgotten or denounced during the 1930s–1950s, became an inspiration in the 1960s to Western filmmakers such as Chris Marker and Jean-Luc Godard.

Vertov's relentless attempts to carry over innovative approaches into the sound era generated mixed reactions, from admiration and astonishment—mostly among leftist filmmakers abroad—to bewilderment and denunciation at home. One of his main goals was to not let sound undo the successfully accomplished emancipation from feature film; however, the realization of his ideas in *Enthusiasm* (Entuziazm, aka *Symphony of Donbass*/Simfoniia Donbassa, 1930) remained a largely quixotic gesture. Vertov's next picture, *Three Songs about Lenin* (Tri pesni o Lenine, 1934), although featuring the innovative inclusion of live interviews, was much more conventional, and his subsequent output became stylistically indistinct.

In the 1930s, a new generation of documentary filmmakers emerged: willing servants of the Soviet establishment whose claim to fame was the documentation of heroic deeds on the "labor front" without risking formal innovations or experimentation. Il'ia Kopalin, **Roman Karmen**, Iakov Posel'skii (1892–1951), and Mikhail

Slutskii (1907–1959) conveyed the pathos of forced industrialization, portraying "heroes of labor," grandiose industrial projects, and the struggle against nature—that ubiquitous enemy of the industrialization period. Other important themes of Soviet documentary filmmaking were the 1936–1939 Civil War in Spain, the revolution in China, the exploration of the Arctic, and the show trials of "enemies of the people." During this period, the harsh everyday reality of Soviet life was utterly purged from the screens. Documentaries had become a closely monitored ideological subgenre devoid of realism, subjective viewpoints, or aesthetic exploration.

The beginning of the Great Patriotic War in 1941 necessitated a logistical and aesthetic reorientation of documentary production. Newsreels were given undisputed priority over all other genres. Over 250 cameramen, including prominent filmmakers such as Medvedkin and Karmen, were drafted to help document the dramatic battles of Moscow, Stalingrad, and Kursk, as well as the activities of partisans behind the front lines. Kopalin's and Leonid Varlamov's (1907–1962) *The Defeat of the German Troops near Moscow* (Razgrom nemetskikh voisk pod Moskvoi, 1942) won their authors a Stalin Prize; when it was released in the United States as *Moscow Strikes Back*, it received an Academy Award as Best Documentary in 1943, the first such sign of distinction for any Soviet picture.

The Politburo of the Communist Party decided that a number of accomplished feature film directors should be assigned the creation of feature-length documentaries depicting major episodes of the war. Thus, **Sergei Iutkevich**—who had prior experience in the documentary genre—made *Liberated France* (Osvobozhdennaia Frantsiia, 1944), **Iosif Kheifits** and **Aleksandr Zarkhi** compiled *The Defeat of Japan* (Razgrom Iaponii, 1945), while **Iulii Raizman** directed *On the Question of the Truce with Finland* (K voprosu o peremirii s Finliandiei, 1944) and *The Fall of Berlin* (1945). Narrative devices such as pathos and irony gave these films a stronger polemical edge and emotional impact than previous mainstream documentaries; **Aleksandr Dovzhenko**'s *The Battle for Our Soviet Ukraine* (Bitva za nashu sovetskuiu Ukrainu, 1943) with its unabashed emotional expressiveness is still considered a masterpiece. Leading feature film directors were assigned large-scale documentary projects in the postwar years as well, including **Sergei Gerasimov** (*Liberated China*/Osvobozhdennyi Kitai, 1951) and **Ivan Pyr'ev** (*We Are for Peace!*, aka *Friendship Triumphs*/My za mir, 1952, with Joris Ivens).

The moderate de-Stalinization of the 1950s left few traces in documentary filmmaking. However, the 1960s brought a veritable blossoming of this genre that led to distinct national phenomena such as the socially alert Riga Documentary School (Hertz Frank, Uldis Brauns, Ivars Seleckis) or the Kyrgyz "New Wave" that astonished international festival audiences with its uncompromising focus on native culture. Thus, **Bolotbek Shamshiev**'s shorts *Manaschi* (1965) and *The Shepherd* (Chaban, 1967) marked the beginning of a self-conscious **Kyrgyz cinema** that soon led to a string of masterpieces in feature film. Armenian director **Artavazd Peleshyan** gained notoriety with radical experiments, demonstrating that the formal potential of nonfiction cinema was far from being exhausted. Still, the majority of Soviet documentaries of the 1960s–1980s were run-of-the-mill propaganda that stayed clear of "unpresentable" aspects of reality and were perceived as a nuisance by regular moviegoers who had to suffer through them prior to every feature film. Karmen continued to travel to the world's hot spots, bringing home footage that was then molded into feature-length narratives about the left in Latin America, the "struggle for peace" in Western Europe, and other such topics. Medvedkin directed a number of remarkable anti-Maoist pamphlets whose unmistakable albeit indirect target was Stalinism.

It may well be that Medvedkin's passionate, sufficiently personal cinematic diatribes were an inspiration to similar experiments undertaken in the 1960s by **Mikhail Romm** and **Fridrikh Ermler**. Yet, while the former's ***Ordinary Fascism*** (aka *Triumph over Violence*/Obyknovennyi fashizm, 1965) became a fascinating lesson in political and media analysis, the latter's *To the Judgment of History* (Pered sudom istorii, 1965) shot itself in the foot, trying in vain to demonstrate the superiority of Communist ideology over the moderate, skeptical conservatism of its main subject, monarchist Vasilii Shul'gin. Other directors who tried their hands at documentaries—or found refuge in that genre—were **Grigorii Chukhrai** (*Memory*/Pamiat', 1970), **Sergei Paradjanov** (*Hakob Hovnatanyan*/Akop Ovnatanian, 1967), and **Arūnas Žebriūnas**. Filming visitors to the Hermitage with a hidden camera produced beautiful effects in *Look at the Face* (Vzglianite na litso, 1966) by Pavel Kogan (b. 1931) and Petr Mostovoi (b. 1938), capturing a rich variety of reactions to Leonardo da Vinci's "Madonna Litta."

Because documentary films were regarded as more politically sensitive than even feature films, the milieu in which they were produced was subject to thorough control by the Communist establishment. It took an outsider, Latvian **Jūris Podnieks**, to break through age-old walls of opportunism—his powerful *Is It Easy to Be Young?* (Vai viegli but jaunam?/Legko li byt' molodym? 1986) signaled the return of honesty to the documentary genre and inspired a series of increasingly radical nonfiction films dealing with the Soviet present and past. Particularly in the Baltic republics, documentaries became a tool of cultural and political emancipation that could react to the profound societal changes much more swiftly than feature films. In the Russian Federation, **Stanislav Govorukhin** turned Shub's montage techniques against the very Communist system that had inspired them, in his radical diatribes *One Cannot Live Like This* (Tak zhit' nel'zia, 1990) and *The Russia That We Have Lost* (Rossiia, kotoruiu my poteriali, 1992).

The post-Soviet 1990s yielded contradictory effects for the documentary genre. While state censorship was abolished, state funding also ran out. The large studios specializing in newsreels and propaganda documentaries lost their major clients and hence their financial backing. Most importantly, the distribution networks broke down, depriving traditional documentaries of their previous viewership. Television replaced cinema as the main market for nonfiction films, shaping their aesthetic parameters and thematic preferences. Leading documentary filmmakers such as Marina Goldovskaia (b. 1932) became independent, securing their funding through international coproductions. The documentary, once considered the most useful genre and all too often force-fed to millions of viewers, has been reduced to a guilty pleasure for connoisseurs and festival audiences.

DOGA, EUGENIU [some Russian sources list the first name and patronymic as Evgenii Dmitrievich] (b. 1 March 1937, Mocra, Ribnita). Moldovan composer. Doga studied at the Chisinau (Kishinev) School of Music in 1951–1955, at the Conservatory of Chisinau in 1955–1960, and at the Chisinau Institute for the Arts in 1960–1965. After working as a teacher of music for some years, he became a freelance artist in 1972. Doga made a name for himself with popular songs, symphonic music, and a ballet, *Morning Star* (Luceafarul, 1973). In the 1970s, he became the leading composer in **Moldovan cinema**.

Doga's first score was for the successful parabolic comedy *Gate-keeper Wanted* (Se cauta un paznic/Nuzhen privratnik, 1967), from Ion Creanga's story. His compositions for influential Moldovan filmmaker **Emil Loteanu** brought him nationwide renown: the melancholic gypsy romance *Fiddlers* (Lautarii/Lautary, 1972), the box-office sensation *The Tabor Leaves for Heaven* (aka *Queen of the Gypsies*/Tabor ukhodit v nebo, 1975), the peculiar Anton Chekhov adaptation *My Loving and Tender Beast* (aka *The Shooting Party*, aka *A Hunting Accident*/Moi laskovyi i nezhnyi zver', 1978), the internationally produced biopic *Anna Pavlova* (aka *The Divine Anna*, aka *Pavlova: A Woman for All Times*, 1983), and *The Morning Star* (Luceafarul, 1987, TV).

Doga predominantly worked with Moldovan directors, including **Valeriu Gajiu** on romanticized revolution stories such as *A Delayed-Action Explosion* (Explozie cu efect intirziat/Vzryv zamedlennogo deistviia, 1971), and with Nicolae Ghibu on the barely released psychological drama *I'll Find a Horseshoe for Luck* (Gaseste potcoava fericirii/Naidu na schast'e podkovu, 1983). Among the Russian directors with whom Doga cooperated repeatedly were **Samson Samsonov** (*Singles Will Get Dorm Space*/Odinokim predostavliaetsia obshchezitie, 1983, and other films) and **Georgii Natanson** (*Valentin i Valentina*, 1985), demonstrating a preference for contemporary subjects treated in a melodramatic fashion. A noteworthy exception is the Romanian-Soviet coproduction *Maria, Mirabella* (1982), a fairy tale combining **animation** and live action, by world-famous director Ion Popescu-Gopo (1923–1989). Doga also contributed the score to the last film of **Vytautas Žalakevičius**, the nightmarish *The Beast That Is Coming Out of the Water* (Zveris iseinantis is juros/Zver', vykhodiashchii iz moria, 1992). Most recently, he wrote the music to the Romanian-Moldovan-Russian art-house success *Procustean Bed* (Patul lui Procust/Prokrustovo lozhe, 2001), a peculiar meditation about love in Bucharest in the 1920s.

Doga, who joined the Communist Party in 1976, was named People's Artist of the Moldavian SSR in 1982 and People's Artist of the USSR in 1987. He won a USSR State Prize in 1984.

Other films: *Queen Margot* (Koroleva Margo, 1996, TV); *Dear Friend of Long Forgotten Years* (Milyi drug davno zabytykh let, 1996); *The Actress* (Artistka, 2007).

DOLIDZE, SIKO [Russian sources list the first name and patronymic as Semen Vissarionovich] (b. 6 February 1903, Ozurgeti–d. 17 June [other sources: July] 1983, Tbilisi). Georgian director and screenwriter. Dolidze studied history and philology at Tbilisi State University, graduating in 1925, and joined the Georgian State Film Industry (Goskinprom) as an administrator and assistant director on the **documentary** *The Law of the Mountains* (Mtis kanoni/Zakon gor, 1928), among others. In 1928, Dolidze initiated the establishment of a Goskinprom office responsible for newsreel and documentary production and was put in charge of it. Together with **Giorgi Mdivani**, he wrote the script for the ill-fated anticorruption satire *My Grandmother* (Chemi bebia/Moia babushka, 1929), directed by Kote Miqaberidze.

Dolidze made his directorial debut with the short documentary *Call of the Soil* (Zov zemli, aka Na shturm zemli, 1929). Characteristic of the filmmaker's nonfictional works is his keen interest in the patriarchal lifestyle of mountain tribes, which he approaches in an ethnographic, descriptive manner. Dolidze's first feature film, *In the Country of Avalanches* (Zvavta mkhareshi/V strane obvalov, 1932), is the dramatic tale of an isolated mountain tribe in Pshavia, its cruel traditions and age-old laws. *The Last Crusaders* (Ukanaskneli djvarosnebi/Poslednie krestonostsy, 1934), about the tribe of Kheruvs, is an attack on anachronistic, sometimes deadly rules that ignite vicious circles of revenge and counterrevenge. Featuring Dolidze's typical directness, the film's didacticism and lack of psychological subtlety today are painfully obvious. Still, *The Last Crusaders* marks the screen debut of splendid actor **Sergo Zakariadze**, whose entire film career was closely intertwined with that of Dolidze.

By critical consent, *Dariko* (1937), freely adapted from stories by Georgian classic author Egnate Ninoshvili, is Dolidze's best film. The tale of a shy peasant girl in the 19th century who grows up to become the leader of an uprising of the poor against landowners successfully combines folklore and social analysis. In the post-Stalinist period, Dolidze returned to the topic of women's emancipation with the lighthearted contemporary musical *The Dragonfly* (Chrichina/ Strekoza, 1954, from a play by M. Baratashvili), which became a huge box-office success throughout the Soviet Union. *Day Last, Day First* (Dge pirveli, dge ukanaskueli/Den' poslednii, den' pervyi, 1960) tells the story of a retiring mail carrier who introduces the inhabitants of a village to his successor.

Dolidze is one of the founders of **Georgian cinema**. For almost two decades, he was the head of the Georgian Filmmakers' Union (1957–1976) and, by many accounts, responsible for the politically and aesthetically stifling activities of that organization. His daughter Ketevan (Keti) Dolidze (b. 1945) is a filmmaker and political activist; she codirected her father's last two pictures, *Is He a Human Being?* (Katsia-Adamiani?/Chelovek li on? 1980) and the tragic prewar story *Kukaracha* (1983).

Dolidze, who joined the Communist Party in 1941, was honored with the title People's Artist of the USSR in 1965. In 1950, he won a First-Class Stalin Prize for *Jurgai's Shield* (Jurgais pari/Shchit Dzhurgaia, 1944, codirected with **Davit Rondeli**), a concert film.

Other films: *Soviet Georgia* (Sovetskaia Gruziia, 1950, doc., with Rondeli); *Encounter with the Past* (Shekhvedra tsarsultan/Vstrecha s proshlym, 1966); *The City Awakens Early* (Qalaqi adre igvidzebs/ Gorod prosypaetsia rano, 1967).

DOLIN, BORIS GENRIKHOVICH (b. 2 August 1903, Sumy, Ukraine–d. 23 November 1976, Moscow). Russian director and screenwriter. After studying law at Khar'kov University in 1919–1921, Dolin enrolled in the film school of **Boris Chaikovskii** in Petrograd, graduating in 1926 as a cinematographer. He joined the laboratory of biologist and microscope film pioneer Vladimir Lebedev (1882–1951), filming silent shorts such as *A Culture of Tissue* (Kul'tura tkani, 1931), *Monocellular Organisms* (Odnokletochnye organizmy, 1932), and *Algae* (Vodorosli, 1935).

After Lebedev's laboratory was turned into a large-scale studio for research and popular science films, Dolin directed **documentaries**, debuting with *Bacteria* (Bakterii, 1936). *In the Depths of the Sea* (V glubinakh moria, 1938, codirected with **Aleksandr Zguridi**) was two years in the making. *The Law of Great Love* (Zakon velikoi liubvi, 1945) analyzes a behavioral peculiarity among animals who grant protection to other's offspring when those lose their parents; it was the first Soviet scientific documentary with a coherent narrative structure and earned Dolin a Stalin Prize in 1946. *Along Animals' Path* (Zverinoi tropoi, 1947) and *The Story of a Ring* (Istoriia odnogo kol'tsa, 1948)—the latter rewarded with another Stalin Prize in 1950—are considered Dolin's highest achievements in the nonfiction genre. However, *Man Follows the Trace* (Chelovek idet po sledu, 1951) about the breeding of sables in Siberia was harshly criticized in a *Pravda* article as "pseudoscientific."

In the mid-1950s, Dolin began to direct feature films for children, focusing on the interaction of juveniles with wild animals. In *Winged Defense* (Krylataia zashchita, 1953) children help endangered birds, while in *Loyal Hearts* (Vernye serdtsa, 1959) a ship is rescued with the help of tamed doves. These films, as well as *The Blind Bird* (Slepaia ptitsa, 1963) about a boy giving his all to restore a pelican's vision, were successful at home and abroad due to their apolitical nature and universal humanist message.

Dolin, along with Zguridi, is credited with founding Soviet biological cinema, a genre he himself defined as "hunting without shooting." The majority of his films are family fare with an unobtrusive, positive message of the need to respect and protect nature and to love animals.

Dolin was in charge of a workshop at the Soviet State Film School **VGIK**, where he began teaching in 1953 and was promoted to the rank of full professor in 1966. He was named People's Artist of the Russian Federation in 1958.

Other films: *Our Invisible Friends* (Nashi nevidimye druz'ia, 1940); *The New Attraction* (aka *A New Number Comes to Moscow*/ Novyi attraktsion, 1958); *King of the Mountains and Others* (Korol' gor i drugie, 1969).

DONSKOI, MARK SEMENOVICH [Samsonovich] (b. 6 March 1901, Odessa–d. 21 March 1981, Moscow). Russian director and scriptwriter. Born into a poor Jewish stove-fitter's family, Donskoi left home at 15 and worked as a professional boxer, among other jobs. During the Civil War he was imprisoned for 10 months by White Army units in the Crimea. He later studied psychiatry and law at Simferopol' University, graduating in 1925, and worked as a criminal investigator and defense lawyer. Also in 1925, Donskoi published *The Inmates* (Zakliuchennye), a volume of stories about his experiences as a prisoner. When his film script *The Last Stronghold* (Poslednii oplot), about the Crimean Bolshevik underground movement, received a favorable review from the Third Moscow Film Factory, Donskoi devoted himself completely to cinema, first as an assistant director to **Grigorii Roshal'**, then as an editor at Belgoskino (**Belarusfilm Studio**).

Donskoi's first directorial effort, the experimental short *Life* (Zhizn', 1927), revealed some stylistic daring, but the director subsequently dissociated himself from all avant-garde trends. He made the anti-NEP films *In the Big City* (V bol'shom gorode, 1928) about a peasant poet, and *The Price of a Human Being* (Tsena cheloveka, 1929), both codirected by Mikhail Averbakh (1904–1980). At Vostokfilm studio, Donskoi shot his first sound picture, *The Song of Happiness* (Pesnia o schast'e, 1934, codirected with Vladimir Legoshin [1904–1954]), a coming-of-age story about a boy from the Mari people, a national minority in the Volga region to whom the Communist regime provided education and industrial development. This film marked the beginning of Donskoi's long-standing interest in the themes of multinationalism and pedagogy.

Donskoi earned lasting critical and popular recognition with his adaptation of Maksim Gor'kii's autobiographical trilogy, **Gor'kii's Childhood** (Detstvo Gor'kogo, 1938), *Among People* (V liudiakh, 1939), and *My Universities* (Moi universitety, 1940). Although on the surface a fictionalized biopic that primarily focuses on the young writer's growing social awareness, Donskoi's genuine artistic achievement lies in the re-creation of the oppressive, philistine merchant milieu in pre-Bolshevik Russia. The film's episodes alternate claustrophobic interiors with vast romantic Volga landscapes that evoke a longing for freedom and social change. Capturing atmosphere through telling details and blending them with a gallery of memorable characters—in particular, the boy's wise, loving grandmother—later served as an inspiration to Italian neorealism and to Satyajit Ray, and secured Donskoi's status as a classic of world cinema. Notably, after the international success of the Gor'kii trilogy, Donskoi's oeuvre received far more critical attention abroad—especially in France—than in the Soviet Union itself.

Parts 1 and 2 of the Gor'kii trilogy were considered superior to the third installment; in 1941, they earned Donskoi his first Stalin Prize. During the Great Patriotic War, he directed the tragic master-piece *The Rainbow* (Raduga, 1943, based on Wanda Wasilewska's novella). This story of a Ukrainian peasant woman who joins the partisans but returns to her village to give birth and is captured, tor-tured, and executed by the German invaders, visualizes Nazi cruelty with passionate directness and shocked audiences worldwide. *The Undefeated* (Nepokorennye, 1945), an artistically remarkable adap-tation of a Boris Gorbatov novel, depicts the holocaust in Ukraine, including the Baby Yar massacre, which was rarely if ever mentioned by Soviet officialdom.

Donskoi then abandoned tragedy for idyll in his hugely popular *The Country Teacher* (Sel'skaia uchitel'nitsa, 1947), which betrays characteristic features of the newly postulated "theory of conflictless-ness." **Vera Maretskaia**, creating a role model for generations to come, displays genuine motherly warmth and believably embodies the pedagogical devotion that endears her to her pupils. But the plot smoothes over any meaningful disagreement or conflict and gives the entire film a rather bland appearance.

Donskoi was a lifelong staunch political dogmatic who even joined the anti-Semitic campaign "against cosmopolitanism" in 1948–1949, publicly denouncing fellow filmmakers such as **Sergei Iutkevich**. It is telling that he did not contribute to the Thaw period following Iosif Stalin's death. Instead, he demonstratively returned to Gor'kii's class struggle tales with the faithful adaptations *The Mother* (aka *1905*/Mat', 1956) and *Foma Gordeev* (1959). The former, which had to compete with **Vsevolod Pudovkin**'s silent classic, has indubitable merits; the latter is one of Donskoi's psychologically and visually most convinc-ing works, a masterpiece that has undeservedly been forgotten.

In the last two decades of his career, Donskoi's unshakeable faith in the Communist mission turned him into an anachronism, respected for his earlier achievements yet hardly taken seriously by the new generation of cinematic innovators who viewed him as a Communist holy fool—a notion that was supported by Donskoi's famously ec-centric behavior. The sentimental dilogy about Vladimir Lenin and his mother, *Heart of a Mother* (Serdtse materi, 1966) and *Devotion of a Mother* (Vernost' materi, 1967), is symptomatic of Donskoi's artistic decline. A fascinating project about legendary émigré singer Fedor Shaliapin, long in the planning stage, never came to fruition. Another Lenin biopic, *Nadezhda* (1973), about Lenin's wife, and a final Gor'kii adaptation, *The Spouses Orlov* (Suprugi Orlovy, 1978), were disconcerting testimony to Donskoi's waning creativity.

Donskoi often worked with first-rate cinematographers who realized his poetic vision, among them **Sergei Urusevskii**, Boris Monastyrskii (1903–1977), and **Margarita Pilikhina**. He was a mentor to Senegalese filmmaker Sembène Ousmane (1923–2007), one of Africa's most accomplished directors. Donskoi's reputation as a champion of poetic realism and a revolutionary romantic rests on his Gor'kii adaptations and his war films; **Sergei Paradjanov** and **Grigorii Chukhrai**, among others, were influenced by this part of his legacy.

The director joined the Communist Party in 1945; he was awarded the title People's Artist of the USSR in 1966 and Hero of Socialist Labor in 1971. In 1984, Chukhrai made a feature-length **documentary** about Donskoi, *I'll Teach You to Dream* (Ia nauchu vas mechtat'). Donskoi's wife, Irina Donskaia, was the coauthor of several of his scripts. The house in Moscow where Donskoi lived from 1974 to 1981 (Bol'shoi Kozikhinskii pereulok, 27) carries a memorial plaque.

Other films: *Alien Shore* (Chuzhoi bereg, 1930); *Fire* (Ogon', 1931); *How the Steel Was Tempered* (aka *Heroes Are Made*/Kak zakalialas' stal', 1942); *Alitet Leaves for the Mountains* (Alitet ukhodit v gory, 1949); *At High Cost* (aka *The Horse That Cried*/Dorogoi tsenoi, 1957).

DORONINA, TAT'IANA VASIL'EVNA (b. 12 September 1933, Leningrad). Russian actress. Doronina studied at the studio school of the Moscow Art Theater (MKhAT), graduating in 1956. Her rise to stardom took her from the theater of Volgograd (1956–1959), to the Gor'kii Grand Drama Theater in Leningrad (1959–1966), to MKhAT (1966–1971) and the Maiakovskii Theater in Moscow (1971–1983). In 1983, Doronina rejoined the troupe of the Moscow Art Theater and became one of the driving forces behind the troupe's split into a Chekhov and a Gor'kii MKhAT; she has been chief director of the latter since 1986.

Doronina made her movie debut in 1956 in **Mikhail Kalatozov**'s inspirational drama about the cultivation of unseeded lands in

Kazakhstan ("virgin soil"), *The First Echelon* (Pervyi eshelon). Following several supporting parts, **Georgii Natanson** entrusted the actress with the lead in the contemporary melodrama *The Older Sister* (Starshaia sestra, 1966), a critical and box-office success. Doronina's performance as the simple but emotionally rich peasant woman Niura in **Tat'iana Lioznova**'s love story *"Three Poplars" at Pliushchikha* ('Tri topolia' na Pliushchikhe, 1967) made her the female idol of a generation—indeed, the chemistry between her and costar **Oleg Efremov** was so convincing that the film's title became forever associated with their names. Natanson capitalized on this success in another romantic melodrama starring Doronina, *One More Time about Love* (Eshche raz pro liubov', 1967), a huge hit with viewers if not critics.

Doronina solidified her popularity with the superhit *The Stepmother* (Machekha, 1973), a family melodrama. With 60 million viewers, it marked the peak of her box-office draw; later attempts to repeat this film's success with similar stories—for example, in *The Drop* (Kapel', 1981)—failed, and the actress largely withdrew from cinema. Doronina's screen image of a strong-willed yet secretly sensitive woman probably had lost its mass appeal. Her egotistical and provocative public behavior as a self-proclaimed cultural activist, legitimized by her position as the leader of the patriotic, nostalgically pro-Soviet half of MKhAT, regularly makes news.

Doronina was named People's Artist of the USSR in 1981.

Other films: *Toward the Clear Fire* (Na iasnyi ogon', 1975); *Valentin and Valentina* (1985).

DOVLATYAN, FRUNZE [some Russian sources list the patronymic Vaginakovich] (b. 26 May 1927, Nor Boyazet [now: Gavar], Armenia–d. 30 August 1997, Yerevan). Armenian director, scriptwriter, and actor. Dovlatyan's career began on the stage of the Azizbek Regional Theater in 1941. In 1944, he joined the troupe of the Sundukyan Theater of Yerevan, simultaneously studying at the affiliated studio school from which he graduated in 1947. The actor's theatrical achievements earned him a Stalin Prize in 1950.

Dovlatyan's film career started with supporting roles in **Hamo Bek-Nazaryan**'s historical epic *David Bek* (1944) and the fairy tale *Anahit* (1947). In 1952, Dovlatyan left the stage and enrolled in

Sergei Gerasimov's and **Tamara Makarova**'s workshop at the Soviet State Film School **VGIK** to become a filmmaker. Upon graduation in 1959, he stayed in Moscow, making his directorial debut with the optimistic contemporary melodrama *Dima Gorin's Career* (Kar'era Dimy Gorina, 1959). Equally successful was the artistically superior drama *Morning Trains* (Utrennie poezda, 1963); both films were codirected with Lev Mirskii (b. 1925). After returning to Armenia, Dovlatyan made *Hello, It's Me* (Barev, yes em/Zdravstvui, eto ia, 1966), a bittersweet story of friendship, loyalty, and love during the Great Patriotic War and the vivid memories of those who survived; the film brought the director critical and popular recognition.

Dovlatyan's subsequent pictures betray an interest in philosophical and historical issues, emphasizing the continuity between past and present. *A Chronicle of Yerevan Days* (Yerevanyan oreri khronikan/Khronika erevanskih dnei, 1974) tells the story of an archivist who feels responsible for everybody around him. Existential questions are the focus of *Live Long* (Apretseq yerkar/Zhivite dolgo, 1980) about a woman who must confront her life after learning that she suffers from a terminal disease.

The openly controversial *A Lonely Nut-Tree* (Menavur enkouzeni/Odinokaia oreshina, 1987) shows Dovlatyan in full form. He plays a teacher who digs more and more deeply into the history of his native mountain village, discovering that the Stalinist decades are still painfully alive in the minds of his fellow villagers. Dovlatyan's last picture, *The Yearning* (Karot/Toska, 1990; begun by **Henrik Malyan**), is the tragic story of a peasant who was forced to flee his homeland after the genocide of 1915. In the 1930s, driven by nostalgia and the duty to visit his parents' graves, he crosses the Soviet border, only to be arrested and deported to Siberia.

Dovlatyan, who joined the Communist Party in 1951, held important positions in the Union of Armenian Filmmakers and headed **Armenfilm Studio** (Hayfilm) in 1988–1992. He was named People's Artist of the Armenian SSR in 1969 and People's Artist of the USSR in 1983. His son Mikael Dovlatyan (b. 1958) is an actor and filmmaker who appeared in several of his father's films and in turn cast him in some of his own. At the international film festival Golden Apricot held in Yerevan, a "Frunze Dovlatyan Award *Hope*" is bestowed annually.

Other films: (as actor) *The Brothers Saroyan* (Saroyan yeghbayr-nere/Brat'ia Saroiany, 1968, codirected with **Khoren Abramyan**); *Labirinthe* (Labirintos/Labirint, 1994); (as director) *The Birth* (Yerkunq/Rozhdenie, 1977). *See also* ARMENIAN CINEMA.

DOVZHENKO, ALEKSANDR PETROVICH [in some sources first name and patronymic are transliterated as Oleksandr Petrovych] (b. 11 September 1894, Sosnytsy, Chernigov [Chernihiv] district, Ukraine–d. 25 November 1956, Moscow). Ukrainian director and screenwriter. Dovzhenko was born into a family of poor, illiterate, and pious peasants. One of two surviving children of a total of 14, in 1911 he enrolled in the Teachers' Institute in the town of Glukhov (Hlukhiv) where his interest in politics and Ukrainian national independence arose. Following graduation in 1914, Dovzhenko taught sciences and sports at a gymnasium in Zhytomir and in 1917 in Kiev. After a brief period of support for the nationalist Petliura, Dovzhenko embraced socialist ideologies, joining the Borot'bist Party in 1919, which advocated an independent Ukraine. (By some accounts, he joined the Communist Party and fought in the Civil War in 1919–1920.) Between 1918 and 1921, he was also active in the People's Commissariat of Education (Narkompros) of Ukraine. In 1921, Dovzhenko joined the diplomatic mission of the Ukrainian Soviet Socialist Republic in Warsaw; the following year, he became secretary of the trade commission of the Ukrainian consulate in Berlin. In 1923, he studied painting in Munich and Berlin with Erich Heckel, supported by a government grant. In 1923–1926, he worked as a cartoonist in Khar'kov (Khar'kiv)—then the capital of Ukraine—and wrote his first screenplay, *Heroes* (Heroi, 1926).

In 1926, Dovzhenko began a full-blown career in **Ukrainian cinema**. His debut at Odessa film studio was the satirical **comedy** *Vasia the Reformer* (Vasia-reformator), featuring a mild critique of the New Economic Policy (NEP), followed by the short comedy *Little Love Berry* (Yahidka kokhannia/Iagodka liubvi) and the thriller *The Pouch of the Diplomatic Courier* (Sumka dipkur'era, 1927), which deals with the "internationalist" underground work of a Soviet diplomatic mission.

With *Zvenigora* (Zvenyhora, 1928), "a panorama of Ukrainian history from the Scythians to the present" and officially presented as a contribution to celebrate the 10th anniversary of the October Revolution, Dovzhenko established his own voice in cinema. The unique blend of revolutionary spirit, folklore, and vitalist mysticism revealed a self-conscious stylistic and thematic approach, distinctly different from the multifaceted Russian avant-garde of **Sergei Eizenshtein**, **Vsevolod Pudovkin**, **Dziga Vertov**, and **Abram Room**. The uncompromising director created a vision of his motherland and its historical transformations that was both solemn and passionate, indulging in a narrative rhythm less explicitly propagandistic than hypnotic. Motifs of universal connectedness—between generations across centuries, between man and nature, and between the nation and its myths—dominate over the factual concreteness of the Civil War. Dovzhenko's surefooted direction engages in aesthetic and philosophical complexity and refuses to give in to mainstream conventions. The unabashed pathos and over-the-top emotional vigor of his film astonished and sometimes alienated viewers at home and abroad, although the director's unique creative power was too obvious to be doubted.

In 1929, Dovzhenko made *Arsenal* about the six-day strike on the Arsenal arms factory in Kiev in January 1918 that was directed against the Petliura administration and the troops of the Central Rada. Dovzhenko continued to experiment with syncretic forms, mixing realistic episodes with allegorical elements in his exploration of the meaning of Ukraine's history. The mythical character of Timosh, who fleetingly appeared in *Zvenigora*, is shown to be immortal, surviving exploitation and violence in various epochs. *Arsenal* also brought out Dovzhenko's satirical gift, especially in his caricatures of bourgeois nationalists and Tsar Nikolai II. The cameraman was **Danylo Demutskii**, who greatly enhanced the visual power of this and subsequent films.

Earth (Zemlia, 1930), by general consensus Dovzhenko's most accomplished picture and one of the crowning achievements of Soviet silent cinema, is an unprecedented tour de force. Although primarily dealing with the transition of individual farming to collectivization and the sabotage of that process by wealthy peasants, the film's most powerful dimension is its praise of the rural world. Unlike other Soviet films, *Earth* depicts peasant culture as a dignified, harmonious, sensual entity in tune with universal cycles of life and death.

No other film expressed the symbiosis of natural and societal life in such pathos-filled cinematic language. In *Earth*, collectivization is interpreted as a quasi-natural process emerging from the depth of the community, an inevitable step in social evolution. The film's drastic humor and shocking erotic candor were perceived as provocations in an increasingly prudish atmosphere in the Soviet Union; not surprisingly, several episodes were cut. In the year of *Earth*'s release, 1930, the first hostile campaign against Dovzhenko was initiated with an article by poet Dem'ian Bednyi in the newspaper *Pravda*.

In 1932, Dovzhenko completed his first sound film, *Ivan*. The name of the title character points to his rank-and-file status: a simple peasant lad who joins the gigantic construction site of the Dnepr Hydroelectric plant (Dneproges) where he undergoes a spectacular transformation from peasant to class-conscious worker and member of the Communist Party. The film was shot in Ukrainian, a daring choice given the increasing suspicions of nationalism raised against the director.

Dovzhenko's move to Moscow in 1934 has been explained as an escape from anti-Ukrainian repressions. But it was Dovzhenko himself who publicly disagreed with A. Lebedev's categorization of his work under the rubric of "national cinematography"; rather, Dovzhenko responded, he wished to be seen as an all-Soviet artist. Iosif Stalin apparently had high hopes for the director, assigning him topics for films and closely scrutinizing his output in the following two decades. The anti-individualistic *Aerograd* (aka *Air City*, aka *Frontier*, 1935), a coproduction between **Mosfilm Studio** and Ukrainfilm about the building of a new city on the shore of the Pacific Ocean, can be understood as a reaction to the criticism launched against *Ivan*. In typical 1930s paranoid fashion, Dovzhenko shows a world populated with saboteurs and formerly rich farmers who dream of returning to the old tsarist order. The central character, Glushak, named "killer of tigers," has an instinct to spot animals as well as "enemies of the people." Yet, despite its romantic ambience and passionate pro-Soviet spirit, the film flopped badly.

Stalin then suggested the topic of a "Ukrainian Chapaev," Mykola Shchors (1895–1919). *Shchors* (1939, codirected with **Iuliia Solntseva**) portrays the legendary Civil War hero who stands for the proclaimed principles of Soviet-style leadership, blending love for his people and strategic intelligence, Communist conviction and romantic affection for native nature. *Shchors* was popular with viewers and stabilized Dovzhenko's position in Soviet cinema; the director was rewarded with a Stalin Prize in 1941. In 1940, he helmed the **documentary** *Liberation* (Osvobozhdenie) about the incorporation of Western Ukraine in the USSR.

During the Great Patriotic War, Dovzhenko worked as a newspaper correspondent and directed documentaries; his first completed effort, *The Battle for Our Soviet Ukraine* (Bitva za nashu Sovetskuiu Ukrainu, 1943), was appreciated by the Communist establishment. However, the script of *Ukraine on Fire* (Ukraina v ohni/Ukraina v ogne, 1943), which focuses on the martyrdom of Ukrainians and alludes to the initial failure of the Red Army to adequately respond to the Nazi invaders, was harshly criticized by Stalin. Its modified version, *The Chronicle of the Flaming Years* (Povist polum'iannykh lit/Povest' plamennykh let), was rejected as well.

Dovzhenko's last completed project was *Michurin* (1949) from his own play, *A Life in Bloom* (Zhyttia v tsvitu/Zhizn' v tsvetu, 1946). This biopic about a canonized horticulturist, Ivan Michurin (1855–1935), was the result of a lengthy, torturous process spanning several years filled with petty criticism and endless revisions. The film was the subject of internal fights in the Communist establishment that viewed questions of species variability and hybridization as central to its dogma. The result was visually interesting—the cameraman, **Leonid Kosmatov**, was a master of color cinematography—but philosophically naïve, even demagogical in its implied affirmation of Trofim Lysenko's pernicious campaigns against genetics. In 1950, Dovzhenko began to work on *Good-bye, America* (Proshchai, Amerika) about a defector from the U.S. embassy in Moscow who embraces the Soviet system. It bears little resemblance to any of his other pictures, except the 1927 diplomatic thriller. A dull product of the Cold War, mixing Soviet hypocrisy and paranoia, its production was stopped without explanation in 1951; only in 1996 was a remastered version with added commentaries released.

Dovzhenko, a forceful myth creator, left behind a complex oeuvre that can be interpreted in a purely pro-Soviet framework, or extrapolated in a wider philosophical perspective. His continuing attempt to blend the forms and sensitivities of age-old Eastern Ukrainian culture with Soviet values seems quixotic after the silent period, but his relentlessness and passion were encouraging examples for individualistic filmmakers such as **Sergei Paradjanov** and **Andrei Tarkovskii**. Dovzhenko's peculiar cinematic poetics implies the compatibility of eternal living nature with modern technology and industry, of patriarchal relations with Soviet collectivism, of atheism with pantheistic awe of a higher power, and of passionate love for the Ukrainian nation with an internationalism bordering on pacifism.

Dovzhenko's second wife was actress and director Iuliia Solntseva, whom he married in 1927; after his passing, Solntseva devoted her life to her husband's legacy, carrying out several projects from unrealized screenplays.

Dovzhenko was honored with the title Merited Artist of Ukrainian SSR in 1940 and People's Artist of the RSFSR in 1950; he was awarded a posthumous Lenin Prize for the screenplay to *Poem of the Sea* (Poema o more, 1958) in 1959. Dovzhenko taught at the Soviet State Film School **VGIK** in 1949–1951 and 1955–1956. The Kiev Film Studio was named after him in 1957. Dovzhenko is buried at Novodevich'e cemetery in Moscow. The house in which he lived since 1942, on Kutuzovskii prospekt 22, carries a memorial plaque.

Other films: *Native Land* (Rodnaia zemlia, 1946; doc.).

DOVZHENKO FILM STUDIO. The studio was founded in 1928 in Kiev (Kyiv) and initially named Kiev Studio of the All-Ukrainian Photo-Cinema Administration (VUFKU).

The roots of filmmaking in Ukraine go back to 1896, when photographer Al'fred Fedetskii began shooting newsreels in Khar'kov (Khar'kiv). In 1907, the first Ukrainian feature film, *Kochubei in the Dungeon* (Kochubei v temnitse) was shot. Between 1911 and 1914, the projectionist D. Sakhnenko in Ekaterinoslav (Katerynoslav) made a number of silent features on subjects such as *Natalka-Poltavka*, from a popular play, and the historical drama *Bohdan Khmelnytskyi*. In 1919, all film theaters and studios in Ukraine were nationalized and put under the command of the Commissariat of Enlightenment (Narkompros). An All-Ukrainian Film Committee was established in Khar'kov, overseeing the production of so-called *agitki*, fictional propaganda shorts of which several dozen were churned out in 1919–1921. VUFKU was founded in 1922 and comprised several studios, most prominently in Yalta and Odessa, where private film production had begun in the 1910s. In 1923, VUFKU invited émigré director **Petr Chardynin**—in a similar fashion as **Mezhrabpomfilm Studio** invited **Iakov Protazanov** back home—to direct silent feature films with national subject matter (*Taras Shevchenko*, 1926; *Taras Triasilo*, 1927, and a dozen others). Georgii Tasin (1896–1956) and Georgii Stabavoi (1894–1968) also directed some noteworthy Ukrainian silents. The country's most famous film actor was **Amvrosii Buchma**, who would later play a leading role in the Ukrainian film industry. Prominent Russian avant-gardist **Dziga Vertov** found temporary shelter at VUFKU's Kiev studio, completing his silent film essay *Man with the Movie Camera* (Chelovek s kinoapparatom, 1929) and the controversial sound experiment *Enthusiasm* (Entuziazm, aka *Symphony of Donbass*/Simfoniia Donbassa, 1930).

In 1930, the studio was renamed Ukrainfilm; in 1939 it was changed to Kiev Film Studio. It attracted artistic innovators such as **Ivan Kavaleridze**, whose *Hard Rain* (Liven', 1929) was the first of a group of radical mise-en-scène experiments that enthused cineastes but disturbed dogmatic cultural bureaucrats. The most important Ukrainian filmmaker, **Aleksandr Dovzhenko**, who directed the silent masterpiece *Earth* (Zemlia, 1930) at the newly built Kiev studio, found himself in a similar situation—celebrated by film buffs but distrusted by Communist hacks. Dovzhenko and his congenial cameraman **Danylo Demutskii** developed a majestically slow yet passionate film language that was as steeped in national tradition as it was open to the changes brought about by the political transformations. The pathos conveyed by *Earth* as well as Dovzhenko's first sound picture, *Ivan* (1932), curiously blended sentimental affection for the country's nature with an unequivocal endorsement of industrialization and progress.

Popular humor, folklore, and a romanticized view of the working class and collectivist peasantry are characteristic of the films of **Ihor' Savchenko**, **Ivan Pyr'ev**, and **Leonid Lukov**. Pyr'ev's comedy *A Rich Bride* (aka *The Country Bride*/Bogataia nevesta, 1938) and Lukov's miner tale *A Great Life* (Bol'shaia zhizn', 1940) were pathbreaking, style-shaping impulses felt across the entire Soviet culture. The fact that Dovzhenko, Pyr'ev, Savchenko, and later Lukov left Ukraine for Moscow caused a serious artistic impoverishment in Ukrainian cinema. The "antinationalist" purges among Ukrainian intellectuals in the 1930s had an equally detrimental effect, while ideological charges against Kavaleridze first neutralized his films stylistically and later led to his departure from cinema altogether.

In 1941, after the beginning of the Great Patriotic War, the Kiev studio was evacuated to Central Asia (to Ashgabat, see **Turkmenfilm Studio**; to Tashkent, see **Uzbekfilm Studio**), where, despite enormous hardships, several feature films were completed, including the partisan tragedy *The Rainbow* (Raduga, 1943) by **Mark Donskoi**, starring Ukraine's leading actress, **Nataliia Uzhvii**. In the postwar years, Savchenko directed two large-scale prestige productions at Kiev Film Studio, the World War II epic *The Third Blow* (Tretii udar, 1948) and the biopic *Taras Shevchenko* (1950), the latter completed by his master class at the Soviet State Film School **VGIK**. The absence of Dovzhenko and other Ukrainian directors from Kiev became painfully obvious in the 1950s, with bland propaganda fare churned out by the likes of **Timofei Levchuk** dominating the output of a studio that, ironically, in 1957 was named after Aleksandr Dovzhenko.

A genuine cinematic revolution occurred in 1964 when Armenian-born **Sergei Paradjanov** gave back to **Ukrainian cinema** its national character with the mythologically inspired *Shadows of Forgotten Ancestors* (Tini zabutykh predkiv/Teni zabytykh predkov) from a novella by Mykhailo Kotsiubynsky. It helped an entire generation of filmmakers formulate their identity, which politically was either neutral or pro-Soviet, yet aesthetically unmistakably Ukrainian. The major representatives of Ukrainian poetic cinema were **Yury Il'enko**, **Ivan Mykolaichuk**, and **Leonid Osyka**. Il'enko in particular remained loyal to his teacher's controversial legacy and followed Paradjanov's stylistic breakthrough with complex masterpieces such as *White Bird with a Black Spot* (Nilyi ptakh z chornoiu oznakoiu/ Belaia ptitsa s chernoi otmetinoi, 1971). Even the brutal official harassment against Paradjanov in the 1970s failed to fully extinguish the spirit of national self-consciousness at Dovzhenko Film Studio.

Other noteworthy directors of Ukrainian cinema on the studio's staff were **Leonid Bykov**, a master of tragicomedies, and **Roman Balaian**, whose unusual literary adaptations and contemporary psychological dramas—most prominently *Flights in Dream and in Reality* (Polety vo sne i naiavu, 1982)—attracted millions of discriminating viewers throughout the USSR and considerably increased their home studio's prestige in the 1970s and 1980s. (**Kira Muratova**, another leading Ukrainian filmmaker, made her creative home at the Odessa Film Studio.)

Despite many setbacks, the Kiev studio has traditionally been open to technical experimentation and consistently developed equipment for the technological advancement of cinema, including sound film (**Aleksandr Shorin**'s *Shorinofon* in the late 1920s) and color film—it was in Kiev that **Nikolai Ekk** made the first Soviet literary adaptation in color, *The Fair of Sorochinsk* (Sorochinskaia iarmarka, 1939), from a Nikolai Gogol' story.

The legacy of the Dovzhenko Film Studio's first eight decades boasts an overall output of about 700 feature films. As a national monument, the studio has remained state owned, sharing the ups and downs of the Ukrainian economy in the 1990s and early 2000s. During those years, all too often salaries were not paid and the large studio halls stood empty. In 1996, the state budget for the needs of cinema was approximately 3.5 million griven (about US$700,000); in 2004, the budget was 19.5 million griven, of which, however, only 11.6 million (about US$2.1 million) were actually released; such amounts allow for a yearly production of two or three feature films. The studio's facilities are often rented by Russian film companies for miniseries and soap operas. A curious exception was *How the Steel Was Tempered*, an 18-part miniseries made for Chinese television from Nikolai Ostrovskii's inspirational Communist novel. Despite many changes, Ukraine's film industry continues to suffer from chronic ailments such as mismanagement and corruption. Thus, prominent new directors in Ukrainian cinema such as Oles Sanin and Taras Tomenko prefer to be independent from traditional entities such as Dovzhenko Film Studio.

DRANKOV, ALEKSANDR OSIPOVICH (b. 1880–d. 1949, San Francisco). Russian producer, cameraman, and director. Drankov, who hailed from a poor Jewish family and had no formal education, founded a photo studio in St. Petersburg together with his younger brother, Lev. After acquiring state-of-the-art equipment in London, Drankov was appointed foreign photo correspondent for the *London Illustrated News*, *L'Illustration*, and other publications. He also became an official photographer for the Russian parliament, the Duma, and for the tsar's court.

In 1907, Drankov announced the opening of the first cinematographic studio in Russia, and in February 1908 released 17 **documentaries**, each about five minutes long, on subjects such as celebrity funerals, life of the homeless, and picturesque views of Moscow and St. Petersburg. He later added shorts about the imperial family, natural disasters, the famine in the Volga region, and visits of foreign dignitaries. The famously entrepreneurial Drankov even secured Lev Tolstoi's consent to being filmed on his 80th birthday, resulting in a sensational film snippet that eventually became a priceless cultural document, tolerated in good humor by the world-famous author who showed genuine curiosity about the new medium.

Creatively responding to foreign competition, Drankov produced the first Russian feature, *Sten'ka Razin* (aka Ponizovaia vol'nitsa, 1908) after an earlier attempt to adapt *Boris Godunov* for the screen—with himself and his brother as cinematographers—remained incomplete. For the lead role in *Sten'ka Razin*, he hired Evgenii Petrov-Kraevskii, who specialized in tragic parts at the Petrograd People's House theater (Narodnyi dom) and later became a leading director in Drankov's studio.

Until 1912, Drankov produced both newsreels—usually with a sensational twist—and features. After 1912, in a joint venture with Aleksei Taldykin, he churned out almost exclusively feature films, including slapstick **comedies**, thrillers, and erotic dramas. The low artistic quality of his productions kept them out of prestigious movie theaters but satisfied less demanding viewers in the poor quarters of Russian cities and provinces. Among Drankov's hits were serials such as *Little Sonia, the Golden Hand* (Son'ka—zolotaia ruchka, 1914–1915), consisting of five films about the infamous criminal Sof'ia Bliuvshtein. His attempts to attract serious theater directors such as Konstantin Mardjanishvili (Mardzhanov) or Aleksandr Tairov failed since these artists found the producer's commercial priorities unacceptable.

One of Drankov's specialties were so-called disruptions (*sryvy*)—a crude method to outfox competitors by releasing an adaptation of the same literary work, or a movie with the same subject matter, just a week earlier. He often used it against producer **Aleksandr**

Khanzhonkov, a man of considerably higher erudition and taste who refused to distribute Drankov's output. Thus, in 1909, Drankov tried to disrupt Khanzhonkov's adaptation of Mikhail Lermontov's *Ballad of the Merchant Kalashnikov* (Pesn' o kuptse Kalashnikove), but Khanzhonkov proved faster, and it took Drankov three years before he was able to release his own made-on-the-cheap version. Drankov's shameless political opportunism, which allowed him to cater to liberal tastes while simultaneously seeking the tsar's favors, in 1916 resulted in the adaptation of Maksim Gor'kii's short story "Konovalov" under the title *Washed in Blood* (Omytye krov'iu). Because of its positive depiction of revolutionaries, the film was banned but later released to great acclaim under the title *A Drama from the Life of Grigorii Rasputin* (Drama iz zhizni Grigoriia Rasputina, 1917). Following the Bolshevik Revolution, Drankov celebrated leftist—to be exact, Social Revolutionary—causes in *The Grandmother of the Russian Revolution* (Babushka russkoi revoliutsii, 1918) and other exploitational fare.

In 1920, the still-wealthy Drankov fled to Constantinople and immigrated to the United States in 1922. According to Jay Leyda, in his later years Drankov operated a boardwalk café in Venice, California, and lived the remainder of his life as the owner of a small photo shop in San Francisco.

Film historians have expressed different views of Drankov's significance for the development of Russian cinema. Despite the fact that he was the country's first film producer, Semen Ginzburg found few redeeming qualities in Drankov and characterized him as a "typical movie business gangster." Rashit Iangirov formulated a more even-handed assessment of Drankov's achievements, stating that he applied aggressive methods typical of Hollywood to the Russian market.

DRUZHNIKOV, VLADIMIR VASIL'EVICH (b. 30 June [other sources: May] 1922, Moscow–d. 20 February 1994, Moscow). Russian actor. Druzhnikov, who performed at the Central Children's Theater in Moscow before embarking on a professional acting career, studied at the studio school of the Moscow Art Theater (MKhAT), graduating in 1945. He then joined the troupe of the Maiakovskii Theater in Moscow.

Druzhnikov's film debut was the part of Neznamov in **Vladimir Petrov**'s *Guilty without Guilt* (Bez viny vinovatye, 1945), from a play by Aleksandr Ostrovskii. His following roles furthered the image of a romantic, strong-willed idealist with manly good looks. This likeable but rather one-dimensional image proved particularly successful in **Ivan Pyr'ev**'s *The Tale of the Siberian Land* (aka *Symphony of Life*/Skazanie o zemle sibirskoi, 1948)—the portrayal of the patriotic composer Andrei Balashov shot Druzhnikov to national stardom and won him a Stalin Prize. The actor portrayed a larger-than-life war hero in **Vladimir Korsh-Sablin** and **Aleksandr Faintsimmer**'s *Konstantin Zaslonov* (aka *The Secret Brigade*/Kanstancin Zaslonau, 1949), which in 1950 earned him another Stalin Prize. He also became a familiar face in Stalinist historical pictures and biopics, including **Grigorii Roshal'**'s *Glinka* and **Mikhail Romm**'s dilogy *Admiral Ushakov* and *Ships Attack the Bastions* (aka *Attack from the Sea*/Korabli shturmuiut bastiony, 1953), as well as in political demagoguery such as **Mikhail Kalatozov**'s *Conspiracy of the Doomed* (Zagovor obrechennykh, 1950).

The qualities embodied by Druzhnikov were less in demand during the mid-1950s, although he found rewarding roles in literary adaptations such as **Samson Samsonov**'s *The Grasshopper* (Poprygun'ia, 1955) from Anton Chekhov's story in which he played the vain painter Riabovskii. However, the more Druzhnikov's screen image became an anachronism, the more his film roles were reduced to episodic parts, often of noble officers. Ironically, one of his last roles was that of a priest in a U.S. production, *Back in the USSR* (1992).

Druzhnikov was named People's Artist of the RSFSR in 1974.

Other films: *The Stone Flower* (Kamennyi tsvetok, 1946); *The Miners of Donetsk* (Donetskie shakhtery, 1950); *A Comrade's Honor* (Chest' tovarishcha, 1953); *Officers* (Ofitsery, 1971).

DUNAEVSKII, ISAAK OSIPOVICH [Iosifovich] (b. 30 January 1900, Lokhvitsa, Poltava province–d. 25 July 1955, Moscow). Ukrainian-Russian composer. Dunaevskii, the son of a clerk, studied violin and composition at Khar'kov (Khar'kiv) Conservatory, graduating in 1919. He subsequently worked as a violinist and musical director at Khar'kov Drama Theater. Dunaevskii moved to Moscow in 1924 and to Leningrad in 1929, composing songs and orchestral pieces for operetta theaters and music halls. He created a dozen operettas, including *We Are for Peace!* (aka *Friendship Triumphs*/My za mir, 1952). Dunaevskii was the conductor when **Sergei Prokof'ev**'s music for **Aleksandr Faintsimmer**'s exceptional satire *Lieutenant Kizhe* (aka *The Czar Wants to Sleep*/Poruchik Kizhe, 1934) was recorded at Belgoskino (**Belarusfilm Studio**) in 1933.

Dunaevskii made his debut as a film composer with a score for **Vladimir Korsh-Sablin**'s World War I drama *The First Platoon* (Pershy uzvod/Pervyi vzvod, 1933), the first Belarusian sound film. He achieved nationwide fame with his tunes for **Grigorii Aleksandrov**'s **comedy** *Jolly Fellows* (Veselye rebiata, 1934), where for the first time he applied his trademark leitmotiv technique suitable both for comical and dramatic situations. Dunaevskii's successful partnership with Aleksandrov continued with the entertaining blockbusters *Circus* (Tsirk, 1936), *Volga-Volga* (1938), *Radiant Path* (aka *Tanya*/Svetlyi put', 1940), and *Spring* (Vesna, 1947). Many of these melodies, perfectly matching Vasilii Lebedev-Kumach's easy-to-remember lyrics, became instant hits and part of a peculiar Stalinist folklore that generations of viewers adored and sang, if only with increasingly ironic undertones. The composer became a veritable star whose name was known to millions.

Dunaevskii also contributed scores to **Semen Timoshenko**'s slightly awkward comedies *Three Comrades* (aka *Three Friends*/Tri tovarishcha, 1935) and *The Goalie* (Vratar', 1936), as well as **Ivan Pyr'ev** first experiment in contemporary musical, *A Rich Bride* (aka *The Country Bride*/Bogataia nevesta, 1938), and to his last effort in the genre, *Cossacks of the Kuban* (Kubanskie kazaki, 1950). Other famous Dunaevskii melodies can be heard in **Vladimir Vainshtok**'s *Children of Captain Grant* (Deti kapitana Granta, 1936) and Korsh-Sablin's *Seekers of Happiness* (aka *Birobidjan, A Greater Promise*/Shukal'niki shchascia/Iskateli schast'ia, 1935).

Dunaevskii's music was influenced by Ukrainian, Russian, Jewish, and Roma (gypsy) folklore, as well as classical Russian music. The composer's intention to convey genuine optimism and patriotism was supported by his keen sense of rhythm—usually waltz or march— and a melodic inventiveness unrivaled among his contemporaries. However, his naïve faith in Soviet-cum-Stalinist ideals made him an easy target for later attacks.

Dunaevskii was honored with the title People's Artist of the RSFSR in 1950. He received Stalin Prizes for *Circus* and *Volga-Volga* in 1941, and for *Cossacks of the Kuban* in 1951. He is buried at Novodevich'e cemetery in Moscow. His brothers were conductor Semen Dunaevskii (1906–1986) and composer Zinovii Dunaevskii (1908–1981).

Other films: *A Concerto by Beethoven* (Kontsert Betkhovena, 1935); *A Girl Rushes to the Rendezvous* (Devushka speshit na svidanie, 1936).

DVORZHETSKII, VLADISLAV VATSLAVOVICH (b. 26 April 1939, Omsk–d. 28 May 1978, Gomel'). Russian actor. Dvorzhetskii was born in Siberia during the political exile of his father, stage and film actor Vatslav Dvorzhetskii (1910–1993). He graduated from Omsk Medical Institute in 1959 and worked as a doctor's assistant in gynecology. In the early 1960s, Dvorzhetskii studied in the studio of the Omsk Theater of Young Viewers (TIuZ), of which he became a member in 1965.

Directors **Aleksandr Alov** and **Vladimir Naumov** came across a photo of Dvorzhetskii and invited him to Moscow, casting him in the role of White Army general Khludov in their impressive Mikhail Bulgakov adaptation *The Flight* (Beg, 1971). Dvorzhetskii's stunning performance—the portrait of an exhausted sadist tormented by inner doubts and nightmares—arguably became *the* discovery of a film that boasted a stellar cast. The only other role of Dvorzhetskii's career that is comparable in quality is the disturbed astronaut Burton in **Andrei Tarkovskii**'s *Solaris* (1972). The hypnotic, burning gaze of Dvorzhetskii's huge eyes that sometimes seem more Martian than human, and his unique, mysterious "foreignness" subsequently attracted directors of second-rate genre fare, while Dvorzhetskii's constant need for money forced him to accept their offers. Soviet moviegoers loved *The Sannikov Land* (Zemlia Sannikova, 1973), a pseudoexotic science fiction attempt in which Dvorzhetskii—wearing a wig—plays an idealistic explorer. The actor's enigmatic persona seemed to be made for embodying utopian dreamers such as Jules Verne's Captain Nemo, and he did so in an acceptable Soviet television version of 1975. In his best performances, Dvorzhetskii was able to prove that he was one of the most intelligent Soviet actors of his day, irradiating an acumen of both vigorous manliness and existential hopelessness.

Dvorzhetskii's death of a heart attack during a concert tour abruptly ended a career that held enormous promise. The actor's half-brother Evgenii Dvorzhetskii (1960–1999) was a prolific film and theater actor who tragically died in a car accident.

Other films: *Behind the Clouds Is the Sky* (Za oblakami nebo, 1973); *Until the Last Minute* (Do poslednei minuty, 1974).

DZHIGARKHANYAN [other spelling: Jigarkhanyan], **ARMEN BORISOVICH** (b. 3 October 1935, Yerevan). Armenian actor. Dzhigarkhanyan attended a Russian high school in the Armenian capital. He then studied with famous director Armen Gulakyan (1899–1960) at the Sundakyan Academic Theater in Yerevan, graduating in 1958, and joined the troupe of the Stanislavskii Russian Drama Theater. In 1967, Dzhigarkhanyan moved to Moscow to work at Lenkom Theater; two years later, he became a member of the Maiakovskii Theater. From the beginning of his stage career, Dzhigarkhanyan has demonstrated an awesome versatility, succeeding in a wide variety of roles in the classical and contemporary repertory, including Shakespeare, Tennessee Williams, and modern Russian authors. In 1996, Dzhigarkhanyan founded his own theater, named "D."

The actor's first movie role was the optimistic young worker Akop in G. Sarkisov's *Landslide* (Obval, 1960). In **Frunze Dovlatyan**'s *Hello, It's Me!* (Zdravstvui, eto ia! 1966), Dzhigarkhanyan impressed viewers with his inspired portrayal of a physicist, Artem Manvelyan; the film gave him national renown and initiated an extremely prolific screen career. Among Dzhigarkhanyan's subsequent roles were Mukuch in **Henrik Malyan**'s *Triangle* (Treugol'nik, 1967), Ovechkin in **Edmond Keosayan**'s *Uncatchable Avengers* (Neulovimye mstiteli, 1966), and Frolovskii in the controversial parable on work ethics, *The Bonus* (Premiia, 1975). By the early 1970s, Dzhigarkhanyan had become one of the most popular Soviet film actors who appeared in more than 200 roles, covering all genres from situational **comedy** to historical adventure, psychological drama, thriller, and quality literary adaptation, moving effortlessly from trivial entertainment to sophisticated art. Dzhigarkhanyan's characters usually are distinguished by stoicism, irony, and a quiet inner strength, irradiating a rough charm that only has grown with age. In **Armenian cinema**, the actor starred as the 18th-century liberation leader Mkhitar Sparapet in Keosayan's epic *The Star of Hope* (Huso astgh/Zvezda nadezhdy, 1979). Some of his best performances, particularly in **Karen Shakhnazarov**'s darkly sarcastic *Zero City* (Gorod Zero, 1989) and *The Assassin of the Tsar* (Tsareubiitsa, 1991), show Dzhigarkhanyan's mellow wisdom and human depth.

Dzhigarkhanyan taught at the Russian State Film School **VGIK** in 1989–1997. He was named People's Artist of the USSR in 1985.

Other films: *The Seagull* (Chaika, 1970); *Teheran-43* (aka *Spy Ring*, aka *Assassination Attempt*, 1980); *What a Mess* (Shirli-myrli, 1995); *Vanechka* (2007).

DZIGAN, EFIM L'VOVICH (b. 14 December 1898, Moscow– d. 31 December 1981, Moscow). Russian director and screenwriter. Dzigan fought with the Red Army in the 1918–1921 Civil War. Following his discharge in 1922, he studied with **Boris Chaikovskii**, whose film school he completed in 1923 (other sources: 1926). Dzigan then worked for **Vsevolod Pudovkin** as assistant director on *The Mechanics of the Brain* (Mekhanika golovnogo mozga, 1924) and also as a newsreel cameraman and actor. As director, he debuted in Tbilisi in 1928 with *First Cornet Streshnyov* (Pirveli korneti Streshniovi/Pervyi kornet Streshnev, aka *The White Horseman*/Tetri mkhedari, codirected with **Mikheil Chiaureli**). In this peculiar paraphrase of Pudovkin's *Mother*, the main character is a father whose son helps him discover his class consciousness. Also at **Gruziya-Film Studio**, Dzigan created the parable *The God of War* (Bog voiny, 1929), with the intention to expose religion as a supporter of war in various times and ages.

Dzigan's next two pictures deal with the transformation of gender roles in a Communist society. *The Court Must Proceed* (Sud dolzhen prodolzhat'sia, 1931) describes a young woman who, after being assaulted by hooligans in contemporary Leningrad, demands in the courtroom a general change in societal attitudes. *A Woman* (Zhenshchina, 1932) focuses on a strong-willed heroine pursuing her dream to become a tractor driver.

Dzigan's most famous picture is the Civil War epic *We Are from Kronshtadt* (My iz Kronshtadta, 1936), from Vsevolod Vishnevskii's screenplay. Its "collective hero"—sailors who defended Petrograd against the White Army siege in 1919—is sufficiently individualized, although the goal was to feature a gallery of social types rather than psychologically unique characters. *We Are from Kronshtadt*, with its tragic and romantic vision of the revolution and groundbreaking synthesis of image and sound, became both a popular and critical success in the Soviet Union and was one of the canonical, style-shaping films of the 1930s; in 1941, Dzigan received a Stalin Prize for it. *If Tomorrow Is War* (Esli zavtra voina, 1938) depicts what a possible military clash with Nazi Germany might look like, but its vision—in accordance with official ideological guidelines—is deceptively harmless and naïve, and the film was criticized for its unrealistic approach in the aftermath of World War II.

Subsequently, Dzigan was assigned tasks in national studios. *Djambul* (1952), made at **Kazakhfilm Studio**, is a typical Stalinist biopic about the Kazakh national poet, while *Fatali-Khan* (1947), produced at Baku Film Studio (**Azerbaijanfilm Studio**) for over seven years, deals with an 18th-century Azeri ruler who promoted a strategic alliance with Russia. *The Prologue* (Prolog, 1956), a reconstruction of the 1905–1907 events featuring Vladimir Lenin, Nadezhda Krupskaia, and Maksim Gor'kii, is of historical interest as one of the first Soviet wide-screen productions. Dzigan then helmed a sensitive project, the Soviet-Chinese *In Unified Formation* (V edinom stroiu, aka *Wind from the East*, 1959, codirected by Sue Wei Gan), about colleagues from both countries who are fighting the elements to build a hydroelectric power plant, developing an inseparable friendship along the way.

In 1967, Dzigan attracted audiences' attention with *The Iron Stream* (Zheleznyi potok), an adaptation of Aleksandr Serafimovich's 1924 novel about the Civil War, characterized by an efficient use of the wide screen format for large-scale battle scenes.

Dzigan became a member of the Communist Party in 1943 and was named People's Artist of the USSR in 1969. He began teaching at the Soviet State Film School **VGIK** in 1937, earning the rank of a full professor in 1965.

Other films: *The Eternal Flame* (Negasimoe plamia, 1964); *North, South, East, West* (Sever, iug, vostok, zapad, 1971).

– E –

EARTH (Zemlia, 1930). VUFKU, Kiev (**Dovzhenko Film Studio**). 89 min., b/w. Directed by **Aleksandr Dovzhenko**. Script: Aleksandr Dovzhenko. Cinematography: **Danylo Demutskii**. Cast: **Stepan Shkurat**, Semen Svashenko, **Iuliia Solntseva**, Elena Maksimova, Ivan Franko, Petr Masokha, Mykola Nademskii. Premiere: 8 May 1930.

In a Ukrainian village in the late 1920s, a group of young peasants led by Vasil' (Svashenko) found a collective farm (kolkhoz) and acquire a tractor. While Vasil''s grandfather Semen (Nademskii) is dying serenely in his apple orchard, Vasil' and his father, Opanas (Shkurat), argue about what constitutes heroism in peasant labor. Eventually, the efficiency of the tractor appeals to the skeptical Opanas. Vasil' clashes with Khoma (Masokha), a wealthy peasant's son who passionately resents the ongoing collectivization. One night, Khoma shoots Vasil' who is returning from visiting his girlfriend (Maksimova) and is dancing proudly. Vasil''s death unites the community, which also rejects traditional religious rituals and ignores Khoma's frenzied confession.

EFREMOV, OLEG NIKOLAEViCH (b. 1 October 1927, Moscow–d. 24 May 2000, Moscow). Russian actor and director. Efremov studied at the studio school of the Moscow Art Theater (MKhAT), graduating in 1949, and stayed on as an acting teacher. In 1956, he was appointed chief director of the newly founded theater The Contemporary (Sovremennik), one of the most innovative troupes in Russia. In 1970, Efremov took over the Moscow Art Theater as executive director.

As a film actor, Efremov made his debut in **Mikhail Kalatozov**'s *The First Echelon* (Pervyi eshelon, 1956). Tall, lean, and far from the typical movie idol appearance, Efremov filled his roles with a high degree of complexity, sometimes reaching a state of inner torment. He worked with leading Soviet directors: as private Ivanov in **Aleksandr Stolper**'s Stalingrad epic *The Living and the Dead* (Zhivye i mertvye, 1964), as the humane attorney in **El'dar Riazanov**'s **comedy** about altruism and selfishness *Watch Out for the Automobile* (Beregis' avtomobilia, 1966), as the flirtatious cab driver in **Tat'iana Liozno-va**'s *"Three Poplars" at Pliushchikha* ('Tri topolia' na Pliushchikhe, 1967), and as Kartsev in **Georgii Natanson**'s blockbuster melodrama *One More Time about Love* (Eshche raz pro liubov', 1968). His memorable interpretation of Dolokhov in **Sergei Bondarchuk**'s Lev Tolstoi adaptation ***War and Peace*** (Voina i mir, 1962–1967) captures that character's vanity and insincerity. In the role of a melancholic militia man in **Vitalii Mel'nikov**'s touching comedy *Hello and Goodbye* (Zdravstvui i proshchai, 1972), he believably portrays a man torn between emotion and law.

Efremov's two attempts in film direction—*A Bridge Is Being Built* (Stroitsia most, codirected by Gavriil Egiazarov, 1965), a coproduction between **Mosfilm Studio** and the Sovremennik theater about a Komsomol brigade, and *The Old New Year* (Staryi novyi god, codirected by Naum Ardashnikov, 1980, TV)—did not leave a deep mark.

In the mid-1980s, Efremov was at the center of an unsightly battle about the future of the Moscow Art Theater that, in 1986, led to the troupe's split. While Efremov remained in charge of the half that named itself after Anton Chekhov, his former costar from *"Three Poplars" at Pliushchikha* and *Once Again about Love*, **Tat'iana Doronina**, took over the other half, which retained the name of Maksim Gor'kii.

Efremov, who joined the Communist Party in 1955, was honored with the title People's Artist of the USSR in 1976 and Hero of Socialist Labor in 1987. He won three USSR State Prizes for his theater work: in 1969, 1974, and 1983. Efremov is buried at Novodevich'e cemetery in Moscow. His son Mikhail Efremov (b. 1963) is a successful film and stage actor and theater director.

Other films: *Rudin* (1976); *Stranded* (Neprikaiannyi, 1989); *An Essay for Victory Day* (Sochinenie ko dniu pobedy, 1998).

EIZENSHTEIN [Eisenstein], **SERGEI MIKHAILOVICH** (b. 22 [other sources: 23] January 1898, Riga, Latvia–d. 10 February 1948, Moscow). Russian director, screenwriter, designer, and film theorist. Eizenshtein was born into a wealthy bourgeois family; his father was a successful architect in the Latvian capital, Riga, and his mother hailed from a Russian merchant family. Eizenshtein's parents provided their only child with a solid education and access to world literature and culture. In 1915, Eizenshtein graduated from Riga gymnasium and enrolled in the Petrograd Institute of Civil Engineering. He was drafted as an ensign into the tsarist army in 1917 and joined the Red Army in 1918.

Following various jobs in the military, including director of amateur theater productions, Eizenshtein was demobilized in 1920 and delegated to Moscow to study Japanese at the Academy of the Red Army's general staff. He joined the ultraleftist organization Proletarian Culture (Proletkul't) that was founded by Aleksandr Bogdanov (1873–1928) as a platform to create an entity radically departing from all preceding cultures. Eizenshtein made his debut as a stage designer at the First Workers' Theater of Proletkul't with *The Mexican* (1921), adapted from a Jack London short story set in the boxing milieu, with **Grigorii Aleksandrov** starring in the title role and **Ivan Pyr'ev** in the supporting cast. Arguably, the deepest influence on Eizenshtein's artistic evolution was exercised by theater innovator Vsevolod Meierkhol'd (1874–1939), whose productions implicitly attacked the schools of naturalism and realism. Together with other future filmmakers such as **Grigorii Roshal'** and **Sergei Iutkevich**, Eizenshtein studied at Meierkhol'd's Supreme Directing Workshops (GVyRM) in 1921–1922.

In 1923, under the impression of the Petrograd FEKS stage productions of **Grigorii Kozintsev** and **Leonid Trauberg**, Eizenshtein directed Aleksandr Ostrovskii's classical comedy *There's Enough Simplicity in Every Wise Man* (Na vsiakogo mudretsa dovol'no prostoty) as a noisy burlesque with elements of circus acrobatics. Together with Iutkevich, he worked as a stage designer for the "Mastfor" workshop of theater avant-gardist Nikolai Foregger (1892–1939).

In his Ostrovskii production, Eizenshtein used a filmed episode, *Glumov's Diary* (Dnevnik Glumova, 1923), in which the stage actors appeared on screen. Deeply impressed by the films of D. W. Griffith and Abel Gance and encouraged by his encounters with **Lev Kuleshov** and **Esfir' Shub**, in 1924 Eizenshtein decided to fully devote himself to cinema. His debut, *Strike* (Stachka, 1924), with the Proletkul't troupe in major roles, was based on the movement's dogma: rather than featuring individuals with unique psychological traits, the film is populated by social "types" (*tipazhi*) involved in class-based conflicts. The rejection of psychological character autonomy and the establishment of socioeconomic determinacy were based on a Marxist sociological approach in which the class origin of a character is primary and individualization or psychological analysis are negligible. In *Strike*, the "collective hero" acts in skillfully staged, quasi-documentary scenes, particularly powerful in the culminating episode of the brutal suppression of the strike by tsarist military.

The Communist cultural establishment was persuaded by Eizenshtein's formal risk-taking and political passion and entrusted the ambitious young director with a large-scale project in celebration of the 20th anniversary of the 1905 revolution. Eizenshtein reduced his initial plan of a grandiose epic to just one episode from **Nina Agadzhanova-Shutko**'s script and presented in record time *Battleship Potemkin* (Bronenosets Potemkin, 1925). Film connoisseurs immediately recognized the unprecedented artistic quality of this work, especially its dynamic, rhythmicized montage and expressive shot compositions created with cinematographer **Eduard Tissé**. Although domestic rank-and-file viewers were more baffled than enthused, international audiences embraced the film as a political and aesthetic revelation. The seven-minute "Odessa steps" scene and metaphors such as the tumbling baby carriage or the roaring lion sculptures became universally recognized, canonized, and, in due course, parodied. *Battleship Potemkin* explored the aesthetic potential of cinema as few other pictures had and demonstrated the extent to which film could shape viewers' political and emotional perceptions. Because of its immense manipulative power, the film was censored in many countries and became a cause for protests and demonstrations.

Eizenshtein decided to further test the limits of cinematic expression, once again by using a government assignment, to create a monumental avant-gardist picture. However, this time the two goals proved incompatible. Although *October* (aka *Ten Days That Shook the World*/Oktiabr'/Desiat' dnei, kotorye potriasli mir, 1927) contains episodes of near-traumatic intensity (the demonstration of 3 July 1917 and the toppling of the monument to Aleksandr III, among others) and a wellspring of aesthetic discoveries, the picture as a whole remains coldly idiosyncratic and excessively intellectualized. Its continuous blending of quasi-documentary scenes with unabashed Communist hagiography and of complex symbolism with demagogical falsification of history reveals its essence as an ideological construct.

Eizenshtein returned to simpler narrative structures with *The Old and the New* (aka *General Line*/Staroe i novoe/General'naia liniia, 1929), the first Soviet full-length feature about the collectivization of agriculture. It juxtaposes the traditional peasant economy in a grotesquely polemical fashion to the officially endorsed methods of modern collective farming. Closely supervised by the Communist cultural establishment and by Iosif Stalin personally, *The Old and the New* is even less convincing than *October*, likely because its milieu was unfamiliar to Eizenshtein and the propaganda concept was too obviously forced upon reality.

In 1929, Eizenshtein was sent to Western Europe, a largely improvised sojourn primarily for the study of sound film technology. Accompanied by Tissé and Aleksandrov, he traveled to Germany, Switzerland, France, Belgium, and Great Britain, giving lectures, participating in film conferences, meeting countless intellectual celebrities, and even filming, always under the keen eyes of state police, who feared the subversive influence of the exotic Soviet trio. Eizenshtein supervised the production of two projects, one helmed by Tissé, the other by Aleksandrov. The feature-length *Women's Misery—Women's Happiness* (Frauennot—Frauenglück, 1929), made in Switzerland and devoted to the problem of abortion, caused an uproar; the surreal sound film experiment *Romance sentimentale*, made in France, was completely apolitical. In 1930, Paramount invited Eizenshtein to Hollywood, where he met Charles Chaplin, Douglas Fairbanks, Robert Flaherty, and other prominent admirers of his work, wrote scripts—none of which came to fruition—and agreed with Upton Sinclair to create a film about Mexico. *¡Que Viva Mexico!* (1932), one of the most severely mutilated of Eizenshtein's films, was meant to capture the soul of an ancient nation, its mysticism and glorious past shining through a miserable present. After months of hard work, Eizenshtein was forced to abandon the project for lack of funding; later, thousands of meters of footage were plundered, rather unceremoniously, by Sol Lesser, Marie Seton, and others for minor films—a blow from which Eizenshtein never recovered.

The Soviet government exercised considerable pressure to persuade Eizenshtein to return to the Soviet Union, which he did in

1932; it took him years to adjust to the country's changed cultural-political climate. With the official endorsement of sound films such as *The Counterplan* (Vstrechnyi, 1934) by Iutkevich and **Fridrikh Ermler** in which dialogues are dominant and the camera work is kept deliberately static, Eizenshtein saw the need to define how exactly the artistic legacy of the 1920s could be upheld. In a compromising approach, he defined the silent montage cinema as "poetry" and the new trend in sound film as "prose." His own first sound film project, *Bezhin Meadow* (Bezhin lug), had little to do with the literary source from which it took its title, Ivan Turgenev's 1850 short story. In the screenplay, which the Communist Party's Central Committee had commissioned, **Aleksandr Rzheshevskii** blended the tale of juvenile serfs with the authentic case of Communist pioneer Pavel (Pavlik) Morozov (1918–1932), who had informed Soviet authorities of his father's anticollectivization activities and was killed by his relatives as a revenge on 3 September 1932. Judging by the few remaining stills, the film would have become visually stunning but politically dubious at best. The campaign unleashed against *Bezhin Meadow* was not caused by any underlying "dissidence"; rather, Communist Party hack **Boris Shumiatskii** and his associates attacked the notion of individual artistry and stylistic experimentation per se. In the summer of 1936, one year after the beginning of the shooting, the leadership of **Mosfilm Studio** refused to accept the completed footage and demanded to restart the shooting from scratch. Another year later, the newly generated footage was rejected again and the work aborted altogether, while the traumatized Eizenshtein engaged in the common ritual of public self-criticism.

With his political situation more precarious than ever, Eizenshtein adjusted to the Stalinist aesthetic doctrine, especially the criteria of popular accessibility and ideological clarity. When *Aleksandr Nevskii* premiered on 1 December 1938, it turned out to be a triumph for its maker and fully rehabilitated him in the eyes of the Soviet establishment. Eizenshtein simplified the hero's personality to the point of fairy-tale, superman quality, and **Nikolai Cherkasov**'s static acting and declarative intonations fit precisely in the monumental shot compositions that visualized the spirit of patriotism and national pride with unprecedented directness. Eizenshtein aptly altered dramatic and comedic episodes, but his greatest achievement is a quasi-operatic synthesis of image and sound in which **Sergei Pokof'ev's** music and his own montage complement each other in rhythmic perfection.

In November 1940, Eizenshtein, by that time appointed artistic director of Mosfilm Studio, agreed to direct Richard Wagner's *Die Walküre* at the Bolshoi Theater, an official nod to Nazi Germany following the Molotov-Ribbentrop Pact. In June 1941, at the outbreak of the Great Patriotic War, he was evacuated to Almaty (Alma-Ata), where he wrote the screenplay and, starting in 1943, shot the first part of *Ivan the Terrible* (Ivan Groznyi), a grandiose epic about the 16th-century ruler who united Russia against internal and external enemies with an iron fist. A comparison of part I (1944) and part II (1945, released 1958) clearly shows that one was an unequivocal apologia for Iosif Stalin and autocracy, while the sequel turns the dictator's triumph into a Shakespearean tragedy. Thus, a possible justification for the demagoguery of part I could be its functioning as a thesis that lay the foundation for the antithesis to follow. In January 1946, the first part was awarded a Stalin Prize; the second was withheld from release and Eizenshtein was told at a meeting with Stalin and other Politburo members to "correct the film's mistakes," an assignment that he could not carry out due to a severe heart ailment leading to his untimely death.

Despite Eizenshtein's unequivocal allegiance to the Communist revolution and the Soviet state, he preserved a degree of inner intellectual freedom unmatched by any other Soviet filmmaker of his day. His theoretical legacy—gigantic in scope, multifaceted, and conceptually contradictory—has only been partially published and researched. Indeed, highly speculative and often playful theoretical searchings accompanied Eizenshtein's creative process throughout, absorbing impulses from Leonardo da Vinci to Karl Marx, from James Joyce to Sigmund Freud, and from Kabuki theater to Walt Disney. In 1919–1920, Eizenshtein penned his first theoretical article on theater; in 1923, the journal *LEF* published "Montage of Attractions" (*Montazh attraktsionov*), in which he emphatically proclaimed montage as the new organizing principle of cinematic narration. During the making of *October*, Eizenshtein developed a theory of "intellectual cinema" in which montage is a synthesizing principle resulting in the emergence of a new notion or idea. In the last years of his life, Eizenshtein worked on a wide range of problems of cinema in the context of culture and aesthetics, including aspects of pathos and the comical, color, and **animation**.

Eizenshtein began to teach at the Soviet State Film School (GTK, later named **VGIK**) in 1932; in 1937, he was promoted to full professor. A lively pedagogue, he made an unforgettable impression on his students, although only a few of them became reputable directors (including **Aleksandr Stolper**, **Stanislav Rostotskii**, **Mikhail Shveitser**, and **Bension Kimyagarov**). Eizenshtein was awarded the title Merited Artist of the RSFSR in 1935. He is buried at Novodevich'e cemetery in Moscow. The house in which he lived in 1920–1934 (Chistoprudnyi bul'var, 23) carries a memorial plaque. In 1966, the apartment of the director's widow, Pera Atasheva, on Smolenskaia ulitsa 10 in Moscow, became a research museum and archive whose director, Naum Kleiman, has worked tirelessly to preserve Eizenshtein's legacy and make it accessible to film scholars from all over the world.

EKK, NIKOLAI VLADIMIROVICH [real surname: Ivakin] (b. 14 June 1902, Riga–d. 14 July 1976, Moscow). Russian director, screenwriter, and actor. Ekk studied with Vsevolod Meierkhol'd (1874–1939) at the Supreme Directing Workshops (GVyRM, aka Workshop of Communist Dramaturgy/Masterskaia kommunisticheskoi dramaturgii) in 1920–1921 and worked as an actor and assistant director at Meierkhol'd's theater while simultaneously studying at the State Film School (GTK, later named **VGIK**) from which he graduated in 1927.

To this day, Ekk's place in film history is secured by being the director of the first Soviet sound feature film, *A Start in Life* (aka *Road to Life*/Putevka v zhizn', 1931). Unimpressed by the ongoing theoretical debates about the effects of sound on the artistic quality of cinema, Ekk applied the technical novelty with the intention of maximizing the effect of each scene, trying out the entire range of opportunities—speeches, dialogues, group cacophony, musical commentary, and diegetic street noise. Most importantly, the various sounds are used to advance the action and to characterize the protagonists psychologically and socially. The film was released in 26 countries and won Ekk the Best Director award at the 1932 Venice Film Festival. Although some critics accused the filmmaker of romanticizing the criminal milieu, *A Start in Life* did provide persuasive arguments for the transformative power of Communist education and voluntary labor in youth communes. Ekk made the film under the guidance and with the practical support of the Soviet secret service, GPU, which ran communes for homeless orphans and instrumentalized *A Start in Life* in its fight against youth gangs and street crime. One of the all-time hits with Soviet audiences, the film's re-release in a slightly altered version in 1957 again proved a popular success. Some film historians credit *A Start in Life* with being among the predecessors to Italian neorealism, an intriguing assumption given the director's mastery of authentic everyday milieu and atmosphere.

Strangely, Ekk then chose the technical advancement of visual media over the development of his artistry, committing his career to achieving primacy in various areas. Thus, he directed a medium-length experimental almanac in color, *Carnival of Colors* (1935), featuring images of Red Square parades, travel in Georgia, and paintings. In 1936, Ekk helmed the first Soviet feature in color, *Grunia Kornakova* (aka *Little Nightingale*/Solovei-Solovushka), about women in a porcelain factory fighting capitalist oppression; yet, due to poor reviews the planned trilogy about the title heroine faltered. In Kiev, Ekk made the Nikolai Gogol' adaptations *The Fair of Sorochinsk* (Sorochinskaia iarmarka, 1939) and *May Night* (Maiskaia noch', 1941), both in color and both critically underrated. After a 20-year hiatus, Ekk directed the first Soviet color television film, *When It Snows* (Kogda idet sneg, 1962). He then helmed the first Soviet stereoscopic film, *The Man in the Green Glove* (Chelovek v zeleneoi perchatke, 1968), about a circus artist who struggles to overcome a hand injury suffered during the war.

Ekk was named Merited Artist of the Russian Federation in 1973. In 2002, Russia issued a stamp in honor of his 100th anniversary.

Other films: *How One Should and How One Should Not* (Kak nado i ne nado, 1929); *Mommy and Two Drones* (Mamochka i dva trutnia, 1963).

END OF ST. PETERSBURG, THE (Konets Sankt-Peterburga, 1927). Mezhrabpom-Rus' (**Mezhrabpomfilm Studio**). 74 min., b/w. Directed by **Vsevolod Pudovkin** (codirector: Mikhail Doller).

Script: **Natan Zarkhi**. Cinematography: **Anatolii Golovnia**. Cast: Ivan Chuvelev, Aleksandr Chistiakov, **Vera Baranovskaia**, **Sergei Komarov**, **Vladimir Fogel'**, Vsevolod Pudovkin. Premiere: 13 December 1927.

When a new baby is born into a large, poor peasant family, the oldest son (Chuvelev) is forced to leave for St. Petersburg to find a job. In the home of a fellow countryman (Chistiakov) and his embittered wife (Baranovskaia), he witnesses the meeting of an illegal strike committee that he later betrays to the authorities. Naïvely, he asks for clemency for his countryman and protests violently when his appeal is ridiculed. After serving a prison sentence, the young man is sent to the front in World War I, where he turns into a class-conscious fighter. In 1917, he actively participates in the Bolshevik Revolution.

ENEI, EVGENII EVGEN'EVICH (b. 9 June 1890, Budapest–d. 6 June 1971, Leningrad). Hungarian-Russian art director and designer. Enei, who studied at the Budapest Academy of Art, served in the Austro-Hungarian army in World War I, was taken prisoner, and decided to stay in Russia, joining the Bolshevik Party in 1920. He then embarked on a career as an art designer with the Petrograd-based Sevzapkino (later: **Lenfilm Studio**).

Enei made his debut in **Viacheslav Viskovskii**'s rather conventional revolutionary action drama *Red Partisans* (Krasnye partizany, 1924). He received more challenging assignments from budding director **Fridrikh Ermler**, working with him on *Little Katia, the Paper Reinette* (aka *Katka's Reinette Apples*/Kat'ka—Bumazhnyi Ranet, 1926), *The House in the Snowdrifts* (Dom v sugrobakh, 1927), and the masterpiece *A Fragment of the Empire* (Oblomok imperii, 1929), whose grandiose images of a radically transforming society owe substantially to Enei's vision. During the mid-1920s, Enei also began to collaborate with **Grigorii Kozintsev** and **Leonid Trauberg**'s Factory of the Eccentric Actor (FEKS). His early sketches for the group's films reveal the influence of German expressionism, with grotesquely distorted shapes of houses and interiors in the controversial Nikolai Gogol' adaptation *The Overcoat* (Shinel', 1926). In the sound period, Enei's vision of Petersburg/Petrograd became more realistic and socially marked, only rarely re-creating the nightmarish cityscapes of his earlier films; the authenticity of Kozintsev and

Trauberg's **Maksim Trilogy** (Trilogiia o Maksime, 1934–1938) is to a large degree the result of Enei's detail-obsessed work.

At different stages of his career, Enei also collaborated with **Semen Timoshenko** (*Napoleon-Gas*/Napoleon-Gaz, 1925; *The Sniper*/ Snaiper, aka Iskusstvo ubivat', 1931), **Mikhail Romm** (*Person #217*, aka *Girl No. 217*/Chelovek No. 217, 1944), **Efim Dzigan** (*Dzhambul*, 1952), **Grigorii Roshal'** (*Academy Member Ivan Pavlov*/Akademik Ivan Pavlov, 1949), and **Aleksandr Faintsimmer** (*The Gadfly*/Ovod, 1955), among others. Yet his most lasting and fruitful collaboration was with Kozintsev, whose loyal, congenial partner he remained for almost half a century. Of particular importance is Enei's architectural design, which fundamentally structured the appearance of Kozintsev's late adaptations: picturesque and warm in *Don Quijote* (Don Kikhot, 1957), grandiose and sternly authoritarian in *Hamlet* (Gamlet, 1964), and gloomily hopeless in *King Lear* (Korol' Lir, 1970).

Enei was named Merited Artist of the RSFSR in 1935 and People's Artist of the USSR in 1969.

Other films: *Devil's Wheel* (Chertovo koleso, 1926); *Young Fritz* (Iunyi Frits, 1943); *A Drama from Old Life* (Drama iz starinnoi zhizni, 1971).

ENTHUSIASM (Entuziasm, aka *Symphony of the Donbass*/Simfoniia Donbassa, 1930). VUFKU/Ukrainfilm (**Dovzhenko Film Studio**). 60 min., b/w. Directed by **Dziga Vertov**. Cinematography: B. Tseitlin. Montage: Dziga Vertov, **Elizaveta Svilova**. Music: Nikolai Timofeev. Sound system: **Aleksandr Shorin** ("Shorinophone"). Premiere: 2 April 1931.

The first Soviet sound **documentary** is a feature-length, associative essay, reflecting on time and rhythm—the foundations of progress and modernity. They are represented by industrial labor, radio communication, political demonstrations of workers and young pioneers, and the symphonic music inspired by them. At the same time, the film shows the steady withdrawal of the "forces of the past"—the Orthodox Church and pious churchgoers, drunkards, and their screaming wives, as well as remnants of the bourgeoisie who secretly dream about the return of tsarism. Vertov experiments with the use of sound in a synchronic and asynchronic manner, including realistic street noise, Communist marches, religious chants, and industrial sounds.

ERDMAN, NIKOLAI ROBERTOVICH (b. 16 November 1900 [other sources: 1902], Moscow–d. 10 August 1970, Moscow). Russian screenwriter and playwright. A descendant of Baltic Germans (his father, Robert Erdman, was an actor who appeared in the role of Robert Karlovich in **Boris Barnet**'s *The Outskirts* [Okraina, 1933]), Erdman began his literary career in 1922 following high school and a brief Red Army service. In the early 1920s, Erdman began to write satirical sketches and a play that became an instant classic—the dark satire *The Mandate* (Mandat, 1924) about the subversion of Communist society by petit-bourgeois values. Another comedy, *The Suicide* (Samoubiitsa, 1928–1931), with an even more grotesque and gloomy outlook, was rehearsed in a number of theaters but prohibited in 1932.

Erdman's screenplay *Mitia* (1927) tells of a naïve, kindhearted young man resisting social pressures, while *The Sold Appetite* (Prodannyi appetit, 1928) is an anticapitalist satire. Both films were directed by **Nikolai Okhlopkov** and enjoyed popular and critical success. Erdman also worked fruitfully with Boris Barnet, whose predominantly soft and forgiving sense of humor was similar to his own. Their first project, *The House on Trubnaia Square* (Dom na Trubnoi, 1928, coauthored with **Viktor Shklovskii** and others), presents a **comedic** portrait of everyday life in the NEP (New Economic Policy) period. Yet only in sound film could Erdman fully realize his potential as a master of witty, fast-paced, and pun-filled dialogues. *Jolly Fellows* (Veselye rebiata, 1934, coauthored with Vladimir Mass and director **Grigorii Aleksandrov**) and *Volga-Volga* (1938) won instant popularity with their blend of antibureaucratic satire and musical revue. The latter, for which Erdman was awarded a Stalin Prize in 1941, marked the beginning of his artistic partnership with screenwriter Mikhail Vol'pin that lasted several decades.

Erdman was arrested on 10 October 1933 after actor Vasilii Kachalov recited some of his satirical poems at a reception in the presence of Soviet hack Kliment Voroshilov; the writer was exiled to Siberia (Eniseisk, Tomsk) and only in 1937 allowed to live in the city of Kalinin (Tver'). From 1940 to 1948, Erdman worked as an author for the Ensemble of Song and Dance of the Soviet secret service (NKVD), writing the script for such concerts as "Native Leningrad" (Rodnoi Leningrad, 1942, directed by **Sergei Iutkevich**). He was allowed to resume his work as a screenwriter, authoring *The Actress* (Aktrisa, 1943) for **Leonid Trauberg** and *The Prince and the Pauper* (Prints i nishchii, 1943) for **Erast Garin**, among others. In 1949, Erdman was permitted to return to Moscow. He wrote four noteworthy screenplays for **Konstantin Iudin**, of which the war adventures *Courageous People* (Smelye liudi, 1950, Stalin Prize) and *Fortress in the Mountains* (Zastava v gorakh, 1953) were box-office hits.

Erdman had a good ear for the tone, ethical foundation, and humor of folktales, which made him the ideal partner for director **Aleksandr Rou** on children's favorites such as *Father Frost* (Morozko, 1964) and *Fire, Water and . . . Brass Pipes* (Ogon', voda, i . . . mednye truby, 1968), and animator **Ivan Ivanov-Vano** on *The Twelve Months* (Dvenadtsat' mesiatsev, 1956), among others. Perhaps the most loved **animation** film based on an Erdman screenplay is **Lev Atamanov**'s *The Snow Queen* (Snezhnaia koroleva, 1957) from Hans Christian Andersen's tale.

Other films: *Sporting Honor* (Sportivnaia chest', 1951); *Tales about Lenin* (Rasskazy o Lenine, 1958); *The City of Masters* (Gorod masterov, 1966).

ERMLER, FRIDRIKH MARKOVICH [real name: Vladimir Markovich Breslav] (b. 13 May 1898, Rechitsa [other sources: Lettonie], Latvia–d. 12 July 1967, Leningrad). Russian director and screenwriter. Ermler came from a petit-bourgeois family and was educated as a pharmacist. During the 1918–1921 Civil War he joined the Red Army and initially acted as a spy behind the Russian-German frontline (at that point, he adopted his pseudonym). Later, he was purportedly captured by White Army soldiers and tortured. Ermler then worked for the Soviet secret police (ChK) and achieved the rank of deputy head of the so-called Special (i.e., secret service) Department of the Red Army. In 1923–1924, he studied acting at the Leningrad Institute for Screen Arts and worked in the scriptwriting department of the film factory North-West Cinema (Sevzapkino, later: **Lenfilm Studio**). In 1924, together with fellow budding director Eduard Ioganson (1894–1942) and actor **Fedor Nikitin**, among others, Ermler organized an experimental cinema workshop (KEM—*kinoeksperimental'naia masterskaia*) and completed his first film project, the eccentric short *Scarlet Fever* (Skarlatina). Originally solicited as a "culture film" (*kul'turfil'm*) by the municipal health department, it has been called the formally most daring of all of Ermler's works.

In *Little Katia, the Paper Reinette* (aka *Katka's Reinette Apples/* Kat'ka—Bumazhnyi Ranet, 1926, codirected with Ioganson), an abused street merchant gets impregnated by a thief but finds genuine love and dignity by adopting the proper Soviet lifestyle. *The House in the Snowdrifts* (Dom v sugrobakh, 1927), based on motifs from Evgenii Zamiatin's story "The Cave," depicts the rebirth of a starving musician once he recognizes the benevolence of the new Communist system. *The Cobbler of Paris* (Parizhskii sapozhnik, 1928), a vigorous attack on sexual promiscuity among Soviet youth, caused controversies because of its subject matter but was generally hailed by the leftist art community.

In 1929, Ermler shot his silent era masterpiece, *A Fragment of the Empire* (Oblomok imperii). A glorification of the deep-running effects of the Bolshevik Revolution both on the human mind and the social environment, it tells the story of a soldier who suffers a concussion on the battlefields of World War I and falls into a coma. Waking up as an amnesiac after several years, he is astonished to see the innovations brought about by the Soviet system. The tormenting process of slowly regaining memory is visualized as an associative chain of metaphors, contrasting the destructive, inhumane past to the positive present.

With the advent of sound, Ermler abandoned artistic experimentation and turned to pure propaganda. In helping define Soviet mainstream, his work in the 1930s and 1940s became both trendsetting and norm shaping. Together with **Sergei Iutkevich**, he created one of the most influential early Soviet sound films, the industrial drama *The Counterplan* (Vstrechnyi, 1932). Its immediate and lasting success put Ermler in a leading position in Soviet cinema that he kept over the following two decades. All of his subsequent films were cleverly conceived, unabashedly affirmative responses to the Communist establishment's political campaigns. Thus, *The Peasants* (Krest'iane, 1935) focuses on a *kulak*—a wealthy farmer—who masquerades as an activist of collectivization yet secretly undermines Iosif Stalin's policies, murdering his own wife in the process and attempting to destroy the Party messenger.

The high point of Ermler's exercises in political demagoguery was his infamous two-part, four-hour diatribe *The Great Citizen* (Velikii grazhdanin, 1937–1939). A barely disguised hagiography of Sergei Kirov whose 1934 murder had been used by the Stalinist leadership as pretext to launch new terror waves, it is an apologia for the paranoid Soviet internal policies in the 1930s; the film won Ermler a Stalin Prize in 1941. Never before were discussions about ideological issues transferred onto the screen with such directness, and never before was the Communist Party itself shown from within, as a locus of "class struggle." The film's official canonization had consequences for the studio too: following the usual inner-bureaucratic debates about the script, those Lenfilm administrators who had raised objections against it were later removed from their positions; Ermler and his coauthors declared their efforts to be part of "the ongoing class struggle in Soviet cinema."

In World War II, Ermler helmed the first full-length feature film after the major studios had been evacuated—under his administrative leadership—to Central Asia. *She Defends Her Motherland* (aka *No Greater Love*/Ona zashchishchaet rodinu, 1943; Stalin Prize 1946) tells the story of partisans led by a heroic woman whose husband and toddler son were murdered by German troops. *The Great Turning Point* (Velikii perelom, 1945) is an attempt to illustrate principles of Soviet military strategy and decision-making processes that had brought about the victory over the Nazi intruders. For this megaproduction, launched during the last year of the war, the director was recognized with another Stalin Prize in 1946 and a Grand Prize at the 1946 Cannes Festival. *The Great Force* (Velikaia sila, 1950, Stalin Prize 1951) thematizes the imminent "dangers of Western genetics" and the Central Committee's vigorous and successful fight against it.

Interestingly, when the official struggle against the previously dominating "theory of conflictlessness" was initiated in 1952, Ermler reacted with a satirical short, *Shattered Dreams* (Razbitye mechty, 1953). But even its mildly critical undertones were considered inappropriate, and the film was released only in 1962 under the title *Dinner by Invitation* (Zvanyi uzhin). During the 1950s Thaw, when Ermler's Stalinist films were hidden in the archives, he turned to private themes. Thus, *Unfinished Story* (Neokonchennaia povest', 1955) is an inspirational melodrama about an incurably ill engineer-activist and his doctor who fall in love. Ermler then made the feature-length semi-**documentary** *To the Judgment of History* (Pered sudom istorii, 1965), centered on interviews with Vasilii V. Shul'gin (1878–1976), a former anti-Bolshevik politician and émigré who was forcibly returned to the USSR, spent decades in GULAG concentration camps, and was expected to admit that his patriotic and bourgeois ideals had suffered a fiasco. However, according to critic Valerii Golovskoi, Shul'gin's impressive personality stole the film, while the conclusions from his discussions with "the Historian" (played by an actor) were ambiguous at best.

Ermler's reputation as a trusted secret service collaborator followed him to the end; his loyalty to the system was unconditional and not at all shaken by the mild revisions occurring during the Thaw—as a matter of fact, he then publicly blamed Stalin for the degeneration of cinema. To be sure, Ermler's innovative talent as a filmmaker in the silent period is also beyond doubt. His early pictures reveal what could have become of this director had he not given in so completely to the demands of the Soviet establishment.

Ermler became a member of the Communist Party in 1919; he was named People's Artist of the Soviet Union in 1948.

Other films: *Children of the Storm* (Deti buri, 1926); *Day One* (Den' pervyi, 1958).

ERMOL'EV, IOSIF NIKOLAEVICH [French: Jacques N. Ermolieff] (b. 24 March 1889–d. 20 February 1962, Los Angeles). Russian-French producer. Ermol'ev was hired by the Moscow branch of Pathé in 1907. In 1912, he became a partner in the distribution company Ermol'ev, Sarkhin, and Segel' in Rostov-on-the-Don. Three years later, Ermol'ev moved to Moscow where he founded his own production company, with an elephant as its emblem. Of particular importance is Ermol'ev's work with **Iakov Protazanov**, for whom he produced two of the most accomplished Russian silents: *Queen of Spades* (Pikovaia dama, 1916) from Aleksandr Pushkin's short story, and *Father Sergius* (Otets Sergii, 1918), an adaptation of Lev Tolstoi's novella, both starring **Ivan Mozzhukhin**. **Aleksandr Ivanovskii** began his film career with Ermol'ev's company, specializing in adaptations of Russian classics such as *The Stationmaster*

(Stantsionnyi smotritel', 1918) after Pushkin, and *Punin and Baburin* (Punin i Baburin, 1919) from a story by Ivan Turgenev. Ermol'ev's output grew exponentially to up to 40 pictures per year. He also produced a pro-Communist *agitka*, solicited by the Moscow Film Committee: **Aleksandr Razumnyi**'s *Comrade Abram* (Tovarishch Abram, 1918).

Not long after the Bolshevik takeover, Ermol'ev relocated his company, including personnel, equipment, and film stock, to Yalta on the Crimean peninsula and subsequently to Paris in 1920. (In 1922, the Soviet government combined the remaining assets with those of his former competitor, **Aleksandr Khanzhonkov**, into Goskino state film factory (*kinofabrika*), which became **Mosfilm Studio** in 1935). In France, Ermol'ev initially worked as executive producer for Gaumont Franco Films before creating his own production company, Les Films Ermolieff, renamed later as Productions Albatros. He hired numerous émigrés but also gave the French film market noteworthy impulses. One of Ermol'ev's trademarks was stories with an exotic background such as *The Tales of a Thousand and One Nights* (Les contes des mille et une nuits, 1921). Ermol'ev gave avant-gardist French filmmakers a chance to create innovative pictures, for example, Jean Epstein, who made *The Lion of the Moguls* (Le Lion des Mogols, 1924) starring Mozzhukhin. Ermol'ev's productions included several successful serials, among them Aleksandr Volkov's nine-hour *The House of Mystery* (La Maison du Mystère, 1923) and Viacheslav Turzhanskii's *Michel Strogoff* (1926). In 1922, Ermol'ev moved to Munich, where he founded yet another studio that turned out Russian-themed pictures such as *Taras Bulba* (1924) and *Wolga-Wolga* (1928), while his Paris enterprise continued to produce pictures for the French market.

In 1937, Ermol'ev moved to the United States, where he produced *Outpost in Morocco* (1948) and *Fort Algiers* (1953).

Other films: *Slums of Petersburg* (Peterburgskie trushchoby, 1915); *Dance of Death* (Pliaska smerti, 1916); *Avoid Blood* (Ne nado krovi, 1917); *Kean* (1923); *Depths of the Big City* (Tiefen der Großstadt, 1924); *The Courier of the Tsar* (Der Kurier des Zaren, 1935).

ESTONIAN CINEMA. *See* ANIMATION; JÄRVET, JÜRI; KIISK, KALJO; KIVI, EVE; LAIUS, LEIDA; PÄRN, PRIIT; PARS,

HEINO; RAPPAPORT, GERBERT; TALLINFILM STUDIO; TU-
GANOV, ELBERT; ULFSAK, LEMBIT.

EVSTIGNEEV, EVGENII ALEKSANDROVICH (b. 9 October
1926, Nizhnii Novgorod–d. 4 March 1992, London). Russian actor. In 1951 Evstigneev, originally a locksmith, graduated from the
theater school in Gor'kii and joined the troupe of the district drama
theater in Vladimir; in 1954–1956, he studied at the studio school of
the Moscow Art Theater (MKhAT). From 1957 to 1970, Evstigneev
belonged to the founding troupe of The Contemporary (Sovremennik). When its leader, **Oleg Efremov**, was appointed chief director
of MKhAT, Evstigneev joined him and became one of the theater's
most recognizable and reliable performers.

In Soviet cinema, Evstigneev debuted in **Vladimir Petrov**'s adaptation of a story by Aleksandr Kuprin, *The Duel* (Poedinok, 1957).
Bald and wiry, with a characteristic hoarse voice, he was particularly
effective in **comedies**, for example, as the malicious bureaucrat Dynin
in **Elem Klimov**'s satire *Welcome, or No Admittance to Strangers*
(Dobro pozhalovat', ili Postoronnim vkhod vospreshchen, 1964).
Evstigneev's sharp characterizations of unlikable people are enriched
by psychological complexity, both in comedy and drama. Even to
the most reprehensible parts, the actor added subtle vulnerability or
melancholy, preventing the viewer from simplistic judgment. That
ability made him particularly valuable in literary adaptations, for
example, as General Pralinskii in **Aleksandr Alov** and **Vladimir
Naumov**'s *A Nasty Anecdote* (Skvernyi anekdot, 1966), a grotesque,
darkly satirical assault on opportunism and kowtowing adapted from
a Fedor Dostoevskii story. With almost 100 movie roles to his credit,
Evstigneev became a household name for Soviet audiences who
enjoyed both his impersonations of naïve, cumbersome intellectuals
and mean administrators.

Evstigneev joined the Communist Party in 1960. He won a USSR
State Prize in 1974 for his stage work and was named People's Artist
of the USSR in 1983.

Other films: *Trust Me, People* (Ver'te mne, liudi, 1965); *The Flight*
(Beg, 1970); *The Black Hen, or The Underground Inhabitants* (Chernaia kuritsa, ili Podzemnye zhiteli, 1981); *Heart of a Dog* (Sobach'e

sertse, 1988); *The Yankees' New Adventures at King Arthur's Court* (Novye prikliucheniia ianki pri dvore korolia Artura, 1989).

– F –

FAINTSIMMER, ALEKSANDR MIKHAILOVICH (b. 31 December 1906, Ekaterinoslav [Dnepropetrovsk, Ukraine]–d. 21 March 1982, Moscow). Russian and Belarusian director and screenwriter. Faintsimmer studied at the State Film School (GTK—later **VGIK**), graduating in 1927, and subsequently worked as an assistant director for **Vsevolod Pudovkin** on *The End of St. Petersburg* (Konets Sankt Peterburga, 1927) and for **Iulii Raizman** on *The Penal Colony* (Katorga, 1928).

Faintsimmer made his directorial debut at Belgoskino (later **Belarusfilm**) with the features *Hotel "Savoy"* (Otel' 'Savoi,' 1930) and *Happiness* (Schast'e, aka *Wind from the East*/Veter s vostoka, 1932). His first major project, *Lieutenant Kizhe* (aka *The Czar Wants to Sleep*/Poruchik Kizhe, 1934), from a screenplay by Iurii Tynianov, was a witty satire of the Russian bureaucracy—embodied by the arrogant stupidity of Pavel I—and its intrinsic absurdity. None of Faintsimmer's subsequent films could match this picture's sharpness and originality. *Tanker Derbent*, which premiered in June 1941, is devoted to the Stakhanov movement of industrial activists at Soviet shipyards. *Kotovskii* (1943) is a conspicuously selective biopic about the legendary, bald-headed Civil War commander. *Konstantin Zaslonov* (aka *The Secret Brigade*/Kanstancin Zaslonau, 1949, codirected with **Vladimir Korsh-Sablin**) won its directors a Stalin Prize in 1950. Two of Faintsimmer's more demagogical pictures are the Cold War litany *They Have a Homeland* (U nikh est' rodina, 1949, codirected by Vladimir Legoshin), rewarded with a Stalin Prize in 1951, and *Dawn over the Neman* (Aušra prie Nemuno/Nad Nemanom rassvet, 1953), touted as a Lithuanian production although made predominantly with **Lenfilm Studio** resources.

Faintsimmer landed a huge hit with *The Gadfly* (Ovod, 1955), a romantic love story (and antireligious diatribe) adapted from Ethel Vojnich's novel. *Night without Mercy* (Noch' bez miloserdiia, 1961) is a patriotic potboiler about an American spy plane pilot who deliberately violates the USSR borders. During the last decade of his career, Faintsimmer devoted himself to the traditionally underrepresented genre of the social thriller with blockbusters such as *No Right to Fail* (Bez prava na oshibku, 1974) and *The Cafeteria on Piatnitskaia Street* (Traktir na Piatnitskoi, 1978).

Faintsimmer, whose solid craftsmanship and political adaptability secured him an exceptionally long career in Soviet cinema, was named Merited Artist of the Belorussian SSR in 1935 and Merited Artist of the Lithuanian SSR (incorrectly listed in some sources as Latvian SSR) in 1954. His son is film director Leonid Kvinikhidze.

Other films: *Baltic Sailors* (aka *Men of the Sea*/Baltiitsy, 1938); *To Those at Sea* (Za tekh, kto v more, 1948); *Girl with a Guitar* (Devushka s gitaroi, 1958); *Far in the West* (Daleko na zapade, 1968). *See also* BELARUSIAN CINEMA; LITHUANIAN CINEMA.

FAIZIEV, LATIF [some Russian sources list the patronymic Abidovich] (b. 2 January 1929, Tashkent). Uzbek director and scriptwriter. Faiziev studied under **Ihor' Savchenko** at the Soviet State Film School **VGIK**, graduating in 1951. He was one of Savchenko's assistants on the monumental World War II picture *The Third Blow* (Tretii udar, 1948) and the biopic *Taras Shevchenko* (1951) in which he also played an episodic part. Faiziev then returned to Uzbekistan, directing newsreels and **documentaries** at the Tashkent film studio (**Uzbekfilm Studio**), before debuting as feature film director with *The Bay and the Farmhand* (Bai i batrak, 1954; codirected with Aleksandr Ginzburg), from a play by Hamza Hakim-zade (1889–1929).

Faiziev's second picture, *The Fall of the Emirate* (Krushenie emirata, 1955, codirected with **Vladimir Basov**), was devoted to the Civil War in Uzbekistan in the 1920s. The dramatic—and sometimes tragic—historical tale *By Order of Lenin* (Po putevke Lenina, 1957) depicts the establishment of the first university in Central Asia and the conflicts that arose from the presence of female students.

The Second Blooming (Vtoroe tsvetenie, 1960) reflects Faiziev's attempt to connect both the private and the professional conflicts of a farm administrator into one coherent story, an approach further developed in *Tiny Bird* (Ptichka-nevelichka, 1961). *The Star of Ulugbek* (Zvezda Ulugbeka, 1965), a biopic about a 15th-century

Central Asian ruler and astronomer, the sultan of Samarkand, Muhammad Ulugbek (1394–1449), focuses on the incompatibility of an enlightened mind and the oppressive political conditions under which he must live. Faiziev landed a huge box-office hit with the colorful Uzbek-Indian coproduction *The Adventures of Ali Baba and the Forty Thieves* (Ali Baba Aur Chalis Chor/Prikliucheniia Ali-Baby i soroka razboinikov, 1979, codirected with Umesh Mehra), the greatest popular success of **Uzbek cinema**. Another coproduction with India, *The Legend of Love* (Sohni mahiwal/Legenda o liubvi, 1984, codirected by Mehra), also became a box-office hit. *By the Law of the Jungle* (Shikari, aka Po zakonu dzhunglei, 1991, with Mehra), an Uzbek-Indian-Russian melodrama with thriller elements, largely follows the aesthetics of Bollywood cinema.

Throughout his career, Faiziev also directed propaganda films such as *Serving the Fatherland* (aka *The Job of Parenthood*/Sluzha otechestvu, 1981), a transparently apologetic tale about Soviet-Afghan ties in the 1930s, and the thriller *The Golden Fleece* (Zolotoe runo, 1982) about foreign coin smugglers, which depicts the role of the KGB in an idealized manner.

Faiziev joined the Communist Party in 1953. He was named People's Artist of the Uzbek SSR in 1979. In 1958–1967, he served as the first secretary of the Uzbek Filmmakers' Union. In 1986, Faiziev was appointed executive director of the Uzbek Hamza Drama Theater.

Other films: *Sacred Blood* (Sviashchennaia krov', 1956); *Born in a Thunderstorm* (Rodivshiisia v grozu, 1966); *Sons of the Fatherland* (Syny otechestva, 1968); *Sunrise over the Ganges* (Vozkhod nad Gangom, 1975); *The Dragon Hunt* (Okhota na drakona, 1986, with Nicaragua).

FALL OF BERLIN, THE (Padenie Berlina, 1949). **Mosfilm Studio**. Two parts: 84 and 83 min., color. Directed by **Mikheil Chiaureli**. Script: Petr Pavlenko, Mikheil Chiaureli. Cinematography: **Leonid Kosmatov**. Music: **Dmitrii Shostakovich**. Cast: **Mikheil Gelovani**, **Boris Andreev**, Marina Kovaleva, Sof'ia Giatsintova, **Nikolai Bogoliubov**, **Maksim Shtraukh**, **Aleksei Gribov**, Grigorii Belov, Ruben Simonov. Premiere: 21 January 1950.

Steelworker Aleksei Ivanov (Andreev) achieves a new record in melting steel, for which Iosif Stalin and other Soviet leaders honor him personally in Moscow. On the day of Aleksei's wedding to country teacher Marina Rumiantseva (Kovaleva), Nazi Germany attacks the Soviet Union. Aleksei, now a Red Army sergeant, participates in the defense of Moscow. He also fights in Stalingrad where the German Sixth Army surrenders to the victorious Soviet troops. In his destroyed native village, Ivanov vows to avenge the murder of his mother (Giatsintova) and the abduction of his wife. At the same time in Yalta, Stalin admonishes Winston Churchill for not opening the second front.

Speaking to the high-level staff, Stalin develops a strategy for the final defeat of Adolf Hitler's armies. Aleksei Ivanov is among the troops preparing the battle at the river Oder. Meanwhile, Hitler and his gang try everything to prevent their downfall, but to no avail. Hitler orders the flooding of the Berlin metro, causing the death of thousands of women and children, and then marries Eva Braun. He and Braun commit suicide, while Aleksei is among the Soviet troops storming the Imperial Chancellery. He also finds his wife, who has been liberated from a concentration camp. Stalin arrives in Berlin on a plane and makes a vow to the cheering crowd that he will protect peace.

FATE OF A MAN, THE (Sud'ba cheloveka, 1959). **Mosfilm Studio**. 103 min., b/w. Directed by **Sergei Bondarchuk**. Script: Iurii Lukin, Fedor Shakhmagonov from Mikhail Sholokhov's 1957 short story. Cinematography: Vladimir Monakhov. Music: **Veniamin Basner**. Cast: Sergei Bondarchuk, Zinaida Kirienko, Pavlik Boriskin, Pavel Volkov, Kirill Alekseev, Iurii Averin. Premiere: 12 April 1959.

In spring 1946, the prematurely aged driver Andrei Sokolov (Bondarchuk) tells a casual acquaintance the tragic story of his life. Before the war, he had fallen in love, started a family, and built a house. German bombs destroyed the house and killed his wife (Kirienko) and two daughters. As a POW, Sokolov goes through the hell of a Nazi concentration camp but upholds his dignity and humanity. Managing to escape, Sokolov hopes to see his son, who serves as an officer, but on the last day of war, the son is killed too. Desperate and lonely, Sokolov encounters an orphaned toddler and takes him in, assuring the boy that he is his real father.

FATHER SERGIUS (Otets Sergii, aka Kniaz' Kasatskii, 1918). **Iosif Ermol'ev** Company. 71 min., b/w. Directed by **Iakov Protazanov**. Script: Aleksandr Volkov from Lev Tolstoi's 1894 novella. Cinematography: Nikolai Rudakov, **Fedor Burgasov**. Cast: **Ivan Mozzhukhin**, Ol'ga Kondorova, **Vladimir Gaidarov**, Nikolai Panov, **Natal'iia Lisenko**, Iona Talanov, **Vera Orlova**. Premiere: 14 May 1918.

The young, hot-headed Prince Stepan Kasatskii (Mozzhukhin), an admirer of Tsar Nikolai I (Gaidarov), falls in love with Meri Korotkova, not suspecting that for years she was the monarch's mistress. After her confession, Kasatskii vows to abandon society and enters a monastery under the name of Father Sergius. A famous recluse, he is visited by numerous people hoping to find spiritual guidance and healing. The moody, rich Madame Makovkina (Lisenko) tries to seduce Sergius, who overcomes the temptation by severing a finger. But he gives in to the charms of a mentally disturbed merchant's daughter (Orlova) and leaves the Church. Arrested as a homeless person, Kasatskii is exiled to Siberia.

FEDOROVA, ZOIA ALEKSEEVNA (b. 21 December 1907–d. 10 December 1981, Moscow). Russian actress. In 1929–1930, Fedorova learned her craft in the theater studio of Iurii Zavadskii (1894–1977) and continued her studies at the drama studio of the Moscow Theater of the Revolution, graduating in 1934.

Fedorova's dashing looks and youthful, unabashed sensuality marked her early movie stardom, beginning with **Ihor' Savchenko**'s musical **comedy** *The Accordion* (Garmon', 1934) and **Leo Arnshtam**'s popular revolutionary drama *Girlfriends* (Podrugi, 1936). Many of Fedorova's roles were politically colored, for example, in **Sergei Iutkevich**'s *Man with a Rifle* (Chelovek s ruzh'em, 1938) and **Fridrikh Ermler**'s *The Great Citizen* (Velikii grazhdanin, 1937–1939), in which she portrayed a devoted youth activist, Nadezhda Kolesnikova. The female lead, Klava Belkina, in **Aleksandr Ivanovskii** and **Gerbert Rappaport**'s apolitical hit *Musical Story* (Muzykal'naia istoriia, 1940) in 1941 won Fedorova her first Stalin Prize, while her performance in *Girlfriends at the Front* (Frontovye prodrugi, 1942) was rewarded with a second one. Yet when her real-life romance with the U.S. Marine attaché Jackson Tate was discovered, it put an abrupt end to her career. Accused of foreign espionage, Fedorova was sent to a GULAG labor camp for nearly 10 years.

After her release in 1955, Fedorova was able to make a modest comeback with episodic parts in **El'dar Riazanov**'s *Girl without Address* (Devushka bez adresa, 1957), **Andrei Tutyshkin**'s *Wedding in Malinovka* (Svad'ba v Malinovke, 1967), and **Vladimir Men'shov**'s *Moscow Does Not Believe in Tears* (Moskva slezam ne verit, 1979), among others. The aged and increasingly rotund actress often portrayed morose teachers, moody neighbors, and gossipy wives, usually in comedies and **children's films**.

Fedorova made news again when her body, shot point blank, was discovered in her classy apartment at Kutuzovskii prospekt in Moscow. The murder was never officially solved, although speculations ranging from an alleged involvement in black market sales of jewelry to tensions with the Leonid Brezhnev clan continue to this day.

Fedorova was named Merited Artist of the RSFSR in 1965.

Other films: *The Honeymoon* (Medovyi mesiats, 1956); *Operation "Y" and Other Adventures of Shurik* (Operatsiia 'Y' i drugie prikliucheniia Shurika, 1965); *The Car, the Violin, and Stain the Dog* (Avtomobil', skripka i sobaka Kliaksa, 1974).

FOGEL', VLADIMIR PETROVICH (b. 1902 [other sources: 1901], Moscow–d. 8 June 1929, Moscow). Russian actor. Fogel' was born into the family of a clerk; he studied at the cinema college (*tekhnikum*) in Moscow before joining **Lev Kuleshov**'s avant-garde film workshop. Kuleshov cast him in several of his pictures—*The Unusual Adventures of Mr. West in the Land of the Bolsheviks* (Neobychainye prikliucheniia mistera Vesta v strane bol'shevikov, 1924), *The Ray of Death* (Luch' smerti, 1925), and, most effectively, *By the Law* (Po zakonu, 1926), where Fogel' proved to be a fine ensemble player, capable of portraying conflicting emotions ranging from friendship, trust, love, and duty to aggressiveness and insanity.

Although his artistic methods were initially shaped by Kuleshov's theories of film acting, Fogel' outgrew the dogma within a few years and adopted a degree of psychological refinement matching that of his partners such as **Nikolai Batalov** of the Moscow Art Theater (MKhAT), particularly in **Abram Room**'s social melodrama ***Third***

Meshchanskaia Street (aka *Bed and Sofa*/Tret'ia Meshchanskaia, aka Liubov' vtroem, 1927). The actor conveyed his character Volodia's strength and inner doubts, charm, and immaturity with rare mastery, and deservedly became one of the admired stars of early Soviet cinema. He subsequently played under the direction of filmmakers such as **Vsevolod Pudovkin**, **Fedor Otsep**, and **Grigorii Roshal'**. Most prominently, Fogel' was one of fellow Kuleshovian **Boris Barnet**'s favorite actors in blockbuster **comedies** such as *The Girl with the Hatbox* (Devushka s korobkoi, 1927) as an honorable yet awkward clerk hopelessly in love, and *The House on Trubnaia Square* (Dom na Trubnoi, 1928), displaying romantic charm and chivalry. He also played one of the leads in **Sergei Komarov**'s action comedy *The Doll with the Millions* (Kukla s millionami, 1928).

Fogel', who suffered from chronic severe depression, committed suicide.

Other films: *Chess Fever* (Shakhmatnaia goriachka, 1925); *Miss Mend* (1926); *Soil in Chains* (aka *The Yellow Pass*/Zemlia v plenu, 1927); *The Salamander* (Salamandra, 1927).

FOUNDLING, THE (Podkidysh, 1939). **Mosfilm Studio**. 76 min., b/w. Directed by **Tat'iana Lukashevich**. Script: Agniia Barto, **Rina Zelenaia**. Cinematography: Semen Sheinin. Music: **Nikolai Kriukov**. Cast: Veronika Lebedeva, **Faina Ranevskaia**, **Rostislav Pliatt**, Ol'ga Zhizneva, Rina Zelenaia, Petr Repnin, **Anatolii Papanov**.

Five-year old Natasha (Lebedeva) runs away from home when her mother (Zhizneva) leaves her with her disinterested brother for a few hours. The charming, trusting girl joins a group of kids in a kindergarten, then a lonely bachelor and geologist (Pliatt), and a bossy lady, Lialia (Ranevskaia) with her husband, Mulia (Repnin), who all become attached to Natasha and want to take care of her. Finally, everybody meets at the militia section for lost children, trying to figure out where the girl might be and to whom she should belong. In the meantime, an official finds Natasha and brings her home to her family.

FREINDLIKH, ALISA BRUNOVNA (b. 8 December 1934, Leningrad). Russian actress. Freindlikh, daughter of famed stage and film actor **Bruno Freindlikh**, studied at the Ostrovskii State Theater

Institute in Leningrad, graduating in 1957. She first worked at the Komissarzhevskaia Theater, then joined the Lensovet Theater in 1961, and in 1983 became a member of the troupe of the Grand Dramatic Theater (BDT, renamed Tovstonogov Theater in 1992). In the 1960s and 1970s, the actress's stage repertory ranged from Shakespeare's Juliet to contemporaries, Russian and international classics, and even Neil Simon **comedies**.

Freindlikh first appeared in cinema in Vladimir Vengerov's *The City Turns on Its Lights* (Gorod zazhigaet ogni, 1958) from a story by Viktor Nekrasov. She gained name recognition with **Elem Klimov**'s satire *Adventures of a Dentist* (Pokhozhdeniia zubnogo vracha, 1965) and roles in musical comedies such as **Giorgi Shengelaia**'s *Melodies of Veris Quarter* (Veris ubnis melodiebi/Melodii Veriiskogo kvartala, 1973) where she portrayed a ballet teacher. Her performance as Liudmila Kalugina in **El'dar Riazanov**'s superhit *Office Romance* (Sluzhebnyi roman, 1978), in which she reveals the emotional depth and inner beauty of an outwardly unremarkable, ordinary woman, shot Freindlikh to national stardom. Her subsequent film roles convey quiet, enigmatic intensity, for example, as the wife in **Andrei Tarkovskii**'s *Stalker* (1979), or power-hungry hysteria—such as Lady Anna Vyrubova in Klimov's *Agony* (aka *Rasputin*/Agoniia, 1975–1981) or the coldhearted wife in **Aleksandr Kaidanovskii**'s *A Simple Death* (Prostaia smert', 1985) from Lev Tolstoi's "The Death of Ivan Il'ich." Among Russian actresses, Freindlikh possesses a unique artistic aura—perhaps comparable to that of Judy Dench—comprising dignified distance, an element of harshness that conceals tenderness and vulnerability, and a complete lack of vanity.

Freindlikh was named People's Artist of the USSR in 1981. She was married to actor and director Igor' Vladimirov (1919–1999).

Other films: *Family Happiness* (Semeinoe schast'e, 1970); *A Cruel Romance* (Zhestokii romans, 1984); *Evenings near Moscow* (Podmoskovnye vechera, 1994); *Female Logic* (Zhenskaia logika, 2001–2004, TV); *On the Upper Maslovka* (Na Verkhnei Maslovke, 2005).

FREINDLIKH, BRUNO ARTUROVICH (b. 10 October 1909, St. Petersburg–d. 9 [other sources: 7] July 2002, St. Petersburg). Russian actor. Freindlikh studied acting at a local theater college (*tekhnikum*) in Leningrad in 1931–1934 and at the Institute for the Increased

Qualification of Art Workers in 1936–1938. Beginning in 1931, he played on the stage of various theaters in Leningrad, Tashkent, and other cities. In 1948, Freindlikh joined the troupe of the Leningrad Academic Pushkin Theater (the former Aleksandrinskii) where, among numerous leads, he was Hamlet in **Grigorii Kozintsev**'s famous production, as well as Ivan Turgenev in the biographical play *Elegy* (Elegiia); he later impersonated the writer in an episode of **Igor' Talankin**'s biopic *Chaikovskii* (1970).

Freindlikh debuted in cinema as Italian inventor Marconi in **Gerbert Rappaport**'s nationalist biopic *Aleksandr Popov* (1949). Although the role was conceptualized with an openly negative bias, Freindlikh offered a differentiated characterization that won him a Stalin Prize in 1951. With stern, authoritarian features and an icy transparency of his eyes, the actor seemed made to play movie villains and often was cast in supporting roles of that type, for example, in **Mikhail Shveitser**'s adventurous blockbuster *The Dagger* (Kortik, 1954), **Nadezhda Kosheverova**'s fairy-tale **comedy** *Kain XVIII* (1963)—as the minister of the secret police—and the spy thriller *The End of "Saturn"* (Konets "Saturna," 1967) where he impersonated Nazi admiral Wilhelm Canaris. But even in second-rate films Freindlikh was able to inform his characters with unexpected depth, and in some pictures he got a chance to transcend the cliché and reveal the psychological and philosophical potential of "negativity," most memorably as the jester in **Ian Frid**'s popular adaptation of Shakespeare's *Twelfth Night* (Dvenadtsataia noch', 1955), as the cynical duke in **Grigorii Kozintsev**'s *Don Quijote* (1957), and as the supreme commander in **Aleksandr Alov** and **Vladimir Naumov**'s *The Flight* (Beg, 1970).

Freindlikh was named People's Artist of the USSR in 1974. His daughter is actress **Alisa Freindlikh**.

Other films: *Rimskii-Korsakov* (1951); *Two Captains* (Dva kapitana, 1955); *Two Tickets for the Daytime Show* (Dva bileta na dnevnoi seans, 1967); *Stalingrad* (1989).

FREZ, IL'IA ABRAMOVICH (b. 2 September 1909, Roslavl', Smolensk district–d. 22 June 1994, Moscow). Russian director and screenwriter. Frez studied in the Cinema Department of the Ostrovskii Theater Institute in Leningrad, graduating in 1932, and subsequently in the same institute's Directing Department, graduating in 1935. He then worked at **Lenfilm Studio** as an assistant to **Grigorii Kozintsev** and **Leonid Trauberg**.

Frez made his directorial debut with the medium-length *The Elephant and the String* (Slon i verevochka, 1945), a naïvely didactic **children's film** from a screenplay by Agniia Barto (1906–1981). *The First-Grader* (Pervoklassnitsa, 1948), the story of a spoiled little brat transformed into a responsible Soviet schoolgirl, also displays an easy resolution of all conflicts. After a hiatus of five years, caused by attacks during the infamous "campaign against cosmopolitanism" during which Frez worked at the studios of **documentary** and popular science films in Kiev and Moscow (1948–1953), he returned to **Gor'kii Studio for Children's and Youth Films** and henceforth made exclusively films about children. His first major successes were the adventurous *Little Vasia Trubachev and His Pals* (Vasek Trubachev i ego tovarishchi, 1955) and its sequel, *Trubachev's Unit Is Fighting* (Otriad Trubacheva srazhaetsia, 1957), about a group of Moscow schoolchildren in the 1930s and during the war. Frez turned to contemporary problems with *I Bought a Dad* (Ia kupil papu, 1963) and *Traveler with Luggage* (Puteshestvennik s bagazhom, 1965) about children in search of a father. The director addressed the problems of a different age group in *I Loved You* (Ia vas liubil, 1967), a serious attempt to discuss the awakening of romantic feelings in teenagers.

Within the framework of children's and youth films, Frez tried a variety of approaches, some targeting young audiences exclusively, others directed toward adult viewers but retaining the child's point of view. Stories such as *The Adventures of the Little Yellow Suitcase* (Prikliucheniia zheltogo chemodanchika, 1971) tend toward the fantastic, while *The Weirdo from 5B Grade* (Chudak iz piatogo "B", 1972; USSR State Prize 1974) describes the relations between children of different age groups in a manner both psychologically realistic and funny. Frez's underlying pedagogical principles, always in tune with official Communist norms, positively emphasize the pure and idealistic elements in children, their sensitivity and vulnerability. In many of Frez's films, children are on their own, facing society's friendly and unfriendly facets, while adult characters are usually judged by the way in which they are able to respond to children's needs. The director's later films, especially *You Couldn't*

Imagine (Vam i ne snilos', 1983)—his greatest critical and popular success—demonstrate a darker outlook on the chances to harmonize generational relations.

Frez was named Merited Artist of the RSFSR in 1968 and People's Artist of the USSR in 1989. His son, Il'ia Frez Jr., is a cinematographer.

Other films: *We Didn't Learn That* (Eto my ne prokhodili, 1976); *Quarantine* (Karantin, 1983).

FRID, IAN BORISOVICH [real name Iakov Borisovich Fridland] (b. 31 May 1908, Krasnoiarsk–d. 21 December 2003, Stuttgart, Germany). Russian director and screenwriter. Frid studied directing at the Leningrad Theater Institute, from which he graduated in 1932, and later at the Soviet State Film School **VGIK** under **Sergei Eizenshtein**, graduating in 1938.

Frid's directorial debut was the short feature *Surgery* (Khirurgiia, 1939) from a story by Anton Chekhov. Over the following five decades, literary adaptations remained one of Frid's domains, with subjects ranging from Soviet revolutionary fare such as *Liubov' Iarovaia* (1953) from Konstantin Trenev's 1926 play—with over 46 million viewers, the highest grossing film of 1953—to Shakespeare's *Twelfth Night* (Dvenadtsataia noch', 1955), perhaps Frid's best-remembered achievement, which stands out for its fine performances by Klara Luchko (1926–2005), **Vasilii Merkur'ev**, and **Bruno Freindlikh**. Other popular adaptations include *Dog on the Manger* (Sobaka na sene, 1977) from Lope de Vega, and *The Honorable Martha* (Blagochestivaia Marta, 1980).

The versatile director joined Stalinist spy mania of the 1930s with *The Patriot* (Patriot, 1939), a film about Japanese undercover operations on the USSR's Far Eastern border. After less successful attempts in the genre of family and social drama such as *The Return* (Vozvrashchenie, 1940) and *Other People's Mischief* (Chuzhaia beda, 1960), Frid carved out a niche for himself with unabashedly entertaining movies, often adapted from operettas such as *The Fledermaus* (Letuchaia mysh', 1979). Many of his films became blockbusters. Of interest is the biographical melodrama *Farewell to Petersburg* (Proshchanie s Peterburgom, 1971) about Johann Strauss's visit to Russia. The director's reliable professionalism, light touch, and openly apolitical demeanor secured him the gratitude of millions of Soviet viewers, if not the appreciation of critics.

Frid, who joined the Communist Party in 1939, was named Merited Artist of the Buriat ASSR in 1951 in appreciation of **documentaries** devoted to that republic. In 1939, he began to teach at Leningrad Conservatory, which promoted him to the rank of full professor in 1970.

Other films: *Soviet Udmurtiia* (Sovetskaia Udmurtiia, 1950); *Soviet Buriat-Mongolia* (Sovetskaia Buriat-Mongoliia, 1951); *The Green Carriage* (Zelenaia kareta, 1967); *Free Wind* (Vol'nyi veter, 1983); *Tartuffe* (Tartiuf, 1992).

– G –

GABRIADZE, REVAZ [also: Rezo; Russian sources list the patronymic Levanovich] (b. 29 June 1936, Kutaisi, Georgia). Georgian screenwriter and director. Gabriadze studied journalism at Tbilisi State University, graduating in 1964. He then enrolled in the Supreme Courses for Screenwriters and Directors (VKSR) in Moscow where his teacher was **Aleksei Kapler**.

Gabriadze's debut as a screenwriter, *An Unusual Exhibition* (Arakhveulebrivi gamopena/Neobyknovennaia vystavka, 1969), was one of the most innovative, thought-provoking Soviet films about the mission of the artist. Directed by **Eldar Shengelaia**, it analyzes the inner conflict of a sculptor who betrays his higher calling for the sake of day-to-day earnings. In effect, Gabriadze made a statement about the chances for individual self-fulfillment in a collectivist society, similar in spirit to films by **Andrei Tarkovskii**, **Sergei Paradjanov**, and **Giorgi Shengelaia**. Also for Eldar Shengelaia, Gabriadze wrote *Crackpots* (Sherekilebi/Chudaki, 1974), a lyrical **comedy** about 19th-century outsiders who are talented and creative yet socially maladjusted.

Together with **Georgii Daneliia**, Gabriadze adapted Claude Tillier's popular novel *My Uncle Benjamin* for the screen, transferring the plot from France to 19th-century Georgia. The result, *Don't Grieve* (Ar daidardo/Ne goriui! 1969), is filled with Gabriadze's typical blend of wise, forgiving humor and bittersweet melancholy. His numerous screenplays of the 1970s include adaptations of Mikhail

Zoshchenko's *Serenade* (Serenada, 1969) and Luigi Pirandello's *The Jug* (Peola/Kuvshin, 1970).

In 1975, Gabriadze made his directorial debut with *A Caucasian Romance* (Kavkasiuri romansi/Kavkazskii romans), a short from the omnibus *Love, Thy Power Is Great*. Gabriadze's work in **Georgian cinema** has contributed to the emergence of a peculiar national style—largely apolitical, deliberately undidactic, with an intense awareness of eternal values such as beauty, love, kindness, and friendship—whose roots lie in Georgian folklore. His subsequent films include the comedic shorts *Conquerors of the Mountains* (Msvervalis dampkrobni/Pokoriteli gor, 1976), *The Lemon Cake* (Limonis torti/Limonnyi tort, 1977), and the experimental puppet film *Dreams of Kojori Forrest* (Kojris tkis sizmrebi/Sny Kodzhorskogo lesa, 1978, TV). By the end of the 1970s, when the stunning inventiveness of his artistry began to clash with cinema's restrictive boundaries, Gabriadze abandoned film direction.

Gabriadze is also known as a painter and sculptor. However, his main field of artistry became puppet theater; in 1981, he founded the Tbilisi Marionette Theater and soon made it world famous. His puppet play *Song of the Volga* (aka *The Battle of Stalingrad*) became a triumphant success and was shown in many countries.

Gabriadze was named Merited Artist of the Georgian SSR in 1979 and People's Artist of Georgia in 1989, the year when he was awarded a USSR State Prize for the puppet play *The Autumn of Our Spring*.

Other films: (as screenwriter) *White Stones* (Tetri qvebi/Belye kamni, 1972); *The Wager* (Nizlavi/Pari, 1974); *The Butterfly* (Pepela/Babochka, 1977); *Mimino* (1977); *Luck* (Sarmateba/Udacha, 1980); *Kin-Dza-Dza* (1986); *The Passport* (Pasport, 1990); *Asphalte* (2005, France).

GABRILOVICH, EVGENII IOSIFOVICH (b. 29 September 1899, Voronezh–d. 6 December 1993, Moscow). Russian screenwriter. After studying law for two years at Moscow University, in 1921 Gabrilovich became a professional writer and joined the Literary Center of Constructivists, staying with that organization until its dissolution by official decree in 1930. In 1930, he was hired by the studio Culture Film (Kul'turfil'm) as an editor; in 1931, he switched to the predecessor of **Mosfilm Studio** as an editor and author of intertitles.

In the mid-1930s, Gabrilovich started writing screenplays. One of them, *The Last Night* (Posledniaia noch', 1937), which describes the eve of the 1917 Bolshevik upheaval, was directed by **Iulii Raizman**. It marked the beginning of a central thematic line in Gabrilovich's work, the romanticized depiction of the October Revolution. It also was the beginning of the author's fruitful partnership with Raizman that lasted for half a century. Arguably, the most famous of their revolutionary tales is *A Communist* (Kommunist, 1957), which revitalized the image of the Bolshevik as a selfless, ascetic leader. A related theme in many of Gabrilovich's screenplays is the life of Vladimir Lenin. Beginning with *Tales about Lenin* (Rasskazy o Lenine, 1957, coauthored with **Nikolai Erdman** and Mikhail Vol'pin) and ending with *Lenin in Paris* (Lenin v Parizhe, 1981)—both directed by **Sergei Iutkevich**—this topic in Gabrilovich's interpretation reflected the changing zeitgeist. While the celluloid Lenin of the 1950s was a down-to-earth friend of rank-and-file people, he became an introspective intellectual in the 1960s (*Lenin in Poland*/Lenin v Pol'she, 1967, USSR State Prize) and a caring internationalist in the 1970s and 1980s détente (*On the Way to Lenin*/Unterwegs zu Lenin/Na puti k Leninu, 1970, a Soviet-East German coproduction).

A third group of Gabrilovich's scripts were devoted to the Great Patriotic War. *Mashen'ka* (1942, Stalin Prize 1943) irradiates genuine human warmth and hope, while *Person #217* (aka *Girl No. 217*/Chelovek No. 217, 1944, directed by **Mikhail Romm**) was an early—and understandably simplified—effort to show the mentality of Nazi Germany from the inside. Gabrilovich also penned a number of polemical screenplays dealing with contemporary problems, including *The Return of Vasilii Bortnikov* (aka *Vasili's Return*/Vozvrashchenie Vasiliia Bortnikova, 1953) for **Vsevolod Pudovkin**, one of the earliest signals of the ensuing Thaw, and the polemical *Your Contemporary* (Tvoi sovremennik, 1968) for Raizman. In a number of screenplays, Gabrilovich revealed an interest in women's emancipation, including *A Lesson in Life* (Urok zhizni, 1955), one of the first Soviet movies to juxtapose societal and private interests, and *A Strange Woman* (Strannaia zhenshchina, 1978), both helmed by Raizman.

Two of his most artistically notable scripts were directed by **Gleb Panfilov**: the Civil War drama *There's No Ford through Fire* (V ogne broda net, 1967) and the peculiar story of personal self-realization, *The*

Debut (Nachalo, 1970), which gave the Joan of Arc story a modern and unexpected twist.

Gabrilovich undoubtedly was the most consistently productive and versatile of all Soviet screenwriters. His longevity made him a witness to—and active participant in—the entire history of Soviet sound cinema, from inception to final fiasco. Gabrilovich's remarkably consistent success was secured by his rare gift for smoothly fitting characters of human interest into the ever-changing ideological framework. Although not a Party member, his political loyalty, professionalism, and genuine talent for conceiving suspenseful plots rendered his screenplays' ideological messages palatable to millions of viewers.

Gabrilovich was awarded the title Merited Artist of the RSFSR in 1969 and Hero of Socialist Labor in 1979. In 1982, he won his third USSR State Prize for *Lenin in Paris.* He began to teach at the Soviet State Film School **VGIK** in 1948 and was promoted to full professor in 1962. His son was the scriptwriter and television director Aleksei Gabrilovich.

Other films: *Two Fighters* (Dva boitsa, 1943); *Two Captains* (Dva kapitana, 1957); *Resurrection* (Voskresenie, 1960–1961); *Monologue* (Monolog, 1972); *Flight of the Bird* (Polet ptitsy, 1988).

GAIDAI, LEONID IOVICH (b. 30 January 1923, Svobodnyi settlement, Amur district–d. 19 November 1993, Moscow). Russian director, screenwriter, and actor. Gaidai, the son of a Ukrainian political activist exiled to Siberia, fought as a soldier in a scouts unit in the Great Patriotic War and was severely wounded. After being discharged in 1944, he studied at the studio school of the Irkutsk District Drama Theater, graduating in 1947, and subsequently acted on stage. He enrolled in **Grigorii Aleksandrov**'s workshop at the Soviet State Film School **VGIK**, which he finished in 1955. Gaidai then worked as an assistant to **Boris Barnet** on the **comedy** *Liana* (1955) in which he also played a supporting role (he continued to appear in minuscule episodic parts in several of his own films too).

After debuting with the Vladimir Korolenko adaptation *The Long Path* (Dolgii put', 1956, codirected with Valentin Nevzorov [1918–1961]), the budding director risked first steps in his trademark genre of comedy. *The Bridegroom from the Otherworld* (Zhenikh s togo sveta, 1958), about a narrow-minded bureaucrat who has to confront his falsely announced passing, was distinguished by wit and precise narrative rhythm but was criticized in the press for the "absence of positive characters." When the Soviet minister of culture, Nikolai Mikhailov, called the film "a lampooning of Soviet reality," it was severely censored and cut down to 47 minutes. In 1961, Gaidai followed with two shorts that made a splash: *Barbos the Dog and an Unusual Cross-Country Race* (Pes Barbos i neobychainyi kross) and *Bootleggers* (Samogonshchiki). They introduced a trio of characters who soon became known nationwide under their screen names "Booby" (*Balbes*), "Experienced" (*Byvalyi*), and "Coward" (*Trus*), as well as under the respective actors' names, **Iurii Nikulin**, Evgenii Morgunov, and **Georgii Vitsin**, forming an integral part of Soviet folklore and appearing in endless variations of jokes.

Gaidai dealt with contemporary Soviet subject matter in three comedies that were phenomenally successful at the box office and made the director's name prominent throughout the USSR. *Operation "Y" and Other Adventures of Shurik* (Operatsiia 'Y' i drugie prikliucheniia Shurika, 1965) consists of three novellas, while *Prisoner of the Caucasus* (aka *Kidnapping Caucasian Style*/Kavkazskaia plennitsa, 1966) and *The Diamond Arm* (Brilliantovaia ruka, 1968) feature one coherent story. Their adventurous plots with thriller and slapstick elements are complemented by satirical asides, sometimes exposing the shallowness of tiresome political rhetoric. Gaidai's ability to create a magnificent chemistry between his protagonists and elicit outstanding supporting performances made him an actors' favorite, although some of them later had to struggle with their persistent comedic image.

In the 1970s, searching for new paths, Gaidai turned to literary adaptations, revealing a preference for satirists of the 1920s New Economic Policy (NEP). Although *The Twelve Chairs* (Dvenadtsat' stul'ev, 1971, from the legendary rogue novel by Il'f and Petrov), *This Can't Be True!* (Ne mozhet byt'! 1975, based on stories by Mikhail Zoshchenko), and especially *Ivan Vasil'evich Changes His Job* (aka *Ivan Vasilievich: Back to the Future*/Ivan Vasil'evich meniaet professiiu, 1973, based on Mikhail Bulgakov's comedy) generated excellent audience responses with 40–60 million viewers each, *Incognito from Petersburg* (Inkognito iz Peterburga, 1978, from Nikolai Gogol''s

1836 *Inspector General*) flopped, probably because it was badly mangled by censors. In 1980, Gaidai helmed the Soviet-Finnish coproduction *Borrowing Matchsticks* (Za spichkami) from stories of leftist classic Maiju Lassila (pseudonym of Algoth Untola [1868–1918]). *Sportloto-82* (1982) marked Gaidai's return to contemporary fun and proved that the filmmaker had kept his prowess. But when the sudden liberalization of the mid-1980s allowed for more open satire, Gaidai's principal benevolence and loyalty toward Soviet society was less in demand. Only in *On Deribasovskaia the Weather Is Fine, or On Brighton Beach It's Raining Again* (Na Deribasovskoi khoroshaia pogoda, ili Na Braiton-Bich opiat' idut dozhdi, 1992), Gaidai took no prisoners, producing a hilarious post-Soviet travesty with fine parodies of Vladimir Lenin, Mikhail Gorbachev, and George Bush Sr. The film proves beyond doubt that this director could have made poignant comedies under neocapitalist conditions too.

Gaidai's best pictures are highly original, fast-paced buffooneries, with visual humor prevailing over the verbal, even though many one-liners from his films did become proverbial among Soviet citizens. The director's humor is enriched with sufficient satirical spice yet never turns bitter. A high-standard professional, Gaidai was a perfectionist with regards to acting and timing of gags—a rarity among Soviet directors. A noteworthy aspect of Gaidai's work is the homegrown nature of his humor: although many gags are inspired by universally appreciated silent classics—especially Charlie Chaplin and Harold Lloyd—Gaidai's films are enjoyed almost exclusively by Soviet and post-Soviet audiences. Sadly, the fact that he was by far the most popular of all Soviet filmmakers has only in post-Soviet times become a compliment. In the decade following his death, the snobbish critical neglect and condescension toward Gaidai were revised and turned into the opposite extreme, proclaiming Gaidai a classic filmmaker. A solid, even-handed assessment of this unique director is still wanting.

Gaidai joined the Communist Party in 1945 and was named People's Artist of the Russian Federation in 1974 and People's Artist of the USSR in 1989. He was married to actress Nina Grebeshkova (b. 1931), who played supporting roles in many of his films.

Other films: *Thrice Resurrected* (Trizhdy voskresshii, 1960); *Dangerous for Life!* (Opasno dlia zhizni! 1985); *The Private Detective, or*

Operation "Cooperation" (Chastnyi detektiv, ili operatsiia 'Kooperatsiia', 1989).

GAIDAROV, VLADIMIR GEORGIEVICH [in European films credited as Wladimir Gaidaroff] (b. 25 July 1893, Poltava–d. 17 December 1976, Leningrad). Ukrainian-Russian actor and director. Gaidarov studied history and philosophy at Moscow University from 1912 to 1917. After meeting Konstantin Stanislavskii in 1912, he became his student and began a stage career with the Moscow Art Theater (MKhAT) in 1914. Gaidarov also became a popular film actor, mostly portraying handsome, romantic young lovers. Thus, he was cast in several films by **Iakov Protazanov**: as Strizhevskii in *Miss Mary* (Panna Meri, 1916), as the student Glagolin in *Avoid Blood* (Ne nado krovi, 1917), but also as an imposing Tsar Nikolai I in the Lev Tolstoi adaptation *Father Sergius* (Otets Sergii, 1918). In several pictures, including Protazanov's *Maid Jenny* (Gornichnaia Dzhenni, 1918), his partner was fellow MKhAT member Ol'ga Gzovskaia (1889 [other sources: 1883]–1962).

In 1920, Gaidarov and Gzovskaia went to Estonia, working in Tallin; in 1921, they moved to Berlin where they settled for the next decade. Gaidarov was a valued performer in numerous German and French silents, including *The Burning Soil* (Der brennende Acker, 1921) and *The Man with the Iron Mask* (Der Mann mit der eisernen Maske, 1923) as the French king and his twin. He also performed in the sound films *Waves of Passion* (Wellen der Leidenschaft, 1930), *Luise, Queen of Prussia* (Luise, Königin von Preußen, 1931), and others.

In 1932, Gaidarov and Gzovskaia returned to what now was the Soviet Union. After being cast in the role of Rogoznyi in *Songs of the Steppe* (Stepnye pesni, 1934), Gaidarov joined the troupe of the Pushkin Theater in Leningrad in 1938, as did Gzovskaia. He made a spectacular movie comeback in **Vladimir Petrov**'s *The Battle of Stalingrad* (Stalingradskaia bitva, 1949), with a portrayal of Nazi commander Friedrich von Paulus that won him a Stalin Prize in 1950. Gaidarov's last screen appearance was in an episodic role in a Soviet-Norwegian coproduction, the biopic *Only One Life* (Vsego odna zhizn', aka Bare et liv—historien om Fridtjof Nansen, 1967).

Gaidarov was honored with the title Merited Artist of the RSFSR in 1940.

Other films: *And the Secret Was Swallowed by the Waves* (I tainu proglotili volny, 1917); *Aroma of Sin* (Aromat grekha, 1917); *Wife and Lover* (Zhena-liubovnitsa, 1918); *The Snowstorm* (Metel', 1918).

GAJIU, VALERIU [also spelled Gagiu; real name: Gaja; Russian sources: Gazhiu, Valerii Georgievich] (b. 1 May 1938, Chisinau [Kishinev]). Moldovan director and screenwriter. Gajiu studied in the Screenwriting Department of the Soviet State Film School **VGIK**, graduating in 1963. His first screenplay, *The Confession of Christian Luka* (Ispoved' Kristiana Luki), was turned into the film *When the Storks Fly Away* (Cind se duc cocorii/Kogda uletaiut aisty, 1963). Gajiu also wrote the screenplays for **Mikhail Kalik**'s poetic childhood meditation *Man Follows the Sun* (aka *Sandu Follows the Sun*/Omul merge dupa soare/Chelovek idet za solntsem, 1961).

Gajiu's directorial debut was the postwar drama *Bitter Grain* (aka *A Taste of Bread*/Gustul piinii/Gor'kie zerna, 1966, codirected with Vadim Lysenko) about three friends fighting for the Communist regime and the collectivization of agriculture in the 1940s. This grittily realistic film gained considerable official recognition and won a number of Soviet prizes. Yet, in 1970, it became the subject of harsh criticism by the Central Committee of the Moldovan Communist Party and was banned from further screenings. Gajiu turned to contemporary themes in *Ten Winters for Just One Summer* (Zece ierni peo vara/Desiat' zim za odno leto, 1970), which consists of several novellas focusing on people searching for a meaningful life; such loose plot structure became typical of his work. He then settled for the relatively safe genre of adventure tales about the Bolshevik movement and the 1918–1921 Civil War, including *A Delayed-Action Explosion* (Explozie cu efect intirziat/Vzryv zamedlennogo deistviia, 1971) about an illegal Bolshevik print shop, *The Last Haiduk* (Ultimul haiduc/Poslednii gaiduk, 1972), and *Along the Wolf's Tracks* (Pe urmele fiarei/Po volch'emu sledu, 1976), the latter two forming a dilogy about legendary cavalry commander Kotovskii.

Where Are You, Love? (Unde esti, iubire?/Gde ty, liubov'? 1980) was an unabashed star vehicle for Moldovan pop singer Sofia Rotaru. *I Am Ready to Take the Challenge* (Ia gotov priniat' vyzov, 1983), a historical musical about the wanderings of a gold coin, is based on works of Vasile Alecsandri and consists of episodes loosely held together by the imagination of a poet and duelist. During the perestroika period, Gajiu returned to the themes of his beginnings. *Kites Don't Share Their Prey* (Corbii prada no impart/Korshuny dobychei ne deliatsia, 1988) depicts the dramatic tensions in a Moldovan village at the end of the 1940s, bringing the hidden skepticism of *Bitter Grain* out into the open. *The Street of Switched-Off Lamps* (Strada felinarelor stinse, 1992) tells the story of a poor barber from Bessarabia who falls victim to Stalinist repressions. In 2004, after a 12-year hiatus, Gajiu helmed the melodrama *Jana* about a young woman who is in love with a worker but marries a rich man.

Gajiu was honored with the title Merited Artist of the Moldavian SSR in 1985.

Other films: *An Alarming Dawn* (Nistrul in flacari/Trevozhnyi rassvet, 1984); *The Mysterious Prisoner* (Detinitul misterios/Tainstvennyi uznik, 1986). *See also* MOLDOVAN CINEMA.

GAL'PERIN, ALEKSANDR VLADIMIROVICH (b. 23 September 1907, Baku–d. 1996, Moscow). Russian cinematographer and pedagogue. Gal'perin started his career in the 1920s as a photographer and correspondent for such magazines as *Ogonek* and *Krasnyi zhurnal*. In 1925, he was sent to Germany to learn the craft of a cameraman. As an extra, he witnessed the making of G. W. Pabst's *The Joyless Street* (Die freudlose Gasse, 1925) and F. W. Murnau's *Der letzte Mann* (Last Laugh, 1925), and became acquainted with Karl Freund, one of the leading German cinematographers. Upon his return to Moscow, Gal'perin published a brochure, *On the Rational Usage of Deep Focus in Cinematographic Objectives* (O ratsional'nom ispol'zovanii kinos"emochnykh ob"ektivov, 1927) with an introduction by **Iurii Zheliabuzhskii**.

Gal'perin made his debut in Georgia where he was hired, jointly with **Mikhail Kalatozov**, by the State Film Industry studio (Goskinprom) to shoot Lev Push's *Gypsy Blood* (Boshuri siskhli/Tsyganskaia krov', 1928). In Armenia, he was behind the camera for **Hamo Bek-Nazaryan**'s *House on the Volcano* (Tune Hrabkhi Vra/Dom na vulkane, 1928), a visually impressive reconstruction of the struggle of oil workers in 1907–1908. This picture is generally acknowledged as the first in which Gal'perin's manner of finding the most effective points of view and his preference for expressive lighting came to the fore.

In 1931, Gal'perin shot a sound film, *Deeds and People* (Dela i liudi), about the construction of a hydroelectric power station, directed by **Aleksandr Macheret**. He then was entrusted with filming a prestigious science fiction tale for director Vasilii Zhuravlev, *Cosmic Journey* (Kosmicheskii reis, 1933–1935). Technically, the story of a rocket journey from Moscow to the moon was highly challenging and gave Gal'perin a chance to demonstrate his inventiveness. Thus, he combined model decorations with live action and synchronized mobile cameras with mobile decorations, creating an effect of weightlessness on the screen.

Gal'perin became known as the cameraman of canonized Stalinist films such as **Ivan Pyr'ev**'s musical **comedy** *Tractor Drivers* (Traktoristy, 1939) and **Abram Room**'s "anticosmopolitan" pamphlet *Court of Honor* (Sud chesti, 1948; Stalin Prize 1949). In 1945, holding the rank of a colonel, he officially served as the emissary of the USSR Ministry of Cinema to Germany. Back in Moscow two years later, he concentrated on his teaching at the Soviet State Film School **VGIK**, which he had begun in 1936. (In 1940, he had earned his PhD with a dissertation *On the Depth of Space Representation*, and was promoted to the rank of full professor in 1960.)

Gal'perin was one of the Soviet film pioneers of the 1920s and 1930s to whom technical innovation primarily was a means to achieve aesthetic ends. At a time when cameras where extremely heavy, he introduced methods for handheld shots and generally achieved a remarkable lightness and flexibility of the camera.

Gal'perin, who joined the Communist Party in 1943, was named Merited Artist of the RSFSR in 1968.

Other films: *The God of War* (Bog voiny, 1929); *Air Chauffeur* (aka *Taxi to Heaven*/Vozdushnyi izvozchik, 1943).

GANIEV, NABI [some sources list the patronymic Ganievich] (b. 15 September 1904, Tashkent–d. 29 October 1952, Tashkent). Uzbek director, screenwriter, and actor. Ganiev, who was also a composer and painter, studied the fine arts at the famous Supreme State Artistic-Technical Workshops (VKhUTEMAS) in Moscow, graduating in 1925. He then worked as a poet and playwright for children and directed some of his plays on stage in Uzbekistan before becoming one of the founders of **Uzbek cinema**.

In 1926, Ganiev was appointed the first director of the Uzbek State Film factory (Uzbekgoskino, later named **Uzbekfilm Studio**). He worked as a consultant, assistant director, and actor, before making his directorial debut with *The Rise* (Pod"em, 1931), a didactic industrialization tale about Komsomol activists at a cotton-cleaning factory. *Ramazan* (1933) delivered a passionate accusation against the persistent, religiously masked feudal exploitation in the Uzbek countryside. *The Djigit* (Egit, 1936), the last silent film of Uzbek cinema, thematized the struggle of Red Army forces against the *basmatchi*, militant groups resisting the Sovietization of their homeland.

During the Great Patriotic War, Ganiev was producing newsreels and dubbing Russian and foreign films. He then turned to Uzbekistan's rich folklore tradition with *Tahir and Zukhra* (1945), his most lasting achievement as director. The tragic story of doomed love between a poor warrior's son and the mighty khan's daughter is set in the 15th century, a time when Uzbekistan was under Mongolian rule. Hailed as the Central Asian *Romeo and Juliet*, its "engaging plot, fine, understated performances, lush set and costume designs make for great entertainment." (Shelley Cameron)

Inspired by **Iakov Protazanov**'s period piece *Nasreddin in Bukhara* (Nasreddin v Bukhare, 1943), in the production of which he participated as second director, Ganiev helmed *The Adventures of Nasreddin* (Pokhozhdeniia Nasreddina, 1947)—not as a sequel but as an original contribution to the continuing process of Uzbek cultural self-discovery. Unlike the Russian director, he used exclusively Uzbek actors. The cinematography in this and the previous film was masterfully executed by Ukrainian exile **Danylo Demutskii**. Yet in the paranoid and malicious atmosphere of the late 1940s, critics viciously attacked Ganiev's work as "ahistorical"—luckily, that accusation did not diminish its popularity with viewers. Ganiev's subsequent return to contemporary subjects with a story about the emancipation of women from patriarchal oppression in the drama *The Daughter of Ferghana* (Doch' Fergany, 1948) proved a similarly unrewarding experience: the film was critically maligned like all his attempts at psychological complexity, modest though they may have been.

Ganiev authored the two earliest monographs on cinema in the Uzbek language, *The Screenplay* and *The Film Actor* (both 1926). He was named Merited Artist of the Uzbek SSR in 1944.

Other films: *A Surprising Case* (Udivitel'noe delo, 1931, short); *The Wellspring of Death* (Kolodets smerti, 1934).

GARDIN [real name: Dobronravov]**, VLADIMIR ROSTISLAV-OVICH** (b. 18 January 1877, Moscow [other sources: Tver']–d. 28 May 1965, Leningrad). Russian director, screenwriter, actor, producer, and pedagogue. Upon graduating from cadet school (1894) and serving in the Russian army in 1896–1897, Gardin set out for an acting career, initially in a laymen troupe that from 1898 to 1904 took him to numerous Russian provincial theaters. He then joined the Komissarzhevskii Drama Theater in Moscow and subsequently toured St. Petersburg, Kiev, London, and Paris, both as an actor and director. His profile as a stage performer was dominated by selfish and pathetic characters.

In 1913, Gardin made his debut as film director with *The Keys to Happiness* (Kliuchi schast'ia, 1913, codirected with **Iakov Protazanov**), a three-hour melodrama from Anastasiia Verbitskaia's bestselling erotic novel. He specialized in literary adaptations, churning out lavish screen versions of Lev Tolstoi's *Anna Karenina* (1914), *Kreutzer Sonata* (Kreitserova sonata, 1914), and ***War and Peace*** (Voina i mir, 1915, with Protazanov); Aleksandr Pushkin's *Lady Peasant* (Baryshnia-krest'ianka, 1915, codirected with **Ol'ga Preobrazhenskaia**); Ivan Turgenev's *Nest of the Gentry* (Dvorianskoe gnezdo, 1914); and Leonid Andreev's *Days of Our Lives* (Dni nashei zhizni, 1914), among others. He also adapted foreign literature, including Henrik Ibsen's *Ghosts* (Privideniia, 1915) and Hermann Bang's *Michael* (under the title *A Shattered Life*/Razbitaia zhizn', 1916), eventually becoming coproducer of many of his own and other directors' films. These prestige projects made Gardin one of the leading filmmakers in Russia. His pictures' artistic worth, however, is subject to debate: some film historians credit Gardin with a considerable degree of taste and respect for the aesthetic peculiarities of literary works, while others find little merit in his speedy plundering of the classical canon. Without doubt, Gardin attracted accomplished theater actors to cinema and put emphasis on the authenticity of locations and details.

Gardin, who served in World War I in 1916–1917, also directed patriotic potboilers such as *Enver-Pasha, the Traitor of Turkey* (Enver-Pasha, predatel' Turtsii, 1914), in which he impersonated German emperor Wilhelm II, and *Glory to the Strong . . . Death to the Weak . . .* (Slava sil'nym . . . gibel' slabym . . . , 1916), a story of two brothers fighting on opposite sides in the war.

In 1918, following the Bolshevik seize of power, Gardin was one of the few Russian film artists who decided to stay in the country. First, he was appointed head of the Newsreel Department of the Moscow Film Committee. In September 1919, he helped organize the State Film School (Gosudarstvennaia shkola kinematografii, later **VGIK**), which attracted numerous young talents, among them **Lev Kuleshov**, **Vsevolod Pudovkin**, and **Evgenii Cherviakov**. Gardin was appointed the school's first director. He was provided with funds to produce features such as *Hammer and Sickle* (Serp i molot, aka V trudnye dni, 1921), an ***agitka*** about a soldier who grows from an exploited farmhand to a conscious builder of Communism, and *Hunger . . . Hunger . . . Hunger* (Golod . . . golod . . . golod, 1921), made in collaboration with Pudovkin and cameraman **Eduard Tissé**. Gardin and his students spent two productive years (1922–1923) on the Crimean peninsula, making films at the Film Factory of the All-Ukrainian Photo-Film Administration (VUFKU). Several of them are attempts to adapt classical literary material for Bolshevik purposes, for example *A Ghost Is Moving across Europe* (Prizrak brodit po Evrope, from Edgar Allen Poe's "The Mask of the Red Death," 1922) and *Locksmith and Chancellor* (Slesar' i kantsler, 1923), from a screenplay by **Anatolii Lunacharskii**.

Gardin's naïve political opportunism aimed at imbuing genre-specific narratives with elements of Bolshevik propaganda. Among his greatest box-office hits was *The Cross and the Mauser* (Krest i mauzer, 1925), a primitive assault on Catholicism that, according to the film, had cooperated with the tsarist secret service. Critical attacks against Gardin's narrative traditionalism escalated after the release of *The Poet and the Tsar* (Poet i tsar', 1927, codirected with Cherviakov) about the final days of Aleksandr Pushkin. The film's popularity did not change the fact that Gardin's reputation had become tainted, effectively ending his directing career two years later, after a brief stint at Belgoskino (the predecessor to **Belarusfilm Studio**).

As a film actor, Gardin reappeared in the early 1930s. He was praised for his performance as the old worker Semen Babchenko in **Sergei Iutkevich** and **Fridrikh Ermler**'s groundbreaking *The Counterplan* (Vstrechnyi, 1932), as cunning diplomat Prince Tolstoi in **Vladimir Petrov**'s *Peter the First* (Petr Pervyi, 1937–1939), and as an American billionaire in **Mikhail Romm**'s Cold War pamphlet *Secret Mission* (Sekretnaia missiia, 1950). The portrayal of a religious hypocrite in **Aleksandr Ivanovskii**'s *Iudushka Golovlev* (aka *Home of Greed*) from Mikhail Saltykov-Shchedrin's 1880 novel was hailed by some critics as a classical achievement, while others dismissed it as exaggerated and cartoonlike.

Gardin was honored with the title People's Artist of the RSFSR in 1935 and People's Artist of the USSR in 1947. His two-volume memoirs were published in 1949.

Other films: (as director) *The Savage Woman* (Dikarka, 1915); *The Burial of Sverdlov* (Pokhorony Sverdlova, 1919, doc.); *Kastus' Kalinovskii* (1928); (as actor) *Dubrovskii* (1935); *The Lights of Baku* (Ogni Baku, 1950).

GARIN, ERAST PAVLOVICH (b. 10 November 1902, Riazan'– d. 4 September 1980, Moscow). Russian actor, director, and screenwriter. Garin was a stage actor with the First Red Army Theater in 1919–1921 and later studied at the State Experimental Theater Workshops of the Commissariat of Enlightenment in Moscow, graduating in 1926. From 1922 to 1936, he was a member of Vsevolod Meierkhol'd's troupe (in 1974 he published memoirs about the director, *With Meyerhold* [S Meierkhol'dom]); from 1936 to 1950 he worked as an actor and director in the Leningrad Comedy Theater, then in the Moscow Theater of the Movie Actor.

Garin debuted in cinema with the part of the kowtowing adjutant Koblukov in **Aleksandr Faintsimmer**'s anti-tsarist farce *Lieutenant Kizhe* (Poruchik Kizhe, 1934). The plum part of pompous chauffeur Al'fred Tarakanov in **Aleksandr Ivanovskii** and **Gerbert Rappaport**'s *Musical Story* (Muzykal'naia istoriia, 1940) won him a Stalin Prize in 1941. Although Garin performed in various genres, his roles in adaptations of Russian classical plays were particularly memorable, including the dense bridegroom in **Isidor Annenskii**'s Anton Chekhov adaptation *The Wedding* (Svad'ba, 1944) and the corrupt postmaster in **Vladimir Petrov**'s *The Inspector General* (Revizor, 1952) from Nikolai Gogol''s satire. The actor's enormous popularity was based on his body language and pantomimic precision, his inimitable high-pitched, nasal, and slightly harsh voice (often used in cartoon films), his peculiarly cadenced speech, and his proclivity for grotesque exaggeration that appealed particularly to juvenile audiences. Thus, the role of the stupid yet decent king in **Nadezhda Kosheverova**'s *Cinderella* (Zolushka, 1947) won him the lasting love of generations of children. Garin was also brilliant in blockbuster **comedies** such as **El'dar Riazanov**'s *Girl without Address* (Devushka bez adresa, 1957) or Aleksandr Seryi's *Gentlemen of Fortune* (Dzhentel'meny udachi, 1973).

Beginning in the 1930s, Garin also worked as a director. He debuted with the refreshingly antistereotypical, albeit critically maligned, Gogol' adaptation *The Marriage* (Zhenit'ba, 1936) and then helmed *Doktor Kaliuzhnyi* (1939), an inspirational tale about a physician who decides to live and work in his native village. *The Prince and the Pauper* (Prints i nishchii, 1943, from Mark Twain), *Sinegoriia* (1946) from a story by Lev Kassil', and *The Little Blue Bird* (Siniaia ptitchka, 1955) were **children's films** and combined realistic and fantasy elements. Garin's humor is kindhearted; satirical assaults are usually directed at human weaknesses, not social or political aspects of Soviet life.

Garin, whose famously eccentric behavior was the subject of countless anecdotes and has often been described in memoirs, was named People's Artist of the USSR in 1977. He was married to Khesia Lokshina (1902–1982), a fellow Meierkhol'd-actress who codirected all of Garin's pictures.

Other films: (as actor) *The Witch* (Ved'ma, 1961); *Kain XVIII* (aka *Two friends*/Dva druga, 1963); (as director) *An Ordinary Miracle* (Obyknovennoe chudo, 1965); *Raspliuev's Days of Fun* (Veselye raspliuevskie dni, 1967).

GELOVANI, MIKHEIL [Russian sources list first name and patronymic as Mikhail Georgievich] (b. 6 January 1893, Lasuria, Qutaisi [Kutaisi] province–d. 21 December 1956, Moscow). Georgian actor and director. Gelovani, offspring of an old aristocratic family, worked on stage in Tbilisi, Kutaisi, Batumi, and Baku and studied in the Aleksandre Djabadari acting school in Tbilisi in 1918–1920. In 1921–1922 and 1936–1939 he belonged to the troupe of the Shota Rustaveli Theater in Tbilisi; from 1942 to 1948 he was a member of the Moscow Art Theater (MKhAT).

Gelovani debuted as a film actor in **Ivan Perestiani**'s historical epic *Three Lives* (Sami sitsotskhle/Tri zhizni, 1924). His interpretation of the male lead, the poor yet ambitious peasant Bahva, brought him considerable critical recognition. He also was convincing in **Mikheil Chiaureli**'s revolutionary epic *The Last Masquerade* (Ukanaskneli maskaradi/Poslednii maskarad, 1934). Together with Patvakan Barkhudaryan (1898–1948), Gelovani tried directing with a melodrama shot in Armenia, *Evil Spirit* (Char vogi/Zloi dukh, 1928), about the plight of a an epileptic girl, in which he also played the girl's grieving father. He went on to direct three more films: *Youth Wins* (Akhalgazrdoba imardjvels/Molodost' pobezhdaet, 1928), a critique of persisting tribal traditions in Georgia; *The Shock-worker* (Damkvreli/Udarnik truda, aka Delo doblesti, 1931), a direct predecessor to **Fridrikh Ermler** and **Sergei Iutkevich**'s industrial drama *The Counterplan* (Vstrechnyi, 1932); and the **comedy** *A Genuine Caucasian* (Namdvili kavkasieli/Nastoiashchii kavkazets, 1934).

Gelovani's name became known to millions of Soviet viewers through his impersonation of Iosif Stalin that he began on stage and continued in a number of prestige films, starting with Chiaureli's *The Great Glow* (aka *They Wanted Peace*/Diadi gantiadi/Velikoe zarevo, 1938). That performance was personally approved by the dictator, and Gelovani became Stalin's de facto cinematic double, being barred from any other roles—a veritable tragedy for this gifted artist. He portrayed Stalin in **Mikhail Romm**'s *Lenin in October* (Lenin v Oktiabre, 1937), **Grigorii Kozintsev** and **Leonid Trauberg**'s *Maksim Trilogy* (Trilogiia o Maksime, 1935–1939), **Mikhail Kalatozov**'s *Valerii Chkalov* (1941), and in the **Vasil'ev brothers'** *The Defense of Tsaritsyn* (Oborona Tsaritsyna, 1942), among others. While these appearances were episodic, Chiaureli's cultish pictures focused solely on the dictator and gave Gelovani's performances maximum representational weight. In *The Oath* (Kliatva, 1946), *The Fall of Berlin* (Padenie Berlina, 1950), and *The Unforgettable Year 1919* (Nezabyvaemyi 1919yi god, 1952), Gelovani defined the official Stalin image—albeit in competition with Russian actor

Aleksei Dikii (1889–1955) who played Stalin in **Ihor' Savchenko**'s *The Third Blow* (Tretii udar, 1948) and **Vladimir Petrov**'s *Battle of Stalingrad* (Stalingradskaia bitva, 1949).

After Stalin's death, Gelovani found himself ostracized; all his scenes in Kalatozov's Dzerzhinskii biopic *Hostile Whirlwinds* (Vikhri vrazhdebnye, 1953) were deleted, new roles were not in sight. The actor's death on Stalin's birthday brought a cruelly ironic conclusion to his career.

Gelovani was named People's Artist of the USSR in 1950; he won Stalin Prizes in 1941, 1942, 1947, and 1950.

Other films: *Two Hunters* (Ori monadire/Dva okhotnika, 1927); *The Golden Valley* (Narindjis veli/Zolotistaia dolina, 1937). *See also* GEORGIAN CINEMA.

GEORGIAN CINEMA. *See* ABASHIDZE, DAVID; ABULADZE, TENGIZ; ANDJAPARIDZE, VERIKO; ANIMATION; BEK-NAZARYAN, HAMO; CHIAURELI, MIKHEIL; CHIAURELI, SOFIKO; CHKHEIDZE, REZO; CHKHIKVADZE, RAMAZ; DANELIIA, GEORGII; DOLIDZE, SIKO; GABRIADZE, REVAZ; GAL'PERIN, ALEKSANDR; GELOVANI, MIKHEIL; GOGOBERIDZE, LANA; GRUZIYA-FILM STUDIO; IOSELIANI, OTAR; KALATOZOV, MIKHAIL; KANCHELI, GIYA; MDIVANI, GIORGI; *ONCE THERE WAS A SINGING THRUSH*; PAATASHVILI, LEVAN; PERESTIANI, IVAN; *PIROSMANI*; *REPENTANCE*; RONDELI, DAVIT; *SALT FOR SVANETIA*; SHENGELAIA, ELDAR; SHENGELAIA, GIORGI; SHENGELAIA, NIKOLOZ; VACHNADZE, NATO; VASADZE, AKAKI; ZAKARIADZE, SERGO.

GERASIMOV, SERGEI APOLLINARIEVICH (b. 21 May 1906, Sarafanovo near Miass, Ural region [other sources: Kundravy, Cheliabinsk province]–d. 28 November 1985, Moscow). Russian director, screenwriter, and actor. Gerasimov was born into the family of a political convict, a former aristocrat turned Social Democrat. With his four siblings, he grew up in the milieu of Orenburg Cossacks.

Gerasimov studied at the Leningrad Art School and subsequently at the Leningrad Institute for Stage Arts, from which he graduated in 1928. As an actor and an assistant director, Gerasimov joined the Factory of the Eccentric Actor workshop (FEKS) of **Grigorii Kozintsev** and **Leonid Trauberg** in 1924, playing supporting parts in their silents such as *The Overcoat* (Shinel', 1926) and *S.V.D.—The Club of Great Deeds* (SVD—Soiuz velikikh del, 1927) in which he was impressive as the traitor Medoks. Gerasimov's acting style was exaggerated, cartoonish, tending toward the grotesque—fully in accordance with the FEKS' iconoclastic theories. However, these early experiences not only laid the groundwork for his episodic roles in sound film but also eventually made him one of the most method-conscious Soviet "actors' directors" who could elicit exquisite performances both from stars and young aspiring artists.

In the late 1920s, Gerasimov emancipated himself from his teachers and began to develop a more realistic style of his own. Although his early directing attempts, produced at **Lenfilm Studio**, are generally regarded as failures, Gerasimov already revealed a heightened interest in contemporary themes that he treated in a deliberately naturalistic manner: *Twenty-two Mishaps* (Dvadtsat'-dva neschast'ia, 1930, codirected with Sergei Bartenev) and especially *Do I Love You?* (Liubliu li ia tebia? 1934), the former starring his wife (since 1928), **Tamara Makarova**.

Three sound films catapulted Gerasimov to the heights of fame in Soviet cinema, indulging audiences with their youthful vigor and formal perfection: *The Bold Seven* (Semero smelykh, 1936, based on a book by explorer Konstantin Zvantsev) about an expedition that builds a station in the Arctic ice; *Komsomol'sk* (aka *City of Youth*, aka *The Frozen North*, 1938), on a topic purportedly suggested by Iosif Stalin himself, the construction of a factory in the Far East; and *The Teacher* (aka *The New Teacher*/Uchitel', 1939), the story of a man who returns to his native village in the Ural mountains to create a high school. The latter won Gerasimov his first Stalin Prize. Few directors have managed to capture the fresh spirit of an emerging society as dynamically as Gerasimov, whose approach seamlessly blends political propaganda with adventure, romantic love story, and even tragedy, always ending on a positive note. Gerasimov's view of the filmmaker as a societal enlightener became his trademark; his films of the 1930s were declared emblematic for Soviet normative cinema and are still unsurpassed in their modernity and freshness, despite early symptoms of an epic breadth consciously borrowed from 19th-century literature.

On the outbreak of the Great Patriotic War, Gerasimov had completed *Masquerade* (Maskarad, 1941), a faithful and visually amazing adaptation of Mikhail Lermontov's play. Both he and Makarova stayed in the Nazi-besieged Leningrad for the semi**documentary** *The Invincible* (Nepobedimye, 1943, codirected with **Mikhail Kalatozov**) about the creation of a new type of tank. After their evacuation to Tashkent in 1943, Gerasimov filmed *Mainland* (aka *The Big Land*/Bol'shaia zemlia, 1944) about an industrial factory in the Urals. He then moved to the **Gor'kii Studio for Children's and Youth Films** in Moscow, which allowed him to combine creative work with increasingly heavy teaching duties. Although he had begun teaching at Lenfilm's directing seminar in 1938, only as head of the Acting and Directing Department at the Soviet State Film School **VGIK** did Gerasimov become the most influential Soviet film pedagogue, a living institution who formed generations of film actors and directors.

Casting his entire class of students, Gerasimov adapted *The Young Guard* (Molodaia gvardiia, 1948) from the just-published novel by Aleksandr Fadeev, filming it on the original location. Due to its open pathos—Jay Leyda called it "grandiose, inflated mock heroics"—it is somewhat atypical of this director who was forced to change the film's first cut (1947) by deleting scenes of panic after the German invasion. However, *The Young Guard* ultimately became a classic, won Gerasimov another Stalin Prize, and literally brought a new guard of film stars to Soviet screens. After a number of political documentaries, the quieter, more intimate *Country Doctor* (Sel'skii vrach, 1952) portrays a woman's growing professional recognition in a Siberian village. Gerasimov's main project in the 1950s was the spectacular Mikhail Sholokhov adaptation *And Quiet Flows the Don* (Tikhii Don, 1957–1958), a monumental historical epic in three parts that was hailed as one of the best Soviet films and became the director's greatest international critical and popular success.

Gerasimov was the rare type of filmmaker who managed to rejuvenate himself several times during a long career, keeping his finger on the pulse of society without ever challenging its fundamental status quo. In the 1960s and 1970s, he made several pictures about Soviet intellectuals such as *People and Beasts* (Liudi i zveri, 1962), *The Journalist* (Zhurnalist, 1967), *At the Lake* (U ozera, 1970), *For the Love of Man* (Liubit' cheloveka, 1973), and *Daughters and Mothers* (Dochki-materi, 1975), touching upon topics such as environmental protection, alienation between generations, and professional ethics. Like his earlier pictures in the 1930s, these films praise modernity and urban civilization and portray Soviet society as profoundly progressive and energetic.

During the last decade of his life, Gerasimov turned toward historical subjects, delivering a hugely popular five-hour TV adaptation of Stendhal's *Red and Black* (Krasnoe i chernoe, 1976, cinema release 1977); the large-scale dilogy *The Youth of Peter* (Iunost' Petra, 1980) and *At the Beginning of Glorious Deeds* (V nachale slavnykh del, 1981) from Aleksei Tolstoi's novel; and a biopic on the last years of *Lev Tolstoi* (aka *The Death of Lev Tolstoi*, 1984), in which the director also impersonated the Russian classic author. Unfortunately, this swan song is painfully lacking in philosophical or psychological depth and avoids most of the complex issues involved with Tolstoi's public and private life, putting a disappointing conclusion to an otherwise outstanding career.

For half a century, Gerasimov's untiring entrepreneurial spirit and vivid political instincts made him one of the most reliable filmmaker functionaries of the Soviet establishment. At the same time, his taste and erudition in classical literature as well as his collegiality in practical matters and fatherly care for his students won him the respect even of those filmmakers who felt uneasy about his political and administrative power. Thus, by broad consensus, VGIK, to which he devoted almost 40 years of his life, was named after Gerasimov following his passing.

The director, who joined the Communist Party in 1943, was honored with the title People's Artist of the USSR in 1948 and Hero of Socialist Labor in 1974. In 1987, Gerasimov's former student Iurii Grigor'ev made a feature-length documentary about his teacher, *There Is but One Life . . .* (Zhizn' odna . . . , codirected with Renita Grigor'eva).

Other films: (as actor) *The Devil's Wheel* (Chertovo koleso, 1926); *A Fragment of the Empire* (Oblomok imperii, 1929); *The Deserter* (Dezertir, 1933); (as director) *The Heart of Solomon* (Serdtse

Solomona, 1932); *Encounter with Maksim* (Vstrecha s Maksimom, 1941, in *War Film Almanac #1*); *Liberated China* (Osvobozhdennyi Kitai, 1951, doc.).

GERMAN, ALEKSEI IUR'EVICH [some sources list the patronymic as Georgievich] (b. 20 July 1938, Leningrad). Russian director, screenwriter, and actor. German's father, the well-known writer Iurii German (1910–1967), won a Stalin Prize in 1948 for the screenplay to **Grigorii Kozintsev**'s *Pirogov*; several of his works were adapted for the screen by **Sergei Gerasimov**, **Leonid Lukov**, **Erast Garin**, and **Iosif Kheifits**, among others. Aleksei German studied in the Directing Department of the Leningrad Institute for Stage Arts, graduating in 1960. After stints at the theater of Smolensk and the Grand Dramatic Theater (BDT) in Leningrad, German joined **Lenfilm Studio** in 1964. He got his first assignment as an assistant director on Vladimir Vengerov's *The Worker's Settlement* (Rabochii poselok, 1965).

German's directorial debut was *The Seventh Companion* (Sed'moi sputnik, 1967, codirected with Grigorii Aronov) from a novella by Boris Lavrenev about a tsarist general turned into a loyal supporter of the Soviet government. In 1971, German completed *Operation "Happy New Year"* (Operatsiia 'S Novym godom'), which was shelved for a long time and only released in 1986 under the title *Road Controls* (Proverki na dorogakh). The story of a Red Army lieutenant who is captured by the Germans—thus categorized as a deserter by Soviet law—and eventually joins a partisan unit only to sacrifice himself to prove his patriotic loyalty, is shot in ascetic black and white. The film's anticlimactic style and "reversed heroism" appear as an implied alternative to the mainstream of Great Patriotic War films. Its unusual plot twists were as disturbing to film officials as the peculiar, "distanced" cinematic style in which the story is told, making it hard to determine any political or moral judgment.

Twenty Days without War (Dvadtsat' dnei bez voiny, 1976), from Konstantin Simonov's World War II diaries, tells the story of a front-savvy journalist who goes on a three-week mission to Tashkent to help with a film based on his script. The loosely connected episodes juxtapose the harsh reality of war to its selective perception by contemporaries and its even more one-sided filmic representation, yet in a nonpolemical, matter-of-fact manner with tragic undertones. *My Friend Ivan Lapshin* (Moi drug Ivan Lapshin, 1984) is perhaps the clearest expression of German's aesthetic searches. This group portrait of men in a barren communal apartment in the 1930s provinces depicts Stalinist everyday life as it had not been shown in Soviet cinema before: as gray, tormentingly slow normalcy. Neither the criminal-hunting investigator nor the depressed journalist nor any other protagonist is able to see through the phenomena surrounding them or the societal processes of which they are part. History appears as the Brownian movement of unsuspecting objects, not active subjects.

In *Khrustalev, the Car!* (Khrustalev, mashinu!, 1998), German took his narrative and stylistic peculiarities to the extreme. If in previous films, conceptually important utterances often were lost in superficial cacophony and symbols appeared almost unnoticeably, in passing, or forlorn in the quasi-**documentary** footage, in *Khrustalev*, even a mere understanding of characters' words is difficult. The grim story of a high-ranking military physician who is arrested during the last days of Iosif Stalin's life, then summoned to the dying dictator whom he cannot save, and finally released into a land of absurdity and complete disrespect for the individual, breathes both atmospheric intensity and utter confusion. *Khrustalev* found a mixed critical response at home and abroad; it did not become the breakthrough in understanding Stalinism that some had expected, but the jury is still out on its intrinsic merits.

German's central theme is the shocking encounter with the gloomy crudeness and cruelty of Soviet life, whether in the 1930s or during the Great Patriotic War. Reality is viewed with a mixture of wonderment and repulsion. Because the director avoids any explicit moral criticism, his indictment against Soviet society emerges slowly and blurred in conceptual vagueness. German's vision of the past is demonstratively emotionless and remains unexplained. Any disillusionment in the Communist utopia is conveyed in an undramatic manner, although it marks the characters' confused sadness that defies the loud optimism of public marches, slogans, and films.

Critics are divided about German; his scarce output makes it hard to determine an evolution of any kind. The hyperbolic judgments of some reviewers cannot refute the fact that German's films are narratively problematic, even if their incoherence and avoidance of focus are intentional. On the other hand, German's taste for neglected aspects of the Soviet past, for unspectacular stories that were overlooked by everyone else, and his uncompromising refusal to cater to viewers' expectations deserve respect. Ultimately, German's primary artistic strength lies in the authentic evocation of eerie atmosphere in an antinostalgic, consistently understated manner.

German also worked as an actor, appearing in episodic roles in made-for-television films such as *Rafferty* (1979) and *The Personal Life of the Director* (Lichnaia zhizn' directora, 1981), as well as in films of **Aleksei Balabanov**, including his darkly funny episode *Trofim"* from the omnibus *The Arrival of a Train* (Pribytie poezda, 1995). In 1985, German was among the driving forces behind the reform of the Cinematographers' Union and was elected to its new board. In 1990, he organized at Lenfilm Studio a workshop for debut films and experimental pictures. He was honored with a belated State Prize of the USSR for *Road Controls* in 1988 and the same year received the title People's Artist of the RSFSR. German is married to screenwriter Svetlana Karmalita (b. 1940), with whom he has coauthored several screenplays. Their son, Aleksei German Jr. (b. 1976), is a filmmaker.

Other films: *The Death of Otrar* (Gibel' Otrara, 1991; screenplay); *It Is Hard to Be a God* (Trudno byt' bogom, 2008).

GIEDRYS, MARIJONAS [other spelling: Marionas Gedris; Russian sources list the patronymic Vintsovich] (b. 16 March 1933, Kaunas). Lithuanian director and screenwriter. Giedrys studied at the Soviet State Film School **VGIK** under **Sergei Gerasimov** and **Tamara Makarova**, graduating in 1964. He began to work at the **Lithuanian Film Studio** in 1959.

Giedrys's directorial debut was the medium-length *We Don't Have To* (Mums nebereikia/Nam ne nuzhno), part of the prize-winning omnibus *Living Heroes* (Gyvieji didvyriai/Zhivye geroi, 1960). In a slow, deliberately prolonged manner, this novella describes the hopeless tribulations of a small boy who seeks employment from a rich peasant. The Lithuanian countryside is also the background for *Alien People* (Svetimi/Chuzhie, 1961), which features Vilkišius, a formerly rich peasant who was exiled and now tries to come to terms with the new Communist order. In a very different vein—with irony and human understanding—Giedrys directed *The Games of Adults* (Suagusių šmonių žaidimai/Igry vzroslykh liudei, 1967), about the romantic adventures of an easygoing chauffeur.

The filmmaker's name is predominantly associated with *Herkus Mantas* (1972), a two-part, action-filled, grand-scale, black-and-white epic about the 13th-century revolt of the Prussians—an ancient Baltic tribe—against invading German crusaders. The film did well at the box office; it was the first picture in **Lithuanian cinema** to deal with this historical period. *The Split Sky* (Perskeltas dangus/Raskolotoe nebo, 1975), from a novel by Vytautas Bubnys, describes the painful process of urbanization, focusing on generational conflicts within the family of an architect whose members are torn between country and city. The extremely pro-Soviet *Dust in the Sunlight* (Dulkės saulėje/Pyl' pod solntsem, 1978) tells of an uprising of Social Revolutionaries (*Esery*) against the Bolsheviks in Siberia shortly after the 1917 revolution that was suppressed under the leadership of the prominent Lithuanian Communist Josef (Iosif) Vareikis (1894–1939). For Soviet national television, Giedrys directed the miniseries *An American Tragedy* (Amerikoniškoji tragedija/Amerikanskaia tragediia, 1981) from Theodore Dreiser's novel. Giedrys also made some **documentaries**, including the critically praised *The Songs of Flax* (Lino daina/Pesni l'na, 1965) about Lithuanian folk art, as well as a film celebrating the 25th anniversary of the establishment of Soviet power in the country.

Giedrys's undeniable artistic versatility and solid professionalism that allowed him to succeed in virtually all film genres were overshadowed by his involvement with the Communist system, which has been judged harshly after the country's liberation. The director, who joined the Communist Party in 1974, was named People's Artist of the Lithuanian SSR in 1983.

Other films: *Summer of Men* (Vyrų vasara/Muzhskoe leto, 1970); *The Wounds of the Land of Ours* (Žaizdos žemės mūsų/Rany zemli nashei, 1971); *Blossoming of the Unsown Rye* (Nesėtų rugių žydėjimas/Tsvetenie neseiannoi rzhi, 1978); *The Prodigal Son* (Sūnus palaidūnas/Bludnyi syn, 1985).

GLUZSKII, MIKHAIL ANDREEVICH (b. 21 November 1918, Kiev–d. 15 June 2001, Moscow). Russian actor. Gluzskii, a factory worker in his youth, studied at the acting school of **Mosfilm Studio**, graduating in 1940, and joined the troupe of the Central Theater of the Red Army. He fought as a soldier in World War II and, upon discharge, worked in various Moscow theaters, including The Contemporary (Sovremennik) and the Theater of the Movie Actor.

In 1939, Gluzskii debuted with episodic roles in three movies: **Grigorii Roshal'**'s *The Oppenheim Family* (Sem'ia Oppengeim), **Konstantin Iudin**'s *A Girl with Personality* (Devushka s kharakterom), and **Vsevolod Pudovkin**'s *Minin and Pozharskii*. Such diverse genres—political pamphlet, romantic **comedy**, historical biopic—remained the actor's trademark, making him one of the most familiar faces on Soviet screens, with a total of more than 130 roles to his credit and continuous employment even in the crisis-ridden 1990s. Gluzskii worked under leading Soviet directors, including **Sergei Gerasimov** (*And Quiet Flows the Don*/Tikhii Don, 1957–1958), **Aleksandr Stolper** (*The Living and the Dead*/Zhivye i mertvye, 1964), and **Gleb Panfilov** (*There's No Ford through Fire*/V ogne broda net, 1967). He was predominantly cast in roles requiring a headstrong temper—military, Party, and state leaders in films such as Vladimir Chebotarev's *Secretary of the District Committee* (Sekretar' obkoma, 1960), Leonid Kvinikhidze's *Mission in Kabul* (Missiia v Kabule, 1971), and Sergei Mikaelian's *The Bonus* (Premiia, 1975).

Gluzskii's ability to transform himself allowed him to play both reflective intellectuals—most prominently, Professor Sretenskii in **Il'ia Averbakh**'s *Monologue* (Monolog, 1972), simple workers, Red Army sergeants, or spies. In later years, his roles became more complex, sometimes subverting the stern, grumpy screen image that had emerged over the decades, for example, as Panteleev in **Vadim Abdrashitov**'s *The Train Halted* (Ostanovilsia poezd, 1982).

Gluzskii was named People's Artist of the USSR in 1983. He was in charge of an acting workshop at the Soviet State Film School **VGIK** in 1988–1996.

Other films: *The Secret of Two Oceans* (Taina dvukh okeanov, 1956); *Kain XVIII* (1963); *The Flight* (Beg, 1970); *A Man for a*

Young Woman (Muzhchina dlia molodoi zhenshchiny, 1996); *The Long-Rangers* (Dal'noboishchiki, 2001).

GOGOBERIDZE, LANA [some Russian sources list the patronymic Levanovna] (b. 13 October 1928, Tbilisi). Georgian director and screenwriter. Gogoberidze's mother, Nina (Nutsu) Gogoberidze, was a folklorist and screenwriter and is considered one of the founders of **Georgian cinema**; in 1933, she directed a feature-length **documentary** dedicated to the 15th anniversary of Communist power in Georgia. Nina Gogoberidze was arrested in 1937 and spent 20 years in GULAG concentration camps. In 1950, Lana, who had been raised by relatives—high-ranking Communist functionaries—graduated from the Department of Romance Languages at the State University of Tbilisi. She then enrolled in the Soviet State Film School **VGIK**, where she studied with **Sergei Gerasimov** and **Tamara Makarova**, graduating in 1959.

Gogoberidze's debut as director was *Under One Sky* (Erti tsis kvesh/Pod odnim nebom, 1961), a compilation of three separate novellas ("Princess Maya," "Doves," and "Fresco") about Georgian women and their plight in various periods of history. The lives of women in specific social circumstances became Gogoberidze's main theme as filmmaker. *Borders* (Peristsvaleba/Rubezhi, 1970) analyzes the hypocrisy of an artist, while *When the Almond Trees Began Blooming* (Rotsa akvavda nushi/Kogda zatsvel mindal', 1972) deals with honesty and honor among contemporary youth, alluding to corrupt privileged families.

Gogoberidze gained international renown with *Several Interviews on Personal Questions* (Ramodenime interviu pirad sakitkhebze/ Neskol'ko interv'iu po lichnym voprosam, 1979). Praised by critics and cinema officials alike, it was viewed as a constructive intellectual contribution to the discourse on female problems in Soviet society and was recognized with a USSR State Prize. In a mosaic-like manner, the film tells the story of a middle-aged journalist in charge of letters to the editor at a newspaper. An outspoken activist for the cause of women's emancipation, she loses her husband to a younger woman in the end. *Waltz at the Pechora* (Valsi Pechoraze/Val's na Pechore, 1992), Gogoberidze's last picture, presents her view of

Stalinism. She also made a number of documentaries, among them *Tbilisi Is 1500 Years Old* (Tbilisi 1500 tslisaa/Tbilisi 1500 let, 1959) and the very personal *Letters to the Children* (Tserilebi shvilebtan/ Pis'ma k detiam, 1981), dedicated to her deceased husband.

Gogoberidze, who has a PhD in literature and published a monograph on Walt Whitman in 1955, also made a name for herself as a translator of foreign poetry into Georgian. She taught film at the Shota Rustaveli Theater Institute in Tbilisi in 1975–1988. Gogoberidze joined the Communist Party in 1965 and was named People's Artist of the Georgian SSR in 1979. In the 1990s, the prominent filmmaker was elected member of parliament and held a number of high official positions. In 1999, she was appointed ambassador of Georgia to the European Council.

Other films: *I See the Sun* (Me vkhedav mzes/Ia vizhu solntse, 1965); *The Little Incident* (Aurzari salkhinetsi/Perepolokh, 1976); *The Day Is Longer than the Night* (Dges game utenebia/Den' dlinnee nochi, 1984); *Rotation* (Oromtriali/Krugovorot, 1986).

GOLOVNIA, ANATOLII DMITRIEVICH (b. 2 February 1900, Kherson, Ukraine–d. 25 June 1982, Moscow). Ukrainian-Russian cinematographer and pedagogue. Golovnia first studied agronomy at Kherson Polytechnical Institute. After moving to Moscow in 1923, he enrolled in the State Cinema College (GTK, later named **VGIK**) and became an assistant to **Aleksandr Levitskii**, one of the most experienced Russian cameramen, on **Lev Kuleshov**'s *The Ray of Death* (Luch smerti, 1925).

Golovnia's encounter with budding filmmaker **Vsevolod Pudovkin** in 1925 marked the beginning of a long and fruitful artistic partnership. The lighthearted *Chess Fever* (Shakhmatnaia goriachka, 1925) combines **documentary** footage and fictitious scenes, while the educational *Mechanics of the Brain* (Mekhanika golovnogo mozga, 1926) applies montage principles in order to visualize Pavlovian theories. *The Mother* (Mat', 1926), a revolutionary drama adapted from Maksim Gor'kii's 1906 novel, caused a sensation; in lucidly composed images, imbued with the pathos of class struggle and romanticized self-sacrifice, Golovnia proved a master whose talent matched that of rival **Eduard Tissé** in originality and inventiveness. Golovnia's ability to add emotional warmth to sequences of political significance distinguishes his work from other cameramen and was in tune with Pudovkin's embracing of psychological acting. In *The End of St. Petersburg* (Konets Sankt Peterburga, 1927), Golovnia alternated majestic, melancholic landscapes of Central Russia with sharply contrasted montage sequences of industrial urbanity. In *The Heir of Chenghiz Khan* (aka *Storm over Asia*/Potomok Chingiz-khana, 1928), quasi-documentary scenes of colonial exploitation and warfare are elevated to a metaphorical level. Golovnia refined his lighting techniques, creating sharply contoured graphic compositions; a major source of inspiration for him was the art of the 19th-century "Wanderers" (*Peredvizhniki*), in particular the social realism of Vasilii Perov (1834–1882).

Over the course of his career, Golovnia also worked with other directors, including **Leonid Obolenskii**, **Iakov Protazanov**, **Fedor Otsep**, and **Vladimir Petrov**. His artistic evolution, however, is inseparably linked to that of Pudovkin, sharing his ups and downs alike: the asynchronic sound experiment *The Deserter* (Dezertir, 1933) and another failure, *Victory* (Pobeda, aka Samyi schastlivyi, 1938); the stylistically less distinct historical epics *Minin and Pozharskii* (1939), *Suvorov* (1941), and *Admiral Nakhimov* (1947), ending, alas, with the lackluster biopic *Zhukovskii* (1950). In later years, Golovnia, by then a celebrated classic film artist of Soviet cinema, devoted most of his time to teaching at VGIK (which he had begun in 1934, since 1939 holding the rank of full professor) and authoring theoretical works on cinematography.

Golovnia, who became a member of the Communist Party in 1944, was honored with the title Merited Artist of the RSFSR in 1935 and Hero of Socialist Labor in 1980. He won Stalin Prizes for *Admiral Nakhimov* in 1947 and *Zhukovskii* in 1951. Golovnia was married to cinematographer Tamara Lobova (b. 1911), with whom he shot all of his films beginning with *Suvorov*.

Other films: *The Man from the Restaurant* (Chelovek iz restorana, 1927); *The Living Corpse* (Zhivoi trup, 1929); *The Elusive Jan* (Neulovimyi Ian, 1943).

GONCHAROV, VASILII MIKHAILOVICH (b. 1861, Voronezh–d. 23 August 1915, Moscow). Russian director and scriptwriter. Goncharov made a career as a railway administrator in the Voronezh district; in his spare time, he wrote theater plays, of which two saw the stage. During a stay in Paris in 1905, he witnessed the Pathé film production, which ignited his interest in the new medium. Upon retiring from railway service in 1908, Goncharov devoted all his energies to cinema, exclusively utilizing Russian subject matter for his numerous projects—which in itself made him a pioneer in the foreign-dominated Russian film scene.

Goncharov wrote the script for the first Russian feature film, *Sten'ka Razin* (Ponizovaia vol'nitsa, 1907), produced by **Aleksandr Drankov**. He then directed a film for Paul (Pavel) Tiemann's Gloria company, *The Death of Ivan the Terrible* (Smert' Ioanna Groznogo, 1909), in which young **Iakov Protazanov** played an episodic role. For **Aleksandr Khanzhonkov**'s company, Goncharov made some rather static historical-ethnographic pictures such as *A Russian Wedding of the XVI Century* (Russkaia svad'ba XVI stoletiia, 1909), as well as contemporary films (*A Drama in Moscow*/Drama v Moskve) that were usually 5 to 10 minutes long.

Goncharov worked for the Moscow branch of Pathé, where he helmed the tremendously successful *Peter the Great* (Petr Velikii, 1910), and for Gaumont, where he made *The Life and Death of A. S. Pushkin* (Zhizn' i smert' A. S. Pushkina, 1910). The director's further efforts were either cinematic illustrations of Russian literary classics rendered naïvely and often quite sloppily (*Crime and Punishment*/Prestuplenie i nakazanie, 1909, and numerous others), or adaptations of folk songs, fairy tales, and legends. But his trademark became patriotic historical pictures officially supported by tsarist military units, featuring extravagant battle scenes. Thus, together with Khanzhonkov, Goncharov undertook in 1911 a grandiose reconstruction of the 1854–1855 defense of Sevastopol in a canvas that became the foundation of an entire new genre. Leaving out any melodramatic plotline, Goncharov created a war chronicle of maximum authenticity, ending **The Defense of Sevastopol** (Oborona Sevastopolia), the world's first full-length feature, with **documentary** footage of contemporary survivors of the events. In this touching scene, Goncharov introduced medium shots, while many battle scenes were realized as high-angle long shots. Following the film's enormous success, Goncharov directed or codirected similar blockbusters: *The Year 1812* (1812 god, 1912), *The Accession of the Romanov Dynasty* (Votsarenie doma Romanovykh, 1913), and *Ermak Timofeevich, the Van-quisher of Siberia* (Ermak Timofeevich—pokoritel' Sibiri, 1914).

As Aleksandr Khanzhonkov testifies in his memoirs, Goncharov tried to create a new type of acting that would be cinema specific: faster than on stage and without paying much attention to psychological subtleties. On the other hand, all sources agree that Goncharov's work with the actors was the weakest aspect of his films. Arguably, his real gift was organizational, not artistic, yet he was inspired by a pure passion for cinema. Goncharov, a "peculiar and partially grotesque character" (Iangirov), at the time of his sudden death left an extremely uneven legacy. Still, referring to his relentless experimentation and exploration of new cinematic means, film historian Romil Sobolev justly called him "a director-innovator."

Other films: *The Song of Merchant Kalashnikov* (Pesn' pro kuptsa Kalashnikova, 1908); *The Sorceress* (Charodeika, 1909); *The Pedlars* (Korobeiniki, 1910); *Eugene Onegin* (Evgenii Onegin, 1911).

GOR'KII STUDIO FOR CHILDREN'S AND YOUTH FILMS [Tsentral'naia kinostudiia detskikh i iunosheskikh fil'mov imeni M. Gor'kogo]. As the official successor to **Mezhrabpomfilm Studio**, the Soviet Children's Film Studio (Soiuzdetfilm) was established after the former's dissolution in 1936. Inspired by a decree of the Council of People's Commissars on the improvement of children's cinema and literature issued in 1935, the studio was charged with the production of quality pictures for young audiences. Initially, these were for the most part didactic, patriotic films with adventurous plots dealing, for example, with foreign spies attempting to violate the Soviet border, such as *Dzhul'bars* (1936) by Vladimir Shneiderov (1900–1973) and *The Locked Border* (Granitsa na zamke, 1938) by Vasilii Zhuravlev (1904–1987). Film industry executive **Boris Shumiatskii** aimed at increasing Soviet cinema's international competitiveness; as a result, directors such as **Vladimir Vainshtok** created superhits adapted from international classics, including *The Children of Captain Grant* (Deti kapitana Granta, 1936) from Jules Verne and *Treasure Island* (Ostrov sokrovishch, 1938) from Robert Louis Stevenson's novel. Vladimir Legoshin (1904–1954) brought an enjoyable version of Valentin Kataev's Civil War yarn *White Sail Gleaming* (Beleet parus odinokii, 1937) to the screen, while **Aleksandr Razumnyi** scored a popular success with *Timur and His Gang* (Timur i ego komanda, 1940), an inspirational tale about children who help adults in their day-to-day duties. Adaptations of Russian folktales, although at first viewed with suspicion by the watchdogs of dialectical materialism, became a mainstay of the studio's production, with **Aleksandr Rou** as the pioneer of the genre.

In accordance with its mission, the studio's production usually featured some quantities of entertainment and humor, but the movies' didactic function and political message were invariably and openly present. Soviet children were encouraged to give their all for the Communist motherland, to learn and work diligently, and to expose enemies of the people, whether homegrown or foreign. However, a number of pictures were not exactly children's films in the narrow sense of the term, an inconsistency that increased in the following decades when leading Soviet directors made the studio their permanent home. Thus, **Mark Donskoi**'s famous trilogy adapted from Maksim Gor'kii's autobiographical novels (*Gor'kii's Childhood*/Detstvo Gor'kogo, 1938, *Among People*/V liudiakh, 1939, and *My Universities*/Moi universitety, 1940) could only be fully appreciated by adult audiences.

Shortly after the beginning of the Great Patriotic War, in November 1941, the studio under the leadership of its executive director **Sergei Iutkevich** was evacuated to Dushanbe, using the facilities of **Tadjikfilm Studio**. It produced several of the so-called *War Film Almanacs*, responding to the needs of troops at the front with compilations of satirical and heroic shorts. At the same time, the production of children's films was continued with pictures such as **Erast Garin**'s charming *The Prince and the Pauper* (Prints i nishchii, 1943, adapted from Mark Twain). *Once There Lived a Girl* (Zhila-byla devochka, 1943) by Viktor Eisymont (1904–1964) and *Zoia* (1944) by **Leo Arnshtam** visualized the harsh reality of the war during the Leningrad siege and the Nazi occupation, respectively.

After the studio's return to Moscow in 1944, **Leonid Lukov** was appointed its executive director. In 1948, it was renamed Moscow Film Studio M. Gor'kii. Its leading directors were Donskoi, who scored a huge success with *The Country Teacher* (Sel'skaia uchitel'nitsa, 1947); **Sergei Gerasimov**, who combined inspiring pedagogy at the State Film School **VGIK** with the immediate application of its lessons in the seminal war tragedy *The Young Guard* (Molodaia gvardiia, 1948); and Lukov, who, despite harsh official criticism for the second part of *A Great Life* (Bol'shaia zhizn', 1946), continued to direct ultraloyal Soviet miners' tales. Among Gor'kii Studio's greatest box-office successes of the postwar years was the Jules Verne adaptation *The Fifteen-Year Old Captain* (Piatnadtsatiletnii kapitan, 1946) by Zhuravlev. **Il'ia Frez** specialized in films about children, beginning with *The Elephant and the String* (Slon i verevochka, 1945), even though the genre of **children's and youth films** as a whole generated considerably fewer movies than in the 1930s.

During the Thaw, an entire generation of new directors came to Gor'kii Studio. Their profile was marked by solid professionalism and moderate innovation but hardly artistic experimentation or sociopolitical daring. **Stanislav Rostotskii** (*It Happened in Penkovo*/Delo bylo v Pen'kove, 1958), **Lev Kulidzhanov** (*The House I Live In*/Dom, v kotorom ia zhivu, 1956, codirected by Iakov Segel' [1923–1995]), and **Tat'iana Lioznova** (*Evdokiia*, 1961) made patriotic melodramas with recognizable elements of Soviet life sufficient in number for the films to pass as realistic. Lukov continued directing blockbusters in a similar vein, including the very popular *Various Destinies* (Raznye sud'by, 1956); Gerasimov helmed the trilogy *And Quiet Flows the Don* (Tikhii Don, 1957–1958) from Mikhail Sholokhov's Cossack epic, while Donskoi added *Foma Gordeev* (1959) to his string of Gor'kii adaptations. The presence of these "living classics" in the studio secured its status in the eyes of the Communist establishment but also maintained an increasingly stifling atmosphere that resulted in the collective discrimination against deviations from the Party-defined status quo. As a result, **Marlen Khutsiev**'s *I Am Twenty* (Mne dvadtsat' let, 1964) suffered from ongoing administrative intrusion, while **Aleksandr Askol'dov**'s *The Commissar* (Komissar, 1968) was ordered destroyed altogether. At the same time, Gerasimov (*The Journalist*/Zhurnalist, 1967; *At the Lake*/U ozera, 1970) and Rostotskii (*Let's See What Monday Brings*/Dozhivem do ponedel'nika, 1968) made some of the highest-grossing films of the decade, dealing with contemporary reality in a lively yet conformist, only modestly critical, manner. **Vasilii Shukshin**'s peculiar films portrayed the tension between countryside and city, featuring a gallery of likeable "weirdoes" who cannot find comfort for their restless souls in either milieu.

In the 1970s, the "classics" had visibly exhausted themselves, returning ad nauseam to their old themes and losing touch with a confusing reality. Donskoi's, Rostotskii's, and Kulidzhanov's films demonstrated their "Party-mindedness" in a hopelessly stale manner, emulated by a cadre of younger opportunists. Lioznova directed the 12-part television series *Seventeen Moments of Spring* (Semnadtsat' mgnovenii vesny, 1973) about a Soviet superspy working in the very center of the Nazi establishment; stylistically, though, this passionately loved and mercilessly mocked cult film was just as retrograde as **Vladimir Rogovoi**'s Red Army blockbusters.

During perestroika, **Vasilii Pichul** made a daring attempt to bring Soviet life in all its unpresentable facets to the screen. His *Little Vera* (Malen'kaia Vera, 1988) pointed out the directions in which a renewed, realistic Soviet cinema could move and how viewers' trust could be won back. But the 1990s were overshadowed by increasing financial problems and scandals, especially during the leadership of Sergei Livnev (1995–1998), an inventive director and imaginative planner whose ideas about producing B-movies as a way to meet the chronic lack of funding ended in a legal and financial fiasco. His successor, Vladimir Grammatikov (1998–2001), who had made a name for himself as a director of children's films, was not much luckier in his attempts to save the studio's legacy while adjusting to market capitalism and government control. The privatization attempts continued into the new millennium, but a planned auction of Gor'kii Studio in 2005 was called off by the Russian government, which declared the studio a national cultural treasure.

GOR'KII'S CHILDHOOD (Detstvo Gor'kogo, 1938). Soiuzdetfilm studio (**Gor'kii Studio for Children's and Youth Films**). 101 min., b/w. Directed by **Mark Donskoi**. Script: Il'ia Gruzdev, Mark Donskoi from Maksim Gor'kii's autobiographical novel. Cinematography: Petr Ermolov. Music: Lev Shvarts. Cast: Aleksei (Alesha) Liarskii, Mikhail Troianosvkii, Varvara Massalitinova, Daniil Sagal, Elizaveta Alekseeva. Premiere: 18 June 1938.

In the 1870s, young Alesha Peshkov and his mother move in with despotic grandfather Kashirin (Troianovskii) and his wife, the kind grandmother Akulina (Massalitinova), in Nizhnii Novgorod on the Volga River. Alesha is very perceptive and learns to see the complexity in human beings, who often become harsh after experiencing hardship. He meets a young gypsy (Sagal) who later dies tragically. Because of a fire in the grandfather's dye works and a general lack of cooperation and solidarity in the family, living conditions worsen. One day, Alesha leaves in order to get to know Russia and to make a living on his own.

GOSTEV, IGOR' ARONOVICH (b. 15 May 1925, Moscow–d. 24 March 1994, Moscow). Russian director, screenwriter, and producer. Gostev began his film career as a producer, after studying economics at the Soviet State Film School **VGIK**, from which he graduated in 1947. He returned to film school in the early 1960s, this time enrolling in **Aleksandr Stolper**'s directing workshop, which he completed in 1963, and then worked as producer and assistant director at **Mosfilm Studio**.

In critic Aleksandr Shpagin's words, Gostev had the reputation of a dutiful executor of official orders who was entrusted with filming the USSR's secret nuclear tests, the footage of which was for Politburo members' eyes only. He also contributed to prize-winning prestige **documentaries** about the Soviet space program such as *The First Trip to the Stars* (Pervyi reis k zvezdam, 1961). As a director of feature films, Gostev debuted with the patriotic spy drama *Radioactive Tracer* (Mechenyi atom, 1972), a box-office success despite its blatant schematism. Gostev's nine-hour trilogy on heroic scouts in the Great Patriotic War, *Front without Flanks* (Front bez flangov, 1974), *Front behind the Front Line* (Front za liniei fronta, 1977), and *Front in the Enemy's Rear* (Front v tylu vraga, 1981), also did well at the box office and won the director numerous national honors. Gostev's subsequent films show a continuing predilection for secret service subject matter marked by harsh Cold War rhetoric and vicious denunciations of the West, for example, in the Soviet-Syrian coproduction *Enclosure* (Zagon, 1987).

Gray Wolves (Serye volki, 1993), made after the breakdown of the Soviet system, is a watchable yarn about the schemes surrounding Nikita Khrushchev's demise in 1964, juxtaposing "good" vs. "evil" Communist hacks.

Gostev, who became a member of the Communist Party in 1962, was named People's Artist of the Russian Federation in 1985.

Other films: *A European Story* (Evropeiskaia istoriia, 1984); *Anarchy* (Bespredel, 1989).

GOVORUKHIN, STANISLAV SERGEEVICH (b. 29 March 1936, Berezniki, Sverdlovsk [now Perm'] district). Ukrainian and Russian director, scriptwriter, actor, and political activist. Govorukhin, a descendant of Don Cossacks whose father perished in 1936, studied geology at Kazan' State University, graduating in 1958. He joined the Kazan' television studio in 1959 as an assistant director and enrolled in the Soviet State Film School **VGIK** in 1961 where he studied with Iakov Segel' (1923–1995). After his graduation in 1967, he worked at Odessa film studio until 1988.

Govorukhin's directorial debut was the mountaineer adventure *The Vertical* (Vertikal', 1967, codirected with Boris Durov), revealing a predilection for locations such as the mountains or the sea where characters have to prove their inner strength. Similarly, *The White Explosion* (Belyi vzryv, 1969) tells about heroic mountaineer troops in the Great Patriotic War, while *Smuggled Goods* (Kontrabanda, 1975) praises Soviet secret service men exposing a group of smugglers on a ship. Govorukhin's adaptations of foreign literary classics hold a particular appeal for young viewers, including *Robinson Crusoe* (Zhizn' i udivitel'nye prikliucheniia Robinzona Kruzo, 1972) and *The Adventures of Tom Sawyer and Huckleberry Finn* (Prikliucheniia Toma Soiera i Gekl'berri Finna, 1981). The director landed a phenomenal hit with the five-part miniseries *The Meeting Place Cannot Be Changed* (Mesto vstrechi izmenit' nel'zia, 1979, TV), starring **Vladimir Vysotskii** as a militia captain who fearlessly and inventively fights criminals in the 1920s. This film elevated the director to the ranks of the most successful populists of Russian cinema. Although the ideological framework of Govorukhin's Soviet movies is far from dissident, their emphasis lies on human virtues such as loyalty and courage, while explicit Communist slogans are usually avoided.

In the post-perestroika period, Govorukhin directed provocative, feature-length **documentaries**. The title of *One Cannot Live Like This* (Tak zhit' nel'zia, 1990) became proverbial, as did *The Great*

Criminal Revolution (Velikaia kriminal'naia revoliutsiia, 1994), which attacks the post-Communist corruption. *The Russia That We Have Lost* (Rossiia, kotoruiu my poteriali, 1992) juxtaposes Tsar Nikolai II and Vladimir Lenin, with a clear preference for the former. Populist attitudes are also reflected in the vigilante drama *The Voroshilov Sniper* (Voroshilovskii strelok, 1999) about an aged marksman who takes merciless revenge for the rape of his granddaughter. In 2005, Govorukhin directed an adaptation of Vladimir Dudintsev's 1956 novel *Not by Bread Alone* (Ne khlebom edinym)—a surprising choice at first sight, but consistent with the filmmaker's sympathy for lonely, idealistic heroes selflessly fighting a cynical establishment.

As a screenwriter, Govorukhin demonstrates a sense for dramatic plot development; he wrote the martial arts superhit *Pirates of the 20th Century* (Piraty dvadtsatogo veka, 1979)—the greatest box-office hit of Russian and Soviet film history—and *A Russian Revolt* (Russkii bunt, 2000), a loyal adaptation of Aleksandr Pushkin's *The Captain's Daughter*. Govorukhin is also a valued actor; among his typically understated performances is Krymov in **Sergei Solov'ev**'s *Assa* (1988), the earl in a 2003 adaptation of *Little Lord Fauntleroy* (Radosti i pechali malen'kogo lorda), and a military instructor in Fedor Bondarchuk's Afghanistan potboiler *The Ninth Company* (Deviataia rota, 2005).

In the early 1990s, Govorukhin's political ambitions got him elected to the Russian parliament. A noble and candid maverick whose positions oscillate between uncompromising anti-Communism and alliances with pro-Communist forces, Govorukhin has also proven a champion for Russian cinema who regularly organizes screenings of new films for deputies and advances legislative projects against pornography.

Govorukhin was named Merited Artist of the Ukrainian SSR in 1986 and People's Artist of Russia in 2006.

Other films: *Angel's Day* (Den' angela, 1968); *Splashes of Champagne* (Bryzgi shampanskogo, 1988); *Bless the Woman* (Blagoslovite zhenshchinu, 2003); *The Actress* (Artistka, 2007).

GREAT CITIZEN, THE (Velikii grazhdanin, 1937–1939). **Lenfilm Studio**. Two parts: 118 and 134 min. Directed by **Fridrikh Ermler**. Script: **Mikhail Bleiman**, Manuel' Bol'shintsov, Fridrikh Ermler.

Cinematography: **Arkadii Kol'tsatyi**. Music: **Dmitrii Shostakovich**. Cast: **Nikolai Bogoliubov**, Ivan Bersenev, **Oleg Zhakov**, **Zoia Fedorova**, Boris Poslavskii, Petr Kirillov, **Boris Chirkov**, Aleksandr Zrazhevskii, Efim Al'tus, **Iurii Tolubeev**. Premiere: Part I: 13 February 1938. Part II: 27 November 1939.

In 1925, at the factory Red Metal Worker (Krasnyi metallist), hidden "enemies of the people" sabotage all attempts to produce tractors more efficiently. Led by a high-ranking official, the manipulative hack Borovskii (Zhakov), they scheme relentlessly to alienate the factory workers from the Communist Party and gain a majority in its leadership. However, the exemplary Communist Petr Shakhov (Bogoliubov) is supported by the workers and publishes an article in the newspaper *Pravda* exposing the enemies' venomous activities. The 14th Party Congress puts an end to Borovskii's subversion; he shows regret and recants. Behind the scenes, though, he and his allies continue their anti-Soviet actions.

In 1934, the enemies' main goal is to eliminate Shakhov. One of their leaders is a Party official, Zemtsov (Tolubeev), the hireling of a foreign secret service. A forest worker accompanying Shakhov—who now serves as the secretary of the CPSU district committee—on a hunt, is supposed to kill him but reveals the scheme to Soviet authorities. The struggle between Shakhov's old foe, Borovskii, and Shakhov gets fiercer. Finally, a follower of Lev Trotskii, Briantsev, kills Shkahov at a workers' meeting, but Shkahov's cause will be carried on by his comrades.

GRIBOV, ALEKSEI NIKOLAEVICH (b. 31 January 1902, Moscow– d. 26 November 1977, Moscow). Russian actor. Gribov studied at the studio of the Moscow Art Theater (MKhAT), graduating in 1924. He became one of the mainstays of the MKhAT for the next half century, especially in plays of Anton Chekhov, Nikolai Gogol', and Mikhail Bulgakov, and received particular official recognition for his roles in Soviet propaganda plays such as Nikolai Virta's *Earth* (Zemlia, 1937) and Nikolai Pogodin's *The Kremlin Bells* (Kremlevskie kuranty, 1941), portraying Vladimir Lenin. The actor also became famous for his inventive, witty, and sometimes daringly original performances in satirical plays.

Gribov made his film debut in **Iosif Kheifits** and **Aleksandr Zarkhi**'s controversial contemporary **comedy** *Hectic Days* (aka *Red Army Days*/Goriachie denechki, 1935). However, his screen reputation mainly rests on adaptations of Russian literary classics. He scored in **Isidor Annenskii**'s versions of Anton Chekhov's *The Man in the Shell* (Chelovek v futliare, 1939) and *The Wedding* (Svad'ba, 1944), as well as **Vladimir Petrov**'s *Guilty without Guilt* (Bez viny vinovatye, 1945) from Aleksandr Ostrovskii's play and *The Inspector General* (Revizor, 1952) from Nikolai Gogol'—all of which were box-office hits. Gribov also played episodic parts in Stalinist fare such as **Mikheil Chiaureli**'s cultish epics *The Fall of Berlin* (aka *Battle of Berlin*/Padenie Berlina, 1949) and **Mikhail Romm**'s exercise in Cold War demagoguery, *Secret Mission* (Sekretnaia missiia, 1950). In the 1950s and 1960s, Gribov was particularly successful in lighthearted comedies, including **Mikhail Kalatozov**'s *Loyal Friends* (Vernye druz'ia, 1954) and **Rolan Bykov**'s *Seven Nurses* (Sem' nianek, 1962).

Gribov joined the Communist Party in 1944. In addition to a 1951 Stalin Prize for *Secret Mission*, he received Stalin Prizes for his theater work in 1942, 1946, and 1952, and the title Hero of Socialist Labor in 1972. He was named People's Artist of the USSR in 1948.

Other films: *The Moor Soldiers* (Bolotnye soldaty, 1938); *Sporting Honor* (Sportivnaia chest', 1951); *People on the Bridge* (Liudi na mostu, 1959); *Dead Souls* (Mertvye dushi, 1960); *Downfall of an Empire* (Krushenie imperii, 1970).

GRICIUS, JONAS AUGUSTINO (b. 5 August 1928). Lithuanian cinematographer. Gricius studied at the Soviet State Film School **VGIK**, graduating in 1954. He was assistant to the famous cameraman **Andrei Moskvin** on **Aleksandr Faintsimmer**'s *Dawn on the Neman River* (Ausra prie Nemuno/Nad Nemanom rassvet, 1953), one of the first post–World War II feature films of **Lithuanian cinema**. Gricius worked at **Lenfilm Studio** as an assistant and second cameraman with directors such as **Mikhail Shveitser** and **Sergei Iutkevich**. His first independent film as cinematographer was Vytautas Mikalauskas's hapless satirical **comedy** *Turkeys* (Indiuki, 1959).

Gricius came into his own with his work on **Arūnas Žebriūnas**'s medium-length *The Last Shot* (Paskutinis šūvis/Poslednii vystrel), a tragic novella from the prize-winning omnibus film *Living Heroes* (Gyvieji didvyriai/Zhivye geroi, 1960). Its bleak, richly contrasted imagery demonstrated for the first time this cameraman's concentrated, original visual approach. Žebriūnas and Gricius continued their partnership for almost three decades, sensitively applying the black-and-white format to masterpieces such as *The Girl and the Echo* (Paskutinė atostogų diena/Devochka i ekho, 1964), and a dramatically dark color spectrum in *Journey to Paradise* (Kelione į rojų/ Puteshestvie v rai, 1980). Gricius worked with other leading Lithuanian directors as well, including **Raimondas Vabalas** (*Steps in the Night*/Žingsniai naktį/Shagi v nochi, 1962; *Staircase to the Sky*/ Laiptai į dangų/Lestnitsa v nebo, 1966), and **Vytautas Žalakevičius** (*Nobody Wanted to Die*/Niekas nenorėjo mirti/Nikto ne khotel umi-rat', 1966). He gained international fame for his brilliant camera work in **Grigorii Kozintsev**'s Shakespeare adaptations *Hamlet* (Gamlet, 1964) and *King Lear* (Korol' Lir, 1970); prior to these achievements, he had already worked as second cameraman on Kozintsev's *Don Quijote* (1957). Ranging from lucid indoor compositions that convey maximum psychological tension, to apocalyptic, grainy landscapes with intense dark tones, Gricius's art proved an ideal match for the director's interpretations.

By the mid-1970s, Gricius had become one of the most respected Soviet cinematographers; thus, he was entrusted with filming George Cukor's high-profile, well-meant, yet ultimately ill-fated U.S.-Soviet coproduction *The Blue Bird* (1976). However, later films shot by Gricius were often disappointing; moreover, he accepted an increasing number of administrative tasks. For several years, Gricius was the first secretary of the Lithuanian Filmmakers' Union and since 1976 a member of the board of the Soviet Filmmakers' Union. In the 1990s, Gricius taught film at the Lithuanian Academy of Music in Vilnius.

Gricius joined the Communist Party in 1960; he was honored with the title People's Artist of the Lithuanian SSR in 1978.

Other films: *Stone upon Stone* (Akmuo ant akmens/Kamen' na ka-men', 1972); *Hour of the Full Moon* (Mėnulio pilnaties metas/Chas polnoluniia, 1988); *Portrait in Profile* (Portret v profil', 1993); *The*

Year of the Dog (God sobaki, 1996); *Antigravitation* (Antigravitacija, 2005, short).

GRIGORIU, GRIGORE [some sources: Grigorii] (b. 4 April 1941, Causeni, Tighina district–d. 20 December 2003, Palanca, Stefan Voda [car accident]). Moldovan actor. Upon finishing high school, Grigoriu made his stage debut at the People's Theater of Causeni without ever having taken acting classes. In 1959, he joined the troupe of the National Theater Vasile Alecsandri in Balti and later worked with other theaters as well.

Grigoriu's screen debut was the role of Sava Milciu in **Emil Loteanu**'s *Red Meadows* (Poienele rosii/Krasnye poliany, 1966), after which he became one of the director's mainstays. The darkly handsome Grigoriu gained nationwide fame—and also became a heartthrob for a generation of female viewers—with his performance as Radu Negostin in Loteanu's bittersweet gypsy tale *Fiddlers* (Lautarii/Lautary, 1972). His reputation was solidified with the role of horse thief Loiku Zobar in the superhit *The Tabor Leaves for Heaven* (aka *Queen of the Gypsies*/Tabor ukhodit v nebo, 1975), also by Loteanu. Following this success, Grigoriu and his female costar, **Svetlana Tomà**, played another romantic couple in the biopic *I Want to Sing* (Ia khochu pet', 1979) about singer Maria Biesu.

Chilean émigré Sebastian Alarcon gave Grigoriu the lead of an architect in his political pamphlet *Night over Chile* (Noch' nad Chile, 1977). Back in Moldova, **Valeriu Gajiu** cast Grigoriu as Victor in the music-filled *Where Are You, Love?* (Unde esti, iubire?/Gde ty, liubov'?, 1980), the thinly veiled life story of famous pop singer Sofia Rotaru portrayed by herself. Grigoriu, who also appeared in Russian films such as **Aleksei Saltykov**'s *Emel'ian Pugachev* (1978), was the most popular male star of **Moldovan cinema** in the 1970s, yet he was unable to maintain that status, and his screen appearances were later reduced to episodic parts. His last screen performance was the supporting role of Misa in Loteanu's little-seen drama *The Suffering* (Durerea, 1989).

Grigoriu was named Merited Artist of the Moldavian SSR in 1976.

Other films: *Bitter Grain* (aka *A Taste of Bread*/Gustul piinii/Gor'kie zerna, 1966); *The Last Haiduk* (Ultimul haiduc/Poslednii gaiduk, 1973); *The Secret Service Agent* (Agent sekretnoi sluzhby, 1978); *The Morning Star* (Luceafarul, 1987, TV).

GRIN'KO, NIKOLAI GRIGOR'EVICH (b. 22 May 1920, Kherson–d. 10 April 1989, Kiev). Ukrainian actor. After military service in the Great Patriotic War, Grin'ko became an actor at the Shchors Dramatic Theater of Zaporozh'e and Uzhgorod in 1946–1955.

His first film role was the supporting part of a mutineer in **Ihor' Savchenko**'s biopic *Taras Shevchenko* (1951). **Aleksandr Alov** and **Vladimir Naumov** repeatedly made use of Grin'ko's ascetic appearance and natural psychological intensity, beginning with the heroic Civil War drama *Pavel Korchagin* (1956) and continuing with such diverse films as the World War II parable *Peace to Him Who Enters* (Mir vkhodiashchemu, 1961) and the espionage thriller *Teheran-43* (aka *Spy Ring*, aka *Assassination Attempt*, 1980).

Internationally, Grin'ko's unique artistry became best known through the films of **Andrei Tarkovskii**, who cast him in mostly small yet conceptually significant parts. In *Ivan's Childhood* (aka *My Name Is Ivan*/Ivanovo detstvo), Grin'ko is a fatherly colonel; in *Andrei Rublev* (1964–1966), the painter-monk Daniil Chernyi; in *Solaris* (1972), Kris Kelvin's father; in *The Mirror* (Zerkalo, 1975), the director of the print shop; and in *Stalker* (1979), the scientist. Grin'ko also played important episodic roles in **Sergei Paradjanov**'s *Shadows of Forgotten Ancestors* (Teni zabytykh predkov, 1964), **Andrei Mikhalkov-Konchalovskii**'s *Romance about Lovers* (Romans o vliublennykh, 1974), **Aleksei German**'s *Twenty Days without War* (Dvadtsat' dnei bez voiny, 1977), and **Yury Il'enko**'s *The Feast of Baked Potatoes* (Prazdnik pechenoi kartoshki, 1977). One of the most remarkable achievements among the actor's over 180 film roles is an authentic portrayal of Anton Chekhov in **Sergei Iutkevich**'s poetic *Plot for a Short Story* (Siuzhet dlia nebol'shogo rasskaza, aka *Lika—Chekhov's Love*/Lika—liubov' Chekhova, 1970).

In the late 1980s, **Ermek Shinarbaev** gave Grin'ko interesting parts in two films adapted from Anatolii Kim's short stories: *My Sister, Liusia* (Sestra moia, Liusia, 1986) and *Stepping Out of the Forest onto the Meadow* (Vyiti iz lesa na polianu, 1988).

Grin'ko was named People's Artist of Ukrainian SSR in 1973.

Other films: *A Dangerous Tour* (Opasnye gastroli, 1969); *The Last Case of Commissar Baerlach* (Poslednee delo komissara Berlakha, 1972); *One-Two, the Soldiers Were Marching* (Aty-baty, shli soldaty, 1975). *See also* UKRAINIAN CINEMA.

GRITSENKO, NIKOLAI OLIMPIEVICH (b. 24 July 1912, Iasinovataia, Ukraine–d. 8 December 1979, Moscow). Ukrainian-Russian actor. Gritsenko worked as a designer at a metallurgic factory and simultaneously studied music and drama at the Worker's Faculty (*rabfak*) until 1934. He then took acting classes in Kiev and Moscow, graduating from the Moscow Shchukin Theater School in 1940, before becoming one of the leading members of the Vakhtangov Theater troupe.

In cinema, Gritsenko debuted in **Iulii Raizman**'s charming melodrama *Mashen'ka* (1942) in the role of the driver Kolia. The beginning of his career was marked by roles in political prestige projects such as Raizman's *Knight of the Golden Star* (aka *Dream of a Cossack*/Kavaler zolotoi zvezdy, 1951), for which he received a Stalin Prize, and **Aleksandr Dovzhenko**'s unfinished Cold War pamphlet *Farewell, America!* (Proshchai, Amerika! 1951, reconstructed 1994). **Iosif Kheifits** cast him as Veniamin Semenovich in his successful working-class saga *The Big Family* (Bol'shaia sem'ia, 1954), one of the earliest attempts to reflect mildly liberal trends in Soviet society.

In later years, Gritsenko developed into a highly prolific supporting actor who excelled in a variety of genres. Even in the briefest of episodes, his performances invariably stood out because of the uncommon complexity and psychological believability that characterized his artistry. Gritsenko was arguably at his best in literary adaptations—outstanding in **Grigorii Roshal'**'s successful trilogy based on Aleksei Tolstoi's *The Calvary* (1957–1959), in **Vladimir Petrov**'s underrated Leonid Leonov adaptation *The Russian Forest* (Russkii les, 1964), and especially as Karenin in **Aleksandr Zarkhi**'s *Anna Karenina* (1968), an impressive impersonation unmatched in its intensity by any other adaptation of that novel. The actor did not shy away from trivial fare, including **Tat'iana Lioznova**'s cult series *Seventeen Moments of Spring* (Semnadtsat' mgnovenii vesny, 1973, TV), elevating the overall quality of such films.

Gritsenko was awarded the title People's Artist of the USSR in 1964. His sister, Liliia Gritsenko (1927–1989), was a well-known opera singer and actress.

Other films: *Anna's Happiness* (Schast'e Anny, 1969); *Father Sergius* (Otets Sergii, 1978).

GRUZIYA-FILM STUDIO. In 1921, the Commissariat of Education of the Georgian Soviet Republic formed a film section that in 1923 was reorganized into a "film trust" called Georgian State Film Industry (Goskinprom) and was provided with professional equipment and facilities. Its first feature films were adaptations of well-known Georgian classics—Aleqsandr Kazbegi, Daniel Chonkadze, Giorgi Tsereteli, and Davit Kladiashvili. Experienced nonnatives such as Vladimir Barskii (1889–1936; *Arsen the Bandit*/Arsena kachagi/ Arsen razboinik, 1923; *Horrors of the Past*/Tsarsulis sashinelebani/ Koshmary proshlogo, 1925), **Hamo Bek-Nazaryan**—who also was the first head of Goskinprom (*Patricide*/Ottseubiistvo, aka *On the Pillory*/Mamis mkvleli/U pozornogo stolba, 1923), and **Ivan Perestiani** (*Arsena Jiorjashvili* aka *The Murder of General Griaznov*, 1921) infused **Georgian cinema** with much-needed professional skills but also the required Communist ideology. Accomplished native theater director Kote Mardjanishvili (1872–1933; *Samanishvili's Stepmother*/Samanishvilis dedinatsvali/Machekha Samanishvili, 1927) and silent film pioneer Aleqsandr Tsutsunava (1881–1955; *Who Is Guilty?*/Vin Aris Damnashave?/Kto vinovat?), used the new medium for formal and narrative experimentation.

Political censors prevented the release of one of the most brilliant Georgian silents, the antibureaucratic satire *My Grandmother* (Chemi bebia/Moia babushka, 1929), directed by Kote Miqaberidze (1896–1973). **Mikhail Kalatozov** (Mikheil Kalatozishvili), who had gained wide recognition with *Salt for Svanetia* (Jim Shvante [marili svanets]/Sol' Svanetii, 1930), was reprimanded for his next project, the satire *A Nail in the Boot* (Gvozd' v sapoge, aka *The Country Is in Danger*/Strana v opasnosti, 1932) and ultimately left Georgia.

In the 1920s, Georgian audiences elevated **Nato Vachnadze** to the rank of a national movie icon; other stars of Georgian cinema were **Veriko Andjaparidze**, **Akaki Vasadze**, and **Sergo Zakariadze**. Among Gruziya-Film's emerging national school of directors were

Nikoloz Shengelaia (*Eliso*, 1928), **Mikheil Gelovani** (*Youth Wins/* Akhalgazrdoba imardjvebs/Molodost' pobezhdaet, 1928), **Mikheil Chiaureli** (*Saba*, 1929), **Davit Rondeli** (*Ugubziara*, 1930), **Siko Dolidze** (*In the Country of Avalanches/*Zvavta mkhareshi/V strane obvalov, 1932), and Leo Esakia (1899–1966), each of whom developed a recognizable cinematic style. Thus, Chiaureli's previous career as a sculptor determined the high level of composition and lighting that stand in peculiar contrast to the openly propagandistic nature of his films, including the famous *Get Out of the Way!* (Khabarda/Postoronites', 1931). Of utmost importance was **Giorgi Mdivani**'s work as a screenwriter.

Chiaureli helmed the first Georgian sound film, *The Last Masquerade* (Ukanaskneli maskaradi/Poslednii maskarad, 1934), a satirical attack on the Georgian bourgeoisie. **Comedies** with a strong populist tendency became one of the mainstays of **Georgian cinema** in the 1930s, including Gelovani's *A Genuine Caucasian* (Namdvili kavkasieli/Nastoiashchii kavkazets, 1934) and Rondeli's controversial *Paradise Lost* (Dakarguli samotkhe/Poteriannyi rai, 1938). Another recurring theme was the country's troubled past, interpreted in a distinctly pro-Russian light, which is typical of Chiaureli's *Arsen* (Arsena Jorjashvili, 1937) and *Georgii Saakadze* (1942–1943), as well as Dolidze's *Dariko* (1937). Chiaureli gained enormous influence by creating a series of monumental films devoted to Iosif Stalin, beginning with *The Great Glow* (aka *They Wanted Peace*/Diadi gantiadi/Velikoe zarevo, 1938, Stalin Prize 1941).

In 1938, the studio was renamed Tbilisi Film Studio. In the 1930s, it began the production of animated films, with Vladimir Mudjiri (1907–1953) as the leading creator of drawn **animation**. The number of feature films made during the Great Patriotic War was negligible, and production did not pick up in postwar years either; the fact that an unremarkable concert film, Dolidze and Rondeli's *Jurgai's Shield* (Jurgais pari/Shchit Dzhurgaia, 1944), won the highest official honors, is telling in itself.

The studio was renamed Gruziya-film in 1953. In the late 1950s, when young directors **Rezo Chkheidze** and **Tengiz Abuladze** joined Gruziya-film and made their joint feature debut with the medium-length *Magdana's Donkey* (Magdanas Lurja/Lurdzha Magdany, 1955), Georgian cinema regained national self-awareness and eventually international stature. Indeed, the 1960s saw a genuine Georgian "film miracle," with the emergence of inimitable masters such as **Otar Ioseliani** (*Fall of the Leaves*/Giorgobistve/Listopad, 1966), **Eldar Shengelaia** (*An Unusual Exhibition*/Arakhveulebrivi gamopena/Neobyknovennaia vystavka, 1969), and **Giorgi Shengelaia** (*Pirosmani*, 1969). Chkheidze celebrated an international triumph with the antiwar parable *Father of the Soldier* (Djariskatsis mama/Otets soldata, 1965), while Abuladze scored a critical success with the dark and mysterious *The Plea* (Vedreba/Mol'ba, 1967). One of the most original cinematographers was **Levan Paatashvili** who worked both in Georgia and Russia, while **Giya Kancheli** became a prominent film composer. Interestingly, the young and the old generations of Georgian filmmakers were able to coexist in the studio—even former ultra-Stalinists such as Chiaureli and Dolidze continued to churn out pictures in regular intervals, some of them aesthetically remarkable.

During the 1970s, Georgian cinema had become a known and valued entity among Soviet and international film connoisseurs. Gruziya-film released art-house hits such as Ioseliani's *Once There Was a Singing Thrush* (Iqo shashvi mgalobeli/Zhil pevchii drozd, 1970), Eldar Shengelaia's *Crackpots* (Sherekilebi/Chudaki, 1974), Abuladze's *The Wishing Tree* (Natris khe/Drevo zhelanii, 1977), and **Lana Gogoberidze**'s distinctly feminist *Several Interviews on Personal Questions* (Ramodenime interviu pirad sakitkhebze/Neskol'ko interv'iu po lichnym voprosam, 1979). However, by the early 1980s, signs of a looming crisis could no longer be ignored. Ioseliani immigrated to France; Chkheidze embarrassed himself with the opportunistic *Your Son, Earth* (Mshobliuro chemo mitsov/Tvoi syn, zemlia, 1980), while Abuladze struggled to complete his anti-Stalinist masterpiece *Repentance* (Monanieba/Pokaianie, 1984). Eldar Shengelaia best expressed the spirit of inevitable reform in his satire *Blue Mountains, or An Unbelievable Story* (Tsisperi mtebi anu arachveulebrivi ambavi/Golubye gory, ili nepravdopodobnaia istoriia, 1984).

Despite serious individual efforts, Georgia was unable to secure its film industry's survival in the 1990s, after the country gained independence. Some filmmakers—among them Lana Gogoberidze and Eldar Shengelaia—became political activists. The studio, in which more than 1,000 feature films had been made, became a stockholding company. State funding barely suffices for one or two feature films annually. Many projects wait for years to be completed. In 2004, businessman Mamuka Hasariadze bought the studio's real estate component, promising to build a "film city." In 2006, Gruziya-film's archive was destroyed by fire in a tragic accident.

GUBENKO, NIKOLAI NIKOLAEVICH (b. 17 August 1941, Odessa). Russian actor and director. Gubenko, who grew up in an orphanage, studied acting under **Sergei Gerasimov** and **Tamara Makarova** at the Soviet State Film School **VGIK**, graduating in 1964. In 1970, he also finished VGIK's Directing Department.

Gubenko's screen debut in the lead role of Nikolai in **Marlen Khutsiev**'s youth drama *I Am Twenty* (Mne dvadtsat' let, aka *Ilyich's Gate*/Zastava Il'icha, 1964) brought him immediate name recognition. He solidified his reputation by working with many of the leading Soviet directors, often displaying an anti-Philistine idealism paired with manly energy and forthright patriotic activism. Thus, he portrayed young Marshall Vasilii Bliukher in the Civil War potboiler *No Password Is Needed* (Parol' ne nuzhen, 1967), the title character in **Aleksei Saltykov**'s *The Director* (Direktor, 1970)—replacing **Evgenii Urbanskii** after his tragic death—about an auto mogul resembling the famous Ivan Likhachev, and Lieutenant Goloshchekov in **Sergei Bondarchuk**'s *They Fought for the Motherland* (Oni srazhalis' za Rodinu, 1975). Gubenko's performance as **Inna Churikova**'s apolitical husband in **Gleb Panfilov**'s provocative social parable *I Wish to Speak* (Proshu slova, 1975) proved that he was capable of capturing less aggressive and even humorous facets as well.

Gubenko directed his first major picture in close cooperation with **Vasilii Shukshin**. *Came a Soldier from the Front* (Prishel soldat s fronta, 1971), adapted from stories by Sergei Antonov, shows the aftermath of the Great Patriotic War in all its tragic gloom. The autobiographically inspired *Orphans* (aka *Winged Birds*/Podranki, 1976) is generally considered Gubenko's best picture, but its gritty subject matter—childhood in an orphanage during the war—is depicted in excessively sentimental, nostalgic colors. *From the Life of Vacationers* (Iz zhizni otdykhaiushchikh, 1980) warns about spreading petit-bourgeois values in contemporary Soviet society; however, its grotesque overtones violate the story's psychological integrity. Gubenko's last film was the alarmist *Forbidden Zone* (Zapretnaia zona, 1988), a curious anticipation of the breakdown of Soviet civilization interpreted as a tragic natural disaster requiring individual heroism.

While making a name for himself in Soviet cinema, Gubenko also pursued a stage career at the Taganka Theater starting in 1964. From 1986–1991, he served as Taganka's chief executive director, but the troupe split after his bitter fallout with the theater's founder, Iurii Liubimov, and Gubenko later established his own Community of Taganka Actors (1993). In the last years of perestroika, Gubenko also became a political activist whose media visibility was boosted by his often extreme viewpoints. He was appointed minister of culture of the USSR in 1989, a position he held until the failed anti-Gorbachev coup in 1991, and was elected to the Russian parliament, the Duma, in 1995–2003, for the faction of the Communist Party. Gubenko is married to actress Zhanna Bolotova (b. 1941), who appeared in a number of his films.

Other films: (as actor) *The Last Crook* (Poslednii zhulik, 1966); *Angel* (1967, released 1987); (as director) *If You Want to Be Happy* (Esli khochesh' byt' schastlivym, 1974); *Life, Tears, and Love* (I zhizn', i slezy, i liubov', 1984).

GUNDAREVA, NATAL'IA GEORGIEVNA (b. 28 August 1948, Moscow–d. 15 May 2005, Moscow). Russian actress. Born into a family of engineers, Gundareva studied at the Moscow Shchukin Theater Institute in 1967–1971. Upon graduation, she joined the troupe of the Maiakovskii Theater, becoming one of its leading stars.

From the beginning, Gundareva's screen image has been that of a rank-and-file working woman endowed with perceptiveness and a big heart, appearing at times headstrong and mean, at times vulnerable, generous, and naïve. Her debut in **Vitalii Mel'nikov**'s charming **comedy** *Hello and Good-bye* (Zdravstvui i proshchai, 1972) was memorable for its naturalness. The lead role in *A Sweet Woman* (Sladkaia zhenshchina, 1977) made headlines, for Gundareva was able to reveal complexity, dignity, and feminine beauty behind the character's deceptive simplicity. Such masterful portrayals turned several of her films into box-office hits and the actress into a loved movie star. While some directors exploited her talent for merely sentimental purposes—in particular **Nikolai Gubenko** in *The Orphans* (Podranki,

1976), others allowed the actress to demonstrate different characteristics such as her gift for parody, for example, **Karen Shakhnazarov** in *A Winter Evening in Gagry* (Zimnii vecher v Gagrakh, 1985) in which Gundareva lampoons pop singer Alla Pugacheva.

Gundareva worked with **Andrei Smirnov** in *Autumn* (Osen', 1975), **Georgii Daneliia** in *Autumn Marathon* (Osennii marafon, 1979), and **El'dar Riazanov** in *Promised Heavens* (Nebesa obetovannye, 1993), but many leading filmmakers avoided her, perhaps fearing Gundareva's powerful, scene-stealing presence. Unsurpassed in Gundareva's film career is the lead role in Leonid Menaker's *Canine Feast* (Sobachii pir, 1990), the fearless, shockingly realistic depiction of a poor, vulgar alcoholic and her attempts to protect her love under the most gloomy of circumstances.

Gundareva was awarded a USSR State Prize in 1984 for her stage work and the title People's Artist of the Russian Federation in 1986. In 1993, she was elected member of the Russian parliament, where she remained until 1996 in the faction of Women of Russia.

Other films: *Citizen Nikanorova Is Expecting You* (Vas ozhidaet grazhdanka Nikanorova, 1978); *The Life of Klim Samgin* (Zhizn' Klima Samgina, 1986, TV); *I Want to Go to Prison* (Khochu v tiur'mu, 1999).

GURCHENKO, LIUDMILA MARKOVNA (b. 12 November 1935, Khar'kiv). Russian actress and singer. Gurchenko studied in **Sergei Gerasimov** and **Tamara Makarova**'s workshop at the Soviet State Film School **VGIK**, graduating in 1958.

As a student, Gurchenko made her debut in **Ian Frid**'s *The Path of Truth* (Doroga pravdy, 1956); that same year, **El'dar Riazanov** gave her the lead in his lighthearted musical **comedy *Carnival Night*** (Karnaval'naia noch'). Gurchenko's inspired performance as club assistant Lena Krylova—elegant, warm, witty, and self-assured—immediately shot her to national stardom. **Aleksandr Faintsimmer** let her reprise that role, now as the singing shop assistant Tania, in *The Girl with a Guitar* (Devushka s gitaroi, 1958). Gurchenko thus was defined early on as a musical entertainer rather than a versatile character actress, a reputation that defied her attempts to break out of the cliché of singing prettiness. Only in the mid-1970s and 1980s did leading Soviet directors cast her in artistically challenging pictures.

Gurchenko raised eyebrows with her top-notch performance as an aging industrial manager suddenly encountering genuine love in Viktor Tregubovich's *Old Walls* (Starye steny, 1974). **Aleksei German** cast her in *Twenty Days without War* (Dvadtsat' dnei bez voiny, 1977), **Nikita Mikhalkov** in *Five Evenings* (Piat' vecherov, 1979), and **Roman Balaian** in *Flights in Dream and in Reality* (Polety vo sne i naiavu, 1982). Riazanov gave her another rewarding task in his crowd-pleaser *A Railway Station for Two* (Vokzal dlia dvoikh, 1983), skillfully combining melodramatic and comedic elements; she played similar roles in films by **Petr Todorovskii** (*The Beloved Woman of Mechanic Gavrilov*/Liubimaia zhenshchina mekhanika Gavrilova, 1981) and **Vladimir Men'shov** (*Love and Doves*/Liubov' i golubi, 1984). In later years, **Mikhail Shveitser** made her the sole focus of his minimalist experiment *Listen, Fellini!* (Poslushai, Fellini! 1993), while Fedor Bondarchuk directed a 50-minute musical video under the title *I Love* (Liubliu) starring Gurchenko.

Despite cinema's general inability to grasp Gurchenko's atypical artistic range, millions of viewers continue to adore the ever-youthful actress for her unparalleled charm, eccentric—sometimes over-the-top—dominance, and tempestuous private life that often enough made for sensational news.

Gurchenko was named People's Artist of the USSR in 1983.

Other films: *Baltic Sky* (Baltiiskoe nebo, 1960–1961); *The Shadow* (Ten', 1971); *White Clothes* (Belye odezhdy, 1992, TV); *Shukshin Stories* (Shukshinskie rasskazy, 2004).

– H –

HEIR OF CHENGHIZ KHAN, THE (aka *Storm over Asia*/Potomok Chingiz-khana, 1928). **Mezhrabpomfilm Studio**. 96 min., b/w. Directed by **Vsevolod Pudovkin**. Script: Osip Brik from the novel by Ivan Novokshenov. Cinematography: **Anatolii Golovnia**. Cast: **Valerii Inkizhinov**, Aleksandr Chistiakov, Vladimir Tsoppi, Anel' Sudakevich, **Boris Barnet**, **Leonid Obolenskii**. Premiere: 11 October 1928. A sound track was added in 1949; the film was restored in 1964.

The young Mongolian hunter Bair (Inkizhinov) rides to a market to sell a silver fox fur. Smith (Tsoppi), a British trader, pays an unfair amount to the outraged Bair, who injures him in the ensuing struggle. Bair flees and joins a partisan unit in the mountains. After being captured, he is about to be executed when the British high command finds an ancient document claiming that he is a direct heir of Chenghiz Khan. The severely wounded Bair gets royal treatment, for the British intend to install him as a puppet ruler. But when Bair witnesses the brutal execution of a prisoner, he erupts in anger and starts a powerful national revolt.

– I –

I AM TWENTY (Mne dvadtsat' let, aka *Ilyich's Gate*/Zastava Il'icha, 1964). **Gor'kii Studio for Children's and Youth Films**. Two parts. 175 min. (original version), b/w. Directed by **Marlen Khutsiev**. Script: **Gennadii Shpalikov**, Marlen Khutsiev. Cinematography: **Margarita Pilikhina**. Music: Nikolai Sidel'nikov. Cast: Valentin Popov, **Nikolai Gubenko**, Stanislav Liubshin, Marianna Vertinskaia, Svetlana Svetlichnaia, Lev Prygunov, **Rodion Nakhapetov**, **Andrei Mikhalkov-Konchalovskii**, **Andrei Tarkovskii**, **Oleg Vidov**. Premiere: 18 January 1965 (abridged version). Reconstructed in 1988.

Sergei (Popov), Nikolai (Gubenko), and Slava (Liubshin) are friends living in the same Moscow street. After Sergei is discharged from the Soviet Army, he wanders through the streets of Moscow where he meets Ania (Vertinskaia) on a bus and falls in love with her. He also attends a party, a public poetry reading at the Polytechnic Museum, an art exhibition, and the May demonstration on Red Square. While Nikolai, a married man, suffers from the suffocating atmosphere in his family, Slava clashes with supervisors whom he suspects of authoritarian tendencies. Sergei dreams about his father who perished in the Great Patriotic War and asks him for advice on how to live.

IAKOVLEV, IURII VASIL'EVICH (b. 25 April 1928, Moscow). Russian actor. Iakovlev studied at the Shchukin Theater School in Moscow. Upon graduation in 1952, he joined the troupe of the Vakhtangov Theater, where he since has become one of Russia's major theater stars.

As a film actor, Iakovlev made his debut in the supporting part of Chakhotkin in **Konstantin Iudin**'s *Behind the Footlights* (Na podmostkakh stseny, 1956). When **Ivan Pyr'ev** cast the virtually unknown actor as Prince Myshkin in his Fedor Dostoevskii adaptation *The Idiot* (Idiot, 1958), he gained immediate nationwide fame. Iakovlev's features were ideally suited to express Myshkin's unworldly purity and tormenting despair. Subsequent roles were in part derivations of that image, showcasing Iakovlev as a noble yet also virile officer-cum-lover, for example, as Lieutenant Rzhevskii in **El'dar Riazanov**'s popular *Husar Ballad* (Gusarskaia ballada, 1962). In the following years, Iakovlev deliberately chose roles that subverted this cliché: in the satirical **comedy** *Easy Life* (Legkaia zhizn', 1964) he played a sleazy crook, and in **Aleksandr Zarkhi**'s Lev Tolstoi adaptation *Anna Karenina* (1968) the unprincipled womanizer Stiva Oblonskii. Although Iakovlev succeeded in virtually all genres, his best performances use his natural aristocratic demeanor, for example, as the writer Potapenko in **Sergei Iutkevich**'s *Plot for a Short Story* (Suzhet dlia nebol'shogo rasskaza, aka *Lika—Chekhov's Love*/Lika—liubov' Chekhova, 1969).

Iakovlev was brilliant in the double role of building manager Bunsha and Tsar Ivan the Terrible in **Leonid Gaidai**'s *Ivan Vasil'evich Changes His Job* (aka *Ivan Vasilievich: Back to the Future*/Ivan Vasil'evich meniaet professiiu, 1973) and as Bi in **Georgii Daneliia**'s grim anti-utopia *Kin-Dza-Dza* (1986). More than 50 million viewers adored his performance in **Evgenii Matveev**'s patriotic, pathos-filled melodramas *Earthly Love* (Liubov' zemnaia, 1974) and *Destiny* (Sud'ba, 1977), which won Iakovlev a USSR State Prize in 1979. In the 1980s and 1990s, he lent his star power to a few daring projects of newcomers, most prominently Sergei Ovcharov's original Nikolai Leskov adaptation *The Left-Hander* (Levsha, 1986).

Iakovlev was named People's Artist of the USSR in 1976. His son Anton, with whom he appeared in the Vladimir Nabokov adaptation *Mashen'ka* (1991), works as an actor.

Other films: *King of the Reindeer* (Korol'-Olen', 1969); *Iuliia Vrevskaia* (1976); *Children of Iron Gods* (Deti chugunnykh bogov,

1993); *East-West* (Vostok-Zapad, 1999); *Irony of Fate: The Sequel* (Ironiia sud'by: Prodolzhenie, 2008).

IANKOVSKII, OLEG IVANOVICH (b. 23 February 1944, Dzhez-kazgan, Karaganda district, Kazakhstan). Russian actor. Iankovskii studied at the theater college of Saratov, graduating in 1965, and was an actor with the Karl Marx Drama Theater in Saratov in 1967–1973. He then joined the troupe of the Moscow Theater of Lenin Komsomol (Lenkom).

Vladimir Basov cast Iankovskii as Genrikh Shvartskopf (Heinrich Schwarzkopf) in his superhit spy adventure *The Shield and the Sword* (Shchit i Mech, 1968), followed by the lead in the romantic Civil War ballad *Once Two Comrades Were Serving* (Sluzhili dva tovarishcha, 1968) and the controversial industrial drama *The Bonus* (Premiia, 1975). Iankovskii also appeared in **Vladimir Motyl'**'s Decembrist saga *Star of Captivating Happiness* (Zvezda plenitel'nogo schast'ia, 1975), **Emil' Loteanu**'s *My Tender and Gentle Beast* (aka *A Hunting Accident*/Moi laskovyi i nezhnyi zver', 1978), **Vadim Abdrashitov**'s *The Turn* (Povorot, 1978), **Mark Zakharov**'s made-for-television hit *An Ordinary Miracle* (Obyknovennoe chudo, 1978), and numerous other films of various genres and quality levels.

Maverick filmmaker **Roman Balaian** gave Iankovskii fine opportunities to demonstrate psychological penetration: in the contemporary tale of hopelessness and depression, *Flights in Dream and in Reality* (Polety vo sne i naiavu, 1982) and in the deeply subversive turn-of-the-century story *The Spy* (Filer, 1987), an unprecedented exposure of the opportunism and cowardice of intellectuals. Iankovskii gained international fame with the lead in **Andrei Tarkovskii**'s *Nostalgia* (1983), the story of a Russian writer in a state of crisis visiting Italy. He starred in a number of international productions while continuing to excel in Russian adaptations of classical literature such as **Mikhail Shveitser**'s *Kreutzer Sonata* (Kreitserova sonata, 1987) from Lev Tolstoi's novella, and historical-philosophical parables such as **Karen Shakhnazarov**'s *The Assassin of the Tsar* (Tsareubi-itsa, 1991). Iankovskii's characteristic blend of intellectual intensity, ascetic nervousness, and restrained sensuality were much in demand in the 1990s when the actor turned into a veritable superstar of post-Communist Russian cinema.

Iankovskii was named People's Artist of the RSFSR in 1984 and People's Artist of the USSR in 1991. His son, Filip Iankovskii, is a successful film director.

Other films: *Other People's Letters* (Chuzhie pis'ma, 1977); *Protect Me, My Talisman* (Khrani menia, moi talisman, 1986); *To Kill the Dragon* (Ubit' drakona, 1989); *First Love* (Pervaia liubov', 1995); *Doktor Zhivago* (2005, TV); *The Chosen One* (Izbrannik, 2007); *Ivan the Terrible and Metropolitan Filipp* (Ivan Groznyi i mitropolit Filipp, 2008).

IBRAHIMBEKOV [other spellings: Ibragimbekov, Ibrahimbeyov], **RUSTAM** [Rustam Mahmed Ibrahim-ogly; Russian sources list the patronymic Ibragimovich] (b. 5 February [other sources: January] 1939, Baku). Azerbaijani screenwriter, director, playwright, and prose writer. Ibrahimbekov majored in cybernetics and initially worked as an engineer. He then studied in the Department of Screenwriting of the Supreme Courses for Screenwriters and Directors (VKSR) where his teacher was **Sergei Gerasimov**, and in the Directing Department under **Leonid Trauberg**, graduating in 1967 and 1974, respectively.

Ibrahimbekov adapted many of his roughly 40 screenplays from his own short stories and novellas, starting with the anticorruption tale *In This Southern City* (V etom iuzhnom gorode, 1970), directed by Eldar Karliev. Equally at home in Russia and Azerbaijan, Ibrahimbekov has made significant contributions to both countries' cultures. His early interest in romantic adventure stories about the Bolshevik Revolution and the ensuing Civil War resulted in potboilers such as *Tale of a Chekist* (Povest' o chekiste, 1970) for action specialist Boris Durov, and the legendary *White Sun of the Desert* (Beloe solntse pustyni, 1969, coauthored with Valentin Ezhov), inventively directed by **Vladimir Motyl'**. Other screenplays evoke more complex and ethically ambiguous notions, including *The Spy* (Filer, 1987, directed by **Roman Balaian**), about a morally spineless intellectual working as a double agent.

After the demise of the Communist system, Ibrahimbekov penned a number of screenplays conveying the disillusionment with the Soviet legacy, including *To See Paris and Die* (Uvidet' Parizh i umeret', 1992), directed by Aleksandr Proshkin, and especially

East-West (Vostok-Zapad, 1999, coauthored with **Sergei Bodrov**), directed by Régis Wargnier. Ibrahimbekov's partnership with **Nikita Mikhalkov** has led to two major international hits, *Close to Eden* (Urga, 1992) and *Burnt by the Sun* (Utomlennye solntsem, 1995). While Ibrahimbekov's own political views seem contradictory and unstable, he succeeded in translating Mikhalkov's "Eurasianism" and neopatriotism into Hollywoodesque drama, most openly in the bloated pseudohistorical epic *The Barber of Siberia* (Sibirskii tsiriul'nik, 1999).

Ibrahimbekov has often worked with Azerbaijani director **Rasim Ojagov**, for whom he authored the screenplays of *The Birthday* (Den' rozhdeniia, 1978), *The Park* (Park, 1983), *Another Life* (Drugaia zhizn', 1987), and *O, Istanbul!* (1995). *The Interrogation* (Istintag/Dopros, 1979), also helmed by Ojagov, is a powerful attack on the shadow economy and state corruption in Azerbaijan; the film won him a USSR State Prize. Ibrahimbekov directed a medium-length **comedy**, *The Suite* (Siuita, 1976), as part of the omnibus *One Fine Day* (V odin prekrasnyi den', 1976), the story of a daydreaming lifeguard. The Russian-Azerbaijani coproduction *The Family* (Sem'ia, 1998), which Ibrahimbekov produced and filmed from his own screenplay, reconstructs the increasingly nationalist and hostile atmosphere in 1990 that ultimately led to the flight of 300,000 Azeri people from their homes in Armenia.

Ibrahimbekov's worldview represents a curious mélange of rational system theory and spirituality, driven by a passionate faith in the mission of intellectuals. As an author, filmmaker, and public figure he became one of the key players in post-Soviet cinema, an authentic representative of its multinational aspects. In 1993, he cofounded the Confederation of Filmmakers' Unions of the Former Soviet Republics and has been its leader since.

Ibrahimbekov won four State Prizes of Russia: a belated one, in 1998, for *White Sun of the Desert*, for *Urga* in 1993, for *Burnt by the Sun* in 1995, and for *The Barber of Siberia* in 1999. He was awarded the title Merited Artist of the Azerbaijanian SSR in 1976. Ibrahimbekov was elected first secretary of the Azerbaijani Filmmakers' Union in 1981. His brother, Maksud Ibrahimbekov (b. 1935), is a well-known author and screenwriter. Both Rustam and Maksud Ibrahimbekov write in Russian.

Other films: *In Front of a Closed Door* (Pered zakrytoi dver'iu, 1981); *Structure of the Moment* (Struktura momenta, 1980); *The Man Who Was Trying* (Chelovek, kotoryi staralsia, 1996, dir.); *Mysteries* (Misterii, 2000); *The Chosen One* (Izbrannik, 2007, screenplay). *See also* AZERBAIJANI CINEMA.

IL'ENKO, YURY HERASYMOVICH (b. 9 May [other sources: 18 July] 1936, Cherkasy, Ukraine). Ukrainian director, cinematographer, screenwriter, and actor. Il'enko, the son of a factory worker, studied cinematography in the workshop of **Boris Volchek** and **Aleksandr Gal'perin** at the Soviet State Film School **VGIK**, graduating in 1960.

In his first feature films as cameraman, including *Farewell, Doves* (Proshchaite, golubi, 1961, directed by Iakov Segel' [1923–1995]), Il'enko revealed a gift for precise shot composition and lighting methods that effectively supported psychological analysis. But only his encounter with filmmaker **Sergei Paradjanov** at the **Dovzhenko Film Studio** fully brought out the cinematographer's artistic potential. *Shadows of Forgotten Ancestors* (Tini zabutykh predkiv/Teni zabytykh predkov, 1964), featuring a free, dynamic camera movement and glowing color spectrum, were groundbreaking for the revival of **Ukrainian cinema**, an impulse so strong its effects can still be felt today. *Shadows*, based on Mykhailo Kotsiubynsky's 1913 story, was an extraordinary critical success worldwide, in large part due to the expressive vigor and picturesque beauty of its cinematography.

One year after *Shadows'* release, Il'enko made his debut as feature film director with *Well for the Thirsty* (Krynytsia dlia sprahlykh/Rodnik dlia zhazhdushchikh). This story of rural decay and subsequent revival was considered nationalistic and only released in 1987. Similarly harsh was the treatment of Il'enko's next project, an inventive, original adaptation of Nikolai Gogol''s story *On the Eve of Ivan Kupala's Day* (Vechir na Ivana Kupala/Vecher nakanune Ivana Kupaly, 1968). After a limited release, it was withdrawn from movie theaters and re-released 20 years later.

White Bird with a Black Spot (Nilyi ptakh z chornoiu oznakoiu/Belaia ptitsa s chernoi otmetinoi, 1971), "a brutal, bloody, and occasionally surreal vision of the events at Bukovina in the years during and immediately after the war" (Liehm and Liehm), has remained Il'enko's most famous picture to this day. His following efforts were aesthetically and politically less remarkable, although *Against All Odds* (V superech vs'omu/Naperekor vsemu, 1973), a Soviet-Yugoslav coproduction about the liberation struggle of Montenegro in the late 18th century under the leadership of the national hero Petar Negosh, can be seen as an allegory of Ukraine's own struggle for independence. Overall, though, the director significantly toned down Ukrainian national elements and opted for subject matter that was more agreeable to the Soviet state, such as in *The Feast of Baked Potatoes* (Prazdnik pechenoi kartoshki, 1977) about a selfless woman who raised 48 children.

After the breakdown of Communism and Ukraine's subsequent independence, Il'enko began to express openly his revulsion toward the old system. But *Swan Lake: The Zone* (Lebedyne ozero. Zona, 1990) is not just an indictment of totalitarian cruelty—it also stands as a monument to his teacher, Paradjanov, whose prison diaries inspired the story. After a decade-long hiatus, Il'enko presented *A Prayer for Hetman Mazepa* (Molitva za hetmana Mazepu, 2002), a lengthy, lavish visual rhapsody that made news because of its iconoclastic depiction of Tsar Peter the First and Muscovy power games against Ukraine.

Il'enko, who has been called a poet-director, relies heavily on the Ukrainian cinematic tradition shaped by **Aleksandr Dovzhenko** and **Ivan Kavaleridze** and nourished by national folklore whose motifs reappear in the most unexpected contexts. With regard to narrative structure, Il'enko's films are deliberately involved, even chaotic, frequently switching back and forth between time levels. Visual associations are more important than plot progression or logic, which makes these pictures challenging to viewers.

Il'enko joined the Communist Party in 1973. He was appointed professor at the Karpenko-Karyi Institute of Theater Arts in Kiev in 1986. In the 1990s, Il'enko became increasingly active in Ukrainian politics. His brothers Vadim (b. 1932) and Mikhail (b. 1947) are well-known cameramen and directors.

Other films: *The Forest Song: Mavka* (Lisova pisnia—Mavka/ Lesovaia pesnia. Mavka, 1981); *The Legend of Princess Olga* (Lehenda pro kniahyniu Olhu/Legenda o kniagine Ol'ge, 1983).

IL'INSKII, IGOR' VLADIMIROVICH (b. 24 July 1901, Moscow–d. 13 January 1987, Moscow). Russian actor and director. Il'inskii learned his craft at the studio of Fedor Kommissarzhevskii (1882–1954) in Moscow and worked in various theaters beginning in 1918. From 1920 to 1935, he belonged to the troupe of Vsevolod Meierkhol'd, where he adopted a sense of comical eccentricity and precise timing. In 1938, he joined the more traditionalist Malyi Theater where for half a century he remained one of the legendary stars.

Iakov Protazanov cast Il'inskii as the narrow-minded investigator Kravtsov in the science fiction extravaganza *Aelita* (aka *Revolt of the Robots*, 1924). The budding actor responded to this challenge with an inventiveness that far surpassed the role's original concept, engraving himself into the memory of both the director and millions of Soviet viewers. Il'inskii subsequently starred as Petia Petelkin in Protazanov's **comedy** *The Tailor from Torzhok* (Zakroishchik iz Torzhka, 1925) and as Franz Schulz in the crassly antireligious *Holiday of St. Iorgen* (aka *St. Jorgen's Day*/Prazdnik sviatogo Iorgena, 1929), exposing the bigotry and primitive vulgarity of his characters. He also appeared in **Iurii Zheliabuzhskii**'s New Economic Policy (NEP) comedy *The Cigarette Girl of Mossel'prom* (Papirosnitsa iz Mossel'proma, 1924) and **Sergei Komarov**'s *The Kiss of Mary Pickford* (Potselui Meri Pikford, 1927).

Il'inskii's 1936 directorial debut with the comedy *Once in the Summer* (Odnazhdy letom), an early attempt to adapt Il'ia Il'f and Evgenii Petrov's satire for the screen, turned out rather lackluster. In 1938, **Grigorii Aleksandrov** gave him the part of the humorless administrator Byvalov in the musical comedy *Volga-Volga*, a role that endeared Il'inskii to generations of viewers and earned him a Stalin Prize in 1941. Twenty years later, following a reasonably amusing lead in **Andrei Tutyshkin**'s *Crazy Day* (Bezumnyi den', 1956), **El'dar Riazanov** cast Il'inskii as yet another unteachable bureaucrat in the smash hit *Carnival Night* (Karnaval'naia noch', 1956). The actor revived the role of Ogurtsov in the successful sequel *An Old Acquaintance* (Staryi znakomyi, 1969), which he also directed. This effectively ended Il'inskii's film career—the hugely popular actor preferred the stage, which offered him genuine artistic challenges such as the role of dying Lev Tolstoi in Ion Druta's *Return to One's Circles* (Vozvrashchenie na krugi svoia, 1978).

Il'inskii joined the Communist Party in 1960. In 1949, he was named People's Artist of the USSR and in 1974, Hero of Socialist Labor. He received Stalin Prizes for his theatrical work in 1942 and 1951 and a Lenin Prize in 1980. Il'inskii is buried at Novodevich'e Cemetery in Moscow.

Other films: *Miss Mend* (1926); *Crime and Punishment* (Prestuplenie i nakazanie, 1940); *Husar Ballad* (Gusarskaia ballada, 1962).

INKIZHINOV, VALERII IVANOVICH (Western sources: Valéry Inkijinoff, also incorrectly credited as Vladimir) (b. 25 March 1895, Irkutsk–d. 26 September 1973, Brunoy, France). Buriat and French actor and director. Inkizhinov, the son of a teacher, grew up in Siberia. He went to Petrograd in 1915 to study at the Polytechnical Institute, while simultaneously working in Vsevolod Meierkhol'd's Theater Studio, where early on he impressed fellow students with his sophisticated, animated body language. In 1920, Inkizhinov moved to Moscow to join **Lev Kuleshov**'s workshop. In 1926, he began to shoot his first movie, *Market of Lust* (Bazar pokhoti), based on a script by **Grigorii Aleksandrov** and **Sergei Eizenshtein**, but the film remained unfinished. However, *The Thief* (Vor, 1927), about a Korean village in the Far East suffering from Japanese assaults, became a critical success.

In 1928, **Vsevolod Pudovkin** cast Inkizhinov as the Mongolian rebel Bair in *The Heir of Chenghiz Khan* (aka *Storm over Asia*/Potomok Chingiz-khana). The actor's restrained performance, conveying burning passion underneath a stoic surface, won enthusiastic reviews all over the world and made Inkizhinov a household name in the international film community; it remained the most accomplished artistic achievement of his career.

In 1929, when Inkizhinov—together with his wife, **Vera Baranovskaia**—was permitted to travel to France to study sound film, he decided to not return to the Soviet Union, a step that practically eradicated his name from the official annals of Soviet cinema. He played some leads in French films such as Julien Duvivier's *The Head of a Man* (aka *A Man's Neck*/La tête d'un homme, 1933), **Fedor Otsep**'s *Amok* (1934), and Viacheslav Turzhanskii's *Volga in Flames* (Volga en flammes, 1934), and later continued his movie career with supporting parts in French and German productions such as G. W. Pabst's *Shanghai Drama* (Le Drame de Shanghaï, 1936) and Fritz Lang's monumental dilogy *The Indian Tomb/The Tiger of Eshnapur* (Das Indische Grabmal/Der Tiger von Eschnapur, 1958–1959). Prolific to the end and never too choosy about genres, Inkizhinov appeared in thrillers, spy spoofs, and television miniseries that often merely used his exotic looks and natural mystique.

In 1994, a foundation devoted to the study of Inkizhinov's life and art began its work in Ulan-Ude, the capital of Buriatia.

Other films: *Matchless* (1966); *The Aeronauts* (Les Chevaliers du ciel, TV, 1967–1968).

IOSELIANI, OTAR [also: Otare Iosseliani] (b. 2 February 1934, Tbilisi). Georgian director and screenwriter. Ioseliani grew up in a highly cultured family with ancient roots. He studied composition and piano at Tbilisi Conservatory, graduating in 1952, and in 1953–1955 applied mathematics at Moscow State Lomonosov University, before enrolling in the Soviet State Film School **VGIK**, where his teachers were **Aleksandr Dovzhenko** and **Mikheil Chiaureli**.

Ioseliani's diploma film, the short feature *April* (Aprili/Aprel', 1961, officially approved in 1965) about the everyday experiences of newlyweds, caused a stir with its unflattering depiction of common consumerist attitudes. *April* carries many of the features that would become mainstays of Ioseliani's peculiar cinematic world: the protagonists are characterized through their actions rather than dialogues; the story tends toward the parabolic and displays both bitterness and a forgiving irony; modernity is depicted as synonymous with chaos and degeneration.

In 1964, Ioseliani made the **documentary** *Molten Iron* (Tudzhi/Chugun), describing one day in the life of workers in a metallurgic factory characterized by the crude pragmatism of the Communist economy. The director's first full-length feature, *Fall of the Leaves* (Giorgobistve/Listopad, 1966), tells the story of a young engineer in a winery whose professional conscientiousness is confronted with common indifference and sloppiness. Superficially seen as a critique of Soviet-style industrial production, the film's implicit criticism points much deeper: the making of wine stands for art per se, to which professional skills and a most serious, loving attitude are vital, whereas a mechanical approach and incompetence prove destructive.

Once There Was a Singing Thrush (Iqo shashvi mgalobeli/Zhil pevchii drozd, 1970) made Ioseliani's name internationally known. It describes the carefree life of a young, talented musician whose sudden death in a traffic accident comes as a shock—as senseless as it is seemingly unmotivated by plot logic. The film presents an unobtrusive, mildly ironic critique of modern urban lifestyle and the inability of city dwellers to concentrate on anything meaningful.

Pastoral (Pastorali, 1976), a story of miscommunication between a vacationing Tbilisi string quartet and residents of a remote village, diagnoses a disturbing alienation between artists and rank-and-file people. However, in later films with different settings—for example, *A Little Monastery in Tuscany* (Un petit monastère en Toscane, 1986) and *Let There Be Light* (Et la lumière est fut, 1988) about a village in Senegal with vital magical traditions not yet distorted by encroaching modernity—Ioseliani seems to assume the possibility of a healthy symbiosis between the realms of the spiritual and the material.

In 1979, Ioseliani moved to Paris and since then has become an "international" filmmaker—comparable to Wim Wenders or Krzysztow Kieslowski—whose specific brand of artistry proves productive within varying national contexts. Ioseliani stated, "I view myself neither as a refugee nor an émigré—after cinema ceased to exist in the Soviet Union and in Georgia, I simply went where it was still doable." *Butterfly Hunt* (La chasse aux papillons, 1989) deals with an old French chateau inherited by a Muscovite and sold to Japanese who, somewhat comically, try to re-create and emulate French aristocratic habits. *Farewell, Home Sweet Home!* (Adieu, plancher des vaches! 1999) is an ironic take on class-conscious France, with a rich offspring pretending to be poor and the poor acting rich. In *Monday Morning* (Lundi matin, 2002) a French factory worker escapes to Venice, experiences the magic of its culture, and quietly returns to the banality of his everyday life.

Ioseliani has not completely abandoned Georgian subjects, as evidenced by the long, made-for-TV documentary *Georgia, Alone* (Seule, Georgie 1994) and the brilliant satire *Brigands—Chapter VII (In vino veritas)* (Brigands—chapitre VII, 1996), perhaps his most open expression of inner torment vis-à-vis his homeland and its troubles: the protagonists are involved in absurd circles of violence that last for centuries and from which apparently no one can escape.

Ioseliani is a cultural preservationist and intellectual aristocrat fully conscious of the futility of his efforts; the origins of his films' deep subversiveness are similar in the Soviet and the modern Western context. In Ioseliani's world, only traditional values that have stood the test of centuries are worthy of their name. His notion of culture implies spiritual cohesion rather than an assembly of artifacts; culture appears as a system of human relations, an organic kinship that, paradoxically, is the fundamental condition for the understanding of other nations. Ioseliani's humor is satirical yet in a tender way, neither destructive nor self-righteous. He relies on the aesthetic perceptiveness of the viewer and rejects intrusive analytical approaches. Among noticeable stylistic influences, critics have pointed to Jean Renoir, Jean Vigo, Luis Buñuel, Jacques Tati, Robert Bresson, **Andrei Tarkovskii**, and **Sergei Paradjanov**. Ioseliani has developed his own brand of melancholic surrealism; his complex **comedies**, often near silent, have consistently won jury prizes at A-festivals (Cannes, Venice, Berlin) but, with their anachronistic worldview, nonlinear plots, and deliberate strangeness and slowness, present considerable difficulties for unprepared viewers, who often react with confusion and anger, finding them monotonous and tedious. The director's no-nonsense elitism may be particularly irritating in the world of cinema, a milieu largely dominated by egalitarian vulgarity.

Other films: *Song of the Forgotten Flower* (Sapovnela, 1959); *Euzkadi Summer 1982* (Euzkadi été 1982, 1983); *The Moon's Favorites* (Les Favoris de la lune, 1984); *Gardens in Autumn* (Jardins en automne, 2006).

ISAEV, KONSTANTIN FEDOROVICH (b. 15 January 1907, Odessa–d. 9 January 1977, Moscow). Russian screenwriter and director. After studying shipbuilding at Odessa Polytechnical Institute in 1927–1930, Isaev became a screenwriter and playwright. He made his debut with *The Big Game* (Bol'shaia igra, 1934, directed by Georgii Tasin) about American engineers working in the Soviet Union. In 1936, Isaev directed an adventure short, *The Fortress at the Devil's Ford* (Zastava u Chertova broda), and a **children's film** from Samuil Marshak's poem "Such an Absent-Minded One" (Vot kakoi rasseiannyi), *Petrushka's Adventures* (Prikliucheniia Petrushki), both at Ukrainfilm studio (**Dovzhenko Film Studio**).

The late 1940s and early 1950s brought Isaev considerable official recognition, primarily for stories about the Great Patriotic War, praising soldiers' selflessness and wit, including *Victorious Return* (Vozvrashchenie s pobedoi, 1948, coauthored with **Mikhail Bleiman**), directed by Aleksandr Ivanov. *The Scout's Quest* (aka *Secret Agent*/Podvig razvedchika, 1947, coauthored with Bleiman and Mikhail Makliarskii [1909–1978] and directed by **Boris Barnet**) won Isaev a Stalin Prize in 1948. A clever adventure tale, it is based on the authentic story of the Soviet scout Kuznetsov and his one-on-one duel with a German spy. *Secret Mission* (Sekretnaia missiia, 1950, Stalin Prize 1951, directed by **Mikhail Romm**), a contribution to Cold War propaganda, depicts an alliance of "U.S. imperialists" with German Nazis designed to carry out subversive acts against the ever-peaceful Soviet Union.

Isaev had a gift for **comedy** that he demonstrated with his popular play *Taimyr Is Calling You* (Vas vyzyvaet Taimyr, 1948, adapted for the screen in 1970) and the charming *Loyal Friends* (Vernye druz'ia, 1954, both coauthored with Aleksandr Galich), the latter directed by **Mikhail Kalatozov**. One of Isaev's lasting accomplishments is the fairy tale *Sadko* (1952), which **Aleksandr Ptushko**'s wizardry turned into a picturesque, colorful medley of folktale motifs, though sadly reduced in the end to a xenophobic message.

Isaev's screenplays are distinguished by clearly drawn plot lines, ultrapatriotic pathos, and an explicit Communist message. Many tales convey a mind-over-matter ideology, most prominently *Pavel Korchagin* (1957), directed with youthful brio by **Aleksandr Alov** and **Vladimir Naumov** from Nikolai Ostrovskii's novel. Isaev's last works were the hugely successful miniseries *Eternal Call* (Vechnyi zov, 1976, TV), a mixture of trivial family saga and heavy-handed Communist nationalism, and the historical epic *Star of Hope* (Zvezda nadezhdy, 1978, directed by **Edmond Keosayan**) about 18th-century Armenian national hero David-Bek.

Other films: *May Night, or The Drowned Woman* (Maiskaia noch', ili utoplennitsa, 1953); *Unfinished Story* (Neokonchennaia povest, 1955); *The First Day* (Den' pervyi, 1958).

ISHMUKHAMEDOV, ELYOR [some Russian sources also list the patronymic Mukhitdinovich] (b. 1 May 1942, Tashkent). Uzbek director and scriptwriter. Ishmukhamedov began to work at **Uzbek-film Studio** as an assistant in 1959 before enrolling in the Soviet State Film School **VGIK**, from which he graduated in 1965. His debut was the short *The Rendezvous* (Svidanie, 1963).

In the mid-1960s, Ishmukhamedov became one of the leading filmmakers of the "New Wave" in **Uzbek cinema**, which creatively absorbed Western European impulses ranging from the French *nouvelle vague* to Federico Fellini. Ishmukhamedov became known for the soft, lyrical flow of his loosely knit, episodic narratives about rank-and-file youngsters capturing the erotic and tragic aspects of their lives. He won critical acclaim and scored a considerable popular success with his diploma film, *Tenderness* (Nezhnost', 1966). The focus on teenagers on the verge of adulthood who experience romantic infatuations, loyal friendship, and betrayal always dominates over the film's undeniable yet mild political propaganda. *Lovers* (Vliublennye, 1969), with its beautiful black-and-white photography, is a feast for the eye and turned out to be a great popular success. In 1973, Ishmukhamedov made *Meetings and Partings* (Vstrechi i rasstavaniia), in which immigration to the West, hopelessness, and longing for one's homeland are central themes. Later pictures such as *What Our Years Were Like* (Kakie nashi gody, 1980) feature adult professionals—mechanics, chauffeurs—who struggle with the prosaic challenges of everyday life while trying to stick to the poetic vision of their youth.

Somewhat alone in the filmmaker's oeuvre stands the biopic *Youth of a Genius* (Iunost' geniia, 1982) about 11th-century scientist and philosopher Avicenna (Ibn Sina); it won Ishmukhamedov a 1984 USSR State Prize. Exotically picturesque, the film visualizes the high level of cultural sophistication and openness to the world of medieval Bukhara but also the isolation of this Renaissance man *avant la lettre*.

In the mid-1980s Ishmukhamedov demonstrated an increasingly critical sociopolitical approach, considerably reducing his earlier indulgence in poetic imagery and romantic feeling. *Farewell, Green Grass of Summer* (Proshchai, zelen' leta, 1985) thematizes the blatant opportunism and materialism of the Brezhnev era that robs the main characters of a meaningful life. Even more radical was *The Shock* (Shok, 1988, TV version *With Affection and Pain*/S liubov'iu i bol'iu, 1990), which reveals the fatal alliance of Communist Party power structures and Mafia crime in Uzbekistan. (It is noteworthy that in the late 1980s, Ishmukhamedov was appointed one of Mikhail Gorbachev's official cultural advisors.) However, when the infamous Sharaf Rashidov—the Communist Party leader of Uzbekistan from 1959 to 1983—was rehabilitated by the country's new government, Ishmukhamedov moved to Moscow, where he has been working since. From 1996–2000 he taught cinema at one of the first private educational institutions in Russia, the Natal'ia Nesterova University, and completed the star-studded melodrama *The Heiresses* (Naslednitsy, 2000). In 2004, he directed a sequel to his earlier hit, *Lovers II* (Vliublennye—2), a Russian-Uzbek coproduction.

Ishmukhamedov was named Merited Artist of Uzbek SSR in 1969 and People's Artist of Uzbekistan in 1983.

Other films: *The Birds of Our Hopes* (Ptitsy nashikh nadezhd, 1975); *An Angel in the Streets* (Angel na dorogakh, 2003, TV miniseries).

IUDIN, KONSTANTIN KONSTANTINOVICH (b. 8 January 1896, Moscow–d. 30 March 1957, Moscow). Russian director. Iudin worked for the Soviet Print Media Agency (Soiuzpechat') in 1923–1926 and subsequently for the All-Russian Photo-Cinema Department. His debut as film director was the **documentary** *Red Crimea* (Krasnyi Krym, 1927), after which Iudin studied at the State Film School (GTK, later renamed **VGIK**), graduating in 1932.

In the 1930s, Iudin worked as an assistant for **Grigorii Aleksandrov** and other directors. Following his first full-length feature, the sleeper hit *A Girl with Personality* (Devushka s kharakterom, 1939), Iudin developed a reputation as a reliable specialist for contemporary **comedies**. His pictures—all of them hugely popular yet often enough critically denounced as "apolitical"—reveal certain similarities to those of Aleksandrov and **Ivan Pyr'ev**, especially their reliance on musical leitmotivs. But they also feature a distinct atmosphere due to the greater intimacy of Iudin's sets—even an air of privacy, as well as genuine kindness regarding human weaknesses. Iudin's central characters usually are energetic young people entangled in mix-ups who in the end meet their great love. Politically naïve but authentic in many details of everyday life in the USSR of the 1930s–1940s, these films are unique as reflections of a civil Soviet mentality blooming behind loud political rhetoric. Thus, *Hearts of Four* (Serdtsa chetyrekh, 1941, released in January 1945) became one of the legendary Soviet romantic comedies, nostalgically remembered to this day.

During World War II, Iudin was allowed to continue making comedies, despite initial doubts about the appropriateness of this genre in times of tragedy and destruction. *Antosha Rybkin*, a 1941 short about a bold army cook, features truly funny situations on an otherwise serious background. It earned Iudin the praise of **Sergei Eizenshtein** and proved so popular with viewers that the director was commissioned to make a medium-length feature under the same title in 1942. In 1950, Iudin won a Stalin Prize for the war adventure *Courageous People* (Smelye liudi) about a young horse breeder fighting Nazi invaders; with more than 40 million viewers it proved a spectacular success at the box office. *The Wrestler and the Clown* (Borets i kloun, 1958), about the friendship between famed wrestler Ivan Poddubnyi and the clown Anatolii Durov, was finished by **Boris Barnet** after Iudin's sudden passing.

Iudin was a critically underrated master of situational comedy. Although the Stalinist underpinnings of his films are in plain view (for example, portraits of "leaders" on the wall, quotes from newspaper articles or newsreel segments, characters' proclamations of political loyalty to Party and government), they never dominate the plots—timeless love stories of a strange purity yet without seeming puritanical—and rarely violate the laws of the genre.

Iudin was named Merited Artist of the RSFSR in 1954.

Other films: *Twins* (Bliznetsy, 1945); *The Fortress in the Mountains* (Zastava v gorakh, 1953); *The Swedish Matchstick* (aka *The Safety Match*/Shvedskaia spichka, 1954); *Behind the Footlights* (Na podmostkakh stseny, 1956).

IUMATOV, GEORGII ALEKSANDROVICH (b. 11 March 1926, Moscow–d. 5 October 1997, Moscow). Russian actor. Born into the family of a professor, Iumatov attended navy school in 1941–1942 and fought in the Great Patriotic War in 1943–1945 where he was repeatedly wounded. Without any formal education, he turned to acting and worked in all leading studios of the USSR, starting with small episodic roles such as a monk in **Sergei Eizenshtein**'s *Ivan the*

Terrible (Ivan Groznyi, 1943–1945), before **Sergei Gerasimov** cast him as one of the underground fighters, Anatolii Popov, in his war drama *The Young Guard* (Molodaia gvardiia, 1948).

By the mid-1950s, Iumatov had become one of the leading Soviet screen idols, adored by millions of viewers. Predominantly employed in contemporary fare, Iumatov was never choosy about his more than 100 movie roles (some accounts claim as many as 150). His lead performances include Ven'ka Malyshev in Vladimir Skuibin's *Cruelty* (Zhestokost', 1959), Zadorov in *Pedagogical Poem* (Pedagogicheskaia poema, 1955), and Stepan Ogurtsov in **Leonid Lukov**'s *Various Fates* (Raznye sud'by, 1956). Iumatov was often cast as a virile, heroic Komsomol activist, KGB agent, officer, or militia man in blockbusters such as *They Were the First* (Oni byli pervymi, 1956), **Gennadii Poloka**'s *One of Us* (Odin iz nas, 1970), **Vladimir Rogovoi**'s *Officers* (Ofitsery, 1971), and the thriller *Petrovka, 38* (1980). By the mid-1980s, his reputation slowly faded, but he continued to work on stage in the Theater of the Film Actor in Moscow (until 1994).

The actor, scandalously known for his hard drinking and womanizing, made news when he shot a building supervisor in 1994 and was granted amnesty the following year.

Iumatov was awarded the title People's Artist of the Russian Federation in 1982.

Other films: *A Dangerous Tour* (Opasnye gastroli, 1969); *Start the Liquidation* (Pristupit' k likvidatsii, 1983); *The Great Ants' Path* (Velikii murav'inyi put', 1992).

IUSOV, VADIM IVANOVICH (b. 20 April 1929, village Klavdino, Leningrad district). Russian cinematographer. Iusov worked at a Moscow metal factory in 1947–1949 before studying at the Soviet State Film School **VGIK** with **Aleksandr Gal'perin**, graduating in 1954. The same year, he joined the staff of **Mosfilm Studio** as an assistant cameraman; in 1957, he began to work as cinematographer.

Iusov developed an intensely meditative visual style during his cooperation with **Andrei Tarkovskii**, starting with *The Steamroller and the Violin* (Katok i skripka, 1960), whose exquisite color images of Moscow add considerably to the film's mysterious charm. The black-and-white imagery of *Ivan's Childhood* (aka *My Name Is Ivan*/Ivanovo detstvo, 1962), contrasting harsh, quasi-documentary, war-torn landscapes with dreamlike idylls, and the broad vistas in the medieval epic *Andrei Rublev* (1966) were essential contributions both to these pictures' historical authenticity and metaphorical grandeur. In *Solaris* (1972), Iusov humanized the science fiction milieu in accordance with Tarkovskii's anthropocentric approach, effectively transforming the technocratic genre. Due to conceptual disagreements about the autobiographical focus of *The Mirror* (Zerkalo, 1975), Iusov and Tarkovskii's partnership broke apart, a step that led to a noticeable change in the director's visual style.

In the 1960s, other filmmakers took notice of Iusov's extraordinary power as cinematographer, among them **Georgii Daneliia** (*Don't Grieve*/Ar daidardo/Ne goriui!, 1969; *Hopelessly Lost*, aka *The Adventures of Huckleberry Finn*/Sovsem propashchii, 1972; *The Passport*/Pasport, 1990) and **Sergei Bondarchuk**, who made use of Iusov's gift for wide-screen compositions—splendidly in *They Fought for the Motherland* (Oni srazhalis' za Rodinu, 1975), grotesquely overblown in *Red Bells* (Krasnye kolokola, 1980–1982), and moderately effective in *Boris Godunov* (1986). At this point, Iusov had almost exhausted the artistic credit accumulated in the first two decades of his career, despite unprecedented official recognition. Then, Ivan Dykhovichnyi offered him rewarding tasks and allowed him to return to the dark mystique of his early pictures, especially in the surreal, visually stunning Anton Chekhov adaptation *The Black Monk* (Chernyi monakh, 1988) and in *Moscow Parade* (Prorva, 1992), where the disjointed plot is somewhat held together by a coherent visual style, mocking the Stalinist "baroque."

Iusov was named People's Artist of the RSFSR in 1979. In 1982, he received a Lenin Prize for shooting **Lev Kulidzhanov**'s seven-part television miniseries *Karl Marx: The Early Years* (Karl Marks: Molodye gody, 1980, TV). He has been a professor at VGIK since 1983.

Other films: *Iuliia Vrevskaia* (1978); *Anna from 6 to 18* (Anna. Ot 6 do 18, 1993, doc.); *The Kopeck* (Kopeika, 2002).

IUTKEVICH, SERGEI IOSIFOVICH [other sources: Osipovich] (b. 28 December [other sources: 15 September] 1904, St. Petersburg– d. 23 April 1985, Moscow). Russian director, screenwriter, art director, art historian, and theorist. In 1919–1920, Iutkevich studied stage design in Kiev and assisted—together with his friend **Grigorii Kozintsev**—theater innovator Kote Mardjanishvili. In 1921–1923, he was enrolled in Vsevolod Meierkhol'd's Supreme Directing Workshops and in the Art Institute VKhUTEMAS. He and **Sergei Eizenshtein** were stage designers in Nikolai Foregger's workshop (Masterskaia Foreggera, or "Mastfor"), lampooning the style of the Moscow Art Theater (MKhAT). Together with Kozintsev and **Leonid Trauberg**, Iutkevich also participated in the creation of FEKS, the Factory of the Eccentric Actor (1922), helping to formulate the group's artistic strategies and programmatic texts. He eventually set up his own group, called Iutkevich's Experimental Film Collective (EKKIu), in 1926.

As an art director, Iutkevich worked on **Abram Room**'s *The Traitor* (Predatel', 1926) and *Bed and Sofa* (aka *Third Meshchanskaia Street*/Tret'ia Meshchanskaia, 1927), adding to the latter film's authentic milieu and atmosphere. His directorial debut, *Conquer Radio* (Daesh' radio, 1924, codirected with S. Griunberg), is a short **comedy** about juvenile delinquents in the streets of Moscow. In *Lace* (Kruzheva, 1928), a successful picture about Komsomol activists fighting hooligans and lackluster work attitudes, Iutkevich used extreme camera angles for seemingly unspectacular phenomena such as rain and machines. Komsomol members fight again in *Black Sail* (Chernyi parus, aka *The Hopper Barge 'Potemkin'*/Shalanda 'Potemkin,' 1929), this time against a private fishmonger.

Golden Mountains (Zlatye gory, aka *The Happy Street*/Schastlivaia ulitsa, 1931) was initially produced as a silent and subsequently given a sound track. This rather schematic story of a peasant who ends up as a politically conscious worker applied asynchronic principles of image and sound that were innovative at the time yet seem imposed and artificial today (budding screenwriter and future director **Leo Arnshtam** was in charge of sound). Iutkevich was then entrusted with *The Counterplan* (Vstrechnyi, 1932, codirected with **Fridrikh Ermler**), one of the groundbreaking cinematic events of the decade. Embedded in an authentic working-class milieu, it tells the story of the first Soviet turbine and was hailed for overcoming the split between avant-garde loftiness and rank-and-file audience expectations. *The Counterplan* represents Socialist Realism *avant la lettre*, with the principles of Party-mindedness, ideological commitment, and populist spirit all enforced. It also marked a revision of the classical silent montage principles that still survived in other early Soviet sound films. Rather, *Counterplan* is overflowing with lengthy dialogues, while its visual level is kept demonstratively simple and pragmatic—a quality that was sharply criticized as retrograde and even bourgeois by champions of the avant-garde such as **Viktor Shklovskii**.

Together with **Esfir' Shub**, Iutkevich then helmed a semi-**documentary**, *Ankara, the Heart of Turkey* (Ankara—serdtse Turtsii, 1934). After his plans to adapt *Crime and Punishment* for the screen failed, he spent three years on *Miners* (Skakhtery, 1937). Its central character is the Party leader of an industrial city in the Donbass region who manages to inspire the local workers to achieving a record-breaking output and defeat sabotage and incompetence. *Man with a Rifle* (Chelovek s ruzh'em, 1938), Iutkevich's first contribution to the cinematic cult of Vladimir Lenin, portrays the Communist leader in a poetic, almost fairy-tale light. *Iakov Sverdlov* (1940), another biopic of a Bolshevik idol, poeticizes its subject in a similar manner and won the director a First-Class Stalin Prize.

In 1939, Iutkevich was put in charge of the Soviet Children's Film Studio (Soiuzdetfilm, later **Gor'kii Studio for Children's and Youth Films**), which at the outbreak of the Great Patriotic War was evacuated to Dushanbe. Iutkevich directed *Schwejk Is Preparing for Battle* (Shveik gotovitsia k boiu, 1942), in which Jaroslav Hašek's immortal rascal frees Czech resistance fighters from the Gestapo. The film was shelved, probably because in the early stages of the war its humor was lost on the military. However, *Schwejk's New Adventures* (Novye pokhozhdeniia Shveika, 1943) fared better—Soviet audiences especially enjoyed the filmic caricature of Adolf Hitler.

Iosif Stalin intensely disliked Iutkevich's first postwar effort, *Light over Russia* (Svet nad Rossiei, 1947), an adaptation of Nikolai Pogodin's *Kremlin Bells* (Kremlevskie kuranty, 1941), which focuses on Lenin's role in supplying the nation with electricity. Despite considerable cuts, it was never released. Iutkevich then won a Stalin Prize for the documentary *The Youth of Our Country* (Molodost' nashei strany, 1947). In the late 1940s, the anti-Semitic campaign "against cosmopolitanism" in which a number of prominent filmmakers played a shameful role, chose Iutkevich among its main targets; as a result, he lost his teaching position at the Soviet State Film School

VGIK. Only after Stalin's death and several unremarkable films was he able to make a comeback with *Othello* (1956), which won him the Best Director award at Cannes in 1956.

During the Thaw when the Communist establishment struggled to prevent complete disillusionment in Communist ideals, Iutkevich continued his Lenin hagiography with *Tales about Lenin* (Rasskazy o Lenine, 1957) in which the politician's image is given emotional warmth and compassion. *Lenin in Poland* (aka *Portrait of Lenin/* Lenin v Pol'she, 1965) intellectualizes this intimate approach; it brought Iutkevich another Best Director award at Cannes in 1966 and a State Prize of the USSR in 1967. The final part of the saga, *Lenin in Paris* (Lenin v Parizhe, 1981), was filmed on location with French beauty Claude Jade as Lenin's love interest Inès Armand and adorned with another State Prize, but it amused rather than enthused its few viewers.

Iutkevich was one of the most consistent experimenters in Soviet cinema, with an interest in formally transgressing film genres, yet without ever challenging the Communist dogma in the slightest. His Vladimir Maiakovskii adaptation *The Bathhouse* (Bania, 1962) combines live action, drawn **animation**, and marionettes. The director also made a number of documentaries, including the official film about Nikita Khrushchev's visit to France (*Encounter with France/*Vstrecha s Frantsiei, 1960) and *About the Most Human of Men* (O samom chelovechnom, 1967), once again devoted to Lenin. A genuinely beautiful picture is *Plot for a Short Story* (Siuzhet dlia nebol'shogo rasskaza, aka *Lika—Chekhov's Love/*Lika—liubov' Chekhova, 1970), a Soviet-French coproduction about a bittersweet episode in the life of Anton Chekhov, using artificial background tableaux in several scenes. Iutkevich followed it with the Maiakovskii adaptation *Bedbug* (Klop), released under the title *Maiakovskii Is Laughing* (Maiakovskii smeetsia, 1975, codirected with Anatolii Karanovich). Last, but not least, in 1967 Iutkevich compiled a montage of stills from Eizenshtein's destroyed *Bezhin Meadow* (Bezhin lug, 1935/37) and in 1973 reconstructed the silent *The Lady and the Hooligan* (Baryshnia i khuligan, 1918), starring Maiakovskii.

Iutkevich left an oeuvre that could not be more motley. Alternating themes such as Sverdlov and Schwejk, Shakespeare and Lenin, Yves Montand and Nikita Khruschev, the director's versatility is unparalleled. Arguably, long-standing political obedience bought Iutkevich the right to experiment aesthetically; it is worth mentioning that he served as principal director of the Ensemble of Song and Dance of the Soviet secret service NKVD in 1939–1946. During his lifetime, he enjoyed the status of a living classic filmmaker as well as the respect of Western European — particularly French — intellectuals.

Iutkevich, who became a member of the Communist Party in 1939, was honored with the title People's Artist of the USSR in 1962 and Hero of Socialist Labor in 1974. He is buried at the Novodevich'e cemetery. The building in Moscow where he lived (Glinishchevskii pereulok 5/7) carries a memorial plaque.

Other films: *Greetings, Moscow!* (Zdravstvui, Moskva! 1945); *Przheval'skii* (1950); *Albania's Great Warrior, Skanderberg* (Velikii voin Albanii Skanderberg, 1953).

IVAN THE TERRIBLE (Ivan Groznyi, 1943–1945). Central United Film Studio for Feature Films (TsOKS: Tsentral'naia ob"edinennaia kinostudiia khudozhestvennykh fil'mov [see **Kazakhfilm Studio**, Alma-Ata]/**Mosfilm Studio**. Two parts, 99 and 85 min., b/w and color. Directed by **Sergei Eizenshtein**. Script: Sergei Eizenshtein. Cinematography: **Eduard Tissé** (exterior scenes), **Andrei Moskvin** (interior scenes). Music: **Sergei Prokof'ev**. Cast: **Nikolai Cherkasov**, **Liudmila Tselikovskaia**, **Mikhail Zharov**, **Serafima Birman**, **Pavel Kadochnikov**, **Amvrosii Buchma**, Andrei Abrikosov, Mikhail Nazvanov, Mikhail Kuznetsov, Aleksandr Mgebrov, **Vsevolod Pudovkin**, **Semen Timoshenko**, **Georgii Iumatov**. Premiere Part 1: 30 December 1944 (other sources: 16 January 1945); Part 2: September 1958.

Part I. 1547. At a lavish ceremony in the Kremlin, 17-year-old Prince Ivan Vasil'evich is crowned to be Russia's first tsar. He declares his intention to unite the country against disloyal nobility and to expand its borders. After marrying Anastasiia Romanova (Tselikovskaia), he defeats the cruel Tartars and conquers Kazan, where he meets Aleksei Basmanov (Buchma), who soon becomes his ardent supporter. Yet his jealous friend Kurbskii (Nazvanov) defects to Poland, Anastasiia is poisoned by Evrosin'ia Staritskaia, the tsar's aunt (Birman), and the external threat from Poland and Lithuania and the internal subversion continue. Ivan withdraws from Moscow, only to be called back to rule by a large procession of rank-and-file Russians.

Part II: The Polish court and their lackey Kurbskii rejoice over the tsar's supposed abdication. Meanwhile, Ivan pursues his policy of centralization with grim determination, ruling with the help of a special force, the *oprichniks*. His former friend, Fedor Kolychev (Abrikosov), by now the metropolitan of Moscow, tries to temper him, but in vain. With his omnipresent "eye," Maliuta Skuratov (Zharov), Ivan preempts a conspiracy led by Evrosin'ia, intended to elevate her son Vladimir (Kadochnikov) to the throne. Ivan manages to outwit the conspirators, leaving Vladimir dead at the end of a mock coronation.

IVANOVSKII, ALEKSANDR VIKTOROVICH (b. 29 November 1881, Kazan'–d. 12 January 1968, Leningrad). Russian director and screenwriter. After graduating from Kazan' University Law School in 1906, Ivanovskii embarked on a career as a stage director, with particular success at the Moscow Zimin Opera Theater, where he worked until 1917. In 1918, Ivanovskii was hired by **Iosif Ermol'ev**'s film company and went through an all-around apprenticeship with leading filmmaker **Iakov Protazanov**. During the first stage of his career, he specialized in adaptations of classical Russian literature, including *The Stationmaster* (Stantsionnyi smotritel', 1918) from Aleksandr Pushkin's short story and *Punin and Baburin* (Punin i Baburin, 1919), an adaptation of an Ivan Turgenev novella.

In the early 1920s, Ivanovskii moved to Sevzapkino (later **Lenfilm Studio**) in Petrograd where he helmed one of Soviet cinema's first international successes, the historical drama *Palace and Fortress* (Dvorets i krepost', 1923) about the anti-tsarist movement of the 1860s. Ivanovskii paid homage to the terrorists of the People's Will organization in *Stepan Khalturin* (1925), describing an assassination attempt against Tsar Aleksandr II in 1880. *The Decembrists* (Dekabristy, 1926) continues the anti-tsarist theme, indulging in the grandiose sets that became the director's trademark, and large numbers of skillfully choreographed extras. However, on the backdrop of the flourishing Soviet film avant-garde, Ivanovskii was labeled "bourgeois" and "reactionary," notwithstanding the popularity of his films. When a sequel to *The Decembrists*, *The Flaming*

Pole (Plameneiushchii polius), was shelved, he returned to literary adaptations with a Marxist-Leninist slant, yet his approach was too transparent to fool dogmatic critics. Of lasting interest is a biopic about 18th-century Renaissance man Mikhailo Lomonosov, *The Fisherman's Son* (Syn rybaka, 1928).

Ivanovskii fared better during the early sound film period. *Iudushka Golovlev* (aka *Home of Greed*), Ivanovskii's 1934 adaptation of Mikhail Saltykov-Shchedrin's gloomy 1880 satire *The Golovlyov Family*, was hailed as exemplary by Soviet critics. Selecting just one of the novel's characters, the off-putting hypocrite Iudushka Golovlev, made for a coherent and lean plotline. The director then adapted *Dubrovskii* (1936) from Pushkin's prose fragment but forced a primitive, class-based message into the original, and ultimately falsified the classic's worldview.

Ivanovskii found his true calling in the genre of musical **comedy**. Thus, *Musical Story* (Muzykal'naia istoriia, 1940, codirected with **Gerbert Rappaport**) became a template for carefree, kindhearted love stories, with legendary tenor Sergei Lemeshev (1902–1977) portraying a driver who is unaware of his singing talent. Despite the film's complete avoidance of political issues, it won Ivanovskii a Stalin Prize in 1941. *Anton Ivanovich Is Angry* (aka *Spring Song*/Anton Ivanovich serditsia, 1941) is equally charming and entertaining. Following other operetta and concert films, Ivanovskii's last major hit was the excellent comedy *Tamer of Tigers* (aka *Tiger Girl*/Ukrotitel'nitsa tigrov, 1955, codirected with **Nadezhda Kosheverova**).

Ivanovskii was a conscientious if pedestrian filmmaker who moderately adjusted his craft to changing political circumstances while maintaining solid professional standards. When sound film initiated a turn toward wordy, slow-paced, theatrical film narration, he made pictures that established a de facto continuity between pre-1917 Russian and 1930s Soviet cinema, with literary adaptations emphasizing the social criticism of Russian classical literature, and vaudeville-type comedies whose sole objective was to enchant and entertain mass audiences. Although Ivanovskii's films often have been described in unflattering terms, the director has defenders such as film historian Romul Sobolev.

Ivanovskii was named Merited Artist of the RSFSR in 1936.

Other films: *A Rude Woman* (Khamka, 1918); *Asia* (1928); *The Prisoner of the Caucasus* (Kavkazskii plennik, 1930); *Silva* (1944); *The Ballet Soloist* (aka *Russian Ballerina*/Solistka baleta, 1947).

IVANOV-VANO, IVAN PETROVICH (b. 8 February 1900, Moscow–d. 20 March 1987, Moscow). Russian **animation** director, screenwriter, and animator. In 1923, Ivanov-Vano graduated from the prestigious Supreme State Workshops for Art and Technology (VKhUTEMAS) and contributed to one of the earliest Soviet animated films, the propaganda short *China on Fire* (Kitai v ogne, 1925) before turning to animation for children. *The Skating Rink* (Katok, 1927, with Daniil Cherkes) features an unexpected graphic approach, drawing white lines on a black background. *Little Simon, the African* (Sen'ka-afrikanets, aka Krokodil Krokodilovich, 1927, from a fairy tale by Kornei Chukovskii) and *Münchhausen's Adventures* (Pokhozhdeniia Miunkhgauzena, 1928), based on G. A. Bürger's novel, "achieved tones and depth that would have surprised foreign audiences" (Jay Leyda).

With the advent of sound film—a critical juncture that made an enormous impact on cartoon films and their reputation as works of cinematic art—Ivanov-Vano gained increasing fame for pictures based on fables, folktales, and fairy tales by Russian writers. Among them were *The Tale of Tsar Durondai* (Skazka o tsare Durondae, 1934, with Valentina and Zinaida Brumberg), *The Dragonfly and the Ant* (Strekoza i muravei, 1935, adapted from Ivan Krylov), *Geese and Swans* (Gusi-lebedi, 1949), *The Twelve Months* (Dvenadtsat' mesiatsev, 1956, from Samuil Marshak's tale), and *How One Peasant Fed Two Generals* (Kak odin muzhik dvukh generalov prokormil, 1965, from Mikhail Saltykov-Shchedrin's satire). Ivanov-Vano is also credited with the first Soviet feature-length animated picture, *The Little Humpbacked Horse* (Konek-Gorbunok, 1947, restored 1975), adapted from a fairy tale by Petr Ershov. It enjoyed international success and was particularly valued by Walt Disney, who bought a copy as a teaching tool for his studios. (Ironically, Ivanov-Vano belonged to those Russian animation artists who had long resisted the powerful stylistic and commercial pressure of Disney productions.)

Snow Maiden (Snegurochka, 1952) from Aleksandr Ostrovskii's tragic tale, incorporated Nikolai Rimskii-Korsakov's opera music, creating a haunting audiovisual fluidity. Other films were centered on a clear political message, for example, the anticolonial *Black-and-White* (1932, codirected by **Leonid Amal'rik**), from a Vladimir Maiakovskii poem, and *The Flying Proletarian* (Letaiushchii proletarii, 1962). Some of Ivanov-Vano's more daring experiments caused controversy, such as his attempt to transform Franz Schubert's "Ave Maria" into a film (1973).

In the majority of his pictures, Ivanov-Vano, who often cooperated with other painters and directors such as **Iurii Norshtein** (on the highly original *Battle of Kerzhenets*/Secha pri Kerzhentse, 1971), combined unobtrusive didacticism with satirical wit and picturesque beauty. The folktale films in particular reveal an extraordinary sense of coordinated body movement and audiovisual rhythm; their images are often stylized after the canonical illustrations of Ivan Bilibin (1876–1942), traditional folk ornaments, and wooden toys, and the popular print series known as *lubok*. Ivanov-Vano's literary adaptations, which demonstrate both a deep respect for the original text and a blooming imagination, entertained generations of children and accompanying adults and served as pleasurable introductions to the world of literature and the intrinsic values of Russian culture.

Beginning in 1939, Ivanov-Vano held a teaching position at the Soviet State Film School **VGIK**; in 1952 he was promoted to full professor. Ivanov-Vano joined the Communist Party in 1951. He was named People's Artist of the Russian Federation in 1969 and People's Artist of the USSR in 1985.

Other films: *The Three Musketeers* (Tri mushketera, 1938); *The Stolen Sun* (Kradenoe solntse, 1944); *Left-Hander* (Levsha, 1964); *The Seasons* (Vremena goda, 1969); *The Tale of Tsar Saltan* (Skazka o tsare Saltane, 1984, codirected by Lev Mil'chin).

IVAN'S CHILDHOOD (aka *My Name Is Ivan*/Ivanovo detstvo, 1962). **Mosfilm Studio**. 97 min., b/w. Directed by **Andrei Tarkovskii**. Script: Vladimir Bogomolov, Mikhail Papava from Bogomolov's novella "Ivan." Cinematography: **Vadim Iusov**. Music: **Viacheslav Ovchinnikov**. Cast: **Nikolai Burliaev**, Valentin Zubkov, Evgenii

Zharikov, Stepan Krylov, **Nikolai Grin'ko**, Valentina Maliavina, Irma Raush, **Andrei Mikhalkov-Konchalovskii**. Premiere: 9 May 1962.

Twelve-year-old Ivan (Burliaev), whose family was killed by German soldiers, helps a Red Army unit as a scout, risking his life by going behind enemy lines and bringing back valuable information. His dreams about childhood frolics turn into nightmares when the barbaric reality of the war intrudes. Officers Kholin (Zubkov) and Gal'tsev (Zharikov) try to protect Ivan, but on a final mission, he is caught and executed by the Nazis. Gal'tsev learns of his fate from a file in the Nazi Imperial Chancellery in Berlin after the end of the war.

IVASHOV, VLADIMIR SERGEEVICH (b. 28 August 1939, Moscow–d. 22 March 1995, Moscow). Russian actor. Ivashov enrolled in the Soviet State Film School **VGIK** in 1958 where he studied under **Mikhail Romm**, graduating in 1963. While still a student, **Grigorii Chukhrai** cast him in the lead role of the Great Patriotic War drama *Ballad of a Soldier* (Ballada o soldate, 1959), a performance that immediately shot Ivashov to national and international stardom. The character, Alesha Skvortsov, imbued with noble principles, youthful sensitivity, and unfailing moral intuition, became emblematic of the interpretation of the Soviet victory over Nazi barbarism and pointed to the tragic, irreplaceable loss of human potential. None of Ivashov's subsequent roles came close to the power of his debut.

Subsequently, directors mostly exploited the actor's name and looks without developing his artistic spectrum. Ivashov was excellent in **comedies** such as **Rolan Bykov**'s *Seven Nurses* (Sem' nianek, 1962) but awfully miscast as the destructive cynic Pechorin in **Stanislav Rostotskii**'s Lermontov adaptation *A Hero of Our Time* (Geroi nashego vremeni, 1965). He appeared in a number of Soviet coproductions with France, Poland, Egypt, and Bulgaria, including the comedy *Leon Garros Is Seeking a Friend* (aka *20000 lieues sur la terre*/Leon Garros ishchet druga, 1960). In the 1970s and 1980s, the actor settled for revolutionary action films (*The New Adventures of the Uncatchable Avengers*/Novye prikliucheniia neulovimykh, 1968, by **Edmond Keosayan**), war and espionage adventures (*Front without Flanks*/Front bez flangov, 1974, by **Igor' Gostev**), as well as contemporary melodramas (*Remember Your Name*/Pomni imia svoe, 1975).

After the breakdown of the Soviet film industry in the early 1990s, Ivashov fell upon hard times. He left the Studio Theater of the Film Actor, of which he had been a member since the 1960s, and was forced to accept jobs such as construction worker to make ends meet. He died of a heart attack, apparently caused by physical exhaustion.

Ivashov was named Merited Artist of the Russian Federation in 1969 and People's Artist of the RSFSR in 1980. He was married to popular film actress Svetlana Svetlichnaia (b. 1940).

Other films: *People on the Nile* (Liudi na Nile, 1972, USSR/Egypt); *Diamonds for the Dictatorship of the Proletariat* (Brillianty dlia diktatury proletariata, 1976); *Across the Gobi and Chingan* (Cherez Gobi i Chingan, 1982).

– J –

JÄRVET, JÜRI [Russian sources list the actor as Iurii Evgen'evich Iarvet] (b. 18 June 1919, Tallin–d. 5 July 1995, Tallin). Estonian actor and screenwriter. Järvet began to work as a stage actor with the Estonian State Artistic Ensemble in 1940. He studied at the Estonian Theater Institute in Tallin from 1945 to 1949. After a three-year engagement as chief director of the Southern Estonian Theater, he joined the troupe of Kingisepp Theater in Tallin (now called National Drama Theater) in 1952. In 1965, Järvet switched to the Estonian Youth Theater.

Järvet's screen debut was the role of Robert in **Gerbert Rappaport**'s *Andrus' Happiness* (Schast'e Andrusa, 1955) from a novel by Hans Leberecht. Among Järvet's noteworthy early performances are Holy Peetrus in the semimythological *The New Devil from the Netherworld* (Põrgupõhja uus Vanapagan/Novyi nechistyi iz preispodnei, 1964) from Anton Tammsaare's novel, the poor peasant Tõnu Prillup in **Leida Laius**'s *The Milkman from Maekula* (Mäeküla piimamees/Molochnik iz Miakula, 1965), and the cold-blooded Gestapo officer Windisch in **Kaljo Kiisk**'s *Insanity* (Hullumeelsus/Bezumie, 1968). When **Grigorii Kozintsev** unexpectedly cast Järvet in the title role of his Shakespeare adaptation *King Lear* (Korol' Lir, 1970), the performance, with an ascetic physique and sharp-lined face, glassy eyes, and pressed-together lips conveying emotional torment and concentrated reflection, made him famous in the Soviet Union and abroad. The only other role matching his Lear is Dr. Snout in **Andrei Tarkovskii**'s science fiction parable *Solaris* (1972), a morally disoriented intellectual whose cynical appearance covers a sensitive, empathetic heart.

Following these two plum parts, Järvet was increasingly typecast as a mysterious, often malevolent foreigner or "grudgy" old man, for example, in *Hotel "At the Lost Climber"* ("Hukkunud Alpinisti" hotell/Otel' "U pogibshego al'pinista," 1978). Among his more interesting roles is Siimon Vaa in Kiisk's rogue adventure *Nipernaadi* (Soviet release title: *Seeker of Adventures*/Iskatel' prikliuchenii, 1983).

Järvet was named Merited Artist of the Estonian SSR in 1964 and People's Artist of the USSR in 1975. He won a USSR State Prize in 1981 for his Count Szegedy in the Georgian historical miniseries *Shores* (Data Tutashkhia/Berega, 1977–1980, TV). After 1984, he was a member of the Supreme Soviet of the USSR. Järvet also made a name for himself as a valued solo performer on stage and regularly published feuilletons in Estonian newspapers. His son is actor Jüri Järvet Jr.

Other films: *Uninvited Guests* (Kutsumata külalised/Nezvanye gosti, 1959); *The Actor Joller* (Laulu sõber/Akter Joller, 1961); *Dead Season* (Mertvyi sezon, 1968); *Forest Violets* (Metskanni kesed/Lesnye fialki, 1980). *See also* ESTONIAN CINEMA.

JOLLY FELLOWS (Veselye rebiata, 1934). Moskinokombinat (**Mosfilm Studio**). 96 min., b/w. Directed by **Grigorii Aleksandrov**. Script: Vladimir Mass, **Nikolai Erdman**, Grigorii Aleksandrov. Cinematography: **Vladimir Nil'sen**. Music: **Isaak Dunaevskii**. Cast: Leonid Utesov, **Liubov' Orlova**, Mariia Strelkova, Elena Tiapkina, Fedor Kurikhin, Robert Erdman. Premiere: 25 December 1934.

The musically gifted shepherd Kostia Potekhin (Utesov), who works at the collective farm Transparent Wells, meets a young woman at the beach. She is the daughter of the director of a boarding house and, enamored by his playing and singing, invites him to perform at her father's restaurant. But Kostia's animals, used to the sound of his music, intrude in the boarding house and make a mess of it. The maid Aniuta (Orlova), a gifted singer, remains loyal to Kostia after the disaster. In Moscow, Kostia pretends to be a conductor but is exposed and must escape. He joins the jazz orchestra Harmony and finally performs on stage together with Aniuta.

– K –

KABALEVSKII, DMITRII BORISOVICH (b. 30 December 1904, St. Petersburg–d. 14 February 1987, Moscow). Russian composer. Kabalevskii, the son of a mathematician, studied at Moscow Conservatory, graduating in 1929. His teachers in composition were Nikolai Miaskovskii (1881–1950) and Georgii Katuar (1861–1926), and in piano, Aleksandr Gol'denveizer (1875–1961). Kabalevskii himself harbored a lifelong love for musical pedagogy, developing didactic principles for children's musical education. At the height of his fame, in 1973, he joined the staff of a Moscow high school in order to teach music to children.

Kabalevskii shared this lively interest in pedagogy with filmmaker **Grigorii Roshal'**, for whom he wrote numerous scores. The composer made his debut in cinema in 1934 with the music for Roshal' and **Vera Stroeva**'s interesting albeit ideologically tainted Fedor Dostoevskii variation *Petersburg Night* (Peterburgskaia noch'). Since its main character is a serf-cum-violinist, the music plays a central conceptual role. Kabalevskii developed a film-specific leitmotiv technique in which natural sounds such as a snowstorm are taken up by a tune that is later sung by a choir. (A distinct element of Kabalevskii's film music is the frequent inclusion of vocal parts.) He contributed the music to **Aleksandr Dovzhenko**'s monumental Communist industrial utopia *Aerograd* (1935), featuring choir songs filled with revolutionary pathos, and the Civil War saga *Shchors* (1939), the score of which is inspired by Ukrainian folklore. Kabalevskii proved his versatility on **Aleksandr Ivanovskii**'s delightful musical **comedy** *Anton Ivanovich Is Angry* (aka *Spring Song*/Anton Ivanovich serditsia, 1941), the plot of which revolves around a clash of classical music and lighthearted operetta. He also provided the required pathos to three stale Stalinist biopics: *Academician Ivan Pavlov* (Akademik Ivan Pavlov, 1949) and *Musorgskii* (1950), both helmed by Roshal', as well as **Mikhail Kalatozov**'s *Hostile Whirlwinds* (Vikhri vrazhdebnye, 1953), devoted to the founder of the Soviet secret police, Feliks Dzierzinski.

Kabalevskii's main cinematic contribution in the 1950s was to Roshal''s historical dramas *Freebooters* (aka *Flames on the Volga*/Vol'nitsa, 1955) about the fate of fishermen in the late 19th century, and the monumental trilogy *Calvary* (Khozhdenie po mukam, 1957–1959) from Aleksei Tolstoi's 1920–1941 novel.

Kabalevskii, who also wrote operas, operettas, and a requiem, taught at Moscow Conservatory from 1932 to 1980. He joined the Communist Party in 1940 and was honored with the titles People's Artist of the USSR in 1963 and Hero of Socialist Labor in 1974. Kabalevskii won three Stalin Prizes (1946, 1949, 1951), a USSR State Prize in 1980, and a Lenin Prize in 1972. The high school where he taught music (#209 Nizhniaia Maslovka Street) now carries his name. The composer is buried at Novodevich'e cemetery.

KADOCHNIKOV, PAVEL PETROVICH (b. 29 July 1915, Bikborda–d. 1 May 1988, Leningrad). Russian actor and director. Kadochnikov studied at the Theater Institute in Leningrad, graduating in 1935, and subsequently joined the troupe of the New Theater of the Young Viewer. He ended his stage career in 1944 in order to fully devote himself to cinema.

Kadochnikov's film debut was a supporting role in the Belarusian revolutionary adventure *Adulthood* (Sovershennoletie, 1934). After various episodic parts, the actor scored a popular success with the romantic lead in **Aleksandr Ivanovskii**'s *Anton Ivanovich Is Angry* (Anton Ivanovich serditsia, 1941). **Sergei Eizenshtein** used Kadochnikov's childlike facial features for the ambiguous role of Vladimir Staritskii in *Ivan the Terrible* (Ivan Groznyi, 1943–1945); in the film's second part, the actor elicited unexpected tragic grandeur from an initially simplified portrait.

The lead in **Boris Barnet**'s *The Scout's Quest* (aka *Secret Agent/* Podvig razvedchika) turned Kadochnikov into a Soviet superstar, a status he solidified a year later as Aleksei Meres'ev in **Aleksandr Stolper**'s *Story of a Real Man* (Povest' o nastoiashchem cheloveke, 1948). Kadochnikov's early screen image was that of a sensitive and bright, morally unshakeable, yet outwardly impenetrable young man who outfoxes the enemy with his endurance and wit and prevails against all odds.

The 1950s were Kadochnikov's most successful decade. He had leading parts in Stalinist propaganda fare such as Stolper's *Far from Moscow* (Daleko ot Moskvy, 1950) and **Mikhail Kalatozov**'s *Conspiracy of the Doomed* (Zagovor obrechennykh, 1950), in apolitical comedy (**Nadezhda Kosheverova** and **Aleksandr Ivanovskii**'s *Tiger Girl*/Ukrotitel'nitsa tigrov, 1955), and in contemporary drama (**Iosif Kheifits**'s *A Great Family*/Bol'shaia sem'ia, 1954). Although Kadochnikov was continually employed in Soviet genre films, he later served more as a monument to his canonized early persona and rarely was given genuine artistic challenges.

In 1965, Kadochnikov debuted as director with a film about the Great Patriotic War, *Musicians of the Same Regiment* (Muzykanty odnogo polka, 1965, codirected with **Gennadii Kazanskii**). His critically underacclaimed *Snow Maiden* (Snegurochka, 1969), a faithful and visually impressive adaptation of Aleksandr Ostrovskii's 1873 play, was an attempt to capture the philosophical depth of Russian fairy tales, focusing on ancient customs and beliefs and avoiding the sugarcoating that was typical of the genre. Kadochnikov also directed the war melodrama *I Shall Never Forget You* (Ia tebia nikogda ne zabudu, 1984) and the biopic *Silver Strings* (Serebriannye struny, 1987) about the founder of the first Russian folk instrument orchestra, Vasilii Andreev.

Kadochnikov, who joined the Communist Party in 1967, was named People's Artist of the USSR in 1979 and Hero of Socialist Labor in 1985. He won Stalin Prizes in 1948, 1949, and 1951.

Other films: *The Defense of Tsaritsyn* (Oborona Tsaritsyna, 1942); *Robinson Crusoe* (1947); *Sibiriade* (Sibiriada, 1979); *Lenin in Paris* (Lenin v Parizhe, 1981).

KAIDANOVSKII, ALEKSANDR LEONIDOVICH (b. 23 June [other sources: July] 1946, Rostov-on-the-Don–d. 3 December 1995, Moscow). Russian actor, director, and screenwriter. Kaidanovskii studied at the college of arts (*tekhnikum iskusstv*) in his hometown Rostov-on-the-Don before joining the local theater troupe. He continued his education at the studio school of the Moscow Art Theater (MKhAT) and the Shchukin Theater School, graduating in 1969.

Kaidanovskii debuted with a small part in **Aleksandr Zarkhi**'s Lev Tolstoi adaptation *Anna Karenina* (1968). In the 1970s, he worked with some of the best Soviet film directors, including **Aleksandr Stolper** (*The Fourth*/Chetvertyi, 1973), **Nikita Mikhalkov** (*At Home among Strangers*/Svoi sredi chuzhikh, chuzhoi sredi svoikh, 1974), and **Ali Khamraev** (*The Bodyguard*/Telokhranitel', 1979). He often was cast in roles of enigmatic, harsh officers, for example, Zimin in Veniamin Dorman's adventurous *The Lost Expedition* (Propavshaia ekspeditsiia, 1975). Kaidanovskii's most significant performance is the title role in **Andrei Tarkovskii**'s gloomy futuristic vision *Stalker* (1979), in which his character's tired gaze conveys total disillusionment with modern civilization and its promises.

Having become a valued—in some circles, even cultishly admired—actor, Kaidanovskii embarked on a career as filmmaker. He enrolled in the Supreme Courses for Screenwriters and Directors in Moscow (**VKSR**) under **Sergei Solov'ev**. After graduation in 1984, he joined the staff of **Mosfilm Studio**.

Following two shorts—*The Garden* (Sad, 1983) from a story by Jorge Luis Borges, and *Jona, or The Artist at Work* (Iona, ili Artist za rabotoi, 1984)—Kaidanovskii made his feature-length debut with a black-and-white adaptation of Lev Tolstoi's "The Death of Ivan Il'ich," *A Simple Death* (Prostaia smert', 1985). Then, free of censorship control, he was able to adapt Borge's mystical story "The Gospel of St. Marcus" under the title *The Guest* (Gost', 1987). In *The Kerosene Seller's Wife* (Zhena kerosinshchika, 1988), Kaidanovskii's further pursued his ominous, mystical style. After the breakdown of the Soviet film industry, he unsuccessfully struggled to get funding for new projects, including a film about Tsar Ivan the Terrible, before succumbing to heart disease.

Kaidanovskii, who remained a sought-after actor in the last decade of his career, appeared in a number of international productions. One of his most impressive later performances was Sir Lancelot in the stylish epic *The Yankees' New Adventures at King Arthur's Court* (Novye prikliucheniia ianki pri dvore korolia Artura, 1989) by Viktor Gres'.

Other films: (as actor) *Story of an Unknown Man* (Rasskaz neizvestnogo cheloveka, 1981); *Confessions to a Stranger* (Confidenze ad uno sconosciuto, 1994, Italy); *The Magic Hunter* (Büvös vadász, 1994, Hungary); (as director) *Maestro* (1992, a medium-length interview film).

KALATOZOV [real name: Kalatozishvili]**, MIKHAIL** [Mikheil] **KONSTANTINOVICH** (b. 28 December 1903, Tbilisi, Georgia–d. 26 March 1973, Moscow). Georgian and Russian director, cinematographer, screenwriter, and film administrator. Kalatozov dropped out of high school at the age of 14 to work as an auto mechanic and film projectionist; he then studied economics at a business school. His career in the movies began in 1923 with a variety of jobs— assistant cutter, cameraman, screenwriter, and actor, all at Tbilisi film studio (later **Gruziya-Film Studio**). For **Ivan Perestiani** he played a supporting part in *The Murder Case of Tariel Mklavadze* (aka *A Hero of Our Time*/Tariel mklavadzis mkvlelobis saqme, 1925), on **Nikoloz Shengelaia**'s *Giulli* (1927) he served as cinematographer, and for *Gypsy Blood* (Boshuri siskhli/Tsyganskaia krov', 1928) he cowrote the script and was the cameraman (jointly with **Aleksandr Gal'perin**); he was also behind the camera in **Lev Kuleshov**'s unfinished project *Locomotive 10006* (Parovoz No. 10006, 1926).

In 1928, Kalatozov made his directorial debut with *Their Kingdom* (Mati samep/Ikh tsarstvo), a compilation **documentary** attacking the Georgian Menshevik Party and depicting the historical development of Georgia between 1918 and 1928 (codirected with Nina [Nutsu] Gogoberidze). Kalatozov achieved prominence with *Salt for Svanetia* (Jim Shvante [marili svanets]/Sol' Svanetii, 1930), a passionate, cinematically sophisticated narrative documentary about a tribe of backward people who are liberated from religious and economic oppression by the Bolshevik revolution. According to one account, it was derived from an earlier project, *Blind Girl* (Usinatlo/Slepaia, 1930), based on an original script by influential avant-garde playwright Sergei Tret'iakov (1892–1937); however, that earlier film was harshly criticized and Kalatozov skillfully remade it into the groundbreaking semifictional masterpiece that has since achieved the status of a classic. Kalatozov's following picture, the 50-minute *A Nail in the Boot* (Gvozd' v sapoge, aka *The Country Is in Danger*/Strana v opasnosti, 1932), which criticized inefficiency in the Red Army, proved equally controversial and was banned.

Kalatozov subsequently studied at the Leningrad Academy of Arts in 1931–1934 and was appointed director of the Tbilisi-based Sakhkinmretsvi film company in 1934 before leaving Georgia in 1936. At **Lenfilm Studio** he directed his first full-length feature, *Courage* (Muzhestvo, 1939), about gangs near the Soviet-Afghan border, foreign spies, and a heroic Soviet pilot who defeats them all. Despite obvious clichés, the director's flare for visual extravagance stood out in a number of scenes. The biopic *Valerii Chkalov*

(1941) about the legendary pilot (1904–1938) and Hero of the Soviet Union famed for his record-breaking long-distance flights, proved tremendously popular.

Following the Leningrad siege drama *The Invincible* (Nepobedi-mye, 1942, codirected with **Sergei Gerasimov**), Kalatozov made a distinguished administrative career. In 1943–1945, he served as the representative of the USSR Film Committee in the United States and in 1945–1948 as deputy minister of cinematography in charge of the production of feature films. After his return to filmmaking, Kalato-zov directed *Conspiracy of the Doomed* (Zagovor obrechennykh, 1950) about a U.S.-inspired anti-Communist coup in a fictitious East-ern bloc country; the film won him a Stalin Prize. The biopic *Hostile Whirlwinds* (Vikhri vrazhdebnye, 1953), devoted to the founder of the Soviet secret police, Feliks Dzierzinski, was released in 1956, with all scenes involving Iosif Stalin deleted. Kalatozov pleasantly surprised audiences with *Loyal Friends* (Vernye druz'ia, 1954), a heartwarming **comedy** sprinkled with a few satirical episodes.

The Cranes Are Flying (Letiat zhuravli, 1957) demonstrated that the director was able to rejuvenate himself as an artist and return to his stylish beginnings. The romantic story of loyalty and tragic loss during the Great Patriotic War revealed a humanity emerging from genuine suffering that spoke to millions of viewers worldwide. Crit-ics particularly lauded **Sergei Urusevskii**'s expressive photography. The picture's international triumph marked the rebirth of Soviet cin-ema as an innovative, artistically noteworthy phenomenon.

Kalatozov attempted an even further-reaching visualization of the human condition in *The Unmailed Letter* (Neotpravlennoe pis'mo, 1960), arguably his most accomplished masterpiece in which all of his preferred themes are expressed in their purest, quasi-parabolic form. Not only is political propaganda absent from the story of a geological expedition—the literal cleansing of the central characters by fire and ice conveys a metaphysical respect for nature, free of any attached optimism from which even *Cranes* had suffered.

The Communist litany *I Am Cuba* (Ia—Kuba/Soy Cuba, 1964) flopped in the USSR and was not shown in the West for several decades owing to its heavy-handed Cold War ideology. Yet, after its endorsement by Francis Ford Coppola and Martin Scorcese in the early 1990s, it has since acquired cult status among Western cinema buffs. Its flamboyant, fluid—at times acrobatic—black-and-white cinematography is undoubtedly spectacular, but the breathtaking imagery cannot outweigh Evgenii Evtushenko's pathos-filled script and insufferable, pseudopoetic commentary.

Kalatozov ended his career with *The Red Tent* (Krasnaia palatka/ La Tenda Rossa, 1969), a Soviet-Italian coproduction about the 1928 Nobile expedition starring Peter Finch, Claudia Cardinale, Sean Connery, and Hardy Krüger, and produced by Franco Cristaldi. Like all of Kalatozov films, it acutely reflected the zeitgeist, in this case, the spirit of peaceful coexistence and cooperation between Communist and capitalist societies, yet artistically it reveals an undeniable decline for the director.

Similar to many of the best Soviet filmmakers, the gap between political obedience and outstanding cinematic vision in Kalatozov is difficult to conceptualize; indeed, there is not a whiff of dissidence in his work, and when criticized, he reacted with complete acquiescence. Kalatozov's image of Soviet society was unconditionally positive: the Communist nation appears as a grandiose sheltering family whose problems are but temporary misunderstandings. Whenever there is decadence—the bohemian milieu in *Cranes*, Havana bars in *Cuba*, Kingsbay in *Red Tent*—it is markedly Western in origin and fundamentally alien to genuine Soviet people.

A member of the Communist Party since 1939, Kalatozov was awarded the title People's Artist of the USSR in 1969. His son, Giorgi Kalatozishvili (1929–1984), was a successful cinematographer and director who brought one of his late father's scripts, *The Café "Izotop"* (Kafe "Izotop," 1976), to the screen. Kalatozov's grandson, Mikhail Kalatozishvili (b. 1959), is also a filmmaker.

Other films: *Giuli* (1927, script and cinematography). *See also* GEORGIAN CINEMA.

KALIK, MIKHAIL [Moisei] **NAUMOVICH** (b. 29 January 1927, Arkhangel'sk). Russian and Moldovan director and screenwriter. In 1949, Kalik enrolled in **Grigorii Aleksandrov**'s directing workshop at the Soviet State Film School **VGIK**. Two years later, he and four fellow students were arrested, convicted of "planning anti-Soviet terrorist acts," and sent to a GULAG concentration camp in the Far

North. Rehabilitated in 1954, Kalik was able to continue his studies with **Sergei Iutkevich**, graduating in 1958.

Kalik's debut was *Ataman Codr* (1958, codirected with Boris Rytsarev after Ol'ga Ulitskaia had abandoned the project), produced by **Moldova-Film Studio**. A fast-paced, action-filled historical adventure, it romanticizes Moldovan Robin-Hood-like outlaws. At the Moscow **Gor'kii Studio for Children's and Youth Films**, Kalik then codirected *The Youth of Our Fathers* (Iunost' nashikh ottsov, 1959, with Rytsarev), a Civil War drama adapted from Aleksandr Fadeev's pro-Bolshevik novel *The Rout* (Razgrom, 1927). With the independently directed *Lullaby* (Kolybel'naia, 1960) Kalik found his own theme and style, focusing on children whose innate goodness and openness to the world defines the film's ethical perspective. Consisting of several novellas, *Lullabye* tells the story of a girl who is orphaned in World War II yet ultimately finds her father.

Kalik's best-known film is *Man Follows the Sun* (Chelovek idet za solntsem, 1961), from a screenplay by **Valeriu Gajiu**, about a six-year-old boy who in one day experiences numerous facets of life, from friendliness and help to heartlessness and rejection. "Sandu discovers a world full of natural light, towards which people gravitate as naturally as sunflowers turn their heads to follow the sun" (Josephine Woll). However, one brief erotic episode caused the indignation of Nikita Khrushchev and led to administrative measures against Kalik. At **Mosfilm Studio**, he directed *Good-bye, Boys!* (Do svidaniia, mal'chiki! 1964), a poetic story of three friends in a port town during the 1930s; the film benefits particularly from **Levan Paatashvili**'s magnificent black-and-white imagery.

To Love (Liubit', 1968), made in Moldova, consists of four shorts adapted from stories by different writers, exploring the nature of affection and mixing fictional and **documentary** scenes. The film was censored, released in a limited number of copies, withdrawn from distribution in the summer of 1969, and restored by the director in 1990. *The Price* (Tsena, 1969, TV, first broadcast in 1989), adapted from an Arthur Miller play about two alienated brothers, was Kalik's last Soviet film. He emigrated in 1971, after which his name was eliminated from all Soviet publications. In Israel, Kalik made one feature film, *Three and One* (Shlosha V'achat, 1974), and worked as a teacher.

In 1991, Kalik came back to Russia and directed *And the Wind Returns . . .* (I vozvrashchaetsia veter . . .), a meditation about his turbulent life and artistic accomplishments, including fictionalized episodes and scenes from his earlier films. *See also* MOLDOVAN CINEMA.

KANCHELI, GIYA [in some Russian sources the first name and patronymic are listed as Georgii Aleksandrovich] (b. 10 August 1935, Tbilisi). Georgian composer. Kancheli studied geology at Tbilisi State University in 1954–1959 before enrolling in Tbilisi State Conservatory where he majored in composition, graduating in 1963.

Kancheli's debut as a film composer was in Konstantine Pipinashvili's *Children of the Sea* (Zgvis shvilebi/Deti moria, 1965). His name is primarily associated with the pictures of leading Georgian directors, beginning with **Eldar Shengelaia**'s *An Unusual Exhibition* (Arakhveulebrivi gamopena/Neobyknovennaia vystavka, 1969), a philosophical reflection on artistic integrity. Kancheli continued to work with Shengelaia, helping to evoke the peculiar atmosphere of Georgia's prerevolutionary gentry milieu in *Crackpots* (Sherekilebi/Chudaki, 1974) and *Samanishvili's Stepmother* (Samanishvili dedinatsvali/Machekha Samanishvili, 1978), and contributing sharp characterizations to the contemporary satire *Blue Mountains, or An Unbelievable Story* (Tsisperi mtebi anu arachveulebrivi ambavi/Golubye gory, ili nepravdopodobnaia istoriia, 1984). Kancheli also struck a lasting creative partnership with **Georgii Daneliia**, significantly contributing to the enormous popularity of his bittersweet **comedy** hits, from *Don't Grieve* (Ar daidardo/Ne goriui! 1969) and the dark anti-utopia *Kin-Dza-Dza* (1986), to his post-Soviet pictures *Heads and Tails* (Orel i reshka, 1995) and *Fortuna* (2000). Interestingly, even in films dealing with the harsh trials and tribulations of the 1990s, Kancheli's music conveys his typical mild, kindhearted melancholy and life-affirming, wise humor.

Although Kancheli's fame mainly rests on comedies, he was successful with scores for contemporary drama too, including Giorgi Kalatozishvili's thriller *I, the Investigator* (Me, gamomdziebeli/Ia, sledovatel', 1971) and **Lana Gogoberidze**'s sociopsychological analysis *Several Interviews on Personal Questions* (Ramodenime interviu pirad sakitkhebze/Neskol'ko interv'iu po lichnym voprosam, 1979). Rarely did Kancheli contribute to propagandistic films, a prominent exception being **Rezo Chkheidze**'s notorious *Your Son, Earth* (Mshobliuro chemo mitsav/Tvoi syn, zemlia, aka *The Story of a Party District Committee Secretary*/Povest' o sekretare raikoma/1980).

Early on, Kancheli developed a unique musical approach characterized by emotional openness, majestic slowness, and tender, prolonged tranquility. Kancheli has written seven symphonies, chamber music, and numerous pieces for stage productions, mostly at the Shota Rustaveli Theater in Tbilisi, particularly in Shakespeare plays. He received a USSR State Prize in 1976 and was honored with the title People's Artist of the Georgian SSR in 1980 and People's Artist of the USSR in 1989. In 1991, Kancheli moved to Germany (Berlin) and Belgium (Antwerp) where he has lived since.

Other films: *A Stray Bullet* (Brma tkvia/Shal'naia pulia, 1980); *The Day Is Longer than the Night* (Dges game utenebia/Den' dlinnee nochi, 1984); *Rotation* (Oromtriali/Krugovorot, 1986); *The Life of Don Quijote and Sancho Panza* (Tskhovreba Don Kikhotisa da Sancho Panchosi/Zhitie Don Kikhota i Sancho, 1988); *Set Me Free* (Emporte-moi, 1999, France); *A National Bomb* (Nastional'naia bomba, 2004). *See also* GEORGIAN CINEMA.

KAPLER, ALEKSEI IAKOVLEVICH (b. 11 October 1904, Kiev–d. 11 September 1979, Moscow). Ukrainian and Russian screenwriter. After finishing the gymnasium in Kiev, Kapler in 1920 organized the theater Harlequin (Arlekin) with his friends, **Grigorii Kozintsev** and **Sergei Iutkevich**, whom he later joined in the legendary FEKS (Factory of the Eccentric Actor) workshop, playing minor roles in their films.

Kapler joined the budding Soviet film industry in 1926 and worked as assistant to **Aleksandr Dovzhenko** on *Arsenal*. He directed the propaganda film *The Right to a Woman* (Pravo na zhenshchinu, 1930), starring his wife, actress and screenwriter Tat'iana Zlatogorova (1912–1950). He also made so-called culture films (*kul'turfil'my*) at the Kiev Film Factory (later: **Dovzhenko Film Studio**) in 1928–1931.

In the 1930s, specializing in screenwriting, Kapler became one of the shooting stars of Soviet cinema with a number of scripts that reveal both a keen sense of drama and unconditional loyalty to the Communist cause: the **comedy** *Three Comrades* (aka *Three Friends*/Tri tovarishcha, 1935), directed by **Semen Timoshenko**, Iutkevich's *Miners* (Shakhtery, 1937, coauthored with Zlatogorova), and especially *Lenin in October* (Lenin v oktiabre, 1937) and *Lenin in 1918* (Lenin v 1918 godu, 1939, with Zlatogorova), both directed by **Mikhail Romm**, for which Kapler received a Stalin Prize in 1941. His original screenplay, *Insurrection* (Vosstanie), had won the first prize in the 1937 nationwide competition for scripts about the October Revolution; its distinctive mark is the humanization of Vladimir Lenin that allowed for a combination of humorous interludes and dramatic pathos. Noteworthy, too, is the emphasis on Iosif Stalin's role, which grew to ludicrous dimensions in the second part of the dilogy.

In winter of 1942, Kapler had a brief affair with Stalin's daughter, Svetlana Allilueva. The Communist leader disapproved of the relationship and had Kapler and his wife arrested and sent to a GULAG concentration camp for 10 years; their names were deleted from all film credits. After his release, though, Kapler was able to continue his career with remarkable success. Thus, **Samson Samsonov**'s comedy *Behind the Show Window* (Za vitrinoi univermaga, 1955) and the spectacular fantasy *Amphibian Man* (Chelovek-amfibiia, 1962, directed by **Gennadii Kazanskii** and Vladimir Chebotarev) proved that the author had not lost his grasp of effective cinematic narration.

Kapler, who has been described as a cynic and a Stalinist falsifier of history, certainly was one of the most savvy Soviet screenwriters. In later years, he deservedly won recognition as an accomplished popularizer of cinema with the television program "Film Panorama" (Kinopanorama). Some of Kapler's scripts were turned into films long after his passing, most notably the nostalgic tragicomedy *Return of the Battleship* (Vozvrashchenie bronenostsa, 1996), directed by **Gennadii Poloka**, about the making of *Battleship Potemkin*.

In the 1960s, Kapler taught screenwriting at the Supreme Courses for Screenwriters and Directors (VKSR); among his students was **Revaz Gabriadze**. Kapler was named Merited Artist of the RSFSR in 1969.

Other films: *Mine 12–28* (Shakhta 12–28; also director); *She Defends the Motherland* (aka *No Greater Love*/Ona zashichaet rodinu,

1943); *First Joys* (Pervye radosti, 1956); *An Unusual Summer* (Neobyknovennoe leto, 1957); *The Blue Bird* (Siniaia ptitsa, 1976).

KARALLI, VERA ALEKSEEVNA [in some sources: Koralli; in German credits: Vera Caroly] (b. 27 July 1889 [other sources: 1888], Moscow–d. 16 November 1972, Baden, Austria). Russian actress. Karalli graduated from the ballet school of the Imperial Bolshoi Theater in 1906 and joined its troupe as a prima ballerina. She also danced with the company of Sergei Diaghilev in 1909 and 1919–1920.

In 1914, producer **Aleksandr Khanzhonkov** persuaded Karalli to try her talent in the movies. According to film historian Romul Sobolev, the star of the Moscow ballet scene was not restricted by the typical theater veto against film work because of her intimate relationship with a grand prince. Endowed with exceptional physical grace, an intricate sense of rhythm, and expressive facial features, Karalli gained the reputation of a powerful screen presence, beginning with her debut in **Petr Chardynin**'s *Do You Recall?* (Ty pomnish' li? 1914), starring with **Ivan Mozzhukhin**, who also was her partner in the farce *Tomboy* (Sorvanets, 1914). **Evgenii Bauer** used Karalli to superb effect in his lavish tales *Burned Wings* (Obozhzhennye kryl'ia, 1915), with **Vitol'd Polonskii** as her partner, and *The Griffon of an Old Fighter* (Grif starogo bortsa, 1916), with **Ivan Perestiani**, among others. Karalli's limited range—she failed in psychological roles—led to a specific screen profile. Thus, she was cast as a ballerina in Chardynin's *Chrysanthemums* (Khrizantemy, 1914), as a blind girl in Bauer's *Bliss of the Eternal Night* (Schast'e vechnoi nochi, 1915), and as a mute dancer in *The Dying Swan* (Umiraiushchii lebed', 1917). Chardynin gave Karalli the plum part of Natasha Rostova in his partial adaptation of Lev Tolstoi's *War and Peace* (*Natasha Rostova*, 1915). The actress also wrote screenplays, including *Kindred Souls* (Rodnye dushi, 1915) and *The Bronsky Sisters* (Sestry Bronskie, 1916).

After immigrating to France in 1918, she settled in Germany and later in Austria, retiring from cinema in the early 1920s. Among Karalli's later roles, her appearance in the German production *Revenge of a Woman* (Die Rache einer Frau, 1921), directed by Robert Wiene of *Caligari* fame, is noteworthy.

Other films: *On the Prisoners' Dock* (Na skam'e podsudimykh, 1914); *Shadows of a Sin* (Teni grekha, 1915); *Alarm* (Nabat, 1917); *Life and Dream* (Mechta i zhizn', 1918).

KARAMYAN [Melik-Karamyan], **ERAZM** [some Russian sources also list the patronymic Aleksandrovich] (b. 15 March 1912, Paris–d. 15 June 1985, Yerevan). Armenian director and scriptwriter. Karamyan worked in theaters of western Siberia and Moscow before studying at the Khar'kov Theater Institute, from which he graduated in 1936. In 1937, he joined the staff of **Armenfilm Studio** (Hayfilm). He was an assistant director to Artashes Aiartyan (1899–1978) on the Civil War-cum-coming-of-age story, *Karo* (1937), and assisted the founder of **Armenian cinema**, **Hamo Bek-Nazaryan**, on the drama *Zangezur* (1938) and the **comedy** *The Girl from Ararat Valley* (Araratyan dashti aghchikr/Devushka s Araratskoi doliny, 1949).

As a director, Karamyan began his career with **documentaries**, including *Armenia's Spas* (Kurorty Armenii, 1940) and *The Architecture of Socialist Yerevan* (Arkhitektura sotsialisticheskogo Erevana, 1952). His feature film debut was *The Mountain March* (Lernayin arshav/Gornyi marsh, 1939, codirected with **Stepan Kevorkov**), followed by *A Family of Patriots* (Sem'ia patriotov, 1941)—an atmospheric description of the first days of the Great Patriotic War, and the documentary *The Soviet Army Enters Iran* (Vstuplenie Sovetskikoi Armii v Iran). From 1947 to 1954, Karamyan directed newsreels.

Together with Kevorkov, Karamyan made the Cold War espionage thriller *The Ghosts Abandon the Peaks* (Urvakannere heranum en lernerits/Prizraki pokidaiut vershiny, 1955) and the fictionalized antiapartheid pamphlet *Along the Path of Thunder* (Ampropi arahetov/Tropoiu groma, 1956). Karamyan independently helmed *Twelve Companions* (Tasnerku ughekitsner/Dvenadtsat' sputnikov, 1962), an attempt to analyze the behavior of plane crash survivors.

Karamyan and Kevorkov gained particular prominence and popular success with their adventurous pictures about famed revolutionary Ter-Petrosyan (1882–1922)—better known under his alias "Kamo"—*Personally Known* (Andzamb tchanachum em/Lichno izvesten, aka Kamo, 1958) and *Extraordinary Assignment* (Artakarg handznararutyun/Chrezvychainoe poruchenie, 1965). In 1959, Karamyan codirected with his mentor of old, Bek-Nazaryan, *Nasreddin in Khodjent, or The Enchanted Prince* (Nasreddin v Khodzhente, ili Ocharovannyi prints, 1959), a somewhat morose attempt to heroicize Nasreddin, the roguish character of folktales. Karamyan's last film was made for television, *An Hour before Dawn* (Lusabatsits mek zham araj/Za chas do rassveta, 1973).

Karamyan, who joined the Communist Party in 1945, was honored with the title People's Artist of the Armenian SSR in 1966 and People's Artist of the USSR in 1971.

Other films: *An Explosion after Midnight* (Paytyun kesgisherits heto/Vzryv posle polunochi, 1969, codirected with Kevorkov).

KARLIEV, ALTY (b. 6 January 1909, Babadaikhan 2, Tedjen district, Turkmenistan–d. 11 December 1973). Turkmen actor, director, and scriptwriter. Karliev studied at the Turkmen Drama studio in Ashgabad (Ashkhabad), graduating in 1929, and began to work on stage. He also studied directing at the Baku Theater College until 1931. The youthful and athletic actor quickly gained fame in comedic parts, especially as Truffaldino in Carlo Goldoni's *Servant of Two Masters* and Khlestakov in Nikolai Gogol''s *The Inspector General.* In 1941–1953 and 1960–1963, he was the chief director of the Turkmen Opera and Ballet Theater named after Makhtumkuli. Karliev's artistic interests were multifaceted; he directed operas and dramas, acted in classical Russian and contemporary Turkmen plays, and also wrote plays and opera libretti.

Karliev's screen debut was the role of a Japanese spy-cum-saboteur, Kelkhan, aka Tanaka, who masks as a friendly tea collector, in Georgii Lomidze's naïve thriller *Soviet Patriots* (Sovetskie patrioty, 1939). In 1940, he gave a more nuanced performance as Nuri, a young *djigit* who is astonished and confused by the professional success of his wife and has to overcome ancient patriarchal norms. For his performance in *Dursun*, directed by one of the founders of **Turkmen cinema**, Evgenii Ivanov-Barkov (1892–1965), Karliev received a Stalin Prize in 1941. For another screen performance, the exemplary soldier Kerim, in Ivanov-Barkov's musical comedy *Faraway Bride* (Dalekaia nevesta, 1948), Karliev was also recognized with a Stalin Prize; however, in the post-Stalinist period, the film was blamed for its conflict avoidance and blatant lies about the reality of Turkmenistan. Unusually relaxed and charming, Karliev appeared as the popular character of Turkmen mythology, Aldar-Kese, leading through the entertaining musical potpourri *The Magic Crystal* (Volshebnyi kristall, 1945). Karliev demonstrated that he was able to master psychologically complex roles as the unhealthily ambitious administrator Bairam Merdanov in the social drama *Family Honor* (Chest' sem'i, 1956).

As a director, Karliev began his career with the Civil War drama *Special Task* (Osoboe poruchenie, 1958, codirected with Ivanov-Barkov). The same theme—the clash between traditional values and the new Soviet order on the backdrop of the Bolshevik Revolution and subsequent Civil War—is interpreted in a less linear and didactic manner in *A Decisive Step* (Reshaiushchii shag, 1966); the film has been compared in scope and controversial approach to Mikhail Sholokhov's *And Quiet Flows the Don*. Karliev's last two significant pictures deal with Turkmen artists: *Makhtumkuli* (1968), a biopic about the 18th-century poet and philosopher, and *The Secrets of Mukam* (Tainy mukama, 1974), about the tragic life of a singer, Karkara, in pre-Soviet times.

Karliev joined the Communist Party in 1948 and was named People's Artist of the USSR in 1955. From 1956 to 1960, he held the position of artistic director of **Turkmenfilm Studio**, which was named after him in 1974.

Other films: (as actor) *The State Attorney* (Prokuror, 1941); *The Shepherd's Son* (Syn pastukha, 1955); *Saltanat* (1955); (as director) *Aina* (1959, codirected with V. Ivanov); *The Border Is behind the River* (Za rekoi granitsa, 1971).

KARMEN, ROMAN LAZAREVICH (b. 29 November 1906, Odessa–d. 28 April 1978, Moscow). Russian **documentary** director, screenwriter, and cinematographer. Karmen, the son of a Bolshevik writer who was killed in prison during the 1918–1921 Civil War, began to work as a photo correspondent for the magazine *Ogonek* in 1922. He studied cinematography at the State Film School in Moscow (GTK, later **VGIK**), graduating in 1931. Karmen was sent out to document major events of Soviet industrialization such as *Volkhovstroi* and the Karakum car race. His debut was the short *Factory-Kitchen* (Fabrika-kukhnia, 1930, codirected with Mikhail Slutskii). Karmen's first major assignment as a political newsreel reporter was the Spanish Civil War, which he observed in 1936–1937, resulting in a special series of newsreels, *On the Events in Spain* (K sobytiiam v Ispanii), of which 22 installments were released. He used the footage shot during those years in several pictures, including *Spain* (Ispaniia, 1939), edited by **Esfir' Shub**.

A Day of the New World (Den' novogo mira, 1940, with Slutskii) was based on a suggestion by writer Maksim Gor'kii to describe a normal day in the life of the Soviet Union, filming it simultaneously in different parts of the country. Thus, on 28 April 1940 numerous crews filmed workers, military personnel, peasants, and intellectuals in various locations all across the USSR at work and at rest. The feature-length documentary premiered to great acclaim on 12 December 1940 and won Karmen his first Stalin Prize in 1942.

Karmen was famous for taking considerable risks. He spent an entire Arctic winter at Tikhaia Bay on Rudolf Island for the picture *Sedovtsy* (1940) about the 1937–1940 expedition of the vessel *Georgii Sedov*. For almost a year, he accompanied Mao's army, resulting in the feature-length *In China* (V Kitae, 1941). During the Great Patriotic War, Karmen was in charge of a unit of cameramen and contributed to a number of prestigious, large-scale documentaries about the 1941 battle of Moscow (*The Defeat of the German Troops near Moscow*/Razgrom nemetskikh voisk pod Moskvoi, 1942), the siege of Leningrad (*Leningrad in Struggle*/Leningrad v bor'be, 1942), and the 1943 battle of Stalingrad; he accompanied the Red Army all the way to the Reichstag in Berlin (*Berlin*, 1945). The aftermath of the war is shown in *Court of Peoples* (Sud narodov, 1946) about the Nuremberg trial; it was recognized with a 1947 Stalin Prize.

In the 1950s, Karmen focused on industrial labor, most prominently in *The Tale of the Oil Workers of the Caspian Sea* (Povest' o neftianikakh Kaspiia, 1953), praising the selfless death of an oil worker on a drilling rig during a heavy storm. In the 1960s and 1970s, Karmen delivered a number of feature-length, essay-type documentaries in which he appears as the personal narrator, remembering events he had witnessed in the past and reflecting on the future of the world. However, these films' pretended subjectivity is dubious and highly selective, never pushing the envelope of Soviet officialdom. Thus, Karmen's dogmatism tainted otherwise fascinating pictures such as his homage to the Spanish Civil War, *My Grenada* (Grenada,

Grenada, Grenada moia . . . , 1968), and the three-hour-long *Continent in Flames* (Pylaiushchii kontinent, 1972) about the political turmoil in Latin America. Karmen's last major project was the 20-hour compilation film *The Great Patriotic War* (aka *The Unknown War*/Velikaia Otechestvennaia, 1979), coproduced with the United States and narrated by Burt Lancaster.

Karmen received his third Stalin Prize in 1952 for *Soviet Turkmenistan* (Sovetskii Turkmenistan), a USSR State Prize in 1975, and a Lenin Prize for *Tale about the Oil Workers of the Caspian Sea* and *Conquerors of the Sea* (Pokoriteli moria, 1959) in 1960. He joined the Communist Party in 1939 and was named People's Artist of the USSR in 1966 and Hero of Socialist Labor in 1976. Karmen taught at VGIK, holding the rank of full professor since 1970.

Other films: *Soviet Georgia Is 15 Years Old* (Sovetskoi Gruzii 15 let, 1936); *Vietnam* (1954); *The Dawn of India* (Utro Indii, 1956); *Comrade Berlin* (Tovarishch Berlin, 1969).

KASYMOV, MUHAMEDJAN [some Russian sources also list the patronymic Mukhitdinovich] (b. 9 May 1907, Kyshlak Rishtan, Fergana district, Uzbekistan–d. 5 July 1971, Dushanbe). Tadjik actor. Kasymov received his education at the Kokand Pedagogical College and at the Tashkent Cooperative College (*tekhnikum*); he also was active in laymen theater groups. In 1931, he joined the troupe of the Lahuti Theater in Dushanbe and became one of its leading stars, excelling in both contemporary drama and the works of William Shakespeare.

Kasymov made his screen debut in the lead role of Hafiz, the loyal friend of fellow scout Ivan, in the patriotic tale *A Son of Tadjikistan* (Syn Tadzhikistana, 1943), followed by the episodic part of Ismail-bek in **Konstantin Iudin**'s adventure hit *A Fortress in the Mountains* (Zastava v gorakh, 1953). One of the remarkable achievements of Kasymov's screen career was the supporting role of Azimsha-bek, a nobleman ruined by the Bolshevik Revolution, in **Bension Kimyagarov**'s *Dokhunda* (1956) from a screenplay by **Viktor Shklovskii** based on the 1930 novel by Tadjik author Sadriddin Ayni (1876–1954). He also appeared as Maimandi in **Kamil Yarmatov**'s biopic *Avicenna* (1957) and in Armenian directors **Ezram Karamyan** and **Hamo Bek-Nazaryan**'s *Nasreddin in Khodjent, or The*

Enchanted Prince (Nasreddin v Khodzhente, ili Ocharovannyi prints, 1959), which was shot at **Tadjikfilm Studio**. Kasymov, who won critical praise for his powerful emotional expression, was one of the preferred actors in the films of Kimyagarov, including the artistically remarkable biopic *A Poet's Destiny* (Sud'ba poeta, 1959) about the 10th-century poet Rudaki, *The Smith's Banner* (Znamia kuznetsa, 1961) from *Shahname* by Firdousi—**Tadjik cinema**'s first wide-screen picture—and the contemporary drama *By Order of the Heart* (Kak velit serdtse, 1968).

Kasymov was honored with the title People's Artist of the USSR in 1941. He joined the Communist Party in 1948.

Other films: *The Legend of Rustam* (Skazanie o Rustame, 1971).

KAVALERIDZE, IVAN PETROVICH (b. 14 April 1887, hutor Lodanskyi [other sources: Romny]–d. 3 December 1979 [other sources: 1978], Kiev). Ukrainian director and screenwriter. A descendant of Georgian peasants who had settled in Ukraine in the 18th century, Kavaleridze studied sculpting at the Kiev Fine Arts School in 1906–1909, then for two semesters at the St. Petersburg Academy of Arts, and later in Paris. Upon his return from France in 1910, Kavaleridze was hired by **Iakov Protazanov** as the art director on the Lev Tolstoi biopic *The Departure of a Great Old Man* (Ukhod velikogo startsa, 1912). He also worked with **Vladimir Gardin**. In 1918, Kavaleridze became a director for the Ukrainian Drama Theater but turned to sculpture again in 1921, creating monuments to Vladimir Lenin, Princess Olga, philosopher Hryhoriy Skovoroda, and national poet Taras Shevchenko in Romny, Kiev, and other Ukrainian cities.

Kavaleridze's background in sculpture—with the noticeable influence of Auguste Rodin—is key to understanding this filmmaker's unique visual style. *Hard Rain* (Liven', 1929), from his own screenplay, immediately catapulted Kavaleridze to the ranks of the most original Soviet filmmakers. A bold attempt to depart from cinematic verisimilitude, the film achieves unprecedented visual concentration through a reduction of decoration to the bare minimum and of acting to a limited number of physical essentials. The plot's six episodes visualize two centuries of Ukrainian liberation struggle through symbolic or allegorical actions, with the performers posing in front of screens. *Hard Rain* was one of the first monumental allegories in the history of cinema and took **Aleksandr Dovzhenko**'s experiments in conflating principles of the fine arts and cinematic forms several steps further.

In *Perekop* (1930), Kavaleridze continued the episodic narration about historical events but gave up on the quasi-sculptural performances. *The Koli Rebellion* (aka *By Water and Smoke*, aka *Mass Struggle*/Koliivshchina, 1933), Kavaleridze's first sound film, depicts the 1767–1768 antifeudal, anti-Polish uprising of Koli serfs who were later betrayed by some of their own leaders and suppressed by Russian troops. The film was planned as the first installment of a trilogy about the Ukrainian people's struggle for liberation. *Prometheus* (Prometei, 1935), which takes place in Ukraine, Georgia, and Russia during the reign of Nikolai I, focuses on a serf named Ivas' who serves in the Russian Army and leads an uprising in the Caucasus. After the film was harshly criticized in an article in *Pravda* on 13 February 1936, it was immediately withdrawn from distribution—a reflection of the repression of all stylistic experimentation, which was flatly denounced as "formalist," no matter how loyal the filmmaker was to the Communist dogma. As a result, Kavaleridze could not finish the third part of the trilogy, *Dnepr*.

Following more critical attacks, Kavaleridze directed a few harmless pictures, including the popular operetta *Natalka, the Girl from Poltava* (Natalka-Poltavka, 1936), that by all accounts do not possess his particular touch, and then abandoned filmmaking altogether. Only in 1960 could he celebrate a comeback with *Grigorii Skovoroda*, a biopic about the 18th-century Ukrainian philosopher, and the historical melodrama *A Loose Woman* (Guliashchaia, 1961) about an 18-year-old peasant girl who is destroyed by human cruelty.

For decades, Kavaleridze remained a singular phenomenon in Soviet cinema. Some film historians rank him close to Dovzhenko, which is problematic insofar as Kavaleridze only could realize a small degree of his creative potential in film. However, his specific impulses in visual experimentation and allegorical narration re-emerged in the later films of **Sergei Paradjanov** and **Yury Il'enko**, among others.

Kavaleridze was named People's Artist of the Ukrainian SSR in 1969. After his passing, a museum was established in his Kiev studio.

Other films: *The Zaparozh Cossack beyond the Danube* (Zaporo-zhets za Dunaem, 1937). *See also* UKRAINIAN CINEMA.

KAZAKH CINEMA. *See* AIMANOV, SHAKEN; ARINBASA-ROVA, NATAL'IA; ASHIMOV, ASANALI; DZIGAN, EFIM; KAZAKHFILM STUDIO; OMIRBAEV, DAREZHAN; ROSHAL', GRIGORII; SHINARBAEV, ERMEK; UMURZAKOVA, AMINA.

KAZAKHFILM STUDIO. In 1934, a studio for newsreel produc-tion was established in Alma-Ata (now: Almaty), the capital of the Kazakh Soviet Socialist Republic. A few years earlier, in 1929, the Moscow-based studio Vostok-kino had produced the documentary *Turksib* by **Viktor Turin**, dealing with the construction of the Turkestan-Siberian railway line—a vitally important project for Kazakhstan's modernization. Already in 1925, **Iakov Tolchan** had made the **documentary** *The Fifth Anniversary of the Kazakh ASSR*/ Piataia godovshchina Kazakhskoi ASSR. Occasionally, Kazakh ac-tors appeared in Russian films with Kazakhstani subject-matter such as **Semen Timoshenko**'s *The Revolt* (Miatezh, 1929).

In 1934, the Alma-Ata Documentary Film Studio was founded. In 1941, at the beginning of the Great Patriotic War, the establish-ment of a Kazakh national feature film studio coincided with the evacuation of **Mosfilm Studio** and **Lenfilm Studio** to Alma-Ata; all three were officially merged in November 1941 and operated until 1944 under the name Central United Film Studio for Feature Films (TsOKS: Tsentral'naia ob"edinennaia kinostudiia khudozhest-vennykh fil'mov). The vast majority of leading Soviet filmmakers, including **Sergei Eizenshtein**, **Vsevolod Pudovkin**, **Abram Room**, **Ivan Pyr'ev**, **Fridrikh Ermler**, **Vladimir Korsh-Sablin**, **Iulii Raiz-man**, **Aleksandr Stolper**, the **Vasil'ev brothers**, **Vera Stroeva**, and **Leonid Trauberg** worked on its premises; their intensive interaction with the native personnel helped create a Kazakh cadre of film spe-cialists. Of the few wartime projects with specific national themes, the concert film *To the Tunes of the Dombra* (Pod zvuki dombry, 1944, by Timoshenko and A. Minkin) features leading Kazakh musi-cians. When the evacuees returned to Moscow and Leningrad, the studio facilities became the basis of the Alma-Ata Studio for Feature and Documentary Films, officially established on 25 January 1944.

After the war, the studio primarily focused on the production of newsreels and **documentaries**. Among the rare feature films was **Grigorii Roshal'**'s *The Songs of Abai* (Pesni Abaia, 1945, codirected with Efim Aron) about the founder of Kazakh literature. **Efim Dzigan** helmed *Djambul* (1952), with **Shaken Aimanov** in the title role of the prominent poet. Both films were typical Stalinist biopics with schematic, heavily didactic plots, black-and-white characterizations, and the obligatory message of the inseparable connection between the artist and the people. Aimanov, who in later years spoke critically of these films, became one of the founders of **Kazakh cinema**. His *Poem about Love* (Poema o liubvi, 1954), the first natively produced Kazakh feature, was a filmed theater production based on the national legend of Kozy-Korpesh and Baian-Sulu. Aimanov's other pictures of the 1950s were harmless propaganda stories that he usually helmed with a Russian codirector, but his later **comedies** and dramas display unmistakable national flavor, especially when featuring folklore motifs. At the same time, non-Kazakh directors came to Alma-Ata to make films about the virgin soil (*tselina*) campaign that gained momentum in the mid-1950s; among them was **Aleksandr Medvedkin** with *Restless Spring* (Bespokoinaia vesna, 1956).

On 9 January 1960, the studio got its current name, Kazakhfilm Studio. Among its leading directors were Efim Aron (1906–1970) and Magit Begalin (1922–1978). One of the most interesting films produced at the studio in the 1960s is the elegiac *Land of the Fathers* (Zemlia ottsov, 1966) about a perished soldier's father who visits his son's grave near Leningrad, and the Civil War thriller *The End of the Ataman* (Konets atamana, 1970); both were directed by Aimanov. In 1967, the studio produced its first animated pictures.

In 1984, Kazakhfilm Studio was named after Shaken Aimanov. In the 1980s, directors such as **Sergei Bodrov** Sr. got a chance to carry out their projects at its premises. During that decade, a large number of Kazakh students graduated from the Soviet State Film School **VGIK** and, after joining the Kazakhfilm staff, created a phenomenon that is referred to as the Kazakh New Wave. Very successful was the dark crime drama *The Needle* (Igla, 1988), directed by Rashid Nugmanov (b. 1954), starring rock legend Viktor Tsoi. Other representatives of the New Wave are Ardak Amirkulov (b. 1955), Serik

Aprymov (b. 1960), **Darezhan Omirbaev**, and **Ermek Shinarbaev**. After a veritable boom in the early 1990s, production volumes shrunk, and many newly founded independent studios disappeared, while Kazakhfilm survived due to considerable investments. A number of Kazakh films of the 1990s were coproductions with Western countries, particularly France. Among Kazakhstan's leading film stars are **Amina Umurzakova**, **Natal'ia Arinbasarova**, and **Asanali Ashimov**, who also embarked on a directing career.

In 2005, Kazakhfilm Studio was transformed into a stockholding company, with the state as the sole owner. The annual production has stabilized at about six to seven feature films, 10 documentaries, and five animated films.

KAZANSKII, GENNADII SERGEEVICH (b. 1 December 1910, Voronezh–d. 14 September 1983, Leningrad). Russian director and scriptwriter. Kazanskii graduated from the Cinema Department of the Advanced Art History Courses in Leningrad in 1930. He was then hired as an assistant director at **Lenfilm Studio**, where he worked with **Fridrikh Ermler**, among others. Kazanskii's directorial debut, the satirical **comedy** *Golden Taiga* (Taiga zolotaia, 1937, codirected with M. Ruf), was considered a failure. During the Great Patriotic War, he worked as a second unit director at Alma-Ata studio (**Kazakhfilm Studio**) in Kazakhstan, where Lenfilm was evacuated.

Kazanskii codirected the prestige biopic *Rimskii-Korsakov* (1952) with **Grigorii Roshal'** before landing his first hit with the three-hour Masterpiece Theater–type film *A Hot Heart* (Goriachee serdtse, 1953) from Aleksandr Ostrovskii's play. A more original and cinematically interesting achievement is *Old Man Khottabych* (Starik Khottabych, 1956), a colorful genie fantasy of lasting popularity with children's audiences in which the didactic purpose is conveyed in a relaxed and humorous fashion. Finally, Kazanskii entered the annals of film history with the romantic science fiction drama *The Amphibian Man* (Chelovek-amfibiia, 1961, codirected with Vladimir Chebotarev), an extraordinary success both in the USSR and abroad. This tragic parable of failed lofty ideals, embodied by the underwater humanoid creature Ikhtiandr who is destroyed by human greed and distrust, won the love of generations of Soviet viewers and has since become a cult film.

Alas, none of Kazanskii's subsequent works—including the stirring antireligious drama *The Sinful Angel* (Greshnyi angel, 1962) and the fairy tale *The Snow Queen* (Snezhnaia koroleva, 1966)—could repeat *Amphibian Man*'s triumph. The biopic *Engineer Graftio* (Inzhener Graftio, 1979), Kazanskii's last film, dealt with the scientist who designed the first Soviet hydroelectric power plant.

Kazanskii joined the Communist Party in 1963; he was named Merited Artist of the RSFSR in 1974.

Other films: *Musicians of the Same Regiment* (Muzykanty odnogo polka, 1965, codirected with **Pavel Kadochnikov**); *The Unknown Heir* (Neznakomyi naslednik, 1974).

KEOSAYAN, EDMOND [Russian sources list the patronymic Gareginovich] (b. 9 October 1936, Leninakan [now: Gjumri], Armenia–d. 21 April 1994, Moscow). Armenian director, screenwriter, and actor. Keosayan was a student at the Moscow Institute of Economics in 1952–1954 when he was selected for the male lead in the contemporary Armenian drama *When Friends Are with You* (Kogda riadom druz'ia, 1956). He subsequently enrolled in the Yerevan Theater Institute, graduating in 1956, and in 1960 joined **Efim Dzigan**'s directing workshop at the Soviet State Film School **VGIK**, graduating in 1964.

While a student, Keosayan helmed two shorts for television, *The Staircase* (Lestnitsa, 1962) and *Three Hours on the Road* (Tri chasa dorogi, 1963). He made his cinema debut at **Mosfilm Studio** with the postwar romance *Where Are You Now, Maksim?* (Gde ty teper', Maksim? 1964). *The Concocter* (Striapukha, 1965), adapted from a **comedy** by ultradogmatic playwright Anatolii Sofronov (1911–1990) about the carefree life of collective farmers in the Kuban' region, attracted an astonishing 30 million viewers. Keosayan landed an even more spectacular hit with *The Uncatchable Avengers* (Neulovimye mstiteli, 1966), a remake of **Ivan Perestiani**'s silent *The Little Red Devils* (Tsiteli eshmakunebi/Krasnye d''iavoliata, 1923). Its Western-style plot about four juvenile "revolutionaries" held special appeal for young audiences, while the Soviet establishment welcomed its romanticized, cleverly encoded Communist message. Such popularity and ideological efficiency inspired a sequel, *The New Adventures of the Uncatchables* (Novye prikliucheniia neulovimykh, 1968), followed by a third installment, *The Crown of the Russian Empire, or About the Uncatchables Again* (Korona Rossiiskoi Imperii, ili Snova o neulovimykh, 1971). However, despite their triumph at the box office, the latter two were criticized for overemphasizing adventure and suspense elements at the expense of ideology.

After moving to Armenia, Keosayan directed the romantic comedy *Men* (Tghamardik/Muzhchiny, 1972), starring **Armen Dzhigarkhanyan** and **Frunze Mkrtchyan**. Back in Moscow, he made *When September Begins* (Kogda nastupaet sentiabr', 1975), a celebration of the Soviet Union's proclaimed multinational harmony packaged as a family melodrama. *The Star of Hope* (Huso astgh/Zvezda nadezhdy, 1979) is an epic about Armenia's 18th-century troubles with the neighboring Ottoman Empire, a conflict in which Russia appeared as the savior (the original Armenian release title, *Mkhitar Sparapet*, refers to one of the leaders in the liberation war). Keosayan's last finished project, *Ascension* (Voznesenie, 1988), deals with the GULAG concentration camps.

Keosayan, who joined the Communist Party in 1963, was honored with the title Merited Artist of the Russian Federation in 1976, Merited Artist of the Armenian SSR in 1977, and Merited Artist of the Georgian SSR in 1979. His son, Tigran Keosayan (b. 1966), is a successful film and television director and screenwriter.

Other films: *The Canyon of the Abandoned Fairy Tales* (Moratsvatz heqiatneri kirtche/Ushchel'e pokinutykh skazok, 1974). *See also* ARMENIAN CINEMA.

KEVORKOV, STEPAN [some Russian sources also list the patronymic Agabekovich] (b. 1 April 1903, Moscow–d. 15 July 1991, Yerevan). Armenian director, scriptwriter, and actor. Kevorkov studied at the State Film College (Gosudarstvennyi Tekhnikum Kinematografii, later **VGIK**) in Moscow, graduating in 1930. At Azerkino studio (later **Azerbaijanfilm**) in Baku, he assisted **Nikoloz Shengelaia** on the stylish *Twenty-six Commissars* (Dvadtsat' shest' komissarov, 1933) and later, at **Mosfilm Studio**, he was an assistant to **Aleksandr Dovzhenko** on *Aerograd* (1935). At **Armenfilm Studio**, Kevorkov worked as an assistant director for **Hamo Bek-Nazaryan** on *The Girl from Ararat Valley* (Araratyan dashti aghchikr/Devushka s Araratskoi doliny, 1949), in which he also played the supporting role of Tatos.

Kevorkov's first picture was *The Mountain March* (Lernayin arshav/Gornyi marsh, 1939, codirected with **Erazm Karamyan**), an adventurous Civil War tale that stood out from other films in this genre because of its folksy sense of humor. After a 15-year hiatus, Kevorkov reappeared with the suspenseful Cold War espionage film, *The Ghosts Abandon the Peaks* (Urvakannere heranum en lernerits/ Prizraki pokidaiut vershiny, 1955, with Karamyan), set in the milieu of geologists. *Along the Path of Thunder* (Ampropi arahetov/Tropoiu groma, 1956, with Karamyan) from the novel *The Path of Thunder* (1948) by South African author Peter Abrahams, is one of the rare attempts in Soviet cinema to illustrate the subject of apartheid. Kevorkov then returned to native soil with the historical thriller *Personally Known* (Andzamb tchanachum em/Lichno izvesten, aka Kamo, 1958, with Karamyan) about legendary revolutionary Ter-Petrosyan (1882–1922), better known under his alias "Kamo." The popular genre of revolutionary action film, which allowed the directors to smoothly combine suspense with Bolshevik propaganda, proved a goldmine since it appealed to viewers of all ages as well as Communist officials. Kevorkov and Karamyan continued the saga with *An Extraordinary Assignment* (Artakarg handznararutyun/Chrezvychainoe poruchenie, 1965). Kevorkov codirected the third installment, *The Last Deed of Kamo* (Kamoyi verjin skhranqe/Poslednii podvig Kamo, 1974), with Grigori Melik-Avakyan.

Kevorkov, who joined the Communist Party in 1945, was named People's Artist of the USSR in 1970. He served as executive director of Armenfilm Studio in 1949–1951 and first secretary of the Armenian Filmmakers' Union from 1956 to 1964.

Other films: *Her Fantasy* (Nra yerevakayutyune, aka Stap gini/Ee fantaziia, 1959); *The Road* (Tchanaparh/Doroga, 1962); *An Explosion after Midnight* (Paytyun kesgisherits heto/Vzryv posle polunochi, 1969, codirected with Karamyan). *See also* ARMENIAN CINEMA.

KHACHATURYAN, ARAM [Russian sources also list the patronymic Il'ich] (b. 6 June 1903, Kodjori near Tbilisi–d. 1 May 1978, Moscow). Armenian composer and conductor. Khachaturyan was born into the family of a bookbinder; in his childhood, he experienced a veritable blend of cultures, including Armenian, Georgian,

Persian, and Azeri. After moving to Moscow in 1921, Khachaturyan studied violoncello and composition at the Gnesin Music College in 1922–1929. In 1929, he enrolled in Moscow Conservatory, where his principal teachers were Reingol'd Glier (1874–1956) and Nikolai Miaskovskii (1903–1963), graduating in 1934.

As a film composer, Khachaturyan made his debut with the score for the first Armenian sound film, **Hamo Bek-Nazaryan**'s social drama *Pepo* (1935), followed by the Civil War tale *Zangezur* (1938). He also wrote the music for the first Tadjik sound film, *The Garden* (Sad, 1938), from which the song "My Garden" gained nationwide popularity.

For several years, Khachaturyan shared an artistic partnership with director **Mikhail Romm**—a curious alliance in which the composer's predilection for strong, ultradramatic contrasts and competing leitmotivs complemented the filmmaker's analytical style. Khachaturyan contributed the music to Romm's anti-Nazi polemic, *Person #217* (aka *Girl No. 217*/Chelovek No. 217, 1944), the Stalinist Cold War pamphlets *The Russian Question* (Russkii vopros, 1947) and *Secret Mission* (Sekretnaia missiia, 1950), and the patriotic maritime dilogy *Admiral Ushakov* and *Ships Attack the Bastions* (aka *Attack from the Sea*/Korabli shturmuiut bastiony, 1953).

In the 1950s, Khachaturyan wrote the scores for some of the most notable films of the decade, among them **Sergei Iutkevich**'s *Othello* (1955) and **Vladimir Petrov**'s adaptation of Aleksandr Kuprin's story *The Duel* (Poedinok, 1957), as well as the first Kyrgyz feature film, the emancipation drama *Saltanat* (1955).

Although Khachaturyan's fame mainly rests on his ballets, three symphonies, and concertos, his film scores display qualities similar to his main body of work: the influence of exotic folklore expressed through motifs and instrumentation, and a spirit of optimism supported by a keen sense of rhythm. Khachaturyan was a pioneer in applying the framework of European musical genres to Armenian and generally Transcaucasian material; several of his film scores reflect such a synthetic approach too.

Khachaturyan, who joined the Communist Party in 1943, held professorships at Moscow Conservatory and Gnesin Music College. He was honored with the title People's Artist of the USSR in 1954 and Hero of Socialist Labor in 1973. He received Stalin Prizes in

1941, 1943, 1946, and 1950, a Lenin Prize in 1959 for the ballet *Spartacus*, and a USSR State Prize in 1971. He lies buried in the pantheon of Yerevan.

Other films: *Salavat Iulaev* (1938); *The Battle of Stalingrad* (Stalingradskaia bitva, 1948); *People and Beasts* (Liudi i zveri, 1962).

KHAMRAEV, ALI [Russian sources list the patronymic Irgashalievich] (b. 19 March [other sources: May] 1937, Tashkent, Uzbekistan). Uzbek director and scriptwriter. Khamraev, the son of Ergash Khamraev, a teacher who became an actor and screenwriter in the 1930s, studied in **Grigorii Roshal'**'s workshop at the Soviet State Film School **VGIK**, graduating in 1961. After the popular romantic **comedy** *Where Are You, My Zul'fiia* (Gde ty, moia Zul'fiia? 1964) he received critical acclaim for *White, White Storks* (Belye, belye aisty, 1966), a contemporary drama in which traditional moral norms clash with passionate love and the desire for self-determination.

Khamraev, a director of extraordinary versatility, made a name for himself with visually intense thrillers set in the 1920s when the establishment of Communist power in Central Asia was met by fierce, militant resistance. *Red Sands* (Krasnye peski, 1969), *The Extraordinary Commissar* (Chrezvychainyi komissar, 1970), *Without Fear* (Bez strakha, 1972), *The Seventh Bullet* (Sed'maia pulia, 1972), and *The Bodyguard* (Telokhranitel', 1979) attracted predominantly young audiences who enjoyed the Western-style action but also the solid performances by Uzbek, Kyrgyz, and Russian stars. Khamraev, ever torn between ideological commitment and artistic ambition, at no point compromised his Communist allegiance, but neither did he deny the tragic aspects of political conflicts, showing a particular interest in the situation of women and children amid brutal clashes.

The director demonstrated an unexpected degree of aesthetic refinement in *A Man Follows the Birds* (Chelovek ukhodit za ptitsami, 1975), a colorful, nonlinear coming-of-age narrative set amid medieval cruelty. However, he also agreed to direct cinematic demagoguery such as the 1983 Soviet-Afghan *Hot Summer in Kabul* (Zharkoe leto v Kabule), which justifies Soviet military aggression.

Another string of Khamraev's films deal with the 1930s and 1940s, especially the impact of the Great Patriotic War on families. Thus, the elegiac *I Remember You* (Ia tebia pomniu, 1986) is dedicated to Khamraev's father, who perished in 1942 as the commander of a scouting unit, while *Garden of Desires* (Sad zhelanii, 1987), produced at **Mosfilm Studio** in the heyday of perestroika, describes the effects of Stalinist persecution.

In 1989, Khamraev founded a private company, Samarkandfilm. The following year, he moved to Italy, where he stayed throughout the 1990s. His only completed film during that period, the controversial tragicomedy *Bo Ba Bu* (1998), was made as an Uzbek-Italian-French coproduction and describes the tribulations of a Western plane crash survivor in the Central Asian desert and her encounter with two native brothers competing for her sexual favors. In 2004, Khamraev returned to Russia to helm a television miniseries, the star-studded thriller *A Place in the Sun* (Mesto pod solntsem).

Khamraev became a member of the Communist Party in 1970 and was named Merited Artist of the Uzbek SSR in 1969.

Other films: *Lenin and Turkestan* (Lenin i Turkestan, 1971); *Lenin and Uzbekistan* (Lenin i Uzbekistan, 1974); *Kim Akhmok* (1990). *See also* UZBEK CINEMA.

KHANZHONKOV, ALEKSANDR ALEKSEEVICH (b. 8 August 1877–d. 26 September 1945, Yalta). Russian producer and screenwriter. Khanzhonkov hailed from an impoverished Cossack family, his father was a retired officer and landowner. He enrolled in an officer's school (*iunkerskoe uchilishche*) in Novocherkassk without having finished gymnasium, and graduated as a cornet (*podkhorunzhii*). Khanzhonkov continued his military career in the First Don Cossack regiment and fought in the Russo-Japanese War of 1904–1905. His first encounter with cinema in 1905 changed his life; he retired and used his payout of 4,000 rubles to finance a small distribution branch, representing the French companies Éclair and Pathé. The Khanzhonkov Trading House (Torgovyi dom Khanzhonkova) began to sell projecting equipment in 1906, expanding into production the following year.

The first picture produced by Khanzhonkov—under his company emblem, the mythical winged horse Pegasus—was *A Drama in a Camp of Gypsies near Moscow* (Drama v tabore podmoskovnykh tsygan, 1908). In 1911, he founded a shareholding company; the production volume increased from about 10 pictures per year to 20 in 1913. Khanzhonkov's instinct for spotting new talents was unmatched; directors **Evgenii Bauer**, **Petr Chardynin**, **Wladyslaw Starewicz**, actors and actresses **Ivan Mozzhukhin**, **Vera Karalli**, **Ivan Perestiani**, and **Vitol'd Polonskii**, and the superstar among Russian actresses, **Vera Kholodnaia**, all began their career in Khanzhonkov's studio.

Together with **Vasilii Goncharov**, Khanzhonkov undertook in 1911 the grandiose reconstruction of the 1854–1855 defense of Sevastopol as an innovative war chronicle. Following the enormous success of *The Defense of Sevastopol* (Oborona Sevastopolia)—the first Russian full-length feature film—Khanzhonkov produced more patriotic blockbusters, among them *The Year 1812* (1812 god, 1912), *The Accession of the Romanov Dynasty* (Votsarenie doma Romanovykh, 1913), and *Ermak Timofeevich, the Vanquisher of Siberia* (Ermak Timofeevich—pokoritel' Sibiri, 1914).

The veritable explosion in production volume that the Russian film industry experienced with the beginning of World War I led to an increased competition among producers in which Khanzhonkov eventually lost his leading position. Star actors and directors moved to better-paying companies. Still, the capital endowment of Khanzhonkov's company increased in 1915 from 500,000 rubles to 1.25 million rubles—an enormous amount at the time.

Together with the majority of Russian film professionals, Khanzhonkov in 1920 went abroad after spending two years on the Crimea; in his absence, the remaining assets of his company were combined with those of **Iosif Ermol'ev** into the State Film Company Goskino (which later became **Mosfilm Studio**) in 1922. Khanzhonkov was one of the few Russian producers who decided to return to his transformed homeland. He was given a chance to work as a production consultant for the company Rusfilm, then for Goskino (since 1924), and as head of production for Proletkino company after 1925. In 1926, Khanzhonkov was arrested and accused of financial embezzlement. There are conflicting accounts of the trial's outcome—some sources claim that Khanzhonkov spent six months in jail and lost his civil rights. Eventually, Khanzhonkov was reinstated in his rights and, by a decision of the Supreme Executive Committee of the USSR, was assigned a prestigious personal pension in 1935.

Later, bound to a wheelchair, he moved to the Crimea, enduring the German occupation, poverty, and starvation.

Khanzhonkov's work in the golden decade from 1907–1918 was characterized by a pioneering entrepreneurial spirit, creativity, experimentation, and an enlightener's drive that was unique among Russian producers. Thus, he financed educational pictures with the intention to visualize physical and biological phenomena, to introduce audiences to various regions of Russia and the world, and to propagate the destructive consequences of alcoholism (although it was unprofitable, he maintained a section of popular science films from 1911 to 1916). Khanzhonkov's company published the journal *Herald of Cinema* (Vestnik kinematografii) since 1910 and *Pegasus* (Pegas) since 1915.

The 1980s and 1990s brought a revision of the artistic merits of his once-ridiculed heritage. Khanzhonkov was turned into an icon of early cultural entrepreneurship, and a monument to him was erected in Moscow. The Khanzhonkov House (Dom Khanzhonkova) in the Russian capital is the only art-house movie theater that exclusively shows national productions.

Khanzhonkov's first wife, Antonina Nikolaevna Khanzhonkova (née Batorovskaia), worked as a screenwriter, director, and producer.

KHEIFITS, IOSIF EFIMOVICH (b. 17 December 1905, Minsk–d. 24 April 1995, St. Petersburg). Russian director and screenwriter. Kheifits was born into the family of a pharmacist. After moving to Petrograd, he joined the Proletarian Culture (Proletkul't) movement and graduated from the Leningrad College (*tekhnikum*) of Screen Arts in 1927. Kheifits then studied at the Department of Cinema in the Institute of Art History, graduating in 1928, and worked in a variety of small jobs in the film factory Sovkino, the later **Lenfilm Studio**, beginning in 1928. Kheifits also joined the Theater of the Workers' Youth (TRAM), which significantly influenced the style and themes of his early, openly propagandistic films.

Kheifits's film career began in earnest as a scriptwriter with *Moon on the Left* (Luna sleva, 1928) and *Transport of Fire* (Transport ognia, 1929), both written with **Aleksandr Zarkhi**, whom he had met in college. In 1929, Kheifits and Zarkhi were put in charge of the first Komsomol Directing Brigade, working as a team from then on. The brigade produced two films, *Facing the Wind* (Veter v litso, 1930) and *Noon* (Polden', 1931), devoted to Komsomol activists fighting against what was declared to be the legacy of pre-Communist society—alcohol abuse, greed, and selfishness. These films also criticize bureaucratic indifference and inefficiency and show a degree of psychological differentiation that was rare at the time. *My Homeland* (Moia Rodina, aka Most, 1933), about a clash between Red Army troops and remnants of the White Army at the Sino-Soviet border, was never released. *Hectic Days* (aka *Red Army Days*/Goriachie denechki, 1935), a popular **comedy** about a charming womanizer, was made in the "American style" and criticized as politically dubious.

The team finally landed a hit with *Baltic Deputy* (Deputat Baltiki, 1937), which won them a Stalin Prize in 1941. For the first time, Kheifits and Zarkhi were able to demonstrate their remarkable gift of turning official political slogans—in this case, the alliance between working class and intelligentsia—into an exciting story populated by largely authentic characters. (This believable human dimension of their films may explain why Western critics and film historians rarely accused them of political opportunism, which was undeniably present.) The title character of *Baltic Deputy*, the biologist Polezhaev, was loosely modeled after biologist Kliment Timiriazev (1843–1920), who had openly supported the Soviet government.

The team's next large-scale picture was *Member of the Government* (aka *The Great Beginning*/Chlen pravitel'stva, 1940) about a kolkhoz peasant who rises to the highest echelons of power. **Vera Maretskaia** gave the title character, Aleksandra Sokolova, feminine grace and warmth in which motherliness and insistence on political principles formed a convincing unity. Just like Polezhaev, Sokolova was an exemplary heroine, embodying the transformation of the Russian village under Soviet power—a politically sensitive task given the brutal history of collectivization and famine.

At the outbreak of the Great Patriotic War in June 1941, Kheifits and Zarkhi were filming a revolutionary epic in Communist Mongolia, *They Call Him Sukhe-Bator* (Ego zovut Sukhe-Bator, 1942). Like other feature directors, the duo was assigned the production of a long **documentary**, in their case *The Defeat of Japan* (Razgrom Iaponii,

1945), which won them another Stalin Prize. After the war, Kheifits and Zarkhi ran into problems caused by ultradogmatic critics, although their films, including *In the Name of Life* (aka *The Miracle of Dr. Petrov*/Vo imia zhizni, 1947) about Soviet scientists and *The Lights of Baku* (Ogni Baku, 1950, released in 1958), apparently contained no ideological heresies.

The Big Family (Bol'shaia sem'ia, 1954) was the first picture that Kheifits directed on his own, after Zarkhi left for **Belarusfilm Studio**. It describes three generations of shipyard workers—a "workers' dynasty," as they were officially called at the time—and conveys a moderate sense of civility that can be viewed as an implied alternative to Stalinism. On the other hand, the film's seamless patriarchal line of succession "misrepresented the reality of Soviet families profoundly injured by wars and political repressions" (Josephine Woll). Kheifits then directed several contemporary melodramas that became trendsetters and box-office hits and have retained their human appeal to this day, particularly *The Rumiantsev Case* (aka *The Case of Sergei Rumyantsev*/Delo Rumiantseva, 1956) and *My Dear Man* (aka *The Cause We Serve*/Dorogoi moi chelovek, 1958).

Kheifits's three Anton Chekhov adaptations—*The Lady with a Lapdog* (Dama s sobachkoi, 1959), *In the Town of S.* (V gorode S., 1967) in which Chekhov himself appears as a narrator, and *A Bad Good Person* (Plokhoi khoroshii chelovek, aka Duel', 1973)—arguably form the most enduring part of his legacy. The first is the most aesthetically perfect among them, characterized by psychologically nuanced acting and visual precision. Admired by cinematic luminaries from George Cukor to Ingmar Bergman, *The Lady with a Lapdog* still holds an exceptional place in the history of Soviet cinema. Its atmosphere and mature attitude toward human desire and the yearning for a meaningful life are utterly Chekhovian, visualized with great tact by **Andrei Moskvin** and supported by **Nadezhda Simonian**'s haunting score. Later literary adaptations such as *Asia* (aka *Love Should Be Guarded*, 1978) from Ivan Turgenev's novella and *Shurochka* (aka *The Duel*, 1983, based on Aleksand Kuprin's story) feature some outstanding performances but leave an overall weaker impression.

The complexity and psychological realism of Kheifits's adaptations also are reflected in his contemporary dramas, including *The*

Only One (aka *Unique*/Edinstvennaia, 1975), *Wife for the First Time* (Vpervye zamuzhem, 1979), and *The Accused* (Podsudimyi, 1986), in which private and societal problems appear closely linked.

It is not easy to categorize this exceptionally versatile, energetic director whose career spanned over half a century and who produced quality work throughout. Kheifits may be the one Russian filmmaker who had his finger on the pulse of Soviet zeitgeist most sensitively and consistently. This granted him both the status of a living classic and consistent success with Soviet audiences. Kheifits's artistic strength became obvious in his films' afterlife, decades after their original release—namely, his ability to narrate stories in purely cinematic ways, more often through telling details than words. The theme of the Russian intellectual connects his revolutionary pictures with the literary adaptations and several of the contemporary films, including his very last one, *The Nomad Bus* (Brodiachii avtobus, 1989), which already breathes perestroika fatigue. But in all of Kheifits's films, workers, peasants, military personnel, and intellectuals are treated with the same genuine respect for their humanity. Perhaps it was this approach that, despite a few episodes of official criticism, secured him one of the longest and happiest careers in Russian and Soviet cinema.

Kheifits's work was recognized with many official honors, most prominently the title People's Artist of the USSR in 1964 and Hero of Socialist Labor in 1975, but he generally tried to stay out of the political limelight and kept a rather low profile. Kheifits became a member of the Communist Party in 1945. In 1987, he made a feature-length documentary, *Let's Remember, Comrade!* (Vspomnim, tovarishch), which tells the story of Lenfilm Studio.

In the 1930s, Kheifits was married to actress **Ianina Zheimo**.

Other films (until 1950 with Zarkhi): *The Song of Metal* (Pesn' o metalle, 1928); *Malakhov Mound* (Malakhov kurgan, aka *The Last Hill*, 1944); *Precious Grain* (Dragotsennye zerna, 1948); *The Horizon* (Gorizont, 1962); *A Day of Happiness* (Den' schast'ia, 1964); *Salute, Maria!* (Saliut, Mariia! 1970); *To Whom Do You Belong, Old Folks?* (Vy ch'e, starich'e? 1988).

KHITRUK, FEDOR SAVEL'EVICH (b. 1 May 1917, Tver'). Russian **animation** director, scriptwriter, animator, and pedagogue. In

1932–1933, Khitruk studied at the Arts and Crafts School in Stuttgart; he then attended the Technical School of the Arts in Moscow (1934–1936) and the Institute for Professional Development of Graphic Artists, graduating in 1938. In 1937, he joined the staff of the newly founded Soiuzmultfilm studio, where he worked until 1984, only interrupted by his service in the Red Army in the Great Patriotic War.

Khitruk, for whom the first screening of a Walt Disney picture in the USSR in 1935 proved an eye-opening experience, soon gained the reputation of a skillful animator whose ability to grasp and visualize a variety of narrative concepts to maximum effect made him one of the most valued artists in drawn animation. Thus, he contributed to *The Tale of Tsar Saltan* (Skazka o tsare Saltane, 1940) and **Lev Atamanov**'s famous *Snow Queen* (Snezhnaia koroleva, 1957), for which he developed the character of Ole Lukoje.

In 1961, Khitruk began to direct, setting a new tone by deliberately turning away from the dominating mainstream, quasi-Disneyan visual style. *Story of a Crime* (Istoriia odnogo prestupleniia, 1962), about a man whose sleep is constantly disturbed by obnoxious neighbors, demonstrates an unprecedented degree of stylistic compression and narrative economy. Each of Khitruk's following films is stylistically unique and targets different audience groups. Thus, *The Holidays of Bonifatius* (Kanikuly Bonifatsiia, 1965) about a circus lion was clearly intended for kids, while *Film! Film! Film!* (1968), a satirical depiction of the insanity in the process of filmmaking with allusions to the classics of Soviet cinema, could only be fully appreciated by culturally erudite adults. Khitruk's stylistic diversity, laconic wit, and authorial independence won him the admiration of several generations of Soviet and post-Soviet animation artists who regard him as their mentor.

The trilogy on *Winnie the Pooh* (Vinni-pukh, 1969–1972) is arguably Khitruk's most popular achievement. He also made some politically hypercorrect films that duly brought him official recognition, including *Young Man Friedrich Engels* (Iunosha Fridrikh Engel's, 1970, with East Germany) and a special contribution to **Iurii Ozerov**'s *Oh Sport—You Are Peace* (O sport, ty—mir! 1981; doc.), which won him a USSR State Prize.

Khitruk, who joined the Communist Party in 1949, was named People's Artist of the Russian Federation in 1977 and People's Artist of the USSR in 1987 (other sources: 1991). Many of Khitruk's films won international prizes. For a number of years, he held high-ranking positions in the Union of Soviet Cinematographers and in the International Association of Animators. In 1993, he founded an independent studio school for animators and animation directors, Shar (together with **Iurii Norshtein**, Eduard Nazarov, and **Andrei Khrzhanovskii**).

Other films: *Little Trampler* (Toptyzhka, 1965); *Man in the Frame* (Chelovek v ramke, 1967); *The Island* (1973, with Nazarov); *I Give You a Star* (Dariu tebe zvezdu, 1975); *Icarus and the Wise Men* (Ikar i mudretsy, 1976); *The Lion and the Bull* (Lev i byk, 1983).

KHOKHLOVA, ALEKSANDRA SERGEEVNA (b. 4 October 1897, Berlin–d. 22 August 1985, Moscow). Russian actress, director, and film pedagogue. Khokhlova debuted in **Wladyslaw Starewicz**'s film *Iola* in 1918. That same year she joined the experimental workshop of budding filmmaker and theorist **Lev Kuleshov** at the First State Film School (Goskinoshkola); Kuleshov soon became her lifelong artistic partner and spouse.

Khokhlova's first role under Kuleshov's direction was in the *agitka At the Red Front* (Na krasnom fronte, 1920). Talented and passionately devoted to cinema, the actress gave her all to successfully applying Kuleshov's theories of film acting, with particular effect in the **comedy** *The Unusual Adventures of Mr. West in the Land of the Bolsheviks*/Neobychainye prikliucheniia mistera Vesta v strane bol'shevikov, 1924, and in the dramatic Jack London adaptation *By the Law* (Po zakonu, 1926). She also had significant roles in *The Ray of Death* (Luch smerti, 1925), *Your Acquaintance* (Vasha znakomaia, 1927), and *The Great Consoler* (Velikii uteshitel', 1933), simultaneously working as Kuleshov's assistant.

Khokhlova directed three features on her own: *The Case with the Clips* (Delo s zastezhkami, 1929), from a short story by Maksim Gor'kii; *Sasha* (1930), a contemporary story of a pregnant peasant girl who is trying to find her husband in the city; and *Toys* (Igrushki, 1931), a semifictitious tale about the production of Russian toys and the children playing with them. The first two films were moderately successful with viewers and critics, but following the third, Khokhlova gave up her directorial ambitions.

As an actress, Khokhlova distinguished herself by a minimalist yet extroverted approach, often bordering on the grotesque, which in the 1930s was defamed as "formalist"; her unusual physique—she was tall, very slender, with supposedly "nonproletarian" features—made Khokhlova a maverick in Soviet cinema. In 1929, British film critic Bryher emphatically defended the actress, writing "how can the superficial prettiness of an average Hollywood heroine be preferred to this creature that has madness and greatness in her face and movements, the quality of snow and the grace of elk scenting storm suddenly among bare branches?"

Khokhlova compensated for lacking artistic opportunities with intense pedagogical activity. For over four decades, she and Kuleshov jointly led a workshop at the Soviet State Film School **VGIK**. Khokhlova was named Merited Artist of the Russian Federation in 1935.

Other films: *The Death of a Sensation* (Gibel' sensatsii, 1935); *Siberians* (Sibiriaki, 1940); *Birch Trees in the Steppe* (Berezy v stepi, 1956).

KHOLODNAIA, VERA VASIL'EVNA [born Levchenko] (b. 1893, Poltava–d. 16 February 1919, Odessa). Russian actress. Kholodnaia, daughter of a high school teacher, enrolled in the Moscow Bolshoi Theater's ballet school at the age of 10 but dropped out after a year. At 17, she married lawyer Vladimir Kholodnyi and became a housewife but kept an early interest in cinema while raising the children.

In 1914, after expressing a desire to act to producer **Aleksandr Khanzhonkov**, she was given the small part of an Italian wet nurse in **Vladimir Gardin**'s adaptation of Lev Tolstoi's *Anna Karenina*. The director did not find Kholodnaia's abilities convincing and advised her to give up her efforts to become a *naturshchitsa*, that is, screen actress. A year later, **Evgenii Bauer** cast Kholodnaia as the lead in his Ivan Turgenev adaptation *Song of Triumphant Love* (Pesn' liubvi torzhestvuiushchei, 1915), which became an enormous success. Viewers of all classes fell in love with the exquisite melancholy of Kholodnaia's large gray eyes and the elegance of her movements, balancing between bashful and erotic. Bauer continued to build his new star in films such as *Beauty Must Rule the World* (V mire dolzhna tsarit' krasota, 1915), *A Lunar Beauty* (Lunnaia krasavitsa, 1915), and the megahit *A Life for a Life* (Zhizn' za zhizn', 1916).

In 1916, Kholodnaia moved with director **Petr Chardynin** from Khanzhonkov's company to that of Dmitrii Kharitonov, where she became the prime star in a series of lavish bourgeois melodramas and was paid the highest salary of all Russian film actors (up to 25,000 rubles per film). Among her greatest successes were *By the Fireplace* (U kamina, 1917), *Forget the Fireplace—Its Flames Are Extinct* (Pozabud' pro kamin, v nem ugasli ogni, 1917), and *Hush, Sadness . . . Hush . . .* (Molchi, grust' . . . molchi . . ., 1918), all directed by Chardynin.

In the spring of 1918, Kholodnaia left Moscow for the Crimea, where she continued to act in movies and also gave concerts for the White Army. Following an accident, she caught the Spanish flu and died within a few days. Her passing at the age of 26 resembled the plots of her films, and so did the rumors following it, including stories surmising that Kholodnaia was a spy for the Bolsheviks and was shot by White Army officers, or that she suffocated from the smell of white lilies sent to her by the French consul. Parallel to the legends, a debate evolved on the nature of Kholodnaia's talent, a discourse that goes to the very heart of the quality of early Russian cinema. Opinions range from allegations that "the queen of the screen" possessed no gift at all and was merely a synthetic creation of her directors who skillfully assembled various poses and facial expressions, to passionate statements about Kholodnaia's unique genius that had impressed Konstantin Stanislavskii and Maksim Gor'kii.

Other films: *Chess of Life* (Shakhmaty zhizni, 1916); *The Woman Who Invented Love* (Zhenshchina, kotoraia izobrela liubov', 1918); *The Last Tango* (Poslednee tango, 1918).

KHOTINENKO, VLADIMIR IVANOVICH (b. 20 January 1952, Slavgorod, Altai province). Russian director, scriptwriter, art director, and producer. Khotinenko worked as a designer at a tractor factory in the 1970s, studied at the Sverdlovsk Institute of Architecture until 1976, and was an art director at Sverdlovsk film studio in 1978–1982. **Nikita Mikhalkov** accepted him into his workshop at the Supreme Directing Courses in Moscow, from which Khotinenko graduated in 1982, and hired him as an assistant on *Oblomov*

(Neskol'ko dnei iz zhizni I.I. Oblomova, 1979), *Five Evenings* (Piat' vecherov, 1980), and *Relatives* (Rodnia, 1982); in the latter, he also played a supporting part.

Khotinenko made his directorial debut with the historical thriller *Alone and Unarmed* (Odin i bez oruzhiia, 1984, codirected with Pavel Fattahutdinov) about the struggle of Soviet police against a criminal gang in the 1920s, followed by the Civil War flick *In the Shooting Wasteland* (V streliaiushchei glushi, 1986). He raised eyebrows with *A Mirror for the Hero* (Zerkalo dlia geroia, 1987), which transforms a time-machine plot into a thorough reflection on the Soviet past and principles of historical judgment.

When Soviet cinema disappeared in the early 1990s, Khotinenko proved one of the few directors unperturbed by the ensuing time of troubles. While other filmmakers suffered from creative paralysis, ideological disorientation, and lack of funding, Khotinenko made two of the most insightful and witty pictures of the decade, *Makarov* (1993) and *The Moslem* (Musul'manin, 1995). The former—paradoxical and sarcastic—is neither the product of nostalgia nor of nihilism, rather showing the incompatibility of cynical reality and cherished humanist ideals of Russia's classical literature. The latter analyzes the Russian patriarchal community with its collectivist comfort and narrow-mindedness, meekness, materialism, and aggressive intolerance.

Khotinenko contributed one of the better episodes to the omnibus *Arrival of the Train* (Pribytie poezda, 1995), which was furnished for the centennial of the invention of cinema. His short, *The Path* (Doroga), describes a talented folksinger on a train station who is exploited by a cruel pimp and touches the heart of a New Russian.

Following an apparent crisis lasting several years, Khotinenko made a comeback with *72 Meters* (72 metra, 2003), loosely based on the catastrophe of the submarine *Kursk*. Although atmospherically convincing, the director's conceptual approach marks a profound departure from the irony and skepticism of the mid-1990s, indulging in patriotic slogans instead. This regrettable trend continues in the popular television miniseries *Death of an Empire* (Gibel' imperii, 2005) about international secret service schemes on the eve of World War I. Its espionage-centered, paranoid view of history reflects Russia's neoimperial spirit in the new millennium.

Khotinenko's ambition has always been to capture his nation's mind-set. Whenever he allows irony and ambiguity to determine the tone of his films, the results are innovative, original, and disturbing. However, when affirmative national pathos appears, the transparent ideological purpose diminishes his pictures' quality. Interestingly, like **Aleksei Balabanov**, Khotinenko is a proud provincialist who wears his non-Muscovite origins like a badge of honor.

In the 1990s, Khotinenko taught directing at the Russian State Film School **VGIK**. His son is filmmaker Il'ia Khotinenko, who made his debut in 1999 with the satire *The News* (Novosti).

Other films: *The Swarm* (Roi, 1990); *A Patriotic Comedy* (Patrioticheskaia komediia, 1992); *Strastnoi Boulevard* (1999); *The Golden Age* (Zolotoi vek, 2003); *1612: Time of Troubles* (1612. Smutnoe vremia, 2007).

KHRENNIKOV, TIKHON NIKOLAEVICH (b. 10 June 1913, Elets—d. 14 August 2007, Moscow). Russian composer, pianist, pedagogue, and cultural administrator. The youngest of 10 children in the family of a petty clerk, Khrennikov was given piano lessons at the age of nine; he composed his first piece at 13. He enrolled in the Gnesin Music College in 1929 studying piano and composition, and in 1932, in Moscow Conservatory where his principal teachers were composer Vissarion Shebalin (1902–1963) and piano virtuoso Genrikh Neigauz (1888–1964). The year he graduated—1936—Khrennikov composed the music for a Vakhtangov Theater production of Shakespeare's *Much Ado about Nothing*, a **comedy** that continued to intrigue him for half a century. He also wrote a successful opera about the Bolshevik Revolution, *Into the Storm* (1939), and soon became a rising star of Soviet culture.

Khrennikov's debut as a film composer, *The Struggle Goes On* (Bor'ba prodolzhaetsia, 1939), from a screenplay by German Communist émigré playwright Friedrich Wolf, proved disappointing: the well-intended tale of antifascist activities in Nazi Germany did not leave a trace in either film or music history. But Khrennikov came into his own with a lighthearted, operetta-type picture, **Ivan Pyr'ev**'s legendary *Swineherd and Shepherd* (aka *They Met in Moscow*/Svinarka i pastukh, 1941). This contemporary fairy tale's vaudeville-like gaiety won the composer a Stalin Prize in 1942. He later wrote the music for Pyr'ev's equally popular *At Six in the Evening after the War* (aka *Six P.M.*/V shest' chasov vechera posle voiny, 1944), which anticipates the coming Soviet victory and was also rewarded by a Stalin Prize.

Khrennikov, who repeatedly professed his passion for writing film music, continued to show his preference for comedy, for example, on **Iulii Raizman**'s *The Train Goes Eastward* (Poezd idet na vostok, 1947). But he also contributed the required official pathos to preposterous Stalinist dramas such as **Leonid Lukov**'s *The Miners of Donetsk* (Donetskie shakhtery, 1950) and Raizman's *Cavalier of the Golden Star* (aka *Dream of a Cossack*/Kavaler zolotoi zvezdy, 1950, Stalin Prize 1952). His gift for writing melodious songs that could be sung by ordinary people accompanied by a guitar was put to good use in **Mikhail Kalatozov**'s charming comedy *Loyal Friends* (Vernye druz'ia, 1954).

For **El'dar Riazanov**, Khrennikov wrote the music for the historical blockbuster *Husar Ballad* (Gusarskaia ballada, 1962) about the 1812 anti-Napoleonic war, synthesizing the patriotic and the lyrical in a way that is typical of his work in general (the film score was turned into a ballet in 1979). He also provided a fine score for the restored version of **Vsevolod Pudovkin**'s silent classic *The Mother* (Mat', 1926) in 1968; the Maksim Gor'kii novel on which that picture was based was the source of the libretto to his own 1951 ill-reputed opera.

Khrennikov authored more than a dozen operas, operettas, and ballets, three symphonies, four concertos for piano and orchestra, and numerous songs. His name is also associated with one of the longest administrative careers in Soviet culture. In 1948, Khrennikov was appointed general secretary of the Soviet Composers' Union, a position that he managed to keep for over 40 years. Curiously, even those who dislike Khrennikov's rather conservative musical approach and find his political career suspicious admitted that he did possess genuine talent and sometimes used his influence to help colleagues. On the other hand, in the 1960s, he authorized a campaign directed against musical innovators such as **Edison Denisov**, **Al'fred Shnitke**, and Sof'ia Gubaidulina, all of whom, incidentally, found a refuge in film music.

In 1961, Khrennikov assumed a teaching position at Moscow Conservatory and was promoted to the rank of full professor in

1966 (among his students was eminent film composer **Viacheslav Ovchinnikov**). Khrennikov joined the Communist Party in 1947 and became a candidate to its Central Committee in 1976. He was named People's Artist of the USSR in 1963 and Hero of Socialist Labor in 1973.

Other films: *Comrade Arsenii* (Tovarishch Arsenii, 1964); *No Password Is Needed* (Parol' ne nuzhen, 1967); *Two Comrades* (Dva tovarishcha, 2001).

KHRZHANOVSKII, ANDREI IUR'EVICH (b. 30 November 1939, Moscow). Russian **animation** director, scriptwriter, and animator. Khrzhanovskii, the son of a painter, studied with **Lev Kuleshov** and **Aleksandra Khokhlova** at the Soviet State Film School **VGIK**, graduating in 1962.

Khrzhanovskii belongs to a group of style-conscious, aesthetically original animation artists whose works are intended for adult, culturally erudite audiences. His insistence on artistic independence in the choice of subject matter and style has earned him respect and success at international festivals. The antibureaucratic satire *Once Lived Koziavin* (Zhil-byl Koziavin, 1966), the script of which was coauthored by Khrzhanovskii and **Gennadii Shpalikov**, uses grotesque exaggeration in order to reveal the pernicious absurdity of Soviet state structures. *The Glass Concertina* (aka *The Glass Harmonica*/Stekliannaia garmonika, 1968) juxtaposes the world of harmony established by art with the destructive energy of money and greed. Both the director's artistic ideal and the forces of destruction are represented by visual quotes from the works of famous painters—including René Magritte, Albrecht Dürer, Pieter Brueghel, and Francisco de Goya—provocatively synthesizing them to an anticommercial, anticapitalist allegory.

Several of Khrzhanovskii's pictures were inspired by classical literature, among them *In the World of Fables* (V mire basen, 1973). He created a trilogy of medium-length animated films based on poems by Aleksandr Pushkin: *I Fly to You by Memory* (Ia k vam lechu vospominan'em, 1977), *And Once Again I Am with You* (I s vami snova ia, 1982), and *Autumn* (Osen', 1982), which bring the poet's own sketches to life and turn them into a coherent, living world. Khrzhanovskii used a similar method in films inspired by drawings of other masters, for example, Federico Fellini in *The Lion with the Silver Beard* (Lev s sedoi borodoi, 1995).

In 1992, Khrzhanovskii was honored with the title Merited Artist of Russia. He teaches at the Russian State Film School **VGIK**. In 1993, he was one of the founders of the independent studio school for animators Shar (together with **Fedor Khitruk**, **Iurii Norshtein**, and Eduard Nazarov). His son is filmmaker Il'ia Khrzhanovskii (b. 1975), whose darkly grotesque *Four* (2004) surprised international festival audiences.

Other films: *The Closet* (Shkaf, 1970); *The Butterfly* (Babochka, 1972); *The House Built by Jack* (Dom, kotoryi postroil Dzhek, 1976); *The Long Sojourn* (Dolgoe puteshestvie, 1997); *A Cat and a Half* (Poltora kota, 2002).

KHUTSIEV, MARLEN MARTYNOVICH (b. 4 October [other sources: December] 1925, Tbilisi). Georgian-Russian director, screenwriter, and pedagogue. Born into the family of a Communist official who perished during the 1937 purges, Khutsiev began to work as an assistant to the special effects designer at Tbilisi film studio (later **Gruziya-Film**) in 1944. He studied directing at the Soviet State Film School **VGIK** under **Ihor' Savchenko**, graduating in 1952. Khutsiev's diploma film, the short *City Builders* (Gradostroiteli, 1950), deals with the lives of Moscow construction workers. In 1954, Khutsiev was an assistant to **Boris Barnet**.

Khutsiev's feature-length debut, ***Springtime on Zarechnaia Street*** (Vesna na Zarechnoi ulitse, 1956), codirected with fellow film student Feliks Mironer (1927–1980), became a sleeper hit. An authentic Thaw picture, its title became a code word for a new, youthful type of cinema that is still sentimentally remembered by those who then were in their 20s. The unobtrusive love story of a cocky steel worker who is eager to learn and a community college teacher who finds the industrial town rough and unwelcoming depicts social frictions with benevolent candor. The protagonists' class and educational differences serve as a source of erotic tension and misunderstandings that are resolved at the end, pointing to a bright future. Khutsiev's following picture, *The Two Fedors* (Dva Fedora, 1958), possesses the same social precision yet added a level of historical depth. Portraying one of the title characters, **Vasilii Shukshin** made his remarkable acting debut in the role of a discharged soldier who grows attached to an orphaned boy. Depicting the postwar poverty with unprecedented honesty, Khutsiev contrasts it with the endearing warmth and generosity in human relations.

Ilyich's Gate (Zastava Il'icha) was a project for which Khutsiev had to endure six years of uncertainty and harassment, beginning in 1959 when the director coauthored the screenplay with **Gennadii Shpalikov**. The title refers to a district in Moscow that is named after Lenin's patronymic, Ilyich—a key detail for the understanding of the underlying concept. Briefly released in 1962, the three-hour, black-and-white picture was shelved and, after being reedited and severely cut, got a limited release under the title *I Am Twenty* (Mne dvadtsat' let, 1964). It aptly reflects the complexity of post-Stalinist Soviet youth looking for spiritual and intellectual orientation, and became the cinematic manifesto of an entire generation. For years, the title served as some sort of parole, especially because of the film's subsequent disappearance from screens (although it was sent to the 1965 Venice Film Festival where it won the Special Jury prize). *I Am Twenty* also marks Khutsiev's turn to less concise plot structures, betraying the influence of Michelangelo Antonioni, Jean-Luc Godard, and Federico Fellini.

Rain in July (Iiul'skii dozhd', 1967), which similarly blends love story and societal panorama, moves even further in loosening the narrative fabric while implicitly warning of an alienation and discontinuity between the generations and possible disintegration of Soviet society.

Following his difficulties with the latter two films, Khutsiev began to work for television. *It Was May* (Byl mesiats mai, 1970, from a Grigorii Baklanov story) thematizes the Great Patriotic War, which had been an implicit topos of Khutsiev's earlier films and denotes a collective heroic act that appears both as a challenge and ethical standard for the searching young. The film is an attempt to capture the essence of Nazism in people's minds, juxtaposing the humanity of a group of Red Army soldiers with the moral compromise and degradation of a German village at the end of World War II. Also for television, Khutsiev made the documentary *The Scarlet Sail of Paris* (Alyi parus Parizha, 1971), devoted to the anniversary of the

Paris Commune, mixing historical footage with images of present-day Paris. He then completed **Mikhail Romm**'s cinematic testament, *And Still, I Do Believe* (I vse-taki ia veriu, with **Elem Klimov** and German Lavrov), the title of which might as well stand for his own life and art.

After a lengthy hiatus, Khutsiev directed the intimate family drama *The Afterword* (Posleslovie, 1983) about an old man and his son-in-law (portrayed by **Rostislav Pliatt** and Andrei Miagkov) whose notions of life and moral values are diametrically opposed. Particularly the young man comes across as a cynic and ultrapragmatist, marking the spiritual numbness of the formerly 20-year-olds who lived through the "age of stagnation."

Actively involved in perestroika debates, and hailed as one of the living classic filmmakers of Soviet cinema, Khutsiev was given the opportunity to reconstruct *Ilyich's Gate*. His next project, *Infinity* (Beskonechnost', 1991), an almost four-hour cinematic autobiography of sorts, is perhaps the most contemplative of Khutsiev's films. Using a "voyage into the past" plot, *Infinity*, which won the director a State Prize of Russia in 1991, is an attempt to make sense of Russia's fate in the 20th century, to transcend hopelessness and find meaning in the country's continued suffering.

Although Khutsiev has always commanded enormous authority in the Russian and post-Soviet film community, his work is much less known abroad. His extraordinary reputation is best understood by viewing his films in the context of their time. In the 1950s, the director's emphasis on simplicity and naturalness marked a refreshing change from the artificiality and dishonest pathos of Stalinist cinema; in the 1960s, Khutsiev expressed the desire of a generation to take charge as sovereign, morally and historically conscious citizens. Khutsiev has a rare sensitivity for central elements of Soviet zeitgeist and a talent for expressing that spirit—including its patriotism and humanism—through the dialogues and the atmosphere of his pictures. Despite his censorial problems and the attacks launched against him by Communist leader Nikita Khrushchev, Khutsiev was never a dissident. Rather, several key scenes in his films feature passionately pro-Soviet, pro-Communist statements that remain visually and verbally unchallenged. The appeal of Khutsiev's films rests on the assumption that a decent individual life is possible within the parameters of post-Stalinist society, a romantic belief that was shared by many Soviet intellectuals of the 1960s and well into the 1980s.

Khutsiev, who has been teaching at VGIK since 1978 (among his students is director **Vasilii Pichul**), was named Merited Artist of the RSFSR in 1965 and People's Artist of the USSR in 1986.

Other films: *An Unusual Sunrise* (Nevecherniaia, 2008).

KIISK, KALJO KARL [spelling in some sources: Kaje Kijsk] (b. 3 December 1925, Voka, Ida-Virumaa [other source: Toila]–d. 20 September 2007, Tallin). Estonian director, actor, and screenwriter. Kiisk studied at the State Institute for Stage Arts (GITIS) in Moscow, graduating in 1953. He then worked as an actor and director at Kingisepp Theater in Tallin until 1955.

Kiisk's first effort in cinema, *In the Background* (Tagahoovis/Na zadvorkakh, 1956, codirected with V. Nevezhin), from a play by prominent Estonian playwright Oskar Luts (1887–1953), betrays strong theatrical influences. The **comedy** *Naughty Curves* (Vallatud kurvid/Ozornye povoroty, 1959, codirected with Iulii Kun) proved so popular that it was remade in 1961 as a technically pioneering panorama screen version under the title *Dangerous Turns* (Ohtlikud kurvid/Opasnye povoroty)—the first Soviet panorama feature film ever.

Kiisk then turned to more serious themes. *Ice Drift* (Jääminek/Ledokhod, 1962) describes two families leading an isolated life on a small island who suddenly have to face Nazi occupation. *Insanity* (Hullumeelsus/Bezumie, 1968), arguably Kiisk's greatest accomplishment as director, was finally released uncut 20 years after its completion. The story of a doctor who saves his patients in a mental asylum by claiming to SS troops that there is a British spy among them is remarkable for its paradoxical, unusual approach to Nazism and as a humanist parable about ethical responsibility.

Kiisk's later works show signs of political resignation. Thus, the staunchly pro-Soviet *Ask the Dead for the Price of Death* (Surma hinda küsi surnutelt/Tsenu smerti sprosi u mertvykh, 1978) about a Communist revolt in 1924 brought Kiisk many official honors but hampered his reputation. *Nipernaadi* (aka *Seeker of Adventures/ Iskatel' prikliuchenii*, 1983) is an entertaining film about the adventures of an Estonian Don Juan—Toomas Nipernaadi—prior to World

War I. Kiisk's last film as director is *The Prompter* (Suflöör, 1993), a triangle love story set in the theater milieu.

Kiisk also had a successful acting career; among his best performances is the part of Kristjan Lible in Arvo Kruusement's three films based on the autobiographical fiction of Oskar Luts: *Spring* (Kevade/Vesna, 1969), *Summer* (Suvi/Leto, 1976), and *Autumn* (Sügis/Osen', 1990). He also appeared in international productions such as the French-Finnish *Rothschild's Fiddle* (Le Violon de Rothschild, 1996).

Kiisk, who joined the Communist Party in 1965 and held high-ranking positions in its apparatus, was named People's Artist of the Estonian SSR in 1980. He served as the first secretary of the Union of Estonian Filmmakers since 1962.

Other films: (as actor) *The Awakening* (Äratus, 1987); *The Old Man Wants to Go Home* (Vana mees tahab kaju, 1991); *The Hostage* (Kilnieks, 2006); (as director) *Turn Around* (Jäljed/Oglianis' v puti, 1964); *Ferry at Noon* (Keskpäevane praam/Poludennyi parom,1967); *Forest Violets* (Metskanni kesed/Lesnye fialki, 1980); *In One Hundred Years in May* (Saja aasta parast mais/Cherez sto let v mae, 1987). *See also* ESTONIAN CINEMA.

KIMYAGAROV, BENSION ARIEVICH (b. 30 September 1920, Samarkand–d. 17 April 1979, Moscow). Tadjik director and screenwriter. Kimyagarov studied at the Soviet State Film School **VGIK** with **Sergei Eizenshtein**. After graduating in 1944 and moving to Tadjikistan, he helmed a number of **documentaries**: *Tadjikistan* (1946, codirected with Lidiia Stepanova), *Sadriddin Ayni* (1949) about the celebrated Tadjik national writer (1876–1954), and *Soviet Tadjikistan* (Sovetskii Tadjikistan, 1951), among others.

Kimyagarov then switched to feature films. His debut was *Dokhunda* (1956) from a screenplay by **Boris Shklovskii**, based on the 1930 novel by Ayni about the political growth of a poor Tadjik man in the 1910s–1920s who eventually joins the Communist movement. Kimyagarov earned high accolades for his inventive biopic *A Poet's Destiny* (Sud'ba poeta, 1959) about the 10th-century poet Rudaki, followed by Tadjikistan's first wide-screen picture, *The Smith's Banner* (Znamia kuznetsa, 1961), adapted from the poem "Shah-Name" by 10th-century Persian writer Firdousi, and the contemporary drama *As the Heart Orders* (Kak velit serdtse, 1968). *A Peaceful Time*

(Mirnoe vremia, 1965) describes the difficult period after the establishment of Soviet power in Dushanbe and the youthful enthusiasm of romantic Communist believers. Similar themes were at the center of *Hasan-Arbakesh* (1966).

In the 1970s, Kimyagarov created the trilogy *The Legend of Rustam* (Skazanie o Rustame, 1970), *Rustam and Zohrab* (1972), and *The Legend of Siiavush* (Skazanie o Siiavushe, 1977). Inspired by Firdousi's works, it represents Kimyagarov's most lasting artistic achievement, and one of the best productions in all of **Tadjik cinema**.

Kimyagarov was one of the leading filmmakers in Tadjikistan who repeatedly and successfully switched genres. Although in his contemporary films a didactic tone and plot structure dominate, the historical and mythological pictures are graced by genuine poetic beauty and an authentic visualization of Tadjik folklore motifs.

Kimyagarov joined the Communist Party in 1944. He won a Stalin Prize in 1952 (for *Soviet Tadjikistan*) and was honored with the title People's Artist of the Tadjik SSR in 1960. In 1958–1975, Kimyagarov served as the first secretary of the Tadjik Filmmakers' Union.

Other films: *In the Mountains of Pamir* (V gorakh Pamira, 1947); *A High Position* (Vysokaia dolzhnost', 1958); *Singer of the Native Land* (Pevets rodnoi zemli, 1968); *One Life Is Not Enough* (Odnoi zhizni malo, 1975).

KIVI, EVE [some Russian sources list the patronymic Iokhannessovna] (b. 8 May 1938, Paide). Estonian actress. Kivi received her education at the studio school of the Estonian Drama Theater, graduating in 1959. She made her film debut in **Kaljo Kiisk**'s *In the Background* (Tagahoovis/Na zadvorkakh, 1956, codirected with V. Nevezhin) from a play by prominent Estonian playwright Oskar Luts (1887–1953). The master of fairy tales and fantasy, **Aleksandr Ptushko**, cast her as Annikki in the lavish Soviet-Finnish coproduction *Sampo* (1959, codirected with Risto Orko), based on the Finnish national epic *Kalevala*. From that point onward, Kivi divided her time between Baltic and Russian studios. Thus, she appeared in **Vladimir Petrov**'s *On the Eve* (Nakanune, 1959) from Ivan Turgenev's novel, as Hilde in Vladimir Vengerov's saga *Baltic Sky* (Baltiiskoe nebo, 1960–1961) about the siege of Leningrad, in **Leonid Gaidai**'s **comedy** *This Can't Be True!* (Ne mozhet byt'! 1975, from stories by

Mikhail Zoshchenko) about the New Economic Policy (NEP), and numerous others. Usually playing supporting parts, Kivi raised eyebrows with her exquisite beauty and atypical elegance.

In her native Estonia, Kivi gained huge popularity as Evi in Kiisk's comedy *Naughty Curves* (Vallatud kurvid/Ozornye povoroty, 1959) and reprised that performance in the film's panorama screen version, *Dangerous Turns* (Ohtlikud kurvid/Opasnye povoroty, 1961). She solidified her star status in **Estonian cinema** with the role of Ursula in the medieval drama and box-office hit *The Last Relic* (Viimne reliikvia/Posledniaia relikviia, 1969) and also appeared in a 2004 **documentary** devoted to that cult film, *Igavene reliikviia*.

Kivi remained one of the most sought-after Estonian actresses well into the 1990s. She was honored with the title Merited Artist of the Estonian SSR in 1983.

Other films: *The "Tobago" Changes Its Course* ('Tobago' meniaet kurs, 1965); *Ruslan and Liudmila* (Ruslan i Liudmila, 1972); *Those Old Love Letters* (Eti starye liubovnye pis'ma, 1992); *Firewater* (Tulivesi, 1994).

KLIMOV, ELEM GERMANOVICH (b. 9 July 1933, Stalingrad [now: Volgograd]–d. 26 October 2003, Moscow). Russian director, screenwriter, and film administrator. The son of devoted Communists (his first name "Elem" is a composite of "Engels, Lenin, Marx"), Klimov graduated from the Moscow Aviation Institute in 1957 before enrolling in the Soviet State Film School **VGIK** where he studied in **Efim Dzigan**'s directing workshop. Upon graduation in 1964, he joined the staff of **Mosfilm Studio**.

Klimov's debut was the **comedy** short *The Bridegroom* (Zhenikh, 1960), followed by two feature-length comedies, *Welcome, or No Admittance to Strangers* (Dobro pozhalovat', ili Postoronnim vkhod vospreshchen, 1964) and *Adventures of a Dentist* (Pokhozhdeniia zubnogo vracha, 1965). While the former lampoons a self-aggrandizing tyrant in charge of a Young Pioneers vacation camp, the latter tells the story of a gifted man who is harassed by his colleagues because of his talent. Sharp satirical wit, a taste for the absurdities of contemporary Soviet reality, and a fearless antibureaucratic stance are characteristic of Klimov's early efforts, which, not surprisingly, caused distrust and animosity toward the director within the film establishment. These comedies were also typical of the spirit of the 1960s with its activist approach to art, pointing out social ills and hoping to cure them. On the other hand, Klimov's satire is unusual due to its unmitigated directness that at times borders on an aesthetic assault on the viewer, leaving little room for subtlety.

Following *Sport, Sport, Sport* (1971), a stylistically unique experiment composed of documentary and fictional episodes from the history of athletics, Klimov raised censorial eyebrows with his large-scale historical drama *Agony* (aka *Rasputin*, Agoniia, 1975, released 1981–1984), a powerful reconstruction of the degeneration and irrationality of the tsarist state during World War I. The film's sympathetic portrayal of Nikolai II and the shocking depiction of Grigorii Rasputin's "supernatural" powers led to a long battle between filmmaker and authorities and delayed the ultimate release of the picture by almost a decade.

In 1976, Klimov helped complete **Mikhail Romm**'s cinematic testament, the feature-length film essay *And Still, I Do Believe* (I vse-taki ia veriu, with **Marlen Khutsiev** and German Lavrov). When Klimov's wife, filmmaker **Larisa Shepit'ko**, died in a car accident at the beginning of the production of *Farewell* (Proshchanie) in 1979, Klimov, grief-stricken, agreed to direct her picture. Adapted from Valentin Rasputin's novella "Farewell to Matera" (Proshchanie s Materoi, 1976), Klimov translated this *memento mori* about a Siberian village that is sacrificed to a hydroelectric power plant into a dark, majestic elegy. He also made a **documentary** about his late wife, *Larisa* (1980).

Come and See (Idi i smotri, 1985), Klimov's last completed picture, is a tour de force both aesthetically and thematically. At a time when the memory of the Great Patriotic War had begun to fade and the pride in the victory over Nazism gave way to a disillusioned and even cynical reassessment of the USSR's achievements, the director confronted viewers with an unprecedented graphic depiction of the horrors experienced by the Soviet people during the war. Moreover, he showed these horrors to be a direct outcome of Nazi ideology, while the Soviet forces act as defenders of humanity. The story of a Belarusian teenager who joins the partisans after his entire village is murdered by an SS unit is both hyperrealistic and meditative, ultimately creating an allegory about the sources of evil and destruction in history. Ending with a low-angle shot of the winter sky accompanied by Mozart's "Requiem," this picture's apocalyptic essence far outweighs any positive considerations and leaves an overall pessimistic impression.

Among Klimov's later projects were adaptations of Fedor Dostoevskii's novel *The Devils* (Besy) and Mikhail Bulgakov's *The Master and Margarita* (Master i Margarita), neither of which came to fruition. In the last decade of his life, Klimov—disenchanted and exhausted—withdrew completely from all matters societal or cinematic into resignation and silence.

Klimov's films represent a peculiar blend of sober, sometimes abstract rationality and metaphysics, even mysticism, especially in his last three pictures. Often, documentary footage is artfully combined with staged scenes, forming polemical sequences with an eye-opening effect. Klimov was a cinematic enlightener with a penchant for elegy. Interestingly, his disrespect for the sacred cows of Soviet bureaucracy never challenged his deeply held belief in the legitimacy and historical mission of the Communist experiment and state.

Klimov joined the Communist Party in 1962. He was named Merited Artist of the RSFSR in 1976. In 1986, he was elected first secretary of the Soviet Filmmakers' Union, a position in which he oversaw the release of dozens of formerly shelved films and the rehabilitation of their makers. However, Klimov was unable to overcome the overt and covert resistance against the planned reforms within the apparatus of the State Cinema bureaucracy (Goskino); sadly, the liberating passions unleashed at the Fifth Congress of Soviet Filmmakers yielded no lasting, constructive transformations, and the hostilities and ensuing disintegration of Soviet cinema as a whole contributed to his ultimate disillusionment. In 1988, Klimov was succeeded by his deputy, **Andrei Smirnov**.

Klimov's brother, German Klimov, is a screenwriter and filmmaker specializing in sports; the two coauthored several scripts.

KOL'TSATYI [sometimes credited as Kal'tsatyi]**, ARKADII NIKO-LAEVICH** [Abram Kopelevich] (b. 14 September 1905, Odessa–?). Russian cinematographer and director. Kol'tsatyi studied at the department of cinematography of the Leningrad Film and Photo College (*kinofototekhnikum*), graduating in 1927. He then joined the staff of Belgoskino (later **Belarusfilm Studio**) as an assistant cameraman.

Kol'tsatyi gave his debut as cinematographer with the documentary *Conquered Soil* (Zavoevannaia zemlia, 1930), directed by **Vladimir Vainshtok**, about the problem of swamp drainage in Belarus. The film's distinct visual style, with extreme angles and expressive montage, betrays avant-garde influences and drew critical attention. A seminal achievement was Kol'tsatyi's camera work in **Aleksandr Faintsimmer**'s anti-tsarist satire *Lieutenant Kizhe* (aka *The Czar Wants to Sleep*/Poruchik Kizhe, 1934). The cinematography in Vainshtok's adventure hit *The Children of Captain Grant* (Deti kapitana Granta, 1936) marked a turn toward a more conventional, albeit atmospherically authentic approach.

Kol'tsatyi became famous for his contribution to **Fridrikh Ermler**'s ultra-Stalinist pamphlet *The Great Citizen* (Velikii grazhdanin, 1937–1939) in which the penetrating spirit of paranoia and distrust was supported by eerily dramatic lighting and slow, smooth tracking shots. He was also responsible for the cinematography in Ermler's World War II epic *The Great Turning Point* (Velikii perelom, 1945) and the antigenetics diatribe *The Great Force* (Velikaia sila, 1949), both of which won him Stalin Prizes (in 1946 and 1951, respectively). Another prestige project, **Ihor' Savchenko**'s biopic *Taras Shevchenko* (1951, Stalin Prize 1952), stands out for its exquisite usage of color.

Kol'tsatyi was adaptable to varying subject matter and directorial approaches; among the filmmakers he worked with were **Vladimir Korsh-Sablin**, **Iulii Raizman**, and **Iosif Kheifits**. His atmospheric cityscapes and psychologically penetrating character portraits won particular praise. Kol'tsatyi demonstrated a talent for effective lighting in musical **comedies** such as **Aleksandr Ivanovskii**'s *Anton Ivanovich Is Angry* (aka *Spring Song*/Anton Ivanovich serditsia, 1941) and **El'dar Riazanov**'s *Carnival Night* (Karnaval'naia noch', 1956). His penultimate work as cinematographer was **Igor' Il'inskii**'s *An Old Acquaintance* (Staryi znakomyi, 1969), a sequel to *Carnival Night*, which he also codirected.

In 1963, Kol'tsatyi made his debut as director with *The Little House in the Dunes* (Domik v diunakh, codirected with A. Markelov). His

Civil War adventure *The Mysterious Monk* (Tainstvennyi monakh, 1968) became a box-office hit.

Kol'tsatyi received the title Merited Artist of the Belorussian SSR in 1935 and Merited Artist of the RSFSR in 1969. In the mid-1970s, he immigrated to the United States, a step that resulted in the deletion of his name from all Soviet publications. He celebrated his 90th birthday in New York in 1995; his further whereabouts could not be established.

Other films: (as cameraman) *The First Platoon* (Pershy uzvod/Pervyi vzvod, 1933); *Film Concert 1941* (aka *Leningrad Concert Hall*, aka *Russian Salad*, 1941); *The Train Goes Eastward* (Poezd idet na vostok, 1947); *The Hottest Month* (Samyi zharkii mesiats, 1974); (as director) *No and Yes* (Net i da, 1966).

KOMAROV, SERGEI PETROVICH [real name: Lavrent'ev] (b. 2 March [other sources: 17 April] 1891, Moscow–d. 23 December 1957, Leningrad). Russian actor, director, and screenwriter. Komarov received a military education, graduating in 1913, and served in World War I. **Lev Kuleshov** was his teacher at the State Film School (Goskinoshkola) in 1921–1923.

As an actor, Komarov made his debut in **Vladimir Gardin**'s *agitka* *Hammer and Sickle* (Serp i molot, 1921). He portrayed the one-eyed crook in Kuleshov's successful slapstick experiment, *The Unusual Adventures of Mr. West in the Land of the Bolsheviks* (Neobychainye prikliucheniia mistera Vesta v strane bol'shevikov, 1924). A psychologically more refined performance was the role of Hans in *By the Law* (Po zakonu, aka *Expiation*, aka *Dura Lex*, 1926). Unlike other members of the group, Komarov remained loyal to the master even when Kuleshov fell from grace in the late 1920s. He played episodic parts in almost all of Kuleshov's projects, including the lesser known sound films *Horizon* (aka *Horizon: The Wandering Jew*/Gorizont, 1932), *The Siberians* (Sibiriaki, 1940), and *We Are from the Urals* (My s Urala, 1944). Komarov was also cast in films by other former Kuleshov group members, including **Boris Barnet**'s *Miss Mend* (1926, codirected with **Fedor Otsep**) and *The Outskirts* (aka *Patriots*/Okraina, 1933), as well as **Vsevolod Pudovkin**'s *The End of St. Petersburg* (Konets Sankt Peterburga, 1927) and *Minin and Pozharsky* (Minin i Pozharskii, 1939).

Komarov's debut as director was the inventive **comedy** *The Kiss of Mary Pickford* (Potselui Meri Pikford, 1927), built around the actual visit of Mary Pickford and Douglas Fairbanks to the Soviet Union. His second—and last—film was the action comedy *The Doll with the Millions* (Kukla s millionami, 1928).

In the 1930s–1950s, Komarov played numerous episodic roles, for example, in **Aleksandr Dovzhenko**'s revolutionary adventure *Shchors* (1939), **Erast Garin**'s Mark Twain adaptation *The Prince and the Pauper* (Prints i nishchii, 1943), **Leonid Lukov**'s anti-Nazi resistance saga *It Happened in the Donbass* (Eto bylo v Donbasse, 1946), **Sergei Gerasimov**'s partisan tragedy *The Young Guard* (Molodaia gvardiia, 1948), and **Samson Samsonov**'s *The Grasshopper* (Poprygun'ia, 1955) from Anton Chekhov's short story. Noteworthy is his performance in the lead role, the scientist Sedykh, in Vasilii Zhuravlev's *Cosmic Journey* (Kosmicheskii reis, 1935), the first Soviet science fiction film.

Komarov, who taught acting at the Soviet State Film School **VGIK** and served as the dean of the Acting Department in 1923–1934, was named Merited Artist of the RSFSR in 1935.

Other films: *The Salamander* (Salamandra, 1928); *Marionettes* (Marionetki, 1934); *By the Bluest of Seas* (U samogo sinego moria, 1936); *The Secret of Two Oceans* (Taina dvukh okeanov, 1956).

KOPALIN, IL'IA PETROVICH (b. 2 August 1900, village Pavlovskaia, Moscow district–d. 12 June 1976, Moscow). Russian **documentary** director and cinematographer. Kopalin began to work under **Dziga Vertov** as a "film scout" (*kinorazvedchik*) in 1925. A member of Vertov's Cine-Eye group (*kinoki*), he codirected the city portrait *Moscow* (Moskva, 1927) with Mikhail Kaufman. In 1927, he directed his first documentaries independently: *A Celebration of Millions* (Prazdnik millionov) and *To the Memory of a Leader* (Pamiati vozhdia).

Kopalin specialized in openly propagandistic films with lyrical elements and pathos-filled comments, spreading the word of the Communist Party on collectivization (*For the Harvest*/Za urozhai, 1929), Vladimir Lenin's leadership (*Along the Path of Lenin*/Po Leninskomu puti, 1929–1937), the Civil War in Spain (*On the Events in Spain*/O sobytiiakh v Ispanii, 1936–1937), and the military clashes in the Far East (*Halchin-Gol*/Khalkhin-Gol, 1939). In 1931, he made his first sound film, *One of Many/The Village* (Odin iz mnogikh/Derevnia), a not altogether successful attempt to apply the new sound-recording technology live.

In 1941, Kopalin received his first Stalin Prize for *On the Danube* (Na Dunae), cementing his reputation of one of the most trusted documentary filmmakers of the Soviet establishment. He served demagogical fare such as *Toward the Sun* (Navstrechu solntsu, 1940), which celebrates the forced incorporation of Latvia into the USSR. During the Great Patriotic War, Kopalin was in charge of front cameramen units; from footage filmed during three months from late 1941 to January 1942, he compiled one of the most important war documentaries, *The Defeat of the German Troops near Moscow* (Razgrom nemetskikh voisk pod Moskvoi, 1942, codirected with Leonid Varlamov [1907–1962]). It won him a second Stalin Prize and, released in the United States under the title *Moscow Strikes Back*, an Academy Award for Best Documentary in 1943. Kopalin's efforts were rewarded with four more Stalin Prizes: for *Liberated Czechoslovakia* (Osvobozhdennaia Chekhoslovakiia, 1946), *A Day in the Victorious Country* (Den' pobedivshei strany, 1947), *The New Albania* (Novaia Albaniia, 1948), and *Rejuvenation of the Soil* (Obnovlenie zemli, 1951). Kopalin sometimes incorporated archival footage, for example, in the seminal *Unforgettable Years* (Nezabyvaemye gody, 1957). Recognized as one of the leading Soviet documentary filmmakers, he was put in charge of prestige projects such as *The First Sojourn to the Stars* (Pervyi reis k zvezdam, 1961, codirected with Dmitrii Bogolepov and G. Kosenko) about Iurii Gagarin's space mission, and *Country of Mine* (Strana moia, 1967), a feature-length, wide-screen production dedicated to the 50th anniversary of the establishment of Soviet power.

In 1950, Kopalin began to teach at the Soviet State Film School **VGIK**, where he was promoted to full professor in 1964. Kopalin joined the Communist Party in 1940. He was named People's Artist of the RSFSR in 1960 and of the USSR in 1968.

Other films: *Renewed Labor* (Obnovlennyi trud, 1930); *Lenin* (1937, codirected with Irina Setkina-Nesterova); *Warsaw Encounters*

(Varshavskie vstrechi, 1955); *A City with a Great Destiny* (Gorod bol'shoi sud'by, 1961); *Pages of Immortality* (Stranitsy bessmertiia, 1965).

KORSH-SABLIN [real name: Sablin], **VLADIMIR VLADIMIROV-ICH** [in Belarusian: Uladzimir Uladzimiravich] (b. 29 March 1900, Moscow–d. 6 July 1974). Belarusian director, actor, and film administrator. Korsh-Sablin was the grandson of famous Russian theater entrepreneur Fedor Korsh (1852–1925). In 1917, after finishing high school, he began to work as a stage actor in Simferopol', Melitopol', and Kazan'. He appeared in supporting roles—and worked as director **Iurii Tarich**'s assistant—in the pictures *Wings of a Serf* (Kryl'ia kholopa, 1926), *Forest Legend* (Liasnaia byl/Lesnaia byl', 1927), *Bulat Batyr* (1928), and *Until Tomorrow* (Do zavtra, 1929). During the Great Patriotic War, Korsh-Sablin and Tarich cooperated once again, codirecting *Belarusian Novellas* (Belorusskie novelly, aka Belorusskii kinosbornik 1942).

Korsh-Sablin made his directorial debut at Belgoskino (later: **Belarusfilm Studio**) in 1930 with the silent epic *Born in the Fire* (U ahni narodzhanaia/V ogne rozhdennaia, aka *The Giant*/Velikan), an attempt to poetically visualize the national history of Belarus from the mythological past to the Bolshevik Revolution. He was assigned an *agitfilm* supporting the official collectivization campaign; however, *The Sun Expedition* (Solnechnyi pokhod, 1931) was declared a failure even by well-wishing critics due to its crude sociological characterizations. Korsh-Sablin turned in a convincingly realistic World War I picture, *The First Platoon* (Pershy uzvod/Pervyi vzvod, 1933), the first Belarusian sound film. *Golden Lights* (Zalatye ahni/Zolotye ogni, 1934) describes the construction of a hydroelectric power station in the Belarusian wilderness, betraying Stalinist paranoia in its treatment of foreign specialists.

Korsh-Sablin's next film is his best known in the West, the **comedy** *Seekers of Happiness* (aka *Birobidjan, A Greater Promise*/Shukal'niki shchascia/Iskateli schast'ia, 1935). This touching story of a Jewish family emigrating in 1934 from Eastern Europe to the Soviet Union and settling in the newly founded Autonomous Region of Birobidzhan in Siberia enjoyed lasting popularity at home and abroad. Another comedy, the superhit *My Love* (Moia liubov', 1940), was a

Soviet-style remake of the popular Franziska Gaál' adoption tale *Little Mother* (Kleine Mutti, 1934); **Isaak Dunaevskii** wrote memorable scores for this and several other of Korsh-Sablin's pictures.

The only time Korsh-Sablin was exposed to harsh criticism during his long career was in 1946 for the comedy *A New House* (Novyi dom, 1946) about two collective farms competing with each other. Although entirely in accordance with official guidelines, the disparity between postwar reality and the shamelessly idyllic on-screen living conditions was so blatant that both audiences and Party officials protested. Korsh-Sablin restored his reputation with the partisan thriller *Konstantin Zaslonov* (aka *The Secret Brigade*/Kanstancin Zaslonau, 1949, codirected with **Aleksandr Faintsimmer**), which won him a Stalin Prize in 1949. In later years, he alternated comedies such as *He Who Laughs Last* (Kto smeetsia poslednim, 1955) with pseudo-historical drama such as *Red Leaves* (Krasnye list'ia, 1958) about the mid-1930s struggle to Sovietize western Belarus. Korsh-Sablin's last film was the revolutionary epic *Downfall of an Empire* (Krushenie imperii, 1970) from the novel by Mikhail Kozakov.

The directorial output of Korsh-Sablin, who is considered one of the founders of **Belarusian cinema**, presents a motley picture. Opportunistic in all political aspects, his films followed the major trends of Soviet mainstream cinema yet also featured entertaining, populist elements—humorous plot turns and attractive props—craved by joy-starved audiences. Korsh-Sablin held leading positions in the Belarusian film industry; among others, he was the artistic director of Belarusfilm Studio in 1945–1960 and 1969–1974. He joined the Communist Party in 1948 and was named People's Artist of the USSR in 1969.

Other films: *Years of Fire* (Vohnennyia hady/Ognennye gody, 1939); *The Nightingales Are Singing* (Poiut zhavoronki, 1953); *First Trials* (Pervye ispytaniia, 1961).

KOSHEVEROVA, NADEZHDA NIKOLAEVNA (b. 23 September 1902, St. Petersburg–d. 22 February 1989, Leningrad). Russian director and screenwriter. Kosheverova graduated from the acting school affiliated with the Petrograd theater Free Comedy in 1923 and worked as an actress in various Leningrad theaters until 1927. Beginning in 1929, she was on the staff of **Lenfilm Studio** as an assistant to **Vladimir Vainshtok** on *Glory of the World* (Slava mira, 1932) and to **Leonid Trauberg** and **Grigorii Kozintsev** on *New Babylon* (Novyi Vavilon, 1929) and the famous *Maksim Trilogy* (1934–1938). Even when Kosheverova had become an established director in her own right, she sometimes served as a so-called second director, for example, on Kozintsev's *Belinskii* (1951).

Kosheverova's directorial debut, the dramatic **comedy** *Arinka* (1939, codirected with I. Muzikant), was an immediate blockbuster. The simple story of a young woman who works as a railway switchman and manages to disarm saboteurs in order to prevent a train wreck was based on a case touted by Soviet newspapers. *Cherevichki*, shot during evacuation in Alma-Ata (1944, with Mikhail Shapiro [1908–1971]) and based on Petr Chaikovskii's rarely played opera, was Kosheverova's first attempt to combine comedy with elements of fantasy.

The film for which the director is still widely remembered is *Cinderella* (Zolushka, 1947, with Shapiro). Although a bit mawkish for today's tastes, it provided to millions of viewers those brief moments of warmth and comfort that were in short supply in an exhausted postwar Soviet Union. Like many of Kosheverova's fairy-tale films, the script for *Cinderella* was written by famed playwright Evgenii Shvarts (1896–1958) whose trademark was the adaptation and modernization of tales by Charles Perrault, Hans Christian Andersen, and folktales. Among Kosheverova's other efforts in this genre are the parable *Kain XVIII* (aka *Two friends*/Dva druga, 1963, with Shapiro), *An Old, Old Tale* (Staraia, staraia skazka, 1968), *The Shadow* (Ten', 1972), and *Tsarevich Proshka* (1977).

One of Kosheverova's best films is the adventurous comedy *Tiger Girl* (Ukrotitel'nitsa tigrov, 1955, codirected with **Aleksandr Ivanovskii**), a box-office hit that she tried to repeat—alas, with less success—in *Today We Have a New Attraction* (Segodnia—novyi attraktsion, 1966). However, the success of *Tiger Girl* was toppled by a delightful comedy that sadly became the most disdained by highbrow critics: *Watch Out, Grandma!* (Ostorozhno, babushka! 1960)—for years, it was cited as an example of thoughtless entertainment, unworthy of Soviet cinema. Kosheverova's last film, *The Tale of a Painter in Love* (Skazka pro vliublennogo maliara), completed at the age of 85, shows this extraordinary woman's sturdiness and undying love for filmmaking.

Among the typical features of Kosheverova's comedies and fairy tales are their kind—rarely satirical—humor, numerous songs, and usually harmless plots with an explicit moral. Kosheverova's cinematic style is sometimes irritatingly theatrical in shot composition and decorations.

Kosheverova was married to cinematographer **Andrei Moskvin**. She was awarded the title Merited Artist of the Russian Federation in 1966.

Other films: *Galia* (1940); *How Ivan the Fool Searched for a Miracle* (Kak Ivanushka-durachok za chudom khodil, 1976); *And There Comes Bumbo . . .* (I vot prishel Bumbo, 1984).

KOSMATOV, LEONID VASIL'EVICH (b. 13 January 1901, Penza–d. 2 August 1977, Moscow). Russian cinematographer and pedagogue. Kosmatov worked as a projectionist in the Russian provinces before enrolling in the Soviet State Film College (GTK, later **VGIK**) where he studied under **Aleksandr Levitskii**, graduating in 1927.

Kosmatov's fame rests on his work for three directors: **Iulii Raizman**, **Grigorii Roshal'**, and **Mikheil Chiaureli**. His partnership with Raizman started with the anti–New Economic Policy (NEP) melodrama *The Circle*—Kosmatov's debut as cinematographer—and continued with the historical drama *Penal Colony* (Katorga, 1928), the semi**documentary** *The Earth Is Thirsty* (Zemlia zhazhdet, 1930) about the Communist transformation of Turkmenistan, the Mikhail Sholokhov adaptation *Virgin Soil Upturned* (Podniataia tselina, 1940), and the aviation melodrama *The Pilots* (aka *Men on Wings/Letchiki*, 1935), combining pathos-filled, declamatory compositions with psychologically nuanced episodes.

For Roshal', Kosmatov shot historical films such as *The Dawn of Paris* (Zori Parizha, 1936), the antifascist drama *The Oppenheim Family* (Sem'ia Oppengeim, 1938), and large-scale literary adaptations, including the trilogy *Calvary* (1957–1959) from the Aleksei Tolstoi epic, all of which are characterized by authentic historical atmosphere.

Kosmatov mostly is remembered for his work with Chiaureli, for whom he created grandiose *tableaux vivants* in infamous Stalin cult superproductions: *The Vow* (Pitsi/Kliatva, 1946), which earned him his first Stalin Prize, *The Fall of Berlin* (Padenie Berlina, 1949, Stalin Prize 1950), and *The Unforgettable Year 1919* (Nezabyvaemyi 1919 god, 1952). A number of images in these films have become synonymous with totalitarian style, combining brazen glorification of the leader, rhetorical megalomania, and blatant falsification of historical facts.

Kosmatov proved his unique grasp of the aesthetics of color on **Aleksandr Dovzhenko**'s *Michurin* (1948, with Iulii Kun)—rewarded with a 1949 Stalin Prize—where the emphasis on certain colors is given conceptual significance, especially in nature scenes. Brutally intense colors are characteristic of *The Fall of Berlin*, reminiscent of the monumental painting style typical of Stalinist art.

Kosmatov gained a reputation as one of the most technically creative Soviet cameramen who held a number of patents—for example, on rendering combined shots—and used color spotlights, rear projection, and self-constructed devices for tracking and aerial shots; he also was among the pioneers introducing the wide-screen format in the USSR. Hailed by **Sergei Eizenshtein** as one of the finest Soviet cinematographers, Kosmatov's style is characterized by rich, baroque compositions inspired by 19th-century Russian realist art. At times, however, he indulged in static, canvaslike shots with an air of representative officialdom, carefully avoiding extreme points of view while striving to achieve majestic grandeur and pathos.

Kosmatov joined the Communist Party in 1941. He was named Merited Artist of the Russian Federation in 1944. Beginning in 1929, he worked as a valued pedagogue at the Soviet State Film School **VGIK**, shaping generations of Soviet cameramen.

Other films: *The Circle: Duty and Love* (Krug. Dolg i liubov', 1927); *People of Baku* (Bakintsy, 1938); *Court of Madmen* (Sud sumasshedshikh, 1962); *They Live Next to Us* (Oni zhivut riadom, 1968).

KOTENOCHKIN, VIACHESLAV MIKHAILOVICH (b. 20 June 1927, Moscow–d. 20 November 2000, Moscow). Russian **animation** director, scriptwriter, and animator. After attending an artillery school during the Great Patriotic War, Kotenochkin studied at the art school affiliated with Soiuzmultfilm studio in Moscow, graduating with a diploma as animator in 1947. Over the next 15 years, he became one of the most prolific artists in Soviet drawn animation, contributing to more than 80 pictures by various directors.

In 1962, Kotenochkin began to direct his own pictures, which are distinguished by fast-paced action and untamed humor, including *We Are Such Masters* (My takie mastera, 1963) and *Traces on the Asphalt* (Sledy na asfal'te, 1963). He also made *The Traveling Frog* (Liagushka-puteshestvennitsa, 1965), adapted from Vladimir Garshin's fairy tale.

In 1969, Kotenochkin was carried to unprecedented heights of success with a series of shorts about a little hare chased by a wolf, *Just Wait!* (Nu, pogodi!). The series became a cultural phenomenon, with each new installment being eagerly awaited by millions of viewers. Altogether, Kotenochkin directed 18 *Just Wait!* films, the last one being released in 1993. The series' unrivaled popularity acquired a dynamic of its own, necessitating sequel after sequel, not all of which could match the charm and originality of the initial four parts. Later episodes rely more heavily on superficial physical humor without paying as much attention to the amusing psychological and social characterizations of earlier films. Interestingly, many children found the antisocial, smoking, and drinking wolf—speaking with **Anatolii Papanov**'s unmistakable bass—more loveable than the half-naïve, half-mean hare whose high-pitched voice was provided by Klara Rumianova (1929–2004), perhaps because the formula of victorious virtue vs. ever-losing vice invited compassion with the dumb underdog.

On rare occasions, Kotenochkin produced political fare such as the pioneer saga *Song of the Young Drummer* (Pesnia o iunom barabanshchike, 1972), but his specialty remained clever, good-natured entertainment for kids, a field in which he was unsurpassed.

Kotenochkin was awarded the title People's Artist of the Russian Federation in 1987; in 1988, he won a USSR State Prize. His son Aleksei Kotenochkin (b. 1958) works as an animator.

Other films: *The Boundary* (Mezha, 1966); *Who'll Win the Prize?* (Kto poluchit priz? 1980); *The Old Record* (Staraia plastinka, 1982); *A Kitten from Liziukov Street* (Kotenok s ulitsy Liziukova, 1988).

KOVAL'-SAMBORSKII, IVAN IVANOVICH (b. 16 September 1893, Moscow–d. 10 January 1962, Moscow). Russian actor. In

1922–1923, Koval'-Samborskii was a member of the troupe of Vsevolod Meierkhol'd's theater in Moscow. He made his film debut in the role of worker Andrei in **Iakov Protazanov**'s pro-Soviet *His Call* (Ego prizyv, 1925) and played episodic parts in **Vsevolod Pudovkin**'s *Chess Fever* (Shakhmatnaia goriachka, 1925) and *The Mother* (Mat', 1926). The male lead of romantic White Army officer Govorukha-Otrok in Protazanov's *Forty-first* (Sorok-pervyi, 1927) shot Koval'Samborskii to national stardom. He landed another hit with **Boris Barnet**'s lottery comedy *The Girl with the Hatbox* (Devushka s korobkoi, 1927) and solidified his fame with Protazanov's social melodrama *The Man from the Restaurant* (Chelovek iz restorana, 1927) and **Fedor Otsep**'s *Soil in Chains* (aka *The Yellow Pass*/Zemlia v plenu, 1927).

As one of the leading stars of the Soviet-German company **Mezhrabpomfilm**, Koval'-Samborskii was given permission to work abroad beginning in the fall of 1927. He appeared in numerous movies, including trivial **comedies** and pseudohistorical adventures, and also acted on stage. After the Nazis seized power in 1933, Koval'-Samborskii returned to the USSR, where he initially continued his career almost seamlessly. Among his many roles, the dashing, self-confident pilot Beliaev in **Iulii Raizman**'s *The Pilots* (Letchiki, 1935) deserves special mentioning. The actor also appeared in **Vladimir Korsh-Sablin**'s contemporary drama about a village teacher, *Daughter of the Homeland* (Doch' rodiny, 1937), and as Walter in **Aleksandr Macheret**'s antifascist pamphlet *The Moor Soldiers* (Bolotnye soldaty, 1938). In 1938, Koval'-Samborskii was arrested and exiled to Central Asia with permission to work in local theaters.

After his rehabilitation and return to Moscow in the mid-1950s, he was cast in supporting roles in Raizman's *A Communist* (Kommunist, 1957), **Grigorii Roshal'**'s *1918* (1958), and Barnet's *Annushka* (1959).

Koval'-Samborskii was named Merited Artist of the Kyrgyz SSR in 1944.

Other films: *Enemies* (Vragi, 1925); *Miss Mend* (1926); *Song of the Don Cossacks* (Das Donkosakenlied, 1930); *Three from the Same Street* (Troe s odnoi ulitsy, 1936); *The Gutta-percha Boy* (Guttaperchevyi mal'chik, 1957); *Catchers of Beasts* (Zverolovy, 1959).

KOZINTSEV, GRIGORII MIKHAILOVICH (b. 22 March 1905, Kiev–d. 11 May 1973, Leningrad). Russian director, screenwriter, film theoretician, and pedagogue. In his youth Kozintsev was close friends with **Sergei Iutkevich** and **Aleksei Kapler**; together they organized a short-lived experimental high school theater, Harlequin (Arlekin). For famous theater innovator Kote Mardjanishvili, Kozintsev worked as an assistant stage designer at the Solovtsov Theater in Kiev in 1919. In 1919–1920, he studied painting (among others, with Aleksandra Ekster) at the Kiev School for Fine Arts, and in 1920–1922, at the Petrograd Academy of Arts.

Of Kozintsev's early undertakings, the Factory of the Eccentric Actor (FEKS), which was cofounded with **Leonid Trauberg** and lasted from 1921 to 1932, is the best remembered today, mainly for its methodological daring and because so many famous actors and directors were shaped by it: **Sergei Gerasimov**, **Oleg Zhakov**, **Sergei Martinson**, **Ianina Zheimo**, **Elena Kuz'mina**, and Andrei Kostrichkin (1901–1973), among others. Iconoclastic, clownish, and provocative to the point of unabashed aesthetic hooliganism, Kozintsev and his group aimed at overcoming the class-based hierarchy within traditional culture, inserting modern elements into performances of canonical texts. Thus, they gave a production of Nikolai Gogol''s *The Wedding* the subtitle "The Electrification of Gogol'." Even though FEKS appeared ultraleftist in its themes and slogans, the underlying aesthetic concept was in essence escapist and elitist. Kozintsev gained inspiration not so much from Soviet reality as from Tatlin's utopian constructions, Maiakovskii's staccato verses, and Vsevolod Meierkhol'd's circuslike stage productions, embracing American industrial civilization and particularly its cinema with demonstrative passion.

The "Feksy" (i.e., members of FEKS) took their theatrical avant-gardism to the movies by joining Sevzapkino (later: **Lenfilm Studio**) in 1924, on invitation of critic, scriptwriter, and administrator Adrian Piotrovskii and studio manager **Fridrikh Ermler**. In close teamwork with Trauberg, Kozintsev directed a number of highly ambitious pictures, starting with the shorts *The Adventures of Oktiabrina* (Pokhozhdeniia Oktiabriny, 1924), about a Komsomol building manager fighting homegrown and foreign bourgeois, and *Mishkas against*

Iudenich (Mishki protiv Iudenicha, 1925) about a Bolshevik reporter in the Civil War.

Kozintsev and Trauberg's first full-length feature, the thriller *Devil's Wheel* (Chertovo koleso, 1926), reflects contemporary urban problems—crime, prostitution, black marketeers—in a manner both grotesque and didactic, describing the implementation of the new Communist morality. *The Overcoat* (Shinel', 1926) is a peculiar, stylistically groundbreaking adaptation of Nikolai Gogol''s novella, the latter being a preferred object of interpretation for scholars of the Formal School such as Iurii Tynianov (1894–1943) and Boris Eikhenbaum (1886–1959), who both took a special interest in cinema and in Kozintsev's work in particular. In short time, Kozintsev and Trauberg managed to mold a team of extraordinary creative personalities, among them cinematographer **Andrei Moskvin** and set designer **Evgenii Enei**, who gave the group's pictures their unusual visual quality.

The duo then turned to Russian history, reenacting an episode from the 1825 Decembrist upheaval in *S.V.D.—The Club of Great Deeds* (SVD—Soiuz velikikh del, 1927). But their genuine triumph during the silent period was *The New Babylon* (Novyi Vavilon, 1929), a grand-scale epic of heroism on the backdrop of the 1870–1871 Paris Commune. Creating a powerful allegorical dimension, the film's finale with its rainy gloom anticipates Kozintsev's Shakespeare adaptations four decades later.

Alone (Odna, 1931), a contemporary drama based on newspaper reports, was Kozintsev and Trauberg's first exercise in sound film, although it was initially shot as a silent. The story of a teacher who is sent to a remote Siberian village thematizes the violent enforcement of collective farms (kolkhoz) and schools for the farmers' children. The peasant community is shown as a threatening, backward entity plotting the central heroine's downfall, while the city and urban technology come to the rescue of the wounded pedagogue.

The staunchly pro-Communist spirit permeating *Alone* became the basis for Kozintsev and Trauberg's so-called ***Maksim Trilogy*** (Trilogiia o Maksime, 1934–1938), a work that catapulted them to the summit of leading Soviet directors. Structured like a novel of education, the *Maksim* films describe the human and political evolution of the title character, a likeable "guy next door" who steadily grows into a Bolshevik leader (the story evolves from 1910 to 1920). The Stalinist establishment particularly valued Maksim's mass appeal who comes across as a political wisecrack, fun-loving, playing the guitar, and singing—but never betraying his loyalty to the Communist Party. *Maksim's Youth* (Iunost' Maksima, 1935), *Maksim's Return* (Vozvrashchenie Maksima, 1937), and *The Vyborg District* (Vyborgskaia storona, 1938) were sensational box-office hits and made a superstar of their lead, **Boris Chirkov**.

After Kozintsev and Trauberg's success was crowned with a Stalin Prize in 1941, a period of thematic misjudgment and bureaucratic harassment commenced; Kozintsev later described it as "the unkind period" (*nedobryi period*). First, a biopic about Karl Marx that had been in preproduction for three years was suddenly stopped. While *An Occurrence at the Telegraph* (Sluchai na telegrafe, 1941), a short film joke about Napoleon sending a cable to Hitler discouraging him from attacking Russia, was released without delay, the following short, *Once at Night* (Odnazhdy noch'iu, 1942), part of the War Film Almanac *Our Girls* (Nashi devushki), was shelved, as was the satire *Young Fritz* (Iunyi Frits, 1943), which Kozintsev directed on his own (Trauberg's name appears erroneously in the credits). The most severe blow was dealt to *Rank-and-file People* (Prostye liudi, 1945), an attempt to visualize Soviet selflessness behind the front lines in harrowing images: people in Central Asia are ordered to erect an airplane factory in the desert, virtually working themselves to death. Sharply criticized for its "unrealistic depiction of Soviet life" and shelved until 1956, it also marked the breakup of the Kozintsev-Trauberg partnership.

In the postwar period, infamous for the minuscule number of movies produced (*malokartin'e*), Kozintsev was commissioned to make two biographical pictures in response to the Stalinist establishment's demand for renewed pride in Russia's achievements of the past. *Pirogov* (1947) deals with a famed surgeon (1810–1881); however, the portrait had to be embellished to an absurd degree, excluding any unappealing features such as Pirogov's well-known bad temper and carelessness in hygienic matters. With *Belinskii* (1951), a biopic about the radical 19th-century literary critic, Kozintsev experienced even more administrative intrusion that turned the production into a torturous process and almost paralyzed the director for good.

The traumatic experiences of the 1940s caused Kozintsev to concentrate on theater projects, simultaneously fighting for the realization of high-brow literary adaptations in cinema. The three pictures that he completed in the last 15 years of his life were accompanied by scholarly research for which Kozintsev found outlets in books and essays. While the Soviet establishment was urging him to create films along the lines of the popular *Maksim* trilogy, Kozintsev, as if to atone for his 1930s flirtations with Stalinism, stubbornly refused and ultimately scored huge critical and popular successes with *Don Quijote* (Don Kikhot, 1957), *Hamlet* (Gamlet, 1964), and *King Lear* (Korol' Lir, 1970). The Cervantes adaptation is distinguished by its exemplary usage of color to create barren landscapes and tense interiors; the two Shakespeare films are kept in gloomy black-and-white. Noteworthy is the director's increasingly tragic worldview: if *Don Quijote* contains some optimistic elements associated with the simple folks who love and protect their utopian idol, *Hamlet* displays a disturbing psychological ambiguity and ethical skepticism, while *King Lear* ends in complete bleakness.

Kozintsev's true utopia was always the realm of human culture, an empire of books and paintings, schools and theaters, juxtaposed to the wilderness of tsarist tyranny, patriarchal peasantry, fascist barbarism, or raw, unrefined nature. The fundamental compromise with the Soviet system that lies at the heart of his entire oeuvre was legitimized by Vladimir Lenin's traditionalist concept of culture that happened to be largely congruent with the filmmaker's own, formed after his avant-garde youth. Indeed, the acceptance and celebration of Kozintsev's films by Soviet officialdom can only be understood with this congruence in mind.

Kozintsev was named People's Artist of the USSR in 1964; he won a Lenin Prize for *Hamlet* in 1965. From 1941 to 1964, he held a professorship at the Soviet State Film School **VGIK** and taught at Lenfilm Studio in 1965–1971. He was married to actress Sof'ia Magarill (1900–1943), who was cast in many of his silent films.

Other films: *Little Brother* (Bratishka, 1927); *Someone Else's Jacket* (Chuzhoi pidzhak, 1927, unreleased); *A Great Heart* (Bol'shoe serdtse, 1952, unfinished).

KRAVCHENKO, GALINA SERGEEVNA (b. 11 February 1905, Kazan'–d. 5 March 1996, Moscow). Russian actress. Kravchenko graduated from the college of the Bolshoi Theater in 1922 and worked as a ballet soloist in the Zimin Theater. She then studied at the State Film College (GTK, Gosudarstvennyi tekhnikum kinematografii, later **VGIK**) in Moscow, graduating in 1927.

Kravchenko made her movie debut in **Aleksandr Razumnyi**'s pro-Bolshevik action **comedy** *The Gang of Father Knysh* (Banda bat'ki Knysha, 1924). She was cast in a supporting role in **Iakov Protazanov**'s *Aelita* (1924), portrayed a film actress in **Iurii Zheliabuzhskii**'s contemporary comedy *The Cigarette Girl from Mossel'prom* (Papirosnitsa ot Mossel'proma, 1924), Vanda in **Iurii Tarich**'s *Forest Tale* (Liasnaia byl/Lesnaia byl'), as well as Blanche in **Sergei Komarov**'s *Puppet with Millions* (Kukla s millionami, 1928). Kravchenko's unusual, exotic beauty and her superb, ballet-trained body language made her one of the most celebrated stars of the company **Mezhrabpomfilm**, but also led to her being typecast in roles of mysterious, often foreign women such as Jeanne de Guelle, the love interest of poet Mikhail Lermontov, in **Aleksandr Ivanovskii**'s exploitational biopic *Prisoner of the Caucasus* (Kavkazskii plennik, 1930).

Lev Kuleshov cast Kravchenko as a femme fatale, the morally dubious dancer Brio who sells her love, in the Civil War espionage thriller *The Cheerful Canary* (Veselaia kanareika, 1929), and as Annabel Adams in his O. Henry adaptation *The Great Consoler* (Velikii uteshitel', 1933). In the 1950s–1970s, Kravchenko appeared in small episodic parts such as Plekhanov's wife in **Leonid Lukov**'s *Two Lives* (Dve zhizni, 1960), but was unable to regain her earlier star status. According to some sources, the long hiatus in her film career from 1941 to 1956 may have been caused by her marriage to the son of the purged Bolshevik hack Lev Kamenev.

Kravchenko was named Merited Artist of the RSFSR in 1980.

Other films: *In the Heat of NEP* (V ugare NEPA, 1925); *The Bear's Wedding* (Medvezh'ia svad'ba, 1926); *The Path of the Vessel* (Shlia karablia/Put' korablia, 1935); *Suvorov* (1941); *War and Peace* (Voina i mir, 1967); *Anna Pavlova* (aka *The Divine Anna*, 1983).

KRIUCHKOV, NIKOLAI AFANAS'EVICH (b. 6 January 1911, Moscow–d. 13 April 1994, Moscow). Russian actor. Originally an engraver, Kriuchkov began acting on stage in 1927 and joined the troupe of the Central Workers' Youth Theater (TRAM) the following year.

Boris Barnet cast Kriuchkov as the cobbler Sen'ka in *The Outskirts* (Okraina, 1933). Due to his natural screen presence and rough, workmanlike charm, Kriuchkov soon became a familiar face in important pictures of the leading Soviet directors. Thus, he appeared in **Grigorii Kozintsev** and **Leonid Trauberg**'s *Maksim Trilogy*, **Sergei Gerasimov**'s *Komsomol'sk* (aka *City of Youth*, aka *The Frozen North*, 1938), **Sergei Iutkevich**'s *Man with the Rifle* (Chelovek s ruzh'em, 1938), and **Ivan Pyr'ev**'s patriotic musical comedy *Tractor Drivers* (Traktoristy, 1939); the role of Klim Iarko in the latter won him a Stalin Prize in 1941.

Kriuchkov's ever-growing popularity lasted for half a century. During the Great Patriotic War, the ultra-Stalinist late 1940s, and the Thaw, he was one of the most trusted and loved actors of Soviet cinema who managed to turn a certain lack of psychological nuance to his advantage, portraying likeable "guys next door" who sang, danced, and played the accordion with uninhibited bravura. This image proved effective both in leading and supporting roles in quality mainstream pictures such as **Aleksandr Stolper**'s *A Lad from Our Town* (Paren' iz nashego goroda, 1942), **Vladimir Petrov**'s *Battle of Stalingrad* (Stalingradskaia bitva, 1949), and **Aleksandr Ptushko**'s *Sadko* (1952). A younger generation of filmmakers relied on Kriuchkov's portrayal of good-natured, rank-and-file Soviet men with humor and generosity, including **Grigorii Chukhrai** and **Andrei Smirnov**. Beginning in the 1950s, Kriuchkov made a noticeable effort to widen his artistic profile, accepting parts of negative characters that subverted his dominant screen image.

Kriuchkov was one of the most prolific Russian screen actors and appeared in more than 130 films. He became a member of the Communist Party in 1953, was named People's Artist of the USSR in 1965, and Hero of Socialist Labor in 1980.

Other films: *By the Bluest of Seas* (U samogo sinego moria, 1936); *Swineherd and Shepherd* (aka *They Met in Moscow*/Svinarka i pastukh, 1941); *Ballad of a Soldier* (Ballada o soldate, 1959); *Your Home Address* (Adres vashego doma, 1972); *Angels of Death* (Angely smerti, 1993).

KRIUKOV, NIKOLAI NIKOLAEVICH (b. 2 February 1908–d. 4 April 1961, Moscow). Russian composer. Kriukov studied at the

Moscow District Music College (*tekhnikum*), graduating in 1932. He made his debut as a film composer with the score for **Aleksandr Macheret**'s *Jobs and People* (aka *Men and Jobs*/Dela i liudi, 1932, with Vissarion Shebalin) about a U.S. specialist who participates in socialist construction in the USSR.

Kriukov then specialized in films about the 1917 Bolshevik Revolution, the 1918–1921 Civil War, and the Great Patriotic War. He developed a style that became normative for the officially favored genre of action-filled, patriotic, inspirational drama, dominated by marching rhythms, sudden dramatic eruptions, and sharp contrasts. Innovative was Kriukov's early cooperation with **Efim Dzigan** on *We Are from Kronshtadt* (My iz Kronshtadta, 1936), where director and composer strove toward a harmonious unity between natural sound elements (sea waves, cries of seagulls, etc.) and musical tunes (traditional revolutionary marches). Kriukov worked with many of the leading Soviet directors: **Iulii Raizman** on *Pilots* (Letchiki, 1935), **Mikhail Romm** on *Lenin in 1918* (Lenin v 1918 godu, 1939), **Aleksandr Stolper** on *Story of a Real Man* (Povest' o nastoiashchem cheloveke, 1948), and **Vsevolod Pudovkin** on *Admiral Nakhimov* (1946), most of which became part of the Socialist-Realist canon. The composer showed a softer, warmer side of his talent with the score for ***The Foundling*** (Podkidysh, 1939), a **comedy** whose leitmotiv structure oscillates between a melancholic longing for affection and cheerful optimism.

Although still maintaining the usual heroic, dramatic intonation, Kriukov applied it with greater differentiation to **Grigorii Chukhrai**'s *The Forty-first* (Sorok pervyi, 1956) and **Mikhail Kalatozov**'s *The Unmailed Letter* (Neotpravlennoe pis'mo, 1960). Similarly, in literary adaptations, Kriukov proved that he was capable of nuanced characterizations, including **Samson Samsonov**'s *The Grasshopper* (Poprygunia, 1955) from Anton Chekhov's story, and **Ivan Pyr'ev**'s *The Idiot* (Idiot, 1958) after Fedor Dostoevskii's novel. Also of lasting value is his music for the 1950 restored version of **Sergei Eizenshtein**'s ***Battleship Potemkin*** (Bronenosets Potemkin, 1925), which has been widely distributed internationally.

Kriukov, one of the most prolific Soviet film composers, received a Stalin Prize for his music to Pyr'ev's *The Tale of the Siberian Land* (aka *Symphony of Life*/Skazanie o zemle sibirskoi, 1946). In 1960, several newspapers launched charges of plagiarism against him. Kriukov's suicide, committed in broad daylight by throwing himself in front of a train at a Moscow station, caused considerable embarrassment for the cultural establishment.

Kriukov's brother was the composer and music critic Vladimir Kriukov (1902–1960).

Other films: *In Search of Joy* (V poiskakh radosti, 1940); *A Lad from Our Town* (Paren' iz nashego goroda, 1942); *Miles of Fire* (Ognennye versty, 1957); *Bread and Roses* (Khleb i rozy, 1960).

KTOROV [real name: Viktorov], **ANATOLII PETROVICH** (b. 24 April 1898, Moscow–d. 30 September 1980, Moscow). Russian actor. Ktorov studied in F. F. Komissarzhevskii's studio until 1919. He was a member of the troupe of Vera Komissarzhevskaia in 1917–1920 and of the Korsh Theater in 1920–1932. After the latter's closure, he joined the Moscow Art Theater (MKhAT) in 1933 where he excelled in classical and modern **comedies**.

As a film actor, Ktorov made his debut as the greedy, cruel émigré Zaglobin in **Iakov Protazanov**'s naïvely pro-Soviet *His Call* (Ego prizyv, 1925). Ktorov's screen image, defined by his tall, impressively controlled physique, was that of an elegant gentleman with dubious moral standards. He was particularly successful in the 1920s in Protazanov's satires *The Tailor from Torzhok* (Zakroishchik iz Torzhka, 1925) and the antibourgeois *The Three Million Case* (aka *Three Thieves*/Protsess o trekh millionakh, 1926), often in a duo with fellow comedian **Igor' Il'inskii**. Budding director **Iulii Raizman** capitalized on Ktorov's stardom in his court drama *The Circle: Duty and Love* (Krug. Dolg i liubov', 1927), casting him as a clichéd class enemy who flourishes during the New Economic Policy (NEP). Ktorov gained immense popularity with the role of the elegant fraud Michael Korkis in Protazanov's crude antireligious comedy *St. Jorgen's Holiday* (Prazdnik sviatogo Iorgena, 1930). His work for Protazanov continued into the sound period, when he gave a top performance as the deceptive landowner Paratov in the Aleksandr Ostrovskii adaptation *The Dowerless Bride* (aka *Without Dowry*/Bespridannitsa, 1936).

Thirty years later, Ktorov delivered an intense portrayal of the ascetic, emotionally restrained old Prince Bolkonskii in **Sergei**

Bondarchuk's monumental Lev Tolstoi adaptation *War and Peace* (Voina i mir, 1962–1967), one of the all-time acting highlights of Russian film history.

Ktorov won a Stalin Prize for his stage work in 1952 and was honored with the title People's Artist of the USSR in 1963. He is buried at Vvedenskoe cemetery in Moscow.

Other films: *Marionets* (Marionetki, 1934); *Ambassador of the Soviet Union* (Posol Sovetskogo Soiuza, 1969).

KULESHOV, LEV VLADIMIROVICH (b. 13 January 1899, Tambov–d. 29 March 1970, Moscow). Russian director, screenwriter, film theorist, and pedagogue. Kuleshov hailed from an impoverished gentry family; his father worked as a painter, his mother as a country teacher. He studied at the Moscow School for Painting, Sculpture and Architecture (MUZhVZ) in 1915–1916. In 1916, Kuleshov began his career in the movie industry as a set designer, assistant director, and occasional actor in **Aleksandr Khanzhonkov**'s company. He worked with **Evgenii Bauer**, beginning with the drama *Alarm* (Nabat, 1916), but also with lesser directors such as **Boris Chaikovskii** (*Miss Meri*, 1918). In Bauer's bohemian melodrama *Toward Happiness* (Za schast'em, 1917) Kuleshov was both responsible for the set design and played the part of the artist Enriko.

Kuleshov, imbued with an innate pioneering spirit, soon began to search for ways to awaken Russia's cinema from its trancelike, self-oblivious, decadent state. Especially the films of David Wark Griffith and Mack Sennett proved genuine revelations, for they made so much more use of cinema's specific properties—movement, rhythm, dynamics—than did their laggard Russian counterparts. As a matter of fact, no other Russian filmmaker embraced the style of American movies as openly as did Kuleshov, who unabashedly praised all aspects of it: fast evolving plotlines, abundance of action sequences with car chases, dynamic editing, and a reduction of the characters' psychological motivation to a bare minimum.

When the 1917 October Revolution drove almost the entire Russian film industry into exile and caused the demolition of studios and equipment, Kuleshov saw a chance to build a new cinema on the tabula rasa left behind. He enthusiastically lent his skills to the Bolsheviks, first reediting old and foreign films according to the

Communist dogma, then shooting newsreels of the 1918–1920 Civil War. Most importantly, Kuleshov gathered other young film buffs around him and organized a workshop intended to put his theoretical assumptions into practice. The so-called Kuleshov Collective at the State Film School (Goskinoshkola—later transformed into the Soviet State Film School **VGIK**) counted soon-to-be classic filmmakers such as **Vsevolod Pudovkin** and **Boris Barnet** among its members and focused on developing a new cinematic language that would adequately express the spirit of the turbulent times.

Emphasizing the physical over the psychological and radically separating film acting from stage acting, actors were expected to master a body language that included acrobatic skills. The editing of a film became the most profound creative act, enabling the filmmaker to determine viewpoint, narrative speed, and emotional impact on the audience. The so-called Kuleshov effect—the result of one shot combined with a number of others, each time producing a different semantic outcome in the mind of the viewer—was to demonstrate the superiority of editing over the intrinsic meaning of the individual shot; moreover, it was declared to be the foundation of an entire film grammar that formalized cinema's functioning principles. This basic film grammar became the point of departure for more sophisticated theories developed thereafter by **Sergei Eizenshtein** and others.

The first film in which Kuleshov applied his theories was the experimental thriller *The Project of Engineer Prite* (Proekt inzhenera Praita, 1918), based on a script by his brother Boris Kuleshov, who also played the lead. Many of its shots were two or three times shorter than was customary in Russia, which caused confusion and irritation among the director's coworkers but apparently did not diminish the enjoyment of regular audiences. After an unremarkable melodrama, *The Unfinished Song of Love* (Pesn' liubvi nedopetaia, 1918), and multiple projects within the Commissariat of Enlightenment, Kuleshov made the *agitka* At the Red Front (Na krasnom fronte, 1920), a simple triangle drama during the Polish-Soviet conflict. In essence, however, the film realized its maker's concept of so-called creative geography by blending fictitious and **documentary** sequences.

When Kuleshov finally got the long-awaited funds, he disguised his avant-garde principles in a satirical **comedy** that, under the baroque title *The Unusual Adventures of Mr. West in the Land of the Bolsheviks*

(Neobychainye prikliucheniia mistera Vesta v strane bol'shevikov, 1924), pleased crowds and made film history. The ideological weight of the story was kept light, effectively mocking common Western misconceptions of Soviet Russia. But the Kuleshov group—with **Aleksandra Khokhlova** (the director's wife), Pudovkin, Barnet, **Sergei Komarov**, Porfirii Podobed, **Vladimir Fogel'**, **Leonid Obolenskii**, and others—proved that their previous "film exercises without film" (due to a lack of film stock) were now paying off. However, Kuleshov's next picture, *The Ray of Death* (Luch smerti, 1925), a suspense story in which Western spies steal a Soviet invention later retrieved by workers, was viciously attacked by critics, who were neither amused nor convinced that the political theme was more than a pretext for a firework of brilliantly staged attractions.

Kuleshov responded with what would soon be seen as his unsurpassed silent masterpiece, *By the Law* (Po zakonu, aka *Expiation*, aka *Dura Lex*, 1926), the minimalist adaptation of a Jack London story that bravely turned its limited budget into cinematic advantage. The gold rush in the Yukon area serves as the framework within which a claustrophobic drama of guilt and retribution unfolds. None of Kuleshov's subsequent pictures could compare to its narrative elegance; indeed, the director failed with his attempt to satisfy critics and master Soviet reality in the contemporary romance *Your Acquaintance* (Vasha znakomaia, aka *Zhurnalistka*, 1927) about a young reporter falling in love with her boss. Here, Kuleshov's conviction that genre principles are universal and can be imposed on any subject matter proved disastrous. Similarly, *The Cheerful Canary* (Veselaia kanareika, 1929) and *Two-Buldi-Two* (Dva-Bul'di-dva), both re-creating adventurous Civil War episodes, were taken to task for being apolitical, ahistorical, petit-bourgeois in taste and, therefore, harmful. By the late 1920s, Soviet leftist dogmatists had chosen Kuleshov as one of their favorite whipping boys. Sadly, Kuleshov was eventually demoralized enough to not only recant but to denounce former colleagues as formalists "as proof of his sincere desire to reform" (Denise Youngblood).

Kuleshov's first sound feature film was *Horizon* (aka *The Wandering Jew*/Gorizont, 1932) about a Jewish émigré from tsarist Russia who is confronted with the horrors of American life and returns to a blooming Soviet Union. The film's caricaturish depiction of America was over the top and failed to win its maker the much-needed political credit. The last time Kuleshov was able to positively surprise Soviet critics was with *The Great Consoler* (Velikii uteshitel', 1933), based on the life of American author O. Henry—one of the most popular foreign writers in Russia—that is blended with two of his stories. Completed in record time, this picture became a lesson in "Americanism" in more than one way, including the perfect planning of its production and the clever juxtaposition of sound film to silent elements.

The Siberians (Sibiriaki, 1940) was meant as a comeback after a hiatus of seven years, and, better still, the story of two boys who are helping hunters proved a success. According to Jay Leyda, "Kuleshov's sound-picture scenario method, an even more precise preparation on paper than was followed in *Nevsky*," was a contributing factor, enabling the ostracized director to return to active filmmaking, albeit for a brief period. *Timur's Oath* (Kliatva Timura, 1942) again was about juveniles, as was Kuleshov's last completed picture, *We Are from the Urals* (My s Urala, 1944). Made among unimaginable hardships in Dushanbe, where the studio for children's films (Soiuzdetfilm, later **Gor'kii Studio for Children's and Youth Films**) had been evacuated, the latter praises the selflessness of children working in factories to help supply the front with weapons.

Almost from the very beginning of his career, Kuleshov churned out theoretical texts about the nature of cinema. His earliest articles, such as "The Art of Light Creation" (Iskusstvo svetotvorchsetva, 1918), betray their author's aesthetic radicalism and his predilection for maximalist statements. Kuleshov overstated the universal power of montage, which he believed could manipulate viewers in an almost arbitrary fashion. Avid technocrat that he was, Kuleshov had little interest in evoking deep emotional reactions from his audience and was content with the elementary excitement gained from good action scenes. Yet such a naïve cinematic pleasure principle was regarded as a dangerous anomaly in Soviet culture and became a liability for Kuleshov, who never fully understood what exactly the Communist establishment wanted him to do, much as he tried to deliver. His attempts to fit in—sometimes clumsily direct, sometimes cunningly— were all doomed to fail, and he remained a marginalized maverick to whom official recognition came only in the last decade of his life.

Kuleshov's work at VGIK, both as administrator and pedagogue, shaped generations of Soviet filmmakers and compensated the living classic director and theorist—recognized as such only by insiders—for being stripped of a chance to make films. He was appointed full professor in 1939 and awarded the degree of a doctor of arts in 1946. Kuleshov joined the Communist Party in 1945. He was named Merited Artist of the Russian Federation in 1935 and People's Artist of the RSFSR in 1969. Kuleshov is buried at Novodevich'e cemetery.

Other films: (as set designer) *The King of Paris* (Korol' Parizha, 1917); *Twilight* (Sumerki, 1917); (as actor); *Black Love* (Chernaia liubov', 1917); (as director) *Theft of Eyesight* (Krazha zreniia, 1934); *Incident in a Volcano* (Sluchai v vulkane, 1941); *Young Partisans* (Iunye partizany, 1942, short, codirected with **Ihor' Savchenko**; unreleased).

KULIDZHANOV, LEV ALEKSANDROVICH (b. 19 March 1924, Tbilisi–d. 18 February 2002, Moscow). Russian director, scriptwriter, and film administrator. Kulidzhanov grew up in Georgia; his father and uncle perished during the purges in the 1930s. He went to Moscow and enrolled in **Sergei Gerasimov** and **Tamara Makarova**'s workshop at the Soviet State Film School **VGIK**, graduating in 1954.

Kulidzhanov's debut was the Anton Chekhov adaptation *Ladies* (Damy, 1955, codirected with Genrikh Oganesian). He addressed the fashionable topic of cultivating virgin soil in Kazakhstan, blending it with a "bad-boss-is-replaced-by-good-boss" plot, in *It Began This Way . . .* (Eto nachinalos' tak . . . , 1956, codirected with Iakov Segel' [1923–1995]). The film's explicit antibureaucratic rhetoric was typical of the Thaw period in Soviet cinema, of which Kulidzhanov became a leading representative.

The House I Live In (Dom, v kotorom ia zhivu, 1956, codirected by Segel') became signature of both the epoch in which it was made and its creators; it secured a minimum of professional respect for Kulidzhanov even in times when he seemed to have completely sold out to Party politics. In typical neorealist manner, the film follows the lives of tenants in a Soviet communal apartment building from before World War II to the Thaw. *The House I Live In* derives its emotional power from the extrapolated family-house metaphor, with tenants being viewed as parts of the grandiose Soviet home that provides shelter, human warmth, and mutual support during the most trying periods. *Our Father's House* (aka *A Home for Tanya*/Otchii dom, 1959), Kulidzhanov's first independently directed picture, uses the house metaphor in relation to a foster child who returns to her biological mother in a village. *When the Trees Were Tall* (Kogda derev'ia byli bol'shimi, 1961), arguably Kulidzhanov's second-most-lasting achievement, focuses—quite daringly—on the problems of a recovering alcoholic and is permeated by a spirit of forgiveness.

The Blue Notebook (Siniaia tetrad', 1963), a contribution to the official Lenin revival caused by the cautious de-Stalinization of the late 1950s, was remarkable for violating some taboos, first and foremost the appearance of Politburo member Grigorii Zinov'ev, who had been executed in 1937 and subsequently purged from all official Soviet history books. However, Soviet audiences hardly noticed this or other "progressive" elements and largely ignored the film as yet another installment of the officially prescribed Lenin cult.

Due to his dramatically increasing administrative workload, Kulidzhanov made fewer and fewer movies. Among those, his most ambitious project was the four-hour b/w Fedor Dostoevskii adaptation *Crime and Punishment* (Prestuplenie i nakazanie, 1969), an uneven, psychologically and philosophically inadequate effort in which only **Innokentii Smoktunovskii**'s investigator Porfirii is artistically convincing. Kulidzhanov also directed the seven-part television miniseries *Karl Marx: The Early Years* (Karl Marks: Molodye gody, 1980, TV), which earned him a Lenin Prize.

With his last two films, *Not Afraid to Die* (Umirat' ne strashno, 1991) and *Forget-me-nots* (Nezabudki, 1994), Kulidzhanov returned to his 1950s roots in historical and social melodrama, with the sole difference that he now was allowed and willing to depict formerly prohibited aspects of Soviet life such as GPU informers and common treason. After these films, he withdrew into complete seclusion.

Kulidzhanov headed the founding committee for the Union of Soviet Filmmakers in 1963–1964 and was elected its first secretary in 1965. Never a die-hard dogmatic, his activities (and passivities) can be characterized as a cautious mediation between filmmakers and power structures interspersed with episodes of decency when the stakes were not too high. Especially during the early years, Kulidzhanov supported reform concepts and values based on a naïve grassroots democratic spirit that was also characteristic of his Thaw films. However, in the 1970s his leadership degenerated into a mere execution of Party orders; his well-known phlegmatic attitude added its share to the artistic decline of Soviet cinema. At the Fifth Congress of Soviet Filmmakers in May 1986, Kulidzhanov was accused of cronyism, servility, and branded the leader of a gang of anti-intellectual hacks; he was subsequently replaced by **Elem Klimov.**

Kulidzhanov undeniably carried unusual political influence as a member of the Soviet *nomenklatura*, simultaneously holding an endless list of offices. Still, there is a certain dignity about this man's return to ordinary directing after his political demise, indicating an authentic love for filmmaking that commands respect.

Kulidzhanov joined the Communist Party in 1962; he was named People's Artist of the USSR in 1976 and Hero of Socialist Labor in 1984. At VGIK, he taught directing in 1970–1995.

Other films: *The Lost Photograph* (Poteriannaia fotografiia, 1960); *Starlit Moment* (Zvezdnaia minuta, 1975).

KULISH, SAVVA IAKOVLEVICH (b. 17 October 1936, Odessa–d. 9 June 2001, Iaroslavl'). Russian director, scriptwriter, and cameraman. Kulish studied in **Leonid Kosmatov**'s cinematography workshop at the Soviet State Film School **VGIK**, graduating in 1959. He worked as an assistant to **Mikhail Romm** on the **documentary *Ordinary Fascism*** (aka *Triumph over Violence*/Obyknovennyi fashizm, 1965). From 1966 to 1968, Kulish studied in the Directing Department of the Shchukin Theater College.

Following a few comedic shorts as cameraman and a prize-winning documentary, *Last Letters* (Poslednie pis'ma, 1966), Kulish made a sensational directorial debut with *Dead Season* (Mertvyi sezon, 1968), a KGB-supported, largely preposterous Cold War conspiracy flick. Based on **Vladimir Vainshtok**'s script, the film evokes the mystique of a lonesome Soviet spy in hostile Western environs, preparing the ground for **Tat'iana Lioznova**'s cult film *Seventeen Moments of Spring* (Semnadtsat' mgnovenii vesny, 1973) and similar fare.

The Committee of Nineteen (Komitet 19-ti, 1972), in many respects a replica of *Dead Season*, is based on the assumption that the United Nations are infiltrated by neo-Nazi forces maintaining a concentration-camp-cum-research-facility in Africa, only to be detected by a Soviet expedition. *The Start* (Vzlet, 1979), an overblown, heavy-handed, and costly epic about space travel pioneer Konstantin Tsiolkovskii—portrayed by poet Evgenii Evtushenko—failed to attract large audiences. Kulish followed up with *The Tales, the Tales, the Tales of Old Arbat* (Skazki . . . skazki . . . skazki Starogo Arbata, 1982) from a play by Aleksei Arbuzov (1908–1986), the sentimental story of a father and his son, both puppetmakers, who compete professionally and for the love of a beautiful woman. The pretentious *Tragedy in the Style of Rock* (Tragediia v stile rok, 1988) juxtaposes the idealism of Soviet youth with the opportunism of the older generation. Kulish's last feature, the four-hour-long, autobiographically inspired *Iron Curtain* (Zheleznyi zanaves, 1994) is a loose reflection about youth in the late 1940s and 1950s. Typical of Kulish's ambitious approach to filmmaking, *Iron Curtain*'s sentiments mostly ring hollow and disingenuous.

Kulish was named Merited Artist of the RSFSR in 1984 and People's Artist of Russia in 1995. He was appointed professor at VGIK in 1986.

Other films: *The First Starts* (Pervye starty, 1980, doc.); *The Icon and the Axe* (1990, doc., Great Britain).

KURAVLEV, LEONID VIACHESLAVOVICH (b. 8 October 1936). Russian actor. Kuravlev studied at the Soviet State Film School **VGIK**, graduating in 1960. He made his screen debut in **Mikhail Shveitser**'s popular Civil War adventure *Warrant Officer Panin* (Michman Panin, 1960); Shveitser later gave him other rewarding roles in *Time, Forward!* (Vremia, vpered, 1966), *The Escape of Mr. MacKinley* (Begstvo mistera Mak-Kinli, 1975), and *Little Tragedies* (Malen'kie tragedii, 1980).

Among Kuravlev's most memorable performances are parts of simple, modest country bumpkins or urban "guys next door"—most prominently, the driver Pashka Kolokol'nikov in **Vasilii Shukshin**'s *There Is Such a Lad* (Zhivet takoi paren', 1964) and Stepan Voevodin in *Your Son and Brother* (Vash syn i brat, 1966). Kuravlev's happy-go-lucky mentality, humor, and decency resonated with millions of Soviet viewers and made him one of the most popular Russian screen actors. He worked for leading Soviet directors, including **Gleb Panfilov** (*The Debut*/Nachalo, 1970), **Aleksandr Mitta** (*Shine, Shine, My Star*/Gori, gori, moia zvezda, 1970), **Iurii Ozerov** (*Liberation*/Osvobozhdenie, 1970–1972), and was particularly effective in **comedies** such as **Leonid Gaidai**'s *Ivan Vasil'evich Changes His Job* (aka *Ivan Vasilievich: Back to the Future*/Ivan Vasil'evich meniaet professiiu, 1973) and **Georgii Daneliia**'s megahit *Afonia* (1975), creating an amusing gallery of recognizable contemporaries.

Kuravlev's popularity grew even more through some of the most successful television miniseries: **Tat'iana Lioznova**'s *Seventeen Moments of Spring* (Semnadtsat' mgnovenii vesny), in which the actor played a high-ranking Nazi official, and **Stanislav Govorukhin**'s thriller *The Meeting Place Cannot be Changed* (Mesto vstrechi izmenit' nel'zia, 1978). An omnipresent artist on screen and television, Kuravlev has remained one of the most bankable Russian film stars in the 1990s and 2000s.

In 1965, Kuravlev was named Merited Artist of the RSFSR, and in 1977, People's Artist of the RSFSR.

Other films: *Vii* (1967); *The Life and Astounding Adventures of Robinson Crusoe* (Zhizn' i udivitel'nye prikliucheniia Robinzona Kruzo, 1973); *Left-Hand* (Levsha, 1987); *What a Mess* (Shirli-myrli, 1995); *The European Convoy* (Evropeiskii konvoi, 2004).

KUZ'MINA, ELENA ALEKSANDROVNA (b. 17 February 1909, Tbilisi–d. 15 October 1979, Moscow). Russian actress. Kuz'mina joined the Factory of the Eccentric Actor (FEKS), led by **Grigorii Kozintsev** and **Leonid Trauberg**, in 1925 and graduated from the Leningrad Institute of Stage Arts in 1930.

The role of Louise in Kozintsev and Trauberg's Paris Commune drama *The New Babylon* (Novyi Vavilon, 1929) became Kuz'mina's successful screen debut. She mastered the transition to sound film in Kozintsev and Trauberg's *Alone* (Odna, 1931), portraying an idealistic teacher in a backward and hostile Siberian village. In **Boris Barnet**'s masterpiece *The Outskirts* (aka *Patriots*/Okraina, 1933) she was cast as the naïve girl Man'ka who falls in love with a German POW during World War I.

Kuz'mina's artistic and private partnership with director **Mikhail Romm** profoundly determined her career in the 1930s and 1940s.

She played leads in Romm's John Ford–inspired Civil War adventure *The Thirteen* (Trinadtsat', 1937), in the antibourgeois melodrama *The Dream* (Mechta, 1941–1943)—as a cumbersome yet kindhearted peasant woman—and in the antifascist *Person #217* (aka *Girl No. 217*/Chelovek No. 217, 1944), a performance that won Kuz'mina her first Stalin Prize in 1946. She also appeared prominently in Romm's Cold War pamphlets *The Russian Question* (Russkii vopros, 1947) as the American Jessy, and *Secret Mission* (Sekretnaia missiia, 1950) as the fearless Soviet spy Masha Glukhova; both roles were adorned with Stalin Prizes in 1948 and 1951, respectively.

In the mid-1950s, following an unofficial Party order that Soviet directors should no longer cast their own wives, Kuz'mina's career nose-dived. Her last role was the mother in **Dinara Asanova**'s drama *Disaster* (Beda, 1978).

Kuz'mina was honored with the title People's Artist of the RSFSR in 1950. In 1976 and 1979, she published two volumes of memoirs that were based on her diaries, begun in the 1920s.

Other films: *By the Bluest of Seas* (U samogo sinego moria, 1936); *Riders* (aka *Guerilla Brigade*/Vsadniki, 1939); *Ships Attack the Bastions* (aka *Attack from the Sea*/Korabli shturmuiut bastiony, 1953).

KYDYKEEVA, BAKEN (b. 20 October 1923, village Oktiabr', Kant district, Kyrgyzstan–d. January 1994). Kyrgyz actress. Kydykeeva began her stage career in 1936 with the Kyrgyz Theater of the Young Viewer. From 1941 to 1944, she worked at the Przheval'skii district theater and the Narynsk theater. In 1944, Kydykeeva joined the troupe of the Kyrgyz Drama Theater in Frunze (now: Bishkek).

The actress's main accomplishments in cinema are two female leads: her debut in Vasilii Pronin's *Saltanat* (1955) as the title heroine, and the role of Tolgonai in Gennadii Bazarov's *Maternal Field* (Materinskoe pole, 1967) from a **Chingiz Aitmatov** story. *Saltanat*, which has the distinction of being the first Kyrgyz full-length feature film, tells the story of a young woman who lives in a rural milieu and has to find her professional and personal calling in a rapidly modernizing world. In *Maternal Field*, Kydykeeva portrays a woman who has lost her husband, three sons, and her daughter-in-law in the Great Patriotic War, and only has her grandson left to live for. Kydykeeva's acting emphasizes the quiet and modest tones, pointing to her characters' shyness and dignity; emotional intensity is mostly revealed through expressive close shots. Kydykeeva also won praise for her introverted performance as Raikhan in Aleksei Sakharov's *The Pass* (Pereval, 1961), from another Aitmatov story.

Kydykeeva, who predominantly worked in **Kyrgyz cinema** and only rarely appeared in Tadjik, Kazakh, and Uzbek films, was cast in numerous memorable episodic roles, including Chernukha in **Andrei Mikhalkov-Konchalovskii**'s *The First Teacher* (Pervyi uchitel', 1965) and Djaidar in **Sergei Urusevskii**'s *Farewell, Gul'sary!* (Proshchai, gul'sary, aka Beg inokhodtsa, 1968). **Elyor Ishmukhamedov** cast her in *Meetings and Partings* (Vstrechi i rasstavaniia, 1973) as Khadicha-khon, an Uzbek émigré in the West, who takes her own life because of her unrealizable longing for her homeland.

Kydykeeva is considered one of the greatest screen and stage actresses of Kyrgyzstan. She was named People's Artist of the USSR in 1970.

Other films: *Toktogul* (1959); *Horsemen of the Revolution* (Vsadniki revoliutsii, 1969); *The Secret of Ancestors* (Taina predkov, 1972); *Aisulu's Field* (Pole Aisulu, 1977); *The Thirteenth Grandson* (Trinadtsatyi vnuk, 1982).

KYRGYZ CINEMA. *See* AITMATOV, CHINGIZ; ASANOVA, DINARA; CHOKMOROV, SUIMENKUL; KYDYKEEVA, BAKEN; KYRGYZFILM STUDIO; OKEEV, TOLOMUSH; SHAMSHIEV, BOLOTBEK.

KYRGYZFILM STUDIO. A decree of the Council of People's Commissars of the Kyrgyz Soviet Socialist Republic, issued on 17 November 1941, turned the Frunze (now: Bishkek) branch of the Tashkent Newsreel Film Studio that had been founded in 1938 into an independent studio. Initially, it specialized in the production of newsreels. (The first issues of *Soviet Kyrgyzstan* [Sovetskaia Kirgiziia] had appeared on a monthly or bimonthly basis beginning in June 1938; although filmed in Kyrgyzstan, they were developed in Tashkent.) The wartime issues—which since 1943 were fully processed in the Frunze studio—called upon the local population to increase the production of coal and mercury, as well as food for the Red Army. In 1941, the country's first feature-length

documentary, *On the High Ground* (Na vysokoi zemle), dedicated to the 15th anniversary of Soviet Kyrgyzstan, was released. To celebrate the 20th anniversary of the Kyrgyz SSR, well-known documentary filmmaker Mikhail Slutskii (1907–1952) worked at Kyrgyzfilm Studio on *Soviet Kyrgyzstan* (Sovietskaia Kirgiziia, 1946). The year 1953 saw the beginning of a regular production of documentaries. Among the leading directors of this early phase of **Kyrgyz cinema** were D. Erdman, Izia Gershtein (b. 1923), Iurii Gershtein, and Lilia Turusbekova (b. 1933).

Russian director Vasilii Pronin (1905–1966) helmed the first full-length feature film with Kyrgyz subject matter, *Saltanat* (1955). Unlike earlier efforts whose plots took place in Kyrgyzstan, the cast consisted of native actors, led by the impressive **Baken Kydykeeva** in the title role. In 1956, the Frunze Studio for Newsreel and Documentary Production embarked on the production of feature films, usually in partnership with **Mosfilm Studio**, **Kazakhfilm Studio**, or **Lenfilm Studio**; the latter, for example, helped create a ballet film, *Cholpon—The Morning Star* (Cholpon—utrenniaia zvezda, 1959). Other early features were *My Mistake* (Moia oshibka, 1957), the first Kyrgyz film in color, and *Toktogul* (1960), a biopic about a prominent oral poet (*aikyn*). Several of Kyrgyzstan's best filmmakers, including **Tolomush Okeev** and **Bolotbek Shamshiev**, began their careers as assistants on **Larisa Shepit'ko**'s *Torrid Heat* (Znoi, 1963).

In 1961, the studio got its present name, Kyrgyzfilm Studio. In the mid-1960s, a new generation of filmmakers appeared who began their careers with poetic documentaries featuring an unmistakable national flavor. Thus, Shamshiev in *Manaschi* (1965) portrayed the renowned myth narrator Saiakbai Karalaev, who was famous for his retelling of the Kyrgyz national epic *Manas*. The film drew international critics' attention to similarly original films, including *These Are Horses* (Eto—loshadi, 1965) by Okeev, and *PSP* (1965) by Algimantas Vidugiris (b. 1932) who was assisted by **Dinara Asanova**, about the search for natural resources in Kyrgyzstan.

Powerful impulses to the development of Kyrgyz cinema came from the writer **Chingiz Aitmatov**, who actively participated in the adaptation of his works for the screen. Thus, *Torrid Heat* was adapted from his story "Camel Eye," while **Andrei Mikhalkov-**

Konchalovskii transformed the novella *The First Teacher* (Pervyi uchitel', 1965) into an impressive drama of modernization, education, and emancipation. Its international triumph encouraged native filmmakers to turn more keenly to the present and past of Kyrgyzstan in films such as Okeev's *The Sky of Our Childhood* (Nebo nashego detstva, 1967), Melis Ubukeev's *White Mountains* (Belye gory, 1966), and *Maternal Field* (Materinskoe pole, 1967), directed by Gennadii Bazarov (b. 1942) from an Aitmatov story.

In the 1970s and 1980s, Tolomush Okeev and Bolotbek Shamshiev became the leading Kyrgyz filmmakers who won national and international praise with sometimes daring, visually stunning dramas focusing on moral and ecological themes. Okeev's *The Red Apple* (Krasnoe iabloko, 1975), *The Ulan* (Ulan, 1977), *Golden Autumn* (Zolotaia osen', 1981), and *The Descendant of the Snow Leopard* (Potomok belogo barsa, 1984) blend the analysis of social transformation with psychological introspection, particularly of complex intellectual characters. Shamshiev's *The White Steamship* (Belyi parakhod, 1976) and *Early Cranes* (Rannie zhuravli, 1979), both adapted from Aitmatov novellas, show the tragic consequences of ethical degeneration.

Since 1953, Kyrgyzfilm Studio has dubbed numerous feature films into Kyrgyz, and since 1977, has also produced **animation** pictures. After Kyrgyzstan gained its independence in 1991, Kyrgyzfilm Studio remained state property. In 2005, it was integrated into the National Trust Kyrgyzkino. The studio's premises and equipment are now leased to various companies. National film production has dwindled considerably, from 12 films in 1992 to roughly one per year after the mid-1990s. Kyrgyz feature films are often financed by foreign companies; thus, Aktan Abdykalykov, who landed an international hit with *Beshkempir—The Adopted Son* (1998), found a French investor for *The Chimp* (Maimal, 2001). In 2005, Ernest Abdyzhaparov's *Saratan* (Aiyl-Okmotu) participated in the Berlin Film Festival and received favorable reviews.

In 2002, Kyrgyzstan's prime minister, Nikolai Tanaev, signed a decree by which Kyrgyzfilm Studio was named after Tolomush Okeev. In 2006, Sapar Koichumanov, executive director of Kyrgyzfilm Studio, announced plans to open a national film school.

– L –

LADYNINA, MARINA ALEKSEEVNA (b. 24 June 1908, village Nazarovo, Krasnoiarsk district–d. 10 March 2003, Moscow). Russian actress. Born into a family of illiterate Siberian peasants, Ladynina became a teacher in her native village and played minor parts in the theater of Achinsk, a nearby town. In 1929, she was accepted into the Moscow State Theater Institute (GITIS), graduating in 1933. She then joined the troupe of the Moscow Art Theater (MKhAT).

After playing supporting parts in films by **Iurii Zheliabuzhskii** and **Ol'ga Preobrazhenskaia**, Ladynina's encounter in 1935 with budding film director **Ivan Pyr'ev** proved fateful professionally and privately. She left the stage for good to play the lead in his collective farm (kolkhoz) **comedy** *A Rich Bride* (Bogataia nevesta, 1937), the first in a series of nine Pyr'ev blockbuster musicals with Ladynina as the female star. These roles include Marianna in *Tractor Drivers* (Traktoristy, 1939), Glasha in *Swineherd and Shepherd* (Svinarka i pastukh, 1941), Natasha in *The Legend of the Siberian Land* (Skazanie o zemle sibirskoi, 1950), and Galina in *The Kuban Cossacks* (Kubanskie kazaki, 1950). All of them represent exemplary peasant or working-class women in artificial Soviet idylls, an image appreciated by huge audiences craving for entertainment, no matter how unrealistic.

Ladynina was awarded five Stalin Prizes and the title People's Artist of the USSR (1950). Her last role, Ol'ga in Pyr'ev's *Test of Loyalty* (aka *Devotion*/Ispytanie vernosti, 1954), shows the actress as a woman of matured beauty who has taken her share of blows and disappointments. After this film—arguably the best of her entire career—she and Pyr'ev split, whereupon Ladynina rejected all offers from other directors. She worked in the Theater Studio of the Movie Actor in Moscow until 1991 and toured with concerts of classical poetry and songs; among others, **Isaak Dunaevskii** set two Robert Burns poems to music for her.

A petite blonde with cheerful, intelligent, and dreamy eyes, Ladynina seemed to overflow with warm energy in both comedic and serious roles. Surprisingly, interviews and memoirs of the 1990s testify that she never believed in the Communist ideology and saw through the hypocrisy of her films from early on.

A son from her marriage to Pyr'ev, Andrei Ladynin (b. 1938), worked as a film director in the 1970s and 1980s.

Other films: *Beloved Girl* (Liubimaia devushka, 1939); *Secretary of the Party District Committee* (aka *We Will Be Back*/Sekretar' raikoma, 1943).

LAIUS, LEIDA [in some sources: Lajus; Russian sources add the patronymic Rikhardovna] (b. 26 March 1923, Khoroshevo, Russia– d. 6 April 1996, Tallin). Estonian director, screenwriter, and actress. Laius graduated from the Tallin Theater Institute in 1950 and worked as an actress on the stage of Kingisepp Theater in Tallin (now called National Drama Theater) in 1951–1955. She subsequently studied at the Soviet State Film School **VGIK**, graduating in 1962.

Laius's first feature was *From Evening till Morning* (Õhtust hommikuni/S vechera do utra, 1962) about the family of a railway man who gives shelter to a Soviet prisoner of war hiding from German troops. In the course of her career, Laius adapted a number of works by Estonian classics. *The Milkman from Maekula* (Mäekūla piimamees/Molochnik iz Miakula, 1965), from a story by Eduard Vilde (1865–1933), tells about a poor peasant in late 19th century who sacrifices his dignity for material gain. *The Master of Korboja* (Kõrboja peremees/Khoziain Kyrboia, 1979), from a short novel by Anton Tammsaare (1878–1940), is about a doomed love affair ending in suicide.

In the 1980s, when the changed atmosphere in Soviet society allowed for a realistic depiction of contemporary life, Laius demonstrated her talent for authentic social drama. *Games for School-Age Children* (aka *Smile, Please*, aka *Well, Come On, Smile*/Naerata ometi/Igry dlia detei shkol'nogo vozrasta, 1985, codirected with Arvo Iho) focuses on a girl who runs from an orphanage. The film presents a sobering depiction of newly built urban environs and addresses formerly taboo problems such as alcoholism. Laius's last film, *Stolen Encounter* (Varastatud kohtumine/Ukradennoe svidanie, 1988), tells the tragic story of a woman who desperately tries to win back her son after her release from prison.

Laius, who also directed several **documentaries** in the 1970s, joined the Communist Party in 1976. She was named Merited Artist of the Estonian SSR in 1979.

Other films: *The Werewolf* (Libahunt/Lesnaia legenda, 1968); *The Spring in the Forest* (Ukuaru/Rodnik v lesu, 1973). *See also* ESTONIAN CINEMA.

LANOVOI, VASILII SEMENOVICH (b. 16 January 1934, Moscow). Russian actor. Lanovoi's first exposure to acting took place at the drama workshop of the Likhachev Factory's Palace of Culture in Moscow in the early 1950s where he worked with **Igor' Talankin**. Lanovoi enrolled in the Shchukin Theater School from which he graduated in 1957 (since 1988, he has held a professorship at this school), and joined the troupe of the prestigious Moscow Vakhtangov Theater, where for half a century he has played the entire classical and modern repertoire while also impressing audiences as a cultured and passionate poetry reciter.

Following his debut as the manipulative and selfish high school student Valentin in **Tat'iana Lukashevich**'s *Graduate Certificate* (aka *Problem Child*/Attestat zrelosti, 1954), Lanovoi later was defined as a strong-willed, noble, ascetic hero and activist, starting with the title role in **Aleksandr Alov** and **Vladimir Naumov**'s *Pavel Korchagin* in 1956. Variations of that image appear in romantic fantasy such as **Aleksandr Ptushko**'s *Scarlet Sails* (Alye parusa, 1961), comedies (*Striped Trip*/Polosatyi reis, 1961), and thrillers (*Petrovka, 38*, 1980). The real scale of his talent became apparent in two adaptations of Lev Tolstoi novels: **Sergei Bondarchuk**'s *War and Peace* (Voina i mir, 1966–1967), with Lanovoi as the coldly handsome Anatole Kuragin, and **Aleksandr Zarkhi**'s *Anna Karenina* (1968), as a torn, virile Vronskii opposite **Tat'iana Samoilova**, Lanovoi's erstwhile real-life spouse.

With over 50 movie roles to his credit, Lanovoi was often typecast as an officer, most prominently as Commander Ivan Varavva in **Vladimir Rogovoi**'s patriotic blockbuster *Officers* (Ofitsery, 1971). He also portrayed the infamous founder of the Soviet secret service, Feliks Dzerzhinzkii, in several films, for example, Iulii Karasik's *Sixth of July* (Shestoe iulia, 1968).

Lanovoi, who became a member of the Communist Party in 1968, was awarded a Lenin Prize in 1980 and the title People's Artist of the USSR in 1985. He is married to actress Irina Kupchenko.

Other films: *Colleagues* (Kollegi, 1962); *I'm Going toward the Thunderstorm* (Idu na grozu, 1964); *A Strange Woman* (Strannaia zhenshchina, 1978); *Lady Peasant* (Baryshnia-krest'ianka, 1995); *The Invisible Traveler* (Nezrimyi puteshestvennik, 1998); *A Golden Head on the Scaffold* (Zolotaia golova na plakhe, 2004).

LAPIKOV, IVAN GERASIMOVICH (b. 7 July 1922, village Gornyi Balyklei, near Tsaritsyn–d. 2 May 1993, Moscow). Russian actor. Lapikov studied for two years at the theater school of Khar'kiv (1940–1941). He was a member of the troupe of Volgograd Theater in 1942–1963 and later joined the Studio Theater of the Film Actor in Moscow.

Lapikov's fame rests on authentic portrayals of rank-and-file Russian men with deep moral convictions. His orientation on traditional national features generated remarkable portrayals such as the skeptic Semen Trubnikov—opponent to **Mikhail Ul'ianov**'s Communist reformer Egor Trubnikov—in **Aleksei Saltykov**'s polemical kolkhoz drama *The Chairman* (Predsedatel', 1964). Lapikov also created numerous recognizable characters in contemporary urban settings, for example, in *Our House* (Nash dom, 1965), or members of rural communities such as in the World War II drama *The Well* (Rodnik, 1981). **Sergei Bondarchuk** entrusted the actor with two superb roles: Sergeant-Major Poprishchenko in the Great Patriotic War epic *They Fought for the Motherland* (Oni srazhalis' za rodinu, 1975), and Pantelei in the atmospherically intense Anton Chekhov adaptation *The Steppe* (Step', 1977).

Lapikov's image of patriarchal authority was used in popular patriotic movies such as **Igor' Gostev**'s *Front behind the Front Line* (Front za liniei fronta, 1977) and in the popular television miniseries *The Eternal Call* (Vechnyi zov, 1976–1983), a performance that was honored with a USSR State Prize in 1979. One of the actor's most memorable achievements was that of the ungifted, jealous monk Kirill in **Andrei Tarkovskii**'s *Andrei Rublev* (1966). He also appeared in adaptations of classical literature such as **Igor' Talankin**'s *Father Sergius* (Otets Sergii, 1978) and **Mikhail Shveitser**'s *Little Tragedies* (Malen'kie tragedii, 1979, TV).

Lapikov was named People's Artist of the USSR in 1982.

Other films: *The Business Trip* (Komandirovka, 1961); *The Journalist* (Zhurnalist, 1967); *Minute of Silence* (Minuta molchaniia, 1971); *What for?* (Za chto? 1991); *House on the Stone* (Dom na kamne, 1994).

LATVIAN CINEMA. *See* ARTMANE, VIJA; CILINSKIS, GŪNARS; LEIMANIS, ALEKSANDRS; LEIMANIS, LEONIDS; PODNIEKS, JŪRIS; RADZIN, ELSA; RIGA FILM STUDIO; SLAPIŅŠ, ANDRIS, TISSÉ, EDUARD.

LAVROV, KIRILL IUR'EVICH (b. 15 September 1925, Leningrad– d. 27 April 2007, St. Petersburg). Russian actor. After graduating from aviation college and army service, Lavrov, the son of prominent stage and film actor Iurii Lavrov (1905–1980), joined the ensemble of the Lesia Ukrainka Russian Theater in Kiev in 1950. In 1955, he moved to Leningrad as a member of the Grand Dramatic Theater (BDT). When the legendary BDT director Georgii Tovstonogov passed away, Lavrov was appointed the theater's executive director in 1990.

As a film actor, Lavrov made his debut in **Nadezhda Kosheverova**'s poetic **comedy** *Honeymoon* (Medovyi mesiats, 1956). **Aleksandr Stolper**'s groundbreaking World War II epic *The Living and the Dead* (Zhivye i mertvye, 1964) about the Battle of Stalingrad shot Lavrov, in the role of journalist Sintsov, to national stardom. An equally complex characterization is Lavrov's portrayal of an escaped prison inmate in Vladimir Berenshtein and Il'ia Gurin's social drama *Believe Me, People!* (Ver'te mne, liudi, 1965). **Ivan Pyr'ev** cast the actor as the ultrarational philosophical seeker Ivan Karamazov in his three-part version of Fedor Dostoevskii's *The Brothers Karamazov* (Brat'ia Karamazovy, 1967–1969), which Lavrov, together with **Mikhail Ul'ianov**, completed after the director's sudden passing.

Lavrov received great acclaim and official recognition—including a USSR State Prize—for the lead role of Bashkirtsev in Daniil Khrabrovitskii's rocket development saga *Taming of Fire* (Ukroshchenie ognia, 1972). In the 1970s, the actor excelled in portrayals of Soviet officials, emphasizing his characters' unconditional duty to the Communist cause. Following the collapse of the Soviet Union, Lavrov's roles were sometimes curious subversions of his earlier authoritarian image, for example, the godfather-like conspirator in *Schizophrenia* (1997). His portrayal of Pontius Pilate in **Vladimir Bortko**'s adaptation of Mikhail Bulgakov's *The Master and Margarita* (Master i Margarita, 2005, TV) focuses on the character's cowardice and repentance.

Lavrov was named People's Artist of the RSFSR in 1969 and People's Artist of the USSR in 1972. He joined the Communist Party in 1946, and received a Lenin Prize in 1982 and the title Hero of Socialist Labor in 1985.

Other films: *The Girl with Whom I Was Not Friends* (Devchonka, s kotoroi ia ne druzhil, 1962); *From Evening till Morning* (Õhtust hommikuni/S vechera do utra, 1962); *The Ocean* (Okean, 1974); *Feedback* (Obratnaia sviaz', 1978).

LEBESHEV, PAVEL TIMOFEEVICH (b. 15 February 1940, Moscow–d. 23 February 2003, Moscow). Russian cinematographer. Lebeshev, son of renowned cinematographer Timofei Lebeshev (1905–1981), studied with **Anatolii Golovnia** at the Soviet State Film School **VGIK**, graduating in 1972. Still a student, he worked with **Andrei Smirnov** on the later banned drama *Angel* (1967) and scored his first success with Smirnov's touching melodrama of war and remembrance ***Belorussian Station*** (Belorusskii vokzal, 1970).

Lebeshev's reputation as an inventive and reliable camera artist stems from his work with **Nikita Mikhalkov**. Using a wide range of artistic means — from documentary-like, handheld camera in the Civil War thriller *At Home among Strangers* (Svoi sredi chuzhikh, chuzhoi sredi svoikh, 1974) to exploitatively nostalgic compositions in *Slave of Love* (Raba liubvi, 1977) — Lebeshev informed Mikhalkov's pictures with a noticeable visual quality. Both for genuine achievements such as the intelligent, stylish Anton Chekhov adaptation *Unfinished Piece for Mechanical Piano* (Neokonchennaia p'esa dlia mekhanicheskogo pianino, 1977) and forgettable fare like the elephantine *Barber of Siberia* (Sibirskii tsiriul'nik, 1999), Lebeshev's art won accolades from critics in Russia and abroad.

The ability to respond with utmost sensitivity to the needs of different directors made Lebeshev an asset to Russian cinema of the 1980s and 1990s. Thus, he was able to visualize the strict asceticism required by **Larisa Shepit'ko** for her ultimate masterpiece

The Ascension (Voskhozhdenie, 1976). Lebeshev also achieved original visual solutions in films by **Georgii Daneliia** (*Kin-Dza-Dza*, 1986), **Roman Balaian** (*Lady Macbeth of Mtsensk*/Ledi Makbet mtsenskogo uezda, 1989; *First Love*/Pervaia liubov', 1995), and **Sergei Bodrov** (*Prisoner of the Caucasus*/Kavkazskii plennik, 1996); the latter won him a State Prize of Russia.

Lebeshev repeatedly was hired for international productions, some with artistic merit such as Peter Fleischmann's German-Russian *It's Not Easy to Be a God* (Es ist nicht leicht, ein Gott zu sein/Trudno byt' bogom, 1990, from a Strugatskii Brothers novel), others of dubious value, for example, the TV miniseries *As Far as the Feet Can Carry You* (So weit die Füße tragen, 2001, Germany). His last work was Jerzy Hoffman's mythical potboiler *An Old Story: When the Sun Was God* (Stara basn. Kiedy slonce bylo bogom, 2003, Poland).

Lebeshev was named Merited Artist of the RSFSR in 1980 and People's Artist of Russia in 1992.

Other films: *Oblomov* (Neskol'ko dnei iz zhizni I.I. Oblomova, 1979); *Without Witnesses* (Bez svidetelei, 1983); *Adam's Rib* (Rebro Adama, 1990); *Mama* (1999); *The Tender Age* (Nezhnyi vozrast, 2001).

LEIMANIS [also spelled Lejmanis], **ALEKSANDRS** [some Russian sources list the patronymic Ottovich] (b. 17 October 1913, Gavrilovo, Smolensk district–d. 17 June 1990, Riga). Latvian director and scriptwriter. Leimanis studied at the Soviet Theater Institute (GITIS) in Moscow, graduating in 1939, and worked as a stage director in Irkutsk, Semipalatinsk, Riga, Elgava, and other cities.

In the early 1960s, when **Latvian cinema** experienced a shortage of film directors, Leimanis switched from theater to film and made a name for himself with pro-Soviet **children's and youth films**, for example, the Civil War flicks *The "Wagtail" Army* (Armiia "Triasoguzka," 1964) and *The "Wagtail" Army Is Fighting Again* (Armiia "Triasoguzka" snova v boiu, 1968), as well as *The "Tobago" Changes Its Course* ('Tobago' meniaet kurs, 1965), a film that depicts the Soviet occupation of Latvia as a necessary and positive change.

In 1970, Leimanis scored one of the greatest box-office hits in the history of Latvian cinema. *The Devil's Servants* (Vella kalpi/Slugi d"iavola), a tale of three fearless young men in 17th-century Riga, blends historical facts with musical **comedy**, providing carefree, largely apolitical entertainment. The film's sequel, *The Devil's Servants at the Devil's Mill* (Vella kalpi vella dzirnavās/Slugi d"iavola na chertovoi mel'nitse, 1972), proved equally successful all over the Soviet Union. Another historical comedy, *In the Claws of the Black Crab* (Melna vîza spiles/V kleshniakh chernogo raka, 1975), tells the story of peasants outwitting the Teutonic knights. These three films, although far from ideologically subversive, conveyed a sense of Latvian national pride and optimistic humor previously unseen on Soviet screens.

Leimanis was in charge of dubbing dozens of films into Latvian and also led a directing workshop at the Latvian State Conservatory. He joined the Communist Party in 1947 and was honored with the title People's Artist of the Latvian SSR in 1973. In 2002, Agita Cane made a **documentary** about the director that premiered at the Riga Cinema Museum.

Other films: *Oleg and Aina* (1974, TV); *Open Country* (Otkrytaia strana, 1979, TV).

LEIMANIS, LEONIDS [Russian sources list the patronymic Ianovich] (b. 16 April 1910, Riga–d. 25 October [other sources: 6 July] 1974, Riga). Latvian director, scriptwriter, and actor. Leimanis gained a solid reputation as an actor and director in the Workers' Theater of Riga and in other Latvian cities. In 1940–1941 and 1944–1946, he worked as the director of the Academic Rainis Theater in Riga. During World War II, Leimanis participated in the anti-Nazi resistance movement. After joining the staff of **Riga Film Studio**, he assisted Russian director Aleksandr Ivanov on *Victorious Return* (Vozvrashchenie s pobedoi, 1948) from a novel by Communist Latvian author Vilis Lacis, and **Iulii Raizman** on the biopic *Rainis* (1949).

Leimanis became one of the founders of postwar **Latvian cinema** with *Spring Frosts* (Salna pavarasi/Vesennie zamorozki, 1955, codirected with Pavel Armand [1902–1962]). The film was adapted from stories by one of the classics of Latvian critical realism, Rūdolfs Blaumanis (1863–1908), and describes the social and economic humiliation experienced by a peasant woman in the 19th century. With *Nauris* (1957), the story of an idealistic high school student, and *The Sword and the Rose* (Šķēps un roze/Mech i roza, 1959), about the conflict between a young construction worker and a conservative house owner, Leimanis turned to contemporary Latvian problems. His directorial style, featuring an uncommon evenhandedness, resulted in nonstereotypical, differentiated portrayals of all characters, an approach that in the part of the "reactionary" house owner even achieves tragic grandeur. *Captain Nulle* (Kapteinis Nulle/Kapitan Nul', 1964) was devoted to the life of Latvian fishermen far away from home. The passionate love story *Edgar and Kristina* (Edgar i Kristina, 1967) marks Leimanis's return to the work of Blaumanis and his tragically tainted social realism; it created a controversy due to its unorthodox approach toward classical literary texts.

Leimanis's films, whether dealing with historical or contemporary subject matter, avoid excessive ideological statements and often juxtapose cynical, materialistic reality to romantic ideals.

Leimanis was honored with the title People's Artist of the Latvian SSR in 1965. In 1980 and 1999, two **documentaries** about the life and work of Leonids Leimanis were released.

Other films: *With a Rich Lady* (Pie bāgātas kundzes/U bogatoi gospozhi, 1969).

LEMBERG, ALEKSANDR GRIGOR'EVICH (b. 22 October 1898–d. 9 June 1974). Russian cinematographer. Lemberg, the son of prominent cameraman Grigorii Lemberg (1873–1945), began working in a film development laboratory in 1914 and as an assistant to his father on silents such as *Chess of Love* (Shakhmaty liubvi, 1916) for producer **Aleksandr Drankov**.

Lemberg specialized on shooting newsreels on the fronts of World War I, during the political unrests in 1917, and the subsequent Civil War (1918–1921). He was among the first film professionals to cooperate with the Bolshevik film committees (*kinokomitety*), regularly contributing to *Film Week* (Kinonedelia, 1918–1919) and *Film Truth* (Kinopravda, 1921–1925). He also was active on propaganda "agit-ships," which he documented in *The Agit-Ship "Red Star"* (Agitparokhod "Krasnaia zevzda," 1919) and "agit-trains" (*The First Agit-Train Named after Comrade Lenin*/Pervyi agitpoezd imeni tovarishcha Lenina, 1922), cruising the Volga and Don regions. In 1920, Lemberg was entrusted with recording the establishment of Communist power in Armenia.

In his early films, Lemberg made attempts to juxtapose old and new technology, as well as traditional and modern methods in agriculture, applying—albeit unsystematically—a polemical type of montage. In 1922, he joined the Cine-Eye (*kinoki*) group led by **Dziga Vertov** as a "film spy" (*kinorazvedchik*), contributing to the feature-length **documentary** pamphlet *One Sixth of the World* (Shestaia chast' mira, 1926), among others. In 1931, he made an attempt to blend document and fiction in *From the Darkness of Time* (Iz t'my vekov), a medium-length "agitprop" film about the plight of the Chuvash people under tsarist exploiters who are assisted by the Orthodox Church.

Lemberg's official claim to fame was his filming of Soviet leader Vladimir Lenin on several occasions in 1918–1921, and of GULAG concentration camps in *The White Sea–Baltic Water Path* (Belo-moro-Baltiiskii vodnyi put', 1932) and *Belomorstroi Is Reporting* (Belomorstroi raportuet, 1933); the latter uses live interviews to authenticate the asserted transformation of former criminals into exemplary Soviet citizens. In later years Lemberg, who wrote noteworthy memoirs about early Russian cinema, worked for military studios and as a newsreel correspondent.

LENFILM STUDIO [*Kinostudiia Lenfil'm*]. The studio's origins date back to the Bolshevik Revolution in November 1917 when the sub-department for cinema ([*kinopodotdel*) of the Petrograd State Commission of Education was founded. One year later, it was renamed "Petrograd Film Committee of the People's Commissariat of Enlightenment"; its first head was Dmitrii Leshchenko. Similar to other Soviet studios, the future Lenfilm underwent numerous restructurings and renamings. In 1920, the Cinema Committee was transformed into the Petrograd District Photo-Cinema Department, which in 1922 was renamed Film Factory North-West Cinema (kinofabrika Sevzapkino). From 1925 to 1926, the studio's name was Leningradkino; from 1926 to 1930, Leningrad Factory Soviet Cinema (Sovkino); from 1930 to 1932, Soiuzkino; from 1932 to 1933, Russian Film (Rosfil'm); and in 1933–1934, Soiuzfil'm, before getting its final name, Lenfilm, in 1934. In the following six decades, minor modifications to that name occurred, in particular the change of "film factory" into "film studio" (*kinostudiia*) and the addition of the "Order of Lenin" to its title in 1935 and the "Order of the Red Banner of Labor" in 1976.

The studio's first picture, the *agitka The Condensation* (Uplotne-nie, 1918), filmed on the premises of the Commissariat of Enlighten-ment from a script by Commissar **Anatolii Lunacharskii**, is consid-ered the first Soviet feature film. Its director, **Aleksandr Panteleev**, subsequently helmed pro-Bolshevik potboilers such as *There Is No Happiness in This World* (Net schast'ia na zemle, 1923), a drama set in contemporary Petrograd. Panteleev had begun his career before the Bolshevik Revolution and brought some professional experience to the studio, as did **Aleksandr Ivanovskii**, whose historical drama *Palace and Fortress* (Dvorets i krepost', 1923) was bought by a number of Western countries. Other directors of the "old school" included **Vladimir Gardin**, who made his Aleksandr Pushkin biopic *The Poet and the Tsar* (Poet i tsar', 1927, with **Evgenii Cherviakov**) at Sevzapkino, and **Viacheslav Viskovskii**, who directed a large-scale reconstruction of the tragic events of 1905, *The Ninth of Janu-ary* (Deviatoe ianvaria, 1925). The willingness of these filmmakers to continue their work under Soviet conditions and contribute to the studio's success initially was appreciated; in the late 1920s, however, when the ideological climate became harsher, their conventional style and transparent political opportunism were no longer tolerated by the Communist administration.

The studio attracted a number of young cinematic iconoclasts whose aesthetic originality was only matched by their professed loyalty to the Communist cause. **Grigorii Kozintsev** and **Leonid Trauberg**, who had developed an original approach to filmmaking in their Factory of the Eccentric Actor (FEKS), got a first chance to put their ideas into practice at the Leningrad studio, as did **Fridrikh Ermler** with his experimental cinema workshop (KEM). Under the energetic leadership of Adrian Piotrovskii (1898–1938), the studio produced avant-garde masterpieces such as Ermler's *A Fragment of the Empire* (Oblomok imperii, 1929), as well as Kozintsev and Trauberg's *The New Babylon* (Novyi Vavilon, 1929). In 1934, the studio's First Artistic Workshop was founded under **Sergei Iutkev-ich**. Its main goal was to emphasize quality acting; the old—and largely Moscow-based—montage school of Soviet cinema was seen as outdated, considering the irreversible advance of sound film. The studio promoted the slogan of "putting the focus on the individual human being." **Iosif Kheifits** and **Aleksandr Zarkhi** were entrusted with creating a Communist Youth (Komsomol) brigade. These and other initiatives made Lenfilm the most successful Soviet studio in the 1930s, turning out classics such as *Alone* (Odna, 1931) and the *Maksim Trilogy* (Trilogiia o Maksime, 1934–1938) by Kozintsev and Trauberg, *The Counterplan* (Vstrechnyi, 1932) by Ermler and Iutkevich, *The Great Citizen* (Velikii grazhdanin, 1937) by Ermler, *Chapaev* (1934) by the **Vasil'ev brothers**, as well as *Baltic Deputy* (Deputat Baltiki, 1937) and *Member of the Government* (Chlen pravitel'stva, 1939) by Kheifits and Zarkhi. **Vladimir Petrov**'s *Peter the First* (aka *Peter the Great*/Petr Pervyi, 1937–1939) was the first of several grandiose, patriotic historical epics.

Following the Great Patriotic War, when Lenfilm was evacuated to Alma-Ata in Kazakhstan, a number of directors left for other studios, among them Iutkevich, Petrov, Zarkhi, and Ermler. The 1950s and 1960s were marked by a turn toward the adaptation of classical literature, among them masterpieces such as *Lady with a Dog* (Dama s sobachkoi, 1959) by Kheifits, as well as *Don Quijote* (1957) and *Hamlet* (1964) by Kozintsev. Subsequently, a number of Lenfilm directors were able to develop a discernable cinematic style and the reputation of auteurs, among them **Il'ia Averbakh**, **Aleksei German**, and **Dinara Asanova**. **Nadezhda Kosheverova** successfully specialized in fairy tales and **comedies**, **Vitalii Mel'nikov** in comedies focusing on everyday life, and **Semen Aranovich** in docudramas. After the breakdown of the Soviet system, **Aleksandr Sokurov** became the most internationally acclaimed filmmaker associated with Lenfilm.

In 1993, the studio was renamed St. Petersburg Studio Lenfilm. In 1998, Lenfilm sold the rights to its entire film archive to the television company NTV for a 10-year duration. The funds from this transaction were invested in modernizing the equipment that is used both for Lenfilm productions and for projects of other companies. In 2004, Lenfilm was transformed into a stockholding company, with the Russian state as the sole stockholder. The average number of films produced by Lenfilm has decreased from about 30 annually in the Soviet era to about two to six in post-Soviet years. The studio's premises are located on Kamennoostrovskii prospect (before: prospekt Kirova).

LEONOV, EVGENII PAVLOVICH (b. 2 September 1926, Moscow– d. 29 January 1994, Moscow). Russian actor. Leonov graduated from the Moscow Theater Studio in 1947. He then worked at Stanislav-skii Theater from 1948–1967 and at Maiakovskii Theater from 1968 to 1971. In 1972, he joined the troupe of the Theater of the Lenin Communist Youth (Lenkom) where he starred in several out-standing productions of classical and contemporary plays directed by **Mark Zakharov**.

Leonov's film career began with episodic roles in *Happy Voy-age* (Schastlivyi reis, 1949) and **Vladimir Petrov**'s soccer **comedy** *Sporting Honor* (Sportivnaia chest', 1951). He proved his talent for dramatic roles as Cossack Iakov Shibalok in Vladimir Fetin's *Don Story* (Donskaia povest', 1964) and in melodramas such as **Iosif Kheifits**'s *The Rumiantsev Case* (Delo Rumiantseva, 1956), as the war veteran and plumber Ivan in **Andrei Smirnov**'s sentimental hit *The Belorussian Station* (Belorusskii vokzal, 1970), and as Potapov in Sergei Mikaelyan's controversial *The Bonus* (Premiia, 1975).

However, Leonov's popularity predominantly rests on the com-edies that made him a national superstar, adored both by children and adults. Short, bald, and rotund, the actor was delightful in carefree, unpretentious crowd-pleasers such as *Striped Trip* (Polosatyi reis, 1961) and *Gentlemen of Luck* (Dzhentel'meny udachi, 1972). In artistically ambitious satires such as **Georgii Daneliia**'s subversive *Thirty-three* (Tridtsat'-tri, 1966), Leonov persuasively embodies outsiders who tend to be misunderstood, abused, and sometimes ostracized. Daneliia gave Leonov some of his most rewarding roles, blending comedy with social analysis in *Afonia* (1975) and *Autumn Marathon* (Osennii marafon, 1979), with tragic undertones in *Tears Were Falling* (Slezy kapali, 1982), and with openly anti-utopian and sarcastic intonations in *Kin-Dza-Dza* (1986). The humanity and tragicomical depth that distinguish Leonov's best work are based on fundamental compassion for human weakness; the humor in his por-trayals is never obnoxious or condescending but always forgiving.

Leonov's extraordinary vocal talent was used in numerous cartoon shorts, for example, in the *Winnie the Pooh* (Vinni-Pukh) series in 1969–1972.

The actor joined the Communist Party in 1955; he was named Peo-ple's Artist of the USSR in 1978. Leonov is buried at Novodevich'e cemetery.

Other films: *Shine, Shine, My Star* (Gori, gori, moia zvezda, 1970); *The Legend of Till* (Legenda o Tile, 1977); *An Ordinary Miracle* (Obyknovennoe chudo, 1978); *To Kill the Dragon* (Ubit' drakona, 1988).

LEVCHUK, TIMOFEI VASIL'EVICH (b. 19 January 1912, village Bystrovka, Zhitomir district, Ukraine–d. 14 December 1998, Kiev). Ukrainian director. Levchuk graduated from the Kiev Film Institute in 1934. He then worked as an assistant to **Ivan Kavaleridze** and **Ihor' Savchenko** and participated in the creation of an early Ukrainian color film, **Nikolai Ekk**'s *May Night* (Maiskaia noch', 1941) from a Nikolai Gogol' story. In 1949, Levchuk made his directorial debut with the educational **documentary** *Dawn on the Carpathian Mountains* (Zaria nad Karpatami). Following other documentary shorts, he helmed his first features, the heavily theatrical *In the Steppes of Ukraine* (V stepiakh Ukrainy, 1952) and *The Snowball Tree Grove* (Kalinovaia roshcha, 1953), from plays by Aleksandr Korneichuk (1905–1972). *The Flame of Fury* (Plamia gneva, 1955), about efforts to unite Ukraine and Russia, and the biopic *Ivan Franko* (1956) were historical pictures with transparent political messages, which became the director's trademark.

Levchuk's main claim to fame is the historical trilogy *The Woman from Kiev* (Kievlianka, 1958–1960), which covers events from the Bolshevik October coup to the late 1950s. Focusing on three generations of a worker's family, it also illustrates the history of the famous weaponry factory Arsenal that had been the subject of a classical silent by **Aleksandr Dovzhenko** three decades earlier. Levchuk landed a hit with *Two Years above the Abyss* (Dva goda nad propast'iu, 1967) about an underground operation in the Great Patriotic War. *The Error of Honoré de Balzac* (Oshibka Onore de Bal'zaka, 1968) is devoted to a Ukraine-related episode from the French author's life. In *A Long Way on a Short Day* (Dlinnaia doroga v korotkii den', 1970), Levchuk polemically juxtaposes the work of Soviet physicists promoting world peace to that of Western scientists whose findings are used for sinister goals. Levchuk followed it with another trilogy, *The Song of Kovpak* (Duma o Kovpake, 1973–1976), about the creation of a guerilla unit in 1941 and its increasing strategic impact under legendary Commander Kovpak. *If the Enemy Does Not Surrender* (Esli vrag ne sdaetsia, 1982), the reconstruction of a large-scale operation in World War II, prominently features Iosif Stalin, whose famous quote inspired the film's title. Levchuk concluded his career with the contemporary thriller *The Bay of Death* (Bukhta smerti, 1991, codirected with Hryhorii Kokhan), an adaptation of a James Chase novel.

A director of thematic versatility, Levchuk exercised enormous administrative and ideological influence on postwar **Ukrainian cinema**. However, the mediocre artistic quality that characterizes his output was admitted even by loyal critics, albeit in somewhat veiled formulations.

Levchuk joined the Communist Party in 1942 and was named People's Artist of the Ukrainian SSR in 1969 and People's Artist of the USSR in 1972. He held high political positions, including candidate member of the Central Committee of the Ukrainian Communist Party since 1973. Beginning in 1957, he was among the driving forces behind the creation of a Ukrainian Filmmakers' Union, an organization that he helmed since 1963.

Other films: *Ukraine Is Singing* (Poet Ukraina, 1954); *The Cosmic Fusion* (Kosmicheskii splav, 1964); *The Kotsiubinsky Family* (Sem'ia Kotsiubinskikh, 1971).

LEVITSKII, ALEKSANDR ANDREEVICH (b. 23 November 1885–d. 4 July 1965, Moscow). Russian cinematographer and pedagogue. Levitskii, son of a professional photographer, became an accomplished photo reporter in the early 1900s before being hired by the Russian branch of Pathé.

Leading directors of early Russian cinema such as **Vladimir Gardin**—for whom Levitskii filmed *Anna Karenina, A Nest of the Gentry* (Dvorianskoe gnezdo, both 1914), and other prestigious literary adaptations—and **Iakov Protazanov** valued Levitskii for his ability to sense the visual dimension of classical texts and preserve some essential elements on screen. Levitskii was famous for a number of technical innovations, including experiments with lenses and lighting techniques creating the illusion of spatial depth. He was the first Russian cameraman to use double exposure—in the final scene of Protazanov's *Departure of a Great Old Man* (Ukhod velikogo startsa, 1912). Although generally considered an adherent to traditional realism, Levitskii did occasionally lend his talent to nonrealistic films such as Vsevolod Meierkhol'd's *Portrait of Dorian Gray* (Portret Doriana Greia, 1915).

Following the 1917 Bolshevik Revolution, Levitskii was much in demand as a newsreel cameraman, an experience that three decades later earned him a Stalin Prize (1949) for being one of the cinematographers who captured Lenin on film. Soviet cinema historians praise his **documentary** work for its intelligent, nonmechanical approach. Levitskii continued to work on features too, among them **Ivan Perestiani**'s *Portrait of a Minister* (Portret ministra, 1917), **Iurii Zheliabuzhskii**'s *Tsarevich Aleksei* (1918), and **Aleksandr Razumnyi**'s adaptation of Maksim Gor'kii's *The Mother* (Mat', 1920). His best-remembered contribution to the Soviet avant-garde is his camera work for **Lev Kuleshov**'s *The Unusual Adventures of Mr. West in the Land of the Bolsheviks*/Neobychainye prikliucheniia mistera Vesta v strane bol'shevikov, 1924). However, when **Sergei Eizenshtein** hired Levitskii to shoot *Battleship Potemkin* (Bronenosets Potemkin, 1925), their cooperation ended prematurely due to aesthetic disagreements.

Many of the leading Soviet cinematographers studied with Levitskii, who began to teach at the State Film School (GTK, later **VGIK**) in 1924 and was promoted to the rank of full professor in 1939. Among his students were **Anatolii Golovnia**, **Leonid Kosmatov**, and **Boris Volchek**.

Levitskii was named Merited Artist of the Russian Federation in 1946.

Other films: *Kreutzer Sonata* (Kreitserova sonata, 1914); *Comrade Elena* (Tovarishch Elena, 1918); *Those Who Were Enlightened* (Te, kotorye prozreli, 1931).

LIOZNOVA, TAT'IANA MIKHAILOVNA [Moiseevna] (b. 20 July 1924, Moscow). Russian director and screenwriter. Lioznova, whose father was killed in action in World War II, studied in **Sergei Gerasimov** and **Tamara Makarova**'s workshop at the Soviet State Film School **VGIK**, graduating in 1949. She worked as Gerasimov's assistant before helming her first feature, *Memory of the Heart* (Pamiat' serdtsa, 1958), featuring a small episode of the Great Patriotic War.

Lioznova came into her own with edifying melodramas, two of which were based on scripts by author Vera Panova (1905–1973): *Evdokiia* (1961) about a married couple raising several adopted children, and *Early in the Morning* (Rano utrom, 1965), in which a community cares for two orphans. She landed a huge hit with *"Three Poplars" at Pliushchikha* ('Tri topolia' na Pliushchikhe, 1967) about a provincial woman on a shopping tour and a Moscow cabdriver who falls in love with her.

Lioznova has a predilection for strong characters committing selfless acts of loyalty and heroism. This was first reflected in *The Sky Submits to Them* (aka *They Conquer the Skies*/Im pokoriaetsia nebo, 1963) about test pilots risking their lives for the motherland. The praise of patriotic virtues also is the foundation of Lioznova's greatest success, the legendary 12-part television series *Seventeen Moments of Spring* (Semnadtsat' mgnovenii vesny), which premiered in August 1973 and has been aired countless times since. **Viacheslav Tikhonov** portrays Soviet agent Shtirlits, whose extraordinary skills and courage enable him to penetrate the Nazi hierarchy, transmit invaluable information to the Soviet high command during the last stages of World War II, and cleverly manipulate the German and American secret services. Lioznova managed to create an atmosphere of continuing suspense, despite remarkably little action and many naïve historical assumptions. The film's romanticized view of spies and the peculiar portrayal of the Nazi establishment made a long-lasting impact on popular historical perceptions in the USSR. The dimension of its popularity can only be compared to that of the **Vasil'ev brothers**' *Chapaev* (1934), which similarly gained entrance into everyday folklore, with countless Chapaev and Shtirlits jokes as illegitimate narrative offsprings.

Seventeen Moments was a near impossible act to follow, and apparently Lioznova refused to even try. After eight years of silence she made the musical melodrama *Carnival* (Karnaval, 1982) about a provincial girl whose dream to become an actress ends in disenchantment. Two television productions—*We, the Undersigned* (My, nizhepodpisavshiesia, 1980) and *The End of the World with a Subsequent Symposium* (Konets sveta s posleduiushchim simpoziumom, 1986, TV)—marked a rather early end to a career that certainly held more potential.

Lioznova's crowd-pleasers have been consistently free of aesthetic ambition; they typically blend quasi-documentary realism and restrained sentimentality, often transcending into the realm of modern fairy tale. The director, who has been called "the Iron Lady of Soviet cinema" for her uncompromising personality and harsh manners on the set, joined the Communist Party in 1962. She was named People's Artist of the USSR in 1984. In 1975–1980, she taught at VGIK (together with **Lev Kulidzhanov**).

LISENKO, NATALIIA [Natal'ia] **ANDRIANOVNA** [French spelling Nathalie Lissenko] (b. 18 August 1884 [other sources: 1886], St. Petersburg–d. 7 January 1969, Paris). Russian-French actress. Lisenko studied acting at the Moscow Art Theater (MKhAT) until 1904 and subsequently joined various theater troupes in the Russian provinces before returning to Moscow as a member of the famous Korsh Theater.

The actress made her film debut in 1915 in the title role of **Petr Chardynin**'s *Katiusha Maslova*, from Lev Tolstoi's novel *Resurrection*. She starred in other literary adaptations such as **Iakov Protazanov**'s *Nikolai Stavrogin* (1915) from Fedor Dostoevskii's *The Devils*, and *Father Sergius* (Otets Sergii, 1918) from Tolstoi's novella, in which she impressed viewers and critics as the lascivious merchant widow Makovkina. Lisenko, whom film historian Semen Ginzburg characterized as "a gifted and experienced professional," was married to the greatest star of the Russian silent period, **Ivan Mozzhukhin**, and costarred in many films with him. Among the directors with whom Lisenko worked were **Evgenii Bauer** (*Leon Drey*, 1915) and Czeslav Sabinskii (*The Hawk's Nest*/Iastrebinoe gnezdo, 1916; *In a Busy Spot*/Na boikom meste, 1916).

In 1918, escaping from the Bolshevik Revolution and subsequent Civil War, Lisenko, together with producer **Iosif Ermol'ev**, Protazanov, and Mozzhukhin, immigrated via the Crimea and Istanbul to France. In films of Russian émigré directors, she managed to maintain her star status in the 1920s. Thus, she appeared in her husband's *Carnival's Child* (L'enfant du carnaval), Aleksandr Volkov's (Alexander Wolkoff) *Kean* (1923), but also worked with French and Italian filmmakers, including Jean Epstein (*The Lion of the Moguls*/Le Lion des Mogols, 1924) and Marcel L'Herbier (*The Night of the Princes*/

Nuit de princes, 1929). In 1927–1928, she spent a year in Berlin, appearing in films such as *Rasputin's Love Adventures* (Rasputins Liebesabenteuer, 1928). After some disappointing attempts to continue her career in sound film, Lisenko retired from the screen in 1939, the year of her husband's passing.

Other films: *The Seagull* (Chaika, 1915); *The Sin* (Grekh, 1916); *Side-Scenes of the Screen* (Kulisy ekrana, 1917); *Little Elli* (Maliutka Elli, 1918); *The Wild Girl* (La fille sauvage, 1922); *Children's Souls Accuse You* (Kinderseelen klagen euch an, 1927).

LITHUANIAN CINEMA. *See* ADOMAITIS, REGIMANTAS; BABKAUSKAS, BRONIUS; BANIONIS, DONATAS; BUDRAITIS, JUOSAS; FAINTSIMMER, ALEKSANDR; GIEDRYS, MARIJONAS; GRICIUS, JONAS; LITHUANIAN FILM STUDIO; *NOBODY WANTED TO DIE*; STROEVA, VERA; VABALAS, RAIMONDAS; ŽALAKEVIČIUS, VYTAUTAS PRANO; ŽEBRIŪNAS, ARŪNAS.

LITHUANIAN FILM STUDIO. The studio's origins go back to the private Kaunas Film Studio, owned by a movie lover, Linartas. In July 1940, under the new Soviet power, it was turned into the Lithuanian Documentary Film Studio. In 1944, when Lithuania was liberated from the German armies and forced into the Soviet Union, the studio was established anew and transferred to Vilnius in 1949. During these years, it exclusively produced newsreels and **documentaries**, some of them made by Lithuanian natives such as Viktoras Starošas and Liudgardas Maciulevičaus. In 1954, the production of feature films began. (Earlier, Russian director **Vera Stroeva** helmed *Maryté* [Marite, 1947] about a martyr of the anti-Nazi struggle, the guerilla fighter Maryté [Maria] Melnikaite [1923–1943]. Although Lithuanian actors starred in the film, the main operations were carried out at **Mosfilm Studio**. In 1951, **Aleksandr Faintsimmer** directed *Dawn over the Neman* [Aušra prie Nemuno/Nad Nemanom rassvet, 1953], touted as a Lithuanian production although made predominantly with **Lenfilm Studio** resources. Featuring a strictly Stalinist point of view, the film schematically juxtaposes the pro-Soviet forces and those resisting them in the Lithuanian countryside, showing how Lithuanians ultimately were overjoyed to live under Iosif Stalin's rule.)

The first Lithuanian director entrusted with a feature film in the new studio was Vytautas Mikalauskas, who made *The Blue Horizon* (Zydrasis horizontas/Goluboi gorizont, 1957). In the 1960s, **Vytautas Žalakevičius** became the leading director of **Lithuanian cinema** and the country's first filmmaker with an international reputation. After completing the Soviet State Film School **VGIK**, he returned to Vilnius and directed **comedies** such as *Before It's Too Late* (Kol nevelu/ Poka ne pozdno, 1958, codirected with Iu. Fogel'man). Together with **Marijonas Giedrys** and **Arūnas Žebriūnas**, Žalakevičius contributed to *Living Heroes* (Gyvieji didvyriai/Zhivye geroi, 1960), a so-called omnibus film consisting of three separate novellas, all dealing with postwar conflicts but allowing for remarkable stylistic diversity, ranging from the poetic to the brutally realistic. Žalakevičius's ***Nobody Wanted to Die*** (Nekas nenorejo mirti/Nikto ne khotel umirat', 1965) for the first time brought to the screen the tragic tornness of the Lithuanian nation after World War II, exemplified by a deadly family conflict in which pro- and anti-Soviet forces clash.

An important theme for Lithuanian filmmakers was the world of children, which permitted a quasi-naïve, nonideological treatment of reality. An outstanding example of this approach is Žebriūnas's *The Girl and the Echo* (Paskutinė atostogų diena/Devochka i ekho, 1964). It was far more difficult to address questions of contemporary social relevance, and directors who attempted such an approach experienced considerable censorship quarrels. Thus, **Raimondas Vabalas**'s *The Summer Begins in June* (Birželis, vasaros pradžia/Iun'-nachalo leta, 1969) was shelved. A particularly dramatic case was that of *Feelings* (Jausmai, 1968) by Algirdas Dausa and Almantas Grikevičius (b. 1935), an intense psychological drama starring two of Lithuania's greatest actors, **Regimantas Adomaitis** and **Juosas Budraitis** as fishermen-twins entangled in a tragic love story. *Feelings* was not cleared for distribution outside Lithuania; many consider it the country's best feature film ever. Lithuanian Film Studio found a politically safe niche in historical epics (*Herkus Mantas*, 1972, by Giedrys) and musicals (*The Devil's Bride* [Velnio nuotaka/Chertova nevesta] by Žebriūnas).

Of the younger generation, Algimantas Puipa (b. 1951) is the most productive filmmaker who has maintained a steady output even in the 1990s; his *Eternal Light* (Amžinoji šviesa, 1988) shows the postwar clashes in a new, poetic vision as the onset of modernity symbolized by the transition from horse to tractor. The more elitist Šarūnas Bartas (b. 1964) has a small, loyal following and has found recognition at international festivals; of importance is the work of Raimundas Banionis (b. 1957) and the documentary director Audrius Stonys (b. 1966).

From 1957 to 1991, Lithuanian Film Studio each year completed about three full-length feature films, 30 documentaries, and 30–40 newsreels. After Lithuania regained its independence in 1991, on average about one film annually was produced by the studio. There is still some state support for national cinema, which funds about two to three full-length features per year, in addition to about 10 documentaries. Since 1992, the Lithuanian Film Studio's facilities and equipment have been leased to foreign companies producing Western television miniseries, costume dramas in particular.

LITTLE RED DEVILS, THE (Tsiteli eshmakunebi/Krasnye d''iavoliata, 1923). State Film Department (Goskinprom) of the Georgian People's Commissariat of Enlightenment (Narkompros). Two parts; 139 min., b/w. Directed by **Ivan Perestiani**. Script: Pavel Bliakhin, Ivan Perestiani. Cinematography: Aleksandr Digmelov. Cast: Pavel Esikovskii, Sofiia Zhozeffi, Kador Ben-Salim, Vladimir Sutyrin. Premiere: 30 November 1923. A sound track was added to an abridged, one-part version in 1943.

During the Civil War in Ukraine in 1918–1921, Red Army commander Semen Budennyi fights the troops of legendary anarchist leader, "father" (*bat'ko*) Makhno (Sutyrin). Young Misha (Esikovskii), a member of the Communist Youth organization Komsomol, and his sister Duniasha (Zhozeffi), who lost their father during a Makhno attack, as well as their friend, African-American Tom Jackson (Ben-Salim), join the First Cavalry Army of Budennyi. After numerous adventures, they manage to capture Makhno.

LITTLE VERA (Malen'kaia Vera, 1988). **Gor'kii Studio for Children's and Youth Films**. 136 min., color. Directed by **Vasilii**

Pichul. Script: Mariia Khmelik. Cinematography: Efim Reznikov. Music: Vladimir Matetskii. Cast: Natal'ia Negoda, Iurii Nazarov, Liudmila Zaitseva, Andrei Sokolov, Aleksandr Alekseev-Negreba. Premiere: October 1988.

In a provincial industrial town in Southern Russia, 17-year-old Vera (Negoda) idles her life away with friends in parks and discotheques, paying no attention to school or the clumsy pedagogical attempts of her working-class parents (Nazarov, Zaitseva) and her older brother Viktor. She falls in love with the arrogant student Sergei (Sokolov), who eventually moves in with the family. Never-ending quarrels between Sergei and Vera's hard-drinking father lead to a fight in which Sergei is severely injured. In court, Vera protects her father but later attempts suicide. Sergei eventually recovers and returns to Vera, while her father suffers a heart attack.

LIVANOV, BORIS NIKOLAEVICH (b. 8 May 1904, Moscow–d. 22 September 1972, Moscow). Russian actor. Livanov studied in the Fourth Studio of the Moscow Art Theater (MKhAT) and joined its troupe in 1924. For almost half a century, he was valued in roles of romantic aristocrats and courageous, noble idealists, sometimes with a satirical penchant.

In Soviet cinema, Livanov debuted with a lead in **Iurii Zheliabuzhskii**'s fairy tale *Father Frost* (Morozko, 1923) and appeared in an episode of **Sergei Eizenshtein**'s *October* (Oktiabr', 1927). Livanov's star status is based on a number of 1930s sound films. He was convincing as the Communist docker Karl Renn in **Vsevolod Pudovkin**'s *The Deserter* (Dezertir, 1933); as an overly self-assured but talented young activist in **Aleksandr Macheret**'s contemporary comedy *The Private Life of Petr Vinogradov* (Chastnaia zhizn' Petra Vinogradova, 1935); as well as the militant Bolshevik administrator supporting frail Professor Polezhaev in **Iosif Kheifits** and **Aleksandr Zarkhi**'s *Baltic Deputy* (Deputat Baltiki, 1937). At times, the actor's declamatory pathos reeked of theatricality, for example, in the lead of **Aleksandr Ivanovskii**'s *Dubrovskii* (1936) from Aleksandr Pushkin's prose fragment. However, Livanov's portrayal of the patriotic Prince Pozharskii in Pudovkin's historical epic *Minin and Pozharskii* (Minin i Pozharskii, 1939) stood out for its natural grace and heroism; it won the actor his first Stalin Prize (1941). The ability to portray genuine leaders made Livanov the preferred choice for roles of captains and admirals in a variety of adventurous pictures; two plum parts were the loud-mouthed Prince Potemkin in **Mikhail Romm**'s *Admiral Ushakov* (1953) and Russian 18th-century scientist Mikhail Lomonosov in Aleksandr Ivanov's 1955 biopic.

Livanov won Stalin Prizes in 1947 for the role of Commander Rudnev in *The Cruiser "Variag"* (Kreiser "Variag"), and in 1942, 1949, and 1950 for stage performances. He was named People's Artist of the USSR in 1948. Livanov is buried at Novodevich'e cemetery. The house in which he lived after 1938 (former Gor'kii Street, now Tverskaia #6) carries a memorial plaque. Livanov's son, Vasilii Livanov (b. 1935), is a popular stage and film actor.

Other films: *Four and Five* (Chetyre i piat', 1924); *The Four Visits of Samuel Wolfe* (Chetyre vizita Samuelia Vul'fa, 1934); *The Blind Musician* (Slepoi muzykant, 1961); *The Bells of the Kremlin* (Kremlevskie kuranty, 1970).

LOPUSHANSKII, KONSTANTIN SERGEEVICH (b. 12 June 1947, Dnepropetrovsk). Russian director and screenwriter. Lopushanskii studied violin at the State Conservatory of Kazan', graduating in 1970, followed by graduate study at Leningrad Conservatory with specialization in the history of music, a field in which he holds a PhD. Lopushanskii studied film direction at the Supreme Courses for Directors and Screenwriters (VKSR) with **Emil Loteanu**, receiving his professional degree in 1978.

After assisting **Andrei Tarkovskii** on *Stalker* (1979), Lopushanskii made his debut in 1980 with the short *Solo* about the siege of Leningrad. He won nationwide acclaim with the alarming anti-utopia *Letters of a Dead Man* (Pis'ma mertvogo cheloveka, 1986). Released in the early days of perestroika, the picture reflected the concerns of many intellectuals about a looming nuclear war. Shot in dark, brownish tones, this cinematic tour de force attempts to visualize the unimaginable horrors of modern warfare and its consequences for future generations. The film conveys a humanist message, conspicuously avoiding Communist propaganda clichés and only rarely slipping into melodramatically enforced sermonizing.

Lopushanskii's following picture was made when the perestroika euphoria had already passed; it reflects the increasing pessimism regarding the improvability of society and humankind as a whole. *The Museum Visitor* (Posetitel' muzeia, aka *Expulsion from Hell/ Izgnanie iz ada*, 1989) intensifies the director's trademark ominous atmosphere but is far from the humanity of Lopushanksii's previous picture. The story of an underwater museum in an ecologically destitute world that is populated by genetically deformed people impressed festival audiences but was hardly seen anywhere else. *Russian Symphony* (Russkaia simfoniia, 1994), the third installment of Lopushanskii's apocalyptic trilogy, departs from the narrative coherence of his earlier films and primarily aims to evoke a mood of despair and hopelessness, contrasting motifs of classical Russian literature against a contemporary setting.

Similar to Tarkovskii, Lopushanskii is driven by the urge to create a "supercinema" (*sverkh-kino*), transcending cinema's conventional paradigm by imbuing it with an explicit spiritual charge and eschatological function. Yet his indulgence in amassing cultural quotations and religious symbols proves burdensome and tends to clash with basic laws of genre and perception, making the viewing experience more trying than enlightening and turning cinema into an elitist pleasure for the initiated few.

Lopushanskii was chairman of the Christian Film Association of St. Petersburg in 1991–1996.

Other films: *Tears in Windy Weather* (Slezy v vetrenuiu pogodu, 1978, short); *End of the Century* (Konets veka, 2001); *The Ugly Swans* (Gadkie lebedi, 2006).

LOTEANU, EMIL [Russian sources: Lotianu, Emil' Vladimirovich] (b. 6 November 1936, Clocusna, Ocnita [Socriani, Chernigov province]–d. 18 April 2003, Moscow). Moldovan director, scriptwriter, and composer. Loteanu, who lost his father and mother in World War II, studied with famed actor Vasilii Toporkov (1889–1970) at the studio school of the Moscow Art Theater (MKhAT) from 1953 to 1956 while also acting on stage at the Moscow Pushkin Theater. He subsequently enrolled in **Grigorii Roshal'**'s directing workshop at the Soviet State Film School **VGIK**, graduating in 1962, and began to work as a director at **Moldova-Film Studio**.

Loteanu began his career with poetic **documentaries**, a genre in which he worked simultaneously with feature films well into the

1980s (*Fresco on White*/Freska na belom, 1967; *My White City*/Moi belyi gorod, 1973, and others). In 1963, he helmed his first full-length feature, which also became his diploma film, *Wait for Us at Dawn* (Asteptati-ne in zori/Zhdite nas na rassvete), set in 1919 in Bessarabia where pro-Bolshevik troops defeated Romanian forces. *Red Meadows* (Poienele rosii/Krasnye poliany, 1966), a simple triangle story set among shepherds in contemporary Moldova, impressed critics with its romantic worldview and expressive use of color.

Loteanu became the leading director of **Moldovan cinema** with three pictures that all combine 19th-century scenery, sophisticated cinematography, and love stories overflowing with uninhibited passion and grand gestures. *Fiddlers* (Lautarii/Lautary, 1972) is a broad canvas about gypsy life, displaying all of the director's strengths—panoramic landscape compositions, sensual music, and a slow narrative rhythm erupting in sudden acts of violence—but also characteristic weaknesses, most frustratingly a plot structure that falls apart due to Loteanu's overindulgence in beautiful imagery and sound. With *The Tabor Leaves for Heaven* (aka *Queen of the Gypsies*/Tabor ukhodit v nebo, 1975), based on early stories by Maksim Gor'kii, Loteanu landed one of the greatest box-office hits of Soviet cinema and made stars of its leads, **Svetlana Tomà** and **Grigore Grigoriu**, who portray a beautiful girl and a horse thief in love. The gypsy milieu and its melodious culture—longtime favorites of Russian audiences—denote both unabashed emotions suppressed in the modern age, and a fatalistic acceptance of the tragic outcome. This holds true, too, for *My Loving and Tender Beast* (aka *The Shooting Party*, aka *A Hunting Accident*/Moi laskovyi i nezhnyi zver', 1978), a picturesque Anton Chekhov adaptation that earned harsh criticism for the liberties taken with the original source.

The 1980s proved a decade of slow decline for Loteanu. His international megaproduction *Anna Pavlova* (aka *The Divine Anna*, aka *Pavlova: A Woman for All Times*, 1983) turned into a commercial disappointment, despite sensational subject matter and a fashionably nostalgic air. (Noteworthy, too, is the appearance of two famous filmmakers in episodic roles, Martin Scorsese and Michael Powell.) The director had obviously lost his feel for viewers' predilections and seemed forlorn in post-Soviet cinema. His last film, *The Shell* (Skorlupa, 1993), is a three-hour requiem mourning the loss of beauty and free bohemian life in a contemporary urban setting. At the time of his death, Loteanu was preparing an international coproduction about legendary singer Maria Cebotari.

Loteanu joined the Communist Party in 1968. In 1969, he was named Merited Artist of the Moldovan SSR, and in 1980, People's Artist of the Russian Federation. He served as president of the Moldovan Filmmakers' Union in 1987–1992.

Loteanu once called himself "a Moldovan Muscovite or a Muscovite Moldovan"; his relations with his motherland were often strained. He was married, among others, to actress Galina Beliaeva (b. 1961), the female lead in *My Loving and Tender Beast* and *Anna Pavlova*.

Other films: *There Once Lived a Boy* (Zhil-byl mal'chik, 1960, short); *This Moment* (Aceasta clipa/Eto mgnovenie, 1968); *The Morning Star* (Luceafarul, 1987, TV); *The Suffering* (Durerea, 1989).

LUKASHEVICH, TAT'IANA NIKOLAEVNA (b. 21 November 1905, Ekaterinoslavl' [Dnepropetrovsk]–d. 2 March 1972, Moscow). Russian director. Lukashevich belonged to the first graduating class of Moscow State Film Technicum (GTK—Gosudarstvennyi tekhnikum kinematografii, later **VGIK**) in 1927, after which she worked as an assistant director and director at **Mezhrabpomfilm Studio**. Her first pictures were instructional shorts and **documentaries** such as the pamphlet *War to Imperialist War* (Voina imperialisticheskoi voine, 1928) and *Care for the Sick* (Ukhod za bol'nym). Her feature film *The Crime of Ivan Karavaev* (Prestuplenie Ivana Karavaeva, 1929) dealt with contemporary social problems, as did the **comedy** *Spring Days* (Vesennie dni, 1934, codirected with Ruben Simonov). Lukashevich's first popular success was *Gavroche* (1937), from motifs of Victor Hugo's *Les Misérables*, about a boy amidst the turmoil of the Paris Commune. The harmless yet profoundly humane and touching urban comedy *The Foundling* (Podkidysh, 1939) became a huge hit, making stars of **Faina Ranevskaia**, **Rostislav Pliatt**, and **Rina Zelenaia**.

Lukashevich, who was generally viewed as a solid craftsman but lacking artistic ambitions, also filmed social dramas (*Certificate of Maturity*, aka *Problem Child*/Attestat zrelosti, 1954) and melodramas, but regularly returned to the genre she knew best. Thus, her comedies of the early 1960s such as *Knight Move* (Khod konem, 1963) were crowd-pleasers, although none of them could outshine *The Foundling*. In the early 1950s, Lukashevich directed a number of screen versions based on celebrated Moscow stage productions: Lope de Vega's *The Dance Teacher* (Uchitel' tantsev, 1952), *Anna Karenina* (1953) with a stellar ensemble of MKhAT performers far beyond their characters' ages, and *Wedding with a Dowry* (Svad'ba s pridanym, 1953, codirected by Boris Ravenskikh), all of which became considerable box-office successes.

Lukashevich never won an award or a title in all of her career, a sad testimony to the lack of official and critical appreciation for the art of entertaining mass audiences in Soviet cinema.

Other films: *Wings* (Kryl'ia, 1956); *The Blind Musician* (aka *Sound of Life*/Slepoi muzykant, 1960); *The Island of Koldun* (Ostrov Koldun, 1964).

LUKOV, LEONID DAVYDOVICH (b. 2 May 1909, Mariupol' [Zhdanov]–d. 24 April 1963, Moscow). Ukrainian-Russian director and screenwriter. In the late 1920s, Lukov studied at a school for workers (*rabfak*) and was a journalist with local newspapers such as *The Komsomol Member of Ukraine* and *Our Truth*. His first screenplay, *Little Ivan and the Avenger* (Van'ka i mstitel'), was made into a film in 1927. He organized the Studio Cinema of the Workers' Youth (*Kinrabmol*) in Khar'kiv, where he directed a cycle of five silent **documentaries** under the title *My Homeland Is the Komsomol* (Rodina moia—komsomol).

After several silent features such as *Scum* (Nakip', 1930) and *Rootlets of the Commune* (Koreshki kommuny, 1931), Lukov helmed his first sound film, *I Love* (Ia liubliu, 1936), devoted to the life of miners in pre-Communist time. He then hit a nerve with the vivacious *A Great Life* (Bol'shaia zhizn', 1940, Stalin Prize 1941). On the surface little more than an unassuming miners' tale, it illustrates the officially propagated Communist work ethics taking root in everyday life. The film also contains a high dosage of Stalinist paranoia, featuring foreign spies undermining Soviet labor. But its authentic atmosphere and rank-and-file worker characters, avoiding the heroic idealization so typical of the 1930s, were genuine achievements.

At the beginning of the Great Patriotic War, Lukov was evacuated to Tashkent (see **Uzbekfilm Studio**) where he directed a short, *The Mother* (Mat', 1941), about a peasant woman who sacrifices all her sons to defeat the enemy, and the Civil War epic *Aleksandr Parkhomenko* (1942). *Two Fighters* (Dva boitsa, 1943), about military buddies, became a hit because of its gentle humor, sense of optimism, and quiet, self-assured patriotism.

It is not entirely clear why Lukov was chosen as the main target for one of the Communist Party's most infamous assault on the arts, "About the Film *A Great Life*, Part 2" (O kinofil'me "Bol'shaia zhizn'," 2-ia seriia)—the Central Committee's verdict on some "dangerous trends" in Soviet cinema, proclaimed on 4 September 1946. The fact that it had the title of Lukov's *A Great Life* in its headline for years gave the director's name a dubious ring, notwithstanding his proven absolute loyalty to the Communist cause and the Soviet state. In actuality, the second part of *A Great Life* features the same characters as its predecessor six years earlier, showing them involved in postwar conflicts, struggling for renewed productivity, and capturing traitors. Paradoxically, in 1952, the director received a Stalin Prize for *The Miners of Donetsk* (Donetskie shakhtery, 1950), a bland and ideologically sanitized rehashing of the plot of *A Great Life*.

In 1953, Lukov helmed two Maksim Gor'kii adaptations, *Barbarians* (Varvary) and *Vassa Zheleznova*. He landed a huge hit with *Various Destinies* (Raznye sud'by, 1956), an openly didactic, yet also romantic contemporary drama focusing on the characters' private lives, followed by the Soviet-Yugoslavian coproduction *Oleko Dundich* (1958) about a Serb fighting with the Red Army in the 1918–1921 Civil War. *Two Lives* (Dve zhizni, 1961), another box-office success, cleverly blends contemporary love melodrama and revolutionary tale. Lukov died during the shooting of *Believe Me, People* (Ver'te mne, liudi), about a criminal who tries to regain the trust of his fellow citizens after his release from prison; the film was finished by Vladimir Berenshtein and Il'ia Gurin and became a major box-office hit in 1964.

Lukov is one of the few regionalists among Soviet filmmakers. He received major impulses from his growing up in the Donetsk coal basin (Donbass), a region that he loved and whose inhabitants he sympathized with. One of Lukov's indubitable directorial strengths was the ability to alter episodes of prosaic everyday life and deft humor with moments of unabashed political pathos during which statements of love for the Soviet motherland and the Communist Party are exclaimed—the believability of the former lent credibility to the latter. The egalitarian spirit and often sincere emotions that pervade Lukov's pictures give them a certain warmth that contemporaries appreciated and that have often been remembered nostalgically.

Lukov, who joined the Communist Party in 1941, was named Merited Artist of the Uzbek SSR in 1942 and People's Artist of the RSFSR in 1957.

Other films: *The Director* (Direktor, 1938); *It Happened in the Donbass* (Eto bylo v Donbasse, 1946); *Private Aleksandr Matrosov* (Riadavoi Aleksandr Matrosov, 1948); *This Must Not Be Forgotten* (Ob etom zabyvat' nel'zia, 1954).

LUNACHARSKII, ANATOLII VASIL'EVICH (b. 23 November 1875, Poltava–d. 26 December 1933, Menton, France). Russian politician, playwright, screenwriter, and film critic. The son of a government official, Lunacharskii developed an early interest in Marxism and joined a Social Democratic organization in 1892. In 1895–1897, he studied philosophy and science at the University of Zurich and subsequently embarked on a career as a "professional revolutionary."

Although Lunacharskii joined the Bolshevik wing of the Social Democratic Russian Worker's Party in 1903, his cultural and philosophical views sometimes deviated substantially from those of Vladimir Lenin and other Bolshevik leaders. Thus, he showed a higher degree of tolerance toward both non-Communist art and artists, and radical leftist cultural organizations such as Aleksandr Bogdanov's Proletarian Culture (Proletkul't), which in the early 1920s had an impact on the development of **Sergei Eizenshtein** and **Dziga Vertov**, among others. After being appointed People's Commissar of Education in 1917, Lunacharskii repeatedly came to the rescue of intellectuals and artists in times of terror.

Lunacharskii was one of the major forces behind the creation of Soviet cinema and was involved in all aspects of financing, production, censorship, and distribution. He was a founding member of the Petrograd Film Committee in May 1918, a supervisory body that served as a template for similar organizations in Moscow and other cities. The decree "On the Transition of the Photo and Film Trade and Industry under the Authority of the People's Commissariat of Education," signed by Lenin into law on 27 August 1919, was formulated under Lunacharskii's auspices. Using his powerful position as well as an undeniable sense for artistic quality, he encouraged traditional filmmakers such as **Vladimir Gardin** to assume an active role in Soviet film production and education, leading to the foundation of the world's first state film school (Gosudarstvennaia shkola kinematografii, later **VGIK**). Following Lenin's instructions, he implemented the obligatory screening of newsreels and educational shorts prior to feature films in movie theaters, as well as the systematic recutting of foreign imports so as to comply with required ideological parameters.

Although Lunacharskii primarily emphasized cinema's propaganda potential, he repeatedly warned against an all-too dogmatic, exclusively politicized approach at the expense of artistry and entertainment. Often, he served as a cultural exegete publicizing and interpreting Lenin's views and statements about art in general and film in particular.

As a screenwriter, Lunacharskii made his debut with the *agitka The Condensation* (Uplotnenie, coauthored with **Aleksandr Panteleev**, 1918), a didactic **comedy** about a pro-Communist scientist who is forced to share his apartment with proletarians. He also authored *The Iron Heel* (Zheleznaia piata, 1919) from Jack London's novel and *The Daredevil* (Smel'chak, 1919), about a circus artist who becomes a Bolshevik fighter in the Civil War. *Locksmith and Chancellor* (Slesar' i kantsler, 1923), directed by Gardin with assistance from **Vsevolod Pudovkin**, is a naïve utopian story about the inevitability of a world revolution. *Poison* (Iad, 1927) pointed to the difficulties of former active revolutionary fighters when trying to blend in the everyday civility of the New Economic Policy (NEP).

Lunacharskii often expressed dismay over the results of his film-related efforts, with the exception of the prestigious German-Soviet coproduction, *The Salamander* (Salamandra, 1928), a somewhat simplified account of Paul Kammerer's genetic experiments that challenged religious dogmas and unleashed a hostile media campaign. Directed by **Grigorii Roshal'**, it starred Lunacharskii's wife, Natalia Rozenel' (1900–1962), among others.

Lunacharskii's aesthetic views present a peculiar blend of traditional populist and avant-garde elements. Thus, he considered *Battleship Potemkin* (Bronenosets Potemkin, 1925) a "plotless film," while *October* (Oktiabr', 1927)—in actuality a far more complex picture—was "an enormous step forward." In his own creative work, Lunacharskii favored traditional plot structures and turned several of his theater plays into screenplays, among them *Bear's Wedding* (Medvezh'ia svad'ba, 1923, after a novella by Prosper Mérimée), filmed in 1926 and attacked by Sergei Eizenshtein as "reactionary."

By the late 1920s, Lunacharskii's role as an empowered, sufficiently tolerant Communist intellectual had become an anachronism. Stripped of his position as commissar in 1929, he concentrated on writing criticism, including articles on Soviet and foreign cinema. In 1933, he was appointed ambassador to Spain but died on his way to Madrid.

LUNGIN [French spelling: Loungine], **PAVEL SEMENOVICH** (b. 12 July 1949, Moscow). Russian director, screenwriter, and producer. Born into the family of well-known screenwriter Semen Lungin, Pavel Lungin studied linguistics at Lomonosov University in Moscow, graduating in 1971. He then began to write screenplays, catering specifically to teenage audiences, including his debut, the high school **comedy** *It's All Because of My Brother* (Vse delo v brate, 1976), as well as action-filled, patriotic adventures such as the Civil War flick *The End of the Taiga Emperor* (Konets imperatora Taigi, 1978) and the historical martial arts drama *The Undefeatable* (Nepobedimyi, 1983); the latter both became blockbusters. In 1980, Lungin graduated from the Supreme Directing and Screenwriting Courses (VKSR) in Moscow, where one of his teachers was **Georgii Daneliia**.

Lungin's impressive directorial debut, *Taxi-Blues* (Taksi-bliuz, 1990), made international headlines and won a prize at Cannes. It was one of the earliest films to reflect the spirit of the new, post-Communist Russia, blending stringent, fast-paced storytelling and poignant social observation with unabashed commercial ambition. Lungin deliberately provoked controversy by reinforcing ethnic and class stereotypes and later subverting them just as forcefully; indeed, he deliberately blurred any ideological patterns that Russian critics in particular were expecting. No less radical was *Luna Park* (1992), which put the emerging radical nationalism and hooliganism among Russian youths within the framework of a father-son conflict, demonstrating the absurdity of anti-Semitic attitudes.

Lungin then moved to Paris and made a number of **documentaries** for French companies, including *Nice: A Little Russia* (Nitstsa: Malen'kaia Rossiia/A propos de Nice, 1993). The feature *Life Line* (Liniia zhizni/Ligne de vie, 1996), intended as a bittersweet comedy about the adventures of a Frenchman in the "Wild East," was all-too predictable in its devices and neither witty nor funny. But Lungin came back with a vengeance in *The Wedding* (Svad'ba, 2000); returning to his beginnings, he describes the clash between upper- and lower-class attitudes in an entertaining and ultimately forgiving manner. *Tycoon* (Oligarkh, 2002), a thinly veiled homage to Vladimir Berezovskii, reveals the corruption and inherent violence of the Russian state but idealizes its central character to a degree bordering on demagoguery. Once again, Lungin came back to form and caused a minor sensation with *The Island* (Ostrov, 2006), a reflection on spirituality and Russian Orthodoxy that became a box-office hit.

Lungin's films derive their considerable energy from the clash of seemingly incompatible sociocultural perceptions; although these clashes can have catastrophic consequences for the protagonists, in the end life always gets the upper hand. The filmmaker usually relies on first-class performers—**Oleg Borisov**, **Nonna Mordiukova**, **Armen Dzhigarkhanyan**, and **Vladimir Mashkov**, among others— whom he presents with gratifying challenges due to the ambivalence of his characters.

Other films: *Maiakovskii* (1995, doc.); *Poor Relatives* (Bednye rodstvenniki, 2005); *The Case of the Dead Souls* (Delo o mertvykh dushakh, 2005, TV); *A Branch of Lilacs* (Vetka sireni, 2007); *Ivan the Terrible and Metropolitan Filipp* (Ivan Groznyi i mitropolit Filipp, 2008).

LUSPEKAEV, PAVEL BORISOVICH (b. 20 April 1927, Lugansk– d. 17 April 1970, Moscow). Ukrainian-Russian actor. Luspekaev studied at the Shchepkin Theater School in Moscow, graduating in 1950. He worked in the theaters of Lugansk and Tbilisi, before joining the troupe of the Russian Dramatic Theater Lesia Ukrainka in

Kiev in 1956. In 1959, famous theater director Georgii Tovstonogov hired him to the Grand Dramatic Theater (BDT) in Leningrad.

Luspekaev made his screen debut in *They Descended from the Mountains* (Oni spustilis' s gor, 1955) and continued to act in adventurous films such as the blockbuster *The Secret of Two Oceans* (Taina dvukh okeanov, 1956), *The Blue Arrow* (Golubaia strela, 1958), and *The Green Chain* (Zelenye tsepochki, 1970). In the 1960s, he was also cast in propaganda movies dealing with the 1917 Bolshevik October Revolution. The actor's legendary fame, however, rests on a supporting role in **Vladimir Motyl'**'s cult hit **White Sun of the Desert** (Beloe solntse pustyni, 1969), in which Luspekaev, already terminally ill, portrays the melancholic yet physically stalwart loner Vereshchagin, conveying a proud, stoic manliness that faces danger and death with a song on his lips (Bulat Okudzhava's bittersweet "Nine Grams of Heart").

Luspekaev was named Merited Artist of the RSFSR in 1965.

Other films: *The Salvo of the Aurora* (Zalp Avrory, 1965); *I'm Moving toward the Thunderstorm* (Idu na grozu, 1965); *Three Fat Men* (Tri tolstiaka, 1966); *The Republic of ShKID* (Respublika ShKID, 1966).

– M –

MACHERET, ALEKSANDR VENIAMINOVICH (b. 27 December 1896, Baku–d. 12 September 1979, Moscow). Russian director, screenwriter, and film theorist. Macheret studied at the Social Science Department of Moscow University, graduating in 1922. The same year, he joined the workshop of avant-gardist Nikolai Foregger (1892–1939), the so-called Mastfor (masterskaia Foreggera), in which the human body and its movements were viewed as functionally similar to mechanical devices and machines. In 1929, he was one of the screenwriters of the celebrated **documentary Turksib**, and in 1930, the sound director on **Iulii Raizman**'s *The Earth Is Thirsty* (Zemlia zhazhdet, 1930).

Macheret made his directorial debut with *People and Deeds* (aka *Men and Jobs*/Dela i liudi, 1932), the story of an American engineer who actively participates in the building of the Dnepr hydroelectric plant (Dneprostroi), competing against a less sophisticated yet ultimately victorious Soviet worker. The film was popular with Soviet viewers and an international success but was taken to task for its crude realism. The theme of personal and political growth is treated in a comedic manner in *The Private Life of Petr Vinogradov* (aka *Peter Vinogradov*/Chastnaia zhizn' Petra Vinogradova, 1935). *The Motherland Calls* (aka *Call to Arms*/Rodina zovet, 1936) became part of a campaign in which filmmakers imagined what a forthcoming war might look like. Macheret then made an attempt to depict the barbaric inside of Adolf Hitler's Germany in *Swamp Soldiers* (aka *Concentration Camp*/Bolotnye soldaty, 1938). He followed it with the more lighthearted espionage thriller *Engineer Kochin's Error* (Oshibka inzhenera Kochina, 1939), a film that was praised for its inventive handling of an otherwise neglected genre in Soviet cinema.

Overall, the 1930s turned out to be the most successful decade of Macheret's career when he entered the ranks of the leading Soviet directors. In 1940, he was commissioned to create a film celebrating the 20th anniversary of Soviet cinema, *Film in Twenty Years* (Kino za dvadtsat' let; codirected with **Vsevolod Pudovkin** and **Esfir' Shub**). The experimental *Color Film Novellas* (Tsvetnye kinonovelly, 1941) consist of two medium-length tales adapted from Prosper Mérimée and Hans Christian Andersen, respectively. During the Great Patriotic War, Macheret helmed *I Am a Sailor of the Black Sea Fleet* (Ia—chernomorets, 1944). Filmed in Novorossiisk, which had just been liberated from Nazi troops, it stood out because of its authentic, war-torn cityscapes.

In 1951, Macheret was appointed research director at the Soviet State Film Archive Gosfil'mofond, a position he held until 1955. Over the following two decades, he published a number of monographs dealing with the aesthetics of cinema.

Macheret was honored with the title Merited Artist of the RSFSR in 1940.

Other films: *Pages of Life* (Stranitsy zhizni, 1948, codirected with **Boris Barnet**).

MAKAROVA, TAMARA FEDOROVNA (b. 13 August 1907, St. Petersburg–d. 19 January 1997, Moscow). Russian actress and screenwriter. Makarova's father, a military doctor, was killed during the

October Revolution in 1917. Beginning in 1924, Makarova studied with the theater avant-gardist Nikolai Foregger (1892–1939) in his Mastfor workshop and graduated from the Leningrad Institute for Stage Art in 1930.

Makarova made her film debut in *Another Person's Jacket* (Chuzhoi pidzhak, based on a story by Veniamin Kaverin, 1927); on its set, she met actor and budding director **Sergei Gerasimov**, whom she married in 1928. For half a century, Makarova played leads in Gerasimov's films, including *Do I Love You?* (Liubliu li ia tebia? 1934), *The Bold Seven* (Semero smelykh, 1936), and *Komsomol'sk* (1938). In *The Young Guard* (Molodaia gvardiia, 1948), she portrayed Elena Koshevaia. Makarova appeared in *People and Beasts* (Liudi i zveri, 1962), whose script she cowrote, and was a wise matriarch in *Daughters and Mothers* (Dochki-materi, 1975). The actress's impressive screen persona for decades defined the ideal, modern Soviet woman—intelligent, strong willed, professionally ambitious, and sensitive, but without sentimentality.

Most of Makarova's characters are socially active, for example, Shumilina in *The Teacher* (Uchitel', 1939), a performance that won her a Stalin Prize, or the physician Kozakova in *The Country Doctor* (Sel'skii vrach, 1952). But she also excelled in **Aleksandr Ptushko**'s picturesque fairy-tale adaptation *The Stone Flower* (Kamennyi tsvetok, 1946) and **Mikheil Chiaureli**'s hagiography of Iosif Stalin *The Oath* (Kliatva, 1946), for which she received another Stalin Prize. Makarova's last role was a cliché-defying, warm impersonation of Sof'ia Andreevna Tolstaia in Gerasimov's *Lev Tolstoi* (1984). However, her arguably highest accomplishment is the vulnerable, trusting Nina in the masterful Mikhail Lermontov adaptation *Masquerade* (Maskarad, 1941) in which insecurity and emotional torment are allowed to prevail over Makarova's typically rational, domineering demeanor.

As a popular pedagogue at the Soviet State Film School **VGIK** since 1943 (appointed to the rank of full professor in 1968), Makarova helped to shape several generations of Soviet filmmakers and actors.

Makarova became a member of the Communist Party in 1943; in 1950, she was awarded the title People's Artist of the USSR and in 1982, Hero of Socialist Labor. Makarova's son Artur Makarov

(d. 1995), adopted from her sister Liudmila who was persecuted under Stalin, worked as a screenwriter specializing in adventures and thrillers.

Other films: *The Deserter* (Dezertir, 1933); *The Invincible* (Nepobedimye, 1942); *The Journalist* (Zhurnalist, 1967).

MAKSIM TRILOGY (Trilogiia o Maksime, 1934–1938). **Lenfilm Studio**. 98, 105, 121 min., b/w. Directed by **Grigorii Kozintsev** and **Leonid Trauberg**. Script: Leonid Trauberg, Grigorii Kozintsev, Lev Slavin. Cinematography: **Andrei Moskvin**. Music: **Dmitrii Shostakovich**. Cast: **Boris Chirkov**, Stepan Kaiukov, Mikhail Tarkhanov, Valentina Kibardina, Boris Blinov, **Maksim Shtraukh**, Aleksandr Chistiakov, Elizaveta Alekseeva, **Mikhail Zharov**, **Vasilii Merkur'ev**, **Mikheil Gelovani**, **Iurii Tolubeev**, **Nataliia Uzhvii**, **Nikolai Kriuchkov**. Premiere: Part 1 — 27 January 1935, Part 2 — 23 May 1937, Part 3 — 2 February 1939.

Part 1, *Maksim's Youth* (Iunost' Maksima): In 1910, a Communist underground group spreads leaflets featuring anti-tsarist slogans. Maksim, a young, happy-go-lucky worker (Chirkov), and his comrades help the teacher Natasha (Kibardina), who was engaged in illegal activities in the factory, hide from the authorities. Maksim's friend Andrei (Kulakov) and another worker lose their lives. Their funeral turns into a huge demonstration at which police arrest numerous people, among them Maksim, who subsequently becomes a propagandist for the Bolshevik Party.

Part 2, *Maksim's Return* (Vozvrashchenie Maksima): In July 1914, Bolsheviks and Mensheviks compete for the representation of the proletariat in the Duma, the Russian parliament. Maksim, who just returned from exile, calls the workers to strike as a protest against the firing of six of their colleagues. The traitor Platon Dymba (Zharov) assaults Maksim, wounding him severely. When the strike unfolds and workers demonstrate by the thousands, the news of the outbreak of World War I suddenly arrives. Maksim gets drafted.

Part 3, *The Vyborg District* (Vyborgskaia storona): Following the 1917 October Revolution, Maksim is appointed state commissar in charge of the national bank. With great efforts, he learns the complexities of the banking trade and begins to fight off sabotaging underlings. Dymba, now a violent enemy of Soviet power, tries to rob a wine store but is arrested with Maksim's help. Maksim also exposes the conspiracy of a group of tsarist officers who prepare an attempt against Vladimir Lenin (Shtraukh). He then joins the Red Army in its fight against German interventionist troops.

MAKSIMOV [real name: Samus'], **VLADIMIR VASIL'EVICH** (b. 27 July 1880, Moscow–d. 22 March 1937, Moscow). Russian actor. Maksimov became a member of the Moscow Art Theater (MKhAT) in 1904, but switched to the Malyi Theater where he worked in 1906–1909 and 1911–1918. After moving to Petrograd in 1919, he joined the Grand Dramatic Theater, staying until 1924.

In 1911, Maksimov made his film debut as Savushka in *Old Times in Kashira* (Kashirskaia starina) about the life of rich Russian merchants. He soon became one of the superstars of early Russian cinema, with more than 60 film roles to his credit. First billed as the Russian competitor for Danish actor Valdemar Psilander, Maksimov appeared in historical frescos such as **Vasilii Goncharov**'s *The Defense of Sevastopol* (Oborona Sevastopolia, 1911). He cultivated an aura of romantic virility in roles of passionate "gentlemen of society" and military men, often battling love-induced neuroses. Maksimov's acting style has been described as "tense and nervous," for example, in **Iakov Protazanov** and **Vladimir Gardin**'s erotic blockbuster *Keys to Happiness* (Kliuchi schast'ia, 1913). He often played opposite the "Queen of the Screen," **Vera Kholodnaia**, helping to turn **Petr Chardynin**'s all-star *By the Fireplace* (U kamina, 1917), where he was cast as Prince Peshcherskii, into one of Russia's greatest blockbusters. Maksimov also was a celebrated master of so-called cinema declamations (*kinodeklamatsii*), silent shorts that were projected on the screen during a concert while the featured performer lip-synched to them, a method that many actors used for profitable solo tours. In Germany, Maksimov starred in Stellan Rye's esoteric *The Satan's Tavern* (aka *The House without Windows and Doors*/Das Haus ohne Tür, 1914).

One of the few movie stars who did not emigrate in 1918, Maksimov continued his career in early Soviet films such as **Aleksandr Panteleev**'s *Infinite Sorrow* (Beskonechnaia skorb', 1922), **Vladimir Gardin**'s *Locksmith and Chancellor* (Slesar' i kantsler, 1923), and **Aleksandr Ivanovskii**'s large-scale historical chronicle *Decem-*

brists (Dekabristy, 1926). The debate over Maksimov's qualities as a screen performer has never been resolved. While the actor's biographer B. Glovatskii maintained that Maksimov was just as nuanced and refined on screen as he was on stage, film historians Semen Ginzburg, Rostislav Iurenev, and others believe that his performances were clichéd and trivial and represent the worst aspects of early Russian cinema.

Maksimov taught acting at the Leningrad Institute of Stage Arts beginning in 1924. He was honored with the title Merited Artist of the Republic in 1925.

Other films: *The Woman Who Invented Love* (Zhenshchina, kotoraia izobrela liubov', 1918).

MALYAN, HENRIK [Russian sources list first name and patronymic as Genrikh Surenovich] (b. 30 September 1925, Telavi–d. 14 March 1988, Yerevan). Armenian director and screenwriter. Malyan, who was born in a small Armenian settlement in Georgia, graduated from the Yerevan Theater Institute in 1951 and from the Supreme Directing Courses of the State Institute of Theater Art (GITIS) in 1953. In 1954, he joined the staff of **Armenfilm Studio**; intermittently, he continued to direct theater productions throughout his career.

Malyan worked as an assistant director on the historical drama *Because of Honor* (Patvi hamar/Iz-za chesti, 1956), before being entrusted with a project of his own, the **comedy** adventure *The Guys from the Army Band* (Nvagakhmbi tghanere/Parni muzkomandy, 1961, codirected with G. Markaryan), about the activities of a Bolshevik musician prior to the establishment of Soviet power. This film and its sequel, *The Road to the Stage* (Tchanaparh depi krkes/Put' na arenu, 1963, with L. Isahakyan), about a circus artist, as well as the medium-length *The Sham Informer* in the satirical omnibus *Monsieur Jacques and Others* (Msyo Zhake yev urishner/Ms'e Zhak i drugie, 1966), demonstrated the director's talent for warm, touching comedy. Malyan's complex worldview became more apparent in *The Triangle* (Yerankyuni/Treugol'nik, 1967), an episodic tale about the friendship of five blacksmiths before and during the Great Patriotic War. His focus in this and subsequent pictures is on human individuality and characters' interaction within a very limited social and geographical space. This approach gives the actors in Malyan's films unusual opportunities to develop their characters through funny and tragic situations. A similar microdrama, *We and Our Mountains* (Menq enq, mer sarere/My i nashi gory, 1970) from Hrant Matevosyan's novel, tells about four shepherds who face trial for thoughtlessly slaughtering another man's sheep.

Malyan then turned to themes of his country's past. *Nahapet* (aka *Life Triumphs*, 1977) is one of the first Armenian pictures to thematize the 1915 Turkish genocide. The melodrama *A Slap in the Face* (aka *A Piece of Sky*; Ktor me yerkinq/Poshchechina, 1980) tells about a man who defends his love—he marries a prostitute—against social pressures. *A Drop of Honey* (Mi katil meghr/Kaplia meda, 1982), an antiwar parable, was Malyan's last completed film. He also wrote screenplays for **documentaries** such as *Immortality* (Bessmertie, 1979) and *Abundance* (Izobilie, 1987), as well as for the satirical almanac *Boomerang* (1988). In 1990, **Frunze Dovlatyan** completed a project begun by Malyan, *The Yearning* (Karot/Toska, 1990), the tragic story of a peasant whose desire for his native place—now part of Turkey—ultimately causes his death.

One of the most respected filmmakers in **Armenia cinema**, Malyan strove to convey through his films a sense of national identity, pushing the envelope as much as the political paradigm allowed him. At the same time, he accentuated universal human values as applied to national specifics, an approach furthered by his theater work to which Shakespeare was of foremost significance.

Malyan was honored with the title People's Artist of the USSR in 1982. In 1997, his memoirs, *Dialogue for a Third Person*, were published in Yerevan.

Other films: *Father* (Hayrik/Airik, 1973).

MANSUROV, BULAT [some Russian sources list the patronymic Bagautdinovich] (b. 7 July 1937, Chardzhou [Chärjew], Turkmenistan). Turkmen director, screenwriter, and producer. Mansurov studied at the conservatory of Frunze (now: Bishkek) in Kyrgyzstan and later was put in charge of music programs at the House of Young Pioneers in his native city in north-western Turkmenistan. In 1959–1963, he studied with **Sergei Gerasimov** and **Tamara Makarova** at the Soviet State Film School **VGIK** in Moscow.

Mansurov made his directorial debut at **Turkmenfilm Studio** with the parable *The Contest* (aka Shukur-Bakshi/Sostiazanie, 1964). It tells the story of a musician in the ancient time of war between Turan (Turkmen) and Tehran (Iranian) tribes who decides to participate in a contest on enemy territory in order to inspire peace and benevolence in the other nation. Visually and conceptually innovative, *The Contest*, in which the lead roles are played by nonprofessionals, presents a stylized yet authentic image of Turkmenistan's cultural heritage and played a groundbreaking role for the development of **Turkmen cinema**. *Quenching of Thirst* (Utolenie zhazhdy, 1966), from Iurii Trifonov's novel, deals with the building of a canal in the Karakum Desert and sheds light on the Stalinist past; the controversial film provided a final plum role for legendary actor **Petr Aleinikov** as the worker Mariutin. Mansurov then turned to a story by Andrei Platonov (1899–1951) about an Austrian prisoner of war who finds shelter in the 1920s in Turkmenistan but falls victim to a Civil War between pro-Bolshevik forces and militant defenders of traditional society, the so-called *basmachi*. This picture, *The Female Slave* (Rabynia, aka *Takyr*, 1969), is regarded by many critics as the director's highest achievement; like its predecessors, it was shot by cinematographer **Khodjakuli Narliev**, who also has played episodic roles in Mansurov's films.

There Is No Death, Pals! (Smerti net, rebiata!, 1970) is an unusual interpretation of the Great Patriotic War, the story of a group of Soviet soldiers confronting Nazi troops in the last days of the war in Germany; one impressive episode describes an eerie encounter with a deserted concentration camp.

In 1972, Mansurov went to **Kazakhfilm Studio** to make *The Funeral Feast* (Trizna) about a 19th-century poet who participates in a horse-riding contest because victory will allow him to free unjustly convicted prisoners. This philosophical reflection on power, opportunism, and the loneliness of the self-sacrificing hero met with stern opposition from local film officials and was only released in 1987. In the mid-1970s, Mansurov moved to Moscow, where he adapted Aleksandr Grin's *The Sparkling World* (Blistaiushchii mir, 1984). Sadly, cut off from his native environment—the primary source of his ascetic visual style with stern compositions of desert landscapes—Mansurov seems to have lost his specific touch. With Kyrgyz director **Tolomush Okeev**, he coauthored the screenplay for the large-scale historical epic *Chingiz Khan* (1990); however, the film was not completed. In the 1990s, Mansurov appeared predominantly as a producer. He also taught at VGIK (1992–1994) and other institutions

Other films: *Parable of Love* (Pritcha o liubvi, 1976); *The Seagulls Did Not Stop Here* (Siuda ne zaletali chaiki, 1977); *The Defeat* (Porazhenie, 1987, TV); *Sultan Beibars* (1989).

MARETSKAIA, VERA PETROVNA (b. 31 July 1906, Moscow—d. 17 August 1978, Moscow). Russian actress. Maretskaia studied with famed theater director Iurii Zavadskii (1894–1977) at the studio school of Vakhtangov Theater, graduating in 1924, and remained in her teacher's—and one-time husband's—troupe after its relocation to Rostov-on-the-Don (1936–1940) and its transformation into the Mossovet Theater.

In cinema, Maretskaia debuted in supporting roles in **Iakov Protazanov**'s peculiar homage to Vladimir Lenin *His Call* (Ego prizyv, 1925) and in the popular comedy *The Tailor from Torzhok* (Zakroishchik iz Torzhka, 1925), as well as films by **Fedor Otsep** (*Soil in Chains*/Zemlia v plenu, 1927; *A Living Corpse*/Zhivoi trup, 1929) and **Lev Kuleshov**. In the late 1930s, Maretskaia became one of the most beloved and officially embraced Soviet screen stars. While her stage reputation was that of a marvelous comedienne with a penchant for farce and eccentrics, in sound film she was cast in roles conveying heroism, pathos, and motherly warmth. The part of Aleksandra Sokolova in **Iosif Kheifits** and **Aleksandr Zarkhi**'s *Member of the Government* (aka *The Great Beginning*/Chlen pravitel'stva, 1939) propelled Maretskaia to national stardom. Her impersonation of an oppressed woman who undergoes a profound evolution, ending up as the leader of her collective farm (kolkhoz) and later a high-ranking Soviet official, became canonical.

During the Great Patriotic War—where Maretskaia's second husband, actor Georgii Troitskii, was killed—she played the stern guerilla leader Praskov'ia Luk'ianova in **Fridrikh Ermler**'s *She Defends Her Motherland* (aka *No Greater Love*/Ona zashchishchaet rodinu, 1943), which won her a Stalin Prize in 1946. **Mark Donskoi** gave Maretskaia the plum part of Varvara Martynova, *The Country Teacher* (Sel'skaia uchitel'nitsa, 1947), whom she believably embodies as a young girl, an adult, and a silver-haired woman, exuding authentic love for her pupils; the role brought her another Stalin Prize in 1948.

Maretskaia interspersed these performances with hilarious **comedies**, for example, as the sensual midwife Zmeiukova in **Isidor Annenskii**'s cult hit *The Wedding* (Svad'ba, 1944, based on an early Anton Chekhov play).

Maretskaia was named People's Artist of the USSR in 1949 and Hero of Socialist Labor in 1976. She is buried at Novodevich'e cemetery.

Other films: *Two-Buldi-Two* (Dva-bul'di-dva, 1929); *The Works of the Artamonovs* (Delo Artamonovykh, 1941); *The Mother* (aka *1905*/Mat', 1956); *Night Call* (Nochnoi zvonok, 1969, TV).

MARTINSON, SERGEI ALEKSANDROVICH (b. 6 February 1899, St. Petersburg–d. 2 September 1984, Moscow). Russian actor. Martinson studied at the Institute for Stage Arts in Petrograd, graduating in 1923. He was also a member of **Grigorii Kozintsev** and **Leonid Trauberg**'s Factory of the Eccentric Actor (FEKS). Over the next three decades, Martinson joined the troupes of various theaters, most significantly that of Vsevolod Meierkhol'd, before becoming a member of the Studio Theater of the Film Actor in Moscow. He was famous as an entertainer who appeared on stage at the Moscow Music Hall and toured the country whenever film roles were in short supply.

Meierkhol'd's methods of sharp, hyperbolic characterization and physical expression bordering on the grotesque, as well as the lessons of FEKS, where cinema was viewed as a close relative of circus, shaped Martinson's art and made him one of the most popular Russian film actors. Because of his peculiar looks, he was usually cast in off-putting roles, for example, in **Iakov Protazanov**'s *Marionettes* (Marionetki, 1934), **Grigorii Roshal'**'s *The Oppenheim Family* (Sem'ia Oppengeim, 1938), and **Ol'ga Preobrazhenskaia** and Ivan Pravov's *Stepan Razin* (1939). A number of **comedies** profited from Martinson's brilliant performances, including harmless musicals such as **Aleksandr Ivanovskii**'s *Anton Ivanovich*

Is Angry (aka *Spring Song*/Anton Ivanovich serditsia, 1941) and political satires, for example, **Sergei Iutkevich**'s *Schwejk's New Adventures* (Novye pokhozhdeniia Shveika, 1943). In 1948, the actor portrayed Adolf Hitler in **Ihor' Savchenko**'s World War II epic *The Third Blow* (Tretii udar).

Martinson was idolized by generations of children for playing hilarious "bad guys" in fairy tales such as the treacherous merchant in **Aleksandr Ptushko**'s *Il'ia Muromets* (aka *The Sword and the Dragon*, 1956). However, his eccentric style was just as effective in literary adaptations, including **Ivan Pyr'ev**'s version of Fedor Dostoevskii's *The Idiot* (Idiot, 1958) in which Martinson chillingly portrayed the servile Lebedev. Altogether, the actor appeared in more than 70 films.

Martinson was named People's Artist of the RSFSR in 1964.

Other films: *Oktiabrina's Adventures* (Pokhozhdeniia Oktiabriny, 1924); *Two Encounters* (Dve vstrechi, 1932); *Ruslan and Liudmila* (1972); *Life, Tears, and Love* (I zhizn', i slezy, i liubov', 1984).

MASHEN'KA (1942). **Mosfilm Studio**. 77 min., b/w. Directed by **Iulii Raizman**. Script: **Evgenii Gabrilovich**, Sergei Ermolinskii. Cinematography: Evgenii Andrikanis. Music: Boris Vol'skii (variations on motifs by Aleksandr Glazunov). Cast: Valentina Karavaeva, Mikhail Kuznetsov, Vera Altaiskaia, Georgii Svetlani, **Nikolai Gritsenko**, **Vladislav Strzhel'chik**. Premiere: 10 April 1942.

Mashen'ka (Karavaeva) works as a telegrapher at a post office and spends her evenings studying to become a nurse. The young, flirtatious cabdriver Alesha (Kuznetsov) is so impressed by Mashen'ka's seriousness and dedication that he decides to enroll in a technical college. Yet the two separate because Alesha is too easygoing with other girls, particularly Mashen'ka's friend Vera (Altaiskaia). Months later, during the Soviet-Finnish war, Mashen'ka and Alesha meet accidentally near the front line where Alesha was wounded. Refusing to take recovery leave, Alesha goes back to the front. He writes a letter to Mashen'ka, convincing her that he deserves her trust. Mashen'ka will wait for Alesha's return.

MASHKOV, VLADIMIR L'VOVICH (b. 27 November 1963, Tula). Russian actor and director. Mashkov's mother was a director in a puppet theater, his father an actor. In 1990, after graduating from the Studio School of the Moscow Art Theater (MKhAT) where he studied under **Oleg Tabakov**, Mashkov joined his teacher's troupe at the Tabakerka theater, occasionally acting and directing at MKhAT as well.

Mashkov's film debut was the lead in *The Goat's Green Fire* (Zelenyi ogon' kozy, 1989), describing one day in the life of a 25-year-old. Since then, the actor has established a screen image conveying dark virility and impulsiveness tending toward physical violence, as demonstrated in the hazing drama *Do It—Once!* (Delai—raz, 1990), in Denis Evstigneev's subversive thriller *Limita* (1994), and in Valerii Todorovskii's *Evenings near Moscow* (Podmoskovnye vechera, 1994), a modern version of Nikolai Leskov's "Katerina Izmailova." The dangerous ambiguity of Mashkov's screen persona is fully revealed in **Pavel Chukhrai**'s anti-Stalinist masterpiece *The Thief* (Vor, 1997), one of Mashkov's most convincing performances, and in **Sergei Bodrov**'s *The Quickie* (Davai sdelaem eto po-bystromu, 2001), a Russian-American drama about loyalty and betrayal. At times, Mashkov's harsh, self-confident manliness degenerates to faux heroism, for example, in the title role of **Pavel Lungin**'s *The Tycoon* (Oligarkh, 2002).

In many performances, Mashkov skillfully conveys a will of iron combined with profound lawlessness and ruthless deceptiveness, making him the ideal choice for 18th-century legendary rogue Emel'ian Pugachev in Aleksandr Proshkin's *A Russian Mutiny* (Russkii bunt, 2000), adapted from Aleksandr Pushkin's *The Captain's Daughter*. The actor mastered an even greater challenge with his portrayal of the murderously passionate Parfen Rogozhin in **Vladimir Bortko**'s *The Idiot* (Idiot, 2003, TV) from Fedor Dostoevskii's novel. These accomplishments stand in strange contrast to the clichéd supporting roles that he has agreed to play in some international thrillers.

In 1997, Mashkov made his directorial debut with the charming New Year's tale *The Orphan of Kazan* (aka *Sympathy Seeker*/Sirota kazanskaia), displaying a rare gift for directing children and creating genuinely comical situations. He followed it with the tragic *Dad* (Papa, 2004) from an Aleksandr Galich play, aptly capturing the mentality of the 1930s. Apart from directing this atmospherically precise picture, Mashkov also delivers a heartbreaking performance in the title role of Abram Shvarts, a provincial Jew who sacrifices everything for the career of his beloved son before perishing in the Holocaust.

Other films: *The American Daughter* (Amerikanskaia doch', 1995); *Mom* (Mama, 2000); *Behind Enemy Lines* (2001, U.S.); *The State Counselor* (Statskii sovetnik, 2005); *The Liquidation* (Likvidatsiia, 2007); *The House Goblin* (Domovoi, 2008).

MATVEEV, EVGENII SEMENOVICH (b. 8 March 1922, Novo-Ukrainka [other sources: Chalbasy], Kherson district, Ukraine–d. 1 June 2003, Moscow). Russian actor, director, and scriptwriter. Matveev hailed from a poor peasant family. As a boy, he joined an acting studio in Kherson, received encouragement from **Nikolai Cherkasov**, and subsequently, with support from **Aleksandr Dovzhenko**, studied at the school for film actors of Kiev Film Studio in 1940–1941. He fought in the Great Patriotic War and, after being discharged, worked in theaters in Tiumen' (1946–1948) and Novosibirsk (1948–1951), upon which he joined the troupe of the Moscow Malyi Theater (1952–1968).

Matveev's film debut was the supporting role of Sud'binin in *Good Morning* (Dobroe utro, 1955), a blend of Soviet industrial propaganda and melodramatic romance that became the actor's trademark genre. He got his first lead in *Searchers* (Iskateli, 1956) from Daniil Granin's inspirational novel, and was cast in **Lev Kulidzhanov** and Iakov Segel''s memorable *The House I Live In* (Dom, v kotorom ia zhivu, 1956). Among Matveev's most interesting achievements as screen actor are such varied roles as Makar Nagul'nov in Aleksandr Ivanov's Mikhail Sholokhov adaptation *Virgin Soil Upturned* (Podniataia tselina, 1959–1961), Prince Nekhliudov in **Mikhail Shveitser**'s Lev Tolstoi adaptation *Resurrection* (Voskresenie, 1960–1961), and Vladimir Fedotov in Mikhail Ershov's blockbuster melodrama *Kindred Blood* (Rodnaia krov', 1963).

After suffering a severe injury on the set, Matveev turned to directing. In his first film, the very successful *The Gypsy* (Tsygan, 1966), he also played the role of Budulai. His biopic of the revolutionary lieutenant Petr Shmidt, *A Postal Affair* (Pochtovyi roman, 1970), demonstrated his ability to convey noble, romantic feelings. Matveev landed huge box-office hits and won a USSR State Prize with two melodramas, *Earthly Love* (Liubov' zemnaia,

1975) and *Destiny* (Sud'ba, 1978), both adapted from novels by Petr Proskurin. The director's approach to filmmaking, based on highly emotionalized patriotism and unabashed pathos, responded with utmost directness to deep-seated needs of tens of millions of Soviet viewers. Consequently, all his films were targeted at domestic audiences and went virtually unnoticed abroad. The actor/director, who played leads in most of his own pictures, also continued to act in other director's films; his performance in the title role of **Aleksei Saltykov**'s *Emel'ian Pugachev* (1978)—which reunited him with **Vija Artmane** of *Kindred Blood* fame—is typical of the passion that he put into his performances.

Mikhail Gorbachev's perestroika was exceptionally hard on Matveev, whom critic Denis Gorelov called "the crying Bolshevik of the Soviet screen." He became a prime target during the Fifth Congress of Soviet Filmmakers in 1986, where his acquiescence to playing Leonid Brezhnev in **Iurii Ozerov**'s pseudomonumental *Soldiers of Freedom* (Soldaty svobody, 1977) was scorned as an example of shameful opportunism. Despite ridicule and attacks, Matveev stuck to his guns. His melodrama *Love, Russian Style* (Liubit' po–russki) was the surprise box-office success of 1995. Matveev hit a nerve when he described the struggle for survival of his 1960s–1970s characters under neocapitalist conditions, praising their naïve insistence on traditional moral principles against cynicism and commercialism. Unperturbed by the scornful media resonance and encouraged by positive viewers' feedback, he churned out two sequels in 1996 and 1999.

Matveev became a member of the Communist Party in 1948 and was named People's Artist of the USSR in 1974. He is buried at Novodevich'e cemetery in Moscow.

Other films: (as director) *Fury* (Iarost', 1967); *Deadly Enemy* (Smertnyi vrag, 1971); *Victory* (Pobeda, 1985); *The Time of the Sons* (Vremia synovei, 1986).

MDIVANI, GIORGI [Russian sources list first name and patronymic as Georgii Davidovich] (b. 26 September 1905, Qutaisi [Kutaisi]–d. 11 October 1981, Moscow). Georgian screenwriter. Mdivani studied at the Law School of Tbilisi University for two years; in 1922, he published his first literary works. In 1928, he joined the Tbilisi-based Georgian State Cinema Industry (Goskinprom) as a screenwriter.

Mdivani's debut in **Georgian cinema**, *Youth Wins* (Molodost' pobezhdaet, 1928, from an idea by **Viktor Shklovskii**, directed by **Mikheil Gelovani**), depicts cruel tribal customs in the province of Adjaria. *My Grandmother* (Chemi bebia/Moia babushka, 1929, coauthored with **Siko Dolidze** and directed by Kote Miqaberidze), a brilliant satire on corruption within the new Soviet bureaucracy, was attacked for "Trotskyite" tendencies and banned until 1976, when film scholars discovered its thematic and formal qualities and declared it a classic. Switching to less dangerous topics, Mdivani thematized revolutionary history in *The American Woman* (Amerikanka, 1930, with Shklovskii and Giorgi Sturua), an adventurous tale about an illegal Bolshevik print shop. *Shakir* (aka *Rote Fahne*/Red Flag, 1932) tells the story of German colonists in the Caucasus and their struggle against rich farmers; it also was the first Georgian film with a sound track.

As his reputation of a versatile and flexible screenwriter grew, Mdivani's scripts were filmed by a number of prominent directors, albeit not always to mutual gain. Thus, *Homeland* (Shamshoblo/ Rodina, 1939), written for **Nikoloz Shengelaia** and featuring a contrived plot about saboteurs undermining a peaceful Georgian farm, turned out a fiasco, as did *In the Mountains of Yugoslavia* (V gorakh Iugoslavii, 1946) for **Abram Room**, a pro-Tito propaganda tale that was shelved when Soviet-Yugoslav relations soured.

In post-Stalinist times, Mdivani, who split his activities between Georgia and Moscow, landed huge box-office hits with the army **comedy** *Soldier Ivan Brovkin* (Soldat Ivan Brovkin, 1955) and its sequel, *Ivan Brovkin on Virgin Soil* (Ivan Brovkin na tseline, 1958). He wrote a fine screenplay for **Rezo Chkheidze**, *Our Court* (Chveni ezo/Nash dvor, 1956), creatively responding to neorealist impulses. As an ideologically reliable professional endowed with artistic originality, Mdivani sometimes came up with unexpected topics; thus, *The Great Path* (Bol'shaia doroga, 1962, directed by **Iurii Ozerov**), coproduced with Czechoslovakia, is a biopic about legendary novelist Jaroslav Hašek. Mdivani contributed prominently to two prestigious international productions: Hungarian director Miklós Jancsó's *Stars and Soldiers* (aka *The Red and the White*/Csillagosok, katonák/ Zvezdy i soldaty, 1967) about Hungarian Communists supporting the Bolshevik forces against the White Army in 1919, and Vittorio de

Sica's star-studded melodrama *Sunflowers* (I Girasoli/Podsolnukhi, 1970, coauthored with Cesare Zavattini and Tonino Guerra), a détente melodrama about the wounds left by World War II and the new chances for love and reconciliation.

Mdivani joined the Communist Party in 1944; he was named Merited Artist of the Georgian SSR in 1961.

Other films: *The Shock-worker* (Damkvreli/Udarnik truda, aka Delo doblesti, 1931); *Lost Paradise* (Dakarguli samotkhe/Poteriannyi rai, 1937); *Khevsur Ballad* (Khevsuruli balada/Khevsurskaia balada, 1965).

MEDVEDKIN, ALEKSANDR IVANOVICH (b. 8 March 1900, Penza–d. 19 February 1989, Moscow). Russian director, scriptwriter, and film administrator. Born into the family of a railway worker and former peasant, Medvedkin joined the Bolshevik First Cavalry Army in 1919, serving in a variety of positions over the next eight years. In 1927, he became an assistant director at the State Military Film Studio (Gosvoenkino), working under **Nikolai Okhlopkov**, among others.

Medvedkin began his career as a scriptwriter, making his debut with *The Bridge across the Vyp'* (Most cherez Vyp', 1928). He then turned to directing satirical shorts, praising the example of conscientious Communist laborers as opposed to sloppy and unqualified workers. Critical assaults contained in *Catch the Thief* (Derzhi vora, 1930), *Moron, You Moron!* (Duren' ty, duren'! 1931), and *Fruits and Vegetables* (Frukty-ovoshchi, 1931), among others, were directed against bureaucratic stupidity, irresponsibility, and other problems that Soviet citizens had to confront daily. The filmmaker's main objective was to use cinema as a productive force that could quickly react to occurring difficulties and help resolve them. Medvedkin's stylistic approach was characterized by eccentric hyperbole and fearless, openly didactic directness.

The tireless filmmaker proved to be an efficient administrator when put in charge of a film train (*kinopoezd*), a mobile studio on wheels that, from January 1932 to 1934, undertook 12 long sojourns to major construction sites in Ukraine, Kuban', Transcaucasia, and the Urals, capturing the accelerated industrial revolution on film. The 32 filmmakers and technicians on board the three train cars sought to convey authenticity and dynamism, as well as to give instantaneous feedback by releasing the resulting shorts—by some accounts, altogether 200, each roughly 10 minutes long—to baffled and agitated audiences. Thus, the filmed opening of the Dneproges Dam on 10 October 1932 was screened the same night at a reception for construction workers and the following day in Moscow and Kiev. The film train was a self-sufficient production unit capable of developing, editing, and copying 2,000 meters of footage daily; particularly surprising is the variety of genres it covered—from newsreels and instructional shorts to "film posters" (*fil'm-plakaty*) and cartoons. Despite some inevitable technical imperfections, this original experiment became a legendary part of Soviet film history.

Back in Moscow, Medvedkin obtained permission to make a full-length feature, albeit without sound, so as to reach audiences in rural locations where the projection technology was still silent. *Happiness* (Schast'e, aka *The Grabbers*/Stiazhateli, 1934) was released in 1935. Featuring an overbearing humor, grotesque hyperbole, and fairy-tale-inspired narrative simplicity, the film was so much outside the paradigm of mainstream cinema that, with the exception of **Sergei Eizenshtein**, **Eduard Tissé**, **Aleksandr Dovzhenko**, and some other connoisseurs, few could fully appreciate its unique quality. The tale of humble peasant Khmyr', who has trouble finding fulfillment under tsarist autocracy and in the Soviet collective farm, interprets Communism not as an ideology-based construct but as the quasi-natural outcome of people's tribulations after centuries of suffering and exploitation. Its unique blend of naïveté and cleverness is matched by an enormous aesthetic inventiveness—episodes such as the dense soldiers marching with puffy heads made of papier-mâché exposing their brainwashed uniformity stunned and enthused discriminating viewers, especially when *Happiness* was rediscovered in 1964 by film historian Viktor Demin.

The Miracle Worker (Chudesnitsa, 1936), Medvedkin's first sound picture, exercises more ideological caution using the typical plot of two competing collective farms and paying propagandistic tribute to an exemplary milkmaid. Medvedkin's unmistakable naïve conformity is still mixed with witty eccentricity and an explosive, unbridled imagination that were a far cry from the opportunistic humor in **Grigorii Aleksandrov**'s and **Ivan Pyr'ev**'s folksy **comedies**. *The*

New Moscow (Novaia Moskva, 1938), another attempt to create an optimistic and honest comedy about the practical building of utopia, was banned.

During the Great Patriotic War, Medvedkin was put in charge of a unit of frontline cameramen; he famously invented an adjusted machine gun equipped with an ultralight camera that could be used even in the heat of the battle. In the mid-1950s, Medvedkin led a group of cinematographers charged with documenting the virgin soil (*tselina*) campaign in Kazakhstan. *Restless Spring* (Bespokoinaia vesna, 1956), Medvedkin's last feature, is an attempt to give the socioeconomic campaign a positive, comedic treatment. While the film was praised for its picturesque beauty, the characters and situations were dismissed by critics as inadequate because of their cartoonlike schematics.

For the last three decades of his career, Medvedkin specialized exclusively in **documentaries**. Some, such as *Reflections on Happiness* (Dumy o schast'e, 1957), were commissioned for official events, while others present a curious continuation of the filmmaker's sharp polemical style of the early 1930s, now attacking Western politics and Mao Tse-tung's Cultural Revolution, as well as the danger of environmental pollution and the global arms race. Particularly effective was a trilogy consisting of *Reason against Insanity* (Razum protiv bezumiia, 1960), *Sclerosis of Conscience* (Skleroz sovesti, 1961), and *The Law of Baseness* (Zakon podlosti, 1968), which Demin characterized as "authorial films in the full and magnificent meaning of the word."

Medvedkin's career is among the most unusual in Soviet film history. An unambiguous loyalist to the Communist cause, his rare artistic creativity and pragmatic adaptability to different genres allowed him to blossom under the most unlikely circumstances. With his unerring ear for popular intonations, Medvedkin's antiauthoritarian humor has been compared to that of Charlie Chaplin and the Marx brothers, although it is undeniably rooted in Russian folklore and, as Eizenshtein put it, possesses "social logic." Medvedkin's art of the 1930s has remained the object of admiration of many cinephiles; his hands-on documentary method, which was aimed at preserving the Communist mission in its ideal, quasi-humanist purity, left deep traces in world cinema. It is also noteworthy that

Medvedkin remained largely outside the Soviet film elite's ivory tower; he stood alone before and after the 1960s rediscovery of his early work. Medvedkin's oeuvre marks a potential alternative direction in which Soviet cinema could have moved had it not been intimidated and trivialized.

A number of Western leftist documentary filmmakers (Jean Rouch, Richard Leacock, and Philippe Garrel, among others) were inspired by Medvedkin's early experiments, which became one of the major sources of cinéma verité and were independent of **Dziga Vertov**'s approach. Chris Marker, an admirer of Medvedkin, devoted two fine documentaries to him: the medium-length homage *The Train Rolls On* (Le Train en marche, 1971) and the three-hour cinematic requiem *Alexander's Tombstone* (Le Tombeau d'Alexandre, aka *The Last Bolshevik*, 1992).

Medvedkin joined the Communist Party in 1920. He was named People's Artist of the Russian Federation in 1969 and People's Artist of the USSR in 1979.

Other films: *The Hole* (Dyra, 1932); *About Love* (Pro liubov', 1932); *Liberated Land* (Osvobozhdennaia zemlia, 1946); *Night over China* (Noch' nad Kitaem, 1971); *Alarm* (Trevoga, 1984).

MEL'NIKOV, VITALII VIACHESLAVOVICH (b. 1 May 1928, Mazanovo, Amur district). Russian director and screenwriter. Mel'nikov was born into a family of Siberian farmers. He studied with **Sergei Iutkevich** and **Mikhail Romm** at the Soviet State Film School **VGIK**, graduating in 1952. Following several years of work at the Leningrad studio for science **documentary** films (Lennauch-film), he joined the staff of **Lenfilm Studio** as a director in 1964.

Mel'nikov's debut was a humorous short about the life of mongrels (*Barbos Visits Bobik*/Barbos v gostiakh u Bobika, 1964). He landed a minor hit with his first full-length feature, the Civil War **comedy** *The Boss of Chukotka* (Nachal'nik Chukotki, 1966). As often in Mel'nikov's pictures, the plot, although never action oriented, centers on an original, anecdotal twist. Mel'nikov eventually became a master of contemporary, so-called lyrical comedies in which Soviet everyday life is presented in a warm, compassionate light. Some of them, like *Mom Got Married* (Mama vyshla zamuzh, 1969) and *Hello and Good-bye* (Zdravstvui i proshchai, 1972), were successful at the box office, while *The Seven Brides of Corporal Zbruev* (Sem' nevest efreitora Zbrueva, 1971) became a veritable hit. Mel'nikov's films betray a particular interest in the private lives and worries of regular citizens and are rich in recognizable details.

A notable counterpoint to Mel'nikov's trademark contemporary tales are his literary adaptations, among them *The Marriage* (Zhenit'ba, 1977) from Nikolai Gogol''s comedy, and *Another Man's Wife and the Husband under the Bed* (Chuzhaia zhena i muzh pod krovat'iu, 1984) from Fedor Dostoevskii's short stories. Two adaptations of plays by Aleksandr Vampilov (1937–1972) also deserve mention: *The Oldest Son* (Starshii syn, 1975, TV) and *Vacation in September* (Otpusk v sentiabre, 1979, based on the play *Duck Hunt*), the latter displaying such an amount of social criticism that it was only released during perestroika, in 1987.

The director's peculiar humanist approach can be detected in his historical films, too, including *Two Lines in Small Print* (Dve strochki melkim shriftom, 1981), *The Tsar's Hunt* (Tsarskaia okhota, 1990) about the famous 18th-century pretender, "Princess" Tarakanova, and especially *Tsarevich Aleksei: A Version* (Tsarevich Aleksei. Versiia, 1997) about the much-maligned son of Peter the Great, an original alternative to **Vladimir Petrov**'s canonized 1937 epic.

After the demise of the Soviet state, Mel'nikov made some hilarious comedies, describing "grandiose" changes from the little man's point of view, poking fun at pro-Soviet nostalgia, and exposing perestroika and free-market illusions. Thus, *Chicha* (1992) is the touching story of a singer in a Soviet Army choir who is forced to hide his powerful bass voice and pretend to be a tenor, while *The Last Case of Vareny* (Poslednee delo Varenogo, 1993) satirizes the political-criminal complex. Both films were appreciated by critics but had difficulty finding viewers because of the disappearance of the Soviet distribution network. In more recent films, the director's typical melancholy at times degenerates into sentimentality, for example, in *The Garden Was Filled with Moonshine* (Lunoi byl polon sad, 2001).

Mel'nikov's most appealing characters seek and find salvation in marriage and family, while society, both in the small community and at large, usually betrays them. His humor does not avoid grotesque colors, although mostly it is tempered by mellowness.

Mel'nikov, who joined the Communist Party in 1973, was named Merited Artist of the RSFSR in 1977 and People's Artist of the RSFSR in 1987.

Other films: *First Meeting, Last Meeting* (Pervaia vstrecha, posledniaia vstrecha, 1987).

MEN'SHIKOV, OLEG EVGEN'EVICH (b. 8 November 1960, Serpukhov, Moscow district). Russian actor. Men'shikov studied at the Shchepkin Theater School, graduating in 1981. He was a member of the troupes of the Moscow Malyi Theater, Ermolova Theater, and Mossovet Theater, among others. Beginning in the early 1990s, Men'shikov appeared in some high-profile stage productions in London and, in 1998, superbly directed Aleksandr Griboedov's *Woe from Wit* with an independent Moscow troupe; the latter enjoyed considerable success on video.

In cinema, Men'shikov debuted with an episodic role in **Nikita Mikhalkov**'s social drama *Relatives* (Rodnia, 1982). Following several supporting parts, for example, in **Roman Balaian**'s *Flights in Dream and in Reality* (Polety vo sne i naiavu, 1982), he landed a minor hit with the title role in the tearjerker *My Beloved Clown* (Moi liubimyi kloun, 1986) and was cast in war films such as **Stanislav Govorukhin**'s *Drops of Champagne* (Bryzgi shampanskogo, 1988) and contemporary psychological dramas such as Aleksei Sakharov's *The Staircase* (Lestnitsa, 1990).

After the end of the Soviet era, Men'shikov was able to demonstrate the true range of his artistic abilities. He gave the chilling portrait of a treacherous, tormented secret service agent in Mikhalkov's peculiar interpretation of Stalinism, *Burnt by the Sun* (Utomlennye solntsem, 1995), and was equally convincing in more straightforward roles such as the domineering ensign Larin in **Sergei Bodrov Sr.**'s pacifist ***Prisoner of the Caucasus*** (aka *Prisoner of the Mountains/Kavkazskii plennik*, 1996) and the husband in Régis Wargnier's Cold War tale *East-West* (East-Ouest/Vostok-Zapad, 1999). Men'shikov's empathetic energy and professional discipline have enabled him to fill even schematic constructions such as Cadet Andrei Tolstoi in Mikhalkov's howler *The Barber of Siberia* (Sibirskii tsiriul'nik, 1999) with color and life. His magnificent performance in Denis Evstigneev's critically maligned *Mom* (Mama, 1999) as the brother who is freed from an insane asylum, reveals that, behind the facade of Men'shikov's otherworldly, romantic heroes loom healthy vitality and humor.

Men'shikov is the recipient of numerous national and international prizes for his stage and screen work, including three State Prizes of Russia (1995, 1997, 1999). Due to his increasing star power—evidenced by his appearance in luxury commercials—he also has become the object of tabloid gossip.

Other films: *Mikhailo Lomonosov* (1986, TV); *Moonzund* (1987); *Doktor Zhivago* (2005, TV); *The Golden Calf* (Zolotoi telenok, 2005, TV).

MEN'SHOV, VLADIMIR VALENTINOVICH (b. 17 September 1939, Baku). Russian actor, director, and screenwriter. Men'shov was born into the family of a sailor and secret service officer; he grew up in Baku and Arkhangel'sk and worked as a turner and a miner while pursuing his dream of an acting career. In 1961, Men'shov enrolled in the studio school of the Moscow Art Theater (MKhAT), graduating in 1965. After a brief stint at Stavropol' Theater, he enrolled in **Mikhail Romm**'s workshop at the Soviet State Film School **VGIK** as a graduate student, completing his education in 1970.

Early on, Men'shov appeared in the lead roles of contemporary films: as a Soviet sailor in a foreign port in *The Salted Dog* (Solenyi pes, 1973), in Boris Buneev's *The Last Encounter* (Posledniaia vstrecha, 1974), and Iulii Karasik's *One's Own Opinion* (Sobstvennoe mnenie, 1975), among others. His understated acting style conveys inner tension and alertness and enables him to carry **comedy**, drama, **children's films**, and horror. It is not surprising that Men'shov has remained one of the mainstays of post-Soviet cinema who lends artistic weight even to artistically mediocre genre fare such as the horror superhit *Night Watch* (Nochnoi dozor, 2004).

Men'shov's considerable popularity as an actor enabled him to embark on a directorial career. His feature-length debut, the high school comedy *A Practical Joke* (Rozygrysh, 1976), keeps a balance between humorous and serious intonations and features very natural performances from laymen; its excellent box-office results proved that Men'shov had a fine sense for the needs of mass audiences. This very intuition explains the unexpected success of his second feature, **Moscow Does Not Believe in Tears** (Moskva slezam ne verit, 1980). With over 80 million viewers, this everyday life comedy about three women struggling to find happiness by balancing professional and private fulfillment became one of the greatest box-office hits in Soviet film history. The sensation was perfect when the unassuming picture won the 1981 Best Foreign Film Academy Award—only the second Russian feature film after **Sergei Bondarchuk**'s *War and Peace*.

Moscow Doesn't Believe in Tears was a hard act to follow. Men'shov settled for a cautious approach with a comedic drama, *Love and Pigeons* (Liubov' i golubi, 1984), a touching story of romantic desire and sobering reality, loyalty and betrayal, married life and maintaining an affair. When Men'shov completed his next picture, the Soviet Union, together with its efficient distribution system, had vanished. Thus, the all-star comedy *What a Mess* (Shirli-myrli, 1995), although more successful than most Russian films of the 1990s, attracted only a fraction of the number of viewers that was typical of Men'shov's earlier films. In addition, few critics recognized the precise timing and inventiveness at work in this burlesque, and even fewer were amused by its blend of social satire and slapstick humor. *The Envy of the Gods* (Zavist' bogov, 2000), a melancholic drama about a Russian woman falling in love with a French journalist in the early 1980s, possesses wit and nostalgia without idealizing the Soviet past. Similar to Men'shov's other films, it celebrates privacy and personal happiness, demonstratively moving societal factors to the background.

As a filmmaker, Men'shov is an unabashed populist. His quality-conscious productions reflect common attitudes and emotions, capturing social milieus and everyday details with astuteness and accuracy. The director's ambition to please large crowds has made him something of a maverick within the profession. His tales are melodramatic yet always psychologically believable; they are funny but in an intelligent way, moderately patriotic—yet never xenophobic.

Men'shov was named People's Artist of Russia in 1991. He is married to actress Vera Alentova (b. 1942), who often plays leads in his films. Their daughter, Iuliia Men'shova (b. 1969), is a popular stage and screen actress and TV personality.

Other films: (as actor) *Spartacus and Kalashnikov* (Spartak i Kalashnikov, 2002); *The Liquidation* (Likvidatsiia, 2007).

MERKUR'EV, VASILII VASIL'EVICH (b. 6 April 1904, Ostrov– d. 12 May 1978, Leningrad). Russian actor. Merkur'ev worked as a carpenter and performed at the Ostrov town theater before studying acting at the Petrograd Institute for Stage Arts in 1923–1926. He joined the Leningrad Academic Pushkin Theater (the former Aleksandrinskii) in 1937 and soon became one of its most versatile and popular stars. Merkur'ev further distinguished himself as an acting teacher heading a workshop at the Leningrad Institute for Theater, Music, and Cinema after 1932.

Merkur'ev's debut in cinema was in the social drama *Engineer Hoff* (Inzhener Goff, 1935), followed by the episodic role of a Menshevik student in **Grigorii Kozintsev** and **Leonid Trauberg**'s *Maksim Trilogy* (Trilogiia o Maksime, 1934–1938). The actor worked with many influential Soviet directors, including **Gerbert Rappaport** in *Professor Mamlock* (1938), **Aleksandr Stolper** in *Story of a Real Man* (Povest' o nastoiashchem cheloveke, 1948—a role that won him a Stalin Prize in 1949), and **Leonid Lukov** in the working class saga *Miners of Donetsk* (Donetskie shakhtery, 1950, Stalin Prize 1952). **Mikhail Kalatozov** gave Merkur'ev two of his most memorable roles. In the **comedy** *Loyal Friends* (Vernye druz'ia, 1954) he was the kind, unpretentious architect Nestratov, and in *The Cranes Are Flying* (Letiat zhuravli, 1957) he portrayed Boris's father Fedor Ivanovich—a benevolent if somewhat hot-tempered doctor and hospital administrator who always finds the right words in trying situations. Managing instant transitions from comic to tragic and from laid-back to lofty with natural ease and irony, Merkur'ev became a household name to Soviet audiences and endeared himself to generations of viewers in numerous supporting parts, including the retired captain in **Georgii Daneliia** and **Igor' Talankin**'s *A Summer to Remember* (Serezha, 1960).

Merkur'ev joined the Communist Party in 1948; he won the second of a total of three Stalin Prizes in 1947 for a supporting part in **Leo Arnshtam**'s *Glinka*. The actor was named People's Artist of the USSR in 1960. He was married to acting teacher Irina Meierkhol'd;

their son, Petr Merkur'ev (b. 1943), is a musicologist and film actor who portrayed his own grandfather, legendary stage director Vsevolod Meierkhol'd, in *I Am an Actress* (Ia—aktrisa, 1980), and played the lead role of soldier Peter Kreutzer in Aleksei German Jr.'s antiheroic war drama *The Last Train* (Poslednii poezd, 2004).

Other films: *People on the Bridge* (Liudi na mostu, 1960); *The Whistle Stop* (Polustanok, 1963).

MEZHRABPOMFILM STUDIO [Mezhrabpom-fil'm]. Mezhrabpom, the acronym of International Workers' Aid (*Mezh*dunarodnaia *rab*ochaia *pom*oshch'), was a branch of the Communist International (Komintern), a conglomerate of Communist Parties that existed from 1919 to 1943. Mezhrabpom was founded in September 1921 in Berlin as an "organization of international proletarian solidarity," initially providing aid to the starving regions of Soviet Russia. Beginning in 1923, Mezhrabpom concentrated on the support of workers' movements and Communist Parties in capitalist countries. The first president of the organization was German Communist leader Clara Zetkin (1857–1933). Its administrative head, Willi Münzenberg (1889–1940), was also in charge of the huge media network of the Communist Party of Germany (he was a member of the German parliament, the Reichstag, for the Communist faction in 1924–1933). As the Komintern saw Germany as its main springboard by which it could spread propaganda all over Western Europe, Mezhrabpom engaged in the distribution of Soviet motion pictures and, in return, acquired precious Western technology and film material for the USSR.

In 1923, the film office of Mezhrabpom formed a joined venture with the private film company Rus'-Film (founded in 1915 by the merchant Mikhail Trofimov); together they became Mezhrabpom-Rus', a German-Soviet stock holding company (*kinematograficheskoe aktsionernoe obshchestvo*). By Soviet standards, it was a rather unique entity that produced and distributed films in the Soviet Union and owned a chain of movie theaters. Thus, the company was ideologically a product of Communist politics, yet economically it enjoyed the moderate liberalism of the New Economic Policy (NEP) of the 1920s that tolerated elements of free market.

The company's main stockholder was Moisei Nikiforovich Aleinikov (1885–1964), one of the founders of Rus'-Film and a highly
adaptable, intellectually gifted entrepreneur who influenced the
company's thematic choices and hires. He understood that films
for export should also generate profits on the domestic market and
therefore had to be entertaining. Thus, in 1923 he invited **Iakov
Protazanov** to return from emigration to direct *Aelita* (1924) in
which commercial and "revolutionary" elements are blended superficially but effectively. Aleinikov also hired avant-garde directors to
Mezhrabpom-Rus'. Thus, **Vsevolod Pudovkin** was able to realize
The Mother (Mat', 1926), *The End of St. Petersburg* (Konets Sankt
Peterburga, 1927), and *The Heir of Chenghiz Khan* (aka *Storm over
Asia*/Potomok Chingiz-khana, 1928); **Boris Barnet** made *Miss Mend*
(1926, codirected with **Fedor Otsep**) and *The Girl with the Hatbox*
(Devushka s korobkoi, 1927); **Sergei Komarov**, like Pudovkin and
Barnet a student of **Lev Kuleshov**, directed *The Kiss of Mary Pick-
ford* (Potselui Meri Pikford, 1927)—films that all skillfully combine
genre features with a clear, albeit unobtrusive pro-Soviet stand, allowing them to fly under the radar of censorship in most Western
countries. The embattled Kuleshov himself eventually found a refuge
at Mezhrabpom-Rus', where he directed one of his best sound films,
The Great Consoler (Velikii uteshitel', 1933).

In 1928, the Council of People's Commissars (SNK) ordered the
withdrawal of all private capital from the company, turning it into
a state-run venture instead. On 30 April 1928, the company was
renamed Mezhrabpomfilm, with the Italian Communist Francesco
Misiano (1884–1936) as director. Responding to its growing success, it churned out coproductions with other countries, among
them the Lev Tolstoi adaptation *The Living Corpse* (Zhivoi trup,
1929). A number of films were coproduced with Prometheus-Film
GmbH in Germany.

In 1932, Iosif Stalin officially confirmed Mezhrabpomfilm Studio's mission to produce films for an international market. However,
in 1933, when the Nazi Party won the German elections, the Berlin
headquarter of Mezhrabpomfilm was closed. Numerous Communist
artists fled to the Soviet Union; many of them found work at Mezhrabpomfilm, which planned to regularly produce anti-Nazi films.

Yet few of these plans came to fruition. When International Workers' Aid, the head organization, was transformed and lowered in status in 1935, the film company was doomed as well. Mezhrabpomfilm was officially closed on 8 June 1936, its assets—studios, bank accounts, machinery—and personnel were transferred to the newly formed Soiuzdetfil'm studio (the later **Gor'kii Studio for Children's and Youth Films**). Shortly thereafter, all foreign employees were fired. Many were accused of espionage and arrested; a number of them perished in GULAG concentration camps.

Since its inception, the legal status of the company as a semiprivate entity had been eyed distrustfully by the Communist establishment. By the mid-1930s, its primary purpose of exporting the revolution using cultural instruments was put on hold. The USSR's internationalist agenda was replaced by a new nationalism that seemed better suited to the political realities of the 1930s; thus, Mezhrabpomfilm became dispensable.

During the 12 years of its existence, Mezhrabpomfilm was one of the most powerful studios in the Soviet Union. According to film historian Günter Agde, it produced a total of 110 feature films, 50 animated pictures, and 65 documentaries, many of which are considered classics of Soviet cinema. In addition to the aforementioned pictures, Protazanov's *The Forty-first* (Sorok-pervyi, 1927) and *Holiday of St. Iorgen* (aka *St. Jorgen's Day*/Prazdnik sviatogo Iorgena, 1929), as well as the first Soviet sound films *A Start in Life* (aka *Road to Life*/Putevka v zhizn', 1931) by **Nikolai Ekk**, *The Outskirts* (aka *Patriots*/Okraina, 1933) by Barnet, the **children's film** *The Torn Shoes* (aka *Broken Shoes*/Rvanye bashmaki, 1933) by **Margarita Barskaia**, and the musical *The Accordion* (Garmon', 1934) by **Ihor' Savchenko** enjoyed lasting critical and popular success.

MIKHALKOV, NIKITA SERGEEVICH (b. 21 October 1945, Moscow). Russian director, actor, screenwriter, producer, and cultural activist. Mikhalkov, the son of poets Sergei Mikhalkov (b. 1913) and Natal'ia Konchalovskaia (1903–1988), takes great pride in his aristocratic pedigree, counting historical painter Vasilii Surikov (1848–1916) among his ancestors. His family also has been closely connected to the Soviet establishment and gained maximum influence under Iosif Stalin and Leonid Brezhnev.

In 1956–1959, Mikhalkov attended a musical school and the Stanislavskii Theater studio. He was cast as a young lad in Konstantin Voinov's postwar drama *The Sun Shines for Everyone* (Solntse svetit vsem, 1959) and Vasilii Ordynskii's antireligious pamphlet *Clouds over Borsk* (Tuchi nad Borskom, 1961). The role of Kolia in **Georgii Daneliia**'s *I Stroll in Moscow* (aka *Meet Me in Moscow*/Ia shagaiu po Moskve, 1963) made the budding actor a household name in the Soviet Union. In 1963–1966, he studied at the Shchukin studio school, but in 1967, he switched to the Soviet State Film School **VGIK**, where he first enrolled in the Acting Department and later in the directing workshop of **Mikhail Romm**. As a student, Mikhalkov already directed numerous shorts for the popular satirical film almanac *The Wick* (Fitil'), of which his father was in charge. The short *A Quiet Day at the End of the War* (Spokoinyi den' v kontse voiny, 1970), about a soldier who sacrifices his life to rescue artwork, was his diploma film. Upon graduation, Mikhalkov was drafted, serving for two years in the Soviet Navy on the Kamchatka Peninsula. In 1973, he joined **Mosfilm Studio**.

After dropping his early screen image of youthful naïveté, Mikhalkov often portrayed ruthless cynics and cold-hearted manipulators whose syrupy talk covers up their sinister intentions. Thus, in his brother **Andrei Mikhalkov-Konchalovskii**'s Ivan Turgenev adaptation *A Nest of the Gentry* (Dvorianskoe gnezdo, 1971) he appeared as Prince Nelidov, in **Sergei Solov'ev**'s *The Stationmaster* (Stantsionnyi smotritel') as hussar officer Minskii, in **El'dar Riazanov**'s picturesque *Cruel Romance* (Zhestokii romans, 1984) as Paratov, and in Andrei Eshpai's Fedor Dostoevskii adaptation *The Humiliated and Insulted* (Unizhennye i oskorblennye, 1991) as Prince Valkovskii. In 2005, Mikhalkov raised eyebrows with the brilliant portrayal of a 1990s vulgar provincial godfather in **Aleksei Balabanov**'s *Blind Man's Bluff* (Zhmurki).

Mikhalkov's major directorial works display genuine professionalism paired with artistic ambition. Skillfully using his connections within the USSR *nomenklatura*, he was allowed to choose topics, projects, and collaborators with a degree of freedom unimaginable for almost any other Soviet filmmaker. Mikhalkov showed his ability to adopt various genres for his purposes, such as the Western *At Home among Strangers* (Svoi sredi chuzhikh, chuzhoi sredi svoikh,

1974) about the 1918–1921 Civil War, or the nostalgic romance *Slave of Love* (Raba liubvi, 1976) about the preemigration, Crimean period of the Russian movie industry; none of these films ever cast a doubt on the director's loyalty to the Soviet cause.

Unfinished Piece for Mechanical Piano (Neokonchennaia p'esa dlia mekhanicheskogo pianino, 1977), from various Anton Chekhov plays, is arguably Mikhalkov's most accomplished picture. Its atmosphere of social paralysis, complemented by a deep longing for meaningful activity, was captured admirably by his longtime cinematographer **Pavel Lebeshev**. The far less cohesive Ivan Goncharov adaptation *Oblomov* (Neskol'ko dnei iz zhizni I.I. Oblomova, 1979) deviates considerably from the novel's concepts, rather illustrating Mikhalkov's own views of the Russian mentality. The controversial contemporary drama *Relatives* (Rodnia, 1982) depicts a country-woman whose complete incomprehension of her children's urban lifestyle borders on the grotesque. Mikhalkov's confident reliance on first-rate actors allowed him to make unusual chamber dramas such as *Five Evenings* (Piat' vecherov, 1978) and *Without Witnesses* (Bez svidetelei, 1983), concentrating on merely two actors in each. However, the Soviet-Italian coproduction *Black Eyes* (Ochi chernye, 1987), an openly exploitative nostalgia piece, revealed the degree of shallow opportunism of which this filmmaker is also capable.

In *Close to Eden* (*Urga*, 1992) Mikhalkov returned to form. The story of a Russian truck driver and his forced stay in the Mongolian steppe with a traditional patriarchal family displays genuine artistry and charm. Only when the underlying "Eurasian" ideology shows through does the film turn into a pamphlet and lose its initial appeal. *Burnt by the Sun* (Utomlennye solntsem, 1995), a simplistic and in some respects falsifying interpretation of the Stalinist regime and its functional mechanisms, became one of the rare Russian blockbusters of the 1990s.

Mikhalkov, a darling of the Moscow glitz society, soberly understood the irreversibility of the end of Soviet cinema. Rather than tilting at windmills, he founded his personal film empire, TriTe, in 1998, making clever use both of the new capitalist conditions and his political connections. *The Barber of Siberia* (Sibirskii tsiriul'nik, 1999), touted as the most expensive Russian film ever, was a box-office hit but an artistic disaster. The fact that the director chose to play the episodic but prominent role of Tsar Aleksandr III—an autocrat who stood for political consolidation and imperial strength—was an unequivocal statement in itself.

Mikhalkov has held numerous administrative positions, of which the chairmanship of the Russian Filmmakers' Union (since 1998) and the presidency of the Russian Culture Foundation (since 1993) are the most significant. A power-conscious man with some dubious administrative decisions to his and his associates' benefit, he is also capable of uncommon collegiality. Qualities such as tireless productivity, independence, intelligence, and pragmatism have made Mikhalkov the most influential Russian filmmaker of the 1990s. He was named People's Artist of the Russian Federation in 1984. Mikhalkov has been in charge of a directing workshop at the Supreme Directing Courses; one of his mentees is **Vladimir Khotinenko**.

Other films: (as actor) *Krosh's Adventures* (Prikliucheniia Krosha, 1962); *Sibiriada* (1978); *Aurora borealis* (Pod severnym sianiem, 1990); *Faith, Hope, Blood* (Vera, nadezhda, krov', 2000); (as director) *The Girl and the Things* (Devochka i veshchi, 1967, short); *Autostop* (1990); *Anna from 6 to 18* (Anna. Ot 6 do 18, 1993, doc.); *Twelve* (Dvenadtsat', 2007); *Burnt by the Sun II* (Utomlennye solntsem—2, 2008).

MIKHALKOV-KONCHALOVSKII, ANDREI SERGEEVICH

[sometimes listed as Andron Konchalovskii] (b. 20 August 1937, Moscow). Russian director and screenwriter. The son of one of the most influential Soviet poets and cultural hacks, Sergei Mikhalkov (b. 1913), first studied piano at Moscow Conservatory from 1953 to 1959 before turning to cinema as a student of **Mikhail Romm** at the Soviet State Film School **VGIK,** from which he graduated in 1964. He penned a superb script for fellow student **Andrei Tarkovskii**'s diploma film *The Steamroller and the Violin* (Katok i skripka, 1960) and played an episodic role in Tarkovskii's feature debut *Ivan's Childhood* (aka My Name Is Ivan/Ivanovo detstvo, 1962). Mikhalkov-Konchalovskii's own debut as director was the poetic short *The Boy and the Dove* (Mal'chik i golub', 1960).

When his diploma feature, *The First Teacher* (Pervyi uchitel', 1965), adapted from a novella by Kyrgyz author **Chingiz Aitmatov**, was released, it became clear that an ambitious new voice had entered Soviet cinema. Shot in expressive black-and-white by **Georgii Rerberg**, its wild yet ascetic vistas form the natural frame for a Communist enlightenment tale with provocative erotic undertones. Sadly, Mikhalkov-Konchalovskii's energetic efforts to further push the aesthetic envelope of Soviet cinema by using contemporary subject matter failed in his following project, *Asia's Happiness* (Asino schast'e, aka Istoriia Asi Kliachinoi, kotoraia liubila da ne vyshla zamuzh, 1967). Made predominantly with amateurs in authentic Russian countryside settings, it was finally released 20 years after its completion. The image of Soviet life presented in this unique film was shocking indeed. No other filmmaker prior to Mikhalkov-Konchalovskii had dared to get as close to raw Russian reality, showing genuine rank-and-file people in their unsightly dusty surroundings, working, flirting, singing, drinking, and remembering the past.

The 1969 Ivan Turgenev adaptation *A Nest of the Gentry* (Dvorianskoe gnezdo) betrays the director's striving for picturesque elegance yet comes across as frustratingly incoherent. Its reflection of 19th-century aristocratic lifestyle overflows with loving detail but overall seems pale and lifeless, except for the psychologically tense finale. *Romance about Lovers* (Romans o vliublennykh, 1974) is a large-scale, romantic-patriotic act of opportunism that did well at the box office but artistically could be saved neither by its superb cast nor by its undeniable visual ingenuity. Mikhalkov-Konchalovskii's most ambitious Soviet project, *Siberiade* (Sibiriada, 1979), a five-hour epic, aimed at grandiosity yet rang hollow. The director's high ambitions were no longer compatible with the state-funded ideological paradigm, and his marriage to a secretary of the French embassy and subsequent departure for Western Europe and the United States (1980) in hindsight appear as a pretext for self-reinvention as a filmmaker under free-market conditions.

The imaginative, sensual Andrei Platonov adaptation *Maria's Lovers* (1984) demonstrated Mikhalkov-Konchalovskii's strategy of blending elements of U.S. mainstream cinema with Russian melancholy and pensiveness. Of his other American pictures, the allegorical thriller *Runaway Train* (1985) was the most critically praised, the Southern drama *Shy People* (1987) the most stylistically solid and psychologically intriguing, and *Tango and Cash* (1989) the most openly commercial. The interesting Julie Andrews vehicle *Duet for One* (1986) flopped badly. All of Mikhalkov-Konchalovskii's American films contain unexpected, atypical plot turns and betray a sensitivity that make them seem "European," albeit lacking a developed, recognizable cinematic style.

When given the chance to tackle Russian subject matter, Mikhalkov-Konchalovskii made the remarkable although critically underrated *Inner Circle* (1991), a chilling melodrama about Iosif Stalin's movie projectionist on the backdrop of ordinary life under totalitarian rule. His ultimate homecoming picture, *The Chicken Riaba* (aka *Ryaba My Chicken*/Kurochka riaba, 1994), a satirical sequel to *Asia's Happiness*, badly misjudged the expectations of Russian audiences and also fell victim to the ruin of the country's distribution system. *The Odyssey* (1997), a lavish, faithful, and artistically convincing adaptation of Homer's epic for U.S. television, was appreciated in many countries around the world. In 2002, the director gave his version of the war in Chechnia in the sentimental farce *House of Fools* (Dom durakov), interspersing the cruel absurdity of war with humane irony and wisdom.

Mikhalkov-Konchalovskii is a prolific screenwriter who has authored or coauthored the scripts to some exceptional pictures, most prominently Tarkovskii's masterpiece **Andrei Rublev** (1966), as well as action-packed historical thrillers such as **Shaken Aimanov**'s *The End of the Ataman* (Konets atamana, 1970) and **Ali Khamraev**'s *The Seventh Bullet* (Sed'maia pulia, 1972), **Tolomush Okeev**'s drama *The Fierce One* (Liutyi, 1975), and his own brother **Nikita Mikhalkov**'s Civil War melodrama *Slave of Love* (Raba liubvi, 1976). Among his recent efforts as scriptwriter is the thriller *Moscow Chill* (2005).

Mikhalkov-Konchalovskii's most serious problem throughout his career has been the inability to define himself as a filmmaker with a coherent aesthetic approach, that is, as a genuine auteur. One can easily trace impulses stemming from world cinema classics—the early Pier Paolo Pasolini, Akira Kurosawa, Federico Fellini, Luis Buñuel, and responses to international phenomena (thus, *Siberiade* was intended as the Soviet answer to—if not imitation of—Bernardo Bertolucci's 1976 Communist monumental epic *Novecento*).

Mikhalkov-Konchalovski was awarded the title People's Artist of the RSFSR in 1980. A son from his marriage to **Natal'ia**

Arinbasarova, Egor Konchalovskii (b. 1966), is a successful director specializing in intellectually complex thrillers.

Other films: *Uncle Vanya* (Diadia Vania, 1974); *Homer and Eddie* (1988); *The Lion in Winter* (2003, TV); *Gloss* (Glianets, 2007).

MIRONOV, ANDREI ALEKSANDROVICH (b. 7 March 1941, Moscow–d. 16 August 1987, Riga). Russian actor. Mironov, the son of the legendary stage duo Mariia Mironova (1911–1997) and Aleksandr Menaker (1913–1982), studied at the prestigious Shchukin Theater School in Moscow, graduating in 1962, and joined the troupe of the Theater of Satire. He became one of its leading stars in productions of Nikolai Gogol', Anton Chekhov, Max Frisch, and especially in the title role of Beaumarchais's *The Wedding of Figaro*.

Handsome, charming, and youthfully energetic, Mironov was first cast as a carefree flirt and guy-next-door in films such as **Aleksandr Zarkhi**'s *My Younger Brother* (Moi mladshii brat, 1963) and Genrikh Oganesian's *Three Plus Two* (Tri plius dva, 1963). Early on directors like **El'dar Riazanov** in *Beware of the Car* (Beregis' avtomobilia, 1966) indicated distrust toward the actor's smooth and elegant surface, letting him play slimy crooks. Mironov himself was able to poke fun at his clichéd narcissism and cockiness, for example, in **Leonid Gaidai**'s *Diamond Arm* (Brilliantovaia ruka, 1969). Thus, he was ideally suited to play Il'f and Petrov's famous rogue Ostap Bender in **Mark Zakharov**'s miniseries *Twelve Chairs* (Dvenadtsat' stul'ev, 1976, TV).

Often, Mironov's "un-Soviet" features led directors to casting him in parts of foreigners such as Orlando in **Aleksandr Mitta**'s fantasy *Story of the Voyages* (Skazka stranstvii, 1982), the American correspondent in **Evgenii Matveev**'s World War II drama *Victory* (Pobeda, 1985), and the film projectionist Mr. First in Alla Surikova's tongue-in-cheek Western *The Man from the Boulevard des Capucines* (Chelovek s bul'vara Kaputsinov, 1987). Few filmmakers allowed Mironov to explore his innate complexity, melancholy, and sadness as did **Aleksei German** in *My Friend Ivan Lapshin* (Moi drug Ivan Lapshin, 1984), where he portrays Khanin, a journalist and widower.

Mironov, who also sang in his films and in concert, was named People's Artist of the Russian Federation in 1980. He died of a heart attack while on stage playing Figaro. His early death set off an unprecedented cult that is reflected in a number of sensationalist memoirs. Mironov is buried at Vagan'kovskoe cemetery; the house on Petrovka Street 22 in which he was born and lived until 1966 carries a commemorative plaque.

Other films: *The Shadow* (Ten', 1971); *Fariat'ev's Phantasies* (Fantazii Fariat'eva, 1979); *The Blonde behind the Corner* (Blondinka za uglom, 1983).

MIRONOV, EVGENII VITAL'EVICH (b. 29 November 1966, Saratov). Russian actor. After graduating from the Saratov theater school, Mironov enrolled in the studio school of the Moscow Art Theater (MKhAT), which he finished in 1990. His teacher, **Oleg Tabakov**, then kept him as a member of his own theater troupe, Tabakerka.

Mironov's screen debut was the supporting role of a flutist in **Aleksandr Kaidanovskii**'s darkly surreal Jorge Luis Borges adaptation *The Kerosene Seller's Wife* (Zhena kerosinshchika, 1988). Early on, the actor cultivated the persona of a naïve young man, a gullible object to various social pressures, for example, in the drama about army hazing *Do It—Once!* (Delai—raz, 1990) and in **Petr Todorovskii**'s revisionist war melodrama *Da capo! Da capo Again!* (Ankor! Eshche ankor! 1992). Mironov's performance in the title role of **Vladimir Khotinenko**'s deeply subversive *The Moslem* (Musul'manin, 1995), about a soldier returning from Afghanistan where he had converted to Islam, solidified his reputation as one of the finest actors of his generation. In the following decade, Mironov became a superstar of post-Soviet cinema whose strong screen presence lends believability both to historical and contemporary stories and who fills even episodic parts such as the hyperactive officer in **Andrei Mikhalkov-Konchalovskii**'s *House of Fools* (Dom durakov, 2002) with a unique, scene-stealing energy. Among Mironov's few failures is a strangely unfunny appearance as the con man Khlestakov in the hapless Nikolai Gogol' adaptation *The Inspector General* (Revisor, 1999); however, he richly made up for that embarrassment with a vibrant portrayal of Prince Myshkin in **Vladimir Bortko**'s Fedor Dostoevskii adaptation *The Idiot* (Idiot, 2003, TV).

Mironov's ability to convey pure, driven idealism troubled by a vague sense of ethical confusion has made him a prime choice for depictions of the Soviet mentality, as evidenced by his outstanding leads in Aleksei Uchitel''s *The Cosmos as an Anticipation* (aka *Dreaming of Space*/Kosmos kak predchuvstvie, 2005) and **Gleb Panfilov**'s *In the First Circle* (V kruge pervom, 2006) from Aleksandr Solzhenitsyn's novel.

In 1996, Mironov was awarded the title Merited Artist of Russia; he also received a State Prize of Russia for his stage work.

Other films: *Burnt by the Sun* (Utomlennye solntsem, 1994); *Mom* (Mama, 2000); *His Wife's Diary* (Dnevnik ego zheny, 2000); *I Feel No Pain* (Mne ne bol'no, 2006); *The Apostle* (Apostol, 2008).

MITTA [real name: Rabinovich], **ALEKSANDR NAUMOVICH** (b. 28 March 1933, Moscow). Russian director, screenwriter, and pedagogue. Mitta was born into a family of high-ranking Communist officials, many of whom were executed in the 1930s purges; he spent part of his childhood in an orphanage. After studying architecture at the Moscow Institute for Construction and Engineering (MISI) until 1955, Mitta worked as a cartoonist and enrolled in **Mikhail Romm**'s workshop at the Soviet State Film School **VGIK**, graduating in 1960.

Mitta's early films reveal a penchant for social didactics. Thus, his diploma feature, *My Friend, Kol'ka!* (Drug moi, Kol'ka! 1961, codirected with **Aleksei Saltykov**), juxtaposes schoolchildren's natural idealism to the insensitivity of school bureaucrats. *No Fear, No Blame* (Bez strakha i upreka, 1962) uses an adventurous plot about children retrieving lost money to espouse values such as honesty and chivalry. The director's consistent humanist message is most openly declared in *Someone Rings, Open the Door* (aka *The Girl and the Burglar*/Zvoniat, otkroite dver', 1965) whose plot (a girl, member of the Young Pioneers, searches for the organization's founding fathers) turns into a parable on mutual support.

Mitta's most artistically convincing picture is the bittersweet *Shine, Shine, My Star* (Gori, gori, moia zvezda, 1970) about a quixotic artist during the 1918–1921 Civil War whose desire to radically transform society is only outweighed by his selflessness and ultimate self-sacrifice. Mitta turned to less complex genre fare with *Moscow, My Love* (Moskva, liubov' moia, 1974, codirected by Kenzi Yesida), a Soviet-Japanese love story with antiwar undertones. *The Tale of How Tsar Peter Married His Moor* (Skaz pro to, kak tsar' Petr arapa zhenil, 1976), adapted from an unfinished novel by Aleksandr Pushkin, is a charming blend of historical **comedy** and musical that particularly gains from **Vladimir Vysotskii**'s lead performance.

If the latter two films, with about 30 million viewers each, can be called box-office hits, they were but a prelude to one of the most spectacular popular successes in Soviet cinema history, *The Crew* (Ekipazh, 1980). Over 70 million people wanted to see this rather tedious melodrama-cum-disaster movie about selfless Soviet pilots and their loving women. Mitta incorporated fantasy in *Tale of Voyages* (Skazka stranstvii, 1983) and détente arguments in the Soviet-Japanese *The Step* (aka *Message from the Future*/Shag, 1988), yet elicited little audience response. *Lost in Siberia* (Zateriannyi v Sibiri, 1991), coproduced with Great Britain, was intended as a visualization of the horrors of GULAG, but Mitta's melodramatic excesses diminish the chilly authenticity achieved in some episodes.

What followed was a decade-long hiatus in which the director worked as a film pedagogue in Hamburg, Germany, and conducted master classes at the Supreme Courses for Screenwriters and Directors (VKSR) in Moscow. In 2001, he helmed a miniseries about the life of Soviet Army officers in the 1970s, *The Border: A Taiga Novel* (Granitsa. Taezhnyi roman, TV), which left a rather incoherent impression.

Mitta is a solid craftsman whose careful calculation of popular effects has hurt his reputation among critics. Still, his crowd-pleasers always come with a distinct morale. During the Soviet period, none of Mitta's films challenged the principles of Communist doctrine, rather romanticizing many of its aspects, while his post-Soviet pictures are critical of the past.

Mitta was named Merited Artist of the Russian Federation in 1974.

Other films: *Period, Period, Comma* (Tochka, tochka, zapiataia, 1972); *Split Saturday* (Raskalennaia subbota, 2002).

MKRTCHYAN, MHER FRUNZE [also: Frunzik; some Russian sources list the patronymic Mushegovich] (b. 4 May [other sources: July] 1930, Leninakan [now: Gyumri], Armenia–d. 29 December 1993, Yerevan). Armenian actor. Mkrtchyan graduated from the

Yerevan Institute of Art and Theater in 1955 and joined the troupe of the Sundukyan Drama Theater in Yerevan in 1956.

Mkrtchyan made his film debut with a small part in the otherwise unremarkable industrial **comedy** *Looking for an Addressee* (Hastseatiroij voronumnere/V poiskakh adresata, 1955). He raised eyebrows with the hilarious performance as a professor in **Georgii Daneliia**'s satire *Thirty-three* (Tridtsat' tri, 1965), creating a comical screen image bordering on the grotesque, which subsequently was employed by various directors and propelled by popular demand. Films that feature Mkrtchyan in effective supporting roles include **Leonid Gaidai**'s superhit *Prisoner of the Caucasus* (aka *Kidnapping Caucasian Style*/Kavkazskaia plennitsa, 1966), **Rolan Bykov**'s extravagant *Aibolit 66* (1966), and **Latif Faiziev**'s Uzbek-Indian fairytale blockbuster *The Adventures of Ali Baba and the Forty Thieves* (Prikliucheniia Ali Baby i soroka razboinikov, 1979). Whether as an obtuse robber or guard, hapless lover or narrow-minded uncle, Mkrtchyan, with his expressive facial features—sad dark eyes and a trademark oversized nose—became a beloved Soviet screen icon.

The actor's appearances in **Armenian cinema** were of a more serious and thoughtful nature and included tragicomical, penetrating characterizations. This is particularly true of **Henrik Malyan**'s *The Triangle* (Yerankyuni/Treugol'nik, 1967), an episodic film about blacksmiths; *We and Our Mountains* (Menq enq, mer sarere/My i nashi gory, 1970) in which Mkrtchyan is cast as a shepherd; *Father* (Hayrik/Airik, 1973); *Nahapet* (aka *Life Triumphs*, 1977), thematizing the 1915 genocide against the Armenian people; and the touching melodrama *A Slap in the Face* (Ktor me yerkinq/Poshchechina, 1980) about a man who defends his love against social pressure. Mkrtchyan also appeared in other Armenian films, including **Erazm Karamyan**'s historical drama *An Explosion after Midnight* (Paytyun kesgisherits heto/Vzryv posle polunochi, 1969), **Edmond Keosayan**'s romantic comedy *Men* (Tghamardik/Muzhchiny, 1972), and the postwar family tragedy *The Tango of Our Childhood* (Mer mankutyan tangon/Tango nashego detstva, 1985).

Mkrtchyan won a USSR State Prize in 1978 for the role of Ruben in Daneliia's mellow comedy *Mimino* and was honored with the title People's Artist of the USSR in 1984.

Other films: *A Matter of Honor* (Patvi hamar/Iz-za chesti, 1956); *Baghdasar Divorces His Wife* (Baghdasare bazhanvum e knojits/ Bagdasar razvoditsia s zhenoi, 1977); *The Breath* (Dykhanie, 1989).

MOLCHANOV, KIRILL VLADIMIROVICH (b. 7 September 1922, Tomsk–d. 14 March 1982, Moscow). Russian composer. Molchanov studied at the Moscow Conservatory, graduating in 1949. In 1950, his first opera premiered at the Stanislavskii and Nemirovich-Danchenko Musical Theater in Moscow: *The Stone Flower* (Kamennyi tsvetok), from a fairy tale by Pavel Bazhov. Other operas include *Del Corno Street* (Ulitsa del' Korno, 1960, from a novel by Vasco Pratolini), and *Romeo, Juliet, and Darkness* (Romeo, Dzhul'etta i t'ma, 1962).

Molchanov's debut in cinema was the score for **Vsevolod Pudovkin**'s last film, the postwar rural tale *The Return of Vasilii Bortnikov* (aka *Vasili's Return*/Vozvrashchenie Vasiliia Bortnikova, 1953). The composer struck a particularly fruitful partnership with **Stanislav Rostotskii** on his blockbusters *It Happened in Pen'kovo* (Delo bylo v Pen'kove, 1958), *Let's See What Monday Brings* (Dozhivem do ponedel'nika, 1968), and *The Dawns Are Quiet Here* (A zori zdes' tikhie, 1972), all of them melodramas whose emotional impact was supported by the composer's harrowing tunes. To some films, he contributed songs, including Rostotskii's hopelessly inadequate adaptation of Mikhail Lermontov's novel *A Hero of Our Time* (Geroi nashego vremeni, 1965) in which Pechorin sings Molchanov's melodies to the guitar.

The composer successfully worked in a variety of genres, from **comedies** such as Iurii Chuliukin's popular *The Unamenables* (Nepoddaiushchiesia, 1959), to family melodramas (**Boris Barnet**'s *Alenka*, 1962), children's Civil War adventures, including **Aleksandrs Leimanis**'s *The "Wagtail" Army* (Armiia "Triasoguzka", 1964), Cold War drama (Vladimir Berenshtein's *Neutral Waters*/Neitral'nye vody, 1969), and biopic (**Sergei Urusevskii**'s Sergei Esenin portrait *Sing a Song, Poet* [Poi pesniu, poet, 1971]), always with a marked preference for patriotic themes.

One of the most prolific film composers of his generation with almost 50 scores to his credit, Molchanov also wrote the music for numerous stage productions, as well as chamber music. He became a member of the Communist Party in 1945 and was named Merited Artist of the RSFSR in 1963. Molchanov was married to Bolshoi Theater ballerina Nina Timofeeva (b. 1935).

Other films: *May Stars* (Maiskie zvezdy, 1959); *Duel in the Taiga* (Poedinok v taige, 1977); *Stove Builders* (Pechniki, 1982, TV).

MOLDOVA-FILM STUDIO. In 1947, a small branch of the Central Studio of Documentary Films was established in Moldova's capital Chisinau (Kishinev) and supervised by the Ukrainian Documentary Studio. In 1949, staff members of the Odessa Film Factory (then called Black Sea Film Factory [Chernomorskaia kinofabrika]) took over, and in 1952, the branch was transformed into the Moldovan Newsreel Documentary Studio. One of its films, *Moldovan Melodies* (Moldavskie napevy, 1955), was an attempt to combine fictional elements and documentary scenes.

In January 1957, the studio was reorganized and renamed Moldovan Studio for Feature and Newsreel Documentary Films, or Moldova-Film Studio. Its first full-length feature films were the agricultural **comedy** *Not in Its Proper Place* (Ne na svoem meste, 1957), directed by Grigorii Komarovskii, and the musical *The White Acacia* (Belaia akatsiia, 1957), helmed by **Georgii Natanson**. The adventure film *Ataman Codr* (1958, codirected by **Mikhail Kalik** and Boris Rytsarev after Ol'ga Ulitskaia [1902–1978] had abandoned the project), became a popular success, introducing the theme of the liberation struggle of the legendary local outlaws, called *haiduks*. Kalik, who developed a poetic, nostalgic style of his own (*Lullaby*/ Kolybel'naia, 1960; *Man Follows the Sun*/Chelovek idet za solntsem, 1961), became one of the studio's leading directors, as did **Vadim Derbenev** (*Last Month of Autumn*/Ultima luna de toamna/Poslednii mesiats oseni, 1965, after Ion Druta), formerly an accomplished cameraman. Ulitskaia directed the first Moldovan full-length **documentary**, *Bloom, Moldova!* (Tsveti, Moldova! 1960).

In the mid-1960s, **Emil Loteanu** helped **Moldovan cinema**—and Moldova-Film Studio—to further emancipate itself, introducing folklore-inspired plots, lavish shot compositions, and scores that drew on gypsy music. The most famous Moldovan composer, **Eugeniu Doga**, contributed the music to numerous Moldovan and

Russian films and became a star in his own right. Loteanu's *Red Meadows* (Poienele rosii/Krasnye poliany, 1966) and *Fiddlers* (Lautarii/Lautary, 1972), filled with unbridled passion and beauty, marked a new level of national self-consciousness. *Bitter Grain* (aka *A Taste of Bread*/Gustul piinii/Gor'kie zerna, 1966) by **Valeriu Gajiu** and Vadim Lysenko attempted an honest depiction of the postwar problems and initially was praised for its unprecedented realism. However, in the early 1970s, the political and cultural atmosphere in Moldova became more oppressive, which led to the shelving of *Bitter Grain*, Kalik's *To Love* (Liubit', 1968), and eventually to the departure of Loteanu, Derbenev, and Kalik.

The complex events of the late 1940s became a taboo, and the remaining Moldovan directors concentrated on less provocative topics, first and foremost the heroism of underground fighters in the Great Patriotic War, as well as the more distant history in films such as *Dimitri Cantemir* (1973). In 1970, famed cameraman and director **Boris Volchek** came to Moldova to make *Accused of Murder* (Obviniaetsia v ubiistve, 1969), a gritty social drama that remained, however, an exception. In the 1970s and 1980s, the most active directors working at Moldova-Film Studio were **Vasile Pascaru**, Nicolae Ghibu, Mikhail Izraelev (b. 1913), and Vadim Lysenko (b. 1932). Its leading stars were **Mihai Volontir**, **Svetlana Tomà**, and **Grigore Grigoriu**, all of whom developed a Soviet-wide reputation and appeared in non-Moldovan films as well.

In the 1990s, film production at the studio stopped. The outdated equipment was not replaced, government funding was scarce (the studio still belongs to the state), and many leading artists had left the now independent country, including Emil Loteanu, Eugeniu Doga, screenwriter Ion Druta, and Svetlana Tomà. Mircea Chistruti, who heads the Moldovan Filmmakers' Union, bitterly stated that there seems to be no need for a Moldovan film industry anymore. One of the three full-length features produced between 1992 and 2006 was the comedy *Danila Prepeleac* (1995) from Ion Creanga's popular story. Moldova-Film also coproduced the art-house success *Procustean Bed* (Patul lui Procust/Prokrustovo lozhe, 2001, directed by Sergiu Prodan and Viorica Mesina) with Romania and Russia. In 2004, Gajiu made *Jana*, a contemporary drama that disappointed both critics and viewers. In 2005, Moldovan President Voronin initiated a restructuring of

Moldova-Film with the intention to enable the studio to lease its facilities to foreign companies.

Between 1957 and 1992, Moldova-Film Studio turned out a total of 160 feature films, 1,500 documentaries and educational shorts, and over 100 **animated** films.

MOLDOVAN [Moldavian] **CINEMA.** *See* DERBENEV, VADIM; DOGA, EUGENIU; GAJIU, VALERIU; GRIGORIU, GRIGORE; KALIK, MIKHAIL; LOTEANU, EMIL; MOLDOVA-FILM STUDIO; PASCARU, VASILE; TOMÀ, SVETLANA; VOLONTIR, MIHAI.

MORDIUKOVA, NONNA [real first name: Noiabrina] **VIKTOROVNA** (b. 25 November 1925, stanitsa Otradnaia [other sources: Konstantinovskaia], Donetsk district–d. 6 July 2008, Moscow). Russian actress. Mordiukova enrolled in **Sergei Gerasimov**'s workshop at the Soviet State Film School **VGIK**, graduating in 1950. Her film debut as the self-sacrificing Ul'iana Gromova in Gerasimov's tragic partisan drama *The Young Guard* (Molodaia gvardiia, 1948) made her famous overnight and won her—still a student at the time—a Stalin Prize at the unprecedented age of 24.

Mordiukova's screen image became that of a rank-and-file Russian woman—passionate yet humble, strong-willed yet craving manly protection. She embodies these features in neorealist Thaw melodramas such as **Vsevolod Pudovkin**'s *The Return of Vasilii Bortnikov* (aka *Vasili's Return*/Vozvrashchenie Vasiliia Bortnikova, 1953) and **Mikhail Shveitser**'s *Alien Kin* (Chuzhaia rodnia, 1956), while the grandiose monumentality of her debut is recapitulated in Nikolai Moskalenko's *The Russian Field* (Russkoe pole, 1971) and **Sergei Bondarchuk**'s *They Fought for the Motherland* (Oni srazahlis' za rodinu, 1975). Mordiukova's unrivalled ability to portray highly emotional peasant women is demonstrated in *The Chairman* (Predsedatel', 1964) by **Aleksei Saltykov**, who later gave her a similar part in *There Is No Return* (Vozvrata net, 1974) in the role of Antonina Kashirina.

One of Mordiukova's greatest and internationally most recognized artistic achievements is the lead in **Aleksandr Askol'dov**'s 1968 *Commissar* (Komissar, released 1988): a woman holding a leadership position in the Red Army who ultimately rejects motherhood for the sake of revolutionary struggle. A curious inversion of that performance, although in a World War II situation, is the part of a mother who puts her son's safety above patriotic duty in **Grigorii Chukhrai**'s *Quagmire* (Triasina, 1977).

Mordiukova proved that she is also capable of biting satire in roles of so-called hack-women (*baby-funktsionerki*) in **Georgii Daneliia**'s *Thirty-three* (Tridtsat'-tri, 1965), **Leonid Gaidai**'s *The Diamond Arm* (Brilliantovaia ruka, 1968), and **Vladimir Men'shov**'s *What a Mess* (Shirli-myrli, 1995). The role of Mariia Konovalova in **Nikita Mikhalkov**'s sharply polemical *Kin* (Rodnia, 1981) demonstrates how the earlier image of strong Russian womanhood had turned into an anachronism under the pressure of modernization. Mordiukova's last major performance, the title role in Denis Evstigneev's *Mom* (Mama, 2000), is a genuine tour de force, despite the harsh criticism launched against the film as a whole.

Mordiukova was named People's Artist of the USSR in 1974. Her son from a marriage to **Viacheslav Tikhonov**, Vladimir Tikhonov (1950–1990), was an actor.

Other films: *War and Peace* (Voina i mir, 1962–1967); *Little Crane* (Zhuravushka, 1969); *Luna Park* (1992).

MOSCOW DOES NOT BELIEVE IN TEARS (Moskva slezam ne verit, 1979). **Mosfilm Studio**. Two parts, 68 and 82 min., color. Directed by **Vladimir Men'shov**. Script: Valentin Chernykh. Cinematography: Igor' Slabnevich. Music: Sergei Nikitin. Cast: Vera Alentova, Irina Murav'eva, Raisa Riazanova, **Aleksei Batalov**, Boris Smorchkov, Iurii Vasil'ev, Natal'ia Vavilova, Aleksandr Fatiushin, **Oleg Tabakov**, Elena Khanaeva, **Zoia Fedorova**, **Innokentii Smoktunovskii**, **Vladimir Basov**, **Garri Bardin**. Premiere: 11 February 1980.

In the late 1950s, Katia (Alentova), Tonia (Riazanova), and Liudmila (Murav'eva), three friends from the Russian provinces, move to Moscow and explore its many promises and temptations. Years later, after some painful private disillusionments, all three have settled socially and professionally, albeit in different positions. Katia has become a major business administrator living with her daughter, whom she raised alone. She encounters Gosha (Batalov), a worker who gives her much-needed affection and care but also insists on patriarchal principles. When he learns of Katia's high-ranking position, he temporarily withdraws from the relationship but eventually returns.

MOSFILM STUDIO [kinostudiia Mosfil'm]. On 15 February 1920, the Bolshevik government nationalized what was left of the studios of leading Russian producers **Aleksandr Khanzhonkov** and **Iosif Ermol'ev**, putting all buildings, equipment, and raw materials in the care of the All-Russian Department of Photography and Cinema (Vserossiiskii fotokinootdel, VFKO). In 1922, VFKO was transformed into the State Cinema enterprise (Goskino). Goskino's structural units were called film factories (*kinofabriki*), with the Khanzhonkov and the Ermol'ev studios representing the First and the Third Film Factories, respectively. Together, they produced their first feature in 1923, Boris Mikhin's *Upwards on Wings* (Na kryl'iakh vvys', released in January 1924). The date of 31 January 1924 is henceforth celebrated as the official date of the foundation of Mosfilm Studio, with Mikhin as its first director. However, in 1926, the two film factories were still named United Moscow Factory Sovkino; one year later, the construction of additional buildings on the Lenin Hills (formerly—and now again—Sparrow Hills/Vorob'evye gory) began. On 9 February 1931, the studio was renamed Moscow United Factory Soiuzkino; in 1932, it became Moscow Factory Rosfil'm; in 1933, Moscow Film Factory Soiuzfil'm; and in 1934, Moskinokombinat. The studio was officially named Mosfilm on 4 January 1936. In the beginning, it produced the entire range of genres, from feature to **animation** and **documentary**; since 1936, it has solely specialized in feature films.

In 1936, one of Mosfilm's major competitors, **Mezhrabpomfilm Studio**, was dismantled. As a result, Mosfilm received some of Mezhrabpomfilm's assets, as well as some leading filmmakers (for example, **Boris Barnet**). The wave of repressions in 1937 had a direct impact on the studio, too: its executive director, Boris Babitskii, was arrested in December 1937, and the production of numerous films came to a halt.

During the Great Patriotic War, Mosfilm Studio was evacuated to Alma-Ata (Almaty), then the capital of the Kazakh SSR, where the production of feature films resumed under the administrative label

Central United Film Studio for Feature Films (TsOKS, Tsentral'naia ob"edinennaia kinostudiia khudozhestvennykh fil'mov). In 1946, upon returning to Moscow, the studio was considerably modernized and enlarged, occupying about 36 hectares (36,000 square meters). *Spring* (Vesna), **Grigorii Aleksandrov**'s 1947 comedy, was the first feature to open with the emblem of Mosfilm, the famous monument "Worker and Peasant Woman" by Vera Mukhina. In 1965, a monument to the Mosfilm workers who lost their lives in the Great Patriotic War was unveiled.

With its gigantic facilities, Mosfilm is one of the largest film studios in the world. In the 1950s–1980s, it churned out about 40 full-length feature films for cinema release and 15 films for television annually. Among the influential filmmakers who spent their entire career or a significant part thereof at Mosfilm Studio, were **Sergei Eizenshtein**, **Vsevolod Pudovkin**, **Lev Kuleshov**, **Abram Room**, **Aleksandr Dovzhenko**, **Ivan Pyr'ev**, **Mikhail Romm**, **Aleksandr Ptushko**, **Vladimir Petrov**, **Mikhail Kalatozov**, **Sergei Iutkevich**, **Sergei Bondarchuk**, **El'dar Riazanov**, **Grigorii Chukhrai**, **Leonid Gaidai**, **Georgii Daneliia**, **Marlen Khutsiev**, **Andrei Tarkovskii**, **Mikhail Shveitser**, **Gleb Panfilov**, **Larisa Shepit'ko**, **Aleksandr Alov** and **Vladimir Naumov**, **Nikita Mikhalkov**, **Andrei Mikhalkov-Konchalovskii**, **Aleksei Saltykov**, and **Vadim Abdrashitov**. In 1965, Chukhrai was put in charge of an experimental production unit (together with Vladimir Pozner) that existed until 1977. Based on the principle of financial self-support (*khozraschet*), it was a curious economic experiment—a studio that maintained a certain artistic independence and produced some of the most interesting Soviet pictures, including blockbusters such as **Vladimir Motyl'**'s *White Sun of the Desert* (Beloe solntse pustyni, 1969). At Mosfilm Studio, Akira Kurosawa was able to realize one of his cherished projects, the Oscar-winning *Dersu Uzala* (1975), after which he again became a bankable filmmaker in his native Japan. **Vladimir Men'shov** won an Oscar for his Mosfilm-produced superhit *Moscow Does Not Believe in Tears* (Moskva slezam ne verit, 1980). Leading directors from national studios, among them Moldovan **Emil Loteanu** and Lithuanian **Vytautas Žalakevičius**, worked at Mosfilm in the 1970s and 1980s.

In June 1987, the creative production units (*khudozhestvennye ob"edineniia*) were transformed into studios, each of which was headed by a prominent director: **Iulii Raizman** was appointed head of the Third Studio, Sergei Bondarchuk was put in charge of the studio Image (Kartina), Georgii Daneliia became head of the studio of **comedies** and musicals, **Sergei Solov'ev** of the studio Circle (Krug), Rolan Bykov of the studio of **children's and youth films**, and Vladimir Men'shov of the studio Genre. In October 1988, the entire Mosfilm Studio, now under the leadership of director Vladimir Dostal', was transferred to the economic principle of financial self-support, with the right to sell its films to foreign distributors and retain the profits.

Mosfilm was the largest Soviet feature film studio and has kept some of its capability even after the breakdown of the Soviet Union, a period marked by endless restructuring, chaotic commercialization, and a drastic decrease in production numbers. Over the years, the studio has produced more than 2,500 pictures. Megaproductions such as Bondarchuk's *War and Peace* (1962–1967) or **Iurii Ozerov**'s *Liberation* (1970–1972) could not have been managed by any other Soviet studio. In the 1990s, Mosfilm was transformed into a film corporation (*kinokontsern*). The question of whether and under which conditions it should be privatized was the subject of controversies throughout the first post-Soviet decade. However, in March 2004, the president of the Russian Federation, Vladimir Putin, issued a decree by which Mosfilm Studio became a "strategic object" that may not be privatized. In close cooperation with Moscow's mayor, Iurii Luzhkov, the executive director of Mosfilm, **Karen Shakhnazarov**, has managed to reestablish the studio as a major player in Russian cinema of the new millennium.

MOSKVIN, ANDREI NIKOLAEVICH (b. 14 February 1901, Tsarskoe Selo–d. 28 February 1961, Pushkin). Russian cinematographer. Moskvin was born into the family of an engineer. He worked as an assistant to **Anatolii Golovnia** on **Vsevolod Pudovkin**'s educational film *Mechanics of the Brain* (Mekhanika golovnogo mozga, 1926) and subsequently joined the Factory of the Eccentric Actor (FEKS), establishing himself as **Grigorii Kozintsev**'s and **Leonid Trauberg**'s reliable artistic partner for many years to come.

Moskvin made his debut on **Viacheslav Viskovskii**'s traditionalist historical epic *The Ninth of January* (Deviatoe ianvaria, 1925). The contemporary criminal drama *Devil's Wheel* (Chertovo koleso, 1926) and the masterful Nikolai Gogol' adaptation *The Overcoat* (Shinel', 1926), directed by Kozintsev and Trauberg, impressed and disturbed viewers with their unusual visual dynamics dominated by a diffuse, instable lighting. Inspired by French impressionism, Moskvin developed a unique, recognizable style; his shot compositions gain their expressive power from extreme points of view and partial opaqueness. The peculiar revolutionary pathos for which Kozintsev and Trauberg were striving found its most original realization in *S.V.D.—The Club of Great Deeds* (SVD—Soiuz velikikh del, 1927) about the 1825 Decembrist upheaval, and *The New Babylon* (Novyi Vavilon, 1929) about the 1870–1871 Paris Commune.

Moskvin mastered the transition to sound film with relative ease, as demonstrated in Kozintsev-Trauberg's antipatriarchal drama *Alone* (Odna, 1931), a furious indictment of the Russian farmers' class. In the famous **Maksim Trilogy** (Trilogiia o Maksime, 1934–1938), Moskvin created a gallery of authentic Petrograd cityscapes, but the visual effects are less emphasized than in his silent pictures. Indeed, realistic understatement became one of Moskvin's trademarks in sound film.

Sergei Eizenshtein's decision to hire Moskvin for the interior scenes of his historical-philosophical epic **Ivan the Terrible** (Ivan Groznyi, 1943–1945) had to do with the cinematographer's "intonation of lighting," which either clarifies the viewer's understanding of a character and the relationship between characters, or blurs it by creating ambiguity. After this artistic triumph, a period of hapless projects began, from the lackluster biopics *Pirogov* (1947) and *Belinskii* (1951) to **Aleksandr Faintsimmer**'s pseudo-Lithuanian *Dawn over the Neman* (Aušra prie Nemuno/Nad Nemanom rassvet, 1953), a low point in Moskvin's career. However, in the post-Stalin period, Moskvin created a picturesque and atmospherically convincing 17th-century Spain for Kozintsev's *Don Quijote* (1957) and a tactful and restrained black-and-white imagery for **Iosif Kheifits**'s Anton Chekhov adaptation *The Lady with a Lapdog* (Dama s sobachkoi, 1959). Moskvin died during preproduction of Kozintsev's *Hamlet* and was replaced by his assistant **Jonas Gricius**.

Moskvin, who in the 1930s also worked as a newsreel cameraman, is credited with founding the "Leningrad School of Cinematography," although he never held a formal teaching position. His poetic style with softened backgrounds that often are filled with dynamic elements such as fog, steam, snowstorms, clouds, or a moving source of light, is markedly different from the rational clarity and linearity of his teacher Golovnia or **Eduard Tissé**. Noteworthy in Moskvin's aesthetic evolution is his movement from early extreme expressiveness toward classical simplicity that renders the camera work almost unnoticeable.

Moskvin was honored with the title Merited Artist of the RSFSR in 1935 and won Stalin Prizes for the first part of *Ivan the Terrible* in 1946 and for *Pirogov* in 1948. He was married to director **Nadezhda Kosheverova**.

Other films: *The Actress* (Aktrisa, 1943); *The Gadfly* (Ovod, 1955); *Tales about Lenin* (Rasskazy o Lenine, 1957).

MOTHER, THE (Mat', 1926). Mezhrabpom-Rus' [**Mezhrabpomfilm Studio**]. 66 min., b/w. Directed by **Vsevolod Pudovkin**. Script: **Natan Zarkhi**, from the 1906 novel by Maksim Gor'kii. Cinematography: **Anatolii Golovnia**. Cast: **Vera Baranovskaia**, **Nikolai Batalov**, Aleksandr Chistiakov, Anna Zemtsova, **Ivan Koval'-Samborskii**, Vsevolod Pudovkin. Premiere: 11 October 1926. A sound track was added in 1935; the film was restored in 1969.

Pavel Vlasov, a young worker and political activist, participates in clandestine operations against the tsarist government. One day his father, a violent drunkard and strikebreaker, gets killed. During a police search, Pavel's mother, Nilovna, a naïve and pious woman hoping to save her son, reveals the place where Pavel and his comrades keep their weapons and other illegal materials. Pavel is tried and incarcerated but uses Nilovna's visits to prison to smuggle information. When a riot breaks out, Pavel is freed and joins a demonstration but eventually is killed by police. His mother picks up the demonstrators' fallen banner and carries it on, until she also is shot.

MOTYL', VLADIMIR IAKOVLEVICH (b. 26 June 1927, Lepel', Belarus'). Russian director and screenwriter. Motyl''s father perished in the Solovki concentration camp in 1931; his mother, a teacher, was exiled to Northern Ural, where she raised the family. Motyl' studied acting at the Ural Theater Institute in Sverdlovsk, graduating in 1948. While working as a stage director, he studied history and philology as an external student at Ural State University, graduating in 1957. He was hired as an assistant director at Sverdlovsk Film Studio and made his first full-length feature, *Children of Pamir* (Deti Pamira), based on the poem "Lenin in Pamir" by M. Mirshakar, at **Tadjikfilm Studio** in 1963.

After censorship problems with his second picture, the antiheroic World War II tragicomedy *Zhenia, Zhenechka, and "Katiusha"* (Zhenia, Zhenechka i "katiusha," 1967) from a script by Bulat Okudzhava, **Grigorii Chukhrai** gave Motyl' a chance to realize his next project at **Mosfilm Studio**'s independent experimental unit. The result, *White Sun of the Desert* (Beloe solntse pustyni, 1969), exceeded all expectations. With its peculiar blend of revolutionary romanticism, irony, and erotic tension, the film became a smash hit and cult classic. *White Sun*'s humorous melancholy resonated perfectly with viewers from all social strata while its basic loyalty to the Bolshevik cause was appreciated by Soviet political leaders; the film was awarded a belated State Prize in 1998. It seems significant that Motyl' was never able—or willing—to re-create a similar mood of melancholic indulgence in any of his subsequent pictures.

The three-hour historical saga *Star of Captivating Bliss* (Zvezda plenitel'nogo schast'ia, 1975) tells the story of the devoted wives of the 1825 Decembrists, noble mutineers who failed to establish a constitutional monarchy in Russia and were hanged or exiled to Siberia. Far more complex than *White Sun of the Desert*, featuring a nonlinear plot with many dialogues in French, the film's irreconcilable ethical dilemmas correspond with its stylistic heterogeneity that is demonstratively different from its predecessor. In essence, Motyl' managed to create a daringly open group portrait of a dissident movement *avant la lettre*.

The Forest (Les, 1980, released in 1987), a seemingly harmless adaptation of a classical Aleksandr Ostrovskii comedy, was shelved for reasons impossible to comprehend in retrospect. In the aftermath, Motyl' was forced to work for television, where he made the Anton Chekhov adaptation *An Incredible Bet, or A True Event That Ended Happily a Hundred Years Ago* (Neveroiatnoe pari, ili istinnoe proisshestvie blagopoluchno zavershivsheesia sto let nazad, 1984), among others. *Gone with the Horses . . .* (Nesut menia koni . . . , 1996), another Chekhov adaptation but transposed to contemporary settings, places a strong emphasis on sexual situations; it failed both critically and commercially.

Motyl' has maintained the reputation of a maverick in Soviet and Russian cinema, never gaining permanent residency in any studio. The main reason for his difficulties with Soviet officialdom likely was his unwillingness to compromise even in the slightest, although in most of his films he appears far from political dissent. The director's sense of artistic integrity prevented him from sacrificing his principles under market conditions and commercial pressures as well.

Motyl', who has been teaching film direction at various institutions, was named Merited Artist of Russia in 1992 and Merited Artist of the Republic of Tadjikistan in 1997.

Other films: *Once Lived Shishlov* (Zhil-byl Shishlov, 1987, TV); *Let's Part While We Are Still Decent* (Rasstanemsia—poka khoroshie, 1991); *The Red Color of Snowfall* (Bagrovyi tsvet snegopada, 2006).

MOZZHUKHIN, IVAN IL'ICH [French spelling: Ivan Mosjoukine] (b. 26 September 1889 [other sources: 1887, 1890], Penza–d. 17 January 1939, Neuilly, France). Russian actor, director, and screenwriter. Born into the family of a small clerk, Mozzhukhin discovered his love for music and theater and acted in amateur stage productions. After studying law at Moscow University for a year, he joined a theater troupe touring the Russian provinces and worked in the Vvedenskii People's House theater and the prestigious Korsh Theater in Moscow. In 1911, after joining **Aleksandr Khanzhonkov**'s company, Mozzhukhin made his film debut with an impersonation of Admiral Vladimir Kornilov in **Vasilii Goncharov**'s *Defense of Sevastopol* (Oborona Sevastopolia, 1911).

The first professional film actor in Russia, Mozzhukhin worked with all leading directors of the 1910s. Thus, he appeared in **Petr Chardynin**'s *The Brothers* (Brat'ia, 1913), in **Wladyslaw Starewicz**'s *Night before Christmas* (Noch' pered rozhdestvom, 1913) impersonating the devil, in **Evgenii Bauer**'s propaganda piece *Glory to Us, Death to the Enemy* (Slava—nam, smert'—vragam, 1914), and numerous others. After joining **Iosif Ermol'ev**'s company in 1915, Mozzhukhin became **Iakov Protazanov**'s principal male actor, with his most impressive performances in *Queen of*

Spades (Pikovaia dama, 1916) and ***Father Sergius*** (Otets Sergii, 1918). His status as Russia's greatest—and most bankable—film star remained unchallenged throughout the decade. As a method-conscious performer, Mozzhukhin elevated the major tools of silent cinema acting—particularly the expression of his eyes—to an unprecedented intensity. What today may appear as an overly dramatic or pompous manner was perceived and admired as a precise language of mimic and gesture in its day. Yet, after the Bolshevik Revolution, Mozzhukhin's name became the avant-garde's code word for everything they despised in pre-Soviet cinema: tearful melodrama and psychological introspection embedded in a luxurious bourgeois or aristocratic milieu.

Together with Ermol'ev's entourage, Mozzhukhin immigrated in 1919 via the Crimea—where he played the lead in Protazanov's *Member of Parliament* (Chlen parlamenta, 1919)—to Paris. In 1921, he made attempts at directing with *Carnival's Child* (L'enfant du carnaval) and *Glowing Fire* (Le Brasier Ardent, 1923), the latter, according to film historian Evgenii Margolit, an example of early film avant-garde. Mozzhukhin also worked in Germany in 1927–1930. Apart from films by émigré directors, he starred in Jean Epstein's *The Lion of the Moguls* (Le Lion des Mogols, 1924) and Marcel L'Herbier's *The Late Mattia Pascal* (Feu Mathias Pascal, 1925). However, with the advance of sound his noticeable accent became a handicap, and the number of leads offered to him dwindled rapidly. He died, impoverished, of tuberculosis.

Mozzhukhin was married to actress **Nataliia Lisenko**. Claims in 1959 by French author Romain Gary that he was Mozzhukhin's illegitimate son have been proven a mystification.

Other films: *Kreutzer Sonata* (Kreitserova sonata, 1911); *Sarra's Grief* (Gore Sarry, 1913); *Nikolai Stavrogin* (1915); *A Giant of the Spirit* (Bogatyr' dukha, 1918); *Kean* (1923); *The White Devil* (aka *Hadzhi Murat*/Der weisse Teufel (1929); *Nitchevo* (1936).

MUNZUK, MAKSIM MUNGUZHUKOVICH (b. 2 May 1910 [other source: 15 September 1912], Mezhegyei, Tyva–d. 28 July 1999, Kyzyl, Tyva). Tuvinian actor. Originally a musician in the military, Munzuk served as the commander of Tyva's Artillery Regiment orchestra and became one of the founders of the Tuvinian

Musical Dramatic Theater in the 1930s. Apart from singing and acting, he also directed, composed, taught, and collected Tuvinian folklore. Munzuk's multifaceted, prolific creativity made him one of the most revered artists in Tyva (Tuva), honored with the titles of People's Artist of Russia and of the Republic of Tyva.

Akira Kurosawa picked Munzuk as the lead in his Soviet-financed epic *Dersu Uzala* (1975), along with **Iurii Solomin** as writer-explorer Vladimir Arsen'ev on whose 1923 book the film was based. Munzuk impersonated the wise hunter and scout Dersu of the Siberian Goldi tribe with such moving authenticity and humanity that the film's international success—it won the 1975 Academy Award as Best Foreign Picture—is undoubtedly owed to a high degree to his performance. Most of Munzuk's other roles in cinema were episodic, usually in adventure movies. However, two literary adaptations in which he participated deserve special mentioning: **Gleb Panfilov**'s *Valentina* (1981, based on a play by Aleksandr Vampilov) and **Ermek Shinarbaev**'s *The Revenge* (Mest', 1989), adapted from a short story by Russian-Korean author Anatolii Kim (b. 1939).

In 2004, the government of Tyva funded a prize for Best Actor named after Munzuk, awarded annually at a national competition; the same year, the Dersu Uzala Foundation, also named in Munzuk's memory and intended to support Tuvinian artists, began its philanthropic work.

Other films: *Disappearance of a Witness* (Propazha svidetelia, 1971); *Preliminary Investigation* (Predvaritel'noe issledovanie, 1978); *The Last Hunt* (Posledniaia okhota, 1979).

MURATOVA [born Korotkova], **KIRA GEORGIEVNA** (b. 5 November 1934, Soroki [Soroca] Romania, now Moldova). Ukrainian-Russian director and screenwriter. Born into a family of Communist functionaries, Muratova studied philology at Moscow Lomonosov University from 1952–1953. She enrolled in **Sergei Gerasimov** and **Tamara Makarova**'s workshop at the Soviet State Film School **VGIK**, graduating in 1959. Her diploma short, *By the Steep Ravine* (aka *The She-Wolf*/U krutogo iara, 1961, was codirected with fellow student Aleksandr I. Muratov (b. 1935), to whom she was married at the time. From that point on, Muratova worked at Odessa Film Studio.

Her first full-length picture, *Our Honest Bread* (Nash chestnyi khleb, 1964, with Muratov), was a rather conventional story of a kolkhoz administrator who seeks rest at a spa. Muratova came into her own with *Brief Encounters* (Korotkie vstrechi, 1967/1987), in which she also played the lead. This love triangle, starring **Vladimir Vysotskii** who is being pursued by two women, conveys such an unusual vision of Soviet reality and human complexity that cultural officials decided to keep it from broad release. *Long Farewells* (Dolgie provody, 1971, released 1987), the story of the difficult relations between a divorced mother and her son, was shelved altogether. While these films fell under the category of "provincial melodramas"—that is, thematically and stylistically unassuming pictures of the kind in which **Vitalii Mel'nikov** and similar directors excelled—Muratova's rendition subverted that genre, making it ideologically slippery, revealing existential abysses and disturbing the viewer instead of praising the comfort of trustworthy small worlds.

Unwilling to compromise either stylistically or conceptually, Muratova agreed to direct *Exploring the Wide World* (Poznavaia belyi svet, 1978) at **Lenfilm Studio**, a seemingly straightforward love story in the milieu of construction workers. Again, the image of reality—and not any explicit anti-Soviet message—caused critical disapproval. *Among the Gray Stones* (Sredi serykh kamnei, 1983), a melodrama adapted from a Vladimir Korolenko story about a widower's son who befriends a group of poor people, suffered official intrusion to a degree that forced Muratova to have her name removed from the credits.

The title of Muratova's next picture, *A Change of Fate* (Peremena uchasti, 1987), from W. Somerset Maugham's play *The Letter*, became a good omen for its maker. When this story of a female murderer premiered, it signaled the beginning of Muratova's recognition as one of the most original contemporary filmmakers. With her older films also being released to great acclaim, she could finally demonstrate her true range. *The Asthenic Syndrome* (Astenicheskii sindrom, 1989), a profound diagnosis of the Soviet mind in a state of catastrophic confusion and insecurity, blends the director's no-nonsense attitude toward existential problems with a playful and at times sarcastic approach toward narrative cohesion and point-of-view consistency. *Asthenic Syndrome* is Muratova's dark farewell to the

Soviet world of repressed aggressions and all-encompassing taboos behind the façade of a seemingly humanist civilization. The main characters, a doctor and a teacher, each dominate one of the film's two parts, the first being shot in black-and-white and the second in color. Both characters are confronted with insurmountable suffering, losing control over their reactions as a result. Muratova's brutal realism, filmed with an unprecedented directness, provoked censorship objections even in the most liberal period of perestroika.

This director had no reason to mourn the breakdown of the Soviet system that had kept her unemployed for so many years. Indeed, freedom has allowed Muratova to flourish, finally giving her sufficient space for cinematic self-realization. Her pictures of the 1990s show diminishing tension and are filled with witty humor and great visual beauty. As if to say that a repressed collective neurosis is more unsightly than liberated individualist insanity, Muratova often focuses on bizarre egomaniacs indulging in their hobbies and talents. *A Sensitive Policeman* (Chuvstvitel'nyi militsioner, 1992) depicts post-Soviet life in a benevolent manner; this ironic cinematic paraphrase of **Tat'iana Lukashevich**'s legendary *The Foundling* shows the people who sometimes are referred to as "trash" as capable of kind and noble feelings. *Passions* (Uvlechen'ia, 1994) takes place among jockeys and circus artists, with Beethoven tunes underlining the beauty of human self-realization. But *Passions* also points to the narcissism that accompanies creative individualism; its characters are devoid of the ability to relate to one another. *Three Stories* (Tri istorii, 1997) is considerably darker, revealing a sense of morbidity and black humor rarely seen in Russian (or Ukrainian) cinema.

The absurdity of contemporary post-Communist life, with an almost universal loss of ethical standards and complete criminalization of society, forms the central theme of *Second-class People* (Vtorostepennye liudi, 2001). *The Tuner* (Nastroishchik, 2004) captures the clash of values of two generations: the elderly traditionalists, nourished by the internalized 19th-century classical literary canon, and the new, pragmatic generation of the 21st century that skillfully uses the self-delusions of a silly old world that is about to abolish itself.

Muratova is one of the few directors of Soviet and post-Soviet cinema who succeeded in developing their own, recognizable poetics. Her films are filled with strange repetitions: of deeds, of words and phrases, and of occurrences. But these repetitions do not conceal any hidden references; rather, they point to the inherent absurdity of the world and the human inability to make sense of it. Muratova opposes pathos as much as ideology; her cinematic world breathes a heightened, quasi-euphoric perception and a unique, unabashed subjectivity. Her characters usually wear verbal masks that hide their true motives. Thus, the communicative function of her dialogues is secondary: people speak without hearing each other or realizing what they themselves are saying. Endless, rhythmic utterances express individual obsessions first and foremost.

The disturbing quality of Muratova's pictures is counterbalanced by their beauty; for example, the gardens and houses in *The Sensitive Policemen* seem to be glowing from secret, inside sources of light, and the hippodrome in *Passions* is a place of inconsequential love where actors and actresses are engaged in balletlike flirtation. Another characteristic feature of Muratova's films is their episodic "novella" structure; furthermore, she has a predilection for lay actors and generally for fragile, sensitive human beings. Muratova indulges in exposing the psychopathology of normalcy. Her approach toward accepted "normal" life also shapes the complex relations between the filmmaker and her audience, whom she provokes, mocks, shocks, leads by the nose, and disrespects, destroying their illusions—and their reliance on common narrative conventions. Along with **Aleksandr Sokurov**, Kira Muratova is indeed the most stubborn aesthetic nonconformist in post-Soviet cinema. She is also a highly cultured director, an erudite in world literature, and she includes allusions to many names and motifs. At the same time, Muratova discloses the unreliable nature of cultural quotes—her characters often deceive each other (and themselves) by exploiting cultural norms and beliefs.

Muratova was named People's Artist of the Ukrainian SSR in 1990.

Other films: *A Letter to America* (1999); *Chekhovian Motifs* (Chekhovskie motivy, 2002); *Two in One* (Dva v odnom, 2007).

MY FRIEND IVAN LAPSHIN (Moi drug Ivan Lapshin, 1984). **Lenfilm Studio**. 100 min., b/w and color. Directed by **Aleksei German**. Script: Eduard Volodarskii from the 1937 short story "Lapshin" by Iurii German. Cinematography: Valerii Fedosov. Music: Arkadii Gagulashvili. Cast: Andrei Boltnev, Nina Ruslanova, **Andrei Mironov**, Aleksei Zharkov, Zinaida Adamovich, Aleksandr Filippenko. Premiere: January 1985.

Ivan Lapshin (Boltnev) works as a criminal investigator in Unchansk, a provincial Russian town, in the mid-1930s. He was a commander during the Civil War and has retained his staunch Communist convictions. In a small, unheated communal apartment, Lapshin lives with colleagues and friends. Among them is journalist Khanin (Mironov), a depressed recent widower who accompanies Lapshin on his pursuits of a criminal gang. Khanin and Lapshin love the same woman, actress Natasha Adashova (Ruslanova). Lapshin, who suffers from nightmares and epileptic fits, is ultimately rejected by Natasha. Khanin recovers from a criminal's assault and moves to Moscow, while Lapshin goes back to professional training.

MYKOLAICHUK, IVAN VASIL'EVICH (b. 15 June 1941, Chertariia, Chernovits district [Bukovina]–d. 3 August 1987). Ukrainian actor, screenwriter, director, and composer. Mykolaichuk studied at the Karpenko-Karyi Institute for Stage Arts in Kiev under Viktor Ivchenko, graduating in 1965.

He made his film debut with the role of national icon, poet Taras Shevchenko, in the unusual biopic *The Dream* (Son, 1964) by Vladimir Denisenko. Mykolaichuk gained international renown with the role of Ivan in **Sergei Paradjanov**'s mythical Carpathian tale *Shadows of Forgotten Ancestors* (Tini zabutykh predkiv/Teni zabytykh predkov, 1964), a film that defined both Mykolaichuk's screen image in most of his subsequent films as well as his own aesthetic development as a screenwriter and filmmaker. After this sensational success, Mykolaichuk became one of the mainstays at **Dovzhenko Film Studio**, working with its leading directors, among them his teacher, Viktor Ivchenko, who cast him in the popular Aleksei Tolstoi adaptation *The Viper* (Gadiuka, 1965). He appeared in the role of Roman in the World War II tragedy (situated in the Hutsul milieu) *Annychka* (1969), as the skeptical Commissar Gromov in Nikolai Mashchenko's *The Commissars* (Komissary, 1971), and as Liubomir in **Leonid Osyka**'s large-scale medieval epic *Zakhar Berkut* (1972) about the struggle of Carpathian peasants against the Mongol-Tatar yoke in the 13th century.

Mykolaichuk's cooperation with **Yury Il'enko**—who responded in a similar creative manner to Paradjanov's early impulses—resulted in their coauthored script for *White Bird with a Black Spot* (Nilyi ptakh z chornoiu oznakoiu/Belaia ptitsa s chernoi otmetinoi, 1971), a dark tale about a family of peasants in the Bukovina torn apart by events surrounding World War II. Mykolaichuk also played a lead in that film and wrote its score. He later appeared in Il'enko's Soviet-Yugoslav *Against All Odds* (V superech vs'omu/Naperekor vsemu, 1973), *The Forest Song: Mavka* (Lisova pisnia—Mavka/Lesovaia pesnia. Mavka, 1981), and *The Legend of Princess Olga* (Lehenda pro kniahyniu Olhu/Legenda o kniagine Ol'ge, 1983). The screenplay for *The Lone Wolf* (Biriuk, 1977), adopted from a story by Ivan Turgenev, was coauthored by Mykolaichuk and **Roman Balaian**, who directed the film.

In 1979, Mykolaichuk made his directorial debut with *Babylon XX* (Vavilon XX) from his own screenplay. In addition, he was the male lead, folk philosopher Fabian who tries to grasp the historical turbulences in Ukraine in the 1920s and 1930s, and wrote the music for this film. His second and, alas, last film as director was *Such a Late, Such a Warm Autumn* (Takaia pozdniaia, takaia teplaia osen', 1981), one of the rare Soviet films made in Ukrainian. It tells the story of an old émigré in Canada who returns to his Bukovina homeland. Like Mykolaichuk's other works, it is characterized by an impressionist narration that puts local metaphors and complex historical allusions above plot coherence and psychological penetration.

Mykolaichuk was named Merited Artist of the Ukrainian SSR in 1968.

Other films: (as actor) *Weeds* (Bur'ian, 1967); *The Stone Cross* (Kamianyi Khrest/Kamennyi krest, 1968); *The Error of Honoré de Balzac* (Oshibka Onore de Bal'zaka, 1968); *The Sea* (More, 1978). *See also* UKRAINIAN CINEMA.

– N –

NAKHAPETOV, RODION RAFAILOVICH (b. 21 January 1944, Piatichatka, Dnepropetrovsk district). Russian actor and director. In his youth, Nakhapetov joined an acting club at the Denopropetrovsk House of Culture before enrolling in the Soviet State Film School

VGIK in 1961. He graduated in 1965 and later enrolled in **Igor' Talankin**'s directing workshop at VGIK which he finished in 1972. Nakhapetov made his acting debut as an engineer in **Vasilii Shukshin**'s *There Is Such a Lad* (Zhivet takoi paren', 1964), followed by another supporting part in **Marlen Khutsiev**'s *I Am Twenty* (aka Zastava Il'icha/Mne dvadtsat' let, 1965). His first lead, a portrayal of young Vladimir Lenin in **Mark Donskoi**'s dilogy *Heart of a Mother* (Serdtse materi, 1966) and *Devotion of a Mother* (Vernost' materi, 1967), radiates genuine humanity and warmth. Uzbek filmmaker **Elyor Ishmukhamedov** used the young actor's romantic aura to fine effect in his popular films *Tenderness* (Nezhnost', 1966) and *Lovers* (Vliublennye, 1969), praising the beauty of youthful devotion and sincerity. Nakhapetov was also convincing as a Latin American revolutionary in **Vytautas Žalakevičius**'s *That Sweet Word: Liberty!* (Eto sladkoe slovo—svoboda! 1973), as a cameraman and Bolshevik sympathizer in **Nikita Mikhalkov**'s *Slave of Love* (Raba liubvi, 1976), and as an officer in the Great Patriotic War in **Semen Aranovich**'s *Torpedo Bombers* (Torpedonostsy, 1983). Typical features of this actor's screen persona were his physically strong yet sensitive manliness, chivalry, and tragically doomed idealism.

Nakhapetov's ambitions as a filmmaker led to mixed results, displaying both consistent productivity and an interest in a variety of genres. Following his diploma, the musical *Wine Made from Dandelion* (Vino iz oduvanchikov, 1972), he scored a moderate box-office success with the drama *With You and Without You* (S toboi i bez tebia, 1974), a love story in a Ukrainian rural setting in the 1930s. *To the End of the World* (Na krai sveta, 1976), a contemporary coming-of-age drama, depicts the experiences of two dropouts, while *Enemies* (Vragi, 1978) is an adaptation of Maksim Gor'kii's play. Nakhapetov's pictures usually feature superb casts, including stars of the 1940s and 1950s, as well as performers from the Baltic republics such as **Juozas Budraitis** and **Regimantas Adomaitis**.

Nakhapetov left the Soviet Union in the late 1980s after marrying a U.S. citizen. He continued to direct, albeit with little resonance; his thrillers *Stir* (1998), *Blood of Success* (2001), and *Border Blues* (2004) went straight to video.

In 1985, Nakhapetov was honored with the title People's Artist of the RSFSR.

Other films: (as actor) *No Password Is Needed* (Parol' ne nuzhen, 1967); *Forgive Us, First Love* (Prosti nas, pervaia liubov', 1984); *Lovers II* (Vliublennye—2, 2004); (as director) *The One Who Followed* (Idushchii sledom, 1985); *An Umbrella for Newlyweds* (Zontik dlia novobrachnykh, 1986); *My Great Armenian Wedding* (Moia bol'shaia armianskaia svad'ba, 2004, TV); *The Contamination* (Zarazhenie, 2008).

NARLIEV, KHODJAKULI (b. 21 January 1937, Station #30 of Ashgabat railway, Turkmenistan). Turkmen director, cinematographer, screenwriter, and actor. Narliev studied at the Soviet State Film School **VGIK** with **Boris Volchek**, graduating in 1960. He began his career with **documentaries** such as *Kara-Bogaz* (1961), *Me and My Brothers* (Ia i moi brat'ia, 1964), and *Three Days of a Year* (Tri dnia odnogo goda, 1968). *Your Eyes* (Tvoi glaza, 1959) is a film essay about Turkmen physicians and their efforts to heal patients with trachoma.

Narliev made a name for himself as the sensitive, visually original cinematographer on **Bulat Mansurov**'s groundbreaking *The Contest* (Shukur-Bakshi/Sostiazanie, 1964), *Quenching of Thirst* (Utolenie zhazhdy, 1966), and *The Female Slave* (Rabynia, 1969). He then turned to directing with *Man Overboard* (Chelovek za bortom, 1970). His second picture, *The Daughter-in-Law* (Nevestka, 1972), about a woman who refuses to believe that her husband, a pilot in World War II, has been killed, became a huge critical success; it was shown at many festivals around the world and won Narliev a USSR State Prize in 1973. In close cooperation with the lead actress, **Maia-Gozel Aimedova**, Narliev then created a series of films focusing on strong-willed women who follow their emotional and ethical instincts despite the resistance of their environment: *When a Woman Saddles the Horse* (Kogda zhenshchina osedlaet konia, 1975), set in the aftermath of the Bolshevik Revolution; *You Must Be Able to Say No* (Umei skazat' net, 1976), a pamphlet against the ancient custom of bride purchasing; and *Djamal's Tree* (Derevo Dzhamal, 1980), which tells about the tribulations of a woman whose husband returns from the Great Patriotic War as an invalid, only to face rumors about his wife's infidelity.

In the 1980s, Narliev became the leading filmmaker in **Turkmen cinema**. He helmed a contemporary industrial drama, *Karakumy,*

45 Degrees in the Shadow (Karakumy, 45 gradusov v teni, 1982), followed by a historical biopic, *Fragi—Separated from Happiness* (Fragi—razluchennyi so schast'em, 1984) about 18th-century poet Makhtumkuli. *Mankurt* (1990), the tragic story of a Turkic warrior captured by Chinese troops and turned into a slave without memory, is a parable about national and cultural identity that is threatened by brutal totalitarian structures. Adapted from a chapter of **Chingiz Aitmatov**'s novel *The Day Lasts Longer than a Century* (I dol'she veka dlitsia den', 1980), this Turkmen-Turkish coproduction is the director's last completed film.

Narliev's style is characterized by quiet psychological intensity and an extremely slow pace, with keen attention to subtle emotions and details of everyday life. Especially his early films give visual grandeur and dignity to landscapes dominated by desert, heat, and blinding sunlight. The pervasive tragic tone of Narliev's films is complemented by a clear, almost linear division of characters into good and evil.

Narliev was named People's Artist of the Turkmen SSR in 1986. He was the first secretary of the Union of Turkmen Filmmakers in 1976–1999. Narliev is married to actress Maia Aimedova; one of his brothers is actor and director Khodjadurdy Narliev.

Other films: (as cameraman) *The Last Road* (Posledniaia doroga, 1962).

NATANSON, GEORGII GRIGOR'EVICH (b. 23 May 1921, Kazan'). Russian director and scriptwriter. Natanson studied at the Soviet State Film School **VGIK** while simultaneously working as an assistant director at **Mosfilm Studio** since 1941. Before and after his graduation (1944), he worked as an assistant with such luminaries of Soviet cinema as **Ivan Pyr'ev**, **Aleksandr Dovzhenko**, **Boris Barnet**, **Konstantin Iudin**, and **Aleksandr Ptushko**. In 1956, Natanson codirected—jointly with legendary puppeteer Sergei Obrastsov (1901–1992)—the feature-length stop-motion picture *A Heavenly Creature* (Nebesnoe sozdanie, 1956), a box-office hit but a critical failure.

Natanson's films hit a nerve with audiences in the 1960s due to their melodramatic structure and open social pathos, blending the propaganda of Soviet values with strong dosages of sentimentality. Following the operetta adaptation *White Acacia* (Belaia akatsiia,

1957) and the harmless family **comedy** *A Noisy Day* (Shumnyi den', codirected with Anatolii Efros [1925–1987]), Natanson landed a huge success with *All Remains to the People* (aka *Legacy*/Vse ostaetsia liudiam, 1963), starring **Nikolai Cherkasov** in his last major role as a terminally ill scientist who continues to work tirelessly despite his nearing end. Even more successful was *One More Time about Love* (Eshche raz pro liubov', 1967) in which a scientist and a stewardess engage in a doomed romance. Natanson praises wise Communist diplomacy in *Ambassador of the Soviet Union* (Posol Sovetskogo Soiuza, 1968), a biopic of the first female USSR diplomat, Aleksandra Kollontai. Pathos-filled patriotic messages are featured in *Answerable for Everything* (Za vse v otvete, 1972), which describes a high school reunion some 30 years after the 1941 graduation, and *They Were Actors* (Oni byli akterami, 1981) about a Crimean theater troupe engaging in underground activities against the Nazi occupants. *The Infuriated Bus* (Vzbesivshiisia avtobus, 1991) deals with the subject of international terrorism; some episodes were shot in Israel. In the 1990s and early 2000s, Natanson worked on a number of projects about author Mikhail Bulgakov (1891–1940); in 2002, the documentary *I Will Be Back!* (Ia vernus'!) about Bulgakov's visits to the Crimea was released.

The fact that almost all of Natanson's films were adapted from successful plays (by prominent Soviet playwrights Samuil Aleshin, Viktor Rozov, Mikhail Roshchin, among others) made him an easy target for accusations of lacking artistic originality and fearing risk. Natanson's films targeted the national market and were hardly seen abroad. They can best be described as stylistically conventional, moderately problem-oriented character studies that proved excellent vehicles for already established stars. Not surprisingly, the director's patriotism proved increasingly out of touch with cynical Soviet perceptions in the late 1970s and 1980s.

Natanson joined the Communist Party in 1947; he was named Merited Artist of the RSFSR in 1981 and People's Artist of Russia in 1994. He received a USSR State Prize in 1977 for his theater work.

Other films: *The Ward* (Palata, 1964); *The Older Sister* (Starshaia sestra, 1966); *Valentin and Valentina* (1985); *Aelita, Don't Pester Men* (Aelita, ne pristavai k muzhchinam, 1989); *Mikhail Bulgakov in the Caucasus* (Bulgakov na Kavkaze, 2007).

NAUMOV, VLADIMIR NAUMOVICH (b. 6 December 1927, Leningrad). Russian director and scriptwriter. Naumov, son of renowned cinematographer Naum Naumov-Strazh (1898–1957), studied with **Ihor' Savchenko** at the Soviet State Film School **VGIK** in 1947–1951 and worked as one of his assistants on the large-scale biopic *Taras Shevchenko* (1951), which he completed with fellow student **Aleksandr Alov** after Savchenko's sudden passing. From that point on, Alov and Naumov became a trademark directorial couple—jokingly named "Alovonaumov" by colleagues—sharing a successful artistic partnership that ended only with Alov's death in 1983. (For their joint films, see the entry on Alov).

Although after 1983 Naumov directed several pictures on his own, he remained loyal to the artistic principles adopted over three decades with Alov. Thus, his first independent picture, *The Choice* (Vybor, 1987), was—just like *The Shore*—based on a novel by Iurii Bondarev and also explored questions of artistry, Cold War, and the impending doom of a nuclear catastrophe in a philosophically reflective, deliberately undramatic manner. In 1989, Naumov completed *The Law* (Zakon) based on a script that had been prohibited more than 20 years earlier. That film and *Ten Years without Permission to Correspond* (Desiat' let bez prava perepiski, 1990) deal with the Stalinist past and aspects of guilt and responsibility.

The script for the 1994 drama *White Feast* (Belyi prazdnik), starring **Innokentii Smoktunovskii** in his last role, was a collaboration between Naumov and prominent Italian screenwriter Tonino Guerra. Another project with Guerra, *The Secret of Nardo, or the Dream of the White Dog* (aka *Marcello's Secret*/Taina Marchello/Taina Nardo, ili son beloi sobaki, 1997/99), was haunted by never-ending financial difficulties and passed several stages before finally being released in 2001 as *Clock without Hands* (Chasy bez strelok). Like Naumov's other films of the 1990s, this story of a widow trying to find the murderers of her powerful husband suffered severely from Russia's cinema crisis and was seen by few.

Naumov, who was named People's Artist of the USSR in 1983, has been teaching at VGIK since 1980; in 1986 he was promoted to the rank of full professor. In 2000, he began to teach at the private Natal'ia Nesterova University in Moscow.

Naumov's wife is actress Natal'ia Belokhostikova (b. 1951), who played the female leads in many of his films. Their daughter Natal'ia is also an actress.

Other films: *La Gioconda on Asphalt* (Dzhokonda na asfal'te, 2007).

NEW GULLIVER, THE (Novyi Gulliver, 1935). **Mosfilm Studio**. 68 min., b/w. Directed by **Aleksandr Ptushko**. Script: **Grigorii Roshal'**, Aleksandr Ptushko, S. Bolotin (dialogues) from Jonathan Swift's novel. Cinematography: Nikolai Renkov. Music: Lev Shvarts. Cast: V. Konstantinov, Ivan Iudin, Ivan Bobrov. Premiere: 25 March 1935. The sound track was restored in 1960.

At the beautiful children's resort Artek on the shores of the Black Sea, Young Pioneers listen to their instructor reading *Gulliver's Travels*. Petia (Konstantinov), who is particularly enamored of the story, falls asleep and dreams that he himself travels to the country of Lilliput. The "new Gulliver's" encounter with the corrupt regime of a grotesquely stupid king and his minions turns dangerous when he refuses to serve his masters as a giant soldier. But the workers at Lilliput's arms factory come to Gulliver/Petia's rescue; together, they overthrow the government and establish a working-class state. Petia wakes up to the laughter of his fellow pioneers.

NIKITIN, FEDOR MIKHAILOVICH (b. 3 May 1900, Lokhvits, Ukraine–d. 17 July 1988, Moscow). Russian actor and director. Prior to getting a professional education at the Second Studio of the Moscow Art Theater (MKhAT), Nikitin had already worked as an actor in Odessa and Kherson and had played a supporting part in **Boris Chaikovskii**'s *Thérèse Raquin* (Tereza Raken, 1918). After graduation in 1922, he acted on stage in Moscow and Iaroslavl' and later in Leningrad's Theater of the Young Viewer (TIuZ).

In 1924, together with directors **Fridrikh Ermler**, Eduard Ioganson, and others, Nikitin organized an experimental film workshop (KEM—*kinoeksperimental'naia masterskaia*); among his students was Uzbek director Yuldash Agzamov. In Ermler's realistic social dramas *Little Katia, the Paper Reinette* (aka *Katka's Reinette Apples/*Kat'ka—Bumazhnyi Ranet, 1926, codirected by Ioganson) and *The*

House in the Snowdrifts (Dom v sugrobakh, 1927), Nikitin plays shy, sensitive, physically almost fragile, yet spiritually strong and reliable men. Most famous of all his roles became the amnesiac sergeant Filimonov in Ermler's masterpiece *A Fragment of the Empire* (Oblomok imperii, 1929), in which Nikitin commanded such a richness of subtle expression, from quiet suffering to tender devotion, that he was likened to Charlie Chaplin and was called "the Prince Myshkin of Russian silent cinema" by critic Neia Zorkaia. In 1928, Nikitin directed the comic short *A Note on Reels* (Nota na kolesakh).

During the 900-day siege of Leningrad by Nazi troops, the actor served as commander of a People's Volunteer Guard platoon. Beginning in 1943, he toured the front with a Red Army theater unit.

After the Great Patriotic War, Nikitin was cast in dozens of supporting parts (teachers, foreign dignitaries, aristocrats, scientists), two of which—both in biopics by **Grigorii Roshal'**—were recognized with Stalin Prizes: Professor Zvantsev in *Academician Ivan Pavlov* (Akademik Ivan Pavlov, 1949) and the composer Aleksandr Dargomyzhskii in *Musorgskii* (1951). His last significant screen appearances were in **Kira Muratova**'s Vladimir Korolenko adaptation *Among Gray Stones* (Sredi serykh kamnei, 1983) and in **Nikolai Gubenko**'s sentimental homage to the acting profession, *Life, Tears, and Love* (I zhizn', i slezy, i liubov', 1984).

In 1969, Nikitin was named People's Artist of the Russian Federation.

Other films: *The Cobbler of Paris* (Parizhskii sapozhnik, 1928); *A White Sail Gleams* (Beleet parus odinokii, 1937); *Leningrad Symphony* (Leningradskaia simfoniia, 1958); *The Gambler* (Igrok, 1972).

NIKONENKO, SERGEI PETROVICH (b. 16 April 1941, Moscow). Russian actor, director, and screenwriter. Nikonenko studied at a so-called evening school (*vecherniaia shkola*) and worked as a bus driver and mail carrier before enrolling at the Soviet State Film School **VGIK** where he first joined **Sergei Gerasimov**'s and **Tamara Makarova**'s acting workshop and subsequently majored in directing, graduating in 1972.

A performer of great versatility, Nikonenko became a master of episodic roles, memorable for their human warmth and behavioral peculiarities. In dozens of films, he was the middle-aged "average citizen," believable both in rural and urban settings, as a tractor driver or policeman, dreamer or drunkard, simpleton or intellectual. Nikonenko made his debut in a social drama, Villen Azarov's *It Happened at the Militia* (Eto sluchilos' v militsii, 1963). Among Nikonenko's more than 100 movie roles, there are several in pictures of leading Soviet directors: in Gerasimov's *People and Beasts* (Liudi i zveri, 1962) and *The Journalist* (Zhurnalist, 1967), **Aleksandr Mitta**'s *Someone Rings, Open the Door* (aka *The Girl and the Burglar*/Zvoniat, otkroite dver', 1965), **Larisa Shepit'ko**'s *Wings* (Kryl'ia, 1966), **Sergei Bondarchuk**'s *War and Peace* (Voina i mir, 1962–1967), **Andrei Mikhalkov-Konchalovskii**'s *A Nest of the Gentry* (Dvorianskoe gnezdo, 1969), and **Gleb Panfilov**'s *The Theme* (Tema, 1979). Remarkable about Nikonenko's artistic profile is not just his untiring productivity but the ease with which he moves from contemporary drama to vaudeville-like **comedy**, from classical adaptation to historical biopic. Thus, he portrayed a Red Army soldier in Hungarian director Miklós Jancsó's *Stars and Soldiers* (aka *The Red and the White*/Csillagosok, katonák/Zvezdy i soldaty, 1967) and the poet Sergei Esenin in **Sergei Urusevskii**'s *Sing a Song, Poet* (Poi pesniu, poet, 1971).

Nikonenko developed a particularly close artistic partnership with **Vasilii Shukshin**, whose view of the Russian mentality he shares. Shukshin cast him in *Strange People* (Strannye liudi, 1970), and Nikonenko years later adapted Shukshin's **comedy** *And in the Morning They Awoke* (A poutru oni prosnulis', 2003). Nikonenko's first directorial effort, the short *Petrukhin's Last Name* (Petrukhina familiia, 1972), was followed by *Birds over the City* (Ptitsy nad gorodom, 1974), *Dawn and Dusk Are Kissing* (Tseluiutsia zori, 1978), *For Heaven's Sake* (Elki-palki, 1988), and numerous other contemporary comedies. These films draw a poetic, slightly melancholic image of Russian everyday life in an unobtrusive and undramatic manner, although featuring some satirical elements as well.

Nikonenko was named People's Artist of the RSFSR in 1991. In 1994, together with his wife, film actress Ekaterina Voronina-Nikonenko, he founded the Sergei Esenin Cultural Center.

Other films: (as actor) *Crime and Punishment* (Prestuplenie i nakazanie, 1969); *Parade of Planets* (Parad planet, 1985); *Tomorrow Was*

War (Zavtra byla voina, 1987); *The Dancer's Time* (Vremia tantsora, 1997); *A Hero of Our Time* (Geroi nashego vremeni, 2006); (as director) *Gypsy Happiness* (Tsyganskoe schast'e, 1981); *Love You. Waiting. Lena* (Liubliu. Zhdu. Lena, 1984); *A Family Man* (Sem'ianin, 1991); *I Don't Want to Marry* (Ne khochu zhenit'sia, 1992); *I Want to Go to America* (Khochu v Ameriku, 1992).

NIKULIN, IURII VLADIMIROVICH (b. 18 December 1921, Demidov, Smolensk district–d. 21 August 1997, Moscow). Russian actor. Nikulin was born into the family of a sketch writer. In 1939, he was drafted and subsequently fought in World War II. After his 1946 discharge, several attempts to enroll at the Soviet State Film School **VGIK** or one of the Moscow theater schools failed. But Nikulin succeeded in fulfilling his childhood dream to become a clown, learning his craft in the studio school of the famous Moscow Circus, whose troupe he joined upon graduation in 1949. In 1982, Nikulin was appointed chief director of Moscow Circus, a position he held until the end of his life.

Nikulin's film debut was the episodic role of a pyrotechnician in **Aleksandr Faintsimmer**'s *Girl with a Guitar* (Devushka s gitaroi, 1958), followed by numerous parts of obnoxious nitwits, drunkards, or somewhat dense, naïve Soviet citizens in popular **comedies** by **Leonid Gaidai**, **El'dar Riazanov**, and **Aleksandr Mitta**. Many Soviet blockbusters owe their success in no small part to Nikulin's hilarious mimicry, among them Gaidai's short *Bootleggers* (Samogonshchiki), where he first created the legendary character of "Booby" (Balbes), the feature-length *Prisoner of the Caucasus* (aka *Kidnapping Caucasian Style*/Kavkazskaia plennitsa, 1966), and *The Diamond Arm* (Brilliantovaia ruka, 1969). At the same time, the actor startled audiences with a contrapunctal line of roles that deliberately subverted his funny clichés by portraying inconsolably sad, vulnerable, and decent men with a child's heart, beginning with the alcoholic Kuz'ma Iordanov in **Lev Kulidzhanov**'s *When the Trees Were Tall* (Kogda derev'ia byli bol'shimi, 1961).

Andrei Tarkovskii took a particular risk by casting Nikulin as the martyred monk Patrikei in *Andrei Rublev* (1966), since it was customary that unsophisticated audiences greeted every screen appearance of the idolized clown with roaring laughter. With similar tragic power, Nikulin revived his war experience in the role of Private Nekrasov in **Sergei Bondarchuk**'s *They Fought for the Motherland* (Oni srazhalis' za rodinu, 1975) and as the journalist Lopatin in **Aleksei German**'s *Twenty Days without War* (Dvadtsat' dnei bez voiny, 1977). In **Rolan Bykov**'s *Scarecrow* (Chuchelo, 1983) he portrayed the fragile, wise grandfather of a girl harassed by her classmates. Viewers could tell that the pain displayed in this role was not just the character's but also reflected the artist's own.

Nikulin joined the Communist Party in 1943; he was named People's Artist of the USSR in 1973 and Hero of Socialist Labor in 1990. He is buried at Novodevich'e cemetery in Moscow. After Nikulin's passing, the Moscow Circus at Tsvetnoi Boulevard was named after him.

Other films: *The Unamenables* (Nepoddaiushchiesia, 1959); *Business People* (Delovye liudi, 1963); *Here, Mukhtar* (Ko mne, Mukhtar, 1965); *Old Men: Robbers* (Stariki-razboiniki, 1972); *The Cable* (Telegramma, 1971).

NIL'SEN, VLADIMIR SEMENOVICH [real name: Al'per, Vladimir Solomonovich] (b. 1906, St. Petersburg–d. 20 January 1938). Russian cinematographer. Nil'sen's father was a successful engineer, his mother a dentist. After studying for one year in the Department of Mathematics at the University of Petrograd in 1923, Nil'sen went to Germany in 1925 to continue his education at the Electrotechnical School in Strelitz/Mecklenburg. While experimenting with cameras and learning the basics of cinematography, he was also active in the German Communist youth movement. Upon his return in 1926, Nil'sen became **Eduard Tissé**'s assistant on **Sergei Eizenshtein**'s *October* (Oktiabr', 1927) and *General Line* (General'naia liniia, aka *The Old and the New*/Staroe i novoe, 1929).

In 1932, Nil'sen joined **Grigorii Aleksandrov** and Tissé on the **documentary** short *Internationale*; the following year, he was hired as the cinematographer on Aleksandrov's hugely popular **comedy** *Jolly Fellows* (Veselye rebiata, 1934), followed by *Circus* (Tsirk, 1936) and *Volga-Volga* (1938). He was assigned professional trips to Germany and France in 1935, and, together with **Boris Shumiatskii** and **Fridrikh Ermler**, traveled to the United States, visiting leading studios in all three countries. In 1936, Nil'sen was entrusted with the documentary *The Report of Comrade Stalin on the Project of the USSR Constitution at the VIII Extraordinary Congress of Soviets* (Doklad tov. Stalina o proekte konstitutsii SSSR na VIII chrez-vychainom s"ezde sovetov), for which he received high honors.

Nil'sen, who had been incarcerated for two years (1929–1931) in a concentration camp in the north of the Soviet Union for alleged border violations, was arrested on 8 October 1937, accused of spying for foreign countries, and executed four months later. His legal rehabilitation, supported by cinematographer **Boris Volchek** and others, came in 1956, after which Nil'sen's name was reinstated in the credits of the films to which he had contributed.

Jay Leyda once called Nil'sen "the most articulate of Soviet cameramen." He certainly was one of the most inventive cinematographers, credited with introducing rear projection, glass shots, and other special effects. Moreover, Nil'sen translated and authored articles and books on technical aspects of cinematography; some of his own works were translated into foreign languages. He taught in the Department of Cinematography at the Soviet State Film School **VGIK** beginning in 1935.

NOBODY WANTED TO DIE (Nekas nenorejo mirti/Nikto ne khotel umirat', 1965). **Lithuanian Film Studio**. 106 min., b/w. Directed by **Vytautas Žalakevičius**. Script: Vytautas Žalakevičius. Cinematography: **Jonas Gricius**. Music: Algimantas Apanavičius. Cast: **Donatas Banionis**, **Regimantas Adomaitis**, **Juosas Budraitis**, Bruno O'Ya, Algimantas Masiulis, Kazimiras Vitkus, Eugenija Shulgajte, **Vija Artmane**, **Bronius Babkauskas**, **Laimonas Noreika**. Premiere: September 1966.

In 1947, amidst war ruins and the beginning Soviet occupation, a small Lithuanian village witnesses a series of murders carried out by a group of nationalists targeting those who cooperate with the Communist system. The Lokys brothers—Donatas (Adomaitis), Bronius (O'Ya), Jonas (Budraitis), and Mykolas (Masiulis)—attend the funeral of their father, the gang's latest victim. Vaitkus (Banionis), a former gang member who has been elected chairman of the village council and wants to break with his past, stands between the clashing groups. He loses his life in a struggle that ultimately brings about the defeat of the anti-Soviet forces. *See also* LITHUANIAN CINEMA.

NOREIKA, LAIMONAS (b. 27 September 1926, Joniskio, Lithuania). Lithuanian actor. Noreika attended for two years the school of the Šiauliai Drama Theater and began to work as an actor at Vilnius Drama Theater in 1944. He later continued his studies at the State Institute for Stage Arts (GITIS) in Moscow. Upon graduation in 1952, Noreika joined the troupe of the Kaunas Dramatic Theater. In 1963, he switched to the Lithuanian State Drama Theater in Vilnius.

Like many Lithuanian actors, Noreika gained fame through **Vytautas Žalakevičius** postwar drama *Nobody Wanted to Die* (Nekas nenorejo mirti/Nikto ne khotel umirat', 1965), where he appeared in the supporting role of the leader of anti-Soviet resistance fighters, the "holy" Juozapas. Noreika's ability to convey the contradictory feelings of a tragic character and his willingness to go against the grain of cliché interpretations soon made him a valued screen actor both in **Lithuanian cinema** and other Soviet republics. Many directors cast him in negative roles such as General Hofman in the Uzbek production *Farhad's Deed* (Podvig Farkhada, 1968) or Rosenberg in *The Moabit Notebook* (Moabitskaia tetrad', 1968), characters that blend cultured manners and refinement with sadism and cynicism. On the opposite end, he portrayed a German pro-Soviet spy in Boris Durov's *Story of a Scout* (Povest' o razvedchike, 1969), displaying discipline and self-control in the most challenging situations. Noreika also excelled in contemporary stories such as *The Last Day of Winter* (Poslednii den' zimy, 1974), where he portrayed the straightforward, competent engineer Ilgunas.

In the 1980s, Noreika was mostly typecast in Cold War espionage thrillers that emphasized his aura of elegant, mysterious manliness and sustained his considerable popularity but rarely allowed him to display other facets of his talent. One of Noreika's latest roles was in *A Knock on the Door* (Stuk v dver', 1989), an account of the Stalinist repressions against Moldova in 1948.

Noreika was named Merited Artist of the Lithuanian SSR in 1976.

Other films: *Dead Season* (Mertvyi sezon, 1968); *The Experiment of Dr. Abst* (Eksperiment doktora Absta, 1968); *Treasure Island* (Ostrov sokrovishch, 1971); *Contract of the Century* (Kontrakt veka, 1985); *Visiting the Minotaurus* (Vizit k minotavru, 1987, TV); *War and Peace* (2007, France).

NORSHTEIN, IURII BORISOVICH (b. 15 September 1941, village Andreevka, Penza province [other sources: Moscow]). Russian **animation** director, scriptwriter, animator, and pedagogue. Norshtein received his education at the school of the animation studio Soiuzmultfilm (1959–1961) and then worked as an animator—first in puppet animation, later in cutout and drawn animation—on more than 40 pictures with directors such as **Leonid Amal'rik**, Vladimir Degtiarev (1916–1974), and Roman Kachanov (b. 1921). His artistic growth was significantly stimulated by the trend toward stylistic and narrative individualization in Soviet animation of the 1960s and the beginning production of shorts for adults by **Fedor Khitruk**, **Andrei Khrzhanovskii**, and Estonian animation artists such as **Elbert Tuganov** and **Heino Pars**. The accompanying genre diversification brought not only more witty **children's films** and nonstereotypical political propaganda to the screens but also philosophical allegories and social satires.

In 1968, Norshtein made his directorial debut with *The 25th Was the First Day* (25-e—den' pervyi, codirected with Arkadii Tiurin), a propaganda short devoted to the 1917 Bolshevik Revolution. Using the music of **Dmitrii Shostakovich**, the film features visual quotes from the works of early revolutionary artists such as Vladimir Tatlin, Kuz'ma Petrov-Vodkin, and Aleksandr Deineka, ending with chronicle footage of a speech by Vladimir Lenin. Together with one of the founders of Soviet animation, **Ivan Ivanov-Vano**, Norshtein then directed the stylistically and conceptually extraordinary *Battle of Kerzhenets*/Secha pri Kerzhentse, 1971), a patriotic medieval parable with music by Nikolai Rimskii-Korsakov. When finally given a chance to direct independently, Norshtein made in quick succession three 10-minute shorts based on Russian fairy-tale motifs. *The Fox and the Hare* (Lisa i zaiats, 1973) from a Vladimir Dal' (1801–1872) folktale collection, is a fable of injustice and the clash between innocence and militancy. *The Heron and the Crane* (Tsaplia i zhuravl', 1974), also adapted from Dal', deals with two birds who are incapable of staying together, no matter how much both long for companionship. *Hedgehog in the Fog* (Ezhik v tumane, 1975) is a simple, touching story about the need for friendship and loyalty. Characteristics of all three films are their noticeable graphic stylization, psychological penetration (the director employed first-rate actors for voiceover, including **Innokentii Smoktunovskii** and **Aleksei Batalov**), and several complex camera movements.

Tale of Tales (Skazka skazok, 1979), arguably Norshtein's greatest achievement, widened the philosophical scope of animation in unprecedented ways. It proved that the plot of an animated picture does not have to be linear—rather, it can operate on various intersecting levels and dimensions and be rich in allusions to myths, as well as to other arts. Norshtein's approach to animation demonstrates that even a theme as existentially serious as the Great Patriotic War can be tackled by a genre that not long ago was seen as exclusive entertainment for children. *Tale of Tales*'s interwoven motifs are multifold and allow for a variety of interpretations. In the context of Norshtein's overall oeuvre, however, it seems likely that the little wolf cub as the film's organizing center symbolizes a universal longing for humanity and civilization just as much as the human fear of our own atavistic elements. *Tale of Tales* can also be seen as a film about the fate of Russia, the hardships its people endured, and the dream of culture and purity that remains its innermost drive.

Since 1981, Norshtein has been working on a feature-length adaptation of Nikolai Gogol''s novella "The Overcoat" (Shinel', 1842); excerpts from this film have been screened at several film festivals. In the 1990s, he also made commercials and worked for television.

Norshtein's art is not so much dominated by stories determining all other aesthetic components but by individual, atmospherically intense visions that are connected in an associative manner and whose transformations are based on aesthetic kinship rather than narrative logic. His films feature a variety of graphic techniques, as well as multifaceted lighting and coloration. Recognizable and reoccurring motifs in Norshtein's pictures are the seasons, leaves, horses, rain, snow, the sun, a broad river, a home with a fireplace, motherhood, and nurturing. Often, nature and domesticity establish a framework that philosophically exceeds the significance of the actual plot and its characters. Even in simple encounters, the earthly and the heavenly dimension meet and gaze at each other in wonderment (thus, the naïve hedgehog and the little wolf perceive the world as a series of miracles). Changes in Norshtein's animated world happen suddenly, at times bringing catastrophes such as war, and at other times the emergence of beauty and love.

After using different animation techniques, from drawn to cutout, Norshtein ultimately developed his own technology of multilayered superimposition. Conspicuously, this master of poetic animation has resisted the temptations of computer animation. For Norshtein, animation is a craft requiring direct manual contact with the material as a precondition of becoming art.

In the 1990s, Norshtein began a pedagogical career that took him to many countries. In 1993, he cofounded an independent studio school for animators, Shar. His work and teaching have found particular appreciation in Japan, where he was awarded the prestigious Order of the Rising Sun in 2004. Norshtein, who has been recognized at numerous international festivals, was awarded a USSR State Prize in 1979 and was named People's Artist of the Russian Federation in 1996. He is married to artist Francheska Iarbusova (b. 1942), a principal contributor to his films.

– O –

OBOLENSKII, LEONID LEONIDOVICH (b. 21 January 1902, Arzamas–d. 17 November 1991, Miassa). Russian director, actor, and sound engineer. Obolenskii hailed from an old aristocratic family; his father, a prince, was active as a lawyer and leftist politician and in the 1920s worked as director of the Hermitage in Leningrad. Upon serving in the political department of the Red Army, young Obolenskii studied with **Lev Kuleshov**—whom he had met at the front—at the First State Film School in 1920–1921. He appeared in his teacher's *agitka On the Red Front* (Na krasnom fronte, 1920) and in *The Unusual Adventures of Mr. West in the Land of the Bolsheviks* (Neobychainye prikliucheniia mistera Vesta v strane bol'shevikov, 1924). It was Obolenskii who acquainted **Sergei Eizenshtein** with Kuleshov's montage experiments.

In 1925–1928, Obolenskii joined the permanent staff of Mezhrabpom-Rus'—later transformed into **Mezhrabpomfilm Studio**—as feature film director. He helmed two **comedies** that took their titles from popular songs: the box-office hit *Little Bricks* (Kirpichiki, 1925) and *Oh, Little Apple . . .* (Ekh, iablochko . . ., 1926), both codirected with Mikhail Doller. After running into censorship problems with the science drama *Al'bidum* (1928), he made one more silent picture, *Merchants of Fame* (Torgovtsy slavoi, 1929). Obolenskii also taught at the **Boris Chaikovskii** Film School in 1925–1927 and at the State Film School—later **VGIK**—in 1922–1941 (with interruptions). He portrayed a film director in **Iakov Protazanov**'s antireligious comedy *St. Iorgen's Holiday* (Prazdnik sviatogo Iorgena, 1930).

In 1929, Obolenskii, known for his thoroughness and technical craftsmanship, was appointed to work with **Pavel Tager** on sound technology; he also went to Berlin in 1929–1930 to study the subject in depth. Obolenskii was a valued sound director on **Boris Barnet**'s *The Outskirts* (Okraina, 1933), Kuleshov's *Horizon* (Gorizont, 1932) and *The Great Consoler* (Velikii uteshitel', 1933), and directed one sound film on his own, *Theft of Eyesight* (Krazha zreniia, 1935) under Kuleshov's supervision. Eizenshtein hired him as sound engineer on his ill-fated *Bezhin Meadow* (Bezhin lug, 1935/37), which got him under fire from the director's powerful nemesis **Boris Shumiatskii**, who deprived Obolenskii of his Moscow apartment and forced him to move to Turkmenistan (Ashkhabad).

In 1941, Obolenskii joined the Soviet home guard troops, was taken prisoner, and survived the Nazi occupation. After the war, he was arrested and sent to a GULAG concentration camp where he worked in a prisoners' theater. Following Iosif Stalin's death, Obolenskii settled in Sverdlovsk and started another film career from scratch, making **documentaries** and educational films both for cinema and television.

In the 1970s, Obolenskii returned to acting, being predominantly cast as an aging aristocrat or distinguished foreigner in numerous second-rate pictures, including **Samson Samsonov**'s *A Purely English Murder* (Chisto angliiskoe ubiistvo, 1974). He had an outstanding part in **Arūnas Žebriūnas**'s *Walnut Bread* (Riešutų duona/Orekhovyi khleb, 1978) and also appeared in quality literary adaptations.

Because of his unusual life experiences, Obolenskii enjoyed extraordinary media attention during perestroika. The title People's Artist of the Russian Federation was awarded to him in 1991.

OJAGOV, RASIM MIRKASUM-OGLY [other spelling: Odjagov] (b. 22 [other sources: 28] November 1933, Shaki [other source: Nuha], Azerbaijan–d. 11 July 2006, Baku). Azerbaijani director and cinematographer. Ojagov studied at the Soviet State Film School **VGIK** in **Anatolii Golovnia**'s workshop from 1951 to 1956 (other sources list **Leonid Kosmatov** as his teacher). Among Ojagov's most interesting works as cinematographer was **Hasan Sayidbey-li**'s *Why Are You Silent?* (San niya sousoursan/Pochemu ty molch-ish'? 1967), betraying strong neorealist influences, a widespread trend in Soviet cinema in the 1960s that was openly acknowledged by Ojagov himself.

After working as a cameraman at **Azerbaijanfilm Studio** for more than a decade, Ojagov enrolled in the Aliev Theater Institute in Baku, graduating in 1967 with a degree that allowed him to direct films. Ojagov's preferred theme as a filmmaker is the clash between idealism and cynicism, most impressively depicted in *The Interroga-tion* (Istintag/Dopros, 1979). Based on a script by Ojagov's frequent collaborator **Rustam Ibrahimbekov**, the picture became a sensation first and foremost due to its subject matter: the connections between Soviet (in this case Azerbaijani) functionaries and the national Mafia. Such an open assault on common Soviet corruption was only made possible through the support of the country's Party leader, Heydar Aliyev (1923–2003). The clash of values is shown as a duel between an investigator who believes in law and a perpetrator who does not. Yet if *Interrogation* conveys mild optimism, *The Air Cathedral* (Khram vozdukha, 1989), which tells the tragic story of a humble soldier returning from the Great Patriotic War only to find himself imprisoned and ostracized, features an atmosphere of overwhelming bleakness and hopelessness.

Among Ojagov's later films, the thriller *Seven Days after the Murder* (Sem' dnei posle ubiistva, 1990), the melodrama *Tahmina* (1993), and the **comedy** *O, Istanbul* (1995) are worth mentioning. Following the independence of Azerbaijan and the privatization of the country's film industry, Ojagov, who described himself as an apolitical person, has repeatedly called for state funding in order to keep the ailing **Azerbaijani cinema** alive.

Ojagov was named People's Artist of the Azerbaijani SSR in 1982. He founded his own studio, Ojag, in 1991.

Other films: *The Avenger from Gyanjebazar* (Mstitel' iz Gian-zhebasara, 1975); *The Birthday* (Den' rozhdeniia, 1978); *The Park*

(Park, 1983); *Another Life* (Drugaia zhizn', 1987); *Hotel Room* (Komnata v otele, 1999).

OKEEV, TOLOMUSH [Russian sources list the patronymic Tolenovich] (b. 11 September 1935, Bokonbaevo, Issyk-Kul' district, Kyrgyzstan–d. 23 December 2001, Ankara, Turkey). Kyrgyz director and screenwriter. Okeev studied at the Leningrad Institute of Film Engineering (LIKI), graduating in 1958, and worked as a sound assistant at **Kyrgyzfilm Studio** in 1958–1962, on **Larisa Shepit'ko**'s *Torrid Heat* (Znoi, 1963) and *Street of Cosmonauts* (Ulitsa kosmonavtov), among others. He then studied with **Leonid Trauberg** at the Supreme Courses for Directors and Screenwriters (VKSR) in Moscow until 1966.

Like other Kyrgyz directors, Okeev started his career with poetic **documentaries** that won him international acclaim: the 10-minute *These Are Horses* (Eto—loshadi, 1965, sometimes translated as *There Are Horses*), *Boom* (1968), *Heritage* (Muras, 1969), and *Hunting Birds* (Lovchie ptitsy, 1970). Already detectable in these meditative cinematic essays is a keen interest in the world of animals, juxtaposed—often in a parabolic manner—to human society. In his first full-length feature, *The Sky of Our Childhood* (Nebo nashego detstva, 1967), Okeev describes the effects of rapid urbanization, especially the painful split between the generations. Although this process is shown as irreversible, the film also appears as an unequivocal homage to the traditional lifestyle of shepherds that had shaped an ethically and ecologically balanced order in harmony with nature. Accordingly, the imperative title of Okeev's next feature, *Worship the Fire* (Poklonis' ogniu, 1972), about the violent and tragic transformations in a 1920s village, is indicative of his worldview.

However, Okeev's position is far from idealizing nature or artificially humanizing it. As he demonstrates in his best film, *The Fierce One* (Liutyi, 1974, based on a script by **Andrei Mikhalkov-Konchalovskii** and produced at **Kazakhfilm Studio**), the laws of nature and of human society are incompatible, and the former cannot be invalidated by the latter. Rather, this dramatic story of a wolf raised in captivity, who later becomes a merciless killer, reveals deep skepticism regarding the taming power of civilization.

Okeev then turned to psychological and social drama. *The Red Apple* (Krasnoe iabloko, 1975), adapted from a story by revered Kyrgyz author **Chingiz Aitmatov**, deals with an artist's creative crisis and its impact on his married life. *The Ulan* (Ulan, 1977), starring Okeev's preferred actor, **Suimenkul Chokmorov**, analyzes the problem of alcoholism. *Golden Autumn* (Zolotaia osen', 1981) deals with the midlife crisis of a journalist trying to come to terms with his native village (*aul*).

The Descendant of the Snow Leopard (Potomok belogo barsa, 1984), which film historian Oksana Bulgakova aptly called "an ecological fairy tale," features a warning that any transgression of natural rules will inevitably cause environmental damage and ultimately destroy human civilization as well. *Mirages of Love* (Mirazhi liubvi, 1986), a Soviet-Syrian coproduction, is the colorful coming-of-age story of a young potter against the backdrop of exotic medieval Bukhara. Okeev wrote a number of scripts, of which the Aitmatov adaptation *Spotted Dog Running on the Edge of the Sea* (Pegii pes begushchii kraem moria, 1989, directed by Karen Gevorkian) became a critical triumph. A large-scale project on Chengiz Khan, for which he wrote the screenplay together with Turkmen director **Bulat Mansurov**, was never completed.

In 1993 Okeev was appointed Kyrgyzstan's ambassador to Turkey. After his official term ended in 1999, he decided to stay with his family in Ankara, teaching film classes at colleges and preparing various projects, before succumbing to a heart attack.

Okeev's means of filmic expression increasingly relied on the purely visual, producing an aesthetic complexity requiring a high degree of concentration. Indeed, Okeev can be called the auteur of **Kyrgyz cinema**; his films always have a personal touch, and several of them are autobiographical. At the same time, Okeev's central themes—the clash of tradition and modern lifestyle initiated by the Bolshevik Revolution and the incompatibility of the laws of nature and human society—are of fundamental importance to his nation's culture, as is the respect for ancient patriarchal wisdom and the torn-ness of his culture in modernity.

Okeev joined the Communist Party in 1975; he was honored with the title People's Artist of the USSR in 1985. Okeev received a state funeral; he is buried at the Ala-Archa cemetery in Bishkek. A monument to the director was erected in front of the film theater October. In 2002, Kyrgyzfilm Studio was named after him.

Other films: *Urkuja* (1972); *Kojojash* (1989).

OKHLOPKOV, NIKOLAI PAVLOVICH (b. 15 May 1900, Irkutsk–d. 8 January 1967, Moscow). Russian actor, director, and screenwriter. Okhlopkov's stage career began in 1918. He studied with Vsevolod Meierkhol'd and joined his troupe in 1923. In 1930, Okhlopkov was put in charge of the Realistic Theater in Moscow. In 1938–1943 he was a member of the Vakhtangov Theater, and in 1943–1966 worked as the chief director of the Maiakovskii Theater in Moscow. He also directed operas at the Bolshoi Theater.

Okhlopkov made his film debut in **Aleksandr Razumnyi**'s Civil War potboiler *The Gang of Father Knysh* (Banda bat'ki Knysha, 1924), playing "the Violinist." He was a scene-stealer as "the sailor in the sweater" (*matros v fufaike*) in **Abram Room**'s *Bay of Death* (Bukhta smerti, 1927) and as a machine operator in **Aleksandr Macheret**'s *People and Deeds* (aka *Men and Jobs*/Dela i liudi, 1932).

In the 1920s, Okhlopkov tried himself out as a director. His first film, the satirical comedy *Mitia* (1927) in which he also played the male lead, is a funny, over-the-top attack on provincial hypocrisy and lack of compassion contrasted to the title character's candor and warmth. *The Sold Appetite* (Prodannyi appetit, 1928), an even more grotesque satire, depicts the absurdities and injustices of capitalism. While these pictures proved successful with viewers and critics alike, Okhlopkov's monumental epic *The Path of Enthusiasts* (Put' entuziastov, 1930), intended as a visualization of the unity between workers and peasants, was a critical and box-office failure and effectively ended his promising career as a filmmaker.

Okhlopkov reappeared in Soviet cinema when it had mastered sound, which added to the actor's strong screen presence. His performances in **Mikhail Romm**'s *Lenin in October* (Lenin v Oktiabre, 1937) and *Lenin in 1918* (Lenin v 1918 godu, 1939) as the worker Vasilii—a "close friend of Lenin"—were rewarded with a Stalin Prize in 1941. **Sergei Eizenshtein** cast Okhlopkov as charming loudmouth Vasilii Buslaev in *Aleksandr Nevskii* (1938), emphasizing his naïve, somewhat cumbersome manliness, generous humor, and selfless heroism—features that would define the actor's screen image for a long time. Other noteworthy roles were the singer in **Sergei Iutkevich**'s biopic *Iakov Sverdlov* (1940), General Barclay de Tolly in **Vladimir Petrov**'s *Kutuzov* (1944), and Commissar Vorob'ev in **Aleksandr Stolper**'s *Story of a Real Man* (Povest' o nastoiashchem cheloveke, 1948, Stalin Prize 1949). Okhlopkov received another Stalin Prize in 1951 for his Batmanov in Stolper's industrialization tale *Far from Moscow* (Daleko ot Moskvy, 1950). In later years, Okhlopkov fully concentrated on his stage work.

For a short period Okhlopkov, who joined the Communist Party in 1952, was appointed deputy USSR minister of culture (1955–1956). He received three more Stalin Prizes for his theater work (in 1947, 1949, and 1951). Okhlopkov was named People's Artist of the USSR in 1948. He is buried at Novodevich'e cemetery.

Other films: *The Traitor* (Predatel', 1926); *The Lights of Baku* (Ogni Baku, 1950).

OMIRBAEV, DAREZHAN (b. 15 March 1958, village Uiuk, Djambul region, Kazakhstan). Kazakh director, scriptwriter, and film theorist. Omirbaev graduated from Kazakh State University, majoring in applied mathematics, in 1980. He worked as a programmer and teacher and later as an editor at **Kazakhfilm Studio** in Almaty. Afterward, he briefly studied directing at the Soviet State Film School **VGIK** before switching to the Department of Film Criticism, graduating in 1987 with a thesis on film semiotics.

The 25-minute-long *July* (Shil'de, 1988) features several of Omirbaev's main themes: childhood memory and dreams of an ideal world, the clash between movie visions and harsh reality, and generational miscommunication. With his first full-length feature, *Kairat* (1991), Omirbaev became one of the founders of the New Wave in **Kazakh cinema** (together with Ardak Amirkulov, Serik Aprimov, and others). The film features a young bus controller who fails in his struggle to overcome alienation and isolation. *Kairat* won Omirbaev a number of international prizes, as did *Cardiogram* (Kardiogramma, 1995), the story of a 12-year-old farm boy suffering from a heart ailment who spends a month in a clinic among people who do not understand his language and whose Russian he does not understand.

The Kazakh-French coproduction *Killer* (Killer/Tueur à gages, 1998) brought Omirbaev further international recognition; however, while the bleak story of everyday brutality under new capitalist conditions in Kazakhstan impressed audiences in many countries, it was hardly seen at home. *The Route* (Jol/La Route, 2001), coproduced with France and Japan, depicts the soul searching of a filmmaker who visits his native village in the steppe. Omirbaev's contribution to the international omnibus project *Digital Sam in Sam Saek 2006: Talk to Her* (2006) is a medium-length adaptation of Anton Chekhov's story "About Love."

Omirbaev is a style-conscious director whose slow-paced, intensely controlled narratives with heightened attention to subtle moral choices reveal the influence of Robert Bresson. Cinematically erudite and artistically uncompromising, Omirbaev has authored several articles on cinema theory. In 1993, he appeared as an actor in Timur Suleimenov's *Stranger*.

Other films: *Life* (Zhizn', 1982; short); *Profession: Controller* (Professiia—kontroler, 1993; doc.); *Shuga* (2007).

ONCE THERE WAS A SINGING THRUSH (Iqo shashvi mgalobeli/Zhil pevchii drozd, 1970). **Gruziya-Film Studio**. 83 min., b/w. Directed by **Otar Ioseliani**. Script: Otar Ioseliani, Dmitrii Eristavi, Otar Mekhrishvili, Il'ia Nusinov, Semen Lungin. Cinematography: Abesalom Maisuradze. Music: Teimuraz Bakhuradze. Cast: Gela Kandelaki, Gogi Chkheidze, Irina Djandieri, Djansug Kakhidze, Marina Kartsivadze, Nugzar Erkumaishvili, Dea Ivanidze. Premiere: 11 July 1972.

Gia Agladze (Kandelaki), a young professional musician who lives in the Georgian capital Tbilisi and plays the kettle drum in an orchestra, is popular and loved by family, friends, and colleagues. Always curious, cheerful, and flirtatious, he rushes from one appointment to the next, be it professional or amorous. However, the orchestra's conductor is irritated by Gia's lack of responsibility—Gia himself does not even make time to write down a melody that he has invented. Suddenly, when hurrying across a street, Gia loses his life in a traffic accident. *See also* GEORGIAN CINEMA.

ORDINARY FASCISM (Obyknovennyi fashizm, 1965). **Mosfilm Studio**. 138 mins., b/w. Directed by **Mikhail Romm**. Script: Mikhail

Romm, Maia Turovskaia, Iurii Khaniutin. Cinematography: German Lavrov. Music: Alembar Karamanov. Premiere: December 1965.

A compilation **documentary**, this grand-scale cinematic essay narrated by Mikhail Romm himself attempts to analyze the nature of National Socialism as an everyday phenomenon, using archival footage of the Weimar Republic, the 12 years of Nazi rule in Germany, and the aftermath of World War II. In 16 chapters, it asks questions rarely before posed in Soviet cinema: about Adolf Hitler's personality, the common mechanisms of brainwashing, the systemic indoctrination of youth with violence, people's leisure activities, fascist "art" and "culture," and the societal system of values, its beneficiaries, and victims. Following the loosely chronological depiction of the rise and fall of the Third Reich, the film also looks at neo-Nazi trends in the West while praising the Soviet Union and the other Communist countries as the vanguard of antifascism.

ORLOVA, LIUBOV' PETROVNA (b. 29 February 1902, Zvenigorod–d. 26 January 1975, Moscow). Russian actress. Orlova's mother and father both hailed from nobility and had their daughter take piano lessons. Orlova studied at Moscow Conservatory in 1919–1922 and in the Choreography Department of Moscow Theatrical College in 1922–1925. From 1926 to 1933, she was employed in the Nemirovich-Danchenko Musical Theater, first as a choir singer and later as a soloist in operettas. At the height of her fame, Orlova would continue her stage career in 1947 in the Mossovet Theater, playing Henrik Ibsen's Nora, among other parts.

After marrying director **Grigorii Aleksandrov** in 1934, Orlova performed the female leads in all of his musical comedies and became the most glamorous Soviet actress of her time. With light blonde hair, delicate features, and a trained physique, Orlova embodied the deepest desires of generations of Soviet men and women and grew into a powerful symbol of Stalinist culture. Whether as a housemaid in *Jolly Fellows* (Veselye rebiata, 1934), a fugitive American circus artist in *Circus* (Tsirk, 1936), a composing mail carrier in *Volga-Volga* (1938), or a Stakhanovite textile worker in *Light Path* (Svetlyi put', 1940), what this Hollywood-type star transplanted into Soviet villages and factories was dancing, singing, and falling in love, always insisting on her right to creative self-realization, and fighting bureaucrats and foreign saboteurs along the way.

An ambitious professional, Orlova did not cope well with aging and was supported by Aleksandrov in her increasingly grotesque denial; thus, in the 1942 war omnibus *One Family* (Odna sem'ia, released 1945), she was cast as student Katia. Orlova's double role of scientist Irina and actress Vera in *Spring* (Vesna, 1947) and her Varvara Komarova in the disastrous *Russian Souvenir* (Russkii suvenir, 1960) proved beyond doubt that the actress's official image had become an anachronism despite the persisting love of millions of viewers. Aleksandrov's final attempt to revitalize Orlova's magic in the spy thriller *Woodpecker and Lyre* (Skvorets i lira, 1973) ended in an unmitigated fiasco.

Orlova repeatedly tried to branch out into genres other than musical. She was cast against type in a tragic role in **Aleksandr Macheret**'s thriller *Engineer Kochin's Error* (Oshibka inzhenera Kochina, 1939), and appeared in **Grigorii Roshal'**'s adaptations *Petersburg Night* (Peterburgskaia noch', 1935) from Fedor Dostoevskii and *The Artamonov Business* (Delo Artamonovykh, 1941) from Maksim Gor'kii, as well as his biopic *Musorgskii* (1950).

Orlova was awarded two Stalin prizes (1941, 1950) and the title People's Artist of the USSR in 1950. In 1983, Aleksandrov devoted a full-length **documentary** to his late wife. The house in Moscow where he and Orlova had lived in 1965–1975 (Bol'shaia Bronnaia, 29) carries a memorial plaque with her portrait.

Other films: *Meeting at the Elbe* (Vstrecha na El'be, 1949).

ORLOVA, VERA GEORGIEVNA (b. 27 May 1894, Riazan' district–d. 28 September 1977, Moscow). Russian actress. Orlova, who hailed from the family of a civil servant, finished the Women's Gymnasium in 1911 and subsequently worked in the State Railway Bureau in Moscow. She took private acting classes before enrolling in the studio school of the Moscow Art Theater (MKhAT), where she studied with Konstantin Stanislavskii, Vladimir Nemirovich-Danchenko, and Evgenii Vakhtangov in 1913–1915. After spending some years in France, Orlova was a member of the second troupe of MKhAT from 1924 to 1936.

Discovered by producer **Iosif Ermol'ev**, Orlova made her screen debut with the female lead in **Iakov Protazanov**'s *The Seagull* (Chaika, 1915—not from Anton Chekhov's play but adapted from a popular romance). Defined as a young ingenue, Orlova was particularly successful in adaptations of Russian classical literature. She portrayed Liza in *Queen of Spades* (Pikovaia dama, 1916) from Aleksandr Pushkin's short story, Masha in *Family Happiness* (Semeinoe schast'e, 1916) from Lev Tolstoi's novella, and Dasha Shatova in *Nikolai Stavrogin* (1915) from Fedor Dostoevskii's *The Devils* (Besy), all helmed by Protazanov, as well as Annushka in Czeslaw Sabinskii's adaptation of Aleksandr Ostrovskii's play *In a Busy Spot* (Na boikom meste, 1916). Orlova often appeared as an erotically challenging nymphet, blending girlish innocence with unabashed sexual temptation—such is her Dunia in **Aleksandr Ivanovskii**'s *The Stationmaster* (Stantsionnyi smotritel', 1918) and especially Mar'ia, the seductive merchant's daughter, in **Father Sergius** (Otets Sergii, 1918), Protazanov's masterful version of Tolstoi's novella. Orlova also participated in the semifictitious anti-tsarist potboiler *Tsar Nikolai the Second, Autocrat of Russia* (1917), where she played Nastia, the lover of a revolutionary.

When Protazanov returned from emigration, he cast Orlova in his utopian extravaganza *Aelita* (1924) as Masha, who engages in exciting duets with **Nikolai Batalov**'s wooden Red Army soldier Gusev. Thereafter, Orlova's film career faded rather quickly, with parts in Oleg Frelikh's *The Prostitute* (Prostitutka, 1927) and *The Young Communards* (Iunye kommunary, 1938) being noticeable exceptions. Her last film, *Two Friends* (Dva druga, 1941), a patriotic spy tale, was never released.

Other films: *Satan Triumphant* (Satana likuiushchii, 1917); *The Power of Darkness* (Vlast' t'my, 1918); *Punin and Barburin* (Punin i Barburin, 1919).

OSYKA, LEONID MYKHAILOVICH (b. 8 March 1930, Kiev–d. 16 September 2001, Kiev). Ukrainian director and screenwriter. Osyka studied at the Odessa Institute of Theater and Art, graduating in 1959. He later enrolled in the Soviet State Film School **VGIK** where he studied under **Boris Dolin**, graduating in 1966.

Osyka's first major film, *Those Who'll Return Shall Love to the End* (Kto vernetsia—doliubit, 1966), is a gloomy tale of loyalty and self-sacrifice during the Great Patriotic War; its main character, a poet, gives his life for his motherland. *The Stone Cross* (Kamennyi krest, 1968), adapted from novellas by Vasyli Stefanik, deals with the hardship endured by the Ukrainian peasantry before 1917. Osyka's early films betray the influence of **Sergei Paradjanov**'s masterpiece *Shadows of Forgotten Ancestors* (Tini zabutykh predkiv/Teni zabytykh predkov, 1964). Like other representatives of the new wave of poetic **Ukrainian cinema** in the 1960s (**Yury Il'enko**, Volodymir Denisenko), Osyka strove for a metaphorical saturation of his cinematic vision in which elements of national folklore and mysticism such as doom and fate abound. These directors' common rejection of narrative coherence, however, renders their films challenging for unprepared viewers.

Zakhar Berkut (1970), a historical epic about the invasion of Mongols and Tatars in the 13th century and the resistance of the Carpathian mountain people, is stylistically less complex than Osyka's previous films, resembling heroic folk legends instead. The director landed a minor box-office hit with *The Troubling Month Veresen'* (Trevozhnyi mesiats Veresen', 1976), a dramatic story about the struggle of pro-Soviet forces against former Nazi collaborators at the end of World War II. Osyka then helmed *The Sea* (More, 1978), a peculiar thriller with ecological notions.

When Mikhail Gorbachev's perestroika gradually abolished censorship, Osyka embarked on a project based on one of Paradjanov's many unrealized screenplays, *Sketches on Vrubel'* (Etiudy o Vrubele, 1989), devoted to Russian painter and mystic Mikhail Vrubel' (1856–1910) and his years in Kiev. Osyka's last film was the historical drama *The Hetman's Treasures* (Getmanskie kleinody, 1993) about the daughter of legendary hetman Bohdan Khmelnytski and her fight for Ukraine's independence. Osyka also directed a **documentary** about actor and filmmaker **Leonid Bykov**, . . . *He Who Was Loved by All* (. . . kotorogo liubili vse, 1982).

Other films: *The Woman Entering the Sea* (Vkhodiashchaia v more, 1965); *Bow to the Ground* (aka *Bow Your Head*/Poklonis' do zemli, 1985); *You, Who Suffer, Enter!* (Voidite, strazhdushchie, 1987).

OTSEP, FEDOR ALEKSANDROVICH (b. 9 February 1895, Moscow–d. 20 June 1949, Beverly Hills, California). Russian director and screenwriter. While attending Moscow University, Otsep also worked as a journalist, film critic, and author of newsreels for **Iosif Ermol'ev**'s company. In 1916, he began writing scripts for prestigious silents such as **Iakov Protazanov**'s *Queen of Spades* (Pikovaia dama, 1916, from Aleksandr Pushkin's story) and **Aleksandr Sanin**'s Lev Tolstoi adaptation *Polikushka* (1919, released in 1922).

In 1919, Otsep was appointed artistic supervisor of Rus' company—later part of **Mezhrabpomfilm Studio**—which produced *Polikushka*, a great domestic and international success. Incidentally, Otsep played an episodic role in **Vsevolod Pudovkin**'s lighthearted debut *Chess Fever* (Shakhmatnaia goriachka, 1925) in which his nephew, **Iulii Raizman**, appeared as well. Otsep was assistant director on the Pushkin adaptation *The Stationmaster* (Kollezhskii registrator, 1925), made from his script by **Iurii Zheliabuzhskii** and Ivan Moskvin.

Together with **Boris Barnet**, he cowrote and codirected *Miss Mend* (1926, adapted from Marietta Shaginian's bestseller *Mess Mend*), a sensational hit. Otsep's first independently directed film was *Soil in Chains* (aka *The Yellow Pass*/Zemlia v plenu, 1927), starring his then-wife **Anna Sten** as a woman who is forced into prostitution. Otsep followed it with the Lev Tolstoi adaptation *The Living Corpse* (Zhivoi trup, 1929), a German-Soviet coproduction. He decided to stay in Germany, where he made a sound adaptation of Fedor Dostoevskii's *Brothers Karamazov* under the title *The Murderer Dmitry Karamazov* (Der Mörder Dimitri Karamasoff, 1930), which, in Jay Leyda's words, "had a greater effect on international films than any Soviet film he directed."

In 1932, Otsep moved to Paris where he helmed *Paris Mirages* (Mirages de Paris, 1932), the Stefan Zweig adaptation *Amok* (1934), *Queen of Spades* (La dame de pique, 1937), and the historical melodrama *Tarakanowa* (1937), among others. As an adaptable and versatile filmmaker and polyglot with uncompromising professional standards but modest artistic ambitions, Otsep was able to efficiently complete versions of the same film in German, French, and English, and shoulder coproductions between various countries.

Lacking a valid citizenship, Otsep was briefly interned at the outbreak of World War II before escaping to Nizza and, via Casablanca, to the United States in 1943. He failed in Hollywood but settled in Canada, where he made features in French and English, codirecting *Three Russian Girls* (aka *She Who Dares*, 1943) with Sten in the lead, *Le père Chopin* (aka *The Music Master*, 1943), and the noirish *Whispering City* (aka *La fortresse*, aka *Crime City*, 1947).

Other films: *Aelita* (script, 1924); *Gibraltar* (1938).

OUTSKIRTS, THE (Okraina, 1933). **Mezhrabpomfilm Studio**. 96 min., b/w. Directed by **Boris Barnet**. Script: Konstantin Finn, Boris Barnet from the 1931 novella by Finn. Cinematography: Mikhail Kirillov, A. Spiridonov. Music: Sergei Vasilenko. Cast: **Elena Kuz'mina**, **Nikolai Bogoliubov**, **Nikolai Kriuchkov**, **Mikhail Zharov**, Robert Erdman, **Sergei Komarov**, Aleksandr Chistiakov, Hans Klering. Premiere: 25 March 1933. The film was restored in 1965.

August 1914: In a provincial Russian town, news of the beginning of World War I disturb the inhabitants' daily routine. The two sons of shoemaker Kadkin—young Sen'ka (Kriuchkov) and Nikolai (Bogoliubov)—are drafted. Kadkin hires a young German POW (Klering) who is allowed to leave prison camp during the day. But when Kadkin learns that Sen'ka has been killed in action, he and other enraged townsfolk beat the prisoner up. The prisoner finds love and shelter with young, naïve Man'ka (Kuz'mina). Meanwhile, Nikolai Kadkin, together with other Bolsheviks, participates in the fraternization at the front; the ensuing October Revolution puts an end to the nightmare of war.

OVCHINNIKOV, VIACHESLAV ALEKSANDROVICH (b. 29 May, 1936, Voronezh). Russian composer and conductor. Ovchinnikov was known as a child prodigy, composing his first pieces at the age of nine. He enrolled in the college of Moscow Conservatory in 1951 and later in the conservatory itself, where he studied composition, graduating in 1962. Among his teachers was **Tikhon Khrennikov**. Ovchinnikov's early compositions, especially his three symphonies, caused a sensation in the Russian music scene and instantly attracted the attention of young filmmakers.

Ovchinnikov debuted as a film composer with *The Cable* (Tele-gramma, 1958, TV) and contributed a psychologically nuanced score to **Andrei Tarkovskii**'s diploma film, *The Steamroller and the Violin* (Katok i skripka, 1960). His music for Tarkovskii's war tragedy *Ivan's Childhood* (aka *My Name Is Ivan*/Ivanovo detstvo, 1962) sensitively supported the contrast between the title character's idyllic dream world and nightmarish reality. Ovchinnikov also wrote the music for another Tarkovskii masterpiece, *Andrei Rublev* (1966), in which the apocalyptic atmosphere is intensified further. At the same time, Ovchinnikov was composing the remarkable score for **Sergei Bondarchuk**'s seven-hour adaptation of Lev Tolstoi's *War and Peace* (Voina i mir, 1962–1967). From the haunting passionate waltz accompanying Natasha Rostova's first ball to the disturbing, dissonant tunes underlying scenes of carnage and destruction, Ovchinnikov gave musical grandeur to this cinematic tour de force. He continued to work with Bondarchuk on the Great Patriotic War epic *They Fought for the Motherland* (Oni srazhalis' za Rodinu, 1975); the quiet, atmospheric Anton Chekhov adaptation *The Steppe* (Step', 1977); and the director's last completed picture, *Boris Godunov* (1986) from Aleksandr Pushkin's tragedy.

Ovchinnikov's ability to translate the spirit of a literary masterpiece into music sometimes exceeds the quality of the film as a whole; such is the case with **Andrei Mikhalkov-Konchalovskii**'s unsatisfactory Ivan Turgenev adaptation *A Nest of the Gentry* (Dvorianskoe gnezdo, 1969). Among Ovchinnikov's other film scores are **Vitautas Žalakevičius**'s *That Sweet Word—Liberty!* (Eto sladkoe slovo—svoboda, 1973) and his Friedrich Dürrenmatt adaptation *The Accident* (Avariia, 1975, TV). The alternation between an intimate, lyrical atmosphere and quasi-official pathos is particularly impressive in Ovchinnikov's scores for remastered versions of **Aleksandr Dovzhenko**'s classics *Zvenigora* (1927), *Arsenal* (1928), and *Earth* (Zemlia, 1930) written in the 1970s; he also contributed the music to **Iuliia Solntseva**'s **documentary** about Dovzhenko, *The Golden Gates* (Zolotye vorota, 1969).

After three decades of prolific work for the cinema, Ovchinnikov made a conscious decision to withdraw from this genre and devote himself entirely to symphonic and choral music. His oeuvre includes violin and piano concertos, symphonic poems and suites, an oratorio

("Sergii Radonezhskii"), an opera, and a ballet, all characterized by a moderately experimental, neoclassical, intensely melodic style. However, considering the supreme quality of the music that Ovchinnikov has contributed to Soviet cinema, he can safely be called one of the most original Russian film composers.

Other films: *The First Teacher* (Pervyi uchitel', 1965); *Such High Mountains* (Takie vysokie gory, 1974).

OZEROV, IURII NIKOLAEVICH (b. 26 January 1921, Moscow– d. 16 October 2001, Moscow). Russian director and scriptwriter. Ozerov was the son of well-known opera singer Nikolai Ozerov (1887– 1953); other family members were stage actors, most prominently among them his brother Nikolai (1922–1997), also a legendary sports anchorman. Ozerov's studies at the Lunacharskii Theater Institute in Moscow were interrupted by military draft in 1939 and his subsequent service as a signal man in the Great Patriot War. Ozerov's experiences as an officer in the battles of Moscow, Königsberg, and others enabled him in the 1960s–1980s to reconstruct these events with a high degree of accuracy on the wide screen. In 1945, Ozerov was discharged at the rank of a major. In 1946 he enrolled at the Soviet State Film School **VGIK** (in **Ihor' Savchenko**'s workshop) and graduated in 1951.

Ozerov's first movies at **Mosfilm Studio** were artistically unremarkable genre works, including the circus drama *Ring of Daring* (aka *Daring Circus Youth*/Arena smelykh, 1953), the moralistic study of juvenile delinquency *The Son* (Syn, 1955), and the Civil War biopic *Kochubei* (1957)—all heavily infused with Communist ideology, and successful crowd-pleasers, too. Ozerov then was entrusted with two coproductions: the World War II guerilla story *Fortuna* (aka *The Storm*, 1959) with Albania and Romania, and *The Great Path* (Bol'shaia doroga, 1962) with Czechoslovakia, a film about legendary novelist Jaroslav Hašek.

Ozerov's all-time achievement is *Liberation* (Osvobozhdenie, 1970–1972), a five-part, eight-hour epic that magnificently recreates major events of the second half of World War II. The film's innumerable episodes combine the political sphere—with Iosif Stalin, Winston Churchill, Franklin Roosevelt, Adolf Hitler, Benito Mussolini, and their respective entourages—and fictitious plotlines whose characters represent the rank-and-file aspects of war. With its unprecedented production values, *Liberation* became a genuine event in the USSR. It marked the official rehabilitation of Marshall Georgii Zhukov, who personally participated in the film's preparation, and, most significantly, of Iosif Stalin who, after a long hiatus in Soviet cinema, once again is portrayed as a wise strategic leader. Effectively using the wide screen, Ozerov's monumental work has undeniable visual merits that endeared it to mass audiences domestically and abroad.

Based on *Liberation*'s success, Ozerov was commissioned to contribute the Soviet episode, *The Beginning* (Start), to the international **documentary** omnibus *Visions of Eight* (1972) about the Olympic Games in Munich; among his codirectors were Claude Lelouch, Kon Ichikawa, and Arthur Penn. However, Ozerov's subsequent attempt to repeat the triumph of *Liberation* with the four-part, seven-hour *Soldiers of Freedom* (Soldaty svobody, 1977) failed miserably. Produced with noticeably less attention to historic detail, this elephantine, tedious mess combines historical demagoguery with kowtowing to the 1970s Communist leaders. The three-hour long *Stalingrad* (1989), coproduced with Warner Brothers, reflected the new politics of glasnost by including facts that were unmentionable before, while *Angels of Death* (Angely smerti, 1993) tells the sniper love story that was later used in Jean-Jacques Annaud's *Enemy at the Gates* (2001). In his last years, Ozerov recycled earlier films for television miniseries, such as *Tragedy of the Century* (Tragediia veka, 1996).

The best of Ozerov's multihour war chronicles satisfied a deep need of several generations of Soviet viewers, not unlike modern-day history channels. The director's artistic ambitions were minimal; as an ever-dutiful Communist Party member, he strictly followed official guidelines. However, it is also worth mentioning that Ozerov never romanticized war as such. Within the Soviet film community, he was regarded as the proverbial political hack, member of countless committees, and recipient of all titles and medals available. Still, in the 1990s his reputation was reevaluated, a trend that became even stronger with the growing neopatriotism in the new millennium.

In 1977, Ozerov was named People's Artist of the USSR. In 1979–1991, he taught at VGIK.

Other films: *Oh Sport—You Are Peace* (O sport, ty—mir! 1981; doc.); *The Battle for Moscow* (Bitva za Moskvu, 1985); *The Great Commander G. K. Zhukov* (Velikii polkovodets G. K. Zhukov, 1996, TV).

–P –

PAATASHVILI, LEVAN [some Russian sources list the patronymic Georgievich] (b. 12 March 1926, Tbilisi). Georgian cinematographer and pedagogue. Paatashvili, whose first specialty is architecture, studied with **Boris Volchek** at the Soviet State Film School **VGIK**, graduating in 1954.

From the beginning of his career, Paatashvili shared his activities between Tbilisi and Moscow, developing a reputation as a sensitive, adaptable cinematographer both in Russian and **Georgian cinema**. His stringent visual style in **Tengiz Abuladze**'s *Somebody Else's Children* (Skhvisi shvilebi/Chuzhie deti, 1958), with a strong emphasis on tension-filled, dramatic black-and-white contrasts, betrays neorealist influences, as do the film's numerous vivacious cityscapes. Paatashvili filmed **Lana Gogoberidze**'s debut, the tripartite *Under One Sky* (Erti tsis kvesh/Pod odnim nebom, 1961), as well as senior filmmaker **Siko Dolidze**'s sentimental *Day Last, Day First* (Dge pirveli, dge ukanaskneli/Den' poslednii, den' pervyi, 1960). His superb camera work on **Mikhail Kalik**'s *Good-bye, Boys!* (Do svidaniia, mal'chiki!, 1965) creates a precious, bittersweet atmosphere.

Paatashvili more than justified **Aleksandr Alov** and **Vladimir Naumov**'s high hopes when they picked him for the historical epic *The Flight* (Beg, 1970) from Mikhail Bulgakov's play. Filmed in color, the cinematographer created a stern, ascetic imagery, especially in a number of nightmarishly bright, extreme long shots. Paatashvili's art gave even questionable films such as **Andrei Mikhalkov-Konchalovskii**'s pathos-filled *Romance about Lovers* (Romans o vliublennykh, 1974) an interesting, at times spectacular, visual appearance. Among his later pictures, two deserve special mentioning: **Eldar Shengelaia**'s biting contemporary satire *Blue Mountains, or An Unbelievable Story* (Tsisperi mtebi anu arachveulebrivi ambavi/Golubye gory, ili nepravdopodobnaia istoriia,

1984) and **Giorgi Shengelaia**'s historical elegy *Sojourn of a Young Composer* (Akhalgarzda kompozitoris mogzauroba/Puteshestvie molodogo kompozitora, 1984).

Paatashvili, who is also valued as a painter and graphic artist, has taught at VGIK and at the Shota Rustaveli Institute of Art in Tbilisi. In the late 1970s, he began to work for television. He was named People's Artist of the Georgian SSR in 1979.

Other films: *Siberiade* (Sibiriada, 1979); *The Nylon Christmas Tree* (Neilonis nadzvis khe/Neilonovaia elka, 1986); *Robinsonade, or My English Grandfather* (Robinzoniada, anu chemi ingliseli Papa/Robinzonada, ili Moi angliiskii dedushka, 1987); *Mado, Poste Réstante* (Mado, do vostrebovaniia, 1990, France); *The Wall* (Kedeli/Stena, 1990); *The Ceiling* (Cheri anu daumtavrebeli pilmis masala, 2003).

PÄRN, PRIIT (b. 26 August 1946, Tallin). Estonian **animation** director, screenwriter, and animator. Pärn initially studied biology at Tartu University, graduating in 1970, and simultaneously made a name for himself as a cartoonist and illustrator. After working at the Botanical Garden in Tallin, he joined the animators' team of director Rein Raamat at **Tallinfilm Studio** in 1976 where he since has worked (the animation studio became independent in 1994 and was renamed Eesti Joonisfilm).

Pärn's debut in drawn animation, the children's short *Is the Earth Round?* (Krugla li zemlia? 1977), an inventive exploration of the circularity of the world and human life, brought him immediate success yet was not permitted for distribution within the entire USSR because of its subversive humor. In this and his following short and medium-length pictures, Pärn indulges in unexpected graphic transformations that at the time were in violation of certain aesthetic and philosophical dogmas of Soviet cinema. Many of his films deal with human weaknesses and are predominantly intended for adult audiences, including *Some Exercises in Preparation for Independent Life* (Nekotorye uprazhneniia dlia samostoiatel'noi zhizni, 1980), *The Triangle* (Kolmnurk/Treugol'nik, 1982), and *Time Out* (Aeg maha/Nebylitsy, 1984). Pärn appears as an insightful critic of modern civilization in prize-winning films such as *Le Dejeuner sur l'herbe*, aka *Breakfast on the Grass* (Eine murul/Zavtrak na trave, 1987) and *Hotel E* (1992). In 1996, Pärn devoted a picture, *1895* (codirected with Janno Põldma) to the Lumière brothers and the 100th anniversary of cinema, the history of which is told in an original, condensed manner.

In the 1990s, Pärn became Estonia's best-known animator whose graphic originality and wit have enthused animation fans all over the world. He has taught at film schools in Scandinavia, Germany, Belgium, Spain, Australia, and Canada, and was appointed head of the Department of Animation of the Turku Arts and Media School in 1994. In the 1990s, he served as head of the Board of the Estonian Film Foundation. Pärn also directs commercials.

Other films: *When Leaving, Turn Off the Light* (Ukhodia, vykliuchi svet, 1988); *Night of the Carrots* (Porgandite öö,1998); *Karl and Marilyn* (Karl ja Marilyn, 2003). *See also* ESTONIAN CINEMA.

PANFILOV, GLEB ANATOL'EVICH (b. 21 May 1934, Magnitogorsk). Russian director and scriptwriter. Panfilov was born into a family of intellectuals. He studied chemical technology at Ural Polytechnical Institute, graduating in 1957, and subsequently worked in Sverdlovsk as an engineer and a Komsomol functionary from 1959 to 1961. Panfilov also organized an amateur filmmakers' club, which turned out so successful that Sverdlovsk television hired him to direct several **documentary** shorts (*The People's Militia*/Narodnaia militsiia, 1958; *Join Our Front!*/Vstavai v nash stroi, 1959), feature shorts (*Nina Melovizinova*; *Not Killed in War*/Ubit ne na voine), and a full-length feature, *The Case of Kurt Clausewitz* (Delo Kurta Klauzevitsa, 1963), in which **Anatolii Solonitsyn** played his first lead. Panfilov enrolled in the Soviet State Film School **VGIK** as an external student in the class of cinematographer **Anatolii Golovnia** in 1960 and then studied with **Leonid Trauberg** in the Supreme Courses for Directors and Screenwriters (VKSR) until 1966.

The Civil War drama *There's No Ford through Fire* (V ogne broda net, 1967), Panfilov's first full-length feature, won instantaneous critical recognition for its innovative depiction of a revolutionary heroine (portrayed by **Inna Churikova**), a nurse who discovers, amidst blood, dirt, and death, her gift for painting. Churikova went on to play the leads in all of Panfilov's following pictures; their partnership, both professional and private, has helped define the idiosyncratic atmosphere and appearance of the filmmaker's oeuvre in a unique way. *There's No Ford through Fire* won a major prize at the Locarno Festival, which—similar in its effect to the careers of **Grigorii Chukhrai** and **Andrei Tarkovskii**—would provide Panfilov with a certain immunity in turbulences to come.

Interestingly, the subtle subversiveness of Panfilov's films does not undermine their underlying faith in the essential cultural mission of the Communist idea. This faith is tested not by explicit dissidence but by the tediousness of everyday reality, as well as sudden, inexplicable turns of fate. Panfilov's obstinate individualism is betrayed by his demonstrative attention to the margins of Russia; significantly, most of his films take place in small towns rather than Moscow or Leningrad. *The Debut* (Nachalo, 1970) contrasts the real life of a gifted provincial weaver to the heroism of Joan of Arc, whom this weaver is to play in a film. (A historical film about Joan of Arc—Panfilov's and Churikova's favorite project and many years in the making—never got past the script stage.) Further developing the awakening-to-self-consciousness motif, *I Wish to Speak* (Proshu slova, 1975) portrays a high-ranking city administrator. In this picture—arguably his most accomplished—Panfilov attempts to assess the maturation of Soviet civil society; indeed, the title itself expresses a call for grassroots democracy a decade before perestroika and glasnost. *I Wish to Speak* is perhaps Panfilov's most ambiguous film, for it directly tackles the question of the functioning of Soviet statehood and its potential, neither glorifying nor dismissing it.

The Theme (Tema, 1979), the sober portrait of an opportunistic playwright, exposes the rottenness of the Soviet cultural establishment as opposed to the idealism of small-town folks; the film remained shelved until 1986. Then, as if to prove the survivability of pure Communist ideology and its compatibility with true art, Panfilov adapted Maksim Gor'kii's play *Vassa Zheleznova* for the screen (*Vassa*, 1983), before turning to Gor'kii's Socialist-Realist, ultracanonical novel *The Mother* (Mat'/aka Zapreshchennye liudi, 1990, also as TV miniseries). On the backdrop of an all-encompassing devaluation of Soviet traditions—including the country's cinematic canon—the latter was perceived as an intentional, quixotic anachronism and provocation. Indeed, Panfilov's only other contributions to the reform-happy perestroika period were the release of

The Theme and a controversial *Hamlet* production at the Moscow Lenkom Theater.

It took Panfilov a decade to complete his next project, *The Romanovs—An Imperial Family* (Romanovy—ventsenosnaia sem'ia, 2000). Typical for the director, the film's narration makes no effort to cater to mainstream expectations, and yet this purportedly objective reconstruction of the last tsar's life is hardly recognizable as the product of an accomplished master: strangely uninspired, tedious, and uncritical of its subject, it marks a low point in Panfilov's career. In 2002–2006, the filmmaker adapted Aleksandr Solzhenitsyn's novel *In the First Circle* (V kruge pervom) for cinema and television.

Throughout his enviably steady yet slow-paced career during the 1960s–1980s, Panfilov managed to maintain a delicate balance between fundamental loyalty to the Soviet state and its ruling Party (of which he became a member in 1961) and his insistence on artistic independence. Like few other directors, Panfilov embodies the dignified, moderate nonconformism of a self-conscious provincial who expertly challenges Muscovite cultural arrogance. Panfilov's ascetic visual style, immediately identifiable, informs his films with a rare intimacy that proves rewarding to the attentive, discriminating viewer.

Panfilov was awarded the title People's Artist of the Russian Federation in 1984.

Other films: *Valentina* (1981).

PANTELEEV, ALEKSANDR PETROVICH (b. 14 July 1874 [other sources: 1872]–d. 1948). Russian director and actor. After finishing modern secondary school (*real'noe uchilishche*) and the imperial dramatic courses, Panteleev worked as a stage actor and member of the prestigious Aleksandrinskii Theater in St. Petersburg from 1893 to 1923. In 1915, he began to direct films, most of them melodramas. Among his approximately 10 movies made until 1918, *The Tree of Death, or The Bloodthursty Susanna* (Derevo smerti, ili Krovozhadnaia Susanna, 1915) stands out as a sensationalist, patriotic espionage drama whose main special effect, according to film historian Semen Ginzburg, was a "vampire tree" used by a spying German biologist to kill his victims.

Panteleev entered the annals of Russian film history as one of the creators of the first Soviet feature film, the ***agitka*** *The Condensation*

(Uplotnenie, codirected with D. Pashkovskii and A. Dolinov, 1918), the title of which refers to the catastrophic shortage of living space in Soviet cities. Produced by the Commissariat of Enlightenment and filmed on its Petrograd premises from a screenplay by Commissar **Anatolii Lunacharskii**, it tells the story of a professor who is forced to admit low-class tenants into his apartment. *Infinite Sorrow* (Beskonechnaia skorb', 1922), devoted to the famine in the Volga region and made with the intention to gather support for the starving population, was shown in a number of foreign countries, impressing audiences with its graphic display of suffering and demoralization. It featured the celebrated star of pre-1917 cinema, **Vladimir Maksimov**, in the role of an intellectual who irresponsibly sends his wife and child to the region. The antireligious satire *The Miracle Worker* (Chudotvorets, 1922), about an act of blasphemy during the reign of Nikolai I, was reportedly enjoyed and praised by Vladimir Lenin. *For the Power of the Soviets* (Za vlast' Sovetov, 1923) deals with the defense of Bolshevik Petrograd against the White Army under General Nikolai Iudenich; the potboiler *Hangmen* (Palachi, 1925) prominently features Tsar Nikolai II and Grigorii Rasputin.

Panteleev paid his dues to the Communist powers by thematizing serious social problems as a framework for conventional melodramas, conveyed in the style of the 1910s. Although audiences responded positively to this approach, in the late 1920s it was branded as anachronistic, and Panteleev, together with **Vladimir Gardin**, **Viacheslav Viskovskii**, and others, was prevented from feature filmmaking. In the 1930s, he worked in educational cinema.

Panteleev was honored with the title Hero of Labor in 1923.

Other films: *The Secret of a Grand Society Romance* (Taina velikosvetskogo romana, 1915); *Blackamoor Passion* (Arapskaia strast', 1915); *Man without Honor* (Chelovek bez chesti, 1917); *Tundra's Song* (Pesn' Tundry, 1926).

PAPANOV, ANATOLII DMITRIEVICH (b. 31 October 1922, Viaz'ma–d. 5 August 1987, Moscow). Russian actor. After a small role in **Tat'iana Lukashevich**'s hit **comedy *The Foundling*** (Podkidysh, 1939) and service in the Great Patriotic War, Papanov studied at the Moscow State Theater Institute (GITIS), graduating in 1946.

He acted on the stage of the Klaipeda Russian Drama Theater and joined the troupe of the Moscow Theater of Satire in 1949.

Papanov's screen image was that of an authentic, rank-and-file Russian with a rough edge; he ably portrayed both petty criminals and experienced, responsible leaders who had weathered many storms. **El'dar Riazanov** cast Papanov in four different roles in his *Man from Nowhere* (Chelovek niotkuda, 1961), while **Leonid Gaidai** shot him to national fame with *The Diamond Arm* (Brilliantovaia ruka, 1968), casting him as the rude, plebeian counterpart to **Andrei Mironov**'s narcissistic crook. Gaidai later gave Papanov more challenging roles such as the mayor in his 1978 Nikolai Gogol' adaptation *Incognito from Petersburg* (Inkognito iz Peterburga, 1978, based on the 1836 satire *Inspector General*).

Aleksandr Stolper recognized Papanov's dramatic potential and cast him as General Serpilin in the famous World War II saga *The Living and the Dead* (Zhivye i mertvye, 1964) and its sequel, *Retribution* (aka *Soldiers Aren't Born*/Vozmezdie, 1969). Papanov's career-long attempts to transcend the limitations of mere comical cliché also were rewarded in **Iosif Kheifits**'s thoughtful Anton Chekhov adaptations *In the Town of S.* (V gorode S., 1967) and *A Bad Good Person* (Plokhoi khoroshii chelovek, 1973), as well as **Andrei Smirnov**'s sleeper-hit drama of war and remembrance *Belorussian Station* (Belorusskii vokzal, 1971).

Papanov concluded his career with a chilling performance as Kopalych, a former GULAG prisoner, in *The Cold Summer of 53* (Kholodnoe leto piat'desiat tret'ego, 1987), for which he was recognized with a posthumous State Prize of the USSR in 1989.

Because of his uniquely hoarse bass voice, Papanov was a favorite in cartoon films, particularly as the wolf in **Viacheslav Kotenochkin**'s hugely successful series *Just Wait!* (Nu, pogodi! 1969–1993).

Papanov was named People's Artist of the USSR in 1973.

Other films: *Aide to His Excellency* (Ad"iutant ego prevoskhoditel'stva, 1970); *Twelve Chairs* (Dvenadtsat' stul'ev, 1977, TV); *Time of Desire* (Vremia zhelanii, 1984).

PARADJANOV [other spellings: Paradzhanov, Parajanov], **SERGEI** [also: Sergo; Russian sources list the patronymic Iosifovich]

(b. 9 January 1924, Tbilisi–d. 20 July 1990, Yerevan). Armenian, Georgian, and Ukrainian director and screenwriter. Paradjanov studied building construction in Tbilisi at the Institute for Railway Engineering from 1942 to 1943 and vocalism at the Tbilisi Conservatory from 1943 to 1944. After moving to Moscow and enrolling in the Soviet State Film School **VGIK** in **Ihor' Savchenko**'s master class, he worked as his teacher's assistant on the large-scale World War II epic *The Third Blow* (Tretii udar, 1948) and the biopic *Taras Shevchenko* (1951).

In 1952, Paradjanov completed his diploma film, the short *A Moldavian Fairy Tale* (Moldavskaia skazka). At Kiev Film Studio (later: **Dovzhenko Film Studio**), he made his feature-length debut, *Andriesh* (1954, codirected by Iakov Bazelyan), the tale of a young shepherd who fights the evil sorcerer Black Whirlwind. In 1957, Paradjanov made three **documentaries** on cultural subjects, among them a portrait of famed Ukrainian actress **Nataliia Uzhvii**. His following film, *The First Guy* (Pervyi paren', 1958), a lighthearted musical **comedy**, tells the love story of a collective farm's Komsomol secretary and a soccer player. *Ukrainian Rhapsody* (Ukrainskaia rapsodiia, 1961) is a melodramatic romance on the backdrop of the Great Patriotic War, while *A Flower on a Stone* (Tsvetok na kamne, 1962) about young miners in the Donbass region features an antireligious slant. Very little in these rather conventional pictures gives an indication of the extraordinary leap forward that took place in Paradjanov's next pictures.

Shadows of Forgotten Ancestors (Tini zabutykh predkiv/Teni zabytykh predkov, 1964), from a 1913 novella by Ukrainian classic Mykhailo Kotsiubynsky, catapulted the director to celebrity status and brought him the reputation of one of the most innovative contemporary filmmakers. This semimythical story of doomed love among two members of the Hutsul people in the Carpathian Mountains boasts an expressive color spectrum and wildly rhythmical camera work. The picture's dark, pessimistic plot is kept deliberately ahistorical; its allusions to the insurmountable power of evil destroying beauty and love through witchcraft and fatal coincidences prove disturbing. *Shadows of Forgotten Ancestors* occupies a unique place in the history of Soviet cinema, marking the rebirth of Ukrainian cinema that shaped a generation of filmmakers—including **Yury**

Il'enko, **Ivan Mykolaichuk**, and **Leonid Osyka**—with a distinct national self-consciousness,.

When the production of Paradjanov's following project, *Kiev Frescoes* (Kievskie freski, 1965) about the contemporary remembrance of World War II, was officially halted, he moved to Armenia where he embarked on *Sayat-Nova* (aka *The Color of Pomegranate* or *The Blood of the Pomegranates*/Nran guyne/Tsvet granata, 1967, released 1969) about the medieval poet Arution Sayadian. A biopic by genre, this highly complex picture is in fact the realization of Paradjanov's own artistic credo in which realistic and parabolic episodes alternate and the plot resembles a loosely assembled patchwork. Achronological and often logic defying, the film's fabric is rich in enigmatic symbols and allusions that are only accessible to viewers familiar with Armenian history and culture. Because of the film's opaque form, administrators on all levels fought against its release; finally, **Sergei Iutkevich** agreed to edit a version that was acceptable to Soviet officials and made a limited distribution possible.

Still considered a powerhouse in Ukraine, Paradjanov was invited to Kiev for a number of projects, among them another adaptation of a Kotsiubynsky story. However, he was reprimanded for a mocking public speech made in Minsk and was prohibited from further working in Ukraine. In December 1974, he was arrested in Kiev, charged with black marketeering and homosexuality, an accusation that already had brought him several months' incarceration in 1947. After three years in prison camps, a personal request from French Communist poet Louis Aragon to Leonid Brezhnev led to Paradjanov's release in December 1977. Another three years later, he was arrested again, this time in Tbilisi on charges of bribing a government official, and spent nine more months in prison.

In 1983, although no longer a member of the Union of Cinematographers, Paradjanov was invited to Georgia on the initiative of **Revaz Chkheidze**. There, he was allowed to make *The Legend of Surami Fortress* (Ambari Suramis tsikhitsa/Legenda o Suramskoi kreposti, 1985, codirected with **David Abashidze**), whose plot is inspired by a folk legend. The film consists of a string of enigmatic episodes featuring silent rituals and static, ornamental shot compositions. However, unlike Paradjanov's previous films, *The Legend of Surami Fortress* carries an affirmative, positive message: the death of a self-sacrificing individual acquires lofty meaning within an allegorical framework. Protected by the might of a fortress in which a young man has been immured, peasants can till the fields and grow grapes—symbol of the eternal survival of the Georgian nation.

Ashik-Kerib (Ashugi Quaribi, 1987), adapted from a poem by Mikhail Lermontov and also codirected with Abashidze, is a fairy tale about a husband who is separated from his wife on their wedding day and has to undergo numerous tribulations before he can return and punish the perpetrators. To a greater extent than even *Legend of Surami Fortress*, this film is carried by the artist's wild, often bizarre imagination. It contains unmistakable allusions to **Andrei Tarkovskii**'s *Andrei Rublev* (1966) as well as to earliest silent cinema with pantomimic acting, interspersed with mysterious artifacts. Like all of Paradjanov's pictures, it is filled with sexual ambivalence situated in a sternly traditional patriarchal framework.

The years of perestroika gave Paradjanov his first chance to see the world. He was a guest of honor at festivals in Berlin, New York, Venice, and Istanbul, among others; his last two films won numerous national and international awards. Suffering from a terminal illness, Paradjanov was unable to embark on his long-cherished project, *Confession* (Ispoved'), which remained unrealized like so many other of his scripts, among them a biopic about Hans Christian Andersen. In 1990, Yury Il'enko, the cameraman on *Shadows of Forgotten Ancestors*, made the grotesque prison tale *Swan Lake: The Zone* (Lebedyne ozero. Zona) from a Paradjanov script, while Leonid Osyka realized *Sketches on Vrubel'* (Etiudy o Vrubele, 1989) about the Russian painter Mikhail Vrubel' (1856–1910) who gained fame with mythological phantasmagorias and spent several years in Kiev.

In the late 1960s and 1970s, Paradjanov acquired the reputation of an uncontrollable maverick, a genius indulging in provocative, unrestrained behavior. His multifaceted talents, especially in the fine arts—he was a master of collage using a motley variety of materials—won him many admirers. Yet Paradjanov's most striking quality was his ability to empathize with national cultures, to sense and enter their deep spiritual and mythological layers. The question whether the mythological elements in his pictures are authentic or rather fruits of the filmmaker's own imagination is open for debate. However, there can be no doubt that Paradjanov's films have given profound impulses to **Ukrainian, Armenian,** and **Georgian cinema,** reflecting and inspiring the search for national identity even under totalitarian conditions. For Paradjanov, whose cinematic vision is that of a free-spirited aesthete, dreamer, and paradoxicalist, cinema was an art that could reach and reveal otherwise invisible mythical depths. Thus, Paradjanov's films are a stand-alone phenomenon not just in Soviet but in world cinema. They reveal an increasing trend toward the static, creating compositions resembling collages rather than moving pictures, a trend that is not only antirealistic, but at times anticinematic. Yet it is also obvious that this creator of unique, never-seen-before images—a cause of fascination to generations of cineastes—was not interested in beautiful games for their own sake but aimed at capturing the aesthetic-spiritual essence of life. The aggressive harassment of this unique artist by Soviet officialdom represents one of the darkest episodes in the history of Soviet cinema.

Paradjanov was honored with the title People's Artist of the Ukrainian SSR in 1990. In 1991, a Paradjanov museum opened its doors in Yerevan.

Other films: *A Ballad* (Dumka, 1957, doc.); *Golden Hands* (Zolotye ruki, 1957, doc.); *Hakob Hovnatanyan* (Akop Ovnatanian, 1967, doc.); *Arabesques on the Theme of Pirosmani* (Arabeski na temu Pirosmani, 1985, doc.).

PARS, HEINO [Russian sources list the first name and patronymic as Kheino Iaakovich] (b. 13 October 1925, Mustla, Viljandimaa). Estonian **animation** director, screenwriter, animator, and cinematographer. Pars studied at Tartu University in 1946–1950. Beginning in 1953, he worked as a camera assistant and cameraman at **Tallinfilm Studio,** particularly on films by the founder of Estonian animation, **Elbert Tuganov,** including *Little Peter's Dream* (Peetrikese Unenägu, 1958).

In 1962, Pars made his debut as animation director with *Little Motor Scooter* (Väike motoroller/Malen'kii motoroller), using stop-motion technology and puppets crafted by the Estonian Puppet Theater. Pars is credited with creating the first animation series in **Estonian cinema;** its central character is "cameraman Kõps." A peculiarity of Pars's films is that many episodes unfold in living nature, for example, in *Cameraman Kops in the Land of Mushrooms* (Operaator Kõps seeneriigis/Operator Kyps v mire gribov, 1964).

Pars achieved international renown with the laconic, humorous *The Nail* (Nael/Gvozd', 1974) and *The Nail II* (Nael II/Gvozd' II, 1981), masterpieces of object animation in which nails act as human beings and feature weaknesses such as disloyalty and alcohol abuse and facing existential situations such as intimacy and death. Other innovative films include *Songs to Spring* (Laulud kevadele/Pesni vesne, 1975), which again combines animated puppets with a live-action background, and the stereoscopic film *When Men Are Singing* (Kui mehed Laulavad/Kogda poiut muzhchiny, 1979).

Pars made his last film in 1990. He was named Merited Artist of the Estonian SSR in 1975.

PASCARU, VASILE [real name Paskar'; Russian sources list first name and patronymic as Vasilii Iakovlevich] (b. 1 January 1937, Vadeni, Belarus–d. 2 October 2004, Chisinau [Kishinev]). Moldovan director and screenwriter. Pascaru studied physics and mathematics at the University of Chisinau in 1955–1958 and briefly worked as an electrician and assistant director at **Moldova-Film Studio**. He then enrolled in the Soviet State Film School **VGIK** where he studied with **Boris Dolin**, graduating in 1965.

Pascaru began his career in Belarus and later directed films in Ukraine, but the main body of his work was made in Moldova. He scored a considerable box-office hit with the adventurous *Marianne* (1967), which is based on the memoirs of journalist Praskovia Didac and describes the fearless pursuits of a female spy behind the frontlines in World War II. Its sequel, *The Risk* (Ruscul/Risk, 1971), which takes place during the Nazi occupation of Poland, was just as popular. The courage and selflessness of simple people in the Great Patriotic War became one of the central themes of Pascaru's films, including *Nobody Replacing You* (Nimeni in locul tau/Nikto vmesto tebia, 1977), about a group of young partisans, and *A Swan Was Swimming in the Pond* (Trecea o lebada pe ape/Lebedi v prudu, 1982), which won critical recognition for its gripping description of a selfless mother of four. The other major theme in Pascaru's career is the establishment of Soviet power in Bessarabia, including the violent collectivization of agriculture, especially in *The Red Blizzard*

(Viforul rosu/Krasnaia metel', 1972) and *Bridges* (Podurile/Mosty, 1974), the chronicle of a village in the 1930s and 1940s. Pascaru's films, always unambiguously pro-Soviet, are effective because of their cleverly built suspense and precisely captured social details.

The Fortress (Cetatea/Krepost', 1979) is the story of a rescue operation for scientists who refuse to cooperate with the Nazis, carried out by the Soviet secret service and Yugoslav partisans. *The Great-Small War* (Bol'shaia–malaia voina, 1981) portrays Soviet military leader Mikhail Frunze and his fight against the troops of anarchist Nestor Makhno. In the early 1980s, Pascaru switched to television, where he helmed a number of miniseries on topics similar to his big-screen pictures. He also directed documentaries.

Pascaru, who joined the Communist Party in 1976, served as first secretary of the Moldovan Filmmakers' Union in 1976–1981. He was named Merited Artist of Moldova in 1994.

Other films: *Little Red Sun* (Soara rasare/Krasno solnyshko, 1972, TV); *Men Go Gray Early* (Barbatii incaruntesc de tineri/Muzhchiny sedeiut rano, 1976); *A Quiet Border Post* (Pichitul linistit, 1985); *Codrii* (1987–1991, TV miniseries).

PELESHYAN, ARTAVAZD [also: Artur; some Russian sources list the patronymic Ashotovich] (b. 22 February [other sources: November] 1938, Leninakan [now: Gyumri]). Armenian **documentary** filmmaker, screenwriter, and film theorist. Peleshyan, who grew up in the town of Kirovakan (now: Vanadzor), studied in the workshop of documentary filmmaker Leonid Kristi (1910–1984) at the Soviet State Film School **VGIK** in 1963–1967.

Beginning with his earliest student films, Peleshyan acquired the reputation of a unique visionary and innovator of cinema. His films blend a carefully crafted sound track with both original footage and newsreels while staying clear of any verbal commentary. The peculiar aesthetic effects are achieved through unusual points of view, unexpected switches in montage rhythm, and sudden frame stops. Peleshyan's art, although dealing with concrete topics and people, reaches beyond common cinematic or political notions, deliberately choosing an approach outside the stylistic mainstream. Thematically, the filmmaker has shown a predilection for strong, selfless, heroic characters such as mountain climbers who prevent avalanches

(*The Mountain Vigil*/Lernayin parek/Gornyi patrul', 1964), shepherds risking their lives to save the livestock (*The Seasons*/Tarva yeghanakner/Vremena goda, 1975), and Soviet cosmonauts (*Our Age*/Mer dare/Nash vek, 1982).

His films, usually about 10 minutes long and, with only one exception, shot in black-and-white, can be described as poetic-philosophical meditations striving for a universal degree of generalization, for example, *People's Earth* (Mardkants yerkire/Zemlia liudei, 1966) or *The Inhabitants* (Obitateli, 1970), about the symbiotic relation between the spheres of animals and humans. *The Beginning* (Skizbe/Nachalo, 1967) is a positive account of the 1917 Bolshevik Revolution, while *We* (Menq/My, 1969) deals with the filmmaker's motherland, Armenia, its past, present, and national mission. *Life* (Kyanq/Zhizn', 1992–1993), Peleshyan's first film in color, describes the birth of a human being and the meaning of this event. Peleshyan's last film to date was released in 1994: *The End* (Verj/Konets).

On a number of projects, Peleshyan worked with cinematographer and director Mikhail Vartanov. He also contributed to **Andrei Mikhalkov-Konchalovskii**'s epic *Siberiade* (Sibiriada, 1979). "Distance montage" is the term that Peleshyan coined in order to pinpoint his artistic method; it also became the title of a programmatic article ("Distantsionnyi montazh," 1974). In 1988, Peleshyan published the book *My Cinema* (Moe kino) in Yerevan. In the mid-1990s, plagued by health problems, Peleshyan withdrew from filmmaking.

Peleshyan was named Merited Artist of the Armenian SSR in 1979 and Merited Artist of Russia in 1995.

Other films: *Autumn Pastoral* (Ashnanayin hovvergutyun/Osenniaia pastoral', 1971, script); *The Star Minute* (Zvezdnaia minuta, 1972, codirected with **Lev Kulidzhanov**); *The Colors of the Autumn Market* (Ashnanayin shukayi guynere/Kraski osennego rynka, 1985, script). *See also* ARMENIAN CINEMA.

PERESTIANI, IVAN NIKOLAEVICH [some Georgian sources list his first name as Ivane] (b. 13 April 1870, Rostov-on-the-Don–d. 14 May 1959, Moscow). Russian-Georgian actor, director, and screenwriter. After finishing gymnasium in 1886, Perestiani entered a moderately successful career as a stage actor and director, touring the country with various troupes. During a chance visit to **Aleksandr**

Khanzhonkov's studio in 1916, **Evgenii Bauer** engaged him on the spot. Perestiani's debut in the melodrama *Coach, Don't Rush the Horses* (Iamshchik, ne goni loshadei, 1916) immediately made him one of the most adored stars of early Russian cinema. Featuring the image of a distinguished, silver-haired gentleman, he played leads and supporting roles for Bauer in *A Life for a Life* (Zhizn' za zhizn', 1916) and *The Revolutionary* (Revoliutsioner, 1917, from Perestiani's own script), for **Vladimir Gardin** in *Satan's Children* (Deti Satany, 1918), for Viacheslav Turzhanskii in *The Shame of the House of Orlov* (Pozor doma Orlovykh, 1918), and many others. He also directed a number of features, among them *Two Hussars* (Dva gusara, 1917), *The Decembrist's Sister* (Sestra dekabrista, 1918), and *In the Days of Thunder* (V dni grozy, 1918).

Following the February Revolution, Perestiani submitted a resolution to the General Assembly of Film Workers on 6 March 1917 that demanded that movies exploiting inflammatory political subjects—such as Grigorii Rasputin or the private life of the Romanovs—should be prohibited. Accepted but largely ignored, the text indicated Perestiani's concern about the quality standards of Russian cinema.

In 1918, Perestiani's opted to stay in the Communist state. He directed pro-Bolshevik *agitka* shorts such as *Father and Son* (Otets i syn, 1919) and *In the Days of Struggle* (V dni bor'by, 1920), and taught at the State Film School. In 1921, Perestiani moved to Georgia, where he had lived before. The film section of the Georgian Commissariat for Enlightenment assigned him to direct its first feature, *Arsena Jiorjashvili* (aka *The Murder of General Griaznov*, 1921) about a mutineer who assassinated a tsarist official in 1905. Made under primitive conditions, the film nonetheless turned out to be a box-office success, and Perestiani was encouraged to adapt important works of Georgian literature for the screen. Thus, *The Suram Fortress* (Suramis tsikhe/Suramskaia krepost', 1923) was based on a story by Davit Chonkadze inspired by an old Georgian legend (many years later, **Sergei Paradjanov** created his own original interpretation of the same legend).

Perestiani's next film became a national and international hit of unexpected proportions. ***The Little Red Devils*** (Tsiteli eshmakunebi/ Krasnye d"iavoliata, 1923), produced without a script from a best-selling story by Pavel Bliakhin (1886–1961), romanticizes the Civil

War in Ukraine. It introduced a new genre, the revolutionary action film. Three juveniles (played by young circus artists) take revenge on the White Army, represented by Nestor Makhno, whose actual historical personality was distorted beyond recognition. The film "manages at the same time to parody and exploit the adventure genre" (Peter Kenez). Perestiani followed it with the more serious historical epic *Three Lives* (Sami sitsotskhle/Tri zhizni, 1924), from Giorgi Tsereteli's celebrated novel, reflecting social transformations in Georgia in the 1880s–1890s.

By the late 1920s, Perestiani's directing career went into decline. Attempts to build upon the triumph of the *Little Red Devils* with similar revolutionary adventure fare—*The Savur Grave* (Savur-mogila), *Illan-Dilli*, *The Crime of Princess Shirvanskaia* (Shirvan-skayas danashauli/Prestuplenie kniazhny Shirvanskoi), and *The Punishment of Princess Shirvanzkaia* (Sasdjeli/Nakazanie kniazhny Shirvanskoi)—were met by critical disdain and diminishing viewer interest. From 1929 to 1932, Perestiani worked in Armenia, where he made *Zamallu* (1930) about a Communist activist, and *Anush* (1931), a drama of love and jealousy ending in murder and revenge, from a poem by Hovhannes Tumanyan.

Perestiani's last directorial effort, *The Outpost* (Forpost, 1941), was a short made at the beginning of the Great Patriotic War. Afterward, he appeared in supporting roles in **Mikheil Chiaureli**'s historical epic *Georgii Zaakadze* (1942–1943) and Konstantin Pipinashvili's *A Poet's Cradle* (Kolybel' poeta, 1947), among others.

Perestiani, one of the founders of **Georgian cinema**, was a solid craftsman with a penchant for spectacular effects. From a political point of view, his films are as naïve as they are stylistically conventional. The fact that Perestiani had discovered a gold mine with his legendary *Little Red Devils* became obvious when in 1966 **Edmond Keosayan** remade it under the title *The Uncatcheable Avengers* (Neulovimye mstiteli, 1966), later adding two equally successful sequels.

In 1935, Perestiani was awarded a prestigious personal pension. He was named People's Artist of the Georgian SSR in 1949. His memoirs are a valuable source on early Russian cinema.

Other films: (as actor) *The Tale of Spring Wind* (Skazka vesennego vetra, 1918); *Arsen* (Arsena Jorjashvili, 1937); (as director) *Man Is Man's Enemy* (Katsi katsistvis mgelia, 1923); *The Case of Tariel*

Mklavadze's Murder (Tariel Mklavadzis mkvlelobis saqme/Delo ob ubiistve Tariela Mklavadze, 1925); *Nest of Wasps* (Krazanas bude/ Dvunogie, 1927); *In the Quagmire* (Gaplangva/V triasine, 1928); *Two Friends* (Ovi megotavi/Dva druga, 1937, short).

PEREVERZEV, IVAN FEDOROVICH (b. 3 September 1914, village Kuz'minki, Orlovo district–d. 23 April 1978, Moscow). Russian actor. Pereverzev, who hailed from a peasant family, moved to Moscow in his youth and became a metalworker before enrolling in the studio school of the Theater of the Revolution, whose troupe he joined in 1938.

Pereverzev's film debut was an episodic part in **Aleksandr Macheret**'s contemporary **comedy** *The Private Life of Petr Vinogradov* (aka *Peter Vinogradov*/Chastnaia zhizn' Petra Vinogradova, 1935). The actor gained wide popularity with the role of Grisha in **Vladimir Korsh-Sablin**'s entertaining *My Love* (Moia liubov', 1940). Tall, handsome, and athletic, Pereverzev became one of the characteristic faces of Stalinist cinema, playing strong-willed superheroes—predominantly Red Army officers—in **Ihor' Savchenko**'s *Ivan Nikulin—A Russian Sailor* (Ivan Nikulin—russkii matros, 1944) and *The Third Blow* (Tretii udar, 1948), **Leonid Lukov**'s *It Happened in the Donbass* (Eto bylo v Donbasse, 1946), **Abram Room**'s *Court of Honor* (Sud chesti, 1948), and **Iulii Raizman**'s *Cavalier of the Golden Star* (aka *Dream of a Cossack*/Kavaler zolotoi zvezdy, 1950), among others. In 1952, the actor won a Stalin Prize for a supporting role in Savchenko's swan song, *Taras Shevchenko* (1951). **Mikhail Romm** cast him as pioneering naval strategist Fedor Ushakov (1744–1817) in his patriotic dilogy *Admiral Ushakov* and *Ships Attack the Bastions* (aka *Attack from the Sea*/Korabli shturmuiut bastiony, 1953).

In post-Stalin years, Pereverzev maintained his star status and managed to continue his career seamlessly. He appeared in fairy tale and fantasy (**Aleksandr Ptushko**'s *Sadko*, 1953), contemporary drama (Raizman's *A Lesson in Life*/Urok zhizni, 1955; **Iosif Kheifits**'s *My Dear Man*, aka *The Cause We Serve*/Dorogoi moi chelovek, 1958; and **Vladimir Basov**'s *Battle Underway*/Bitva v puti, 1961), and monumental chronicles of the Great Patriotic War (**Iurii Ozerov**'s *Liberation* [Osvobozhdenie, 1970–1972]).

Pereverzev, a member of the Communist Party since 1953, was named People's Artist of the Russian Federation in 1966 and of the USSR in 1975.

Other films: *Heroes of Shipka* (Geroi Shipki, 1955); *Meet Baluev* (Znakom'tes'—Baluev, 1963); *Angel's Day* (Den' angela, 1967); *A Purely English Murder* (Chisto angliiskoe ubiistvo, 1974).

PETRENKO, ALEKSEI VASIL'EVICH (b. 26 March 1938, village Chemer, Chernigov district, Ukraine). Ukrainian-Russian actor. Petrenko studied at the Theater Institute of Khar'kiv, graduating in 1961. He worked for various theaters in Ukraine before joining the troupe of Lensovet Theater in Leningrad in 1964. In 1978, he became a member of the Moscow Art Theater (MKhAT).

Petrenko made his film debut with the role of a black marketeer in the **children's film** *A Day of Sun and Rain* (Den' solntsa i dozhdia, 1968). His screen career started in earnest when **Grigorii Kozintsev** cast him as Oswald in his *King Lear* (Korol' Lir, 1970). **Elem Klimov** then gave Petrenko the plum part of infamous monk Grigorii Rasputin in *Agony* (aka *Rasputin*/Agoniia, 1975, released 1985), in which the actor's expressive power came out in full for the first time. This performance represented a novelty in Soviet cinema and raised eyebrows nationally and internationally with its air of sinister obsession and scenes of suddenly erupting irrationality and violence.

Petrenko's appearance in **Dinara Asanova**'s *Private Key* (Kliuch bez prava peredachi, 1977), in which he portrayed a school headmaster, proved that he was capable of psychological subtlety and self-control. The actor created fine portraits of Peter the Great in **Aleksandr Mitta**'s *The Tale of How Tsar Peter Married His Moor* (Skaz pro to, kak tsar' Petr arapa zhenil, 1976), of an air force officer in **Aleksei German**'s *Twenty Days without War* (Dvadtsat' dnei bez voiny, 1977), and, with chilling power, of Iosif Stalin in **Iurii Kara**'s *Balthazar's Feasts, or A Night with Stalin* (Piry Valtasara, ili Noch' so Stalinym, 1990). In some roles, Petrenko's habit to push the emotional expression over the top resulted in less persuasive performances, for example, as a street artist in the social parable *Agape* (1996) or as an "ultra-Russian" general in **Nikita Mikhalkov**'s patriotic megashow *The Barber of Siberia* (Sibirskii tsiriul'nik, 1999), a role that won him a State Prize of Russia. Less spectacular but more harrowingly intense, realistic impersonations are his portrayal of writer Iurii Kazakov in *Listen, Is It Not Raining . . .* (Poslushai, ne idet li dozhd' . . . , 1999), and as General Ivolgin in **Vladimir Bortko**'s Fedor Dostoevskii adaptation *The Idiot* (Idiot, 2003, TV).

Petrenko was named People's Artist of the RSFSR in 1988.

Other films: *Farewell* (Proshchanie, 1981); *Day of Wrath* (Den' gneva, 1985); *The Servant* (Sluga, 1989); *Not by Bread Alone* (Ne khlebom edinym, 2005); *Doktor Zhivago* (2005, TV); *The House on the Embankment* (Dom na naberezhnoi, 2007, TV).

PETROV, VLADIMIR MIKHAILOVICH (b. 22 July 1896, St. Petersburg–d. 7 January 1966, Moscow). Russian director and screenwriter. Petrov studied law at the University of St. Petersburg and was simultaneously enrolled in the School of the Aleksandrinskii Theater. During World War I, he attended the Odessa officers' school and later fought at the front. Petrov's acting career began on the stage of the Lesnoi Zimnii Teatr in Petrograd in 1917. In 1918, he was permitted to go to England, where he worked in Gordon Craig's company both as an actor and director. Upon returning to Russia in 1920, he studied in **Viacheslav Viskovskii**'s cinema school. Beginning in 1925, Petrov worked as assistant director at Sevzapkino studio in Leningrad on **Grigorii Kozintsev** and **Leonid Trauberg**'s *The Overcoat* (Shinel', 1926), among others.

As a director, Petrov initially made a name for himself with **children's movies**: *Golden Honey* (Zolotoi med, 1928, codirected by Nikolai Beresnev [1893–1965]), which addresses the problem of juvenile delinquency and uses real street children as actors; *Joy and Buddy* (Dzhoi i druzhok, 1928, codirected by M. Khukhunashvili); *Lenin's Address* (aka *Children of the New Day*/Adres Lenina, 1929), which tells the story of a Young Pioneer community and was praised by the commissar of enlightenment, **Anatolii Lunacharskii**; and *Fritz Bauer* (1930), about German working-class kids helping their parents in their daily political struggle. *The Dam* (Plotina, 1931) revealed Petrov's increasing interest in visual expressiveness. *The Fugitive* (Beglets, 1932), his first sound film, tells the story of a German Communist activist who uses his volunteer appearance in court as a propaganda vehicle.

The Thunderstorm (Groza, 1934), an adaptation of Aleksandr Ostrovskii's famous 1859 play, brought the director national and international fame. Petrov deliberately chose actors from the Moscow Art Theater (MKhAT) for all major parts and created a gallery of psychological portraits that gave the protagonists an unprecedented chance to bring their art to the screen. At the same time, the picture was conceived in a sufficiently cinematic style, achieving an organic unity of visual and audial elements. Group compositions in a variety of long shots—some resembling canvases of the 19th-century *Peredvizhniki* painters—are interspersed with dramatically lit close shots. The overall effect, an authentic depiction of Russia's depressing merchants' milieu, was staggering.

Over the following three decades, Petrov kept alternating overt political assignments with classical adaptations, among them another Ostrovskii adaptation, *Guilty without Guilt* (Bez viny vinovatye, 1945), the greatest box-office hit of the year, honored with a First-Class Stalin Prize. The monumental two-part biopic *Peter the First* (aka *Peter the Great*/Petr Pervyi, 1937–1939) proved that Petrov could also shoulder a big-budget epic, combining expertly staged battle scenes with tense personal drama. A loose adaptation of Aleksei Tolstoi's novel, the film interprets Peter as political reformer and benevolent autocrat who inflicts pain on his people because he means well—an exact reflection of Iosif Stalin's image of himself. Apart from its underlying statist concept, Petrov's *Peter* was also the first to signal Soviet society's turn from internationalist to patriotic values, which at times could override the previously dominating class-based view of history. As usual, Petrov cast top-notch performers even in supporting roles; however, it fell upon **Nikolai Simonov** to create the tsar's canonical film persona with verve, pathos, and humor, defining the modernizer's and nation-builder's image for millions of viewers.

At the outbreak of the Great Patriotic War, Petrov made a short about the Civil War hero Vasilii Chapaev, derived from the **Vasil'ev brothers'** blockbuster (*Chapaev Is with Us*/Chapaev s nami, 1941). After an adventure movie shot for **Gruziya-Film Studio**, *The Elusive Jan* (Neulovimyi Ian, 1943, codirected by **Isidor Annenskii**), and a Chekhov comedy, *The Jubilee* (Iubilei, 1944), Petrov directed *Kutuzov* (1944), a monumental historical epic about the field marshal under whose command Russia defeated Napoleon; the film won a

Stalin Prize in 1946. *Kutuzov* mainly focuses on aspects of military strategizing, that is, the leader's point of view. This tendency toward deindividualization of "the masses" in favor of a leader grew even stronger in the 1949 three-hour, elephantine *Battle of Stalingrad* (Stalingradskaia bitva; its first part was released in the United States as *The First Front*, the second as *The Victors and the Vanquished*). Although its style is visibly inspired by newsreels and the director had more army units at his disposal than any filmmaker before him, numerous historical facts are distorted according to Stalin's instructions (the film won Petrov his fourth Stalin Prize).

Following a color **comedy** about soccer players (*Sporting Honor/* Sportivnaia chest', 1951), Petrov returned to form in a fine adaptation of *The Inspector General* (Revizor, 1952), preserving the original's theatrical effects and eliciting first-rate performances from his stars. Yet, in the last decade of his career, Petrov seemed to lose touch with audiences. None of the literary adaptations he delivered—*The Duel* (Poedinok, 1957) based on a story by Aleksandr Kuprin, *On the Eve* (Nakanune, 1959) adapted from an Ivan Turgenev novel, and *The Russian Forest* (Russkii les, 1964) from Leonid Leonov's 1953 ecological epic—found large audiences or critical appreciation.

In Russian and Soviet film history, Petrov occupies an isolated place. He never belonged to any particular group or school and seemed uninterested in discussing theoretical aspects of filmmaking. A highly cultured and erudite artist, Petrov conveys in his films an original image of the Russian past dominated by grim and dark tones, softened only by deft humor and the innate kindness of people. The director's political position seems to have been one of enlightened, promodern, authoritarian nationalism. However, what attracted viewers—if not critics and scholars—were the gripping stories that Petrov told so impressively, centered on exquisite ensembles of actors.

Petrov was named People's Artist of the Soviet Union in 1950.

Other films: *Three Hundred Years Ago* (Trista rokiv tomu . . . , 1956).

PICHUL, VASILII VLADIMIROVICH (b. 15 June 1961, Zhdanov [Mariupol']). Russian director and screenwriter. Pichul studied with **Marlen Khutsiev** at the Soviet State Film School **VGIK**, graduating in 1983.

With his big-screen debut, *Little Vera* (Malen'kaia Vera, 1988), Pichul delivered the right film for the right moment. The story of a rank-and-file provincial family and its everyday plights—alcoholism, generational estrangement, lack of purpose—exposes the reality of life in Communism like no other film before. Pichul's sober precision in diagnosing the state of affairs in Soviet society came at a point when it had already lost its "little faith" in self-reformation. Indeed, much to audiences' shock and chagrin, the director presented them with a mirror image that defied reformation. Thus, *Little Vera* anticipated the sad fiasco of the perestroika experiment when its proponents were yet unaware of it. The picture's harsh realism remained unmatched in Soviet and post-Soviet cinema. Pichul's ability to re-create on the screen the authentic atmosphere of Soviet normalcy bore a genuine promise, and the film's style—quasi documentary, with dominating handheld camera and diegetic sound—might have carried many other films, serving as a valuable barometer of this society's evolution for years to come.

But when the sensation caused by his rigorous, disillusioned realism had subsided, Pichul's artistic ambition moved in the direction of satire and hyperbole. As his independently produced **comedy** *In the City of Sochi, the Nights Are Dark* (V gorode Sochi temnye nochi, 1989) shows, such a change led to a loss in human interest and viewers' interest as well. This holds even more true of *Dreams of an Idiot* (Mechty idiota, 1993), an adaptation of Il'ia Il'f and Evgenii Petrov's cult novel *The Golden Calf* (Zolotoi telenok). The film takes the absurdness of the *homo sovieticus* and his lifestyle to the extreme, deliberately deromanticizing the canonical text but also stripping it of all charm and leaving the viewer befuddled and confused.

Pichul, who had already gained some television experience after graduation, went on to direct the popular series *Marionettes* (Kukly, 1994–1998), which poked fun at post-Communist politicians, pointing to their stupidity and corruption. In the late 1990s, he switched to **documentaries** in which it was his declared goal to go against all political taboos.

Pichul is married to screenwriter Mariia Khmelik.

Other films: *Mitia's Love* (Mitina liubov', 1981, short); *I Want to Tell You* (Khochu tebe skazat', 1985, TV); *Old Songs about the Main*

Thing III (Starye pesni o glavnom 3, 1998, TV); *The Diamond-Filled Sky* (Nebo v almazakh/Un ciel parsemé de diamants, 1999, Russia/France); *The Film Festival* (Kinofestival', 2007).

PILIKHINA, MARGARITA MIKHAILOVNA (b. 30 June 1926–d. 13 March 1975, Moscow). Russian cinematographer. Pilikhina studied at the Soviet State Film School **VGIK** under **Boris Volchek**, graduating in 1950. Already in her first pictures she proved to be remarkably flexible in adjusting to a variety of directorial styles, while noticeably enriching the films' visual expressiveness. Thus, her camera work in Ajdar Ibragimov's Nazim Hikmet adaptation *Two from One District* (Dvoe iz odnogo kvartala, 1957) has been described as neorealist, while the austere, lucidly structured black-and-white compositions in **Mark Donskoi**'s superb Maksim Gor'kii adaptation *Foma Gordeev* (1959) convey epic breadth and classical simplicity. The originality of Pilikhina's artistic contribution to this film is corroborated by the fact that Donskoi's subsequent output lacks such high visual quality.

Pilikhina's best-remembered achievement is **Marlen Khutsiev**'s *I Am Twenty* (Mne dvadtsat' let, 1965), where her vivid, quasi-documentary manner captures the emotional turmoil of the young, post-Stalinist generation, rendering atmospherically rich images of Moscow's interiors and exteriors. In **Igor' Talankin**'s *Day Stars* (Dnevnye zvezdy, 1966/69), Pilikhina creates visions of solemn beauty and tragic depth, using an original, associative color principle that corresponds with the film's underlying philosophical concept. Her last work, which she also directed, was the ballet film *Anna Karenina*—a daring, unique interpretation of Lev Tolstoi's novel starring Maia Plisetskaia and Aleksandr Godunov, supported by the inventive shot compositions, psychological usage of color, and daring viewpoints that are generally characteristic of this cinematographer.

Pilikhina, who joined the Communist Party in 1956, was named Merited Artist of the RSFSR in 1965. She taught at VGIK, beginning in 1959.

Other films: *Night Guard* (Nochnoi patrul', 1957, with Vasilii Dul'tsev); Chaikovskii (1970); *Matters of the Heart* (Dela serdechnye, 1974).

PIRMUKHAMEDOV [other sources: Pir-Mukhamedov], **RAKHIM** (b. 1 January 1897, Tashkent–d. 16 February 1972, Tashkent). Uzbek actor. Pirmukhamedov began his acting career in 1918. He worked in various Uzbek theaters—Samarkand, Namangan, and the Karl Marx Theater in Tashkent—and organized theater groups in Tashkent in 1923–1927. He then studied at the Uzbek Drama Studio in Moscow, graduating in 1930, and joined the troupe of the Hamza Theater in Tashkent.

Pirmukhamedov was primarily a screen actor who quickly gained a reputation as one of the most versatile and prolific artists in **Uzbek cinema**, with roles ranging from dramatic to comedic. He made his debut playing the leader of a gang of *basmachi* (organized opponents of the Soviet order who were declared criminals by the Bolsheviks), Kurbashi Akramkhan, in the political thriller *The Jackals of Ravat* (Shakaly Ravata, 1927). In Oleg Frelikh's *The Covered Van* (Krytyi furgon, 1927) he was cast in a similarly negative role, the rich Jurabai.

In the mid-1930s, when **Uzbekfilm Studio** prepared its first sound film, Pirmukhamedov was one of the acting teachers in the newly established local studio school. In the finished picture, *The Oath* (Kliatva, aka Ia ne predatel', 1937), he was cast as the militia man Rakhim. Pirmukhamedov revealed his talent for eccentric **comedy** as the emir's guard in **Iakov Protazanov**'s *Nasreddin in Bukhara* (Nasreddin v Bukhare, 1943). He again played a guard, although this time as part of a tragic Romeo-and-Juliet plot, in one of the most beautiful Uzbek films, **Nabi Ganiev**'s *Tahir and Zukhra* (1945). Ganiev then entrusted Pirmukhamedov with a lead in his inventive *Nasreddin's Adventures* (Pokhozhdeniia Nasreddina, 1947), where he portrayed Nasreddin's loyal albeit morally ambiguous companion, a thief named "Beardless." Among Pirmukhamedov's later performances, the part of Abdul-Malik in **Kamil Yarmatov**'s biopic *Alisher Navoi* (1948), the henpecked husband Arslan in **Shukhrat Abbasov**'s successful comedy *The Entire Makhalia Is Talking about This* (Ob etom govorit vsia makhallia, 1961), and a lead in **Ali Khamraev**'s poetic *White, White Storks* (Belye, belye aisty, 1966) are worth mentioning.

Pirmukhamedov, who joined the Communist Party in 1945, was honored with the title People's Artist of the USSR in 1967.

Other films: *From under the Vaults of the Mosque* (Iz-pod svodov mecheti, 1928); *Avicenna* (1957); *The Sons Go Further* (Synov'ia idut dal'she, 1959); *Hamza* (1961); *Poem of Two Hearts* (Poema dvukh serdets, 1968).

PIROSMANI (1969). **Gruziya-Film Studio**. 87 min., color. Directed by **Giorgi Shengelaia**. Script: Erlam Akhvlediani, Giorgi Shengelaia. Cinematography: Konstantin Apriatin. Music: Vakhtang Kukhianidze. Cast: Avtandil Varazi, **David Abashidze**, Zurab Kapianidze, Maria Gvaramadze, Boris Cipuria, Givi Alexandria. Premiere: February 1972.

The self-taught painter Nikoz Pirosmanishvili (1862–1918), although born into a wealthy family, embarks on a life as a social outcast, relentlessly pursuing his aesthetic ideal and creating a naïve, spiritual, humble universe in tune with the ancient rural culture of his native land. Despite an increasing number of admirers, Pirosmani never manages to build a career for himself; he remains poor and often pays for his meals by painting the walls of the inn where he is staying. The urban artistic establishment begins to recognize Pirosmani's works as genuine art, while the painter, haunted by alcoholism, escapes into a world of imagination. *See also* GEORGIAN CINEMA.

PLIATT, ROSTISLAV IANOVICH (b. 13 December 1908, Rostov-on-the-Don–d. 30 June 1989, Moscow). Russian actor. Pliatt studied with influential theater director Iurii Zavadskii (1894–1977) at the studio school of Vakhtangov Theater, graduating in 1928, and remained in his teacher's troupe after its relocation to Rostov-on-the-Don (1936–1938). He returned to this theater after stints at Lenkom (1938–1941) and Moscow Drama Theater (1941–1943), following its transformation into Mossovet Theater in 1943.

Pliatt's film debut as an unmarried geologist in **Tat'iana Lukashevich**'s seminal **comedy *The Foundling*** (Podkidysh, 1939) made him a star, respected by critics and adored by millions of viewers for his ability to convey genuine intelligence, decency, and helpless naïveté. Together with legendary comedienne **Faina Ranevskaia**, he poured some life into **Grigorii Aleksandrov**'s rather uninspired comedy *Spring* (Vsena, 1947), portraying—against type—the ruthless careerist Bubentsov.

Mikhail Romm recognized the enormous artistic potential in Pliatt and cast him in supporting roles in *The Dream* (Mechta, 1941–1943) and *Murder on Dante Street* (Ubiistvo na ulitse Dante, 1956). Memorable episodic appearances remained the actor's forte, for example, in **Il'ia Frez**'s benevolent children's tales *The Elephant and the Little Rope* (Slon i verevochka, 1946) and *The First-Grade Girl* (Pervoklassnitsa, 1948). Often enough, mediocre fare—including Cold War espionage flicks and television thrillers—profited from Pliatt's artistry. One of his better achievements in this genre is his portrayal of courageous, anti-Nazi pastor Schlag in **Tat'iana Lioznova**'s television cult series *Seventeen Moments of Spring* (Semnadtsat' mgnovenii vesny, 1973). **Marlen Khutsiev** offered the actor a late triumph in his microdrama *The Afterword* (Posleslovie, 1984) in which Pliatt portrays an aged father-in-law who is left one-on-one with his daughter's pragmatic, rationalist husband. Overall, Pliatt's screen persona was defined by soft irony and a kindhearted intellectualism, implying a certain resistance to the common anti-intellectual attitudes of the 1930s–1950s.

Pliatt was honored with the title People's Artist of the USSR in 1961. He won a USSR State Prize in 1982 for his stage work. The actor is buried at Novodevich'e Cemetery; the Moscow house in which he lived (Bronnaia ulitsa 2/6) carries a memorial plaque.

Other films: *Conspiracy of the Doomed* (Zagovor obrechennykh, 1950); *The Bridegroom from the Otherworld* (Zhenikh s togo sveta, 1958); *I'm Going toward the Thunderstorm* (Idu na grozu, 1964); *Visiting the Minotaur* (Vizit k minotavru, 1987, TV).

PLOTNIKOV, NIKOLAI SERGEEVICH (b. 5 November 1897, Viaz'ma–d. 5 February 1979, Moscow). Russian actor. After two years on the stage of Viaz'ma People's Theater (1920–1922), Plotnikov studied in the studio school of the Moscow Art Theater (MKhAT) in 1922–1926. In 1938, he became a member of Moscow Vakhtangov Theater.

Beginning in the early 1930s, Plotnikov regularly appeared in Soviet movies as a scene-stealing supporting actor who imbued his characters with sly wit and optimism. One of his memorable roles is the naïve idealist Edgar Oppenheim in **Grigorii Roshal'**'s *The Oppenheim Family* (Sem'ia Oppengeim, 1938), a film that Plotnikov also codirected. After several parts in Stalinist epics, one of which—the worker Ermilov in **Mikheil Chiaureli**'s *The Oath* (Kliatva, 1946)—won him a Stalin Prize in 1947, Plotnikov prominently reappeared in the 1960s as a bold, cranky, but optimistic old man obsessed by socially useful ideas: as the selfless physicist Professor Sintsov in **Mikhail Romm**'s *Nine Days of a Year* (Deviat' dnei odnogo goda, 1962) and as Professor Nitochkin in **Iulii Raizman**'s *Your Contemporary* (Tvoi sovremennik, 1968), for which he won a Best Actor award in Karlovy Vary. Plotnikov was famous for the thorough, conscientious preparation of even the smallest roles; the intensity of his performances is immediately noticeable on screen. He was also a successful acting teacher at the Soviet State Film School **VGIK** and at **Mosfilm Studio**.

Plotnikov joined the Communist Party in 1954; he was named People's Artist of the USSR in 1966.

Other films: *Lenin in 1918* (1936); *Marite* (1947); *Musorgskii* (1950); *The Prologue* (Prolog, 1956); *The Seagull* (Chaika, 1970).

PODNIEKS, JŪRIS (b. 5 December 1950, Riga–d. 23 June 1992, Lake Zvirgzdu). Latvian director, cinematographer, and scriptwriter. Podnieks, whose father Boriss Podnieks was on the staff of **Riga Film Studio**, began as an assistant cameraman at that studio in 1967 and studied cinematography as an extern at the Soviet State Film School **VGIK**, graduating in 1975. In the 1970s and 1980s, he became one of the most valued Latvian cameramen, contributing to numerous **documentaries**, popular science films, and newsreels.

As documentary director, Podnieks developed a peculiar style of indirect narration, achieving powerful effects through imagery and music and avoiding verbal commentary. He won national prizes with *Constellation of Riflemen* (aka *Under the Sign of Sagittarius*, Sozvezdie strelkov 1982), a group portrait of former Latvian snipers who had played a major role in the 1917 Bolshevik Revolution. *Sisyphus Is Rolling the Stone* (Vel Sīzifs akmeni/Katit Sizif kamen', 1985) tells about nonconformist sculptors boldly searching for new ways of artistic expression. Podnieks also made films about actress **Vija Artmane** (1980) and pop singer Alla Pugacheva (1982).

After he filmed a rock concert in July 1985, the resulting footage became the core of the most famous Soviet documentary of the decade, the feature-length *Is It Easy to Be Young?* (Vai viegli but jaunam?/Legko li byt' molodym? 1986). Although not intended as a taboo-breaking sensation, and rather quiet and reflective in tone, the film turned out to be the right picture at the right moment, a crucial cultural event of perestroika that attracted millions of viewers in the USSR and worldwide. With Podnieks's typical blend of confessional interviews, revealing details, emotionally gripping music, and the conspicuous absence of voiceover narration, the film opened viewers' eyes to the existential frustration of the young in the USSR, a generation shockingly antisocial, artistically sensitive, and immune to all attempts of brainwashing.

The worldwide respect that Podnieks won with his nonjudgmental honesty and ability to expose the essence of social phenomena legitimized him as a chronicler of the Soviet Union's disintegration. In his five-part *We* (aka *Hello, Do You Hear Us?* aka *Soviets*, 1990), coproduced with British television companies, the director visualized the dangerous fragility of the Communist system by connecting a long line of critical hot spots such as Chernobyl and Armenia. After founding his own studio in 1990, Podnieks made the moving *Homeland* about the three Baltic nations Latvia, Lithuania, and Estonia as they were rediscovering and reclaiming their long-suppressed cultures.

Podnieks witnessed—and filmed—the gruesome deaths of his close collaborators **Andris Slapiņš** and Gvido Zvaigzne (1958–1991) on 24 January 1991 at the hand of snipers, a scene that became part of *Homeland: PostScript*. The filmmaker's own untimely death in a diving accident put an abrupt end to his exceptional career. The Jūris Podnieks Studio in Riga continues to produce documentaries and features.

Other films: *The Brothers Kokar*s (Brāļy Kokari/Brat'ia Kokary, 1978); *Commander* (Komandieris/Komandir, 1984).

POLIKUSHKA (1919). Rus' studio. 51 min., b/w. Directed by **Aleksandr Sanin**. Script: Valentin Turkin, **Fedor Otsep**, Nikolai Efros from Lev Tolstoi's 1862 story. Cinematography: **Iurii Zheliabuzhskii**. Cast: Ivan Moskvin, Vera Pashennaia, Evgeniia Raevskaia, Varvara Bulgakova, Sergei Aidarov, Dmitrii Gundurov, Varvara Massalitinova. Premiere: 23 October 1922.

The peasant Polikei, called Polikushka (Moskvin), is a poor serf and also a drunkard and ne'er-do-well with numerous children, respected by neither his wife, Akulina (Pashennaia), nor anyone else. One day, he is sent to the city by his female owner (Raevskaia) to fetch a large sum of money. On his way home, while Polikushka is asleep and dreaming, he loses the envelope with the money that had been stored in his hat. When Polikushka realizes what has happened, he hangs himself. His little son, left alone with no one to watch over him, drowns. During the funeral of the two, a group of merry people drives by—they are the lucky finders of the envelope with the money.

POLOKA, GENNADII IVANOVICH (b. 15 July 1930, Kuibyshev). Russian director, scriptwriter, actor, and producer. After graduating from the Moscow Shchepkin Theater Institute in 1951, Poloka enrolled in the Soviet State Film School **VGIK** where he studied with **Lev Kuleshov** and **Aleksandra Khokhlova**, graduating in 1957.

Poloka's directorial debut was a **documentary**, *Our Guests from Faraway Countries* (Nashi gosti iz dalekikh stran, 1957). His first full-length feature, *Kapron Nets* (Kapronovye seti, codirected with Levan Shengeliia), was released in 1963. The popular youth film *Republic of SHKID* (Respublika ShKID, 1966) offers a greatly romanticized view of a 1920s school for juvenile delinquents and the efforts of a humanist teacher to imbue students with ethical and cultural values, invoking the name of Fedor Dostoevskii. Poloka's subsequent attempt to challenge stereotypes of the Bolshevik Revolution and depict events in a manner blending pathos and farce in *The Intervention* (Interventsiia, 1967) caused an uproar. He was prevented from completing the picture, the footage was shelved, and the film could only be finished and released 20 years later, during perestroika. Poloka followed this traumatic experience with a thriller fully in compliance with the official political parameters, *One of Us* (Odin iz nas, 1971), about courageous secret service agents on the eve of the Great Patriotic War; it proved a hit at the box office. *One Time One* (Odinazhdy odin, 1975) tells the story of a man and his various marriages in a comedic tone.

Poloka often was the target of censorial harassment and as a result switched studios a number of times; more than other directors, he benefited from the liberalization in the mid-1980s. However, he retained a peculiar nostalgic loyalty toward the Soviet lifestyle and Communist values, as demonstrated in *Was There a Karotin at All?* (A byl li Karotin? 1989), a mildly satirical detective story set in the paranoid 1930s. The charming *Return of the Battleship* (Vozvrashchenie bronenostsa, 1996) is a three-hour long, tongue-in-cheek fictitious reconstruction of **Sergei Eizenshtein**'s work on *Battleship Potemkin*, evoking the carnivalesque atmosphere in 1920s Odessa.

Poloka has been in charge of a directing workshop at VGIK since 1988. He was named People's Artist of Russia in 1998.

Other films: *Our Calling* (Nashe prizvanie, 1981, TV; first shown 1986).

POLONSKII, VITOL'D AL'FONSOVICH (b. 1879, Moscow–d. 5 January 1919). Russian actor. Polonskii studied acting at the Moscow Theater College, graduating in 1907. He then joined the troupe of the prestigious Malyi Theater, where he stayed until 1916.

Polonskii made his screen debut in **Petr Chardynin**'s Lev Tolstoi adaptation *Natasha Rostova* (1915), a compilation of episodes from *War and Peace* with him portraying Prince Andrei Bolkonskii. After roles in *The Brothers Boris and Gleb* (Brat'ia Boris i Gleb, 1915) and *Irina Kirsanova* (1915), he had two major hits: **Evgenii Bauer**'s Ivan Turgenev adaptations *Song of Triumphant Love* (Pesn' liubvi torzhestvuiushchei, 1915) and *After Death* (Posle smerti, 1915). The role of Prince Bartinskii, a bankrupt aristocrat who decides to marry a rich woman, in Bauer's *A Life for a Life* (Zhizn' za zhizn', 1916) best defined Polonskii's screen persona: elegant, graceful, and sentimental, an image that he also conveyed in several other Bauer films such as *The Bliss of Eternal Night* (Schast'e vechnoi nochi, 1915). Along with **Vera Kholodnaia** and **Vladimir Maksimov**, Polonskii was part of the stellar cast in Chardynin's mega-hit *By the Fireplace* (U kamina, 1917) and its sequel, *Forget the Fireplace—Its Flames Are Dead* (Pozabud' pro kamin, v nem ugasli ogni, 1917). Polonskii's characters often display a certain gentleness; thus, the civil servant Lanin in the *Fireplace* dilogy accepts his wife's infidelity with the aristocrat Pecherskii, whom he finally meets at her grave. In *Queen of the Screen* (Koroleva ekrana, 1916), Polonskii's character Antek Galsen, a screenwriter who churns out faddish scripts catering to low tastes, comes to an understanding of his superficial ways. Polonskii was the male lead, pianist Vitol'd Dal'k, in Viacheslav Turzhanskii's *The Lord's Ball* (Bal Gospoden', aka K bogu na bal, 1918), from a song by Aleksandr Vertinskii.

The actor died of typhoid fever. His daughter, Veronika Polons-kaia (1909–?), was a theater and film actress who became famous as Vladimir Maiakovskii's last love.

Other films: *Shadows of Sin* (Teni grekha, 1915); *The Dying Swan* (Umiraiushchii lebed', 1917); *Hush, Sadness . . . Hush . . .* (Mol-chi, grust' . . . molchi . . ., 1918); *The God of Revenge* (Bog mesti, 1918).

POPOV, ANDREI ALEKSEEVICH (b. 12 April 1918, Kostroma–d. 10 June 1983, Moscow). Russian actor. Popov was born into the family of well-known theater director and scholar Aleksei Popov (1892–1961). He studied at the acting school of the Theater of the So-viet Army in Moscow and joined its troupe after graduation in 1939. From 1963 to 1973, he was the executive director of that theater. In 1974, he joined the Moscow Art Theater (MKhAT).

Popov's film debut was the role of Mikolas in **Vera Stroeva**'s World War II drama *Marite* (1947) about a young Lithuanian resis-tance martyr. Subsequently he played under leading Soviet directors: a supporting role in **Grigorii Roshal'**'s *Musorgskii* (1950) and the title role in *Rimskii-Korsakov* (1952), in **Mikheil Chiaureli**'s *The Unforgettable Year 1919* (Nezabyvaemyi 1919yi god, 1952), and in **Mikhail Kalatozov**'s *Hostile Whirlwinds* (Vikhri vrazhdebnye, 1953/1956). He was outstanding in two Shakespeare adaptations: as Jago in **Sergei Iutkevich**'s *Othello* (1956) and as Petrucchio in Ser-gei Kolosov's *Taming of the Shrew* (Ukroshchenie stroptivoi, 1961). Because of Popov's ability to believably convey aristocratic ennui and cultured melancholy, several filmmakers cast him in adaptations of 19th-century Russian classics, including **Vladimir Petrov** in *The Duel* (Poedinok, 1957), from Aleksandr Kuprin's story, and **Iosif Kheifits** in *In the Town of S.* (V gorode S., 1967), in which Popov impersonates Anton Chekhov as the film's narrator. One of his most memorable performances was the male lead in **Igor' Talankin**'s *Daytime Stars* (Dnevnye zvezdy, 1966–1969), oscillating between soft-spoken humanism and dignified intellectual resignation. **Nikita**

Mikhalkov cast Popov to great effect as the dense but loyal servant Zakhar in his Ivan Goncharov adaptation *Oblomov* (Neskol'ko dnei iz zhizni I.I. Oblomova, 1979).

Popov, who joined the Communist Party in 1946, received a Stalin Prize in 1950 and was named People's Artist of the USSR in 1965. He held a professorship at the State Institute for Stage Arts (GITIS) after 1973.

Other films: *The Composer Glinka* (aka *Man of Music*/Kompozitor Glinka, 1952); *The Swedish Matchstick* (Shvedskaia spichka, 1954); *A Gentle Creature* (Krotkaia, 1960); *All Remains to the People* (aka *Legacy*/Vse ostaetsia liudiam, 1963).

PREOBRAZHENSKAIA, OL'GA IVANOVNA (b. 24 July 1881 [other sources: 1884], Moscow–d. 31 October 1971, Moscow). Russian actress and director. A student of Konstantin Stanislavskii, Preobrazhenskaia was a member of the studio of the Moscow Art Theater (MKhAT) in 1905–1906, after which she worked on provincial stages until 1913. Her first film role was that of Mania El'tsova in **Iakov Protazanov** and **Vladimir Gardin**'s erotic blockbuster *Keys to Happiness* (Kliuchi schast'ia, 1913), from Anastasia Verbitskaia's risqué best-seller. Preobrazhenskaia quickly became a star of Russian silent cinema, mostly appearing in prestigious adaptations of Russian classics: as Liza in *Nest of the Gentry* (Dvorianskoe gnezdo, 1914) and Elena in *On the Eve* (Nakanune, 1915), both based on Ivan Turgenev novels, and as the title heroine in *Anna Karenina* (1914) and as Natasha Rostova in *War and Peace* (Voina i mir, 1915), two Lev Tolstoi adaptations. Preobrazhenskaia then codirected the Aleksandr Pushkin adaptation *Lady Peasant* (Baryshnia-krest'ianka, 1915, with Gardin). Her first independent project as director was *Viktoria* (1917), based on a Knut Hamsun novel.

After the Bolshevik Revolution, Preobrazhenskaia founded a workshop for film actors as part of the State Film School in 1919 and was among the first filmmakers to join the Bolshevik Moscow Film Committee. She began to direct **children's films** that were moderately budgeted but critically and commercially successful. *Fedka's Truth* (Fed'kina pravda, 1926), the tragic story of a poor boy in pre-Bolshevik time who sacrifices his life for a drowning rich kid, caused controversies because of its harsh naturalism. The Anton

Chekhov adaptation *Kashtanka* (1927) was also made for young audiences, while the circus film *The Last Attraction* (Poslednii attraktsion, 1929), based on a story by Marietta Shaginian, pleased viewers of all ages.

Upon marrying director **Ivan Pravov**, Preobrazhenskaia helmed several pictures jointly with her husband, some featuring adventurous plots, others focusing on social problems. Best remembered is their *Peasant Women of Riazan'* (Baby riazanskie, 1927), which re-creates the situation in the Russian countryside prior to 1917. The story of young Anna who is raped and impregnated by her own father-in-law and later drowns herself after her husband's return from World War I, impressed audiences by its gritty authenticity and genuine respect for the peasant characters. However, Soviet critics were less endeared by the filmmakers' overall acceptance of the patriarchal milieu. The film—"this best example of Russian rural exotica" (Leyda)—enjoyed such immense success nationally and worldwide (with a budget of 46,000 rubles, it grossed 210,000 rubles within little more than a year) that inventor **Aleksandr Shorin** produced a partial sound track for it in 1929, securing its continuing distribution into the 1930s.

And Quiet Flows the Don (Tikhii Don, 1930), based on the first volume of Mikhail Sholokhov's Civil War epic—not yet finished at the time—continues the exploration of Russia's rural life. The adaptation, in which Sholokhov participated as a consultant, focuses on the love between Grigorii Melekhov and Aksin'ia. Like *Peasant Women of Riazan'*, *And Quiet Flows the Don* became an international hit and was also provided with a sound track in Paris in 1932.

Preobrazhenskaia's following picture, *Enemies' Paths* (Vrazh'i tropy, 1934), based on I. Shukhov's novel *Hatred*, is a drama on the backdrop of collectivization in Kazakhstan; it marked the beginning of the hard-to-explain decline in Preobrazhenskaia's career. At the height of her fame—she was awarded the title Merited Artist of the Russian Federation in 1935—Preobrazhenskaia turned to a legendary figure, *Stepan Razin* (1939), leader of a 17th-century peasant upheaval. Scripted by Aleksandr Chaplygin after his own novel, the film, sadly, shows all the features of Stalinist historical lore, with simple peasants discussing the class essence of their activities and pointing toward a happier future.

Preobrazhenskaia, the first Russian female director and one of the founders of Soviet cinema for children, taught at the State Film School (Goskinoshkola, later **VGIK**) from 1927 to 1941. *Peasant Women of Riazan'* has been called "one of the greatest and most beautiful films that has been made," combining "construction, beauty and dramatic power together with beautiful photography" (Bryher).

Other films: (as actress) *The Garnet Bracelet* (Granatovyi braslet, 1915); (as director) *Ania* (1927); *Bright City* (Svetlyi gorod, 1928); *One Joy* (Odna radost', 1933); *Prairie Station* (1941); *A Lad from the Taiga* (Paren' iz taigi, 1944).

PRISONER OF THE CAUCASUS, THE (aka *Prisoner of the Mountains*/Kavkazskii plennik, 1996). Karavan Productions. 96 min., color. Directed by **Sergei Bodrov**. Script: Arif Aliev, Sergei Bodrov, Boris Giller, from Lev Tolstoi's story (uncredited). Cinematography: **Pavel Lebeshev**. Music: Leonid Desiatnikov. Cast: **Oleg Men'shikov, Sergei Bodrov Jr.**, Susanna Mekhralieva, Djamal Sikharulidze, Aleksei Zharkov, Aleksandr Bureev, Valentina Fedotova.

The newly drafted Ivan Zhilin (Bodrov) and the experienced ensign Aleksandr Larin (Men'shikov) are stationed in a remote region of the Caucasus that has been shattered by an ongoing conflict between the Russian Army and the local Muslim population. When their armored vehicle is attacked, Zhilin and Larin are taken hostage so that old Abdul Murad (Sikharulidze) can exchange them for his son held in prison. But Abdul's son is shot during an escape attempt; in turn, Larin is killed after his and Zhilin's failed escape during which Larin had killed two locals. Abdul Murad's teenage daughter Dina (Mekhralieva) implores her father not to shoot Ivan. He is set free and witnesses how Russian helicopters attack the village.

PROKOF'EV [Prokofiev]**, SERGEI SERGEEVICH** (b. 23 April 1891, Sontsovka estate, Ekaterinoslav province–d. 5 March 1953, Moscow). Russian composer. The son of an agricultural specialist and a highly cultured mother who provided their offspring with an early, intensive education in music, Sergei studied with Reingol'd Glièr as a child and began to compose operas and chamber music under his guidance. From 1904–1914, he studied at St. Petersburg Conservatory under Nikolai Rimskii-Korsakov and Anatolii Liadov, among others. Upon graduation, Prokof'ev toured Western Europe as a pianist and lived there in 1918–1932, occasionally visiting Soviet Russia for concerts.

After permanently settling in the USSR in 1933, the already world-famous composer agreed to score **Aleksandr Faintsimmer**'s anti-tsarist satire *Lieutenant Kizhe* (aka *The Czar Wants to Sleep*/Poruchik Kizhe, 1934) from a story by Iurii Tynianov. The music was recorded at Belgoskino Studio in Leningrad (the later **Belarusfilm Studio**) and conducted by **Isaak Dunaevskii**, who shortly thereafter made his own debut as a film composer. Prokof'ev's keen sense of rhythm and colorful instrumentation were ideally suited to match grotesque visual exaggerations; the film music revealed this composer's rare gift of fully empathizing with the underlying aesthetic concept of a moving picture.

In 1938, **Sergei Eizenshtein** approached Prokof'ev with the proposal to write the score for his 13th-century epic *Aleksandr Nevskii*. The artistic partnership between director and composer proved one of unique mutual comprehension and yielded some of the most perfectly scored episodes in film history. Prokof'ev decided to not emulate period music but to create a sound that would evoke medieval atmosphere in the modern mind, that is, quasi-historical music. While the Teutonic knights are characterized by soulless, dull tunes of trumpets and horns, the Russian defenders of the motherland are accompanied by soft, romantic melodies. The "Battle on the Ice" culminates in a fast, overjoyed frenzy, and Prince Aleksandr's final speech boasts a musical commentary of proud triumph and patriotic pathos. The complementarity of shot composition, montage, actors' movements, and music achieved a degree of perfection previously unseen in cinema, which led some critics to define the picture as a "filmed opera."

During the Great Patriotic War, Prokof'ev and his family were evacuated to Nal'chik and then Tbilisi, Georgia. He contributed a score to **Ihor' Savchenko**'s war movie *Partisans in the Ukrainian Steppes* (Partizany v stepiakh Ukrainy, 1942) and, in 1943, again worked with Faintsimmer on *Kotovskii*, a Civil War potboiler about the legendary Red Army commander. He also wrote the music for the biopic *Lermontov* by Al'bert Gendel'shtein (1906–1981). Alas, none of these pictures left a mark in film history.

However, Prokof'ev's next—and final—effort in film music proved to be of lasting grandeur. For Eizenshtein's prestige film *Ivan the Terrible* (Ivan Groznyi, 1943–1945), he composed a hauntingly beautiful and disturbingly complex score, equally convincing in its first part (1945) in which the idea of centralized Russian statehood triumphs, and the second (released 1958), which depicts the psychological and moral disintegration of the tyrant with frightening precision. Intensely involved in the recording process, Prokof'ev tried to achieve specific sound effects, going far beyond mere musical techniques; thus, he used an early form of multiple-microphone recording.

Similar to **Dmitrii Shostakovich**, Prokof'ev later transformed his film scores into other pieces—for example, the *Nevskii* score became a cantata. Moreover, numerous film directors eventually used Prokof'ev's music in their pictures, among them Pier Paolo Pasolini in *The Gospel According to St. Matthews* (Il Vangelo Secondo Matteo, 1964) or Woody Allen in *Love and Death* (1975), the latter score derived from *Lieutenant Kizhe* and *Aleksandr Nevskii.* Prokof'ev's ballets *Romeo and Juliet* (1936) and *Cinderella* (1944) were repeatedly turned into films, as was the children's opera *Peter and the Wolf.*

Prokof'ev received a Stalin Prize for his music for *Ivan the Terrible* in 1946 (of altogether six Stalin Prizes in his career); he was awarded the title People's Artist of the RSFSR in 1947. The composer is buried at Novodevich'e cemetery in Moscow.

PROTAZANOV, IAKOV ALEKSANDROVICH (b. 4 February 1881, Moscow–d. 8 August 1945, Moscow). Russian director and screenwriter. Protazanov was born into a cultured merchant family with a lively interest in literature and theater. After finishing the Moscow Commercial School in 1900, he worked as a salesman. An inheritance allowed him to travel to France and Italy in 1904 to broaden his education. Upon returning to Russia in 1907, Protazanov was hired by the short-lived film company Gloria as an interpreter; he also learned the intricacies of filmmaking, gaining experience as a screenwriter and assistant director. His first accepted screenplay was the Aleksandr Pushkin adaptation *The Fountain of Bakhchissarai* (Bakhchisaraiskii fontan, 1909), directed by **Vasilii Goncharov**. Protazanov also played a supporting part, the Polish envoy Garaburda, in Goncharov's sensational *Death of Ivan the Terrible* (Smert' Ioanna Groznogo, 1909).

In 1911, Protazanov began to work for Gaumont's former representative Paul Thiemann and his companion, F. Reinhardt. His first independently directed film, *The Prisoner's Song* (Pesn' katorzhanina, 1911), was a commercial success. In 1912, Protazanov cooperated with famous writer Leonid Andreev on the script for *Anfisa*. Another Protazanov film caused a veritable sensation—*The Departure of a Grand Old Man* (Ukhod velikogo startsa, 1912), a surprisingly authentic chronicle of the turbulent last months of Lev Tolstoi's life. However, Tolstoi's family asked for the film not to be released, and Thiemann acquiesced. Some sources claim that the film's withdrawal was due to a court order; ultimately, it was successfully released abroad.

Protazanov soon developed a reputation as one of the most versatile and reliable Russian filmmakers who managed to churn out up to a dozen features per year. Even when following profitable trends—for example, with the melodramatic potboiler *Keys to Happiness* (Kliuchi schast'ia, 1913, codirected with **Vladimir Gardin**)—he turned in respectable fare that helped increase cinema's overall standing in Russia. But despite the wide variety of genres in which Protazanov excelled, it was literary adaptations whose inherent challenge inspired him the most, including ***War and Peace*** (Voina i mir, 1915, codirected with Gardin) from Tolstoi, *Nikolai Stavrogin* (1915) from Fedor Dostoevskii's *The Demons*, *The Queen of Spades* (Pikovaia dama, 1916) from Aleksandr Pushkin's short story, and ***Father Sergius*** (Otets Sergii, 1918), based on a late Tolstoi novella and, by general consensus, the greatest artistic achievement of pre-Soviet silent cinema.

Protazanov also demonstrated an interest in mysticism, for example, in *Satan Triumphant* (Satana likuiushchii, 1917), thematizing the interference of supernatural evil leading decent people astray. In 1917, he joined **Iosif Ermol'ev**'s company. There, he helmed films with openly leftist tendencies such as *Andrei Kozhukhov*, based on a novel by terrorist Sergei Stepniak-Kravchinskii. The following year, as a member of Ermol'ev's entourage, Protazanov fled from the Bolsheviks to the Crimea, continuing to film along the way. Thus, *The*

Queen's Secret (Taina korolevy) was begun in Moscow and finished in 1919 in Yalta. In 1920, aboard a British ship, he went with the company to Constantinople and later to France, where he appeared in credits as Jacques or Jacob Protozanoff. After several successful French pictures he accompanied Ermol'ev to Germany and made *Love's Pilgrimage* (Der Liebe Pilgerfahrt) for Universum Film AG (UFA), among others.

In 1923, while in Berlin, Protazanov was approached with an offer to return to Russia under favorable conditions and to work for the newly formed joint venture **Mezhrabpomfilm Studio**. He accepted the offer and was provided with unprecedented funds for the lavish, naïvely pro-Communist utopia *Aelita* (aka *Revolt of the Robots*, 1924). Protazanov used constructivist set designs but interspersed the pompous, quasi-Marxist Mars episodes with impressively atmospheric scenes from neobourgeois Moscow. (Andrew Horton pointed out that *Aelita* influenced Fritz Lang's *Metropolis* and **Andrei Tarkovskii**'s later approach to science fiction, in which philosophical and ethical questions dominate technical aspects.)

His Call (Ego prizyv, 1925), referring to Vladimir Lenin's legacy, proved that Protazanov intended to continue directing pro-Soviet films and that his return was not just a temporary flirtation with the new power. His professional skills were particularly valued during the 1920s, the period of the New Economic Policy (NEP), which allowed for some thematic and aesthetic diversity and rewarded commercially successful productions. Viewed as a bourgeois relic by the avant-garde, the unperturbed Protazanov directed popular **comedies** such as *The Tailor from Torzhok* (Zakroishchik iz Torzhka, 1925) and melodramas, including *The Forty-first* (Sorok-pervyi, 1926), from a story by Boris Lavrenev. The crudely antireligious *Holiday of St. Iorgen* (aka *St. Jorgen's Day*/Prazdnik sviatogo Iorgena, 1929)—sheer cinematic blasphemy to some and a valid critique of shameless hypocrisy and moneymaking by the Church to others—became a superhit; it was provided with a sound track in 1935.

Tommy (aka *Siberian Patrol*, 1931), Protazanov's first sound film, was based on episodes from Vsevolod Ivanov's play *Armored Train 14-69* and tells the story of a British POW who converts to Communism. Protazanov's most famous sound picture sensitively reflects the neoclassical turn in Soviet culture: *The Dowerless Bride* (aka *Without Dowry*/Bespridannitsa, 1936) from a play by 19th-century classic Aleksandr Ostrovskii, which "has a film life outside its dependence on a well-known play" (Leyda). Among Protazanov's later efforts, *Savalat Iulaev* (aka *Eagle of the Steppe*, 1940) about the Bashkir liberation struggle, and *Nasreddin in Bukhara* (Nasreddin v Bukhare, 1943), a colorful, witty rogue tale made during evacuation at the Tashkent studio (later: **Uzbekfilm Studio**), are worth mentioning. The director died during the preparations for another Ostrovskii adaptation, *Wolves and Sheep* (Volki i ovtsy).

Protazanov can be called Russian cinema's "man for all seasons" who weathered numerous political storms while maintaining his keen sense for the taste of large audiences and his ability to satisfy changing cultural needs. The director readily agreed to political compromises before and after the Bolshevik Revolution and displayed no independent, or even minimally consistent, worldview. Yet Protazanov possessed a profound respect for the viewer and in his best pictures put formal brilliance in perfect balance with commercial considerations. Neither elitist nor avant-gardist, Protazanov defined Russian cinema's quality mainstream and became its lifelong representative. Moreover, deliberately or unintentionally, he upheld the primacy of Russian classical literature within the arts, neutralizing cinema's attempts at emancipation and effectively supporting the anti–avant-garde "rollback" tendencies of the 1930s.

Protazanov's personality and directorial methods are surrounded by legends that were enhanced by the filmmaker's well-known discretion. Thus, he was admired and feared for his enormous efficiency—French studio workers called him "Jacques le Terrible." On the set, he always wore white gloves, and, in order to determine the rhythms of actors' movements, used a conductor's baton while shooting.

Protazanov was honored with the titles Merited Artist of the Russian Federation in 1935 and Merited Artist of the Uzbek SSR in 1943.

Other films: *How the Child's Soul Cried* (Kak rydala dusha rebenka, 1913); *Drama on the Telephone* (Drama u telefona, 1914); *For a Night of Love* (Pour Une Nuit d'Amour, 1923); *The Three Million Case* (aka *Three Thieves*/Protsess o trekh millionakh, 1926); *The Man from the Restaurant* (Chelovek iz restorana, 1927); *Don Diego and Pelageia* (Don Diego i Pelageia, 1928); *Marionettes* (Marionetki, 1934).

PTUSHKO, ALEKSANDR LUKICH (b. 19 April 1900, Lugansk–d. 6 March 1973, Moscow). Ukrainian-Russian director, screenwriter, painter, sculptor, and designer. According to Ptushko's own account, it was his mother who made a lasting impact on his perceptiveness and imagination by telling him countless fairy tales in his childhood. In 1923, he moved to Moscow, studying at the Plekhanov Institute of National Economy, while simultaneously supporting himself as a newspaper correspondent, actor, and set designer for the stage. In 1927, Ptushko began to design and build puppets. As early as 1928, he directed a series of **animated** shorts centered on one character, Bratishkin, whom Ptushko initially had created for Iurii Merkulov's *Bratishkin's Adventures* (Prikliucheniia Bratishkina, 1928): *Incident at the Stadium* (Sluchai na stadione, 1928), *One Hundred Adventures* (Sto prikliuchenii, 1929), and *Cinema to the Countryside!* (Kino v derevniu! 1930).

In 1932, Ptushko made his first stop-motion sound film, *The Master of Daily Life* (Vlastelin byta). Then, for over three years he pursued a project of unprecedented dimensions: ***The New Gulliver*** (Novyi Gulliver, 1935), the world's first feature-length stop-motion picture, boasting 1,500 puppets combined with live actors and numerous special effects. **Grigorii Roshal'**'s script had significantly modified Jonathan Swift's novel, yet the crude Marxist message could not diminish the film's charm for audiences worldwide. Its extraordinary national and international success—Charlie Chaplin was among the admirers—paid off: Ptushko was among the first Soviet directors to be honored with the title Merited Artist of the Russian Federation in 1935. Other animated pictures followed: *The Tale of the Fisherman and the Fish* (Skazka o rybake i rybke, 1937, short), *Jolly Musicians* (Veselye muzykanty, 1938, short), and the full-length *The Golden Key* (Zolotoi kliuchik, 1939), an adaptation of Aleksei Tolstoi's Pinocchio variation in which the special effects were perfected further. At the same time, Ptushko created new special effects for such non-animated crowd-pleasers as **Vladimir Vainshtok**'s *The Children of Captain Grant* (Deti kapitana Granta, 1936).

By the late 1930s, Ptushko had made a name for himself as the most accomplished technical innovator of Soviet cinema, named the "Red Méliès" or "Soviet Walt Disney." During World War II, he was responsible for the special effects in battle scenes of such films as **Aleksandr Stolper**'s *A Guy from Our Town* (Paren' iz nashego goroda, 1942), while also supporting his family as a shoemaker. In 1944, he was temporarily put in charge of Soiuzmultfilm studio.

The most prolific phase of Ptushko's career started in 1945 when he abandoned stop-motion animation and fully devoted himself to the live-action adaptation of fairy tales and legends. His first effort made a splash at Cannes in 1946 because of its rich spectrum of colors inspired by Russian folk art. *The Stone Flower* (Kamennyi tsvetok, 1946), shot partly in Prague on Agfa material, was an adaptation of the Ural fairy tales of Pavel Bazhov (1879–1950) and a genuine feast for the eye; it won Ptushko a First-Class Stalin Prize. *Sadko* (1952) received a Silver Lion at the Venice Film Festival in 1953 and became one of the greatest box-office hits in the Soviet Union. In 1956, Ptushko helmed the first Soviet wide-screen picture with stereo sound, the epic *Il'ia Muromets* (aka *The Sword and the Dragon*), which uses the new format to maximum effect, especially in gigantic battles between peaceful Russians and evil "Tugars," as well as panoramic landscape shots. Noteworthy, too, was the film's inherent antityranny message and delightful satirical overtones that tempered the sometimes heavy-handed patriotic rhetoric. *Sampo* (1959, codirected with Risto Orko), another larger-than-life project, based on the Finnish national epic *Kalevala*, was coproduced with Finland. *Crimson Sails* (Alye parusa, 1962), a somewhat sugary tale of true love and the necessity of relentlessly pursuing one's dream, was adapted from Aleksandr Grin's sentimental classic and became a huge success. In *The Tale of Lost Time* (Skazka o poteriannom vremeni, 1964)—based on Evgenii Shvarts's play—Ptushko demonstrated his penchant for satire. As a member of the creative group Youth (Iunost', a branch of **Mosfilm Studio**), Ptushko declared that his pictures were meant both for children and adults; indeed, numerous puns and satirical details in all of his films work better for perceptive, educated grown-ups.

Ptushko's penultimate project, *The Tale of Tsar Saltan* (Skazka o tsare Saltane, 1966), adapted from Aleksandr Pushkin's timeless fairy-tale poem, is one of the most pure and picturesque films of Russian cinema. *Ruslan and Liudmila* (1972), also adapted from a Pushkin narrative poem, became Ptushko's swan song. In both of these delightful pictures, not only did the filmmaker leave the integrity of the original Pushkin verse untouched—he allowed their rhythm to determine the cinematic narration as a whole.

Ptushko taught at the Soviet State Film School **VGIK** from 1932 to 1949 as an "acting chairman" of the Arts Department. During those years, he wrote a number of monographs on technical aspects of cinema.

Because of the genre designation as "**children's films**," Ptushko's creative uniqueness remained insufficiently recognized by contemporary critics. While his technical wizardry was valued and appreciated by colleagues, the stylistic consistency and epic grandeur that distinguish Ptushko's overall output from the majority of comparable works received hardly any notice. This neglect finally changed in the 1990s when increased Western esteem for technical innovation and special effects forced Russians to take another look at their own masters, whose achievements had somehow been taken for granted. As a matter of fact, Western directors and critics were the first to express their high regard for Ptushko's oeuvre. Sadly though, in the 1950s and 1960s, Ptushko's films had been "adapted" in the United States beyond recognition in such shameful acts of butchery as *The Magic Voyage of Sinbad* (from *Sadko*) and *The Day the Earth Froze* (from *Sampo*). Today, the originals have been restored laboriously and released on pristine DVD editions, bringing late justice to one of Russian cinema's unsurpassed original creators.

Ptushko was awarded the title People's Artist of the USSR in 1969.

Other films: *The Coded Document* (Shifrovannyi dokument, 1928); *Three Encounters* (Tri vstrechi, 1948, codirected with **Sergei Iutkevich** and **Vsevolod Pudovkin**).

PUDOVKIN, VSEVOLOD ILLARIONOVICH (b. 28 February 1893, Penza–d. 30 June 1953, Dubolty, Latvia). Russian director, screenwriter, actor, and film theorist. Born into the family of a well-to-do traveling salesman, Pudovkin pursued a natural science degree in the Department of Physics and Mathematics at Moscow University. Before graduating, he volunteered as an artillery soldier in World War I and was injured and taken prisoner by German troops in 1915. In a POW camp in Germany, Pudovkin staged plays and experienced lifesaving international solidarity, a value he upheld throughout his life.

Upon returning to Russia in 1918, Pudovkin worked as a chemist. In 1920, profoundly impressed by D. W. Griffith's *Intolerance*, he enrolled in the State Film School—the later **VGIK**—where he studied with the traditionalist **Vladimir Gardin** and contributed to important projects of his teacher, especially *Hammer and Sickle* (Serp i molot, 1921). In this feature-length *agitka*, Pudovkin played one of the leads, Andrei Krasnov, who undergoes an evolution from a kulak's farmhand to factory worker, ending up as a soldier in the Red Army and active Bolshevik. According to various film historians, he brought to the part an authenticity that was unusual in early Soviet cinema (he had made his acting debut in **Ivan Perestiani**'s *In the Days of Struggle*/V dni bor'by, 1920).

In 1922, Pudovkin joined **Lev Kuleshov**'s workshop, where he encountered a new approach to the cinematic crafts while continuing to write screenplays, acting, directing, editing, and designing sets. In Kuleshov's *The Extraordinary Adventures of Mr. West in the Land of the Bolsheviks* (Neobychainye prikliucheniia mistera Vesta v strane bol'shevikov, 1924), Pudovkin portrayed the devious criminal Zhban ("the Count") with satirical poignancy and visible enjoyment. In 1925, Pudovkin left the Kuleshov workshop and joined Mezhrabpom-Rus' studio (later: **Mezhrabpomfilm Studio**). His first attempt to creatively apply Kuleshov's innovative montage theories was the short *Chess Fever* (Shakhmatnaia goriachka, 1925), a lighthearted, clownesque sketch, blending **documentary** footage and staged scenes that starred many of Pudovkin's fellow budding filmmakers in episodic roles. But neither this cinematic joke nor the educational *Mechanics of the Brain* (Mekhanika golovnogo mozga, 1926), a popular explanation of physiologist Ivan Pavlov's theories, gave any indication of the filmmaker's subsequent sensational breakthrough.

The Mother (Mat', 1926), an adaptation of Maksim Gor'kii's 1906 novel, was produced from **Natan Zarkhi**'s first-rate script and filmed by cinematographer **Anatolii Golovnia**, two artistic partners who would accompany Pudovkin's career for years to come. In *The Mother*, for the first time, Pudovkin openly challenged Kuleshov's nonpsychological concept of cinema acting that called for an extreme simplification and reduction of expressive elements. Instead, the director hired actors steeped in the Stanislavskii method that was abhorred by Soviet film avant-gardists. Unlike **Sergei Eizenshtein**, Pudovkin concentrated on the personality of individual characters, not social "types" or a "collective hero"; unlike **Dziga Vertov**, he believed in fictitious emotional stories and pathos-filled gestures, moving in a direction profoundly different from Kuleshov's cinema where the experiment as such was the primary purpose while ideology and catharsis were nonessential side effects. *The Mother* made Pudovkin world famous, and his two subsequent pictures solidified his position; all three were aimed first and foremost at achieving a deep catharsis in the viewer. Still, each of Pudovkin's individual stories was intended for ideological and political extrapolation. Thus, Nilovna, the deprived title heroine, stood for all exploited women; the young peasant ("the lad") in *The End of St. Petersburg* (Konets Sankt Peterburga, 1927) for the entire peasant class; and the Mongolian shepherd Bair in *The Heir of Chenghiz Khan* (aka *Storm over Asia*/Potomok Chingiz-khana, 1928) for the oppressed peoples of the developing world.

Pudovkin enriched the possibilities of montage by centering on psychologically sophisticated acting and emotionally charged close-ups, nature and architecture metaphors, and lyrical similes. Thus, if Eizenshtein's artistic method can be defined as analytical, Pudovkin's tends toward the synthetic. The most perfect balance between an individual case and historical generalization is arguably achieved in *The End of St. Petersburg*, whose initial title was *Petersburg-Petrograd-Leningrad*. A chronicle of Russia from before World War I to 1917, it is interwoven with the portrait of an individual and the two social classes of which he is part—the peasantry and the proletariat.

Pudovkin's loosely connected trilogy marks the artistic peak of his career. The primacy of the human consciousness conveyed in these films represents a deeply humanistic fundament: it is not the revolution that transforms peoples' minds but life experiences that gradually transform their consciousness and in turn lead to revolution.

Pudovkin's last silent picture was the controversial *A Common Case* (aka *Life Is Beautiful*/Prostoi sluchai, 1932), based on a so-called emotional script by **Aleksandr Rzheshevskii** that was originally entitled *Life Is Very Good* (Ochen' khorosho zhivetsia, 1930).

The story of a Red Army commander who returns from the front and falls in love with a petit-bourgeois girl, betraying his wife (and Civil War comrade) as well as his Communist principles, was meant as an antiphilistine warning. However, Pudovkin's attempts to further develop film language by using slow motion and other innovations made the film incomprehensible to regular viewers and suspicious to the ever-stiffening cultural bureaucracy.

Similar to most Soviet avant-gardists, the transition to sound film was a tormenting, complex experience for Pudovkin. He armed himself with theories, demanding that the level of artistry that was reached in silent cinema not be sacrificed for the elementary technical innovation of a sound track. However, when testing his own theses about asynchronic sound in *The Deserter* (Dezertir, 1933), the story of a German worker who attempts to stay in the exploitation-free USSR, the result seemed awkward and arbitrary and once again alienated audiences. This partial failure threw the filmmaker into a lingering crisis, worsened by a severe car accident in 1935 that killed Zarkhi and left Pudovkin—the driver—injured.

When in the late 1930s the Soviet establishment turned away from proletarian internationalism and integrated Russian nationalism as a pillar into its official ideological arsenal, Russian history had to be interpreted from a patriotic point of view. Like Eizenshtein, and in accordance with official Party guidelines, Pudovkin was encouraged to try his hand at historical subject matter with the focus on great personalities. Abandoning formal experimentation almost completely, Pudovkin helmed *Minin and Pozharskii* (Minin i Pozharskii, 1939) and *Suvorov* (aka *General Suvorov*, 1941), illustrating the Russian struggle against Polish invaders in the 17th century and the early stages of the war against Napoleon, respectively. According to film historian Oksana Bulgakowa, the latter film was inspired by Iosif Stalin's pre-1941 doctrine that the coming war would be fought on foreign territory—which made Suvorov, whose celebrated victories took place in Italy and Switzerland, the hero of the day. Both pictures were popular with audiences and won the director his first Stalin Prize in 1941. *Suvorov* is also remarkable for its lead, Nikolai Cherkasov-Sergeev (1884–1944), who embodies the legendary strategist as a quasi-Chapaevian flamboyant leader, father to his soldiers and unafraid of tsars or courtiers.

In 1941, Pudovkin reacted to the outbreak of the war with the short *Feast in Zhirmunka* (Pir v Zhirmunke, 1941), a contribution to War Film Almanac #6, which praises the superiority of the Russian people over the German aggressors because of their ability to sacrifice themselves. He followed with a surprisingly lucid adaptation of Bertolt Brecht's *Fear and Misery of the Third Reich* (Furcht und Elend des Dritten Reiches), entitled *Murderers Are on Their Way* (Ubiitsy vykhodiat na dorogu, 1942, codirected with **Iurii Tarich**). The picture, breathtakingly modern in its analysis of the inner workings of a totalitarian society, turned out deeply subversive rather than patriotic and was never released. *Admiral Nakhimov* (1946), another commissioned biopic about a military leader famed for the defense of Sevastopol during the Russian-Turkish war, was first criticized for "historical inaccuracies," then, after numerous changes, rewarded with a Stalin Prize. Finally, *Zhukovskii* (1951) seemed to give the director a chance to return to his beginnings—science and technology—but the life of the founder of Russian aerodynamics turned out to be a lackluster experience both for the filmmaker and audiences. Overall, Pudovkin's biopics meant several steps back from the artistic achievements of the 1920s and today are of mere historical interest.

The Return of Vasilii Bortnikov (aka *Vasili's Return*/Vozvrashchenie Vasiliia Bortnikova, 1953), Pudovkin's last picture, literally marked a return to contemporary problems and is sometimes seen as a predecessor to the Thaw period. Given the filmmaker's energy and sincerity and indicators such as *Murderers Are on Their Way*, Pudovkin may well have surprised his contemporaries with truly innovative dramas of consciousness had his life not been cut short by a heart attack.

Throughout his career, Pudovkin never completely abandoned acting; he obviously found enormous joy in the craft, which shows even in minuscule episodic roles. Thus, he played the lead, Fedor Protasov, in **Fedor Otsep**'s successful Lev Tolstoi adaptation *The Living Corpse* (Zhivoi trup, 1928), sadistic officers in his own *The Mother* and *In the Name of the Motherland* (Vo imia Rodiny, 1943, codirected by P. Vasil'ev) and in **Grigorii Kozintsev**'s *Young Fritz/* Iunyi Frits, 1943), as well as a holy fool in Eizenshstein's *Ivan the Terrible* (Ivan Groznyi, 1943–1945), among others.

Pudovkin's legacy includes a number of articles and monographs on practical and theoretical aspects of cinema, among them *The Film Director and the Film Material* (Kinorezhisser i kinomaterial, 1926), several of which were translated into English. Never a theoretical risk taker or flamboyant aesthetic explorer as was Eizenshtein, Pudovkin's texts are less speculative and more empirical in nature and abound with practical, helpful observations.

Pudovkin joined the Communist Party in 1939. He was named People's Artist of the USSR in 1948. In 1924, Pudovkin married actress Anna Zemtsova (1893–1966), also known under her pseudonym Anna Li. He is buried at Novodevich'e cemetery in Moscow. The house in which he lived (Povarskaia ulitsa 29/31) carries a memorial plaque; in 1961, a Moscow street was named after him.

Other films: (as actor) *Hunger . . . Hunger . . . Hunger* (Golod . . . golod . . . golod, 1921); *Locksmith and Chancellor* (Slesar' i kantsler, 1923); *The Ray of Death* (Luch smerti, 1925); (as director) *Victory* (Pobeda, aka Samyi schastlivyi, 1938); *Three Encounters* (Tri vstrechi, 1948, omnibus film with **Sergei Iutkevich** and **Aleksandr Ptushko**).

PYR'EV, IVAN ALEKSANDROVICH (b. 17 November 1901, Kamen'-na-Obi, Altai district–d. 7 February 1968, Moscow). Russian director and screenwriter. Pyr'ev grew up in a Siberian peasant family, was drafted in 1916, and served in the tsar's army during World War I, where he was awarded several medals. In the ensuing Civil War, he joined the Red Army as a propaganda officer. After being discharged in 1920, he studied at the State Experimental Theater Workshops (GEKTEMAS), graduating in 1923. Pyr'ev then was an actor at the First Workers' Theater of the Proletarian Culture organization (Proletkul't), appearing in **Sergei Eizenshtein**'s production of *The Mexican*, and also worked in Vsevolod Meierkhol'd's troupe. The lessons in eccentric, clownesque acting learned in those years would later serve him well, both in his **comedies** and in real-life situations, as numerous memoirs confirm.

In 1925, Pyr'ev started his movie career, first as assistant director to **Iurii Tarich** on period pieces such as *Wings of a Serf* (Kryl'ia kholopa, 1926) and *Bulat Batyr* (1928). He also coauthored a number of screenplays, for example, *Torn-off Sleeves* (Otorvannye rukava, 1928) and *Turner Alekseev* (Tokar' Alekseev, 1931).

An Alien Woman (Postoronniaia zhenshchina, 1929), based on a script by **Nikolai Erdman** and Anatolii Mariengof, was Pyr'ev's first directorial effort; it attacked petit-bourgeois hypocrisy and outdated moral standards in a manner tending toward the grotesque. While Pyr'ev's debut film offered some positive alternative, his next project, the satire *The Civil Servant* (Gosudarstvennyi chinovnik, 1931) about embezzlement in the railway industry, painted a rather gloomy picture; it was temporarily prohibited and later substantially modified. After this experience, Pyr'ev abandoned social criticism for good; had he continued to move in the direction of gogolesque satire, as indicated in a screenplay based on *Dead Souls* (1842) written with Mikhail Bulgakov in the mid-1930s, Pyr'ev's evolution might have yielded some surprising results. Instead, he made the political drama *Conveyer Belt of Death* (Konveier smerti, 1933) about three German girls fighting National Socialism. Even more dark in style, yet utterly demagogical in its paranoid message, is *The Party Membership Card* (aka *Anna*/Partiinyi bilet, 1936), a suspenseful story about a saboteur masking as a loyal Communist and husband—an implied justification of the purges.

A Rich Bride (aka *The Country Bride*/Bogataia nevesta, 1938) was the first of several lavish film operettas that are still most often associated with Pyr'ev's name. Set in contemporary Ukraine, it creates a bucolic idyll of nutritional abundance supposedly enjoyed in collective farms, only five years after the deadly famines that left millions dead. Yet *Rich Bride* and its successors fulfilled both a need of the Soviet state and of mass audiences. For *Tractor Drivers* (Traktoristy, 1939), a harmless love triangle that applied the same basic formula, Pyr'ev received his first Stalin Prize. *Beloved Girl* (Liubimaia devushka, 1940), although a brief detour to the urban milieu of industrial workers, centers on similar pseudo conflicts (silly misunderstandings, unfounded jealousy) and their quick "resolution." *Swineherd and Shepherd* (aka *They Met in Moscow*/Svinarka i pastukh, 1941), the title of which became proverbial, continued the line of kolkhoz vaudevilles-cum-operettas, illustrating the Soviet-style multinationalism in a Russian-Dagestan romance and winning the director another Stalin Prize in 1942.

With habitual efficiency, Pyr'ev reacted to the outbreak of the Great Patriotic War by delivering an adventurous drama, *The Secretary of the Party District Committee* (aka *We Will Come Back*/Sekretar' raikoma, 1942), that is devoted to the underground struggle in the Nazi-occupied territories (Stalin Prize 1943). *At Six in the*

Evening after the War (aka *Six P.M.*/V shest' chasov vechera posle voiny, 1944) blends operetta elements with a dramatic war story, ending its many illogical and unbelievable plot turns on a genuinely touching, inspirational note. *The Tale of the Siberian Land* (aka *Symphony of Life*/Skazanie o zemle sibirskoi, 1946), shot in color, again centers on a simple love story but also makes a conspicuous case for nonelitist art. *Cossacks of the Kuban* (Kubanskie kazaki, 1950) concluded Pyr'ev's Soviet musical variations.

A masterpiece in its own right is the drama *Test of Faithfulness* (aka *Devotion*/Ispytanie vernosti, 1954), perhaps the most sincere and mature of Pyr'ev's films and one of the few revealing genuine human depth and even sadness. It shows the director's invariable female lead and long-term wife, **Marina Ladynina**, parting with her usual singing and giggles, as a mature woman who has to cope with spousal disloyalty.

One of the great enigmas of Russian film history is Pyr'ev's subsequent turn from Stalinist comedy to the works of Fedor Dostoevskii. *The Idiot* (Idiot, aka Nastas'ia Filippovna, 1958), a faithful and at times haunting adaptation of the novel's first part, emphasizes the text's anticapitalist tendencies. After such a promising beginning, *White Nights* (Belye nochi, 1960) came as a disappointment and could not stand up to Luchino Visconti's beautiful 1958 version. Following an unremarkable intermission with the kolkhoz melodrama *Our Common Friend* (Nash obshchii drug, 1962) and the wartime romance *Light from a Faraway Star* (Svet dalekoi zvezdy, 1965), the director staged his most daring coup: *The Brothers Karamazov* (Brat'ia Karamazovy, 1967–1969, completed by actors **Kirill Lavrov** and **Mikhail Ul'ianov**). Despite some controversial casting decisions and an at times pedestrian approach, Pyr'ev's four-hour adaptation compares favorably to the 1957 U.S. version and has undeniable merits that deserve critical reexamination.

Within Stalinist culture, Pyr'ev deliberately promoted a cinema of wishful thinking, sugary optimism, and a depiction of life not as it is commonly experienced but as it is supposed to be. Most of his earlier films feature an oppressive cheerfulness, an often heavy-handed humor, and a simplistic plot structure. However, Pyr'ev also strove for narrative stringency, a quality of his films that was pointed out by Béla Bálasz, who praised *Conveyer Belt of Death*.

As the winner of six Stalin Prizes and deputy of the Supreme Soviet, Pyr'ev for 30 years carried enormous authority within the Soviet political and cultural establishment. He did use his influence for the advancement of Soviet cinema, especially as executive director of **Mosfilm Studio** in 1954–1957 and head of one of its major production units, supporting young filmmakers such as **El'dar Riazanov**, **Aleksandr Alov** and **Vladimir Naumov**, **Grigorii Chukhrai**, **Leonid Gaidai**, **Georgii Natanson**, and others who enjoyed his mentoring protection during difficult career phases. Josephine Woll pointed out how "adroit at maneuvering within the system" Pyr'ev was, and how he "took risks for projects he had faith in and . . . trusted people, especially young people, whom he respected." For many years (1957–1965) Pyr'ev relentlessly fought for the creation of a Union of Soviet Filmmakers. Still, in the eyes of highbrow filmmakers and critics, Pyr'ev symbolizes everything they resent about Soviet cinema—proud ignorance, dishonesty, and vulgarity. On the other hand, many people in the film community who found Pyr'ev's movies insufferable were impressed by his genuine passion for cinema, his collegiality, and his human decency. In the 1990s, an increasing—and not altogether rational—admiration for Pyr'ev's Stalinist folklore was noticeable among film critics and historians.

Pyr'ev joined the Communist Party in 1956. He was named People's Artist of the USSR in 1948. Pyr'ev was married to actresses Ada Voitsik (1905–1982), Marina Ladynina, and Lionella Skirda-Pyr'eva. He is buried at Novodevich'e cemetery. The Moscow house in which he lived from 1962–1968 (Smolenskaia Street 10) carries a memorial plaque.

Other films: *Song of Youth* (Pesnia molodosti, 1951; doc.); *We Are for Peace!* (aka *Friendship Triumphs*/My za mir! 1952, with Joris Ivens, doc.).

– R –

RADZIN, ELSA [real name Szolkonis; some sources list her name as Elze Radzinya; Russian sources also include the patronymic Ianovna] (b. 10 February 1917, Khar'kiv–d. 18 August 2005, Riga). Latvian actress. In 1936, after jobs as a book salesperson and librarian, Radzin became a member of the theater of Elgava—first as a dancer, then as a dramatic actress—until 1953. In 1954, she joined the Upits Theater in Riga.

Radzin made her debut in **Latvian cinema** with the role of Dora in **Iulii Raizman**'s Stalin Prize–winning biopic *Rainis* (1949) about a canonized Communist poet. Fifteen years later, the actress gained international fame through her energetic portrayal of Getrude in **Grigorii Kozintsev**'s *Hamlet* (1964). That tour-de-force performance and an equally impressive Honerile in Kozintsev's *King Lear* (1971) remain the best-remembered achievements in Radzin's screen career. However, she was willing to demonstrate the breadth of her artistic potential in lighter fare as well, making appearances in Grigorii Kromanov's adventurous superhit *The Last Relic* (Viimne relikviia/Posledniaia relikviia, 1969) where she was cast as the abbess, and **Aleksandrs Leimanis**'s historical musical *The Devil's Servants* (Vella kalpi/Slugi d"iavola, 1970) and its sequel, *The Devil's Servants at the Devil's Mill* (Vella kalpi vella dzirnavās/Slugi d"iavola na chertovoi mel'nitse, 1972), as well as the medieval **comedy**, *In the Claws of the Black Crab* (Melna vîza spiles/V kleshniakh chernogo raka, 1975).

In several productions, Radzin was cast in roles of upper-class ladies, including Madame Horst in **Leonids Leimanis**'s *Edgar and Christina* (1967) and Dolly in Jānis Streičs's *Theater* (Teātris/Teatr, 1978) from Somerset Maugham's novel. Her last screen appearance was in Gunnar Piesis's fairy tale *Maija and Paija* (1990).

Radzin was honored with the title People's Artist of the USSR in 1976.

Other films: *Sergei Ivanovich Is Retiring* (Sergei Ivanovich ukhodit na pensiiu, 1981); *The Last Visit* (Poslednii vizit, 1984, TV).

RAINBOW, THE (Raduga, 1943). Kiev film studio (**Dovzhenko Film Studio**). 91 min., b/w. Directed by **Mark Donskoi**. Script: Vanda Vasilevskaia (Wanda Wasilewska). Cinematography: Boris Monastyrskii. Music: Lev Shvarts. Cast: **Nataliia Uzhvii**, Nina Alisova, Elena Tiapkina, Valentina Ivasheva, Anton Dunaiskii, Anna Lisianskaia, Hans Klering. Premiere: 26 January 1944.

Olena Kostiuk (Uzhvii), a member of the Ukrainian partisans in the Great Patriotic War against the German occupying forces, returns to her native village, Novaia Lebedivka, to give birth to a son. A traitor from the village surrenders Olena to the Nazis, who interrogate her in order to find out the partisans' location. When Olena refuses to talk, the German commander (Klering) first shoots her baby and later orders her execution too. The commander's lover, Pusia (Alisova), tries to get information about the partisans but fails. When Soviet troops liberate the village, Pusia's husband shoots his treasonous wife. An emerging rainbow is seen as a sign that the victory is near. *See also* UKRAINIAN CINEMA.

RAIZMAN, IULII IAKOVLEVICH (b. 15 December 1903, Moscow–d. 11 December 1994, Moscow). Russian director and screenwriter. Raizman, son of a well-to-do tailor, studied art and literature at Moscow University, graduating in 1924, and then acting with the Supreme Theater Workshops. In 1924, he was hired as a literary consultant for Mezhrabpom-Rus' (later: **Mezhrabpom-film Studio**). In 1926–1927, he worked as an assistant director to Konstantin Eggert and **Iakov Protazanov**. Raizman's first film as director, made for Gosvoenkino studio, was the court drama *The Circle: Duty and Love* (Krug. Dolg i liubov', 1927, codirected with A. Gavronskii), in which a pre-1917 "class enemy" reappears as a NEP (New Economic Policy) profiteer. Although critics found it unremarkable, the film displays certain characteristics of all of Raizman's later works: concentration on only a few characters bound together by a melodramatic plot, individual behavior shown as class-determined, and the interference of chance.

The Penal Colony (Katorga, 1928), a visually stylish tale about the sadistic treatment of political prisoners in Siberia in the 19th century, brought Raizman name recognition at home and abroad. *The Earth Is Thirsty* (Zemlia zhazhdet, 1930), filmed and released as a silent, was re-released a year later with sound effects and a musical score. The story of five Komsomol enthusiasts who give their all to fertilize the desert in Turkmenistan demonstrates how romantic idealism overcomes the passiveness and indifference of the native population. Fighting nature—one of the declared enemies of Communist construction—is as fundamental as eliminating the exploiters.

Although Raizman's silent pictures were not groundbreaking, they put the achievements of Soviet classical montage to good use, enriching otherwise simple plots by a quality visual dimension. *The Pilots* (aka *Men on Wings*/Letchiki, 1935), Raizman's first sound feature, was yet again a seemingly private story: two men, one old and heavy, one young and dashing, are competing for the same woman—but the real "message" was the fashionable military milieu. The film's carefully crafted imagery and its joyful, enthusiastic atmosphere made it a hit. *The Last Night* (Posledniaia noch', 1937), which won Raizman his first Stalin Prize (of a staggering seven altogether), brings to life the Moscow uprising, part of the 1917 October Revolution. Bourgeois and proletarian family members are connected through private and professional ties; as the political events unfold, the capitalists reveal their murderous resentment against the underdogs. The film marked the beginning of a long-lasting partnership between Raizman and scriptwriter **Evgenii Gabrilovich**.

Virgin Soil Upturned (Podniataia tselina, 1940) was the partial adaptation of Mikhail Sholokhov's collectivization epic, while *Mashen'ka* (1942, Stalin Prize 1943) aimed at conveying the beauty of new Soviet human relations and became one of Raizman's most fondly remembered films. It owes much of its charm to Valentina Karavaeva's refreshing performance as the kind, somewhat naïve title heroine.

At this point, Raizman's reputation as one of the politically most loyal and professionally reliable Soviet filmmakers had become solid. After the Politburo decided in 1944 that leading feature film directors be assigned the production of important **documentaries**, Raizman made *On the Question of the Truce with Finland* (K voprosu o peremirii s Finlandiei, 1944) and the feature-length *Berlin* (1945); both were adorned with Stalin Prizes in 1946. He returned to narrative films with the romantic **comedy** *The Train Goes Eastward* (Poezd idet na vostok, 1947), a rather monotonous and not very funny love story intended as a reflection of the new optimism after the Great Patriotic War. Like other leading directors, Raizman was then sent to a local studio in one of the newly occupied republics, Latvia. The result, *Rainis* (1949, Stalin Prize 1950) was a pompous, stale biopic of a revolutionary Latvian poet, meant to give a boost to film production at **Riga Film Studio**. Raizman subsequently was entrusted with another prestige project, the adaptation of Semen Babaevskii's ultra-Stalinist *Cavalier of the Golden Star* (aka *Dream* *of a Cossack*/Kavaler zolotoi zvezdy, 1950, Stalin Prize 1952) whose over-the-top depiction of postwar wealth in the Russian countryside today appears like mockery.

Raizman's next film was more realistic and, anticipating the spirit of the ensuing Thaw, moderately daring. *A Lesson in Life* (aka *Conflict*/Urok zhizni, 1955) shows the attempt of a woman to liberate herself from an abusive husband, a theme that the director would develop more uncompromisingly in his films of the 1970s. *A Communist* (Kommunist, 1957) is filled with drama and pathos and implicitly praises its title character, the larger-than-life hero Gubanov, as an implicit antidote against post-Stalinist disenchantment. *And What if It Is Love* (A esli eto liubov'? 1962), about the romantic aspirations of 10th-graders that are destroyed by gossip and parental distrust, caused controversy and can be interpreted as an indictment of rampant Soviet puritanism. *Your Contemporary* (Tvoi sovremennik, 1968), the script of which was originally called *The Communist's Son*, referred to Gubanov's child of 10 years earlier. It contains explicit criticism of Soviet bureaucratic incompetence and brings some burning social questions to the big screen.

Three mildly controversial melodramas concluded Raizman's career: *A Strange Woman* (Strannaia zhenshchina, 1978), *Private Life* (Chastnaia zhizn', 1982, USSR State Prize 1983), and *Time of Desire* (Vremia zhelanii, 1984). Like all of Raizman's films, they are held together by a strictly didactic strategy underneath the quasi-psychological surface; indeed, the conflicts often seem preconceived, with the possible exception of *Private Life*, in which the problems of a retired high-ranking Muscovite are described with knowledge of detail, albeit little compassion.

In retrospect, Raizman's artistic originality appears to have been substantially overrated by contemporary critics. In post-Soviet times, his films have been largely forgotten and, with the exception of *Mashen'ka*, have not regained viewers' affection through patriotic nostalgia. Still, Raizman's longevity as a leading director despite changing political conditions is remarkable, based on a brand of opportunism both competently cautious and socially energetic. Indeed, without being a Party member, Raizman untiringly centered his films around Communist Party policies, making him one of the most influential activists of Soviet cinema whose pictures reflect societal trends in a semiofficial manner.

For many years, Raizman taught at the Soviet state film school **VGIK**, after 1960 at the rank of full professor. He was honored with the title People's Artist of the USSR in 1964 and Hero of Socialist Labor in 1973. He was the first Russian filmmaker to win a Nika prize in the category "Honor and Dignity" (1987).

Other films: *The Tale of Umara Khantsoko* (Rasskaz ob Umare Khantsoko, 1932); *Moscow Sky* (Nebo Moskvy, 1944); *Courtesy Call* (Vizit vezhlivosti, 1973).

RANEVSKAIA, FAINA GRIGOR'EVNA [real name: Fanni Fel'dman; some sources list the patronymic Georgievna] (b. 27 August 1896, Taganrog–d. 19 July 1984, Moscow). Russian actress. Ranevskaia, who took her pseudonym from a character in Anton Chekhov's *Cherry Orchard*, hailed from the family of a wealthy entrepreneur. She attended a private acting school before joining various provincial theater troupes in Southern Russia, beginning in 1915. In 1931, Aleksandr Tairov invited her to become a member of the Moscow Chamber Theater (Kamernyi teatr). Her main artistic home was the Mossovet Theater where she worked in 1949–1955 and after 1963.

Ranevskaia made her movie debut with the episodic part of Madame Loiseau in **Mikhail Romm**'s *Boule de Suif* (Pyshka, 1934). Her penchant for depicting obnoxious characters, supported by a hoarse voice, plain features, and a heavy albeit mobile physique became the actress's trademark and soon won her immense popularity. Ranevskaia's specialty were loudmouth, street-smart ladies, usually eloquent, boorish, and often endowed with a golden heart. Especially her portrait of the domineering Lelia who bosses her husband, Mulia, in **Tat'iana Lukashevich**'s cult **comedy** *The Foundling* (Podkidysh, 1939) became an oft-quoted classic. Her acting, however, could also betray a certain tenderness and vulnerability that she used to great tragicomical effect. In particular, her Roza Skorokhod in Romm's *The Dream* (Mechta, 1941/1943) demonstrated Ranevskaia's unique talent, ranging from grotesque, off-putting hyperbole to tragic subtlety.

Ranevskaia's supporting roles proved scene-stealers in **Ivan Pyr'ev**'s *Beloved Girl* (Liubimaia devushka, 1940), **Semen Timoshenko**'s *The Sky Sloth* (Nebesnyi tikhokhod, 1945), and **Girgorii Aleksandrov**'s *Spring* (Vesna, 1947). Even demagogical fare such as the Cold War extravaganzas *Meeting at the Elbe* (Vstrecha na El'be, 1949) by Aleksandrov, where she mocked American manners as "General McDermott's wife," and **Aleksandr Faintsimmer** and Vladimir Legoshin's *They Have a Homeland* (U nikh est' rodina, 1950, as Frau Wurst) were partially saved by Ranevskaia's acting (she received a Stalin Prize for the latter part). In later years, **Nadezhda Kosheverova** gave her some memorable roles, among them the lead in the critically maligned comedy hit *Watch Out, Grandma!* (Ostorozhno, babushka!, 1960).

Ranevskaia was named People's Artist of the USSR in 1961; she was awarded Stalin Prizes for her stage work in 1949 and 1951.

Other films: *The Man in the Shell* (Chelovek v futliare, 1939); *An Easy Life* (Legkaia zhizn', 1965).

RAPPAPORT, GERBERT (Herbert) **MORITSEVICH** (b. 7 July 1908, Vienna–d. 5 September 1983, Moscow). Austrian-Russian director and screenwriter. Rappaport studied law at Vienna University in 1927–1929. He worked in the studios of Berlin, Paris, and Hollywood from 1928 to 1936, most notably as an assistant to Georg Wilhelm Pabst on 10 of his pictures, including *Kameradschaft* (1931) and *L'Atlantide* (1932).

After immigrating to the USSR, Rappaport, a "serious, quiet, experienced artist" (Jay Leyda), began his Soviet career at **Lenfilm Studio** with the political drama *Professor Mamlock* (1938, codirected with A. Minkin) from German émigré Friedrich Wolf's powerful anti-Nazi play. This tragic story of a Jewish doctor who pays dearly for his illusions about the racist nature of the National Socialist regime won critical praise but was withdrawn from Soviet screens after the signing of the Molotov-Ribbentropp Pact in 1939. Rappaport turned to lighter fare such as the **comedy** *Musical Story* (Muzykal'naia istoriia, 1940, codirected with **Aleksandr Ivanovskii**), as well as so-called concert films (for example, *Film Concert 1941*), which satisfied an urgent need for low-budget, quality entertainment.

During the Great Patriotic War, Rappaport directed several shorts for War Film Almanacs. In Alma-Ata, where most of the Soviet film industry had been evacuated, he also helmed the musical comedy *Airchauffeur* (aka *Taxi to Heaven*/Vozdushnyi izvozchik, 1943), a romantic love story about a pilot and a Bolshoi theater soloist on the backdrop of the beginning Great Patriotic War; the film was officially criticized for its overly lighthearted attitude but was extremely popular with audiences even years after its initial release. In the war's aftermath, Rappaport was commissioned to help create a Communist film industry in Soviet-occupied Estonia, mainly using Lenfilm resources but employing native actors, as well as specialists from **Tallinfilm Studio**. *Life in the Citadel* (Elu tsidallis/Zhizn' v tsitadeli, 1948), an adaptation of August Jakobson's play of the same title, won Rappaport a Stalin Prize, as did *Light in Koordi* (Svet v Koordi, 1951), the story of the new collective farms in the Estonian Soviet Republic. *Aleksandr Popov* (1949), codirected with Viktor Eisymont (1904–1964) and honored with another Stalin Prize, is an ultrapatriotic biopic about a Russian scientist whom official Soviet historiography credited with inventing the radio. *Cheremushki* (aka *Song Over Moscow*, 1963), one of the rare Soviet operetta films, in which shortage of living space unleashes comedic confusion, was adapted from **Dmitrii Shostakovich**'s piece and became a huge crowd-pleaser, as were almost all of Rappaport's films.

In the 1960s and 1970s, Rappaport directed a number of successful thrillers, a genre that occupied a marginal position in Soviet cinema: *Two Tickets for the Daytime Show* (Dva bileta na dnevnoi seans, 1967), its sequel *The Circle* (Krug, 1973), *This Doesn't Concern Me* (Menia eto ne kasaetsia, 1977), and others. He was also assigned a coproduction with East Germany, *Black Rusks* (Chernye sukhari, 1971), an internationalist drama about Bolshevik food aid for starving German proletarians in 1918.

In 1947, Rappaport was named Merited Artist of the Estonian SSR, and in 1980, People's Artist of the Russian Federation. A number of sources indicate that Rappaport intended to return to Austria by the end of his life but died under suspicious circumstances.

Other films: *A Hundred for One* (Sto za odnogo, 1941, short); *Andrus's Happiness* (Schast'e Andrusa, 1955); *In Rain and Sun* (V dozhd' i v solntse, 1960); *The Militia Sergeant* (Serzhant militsii, 1974).

RAZUMNYI, ALEKSANDR EFIMOVICH (b. 1 May 1891, Eliza-
vetgrad–d. 16 November 1972, Moscow). Russian director and
scriptwriter. Razumnyi was an apprentice in a photo store, then attended the Odessa School of Arts where he studied until 1914, before
working as a decoration and costume designer on stage and in the
movies. A member of the Communist Party since 1919, Razumnyi
commanded considerable political influence in the People's Commissariat of Enlightenment (Narkompros), which oversaw the Moscow Cinema Committee (*kinokomitet*) since August 1918. However,
he never joined the film avant-garde of the 1920s, as his views on
film aesthetics were rather conservative and remained such throughout his long career.

Razumnyi was particularly productive in the years following
the Bolshevik Revolution. After *The Life and Death of Lieutenant
Shmidt* (Zhizn' i smert' leitenanta Shmidta, 1917)—his directorial
debut—he made *agitka* shorts such as *The Uprising* (Vosstanie,
1918), describing the Communist transformations in the countryside
by using both **documentary** and fictitious footage, and *Comrade
Abram* (1919), which tells the story of "a Jew who has survived the
miseries of Imperialist war and the horror of the pogrom, takes his
place beside the Bolsheviks and volunteers in a Red Army detach-
ment that beats the Whites in a battle" (Leyda). *The Mother* (Mat',
1920), the first of altogether four Soviet adaptations of Maksim
Gor'kii's 1906 novel about awakening class consciousness, was
also the first feature completely realized by the Cinema Committee,
avoiding private investors.

In 1923, Razumnyi shot the naïve **comedy** *Kombrig Ivanov* (released in the United States as *The Beauty and the Bolshevik*), made
with Red Army support. A box-office success, it was based on a contemporary poem of which some lines were used for intertitles, telling
the story of a Bolshevik commander who falls in love with the daughter of a priest, ultimately persuading her to read Nikolai Bukharin and
to get married not in a church but in a Soviet registration office.

In 1926, the director was sent to Berlin where he helmed, among
others, two literary adaptations, *Superfluous People* (Überflüssige
Menschen, based on an Anton Chekhov story), as well as *Prince
or Clown* (Fürst oder Clown, 1927). In 1940, Razumnyi made the
hugely popular *Timur and His Gang* (Timur i ego komanda, remas-

tered 1965), for which Arkadii Gaidar, the classic of inspirational Communist children's literature, wrote the script. The film initiated an entire youth movement supporting adults in their daily trials and tribulations. After World War II, Razumnyi was sent to Lithuania to support the local film industry (however, most of these films were shot in Riga or Leningrad). His last notable films were the biopic *Miklukho-Maklai* (aka *Without Prejudice*, 1947) about the 19th-century Russian scientist and explorer, featuring an explicit antiracist and anti-Western message, and *The Case of Private First Class Kochetkov* (Sluchai s efreitorom Kochetkovym, 1955), the story of a young man who exposes his girlfriend and her grandmother as foreign spies. In the last decade of his life, Razumnyi directed educational shorts on Russian art and theater.

Razumnyi's talent had clear limitations, which explains the lack of attention paid to him by historians of cinema. However, as an example of steadfast Soviet mainstream in all its ups and downs, Razumnyi's intriguing career deserves a closer look. The director was named Merited Artist of the Russian Federation in 1957.

Other films: *The Gang of Father Knysh* (Banda bat'ki Knysha, 1924); *Personal File* (Lichnoe delo, 1937); *Ignotas Returned Home* (aka *Homecoming*/Ignotas vernulsia domoi, 1956); *Sergeant Fetisov* (Serzhant Fetisov, 1962).

RED SNOWBALL TREE (Kalina krasnaia, 1973). **Mosfilm Studio**. 108 min., color and b/w. Directed by **Vasilii Shukshin**. Script: Vasilii Shukshin. Cinematography: Anatolii Zabolotskii. Music: Pavel Chekalov. Cast: Vasilii Shukshin, Lidiia Fedoseeva-Shukshina, **Ivan Ryzhov**, Aleksei Vanin, Mariia Skvortsova, Zhanna Prokhorenko, Georgii Burkov, Lev Durov. Premiere: 25 March 1974.

After his release from prison, career criminal Egor Prokudin (Shukshin) moves to a remote village in order to meet a woman, Liuba Baikalova (Fedoseeva-Shukshina), with whom he had corresponded. Liuba's parents (Ryzhov, Skvortsova) are as distrustful of the shady visitor as are most villagers, but Egor also finds friends such as Liuba's brother Petr (Vanin), who helps him get a job as a tractor driver. Egor decides to abandon his criminal past and begin an honest life. However, members of his former gang find him and kill him after an argument.

REPENTANCE (Monanieba/Pokaianie, 1984). **Gruziya-Film Studio**. 153 min., color. Directed by **Tengiz Abuladze**. Script: Nana Janelidze, Tengiz Abuladze, Rezo Kveselava. Cinematography: Mikhail Agranovich. Music compilation: Nana Janelidze. Cast: Avtandil Makharadze, Edisher Giorgobiani, Ketevan Abuladze, Zeinab Botsvadze, Kakhi Kavsadze, Nino Zakariadze, **Sofiko Chiaureli**, Merab Ninidze, **Veriko Andjaparidze**. Premiere: March 1987.

Varlam Aravidze (Makharadze) rules the city as an unchallenged dictator; his public appearances are celebrated by cheering crowds, while countless innocents are arrested, accused of absurd crimes, and executed or put in concentration camps. The artist Sandro Barateli (Giorgobiani) and his wife, Nino (Abuladze), are among the victims; their daughter Ketevan (Botsvadze) is raised as an orphan. Many years later, upon learning of Varlam's death, Ketevan unearths his remains three times in a row and finally is tried in court, where she tells about the late tyrant's totalitarian rule. Varlam's son, Avel (Makharadze), denies the charges, but his own son, Tornike (Ninidze), is so appalled that he commits suicide. Avel, in despair, himself digs up the dictator's corpse and throws it into an abyss.

RERBERG, GEORGII IVANOVICH (b. 28 September 1937, Moscow–d. 25 July 1999, Moscow). Russian cinematographer. Rerberg, the offspring of an old artistic family—his grandfather was the well-known Moscow architect Ivan Rerberg (1869–1932)—studied at the Soviet State Film School **VGIK** with **Boris Volchek**, graduating in 1960. **Andrei Mikhalkov-Konchalovskii** hired him for his debut feature, *The First Teacher* (Pervyi uchitel', 1965), a powerful black-and-white adaptation of **Chingiz Aitmatov**'s novella about a Communist educator in Kyrgyzstan in the aftermath of the 1918–1920 Civil War. This picture immediately revealed Rerberg's extraordinary talent, equally persuasive in capturing the dreamlike beauty of wilderness and the claustrophobia of filthy interiors. The creative partnership between director and cinematographer continued with the even more ambitious, albeit ill-fated, *Asia's Happiness* (Asino schast'e, 1966, released in 1988) in which neorealist principles to expose the shocking living conditions of people in the Russian countryside were applied. After the film's ban, Mikhalkov-Konchalovskii and Rerberg moved to safer grounds with the openly nostalgic, elegant, albeit somewhat erratic—and certainly escapist—Ivan Turgenev adaptation *A Nest of the Gentry* (Dvorianskoe gnezdo, 1969), a work that particularly gained from Rerberg's visual taste. In Mikhalkov-Konchalovskii's Anton Chekhov adaptation *Uncle Vanya* (Diadia Vania, 1970), Rerberg used contrasting black-and-white and color images to achieve a psychologically illuminating effect.

An ardent, strong-willed individualist, Rerberg soon became the darling of the most artistically ambitious directors of the 1970s and 1980s. Among others, **Andrei Tarkovskii** hired him for his autobiographical extravaganza *The Mirror* (Zerkalo, 1975), and **Vadim Abdrashitov** for the provocative *Plumbum, or a Dangerous Game* (Pliumbum, ili opasnaia igra, 1986). Yet Rerberg also worked for the traditionalist **Igor' Talankin** (*Father Sergius*/Otets Sergii, 1978; *Starfall*/Zvezopad, 1981; *The Time to Rest Is from Saturday to Monday*/Vremia otdykha s subboty do ponedel'nika, 1984). In 1995 Rerberg shot *Waati* by Moscow-trained African filmmaker Souleymane Cissé. He also made documentaries about the philosopher Aleksei Losev (1989) and violinist Oleg Kagan (1995), as well as a number of video clips. Referring to Rerberg's stylistic multifacetedness, critic Irina Shilova aptly called him "a cinematographer with a thousand eyes."

Rerberg was named Merited Artist of the Russian Federation in 1980 and People's Artist of the RSFSR in 1988.

Other films: *Arrival of a Train* (Pribytie poezda, 1995, segment "The Path" [Doroga]).

RIAZANOV, EL'DAR ALEKSANDROVICH (b. 18 November 1927, Samara [other sources: Moscow]). Russian director and scriptwriter. Riazanov grew up in the family of a Soviet industrial executive who perished in the 1930s purges. He studied at the Soviet State Film School **VGIK** with **Grigorii Kozintsev**, graduating in 1950 with a **documentary** short. His filmmaking career took off at the Central Studio for Documentary Films, where he turned out regular Socialist Realist fare, hardly betraying his extraordinary talent.

In 1955, Riazanov joined the staff of **Mosfilm Studio**. Following an unremarkable debut, the musical revue *Spring Voices* (Vesennie golosa, codirected by S. Gurov), Riazanov's perceptive mentor **Ivan Pyr'ev** helped him discover his true calling: **comedy**. Riazanov's first attempt in this genre, **Carnival Night** (Karnaval'naia noch', 1956), was an immediate triumph. Indeed, the film's success was so spectacular and lasting that many quotes from it became proverbial. The chain of blockbusters continued with *Girl without Address* (Devushka bez adresa, 1957), the gender-crossing adventure *Husar Ballad* (Gusarskaia ballada, 1962), based on a true story from the 1812 anti-Napoleonic war, and *Hand Me the Complaint Book* (Daite zhalobnuiu knigu, 1964), only interrupted by the subversive *Man from Nowhere* (Chelovek niotkuda, 1961), which was given a limited release due to its satirical daring.

The clash of quixotic idealism and bureaucratic harshness that became a typical theme of Riazanov's pictures is best realized in *Watch Out for the Automobile* (Beregis' avtomobilia, 1966), a modern classic about a Robin Hood–type, youthfully naïve insurance agent inventively fighting consumerism and greed in Moscow. The intelligent, bittersweet humor and the outstanding performances provide the film with a rare originality, making it one of the best in Soviet cinema history.

Unfortunately, the formula was applied with far less depth in *Zigzag of Luck* (Zigzag udachi, 1968) and *Old Men: Robbers* (Starikirazboiniki, 1972). Riazanov reached an all-time artistic low with the slapstick hit *The Unbelievable Adventures of Italians in Russia* (Neveroiatnye prikliucheniia ital'iantsev v Rossii, 1974, coproduced with Dino de Laurentiis), but returned to form in the made-for-TV *Irony of Fate* (Ironiia sud'by, ili S legkim parom, 1975), the success of which was so immense that it subsequently was released in movie theaters. The genuinely touching crowd-pleaser *Office Romance* (Sluzhebnyi roman, 1978) was followed by a daring assault on Soviet-style materialism and hypocrisy, *The Garage* (Garazh, 1979), perhaps the only satire in which Riazanov took no prisoners and presented a devastating diagnosis of society's ills. *A Railway Station for Two* (Vokzal dlia dvoikh, 1983) was far softer and far more successful at the box office, while *A Cruel Romance* (Zhestokii romans, 1984), the hauntingly beautiful adaptation of *Without Dowry* (Bespridannitsa) by 19th-century classic playwright Aleksandr Ostrovskii, could be interpreted as escapist if it were not such a masterpiece in its own right.

Critics have long been trying to make sense of the Riazanov phenomenon. The most common view is that his films are melodramatic fairy tales transplanted into a recognizable, modern urban environment. Indeed, typical of his stories (mostly created with scriptwriter Emil' Braginskii [1921–1998]) is the significance of chance. What Riazanov certainly shares with his predecessors in melodramatic comedy-making (first and foremost **Grigorii Aleksandrov** and **Konstantin Iudin**) is professional perfectionism, musicality, wit, and a fundamental loyalty to the ideals of Soviet society; often, sentimentality and pathos are ingredients as well. However, unlike his rival in popularity, **Leonid Gaidai**, Riazanov devotes a great deal of attention to psychologically subtle acting and rarely uses physical humor. For half a century, this blend has been appreciated by viewers of all social strata, including intellectuals who indulge in Riazanov's mildly subversive wit.

Paradoxically, perestroika was no cause for euphoria to this filmmaker; rather, he reacted with confusion and sadness, as evidenced by the rather weak and undecided *Forgotten Tune for Flute* (Zabytaia melodiia dlia fleity, 1987). Even less comforting was *Dear Elena Sergeevna* (Dorogaia Elena Sergeevna, 1988), an alarmist drama about the cynicism and brutality of contemporary youth with strong dosages of didacticism. Riazanov's post-Soviet films demonstrate an honest, slightly desperate effort to keep the old spirit and narrative formula alive, with mixed results since the Soviet distribution system had dissembled and directors were left without a regular audience. However, it is noteworthy that the overall mood, speed, and timing of his latest comedies have improved again, abandoning the melancholy and underlying horror that could be sensed in his films of the mid-1990s.

This prolific filmmaker—a real superstar known to virtually everybody in Russia—is also a prominent TV personality: Riazanov's numerous programs about outstanding people in culture and history profit from his erudition, personal warmth, and natural tact, as well as sincere collegial respect for his subjects. Riazanov has written the lyrics to many songs in his films; he easily crosses the lines between highbrow and lowbrow, pleasing a variety of viewers as a result. Riazanov's specific demeanor could be described as "melancholic loyalty"; it proved an acceptable common denominator for Soviet society. And yet, despite official recognition—Riazanov won State Prizes and medals and was awarded the highest title, People's Artist of the USSR, in 1984—he was forced to abandon some cherished projects, most prominently a *Cyrano de Bergerac* adaptation in the late 1960s, a story that seems tailored for Riazanov and could have become one of his most interesting films.

Other films: *How Robinson Was Written* (Kak sozdavalsia Robinzon, 1961, from the five-part omnibus *Absolutely Serious*/Soversh-enno ser'ezno, 1961); *The Prophecy* (Predskazanie, 1991); *Promised Heavens* (Nebesa obetovannye, 1993); *Hi There, Fools!* (Privet, duralei! 1996); *Old Hags* (Starye kliachi, 2000); *Keys to the Bedroom* (Kliuchi ot spal'ni, 2003); *Andersen: A Life without Love* (Andersen. Zhizn' bez liubvi, 2007).

RIGA FILM STUDIO. In July 1940, with the establishment of a Communist government in Latvia, the Riga Feature Film Studio and the Riga Documentary Film Studio were founded. In 1948, they were unified as Riga Film Studio, which to some extent could draw from a legacy of bourgeois professional filmmaking of the 1930s. From the very beginning, Latvian films featured actors and actresses from the nation's leading theaters, including the country's first full-length feature, *The Fisherman's Son* (Zvejnieka Dels, 1939), directed by Vilis Lapinieks from a novel by Communist writer Vilis Lacis.

After World War II, politically reliable Soviet directors were assigned to "national" films, usually inspirational pro-Communist tales with a clear didactic message. Thus, Leningrad director Aleksandr Ivanov was entrusted with quasi-Latvian productions such as *The Sons* (1946) and *Victorious Return* (Vozvrashchenie s pobedoi, 1948). In a similar spirit, **Iulii Raizman** directed the biopic *Rainis* (1949, Stalin Prize 1950) about a Latvian revolutionary poet.

The Thaw allowed for a less blatant propagandistic approach and brought opportunities for native filmmakers to address questions of national importance. Thus, **Leonids Leimanis** adapted *Spring Frosts* (Salna pavarasi/Vesennie zamorozki, 1955, codirected with Pavel Armand [1902–1964]) from stories by one of the classic authors of 19th-century Latvian literature, Rūdolfs Blaumanis (1863–1908), about the social and economic exploitation in the 19th century. Leimanis became one of Latvia's most artistically versatile filmmakers who particularly excelled in historical and neorealist drama (*Edgar* *and Kristina*/Edgar i Kristina, 1967; *At the Rich Lady's*/Pie bāgātas kundzes/U bogatoi gospozhi, 1969).

Aleksandrs Leimanis made **Latvian cinema** popular—and Riga Film Studio a favorite of Soviet audiences—with two blockbusters, the historical adventure **comedies** *The Devil's Servants* (Vella kalpi/Slugi d"iavola, 1970) and *The Devil's Servants at the Devil's Mill* (Vella kalpi vella dzirnavās/Slugi d"iavola na chertovoi mel'nitse, 1972), from stories by Rutku Tevs. Another great success was Roland Kalnins's antibourgeois satire *Ceplis* (Afera Tseplisa, 1972), about a ruthless businessman in the 1930s, with the popular Eduard Pavuls (1929–2006) in the title role. *A Limousine in the Color of St. John's Night* (Limuzins Janu Nakts Krasa/Limuzin tsveta beloi nochi, 1981), a contemporary comedy about greed among family members, one of whom wins the lottery, was directed by Jānis Streičs (b. 1936), and became one of the most popular of all Latvian pictures. Other noteworthy directors working at Riga Film Studio were Gunārs Piesis (*In the Shadow of Death*/Naves Ena, 1971) and former actor **Gunārs Cilinskis** (*Sonata at the Lake*/Ezera sonāte/Sonata nad ozerom, 1976, codirected with Varis Brasla). Among the studio's stars were **Vija Artmane** and **Elsa Radzin**.

Riga Film Studio gained international recognition for its **documentaries**, a tradition begun in the early 1960s when filmmakers such as Uldis Brauns (b. 1932) and Hercs Franks (Herz Frank, b. 1926) creatively applied the principles of cinéma vérité of the 1920s (**Dziga Vertov, Aleksandr Medvedkin**). Other important Latvian documentalists associated with the so-called Riga School of Poetic Documentary are Ivars Seleckis (*Crossroad Street*/Skérsielá/Ulitsa poperechnaia, 1988) and Ansis Epners. During the years of perestroika, **Jūris Podnieks** scored a huge national and international success with the feature-length *Is It Easy to Be Young?* (Vai viegli but jaunam?/Legko li byt' molodym?, 1986), a documentary that implicitly questioned the moral legitimacy of the Soviet system. **Andris Slapiņš**, who specialized in ethnographic documentaries, became a symbol of Latvia's struggle for independence when he was shot by snipers on 21 January 1991.

Among the directors who continued their work into the 1990s is Streičs, as well as Ivars Freimanis who made *Life* (Dzivite, 1990), a biopic about Krisjans Barons, a famous folklorist, and Arvids Krievs (b. 1944), a specialist in detective films such as *Eve's Garden of Paradise* (Ievas Paradīzes Dārzs, 1990). Since the 1990s, 31 percent of the Riga Film Studio has belonged to the Latvian state represented by the Latvian Film Corporation, and the rest is owned by private business. Film production came to a halt in 1994; since then, the studio's facilities have been rented out to foreign companies for film and television productions.

ROGOVOI, VLADIMIR AVRAAMOVICH [other sources: Abramovich] (5 February 1923, Kiev–d. 20 February 1983, Moscow). Russian director. Rogovoi graduated from the Economics Department of the Soviet State Film School **VGIK** in 1950 and began to work as a producer at **Gor'kii Studio for Children's and Youth Films** in Moscow in 1953. In later years, he was an assistant for **Mark Donskoi**, **Il'ia Frez**, and other leading directors.

In 1968, Rogovoi was given a chance to helm his first feature, *Fit for Noncombatant Service* (Goden k nestroevoi), a military **comedy** in which an awkward draftee proves his prowess as a soldier. With 28 million viewers, the film became Rogovoi's first blockbuster. *Officers* (Ofitsery, 1971) outdid its predecessor, attracting a sensational 53.4 million viewers. A blend of historical adventure and tearjerking melodrama, it consists of loose episodes ranging from the heroicized Bolshevik oppression of Muslim rebels during the Civil War in 1919 to life in military barracks in the present. The main underlying message is one of unconditional loyalty to the Communist homeland; any facts that might have contradicted that notion—for example, the purges in the Red Army in the late 1930s—are omitted.

Minors (Nesovershennoletnie, 1976) addresses problems of juvenile delinquency in a similarly patriotic fashion and was viewed by more than 44 million viewers. Rogovoi's last movie, the comedy *The Married Bachelor* (Zhenatyi kholostiak, 1983), features all of his films' typical ingredients—chance encounters with subsequent romantic involvement, unquestioned Soviet loyalty—and attracted 35 million viewers.

Rogovoi had an unfailing instinct for popular tastes and patriotic themes. Thus, it is no coincidence that his melodramas were repeatedly among the highest grossing box-office hits in the USSR. However, statistical data on film attendance were neither publicly accessible nor discussed until the late 1980s. Although studio officials and the filmmakers themselves knew which films were *lidery prokata* (literally: leaders of distribution) and which ones flopped, only in post-Soviet years, when the previously confidential statistics were made public, did it become clear that the taste of "the masses"—that is, rank-and-file viewers—rarely coincided with that of critics, who mostly disdained box-office success per se. Consequently, Rogovoi's films were critically ignored; the honorable title he received three years before his passing—Merited Artist of the Russian Federation—was the lowest on the scale.

Rogovoi joined the Communist Party in 1944.

Other films: *City Dwellers* (Gorozhane, 1975); *The Troublemaker* (Balamut, 1978); *Sailors Ask No Questions* (U matrosov net voprosov, 1980).

ROGOZHKIN, ALEKSANDR VLADIMIROVICH (b. 3 October 1949 [other sources: 1950], Leningrad). Russian director, scriptwriter, cutter, and production designer. Rogozhkin majored in history at Leningrad University, graduating in 1972. He then switched to graphic arts, which he studied at Hertsen Pedagogical Institute. Subsequently Rogozhkin worked as a production designer at Leningrad TV and **Lenfilm Studio** before completing his studies at the Soviet State Film School **VGIK** in 1982, where **Sergei Gerasimov** was his teacher.

In Rogozhkin's debut picture, *For a Few Lines* (Radi neskol'kikh strochek, aka Divizionka, 1985), some of this director's specific features are already discernible: a predilection for "small," rank-and-file characters who are thrown into the whirlwinds of history by an undiscriminating fate; paradoxical plot turns with tragicomical effects; focus on a minute episode on the margins of World War II (in this case, in the Carpathian Mountains in 1944), where the characters, faced with bad luck and social pressures, prove their humanity in the most unspectacular way.

Two gripping dramas, *The Guard* (Karaul, 1989) and *The Chekist* (Chekist, 1991) brought Rogozhkin international renown. While the former deals with the long tabooed harassment of young recruits in the Russian Army (the so-called *dedovshchina*), the latter shocked audiences with its graphic images of systematic, conveyer-belt-like executions in the name of the Communist revolution. The film's drastic depiction of Bolshevik terror, adapted from a little-known short story by Vladimir Zazubrin (1895–1937), attempts to radically destroy the myth of humanist values that are usually claimed for the Bolshevik coup. *The Chekist* has been justifiably compared to Bernardo Bertolucci's *The Conformist* and Pier Paolo Pasolini's *Salò, or The 120 Days of Sodom* and their uncompromising antitotalitarian vigor. In a similar vein, *Living with an Idiot* (Zhizn' s idiotom, 1993, based on a satirical short story by Viktor Erofeev) portrays liberal intellectuals' illusions about the "noble, simple folk."

Rogozhkin's **comedy** *Peculiarities of the National Hunt* (Osobennosti natsional'noi okhoty, 1995), the title of which has since become proverbial, gained him nationwide popularity. Characters such as the pensive hunter Kuz'mich and General Mikhalych immediately became favorites of Russian viewers. The film's underlying bitterness and disenchantment with Russian self-serving myths were all too often conveniently ignored. Still, in the existential crisis of the Russian film industry, the sudden success of Rogozhkin's *Peculiarities* inevitably developed a dynamic of its own, inspiring a number of sequels. *Checkpoint* (Blokpost, 1998) is a serious, humane interpretation of the Chechen war, with emphasis on soldiers' naïveté, the corruption of their commanders, and the conflict's absurdity and mercilessness. *The Cuckoo* (Kukushka, 2002), a minimalist triangle love story set in the Finno-Soviet "Continuation" War in 1944, marked a return to the themes of Rogozhkin's first features, now treated in a revisionist manner; the film became an international triumph.

Rogozhkin is a solid craftsman who brings fresh ideas to worn-out themes; he can tackle a made-for-TV thriller as expertly as a contemporary comedy-drama with tragic undertones. The one concept that is addressed more or less openly in most of his films is the innate kinship between all people, regardless of their national or class origins. It is this heartwarming appeal, enriched by alternating melodramatic, romantic, or satirical elements, that has won Rogozhkin the affection of festival juries and audiences worldwide. Some minor but noticeable deficiencies even in the best of his films are likely the result of rushed production methods, perhaps adopted from television.

Other films: *Miss Millionaire* (Miss millionersha, 1988); *The Span* (Peregon, 2006); *Where the Russian Land Came From* (Otkuda est' poshla russkaia zemlia, 2007).

ROMM, MIKHAIL IL'ICH (b. 18 February 1901, Zaigraievo, Buriatia [other sources: Irkutsk]–d. 1 November 1971, Moscow). Russian director, screenwriter, and pedagogue. Romm, the son of an exiled physician and political activist, grew up in the Irkutsk region of Siberia. In 1918–1921, he served in the Red Army holding a number of commanding ranks and participating in War Communism's food requisitions. He studied sculpture with Anna Golubkina (1864–1927) at the Supreme Institute of Art and Technology, graduating in 1925. Romm also translated fiction from French and was a scholar at the Institute for Extracurricular School Work (1928–1930).

In 1929, Romm joined the Soviet film industry, first as a screenwriter on *The Revenge* (Revanch, 1930), *Next to Us* (Riadom s nami, 1931), and **Ivan Pyr'ev**'s *Conveyor Belt of Death* (Konveier smerti, 1933). He learned the director's craft as an assistant to **Aleksandr Macheret** on one of the first Soviet sound films, *People and Deeds* (aka *Men and Jobs*/Dela i liudi, 1932), about an American who comes to work on a Soviet construction site. Romm's own directorial debut was a late silent, the Guy de Maupassant adaptation *Boule de Suif* (Pyshka, 1934). This grotesque story of a prostitute who saves a group of passengers on a coach during the 1870 Franco-Prussian war demonstrated Romm's ability to believably depict antagonistic group relations, and to finish a project on a shoestring budget in very little time. After praise from Romain Rolland and Maksim Gor'kii, the film was shown to Iosif Stalin, who liked it and later entrusted the director with political prestige projects.

The Thirteen (Trinadtsat', 1937), purportedly assigned to Romm by **Boris Shumiatskii** after having watched John Ford's *The Lost Patrol*, is a brilliantly executed adventurous border drama about Soviet soldiers fighting Islamist intruders. Romm gained fame with *Lenin in October* (Lenin v Oktiabre, 1937), the first in a long line of Soviet hagiographical pictures about the USSR's founding father (together, these films represent the so-called "Leniniana"). Completed in a record three months and followed by *Lenin in 1918* (Lenin v

1918 godu, 1939), it depicts Vladimir Lenin at crucial points of his political career. Boris Shchukin's (1894–1939) impersonation shows the Bolshevik leader as a dynamic, nervous, and humane populist, often accompanied by Stalin as his sidekick. The film's episodic structure connects a series of anecdote-like scenes—many of them funny albeit unmistakably didactic—meant to endear their subject to Soviet viewers. The third installment of the planned trilogy could not be completed because of Shchukin's sudden death. Romm was rewarded with a First-Class Stalin Prize in 1941. In 1957, he deleted all scenes involving Stalin.

The director also garnered much praise for *The Dream* (Mechta), completed in 1941 and released in 1943. This melodrama, with Romm's wife, **Elena Kuz'mina**, as An'ka, an oppressed peasant girl in a shabby hotel populated by exploitative cynics and disoriented underdogs, takes place in Lviv in Western Ukraine, then still part of Poland. An'ka ends up fleeing to the Soviet Union and triumphantly returns with the Red Army. In *Person #217* (aka *Girl No. 217/ Chelovek No. 217*, 1944), Kuz'mina portrays a young woman deported by the Nazis to do forced labor for a butcher's family in Germany. The film marks the beginning of Romm's fruitful partnership with screenwriter **Evgenii Gabrilovich**.

The Russian Question (Russkii vopros, 1947; First-Class Stalin Prize 1948), from a play by Konstantin Simonov, tells the story of an American journalist who travels to the Soviet Union in search of slanderous material but returns as a convert and spreads the good news of Communism to U.S. audiences. The deeply paranoid spy thriller *Secret Mission* (Sekretnaia missiia, 1950; First-Class Stalin Prize 1951) is based on the assumption of a secret alliance between the U.S. and Nazi German secret services forged before the end of World War II. While these prime examples of Cold War demagoguery disappeared after Stalin's death, the two-part crowd-pleaser *Admiral Ushakov* and *Ships Attack the Bastions* (aka *Attack from the Sea*/Korabli shturmuiut bastiony, 1953), about an 18th-century military leader, contains many colorful scenes of naval clashes and had a more lasting screen life than any of Romm's other works (despite being dismissed by the director himself).

Murder on Dante Street (Ubiistvo na ulitse Dante, 1956) was received as an anachronism at the time of its release, although its

French milieu and the suspenseful story attracted a large viewership. Yet this drama of a resistance fighter whose own son denounces her to the Nazis uses black-and-white characterizations typical of Romm's Stalinist films, as pointed out by his own students. The director, pained by this critical failure, and after much soul searching, followed it with a deliberately modern, provocative picture, *Nine Days of a Year* (Deviat' dnei odnogo goda, 1962), about two nuclear physicists with incompatible outlooks on life and the same love interest. The film's vibrant intellectualism endeared it to the generation of the 1960s (*shestidesiatniki*) and proved Romm's stunning ability to self-rejuvenate.

The feature-length **documentary *Ordinary Fascism*** (aka *Triumph over Violence*/Obyknovennyi fashizm, 1965), which Romm himself narrates, caused a sensation. Arguably the director's most persuasive, personal, and artistic work, this cinematic essay attempts to analyze the emergence of National Socialism, its underlying mentality, manipulative techniques, ideology, and art. The main object of attention is the documentary image as such—Romm teaches the viewer a practical lesson in visual analysis and manipulative techniques. The film gains considerably from the director's natural talent as a storyteller, using irony, pathos, sarcasm, and moral appeal. After a little-seen documentary about Lenin (*The First Pages*/Pervye stranitsy, 1967), Romm began to work on another compilation pamphlet, *And Still, I Do Believe* (I vse-taki ia veriu), an overall assessment of contemporary global dangers and the forces withstanding them. After Romm's passing, it was completed by his former students **Marlen Khutsiev**, **Elem Klimov**, and German Lavrov, and released in 1974, albeit to much less acclaim than *Ordinary Fascism*.

Romm was a profoundly political director who viewed the individual as determined by societal factors. This worldview allowed him to adapt to all changes in the Soviet doctrine, from Lenin cult to Stalin imperialism and Thaw-induced liberalization. Romm's devotion to the ideals of Communism is beyond doubt. However, by numerous accounts, as a private man he came across as extremely honest and was able to distance himself from his role in the regime. Despite the vicious anti-Americanism of his films, he returned from a trip to the United States enamored by the country, its people, and quality of life, and spoke candidly about his impressions, much to the annoyance of

Party watchdogs. Romm's memoirist notes, published long after his death, reveal an alert, perceptive mind that masterfully exposes the brutal essence of Stalin, Nikita Khrushchev, and their minions. Indeed, an undeniable antitotalitarian undercurrent was already detectable in *Person #217*; it becomes a major focus in *Ordinary Fascism*, the title and concept of which correspond—perhaps unconsciously so—with Hannah Arendt's "banality of evil."

Romm joined the Communist Party in 1939; in 1950, he was awarded the title People's Artist of the USSR. In 1938, he began to teach at the Soviet State Film School **VGIK**; in 1948, he was appointed head of an acting/directing workshop, and in 1958 promoted to full professor. Romm was an extraordinary pedagogue who allowed his students to realize their individuality. Filmmakers such as **Andrei Tarkovskii**, **Tengiz Abuladze**, **Vasilii Shukshin**, and **Grigorii Chukhrai** later warmly remembered their teacher as an open-minded, inspiring father figure.

RONDELI [real name: Tsagareishvili], **DAVIT** [Russian sources list the patronymic Evgen'evich] (b. 11 April 1904, Kutaisi, Georgia– d. 12 March 1976, Tbilisi). Georgian director and screenwriter. Rondeli began his career as a writer and film critic associated with various proletarian cultural organizations. He regularly published reviews in the Bolshevik monthly *Dynamite*, before being hired as an assistant on **Mikheil Gelovani**'s *Youth Wins* (Akhalgazrdoba imardjvebs/Molodost' pobezhdaet, 1928) and Lev Push's *The Doomed* (Gantsirulni/Obrechennye, 1930).

Rondeli's directorial debut was *Ugubziara* (1930) from a screenplay by **Giorgi Mdivani**, a critical account of superstition and unscientific healing practices in the countryside. The film was popular with audiences and hailed by critics for its authentic depiction of the rural milieu and some episodes shot in an expressive montage style. Rondeli's next picture, a semi**documentary** film essay about the mountain tribe of Svans, *The Second Factor* (Vtoroe slagaemoe), was influenced by **Mikhail Kalatozov**'s masterpiece *Salt for Svanetia* (Jim Shvante [marili svanets]/Sol' Svanetii, 1930). The same theme—the onset of modernization in remote regions of Georgia—is the focus of the country's first independently produced sound feature film, Rondeli's *The Arshaula Mountain* (Arshaula/Skala Arshaula,

1935). The director's most lasting contribution to **Georgian cinema** is the **comedy** *Paradise Lost* (Dakarguli samotkhe/Poteriannyi rai, 1938), a hilarious satire loosely adapted from Davit Kldiashvili's classical stories about the parasitic lifestyle of impoverished nobility. Misconstrued by some officials as "anti-Georgian," the film's production was repeatedly interrupted; however, Rondeli in the end won critical recognition for his superb capturing of characters and situations. *Paradise Lost* is still called the best Georgian comedy of the 1930s.

Among later highlights of Rondeli's career is the concert film *Djurgai's Shield* (Jurgais Pari/Shchit Dzhurgaia, 1944, codirected with **Siko Dolidze**), which won him a First-Class Stalin Prize in 1950 but has been thoroughly forgotten since. *Conquerors of Peaks* (Mtsvervalta dampkrobni/Pokoriteli vershin, 1951), the only Georgian film allowed for release in the years of stifled production ("*malokartin'e*"), was devoted to a famous, real-life family of mountain climbers and their adventures in Svanetia but suffered from conflict avoidance typical of those years. Rondeli subsequently worked in various genres, including adventure (*A Shadow on the Street*/Chrdili gzaze/Ten' na doroge, 1956), historical tale (*On the Shores of Enguri*/Enguris napirebze/Na beregakh Inguri, 1961), and comedy (*Pierre, the Militia Man*/Pieri—militsis tanamshromeli/P'er—sotrudnik militsii, 1965, and *My Best Friend Nodar*/Chemi megobari Nodari/Moi drug Nodar, 1967). Intermittently with his features, Rondeli also helmed a number of documentaries, including *To the Memory of Jose Diaz* (Pamiati Khoze Diasa, 1942) and *Soviet Georgia* (Sovetskaia Gruziia, 1950, doc., with Dolidze).

Rondeli, who joined the Communist Party in 1939, was named People's Artist of the Georgian SSR in 1961. For many years, he was on the faculty of the acting school of **Gruziya-Film Studio**.

Other films: *The Lights of Kolkhis* (Kolkhetis chiraqdnebi/Ogni Kolkhidy, 1941); *The Air Bridge* (Sahaero khidi/Vozdushnyi most, 1974).

ROOM, ABRAM MATVEEVICH (b. 28 June 1894, Vilnius [Vil'no]– d. 26 July 1976, Moscow). Russian director and screenwriter. Upon finishing gymnasium in Vilnius, Room studied at the Psychoneurological Institute in Petrograd in 1914–1917, where he also was head of the student theater. From 1917 to 1922, Room continued his studies at the Medical School of the University of Saratov, only interrupted by his service as a military doctor in the Red Army. In 1923, Vsevolod Meierkhol'd invited Room to Moscow, where he directed a number of plays at the Theater of the Revolution before switching to filmmaking.

In 1924, Room became a member of the Association of Revolutionary Cinematography (ARK), holding leading administrative positions and debuting with a commissioned short intended to publicize the work of the Moscow Office of Advertising (MOS): *What Mos Is Saying, You Should Guess* (Chto govorit 'Mos', sei otgadaite vopros, 1924), with the prominent Louis Forrestier (1892–1954) as cinematographer. Room also directed a provocative short about alcoholism and bootleggers, *The Hunt for Bootleg* (Gonka za samogonkoi, 1925), which won him critical attention. The **documentary** short *Jews on the Land* (Evrei na zemle, 1926), which he shot at the Crimea with Vladimir Maiakovskii, Lilia Brik, and **Viktor Shklovskii** as collaborators, deals with Jewish settlers who were beginning a new life as farmers.

Room became known as an original filmmaker with his first full-length feature, *Bay of Death* (Bukhta smerti, 1926), dramatically describing the political growth of a ship mechanic during the 1918–1921 Civil War. The film impressed and even shocked audiences with graphic details and became a critical and popular success at home and abroad. Room continued to explore revolutionary subject matter in *The Traitor* (Predatel', 1926), the story of a tsarist secret police informer who is brought to justice. According to film historian Irina Grashchenkova, the ability to combine a quasi-detective plot structure with complex psychological insight was a reflection of Room's expertise in psychology and psychiatry, including the theories of Sigmund Freud, which he had studied in depth.

Continuing the themes of his first documentaries, Room turned to contemporary urban life with ***Third Meshchanskaia Street*** (aka *Bed and Sofa*/Tret'ia Meshchanskaia, aka Liubov' vtroem, 1927), a story based on a newspaper article about a ménage-à-trois, Soviet style. Room's flamboyant direction sharply contrasts the male protagonists' "my-home-is-my-castle" mentality to the open urbanity of Moscow with its wide streets and gigantic construction sites. The film's antipuritanical stance seems daring even today; it caused considerable controversies at the time of its release. The interaction between the members of the triangle — the increasingly self-conscious and self-assertive wife, her husband, and her lover — is unsurpassed in Soviet cinema in its provocative realism and maturity.

After the failure of a project in Germany, the adaptation of Guy de Maupassant's "Boule de suif" (*Pyshka*, realized six years later by **Mikhail Romm**), Room made his last great silent, the stylish *The Ghost That Does Not Return* (Prividenie, kotoroe ne vozvrashchaetsia, 1930) about struggling oil workers in a vaguely defined Latin American country. He then directed *The Plan of the Great Works* (Plan velikikh rabot, aka *Five-Year Plan*/Piatiletka, 1930), the first Soviet sound film, a long documentary compiled from footage made by other directors, with a soundtrack consisting of music and verbal comments. While this was a predominantly technical experiment, Room's next two pictures, the "agitprops" *Manometer No. 1* (1930) and *Manometer No. 2* (1932), daringly blended documentary elements with a semifictitious plot. Here, film in itself became a tool actively intruding in the day-to-day battle for increased industrial production in a Moscow factory, with an intelligent film-in-film structure reminiscent of **Dziga Vertov**.

In 1932, Room was delegated to Ukrainfilm studio in Kiev, where he worked until 1941. His lyrical comedy *A Strict Young Man* (Strogii iunosha, 1934–1937) was based on a script by Iurii Olesha (1899–1960) and his peculiar vision of the Soviet "New Man": athletic, rational, and in absolute control of all emotions. The film, philosophically ambivalent, visually stunning, and as unique for early Soviet sound film as *Third Meshchanskaia* was for the silent era, was accused of formalism and shelved; it got a limited art-house and film club release in the 1960s and 1970s. Interestingly, American film historian Jay Leyda dismissed it too, and commented that, although there was sympathy for the director, "for once the punishment fitted the crime." Certainly, the years of debates and harsh administrative attacks left Room traumatized for good — never again would he challenge official aesthetic norms.

The first symptom of his partial resignation was *Squadron No. 5* (Eskadril'ia No 5, 1939), which depicts the assumed ease of a Soviet victory if a war were to start. *Wind from the East* (Veter s vostoka,

1940) focuses on the occupation—then called liberation—of Western Ukrainian territory by Soviet troops after the Hitler-Stalin pact in September 1939. Room made a noteworthy picture on loyalty, betrayal, and self-sacrifice in the Great Patriotic War, *The Invasion* (Nashestvie, 1944), based on a play by Leonid Leonov (1899–1994), for which he won a Stalin Prize in 1946. Thus rehabilitated, he was entrusted with the pro-Tito epic *In the Mountains of Yugoslavia* (V gorakh Iugoslavii, 1946), a huge box-office hit but withdrawn from screens when Soviet-Yugoslavian relations went sour. The moral low point of Room's career is marked by *Court of Honor* (Sud chesti, 1948, Stalin Prize 1949), a vicious attack on so-called cosmopolitanism among intellectuals, launched at a time when many of Room's colleagues—such as his former assistant **Sergei Iutkevich**—were harassed and threatened. *Silvery Dust* (Serebristaia pyl', 1953) is a fantastic Cold War yarn about a new weapon of mass destruction—"radioactive silvery dust"—that destroys first the U.S. scientist who invented it, then his family.

Room concluded his career with a trilogy of literary adaptations: *The Garnet Bracelet* (Granatovyi braslet, 1964), based on a classical story by Aleksandr Kuprin; *Belated Flowers* (Tsvety zapozdalye, 1970), from an Anton Chekhov story; and *A Premature Man* (Prezhdevremennyi chelovek, 1972), from a Maksim Gor'kii play. With their cultivated acting and picturesque beauty, these films form a serene, dignified epilogue to an extraordinary career marked by turbulence, creative originality, and self-destructive opportunism.

In the 1920s, Room was one of the great hopes of modern Soviet cinema, not so much as a formal innovator but as a socially sensitive, analytical narrator whose films were breathing the optimistic air of modernization. Indeed, there is a genuine democratic, egalitarian spirit at the heart of his best pictures, and the adventurousness and curiosity of an explorer. These qualities made him a maverick, similar to Vertov, but with more flexibility that allowed him to adjust and transform himself when under pressure.

Room joined the Communist Party in 1949; he was named People's Artist of the Russian Federation in 1965. He taught at the State Film College (*tekhnikum*)—predecessor to the Soviet State Film School **VGIK**—in 1925–1934. Room was married to actress Ol'ga Zhizneva (1899–1972), who played leads in several of his films.

Other films: *Pits* (Ukhaby, 1928); *Our Girls* (Nashi devushki, 1942, short in a War Film Almanac); *The School of Calumny* (Shkola zloslo-viia, 1952); *The Heart Beats Anew* (Serdtse b'etsia vnov', 1956).

ROSHAL', GRIGORII L'VOVICH (b. 21 October 1899 [other sources: 1898], Novozybkov, Orel province–d. 11 January 1983, Moscow). Russian director and screenwriter. Roshal' began his career as an educator and administrator for the Commissariat of Enlighten-ment (Narkompros) in various cities in Ukraine and Azerbaijan in 1918–1920. In 1921, he was appointed head of the Arts Council for Children's Education at Narkompros. At the same time, he studied at the Supreme Directing Workshops of Vsevolod Meierkhol'd (GVyRM) and worked as a director in the Central Pedagogical The-ater in Moscow (the former Experimental Theater of Narkompros, which he also headed).

In 1925, Roshal' switched to filmmaking. His directorial debut was a silent screen version of Denis Fonvizin's classical pro-Enlighten-ment satire *The Minor* (Nedorosl', 1782) under the title *The Skotinin Masters* (Gospoda Skotininy, 1927). Roshal''s best-known silent, the German-Russian coproduction *The Salamander* (Salamandra, 1928), was directed against obscurantism and ignorance too, albeit in a less grotesque rendition than its predecessor. *Salamander* depicts the plight of a biologist (based on Austrian scientist Paul Kammerer) whose experiments cause outrage among Church authorities and who is finally driven to suicide. The film was prohibited in Germany; it starred, among others, Natal'ia Rozenel' (1900–1962), wife of Com-missar **Anatolii Lunacharskii**, who had supplied the script.

In his first sound film, *Petersburg Night* (Peterburgskaia noch', 1934, codirected with **Vera Stroeva**), Roshal' freed Fedor Dos-toevskii's novellas "White Nights" and "Netochka Nezvanova" (both 1848) of their rapturous Romantic rhetoric and turned them into Marxist commentaries on the mission of the artist in society. Its central character, serf violinist Egor Efimov (modeled after Modest Musorgskii) painfully learns the lesson that what truly matters is not his individuality but the popular appreciation of his art that will ulti-mately immortalize it as folk music. The adaptation preserved some original Dostoevskian notions for which it was criticized in the USSR and praised abroad.

The Oppenheim Family (Sem'ia Oppengeim, 1938, codirected by **Nikolai Plotnikov**), based on a novel by Lion Feuchtwanger, was a noteworthy attempt to interpret the emergence of National Socialism in Germany, featuring first-rate actors such as Solomon Mikhoels who plays the harassed Jewish doctor Jacobi. *The Songs of Abai* (Pesni Abaia, 1945, codirected with Efim Aron [1906–1970]), made at **Kazakhfilm Studio**, again illustrates the thesis of a nation's unity with its artists, in this case, using Kazakh subject matter. Roshal' then helmed a trilogy of biopics characterized by pedestrian cinematic language, openly didactic dialogues, and dogmatic statements about contemporary art and science, including approving allusions to the campaign against "cosmopolitanism." *Academy Member Ivan Pavlov* (Akademik Ivan Pavlov, 1949) in 1950 won the director his first Stalin Prize; *Musorgskii* (1950) in 1951 the second; the third part was *Rimskii-Korsakov* (1952, codirected by **Gennadii Kazanskii**), which came too late for another prize.

Unperturbed by Thaw liberalization, Roshal' made traditionalist historical dramas, starting with *Freebooters* (aka *Flames on the Volga*/Vol'nitsa, 1955) about the exploitation of fishermen in late 19th century. Another period piece, and arguably Roshal's most enduring achievement, is the adaptation of Aleksei Tolstoi's epic *Calvary* (1920–1941), a monumental film trilogy consisting of *The Sisters* (Sestry, 1957), *1918* (1958), and *Gloomy Morning* (Khmuroe utro, 1959). It became a box-office hit, mainly because of its superb performances and the picturesque, in many parts authentic, reconstruction of the 1918–1921 Civil War.

Roshal''s efforts in the 1960s betray a lessening contact with reality and viewers. He returned to the topic of *Salamander* with the political pamphlet *Court of Madmen* (Sud sumasshedshikh, 1962) and to his didactic biopics with the Karl Marx chronicle *A Year Like a Life* (God kak zhizn', 1965). Neither of them left a lasting impression, and Roshal''s swan song, *They Live Next to Us* (Oni zhivut riadom, 1968), about Soviet scientists, was hardly noticed at all.

Roshal' wrote some original screenplays, among them *The New Gulliver* (Novyi Gulliver, 1934), which today is viewed as a classic of stop-motion **animation**. A humanist at heart, but also an extremely cautious man, Roshal''s method of "modernizing" classical literature for propaganda purposes was of crude directness. Apart from films,

Roshal' applied his pedagogical passion at **VGIK**, where he taught for over 30 years, and in the international film amateur movement that he helped organize and administer.

In 1967, Roshal' was awarded the title People's Artist of the USSR. He was married to director Vera Stroeva. His sister, Serafima Roshal' (1906–?), was a screenwriter.

Other films: *His Excellency* (Ego prevoskhoditel'stvo, 1927); *A Man from the Shtetl* (aka *A Jew at War*/Chelovek iz mestechka, 1930); *In Search of Joy* (V poiskakh radosti, 1940); *The Works of the Artamonovs* (Delo Artamonovykh, 1941).

ROSTOTSKII, STANISLAV IOSIFOVICH (b. 21 April 1922, Rybinsk–d. 10 August 2001, Vyborg). Russian director and screenwriter. Rostotskii studied philology at the Moscow Literature Institute in 1940–1942. He fought in the Great Patriotic War where he was severely wounded (he lost a leg). In 1946, Rostotskii became an intern at **Lenfilm Studio** and subsequently enrolled in the Soviet State Film School **VGIK** in the directing workshops of **Sergei Eizenshtein** and **Grigorii Kozintsev**, graduating in 1952.

Rostotskii made his debut with a film about a contemporary Soviet village, *Soil and People* (Zemlia i liudi, 1955), based on essays by Gavriil Troepol'skii. Critics took note of the gritty, problem-oriented realism, avoiding the usual idealization and romanticization. This was even more true of the drama *It Happened in Pen'kovo* (Delo bylo v Pen'kove, 1958), another rural tale that made a star of **Viacheslav Tikhonov**, who subsequently played the male lead in several of Rostotskii's pictures.

May Stars (Maiskie zvezdy, 1959), a Soviet-Czechoslovakian coproduction, marked the first time that Rostotskii dealt with his war experience. He developed that theme in *Out in the Seven Winds* (aka *Four Winds of Heaven*/Na semi vetrakh, 1962), a love story on the backdrop of the German occupation. Rostotskii's self-assertive attempt to adapt Mikhail Lermontov's *A Hero of Our Time* (Geroi nashego vremeni, 1965), with Pechorin singing to the guitar, turned out to be an embarrassment. He fared much better with *Let's See What Monday Brings* (Dozhivem do ponedel'nika, 1968); rewarded with a USSR State Prize in 1970, this contemporary story of a noble high school teacher became a huge blockbuster. The year 1972 marked the peak of Rostotskii's career when he adapted Boris Vasil'ev's tragic novella *The Dawns Are Quiet Here* (A zori zdes' tikhie). Praising youthful beauty and selflessness, this story of five inexperienced female soldiers who sacrifice their lives in the war against Nazi intruders attracted 66 million viewers and won a USSR State Prize in 1975. Rostotskii followed it with a sentimental ballad about canine loyalty, *White Bim Black Ear* (Belyi Bim Chernoe Ukho, 1977), that was crowned, rather surprisingly, with a Lenin Prize in 1980.

Rostotskii irritated many critics with his escapist historical action films *Squadron of Flying Hussars* (Eskadron gusarov letuchikh, 1981, under the pseudonym "Stepan Stepanov") about the hero of the 1812 anti-Napoleonic war, poet Denis Davydov, and *Trees Grow on Stones, Too* (I na kamniakh rastut derev'ia, 1985), a moderately successful Soviet-Norwegian coproduction about the Vikings. Both seemed to prove that the director had lost touch with his audience and with society as well. In the mid-1980s, Rostotskii was one of the few outspoken perestroika skeptics and was attacked as an opportunistic hack at the 1986 Fifth Congress of Soviet Filmmakers. *From the Life of Fedor Kuz'kin* (Iz zhizni Fedora Kuz'kina 1989), from Boris Mozhaev's satire, showed some formerly taboo aspects of rural life in the 1950s but otherwise proved an overly long, uninspiring exercise. Rostotskii spent the last 15 years of his life as a recluse on a Karelian island. In interviews, he expressed his incomprehension and rejection of the changes that Soviet and post-Soviet society was undergoing and viewed the crisis of Russian cinema in the 1990s as a vindication of his stubbornly pro-Soviet attitude.

With his trademark blend of melodramatic plots, open patriotic pathos, and occasional mild humor, Rostotskii's films found the greatest appreciation on the domestic market. A lifelong favorite of the Communist establishment, the director belonged to the category of populists who took pride in their ability to satisfy the emotional needs of the "mass viewer" (*massovyi zritel'*). Such directors proudly juxtaposed their own productions to the popular "low" genre films (thrillers, musicals), on the one hand, and the aesthetically ambitious pictures for a minority of connoisseurs, on the other.

Rostotskii joined the Communist Party in 1951; he was named People's Artist of the USSR in 1974. He held influential administrative posts such as longtime president of the jury of the Moscow Film

Festival. The director's son, actor Andrei Rostotskii (1957–2002), worked in action movies.

ROU, ALEKSANDR ARTUROVICH (b. 8 March 1906, Sergiev Posad [Zagorsk]–d. 28 December 1973, Moscow). Russian director. Rou was of Irish descent; his father worked as a foreign specialist and consultant in the Russian flour-grinding industry and left the country—and his wife and children—at the outbreak of World War I. Young Aleksandr Rou helped support the family in a variety of jobs while also studying accounting. In 1921, he joined the political theater troupe The Blue Blouse (Siniaia bluza) and later enrolled in the Acting Department of **Boris Chaikovskii**'s film school, graduating in 1930. He became an assistant director at **Mezhrabpomfilm Studio**, working for **Iakov Protazanov** and Vladimir Legoshin (1904–1954).

When Rou decided to debut as a filmmaker with a fairy tale, the genre itself had not been established in Soviet cinema and was viewed with suspicion by Marxist dogmatics. However, *On the Pike's Order* (Po shchuch'emu veleniiu, 1938) persuaded many skeptics, demonstrating that miracles, witches, and kings were compatible with the educational needs of a Communist society. Rou thus became the pioneer of a genre; his naïve inventiveness and keen sense of traditional Russian folk humor endeared his pictures to millions of viewers.

Rou also was able to prove that fairy tales were elastic enough to adapt to a variety of circumstances. Thus, his version of *The Immortal Kashchei* (Kashchei bessmertnyi, 1944) features stylized soldiers who closely resemble Nazi troops. With only two exceptions—the adventure *The Secret of the Mountain Lake* (Taina gornogo ozera, 1954), set in Armenia, and the contemporary yarn *A Valuable Gift* (Dragotsennyi podarok, 1956)—Rou managed to stay within his self-carved niche of fantasy, being recognized as a living classic of sorts. Indeed, many of his pictures have retained their freshness and appeal. Not all of Rou's plots were derived from Russian folktales—*The New Adventures of Puss-in-Boots* (Novye pokhozhdeniia Kota v Sapogakh, 1958), for example, used motifs from Charles Perrault. Rou also helmed the ballet film *The Crystal Shoe* (aka *Cinderella*/Khrustal'nyi bashmak, 1960, after **Sergei Prokof'ev**) and the Nikolai Gogol' adaptations *May Night, or the Drowned Woman* (Maiskaia noch', ili utoplennitsa, 1953) and *Evenings on a Farm near Dikanka* (aka *The Night before Christmas*/Vechera na khutore bliz Dikanki, 1961).

Rou's best fairy-tale films feature a clear ethical message but also a weird sense of humor; however, they are cleansed of folklore aspects that were considered embarrassing, such as mysticism and sexual vulgarity. Less visually inventive than his great competitor, **Aleksandr Ptushko**, some of Rou's color pictures unpleasantly smack of studio façade (for example, the otherwise funny *Kingdom of Crooked Mirrors*/Korolevstvo krivykh zerkal, 1963). Especially in the late 1950s–early 1960s, the essential folklore elements were artificially complemented by frame narratives with Pioneers in red ties announcing trivial Soviet morals. Overall, though, Rou's profound respect for the Russian cultural heritage is beyond doubt. In his best adaptations, the tales' stylistic, mythical, and moral integrity is fully intact.

In almost every one of his pictures, Rou cast a group of preferred actors such as Georgii Milliar (1903–1993), who was unsurpassed as the witch Baba Yaga; Anatolii Kubatskii (1908–2001) who specialized in dim-witted robbers; and **Anastasia Zueva** as the wise old narrator introducing and concluding the stories from the window of her hut. Even at the height of the Cold War, when the USSR's cultural exchange with the West was reduced to a minimum, Rou's films were sold to countries all over the world, enchanting and surprising viewers by their wisdom and optimism. Some of Rou's works, in particular the delightful *Father Frost* (aka *Jack Frost*, aka *The Crystal Star*/Morozko, 1964), won reputable international festival prizes.

Rou joined the Communist Party in 1943; he was named People's Artist of the RSFSR in 1968.

Other films: *Vasilisa the Beautiful* (Vasilisa Prekrasnaia, 1939); *The Little Humpbacked Horse* (Konek-Gorbunok, 1941); *Barbara the Fair with the Silken Hair* (Varvara-krasa, dlinnaia kosa, 1969); *The Golden Horns* (Zolotye roga, 1972).

RUMIANTSEVA, NADEZHDA VASIL'EVNA (b. 9 September 1930, Potapovo, Smolensk district–d. 8 April 2008, Moscow). Russian actress. While studying at the Lunacharskii State Theater Institute, Rumiantseva joined the troupe of the Central Children's Theater in Moscow, where she worked from 1948–1950. In 1950, she enrolled in the Soviet State Film School **VGIK**, graduating in 1955, and subsequently became a member of the Theater of the Film Actor.

Petite, sensitive, irresistibly funny, and imbued with an innocent sincerity, Rumiantseva initially was cast in numerous minor roles in second-rate films—for example, as the student Marusia Rodnikova in Nikolai Lebedev's *Toward Life* (Navstrechu zhizni, 1952)— before becoming one of the most popular faces of the 1960s. As one of Soviet cinema's few comediennes, Rumiantseva embodied the spirit of feminine strength and sensitivity in such crowd-pleasers as Iurii Chuliukin's *The Defiant Ones* (Nepoddaiushchiesia, 1959) and *The Gals* (Devchata, 1962), as well as *Queen of the Dispensing Pump* (Koroleva benzokolonki, 1963). Her "cute" screen image was balanced by a strong personality and stubbornness in defending moral and social principles. The gullibility of Rumiantseva's heroines to romantic advances made for exciting chemistry with her—often sexist—male partners, such as **Nikolai Rybnikov**. Subsequent films, including **Boris Barnet**'s *The Whistle Stop* (Polustanok, 1963), *The Stubborn Girl* (Upriamaia devchonka, 1964), and *An Easy Life* (Legkaia zhizn', 1965), solidified Rumiantseva's reputation as a charming scene-stealer.

In the 1970s, the number of roles that were offered to this endearing actress dwindled; living with her husband, a diplomat, abroad for several years, Rumiantseva practically disappeared from Soviet screens. As a film actress, her name remains associated with the 1960s and the hopes and youthful optimism of that decade.

Rumiantseva was named Merited Artist of the RSFSR in 1963.

Other films: *Alyosha Ptitsyn Develops Personality* (Alesha Ptitsyn vyrabatyvaet kharakter, 1953); *The Mexican* (Meksikanets, 1956); *A Tough Cookie* (Krepkii oreshek, 1968); *The Married Bachelor* (Zhenatyi kholostiak, 1983); *Carrion-Eagles on the Roads* (Sterviatniki na dorogakh, 1990); *A Chance Joy* (Nechaiannaia radost', 2005, TV).

RUSSIAN ARK (Russkii kovcheg, 2002). Russia/Germany. 96 min., color. Directed by **Aleksandr Sokurov**. Script: Anatolii Nikoforov, Boris Khaimskii, Svetlana Proskurina, Aleksandr Sokurov. Cinematography: Tilman Büttner. Music: Sergei Evtushenko. Cast: Sergei

Dontsov, Mariia Kuznetsova, Leonid Mozgovoi, David Giorgobiani, Maksim Sergeev.

A refined 19th-century French aristocrat and intellectual (Dontsov) who has studied Russia embarks on a fantastic tour of the Hermitage museum in St. Petersburg, commenting on the peculiarities of Russian history, culture, and mentality, as well as the nation's troubled relationship with the West. On his tour, he passes a private theater and galleries and encounters a variety of historical figures, including Peter the Great (Sergeev), Catherine II (Kuznetsova), and Nikolai II and his family. A large ball—the last royal gala of 1913—concludes the film, celebrating the grandeur of the Russian Empire, which is condensed in this "Noah's ark" of culture and saved from the bestialities of the past.

RYBNIKOV, NIKOLAI NIKOLAEVICH (b.13 December 1930, Borisoglebsk, Voronezh district–d. 28 July 1990, Moscow). Russian actor. Rybnikov studied at the Stalingrad (later: Volgograd) Medical Institute and worked on stage at the Stalingrad Drama Theater before enrolling in the Soviet State Film School **VGIK** in the workshop of **Sergei Gerasimov** and **Tamara Makarova**, graduating in 1953. He made his movie debut with supporting parts in **Semen Timoshenko**'s unusual soccer **comedy** *The Reserve Player* (Zapasnoi igrok) and the **children's film** *The Team from Our Street* (Kommanda s nashei ulitsy), both 1954.

In the mid-1950s, Rybnikov became a cult star with roles of raw young men—usually workers—whose forthrightness and idealism reflected the spirit of the post-Stalinist Thaw, and whose open erotic drive marked a change from bloodless, Stalinist puritans. The actor was effective in contemporary dramas such as **Mikhail Shveitser**'s *Alien Kin* (Chuzhaia rodnia, 1955), **Marlen Khutsiev**'s *Springtime on Zarechnaia Street* (Vesna na Zarechnoi ulitse, 1956), and **Aleksandr Zarkhi**'s *The Height* (Vysota, 1957), yet also in comedies, including **El'dar Riazanov**'s *Girl without Address* (Devushka bez adresa, 1957) and Iurii Chuliukin's megahit *The Gals* (Devchata, 1962). Whether in dramatic or comedic parts, Rybnikov's natural talent and romantic aura of a flirtatious womanizer with a golden heart never failed to enchant millions of Soviet viewers, perhaps because

he was "one of the first Soviet actors to embody individual empower-
ment" (Josephine Woll).

Rybnikov's fame began to fade in the mid-1960s when the euphoria of the Thaw was over. By the early 1970s, he was reduced to
supporting parts, predominantly workers' characters in films such as
Aleksei Saltykov's *The Ivanov Family* (Sem'ia Ivanovykh, 1975),
still recognized but no longer idolized.

Rybnikov was honored with the title Merited Artist of the RSFSR
in 1964 and People's Artist of the Russian Federation in 1981. He
was married to popular actress Alla Larionova (1931–2000), who
costarred with him in a number of films.

Other films: *Kochubei* (1956); ***War and Peace*** (Voina i mir,
1962–1967).

RYZHOV, IVAN PETROVICH (b. 25 January 1913, Zelenaia slo-
boda, Ramensk district–d. 15 March 2004, Moscow). Russian actor.
Ryzhov grew up in a rural area and worked in a collective farm
(kolkhoz). He studied at the school of the Theater of the Revolution
in Moscow, graduating in 1935, and joined the theater's troupe the
same year. In 1940, he became a member of Soiuzdetfilm studio (the
later **Gor'kii Studio for Children's and Youth Films**), and in 1945,
of the Studio Theater of the Movie Actor in Moscow.

After debuting with the role of a Cossack leader in *People from
Kuban'* (Kubantsy, 1939), Ryzhov became a valued supporting actor who informed seemingly unremarkable episodic characters with
color and unexpected depth. Some of his more than 80 film roles are
in literary adaptations such as Svistunov in **Vladimir Petrov**'s loyal
version of Nikolai Gogol''s *The Inspector General* (Revizor, 1952),
and the conservative boyar Gavrila Rtishchev in **Aleksandr Mitta**'s
popular *The Tale of How Tsar Peter Married His Moor* (Skaz pro
to, kak tsar' Petr arapa zhenil, 1976), adapted from an Aleksandr
Pushkin fragment.

Ryzhov gained great popularity in 1964 when **Vasilii Shukshin**
cast him as the boss of a car depot in *There Is Such a Lad* (Zhivet
takoi paren'). It marked the beginning of an artistic partnership that
continued with the funny part of a train steward in *Happy Go Lucky*
(Pechki-lavochki, 1972) and the impressive performance as Fedor

Baikalov, the somewhat naïve, utterly decent old father of Liuba, in *Red Snowball Tree* (Kalina krasnaia, 1974), Shukshin's tragic swan song. Ryzhov embodied the positive appeal of rural Russians—sincerity, trust, wit, and generosity of the heart—without ever degenerating into nationalist clichés. He seemed an organic part of Shukshin's world, and when other directors adapted the late writer's stories for the screen, their casting of Ryzhov signified continuity, for example, in **Sergei Nikonenko**'s *For Heaven's Sake* (Elki-palki, 1988).

Ryzhov was awarded the title People's Artist of the Russian Federation in 1980.

Other films: *Kutuzov* (aka *1812*, 1944); *The Tale of Time Lost* (Skazka o poteriannom vremeni, 1964); *Dawns Are Kissing* (Tseluiutsia zori, 1978); *He's a Good Grandfather but Doesn't Say Where the Money Is Hidden* (Ded khoroshii, no . . . ne govorit gde spriatal den'gi, 1993).

RZHESHEVSKII, ALEKSANDR GEORGIEVICH (b. 12 September 1903, St. Petersburg–d. 19 January 1967, Moscow). Russian screenwriter. Rzheshevskii was a sailor in the Baltic fleet and participated in Civil War battles in Kronshtadt, Southern Russia, and Central Asia, before joining the Soviet secret service (GPU) in Leningrad. He also started an acting career with episodic roles in silent movies in 1923, studied acting at the Leningrad Institute for Screen Art in 1924–1926, and began to write screenplays.

In the late 1920s, faced with the ongoing, stale theatricality of mainstream cinema and the petit-bourgeois atmosphere of the New Economic Policy (NEP), leading Soviet avant-garde directors found a congenial author in Rzheshevskii, whose unusual scripts were perceived by many as genuine, revolutionary revelations. Full of unabashed pathos and often achronological in structure ("loose narration"), Rzheshevskii's so-called emotional scripts (*emotsional'nye ststenarii*) were intended to evoke an emotion-filled atmosphere and to describe the anticipated impact on the viewer rather than capturing details.

The already well-established filmmaker **Iurii Zheliabuzhskii** was the first to direct one of Rzheshevskii's peculiar screenplays, *The City Cannot Be Entered* (V gorod vkhodit' nel'zia, 1929), a melodramatic spy story in which a loyal Soviet professor is forced to confront his treacherous son. **Vsevolod Pudovkin** publicly endorsed Rzheshevskii's theoretical assumptions and chose the 1928 script *Life Is Very Good* (Ochen' khorosho zhivetsia, 1930, released in 1932 as *A Simple Case*/Prostoi sluchai, 1932). Yet the final product was neither accepted nor understood by viewers in the Soviet Union or abroad: "The problem of ethics that Pudovkin declared to be his foremost aim was actually submerged in a splendor of sensual experiments that always moved their maker more than they did any audience" (Leyda).

Twenty-six Commissars (1933, coauthored by Rzheshevskii with A. Amiragov and the director, **Nikoloz Shengelaia**) tells the story of Bolshevik activists murdered by occupational forces in Baku in 1918 in a pathos-filled, emotionally overbearing manner. Two years after its successful—albeit controversially received—release, **Sergei Eizenshtein**, who had just returned to the USSR after years abroad and was looking for an ambitious project, began to shoot *Bezhin Meadow* (Bezhin lug, 1935). Rzheshevskii's script— commissioned by the Central Committee of the Komsomol—took extreme liberties with its source, Ivan Turgenev's 1850 short story, giving it a militantly antipatriarchal and antireligious slant. The ensuing disaster harmed both the director's and his scriptwriter's reputations; the latter never recovered from the blow. Although Rzheshevskii continued to write scripts, the label "formalist"— attached to him by relentless dogmatics—stuck and turned him into a persona non grata in Soviet cinema. As a result, this father of 10 children could barely make ends meet in subsequent decades, living in extreme poverty in the Moscow suburbs.

Rzheshevskii, who at one point harbored hopes for directing his own films, regarded the screenwriter as a close artistic partner of the director. In hindsight, he can be described as a hapless radical innovator, one of the first who dared to focus a film plot on the author's subjective emotional attitude toward it, thus deviating from traditional descriptive, chronological, event-based storytelling.

Other screenplays (all unfilmed): *The Year 1916* (Tysiacha deviat'sot shestnadtsatyi god, 1928); *There Is Talk in the Mountains* (V gorakh govoriat, 1930); *The Ocean* (Okean, 1931); *World and Man* (Mir i chelovek, 1936); *Nobody Is Merrier Than Us* (Veselei nas net, 1940).

– S –

SALT FOR SVANETIA (Jim Shvante [marili svanets]/Sol' Svanetii, 1930). State Film Department (Goskinprom) of the Georgian People's Commissariat of Enlightenment (Narkompros). 62 mins., b/w. Directed by **Mikhail Kalatozov**. Script: Mikhail Kalatozov from an article by Sergei Tret'iakov. Cinematography: Mikhail Kalatozov, M. Gegelashvili. Premiere: November 1931.

The **documentary** tells about the proud yet poor and backward tribe of the Svans in the mountains of Svanetia who live under constant threat, defending themselves from the greedy landowners in the valleys. Nature, wild and unpredictable, is another foe. Because of a lack of water and salt, the Svans and their livestock suffer from numerous health problems. Religious faith and ancient superstition keep the people under the yoke of exploiters and priests, to whom the burial of a rich man is more important than the birth of a child. Only when the Bolsheviks build a road through the mountains is Svanetia finally connected with the outside world and able to solve its problems.

SALTYKOV, ALEKSEI ALEKSANDROVICH (b. 13 May 1934, Moscow–d. 8 April 1993, Moscow). Russian director and screenwriter. In the late 1940s, Saltykov worked in a variety of jobs such as electrician in the building of the newspaper *Pravda*. He studied economics in 1951–1952 and then enrolled in **Sergei Gerasimov** and **Tamara Makarova**'s workshop at the Soviet State Film School **VGIK**. After his graduation in 1959, Saltykov joined **Mosfilm Studio**.

Saltykov debuted with two **children's films**, *The Kids from Our Block* (Rebiata s nashego dvora, 1959, codirected with A. Iastrebov) and the popular *My Friend, Kol'ka!* (Drug moi, Kol'ka! 1961, codirected with **Aleksandr Mitta**), which contains a critical, differentiated depiction of Soviet society. Saltykov's first independently directed feature, *Bang, Drum* (Bei, baraban, 1962), deals with orphans who became Young Pioneers in the 1920s.

Saltykov then was entrusted with a major project, the three-hour drama ***The Chairman*** (Predsedatel', 1964), about an administrator in a barren, postwar village whose willpower and leadership abilities raise the peasants from their lethargy. The picture was controversial already at the script stage, yet its makers ultimately managed to bring to the screen some grittily realistic and anti-Stalinist elements that were met with critical and popular approval. In Saltykov's view, the country's agriculture could be rescued from its continuing misery only by authoritarian methods exercised by a stern, ascetic type of leader. Thus, *The Chairman* demonstrates a principal reliance on personality, not structural economic changes. This concept is also characteristic of *The Director* (Direktor, 1970) about an automobile industry manager modeled after the legendary Ivan Likhachev (1896–1956); like Saltykov's previous film, it was based on a script by Iurii Nagibin (1920–1994). The production was interrupted by the tragic death of its lead, **Evgenii Urbanskii**, on location in Turkmenistan.

Another important theme in Saltykov's work was the Great Patriotic War, starting with *Women's Kingdom* (Bab'e Tsarstvo, 1966), about a widow whose husband and son were killed in action and who provides leadership and orientation to her fellow villagers under German occupation; this film became an even greater blockbuster than *The Chairman*. Heroism and betrayal on the backdrop of the war are also at the center of the tragic romance *There Is No Return* (Vozvrata net, 1973), another box-office hit, and *Test for Immortality* (Ekzamen na bessmertie, 1983) about a unit of ensigns defending Moscow against the Nazi onslaught in 1941. *Emel'ian Pugachev* (1978), a two-part epic about the 18th-century uprising of serfs and Cossacks that shook up the Russian Empire, continued the theme of leadership and statism. Saltykov's last picture, the four-hour epic *Thunder over Russia* (Groza nad Rus'iu, 1992), an adaptation of Aleksei K. Tolstoi's novel *The Silver Prince* (1862), was inspired by the crisis and ultimate demise of Soviet statehood, albeit in historical, mid-17th-century disguise.

Saltykov was a prolific filmmaker with a reliably realistic style whose output showed confidence in a diversity of genres with a penchant for strong, passionate characters driven by a cause. Stylistically unpretentious, critically underrated, and almost exclusively targeting domestic audiences, the majority of Saltykov's pictures combine Communist ideology with a sincere concern for the well-being of Russia.

Saltykov was awarded the title Merited Artist of the RSFSR in 1969 and People's Artist of the Russian Federation in 1980.

Other films: *And It Was Evening, and It Was Morning* (I byl vecher, i bylo utro, 1971); *The Ivanov Family* (Sem'ia Ivanovykh, 1975); *Lord Great Novgorod* (Gospodin Velikii Novgorod, 1984); *Everything Has Been Paid For* (Za vse zaplacheno, 1988, TV miniseries).

SAMOILOV, EVGENII VALERIANOVICH (b. 16 April 1912, St. Petersburg–d. 17 February 2006, Moscow). Russian actor. Born into the family of a factory worker, Samoilov began to study acting in Nikolai Khodotov's studio in Leningrad in 1928 and continued at the Arts Polytechnicum, graduating in 1930. In 1934, Vsevolod Meierkhol'd invited him into his Moscow troupe; in 1940, he joined the Theater of the Revolution, and in 1968, the Malyi Theater.

Samoilov debuted in the movies in **Ihor' Savchenko**'s little-seen **comedy** *Chance Encounter* (Sluchainaia vstrecha, 1934–1936). When **Aleksandr Dovzhenko** cast him as the revolutionary leader Shchors in his 1939 biopic, Samoilov became a star, adorned with a Stalin Prize in 1941 and cast in films of **Grigorii Aleksandrov**, **Iulii Raizman**, **Vladimir Petrov**, and **Mikhail Romm**. His best performances in the 1940s were in roles of charming, chivalrous young men, usually officers in shining uniforms, whose professional devotion is only matched by their unconditional affection for the woman they love. Especially the parts of Lieutenant Kolchin in **Konstantin Iudin**'s hit *Hearts of Four* (aka *Four Hearts*/Serdtsa chetyrekh, 1941, released 1945) and of Kudriashov in **Ivan Pyr'ev**'s *At Six in the Evening after the War* (aka *Six P.M.*/V shest' chasov vechera posle voiny, 1944, Stalin Prize 1946) enchanted viewers with their irresistible friendliness, optimism, decency, and Samoilov's trademark dashing smile.

The actor's popularity was exploited for Stalinist demagoguery in films such as **Abram Room**'s "anticosmopolitan" *Court of Honor* (Sud chesti, 1948) and **Mikheil Chiaureli**'s *Unforgettable Year 1919* (Nezabyvaemyi 1919i god, 1952). In later years, Samoilov continued both his carefree comedic line—among others, in **Andrei Tutyshkin**'s *To the Black Sea* (K Chernomu moriu, 1957)—and the pathos-filled patriotic image, for example, in **Sergei Bondarchuk**'s *They Fought for the Motherland* (Oni srazahlis' za rodinu, 1975). His last film role was the monk and chronicler Pimen in Bondarchuk's adaptation of Aleksandr Pushkin's *Boris Godunov* (1986).

Samoilov joined the Communist Party in 1951; he was named People's Artist of the Russian Federation in 1954 and People's Artist of the USSR in 1974. Samoilov's daughter is **Tat'iana Samoilova** with whom he starred in *A Long Path on a Short Day* (Dlinnaia doroga v korotkii den', 1972); his son Aleksei (b. 1945) is an actor at Malyi Theater.

Other films: *The Radiant Path* (aka *Tanya*/Svetlyi put', 1940); *Mashen'ka* (1942); *Admiral Nakhimov* (1947); *Heroes of Shipka* (Geroi Shipki, 1956); *Waterloo* (1971).

SAMOILOVA, TAT'IANA EVGEN'EVNA (b. 4 May 1934, Leningrad). Russian actress. Samoilova was born into the family of popular film and stage actor **Evgenii Samoilov**. She studied at the Shchukin theater school in Moscow, graduating in 1956, and the State Theater Institute (GITIS), graduating in 1962.

Samoilova made her film debut with the role of Mariia in Vladimir Kaplunovskii's *The Mexican* (Meksikanets, 1956). Her performance as Veronika in **Mikhail Kalatozov**'s World War II drama *The Cranes Are Flying* (Letiat zhuravli, 1957) catapulted her to international fame. The actress provided this character with a passion and a feminine enigma unprecedented in Soviet cinema, stunning critics and viewers alike. Her star status, resulting from the film's triumph at the 1958 Cannes Film Festival, was used in foreign productions such as the Hungarian *Alba Regia* (1961), directed by Mihály Szemes, the French-Soviet coproduction *Leon Garros Is Seeking a Friend* (aka *20000 lieues sur la terre*/Leon Garros ishchet druga, 1960), and the joint Italian-Soviet project *They Went Eastward* (aka Italiani brava gente/Oni shli na vostok, 1964), helmed by Giuseppe di Santis.

Kalatozov cast Samoilova in an interesting variation of her Veronika image, putting more emphasis on the heroic aspect, in the powerful yet critically underrated existential drama *The Unmailed Letter* (Neotpravlennoe pis'mo, 1960). **Aleksandr Zarkhi** drew on the actress's sensuality and unbridled emotionality when he gave her the title role of his Lev Tolstoi adaptation *Anna Karenina* (1968), a choice that was controversial at the time but seems more than justified in hindsight. Due to health problems, Samoilova was unable to continue her film career in later years; her appearances after the 1960s were sporadic and unremarkable.

Samoilova was named Merited Artist of the Russian Federation in 1965 and People's Artist of Russia in 1993. In the late 1950s, she was married to actor **Vasilii Lanovoi**, who portrays Count Vronskii in *Anna Karenina*.

Other films: *There Is No Return* (Vozvrata net, 1974); *The Ocean* (Okean, 1974); *Diamonds for the Dictatorship of the Proletariat* (Brillianty dlia diktatury proletariata, 1976); *Mars* (2004); *Nirvana* (2008).

SAMSONOV [real name: Edel'shtein]**, SAMSON IOSIFOVICH** (b. 23 February 1921, Novozybkovo, Briansk district–d. 31 August 2002, Moscow). Russian director, screenwriter, and actor. Samsonov began his career as an actor at **Mosfilm Studio** in 1939, specializing in episodic parts, while simultaneously studying at the Moscow District Art College "To the Memory of 1905" and also working as a stage actor. He enrolled in the Soviet State Film School **VGIK**, where he studied with **Sergei Gerasimov** and **Tamara Makarova**, graduating in 1949, and was Gerasimov's assistant on the Great Patriotic War tragedy *The Young Guard* (Molodaia gvardiia, 1948). Samsonov then worked as a stage director at Vakhtangov Theater (1951–1952) and the Studio Theater of the Film Actor (1949–1954).

Samsonov made his directorial debut in 1955 with an adaptation of Anton Chekhov's short story *The Grasshopper* (Poprygun'ia, 1955), which he had already directed on stage. The film, with quality performances by **Sergei Bondarchuk** and **Liudmila Tselikovskaia**, won a Silver Lion in Venice and was praised, among others, by François Truffaut, who wrote, "The delightful direction, a bit in the manner of Max Ophüls, these beautiful colors, and the excellent acting—an intelligent and delicate picture!" Inexplicably, over the following four decades Samsonov did not quite meet the high expectations established by his debut, including his disappointing return to Chekhov, *The Three Sisters* (Tri sestry, 1965). Samsonov scored a major box-office success with *An Optimistic Tragedy* (Optimisticheskaia tragediia, 1963), a dynamic Civil War drama adapted from Vsevolod Vishnevskii's play. He became a prolific, reliable all-around professional who could pull off everything from war drama to sports **comedy**, countryside melodrama, foreign mystery, William Shakespeare, and J. B. Priestley.

In the 1980s, Samsonov proved his talent for contemporary social themes with *Singles Will Be Provided with Dorm Space* (Odinokim predostavliaetsia obshchezhitie, 1983) and *The Dancing Floor* (Tantsploshchadka, 1985), both taking place in provincial towns. *The Man Out of Place* (Neprikaiannyi, 1989), about a choreographer who at the end of his life realizes the futility of his efforts, likely has autobiographical significance. Two openly commercial thrillers, *The Mousetrap* (Myshelovka, 1990) from Agatha Christie, and *Casino* (1992) from a D. H. Chase novel, show an unusual adaptability to different milieus but scarce artistic ambition. Samsonov concluded his career with a literary adaptation, *Dear Friend of Long Forgotten Years* (Milyi drug davno zabytykh let, 1996), from a short story by Aleksei Tolstoi.

Samsonov was named Merited Artist of the RSFSR in 1965 and People's Artist of the RSFSR in 1978.

Other films: *Behind the Window of the Store* (Za vitrinoi univermaga, 1956); *Miles of Fire* (Ognennye versty, 1957); *The Arena* (Arena, 1967); *A Purely English Murder* (Chisto angliiskoe ubiistvo, 1974); *The Eighth World Wonder* (Vos'moe chudo sveta, 1981).

SANIN, ALEKSANDR AKIMOVICH [real name: Shenberg; an earlier pseudonym was Bezhin] (b. 3 April 1869, Moscow–d. 7 May 1956, Rome). Russian director. Born into the family of russified Germans, Sanin studied history and philology at Moscow University and simultaneously began to act in amateur theater ventures. After meeting Konstantin Stanislavskii in 1887, he devoted his life to theater, performing various functions and finally joining the troupe of the Moscow Art Theater (MKhAT) in 1898. Apart from appearing in supporting roles, Sanin was Stanislavskii's codirector in productions of historical plays by Aleksei K. Tolstoi, among others. In 1902–1907, he worked at the Aleksandrinskii Theater in St. Petersburg as a director, actor, and acting teacher. He then joined the troupe of Sergei Diagilev, directing Russian operas in Paris and London. Following the 1917 Bolshevik Revolution, Sanin worked as an opera director at the Bolshoi Theater in Moscow.

Sanin's cinema debut, *Tsarevich Aleksei* (1918), from a historical play by Dmitrii Merezhkovskii (1869–1941) about Peter I and his pious son, revealed a profoundly conservative political approach.

Virgin Hills (aka *Maiden's Mountains*/Dev'i gory, aka *Legend of the Antichrist*/Legenda ob antikhriste, 1918), starring a number of MKhAT artists, features an apocalyptic plot loosely based on a Merezhkovskii novel and elements of apocryphal legends from the Volga region. The film was produced by the company Rus'—the later **Mezhrabpomfilm Studio**—with **Iurii Zheliabuzhskii** as cinematographer; its underlying mystical concept was interpreted as reactionary by pro-Soviet critics. Sanin's foremost achievement in cinema is the Lev Tolstoi adaptation *Polikushka* (1919). This tragedy of a pathetic, small man whose life is destroyed by his own passiveness and a stroke of bad luck became a worldwide success after its delayed release in 1922. Particularly the expressive power of theater legend Ivan Moskvin (1874–1946) in the title role turned the film into a genuine cultural event. Sanin's last picture was *The Thieving Magpie* (Soroka-vorovka, 1920), an adaptation of a story by Aleksandr Hertsen about the hardships suffered by a serf working as an actress. All of Sanin's films reveal a keen sense of rhythm and an extraordinary ability to direct viewers' emotions.

Sanin left the Soviet Union in 1922, never to return to Russian soil—or to cinema, for that matter. He continued his successful career as an opera director in Italy, France, Spain, Latin America, and the United States.

SAPAROV, USMAN (b. 19 February 1938, village Peshai-Ali, Turkmenistan). Turkmen director, screenwriter, and cinematographer. After graduating from the Soviet State Film School **VGIK** in 1963, where he had studied with **Boris Volchek**, Saparov worked as a cameraman at **Turkmenfilm Studio**. He then enrolled in the Supreme Directing and Screenwriting Courses (VKSR) in Moscow, where **Aleksandr Mitta** was his teacher, graduating in 1979.

Saparov's full-length feature debut, *The Upbringing of a Man* (Muzhskoe vospitanie, 1983), was a triumphant success, winning him a USSR State Prize in 1984, as well as international recognition. This poetic story of a seven-year-old and his eye-opening experiences when living with his grandfather, a shepherd, sensitively captures the psychology of a child. Saparov's later films, including the fact-based thriller *Halima* (1989), display a gritty, harshly realistic view of contemporary Turkmen life characterized by corruption, crime, and moral decay. *Little Angel, Bring Me Joy* (Angelochek, sdelai radost', 1992) tells the story of a six-year-old German boy who is left to himself after the forced resettling of his community from Turkmenistan and creates a better world in his own imagination.

Following the breakdown of the **Turkmen cinema** industry, Saparov settled in Moscow, where he works for Russian television, in particular children's programs such as *Sesame Street.*

Saparov was named People's Artist of Turkmenistan in 1994.

Other films: *The Little Camel* (Verbliuzhonok, 1979, short); *Adventures on Small Islands* (Prikliucheniia na malen'kikh ostrovakh, 1985); *The Madwoman* (Beshenaia, 1987); *Karakum* (1997).

SAVCHENKO, IHOR' ANDREEVICH (b. 11 October 1906, Vinnitsa, Ukraine–d. 14 December 1950, Moscow). Ukrainian director, screenwriter, and actor. In 1918, Savchenko joined various tour theaters working as a child actor and later as a costume and set designer; he also attended the private acting studio of Ol'ga Ordi-Svetlova. Savchenko studied at the Leningrad Theater Institute from 1926 to 1929 and then headed the Baku Theater of Workers' Youth (TRAM) until 1932 and the Moscow Theater of Workers' Youth until 1935.

Savchenko's movie career began with two agitprop shorts: *Nikita Ivanovich and Socialism* (Nikita Ivanovich i sotsializm, 1931), adapted from his own stage play, and *People without Hands* (Liudi bez ruk, 1932). *The Accordion* (Garmon', 1934) was categorized as a "film operetta" and became the first Soviet musical **comedy**; it deals with Komsomol youths fighting for Communism in a culturally resistant village. Characteristic of Savchenko's visual style are romantic grand vistas in which the rural communities are embedded. Produced for **Mezhrabpomfilm Studio**, *The Accordion* was popular with audiences but loathed by critics. "Compared with the huge musical comedy machines to come, *Accordion* is a real credit to the Soviet film, despite its neglect then and since" (Jay Leyda).

Savchenko's comedy *The Month of May* (Mesiats mai, 1934–1936) was severely criticized for its supposed "formalism" and butchered by censors. Soon after its release under the alternate title *Chance Encounter* (Sluchainaia vstrecha), following a yearlong dispute, it disappeared from the screens and was forgotten. The director was more successful with films about the Bolshevik Revolution and the ensuing Civil War, including *The Song of Cossack Golota* (aka *The Ballad of Cossack Golota*/Duma pro kazaka Golotu, 1937) in which the brutal clash between Reds and Whites is portrayed as an adventure with heroic youngsters as participants. The little-seen *Riders* (aka *Guerilla Brigade*/Vsadniki, 1939) operates on similar ground, blending peasants' patriotism, folklore, and humor directed against inept German aggressors. All of these films are distinguished by Savchenko's deliberately nonintellectual approach to cinema and his preference for optimistic plots with energetic, rank-and-file characters who are unperturbed by doubts or hesitation and rather sing and joke together.

Savchenko won critical praise and official recognition for his keen attention to historical detail in the monumental 17th-century epic *Bohdan Khmel'nitskii* (1941) about Ukraine's resistance against Polish occupation. The film earned the director his first Stalin Prize, largely for its positive emphasis on Ukraine's 1654 union with Russia. The World War II adventure *Young Partisans* (Iunye partizany, 1942), however, which Savchenko codirected with **Lev Kuleshov**, was shelved, supposedly because it showed Soviet children too actively participating in anti-Nazi combat. *Partisans in the Ukrainian Steppes* (Partizany v stepiakh Ukrainy, 1942) and *Ivan Nikulin, Russian Sailor* (Ivan Nikulin—russkii matros, 1944)—Savchenko's first film in color—tell episodes of the Great Patriotic War, singing praise to regular people's courage and selflessness. The comedy *An Old Vaudeville* (aka *The Lucky Bride*/Starinnyi vodevil', 1946), which—together with similar efforts by **Ivan Pyr'ev** and **Konstantin Iudin**—responded to Soviet viewers' need for populist, carefree entertainment, was a huge hit with audiences, if not with critics.

Savchenko's last completed project, *The Third Blow* (Tretii udar, 1948), was part of a series of cinematic re-creations of the major battles of the Great Patriotic War made at Iosif Stalin's order. A monumental account of World War II events, the film heavily focuses on the Soviet leader amidst expertly staged battle scenes. Yet Savchenko also managed to insert his usual populism—apparently too much for the dictator's taste, so that the film only received a Second-Class Stalin Prize, an anomaly given its prestige status.

Savchenko's life ended suddenly before he was able to finish *Taras Shevchenko* with **Sergei Bondarchuk** in the title role of Ukraine's national poet in the 1840s and 1850s. Completed by Savchenko's students at the Soviet State Film School **VGIK**, where he had been in charge of a directing workshop since 1946, the film was awarded a posthumous Stalin Prize in 1952. Despite numerous interferences by censors, the final version conveys liveliness and artistry, which were rare in those days.

Savchenko counted among his students **Sergei Paradjanov**, **Aleksandr Alov**, **Vladimir Naumov**, **Marlen Khutsiev**, Feliks Mironer, **Latif Faiziev**, and **Iurii Ozerov**, who in later years praised their teacher's impeccable professionalism and personal warmth. Soviet film historians, too, have always regarded Savchenko with reverence, while he is almost unknown abroad.

Savchenko joined the Communist Party in 1944 and was awarded the title Merited Artist of the Russian Federation the same year. *See also* UKRAINIAN CINEMA.

SAVEL'EVA, LIUDMILA MIKHAILOVNA (b. 24 January 1942, Leningrad). Russian actress. Savel'eva was educated as a ballerina and made her stage debut with the Kirov Theater ballet troupe in Leningrad in 1961. **Sergei Bondarchuk** discovered Savel'eva's acting talent and focused on her youthful, at times even childlike, emotionality and purity in his mega-epic *War and Peace* (Voina i mir, 1962–1967) from Lev Tolstoi's novel. Savel'eva, portraying Natasha Rostova, stood her ground next to the crème de la crème of Russian actors and actresses. The unprecedented international success of that film shot the novice actress to stardom. As a result, she was cast as the Russian wife of Marcello Mastroianni in Vittorio de Sica's Italian-Soviet coproduction *Sunflowers* (I girasoli/Podsolnukhi, 1969). She also played the lead in the Bulgarian-Soviet historical drama *Iuliia Vrevskaia* (1978).

Subsequently, Savel'eva worked with leading Soviet directors in quality productions, among them **Aleksandr Alov** and **Vladimir Naumov**'s *The Flight* (Beg, 1970) from Mikhail Bulgakov's play, and also in lighter entertainment fare such as **Vladimir Vainshtok**'s *Horseman without Head* (Vsadnik bez golovy, 1973) or *The Hat* (Shliapa, 1982). However, none of Savel'eva's later roles could match her memorable debut.

Savel'eva was named People's Artist of the RSFSR in 1985.

Other films: *Chaika* (The Seagull, 1970); *Success* (Uspekh, 1985); *The Tender Age* (Nezhnyi vozrast, 2000); *Anna Karenina* (2008, TV).

SAVVINA, IIA SERGEEVNA (b. 2 March 1936, Voronezh). Russian actress. Savvina, the daughter of a country doctor, graduated from the Department of Journalism at Moscow Lomonosov University in 1960, where she also had worked in the famous student theater. Her superb performance in the title role of **Iosif Kheifits**'s Anton Chekhov adaptation *The Lady with a Lapdog* (Dama s sobachkoi, 1960) forever defined the screen image of this actress, although subsequent pictures, as well as numerous stage roles at the Mossovet Theater (1960–1977) and Moscow Art Theater (MKhAT, since 1977) proved that her range is broader than a sensitive ingenue.

Savvina played leads in a number of contemporary dramas, among them the antireligious *The Sinner* (Greshnitsa, 1962) and *Every Day of Doctor Kalinnikova* (Kazhdyi den' doktora Kalinnikovoi (1973). In **Andrei Mikhalkov-Konchalovskii**'s ill-fated masterpiece *Asia's Happiness* (Asino schast'e, aka Istoriia Asi Kliachinoi, kotoraia liubila, da ne vyshla zamuzh, 1967; released 1988) Savvina seamlessly blends in with a crowd of authentic country folk; the role brought her renewed recognition in the time of perestroika. However, she refused to play the aged Asia in a sequel, *Riaba My Chicken* (Kurochka Riaba, 1994), charging that the film was essentially anti-Russian; the part went to **Inna Churikova** instead.

Savvina's delicate features and calm sensuality lent themselves to adaptations of 19th-century classics such as **Aleksandr Zarkhi**'s *Anna Karenina* (1968), where she played Dolly, and **Aleksandr Borisov**'s *A Gentle Creature* (Krotkaia, 1960) from Dostoevskii's short story. She portrayed Chekhov's sister, Mariia Pavlovna, in **Sergei Iutkevich**'s poetic *Plot for a Short Story* (Siuzhet dlia nebol'shogo rasskaza, 1969). As a brutally obnoxious schemer in **El'dar Riazanov**'s satire *The Garage* (Garazh, 1982) and an unfeeling wife in **Iulii Raizman**'s *Private Life* (Chastnaia zhizn', 1983), Savvina was cast against type, much to the amazement of fans who were used to her aura of romantic vulnerability.

In 1983, Savvina received a USSR State Prize for her performance in *Private Life*, and in 1990 the same award for *Asia's Happiness*.

She was named People's Artist of the Russian Federation in 1977 and People's Artist of the USSR in 1990.

Other films: *In the Town of S.* (V gorode S., 1967); *Diary of a School Headmaster* (Dnevnik direktora shkoly, 1976); *Trotskii* (1993); *A Place in the Sun* (Mesto pod solntsem, 2004, TV); *Listening to Silence* (Slushaia tishinu, 2007).

SAYIDBEYLI, HASAN MEHDI-OGLY [other spellings: Seyidbeyli, Seydbely] (b. 22 December 1920, Baku–d. 25 June 1980). Azerbaijani director and screenwriter. In 1943, Sayidbeyli graduated from the Soviet State Film School **VGIK**, where he studied with **Sergei Eizenshtein**. He initially worked as a writer of fiction; in the 1950s, he turned some of his stories and novels into scripts and also directed **documentaries**. One of his most successful screenplays was the World War II adventure story *On Faraway Shores* (Uzag Sahillarda/Na dal'nikh beregakh, 1957, directed by Tofig Tagi-zade) about the famous Azeri fighter Mehdi Husein-zade who, after being captured by the Nazis, escaped and became a prominent partisan in the Trieste region in Italy.

As a feature film director, Sayidbeyli debuted with *The Telephone Operator Girl* (Telefonchu Giz/Telefonistka, codirected with Iurii Fogel'man, 1962), starring Raisa Nedashkovskaia of later *Commissar* fame as a young woman in search of a dignified place in society. His second film, *There Is Such an Island* (Est' takoi ostrov, 1964), praising the heroism of oil workers, was criticized for its superficial treatment of conflicts. In the short *Force of Attraction* (Sila pritiazheniia, 1965), Sayidbeyli tells the story of a peasant girl who becomes a successful athlete.

Why Are You Silent? (San niya sousoursan/Pochemu ty molchish'? 1967), arguably Sayidbeli's most interesting picture, blends a detective plot about poachers and fish trafficking with a psychologically complex love story. *My Teacher Jabish* (Our Jabish Muallim/Moi uchitel' Dzhabish, 1970, TV), shot in black and white, tells about an aging pedagogue whose failing eyesight prevents him from fighting in the Great Patriotic War but whose passionate desire to help the troops results in the production of much-needed soap. The director's last major picture was *Nasimi* (1974), a biopic about the great Azerbaijani philosopher and poet.

Pursuing a successful administrative career in **Azerbaijani cinema**, Sayidbeyli acquired the reputation of a state hack. However, in the 1990s, his work underwent a reevaluation among film historians, who acknowledged his ability to create authentic atmosphere in scenes of everyday life. In his best work, Sayidbeyli transcended schematic Socialist-Realist patterns by believably depicting societal alienation.

Sayidbeyli joined the Communist Party in 1955; he was named People's Artist of the Azerbaijani SSR in 1976 and served as chairman of the Azerbaijani Filmmakers' Union in 1975–1980.

Other films: *Under the Burning Sky* (Pod znoinym nebom, 1956, script); *The Price of Happiness* (Tsena schast'ia, 1976).

SEMENOVA, LIUDMILA NIKOLAEVNA (b. 17 February 1899, St. Petersburg–d. 25 May 1990, Moscow). Russian actress. Semenova studied in **Boris Chaikovskii**'s private film school, graduating in 1919, and in the Lunacharskii dance studio until 1921. She then joined the workshop of avant-gardist Nikolai Foregger (1892–1939), the so-called Mastfor (masterskaia Foreggera), in which the human body and its movements were viewed as related to mechanical devices and machines. Foregger also became Semenova's husband.

In 1926, **Grigorii Kozintsev** and **Leonid Trauberg**, impressed by Semenova's stage performances, gave her the lead of a young woman who inadvertently gets involved with the Petrograd underworld, in their thriller *Devil's Wheel* (Chertovo koleso)—a role that propelled the actress to stardom. She also played a supporting part in their *S.V.D.—The Club of Great Deeds* (SVD—Soiuz velikikh del, 1927). Semenova is best remembered for her extraordinary performance in **Abram Room**'s provocative socioerotic drama *Third Meshchanskaia Street* (aka *Bed and Sofa*/Tret'ia Meshchanskaia, 1927). In the role of Liudmila, she portrays a modern, mature, intelligent woman who suffers from her enslavement in anachronistic patriarchal relations and in the end finds the strength to free herself. This character, already controversial at the time of the picture's release, remained a singular occurrence in Soviet cinema and only found a continuation in some of the female portraits in **Iulii Raizman**'s films of the 1970s.

Semenova then played the wife of a wounded soldier suffering from amnesia in **Fridrikh Ermler**'s *A Fragment of the Empire*

(Oblomok imperii, 1929). With the advent of sound film and the official discrediting of the 1920s avant-garde, Semenova's career went downhill. She appeared on stage—first in Leningrad Music Halls, later in the Studio Theater of the Film Actor in Moscow (1945–57)—but her film roles became more and more minuscule, and she worked as an administrator in culture clubs to make ends meet. **Aleksandr Zarkhi**, who had cast Semenova in his 1933 sound film *My Homeland* (Moia rodina; not released), gave her a small part in his 1968 Lev Tolstoi adaptation *Anna Karenina*. In the 1970s, the actress published memoirist articles, for example, about **Nikolai Batalov**, her costar in *Bed and Sofa*.

Other films: *My Son* (Moi syn, 1928); *New Babylon* (Novyi Vavilon, 1929); *Alien Shore* (Chuzhoi bereg, 1930); *Anna on the Neck* (Anna na shee, 1954).

SEROVA, VALENTINA VASIL'EVNA [b. Polovikova] (b. 23 December 1917, Khar'kov–d. 12 December 1975, Moscow). Russian actress. Serova grew up with her mother, actress Klavdiia Polovikova, who, after moving to Moscow, made her a child performer on stage. In 1934, **Abram Room** gave Serova—then still appearing under the name Polovikova—the supporting role of the self-assured, flirtatious Komsomol girl Lizochka in *A Strict Young Man* (Strogii iunosha, 1934–1937), but the film was shelved. Serova's real movie career started only five years later, with the lead in **Konstantin Iudin**'s *A Girl with Personality* (Devushka s kharakterom, 1939), a **comedy** about an active, uncompromising young woman. The film made Serova a star overnight—her unabashed sensuality, unpredictable naughtiness, and optimistic vigor resonated with millions of Soviet viewers.

The lead in Iudin's lovely and surprisingly apolitical *Hearts of Four* (aka *Four Hearts*/Serdtsa chetyrekh, 1941, released 1945) cemented Serova's fame, as did her tumultuous private life and love affairs with military and literary celebrities. Her first husband, the test pilot Anatolii Serov, was a darling of the Soviet establishment; after his death in a plane crash (1939), Serova remained part of the Kremlin's inner circle and a favorite of Iosif Stalin's. In 1942, writer Konstantin Simonov dedicated the legendary poem "Wait for Me" (Zhdi menia) to Serova; in **Aleksandr Stolper**'s film *Wait* *for Me*, released in 1943, the actress plays the lead. In 1946, she received a Stalin Prize for her role as Mikhail Glinka's wife in **Leo Arnshtam**'s biopic about the composer (released in the United States as *The Great Glinka*).

Early in her life, Serova began to suffer from alcoholism, which caused her rapid physical and artistic decline and was a constant source of malicious gossip. Moving from one Moscow theater to another, this uniquely gifted actress got fewer and fewer roles and soon lost her superstar status, thus remaining forever associated with Stalinist cinema. Impoverished and hardly recognizable, Serova died in an accident in her apartment.

Serova was named Merited Artist of the Russian Federation in 1946. In 2005, director Iurii Kara made a television miniseries about the actress, *Star of the Epoch* (Zvezda epokhi).

Other films: *The Immortal Garrison* (Bessmertnyi garnison, 1956).

SHADOWS OF FORGOTTEN ANCESTORS (Tini zabutykh predkiv/Teni zabytykh predkov, 1964). **Dovzhenko Film Studio**. 97 min., color. Directed by **Sergei Paradjanov**. Script: Sergei Paradjanov, Ivan Chendei from the 1913 novella by Mykhailo Kotsiubynsky. Cinematography: **Yury Il'enko**. Music: Miroslav Skorik. Cast: **Ivan Mykolaichuk**, Larisa Kadochnikova, Tat'iana Pestaeva, Spartak Bagashvili, **Nikolai Grin'ko**, Nina Alisova. Premiere: 18 October 1965.

Little Ivan Palyichuk, a member of the Hutsul tribe in the Carpathian Mountains, is saved by his older brother who sacrifices his own life when a huge tree falls on them. Ivan befriends Marichka Hutenok, the daughter of a rich peasant. Following an argument in church, Marichka's father kills Ivan's father. Despite the hatred between the two families, the grown-up Ivan (Mykolaichuk) and Marichka (Kadochnikova) love each other dearly. One day, Marichka falls to her death when trying to save a lost lamb. Ivan is inconsolable and only after several years of wanderings marries Palagna (Pestaeva). The marriage is without love and remains childless. Iurko (Bagashvili), who is interested in Palagna, kills Ivan during a fight. *See also* UKRAINIAN CINEMA.

SHAKHNAZAROV, KAREN GEORGIEVICH (b. 8 July 1952, Krasnodar). Russian director, scriptwriter, and producer. Shakhnazarov's Armenian-born father, Georgii Shakhnazarov (1924–2001), a high-ranking Communist Party functionary, was an erudite international affairs analyst and one of Mikhail Gorbachev's closest advisors. The privileged pedigree eased his son's entrance into the movie world—he studied with **Igor' Talankin** at the Soviet State Film School **VGIK** from 1969 to 1975 and was hired to be his teacher's assistant in 1973–1975.

At **Mosfilm Studio**, Shakhnazarov made his debut—after several short features—with the **comedy** *Kind Fellows* (Dobriaki, 1980) about conflicts in a humanities institute. He landed his first hit with *We're from Jazz* (aka *Jazzmen*/My iz dzhaza, 1983), a charming homage to 1920s fans trying to establish jazz in a politicized, dogmatic environment. *A Winter Evening in Gagry* (Zimnii vecher v Gagrakh, 1985) used the successful formula again, this time dealing with step-dancing in the USSR but lacked the previous film's irresistible lure.

The Messenger Boy (Kur'er, 1987), an intelligent, vivid contribution to perestroika and glasnost—albeit with noticeable undertones of skepticism—aptly analyzes generational behavior; it became a blockbuster. *Zero City* (Gorod Zero, 1989) is a sarcastic, darkly surreal farce in which social satire turns sharp and bitter. This brilliant film, arguably the director's best, reflected the Soviet intelligentsia's dimming perestroika hopes and presented a disenchanted farewell to Communist ideology and cultural myths that left behind ruins and mockery. Shakhnazarov's emphasis on the absurdity of Russian history became a leitmotiv in *The Assassin of the Tsar* (Tsareubiitsa, 1991), which features a bleak insane asylum as a metaphor for society at large. One of its patients claims to have killed both Nikolai II in 1918 and Aleksandr II in 1881 and discusses his purported crimes with a bewildered psychiatrist. Yet, despite featuring Malcolm McDowell in the title role, *Assassin* impressed neither critics nor audiences, being too obviously the product of crisis and deep disorientation—the director's own, Russian cinema's, and post-Soviet society's as a whole.

Shakhnazarov then switched from historical-philosophical musings to modern melodrama, using a scandal from his own past (his second wife had eloped to the United States, taking their four-year-old daughter with her). Unfortunately, *The American Daughter* (Amerikanskaia doch', 1995) fails to make this story believable on screen, despite a few fascinating scenes in which the awkward Russian father explores American life. *A Horseman Named Death* (Vsadnik po imeni smert', 2004) is an adaptation of anarchist Boris Savinkov's novel *The Pale Horse* (Kon' blednyi), another attempt to make sense of the vicious circle of revolutionary fervor and violence.

Besides being one of the most prominent contemporary directors in Russia, Shakhnazarov was appointed one of the executive artistic directors at Mosfilm, and in 1998 became president of the entire studio. In that capacity, he has shown remarkable entrepreneurial spirit and proven a genuine modernizer and enabler who brought the moribund giant back to life with a production volume steadily bouncing back to that of Soviet years. As producer, he has helmed some of the most interesting recent Russian films, among them Tamás Thót's *Children of Iron Gods* (Deti chugunnykh bogov, 1993). In 2002, Shakhnazarov made headlines by demanding quotas for foreign films released in Russia.

Shakhnazarov was awarded the title Merited Artist of Russia in 1997 and People's Artist of Russia in 2002.

Other films: *Stride Wider, Maestro* (Shire shag, maestro, 1975); *Dreams* (Sny, 1993); *Day of the Full Moon* (Den' polnoluniia, 1998); *Poisons, or the World History of Poisoning* (Iady, ili mirovaia istoriia otravlenii, 2001).

SHAMSHIEV, BOLOTBEK [some sources list the patronymic Tolenovich] (b. 12 January 1941, Frunze [now Bishkek]). Kyrgyz director, screenwriter, producer, and politician. Shamshiev studied in the workshop of **Aleksandr Zguridi** at the Soviet Film School **VGIK** in 1959–1964. In 1963, still a student, he played one of the leads (Kemel) in **Larisa Shepit'ko**'s *Torrid Heat* and also worked as a sound assistant on that picture.

Shamshiev's **documentary** *Manaschi* (1965), a poetic portrait of the famous myth-narrator Saiakbai Karalaev who retells the Kyrgyz national epic *Manas*, won the Grand Prize at the 1966 Short Film festival in Oberhausen. Another documentary, *The Shepherd* (Chaban, 1967), about the harsh life of nomads in the mountains of Kyrgyzstan, also became an international success. These documentaries were welcomed as true revelations, visualizing the magic of an ancient oral culture under a thin Soviet veil and conveying the pulsating vitality of national archetypes and symbols.

Shamshiev's first feature, *The Shot at Karash Passing* (Vystrel na perevale Karash, 1969), is in essence a drama of modernization, showing the clash between internalized tribal values such as respect for elders, nature, and community, and ruthless exploitation in early 20th century. The director followed it with the action-filled *Scarlet Poppies of Issyk-Kul'* (Alye maki Issyk-Kulia, 1972), a thriller set in the 1920s, with pro-Soviet forces trying to stop opium trafficking.

Only with his next film did Shamshiev rise to the artistic level of his documentaries, likely due to the inspiration coming from an outstanding literary source: the script for *The White Steamship* (Belyi parakhod, 1976) was penned by Kyrgyzstan's greatest contemporary author, **Chingiz Aitmatov**, who developed it from his own seminal novel. This drama turns into bleak tragedy when the abandonment of ancient laws—conveyed through beliefs and myths—leads a trusting little boy to commit suicide in the end. The film, which won Shamshiev a USSR State Prize in 1977, is generally seen as the director's greatest artistic accomplishment. *Early Cranes* (Rannie zhuravli, 1979), also from an Aitmatov story, was similarly stylish and dark, suggesting an analogy between Nazi invaders and the brutal thugs terrorizing the population on the home front in World War II. An interesting counterpoint to *Early Cranes* is *Snipers* (Snaipery, 1985), a box-office hit about Aliia Moldagulova, the most famous of a cohort of Kazakh female snipers in the Great Patriotic War. Shamshiev's last film, a contribution to the perestroika discourse on Stalinism, was again based on an Aitmatov script from his own play. *The Climb to Fujiyama* (Voskhozhdenie na Fudziiamu, 1988) explores questions of guilt and responsibility, drawing a connection between the disrespect for ancient ethical rules and moral transgressions.

In the 1990s, Shamshiev retired from filmmaking, although officially he was on staff with **Kyrgyzfilm Studio** until 1999. He turned to politics, serving as a member of the parliament of Kyrgyzstan—the Zhogorgu Kenesh—from 1985 to 1995, and was appointed director of the Kyrgyz State Agency for Tourism and Sport and ambassador to the United Arab Emirates. The versatile Shamshiev also excelled as a businessman, head of a private film studio (Salamalik), and author of books dealing with various aspects of Islam. In 2005, he was appointed advisor to President Kurmanbek Bakiev.

In his relatively few films Shamshiev was able to capture the fundamental conflict between Kyrgyzstan's native cultural and spiritual heritage and the intrusion of Soviet-style modernity, showing how this process was bringing not only education and technology but also blasphemy, moral degradation, and disintegration of the traditional societal fabric. Such an approach reflected a general unease about the increasingly nonpatriarchal civilization, Communist atheism, and Westernization in all Central Asian nations. Once the emancipation of his homeland from the Soviet state system was formally achieved, such a critique of modern conditions from an archaistic and humanistic foundation lost its justification, which might explain this filmmaker's regrettable withdrawal from **Kyrgyz cinema**.

Shamshiev joined the Communist Party in 1972; he was named People's Artist of the Kyrgyz SSR in 1975 and People's Artist of the USSR in 1991.

Other films: *Echo of Love* (Ekho liubvi, 1974, TV); *Among People* (Sredi liudei, 1979); *Wolf Pit* (Volch'ia iama, 1983).

SHENGELAIA, ELDAR [Russian sources list the patronymic Nikolaevich] (b. 26 January 1933, Tbilisi). Georgian director, screenwriter, and actor. The son of filmmaker **Nikoloz Shengelaia** and famed actress **Nato Vachnadze** was educated at the Soviet State Film School **VGIK** where he studied with **Sergei Iutkevich**, graduating in 1958. At **Mosfilm Studio**, he and fellow graduate Aleksei Sakharov directed *Legend of the Ice Heart* (Legenda o ledianom serdtse, 1958) from a fairy tale by Wilhelm Hauff, and *Snow Tale* (Snezhnaia skazka, 1960), an allegory about the Old Year trying to stop the clock so that the progression of time could be halted. It is noteworthy that Shengelaia's two earliest pictures place a miraculous dimension in the very middle of everyday life—an approach that the director continued throughout his career.

In Georgia, Shengelaia directed the provocative full-length feature *An Unusual Exhibition* (Arakhveulebrivi gamopena/Neobyknovennaia vystavka, 1969), offering peculiar parallels to his brother **Giorgi Shengelaia**'s masterpiece *Pirosmani*. Both pictures are reflections on the conditions of artistic creativity, juxtaposing the needs of the family and society at large to the demands of pure artistry. The main character, sculptor Aguli Eristavi, makes money by churning out lucrative tombstone busts, but in the end has created nothing but a monstrous cemetery, a sad symbol of his own buried talent.

Following such sarcastic rejection of pragmatism and compromise, *Crackpots* (Sherekilebi/Chudaki, 1974) sings praise to those loveable albeit slightly deranged outsiders who give up their earthly possessions to make a sojourn of personal self-realization. *Samanishvili's Stepmother* (Samanishvili dedinatsvali/Machekha Samanishvili, 1978) depicts the life of prerevolutionary Georgian rural gentry in a bittersweet, tragicomical manner that is characteristic of Shengelaia's oeuvre as a whole.

On the advent of perestroika, this filmmaker was one of the first to subtly but unmistakably delegitimize the Soviet system by pointing to its incurable inefficiency and common procrastination in the daring satire *Blue Mountains, or An Unbelievable Story* (Tsisperi mtebi anu arachveulebrivi ambavi/Golubye gory, ili nepravdopodobnaia istoriia, 1984). Apart from its remarkable sociopolitical insights, this picture continues Shengelaia's longtime musings about the threats to which human creativity is subjugated. In *Blue Mountains*, it is a literary manuscript that is virtually annihilated by bureaucratic indifference and stupidity.

Because of their sophisticated comedic elements and playful subversiveness, Shengelaia's films have always appealed to a select audience of connoisseurs, both at home and abroad; their plots were deliberately kept slow-paced and undramatic, putting parabolic signification above storytelling per se. Such pictures were festival favorites and increased the international prestige of **Georgian cinema** but enjoyed scarce success at the box office.

Shengelaia joined the Communist Party in 1965; he was named People's Artist of the Georgian SSR in 1979 and People's Artist of the USSR in 1988. In 1976, Shengelaia was elected first secretary of the Union of Georgian Filmmakers, a position he still holds (since 1991 in the rank of chairman). From 1989 to 1991, he also served as member of the USSR Supreme Soviet. In the late 1980s, Shengelaia's political interests became more dominant. Thus, he cofounded the movement People's Front in 1989 and was one of the leaders of the Citizens'

Union of Georgia; moreover, he has served as a member of Georgian parliament since 1992 and also as its deputy chairman. Shengelaia's absurdist comedy *Express Information* (Expres-Informatsia), a Georgian-German coproduction, was completed in 1993 after seven years of struggles. Another project, *Kutaisi Kalaika*, was begun in 2001 and has been in production for several years.

Other films: *The White Caravan* (Tetri karavani/Belyi karavan, 1964, codirected with T. Meliava); *Miqela* (1965, short).

SHENGELAIA, GIORGI [Russian sources list name and patronymic as Georgii Nikolaevich] (b. 11 May 1937, Moscow). Georgian director, screenwriter, and actor. Shengelaia, the son of **Nikoloz Shengelaia** and famed actress **Nato Vachnadze**, studied at the Soviet State Film School **VGIK** with **Aleksandr Dovzhenko** and **Mikhail Romm**, graduating in 1961.

As a student, Shengelaia appeared in significant pictures, starting with the role of Dato in **Revaz Chkheidze**'s modern youth story *Our Court* (Chveni ezo/Nash dvor, 1957)—along with his future wife, actress **Sofiko Chiaureli**—and continuing with parts such as Giorgi in his father-in-law **Mikheil Chiaureli**'s *Otar's Widow* (Otaraant qvrivi/Otarova vdova, 1958). (Interestingly, Chiaureli also was one of Shengelaia's professors at VGIK.)

As a director, Shengelaia debuted with a **documentary** about Georgian primitivist painter Nikos Pirosmanishvili (1863–1918) in 1960. His first feature was the 43-minute-long *Alaverdoba* (1963), a pensive depiction of the ancient tradition of wildly celebrating Thanksgiving near the Alaverdi monastery. The film raised eyebrows because of its candor and complex, even-handed approach. Shengelaia then contributed the short *The Prize* (Djildo/Nagrada) to the omnibus project *Pages of the Past* (Stranitsy proshlogo, 1965), made jointly with his brother, **Eldar Shengelaia**. In 1966, he helmed the adventure movie *Matsi Kvitia* (aka *He Did Not Mean to Kill*/On ubivat' ne khotel, 1966) about a 13th-century Georgian Robin Hood.

Shengelaia's most important film is *Pirosmani* (1969), an outwardly calm, unspectacular biopic about Nikos Pirosmanishvili. Originally made for television, it proved a veritable cinematic gem that won its maker several international prizes and was released in movie theaters in 1972. From its lucid, ascetic shot compositions—stylized after the master's own paintings—and understated acting emerges a powerful, uncompromising credo about the artist's divine duty and national mission that must be followed, regardless of societal resistance and ignorance. Within Shengelaia's oeuvre, *Pirosmani* is unsurpassed in its stylistic homogeneity and philosophical stringency; it remains one of the all-time masterpieces of **Georgian cinema**.

Somewhat unexpectedly, Shengelaia then turned to the genre of musical with *Melodies of Veris Quarter* (Veris ubnis melodiebi/ Melodii Veriiskogo kvartala, 1973), a loving portrait of prerevolutionary Tbilisi populated by a gallery of colorful characters. *Come to the Valley of Grapes* (aka *Our Daily Water*/Kvishani darchebian/ Pridi v dolinu vinograda, 1977), in which Shengelaia and his wife played the leads, tells the contemporary story of an ancient house that is an obstacle to the construction of a canal. The gloomy *Sojourn of a Young Composer* (Akhalgarzda kompozitoris mogzauroba/Puteshestvie molodogo kompozitora, 1984) is set in the restoration period after the 1905–1907 revolution and shows the intellectual principles of a folklore collector to be incompatible with revolutionary fervor. Shengelaia's last full-length feature to date, *The Death of Orpheus* (Orpeosis sikudili/Smert' Orfeia, 1996), a Georgian-Russian coproduction, is a grim depiction of the state of affairs in Georgia, where humanist values are destroyed by partisan fanaticism. Both the main character—a professor who publishes antinationalist articles—and his love interest are murdered in the end.

Throughout his career and in an impressive variety of genres, Shengelaia has been consistent in his attention to the national specifics of Georgian culture. He observes contemporary society with melancholic distrust, telling deeply subversive, antimodern stories and insisting on the autonomy of art and the artist.

The director, who is also a successful vintner, made news by reporting that the profits from his 2004 wine sales will finance his new film project.

Shengelaia was named People's Artist of the Georgian Republic in 1985. He was one of the founders of the Georgian Society of Audiovisual Authors and Producers in 1999. As head of the Creative Council of **Gruziya-Film Studio**, he has been at the center of controversies in the 1990s and early 2000s. In 2007–2008, he publicly supported the opposition movement against President Mikheil Saakashvili.

Shengelaia is not to be confused with the filmmaker and action specialist Georgii Shengeliia (b. 1960), as is inaccurately stated in some publications.

Other films: (as actor) *Story of a Young Girl* (Ambavi erti kalishvilisa/Povest' ob odnoi devushke, 1960); *The General and the Daisies* (Generali da zizilebi/General i margaritki, 1963); (as director) *The Girl with the Sewing Machine* (Sikvaruli kvelas unda/Devushka so shveinoi mashinkoi, 1980, codirected with Mikheil O. Chiaureli); *Khareba and Gogi* (Khareba da Gogia, 1987); *Georgian Grapes* (Sikvaruli venakshi/Georgische Trauben, 1996, short, Germany); *The Train Moved on and on* (Midioda matarebeli, 2005).

SHENGELAIA, NIKOLOZ [Russian sources list first name and patronymic as Nikolai Mikhailovich] (b. 19 August 1903, Obuji, Zugdid district, Mingrelia–4 January 1943, near Tbilisi). Georgian director and screenwriter. After studying at the University of Tbilisi, Shengelaia, heavily influenced by Vladimir Maiakovskii (1893–1930), made a name for himself in the 1920s as a leftist avant-garde poet; his texts appeared in the journals of proletarian and futurist groups. Shengelaia worked as an assistant to Kote Mardjanishvili (1873–1933) on his film *Before the Storm* (Nakanune grozy, aka Burevestnik, 1925), about the revolutionary underground movement in Tbilisi, and on **Iurii Zheliabuzhskii**'s *Dina Dza-Dzu* (1926), which was filmed in Svanetia. He also worked as a scriptwriter for Mardjanishvili's satirical **comedy** *Samanishvili's Stepmother* (Samanishvilis dedinatsvali/Machekha Samanishvili, 1927)—based on the story of 19th-century Georgian classic Davit Kldiashvili—and for **Ivan Perestiani**'s *In the Quagmire* (Gaplangva/V trsiasine, 1928).

In 1927, Shengelaia codirected with Lev Push *Giuli*, the adaptation of Shio Aragvispireli's tragic story about a love destroyed by the cultural and religious rift between Muslims and Christians. The film was a success; it is also noteworthy as **Mikhail Kalatozov**'s debut as cameraman. Under the influence of **Lev Kuleshov**'s teachings about the nature of film acting, Shengelaia abandoned Mardjanishvili's theatrocentric concepts and attempted new paths in **Georgian cinema**. His first independently directed picture, *Eliso* (1928), became an instant classic. Following the 1920s avant-garde view that Communist films should focus on a collective rather than individual heroes, *Eliso* portrays a Chechen village (*aul*) in the Caucasus that faces forced resettlement to Turkey in 1864. The central plotline of a Muslim girl who is in love with a Christian man is reduced to a minor component. The fiery indictment of tsarist injustice toward the poor Muslim population was given a passionate cinematic form, alternating episodes of majestic calm with eruptions of violence. Shengelaia's film stunned audiences, won critical praise at home and abroad, and made its director a respected brother-in-arms for fellow film pioneers **Sergei Eizenshtein**, **Vsevolod Pudovkin**, and **Aleksandr Dovzhenko**.

In 1932, Shengelaia went to the film factory of Azerbaijan, Azerkino (later: **Azerbaijanfilm Studio**), to direct *Twenty-six Commissars* (Dvadtsat' shest' komissarov, 1933, assisted by **Stepan Kevorkov**) about the 1918 defeat of pro-Soviet forces in Baku, an event that had opened the doors for British and Turkish occupants. The film continued the deindividualized approach toward characters, centering on classes and political groups instead. The critical response was mixed, although the picture's stylish pathos and ritualism preceded the monumentalism of the late 1930s–1940s and secured it a place in the annals of Soviet cinema. Shengelaia then began to work with writer Mikhail Sholokhov (1905–1984) on the adaptation of his epic *Virgin Soil Upturned* (Podniataia tselina), which at that point was only partially published; however, after the shooting had already commenced, the work was stopped without explanation by a decree from Moscow—a severe blow from which the director never fully recovered.

Back in Georgia, Shengelaia made *The Golden Valley* (Narindjis veli/Zolotistaia dolina, 1937), a light-spirited film about the establishment of collective farms in western Georgia that won him a Stalin Prize in 1941. *Homeland* (Shamshoblo/Rodina, 1939), intended as a warning about the danger of foreign agents and traitors undermining the security of the Soviet state, arguably marks the lowest point in Shengelaia's career, coming across as a mere illustration of paranoid political slogans. Shengelaia's last completed picture was the 1941 short *In the Black Mountains* (Shav mtebshi/V chernykh gorakh, 1941) about the struggle of Serbian guerilla fighters against Nazi invaders; the script was authored by famous Hungarian film theoretician Béla Bálasz. The production of *He Will Come Back* (Is kidev dabrundeba/On eshche vernetsia, 1943), also about the Great Patriotic War, was interrupted by the director's death in a car accident.

Shengelaia was named Merited Artist of the Russian Federation in 1935. He was elected to the USSR Supreme Soviet in 1938. Shengelaia was married to famous actress **Nato Vachnadze**; their sons **Eldar** and **Giorgi Shengelaia** became prominent filmmakers.

SHEPIT'KO, LARISA EFIMOVNA (b. 6 January 1938, Artemovsk, Ukraine–d. 2 July 1979, Tver' province). Russian director and screenwriter. Born into the family of an officer and a teacher, Shepit'ko studied directing at the Soviet State Film School **VGIK** with **Aleksandr Dovzhenko** and **Mikhail Romm**, graduating in 1963. Shepit'ko's teachers in many ways defined her artistic approach: Dovzhenko informed it with a sense of lofty poetic pathos, whereas Romm imbued it with an interest in the cinematic reflection of contemporary societal conflicts. In 1958, Shepit'ko worked as assistant to **Iuliia Solntseva** on *Poem about the Sea* (Poema o more), which was based on a Dovzhenko script praising the erection of the gigantic Kakhovsk hydroelectric power plant (ironically, the last project of Shepit'ko's career bitterly mourns the environmental, sociocultural, and spiritual consequences of such plants).

Shepit'ko's diploma film, *Torrid Heat* (Znoi, 1963), an adaptation of **Chingiz Aitmatov**'s story "Camel Eye," was produced at **Kyrgyzfilm Studio** and won several national and international prizes, mainly for its impressive visual qualities. The plot was typical of the Thaw period: two men—the older, more conservative Abakir and the younger, innovative Kemel—work on a collective farm and clash over the correct methods to run it. Young **Bolotbek Shamshiev** played Kemel and also was the film's sound assistant; another assistant was **Dinara Asanova**. *Wings* (Kryl'ia, 1966, originally titled *The Guards Captain*/Gvardii kapitan) continued the exploration of generational relations. Nadezhda, a famed female war pilot, is trying to find a new purpose for her life in a provincial town. Torn between idealistic aspirations and internalized authoritarian military methods, she must face the challenges of administering a civilian professional school.

The Homeland of Electricity (Rodina elektrichestva, 1967) was banned and released only 20 years later during perestroika. Shot at the Experimental Creative Film Studio, a branch of **Mosfilm Studio** run by **Grigorii Chukhrai**, this 40-minute feature was part of an omnibus project, *The Beginning of an Unknown Century* (Nachalo nevedomogo veka). Based on a short story by Andrei Platonov (1899–1951), one of the most complex Russian authors whose narratives describe the "common cause" of Communist construction with disturbing ambiguity, *The Homeland of Electricity* portrays starving villagers who are naïvely expecting salvation and—literally—ultimate enlightenment from electricity.

You and I (Ty i ia, 1972) is a highly original contemporary drama about three intellectuals trying to overcome their inner resignation and resist society's seemingly insurmountable corruption. The film was severely mutilated by censors; its open antididactic narration and shocking depiction of an existential crisis broke through the façade of normative cinematic representation and allowed its characters an unprecedented freedom of decision making and humanity. Shepit'ko's last completed picture, ***The Ascension*** (Voskhozhdenie, 1976), adapted from Belarusian author Vasil' Bykau's masterpiece *Sotnikau*, was saved from being shelved through the direct interference of Belarus's Party leader, Petr Masherov. It made headlines when it won the Golden Bear at the 1977 Berlin Film Festival, against the noisy protests of some jury members, including Rainer Werner Fassbinder. Stringently composed black-and-white imagery and astoundingly open biblical allusions gave this tense war story about the choices between loyalty, betrayal, self-sacrifice, and the gray areas between them a powerful allegorical dimension.

Shepit'ko died in a car accident, along with cinematographer Vladimir Chukhnov (1946–1979) and painter Iurii Fomenko (1942–1979), on the first day of location shooting of *Farewell* (Proshchanie). The film was completed by her husband, **Elem Klimov**, and released in 1981. Based on Valentin Rasputin's controversial novella "Farewell to Matyora" (1976), it describes the destruction of a Siberian village that has to make room for an artificial lake and hydroelectric power plant. Instead of justifying the project as necessary and inevitable, *Farewell*—conceptualized by Shepit'ko as a darkly majestic and tormentingly slow visual requiem—emphasizes the tragic consequences of industrialization and mourns the aborted, time-honored cultural and religious traditions.

With the exception of *Wings* and *You and I*, all of Shepit'ko's works use high-quality literary sources as their point of departure but transform the plots in a distinctly cinematic fashion, showing stylistic ambition, a predilection for ascetic landscape compositions (deserts, steppe, deep winter), taciturn characters, and a sharp contrast between long quiet episodes and sudden collisions.

Shepit'ko was awarded the title Merited Artist of the Russian Federation in 1974. In 1980, Elem Klimov made a documentary, *Larisa*, about his late wife.

Other films: *The Blind Cook* (Slepoi kukhar', 1956, short); *Living Water* (Zhivaia voda, 1957, short); *In the Thirteenth Hour of the Night* (aka *13PM*/V trinadtsatom chasu nochi, 1968, TV).

SHINARBAEV, ERMEK (b. 24 January 1953, Almaty, Kazakhstan). Kazakh director and screenwriter. Shinarbaev studied in **Boris Babochkin**'s acting workshop at the Soviet State Film School **VGIK**, graduating in 1974, and, after working at **Kazakhfilm Studio** as an actor and assistant director, enrolled in **Sergei Gerasimov**'s directing workshop, graduating in 1981.

Following the short *The Beauty in Mourning* (Krasavitsa v traure, 1981) and two **documentaries**, one of which was devoted to the late director Magit Begalin (1922–1978), Shinarbaev achieved critical and popular success with an adaptation of Russian-Korean author Anatolii Kim's short story *My Sister, Liusia* (Sestra moia, Liusia, 1985). Situated in postwar Kazakhstan, where the Soviet Korean minority had been exiled by force in 1939, the film evokes both the experience of incredible hardships and human warmth of those years in intensely poetic, melancholic images. Although produced for television, this thoughtful picture also had a theatrical release. Shinarbaev then adapted two other Kim stories: in 1987, *To Exit the Forest and Enter a Meadow* (Vyiti iz lesa na polianu), and in 1989, *The Revenge* (Mest'). The latter, a historical parable about the futility of trying to achieve earthly justice, demonstrates the director's psychologically tactful, metaphorically saturated, yet always grittily realistic style in near perfection. Shinarbaev followed this film's international success with a drama about the life of modern Kazakh youth, *A Spot on the Cocked Hat* (Mesto na seroi treugolke, 1993). *A Tender Heart* (Alciz Shurek/Coeur fragile, 1994), a French-Kazakh coproduction starring **Natal'ia Arinbasarova**, tells the story of an aging ballerina and her romantic involvement with a younger man.

In 1989–1996, Shinarbaev was the artistic director of the group Alem at Kazakhfilm. Since the mid-1990s, the filmmaker has been concentrating on documentaries, several of which are dealing with musical themes. He also works as a producer, sometimes together with Ardak Amirkulov.

Shinarbaev was named Merited Artist of Kazakhstan in 1997.

Other films: *Monologues at the Piano* (Monologi u roialia, 1986, doc.); *The Duet* (1998, doc.); *We Are Playing Brahms* (Igraem Bramsa, 1998, doc.); *The Master Class* (Master-klass, 1999, doc.). *See also* KAZAKH CINEMA.

SHKLOVSKII, VIKTOR BORISOVICH (b. 6 February 1893, St. Petersburg–d. 5 December 1984, Moscow). Russian screenwriter, film theorist, critic, and author. The son of a mathematics teacher, Shklovskii studied philology at the University of St. Petersburg/Petrograd in 1912–1914. Toward the end of World War I, Shklovskii served as a sergeant in an automobile unit in the tsar's army, switching to the Bolsheviks after the 1917 October Revolution. In 1922, he immigrated to Germany but was allowed to return to Soviet Russia following an amnesty in 1923. A highly prolific author, Shklovskii produced numerous volumes of criticism and prose over the next six decades, featuring a unique syncretic style in which fictitious elements, markedly subjective statements, and scholarly analyses are mixed.

As one of the founders of the so-called Formal School, Shklovskii's approach to literature was defined by the Society for the Study of Poetic Language (OPOIAZ, 1914–1923), in which the specificity of poetic texts was viewed as a system of devices (see, for example, *Art as Device*, 1917). His early interest in cinema emerged from similar assumptions, emphasizing the formal, technical side of film rather than its underlying ideology. Since Shklovskii proved to be an inventive, original screenwriter, many of his ideas and theoretical constructs are based on practical experience and found a vivid response among the Soviet film avant-garde. In the 1920s, Shklovskii's major partners in the critical discourse on cinema were **Sergei Eizenshtein**, **Vsevolod Pudovkin**, **Aleksandr Dovzhenko**, **Dziga Vertov** (whom he vigorously opposed), **Esfir' Shub**, and **Grigorii Kozintsev**.

As the head of the Screenplay Department of the Leningrad film factory Sovkino (later: **Lenfilm Studio**), Shklovskii demonstrated a feel for the specifics of silents in such diverse screenplays as *Wings of a Serf* (aka *Ivan the Terrible*/Kryl'ia kholopa, 1926), an unusual historical drama directed by **Iurii Tarich**, the contemporary romantic comedy *The House on Trubnaia Square* (Dom na Trubnoi, 1928, coauthored with **Nikolai Erdman**, directed by **Boris Barnet**), and the drama about soldiers who take the side of the Bolsheviks, *Two Armored Cars* (Dva bronevika, 1928, directed by **Semen Timoshenko**). Shklovskii showed thematic and narrative originality in a number of scripts that he penned for leading avant-garde filmmakers, beginning with superb material for **Lev Kuleshov**—the austere *By the Law* (Po zakonu, aka *Expiation*, aka *Dura Lex*, 1926) from a Jack London story, as well as the sensational socioerotic drama *Third Meshchanskaia Street* (aka *Bed and Sofa*/Tret'ia Meshchanskaia, aka Liubov' vtroem, 1927) for **Abram Room**. Following an initial radical opposition to sound film, he wrote the script for Kuleshov's *Horizon* (aka *The Wandering Jew*/Gorizont, 1932), a polemical juxtaposition of American and Soviet life. When the Communist establishment hit hard on "formalism" in the early 1930s, Shklovskii was among the first to recant, although at heart he remained an avant-gardist, admiring more consistently radical screenwriters such as **Aleksandr Rzheshevskii**.

Adjusting to the new spirit of nationalism propagated in the late 1930s, Shklovskii became a specialist in period pieces, gaining official recognition for *Minin and Pozharskii* (1939, directed by Pudovkin). He contributed to the Uzbek biopic *Alisher Navoi* (1948), directed by **Kamil Yarmatov**, and to the Tadjik revolutionary epic *Dokhunda* (1953, directed by **Bension Kimyagarov**). Shklovskii arguably reached the moral low point in his career when he agreed to write the screenplay for the propaganda piece *The Belomor-Baltic Canal* (Belomorsko-Baltiiskii vodnyi put', 1932, directed by **Aleksandr Lemberg**), a shamelessly demagogical **documentary** praising the GULAG concentration camps as institutions of social education.

Shklovskii authored several literary adaptations, from the controversial *The Captain's Daughter* (Kapitanskaia dochka, 1928, for Tarich), which consciously betrayed the spirit of Aleksandr Pushkin's humanist novel for the sake of Marxist vulgarization, to the daring *House of the Dead* (Mertvyi dom, 1932) from Fedor Dostoevskii's semifictitious memoir. A late triumph for the screenwriter was the success of **Aleksei Batalov**'s *Three Fat Men* (Tri tolstiaka, 1966), which Shklovskii adapted from Iurii Olesha's fairy tale.

As an insightful if often confrontational critic, Shklovskii managed to secure for himself the position of a unique, almost untouchable intellectual maverick and living classic. His dynamic, montagelike essayistic style, too, betrays cinematic influences. Shklovskii won three Stalin Prizes: for *Minin and Pozharskii* in 1941, *Alisher Navoi* in 1948, and *Faraway Bride* in 1949. In 1979, he was awarded a USSR State Prize for the second edition of his monograph *Eizenshtein* (1973).

Other films: *Jews on the Land* (Evrei na zemle, 1926, short); *The Gadfly* (Krazana/Ovod, 1928); *Chuk and Gek* (Chuk i Gek, 1953); *The Ballad of Bering and His Friends* (Ballada o Beringe i ego druz'iakh, 1970).

SHKURAT, STEPAN IOSIFOVICH (b. 8 January 1886, Kobeliaki, Ukraine–d. 26 February 1973, Kiev). Ukrainian actor. Shkurat was born into a peasant family and worked as a farmhand and a stove maker before joining rural theater groups. In 1910, he met sculptor and theater avant-gardist **Ivan Kavaleridze** and became a member of his amateur theater in Romny.

Shkurat made his debut in **Ukrainian cinema** with the role of the peasant Ivan in Kavaleridze's debut, the allegorical *Hard Rain* (Liven', 1929). The actor's artistic partnership with this director continued for more than three decades, including performances in *Storm Nights* (Shturmovye nochi, 1931), *Natalka, the Girl from Poltava* (Natalka-Poltavka, 1936), and *A Loose Woman* (Guliashchaia, 1961). **Aleksandr Dovzhenko** cast Shkurat as father Opanas in his masterpiece *Earth* (Zemlia, 1930); he delivered one of the film's central performances, conveying immense concentration and dignity with an uncompromising slowness and almost hypnotic power. Shkurat continued to appear in Dovzhenko's pictures, including *Ivan* (1932) as the slacker Guba, *Aerograd* (1935), and *Shchors* (1939), in which he was cast as the old, patriotic hunter Glushak. Shkurat's dark, wordless intensity impressed viewers and critics and often proved scene-stealing, for example, as the Cossack Potapov opposite the masterful theater actor Illarion Pevtsov's Colonel Borozdin in the **Vasil'ev brothers'** *Chapaev* (1934). Other memorable roles include the old Buntsevich in **Vladimir Korsh-Sablin**'s industrialization tale *Golden Lights* (Zalatye ahni/Zolotye ogni, 1934) and Iakim Nedolia in **Ihor' Savchenko**'s Civil War tale *Riders* (aka *Guerilla Brigade/ Vsadniki*, 1939).

Shkurat was named Merited Artist of the Ukrainian SSR in 1935 and People's Artist of the Ukrainian SSR in 1971.

Other films: *Fata Morgana* (1931); *The Swallow* (Lastochka, 1958); *Ukrainian Rhapsody* (Ukrainskaia rapsodiia, 1961); *Vii* (1967).

SHNITKE [other spelling: Schnittke], **AL'FRED GARRIEVICH** (b. 24 November 1934, Engel's [now: Pokrovsk, Saratov district]– d. 3 August 1998, Hamburg, Germany). Russian composer. Shnitke's father, a journalist, emigrated from Germany to the Soviet Union in 1926. The family lived in Vienna in 1946–1948. Shnitke enrolled in Moscow Conservatory in 1953, graduated in 1958, and later stayed on as a teacher of instrumentation, composition, and polyphony (1961–1972). Influenced by Anton Webern, **Dmitrii Shostakovich**, Igor' Stravinskii, **Sergei Prokof'ev**, and **Edison Denisov**, Shnitke was a theoretically conscious explorer who at the same time maintained utmost spiritual standards in his art. Although his talent was recognized early, Shnitke's music found more appreciation in the West than in his homeland. Antimodernist campaigns launched under the leadership of **Tikhon Khrennikov** in the 1960s forced Shnitke to seek refuge in film music, a less regimented genre that gave him an uncommon degree of creative freedom and access to huge audiences.

Writing scores for feature films became a major area of artistic activity and a significant source of income for the ostracized composer. His debut in cinema was the music to **Igor' Talankin**'s war drama *The Entry* (Vstuplenie, 1962). Shnitke continued to work with Talankin on such diverse projects as the stern yet highly poetic account of the siege of Leningrad, *Daytime Stars* (Dnevnye zvezdy, 1966–1969), the noteworthy Igor' Kurchatov biopic *Choice of the Goal* (Vybor tseli, 1975), and the Lev Tolstoi adaptation *Father Sergius* (Otets Sergii, 1978). Atmospheric perceptiveness and philosophical depth were also characteristic of Shnitke's music for the contemporary existential drama *You and I* (Ty i ia, 1972) and the war parable *The Ascension* (Voskhozhdenie, 1976), both directed by **Larisa Shepit'ko**.

Shnitke's original approach to film music, combining traditional "high-brow" forms with elements of trivial genres as well as direct quotes and allusions, constitutes the "polystylistic technique," which allowed him enough flexibility to adjust to different directorial styles and to work in a variety of genres. Polystylism yielded particularly powerful results in historical pictures such as **Aleksandr Askol'dov**'s *The Commissar* (Komissar, 1968, released 1988) and **Elem Klimov**'s *Agony* (aka *Rasputin*/Agoniia, 1975/81), whose richness of musical motifs, diverse allusions, and psychological penetration skillfully blend with diegetic sounds. This quality can also be found in Shnitke's music for intimate contemporary dramas such as **Andrei Smirnov**'s *Belorussian Station* (Belorusskii vokzal, 1970) and *Autumn* (Osen's, 1975). Although Shnitke was capable of conveying grotesquely funny moods—for example, in **Aleksandr Mitta**'s *The Tale of How Tsar Peter Married His Moor* (Skaz pro to, kak tsar' Petr arapa zhenil, 1976)—his forte were pensive, tragic, and even apocalyptic tones such as in **Bolotbek Shamshiev**'s *The White Steamship* (Belyi parakhod, 1976). Shnitke also contributed masterful, sensitive scores to adaptations of classical literature, including **Mikhail Shveitser**'s *Little Tragedies* (Malen'kie tragedii, 1980) from Aleksandr Pushkin's plays, and *Dead Souls* (Mertvye dushi, 1984) from Nikolai Gogol''s novel.

In animation, Shnitke worked particularly well with **Andrei Khrzhanovskii** (*The Glass Concertina*, aka *The Glass Harmonica*/Stekliannaia garmonika, 1968, and others), whose refined intellectual concepts and visual motifs quoting artifacts of world culture found a perfect audial match in Shnitke's polystylism.

The cultural liberalization of Soviet society in the mid-1980s finally brought Shnitke the official recognition he deserved. Performances of his operas, ballets, and symphonic music became public events. In 1987, Shnitke was named Merited Artist of the RSFSR. In 1990, he moved to Germany. He is buried at Novodevich'e cemetery in Moscow.

Other films: *The Sixth of July* (Shestoe iulia, 1968); *Cities and Years* (Goroda i gody, 1973); *Farewell* (Proshchanie, 1982); *The Master and Margarita* (Master i Margarita, 1994, unreleased).

SHORIN, ALEKSANDR FEDOROVICH (b. 5 December 1890, St. Petersburg–d. 21 October 1941, Ul'ianovsk). Russian inventor in the field of telegraph and sound recording technology. Shorin enrolled in the St. Petersburg Institute of Electrical Technology in 1911. He interrupted his studies to serve in World War I at the Tsarskoe Selo Radio Station, where he began to experiment with radio technology. Shorin graduated in 1919, worked at the radio laboratory in Nizhnii Novgorod from 1919 to 1922, and then joined the staff of various institutes. He was promoted to full professor in 1933 and appointed director of the Institute of Automatics and Telemechanics of the Academy of Sciences of the USSR in 1934. Many of Shorin's inventions were made in the field of telegraphic transmission, loudspeaker technology, and sound recording. The "Shorin telegraph"—one of the first Soviet so-called start-stop telegraphic devices in which a message is transmitted with a five-signal code that is then printed on a tape—was first used in 1929 but later replaced by more efficient devices.

When the Soviet film industry was in urgent need of its own sound film technology because Western patents proved too costly, Shorin, simultaneously with his Moscow-based competitor **Pavel Tager**, developed a system to record and reproduce sound on film. The first results of his efforts were publicly demonstrated in 1929. He called his device a "Shorinophone" (*shorinofon*) and worked closely with Sovkino (later: **Lenfilm Studio**) in Leningrad on its application. Most prominently, it was used by **Dziga Vertov** for the feature-length **documentary** *Enthusiasm* (Entuziazm, aka *Symphony of Donbass*/Simfoniia Donbassa, 1930), which includes live recordings. **Grigorii Kozintsev** and **Leonid Trauberg** used it for their drama *Alone* (Odna, 1931), as did **Aleksandr Dovzhenko** for *Ivan* (1932). According to Jay Leyda, the Shorin system applied in *Alone* "did enough justice to the exciting score by Shostakovich for the film to gain an international audience largely on the strength of its music."

Shorin received a Stalin Prize in 1941.

SHOSTAKOVICH, DMITRII DMITRIEVICH (b. 25 September 1906, St. Petersburg–d. 9 August 1975, Kuntsevo). Russian composer. Shostakovich was born into the cultured family of a chemical engineer. He enrolled in Petrograd Conservatory in 1919 and graduated with degrees in piano (1923) and composition (1925). In 1923, to make ends meet, he began to work as a piano accompanist in the Petrograd movie theater Light Tape (Svetlaia lenta). Critical recognition came early to Shostakovich—his *First Symphony* was performed under Bruno Walter in Berlin in 1927, and his interest in film soon became a genuine artistic challenge, although financial aspects did retain their importance for some time.

Shostakovich wrote his first film score for **Grigorii Kozintsev** and **Leonid Trauberg**'s *The New Babylon* (Novyi Vavilon, 1929) about the 1870–1871 Paris Commune. The music was controversial at the time, blending revolutionary tunes with period pieces such as waltzes and the can-can in accordance with the iconoclastic aesthetic concepts of the FEKS group. He continued his partnership with the directors on the early sound film *Alone* (Odna, 1931), an original, leitmotiv-based score that helped deepen the picture's characterizations. Shostakovich scored a tremendous success with the music for the *Maksim Trilogy* (Trilogiia o Maksime, 1934–1938), which expressed pro-Bolshevik sentiments through folklore motifs and revolutionary songs. Other directors with whom Shostakovich worked in the 1930s were **Sergei Iutkevich**, whose *Golden Mountains* (Zlatye gory, aka *The Happy Street*/Schastlivaia ulitsa, 1931) features the popular song "If Only I Had Mountains of Gold," and **Fridrikh Ermler**, whose industrialization tale *The Counterplan* (Vstrechnyi, 1932) also contains a memorable song that forms the score's center.

Deviating from the more conventional stylistic direction that his film music had taken, Shostakovich embarked on an **animation** project with **Mikhail Tsekhanovskii**, *The Tale of the Priest and His Worker, Blockhead* (Skazka o pope i rabotnike ego Balde), adapted from a poem by Aleksandr Pushkin. Yet the film's first episodes turned out so unusual and satirically irreverent that the production was stopped. Some years later, the composer worked with Tsekhanovskii again, on the more fortunate *The Tale of the Stupid Little Mouse* (Skazka o glupom myshonke, 1940).

On 28 January 1936, Shostakovich's opera *Lady Macbeth of Mtsensk* was chosen as the target of a *Pravda* attack that rendered the composer's situation precarious for years to come and forced him to defend himself against accusations of "elitism" and "formalism"; subsequently, his work in cinema was one way of proving his political reliability to the Communist establishment. For his fellow student from the conservatory **Leo Arnshtam**, Shostakovich contributed the score for the revolutionary melodrama *Girlfriends* (Podrugi, 1936) as well as for *Friends* (Druz'ia, 1938), about the complex relations between different ethnic groups. Among the most openly pro-Stalinist films for which Shostakovich composed the music is Ermler's *The Great Citizen* (Velikii grazhdanin, 1937–1939), an implicit justification of the purges. Other politically important scores include Iutkevich's cult picture *Man with a Rifle* (Chelovek s ruzh'em, 1938), featuring Iosif Stalin as the heir apparent to Vladimir Lenin, and the **Vasil'ev brothers'** *Volochaev Days* (Volochaevskie dni, 1937) about the struggle against Japan during the Civil War.

Shostakovich continued to be one of the most prolific Soviet film composers even during the late 1940s, a period of artificially reduced production numbers (*malokartin'e*), writing the scores for prestige biopics such as Kozintsev's *Pirogov* (1947) and *Belinskii* (1950), and **Aleksandr Dovzhenko**'s *Michurin* (1948). His talent for capturing heroism was put to effective use in **Sergei Gerasimov**'s Great Patriotic War tragedy *The Young Guard* (Molodaia gvardiia, 1948). Still politically vulnerable, he agreed to cooperate on morally questionable projects such as **Grigorii Aleksandrov**'s demagogical Cold War fantasy *Meeting at the Elbe* (Vstrecha na El'be, 1949) and **Mikheil Chiaureli**'s grotesque Stalin homages *The Fall of Berlin* (aka *Battle of Berlin*/Padenie Berlina, 1949) and *The Unforgettable Year 1919* (Nezabyvaemyi 1919 god, 1952).

Among Shostakovich's outstanding post-Stalinist film scores are the hauntingly beautiful tunes for **Aleksandr Faintsimmer**'s romantic hit *The Gadfly* (Ovod, 1955), for Arnshtam's *Five Days, Five Nights* (Piat' dnei, piat' nochei, 1960) about the rescue of art work from the Dresden Gallery by Red Army units, and *Cheremushki* (aka *Song Over Moscow*, 1963), adapted from his own operetta and directed by **Gerbert Rappaport**. Shostakovich's crowning achievements in film music are his dark, disturbing scores for Kozintsev's Shakespeare adaptations *Hamlet* (Gamlet, 1964) and *King Lear* (Korol' Lir, 1970), plays for which he had written theater music in 1931 and 1940, respectively. Yet even during the years when his status in Soviet music and society was safe, Shostakovich acquiesced to work on mediocre fare such as **Grigorii Roshal**'s Karl Marx biopic *A Year Like a Life* (God kak zhizn', 1965).

Shostakovich is recognized as one of the founders of Soviet film music. His 36 scores span a whole era, beginning with the classical silent avant-garde, reaching its peak during Stalinism, and ending with superb literary adaptations of the 1960s. Shostakovich, who joined the Communist Party in 1960, was named People's Artist of the USSR in 1954 and Hero of Socialist Labor in 1966. He won Stalin Prizes in 1941, 1942, 1946, 1950, and 1952, and a USSR State Prize in 1968, as well as a Lenin Prize in 1958. He is buried at Novodevich'e cemetery in Moscow. In 1980, **Aleksandr Sokurov** and **Semen Aranovich** devoted an unusual **documentary** to the composer, *Dmitrii Shostakovich: Sonata for Alto* (Dmitrii Shostakovich: Al'tovaia sonata, 1980).

Other films: *Love and Hatred* (Liubov' i nenavist', 1934); *Korzinkin's Adventures* (Prikliucheniia Korzinkina, 1940); *Song of Rivers* (Lied der Ströme, 1954).

SHPALIKOV, GENNADII FEDOROVICH (b. 6 September 1937, Segezh, Karelo-Finnish SSR–d. 1 November 1974, Peredelkino near Moscow). Russian screenwriter, director, and poet. Shpalikov finished an officers' school in Kiev before enrolling in the Soviet State Film School **VGIK**, graduating in 1964.

Shpalikov's screenplay *Ilyich's Gate* (Zastava Il'icha), thematizing his own generation's frustrations in post-Stalinist society, was accepted for production while the author was still a student, and filmed by **Marlen Khutsiev** in 1961. Both the script and the picture were attacked by Communist Party officials, resulting in numerous cuts before the abridged version was released in 1964 as *I Am Twenty* (Mne dvadtsat' let). Shpalikov authored the screenplay for **Georgii Daneliia**'s popular youth **comedy** *I Stroll in Moscow* (aka *Meet Me in Moscow*/Ia shagaiu po Moskve, 1963), a harmless story that captured some of the upbeat atmosphere of its time. He adapted a story by Ales' Adamovich, a tragic account of the aftermath of the Great Patriotic War, for the Belarusian film *I Hail from Childhood* (Ia rodam z dziacinstva/Ia rodom iz detstva, 1966), directed by **Viktor Turov**. **Larisa Shepit'ko**'s remarkable contemporary psychological drama *You and I* (Ty i ia, 1972), the script of which was coauthored by Shpalikov, lucidly diagnoses the state of depression and resignation experienced by many Soviet intellectuals during the Leonid Brezhnev era. His attempt to convey the passion and self-destructiveness of legendary poet Sergei Esenin (1895–1925) in *Sing a Song, Poet* (Poi pesniu, poet, 1971), directed by **Sergei Urusevskii**, caused a critical controversy.

Shpalikov also wrote screenplays for **animated** films, including **Andrei Khrzhanovskii**'s *Once Lived Koziavin* (Zhil-byl Koziavin, 1966) and *The Glass Concertina* (aka *The Glass Harmonica*/Stekliannaia garmonika, 1968), attacking Western materialism in a manner blending the grotesque with the romantic. In 1966, Shpalikov directed *A Long, Happy Life* (Dolgaia, schastlivaia zhizn'), the title of which reveals deep sarcasm since the tribulations of its young protagonists are depicted in dark, sad tones.

Despite his considerable early success and critical recognition, Shpalikov never accepted the cynical status quo of the 1960s and 1970s; in fact, his famously eccentric behavior and severe alcoholism were later interpreted as reactions to the bleakness and hopelessness of that time. Following Shpalikov's suicide, his image in memoirs and articles acquired an aura of dissidence, martyrdom, and doom.

Shpalikov was married to actress Inna Gulaia (1941–1989).

Other films (as screenwriter): *A Streetcar to Other Cities* (Tramvai v drugie goroda, 1962, short); *Star on a Buckle* (Zvezda na priazhke, 1963); *The Day of a Charming Person* (Den' obaiatel'nogo cheloveka, 1994; short).

SHTRAUKH, MAKSIM MAKSIMOVICH (b. 24 February 1900, Moscow–d. 3 January 1974, Moscow). Russian actor. Shtraukh joined the First Workers' Theater of Proletarian Culture (Proletkul't) in 1921, where he met **Sergei Eizenshtein** who exercised a profound influence on his career. In 1929–1931, Shtraukh was a member of Vsevolod Meierkhol'd's theater and in 1932 joined the troupe of the Theater of the Revolution (renamed Maiakovskii Theater in 1954) in Moscow, where he remained, with one interruption at Malyi Theater (1950–1957), until the end of his life.

Shtraukh's screen debut was the role of a police informer in Eizenshtein's *Strike* (Stachka, 1925). He also worked as an assistant to the director on this and all of Eizenshtein's other silent pictures. In the 1940s, the actor was cast in ultra-Stalinist films, including **Abram Room**'s "anticosmopolitan" *Court of Honor* (Sud chesti, 1948) and **Mikhail Kalatozov**'s anti-American *Conspiracy of the Doomed* (Zagovor obrechennykh, 1950); for his portrayal of the American McHill, Shtraukh received a Stalin Prize in 1951.

Shtraukh's main claim to fame is his portrayal of Vladimir Lenin, starting with **Grigorii Kozintsev** and **Leonid Trauberg**'s *Maksim Trilogy* (Trilogiia o Maksime, 1934–1938) and **Sergei Iutkevich**'s *Man with a Rifle* (Chelovek s ruzh'em, 1938). His competitor in that role was Boris Shchukin (1894–1939), who won enthusiastic acclaim for **Mikhail Romm**'s cultish dilogy *Lenin in October* (Lenin v Oktiabre, 1937) and *Lenin in 1918* (Lenin v 1918 godu, 1939). After Shchukin's passing, Shtraukh portrayed Lenin in Iutkevich's *Iakov Sverdlov* (1940), *Tales about Lenin* (Rasskazy o Lenine, 1957; Lenin Prize, 1959), as well as **Mikheil Chiaureli**'s *The Oath* (Pitsi/Kliatva, 1946) and other devotional fare. While in the 1930s and 1940s Shtraukh's Lenin image was populist and down to earth, and at times merely complementary to the dominating portrayals of Iosif Stalin, his post-Stalinist performances painted a character of greater intellectual complexity, especially in Iutkevich's *Lenin in Poland* (aka *Portrait of Lenin*/Lenin v Pol'she, 1965).

Shtraukh received two Stalin Prizes for his stage work in 1949 and 1951. He was named People's Artist of the USSR in 1965.

Other films: *The Fall of Berlin* (aka *Battle of Berlin*/Padenie Berlina, 1949); *Murder on Dante Street* (Ubiistvo na ulitse Dante, 1956).

SHUB, ESFIR' IL'INICHNA (b. 16 March 1894, Chernigovsk–d. 21 September 1959, Moscow). Russian documentary director, screenwriter, and editor. After finishing the Supreme Women's Courses in Moscow, Shub worked in the administration of the theater section of the Commissariat of Enlightenment (Narkompros) in 1919–1921.

In 1922, Shub joined the State Cinema (Goskino) film factory as an editor of foreign films—according to Jay Leyda, Shub worked on about 200 of them—which were changed so as to comply with Soviet political requirements. Shub became one of the most respected cutters of Soviet feature films, editing **Iurii Tarich**'s *Wings of a Serf*

(Kryl'ia kholopa, 1926) and **Grigorii Roshal'**'s *The Skotinin Masters* (Gospoda Skotininy, 1927), among others. In the early 1920s, Shub joined a group of artists close to the organization LEF (Left Front of the Arts/*Levyi Front Iskusstv*); its founder, poet Vladimir Maiakovskii (1893–1930), had a passionate interest in modern cinema and became one of Shub's vocal allies. However, Shub's own artistic evolution and her understanding of what defines film both as document and artifact were most profoundly shaped by **Dziga Vertov**.

As part of an original project to celebrate the 10th anniversary of the October Revolution, Shub began to sort through **documentary** footage shot before 1917, a process that ultimately turned into the discovery of a new film genre, the historical compilation documentary. Recycling surviving visual materials and organizing it according to **Sergei Eizenshtein**'s dialectical montage principles, Shub created the full-length documentary *The Fall of the Romanov Dynasty* (Padenie dinastii Romanovykh, 1927), a literal eye-opener both to filmmakers and audiences, and an undisputed classic today. Shub later described the laborious research, "not in film libraries or archives, for there were no such things then. In the damp cellars of Goskino, in 'Kino Moskva,' in the Museum of the Revolution lay boxes of negatives and random prints." She turned seemingly irrelevant or outdated material, such as the late tsar's home movies, into a highly effective instrument of cinematic polemics, creating a discourse that constantly transcends the literal meaning of images. Ultimately, the material is structured in such order that class society as a whole is delegitimized.

Shub followed her success with *The Great Path* (Velikii put', 1927), documenting the Bolshevik Revolution and subsequent New Economic Policy (NEP). Because of Shub's necessarily affirmative attitude, the director predominantly takes the role of a chronicler of events, save for some anti-Western attacks. *The Russia of Nikolai II and Lev Tolstoi* (Rossiia Nikolaia II i Lev Tolstoi, 1928) became the third part of the trilogy—although chronologically the first—focusing on the period before World War I. *Today* (aka *Cannons or Tractors*/Segodnia, 1930), a polemical statement about the direction in which the modern world was moving, shows parasitic American capitalism and dynamic Soviet Communism as the main opposing poles. It was a film of transition in Shub's career, for she was aspiring to stronger authorial control. *Komsomol—the Patron of Electrification* (KShE—Komsomol Shef Elektrifikatsii, 1932), her first sound documentary, tells about a hydroelectric power station, depicting Soviet workers with as much proximity as possible; the filmed dialogues and meetings are obviously unrehearsed, while the camera's presence is never denied, creating an atmosphere of immediacy and authenticity.

In 1939, Shub made another full-length documentary, *Spain* (Ispaniia, 1939), entirely consisting of footage filmed in 1936–1937 by Soviet cameramen. *The Land of Bessarabia* (Zemlia Bessarabskaia, 1940), with **Eduard Tissé** as cameraman, was intended as a justification of recent Soviet occupations but remained unfinished. Shub compiled *Fascism Will Be Destroyed* (Fashizm budet razbit, 1941) from British footage before joining the Central Studio of Documentary Films to take the post of chief editor of *News of the Day* (Novosti dnia) in 1942. In her later films, the subjective, passionate rhetoric of the 1920s–1930s is missing and Shub's style becomes virtually unrecognizable. *Beyond Araks* (Po tu storonu Araksa, 1946–1947), Shub's last completed project, criticizes the terrible living conditions of Azeri people in Iran. In her final years, Shub, severely ill and permanently bedridden, wrote memoirs.

The documentary compilation technique developed by Shub is a direct derivate of the 1920s montage theories and the declared dominance of fact over fiction. However, the establishment of documentary editing as a principally creative and even authorial act goes beyond ideology and has remained Shub's true legacy. Shub taught at the Soviet State Film School **VGIK** in 1933–1935; her decisive influence upon documentary auteurs such as **Roman Karmen** is undeniable, as is her impact on **Mikhail Kalatozov** in the 1920s and **Mikhail Romm** and **Fridrikh Ermler** in the 1960s. Moreover, in Eric Barnouw's words, Shub's "scholarly achievement played an important role in encouraging the development of film archives."

Shub was named Merited Artist of the Russian Federation in 1935.

Other films: *Land of the Soviets* (Strana sovetov, 1937); *Turkey on the Rise* (Turtsiia na pod"eme, 1938); *Twenty Years of Soviet Cinema* (Dvadtsat' let sovetskogo kino, 1940, codirected with **Vsevolod Pudovkin**); *Native Land* (Strana rodnaia, 1942).

SHUKSHIN, VASILII MAKAROVICH (b. 25 July 1929, Srostki, Altai district–d. 2 October 1974, stanitsa Kletskaia, Volgograd district). Russian director, screenwriter, and actor. Shukshin hailed from a Siberian village; his father was arrested by the Soviet secret police (OGPU) in 1933 and later perished in a GULAG concentration camp, his stepfather was killed in action in World War II. Shukshin first worked as an auto mechanic, then as a village scribe and a teacher. He served four years in the Baltic navy before enrolling in **Mikhail Romm**'s directing workshop at the Soviet State Film School **VGIK** in 1954.

Shukshin's diploma short, *Reporting from Lebiazh'e* (Iz Lebiazh'ego soobshchaiut, 1960), about administrators overseeing the harvest on a hot summer day, was based on his own script. In addition to directing, Shukshin played the lead—a threefold creative combination that became his trademark. As an actor, Shukshin had debuted in 1959 in **Marlen Khutsiev**'s touching neorealist drama *The Two Fedors* (Dva Fedora) in which the portrayal of a man who takes care of an orphaned boy conveys laconic intensity and depth.

From the beginning of his career, Shukshin was a genuine auteur, albeit in nonintellectual, "peasant" disguise. His full-length feature debut, *There Is Such a Lad* (Zhivet takoi paren', 1964), portrays a young truck driver whose decency and uninhibited shyness win him the friendship and sympathy of numerous rank-and-file people, and who at the end proves that he is capable of selfless, heroic behavior. The film's loose, episodic structure resembles the director's own short stories, complemented by improvised scenes. The natural warmth and candor of its characters and the humor in its view of contemporary reality brought it critical and popular success.

In 1966, Shukshin directed *Your Son and Brother* (Vash syn i brat), the story of an old peasant and his four sons, each of whom embarks upon a different path in life. *Strange People* (Strannye liudi, 1970), consisting of three independent novellas, was a box-office failure and caused Shukshin fears of having lost touch with Soviet audiences. *Happy Go Lucky* (Pechki-lavochki, 1972), about a tractor driver from an isolated rural area who goes on a vacation and discovers the world at large, was appreciated by larger numbers of viewers, perhaps because of its bittersweet, comedic spirit. Generally, Shukshin's films were highly atypical compared to the Soviet mainstream, marked by an inherent complexity, despite their concentration on "simple folk" and intrinsic popular humor. Narratively, they resemble galleries of colorful, awkwardly funny characters who often experience a culture shock generated by the confrontation of urban and rural lifestyles. Many of Shukshin's central characters seek truth and genuine happiness; they encounter abuse because of their naïve and uncompromising nature and suffer from their sensitivity and unpolished directness. Shukshin's mavericks (*chudiki*) believe in the promises of Communism and education, consequently clashing with the system's heartless bureaucracy. The author neither idealizes the countryside nor vilifies the city per se. Rather, Shukshin shows their mutual incomprehension and alienation that the Soviet state and its dominating urban culture fail to overcome.

Shukshin's ultimate triumph as filmmaker came a year before his death. *Red Snowball Tree* (Kalina krasnaia, 1974), the tragic story of a criminal who finds love and kindness in a small Russian village but who must also confront his guilt and dies by the hands of his former gang members, was an outcry of genuine, existential torment. Shukshin's portrayal of the central character achieves a level of raw, unrestrained emotional power unprecedented in Soviet cinema. The cinematography, with a mostly handheld camera, provides a sobering counterbalance to the plot's melodramatic pressures that at times slip into sentimentality. With over 60 million viewers, *Red Snowball Tree* finally brought Shukshin the national response he had been yearning for all his life.

Simultaneously with his own filmmaking, Shukshin was a sought-after actor in other directors' pictures, an impersonator of genuinely popular characters. Thus, he appeared in episodic roles in **Boris Barnet**'s *Alenka* (1962, as the driver Stepan), **Lev Kulidzhanov**'s *When the Trees Were Tall* (Kogda derev'ia byli bol'shimi, 1961), **Sergei Gerasimov**'s *The Journalist* (Zhurnalist, 1967), and **Gleb Panfilov**'s *I Wish to Speak* (Proshu slova, 1975). His sometimes minute episodic performances are memorable due to their believability and vivaciousness, for example, as the sarcastic commander in **Aleksandr Askol'dov**'s *The Commissar* (Komissar, 1968). Shukshin's last role was Private Petr Lopakhin in **Sergei Bondarchuk**'s World War II epic *They Fought for the Motherland* (Oni srazhalis' za Rodinu, 1975). He died of a heart attack on location near the Don River.

As a filmmaker, Shukshin stands alone in Russian cinema. His unpretentious yet stubborn individualism and artistic originality long went unnoticed and are still critically underestimated, perhaps because Shukshin preferred the mask of a simpleton and nonintellectual. Notwithstanding the two predominant critical poles of either nationalist reverence or high-brow condescension, it is beyond doubt that Shukshin has created a peculiar oeuvre driven by an authentic and powerful artistry. He was not protected from hurtful setbacks by Soviet cinema officialdom, most significantly the continued rejection of his favorite project, a large-scale biopic of 17th-century peasant mutineer Stepan Razin to whom he had devoted a novel (*I Came to Give You Freedom*/Ia prishel dat' vam voliu, 1971). Some of Shukshin's short stories and novels were adapted for the screen by other directors, for example, **Sergei Nikonenko** (*And in the Morning They Awakened*/A poutru oni prosnulis', 2003).

Shukshin joined the Communist Party in 1955; he was named Merited Artist of the Russian Federation in 1969. In 1970, he was awarded a USSR State Prize for the role of a factory director in Gerasimov's *At the Lake*; in 1976, he received a posthumous Lenin Prize. Shukshin is buried at Novodevich'e cemetery in Moscow. The house in which he lived in 1972–1974 (Bochkova street, 5) carries a memorial plaque. Shukshin's last wife was actress Lidiia Fedoseeva-Shukshina (b. 1938), who played female leads in three of his films; one of their daughters is the successful film actress Mariia (Masha) Shukshina (b. 1967).

Other films: (as actor) *A Simple Story* (Prostaia istoriia, 1960); *What Is the Sea Like?* (Kakoe ono, more? 1965); *If You Want to Be Happy* (Esli khochesh' byt' schatslivym, 1974).

SHUMIATSKII, BORIS ZAKHAROVICH (b. 16 November 1886, Verkhne-Udinsk [Ulan-Ude]–d. 1 August [other sources: 29 July] 1938, Moscow). Russian film industry executive. Shumiatskii, who hailed from a Jewish proletarian family, became a member of Lenin's Social Democratic Workers' Party in 1903. He was a prominent activist in the underground anti-tsarist movement in Siberia, later fought against the White Army and, in 1918, was briefly prime minister of the Far Eastern Republic. In 1920–1922, he served as a commissar in the Red Army and in 1922–1925 as envoy of the Russian Federation to Persia. In the late 1920s, he held administrative positions in Siberia, simultaneously publishing accounts about his role in the Bolshevik Revolution.

In December 1930, with no previous experience in cinema or the arts, Shumiatskii was appointed head of the newly established Soiuz-kino conglomerate, and in 1933, chairman of its derivative, the Main Administration of the Cinema-Photo Industry, overseeing the entire production of Soviet feature films.

In his conceptual approach to cinema, Shumiatskii was an uncom-promising populist. He promoted films that turned basic Marxist-Leninist concepts into entertaining stories, such as **Grigorii Kozint-sev** and **Leonid Trauberg**'s *Maksim Trilogy* (1934–1938) and the **Vasil'ev brothers**' *Chapaev* (1934); large-scale, monumental his-torical epics such as **Vladimir Petrov**'s *Peter the First* (Petr Pervyi, 1937–1939); lighthearted **comedies** such as **Grigorii Aleksandrov**'s *Jolly Fellows* (Veselye rebiata, 1934), and Communist cult fare such as **Mikhail Romm**'s *Lenin in October* (1937). However, the 1920s avant-garde legacy, as well as any sort of formal innovations, was suspicious to him—which explains his open hostility to and harass-ment of **Sergei Eizenshtein** before and during the production of *Bezhin Meadow* (Bezhin lug, 1935–1937). A loyal Party soldier all his life, Shumiatskii carried out the will of the Soviet establishment, namely Iosif Stalin's, as stated during screenings in the Politburo at which Shumiatskii was invariably present.

Regarding his administrative style, a number of testimonies agree that Shumiatskii was a strong leader who rewarded efficiency and came across as energetic and unbureaucratic. His correspondence with directors such as Kozintsev reveals an unusual erudition and wit—especially when one compares him to his successors, Semen Dukel'skii and **Ivan Bol'shakov**. At the same time, Shumiatskii ruled in a crude and autocratic manner, interrupting the production of numerous pictures and arbitrarily handing out assignments, ulti-mately causing chaos and overspending. Shumiatskii has been cred-ited with improving the quality of Soviet film stock so that it became competitive with expensive imports, and for making every effort to raise the international prestige of Soviet cinema. Thus, he headed the large Soviet delegation to the 1934 Venice Film Festival where the USSR collective program won a major prize. In 1935, he traveled to

Hollywood with two of his young protégés, **Fridrikh Ermler** and **Vladimir Nil'sen**, to study organizational structures. American efficiency made a deep impression on Shumiatskii and likely inspired his plan to profoundly transform the Soviet movie industry, a plan that he introduced at a special congress devoted to administrative and thematic problems of cinema (13–15 December 1935). He announced the goal of increasing the national production of full-length feature films from 40 to 360 per annum. Similar to Hollywood practice, powerful producers would oversee four or five pictures simultaneously, cutting production time from 15 to 5 months per film. Enthused by Walt Disney's **animation**, he also ordered the creation of Soiuzmultfilm studio in Moscow, centralizing all Soviet efforts in drawn animation and increasing the output of animated films but also effectively destroying any stylistic originality and diversity that had emerged in Soviet animation.

Shumiatskii's grandiose vision of building a "Soviet Hollywood" at the Black Sea that alone would churn out 200 pictures per year proved sheer megalomaniac fantasy. The USSR movie industry released a third of the movies promised by Shumiatskii for 1935–1936 (59 instead of 165; 25 instead of the planned 62 in 1937). After sacrificing several of his deputies and coworkers, Shumiatskii himself was criticized in a *Pravda* article on 8 January 1938 and demoted the following day. In historian Richard Taylor's words, "if at the height of the purges even success was punished, then failure did not stand a chance." Together with his wife, Shumiatskii was arrested on 17 January 1938, accused of espionage for Great Britain and Japan, and executed. His official rehabilitation, supported by filmmakers such as Romm, came in 1956. (The recently publicized version that Shumiatskii was put to death for refusing to join in a toast at Stalin's New Year's reception, implying that this was a gesture of antityrannical protest, is absurd: Shumiatskii was known to be a teatotaller, and his entire career proves the unimaginability of insubordination.)

SHURANOVA, ANTONINA NIKOLAEVNA (b. 30 April 1936, Sevastopol'–d. 5 February 2003, St. Petersburg). Russian actress. Shuranova graduated from the Leningrad Technical School for Tree Planting in 1955 and worked as a gardener for three years; she then enrolled in the Leningrad State Institute of Theater, Music, and Cinema. Upon graduation in 1962, she joined the troupe of the Leningrad Theater for the Young Spectator, where she appeared in numerous leading roles. From 1996 until her death, she worked at the Petersburg Theater of Satire.

Shuranova's memorable debut as the morose, unattractive, suffering Princess Mar'ia Bolkonskaia in **Sergei Bondarchuk**'s monumental Lev Tolstoi adaptation *War and Peace* (Voina i mir, 1962–1967) became one of the most acclaimed performances in that epic. No less intense was Shuranova's impersonation of Nadezhda von Meck in **Igor' Talankin**'s *Chaikovskii* (1970). The actress's ascetic features, penetrating gaze, and restrained yet energetic body language express a richness of emotions rarely seen on Soviet screens before. Another noteworthy part was Voinitskaia in **Nikita Mikhalkov**'s Anton Chekhov adaptation *Unfinished Piece for Mechanical Piano* (Neokonchennaia p'esa dlia mekhanicheskogo pianino, 1977). In later years, however, even quality roles such as Rosa Luxemburg in Viktor Tregubovich's *Trust* (Doverie, 1976) could not match the 19th-century-related parts that marked the spectacular beginning of her film career.

Shuranova joined the Communist Party in 1971. She was named People's Artist of the RSFSR in 1980.

Other films: *On the 22 June, at Four O'clock Sharp* (22 iunia, rovno v chetyre chasa, 1992); *Street of Broken Lanterns* (Ulitsa razbitykh fonarei, 1999, TV).

SHVARTS, ISAAK IOSIFOVICH (b. 13 May 1923, Romny, Ukraine). Ukrainian-Russian composer. Shvarts studied at the Rimskii-Korsakov State Conservatory in Leningrad, graduating in 1951. He made his debut as a film composer in 1958 with the contemporary tale of a female journalist, *Our Correspondent* (Nash korrespondent). Vladimir Vengerov's epic about the siege of Leningrad, *Baltic Sky* (Baltiiskoe nebo, 1960/61), and Iulii Karasik's youth romance *The Wild Dog Dingo* (Dikaia sobaka Dingo, 1962) brought Shvarts popular and critical recognition and initiated one of the most prolific careers in Soviet film music.

Shvarts was particularly successful with his scores for literary adaptations, demonstrating stylistic flexibility, psychological penetration, and precise timing. He worked on **Ivan Pyr'ev**'s three-part

Fedor Dostoevskii adaptation *The Brothers Karamazov* (Brat'ia Karamazovy, 1966–1968), Vengerov's *A Living Corpse* (Zhivoi trup, 1969) from Lev Tolstoi's play, and **Sergei Solov'ev**'s *The Stationmaster* (Stantsionnyi smotritel', 1972) from Aleksandr Pushkin's short story; for the latter, he wrote romantic songs based on Pushkin poems. Although Shvarts's music betrays a preference for melodramatic approaches and avoids experimentation, he did achieve remarkable tragic and heroic grandeur in **Vladimir Motyl'**'s historical epic *Star of Captivating Bliss* (Zvezda plenitel'nogo schast'ia, 1975), about the wives of the Decembrists who followed their husbands to Siberian exile, and Akira Kurosawa's Oscar-winning ecological parable *Dersu Uzala* (1975). Shvarts worked with Motyl' on the legendary Civil War ballad *White Sun of the Desert* (Beloe solntse pustyni, 1969), a sleeper hit whose inimitable irony and melancholic atmosphere owes considerably to his tunes.

Other directors with whom Shvarts cooperated include **Vladimir Shveitser** (*The Escape of Mr. MacKinley*/Begstvo mistera MakKinli, 1975; *Listen, Fellini!*/Poslushai, Fellini! 1993) and **Aleksei German** (*Road Control*/Proverka na dorogakh, 1971/1986). He contributed the score to Michael Anderson's television miniseries *Young Catherine* (1991), a star-studded American-Russian coproduction.

Shvarts, who also wrote symphonic and ballet music, was honored with the title People's Artist of Russia in 1996.

Other films: *Gone with the Horses* . . . (Nesut menia koni . . . , 1996); *Listen, Is It Not Raining* . . . (Poslushai, ne idet li dozhd' . . . , 1999); *True Events* (Istinnye proishestviia, 2002); *The House on the Embankment* (Dom na naberezhnoi, TV, 2007).

SHVEITSER, MIKHAIL [Moisei] **ABRAMOVICH** (b. 16 March 1920, Perm'–d. 2 June 2000, Moscow). Russian director and scriptwriter. Shveitser was a student of **Sergei Eizenshtein** at the Soviet State Film School **VGIK**. After his graduation in 1943, he worked as an assistant to **Mikhail Romm** on *Person #217* (aka *Girl No. 217*/Chelovek No. 217, 1944) and, in 1951–1953, as a **documentary** filmmaker at Sverdlovsk film studio.

In feature films, Shveitser debuted with *Path of Glory* (Put' slavy, 1949, codirected with his fellow Eizenshtein students Boris Buneev [b. 1921] and Anatolii Rybakov [1919–1962]). *The Dagger* (Kortik,

1954, codirected with Vladimir Vengerov) was a solidly narrated juvenile Civil War adventure based on a popular novel by Anatolii Rybakov that became a box-office hit.

During the Thaw, Shveitser explored new territory with two controversial social melodramas set in the Soviet countryside, both based on stories by Vladimir Tendriakov (1923–1984). *Alien Kin* (Chuzhaia rodnia, 1956) was aimed at exposing the mentality of greed and selfishness among farmers, while *Sasha Steps into Life* (Sasha vstupaet v zhizn', aka *Tight Knot*/Tugoi uzel, 1957, reconstructed and released in 1988) conveys an unflattering picture of provincial Party hacks. Following the censors' mutilation of that film, Shveitser turned to less provocative material with the revolutionary yarn *Warrant Officer Panin* (Michman Panin, 1960), to this day his best-remembered movie.

Shveitser then helmed a two-part black-and-white version of Lev Tolstoi's *Resurrection* (Voskresenie, 1960–1961), rendered with erudition and respect for the literary text—a quality interpreted by some critics as "academic dryness" and "theatricality." While undoubtedly implying a certain avoidance of more original experimentation of which this serious, ambitious artist was capable, literary adaptations allowed Shveitser to maintain sufficiently high aesthetic standards. In the 1980s, he directed excellent adaptations for television, effectively casting many of Russia's leading actors in starring and supporting roles. *Little Tragedies* (Malen'kie tragedii, 1980), from Aleksandr Pushkin's plays, presents the high point of Shveitser's mastery in transferring literature onto the screen; with its stylishly designed sets and extraordinary impersonations, it breathes a modernity and freshness of perception unparalleled by any other Pushkin adaptation.

Shveitser earned the highest official recognition of his career for *The Escape of Mr. MacKinley* (Begstvo mistera Mak-Kinli, 1975), based on a novella by Leonid Leonov, a satirical anti-utopia and critique of bourgeois civilization; it won the director a USSR State Prize in 1977.

After 1991, Shveitser was able to complete two more feature films, adapting his work to increasingly tight budgets. *How Is It Going, Crucians?* (Kak zhivete, karasi? 1992) is a sarcastic, fearless, albeit somewhat incoherent attack on the corruption of Soviet intellectuals. Told in the unassuming, chamberlike manner typical of

Shveitser, it represents a rarity for its time, confronting the viewer with a completely disillusioned image of society and taking apart common self-serving myths of the Soviet intelligentsia. *Listen, Fellini!* (Poslushai, Fellini! 1993), a tragicomical monologue starring **Liudmila Gurchenko**, applies minimalist methods with utmost efficiency and gives an idea of what could have become of this director had he been able to work without censorial obstacles. Indeed, Shveitser was one of the most aesthetically conscious filmmakers of his generation, rendering even propaganda fare such as *Time, Forward!* (Vremia, vpered, 1966), a revival of Eizenshtein's forgotten "montage of attractions," digestible.

Shveitser worked on most of his projects with his wife and creative partner, Sof'ia Mil'kina (1922–1997). He was named People's Artist of the Russian Federation in 1977 and People's Artist of the USSR in 1990.

⟶Other films: *The Golden Calf* (Zolotoi telenok, 1968); *Funny People* (Smeshnye liudi, 1977); *Dead Souls* (Mertvye dushi, 1984, TV); *Kreutzer Sonata* (Kreitserova sonata, 1987).

SIMONIAN, NADEZHDA [Shogakat] **SIMONOVNA** (b. 22 June 1922, Rostov-on-the-Don–d. 7 June 1997, St. Petersburg). Russian composer. Simonian graduated from the School of Music of Leningrad Conservatory, specializing in piano, and afterward enrolled in Leningrad Conservatory in composition; one of her teachers was Oles' Chishko (1895–1976). After her graduation in 1950, she wrote chamber music, romances, and songs, as well as symphonies and pieces for radio programs and circus performances.

In 1956, Simonian made her debut as a film composer with the colorful, dynamic score to **Gennadii Kazanskii**'s **children's film** *Old Man Khottabych* (Starik Khottabych, 1956), which became a classic in its own right. Simonian continued to provide the music for other films by Kazanskii, ranging from the contemporary drama *The Sinful Angel* (Greshnyi angel, 1962) and the fairy tale *The Snow Queen* (Snezhnaia koroleva, 1966) to the biopic *Engineer Graftio* (Inzhener Graftio, 1979). These pictures benefited from Simonian's strength—a stringently developed, warm melodiousness that equally energizes cheerful, dramatic, and tragic episodes, with a pragmatic, flexible approach to instrumentation.

Simonian's greatest achievements in film music were her scores for **Iosif Kheifits**, beginning with *The Lady with a Lapdog* (Dama s sobachkoi, 1959). Without dominating any episode, Simonian's bittersweet, romantic tunes, structured in a lucid leitmotiv manner, convey powerful, barely restrained desire that is fully in accord with this tale of forbidden love. The score for *Lady with a Lapdog* became a rare aesthetic match to the film's superb acting and camera work and can be considered a classic. Simonian's partnership with Kheifits continued on two other Anton Chekhov adaptations—*In the Town of S.* (V gorode S., 1967) and *A Bad Good Person* (Plokhoi khoroshii chelovek, aka Duel', 1973)—as well as contemporary stories such as *A Day of Happiness* (Den' schast'ia, 1964) and *The Only One* (aka *Unique*/Edinstvennaia, 1975), and a touching film about the 1936–1937 Civil War in Spain, *Salute, Maria* (1970). The composer's ability to convey authentic emotion also shows in films by **Vitalii Mel'nikov**, among them *The Boss of Chukotka* (Nachal'nik Chukotki, 1966) and *Two Lines in Small Print* (Dve strochki melkim shriftom, 1981), which are characterized by a blend of melodramatic and comedic elements.

Despite numerous other compositions for cinema and television, Simonian's work found scarce official appreciation during her lifetime.

Other films: *Stepan Kolchugin* (1957); *Without Visible Reasons* (Bez vidimykh prichin, 1982).

SIMONOV, NIKOLAI KONSTANTINOVICH (b. 4 December 1901, Samara–d. 20 April 1973, Leningrad). Russian actor. Simonov studied painting at the Petrograd Academy of Arts in 1919–1922 and the Leningrad Institute of Fine Arts, graduating in 1924. From 1924 on, he was a member of the Pushkin Drama Theater in Leningrad.

Simonov made his film debut in 1924 in **Viacheslav Viskovskii**'s *Red Partisans* (Krasnye partizany) and subsequently was cast in numerous movies, among them in the title roles of **Vladimir Gardin**'s controversial historical epic *Kastus' Kalinovskii* (1928) and **Aleksandr Ivanovskii**'s *The Fisherman's Son* (Syn rybaka, 1928) about 18th-century Renaissance man Mikhailo Lomonosov. An interesting episodic part in the early sound period was the undisciplined Commander Zhikharev in the **Vasil'ev brothers**' *Chapaev* (1934).

Simonov is best remembered for his vivid, temperamental performance in the title role of **Vladimir Petrov**'s two-part historical epic *Peter the First* (aka *Peter the Great*/Petr Pervyi, 1937–1939), a unique characterization oscillating between paternalistic statesmanship and wisdom, harshness and humor, decisiveness and pain. Not only did this role win Simonov a Stalin Prize in 1941, but his portrait of the innovative autocrat also defined his own cinematic image over the following decade, marked by a grandiose voice, physical dominance, and the absence of inner doubts. In another Petrov film, *The Battle of Stalingrad* (1949), Simonov played famous General Chuikov, a role that also was rewarded with a Stalin Prize.

In later years, Simonov's performances exuded more warmth and fatherly care, for example, as Montanelli in **Aleksandr Faintsimmer**'s crowd-pleaser *The Gadfly* (Ovod, 1955) and Professor Salvator in **Gennadii Kazanskii** and Vladimir Chebotarev's fantasy hit *Amphibian Man* (Chelovek-amfibiia, 1962).

Simonov was honored with the title People's Artist of the USSR in 1950 and Hero of Socialist Labor in 1971. The actor remained a lifelong religious believer at a time when loyalty to the Orthodox Church was not officially approved.

Other films: *Hard Years* (Tiazhelye gody, 1925); *The Return* (Vozvrashchenie, 1940); *The Living Corpse* (Zhivoi trup, 1952); *The Knight of Dream* (Rytsar' mechty, 1969).

SLAPIŅŠ, ANDRIS (b. 29 December 1949, Riga–d. 20 January 1991, Riga, Bastejkalns). Latvian documentary director, cinematographer, and scriptwriter. Slapiņš began work as a newsreel cameraman at **Riga Film Studio** in 1971 and subsequently studied in an experimental workshop for cinematographer-journalists at the Soviet State Film School **VGIK**, graduating in 1976.

Slapiņš's debut as **documentary** director, *Latvian Song* (Livu dziesma/Pesnia livov, 1976), featured famous folk singer Katrina Krasone (1890–1979) and introduces the theme of native Latvian culture that the director continued to explore in films such as *Latvian Folklore* (Latviesu folklora. Gadskatu dziesmas/Latyshskii fol'klor, 1983). However, the main focus of his career was ethnographic film, most prominently in *Time of Dreams: The Art of Shamans* (1984), a feature-length introduction to Siberian shamanic practices, including healing ceremonies and reindeer sacrifices. Other pictures of Slapiņš's in that genre deal with the Mansi and the Eskimos and their mythologies.

While filming dramatic events during his country's struggle for independence, Slapiņš and fellow cameraman Gvido Zvaigzne (1958–1991) were hit by snipers. Slapiņš's death in front of the camera became part of director **Jūris Podnieks**'s *Homeland: PostScript*, as Slapiņš himself had requested. His film *Baltic Saga* (Baltiiskaia saga) remained unfinished. Slapiņš was also an accomplished poet. A monument in his honor has been erected in Bastejkalns Park in Riga.

Other films: *The Night before the Song* (Noch' pered pesnei, 1979); *Dedication* (1980); *Fields of Hopes* (Polia nadezhd, 1988); *Letters from Latvia* (Pis'ma iz Latvii, 1989). *See also* LATVIAN CINEMA.

SMIRNOV, ANDREI SERGEEVICH (b. 12 March 1941, Moscow). Russian director and actor. The son of prominent Soviet writer Sergei Smirnov (1915–1976) studied under **Mikhail Romm** at the Soviet State Film School **VGIK**, graduating in 1962. He made his acting debut in an episodic role of his teacher's *Nine Days of a Year* (Deviat' dnei odnogo goda, 1962).

As a director, Smirnov debuted with the short *Listen, Anybody* (Ei, kto-nibud', 1962, codirected with Boris Iashin) from a William Saroyan story, followed by the unremarkable *An Inch of Land* (Piad' zemli, 1964, with Iashin), a war drama based on a Grigorii Baklanov novel. *Angel* (Angel, 1967), a medium-length feature, was banned and released 20 years later, during perestroika. This adaptation of a Civil War story by Iurii Olesha was shot at the Experimental Creative Film Studio, a branch of **Mosfilm Studio** run by **Grigorii Chukhrai**. Part of an omnibus project, *The Beginning of an Unknown Century* (Nachalo nevedomogo veka), its antiheroic interpretation of the Bolshevik Revolution marked the beginning of Smirnov's revisionist approach toward the Soviet canon, which repeatedly got him into censorship trouble. *Belorussian Station* (Belorusskii vokzal, 1970) shows survivors of the Great Patriotic War entangled in everyday banalities. Their ultimate bonding on a day of mourning and remembrance points to their shared humane mission that was buried under the common middle-class malaise of postwar decades. The film, whose quiet yet intense probing of various life models is carried by an excellent ensemble performance, was hugely popular and became a classic.

Autumn (Osen', 1974), one of the rare psychological dramas with erotic undertones of Soviet cinema, depicts an extramarital affair with uncommon candor. Visibly inspired by Ingmar Bergman's 1960s minimalism, Smirnov captures images of intimacy amid rural settings with the gaze of an adult observer who sees through societal clichés and ethical common places. Had Smirnov been able to continue in the same vain, his contribution to Soviet cinema could have become an outstanding one. Alas, following his next film, the social drama *Loyal Service* (Veroi i pravdoi, 1979) set in the milieu of architects, he withdrew from directing, apparently exhausted by endless battles with cinema officials. Surprisingly, in the summer of 2008, Smirnov returned to directing with *Once There Lived an Old Woman* (Zhila-byla odna baba), a film about an anti-Soviet peasant revolt in 1919–1921. In 1988–1990, though, he returned with a vengeance, only this time as an administrator—the acting head of the Soviet Filmmakers' Union, temporarily replacing **Elem Klimov** during a crucial period of deconstruction.

After the breakdown of the Soviet film industry, Smirnov concentrated on acting and screenwriting. He delivered powerful performances in the lead role of Efim Uchitel''s *His Wife's Diary* (Dnevnik ego zheny, 2001) about Russian émigré writer Ivan Bunin, and as the slimy, sensual cynic Totskii in **Vladimir Bortko**'s *The Idiot* (Idiot, 2003, TV) from Fedor Dostoevskii's novel. Smirnov's daughter, Dunia Smirnova, has made a name for herself as a screenwriter.

Other films: (as director) *Somebody Else's Pain* (Chuzhaia bol', 1967, TV); (as actor) *The Red Arrow* (Krasnaia strela, 1987); *Moscow Saga* (Moskovskaia saga, 2004, TV); *The First Circle* (V kruge pervom, 2006); *The Apostle* (Apostol, 2008, TV).

SMOKTUNOVSKII, INNOKENTII MIKHAILOVICH (b. 28 March 1925, Tat'ianovka, Tomsk district–d. 3 August 1994, Moscow). Russian actor. In 1943–1945, Smoktunovskii fought as a soldier in the Great Patriotic War, was briefly a POW, and after managing to escape, joined a Soviet partisan unit. He studied acting at the studio school of the Pushkin Theater in Krasnoiarsk in 1946 and worked on the stages of Noril'sk, Makhachkala, Stalingrad, and

Moscow. In 1957, Georgii Tovstonogov invited him to the Leningrad Grand Dramatic Theater (BDT) for the role of Prince Myshkin in *The Idiot*, a performance that caused a sensation. In 1971, Smoktunovskii became a member of the Malyi Theater in Moscow and, in 1976, of the Moscow Art Theater (MKhAT).

Smoktunovskii's prolific film career began with an episodic role in **Mikhail Romm**'s *Murder on Dante Street* (Ubiistvo na ulitse Dante, 1956). **Mikhail Kalatozov** then gave him a lead in *The Unmailed Letter* (Neotpravlennoe pis'mo, 1960), while Romm cast him as the eloquent scientist Kulikov in *Nine Days of a Year* (Deviat' dnei odnogo goda, 1961). The role of Hamlet in **Grigorii Kozintsev**'s 1964 Shakespeare adaptation brought the actor international renown. Several of Smoktunovskii's contemporary parts, oscillating between a rational, analytical worldview and childlike purity, allude to central motifs of Russian classical literature, for example, the naïve fighter for justice Detochkin in **El'dar Riazanov**'s *Watch Out for the Automobile* (Beregis' avtomobilia, 1966), one of the actor's finest accomplishments. Smoktunovskii's stunning ability to transform was used in biopics where he played, among others, Petr Tchaikovskii in **Igor' Talankin**'s 1970 picture, Vladimir Lenin in *On One Planet* (Na odnoi planete, 1966), and Roosevelt in *Choice of the Goal* (Vybor tseli, 1975).

Smoktunovskii, a master of cultured understatement, excelled in adaptations of classical literature, among them **Andrei Mikhalkov-Konchalovskii**'s *Uncle Vanya* (Diadia Vania, 1971) from Anton Chekhov's play, **Lev Kulidzhanov**'s *Crime and Punishment* (Prestuplenie i nakazanie, 1970) in which his performance as investigator Porfirii is one of the rare highlights, and **Mikhail Shveitser**'s Aleksandr Pushkin extravaganza *Little Tragedies* (Malen'kie tragedii, 1980, TV) as Salieri. At the same time, he accepted numerous roles in second-rate movies, both genre fare and political propaganda, that could not be saved even by his contribution.

Smoktunovskii was named People's Artist of the USSR in 1974. He was awarded a Lenin Prize for his work in *Hamlet* in 1965.

Other films: *They Fought for the Motherland* (Oni srazhalis' za rodinu, 1975); *Primordial Russia* (Rus' iznachal'naia, 1986); *Mother* (Mat', 1990).

SOKUROV, ALEKSANDR NIKOLAEVICH (b. 14 June 1951, village Podorvikha, Irkutsk region). Russian director and screenwriter.

Sokurov, the son of an officer, began his professional career at the local television station of Gor'kii (now: Nizhnii Novgorod), where he worked as an assistant director while also studying in the History Department of Gor'kii University, from which he graduated in 1974. Later, he studied at the Soviet State Film School **VGIK** with **Aleksandr Zguridi**, graduating in 1978.

Sokurov's debut, the **documentary** *Maria* (aka Leto Marii Voinovoi, 1978 [other sources: 1975]), was shelved and only released a decade after its completion. Other documentary shorts were treated with similar harshness, including *Sonata for Hitler* (Sonata dlia Gitlera, 1979) and *Dmitrii Shostakovich: Sonata for Alto* (**Dmitrii Shostakovich**: Al'tovaia sonata, 1980, codirected with **Semen Aranovich**), the latter an unusually intimate and warm portrait of the great composer. Sokurov's first feature film, *Man's Lonely Voice* (Odinokii golos cheloveka, 1979), adapted from stories by Andrei Platonov (1899–1950), won a Jury prize at Locarno but was not released in the USSR.

Mournful Anesthesia (Skorbnoe beschuvstvie, 1987) is a peculiar adaptation of George Bernard Shaw's play *Heartbreak House* that also brings the playwright himself to the screen. This picture for the first time revealed the richness of Sokurov's potential, the many facets of his artistry, and the paths that he might choose to pursue. Through unexpected montages, sound manipulation, juxtaposition of chronicle footage, and staged scenes mixed with quotations from various epochs, the play's original subversive, antibourgeois message is itself subverted, by implicit and explicit allusions to the 20th-century experience and its totalitarian and consumerist promises. Indeed, this bitter satire of *all* Western-type civilizations erupts with historical and cultural meaning, pointing to the profound crisis of modernity as it approaches self-extinction. Such an intellectual and aesthetic eruption was not only disturbing, it was also hard to fathom, marking the beginning of Sokurov's uneasy relationship with the general viewership as well as populist film critics.

Days of Eclipse (Dni zatmeniia, 1988) brought Sokurov's unique cinematic vision for the first time to the attention of a broader audience. It is the story of a young doctor whose alienated, scarce interaction with the inhabitants of a Central Asian village inspires a spiritual search with an uncertain outcome. The film carries a theme that has haunted Sokurov's cinema from the beginning: the principal inexplicability of the world in purely rational terms and, at the same time, the inevitability of human self-positioning within the world. The film's hypnotic pace and its alternation of vast, empty landscapes with close shots of the main protagonist visualize man's confrontation with a dangerous, apocalyptic reality. *The Second Circle* (Krug vtoroi, 1990) and *Mother and Son* (Mat' i syn, 1997) probe deeply into the substance of filial love. Sokurov consciously avoids violating the unspeakable, treating the mysteries of dying and death and the act of burial with extreme, sometimes tormentingly tactful distance. But the minimalist acting style and the manipulation of the color spectrum that characterize these pictures lead to an unprecedented capturing of emotions and mystical perceptions, making the viewing itself uncomfortably intense, turning it into a difficult spiritual experience for the viewer. How disquieting and potentially misleading the visualization of the intimate bond between a parent and a child can be shows in the case of the beautiful, dreamlike *Father and Son* (Otets i syn, 2003), which many critics, especially in the West, misunderstood with an irritating narrow-mindedness.

In the 1990s, Sokurov became Russia's foremost auteur filmmaker, whose astounding productivity is rooted in his unabashed subjectivity, allowing him to express himself both in minimalist, quasi-documentary film essays and feature-length literary adaptations and biopics. It seems that Sokurov's keen sense of personal and artistic independence necessitates the regular reestablishment of his authorial autonomy, which might be "threatened" by larger-scale productions. His short- or medium-length pictures, made at minimal cost, often with his own voiceover, achieve unique cinematic effects because they are based both on a firm aesthetic foundation and untiring philosophical searching. Not content to wait until an opportunity (and funding) arises, Sokurov seems to live with the camera when creating fictional and nonfictional narratives. Strangely, this uncompromising attitude propelled his career rather than slowed it down. His peculiar cycle of cinematic elegies that opened with *Elegy* (Elegiia, 1986) and includes *Moscow Elegy* (Moskovskaia elegiia, 1986), *Petersburg Elegy* (Peterburgskaia elegiia, 1989), *Soviet Elegy* (Sovetskaia elegiia, 1989), *Eastern Elegy* (Vostochnaia elegiia, 1996), *Elegy of a Voyage* (Elegiia dorogi, 2001), and *Elegy of Life: Rostropovich, Vishnevskaia*

(Elegiia zhizni. Rostropovich. Vishnevskaia, 2006) demonstrates an individualistic approach to filmmaking never before seen in Russian cinema. In these films, Sokurov uses the medium to carry out a quasi-meditative act: filming turns into contemplation, of which viewers may become part if they so choose.

Sokurov's most controversial pictures were "antibiopics," full-length feature films portraying totalitarian rulers: *Moloch* (1999) about Adolf Hitler, *Taurus* (Telets, 2001) about Vladimir Lenin, and *The Sun* (Solntse, 2005) about Japanese Emperor Hirohito. In all three, Sokurov's approach to his protagonists, their power, and their actions may be called *transpolitical*: political facts are neither denied nor focused on. Rather, Sokurov explores physical and metaphysical aspects of the lives of those who hold absolute power. The Hitler film is curiously inspired by the imagery of Leni Riefenstahl's staged Nazi documentaries and chooses as its focus Hitler's lover, Eva Braun, who appears as the lively antithesis vis-à-vis the grotesque dictator and his morbid entourage. Lenin's portrayal, in particular, had to come up against a whole series of hagiographical falsifications in classical Soviet biopics—the so-called Leniniana—made by **Mikhail Romm**, **Sergei Iutkevich**, **Lev Kulidzhanov**, and other former luminaries. Sokurov, rather than showing Lenin's intellectual and strategic dominance as had been the rule in the past, emphasizes the leader's unstoppable physical and mental decline, his embarrassing fragility, disorientation, and helplessness. Rejecting both the overblown idolatry of the Communist age and the cynical mockery of post-Communism, Sokurov gives back to Lenin the humanity of an individual, reintegrating him into a Christian framework and even hinting at salvation in the very end. *The Sun* depicts Japan's catastrophic defeat in World War II as originating from the nation's ideology of innate superiority, embodied by the sophisticated rituals surrounding the Tenno, a fatal cluster that almost leads to national self-annihilation. Only when Hirohito renounces his status and the notion of absolute, quasi-natural (or quasi-divine) power can life and peace reemerge.

In 2002, Sokurov created an international art-house sensation with ***Russian Ark*** (Russkii kovcheg), predominantly because of its technical daring as a full-length feature that was shot in one single, uninterrupted take through the Hermitage. The symbolic relevance of the absence of cuts is clear—Russia's history until 1917 represents one entity, regardless of its repeated cataclysms and claims to start societal evolution all over again. But other aspects of the film—its quasi chronology from Peter the Great to Nikolai II, the provocative and sarcastic comments of the foreign "guide" through the centuries—remain in part enigmatic and received far less critical attention than the camera work.

Sokurov's meditative slowness is reminiscent of **Andrei Tarkovskii**, to whom he has been linked by many critics, but his overall artistic priorities are very different from the older master's. Indeed, Sokurov's concentration on the metaphysical foundations of being and his conscious neglect of social relevance are unique in the history of Russian cinema. Fearless of current tastes and viewers' expectations, this filmmaker explores the potentials of the cinematic medium per se. He is equally savvy at making low-budget documentaries and international coproductions. While mainstream cinema indulges in technological perfection, gigantic budgets, and global distribution schemes, Sokurov's art is deliberately ascetic and individualistic, an attitude so rare in cinema today that it is bound to cause misunderstandings and irritation. Sokurov's understanding of cinema and its aesthetics is related to the greatest achievements of the other arts, which in his view hold the standards of genuine art. For Sokurov, cinema in principle can achieve the depth of Rembrandt and Johann Sebastian Bach, the grandiosity of Michelangelo and Ludwig van Beethoven, and the refinement of Wolfgang Amadeus Mozart, once it frees itself from the commercial paradigm.

Sokurov's oeuvre has attracted the attention of critics worldwide. However, his outwardly humble yet utterly subversive worldview sometimes provokes strong negative reactions, especially when he turns to political and historical themes such as totalitarianism. Russian critics in particular have often been militantly unkind toward this filmmaker, refusing to accept his seemingly unobtrusive yet inimitable simplicity as the mark of a genius. Western reviewers in general hold Sokurov in higher esteem; not surprisingly, many of his films were funded by non-Russian companies and institutions.

With more than 50 pictures to his credit, Sokurov's productivity is immense. One of the reasons is his flexibility, allowing him to switch from large to small formats anytime and to use his creative resources with utmost efficiency. A major role, too, is played by his thematic versatility—he feels equally at home with contemporary issues, including current political events and leaders such as Boris El'tsin, as with "eternal" themes. Because of Sokurov's uniquely "holistic" approach to cinema, whatever object he may direct his camera to—whether **Grigorii Kozintsev**'s apartment in St. Petersburg or one of the barracks of the Russian Army, the face of writer Aleksandr Solzhenitsyn or that of rank-and-file peasants—is turned into art.

Sokurov was honored with the title Merited Artist of Russia in 1997.

Other films: *Allies* (Soiuzniki, 1982, doc., released 1987 as *And Nothing More*/I nichego bol'she); *Salute* (Saliut, 1984, doc., released 1987 as *Evening Sacrifice*/Zhertva vecherniaia); *Save and Protect* (Spasi i sokhrani, 1989); *The Stone* (Kamen', 1992); *Quiet Pages* (Tikhie stranitsy, 1993); *Spiritual Voices* (Dukhovnye golosa, 1995); *Petersburg Diary: Dedication of a Dostoevskii Monument* (Peterburgskii dnevnik. Otkrytie pamiatnika Dostoevskomu, 1997); *The Knot: Conversations with Solzhenitsyn* (Uzel. Besedy s Solzhenitsynym, 1998, doc.); *Aleksandra* (2007).

SOLNTSEVA, IULIIA IPPOLITOVNA (b. 7 August 1901, Moscow–d. 28 October 1989, Moscow). Russian director and actress. Solntseva briefly studied history and philology at Moscow University and acting at the State Institute of Musical Drama, graduating in 1924. An attempt to start a stage career with the Moscow Chamber Theater studio failed. However, Solntseva's performance in the title role of **Iakov Protazanov**'s megaproduction *Aelita* (1924), an adaptation of Aleksei Tolstoi's proto-Communist utopia, brought her fame. Despite the static nature of the Mars scenes and Solntseva's exotic makeup, she delivered what Protazanov needed: a proud, ruthless, and gorgeous queen who lusts after a space-traveling earthling while sticking to her power over the exploited Martians.

Capitalizing on that success, Solntseva won another lead, the part of Zina Vesenina in **Iurii Zheliabuzhskii**'s charming **comedy** *The Cigarette Girl of Mossel'prom* (Papirosnitsa iz Mossel'proma, 1924). Extraordinarily beautiful and a genuine celebrity of the New Economic Policy (NEP) era whose star postcards were collector items throughout the USSR, Solntseva became a member of the capital's bohemian circles and counted legends such as Andrei Belyi and Vladimir Maiakovskii among her acquaintances.

While filming on location in Odessa for Georgii Tasin's Upton Sinclair adaptation *Jimmy Higgins* (from a script by Isaak Babel'), Solntseva met budding Ukrainian director **Aleksandr Dovzhenko**. They married in 1928, after which Solntseva gave up her acting ambitions and dedicated herself to her husband; her last role in a motion picture was Krekshina in **Grigorii Roshal'**'s *Two Women* (Dve zhenshchiny, 1930). Initially, Solntseva worked as an assistant on Dovzhenko's pictures *Earth* (Zemlia, 1930) in which she also played the episodic role of Opanas's daughter, *Ivan* (1932), and *Aerograd* (1935). She then was promoted to the rank of codirector on *Shchors* (1939), several compilation **documentaries** about Ukraine in the Great Patriotic War, and *Michurin* (1949). For the latter, Solntseva won a Stalin Prize. As an independent director, she shot a documentary, *Bukovina, a Ukrainian Land* (Bukovina—zemlia ukrainskaia, 1940), and filmed a stage production of Maksim Gor'kii's *Egor Bulychev and Others* (Egor Bulychev i drugie, 1953).

Only following Dovzhenko's sudden death in 1956 did Solntseva's artistic energy, willpower, and loyalty came fully to the fore. She completed several of his planned projects, including *Poem of the Sea* (Poema o more, 1958); *Chronicle of the Flaming Years* (Istoriia plamennykh let, 1960)—the first Soviet 70mm film with stereo sound, for which she won the Best Director award at the Cannes festival in 1961; *The Enchanted Desna* (Zacharovannaia Desna, 1964); *The Unforgettable* (Nezabyvaemoe, 1968, based on Dovzhenko's short stories); and the documentary biopic *The Golden Gates* (Zolotye vorota, 1969) about her late husband. A picture completely unrelated to Dovzhenko, *Such High Mountains* (Takie vysokie gory, 1974), proved neither a critical nor a popular success, despite the fact that **Sergei Bondarchuk** played the lead, an idealistic village teacher. Similarly, Solntseva's last project, *The World in Three Dimensions* (Mir v trekh izmereniiakh, 1979), about a worker aspiring to become a scientist, failed to make a lasting impression.

Both in the pictures based on Dovzhenko's scripts and in those independently conceived, Solntseva tried to apply the same filmmaking principles as her husband, striving for poetic generalization and emotional pathos. Her films are also characterized by a deep concern for the fate of Ukraine, although all of them were realized at **Mosfilm Studio**. Rob Edelman aptly wrote that Solntseva "viewed herself as an interpreter of Dovzhenko's aesthetic vision." As a result, Dovzhenko's cult status extended to Solntseva as well and enabled her to carry out projects of her own. She played a major role in the edition of Dovzhenko's *Collected Works* (1964–1966 in Ukrainian, 1966–1969 in Russian).

In 1935 Solntseva was awarded the title Merited Artist of the Russian Federation, and in 1981, People's Artist of the USSR.

Other films: (as actress) *Leon Couturier* (1927); *The Eyes That Saw* (Glaza, kotorye videli, 1928); (as director) *Liberation* (Osvobozhdenie, 1940, codirected with Dovzhenko); *The Battle for Our Soviet Ukraine* (aka *Ukraine in Flames*/Bitva za nashu Sovetskuiu Ukrainu, 1943, codirected with Dovzhenko).

SOLOMIN, IURII MEFOD'EVICH (b. 18 June 1935, Chita). Russian actor and director. Solomin enrolled in the Shchepkin Theater School in Moscow in 1953. Upon graduation in 1957, he joined the troupe of the Malyi Theater where he since has been one of the leading actors. In 1988, Solomin was appointed chief executive director of the Malyi.

Solomin's film career began with the lead role of engineer Kaurov in **Isidor Annenskii**'s *Sleepless Night* (Bessonnaia noch', 1960). He played supporting roles for **Mark Donskoi** in the dilogy *Heart of a Mother* (Serdtse materi, 1966) and for **Mikhail Kalatozov** in *The Red Tent* (Krasnaia palatka/La Tenda Rossa, 1969). Solomin became a national superstar as Bolshevik double agent Pavel Kol'tsov in Evgenii Tashkov's entertaining television miniseries *Aide to His Excellency* (Ad"iutant ego prevoskhoditel'stva, 1970). The actor's gentle, sensitive features and aura of a cultured, noble intellectual were ideally suited for the part of writer-ethnographer Vladimir Arsen'ev in Akira Kurosawa's Oscar-winning *Dersu Uzala* (1975), portraying a man who embodies ecological conscientiousness, decency, and genuine respect for other cultures.

Solomin directed three films: a television adaptation of J. B. Priestley's *A Scandalous Event in Brickmille* (Skandal'noe proisshestvie v Brikmille, 1981); *The Shore of His Life* (Bereg ego zhizni,

1985, TV), a biopic about Russian 19th-century explorer Nikolai Miklukho-Maklai; and *In the Beginning Was the Word* (V nachale bylo slovo, 1992), a Ukrainian-Russian coproduction devoted to the creation of the national epic *Song of Prince Igor's Campaign*.

Solomin served as minister of culture of the Russian Federation from 1990 to 1992, a position in which he displayed tolerance and tact. His brother, actor Vitalii Solomin (1941–2002), had a successful career at Malyi Theater and in Soviet cinema, especially in the role of Dr. Watson in a number of Sherlock Holmes films by Igor' Maslennikov in 1979–1986. His sister-in-law is film and theater actress Mariia Solomina (b. 1949).

Solomin, who joined the Communist Party in 1966, was named People's Artist of the Russian Federation in 1974 and People's Artist of the USSR in 1988. He also holds the title People's Artist of Kyrgyzstan.

Other films: *Those Who Are Strong in Spirit* (Sil'nye dukhom, 1968); *Blockade* (Blokada, 1975–1978; USSR State Prize); *Anna Karamazoff* (1991, France); *The Dream of Russia* (Khodayo, 1992, Japan); *Moscow Saga* (Moskovskaia saga, 2004, TV); *The Maltese Cross* (Mal'tiiskii krest, 2007).

SOLONITSYN, ANATOLII [real first name: Otto] **ALEKSEEVICH** (b. 30 August 1934, Bogorodsk [other sources: Nizhnii Tagil]–d. 11 June 1982, Moscow). Russian actor. Solonitsyn began his career at the studio of Sverdlovsk Theater, where he studied until 1960 and stayed with its troupe for some years, subsequently moving to Tallin, Novosibirsk, Minsk, Leningrad, and Moscow, often for just one artistically challenging stage role. His first movie part was for Sverdlovsk television in *The Case of Kurt Clausewitz* (Delo Kurta Klauzevitsa, 1963, first broadcast 1988) by **Gleb Panfilov**, who later entrusted him with the role of Commissar Evstriukov in the seminal *There's No Ford through Fire* (V ogne broda net, 1968).

Solonitsyn's most memorable parts are in the pictures of **Andrei Tarkovskii** who first cast him in the title role of *Andrei Rublev* (1966). Curiously, Solonitsyn had read the published script in a journal, traveled to Moscow, and managed to persuade the director that he would be the right choice for this role. For Tarkovskii he also played the ultrarational scientist Sartorius in *Solaris* (1972), the cynical writer in *Stalker* (1979), and Hamlet in the 1977 production at the Moscow Theater of the Lenin Komsomol (Lenkom).

Solonitsyn's ascetic features and intense acting style—profoundly intellectual, restrained as if tormented by constant pain or revulsion, morose, and often harsh—helped to shape some of the best Russian films of the 1970s, among them **Aleksei German**'s *Check-up on the Roads* (Proverki na dorogakh, 1971, released 1985), **Sergei Gerasimov**'s *To Love a Man* (Liubit' cheloveka, 1973), and **Larisa Shepit'ko**'s *The Ascension* (Voskhozhdenie, 1976), in which he played the Nazi collaborator and investigator Portnov with chilling precision. The masterful impersonation of Fedor Dostoevskii in **Aleksandr Zarkhi**'s biopic *Twenty-six Days from the Life of Dostoevskii* (26 dnei iz zhizni Dostoevskogo, 1980) won Solonitsyn the Silver Bear as Best Actor at the 1981 Berlin Film Festival. He also accepted numerous episodic roles in mediocre movies, informing them with depth and raising their overall artistic level.

In 1981, Solonitsyn was awarded the title Merited Artist of the Russian Federation. His younger brother Aleksei has made a name for himself as a religious writer.

Other films: *The Mirror* (Zerkalo, 1975); *The Train Stopped* (Ostanovilsia poezd, 1982).

SOLOV'EV, SERGEI ALEKSANDROVICH (b. 25 August 1944, Kem', Karelian ASSR). Russian director and screenwriter. Solov'ev worked at Leningrad television in 1960–1962 and subsequently studied at the Soviet State Film School **VGIK** with **Mikhail Romm** and **Aleksandr Stolper**, graduating in 1968.

Solov'ev's directorial career began with adaptations of two short stories by Anton Chekhov, "From Nothing Else to Do" (Ot nechego delat') and "The Proposal" (Predlozhenie), which became part of the omnibus *Family Happiness* (Semeinoe schast'e, 1970). *Egor Bulychev and Others* (Egor Bulychev i drugie, 1971, released 1973) from a play by Maksim Gor'kii, and *The Stationmaster* (Stantsionnyi smotritel', 1972, TV) from Aleksandr Pushkin's story both featured star-studded casts. Solov'ev then scored a remarkable success with the coming-of-age tale *One Hundred Days after Childhood* (Sto dnei posle detstva, 1975), a rather static, more picturesque than analytical depiction of relations among Soviet youths, filmed in beautiful landscapes. Solov'ev's tendency to turn contemporary life into a pretty idyll and season it with sentimentality became even stronger in *Melodies of the White Night* (Melodii beloi nochi, 1976), a Soviet-Japanese coproduction about the love between a Russian conductor and a widowed Japanese pianist. Another coproduction helmed by Solov'ev, with Colombia, was *The Chosen Ones* (Los Elegidos/ Izbrannye, 1983) from a novel by the country's prime minister, A. López Michelsen.

Solov'ev achieved stardom during the cultural liberalization of Mikhail Gorbachev's perestroika with his impressive depiction of a postwar childhood in Kazakhstan, *The Alien White and the Speckled* (Chuzhaia Belaia i Riaboi, 1986), blending authentic bitterness and nostalgia. However, the director's instinct for what is en vogue and his opportunistic stylization got the better of him in *Assa* (1987), an attempt to express the nihilistic mood of Soviet youth, featuring rock stars such as Viktor Tsoi and Boris Grebenshchikov. The peak of kitsch and pretension was reached in *The Black Rose Is an Emblem of Sorrow, the Red Rose Is an Emblem of Love* (Chernaia roza— emblema pechali, krasnaia roza—emblema liubvi, 1989), a film bordering on self-parody.

Despite his proven adaptability, Solov'ev had difficulties adjusting to the brutal conditions in the post-Soviet movie market. *Three Sisters* (Tri sestry, 1994) was ridiculed by critics for its amateurish acting, while *The Tender Age* (Nezhnyi vozrast, 2001) suffered from plot incoherence and all-too-obvious stylistic borrowings. Solov'ev finally came into his own with *About Love* (O liubvi, 2004), a Chekhov adaptation of considerable visual refinement and genuine psychological penetration.

Almost all of Solov'ev's films are dominated by escapism and nourished by sometimes vulgarized 19th-century Russian classics. Just as his characters prefer book-inspired dream worlds to the gritty reality surrounding them, so does the director.

In the 1990s, Solov'ev accepted a number of administrative positions; thus, he chaired the Russian Filmmakers Union in 1994–1997 and was in charge of the Moscow Film Festival in 1994–1998. He has been teaching at VGIK since 1986. Solov'ev was named Merited Artist of the RSFSR in 1976 and People's Artist of the RSFSR in

1989. He won a USSR State Prize in 1977 for *One Hundred Days after Childhood*. Solov'ev was married to the actress—and often lead in his films—Tat'iana Drubich (b. 1959). His son Dmitrii Solov'ev, from a liaison with actress Marianna Kushnirova, is a screenwriter who collaborated with his father on several projects.

Other films: *The Rescuer* (Spasatel', 1980); *The House under the Starry Sky* (Dom pod zvezdnym nebom, 1991); *Anna Karenina* (2008, TV); *2—Assa—2* (2008).

SPRINGTIME ON ZARECHNAIA STREET (Vesna na Zarechnoi ulitse, 1956). Odessa film studio. 96 min, b/w. Directed by **Marlen Khutsiev** and Feliks Mironer Script: Feliks Mironer. Cinematography: Radomir Vasilevskii, **Petr Todorovskii**. Music: Boris Mokrousov. Cast: **Nikolai Rybnikov**, Nina Ivanova, Vladimir Guliaev, Valentina Pugacheva, Gennadii Iukhtin, Rimma Shorokhova. Premiere: 26 November 1956.

Tania Levchenko (Ivanova), a budding teacher of Russian literature who just graduated from college, arrives in a forlorn industrial settlement to teach at a night school for workers. Her clientele's rough manners and the provincial backwardness of life set her aback. A beginning relationship with a steelworker, Sasha Savchenko (Rybnikov), goes through a period of turbulence because of their mutual prejudices. After a fallout, Sasha abandons school altogether. However, when Tania visits the factory, she begins to feel respect for the hard work and commitment of the people. Sasha realizes who his true friends are and who had betrayed him, and makes the first step toward reconciliation with Tania.

STAREWICZ, WLADYSLAW ALEKSANDROVICH [other spellings: Ladislas Starewitch, Starevich] (b. 8 August 1882, Moscow [other sources: Vilnius]–d. 26 [other sources: 28, 30] March 1965, Fontenay-sous-Bois, France). Russian-French **animation** and feature film director, scriptwriter, cinematographer, animator, and actor. Of Polish descent, Starewicz grew up in Kovno, Lithuania, and attended high school in Dorpat, Estonia. He worked as a civil servant and in his spare time collected butterflies, drew cartoons, and acted in amateur stage productions. According to some sources, Starewicz, who also was an avid photographer with a keen interest in new technical developments, shot a documentary short, *Above the Neman* (Nad Nemanom), in 1909 for the Kovno Ethnographic Museum.

Producer **Aleksandr Khanzhonkov** heard about Starewicz's talent as a designer and invited him to Moscow, where soon he proved to be an apt pupil in all aspects of filmmaking, including cinematography. As one of Khanzhonkov's most creative collaborators, Starewicz became a sought-after director and cameraman; however, his reputation rests mainly on his pioneering work in animation.

Starewicz began to experiment with stop-motion techniques in 1910 and made his first full-fledged pictures in 1912, putting his expertise in entomology to good use. In his debut film, *Christmas of the Forest Dwellers* (Rozhdestvo obitatelei lesa, 1912), Santa Claus distributes gifts among animals—a plot to which Starewicz would eventually return at the end of his life. *The Beautiful Leukanida, or The War between the Stag Beetles and the Capricorn Beetles* (Prekrasnaia Liukanida, ili Voina rogachei i usachei, 1912), in which beetles, ants, and bugs play the main parts, stunned Russian and international audiences.

Apart from his restless, inventive mind, Starewicz possessed an exquisite visual sense and aesthetic taste. Film historian Semen Ginzburg regards the lampooning of film clichés in Starewicz's animation as his greatest artistic accomplishment—for example, in *The Revenge of a Cinematographer* (Mest' kinematograficheskogo operatora, 1912), which mocks cinema's predilection for silly harlequin romances, and *Four Devils* (Chetyre cherta, 1913), a parody of popular Danish movies. The usage of insects as "actors" and "actresses," whose appearance was both stunningly realistic and sufficiently individualized, fooled many contemporaries who believed that genuine insects had been filmed. Interestingly, in the 1920s and 1930s, Starewicz satirized Hollywood stereotypes in a similar fashion, for example, in the nine-minute *Black Love and White Love* (Amour noir et amour blanc). Starewicz also lent his talent to educational efforts, as evidenced by *Alcoholism and Its Consequences* (P'ianstvo i ego posledstviia, 1912), in which animation sequences are used to visualize a drunkard's nightmares.

Like other filmmakers in Russia, Starewicz was attracted to classical works of Russian literature, giving preference to those that were considered "unfilmable." Brilliantly overcoming technical challenges, he demonstrated the artistic potential of animation in the short *The Grasshopper and the Ant* (Strekoza i muravei, 1913) from Ivan Krylov's fable. Starewicz temporarily focused on live-action films, revealing a particular penchant for the eerie and supernatural in fairy tales such as *The Snow Maiden* (Snegurochka, 1914) and *Ruslan and Liudmila* (1915, from Aleksandr Pushkin's poem), as well as the Nikolai Gogol' adaptations *The Terrible Vengeance* (Strashnaia mest', 1913), *The Night before Christmas* (Noch' pered Rozhdestvom, 1913), which combined animated and live action, *The Portrait* (Portret, 1915), and *Vii* (1918). Starewicz's feature films are distinguished by fast-paced action, avoidance of psychological subtlety, optimism, and a drastic sense of humor, often bordering on the grotesque, for example, in *Women in the Spa Don't Even Fear the Devil* (Zhenshchiny kurorta ne boiatsia dazhe cherta, 1916). During World War I, Starewicz contributed to Russian patriotic propaganda efforts with *Flight to the Moon* (Polet na lunu, aka *How a German General Signed a Contract with the Devil*/Kak nemetskii general s chertom kontrakt podpisal, 1914) and similar pictures. Starewicz also excelled in drawn animation, initially in short episodes for Khanzhonkov's satirical almanac *The Mockingbird* (Peresmeshnik). His drawn animation film *The Rooster and Pegasus* (Petukh i Pegas, 1914) poked fun at the Pathé brothers' company and their Russian competitors.

In 1919, Starewicz immigrated via Odessa and Yalta to France where he created a small, home-based studio in Fontenay-sous-Bois that allowed him to continue the production of stop-motion shorts, including commercials. Among his pictures were adaptations of fables such as *The Frogs Who Demanded a King* (Les Grenouilles qui demandent un roi, 1922), fairy tales (*The Little Parade*/La Petite Parade, 1930, from Hans Christian Anderson's "The Little Tin Soldier"), and animation for adult viewers. In *The Magic Clock* (L'Horloge magique, 1928), shot in Nice and surrounding areas, live action and animation are combined in a medieval tale. Starewicz's most accomplished project after his emigration was *Le Roman de Renard* (aka *Reineke-Fuchs*, 1939), a feature-length adaptation of the classical text that took a decade to complete. In 1949, Starewicz made his first picture in color, *The Fern Flower* (Fleur de fougère).

Russian sources credit Starewicz with inventing stop-motion animation, a claim that is disputed by Western historians who give priority to Émile Cohl (1857–1938). However, there is no doubt that it was Starewicz who informed animation with an unprecedented artistic quality, advancing it far beyond mere trickery. Throughout his life, Starewicz managed to keep control of all phases of the film-making process, functioning as animator, set designer, cinematographer, and director at a time when professional specialization and division of labor in cinema made such individualistic self-reliance increasingly uncommon. His influence on world cinema is immense and lasting, ranging from **Aleksandr Ptushko** to Terry Gilliam and Jan Svankmajer.

Starewicz's daughter Irina (Irène) (1907–1992) acted in some of her father's films, for example, as the little girl in the World War I propaganda vehicle *The Lily of Belgium* (Liliia Bel'gii, 1915). In later years, she assisted Starewicz on his productions and worked to preserve her father's legacy after his passing. The younger daughter Jeanne (1913–1984) was an actress who worked under the pseudonym "Nina Star."

Other films: *The Flight Show Week of Insects* (Aviatsionnaia nedelia nasekomykh, 1912); *Taman'* (1916, after Lermontov); *The False Masons* (Lzhemasony, aka *Cagliostro*, 1917); *People's Power* (Narodnaia vlast', 1917); *The Star of the Sea* (Zvezda moria, 1918); *Two Fables of La Fontaine* (Deux fables de La Fontaine, 1932); *Forest Carousal* (Carrousal borreal, 1958).

START IN LIFE, A (aka *Road to Life*/Putevka v zhizn', 1931). **Mezhrabpomfilm Studio**. 96 min., b/w. Directed by **Nikolai Ekk**. Script: Nikolai Ekk, Regina Ianushkevich, **Aleksandr Stolper**. Cinematography: Vasilii Pronin. Music: Iakov Stolliar. Cast: **Nikolai Batalov**, **Mikhail Zharov**, Jyvan Kyrla, Regina Ianushkevich, Vladimir Vesnovskii, **Rina Zelenaia**. Premiere: 1 June 1931.

One day in 1923, Kolka, a happy teenager, suddenly loses his mother (Ianushkevich) in an accident caused by juvenile delinquents. Kolka's father becomes a drunkard, while the boy joins one of the city's many youth gangs. Following a police raid, the educator Nikolai Sergeev (Batalov) takes a group of arrested thugs to a youth commune that transforms them through labor and self-governing into responsible citizens. Mustafa, a clownish thief (Kyrla), turns into an exemplary worker but eventually is killed by the leader of his former gang, Zhigan (Zharov), who attempts to sabotage the completion of a railroad leading to the commune.

STEN, ANNA [Annushka Stenski Sudakevich] (b. 3 December 1903 [other sources: 29 June 1908], Kiev–d. 12 November 1993, New York). Russian-American actress. Sten, the daughter of a Ukrainian actor and a Swedish dancer, came to Moscow in 1926, working in a variety of jobs. She briefly studied with Konstantin Stanislavskii and at the State Film School (the later **VGIK**) and made her screen debut in a episode of **Boris Barnet**'s *Moscow in October* (Moskva v oktiabre, 1927), dedicated to the 10th anniversary of the Bolshevik Revolution.

The role of Natasha in Barnet's funny *The Girl with a Hatbox* (Devushka s korobkoi, 1927) turned her into a superstar overnight and was followed by other leads, for example, in her husband **Fedor Otsep**'s peasant drama *Earth in Chains* (Zemlia v plenu, 1927), **Iakov Protazanov**'s Leonid Andreev adaptation *White Eagle* (Belyi orel, 1928), and **Evgenii Cherviakov**'s melodrama *My Son* (Moi syn, 1928). In 1929, Sten accepted an offer from Germany, never to return to the Soviet Union. She was particularly successful as Grushenka in her husband Otsep's Fedor Dostoevskii adaptation *The Murderer Dmitri Karamazov* (Der Mörder Dmitri Karamasoff, 1931) and its French version, *Les Frères Karamazoff*. By now an international star, she also got top billing in the German drama *Salto mortale* (1931), the comedy *Bombs on Monte Carlo* (Bomben auf Monte Carlo, 1931), and *Storms of Passion* (Stürme der Leiden-schaft, 1931), costarring with Emil Jannings in the latter.

Samuel Goldwyn, hoping to turn Sten into another Greta Garbo or Marlene Dietrich, invited her to Hollywood. However, Sten's perfor-mances in Dorothy Arzner's version of Emile Zola's *Nana* (1933), Rouben Mamoulian's *We Live Again* (1934; an adaptation of Lev Tolstoi's *Resurrection*), and King Vidor's *The Wedding Night* (1935) did not have the expected box-office effect, after which the actress only got a few more leads, for example, in the war drama *Chetnics* (1943) and in Otsep's *Three Russian Girls* (1943).

Anna Sten is not to be confused with the Russian actress and stage designer Anel' Sudakevich (1906–2002), as erroneously claimed in some reference works.

Other films: *Let's Live a Little* (1948); *The Nun and the Sergeant* (1962).

STOLIAROV, SERGEI DMITRIEVICH (b. 1 November 1911, village Bezzubovo, Tula province–d. 9 December 1969, Moscow). Russian actor. Stoliarov was born into the family of a forester. In the 1920s, he worked as a railway mechanic while simultaneously studying in **Aleksei Dikii**'s Proletkul't theater acting studio. In 1931, Stoliarov joined the troupe of the Moscow Art Theater (MKhAT); in 1934 he switched to the Theater of the Red Army, in 1940 the Mossovet Theater, and in 1944 the Studio Theater of the Film Actor.

Stoliarov's movie debut was a supporting part in the first Soviet science fiction film, *Cosmic Voyage* (Kosmicheskii reis, 1935), directed by Vasilii Zhuravlev (1904–1987). That same year, **Aleksandr Dovzhenko** entrusted him with the lead of heroic pilot Vladimir in *Aerograd* (1935), a performance that in turn convinced **Grigorii Aleksandrov** to cast him as the artist Ivan Martynov in *Circus* (1936), a chivalrous, physically trained and patriotic man with fair hair and a dashing smile who takes fugitive American Marion Dixon and her illegitimate black toddler under his wings and introduces them to the blessings of Communist togetherness. This role made Stoliarov a cult star.

Because of his striking looks and natural egalitarian demeanor, Stoliarov seemed the ideal choice for noble characters—"positive heroes," in the doctrine of Socialist Realism—in Stalinist fare such as **Aleksandr Stolper**'s *Far from Moscow* (Daleko ot Moskvy, 1950), which earned him a Stalin Prize, but also fairy-tale impersonations such as Ivanushka in **Aleksandr Rou**'s *Vasilisa the Beautiful* (Vasilisa prekrasnaia, 1940) and the title character in **Aleksandr Ptushko**'s *Sadko* (1954). He demonstrated a gift for **comedy** in **Ihor' Savchenko**'s hugely popular *Old Vaudeville* (Starinnyi vodevil', 1947) and for drama in the Cold War potboiler *The Secret of Two Oceans* (Taina dvukh okeanov, 1956). Incidentally, Stoliarov's last role was—just like his first—in a science fiction movie, the underrated *Andromeda Nebula* (Tumannost' Andromedy, 1967).

Stoliarov, who joined the Communist Party in 1958, was named People's Artist of the Russian Federation in 1969. His son Kirill Stoliarov (b. 1937) was a film actor who starred in *When the Fog*

Disappears (Kogda raskhoditsia tuman, 1972), made from his father's script. He heads a cultural foundation named after Sergei Stoliarov.

Other films: *Kashchei the Immortal* (Kashchei bessmertnyi, 1945); *Ilya Muromets* (1956).

STOLPER, ALEKSANDR BORISOVICH (b. 12 August 1907, Dvinsk [Daugavpils, Latvia]–d. 11 January 1979, Moscow). Russian director and screenwriter. After attending **Lev Kuleshov**'s workshop in 1923–1925 and simultaneously working as a newspaper correspondent specializing in problems of rural life, Stolper studied in the acting workshop of the organization Proletarian Culture (Proletkul't) and in 1927 was admitted as an intern to the Scriptwriting Department of **Mezhrabpomfilm Studio**. Together with **Nikolai Ekk** and Regina Ianushkevich, Stolper authored the screenplay for the first Soviet sound feature, *A Start in Life* (aka *Road to Life*/Putevka v zhizn', 1931). His directorial debut was the agitprop short *A Simple Story* (Prostaia istoriia, 1930). He then studied with **Sergei Eizenshtein** at the Soviet State Film School **VGIK**, graduating in 1938.

Stolper gained a lasting reputation through his long-term association with author Konstantin Simonov (1915–1979), whose plays and novels about the Great Patriotic War he adapted for the screen: *A Lad from Our Town* (Paren' iz nashego goroda, 1942, codirected with Boris Ivanov [1908–1964]), *Wait for Me* (Zhdi menia, 1943), *Days and Nights* (Dni i nochi, 1945), *The Living and the Dead* (Zhivye i mertvye, 1964) about the battle of Stalingrad, and its sequel, *Retribution* (aka *Soldiers Aren't Born*/Vozmezdie, 1969), as well as *The Fourth* (Chetvertyi, 1973); all enjoyed considerable critical and popular success. Without doubt, Stolper's highest artistic accomplishment is *The Living and the Dead*; its gritty black-and-white compositions, deliberate lack of music, and fearless description of the chaos at the beginning of the war impressed tens of millions of viewers and introduced a new degree of verisimilitude to Soviet cinema about the war. However, a trend toward romantization and idealization of the military can be detected in all of Stolper's films.

Stolper was a solid craftsman with a long list of box-office hits to his credit. Ideologically, he easily adjusted to changing Party policies and generally avoided risks. The fact that his Komsomol drama *The Law of Life* (Zakon zhizni, 1940, codirected with Ivanov) was harshly

STRIZHENOV, OLEG ALEKSANDROVICH • 669

attacked by *Pravda* ("A Disingenuous Film"/"Fal'shivyi fil'm") and subsequently withdrawn from distribution is hard to explain, considering its unconditional political loyalty to the Communist cause. A major success—and winner of a 1949 Stalin Prize—was *Story of a Real Man* (Povest' o nastoiashchem cheloveke, 1948, based on a true case and adapted from Boris Polevoi's nonfiction novella), about a fighter pilot who loses both legs in battle yet by sheer willpower learns to walk and ultimately to fly planes again. *Far from Moscow* (Daleko ot Moskvy, 1950) depicts, in a blatantly demagogical, apologetic manner, GULAG convicts in Siberia building an oil pipeline. This adaptation of Vasilii Azhaev's novel won Stolper his second Stalin Prize.

Stolper taught film direction at VGIK after 1964. In 1977, he was awarded the title People's Artist of the USSR.

Other films: *The Four Visits of Samuel Wolfe* (Chetyre vizita Samuelia Vul'fa, 1934); *Our Heart* (Nashe serdtse, 1946); *The Road* (Doroga, 1955); *A Unique Spring* (Nepovtorimaia vesna, 1957); *Slope: Zero* (Otklonenie—nol', 1977).

STRIZHENOV, OLEG ALEKSANDROVICH (b. 10 August 1929, Blagoveshchensk). Russian actor. Strizhenov studied at the Shchukin Theater School in Moscow. He made his film debut with the role of Arthur in **Aleksandr Faintsimmer**'s successful Ethel Voynich adaptation *The Gadfly* (Ovod, 1955), a performance that turned the young actor into a national superstar. When **Grigorii Chukhrai** cast him as Govorukha-Otrok in his masterful Civil War drama *The Forty-first* (Sorok pervyi, 1956), the audiences at Cannes Festival and later in many countries of the world paid special attention to the fair-haired actor, whose striking looks went along with considerable acting talent. Because of his aura of romantic chivalry and manly refinement, Strizhenov was often cast in adaptations of classical Russian literature. Thus, he played Petr Grinev in Vladimir Kaplunovskii's *The Captain's Daughter* (Kapitanskaia dochka, 1958) from Aleksandr Pushkin's novel, and the dreamer in **Ivan Pyr'ev**'s Fedor Dostoevskii adaptation *White Nights* (Belye nochi, 1961).

Strizhenov's exceptional star power was also used in travel adventures such as the Indian-Soviet coproduction *Sojourn beyond the Three Seas* (Khozhdenie za tri moria, 1958) in which he portrayed 15th-century explorer Afanasii Nikitin. He carried revolutionary drama such as **Samson Samsonov**'s superhit *Optimistic Tragedy* (Optimisticheskaia tragediia, 1965), or patriotic spy thrillers, for example, *Earth, Post Restante* (Zemlia, do vostrebovaniia, 1973). Some films with an underlying propaganda agenda exploited the actor in order to romanticize Communist hacks, Red Army officers, and militia men. Along with entertaining but artistically mediocre fare, Strizhenov played under some of Russia's leading directors, including **Vladimir Motyl'** (*Star of Captivating Bliss*/Zvezda plenitel'nogo schast'ia, 1975), and **Sergei Gerasimov** (*Peter the Great—The Youth of Peter*/Iunost' Petra, 1980).

Strizhenov was named Merited Artist of the Russian Federation in 1964 and People's Artist of the USSR in 1988. His brother was renowned film actor Gleb Strizhenov (1925–1985).

Other films: *The Mexican* (Meksikanets, 1956); *They Called Him Robert* (Ego zvali Robert, 1967); *Mission in Kabul* (Missiia v Kabule, 1971); *Start the Liquidation* (Pristupit' k likvidatsii, 1984); *Instead of Me* (Vmesto menia, 2000).

STROEVA, VERA PAVLOVNA (b. 4 October 1903, Kiev–d. 26 August 1991 [other sources: 1988, 1992], Moscow). Russian director and screenwriter. Stroeva studied at the Lysenko Institute for Theater and Drama in Kiev in 1920–1922 and in the Workshop of the Pedagogical Theater, a branch of the People's Commissariat of Enlightenment (Narkompros), until 1924. In 1925–1927, she was an actress and teacher at the Experimental Pedagogical Theater in Moscow.

Stroeva began writing film scripts in 1925 and directed her first movie in 1930. The Fedor Dostoevskii adaptation *Petersburg Night* (Peterburgskaia noch', 1934, codirected with her husband **Grigorii Roshal'**, reconstructed in 1968) took considerable liberties with the original stories ("White Nights" and "Netochka Nezvanova") in order to make the "reactionary" texts more palatable for Soviet viewers. Yet, despite its open social didactics, the picture evokes an authentic Dostoevskian atmosphere and was attacked by ultradogmatic critics. This notwithstanding, it won international praise and is seen by Italian film historians as an important predecessor to Luchino Visconti's classic, *Le Notti Bianche* (1958).

As a reaction to the critical debacle, Stroeva moved into politically safer waters and delivered pictures such as the 1936 *Generation of*

Victors (Pokolenie pobeditelei) about events leading to the revolution of 1905. In 1941, Stroeva was evacuated to Kazakhstan, where she made two shorts in the Alma-Ata (Almaty) studio (**Kazakhfilm Studio**) about the heroic deeds of Kazakh soldiers, *Son of a Fighter* (Syn boitsa) and *Song of a Giant* (Pesnia o velikane). In 1947, Stroeva was commissioned to direct the first Lithuanian feature after the country was forced into the USSR: *Maryté* (Marite), the story of the legendary Lithuanian guerilla fighter, Maryté Melnikaite (1923–1943). In the 1950s, Stroeva specialized in opera and concert films, several of which were released in the United States: *The Grand Concert* (Bol'shoi kontsert, 1951), in which a group of kolkhoz peasants celebrates with Bolshoi Theater artists, as well as, the Bolshoi productions of Modest Musorgskii's *Boris Godunov* (1955) and *Khovanshchina* (1959), and others.

Toward the end of her career, Stroeva again turned to Soviet history, dutifully producing officially approved cinematic versions full of omissions and distortions such as *We, the Russian People* (My, russkii narod, 1965), an account of the creation of the Red Army and its first victories. *The Heart of Russia* (Serdtse Rossii, 1970) chronicles the events surrounding the 1917 Bolshevik Revolution, with particular emphasis on Iakov Sverdlov and Feliks Dzerzhinskii.

Stroeva was awarded the title Merited Artist of the Kazakh SSR in 1944 and People's Artist of the Russian Federation in 1973.

Other films: *The Fathers' Right* (Pravo ottsov, 1930); *Searching for Joy* (V poiskakh radosti, 1940, codirected with Roshal'); *Jolly Stars* (aka *Variety Stars*/Veselye zvezdy, 1955); *A Bunch of Violets* (Buket fialok, 1983, codirected with O. Bondarev).

STRZHEL'CHIK, VLADISLAV IGNAT'EVICH (b. 31 January 1921, Petrograd–d. 1 September 1995, St. Petersburg). Russian actor. Strzhel'chik became a member of the troupe of the Grand Dramatic Theater (BDT) in Leningrad in 1938. Later, he studied with **Boris Babochkin** at the theater's studio school, graduating in 1947. Strzhel'chik's reputation as one of the most accomplished and versatile Soviet stage actors rests on his work with Georgii Tovstonogov, who for decades gave him a wide variety of challenging roles.

In cinema, Strzhel'chik made his debut with the episodic role of a Finnish officer in **Iulii Raizman**'s legendary wartime romance

Mashen'ka (1942). He continued to be cast in roles of foreigners, particularly high-ranking officials, officers, and aristocrats with an authoritarian streak. Some of his most interesting portrayals are in Lev Tolstoi adaptations: Count Shenbrok in **Mikhail Shveitser**'s *Resurrection* (Voskresenie, 1960–1961), Napoleon Bonaparte in **Sergei Bondarchuk**'s *War and Peace* (Voina i mir, 1962–1967), and Nikolai I in **Igor' Talankin**'s *Father Sergius* (Otets Sergii, 1978). The "foreignness" of Strzhel'chik's screen image also led him to be typecast as a stock evil character in scout thrillers such as *How Shall You Be Called Now?* (Kak vas teper' nazvat? 1965), *Major Whirlwind* (Maior Vikhr', 1967), and **Shaken Aimanov**'s *The End of the Ataman* (Konets atamana, 1970), all of which were major blockbusters. On the other hand, the prolific actor delivered an unusually lively, moving performance as composer and pianist Nikolai Rubinshtein in Talankin's biopic *Chaikovskii* (1970), blending features such as benevolence and vanity with posing and genuine artistry. Still, Strzhel'chik's talent was used most efficiently in literary adaptations; examples include **Abram Room**'s *The Garnet Bracelet* (Granatovyi braslet, 1964) from Aleksandr Kuprin's story; **Vitalii Mel'nikov**'s *The Wedding* (Zhenit'ba, 1977), an original interpretation of Nikolai Gogol''s **comedy**; and **Ian Frid**'s *Tartuffe* (1992) from Molière.

Strzhel'chik was named People's Artist of the USSR in 1974.

Other films: *Aide to His Excellency* (Ad"iutant ego prevoskhoditel'stva, 1970); *Front without Flanks* (Front bez flangov, 1974); *Poem of Wings* (Poema o kryl'iakh, 1978); *Time of Desire* (Vremia zhelanii, 1984).

STUPKA, BOHDAN [Bogdan] **SIL'VESTROVICH** (b. 27 August 1941, Kulykiv, L'viv region). Ukrainian actor and politician. Stupka, the son of a choir singer in the opera theater of L'viv, studied at the studio of the Zan'kovetskaia Drama Theater in L'viv in 1959–1961 and after graduation joined its main troupe. Simultaneously, he continued his education in Ukrainian philology at L'viv State University (1963–1965), and in 1984 graduated from the Karpenko-Karyi Theater Institute in Kyiv (Kiev). In 1978, Stupka became a member of the Ivan Franko Academic Theater in Kyiv and was appointed its artistic director in 2001.

Stupka had an impressive screen debut with the tragic role of Orest Dzvonar' in **Yury Il'enko**'s subversive World War II drama *White Bird with a Black Spot* (Bilyi ptakh z chornoiu oznakoiu/ Belaia ptitsa s chernoi otmetinoi, 1971). He showed great talent in portraying historical figures, including Aleksandr Kerenskii in **Sergei Bondarchuk**'s chronicle *Red Bells* (Krasnye kolokola, 1980–1982), the head of the KGB and anti-Khruschev schemer Semichastnyi in **Igor' Gostev**'s *Gray Wolves* (Serye volki, 1993), and the infamous pseudobiologist Trofim Lysenko in the TV miniseries *Nikolai Vavilov* (1990).

Only in the late 1990s was Stupka's reputation of being predominantly a stage actor superseded by his work in cinema. His performances as Cossack leader Bohdan Khmelnitski in Jerzy Hoffman's 17th-century epic *With Fire and Sword* (Ogniem i mieczem, 1999, Poland) and in the title role of Il'enko's iconoclastic *A Prayer for Hetman Mazepa* (Molitva za hetmana Mazepu, 2002) focus on the characters' physical prowess and willpower. Stupka's portrayal of a Soviet general who is torn between duty and personal allegiance in **Pavel Chukhrai**'s *A Driver for Vera* (Voditel' dlia Very, 2004) reveals psychological nuance and genuine tragic grandeur. Similarly complex is his performance as the village elder in Dmitrii Meskhiev's disturbing war drama *Our Own* (aka *Us*/Svoi, 2004), oscillating between patriarchal care and remorseless cruelty.

Stupka won a USSR State Prize for his theater work in 1980 and was named People's Artist of the Ukrainian SSR in 1980 and People's Artist of the USSR in 1991. He has held a number of official positions following Ukraine's independence, most prominently minister of culture in 1999–2001. Stupka's son, Ostap Stupka (b. 1967), is a successful actor.

Other films: *Against All Odds* (V superech vs'omu/Naperekor vsemu, 1973); *Glory to You, Son of Man* (In nini proslavsia, sin liud'ski/Nyne proslavisia, syn chelovecheskii, 1990); *Two in One* (Dva v odnom, 2006); *1814* (2007); *Son'ka, the Golden Hand* (Son'ka—zolotaia ruchka, 2007); *Taras Bul'ba* (2008). *See also* UKRAINIAN CINEMA.

SVERDLIN, LEV NAUMOVICH (b. 16 November 1901, Astrakhan'–d. 28 August 1969, Moscow). Russian actor. In 1921, Sverdlin enrolled in Vsevolod Meierkhol'd's class at the Lunacharskii Theater College (*tekhnikum*). He joined the troupe of Meierkhol'd's theater in 1926, applying theoretical principles of biomechanics with particular emphasis on eccentric means of expression. After Meierkhol'd's arrest and the forced closure of his theater in 1938, Sverdlin became a member of the Vakhtangov Theater and later of the Maiakovskii Theater in 1943.

Sverdlin debuted as a movie actor in the revolutionary adventure *On the Right Track* (Na vernom sledu, 1925). In 1936, he played the thoughtful fisherman Iusuf in **Boris Barnet**'s romantic comedy *By the Bluest of Seas* (U samogo sinego moria); that same year, he portrayed the father in **Margarita Barskaia**'s psychological drama *Father and Son* (Otets i syn, 1936). Sadly, the former film was released only in a few copies, the latter was destroyed altogether.

Sverdlin gained a reputation for impersonating negative Asian characters whose accent and mimics he skillfully imitated: the mischievous Japanese Colonel Usizhima in *Volochaevsk Days* (Volochaevskie dni, 1937) by the **Vasil'ev brothers**; the Japanese spy Tsoi in *In the Far East* (Na dal'nem vostoke, 1937), and the repulsive, greedy Chukcha title character in **Mark Donskoi**'s *Alitet Leaves for the Mountains* (Alitet ukhodit v gory, 1950). With their heavy makeup and weird body language, these characterizations, depicting foreigners as suspicious aliens, cemented questionable ethnopolitical stereotypes.

Among Sverdlin's "positive" roles was a Mongolian revolutionary leader in **Aleksandr Zarkhi** and **Iosif Kheifits**'s *His Name Was Sukhe Bator* (Ego zvali Sukhe Bator, 1942) and Hodzha Nasreddin in **Iakov Protazanov**'s comedy *Nasreddin in Bukhara* (Nasreddin v Bukhare, 1943). Jay Leyda wrote about the latter, "Without the athletic quality of Douglas Fairbanks, Sverdlin, with more wit, was able to rival *The Thief of Baghdad* himself." One of Sverdlin's specialties was his portrayal of legendary Marshall Semen Budennyi (1881–1971) in **Leonid Lukov**'s *Oleko Dundich* (1954) and in **Edmond Keosayan**'s popular Civil War yarn *The Uncatchable Avengers* (Neulovimye mstiteli, 1966), among others.

Sverdlin won two Stalin prizes for his stage work and one for his performance as Party secretary Zalkind in **Aleksandr Stolper**'s *Far from Moscow* (Daleko ot Moskvy, 1950). He was named People's Artist of the USSR in 1954.

Other films: *Guerilla Brigade* (Vsadniki, 1939); *Wait for Me* (Zhdi menia, 1943); *Various Destinies* (Raznye sud'by, 1956); *Two Lives* (Dve zhizni, 1961).

SVILOVA [married name: Vertova], **ELIZAVETA IGNAT'EVNA** (b. 5 September 1900–d. 11 November 1975, Moscow). Russian **documentary** director and editor. Svilova, daughter of a worker who perished in the 1918–1921 Civil War, began her career in 1914 as a cutter and photo printer for the Pathé brothers in Moscow, as well as other foreign studios. After the 1917 Bolshevik Revolution, she joined the Moscow Film Committee, then Goskino, and in 1928 Ukrainfilm studio.

In 1918, Svilova met budding documentary innovator **Dziga Vertov** and became his wife and closest collaborator. As a member of Vertov's groups Council of Three and Cine-Eyes (*kinoki*), she was the editor and codirector of a number of his major pictures. In 1921, Svilova was assigned the collection of all preserved footage of Vladimir Lenin that she then compiled into a newsreel (released in 1922).

In 1944, Svilova assumed a position at the Central Studio of Documentary Films. She worked with **Iulii Raizman** on *Berlin* (aka *The Fall of Berlin*, 1945), which won her a Stalin Prize, and with **Roman Karmen** on *The Trial of Nations* (Sud narodov, 1946). She also directed numerous films on her own, for example, *On Transportation* (O transporte, 1939), *Auschwitz* (Osventsim, 1945), and *Bestialities of the Fascists* (Zverstva fashistov, 1946). Svilova, in Annette Michelson's words, "is an outstanding example of the interesting development and realization of careers for women in a cinematic tradition which was grounded in an aesthetically innovative and politically revolutionary era." Despite her overall remarkable career, Svilova experienced collegial hostilities, marginalization, and administrative harassment in the 1930s similar to those that befell Vertov.

After her husband's death in 1954, Svilova helped edit and publish Vertov's writings and a collection of memoirs about him.

Other films: *The Fifth Anniversary of the Metro* (Piatiletie metro, 1940); *For You, Front* (Tebe, front, 1943); *Parade of Youth* (Parad molodosti, 1946); *The Slavic Congress in Belgrad* (Slavianskii kongress v Belgrade, 1947).

– T –

TABAKOV, OLEG PAVLOVICH (b. 17 August 1935, Saratov). Russian actor and pedagogue. Tabakov studied at the studio school of the Moscow Art Theater (MKhAT), graduating in 1957—30 years later, he would return to his alma mater as professor and president (*rektor*). Tabakov was a founding member of The Contemporary (Sovremennik) theater, one of the most daring experimental troupes of the 1960s. He switched to MKhAT in 1983, taking over as artistic director in 2000.

Tabakov debuted in the movies in 1957 with the lead, Sasha Komelev, in **Mikhail Shveitser**'s *Sasha Steps into Life* (Sasha vstupaet v zhizn', aka *Tight Knot*/Tugoi uzel). From early on he worked with leading Soviet directors such as **Aleksandr Zarkhi**, **Grigorii Chukhrai**, **Vladimir Petrov**, and **Aleksandr Stolper**. Tabakov excelled both in contemporary roles and in literary adaptations, often blending remnants of childish purity with immature selfishness and an egocentric demeanor that could transcend into hysteria, for example, as Petia Rostov in **Sergei Bondarchuk**'s *War and Peace* (Voina i mir, 1962–1967) and in the title role of **Nikita Mikhalkov**'s peculiar Ivan Goncharov interpretation, *Oblomov* (Neskol'ko dnei iz zhizni I.I. Oblomova, 1981). Narcissism and moral ambiguity were prominent in Tabakov's impersonation of Nazi hack Schellenberg in **Tat'iana Lioznova**'s cult miniseries *Seventeen Moments of Spring* (Semnadtsat' mgnovenii vesny, 1973); many of his impersonations tend toward the grotesque or even clownish.

One of Tabakov's most memorable achievements among his almost 100 movie roles is the part of avant-garde artist Iskremas (acronym of "Revolutionary Art for the Masses") in **Aleksandr Mitta**'s *Shine, Shine, My Star* (Gori, gori, moia zvezda, 1970). In Istvan Szabo's thought-provoking postwar drama *Taking Sides* (2002) the actor proved a veritable scene-stealer as a manipulative Soviet colonel.

Tabakov, who joined the Communist Party in 1965, won a USSR State Prize for his theatrical work in 1967 and a State Prize of Russia in 1998; he was named People's Artist of the Russian Federation in 1977 and People's Artist of the USSR in 1987. His work as an acting teacher in his own studio theater (founded in 1974, nicknamed

"Tabakerka" [Snuffbox]) has shaped a generation of eminent actors of the 1990s.

Other films: *A Noisy Day* (Shumnyi den', 1960); *The Shot* (Vystrel, 1966); ***Moscow Does Not Believe in Tears*** (Moskva slezam ne verit, 1979); *Stalin* (1992, TV, U.S./Great Britain); *Three Stories* (Tri istorii, 1997); *The President and His Granddaughter* (President i ego vnuchka, 2000); *Rokonok* (2006, Hungary).

TADJIK CINEMA. *See* KASYMOV, MUHAMEDJAN; KIMYAGAROV, BENSION; MOTYL', VLADIMIR; TADJIKFILM STUDIO; YARMATOV, KAMIL.

TADJIKFILM STUDIO. The studio was founded under the name Tadjikkino in January 1930 in Dushanbe, the capital of Tadjikistan (since 1929: Tadjik Soviet Socialist Republic), where the first movie theaters had been established in 1927. Initially, Tadjikkino produced **documentary** shorts and newsreels with the intention to propagate the country's industrial and agricultural achievements under Bolshevik rule. A number of early documentaries, so-called *kul'turfil'my*, were shot by Russian cinematographers and generated considerable attention for Tadjikistan's traditional culture, its nature, and history. Although the dominating genre in **Tadjik cinema** during its first 25 years were documentaries, **Kamil Yarmatov**, originally an actor and one of the founders of Tadjik cinema, also directed *Right of Honor* (Pochetnoe pravo, 1932), a blend of documentary and fictional episodes about the military draft. The silent *When the Emirs Die* (Kogda umiraiut emiry, 1932) by Liudmila Pechorina was devoted to the violent collectivization in the countryside. Other films denounced Islam, for example, *The Living God* (Zhivoi bog, 1935). In 1938, the studio turned out its first sound feature film, *The Garden* (Sad), directed by Nikolai Dostal', with a memorable score by **Aram Khachaturyan**. It was followed by Yarmatov's *Friends Meet Anew* (Druz'ia vstrechaiutsia vnov', 1939).

In November 1941, the Moscow studio Soiuzdetfilm (later: **Gor'kii Studio for Children's and Youth Films**) was evacuated to Stalinabad (Dushanbe) because of the Great Patriotic War. Jointly, the studios produced *The Son of Tadjikistan* (Syn Tadzhikistana)—the only

Tadjik war film—and *Tadjik Film Concert* (Tadzhikskii kinokont-sert). On other projects, directors such as **Sergei Iutkevich** (*Schwejk's New Adventures*/Novye pokhozhdeniia Shveika, 1943) and **Lev Kule-shov** (*Timur's Oath*/Kliatva Timura, 1942) worked together with local film professionals.

In the first postwar decade, no more feature films were produced at Tadjikfilm Studio; its staff concentrated exclusively on newsreels and documentaries, some of which were feature length. The leading Tadjik filmmaker from the mid-1950s to the late 1970s was **Bension Kimyagarov**, who began his career with documentaries, including *Tadjikistan* (1946, codirected with Lidiia Stepanova) and *Soviet Tadjikistan* (Sovetskii Tadjikistan, 1951). In 1956, Kimyagarov directed *Dokhunda* (1956), from a screenplay by **Viktor Shklovskii** based on the 1930 novel by Tadjik author Sadriddin Ayni (1876–1954), to whom the director had devoted a documentary in 1949. In *Dokhunda*, the best-known Tadjik film actor, **Muhamedjan Kasymov**, impressively portrays a landowner who loses everything because of the revolution. Rafail Perel'shtein's musical **comedy** *I Met a Girl* (Ia vstretil devushku, 1957) about an aspiring pop singer was very successful throughout the Soviet Union. Perel'shtein also directed the three-hour epic *Man Changes His Skin* (Chelovek meniaet ko-zhu, 1960) from a novel by Bruno Jasienski (1901–1938) about an American engineer traveling through Soviet Tadjikistan. Takhir Sabirov (b. 1929) is a prolific actor who made his directorial debut in 1960 with the comedy *It's Time for the Son to Get Married* (Synu pora zhenit'sia), followed by a large number of films in a variety of genres, including *The Pawnbroker's Death* (Smert' rostovshchika, 1966) from a novel by Ayni.

It is noteworthy that the studio gave non-Tadjik directors a chance to carry out their projects, among them prominent filmmakers such as Armenian **Hamo Bek-Nazaryan** and **Ezram Karamyan**, who helmed *Nasreddin in Khodjent, or The Enchanted Prince* (Nasreddin v Khodzhente, ili Ocharovannyi prints, 1959), and Russian **Vladimir Motyl'**, who directed the poetic *Children of Pamir* (Deti Pamira, 1963).

Among the most important Tadjik films of the 1970s were Kimyagarov's *The Legend of Rustam* (Skazanie o Rustame, 1970), *Rustam and Zohrab* (1972), and *The Legend of Siiavush* (Skazanie o Siiavushe, 1977), a trilogy from Firdousi's classical epic poem *Shahname*. Also successful was Margarita Kasymova (b. 1938) who specialized in **children's and youth films** but moved to Belarus in the 1980s. The studio has been dubbing foreign films into Tadjik since 1938, including its own productions of the 1930s that were shot in Russian; about 30–40 full-length features were dubbed per year, in addition to a number of documentaries.

After Tadjikistan gained its independence in 1991, Tadjikfilm Studio leased its premises and equipment to foreign productions and has not completed any feature film since 1993. In 2005, when a new law on national cinema was issued, the production of a large-scale historical film about Shamsiddhin Shokhin began.

TAGER, PAVEL GRIGOR'EVICH (b. 1 October 1903, Moscow– d. 30 June 1971, Moscow). Russian inventor in cinema and television technology. Tager graduated from Moscow University in 1926 and from the Lomonosov Institute of Mechanics in Moscow in 1929; that same year he was hired by **Mezhrabpomfilm Studio**, where he worked closely with director **Leonid Obolenskii**.

From 1926 on, Tager and his group devoted themselves to the problem of sound film and regularly presented their findings to the public, including nine models of sound recording and six models of sound reproduction. Tager's ultimate sound-on-film system was based on an approach similar to the German "Tri Ergon" that was demonstrated in Moscow in 1926 using a Kerr cell. Tager's device was ready in 1928 when the first experimental shorts with sound were screened. By the late 1920s, it became clear that the days of silent cinema were numbered and that the USSR was not willing to buy (or able to pay for a license) the expensive U.S. or German sound film patents. At this point, the experiments of Tager and his Leningrad competitor **Aleksandr Shorin** attracted the Soviet film industry's attention in earnest.

Tager named his device "Tagephone" (Tagefon SGK-7). It was used for the first Soviet sound documentary, **Abram Room**'s feature-length *The Plan of the Great Works* (Plan velikikh rabot, aka *Five-Year Plan*/Piatiletka, 1930), compiled from footage made by other directors with a soundtrack consisting of music and spoken commentary. The film was completed in record time in 1930 and demonstrated at the October Revolution celebrations. The Tagephone was also used for the first sound feature film, **Nikolai Ekk**'s *A Start in Life* (aka *Road to Life*/Putevka v zhizn'), released on 1 June 1931, and for **Vsevolod Pudovkin**'s *The Deserter* (Dezertir, 1933).

Later inventions made by Tager included a system for the transposition of television programs onto film (1957), as well as a device for video magnetic recording (1957–1960). From 1932 to 1939 and 1947 to 1969, Tager worked at the Soviet Research Institute of Cinema and Photography and, from 1939 to 1947, at the Institute for Automatics and Telemechanics. He was appointed full professor in 1937.

Tager received the Order of Lenin in 1935 and a Stalin Prize in 1950. He was named Merited Activist of Science and Technology in 1947.

TALANKIN, IGOR' [real first name: Industrii] **VASIL'EVICH** (b. 3 October 1927, Noginsk near Moscow). Russian director and scriptwriter. Talankin studied acting at the Glazunov School for Theater and Music until 1950; he graduated from the State Institute for Stage Arts (GITIS) in 1956 and from **Mosfilm Studio**'s Supreme Directing Courses (VKSR), where he studied with **Iulii Raizman**, in 1959.

Talankin's directorial debut, the touching childhood drama *Seryozha* (aka *A Summer to Remember*/Serezha, 1960, codirected with **Georgii Daneliia**), was popular at home and abroad. A warm, empathetic portrayal of family relations from the viewpoint of a perceptive toddler pointed—however mildly—to existing painful contradictions between private and societal interests in Soviet society and thus signaled a shift away from exclusively collectivist positions. Talankin helmed another coming-of-age picture, *The Entry* (Vstuplenie, 1962), once again addressing the problem of a boy's need for a father. However, the film's atmosphere, defined by the chaos of the Great Patriotic War, was noticeably gloomier and the problem constellation harsher than in the more lighthearted *Seryozha*.

Daytime Stars (Dnevnye zvezdy, 1966–1969), inspired by the life of poet Ol'ga Berggol'ts (1910–1975), a survivor of the 900-day Nazi siege of Leningrad, was a serious attempt to introduce to Soviet cinema modern narrative structures based on poetic and philosophical association rather than plain chronology. Intended as an intellectual-cinematic credo, the film, however, turned into a fiasco for its maker; officially denounced as overly cerebral and incomprehensible to Soviet viewers, it was severely censored and only permitted for limited release. Yet its mutilated shape notwithstanding, Talankin's sensitive direction, together with **Margarita Pilikhina**'s superb cinematography, make *Daytime Stars* this filmmaker's purest achievement in artistic terms.

The grand-scale biopic *Chaikovskii* (1970) operated on politically and aesthetically safer ground and delivered a dignified if somewhat static illustration of the composer's life, avoiding its more controversial aspects. This trend continued in *Choice of the Goal* (Vybor tseli, 1975), which was devoted to the life of Igor' Kurchatov (1903–1960), the physicist officially credited with the invention of the Soviet nuclear bomb. However, while demonstrating unequivocal loyalty to the Communist military strategies, the film stunned attentive viewers with its unflattering depiction of Soviet leaders, among them a chilling portrayal of Lavrentii Beriia.

Talankin's adaptation of Lev Tolstoi's novella *Father Sergius* (Otets Sergii, 1978), about a nobleman so disenchanted with tsarist corruption that he decides to become a hermit, is more truthful to the letter of the original than **Iakov Protazanov**'s famous 1918 silent version. In hindsight, it can be interpreted as a parable about the resignation and inner withdrawal of Soviet intellectuals during the 1970s. After the breakup of the USSR, Talankin adapted Fedor Dostoevskii's *The Devils* (Besy/aka Nikolai Stavrogin, 1992, codirected with his son, Dmitrii Talankin) and made *The Invisible Traveler* (Nezrimyi puteshestvennik, 1998), based on a legend about Tsar Aleksandr I.

Talankin is an ambitious filmmaker with a preference for serious themes, often with tragic overtones and handled in a rather austere manner. Most of his films deal with the individual suffering from the mercilessness of historical necessity.

Talankin was named Merited Artist of the RSFSR in 1965 and People's Artist of the USSR in 1988. He joined the Communist Party in 1978. From 1964 to 1989, Talankin was in charge of a directing workshop at the Soviet State Film School **VGIK**; in 1976, he was promoted to the rank of full professor.

Other films: *Starfall* (Zvezdopad, 1982); *The Time to Rest Is from Saturday to Monday* (Vremia otdykha s subboty do ponedel'nika, 1984); *Autumn, Chertanovo* (Osen', Chertanovo, 1988).

TALLINFILM STUDIO [Filmistuudio Tallinnfilm]. The studio was founded in 1940 and originally called Tallin Studio for Newsreels and Documentaries (Dokumentaalfilmide Tallinna Kinostuudio). It was created on the basis of the private company Estonian Culture Film (Eesti Kultuurfilm, 1931–1940), which had produced some feature films using government subsidies. The studio was "nationalized" after the country had been forced into the USSR in 1940. In 1963, it was renamed Tallinfilm Studio.

Initially specializing in documentaries and newsreels, as well as dubbing foreign films into Estonian since 1946, Tallinfilm began the production of feature films in 1954. Prior to that, so-called Estonian films were produced at **Lenfilm Studio** by **Gerbert Rappaport**, including the Stalin Prize–winning *Life in the Citadel* (Elu tsidallis/ Zhizn' v tsitadeli, 1948), an adaptation of August Jakobson's play. *When the Evening Begins* (Kogda nastupaet vecher, 1955) and *Yachts at Sea* (Iakhty v more, 1956) were made locally, but predominantly by non-Estonian crews. Gradually, Tallinfilm came into its own and landed a Soviet-wide hit with the **comedy** *Naughty Curves* (Vallatud kurvid/Ozornye povoroty, 1959, directed by **Kaljo Kiisk** and Iulii Kun), which two years later was remade as a wide-screen/panorama version. Estonian directors such as Kiisk, Arvo Kruusement (b. 1928), Jüri Müür (1929–1984), **Leida Laius**, and, in the 1980s, Peeter Simm (b. 1953) and Arvo Iho (b. 1949) tried hard to capture specific national values, subverting the required Socialist-Realist norms to some degree. Thus, the studio produced adaptations of prominent works of Estonian literature such as *The New Devil from the Netherworld* (Põrgupõhja uus Vanapagan/Novyi nechistyi iz preispodnei, 1964), from Anton Tammsaare's novel. However, iconoclastic or ambiguous approaches to the country's past, for example, in Kiisk's allegory on violence and humanity, *Insanity* (Hullumeelsus/Bezumie, 1968), were heavily censored or prohibited. Harmless contemporary comedies such as Kruusement's *Don Juan from Tallin* (Don Juan Tallinnas/Don Zhuan v Talline, 1971) fared much better with the Goskino censors in Moscow. The historical adventure movie *The Last Relic*

(Viimne relikviia/Posledniaia relikviia, 1969) by Grigorii Kromanov (1926–1984) became the biggest box-office success in the history of **Estonian cinema**; it was sold to over 60 countries. Among the studio's stars who also developed an international reputation were **Jüri Järvet**, **Eve Kivi**, and **Lembit Ulfsak**.

On average, Tallinfilm Studio produced three to five full-length pictures per year. For financial and logistical reasons, the number of documentaries was much higher than that of feature films. In 1958, **Elbert Tuganov** created the first Estonian **animated** film, *Little Peter's Dream* (Peetrikese Unenägu/Son Petrika, 1958), a stop-motion picture. In 1972, the production of drawn animation at Tallinfilm Studio began. Among the best-known Estonian animators are Rein Raamat (b. 1931), **Heino Pars**, and **Priit Pärn**.

After the Republic of Estonia declared its independence on 24 August 1991, film production was decentralized. In May 1994, the animation studio and stop-motion studio were separated from Tallinfilm, the former as Eesti Joonisfilm, the latter as Nukufilm (Puppet Animation Film Studio). In 1995, the production of feature films at Tallinfilm Studio came to a halt, although the Ministry of Culture continues to fund culturally valuable Estonian films. The studio's archive became part of the Estonian Film Foundation, established in 1997, while the building and the technical equipment were leased to private companies. The last newsreel was produced in 1998. In 2000, Tallinfilm was closed down; its building became a hotel.

From 1941 to 1994, Tallinfilm Studio produced 116 feature films and about 900 **documentary** and educational shorts, as well as 194 animated films, of which 128 are stop-motion pictures.

TARICH [also: Tarych; real name: Alekseev], **IURII VIKTOROVICH** (b. 24 January 1885, Polotsk, Western Belarus–d. 21 February 1967, Moscow). Belarusian director, scriptwriter, and actor. Tarich, who hailed from an old military family, served in the Russian Army as a paramedic, studied at the Law School of Moscow University from 1903 to 1905, and became involved in leftist activities for which he was sentenced to one year in prison and three years of exile to Siberia. From 1907 to 1917, he acted on the stage of various provincial theaters and, in 1914, began to write screenplays, among them *The Tragedy of the Nabatov Family* (Tragediia sem'i Nabatovykh,

1915). Tarich also fought in the tsarist army in World War I and later joined Bolshevik troops. After his demobilization, he worked as an actor and director with a number of Moscow troupes, among them Vsevolod Meierkhol'd's theater.

Tarich wrote several scripts for early Soviet silents, most of them action-filled revolutionary thrillers, of which *The Gang of Father Knysh* (Banda bat'ki Knysha, 1924) for director **Aleksandr Razumnyi** was the most successful. He debuted as film director in 1925 with a movie about the contemporary Russian countryside, *Moroka* (codirected with Evgenii Ivanov-Barkov). Tarich won considerable critical recognition for *Wings of a Serf* (aka *Ivan the Terrible*/Kryl'ia kholopa, 1926), an epic set in the 16th century that avoided typical clichés of the historical genre by emphasizing socioeconomic factors rather than love intrigues. According to Jay Leyda, *Wings* remained Tarich's best picture because of its exceptional crew, including **Viktor Shklovskii** as scriptwriter, **Ivan Pyr'ev** as assistant, and **Esfir' Shub** as editor. However, the director's attempt to repeat this accomplishment and apply Marxist doctrines to classical literature in *The Captain's Daughter* (Kapitanskaia dochka, 1928) was derided by critics because of its vulgarization of Aleksandr Pushkin's novel.

In 1927, Tarich directed the first Belarusian feature, the anti-Polish Civil War drama *Forest Tale* (Liasnaia byl/Lesnaia byl'). Also at Belgoskino—the later **Belarusfilm Studio**—he made *Till Tomorrow* (Da zautra/Do zavtra, 1929) about a group of Belarusian youngsters in a small town engaged in illegal political activities against Polish occupants. Under the title *Upheaval* (Perevorot), Tarich compiled sound film bites for the opening of the first sound movie theater in Minsk in 1930. Noteworthy among his own sound pictures are the maritime adventure *The Path of the Vessel* (Shlia karablia/Put' korablia, 1935) and *The 11th of July* (Adzinaccataha lipenia/Odinnadtsatoe iiulia, 1938), a chronicle of events that led to the establishment of Soviet power in Belarus. Not as successful was his attempt to make a **comedy**, *The Skies* (Nebesa, 1940), the tale of a farmer who distrusts modern technology before being converted.

Following the evacuation of the Belarusian film studio to Alma Ata, Tarich directed, together with **Vladimir Korsh-Sablin**, *Belorussian Novellas* (Belorusskie novelly, 1942), about rank-and-file people who fight Nazi occupation. By far the most interesting of his wartime pictures, however, is the thought-provoking Bertolt Brecht adaptation *Murderers Are on Their Way* (Ubiitsy vykhodiat na dorogu, 1942), codirected with **Vsevolod Pudovkin**. This intelligent, perhaps inadvertently subversive depiction of life under totalitarian rule was shelved because it rang too close to home.

In 1943–1945, Tarich helped develop film production in Mongolia, codirecting the feature *Prince Tsogt* (Tsogt taij, 1945), as well as a number of **documentaries**. In the 1940s and 1950s he worked as a consultant for **children's films** and made documentary shorts popularizing the sciences both at Belarusfilm Studio and at Mosnauchfilm in Moscow.

Tarich, one of the founders of **Belarusian cinema**, was named Merited Artist of the Russian Federation in 1935. The Ministry of Culture of Belarus awards a Tarich Prize to its country's accomplished filmmakers.

Other films: *First Lights* (Pervye ogni, 1925); *Bulat Batyr* (1927); *Hatred* (Nenavist', 1930); *Fugitives* (Begletsy, 1932).

TARKOVSKII, ANDREI ARSEN'EVICH (b. 4 April 1932, Zavrazh'e, Ivanovo district–d. 29 December 1986, Paris). Russian director and screenwriter. Tarkovskii's father, eminent poet Arsenii Tarkovskii (1907–1989), left the family when his children were still infants. Tarkovskii grew up with his mother in a village near the town of Iur'evets on the Volga River. After moving to Moscow in 1939, he attended a music school and took drawing lessons. In 1951, Tarkovskii enrolled in the Moscow Institute for Oriental Studies, where he specialized in Arabic; the following year, he left the institute because of an accident and worked as a geologist in Siberia (Turukhansk region) until 1953.

Tarkovskii enrolled in the Soviet State Film School **VGIK** in 1954 as a member of **Mikhail Romm**'s directing workshop, and graduated in 1960. Together with Aleksandr Gordon (b. 1931), he directed the television film *Today, There Will Be No Firing* (Segodnia uvol'neniia ne budet, 1959) about the disposal of landmines from World War II. His diploma film, the medium-length *The Steamroller and the Violin* (Katok i skripka, 1960), won praise for its unusual plot—the script was coauthored by Tarkovskii's fellow student **Andrei Mikhalkov-Konchalovskii**—describing the friendship of a little boy and a worker, as well as for **Vadim Iusov**'s exquisite color photography and **Viacheslav Ovchinnikov**'s complex, haunting score. Tarkovskii's extraordinary ability to direct children, as demonstrated in his debut, was among the reasons why the administration of **Mosfilm Studio** assigned the novice to complete *Ivan*, a war film that had been abandoned by another director, Eduard Abalov.

The resulting picture, ***Ivan's Childhood*** (aka *My Name Is Ivan*/ Ivanovo detstvo), which premiered in April 1962, exceeded all expectations. Not only did Tarkovskii radically change the original script from a conventional, pedestrian scout tale to a philosophical parable, he elevated the story of a 12-year-old orphan who is captured and executed by the Nazis to a cinematic meditation on war and human values unseen before in world cinema. The innovative interpretation of the Soviet Union's Great Patriotic War contains implicit polemics with earlier propagandistic and romanticized war films. In accordance with its underlying parabolic concept, the film gives the Soviet military an aura of nobility, chivalrous generosity, and decency, which are emphasized as the ultimate reasons enabling them to defeat an all-destructive enemy whose goal is to annihilate culture and spirit. **Nikolai Burliaev** in the title role astounded Soviet and international critics, although his portrayal of fragility and fanatical devotion to the cause of revenge and victory garnered considerable controversy. Of all of Tarkovskii's films, *Ivan's Childhood* has remained the most narratively coherent and accessible. When it won the Golden Lion at the Venice Film Festival in 1962 and the Golden Gate Award at the San Francisco Film Festival, Tarkovskii became a household name for discriminating audiences all over the world.

Emboldened by the triumph of *Ivan's Childhood*, Tarkovskii embarked on a project of unprecedented thematic and stylistic daring—***Andrei Rublev*** (1964–1966), which can be viewed as the director's credo. Rather than attempting a standard biopic of the icon painter Rublev (1360–1430) of whom only scarce factual information is available, Tarkovskii created a parable of the artist as a captive of time whose mission it is to transcend societal boundaries. In the resulting three-hour epic, Russia's medieval genius never once is shown at work, suggesting that the creative act itself lies beyond cinematic re-creation. The film's ascetic black-and-white imagery, with hypnotic rhythmic fluency, evokes an authentic period atmosphere interspersed only by eruptions of apocalyptic violence. The artist's mission to create cultural-spiritual values and uphold them even in the face of grave barbarity is given universal validity.

Tarkovskii had to endure years of exhausting struggles to save the essential components of his film from unending censorial intrusions. After a brief release in 1969, *Andrei Rublev* was withdrawn from theaters and re-released in 1971. The film was legendary among international cineastes long before its international distribution in 1973 and further enhanced the filmmaker's reputation as a living classic filmmaker.

Solaris (1972), on the surface the adaptation of a science fiction novel by Polish author Stanisław Lem, deviates significantly from the literary source. Its plot and haunting imagery influenced the science fiction genre as a whole by humanizing it and giving it anthropocentric gravity. Despite a philosophical foundation incompatible with the Marxist-Leninist doctrine, the picture, surprisingly, was welcomed by Soviet officialdom, unlike die-hard sci-fi fans who missed the typical action plot.

If *Solaris* at least partially responded to conventional viewing habits, Tarkovskii's next film, the autobiographical *Mirror* (Zerkalo, 1975), was kept deliberately opaque and could not be adjusted to the paradigms of Soviet mainstream cinema. The idea of making an autobiographical film in a profoundly anti-individualistic society in itself was provocative, but Tarkovskii's arbitrary transitions between different levels of time, reality, and subjective consciousness gave the picture an openly elitist quality, rendering futile all attempts to simply "understand" and "explain" its meaning or message. *Stalker*, labeled the adaptation of a science fiction novella by Arkadii and Boris Strugatskii, is a slow-moving semi-utopian travelogue of three desperate, exhausted men who journey into a zone that supposedly had been visited by aliens. At the time of its release, the film's bleak color spectrum and indecisive conclusion indicated a state of profound crisis, both philosophical and ecological, implicitly reflecting a society in decline.

In 1982, Tarkovskii went to Italy to make *Nostalgia* (Nostalghia), about a Russian writer's research abroad that turns into a self-finding mission. When the Soviet government refused to prolong Tarkovskii's visa, he decided to stay in the West for good. His last picture, *Sacrifice* (Offret, 1986), was made in Sweden with funds of the Svenska Filminstitutet. At the time, Tarkovskii knew he was suffering from a terminal illness and thus conceived the picture as a testament, ending it with a dedication to his youngest son. Reaching back to an idea expressed in *Andrei Rublev*, the artist is the one person capable of saving the world—if only he realizes his calling and sacrifices himself by cutting all social ties.

On two occasions Tarkovskii worked for the stage: he directed Shakespeare's *Hamlet*, starring his favorite protagonist **Anatolii Solonitsyn**, at the Lenkom Theater in Moscow in 1976, and Modest Musorgskii's opera *Boris Godunov* at Covent Garden Theater in London in 1983, with Claudio Abbado as conductor. Tarkovskii also made brief stints as an actor: in **Marlen Khutsiev**'s 1964 *I Am Twenty* (Mne dvadtsat' let), in which he portrayed a snobbish young intellectual, and in Aleksandr Gordon's 1967 *Sergei Lazo*.

Tarkovskii is one of the few Russian filmmakers of the postwar period who created a recognizable poetics. The world of his films is permeated with reappearing motifs of hope such as trees, water, fire, wind, and bells, as well as artifact quotes from the world's humanistic heritage. Indeed, Tarkovskii took the realization of his personal, subjective, and sometimes mystical vision to an extreme level that was unprecedented in Soviet cinema and incompatible with its collectivist, materialist assumptions. Like few other directors, he freed himself from the ties of narrative conventions and became one of the most enigmatic filmmakers whose apocalyptic parables continue to challenge regular viewers, film critics, and philosophers alike. His poles of orientation were the majestic intensity, unhurried narration, and spiritual searching of Robert Bresson, Akira Kurosawa, and Ingmar Bergman.

To understand the enormity of Tarkovskii's aesthetic deviation from the mainstream, it is necessary to realize what the common parameters of Soviet film production were. None of Tarkovskii's pictures—not even his diploma and debut film—show an iota of the officially required Party-mindedness, ideological commitment, or "popular spirit." Rather, Tarkovskii developed a highly personal alternative to the official worldview that with each picture became more and more apparent and disconcerting for Soviet officialdom.

Tarkovskii is generally seen as a poet and a philosopher of cinema whose personal example of uncompromising artistic courage has become exemplary in itself. However, for Tarkovskii, cinema was neither "poetry" nor "philosophy," although his films contain elements of both. Rather, as expressed in his writings, film is a medium of spirituality, and the filmmaker's highest mission is the discovery of a spiritual dimension through cinematic means, be it in nature or society, family or the individual. Unlike the majority of his colleagues, Tarkovskii cared little about politics, although the bureaucratic control network of the Communist Party and the Soviet state caused endless frustration to this filmmaker whose unabashed individualism, self-conscious dignity, and pride were a constant provocation to the authorities. Tarkovskii thematized artistry and its metaphysics in several of his pictures, most prominently in *Andrei Rublev*, *Nostalgia*, and *Sacrifice*, where the artist appears as a quasi prophet, miraculously, or divinely, chosen and inspired, his work not fully explicable through rational concepts. At the same time, society—regardless of its name, self-image, and epoch—is an agent of materialism, power, and crude suppression of the spiritual, an agent that the artist has to resist in order to fulfill his calling.

Tarkovskii's influence on Russian and world cinema has been enormous, although more stylistically than philosophically. With the advent of perestroika in the mid-1980s and the official regret over the filmmaker's abysmal treatment in his own country, his films became objects of cultlike veneration and imitation, sometimes called "Tarkovshchina." The implied cinematic self-aggrandizement by epigones that can be found in a number of films of the late 1980s and early 1990s lacks the innovative force and originality that Tarkovskii's oeuvre doubtlessly possesses, and took the intellectualization of Russian cinema to an absurd extreme. Thus, on the one hand, it is Tarkovskii who most poignantly marks the split between mass and elitist approaches in Soviet cinema, introducing the filmmaker as an author/individual and overcoming the postulate of populism. On the other, Tarkovskii's approach to film demonstrates an alienation from popular viewership that in cinema is more problematic than in other arts.

Tarkovskii was named People's Artist of the RSFSR in 1980. He is buried at Sainte Geneviève des Bois cemetery in Paris. Tarkovskii's first marriage was to director Irma Raush, who appeared as the mother in *Ivan's Childhood* and as the "holy fool" in *Andrei Rublev*; his second wife, Larisa Pavlovna Tarkovskaia, has devoted herself to her late husband's legacy.

Other films: *Tempo di viaggio* (doc., Italy, 1983); *De weg naar Bresson* (doc., Netherlands, 1984).

TEREKHOVA, MARGARITA BORISOVNA (b. 25 August 1942, Turinsk, Sverdlovsk district). Russian actress. The daughter of a stage actress, Terekhova studied at the University of Tashkent in 1959–1961. She then enrolled in the studio school of Mossovet Theater in Moscow, where her teacher was the legendary Iurii Zavadskii (1894–1977), and joined its troupe upon graduation in 1964.

In 1966, Terekhova made her movie debut with the role of Tania in **Frunze Dovlatian**'s *Hello, It's Me!* (Zdravstvui, eto ia!). After important supporting roles in **Igor' Talankin**'s *Day Stars* (Dnevnye zvezdy, 1966–1969), **Il'ia Averbakh**'s *Monologue* (Monolog, 1972), and **Andrei Smirnov**'s *Belorussian Station* (Belorusskii vokzal, 1971), **Andrei Tarkovskii** cast Terekhova as both the mother and Natal'ia in his visually stunning autobiographical meditation *The Mirror* (Zerkalo, 1975). This performance for the first time revealed her artistic capacity in full, conveying a rare, enigmatic sensuality, emotional unpredictability, vulnerability, and tender beauty.

Following Tarkovskii's critical triumph, various directors used Terekhova's star status and exquisite femininity rather than her talent for psychological introspection. Thus, although her performances in a number of film and television productions—including literary adaptations and historical potboilers—were usually interesting, the actress found more challenging tasks in the theater, especially in productions of George Bernard Shaw and Shakespeare. One of the few exceptions is Estonian filmmaker Arvo Iho, who gave her a challenging role as a nurse who is trying to save an imbalanced young man in *Only for the Insane* (Tol'ko dlia sumasshedshikh, 1990).

Terekhova, whom critic Elena Gorfunkel' once aptly called "the muse of intellectual cinema," was awarded the title Merited Artist of the RSFSR in 1976 and People's Artist of Russia in 1996. Her daughter Anna Terekhova (b. 1967) is a valued stage and film actress.

Other films: *The Blue Bird* (Siniaia ptitsa, 1976); *Mama, I'm Alive* (Mama, ich lebe, 1977, East Germany); *Primordial Russia* (Rus' iznachal'naia, 1986); *The Dissident* (Dissident, 1988); *It* (Ono, 1990); *The Kings of Russian Criminal Investigation* (Koroli rossiiskogo syska, 1996).

THIRD MESHCHANSKAIA STREET (aka *Bed and Sofa*/Tret'ia Meshchanskaia, 1927). Goskino. 74 min., b/w. Directed by **Abram Room**. Script: **Viktor Shklovskii**, Abram Room. Cinematography: Grigorii Giber. Cast: **Liudmila Semenova**, **Nikolai Batalov**, **Vladimir Fogel'**, Mariia Iarotskaia, Leonid Iurenev. Premiere: 15 March 1927.

Nikolai (Batalov), a happy-go-lucky construction worker, lives with his wife, Liudmila (Semenova), in a one-room apartment on the quiet Third Meshchanskaia (literally: Petit-Bourgeois) Street in Moscow. When Nikolai's friend, Vladimir (Fogel'), a printer, arrives and needs a place to stay, he is offered the couple's sofa. Yet once Nikolai goes on a business trip, Liudmila and Vladimir fall in love, and Nikolai has to occupy the sofa after his return. Liudmila gets pregnant, and the two men insist on her having an abortion. However, after a visit to a clinic, Liudmila decides to keep the baby and to leave both Nikolai and Vladimir.

THUNDERSTORM, THE (Groza, 1934). Soiuzfilm studio. 85 min., b/w. Directed by **Vladimir Petrov**. Script: Vladimir Petrov from Aleksandr Ostrovskii's play. Cinematography: Viacheslav Gardanov. Music: Vladimir Shcherbachev. Cast: Alla Tarasova, Ivan Chuvelev, Mikhail Tarkhanov, Varvara Massalitinova, Irina Zarubina, **Mikhail Zharov**, Mikhail Tsarev. Premiere: 25 March 1934.

In a provincial town on the Volga River, the young and sensitive Katerina (Tarasova) marries Tikhon (Chuvelev), a violent drunkard, and thus enters the crude milieu of greedy salesmen, the "dark kingdom" (*temnoe tsarstvo*). Her mother-in-law, Kabanikha (Massalitinova), rules the family with an iron fist and endlessly harasses Katerina. One day, when Tikhon is away, she meets Boris, a man who embodies everything Katerina is longing for. After their love is consummated, Katerina is tormented by her conscience and cries out her secret in church, while a thunderstorm is raging outside. She becomes an outcast, beaten by Tikhon and betrayed by Boris, and eventually commits suicide by drowning herself in the Volga.

TIKHONOV, VIACHESLAV VASIL'EVICH (b. 8 February 1928, Pavlovo-Posad, Moscow district). Russian actor. Tikhonov studied at the Soviet State Film School **VGIK** in the workshop of **Sergei Gerasimov** and **Tamara Makarova**, graduating in 1950. His teacher Gerasimov gave him the memorable part of Volodia Os'mukhin in the Great Patriotic War tragedy *The Young Guard* (Molodaia gvardiia, 1948). The lead in **Stanislav Rostotskii**'s rural drama *It Happened in Pen'kovo* (Delo bylo v Pen'kove, 1958) shot Tikhonov to national stardom. In later years, Rostotskii also cast him in rewarding roles of thoughtful, reliable, manly intellectuals in *Out in the Seven Winds* (aka *Four Winds of Heaven*/Na semi vetrakh, 1962), *Let's See What Monday Brings* (Dozhivem do ponedel'nika, 1968)—which won Tikhonov a 1970 USSR State Prize—and in the sentimental ballad about canine loyalty *White Bim Black Ear* (Belyi Bim Chernoe Ukho, 1977), an achievement that was crowned with a Lenin Prize in 1980. Furthermore, Rostotskii shot the **documentary** *Profession: Film Actor* (Professiia: kinoakter, 1980) about Tikhonov.

The actor proved his extraordinary artistic range most fully in **Sergei Bondarchuk**'s Lev Tolstoi adaptation *War and Peace* (Voina i mir, 1962–1967) as Prince Andrei Bolkonskii, whom he portrayed with noble dignity and pensiveness. He gained unprecedented cult fame as Colonel Shtirlits in **Tat'iana Lioznova**'s legendary television miniseries *Seventeen Moments of Spring* (Semnadtsat' mgnovenii vesny, 1973). Tikhonov informed the fictitious spy-genius—who manages to outwit the entire Nazi leadership—with intelligence, stoicism, self-discipline, and unconditional loyalty to his country, features that gave espionage the air of a chivalrous vocation for generations of youngsters. Capitalizing on his star power, other directors cast Tikhonov in similar roles ad nauseam, for example, **Igor' Gostev** in his World War II scout trilogy *Front without Flanks* (Front bez flangov, 1974–1981), turning the actor's image into a patriotic—and covertly sexual—cliché rather than using his talent for greater psychological differentiation.

Tikhonov was named People's Artist of the USSR in 1974 and Hero of Socialist Labor in 1982. He joined the Communist Party in 1976.

For a number of years Tikhonov was married to actress **Nonna Mordiukova**; their son, Vladimir Tikhonov (1950–1990), also worked as an actor.

Other films: *Optimistic Tragedy* (Optimisticheskaia tragediia, 1963); *They Fought for the Motherland* (Oni srazhalis' za Rodinu, 1975); *To Kill the Dragon* (Ubit' drakona, 1988); *Burnt by the Sun* (Utomlennye solntsem, 1995); *An Essay for Victory Day* (Sochinenie ko dniu pobedy, 1998); *Andersen: A Life without Love* (Andersen. Zhizn' bez liubvi, 2007).

TIMOSHENKO, SEMEN ALEKSEEVICH (b. 18 January 1899, St. Petersburg–d. 13 November 1958, Leningrad). Russian director, screenwriter, actor, and film theorist. Timoshenko studied civil engineering in 1918–1920. In 1920, he also finished the directing courses offered by the Petrograd Theater Department of the Commissariat of Enlightenment (Narkompros); one of his teachers was Vsevolod Meierkhol'd. From 1919 to 1924, Timoshenko worked as an actor at the Grand Dramatic Theater in Petrograd.

After joining Sevzapkino—the later **Lenfilm Studio**—in Leningrad in 1925, Timoshenko made a film critical of private entrepreneurs during the New Economic Policy (NEP) period, *A Coupon for a Life* (Order na zhizn', 1927). Trying to apply theoretical concepts of **Sergei Eizenshtein** and other avant-gardists, Timoshenko then turned to reconstructions of major political events in Petrograd of 1917–1919 in *Two Armored Cars* (Dva bronevika, 1928), *The Revolt* (Miatezh, 1929), and *Conspiracy of the Dead* (Zagovor mertvykh, 1930). These films were criticized for their neglect of individual characters in favor of mass action scenes.

Timoshenko played a pioneering role as the creator of two early sound **comedies**, *Three Comrades* (aka *Three Friends*/Tri tovarishcha, 1935) and *The Goalkeeper* (Vratar', 1936). The former was devoted to the problem of industrial leadership, juxtaposing different methods of administration. Although *Three Comrades* appears rather naïve and didactic, the lively acting of **Mikhail Zharov** and **Nikolai Batalov** as the friends/antagonists made this early effort a success. *The Goalkeeper*, mildly amusing and rather awkward in its acting and camera work, enjoyed a long life on television and video, perhaps because its subject matter—soccer—was rarely thematized by Soviet cinema.

Timoshenko also stood at the cradle of another genre, the so-called film concert, an inexpensive solution to the problem of providing quality entertainment for Soviet mass audiences. Among his efforts was *Concert on the Screen* (Kontsert na ekrane, 1940) and, during the Great Patriotic War, a concert film with Kazakh themes, *To the Tunes of the Dombra* (Pod zvuki dombry, 1944, codirected with A. Minkin). One of Timoshenko's best-remembered pictures is the wartime comedy *The Sky Sloth* (Nebesnyi tikhokhod, 1945), a lighthearted, optimistic musical about the competition between a female and a male pilot unit. The star-studded soccer comedy *The Reserve Player* (Zapasnoi igrok, 1954) became Timoshenko's swan song.

Timoshenko wrote several monographs on theoretical and practical problems of cinema, among them *Cinema Art and the Montage of a Film* (Iskusstvo kino i montazh fil'ma, 1926) and *The Engineer of a Film: What a Film Director Needs to Know* (Inzehener fil'ma. Chto dolzhen znat' kinorezhisser, 1929). According to some sources, he played a particularly reprehensible role during the anti-Semitic campaign "against cosmopolitanism" in the late 1940s.

Other films: *Napoleon-Gas* (Napoleon-Gaz, 1925); *Turbine #3* (Turbina 3, 1927); *The Sniper* (Snaiper, aka Iskusstvo ubivat', 1931); *To Live* (Zhit', 1933); *The Forest* (Les, 1953, codirected with Vladimir Vengerov).

TISSÉ, EDUARD KAZIMIROVICH (b. 13 April 1897, Stockholm, Sweden [other sources: Litan, Latvia, or Libau/Liepa, Lithuania]– d. 18 November 1961, Moscow). Russian cinematographer and director. Tissé, the son of a Russian mother and a Swedish father, studied painting and photography at a private school for fine arts in Liepa from 1914 to 1916. In 1917, he began shooting World War I newsreels and became a full-time correspondent, traveling the country and eventually documenting the Bolshevik Revolution and the ensuing Civil War. In 1919, Tissé joined the All-Russian Department of Photography and Cinema, where he specialized in short **documentaries** and features with a didactic twist. His debut was *The Signal* (Signal, 1918), directed by Aleksandr Arkashov, the adaptation of a Vladimir Garshin short story about a railway worker who prevents a collision. Subsequent films had a more explicit political message, among them **Vladimir Gardin**'s *Hunger . . . Hunger . . . Hunger* (Golod . . . golod . . . golod, 1921) and **Boris Chaikovskii**'s *It Must Not Be Thus!* (Tak byt' ne dolzhno!).

Tissé's encounter with **Sergei Eizenshtein** in 1924 had momentous significance for both men's careers. Although the cinematographer remained mostly in the shadow of the director, it was Tissé who congenially responded to Eizenshtein's ideas and translated them into a radically new cinematic vision, beginning with *Strike* (Stachka, 1924), which strove to generate strong emotional effects through a blend of seemingly unstaged, newsreel-like shots. A similar visual structure is characteristic of *October* (Oktiabr', 1927), whose patchwork narrative corresponds to its stylistic heterogeneity, alternating complex metaphors and symbols with quasi-documentary scenes. The cinematography in ***Battleship Potemkin*** (Bronenosets Potemkin, 1925) and *The Old and the New* (Staroe i novoe, aka *General Line/ General'naia liniia*, 1929), although similarly montage oriented, was more fluid and accessible.

In 1929, Tissé traveled with Eizenshtein and his assistant **Grigorii Aleksandrov** to Western Europe and the United States to study sound film technology. While in Switzerland, he directed a noteworthy feature of his own, *Women's Plight, Women's Happiness* (Frauennot, Frauenglück) about social and psychological aspects of abortion. In France, the three made a boldly surrealist short, *Romance sentimentale* (1930), their first experimental sound film. The ill-fated *¡Que Viva Mexico!* (Da zdravstuet Meksika!, 1931–1932, unfinished), a work of picturesque grandeur, features sunbathed, soft-contoured images, some of which have become classics as stills. An extraordinary visual quality was also achieved in another failed Eizenshtein project, the collectivization tragedy *Bezhin Meadow* (Bezhin lug, 1935–1937); its few surviving stills give an idea of the director's and his cinematographer's stylistic audacity.

Tissé once again proved his adaptability with the monumental, predominantly static and stringent compositions of *Aleksandr*

Nevskii (1938) and the external shots of *Ivan the Terrible* (Ivan Groznyi, 1943–1945). Perhaps because of his ethnic origins, he then was commissioned to film Aleksandr Ivanov's 1947 *Victorious Return* (Vozvrashchenie s pobedoi), one of the first full-length features in Latvia under the Soviet regime. He also shot *In the Mountains of Yugoslavia* (V gorakh Iugoslavii, 1947) and the anti-American *Silver Dust* (Serebristaia pyl', 1953) for **Abram Room**—both of them Stalinist prestige films. In 1956, Tissé codirected the war drama *The Immortal Garrison* (Bessmertnyi ganizon, with Zakhar Agranenko [1912–1960]) about the troops of Brest fortress who had heroically resisted invading German troops for months.

Tissé, a genuine author-cinematographer, was one of the most respected and influential Soviet cameramen. His unfailing sense of measure, narrative rhythm, and harmony, as well as his personal modesty, neatness, and professionalism, made him a sought-after partner for leading Soviet directors. Tissé began to teach at the State Film School in Moscow (renamed **VGIK** in 1934) in 1921 and was promoted to full professor in 1943. He won three Stalin Prizes: for part 1 of *Ivan the Terrible* in 1946; in 1949 for footage of Lenin that he had filmed between 1918 and 1924 (the compilation film, *Vladimir Il'ich Lenin*, was released in 1948); and for *Meeting at the Elbe* (Vstrecha na El'be) in 1950. He was named Merited Artist of the Russian Federation in 1935 and of the Latvian SSR in 1947. Tissé joined the Communist Party in 1940. He is buried at Novodevich'e cemetery in Moscow.

Other Films: *Hammer and Sickle* (Serp i molot, 1921); *Jewish Luck* (Evreiskoe schast'e, 1925); *Aerograd* (1935).

TODOROVSKII, PETR EFIMOVICH (b. 26 August 1925, Bobrinets, Kirovgrad district, Ukraine). Ukrainian-Russian director, screenwriter, cinematographer, and composer. Following military school, in 1944–1945 Todorovskii was a Red Army officer in the Great Patriotic War. After his demobilization in 1949, he enrolled in **Boris Volchek**'s workshop for cameramen at the Soviet State Film School **VGIK**, from which he graduated in 1954.

Todorovskii's style as cinematographer in capturing different social milieus was primarily influenced by the sobriety and authenticity of neorealism. His work on **Marlen Khutsiev**'s *Springtime on*

Zarechnaia Street (Vesna na Zarechnoi ulitse, 1956, with Radomir Vasilevskii) proved to be literally an eye-opener in regards to Soviet postwar reality, an effect even more intensified in Khutsiev's next picture, *The Two Fedors* (Dva Fedora), also filmed by Todorovskii. *Thirst* (Zhazhda, 1960), about the defense of Odessa against Nazi troops, revealed the full range of emotional expression and mobility of which Todorovskii's camera was capable.

In 1963, Todorovskii made his directing debut with *Never* (Nikogda, with V. D'iachenko), a rather gloomy film about loneliness that "anticipates the nearing end of the Thaw" (Andrei Plakhov). Todorovskii's first independently directed picture, *Loyalty* (Vernost', 1964), deals with the generation that was drafted to fight in the Great Patriotic War. Its soft, poetic intonations and apolitical stance stood out favorably and won the director the Best Debut prize at the 1965 Venice Film Festival.

Social awareness and sentimentality, with the latter usually outweighing the former, characterize Todorovskii's directorial approach, blending an overall melodramatic structure with elements of burlesque humor, sudden tragic turns, and nonideological patriotic pathos. *Urban Romance* (Gorodskoi romans, 1970) and *Mechanic Gavrilov's Beloved Woman* (Liubimaia zhenshchina mekhanika Gavrilova, 1981), which aptly convey the atmosphere of the Brezhnev years, are typical of the filmmaker's keen sense of contemporaneity. *On the Holiday* (V den' prazdnika, 1978) and *Frontline Romance* (Voenno-polevoi roman, 1983), both invoking memories of the war and postwar period, as well as *Along the Main Street with an Orchestra* (Po glavnoi ulitse s orkestrom, 1986), are dominated by melancholy and nostalgia.

Todorovskii achieved his greatest box-office success with *Intergirl* (Interdevochka, 1989), the story of a Moscow prostitute, meant to drastically showcase the dangers of selling out to Western commercial temptations. After the end of the Soviet era, Todorovskii struck a cord with *Da capo! Da capo Again!* (Ankor! Eshche ankor! 1992) and *Such a Wonderful Game* (Takaia chudnaia igra, 1995), set in the military and the student milieu of the postwar period, respectively. The destructive effect of GPU informers on love and friendship, which are also featured, adds a bitter taste but does not principally disturb the affectionate look at the Soviet past. *A Retro Threesome*

(Retro vtroem, 1998) is a remake of **Abram Room**'s silent classic *Third Meshchanskaia Street* (aka *Bed and Sofa*/Tret'ia Meshchanskaia, aka Liubov' vtroem, 1927).

Occasionally dabbling in composition, Todorovskii has written several pleasant scores and theme songs for his own films, as well as those of other directors. Todorovskii's wife, Mira Todorovskaia (b. 1933), is a screenwriter and producer; his son, Valerii Todorovskii (b. 1962), a talented director and successful producer whose *Evenings near Moscow* (Podmoskovnye vechera, 1994) and *Land of the Deaf* (Strana glukhikh, 1998) were among the most interesting films of the 1990s.

Todorovskii, a member of the Communist Party since 1945, was named Merited Artist of the Ukrainian SSR in 1967 and People's Artist of the RSFSR in 1985.

Other films: (as cameraman) *Moldovan Tunes* (Moldavskie napevy, 1955); (as director) *The Trickster* (Fokusnik, 1967); *One's Own Land* (Svoia zemlia, 1973, TV); *In the Taurus Constellation* (V sozvezdii Byka, 2004).

TOLCHAN, IAKOV MOISEEVICH (b. 13 August 1901–d. 1993, Moscow). Russian documentary director and cinematographer. Tolchan began to work in the movies in 1924, initially in Sovkino's Third Film Factory in Moscow where he made so-called *kul'turfil'my* (literally, "culture films," i.e. shorts with an educational purpose). The same year, while studying at the Cinema Technical School (*kinotekhnikum*), Tolchan joined **Dziga Vertov**'s group as a cinematographer on *A Sixth of the World* (Shestaia chast' mira, 1926) and others projects.

A versatile cameraman, Tolchan shot a number of features before turning to **documentaries** on science and nature in 1938. In later years Tolchan's specialty became shorts dealing with the fine arts: *In the Tretiakov Gallery* (V Tret'iakovskoi galeree, 1956), *Rockwell Kent* (1959) about the American painter and friend of the USSR, *The Painter N. Iaroshenko* (Khudozhnik N. Iaroshenko, 1964), and numerous others. Tolchan also directed propaganda fare such as *Atoms for Peace* (Atomnaia energiia dlia mira, 1956).

In 1976, Tolchan published his *Visible Memoirs* (Zrimye vospominaniia). He also authored several monographs on film technology.

Toward the end of his life, frail, disillusioned, somber, but mentally alert, he was prominently featured as a witness to Soviet film history in *The Last Bolshevik* (1993, aka *Le Tombeau d'Alexandre*), French filmmaker Chris Marker's melancholic requiem for the Soviet Communist utopia and its most important art. He also appeared in Rasmus Gerlach's *Operator Kaufman* (Germany, 1999).

Tolchan taught at the Soviet State Film School **VGIK** in 1931–1957.

Other films: *Pamir* (1928); *Apartheid Is a Crime* (Aparteid—prestuplenie, 1965).

TOLUBEEV, IURII VLADIMIROVICH (b. 1 May 1905 [other sources: 1906], St. Petersburg–d. 28 December 1979, Leningrad). Russian actor. An active stage performer since 1926, Tolubeev studied at the Institute for Stage Arts in Leningrad, graduating in 1929. After working with various troupes, the actor joined the Leningrad Academic Pushkin Theater—the former Aleksandrinskii—in 1942 and soon became one of its leading stars.

In the movies, Tolubeev debuted in 1935 in the Belarusian revolutionary drama *Full Age* (Sovershennoletie). He played episodic roles in some of the most important films of the 1930s, demonstrating versatility both in markedly negative and positive parts: in **Grigorii Kozintsev** and **Leonid Trauberg**'s *Maksim Trilogy* (Trilogiia o Maksime, 1935–1939) portraying a strikebreaker, as well as in **Gerbert Rappaport**'s *Professor Mamlock* (1938) and **Fridrikh Ermler**'s *The Great Citizen* (1938–1939), in which he played an "enemy of the people," Zemtsov. In devotional Stalinist fairy tales such as **Erast Garin**'s *Doktor Kaliuzhnyi* (1939), Ermler's *The Great Turning Point* (Velikii perelom, 1945) where he played General Lavrov, or **Aleksandr Faintsimmer** and **Vladimir Korsh-Sablin**'s guerilla epic *Konstantin Zaslonov* (aka *The Secret Brigade*/Kanstancin Zaslonau, 1949), Tolubeev portrayed strong-willed characters intended as typical representations of the Russian people and their "natural" pro-Soviet loyalty.

Tolubeev, who used his corpulent physique to great comical or tragicomical effect, was outstanding in adaptations of classical literature, particularly as the mayor in **Vladimir Petrov**'s *The Inspector General* (Revizor, 1952, after Nikolai Gogol') and Sancho Panza in

Kozintsev's *Don Quijote* (1957), displaying enormous emotional and physical energy and drive. He also excelled as the VIP in **Aleksei Batalov**'s *The Overcoat* (Shinel', 1960) and Polonius in Kozintsev's *Hamlet* (Gamlet, 1964). In later years, he often appeared in less challenging genres, particularly espionage and war films.

Tolubeev received a Stalin Prize for his stage work in 1947 and a Lenin Prize in 1958. He was awarded the title People's Artist of the USSR in 1956 and Hero of Socialist Labor in 1976. His son Andrei Tolubeev (b. 1945) is a stage and film actor.

Other films: *The Battle of Stalingrad* (Stalingradskaia bitva, 1949); *Radioactive Tracer* (Mechenyi atom, 1972); *Front behind the Front Line* (Front za liniei fronta, 1977).

TOMÀ [real name Fomicheva], **SVETLANA ANDREEVNA** (b. 24 March 1947, Chisinau [Kishinev]). Moldovan actress. Tomà, who adapted her stage name from her French great-grandmother, studied at the Chisinau Institute for the Arts, graduating in 1969. She joined the troupe of the Chekhov Theater in Chisinau, staying until 1976, and thereafter the Studio Theater of **Moldova Film Studio**.

Emil' Loteanu cast Tomà in the role of Ioanna in the colorful, sentimental rural romance *The Red Meadows* (Krasnye poliany, 1966). Subsequently, Loteanu became Tomà's mentor and partner, both professionally and privately, and gave her leads in his following three blockbusters: *Fiddlers* (Lautarii/Lautary, 1972), *The Tabor Leaves for Heaven* (aka *Queen of the Gypsies*/Tabor ukhodit v nebo, 1975), and *My Tender and Gentle Beast* (aka *A Hunting Accident*/Moi laskovyi i nezhnyi zver', 1978), in which Tomà embodied dark-haired, enigmatic, unpredictable women of few words driven by uncontrollable erotic passion. These films proved hugely popular with Soviet audiences and made Tomà a star whose prominence eventually survived her split from Loteanu and transition to roles in other genres and even in fashion shows.

Tomà's daughter, Irina Lachina (sometimes credited as Irina Tomà), is a successful actress at the Moscow theater The Contemporary (Sovremennik). In recent years, Tomà has appeared in supporting roles in a number of films in which her daughter played the leads, for example, the Sholem Aleichem adaptation *Wandering*

Stars (Bluzhdaiushchie zvezdy, 1991) and in television miniseries such as *Lady Boss* (2001).

Tomà became a member of the Communist Party in 1978; she was awarded the title Merited Artist of the Moldavian SSR in 1979.

Other films: *A Living Corpse* (Zhivoi trup, 1968); *Anna Pavlova* (1983); *Morning Star* (Luceafarul, TV, Moldova); *A Train to Brooklyn* (Poezd do Bruklina, 1994); *Poor Nastia* (Bednaia Nastia, 2003, TV). *See also* MOLDOVAN CINEMA.

TRAUBERG, LEONID ZAKHAROVICH (b. 17 January 1902, Odessa–d. 14 November 1990, Moscow). Russian director, screenwriter, and pedagogue. Trauberg hailed from a bourgeois, intellectual family. He studied at the studio school of the Comical Opera Theater in Odessa, started a studio theater of his own, and worked as a journalist. In 1921, he moved to Leningrad and founded, together with **Grigorii Kozintsev**, the avant-gardist Factory of the Eccentric Actor (FEKS).

Trauberg formed a close artistic partnership with Kozintsev, codirecting all major pictures with him until 1945 (for their jointly directed films, see the entry on Kozintsev). Recently published documents indicate that Trauberg dominated the scriptwriting process, while Kozintsev's forte was the work on the set.

In 1943, after Kozintsev directed *Young Fritz* (Iunyi Frits) by himself—the credits list Trauberg incorrectly as codirector—Trauberg also helmed a project of his own, *The Actress* (Aktrisa), a musical melodrama about a selfless entertainer who falls in love with a blinded officer. The film was criticized mercilessly, apparently with some justification, for its melodramatic indulgence. After *Simple People* (Prostye liudi, 1945), their last codirected film, Kozintsev and Trauberg separated.

Trauberg was singled out by the minister of cinematography, **Ivan Bol'shakov**, at a conference in the House of Cinema in February 1949 as "the leader of an antipatriotic group of cosmopolitans in the movie industry." As a result, he was fired from **Lenfilm Studio** and moved to Moscow. After a long hiatus during which Trauberg struggled to make ends meet, he directed *The Soldiers Were Marching* (Shli soldaty, 1958), starring **Sergei Bondarchuk**, about the fraternization of Russian and German soldiers in World War I; the film was a critical flop.

While Kozintsev, after a decade of trouble, managed to furnish a new career for himself, gaining international fame as the creator of outstanding Cervantes and Shakespeare adaptations, Trauberg never regained his previous momentum. His last projects were artistically unremarkable: an adaptation of Mikhail Bulgakov's MKhAT production of Nikolai Gogol''s *Dead Souls* (Mertvye dushi, 1960), *Free Wind* (Vol'nyi veter, 1961, codirected with **Andrei Tutyshkin** from a political operetta by **Isaak Dunaevskii**), and the script to the historical operetta *The Serf Actress* (Krepostnaia aktrisa, 1963). In the last two decades of his life, Trauberg was the guest of honor of numerous film festivals and retrospectives in Western Europe and was frequently interviewed by grateful film historians.

Trauberg was famed as an inventive and generous teacher; indeed, the FEKS workshop was a school for such actors and directors as **Sergei Gerasimov** and **Elena Kuz'mina**. Trauberg also taught at the Leningrad Institute for Stage Arts (1926–1934) and was in charge of the Supreme Directing and Screenwriting Courses (VKSR) in Moscow in 1962–1968. He was named Merited Artist of the RSFSR in 1967 and People's Artist of the Russian Federation in 1987. His brother was film director Il'ia Trauberg (1905–1948).

TSEKHANOVSKII, MIKHAIL MIKHAILOVICH (b. 6 June 1889, Proskurov, Podol'sk district [now: Khmel'nitskii, Ukraine]–d. 22 June 1965, Moscow). Russian **animation** director, screenwriter, and animator. After finishing gymnasium, Tsekhanovskii studied sculpture in Paris in 1908–1910 and then at the St. Petersburg Academy of Arts. In 1914, he enrolled in the Moscow School for Painting, Sculpture, and Architecture, graduating in 1918. During the Civil War, he served in the Red Army. In 1923, Tsekhanovskii began a career as a designer of movie posters in Petrograd and later as an illustrator for children's books. Some of his books were so-called cine-books (*kinoknizhki*, a Russian version of flip books).

Tsekhanovskii's decision to create "graphic films" (*graficheskie fil'my*) was thus a logical step. His debut, *Mail* (aka *Post*/Pochta, 1928), was made from a tale in verse by Samuil Marshak (1887–1964) about a letter's journey around the globe, which Tsekhanovskii had already illustrated in a 1927 book edition. The characters were brought to life with flat puppets, creating movements of perfect fluidity. When a soundtrack was added in 1930, *Mail* became an international success and was sold to many countries. Interestingly, absurdist poet Daniil Kharms (1905–1942) contributed to it as a screenwriter.

Even more ambitious was *Pacific 231* (1930), an attempt to illustrate the "Symphonic Movement #1" by Swiss avant-garde composer Arthur Honegger (1892–1955), a piece that was recorded prior to the drawing and filming process, to ensure perfect synchronicity. The composer had intended to capture the sound patterns of a steam locomotive, which in the picture were visualized by Tsekhanovskii on three levels: images of a locomotive, the orchestra musicians, and the conductor. *Pacific 231* gained immediate recognition as a pioneering work of art and gave the filmmaker enough prestige to tackle a full-length animation feature, the adaptation of Aleksandr Pushkin's *Tale of the Priest and His Worker, Blockhead* (Skazka o pope i rabotnike ego Balde). It was to be executed in drawn animation technique, using **Dmitrii Shostakovich**'s score specifically written for the film. However, Tsekhanovskii's resistance to industrial animation technology, as well as the increasing political pressure against Shostakovich and so-called formalism put an end to the project after three years of struggle. Only a two-minute scene of the film has survived, indicating that "the Soviet animated cartoon of today might look very different" had Tsekhanovskii succeeded (Jay Leyda).

During World War II, Tsekhanovskii was evacuated to Ashkhabad, where he contributed to film medleys such as *Film Concert 1941* (Kinokontsert 1941, aka *Leningrad Concert Hall*). In 1945, he moved to Moscow and joined the staff of Soiuzmultfilm studio. He landed an international success with *The Tale of the Fisherman and the Little Fish* (Skazka o rybake i rybke, 1949), one of his most perfect achievements, creating psychologically believable fairy-tale characters.

Today, Tsekhanovskii is recognized as a founder of Soviet animation who early on fought the trivialization and "Disneyization" of animation, which he considered technically flawless but antiartistic. At a time when few people took animation seriously, Tsekhanovskii believed in its potential as a high art form—indeed, one that may be closer to the fine arts than to cinema proper.

In 1964, Tsekhanovskii was awarded the title Merited Artist of the RSFSR. His wife was animation director Vera Tsekhanovskaia (1902–1977), who worked with him on a number of films, among them *The Wild Swans* (Dikie lebedi, 1963) and a remake of his first film, *Mail* (Pochta, 1964).

Other films: *Gopak* (1931); *The Tale of the Stupid Little Mouse* (Skazka o glupom myshonke, 1940); *The Christmas Tree* (Elka, 1943); *The Frog Queen* (Tsarevna-liagushka, 1954); *The Tale of Chapaev* (Skaz o Chapaeve, 1958).

TSELIKOVSKAIA, LIUDMILA VASIL'EVNA (b. 8 September 1919, Astrakhan'–d. 4 July 1992, Moscow). Russian actress. Born into the family of a conductor, Tselikovskaia studied piano before switching to acting at the Moscow Shchukin Theater School, which she attended in 1937–1941. Upon graduation, she joined the prestigious Moscow Vakhtangov Theater, gaining fame in the classical repertoire, notably as Shakespearean ingenues.

Tselikovskaia's second role in the movies, the gorgeous soprano soloist Sima Voronova in **Aleksandr Ivanovskii**'s charming musical **comedy** *Anton Ivanovich Is Angry* (aka *Spring Song*/Anton Ivanovich serditsia, 1941), propelled her to national stardom. It defined an image that millions of Soviet viewers came to adore: ever-shining, friendly eyes with huge dark eyelashes, blonde curls, and a petite, athletic physique irradiating a unique blend of bashful sweetness and sensuality. No matter how often that image was re-created—and derided by critics—Soviet viewers could not get enough of it and even decades later raved about Tselikovskaia's performances, for example, in **Konstantin Iudin**'s *Hearts of Four* (Serdtsa chetyrekh, 1941, released 1945) and **Gerbert Rappaport**'s *Airchauffeur* (aka *Taxi to Heaven*/Vozdushnyi izvozchik, 1943), where she starred with her then-husband, **Mikhail Zharov**. As various memoirists testify, Tselikovskaia's persona was the ideal of femininity in the 1940s and essential in supplying hope for a better life on the backdrop of political terror and a horrendous war.

Sergei Eizenshtein gave the actress a chance to demonstrate other facets of her talent in *Ivan the Terrible* (Ivan Groznyi, 1943–1945) as Ivan's wife Anastasiia, as did **Samson Samsonov** in his Anton Chekhov adaptation *The Grasshopper* (Poprygunia, 1955) as the flighty, confused, yet well-meaning Ol'ga Ivanovna.

Although Tselikovskaia's immense popularity never waned, she remained strangely underemployed in Soviet cinema, which led to speculations that Iosif Stalin may have disliked her. Unlike many of her peers, Tselikovskaia never received any medals or the title People's Artist of the USSR, which few deserved as much as she did.

Tselikovskaia was named People's Artist of the Russian Federation in 1963. She was married to the leading Moscow architect Karo Alabian (1897–1959), and to the founder of Taganka Theater, Iurii Liubimov (b. 1918).

Other films: *Story of a True Man* (Povest' o nastoiashchem cheloveke, 1948); *We Must Have Met Somewhere Before* (My s vami gde-to vstrechalis', 1954); *The Forest* (Les, 1980, released 1987).

TUGANOV, ELBERT (b. 22 February 1920, Baku). Estonian **animation** director, screenwriter, and animator. Tuganov was born in Azerbaijan to an Estonian mother and an Ossetian father. He learned his craft in Germany in the 1930s where he was employed by commercial studios. During World War II, Tuganov served in the Estonian Army and was discharged in 1946 after the country had already been forced into the Soviet Union. Tuganov was hired by **Tallinfilm Studio** as an assistant cameraman responsible for titles and credits, a position he held until 1957.

In 1958, Tuganov made the first animated picture in **Estonian cinema**, *Little Peter's Dream* (Peetrikese Unenägu/Son Petrika, 1958), adapted from a popular Danish children's tale about a mischievous boy who learns the hard way the importance of kindness toward others. Using stop-motion technology with puppets crafted by the Estonian Puppet Theater, Tuganov continued to make puppet and cutout ("flat") animation films for children such as *Ott in Outer Space* (Ott kosmoses/Ott v kosmose, 1961). Eventually, he began to explore new territories with satirical animated shorts for adults, including *The Talent* (Talent/Talant, 1963), *Cats and Mice* (Lapsed ja puu/Koshki-myshki, 1965), *Just So* (Just nii!/Prosto tak, 1963), *The Park* (1966), *Cogwheel* (Hammasratas, 1968), *Pedestrians* (Jalakäijad/Peshek-hody, 1971), and *Car Drivers* (Autosõitjad/Avtomobilisty, 1972), all characterized by generally mild, kindhearted humor.

Inspiration (Inspiratsioon/Vdokhnovenie, 1975), about the Estonian Song Festival, was perceived as a semisubversive homage to the country's national and cultural independence: "it stands as a subtle, yet ultimately overwhelming, celebration of Estonian culture in firm defiance of Soviet occupation" (Chris Robinson). Tuganov also experimented with new cinematic technologies and as a result created *The Souvenir* (Suveniir, 1977), the first Soviet stereo animation film. His last film was made for children, *The Dappled Colt* (Õunkimmel/ Zherebenok v iablokakh, 1981).

Other films: *A Forest Tale* (Metsamuinasjutt, 1959); *Mina and Murri* (Mina ja Murri, 1961); *The Donkey, the Herring, and the Broom* (Eesel, heeringas ja nõialund/Osel, seledka i metla, 1969); *Bloody John* (Verine John/Krovavyi Dzhon, 1974); *The Captain from Köpenick* (Köpenicki kapten, 1978); *Djufa* (Giufa/Dzhufa, 1979).

TURIN, VIKTOR ALEKSANDROVICH (b. 1895, St. Petersburg– d. 1945, Moscow). Russian director, screenwriter, and editor. Turin, born into an affluent family, joined a leftist political group in high school. He attended a theater school in St. Petersburg before moving to the United States in 1912, where he studied at the Massachusetts Institute of Technology in Boston, graduating with a degree in engineering in 1916. He then worked in Hollywood for Vitagraph and other studios as an actor, scriptwriter, and assistant director.

Upon his return to Russia in 1922, Turin directed his first picture at the Yalta film studio, *The Slogans of October* (Lozungi Oktiabria, 1925), which blends **documentary** and fictional scenes. The feature *Battle of Giants* (Bor'ba gigantov, 1926) was inspired by Turin's American experiences and depicts the class struggle in a fictitious capitalist country. Critics noticed the parallel montage juxtaposing the lavish life of exploiters to the outrageous poverty of the exploited, a cinematic tool that became characteristic of all of Turin's films. His next feature, *The Provocateur* (Provokator, 1928), deals with illegal political organizations in pre-1917 Russia.

Turin created an international sensation with his hour-long documentary ***Turksib*** (aka *The Steel Road*/Stal'noi put', 1929), made for Vostok-kino studio, which specialized in Central Asian subject matter. The film's screenplay was coauthored by the director with **Aleksandr Macheret** and **Viktor Shklovskii**, among others, and describes the conditions under which the 1,000-mile-long Turkestan-Siberian railway line was built. The dramatic narration emphasizes the heroic efforts in overcoming extreme heat and cold, as well as the isolation of people in remote desert areas. As a passionate promodernization pamphlet, *Turksib* betrays the influence of the masters of avant-garde montage, from **Sergei Eizenshtein** to **Esfir' Shub** and **Dziga Vertov**. However, the film's narrative structure with its logical lucidity, sense of measure, pulsating rhythm, and "Whitmanesque style of subtitles" (Erik Barnow) were universally recognized as a unique achievement influencing the art of documentary filmmaking all over the world.

Turin subsequently worked as a producer and consultant; several of his projects—among them the story of a "Soviet Don Quijote" conceived with **Anatolii Lunacharskii**—remained in the planning stage. In 1935, Turin embarked on creating the first Azerbaijani sound film, *The People of Baku* (Bakintsy, 1938), about the participation of oil workers in the 1905 political turmoils. Despite the film's superb imagery, its schematic plotline echoing **Grigorii Kozintsev** and **Leonid Trauberg**'s *Maksim Trilogy* (Trilogiia o Maksime, 1934–38) was all too obvious. Subsequently, serious health problems prevented Turin from returning to directing.

TURKMEN CINEMA. *See* AIMEDOVA, MAIA-GOZEL; KARLIEV, ALTY; MANSUROV, BULAT; NARLIEV, KHODJAKULI; SAPAROV, USMAN; TURKMENFILM STUDIO.

TURKMENFILM STUDIO. Founded through a decree of the Council of People's Commissars of the Turkmen SSR in Ashgabat (Ashkhabad) in 1926, the studio was first designated as a "film factory." It initially produced **documentaries**, educational films, and newsreels. In 1929, the first Turkmen feature film, *White Gold* (Beloe zoloto) about the collectivization of cotton production was released. In the following decades, non-Turkmen directors such as Mikhail Bystritskii, Dmitrii Poznanskii, Aleksandr Ledashchev, and Georgii Lomidze provided the required didactic films about the socioeconomic transformation of villages (*auls*) and the struggle against anti-Communist, Muslim rebels (the so-called *basmachi*). The most acclaimed of those films was *I'll Come Back* (Ia vernus', 1935).

In 1938, the studio's name was changed to Ashkhabad Film Studio. On its premises, Russian director Evgenii Ivanov-Barkov (1892–1965) made *Dursun* (1940) about a young Turkmen woman—portrayed by

Russian actress Nina Alisova—who emancipates herself from the traditional gender concepts. More and more often, Turkmen performers were cast in roles of Turkmen people, most prominently **Alty Karliev**, who played a supporting role in *Dursun*, for which he was recognized with a 1941 Stalin Prize.

During the Great Patriotic War, the Kiev film studio (later **Dovzhenko Film Studio**) was evacuated to Ashgabat where it completed two features. After the war, Ivanov-Barkov won accolades for the musical comedy *Faraway Bride* (Dalekaia nevesta, 1948), made in the spirit of **Ivan Pyr'ev**'s cheerful Stalinist entertainment. A severe earthquake in 1948 destroyed the studio completely and took the lives of a considerable number of film artists and technical personnel. It took several years before the facilities were rebuilt and feature film production could resume.

In 1958, the studio's official name was changed back to Turkmenfilm. On its staff was Rafail Perel'shtein, whose *Son of a Shepherd* (Syn pastukha, 1955) about a man from the country who becomes a surgeon, as well as the musical *Old Ashir's Trick* (Khitrost' starogo Ashira, 1956), marked the beginning of a new era in **Turkmen cinema**; other prominent filmmakers were Alty Karliev who embarked on a directing career, and Tahir Sabirov. In 1961, the Central Committee of the Turkmen Communist Party issued a decree, "On Major Insufficiencies in the Work of Turkmenfilm" (O krupnykh nedostatkakh v deiatel'nosti Turkmenfilma) that shook up film production and likely opened the doors for a new generation of filmmakers. Best known among them are directors and cameramen **Bulat Mansurov**, **Khodjakuli Narliev**, Khodjadurdy Narliev, **Usman Saparov**, Khalmamed Kakabaev, and actress **Maia-Gozel Aimedova**, who brought Turkmen cinema national and international recognition. In 1974, the studio was renamed after Alty Karliev. In the 1960s–1980s, Turkmenfilm Studio produced about five full-length features annually (including some for television), as well as documentaries and **animated** shorts for children. It dubbed about 50 Russian and foreign films per year and produced a monthly news almanac, *Soviet Turkmenistan*, as well as a satirical almanac, *The Spear* (Kop'e).

In 1989, the studio received a large piece of land outside of Ashgabat that was intended for the re-creation of an authentic 19th-century *aul*. However, this and numerous other projects such as film festivals came to a halt by the early 1990s. In 1992, the Turkmen government issued a law that all films had to be made in the Turkmen language. Although they had been promised the funding of noncommercial films on a regular basis, Turkmen filmmakers encountered both financial problems and political harassment. The studio stopped producing 35mm films and only occasionally released video productions. Among its noteworthy pictures are *The Legend of My Youth* (Destan moei iunosti, 1992) by Biul-Biul Mamedov and *The Soul Is Burned Out* (Yandim, 1995) by Bairam Abdullaev and Laura Stepanskaia. In 1996, the studio was closed down, supposedly for the construction of a highway, or by other accounts, to be replaced by a sports stadium. According to critic Gulnara Abikeyeva, the films made in the years of independence have been prohibited by the country's administration. Cinema, along with theater and the circus, were declared incompatible with Turkmenistan's national traditions. In December 2003, Turkmenfilm, downgraded to a "film production association," was merged with Turkmen television. In an atmosphere of religious and cultural intolerance, corruption, and distrust, promising filmmakers such as Shikhmurat Annamuratov and Kerim Annanov can no longer rely on state support or the country's once prestigious film studio, which is now defunct.

TURKSIB (aka *The Steel Road*/Stal'noi put', 1929). Vostok-kino Studio. 61 mins., b/w. Directed by **Viktor Turin**. Script: Viktor Turin, Efim Aron, **Viktor Shklovskii, Aleksandr Macheret**. Cinematography: Evgenii Slavinskii, Boris Frantsisson. Premiere: 15 October 1929.

The documentary is devoted to the construction of a railway connecting Turkestan with Siberia, as outlined by the Soviet Union's first five-year plan. The economic rationale behind this project is the urgent necessity to transport grain to Central Asia and cotton to factories in the north. Nature is perceived as a cruel, merciless enemy that needs to be defeated by machinery, communication, and human sacrifice.

TUROV [also: Turau], **VIKTOR TIMOFEEVICH** (b. 25 October 1936, Mahilyow [Mogilev], Belarus–d. 31 October 1996, Minsk). Belarusian director and screenwriter. In his childhood, Turov experienced the horrors of war, surviving in a partisan unit in the Belarusian forests. The Great Patriotic War became a central theme for him, as for **Belarusian cinema** in general; however, in his films, war is often shown from a child's point of view. In 1960, Turov graduated from the Soviet State Film School **VGIK**, where he had studied with **Aleksandr Dovzhenko**.

Turov's diploma film was *Communist Construction Site* (Komstroi, 1959), released as part of the almanac *Young Heroes* (Iunye geroi, 1959). He made his directorial debut with the medium-length *The Star on the Belt Buckle* (Zvezda na priazhke, 1963) from a story by well-known Belarusian author Yanka Bryl'. This short tells about a group of children who begin to treat an unassuming man in their neighborhood with respect after learning that he was a soldier with a distinguished service record in World War II. In Turov's first full-length feature, *Across the Cemetery* (Praz mohilki/Cherez kladbishche, 1964), war is the backdrop for a drama about life in the underground during Nazi occupation. Its oppressive atmosphere and anticlimactic narration reminded contemporary critics of **Andrei Tarkovskii**'s influential *Ivan's Childhood* (aka *My Name Is Ivan*/ Ivanovo detstvo, 1962).

I Hail from Childhood (Ia rodam z dziacinstva/Ia rodom iz detstva, 1966), from a screenplay by **Gennadii Shpalikov**, continues the exploration of the tragic impact of war on the lives of adolescents and their families. Turov then directed two films based on works by leading Belarusian author Ales' Adamovich (1927–1994), whose experiences in the Great Patriotic War were similar to his own and whose worldview underwent a comparable evolution, ultimately resulting in a passionate endorsement of humanist values: *The War under the Roofs* (Voina pod kryshami, 1967), which deals with a village occupied by Nazi troops, and *The Sons Leave for Battle* (Synov'ia ukhodiat v boi, 1969), in which the dividing lines between the enemy and Soviet forces are blurred, since both attack the partisan units. These films were released in 1971, following considerable controversy.

Sunday Night (Voskresnaia noch', 1977) is one of the few Turov films dealing with contemporary problems, in this case alcoholism and its social ramifications. *Point of Reading* (Tochka otscheta, 1979), about a juvenile criminal who has to prove his character strength when drafted to the Soviet Army, became a box-office success. The two-part, six-hour-long *Chronicle of Polesye* (Polesskaia khronika) from Ivan Melezh's classical epic, consisting of *People at the Swamps* (Liudi na bolote, 1981) and *Breath of Thunder* (Dykhanie grozy, 1982), describes the establishment of the Communist system in Belarus in the 1920s and won Turov a USSR State Prize in 1984; it was also released as a television miniseries. *The Black Stork* (Chernyi aist, 1993), a gloomy drama taking place in a forlorn village, deals with the effects of the Chernobyl' nuclear power plant disaster on rank-and-file people.

Although Turov's films are not well known abroad, he is considered the leading Belarusian filmmaker of the 1960s–1980s whose work reflects the nation's historical traumas. Early on, he developed a recognizable narrative manner in which visual and audial aspects of a scene dominate over plot linearity and dramatic buildup, an ascetic style that brought him more critical recognition than popular appreciation.

Turov, who joined the Communist Party in 1977, was named People's Artist of the Belarusian SSR in 1979 and People's Artist of the USSR in 1986. From 1976 to 1981, he was the first secretary of the Belarusian Filmmakers' Union.

Other films: *The Time of Her Sons* (Vremia ee synovei, 1975); *The Least among Brothers* (Men'shii sredi brat'ev, 1984, TV); *The Crossing* (Pereprava, 1987, TV); *Shlyakhta Member Zavalnya, or Belarus in Fantastic Stories* (Shliakhtich Zaval'nia, ili Belarus' v fantasticheskikh rasskazakh, 1994).

TUTYSHKIN, ANDREI PETROVICH (b. 24 January 1910, Kishinev–d. 1 December [other sources: 30 October] 1971, Leningrad). Russian actor, director, and screenwriter. After studying at the school of the Vakhtangov Theater in Moscow in 1927–1931, Tutyshkin joined its troupe, later switching to musical theaters in Moscow and Leningrad both as an actor and director.

Tutyshkin's screen career began in the late 1930s. In **Grigorii Aleksandrov**'s *Volga-Volga* (1938) and **Konstantin Iudin**'s *A Girl with Personality* (Devushka s kharakterom, 1939), Tutyshkin proved an effective male lead and quickly rose to national stardom. Playing kindhearted, slightly stubborn but likeable young men, he served as the comedic sounding board to **Liubov' Orlova**'s and **Valentina Serova**'s strong-willed female characters. A fine supporting performance in Iudin's charming *Hearts of Four* (Serdtsa chetyrekh, 1941, released 1945) and a lead in Vladimir Legoshin's military spy thriller *The Duel* (Poedinok, 1944) further solidified Tutyshkin's fame. However, in the mid-1940s his acting career came almost to a halt; subsequently, he was merely given episodic assignments, performing honorably but far from the promise that his first roles had held.

In 1954, Tutyshkin began a directing career specializing in musical comedies, often with love triangle plots evolving in some picturesque Black Sea spa. *You and I Have Met Somewhere* (My s vami gde-to vstrechalis', 1954, codirected by Nikolai Dostal'), with legendary standup comedian Arkadii Raikin in the lead, *A Crazy Day* (Bezumnyi den', 1956, from a play by Valentin Kataev), and *To the Black Sea* (K Chernomu moriu, 1957) entertained tens of millions with a mix of friendly characterizations, satirical bits, and a harmless—but considered risqué at the time—erotic atmosphere. Tutyshkin followed up with the antifascist **Isaak Dunaevskii** operetta *Free Wind* (Vol'nyi veter, 1961, codirected with **Leonid Trauberg**) and his greatest box-office success, the musical *Wedding in Malinovka* (Svad'ba v Malinovke, 1967), which attracted almost 80 million viewers in the first year of its release. A buffoonery set during the 1918–1921 Civil War in rural Ukraine, it features the director's usual trademarks: well-timed dialogues, a naïve plot, openly theatrical singing and dancing scenes, and conciliatory humor. Loved by audiences but critically ignored, Tutyshkin has the distinction of not being mentioned even once in the official four-volume *History of Soviet Cinema*.

Tutyshkin was awarded the title Merited Artist of the Russian Federation in 1946.

Other films: (as actor) *Twins* (Bliznetsy, 1945); *Carnival Night* (Karnaval'naia noch', 1956); (as director) *Shel'menko the Batman* (Shel'menko-denshchik, 1971).

– U –

UKRAINIAN CINEMA. *See* BALAIAN, ROMAN; BARSKAIA, MARGARITA; BUCHMA, AMVROSII; BYKOV, LEONID; CHARDYNIN, PETR; DEMUTSKII, DANYLO; DONSKOI, MARK; DOVZHENKO, ALEKSANDR; DOVZHENKO FILM

STUDIO; *EARTH*; GAIDAROV, VLADIMIR; GRIN'KO, NIKO-
LAI; KAPLER, ALEKSEI; KAVALERIDZE, IVAN; LEVCHUK,
TIMOFEI; LUKOV, LEONID; MURATOVA, KIRA; MYKOLAI-
CHUK, IVAN; OSYKA, LEONID; *RAINBOW, THE*; SAVCHENKO,
IHOR'; *SHADOWS OF FORGOTTEN ANCESTORS*; SHKURAT,
STEPAN; SOLNTSEVA, IULIIA; TODOROVSKII, PETR; UZH-
VII, NATALIIA.

ULFSAK, LEMBIT (b. 4 July 1947, Koerus [Kõõru]). Estonian actor and director. Ulfsak studied acting at Tallin Conservatory. In
1969–1978, he was a member of the troupe of the Tallin Youth Theater (Noorooteatris). From 1978 to 1985 and again since 1994, he has
been one of the leading actors of the Estonian Drama Theater (Eesti
Draamateatri), where he stars in plays by Tom Stoppard and Edward
Albee, among others.

Ulfsak made his movie debut with a supporting role in Boris
Durov's World War II spy drama *Story of a Chekist* (Povest' o
chekiste, 1969). He gave a fine performance in the title role of Arvo
Kruusement's entertaining *Don Juan from Tallin* (Don Juan Tallin-
nas/Don Zhuan v Talline, 1971), before gaining enormous popularity
throughout the Soviet Union with the title role of **Aleksandr Alov**
and **Vladimir Naumov**'s *The Legend of Till* (Legenda o Tile, 1977),
in which he displayed wit and youthful, antiauthoritarian vivacity. Another memorable film, with Ulfsak starring as Paganel, is
Stanislav Govorukhin's popular Jules Verne adaptation *In Search
of Captain Grant* (V poiskakh kapitana Granta, 1985). He also appeared in artistically more ambitious pictures such as **Leida Laius**'s
The Spring in the Forest (Ukuaru/Rodnik v lesu, 1973), **Elyor
Ishmukhamedov**'s *What Our Years Were Like* (Kakie nashi gody,
1980), and **Dinara Asanova**'s *"My Sweet, Dear, Beloved, Only One
. . ."* ("Milyi, dorogoi, liubimyi, edinstvennyi . . . ," 1984).

Ulfsak is particularly successful in **comedies** with a tragicomical
slant, using his tall, bony, somewhat cumbersome physique to good
effect, such as in Peeter Simm's Estonian-Latvian coproduction
Good Hands (Head käed/Labas rokas, 2001) in which he portrays
an engineer who loses his professional and social status. He also
impersonated Hans Christian Andersen in the Polish children's film
Mr. Kleks's Academy (Akademiya pana Kleksa, 1984). In the 1990s

and early 2000s, he appeared in several Swedish and Russian television miniseries.

Ulfsak, one of the undisputed stars of **Estonian cinema**, directed two pictures, *The Joys of Midlife* (Keskea rõõmud/Radosti srednego vozrasta, 1986) and *The Secret Lamb* (Lammas all paremas nurgas, 1992). The former is a tragicomedy about five middle-aged city-dwellers who seek relief from urban boredom and alienation by going out to the countryside to consult an alternative healer.

Ulfsak was named Merited Artist of the Estonian SSR in 1989. His son, Juhan Ulfsak (b. 1973), is also a film actor; both appeared in the Estonian comedy *Röövlirahnuu Martin* (2005).

Other films: *Mary Poppins, Good-bye!* (Meri Poppins, do svidaniia! 1983); *The Hunt for the Dragon* (Okhota na drakona, 1986); *Firewater* (Tulivesi, 1994); *Heart of a Bear* (Karn Süda, 2001).

UL'IANOV, MIKHAIL ALEKSANDROVICH (b. 20 November 1927, village Bergamak, Omsk district–d. 26 March 2007, Moscow). Russian actor and director. Ul'ianov studied at the Shchukin Theater School—attached to the famous Moscow Vakhtangov Theater—in 1946–1950 and joined its troupe after graduation.

In cinema, Ul'ianov debuted in 1953 in **Iuliia Solntseva**'s filmed stage production of Maksim Gor'kii's *Egor Bulychev and Others* (Egor Bulychev i drugie, 1953), followed in 1956 by the supporting part of Kashirin in **Lev Kulidzhanov**'s and Iakov Segel''s *The House in Which I Live* (Dom, v kotorom ia zhivu, 1957). The 1960s for Ul'ianov turned out to be a decade of eminent cinematic accomplishments, starting with the lead part of Bakhirev in **Vladimir Basov**'s *Battle Underway* (Bitva v puti, 1961) and the kolkhoz director Egor Trubnikov in **Aleksei Saltykov**'s *The Chairman* (Predsedatel', 1964), an openly polemical, programmatic picture in which the spirit of a new beginning after the Stalinist trauma found its authentic expression. Tempestuous emotion unbridled by rational considerations characterizes Ul'ianov's interpretation of Dmitrii Karamazov in **Ivan Pyr'ev**'s adaptation of Fedor Dostoevskii's *The Brothers Karamazov* (Brat'ia Karamazovy, 1966–1968). After Pyr'ev's passing, Ul'ianov, together with **Kirill Lavrov**, brought the project to completion. His only other attempt in film direction was the 1973 *The Very Last Day* (Samyi poslednii den'), a tragic story about a police officer killed on duty a day before his retirement.

Based on an astounding resemblance, Ul'ianov portrayed Soviet Marshal Georgii Zhukov (1896–1974) in numerous large-scale World War II epics such as **Iurii Ozerov**'s *Liberation* (Osvobozhde-nie, 1971) and *Stalingrad* (1989).

Among Ul'ianov's most interesting achievements are the part of Sergei Abrikosov in **Iulii Raizman**'s *Private Life* (Chastnaia zhizn', 1982)—which won him a prize at the Venice Film Festival in 1982 and a USSR State Prize in 1983—and the lead in **Nikita Mikhalkov**'s shocking intimate drama *Without Witnesses* (Bez svi-detelei, 1983). Using Ul'ianov's traditional image of a strong, digni-fied Soviet patriarch, **Stanislav Govorukhin** cast him as a former World War II fighter whose granddaughter is raped by three nouveau riche thugs in the vigilante drama *The Voroshilov Sniper* (Voroshi-lovskii strelok, 1999).

An original stage director open to innovation and experimentation, Ul'ianov was appointed artistic director of the Vakhtangov Theater in 1987, where he proved to be an energetic if headstrong administra-tor. He also held high positions within the Communist Party, which he joined in 1951. He was awarded a Lenin Prize in 1966 for *The Chairman*, and named People's Artist of the USSR in 1969 and Hero of Socialist Labor in 1986.

Other films: *Volunteers* (Dobrovol'tsy, 1958); *The Silence* (Tishina, 1963); *The Flight* (Beg, 1970); *The Theme* (Tema, 1979); *The Master and Margarita* (Master i Margarita, 1994, unreleased).

UMURZAKOVA, AMINA [some Russian sources list the patronymic Ergozhaevna] (b. 8 March 1919, Abai, Semipalatinsk district–d. 28 September 2006, Almaty, Kazakhstan). Kazakh actress. In 1934, Umurzakova ran away from home and went to Leningrad to study acting at the Theater Institute with **Vasilii Merkur'ev**. After gradu-ation in 1938 she worked as a stage actress at the Mukhtar Auezov Theater and, from 1940–1946, as a film editor in Almaty (Alma-Ata). In 1946, she joined the troupe of the Almaty Theater of the Young Viewer (TIuZ).

Following minor parts in **Sergei Gerasimov**'s *Komsomol'sk* (1938) and Moisei Levin's revolutionary biopic *Amangel'dy* (1938), **Grigorii Roshal'** entrusted Umurzakova with the female lead in his biopic *The Songs of Abai* (Pesni Abaia, 1945, codirected with Efim Aron), the success of which paved the way for the actress both on stage and in the movies, making her one of the stars of **Kazakh cinema**. Thus, Umurzakova's heart-wrenching performance as a mother waiting for her son to return from the front in the Great Patriotic War in Aleksandr Karpov's *Legend of a Mother* (Skaz o Materi, 1963) was a national triumph. In a number of pictures, the actress was cast in similar roles, irradiating warmth, compassion, and quiet spiritual strength: in the Chukotka drama *The Most Beautiful Ships* (Samye krasivye korabli, 1973, from Yuri Rytkhëu's story), in the fairy tale *Enemy, Fear the Ninth Son* (Boisia, vrag, deviatogo syna, 1986), and in the drama *Mama Roza* (1991), which won several international prizes.

Leading Kazakh director **Shaken Aimanov** gave Umurzakova roles that allowed her to demonstrate various facets of her talent, including parts in the **comedy** *Beardless Swindler* (Bezborodyi obmanshchik, 1965) and the popular musical *Angel in a Cap* (Angel v tiubeteike, 1969). Her last role was in the contemporary urban drama *Shanghai* (1996). The actress also worked in children's programs on television.

Umurzakova was named People's Artist of the Kazakh SSR in 1965.

Other films: *Djambul* (1952); *In One District* (V odnom raione, 1960); *The Scarlet Poppies of Issyk-Kul'* (Alye maki Issyk-Kulia, 1972).

URBANSKII, EVGENII IAKOVLEVICH (b. 27 February 1932 Inta, Komi ASSR [other sources: Moscow]–d. 5 November 1965, near Bukhara). Russian actor. Urbanskii's father, a high-ranking Communist functionary, was arrested in 1937 and spent 17 years in GULAG concentration camps in the north of the USSR; his family was exiled to Alma-Ata. After studying at the Institute of Transportation and at the Institute of Mining in Moscow, Urbanskii enrolled in the studio school of the Moscow Art Theater (MKhAT) in 1952, graduating in 1957. That same year, he joined the troupe of the Stanislavskii Drama Theater.

Urbanskii's movie debut took place during his last year of study and was nothing short of sensational. In **Iulii Raizman**'s drama *A Communist* (Kommunist, 1957) the actor informed the title role of Vasilii Gubanov with noble, manly stoicism, modesty, and passion previously unseen in Soviet cinema. He believably embodied the very traits that Soviet society was craving when the Thaw shock waves threatened to delegitimize Communist ideals altogether: selflessness, unconditional faith in Leninism, and indestructible integrity. While *A Communist* propelled Urbanskii to national fame, the film's pathos looks rather dated today. However, **Grigorii Chukhrai**'s *Ballad of a Soldier* (Ballada o soldate, 1959) has kept its emotional grip; Urbanskii, who carried just one episode—about a self-doubting soldier who lost a leg in the Great Patriotic War and waits for his wife at the train station—conveys unforgettable emotional intensity. **Mikhail Kalatozov** shows a variation of Urbanskii's heroic charisma in the gripping drama *The Unmailed Letter* (Neotpravlennoe pis'mo, 1960), while Chukhrai cast him as the maligned pilot Aleksei Astakhov in his anti-Stalinist pamphlet *Clear Skies* (Chistoe nebo, 1962). Urbanskii also appeared in **Andrei Mikhalkov-Konchalovskii**'s diploma short *The Boy and the Dove* (Mal'chik i golub', 1960).

At the height of his fame, Urbanskii died in a car accident while shooting a stunt for **Aleksei Saltykov**'s *The Director* (Direktor, 1965) in the Turkmen desert.

Urbanskii joined the Communist Party in 1962; the same year, he was named Merited Artist of the Russian Federation. He was married to Latvian actress and director Dzidra Ritenberga (1928–2003). In 1968, Elena Stashevskaia-Naroditskaia made a feature-length **documentary** about the actor.

Other films: *The Great Ore* (Bol'shaia ruda, 1964); *An Inch of Land* (Piad' zemli, 1964).

URUSEVSKII, SERGEI PAVLOVICH (b. 23 December 1908, Moscow–d. 12 November 1974, Moscow). Russian cinematographer, director, and screenwriter. Urusevskii studied at the Leningrad college (*tekhnikum*) for industrial design until 1929, and at the Institute for Fine Arts (VKhUTEIN) with Vladimir Favorskii (1886–1964). There, he began to practice photography and painting, which remained lifelong passions. After a number of unsuccessful attempts, Urusevskii joined the Soviet film industry in 1935, initially as an assistant cameraman at **Mezhrabpomfilm Studio**. His first independent work as cinematographer was the inconsequential Nikolai Gogol' adaptation *How Ivan Ivanovich and Ivan*

Nikiforovich Quarreled (Kak possorilis' Ivan Ivanovich s Ivanom Nikiforovichem, 1941). During the Great Patriotic War, Urusevskii filmed at the front lines.

Urusevskii's encounter with **Mark Donskoi**, who shared his interest in a poetic, pristine reflection of reality, proved decisive. *The Country Teacher* (Sel'skaia uchitel'nitsa, 1947), which won Urusevskii a Stalin Prize in 1948, immersed the harsh reality of a Soviet village before and after World War II in tender, impressionistic light reflecting the heroine's humane pedagogical intentions. Urusevskii's first film in color, **Iulii Raizman**'s *Cavalier of the Golden Star* (aka *Dream of a Cossack*/Kavaler zolotoi zvezdy, 1950), which earned the cameraman his second Stalin Prize, presented a challenge with regard to the control of the color spectrum, especially in landscape shots. Urusevskii's ambition to mellow colors and achieve a quasi-pastel dissolution is essential for **Vsevolod Pudovkin**'s *The Return of Vasily Bortnikov* (Vozvrashchenie Vasiliia Bortnikova, 1953). As this picture blends intimate drama with social collision in a new, undogmatic way, Urusevskii responded by using image softeners, infusing the film's atmosphere with a promising benevolence that literally seems to anticipate the coming Thaw.

For **Grigorii Chukhrai**'s unorthodox Civil War romance *The Forty-first* (Sorok pervyi, 1956) Urusevskii provided gentle compositions in perfect agreement with the psychological state of the two main characters. Yet, despite remarkable innovations, it is still a far cry from the radical aesthetic solutions that Urusevskii risked in his partnership with **Mikhail Kalatozov**, whose own expressive camera ambitions are revealed in *Salt for Svanetia* (1930). In the war drama *The Cranes Are Flying* (Letiat zhuravli, 1957), Urusevskii's passionately mobile, handheld camera achieves the status of an active participant in the unfolding story, with a near-independent subjectivity, incessantly interacting with the main characters yet seemingly following a plotline of its own, sometimes transcending the realistic dimension and reaching a metaphysical level. *The Unmailed Letter* (Neotpravlennoe pis'mo, 1960) and *I Am Cuba* (Ia—Kuba, 1962) took the camera's freedom of mobility even further, which led to accusations of experimentation for experimentation's sake. In the former, the shot compositions give the fateful expedition of four geologists a quasi-philosophical framework, while in the latter, the cinematic acrobatics often go over the top, revealing the film's ideological, formulaic blandness.

In hindsight, there can be no doubt that Urusevskii's camera art not only stunned international audiences and raised the prestige of Soviet cinema worldwide but also helped untie the hands of young Soviet cinematographers such as **Vadim Iusov**, **Jonas Gricius**, **Margarita Pilikhina**, **Levan Paatashvili**, **Yury Il'enko**, and **Vadim Derbenev**. Indeed, Urusevskii inspired a number of national poetic schools of filmmaking that emerged in the early 1960s.

Urusevskii's directorial debut was *Farewell, Gul'sary!* (Proshchai, gul'sary, aka Beg inokhodtsa, 1968), an emotion-filled war film adapted from **Chingiz Aitmatov**'s story. It won accolades for its visually intensity but was criticized for the unevenness of its plot and awkward characterizations. Urusevskii followed with *Sing a Song, Poet* (Poi pesniu, poet, 1971), an episodic biopic about cult poet Sergei Esenin (1895–1925), the script of which the director coauthored with **Gennadii Shpalikov**. More than any previous works, it earned Urusevskii both respect and scorn, as well as accusations of visual mannerism and negligence of psychological and historical aspects. In spite of such a hapless ending to his career, Urusevskii deservedly has retained his reputation as one of the few Soviet cameramen with a recognizable individual style.

Urusevskii, a member of the Communist Party since 1942, was honored with the title Merited Artist of the RSFSR in 1951.

Other films: *The Duel* (Poedinok, 1945); *Alitet Leaves for the Mountains* (Alitet ukhodit v gory, 1948); *The First Echelon* (Pervyi eshelon, 1956, with Iurii Ekel'chik).

UZBEK CINEMA. *See* ABBASOV, SHUKHRAT; FAIZIEV, LATIF; ISHMUKHAMEDOV, ELYOR; KHAMRAEV, ALI; PIRMUKHAMEDOV, RAKHIM; UZBEKFILM STUDIO.

UZBEKFILM STUDIO. The studio was founded in Tashkent in 1925 as film factory Star of the East (Shark Yulduzi) and belonged to the Uzbek State Film Company (Uzbekgoskino). Its first silent feature films dealt with the Civil War in Central Asia, denouncing those who resisted the Bolshevik forces as gangsters, for example, *The Jackals of Ravat* (Shakaly Ravata), starring **Kamil**

Yarmatov. Later feature films reflected the Communist transformation of Uzbek society, depicting the traditional, religiously determined lifestyle as a negative burden that had to be disposed of. The films of the 1920s were exclusively directed by nonnative—mostly Russian—filmmakers such as **Viacheslav Viskovskii** (*Minaret of Death*/Minaret smerti, 1925). **Nabi Ganiev**, one of Uzbekistan's first native directors, addressed problems of the country's industrialization in *The Rise* (Pod"em, 1931) and its so-called religious superstition in *Ramazan* (1933).

In 1936, the studio was renamed Uzbekfilm; a year later, it released the first Uzbek sound film, *The Oath* (Kliatva), directed by Aleksandr Usol'tsev (1901–?). Native Uzbek directors who began their careers in the 1930s were Iuldash Agzamov (1909–1985) and Zagid Sabitov (1909–1982).

In 1941, at the beginning of the Great Patriotic War, the studio was renamed Tashkent Film Studio and hosted a large number of evacuated filmmakers from various national studios. It was here that **Leonid Lukov** made the famous patriotic **comedy** *Two Fighters* (Dva boitsa, 1943) and **Mikhail Romm** the anti-Nazi drama *Person #217* (aka *Girl No. 217*/Chelovek No. 217, 1944). Of particular importance was **Iakov Protazanov**'s work on *Nasreddin in Bukhara* (Nasreddin v Bukhare, 1943), because it used local talent to a greater extent than other productions. Indeed, for a number of years Uzbek filmmakers were marginalized: Yarmatov could only make the short *We Shall Prevail* (My pobedim, 1941) and the concert film *A Gift from the Homeland* (Podarok Rodiny, 1943), while Ganiev was occupied with dubbing Russian films.

At the end of the war, Uzbek filmmakers turned to their country's rich folklore, delivering some of the most accomplished national pictures, particularly *Tahir and Zukhra* (1945) and *The Adventures of Nasreddin* (Pokhozhdeniia Nasreddina, 1947), both directed by Ganiev with excellent cinematography of **Danylo Demutskii**, who had been exiled to Central Asia. Ganiev's attempt to create a realistic film about contemporary Uzbekistan was attacked by dogmatic critics; as a result, *The Daughter of Ferghana* (Doch' Fergany, 1948), remained a stand-alone experiment. With grandiose biopics such as *Alisher Navoi* (1948) and *Avicenna* (1957), Yarmatov became the country's leading filmmaker.

In 1958, the studio was again renamed Uzbekfilm. A new generation of directors—graduates from the Soviet State Film School **VGIK**—appeared in **Uzbek cinema**, including **Latif Faiziev**, a versatile filmmaker who gained fame through exotic coproductions with India such as *The Adventures of Ali Baba and the Forty Thieves* (Ali Baba Aur Chalis Chor/Prikliucheniia Ali-Baby i soroka razboinikov, 1979, codirected with Umesh Mehra), an enormous box-office hit. Among Uzbekistan's other leading directors who emerged in the 1960s, were **Shukhrat Abbasov**, **Ali Khamraev**, and **Elyor Ishmukhamedov**, whose themes transcended national borders and whose stylistic innovations gained recognition among Soviet and international critics. The most popular genres were action-filled adventure films such as Khamraev's *The Seventh Bullet* (Sed'maia pulia, 1972), lyrical youth romances such as Ishmukhamedov's *Lovers* (Vliublennye, 1969), and biopics about great poets and scientists, for example, Abbasov's *Abu-Raikhan Beruni* (1975). The most important Uzbek **documentary** filmmaker was Malik Kaiumov. In 1965, Uzbekfilm Studio began the production of **animated** films.

In 1979, the studio was named after Kamil Yarmatov, who had been its artistic director for over two decades. In the 1970s and 1980s, the annual production volume was 10 to 12 full-length features, in addition to satirical almanacs (*The Spear*/Nashtar) and animated shorts. Also, more than 60 films were dubbed into Uzbek every year.

In the 1990s, Uzbekfilm Studio was transformed into a joint stock association, with the Uzbek state holding 51 percent of stocks, lending its facilities to Russian, British, French, Pakistani, Indian, and Turkish film companies. In 2005, President Karimov issued a decree criticizing the lack of optimism and positive values in recent Uzbek productions; the director of Uzbekfilm was replaced by an administrator close to the president. In 2006, the government announced plans to fund 15 feature films, 20 documentaries, and 10 animated films annually. Overall, Uzbekfilm studio produced about 300 full-length feature films, hundreds of documentaries and instructional films, and about 150 animated pictures.

UZHVII, NATAL'IA MIKHAILOVNA (b. 8 September 1898, Liuboml'–d. 30 July 1986, Kyiv [Kiev]). Ukrainian actress. Uzhvii began her career in amateur theater productions in 1918. In 1922, she enrolled in the studio of the Taras Shevchenko First State Drama Theater of the Ukrainian SSR in Kyiv and joined its troupe after graduation in 1923. In 1925, she worked with the Derzhdrama theater in Odessa, in 1926, in the theater Berezil' in Kharkiv, and after 1936, she was one of the leading stars of the Ivan Franko Ukrainian Drama Theater in Kyiv. An actress of great emotional intensity and passion, Uzhvii excelled in classical works of Shakespeare, Anton Chekhov, Ivan Franko, and Aleksandr Ostrovskii, as well as revolutionary and contemporary plays.

As a film actress, Uzhvii made her debut in **Ukrainian cinema** in 1926 with the role of Galia Dombrovskaia in the revolutionary adventure *PKP*, directed by Georgii Stabavoi. Another noteworthy silent role is that of Marina in **Petr Chardynin**'s historical picture *Taras Triasilo* (1927). During the sound period, Uzhvii worked with leading Ukrainian and Russian directors, among them **Ivan Kavaleridze** (Nastas'ia Makarovna in the historical parable *Prometheus*/Prometei, 1935), **Leonid Lukov** (Gorpina, the main character's wife, in the drama about pre-1917 Donbas miners, *I Love*/Ia liubliu, 1936), and **Grigorii Kozintsev** and **Leonid Trauberg** (the soldier's wife, Evdokiia, in *The Vyborg District*/Vyborgskaia storona, 1938, the third part of the *Maksim Trilogy*). She gained national fame with her performance as the partisan martyr Olena Kostiuk in **Mark Donskoi**'s war tragedy *The Rainbow* (Raduga, 1944), an achievement that won her a Stalin Prize in 1946.

Later movie appearances were either in filmed stage productions or episodic, for example, in **Ihor' Savchenko**'s celebrated biopic *Taras Shevchenko* (1951) and **Sergei Paradjanov**'s *Ukrainian Rhapsody* (Ukrainskaia rapsodiia, 1961). One of Uzhvii's last film roles was the mother of poet Sergei Esenin in **Sergei Urusevskii**'s controversial biopic *Sing a Song, Poet* (Poi pesniu, poet, 1971).

Uzhvii joined the Communist Party in 1945. She was honored with two more Stalin Prizes—in 1949 and 1951—for her stage work, and the titles People's Artist of the USSR in 1944 and Hero of Socialist Labor in 1973. In 1957, Paradjanov made a documentary about the actress.

Other films: *Nazar Stodolia* (1937); *Karmeliuk* (1939); *May Night* (Maiskaia noch', 1941); *The Snowball Tree Grove* (Kalinovaia roshcha, 1953).

– V –

VABALAS, RAIMONDAS [Raimondas-Piatras; Russian sources list the patronymic Al'fonsovich] (b. 5 March 1937, Paris). Lithuanian director and screenwriter. Vabalas was a stage actor in the town of Panevėžys in 1952–1956. His career in **Lithuanian cinema** began in 1960; at the same time, he studied with **Lev Kuleshov** at the Soviet State Film School **VGIK**, graduating in 1964.

Vabalas's directorial debut was *The Cannonade* (Kanonada, 1961, codirected with **Arūnas Žebriūnas**) about conflicts in a Lithuanian village in the aftermath of World War II. *Steps in the Night* (Žingsniai naktį/Shagi v nochi, 1962), distinguished by the masterful camera work of **Jonas Gricius** evoking a quasi-documentary effect, is devoted to a group of young anti-Nazi fighters who manage to escape from captivity. Vabalas followed it with a satire that was generally seen as a failure, *March, March! Tra-ta-ta!* (Marš, marš, tra-ta-ta, 1964), attacking pre–World War II Lithuanian militarism and nationalism. He then made a **documentary**, *All They Need Is a Fuehrer* (Stinga tik fiurerio/Ne khvataet tol'ko fiurera, 1965, doc.), a political pamphlet. The feature *A Staircase to the Sky* (Laiptai į dangų/Lestnitsa v nebo, 1966), from the novel by Mykolas Sluckis, was a critical success, demonstrating the filmmaker's ability to blend intimate psychological and historical aspects with a deliberately objective description of postwar clashes.

When Vabalas turned to contemporary problems, he encountered administrative harassment—thus, his film *The Summer Begins in June* (Birželis, vasaros pradžia/Iun'- nachalo leta, 1969) was not released. The historical picture *Stone upon Stone* (Akmuo ant akmens/Kamen' na kamen', 1971) turned to safer ground, telling about the hardships of serfdom. *At the Border* (Ties riba/Podvodia chertu, 1972), from a book by Grigorijus Kanovicius, is a thriller about greed and betrayal on the backdrop of the 1970s. *The Exchange* (Mainai/Obmen, 1977), the story of a man who has to choose between his materialistic wife and another woman, visualizes a deep existential crisis resulting from conflicting values; it was adapted from a controversial novella by Russian author Iurii Trifonov. Like other Lithuanian directors (Žebriūnas, **Marijonas Giedrys**), Vabalas turned to television in the mid-1970s, helming a four-part miniseries,

Smoke and the Toddler (Smokas ir Mažylis/Smok i malysh, 1975), from a Jack London story.

Vabalas has the distinction of making the most successful Lithuanian feature film, *Flight across the Atlantic* (Skrydis per Atlantą/ Polet cherez Atlanticheskii okean, 1983), about legendary pilots Steponas Darius (1896–1933) and Stasys Girėnas (1893–1933). *Autumn Comes through the Forest* (Miškais ateina ruduo, 1991) synthesizes themes that had occupied Vabalas throughout his career: Lithuanian rural society in the 1930s, gender relations, and the roots of antisocial behavior.

Vabalas, who held the position of first secretary of the Lithuanian Filmmakers' Union in 1968–1973, was honored with the title Merited Artist of the Lithuanian SSR in 1969.

VACHNADZE, NATO [b. Andronikashvili; Russian sources list her first name and patronymic as Natal'ia Georgievna] (b. 3 April 1904, Warsaw–d. 14 June 1954). Georgian actress. The daughter of a Georgian father and a Polish mother, Vachnadze made her screen debut in the adventurous *Arsen the Bandit* (Arsena kachagi/Arsen razboinik, 1923) by Vladimir Barskii (1889–1936). In **Hamo Bek-Nazaryan**'s peasant drama *Patricide* (Ottseubiistvo, aka *On the Pillory*/U pozornogo stolba, 1923) she portrayed the young woman Nunu who is wrongly accused of murdering her father. This highly expressive performance, together with the subsequent role of Esma, a poor seamstress, in *Three Lives* (Sami sitsotskle/Tri zhizni, 1924), directed by **Ivan Perestiani**, catapulted Vachnadze to national fame. Her screen image as a pure and passionately devoted ingénue was further solidified by the part of Despine in Perestiani's *The Case of Tariel Mklavadze's Murder* (Tariel Mklavadzis mkvlelobis saqme/ Delo ob ubiistve Tariela Mklavadze, 1925).

Kote Mardjanishvili (1872–1933) gave Vachnadze two challenging roles in experimental literary adaptations: *The Gadfly* (Krazana/Ovod, 1926) from Ethel Vojnich's popular novel, and *Amok* (Amoki, 1927), an adaptation of Stefan Zweig's novella. **Fedor Otsep** cast Vachnadze—by now an internationally recognized star—as the gypsy Masha in his 1928 German-Soviet Lev Tolstoi adaptation *The Living Corpse* (Zhivoi trup). In the 1930s, the actress appeared in some of the earliest Georgian sound films, among them

Siko Dolidze's antitribal drama *The Last Crusaders* (Ukanaskueli djvarosuebi/Poslednie krestonostsy, 1934) and **Mikheil Chiaureli**'s anti-Menshevik *The Last Masquerade* (Ukanaskneli maskaradi/Poslednii maskarad, 1934).

Vachnadze was also the star in the directorial debut of her second husband, **Nikoloz Shengelaia**, *Giuli* (1927). Her performance as Nani in Shengelaia's *The Golden Valley* (Narindjis veli/Zolotistaia dolina, 1937)—a cheerful account of collectivization in the Georgian countryside—was recognized with a Stalin Prize in 1941. Vachnadze's last role was in **Davit Rondeli**'s *Conquerors of the Peaks* (Mtsvervalta damkrobni/Pokoriteli vershin, 1952).

Vachnadze is the first superstar of **Georgian cinema** whose cult status survived the transition from silent to sound film; she became a veritable legend after her tragic death in a plane crash.

The actress joined the Communist Party in 1943 and was named People's Artist of the Georgian SSR in 1941. Her sons are filmmakers **Eldar** and **Giorgi Shengelaia**. In Gurdjaani, a Nato Vachnadze Memorial museum was established in 1981.

Other films: *Natela* (1926); *Who Is to Blame?* (Vin Arils Damnashave?/Kto vinovat?); *He Will Come Back* (Is kidev dabrundeba/On eshche vernetsia, 1943); *A Cradle for Akaki* (Akakis akvoni/Kolybel' poeta, 1947).

VAINSHTOK, VLADIMIR PETROVICH (b. 11 March 1908, St. Petersburg–d. 18 October 1978, Moscow). Russian director, screenwriter, and film administrator. Vainshtok studied at the Leningrad Institute for Screen Arts in 1924–1927. His first feature film, the comedy *Actor against Will* (Akter ponevole, 1927), was shelved for unknown reasons. Vainshtok then made the **documentaries** *Save the Millions* (Spasaite milliony, 1928) and *About Two Factories* (O dvukh zavodakh, 1930). *Glory of the World* (Slava mira, 1932), a feature, tells the heart-wrenching story of American Communists disrupting the transportation of weapons intended for war against the Soviet Union.

Vainshtok is best remembered for directing two adventure films, the 1936 *Children of Captain Grant* (Deti kapitana Granta) and the 1938 *Treasure Island* (Ostrov sokrovishch), adapted from novels by Jules Verne and R. L. Stevenson, respectively. Today, these movies' painted sets, simple "special effects," and plain and theatrical acting, together with their ideological kowtowing, may seem embarrassing, yet generations of Soviet viewers rejoiced over these attempts to provide genuine entertainment and gladly ignored the technical crudeness and anachronisms, grateful for wanderlust-inspiring plots and memorable, enthusiastic songs. Vainshtok's foreign adventure fantasies reflected a trend encouraged by the 1930s film industry leader, **Boris Shumiatskii**, who wanted to increase Soviet cinema's entertainment value and international appeal. After Shumiatskii's demise, such films were attacked as "unhealthy" and "misguided" (thus, *Treasure Island* was torn apart by *Pravda* in January 1938). As an effort to recant, Vainshtok made *The Youth of Army Commanders* (Iunost' komandarmov, 1939), an optimistic picture about Red Army ensigns and the might of the Soviet armed forces.

In 1940, Vainshtok was appointed to a number of high-ranking administrative positions in the Soviet film industry and, according to some sources, also became a NKVD (later KGB) agent. In the 1960s, Vainshtok worked as a journalist and screenwriter under the pseudonym Vladimir Vladimirov, showing a thematic preference for secret service and anti-Western tales, among them the very successful *Dead Season* (1968, directed by **Savva Kulish**).

After an intermission of almost four decades, Vainshtok returned to directing, adapting a novel by American author Mayne Reid, who enjoyed cult status in Russia, *Horseman without Head* (Vsadnik bez golovy, 1973). He followed it with *Armed and Very Dangerous: The Time and Heroes of Bret Harte* (Vooruzhen i ochen' opasen: Vremia i geroi Bret Garta, 1977). Both films became huge blockbusters, despite their many painfully obvious weaknesses.

Vainshtok was named Merited Cultural Worker of the RSFSR in 1969 and Merited Artist of the Russian Federation in 1978.

Other films: *Rubikon* (1931).

VASADZE, AKAKI [Russian sources list the patronymic Alekseevich] (b. 6 August 1899, Kutaisi–d. 23 March [other sources: 3 April] 1978, Tbilisi). Georgian actor and pedagogue. Vasadze began his career as a stage decorator in 1917 in the theater of Kutaisi, where he also tried acting. In 1918–1920, he studied at the dramatic studio of Aleksandr Jabadari in Tbilisi. In 1920, Vasadze joined the troupe of the Shota Rustaveli Theater in Tbilisi as an actor and, beginning in 1926, as a director; from 1935 to 1955 he was the theater's executive artistic director. In 1958, he switched to the Meskhiashvili Theater in Kutaisi.

Although primarily a stage actor, Vasadze left notable marks in **Georgian cinema** as well. In early silents, his deliberate emphasis on the social origins of a character outweighed their psychological differentiation, for example, portraying the ruthless policeman Grigola in **Hamo Bek-Nazaryan**'s *Patricide* (Ottseubiistvo, aka *On the Pillory*/Mamis mkvleli/U pozornogo stolba, 1923). Vasadze was famous for his comical characterizations such as the role of Platon in Kote Mardjanishvili's *Samanishvili's Stepmother* (Samanishvili dedinatsvali/Machekha Samanishvili, 1927) about the life of the pre-Soviet gentry. He also appeared in **Iuri Zheliabuzhskii** and **Nikoloz Shengelaia**'s *Dina Dza-dzu* (1926), **Mikheil Chiaureli**'s heroic epic about Georgia in the 17th century, *Georgii Saakadze* (1942–43), **Tengiz Abuladze** and **Revaz Chkheidze**'s successful feature debut *Magdana's Donkey* (Magdanas Lurja/Lurdzha Magdany, 1955), and **Siko Dolidze**'s *Day Last, Day First* (Dge pirveli, dge ukanaskueli/ Den' poslednii, den' pervyi, 1960).

Vasadze, who became a member of the Communist Party in 1939, was named People's Artist of the USSR in 1936. He was awarded three Stalin Prizes for his theater work. For more than 30 years, Vasadze was a successful acting teacher at the Rustaveli Theater Institute in Tbilisi.

Other films: *I Shall Tell the Truth* (Me vitkvi simarrles/Ia skazhu pravdu, 1958); *The Master's Right Hand* (Didostatis Marjvena/Desnitsa velikogo mastera, 1969); *The Kidnapping of the Moon* (Mtvaris motatseba/Pokhishchenie luny, 1973); *Shores* (Data Tutashkhia/ Berega, 1977/80, TV).

VASIL'EV BROTHERS (pseudonym of the unrelated **Georgii Nikolaevich Vasil'ev** [b. 25 November 1899, Vologda–d. 18 June 1946, Leningrad] and **Sergei Dmitrievich Vasil'ev** [b. 4 November 1900, Moscow–d. 16 December 1959, Leningrad]). Russian directors, screenwriters, and film administrators. Georgii Vasil'ev was born into the family of a lawyer and studied at the polytechnic school in Astrakhan'. In the 1918–1920 Civil War, he served in the Red Army and then studied at the Moscow theater studio Young Masters under the actor Illarion Pevtsov (1879–1934). There, he met his lifelong artistic partner and codirector, Sergei Vasil'ev. In 1923, Georgii Vasil'ev began to work as a film critic and, in 1924, as a cutter at Goskino studio.

Sergei Vasil'ev's father was a high-ranking tsarist officer who in later years worked as the archivist of the Russian Army. In 1916, Sergei Vasil'ev volunteered to fight in World War I. After the 1917 Bolshevik Revolution, he joined the guard at the Petrograd Smol'nyi and also worked as a courier, coming in regular contact with Vladimir Lenin and Commissar **Anatolii Lunacharskii**. In fall 1921, Vasil'ev enrolled in the Institute for Screen Arts; in 1923, he began to work as an editor at the Moscow branch of Sevzapkino (later **Lenfilm Studio**). For both Georgii and Sergei, years of reediting films—among them masterpieces by D. W. Griffith and Fritz Lang—adjusting them to Soviet propaganda standards, became the foundation of their own craftsmanship as directors.

In 1924, Georgii and Sergei studied in **Sergei Eizenshtein**'s workshop at the State School of Theater and Cinema (GTK, later **VGIK**). They became friends and were jointly put in charge of a compilation film for Sovkino in Leningrad, *A Heroic Deed in the Ice* (Podvig vo l'dakh, 1928), about the rescue of the Umberto Nobile expedition by the Soviet icebreakers *Krasin* and *Malygin*. The film's considerable resonance helped the duo in getting their first feature assignment, a flamboyant cinematic pamphlet with the ironic title *Sleeping Beauty* (Spiashchaia krasavitsa, 1930). Most critics viewed this polemical juxtaposition of the "arcane" art of ballet to the groundbreaking events of the October Revolution and Civil War as an interesting failure at best. But it was on that picture that the "Vasil'ev brothers" began the practice of creating a director's script, or story board, containing drafts and descriptions of every shot of the planned film. Although various filmmakers claim primacy to this method, French film historian Georges Sadoul credited the Soviet duo with the idea.

Their next project, *Personnel File* (which can also mean *Personal Cause*/Lichnoe delo, 1932), is the story of a pious worker at a dockyard who melts a church bell into a ship's propeller when an urgent metal shortage occurs. Although the film lacks the visual inventiveness of *Sleeping Beauty*, it features one of the earliest worker's characters in Soviet sound cinema.

In 1934, the Vasil'ev brothers shot their most famous—and arguably their only lasting—picture, the Civil War drama ***Chapaev***. Completed two years after the official definition of Socialist Realism as the binding dogma for all Soviet artists, and released the year that the dogma was officially proclaimed at the First Congress of Soviet Writers, *Chapaev* was immediately touted as triumphant proof that the method works for cinema. Indeed, the film met all required criteria: Party-mindedness, ideological commitment, popular appeal, and a positive hero at its center. But apart from its absolute loyalty to the Bolshevik cause, *Chapaev* was a genuine trendsetter in Soviet cinema, expertly blending comedic and tragic elements and cleverly using sound effects. It made stars of its protagonists—**Boris Babochkin** in the title role, Leonid Kmit (1908–1982) as his adjutant Pet'ka, and Varvara Miasnikova (1900–1978) as An'ka the machine-gunner—a trio that became the butt of countless jokes and an integral part of Soviet folklore. Although the official cult surrounding *Chapaev* bordered on the grotesque (large groups of viewers would march in the streets with banners saying "We are going to watch *Chapaev!*"), the success was not entirely orchestrated but due to the film's genuine narrative qualities.

None of the Vasil'ev brothers' subsequent pictures came close to the triumph of *Chapaev*. Sadly, these gifted filmmakers continued within the paradigm of monumental battlefield choreography, reconstructing events of the Civil War and World War II without ever achieving the human warmth of their earlier picture. *Volochaev Days* (Volochaevskie dni, 1937), which applied the *Chapaev* formula to the 1918 Soviet-Japanese border conflict in the Vladivostok region, was received lukewarmly, primarily because of its incoherent plot. *The Defense of Tsaritsyn* (Oborona Tsaritsyna, 1942) retroactively projected the Stalin cult onto another Civil War chapter; why the film's second part was not released has yet to be explained. In 1943, the Vasil'ev brothers adapted Aleksandr Korneichuk's play *Front*, which contained some harsh criticism of the Red Army leadership at the outbreak of the Great Patriotic War. In 1946, they began preproduction of an adaptation of Aleksandr Pushkin's "Queen of Spades," when Georgii Vasil'ev suddenly died. It was not until 1955, when Sergei Vasil'ev held the position of executive director of Lenfilm Studio, that he was able to make a picture on his own, the Soviet-Bulgarian coproduction *Heroes of Shipka* (Geroi Shipki). Interestingly, the film's underlying Pan-Slavism allowed him to portray tsarist generals in a surprisingly even-handed manner; it won Vasil'ev the Best Director award at Cannes in 1955. Sergei Vasil'ev's career ended with a superficial reenactment of the October 1917 events, *In the Days of October* (V dni oktiabria, 1958).

Georgii Vasil'ev was named Merited Artist of the Russian Federation in 1940; Sergei Vasil'ev became People's Artist of the USSR in 1948. The filmmakers are buried together at Novodevich'e cemetery in Moscow. The house in which Sergei Vasil'ev was born (Moscow, Second Bauman Street 3) carries a memorial plaque, as does the house in Astrakhan' in which Georgii Vasil'ev lived in 1904–1920.

Other films: *Unbelievable—But True!* (Neveroiatno—no fakt! 1933, short); *Our Songs* (Nashi pesni, 1950, unfinished).

VERTINSKAIA, ANASTASIIA ALEKSANDROVNA (b. 19 December 1944, Moscow). Russian actress. Vertinskaia, daughter of legendary songwriter, singer, and actor Aleksandr Vertinskii (1889–1957) who had returned to the USSR from emigration in 1943, studied at the Shchukin Theater School in Moscow, graduating in 1967. She joined the troupe of the theater The Contemporary (Sovremennik) but switched to the Moscow Art Theater (MKhAT) in 1978.

As a student, Vertinskaia made her film debut in **Aleksandr Ptushko**'s *Crimson Sails* (Alye parusa, 1961). Her portrayal of the angelic, pure Assol' who overcomes crudeness and cruelty and finds love by believing in her dream made Vertinskaia—imbued with tender, almost transparent features—a star overnight. Her otherworldly beauty also contributed to the success of the fantasy megahit *The Amphibian Man* (Chelovek-amfibiia, 1961), directed by **Gennadii Kazanskii** and Vladimir Chebotarev. **Grigorii Kozintsev** then cast her as Ophelia in his version of *Hamlet* (Gamlet, 1964), in which Vertinskaia renders the doomed heroine's vulnerability almost tangible. The 1960s continued to be Vertinskaia's most successful creative decade with parts in **Sergei Bondarchuk**'s *War and Peace* (Voina i mir, 1962–67) as Liza Bolkonskaia, **Aleksandr Zarkhi**'s Lev Tolstoi adaptation *Anna Karenina* (1968) as Kitty, **Georgii Daneliia**'s *Don't Grieve* (Ar daidardo/Ne goriui! 1969) as Levan's daughter, and **Elyor Ishmukhamedov**'s *Lovers* (Vliublennye, 1969) as Tania, all of which capitalized on the actress's romantic aura.

In the 1970s and 1980s, Vertinskaia's screen and television appearances became rarer, perhaps because the type of lofty idealism and childlike decency that she embodied seemed out of date. In the 1990s, when her once ostracized father was rediscovered by post-Soviet media, Vertinskaia appeared with a solo program of Aleksandr Vertinskii's texts and songs.

Vertinskaia's mother, Lidiia Vertinskaia (b. 1923), made some memorable screen appearances, including as the Phoenix in Ptushko's *Sadko* (1953) and the duchess in Kozintsev's *Don Quijote* (1957). Anastasiia's sister, Marianna Vertinskaia (b. 1943), is also a stage and film actress.

Vertinskaia was named Merited Artist of the RSFSR in 1980 and People's Artist of the RSFSR in 1988.

Other films: *The Shadow* (Ten', 1971); *The Gadfly* (Ovod, 1980, TV); *The Theft* (Krazha, 1982); *The Life of Don Quijote and Sancho Panza* (Tskhovreba Don Kikhotisa da Sancho Panchosi/Zhitie Don Kikhota i Sancho, 1988); *The Master and Margarita* (Master i Margarita, 1994, unreleased).

VERTOV, DZIGA [real name: Denis Arkad'evich—originally Abramovich—Kaufman] (b. 2 January 1896, Białystok–d. 12 February 1954, Moscow). Russian **documentary** director, screenwriter, and film theorist. The son of a book dealer (other sources: librarian), Vertov attended a military music school in Białystok, Poland. In World War I, the family fled to Petrograd, where Vertov studied at the Institute for Psychoneurology. In 1916, he started an experimental sound studio—an early indicator of his interests both in art and technology and a prelude to his innovative work in cinema. The leading Communist journalist Mikhail Kol'tsov (1898–1940) invited Vertov to join the Moscow Committee for Cinematography (*kinokomitet*) in 1918; for the following two years, Vertov worked on the first Soviet newsreel *Film Week* (Kinonedelia) as an editor and author of intertitles. Inspired by his colleague **Lev Kuleshov**, Vertov began to explore the artistic and propaganda potentials of cinema, in particular montage.

Vertov made his directorial debut in 1918 with the documentary *Anniversary of the Revolution* (Godovshchina revoliutsii, 1918, together with A. I. Savel'ev). During the 1918–1921 Civil War, he demonstrated his versatility with a number of documentary shorts on major military events; while these films were based on the notion of the filmmaker as a reporter, the subsequent feature-length *History of the Civil War* (Istoriia grazhdanskoi voiny, 1921) transformed the artist's function into that of a chronicler with the distinct mission to shape society's view of history. During the reconstructive period of the New Economic Policy (NEP, 1921–1928), Vertov conceived a cinematic parallel to the Communist Party newspaper *Pravda* under the title *Cine-Truth* (Kino-Pravda, begun in 1922)—monthly almanacs consisting of several "news stories."

Important sources for Vertov's emerging concepts were Russian Futurism and the Proletkul't theories of Aleksandr Bogdanov (1873–1928); the latter assumed the "objectively inevitable" birth of a proletarian culture to be so profoundly new that it has virtually nothing in common with all preceding class-based cultures. In the same spirit, Vertov saw a particular role for cinema as the most recent art and the only one entirely based on technology, that is, one largely independent of human physical and mental restrictions. Already at this early stage of his career Vertov formulated an increasingly hyperbolic view of the camera, concluding that it is superior to the human eye in providing a "pure" and exact image of reality, and that Soviet cinema must make conscious use of this superiority. According to Vertov, the epistemological potential of the camera makes it particularly efficient for Communist purposes, effectively eliminating personal bias and subjectivity. Cinema could thus contribute invaluable insight to the ongoing Communist exploration of the world, ultimately helping define Marxist-Leninist truth and spreading it too. In order to achieve this goal, film had to completely emancipate itself from literature and theater, which Vertov and his followers viewed as obstacles on the road to unadulterated, modern, genuinely Communist cinema.

Vertov followed the common trend toward collectivism by founding a group, with his brother Mikhail Kaufman and his wife, **Eliza-**

veta Svilova. Initially, it called itself Committee of Three (*troika*), then Cine-Eyes (*kinoki*). Vertov's iconoclastic concepts of cinema as part of a cultural revolution were put into practice in the feature-length documentaries *Forward, Soviet!* (Shagai, Soviet! 1926), *One Sixth of the World* (Shestaia chast' mira, 1926), and *The Elevenths* (Odinnadtsatyi, 1928, referring to the 11th year since the October Revolution). In order to maximize the films' emotional impact without resorting to fictionalization, the *kinoki* demonstrated an enviable inventiveness in manipulating the image—from using unexpected camera angles to a rhythmic coordination of the material through montage and intertitles.

Still, with his loud and uncompromising claims to methodological superiority over all other Soviet filmmakers, Vertov made more enemies than friends and found less and less support within the industry, despite his international reputation as one of the world's true film pioneers. Astute critics such as Ippolit Sokolov (1902–1974) pointed to violations of the director's dogmas within his own films, which partially discredited Vertov within the artistic community.

Vertov was forced to accept the invitation of the All-Ukrainian Photo-Cinema Administration (VUFKU) and moved to Kiev, where he completed his masterpiece, *Man with the Movie Camera* (Chelovek s kinoapparatom, 1929). In this feature-length cinematic poem, Vertov's theories are translated into film in the most playful and original manner. Organized by the structure of a day—awakening of a city in the morning, reaching the pinnacle of activities, and going to rest at night—and observed by actively involved cameras that never rest, the film displays an insatiable curiosity for human events ranging from birth to wedding and funeral.

Creatively responding to the challenge of emerging sound technology, Vertov suggested an original audio montage that would avoid the simple acoustic illustration of the image flow. However, this innovation added even more complexity to the cinematic texture; as a result, *Enthusiasm* (Entuziazm, aka *Symphony of Donbass*/Simfoniia Donbassa, 1930) alienated audiences, requiring multiple viewings to grasp the semantics both on the visual and audial levels.

Perhaps because of the shock from the hostile reception of *Enthusiasm* in the USSR, Vertov made a drastic turn toward linearity and comprehensibility with *Three Songs about Lenin* (Tri pesni o

Lenine, 1934), a lamentable regression both in form and message. Part of the growing idolatry of Vladimir Lenin, grandiose in tone and pathos-filled in style, this film stands in sharp, unfavorable contrast to Vertov's lively, dynamic narration of the 1920s. It is overflowing with ludicrous statements about Lenin's postmortal power as a panacea against depression and lack of productivity, although it does contain some worthwhile sequences, including two live interviews. The 1937 *Lullaby* (Kolybel'naia), Vertov's last feature-length effort, was even more bombastic and later led to accusations of cinematic totalitarianism and Stalinism that are not altogether unfounded.

Eventually Vertov's reputation as the most radical of all Soviet film avant-gardists turned into a curse, as did his earlier verbal self-righteousness and intolerance. His attempts to adjust to the new requirements defined by the Soviet establishment in the 1930s—a painful process that all leading filmmakers were undergoing—were met with fierce resistance by administrators such as **Boris Shumiatskii** and by colleagues alike; Vertov was deliberately marginalized and never given a second chance. Indeed, while most Soviet filmmakers habitually competed with each other, and such competition for Party and audience recognition could sometimes become militant in tone, no other director consistently denied the artistic and ideological legitimacy of all other filmmakers as did Vertov. He ended his days as a tragic has-been, editing dull newsreels, asking in vain for funding for larger projects, and complaining in his diaries about the countless missed opportunities in his career.

Years after Vertov's death, his work found new appreciation among the cultural left in the 1960s, particularly in France and Great Britain, and in academic circles where he is sometimes viewed as a martyr of modern cinema. Ironically, in post-Communist Russia, he has been denounced as one of the founding fathers of cinematic manipulation and totalitarian demagoguery. Filmmakers who were influenced by Vertov's art and doctrine were the so-called Riga School of Poetic Documentary, which emerged in the early 1960s with directors such as Uldis Brauns (b. 1932), Hercs Franks (Herz Frank, b. 1926), and **Jūris Podnieks**.

Vertov's brother Boris Kaufman (1906–1980) studied in France and became a leading Hollywood cinematographer; a third brother,

Mikhail Kaufman (1897–1980), after splitting with Vertov in 1929, pursued a successful career as documentary filmmaker.

Other films: *The Battle near Tsaritsyn* (Boi pod Tsaritsinym, 1919); *The Trial of the Social Revolutionaries* (Protsess eserov, 1922); *Sergo Ordzhonikidze* (1937); *Blood for Blood, Death for Death!* (Krov' za krov', smert' za smert'! 1941).

VGIK, acronym of Vserossiiskii Gosudarstvennyi Institut Kinematografii, the All-Russian State Institute of Cinema. VGIK, the world's first State Film School (*goskinoshkola*), was officially founded on 1 September 1919 in Moscow under the directorship of renowned filmmaker **Vladimir Gardin**. Later that year, budding avant-garde artist **Lev Kuleshov** joined the school's faculty, forming his own workshop for the development and practice of innovative approaches to all aspects of filmmaking. Other faculty were the cameramen **Eduard Tissé**, **Aleksandr Levitskii**, and Grigorii Giber (1891–1951), as well as screenwriter Valentin Turkin (1887–1957). Faculty and students were involved in the production of *agitka* films such as Kuleshov's short *At the Red Front* (Na krasnom fronte, 1920), *In the Days of Struggle* (V dni bor'by, 1920, starring **Vsevolod Pudovkin**), and Gardin's full-length feature *Hammer and Sickle* (Serp i molot, aka V trudnye dni, 1921). In 1922, the school was restructured as a conglomerate of workshops (*masterskie*) specializing in film direction (since 1924), screenwriting, acting, and set design. Another transformation took place in 1925 when the institution was named State College of Cinema (Gosudarstvennyi tekhnikum kinematografii, GTK). The first graduates received their diplomas in May 1927, among them 71 actors and actresses, 15 directors, and 19 cinematographers. On 5 August 1930, the school became the State Institute of Cinema, and in 1934, the All-Soviet State Institute of Cinema (Vsesoiuznyi gosudarstvennyi institut kinematografii).

Among VGIK's most respected teachers were directors **Sergei Eizenshtein**, who created a systematic curriculum for film directors in 1932, Vsevolod Pudovkin, **Aleksandr Dovzhenko, Ihor' Savchenko, Mikhail Romm, Aleksandr Zguridi, Efim Dzigan, Sergei Gerasimov, Sergei Iutkevich**, and **Sergei Bondarchuk**; actors and actresses **Boris Babochkin, Aleksei Batalov, Aleksandra**

Khokhlova, **Tamara Makarova**, and Irina Skobtseva; cinematographers **Iurii Zheliabuzhskii**, **Vladimir Nil'sen**, **Anatolii Golovnia**, **Leonid Kosmatov**, **Aleksandr Gal'perin**, and **Boris Volchek**; **documentary** filmmaker **Roman Karmen**, **animation** director **Ivan Ivanov-Vano**, and screenwriters **Evgenii Gabrilovich** and **Aleksei Kapler**. Many of them left a distinct mark on younger generations of Soviet filmmakers; some even founded veritable "schools." Film-specific acting was taught by such prominent actors and actresses as Boris Babochkin, **Boris Chirkov**, and Tamara Makarova. In some cases, the institute provided ostracized avant-gardists, including Kuleshov and his wife, Aleksandra Khokhlova, a venue to pass on their insights to new generations of Russian and international film artists. Although the curriculum was heavily politicized on the surface, the school managed to familiarize its students with the true achievements of world cinema and imbue them with a genuine passion for filmmaking. Thus, many VGIK graduates retain a nostalgic love and gratitude for this institution, its teachers, and benevolent atmosphere. Among the school's foreign, internationally renowned teachers was Hungarian-German film theorist Béla Bálasz; among foreign VGIK graduates are Hungarian director Martha Mészáros and East German filmmaker Konrad Wolf. VGIK also has a prestigious department of film criticism.

In 1986, the institute was given the name of one of its most influential pedagogues, Sergei Gerasimov. In 1992, the "Soviet" part of its title was replaced by "Russian." In 2003, a Department of Animation and Multimedia was founded. The school continues its tradition of hiring leading film artists to its faculty, among them actor Aleksei Batalov, cinematographer **Vadim Iusov**, screenwriter Iurii Arabov, and animator **Andrei Khrzhanovskii**.

VIDOV, OLEG BORISOVICH (b. 11 June 1943, Filimonki, Moscow district). Russian-American actor, director, and producer. Vidov was a construction worker, forest ranger, and locksmith before enrolling in **Boris Babochkin**'s acting workshop at the Soviet State Film School **VGIK**, from which he graduated in 1966. In 1974, Vidov again enrolled in VGIK, this time in the Directing Department, where he studied with **Efim Dzigan** and graduated in 1978.

Vidov made his movie debut with a small part in **Aleksei Saltykov** and **Aleksandr Mitta**'s popular **children's film** *My Friend, Kol'ka!* (Drug moi, Kol'ka! 1961). Fair-haired, blue-eyed, and athletic, Vidov specialized in romantic and adventurous roles and soon became the object of semiofficial, cultish admiration for millions of mostly female viewers. He won enormous popularity with the lead in **Vladimir Vainshtok**'s pseudo-Western *Horseman without Head* (Vsadnik bez golovy, 1973). However, at times he was cast in more artistically ambitious pictures, for example, as Prince Gvidon in **Aleksandr Ptushko**'s *The Tale of Tsar Saltan* (Skazka o tsare Saltane, 1966), and in Mitta's Soviet-Japanese love story *Moscow, My Love* (Moskva, liubov' moia, 1974). Judged unfit for psychological roles, Vidov did excel in numerous genre fare, from Cold War thrillers such as *Mission in Kabul* (Missiia v Kabule, 1971) to slapstick **comedies** (*Gentlemen of Luck*/Dzhentel'meny udachi, 1972) and musicals.

Vidov was one of the few Soviet actors with permission to work abroad. Thus, he played the male lead, Viking Hagbard, in Danish director Gabriel Axel's *Red Shawl* (Den rode kappe, 1967) and was prominently cast in the Yugoslav-Italian coproduction *Battle at the River Neretva* (Bitka na Neretvi, 1969) by Veljko Bulajić. In 1983, while on location in Yugoslavia, Vidov escaped to Austria. He moved to Hollywood and—an exception among expatriate Russian actors—was able to continue his acting career. Among his roles are a militia man in *Red Heat* (1988), Otto in *Wild Orchid* (1989), and Soviet UN Ambassador Valerian Zorin in *Thirteen Days* (2001). Together with his American wife, Vidov owns the company Films by Jove, which acquired the rights to numerous Soviet **animated** films, distributing them in the United States. In the 1990s, he was entangled in legal battles over these copyrights.

Vidov was named Merited Artist of the Russian Federation in 1974.

Other films: *Karolina of Rijeka* (Karolina Riječka, 1961, Yugoslavia); *The Ivanov Family* (Sem'ia Ivanovykh, 1975); *The Demidovs* (Demidovy, 1983, TV); *The West Wing* (2005, TV).

VISKOVSKII, VIACHESLAV KAZIMIROVICH (b. 1881, St. Petersburg–d. 1933, Moscow). Russian director, scriptwriter, and actor.

Viskovskii worked as a stage actor and director before turning to cinema in 1913, first as a screenwriter.

Viskovskii made his directing debut with *The White Colonnade* (Belaia kolonada, 1915) and subsequently churned out literary adaptations such as *First Love* (Pervaia liubov', 1915, from Ivan Turgenev's novella), **comedies** such as *Happiness Is for Fools* (Durakam schast'e, 1915), and numerous melodramas, including *The Last Tango* (Poslednee tango, 1918) and *The Woman Who Invented Love* (Zhenshchina, kotoraia izobrela liubov', 1919).

Viskovskii demonstrated his approval of the bourgeois February Revolution with *Under the Ruins of the Empire* (Pod oblomkami samoderzhaviia, 1917) and *The Great Days of the Russian Revolution from 28 February to 4 March 1917* (Velikie dni rossiiskoi revoliutsii s 28 fevralia po 4 marta 1917 goda, doc.). In 1919 (other sources: 1922), he immigrated to the United States and worked in Hollywood in various capacities. Viskovskii returned to Russia in 1923 and made traditional genre films with an ideological icing, including *Red Partisans* (Krasnye partizany, 1924), *The Ninth of January* (Deviatoe ianvaria, 1925)—which contained some interesting mass scenes illustrating the political turmoil of 1905—and *Minaret of Death* (Minaret smerti, 1925), produced for **Uzbekfilm Studio** in Tashkent. Yet despite their blatant political opportunism, these films were torn apart by Communist critics as "petit-bourgeois," "unhealthy," and "decadent." After a few more attempts to combine mass appeal with politically correct messages—*The Mullah's Third Wife* (Tret'ia zhena mully, 1928) and *Kabu* (1929)—Viskovskii was prevented from further directing and made a living as an acting teacher and supporting actor, appearing in **Fridrikh Ermler**'s *A Fragment of the Empire* (Oblomok imperii, 1929) and *The Fugitive* (Bezhenets, 1932).

Other films: *Elena Pavlovna and Little Sergei* (Elena Pavlovna i Serezhka, 1915); *Thou Shall Not Kill* (Ne ubii, 1916); *The Battalion of the First of March* (Batal'on pervogo marta, 1917); *Tea* (Chai, 1924).

VITSIN, GEORGII MIKHAILOVICH (b. 23 April 1917, Petrograd–d. 23 October 2001, Moscow). Russian actor. Vitsin enrolled in the Vakhtangov Theater School in Moscow in 1934 but switched to the Second Moscow Art Theater (MKhAT) studio the following year. Although he subsequently was active in a number of minor theater troupes, the actor's fame is based exclusively on his more than 100 film roles.

Vitsin's characteristic lanky physique and face can be spotted among the dancing *oprichniks* in the second part of **Sergei Eizenshtein**'s *Ivan the Terrible* (Ivan Groznyi, 1943–45)—his screen debut. Because of a likeness to Nikolai Gogol', he portrayed the writer in several biopics such as **Grigorii Kozintsev**'s *Belinskii* (1951). **Semen Timoshenko** cast Vitsin in his first lead role, Vasia Vesnushkin, in the popular soccer tale *The Substitute Player* (Zapasnoi igrok, 1954), creating the image of a noble loser who is naïve and lacking social skills.

Vitsin became a national celebrity with the part of "Coward" (Trus) in **Leonid Gaidai**'s 1961 **comedy** shorts *Barbos the Dog and an Unusual Cross-Country Race* (Pes Barbos i neobychainyi kross) and *Bootleggers* (Samogonshchiki). In these fast-paced, hilarious slapstick satires, the actor portrayed a self-pitying, daydreaming, often victimized pseudointellectual. Part of a peculiar trio that consisted of "Coward," "Booby" (Balbes, played by **Iurii Nikulin**), and "Experienced" (Byvalyi, performed by Evgenii Morgunov), Vitsin's character somewhat resembles Stan Laurel's screen persona. "Coward" also appeared in Gaidai's cult blockbusters *Operation "Y" and Other Adventures of Shurik* (Operatsiia 'Y' i drugie prikliucheniia Shurika, 1965) and *Prisoner of the Caucasus* (aka *Kidnapping Caucasian Style*/Kavkazskaia plennitsa, 1966). In later years, Gaidai gave Vitsin funny yet more differentiated roles in *The Twelve Chairs* (Dvenadtsat' stul'ev, 1971, from the rogue novel by Il'f and Petrov), *This Can't Be True!* (Ne mozhet byt'! 1975), and *Borrowing Matchsticks* (Za spichkami, 1980). Other directors used the actor's immense popularity to more superficial comedic effect. Vitsin was also cast in fairy tales where he portrayed picture-book "baddies," for example, in **Aleksandr Ptushko**'s *The Tale of Lost Time* (Skazka o poteriannom vremeni, 1964). His characteristic nasal voice can be heard in countless **animated** films.

Vitsin was named People's Artist of the USSR in 1990.

Other films: *She Loves You* (Ona vas liubit, 1956); *The Bridegroom from the Otherworld* (Zhenikh s togo sveta, 1958); *Bal'zaminov's*

Wedding (Zhenit'ba Bal'zaminova, 1964); *Gentlemen of Luck* (Dzhentel'meny udachi, 1972); *Good Guys* (Bravye parni, 1993).

VOLCHEK, BORIS IZRAILEVICH (b. 6 December 1905, Vitebsk–d. 15 May 1974, Moscow). Russian cinematographer, director, screenwriter, and pedagogue. In his youth, Volchek worked as a film projectionist in Vitebsk. The local trade union sent him to Moscow, where he studied at the State Film College (later renamed **VGIK**) in 1927–1931.

Following two insignificant projects, Volchek made a name for himself with **Mikhail Romm**'s peculiar adaptation of Guy de Maupassant's story *Boule de Suif* (Pyshka, 1934), one of the last Russian silent pictures. Its ideological coloration as an antibourgeois social satire was strongly supported by the domination of sharply focused, close shots of a group of passengers within the minimal space of a carriage. Volchek continued to work with Romm, refining his art of cinematic portraiture and developing lighting techniques that aimed to achieve three-dimensional depth. Volchek added a strong documentary flavor to the celebrated dilogy *Lenin in October* (Lenin v Oktiabre, 1937) and *Lenin in 1918* (Lenin v 1918 godu, 1939), providing semifictitious, hagiographic plots with a degree of authenticity. Such stylization, inspired by historical photos and newsreels, became even more characteristic of Romm's Cold War pamphlets *The Russian Question* (Russkii vopros, 1947) and *Secret Mission* (Sekretnaia missiia, 1950), in which Western nighttime cityscapes are endowed with frightening contrasts, adding to the prevailing atmosphere of Soviet paranoia and distrust toward the West. On the other hand, the surreal melancholy and poetic intimacy of the prewar drama *The Dream* (Mechta, 1941–1943) demonstrates less didactic and politically manipulative facets of Volchek's cinematography.

Volchek brilliantly filmed **Vsevolod Pudovkin**'s subversive—and unreleased—analytical look behind the scene of the Third Reich, *Murderers Are on Their Way* (Ubiitsy vykhodiat na dorogu, 1942, with Era Savel'eva) and the war drama *In the Name of the Motherland* (Vo imia rodiny, 1943), as well as **Aleksandr Zguridi**'s Jack London adaptation *White Fang* (Belyi klyk, 1944–1946).

Dissatisfied with the dependence of a cameraman, Volchek embarked on a directing career, following his last film for Romm,

Murder on Dante Street (Ubiistvo na ulitse Dante, 1956). His first independent project was the patriotic Civil War thriller *Member of the Secret Service* (Sotrudnik ChK, 1964), a smash success that attracted more than 30 million viewers. Volchek landed another critical and popular hit with *Accused of Murder* (Obviniaetsia v ubiistve, 1969). Made at **Moldova-Film Studio**, this court drama about juvenile delinquents was recognized with a USSR State Prize in 1970. Volchek's last completed film was the World War II adventure *The Commander of the Happy "Pike"* (Komandir schastlivoi "shchuki," 1973). The director also was responsible for the cinematography on the last two films.

Volchek earned high accolades with his outstanding pedagogical work. He began to teach at VGIK as a fourth-year student, in 1931. In 1943, he was promoted to the rank of full professor. Among his students were such distinct masters of cinematography as **Levan Paatashvili**, **Margarita Pilikhina**, **Georgii Rerberg**, **Vadim Derbenev**, **Yury Il'enko**, and **Petr Todorovskii**.

Volchek, who joined the Communist Party in 1925, was named Merited Artist of the RSFSR in 1958. He won three Stalin Prizes for his camera work: on Romm's *Person #217* (aka *Girl No. 217/ Chelovek No. 217*, 1944), *The Russian Question* (1947), and *Secret Mission* (1950).

Other films: *Celebrity* (Znamenitost', 1929); *The Thirteen* (Trinadtsat', 1937); *Vladimir Il'ich Lenin* (1948, doc.).

VOLONTIR, MIHAI [some sources list name and patronymic as Mikhail Ermolaevich] (b. 9 March 1934, Glinjeni, Rezina district). Moldovan actor. Volontir studied at Orhei Pedagogical Institute in 1952–1955 before joining the troupe of the National Theater of Music and Drama Vasile Alecsandri in Balti (Bel'tsy) in 1957.

Volontir made his screen debut with the lead role of the brave, rebellious soldier Ivan Turbinca in the parabolic **comedy** *Gatekeeper Wanted* (Se cauta un paznic/Nuzhen privratnik, 1967), from Ion Creanga's story. He followed it with another lead, pilot Mihai Adam, in **Emil Loteanu**'s homage to the Civil War in Spain, *This Moment* (Aceasta clipa/Eto mgnovenie, 1968). The latter role, as well as the part of Ilie in **Valeriu Gajiu**'s *Ten Winters for Just One Summer* (Zece ierni penrtu o vara/Desiat' zim za odno leto, 1970) and an episodic part in **Aleksandr Stolper**'s World War II drama *The Fourth* (Chetvertyi, 1972), brought Volontir wide attention. Lithuanian filmmaker **Vytautas Žalakevičius** cast him as the Latin American revolutionary Carlos in his political thriller *That Sweet Word: Liberty!* (Eto sladkoe slovo—svoboda, 1973) and in *Centaurs* (Kentaurai/Kentavry, 1978). One of Volontir's most prestigious screen accomplishments is the title role in the biopic *Dimitrie Cantemir* (Dmitrii Kantemir, 1973) about the 18th-century enlightener and statesman.

Volontir's manly charisma, conveying courage, honesty, seriousness, and a noble mind-set, made him a preferred candidate for the portrayal of exemplary Red Army officers in ultrapatriotic blockbusters such as *Response Move* (Otvetnyi khod, 1981) and *Incident at Map-Grid 36–80* (Sluchai v kvadrate 36–80, 1982). The actor often embodied police investigators or professionals with high moral standards, especially in contemporary dramas, including *The Accusation* (Obvinenie, 1984) and *I Am Responsible for You* (Ia za tebia otvechaiu, 1984). He also gained huge popularity as Budulai in the miniseries *The Gypsy* (Tiganul/Tsygan, 1979, TV) and its sequel, *Budulai's Return* (Vozvrashchenie Budulaia, 1985). Among his latest films is the international coproduction about the Spanish Civil War *Faithfulness We Pledge* (Vernymi ostanemsia, 1989) and the American-Russian-Moldovan *Am I Guilty* (Vinovata li ia, 1992), directed by Nicolae Ghibu, about the disastrous effects of alcoholism on a family.

Volontir was named People's Artist of the USSR in 1984.

Other films: *Steepness* (Povirnisul/Krutizna, 1970); *Bridges* (Podurile/Mosty, 1973); *Be Happy, Julia* (Fii fericita, Iulia/Bud' schastliva, Iuliia, 1983); *A Knock on the Door* (Stuk v dver', 1989); *Chandra* (2006). *See also* MOLDOVAN CINEMA.

VYSOTSKII, VLADIMIR SEMENOVICH (b. 25 January 1938, Moscow–d. 25 July 1980, Moscow). Russian actor, poet, composer, and singer. Vysotskii, the son of a Red Army officer, enrolled in the studio school of the Moscow Art Theater (MKhAT), graduating in 1960. He joined the troupe of the Taganka Theater in 1964 and became one of its legendary stars. In 1961, in small private circles, Vysotskii began to perform his own songs, many of which were later distributed through countless homemade tapes. His career as a guitar-playing singer in clubs and on stage across the Soviet Union started in 1965 and propelled him to superstardom. But Vysotskii's status remained ambiguous: continuously harassed and humiliated by cultural watchdogs, he was revered by tens of millions across all social strata, including the highest echelons of the Soviet establishment—and even more idolized after his untimely passing from a heart attack.

The actor made his screen debut with the minute part of a student in Vasilii Ordynskii's contemporary tale *Girls of the Same Age* (Sverstnitsy, 1959). **Frunze Dovlatyan**'s love story *Dima Gorin's Career* (Kar'era Dimy Gorina, 1961) and the antireligious *The Sinner* (Greshnitsa, 1962) won him a reputation as a reliable supporting performer whose hoarse voice and rough, virile charm appealed to audiences of all ages. In *The Vertical* (Vertikal', 1967), as radio operator Volodia, Vysotskii also sang his own songs, which added to the film's popularity. Thereafter, many directors used Vysotskii songs as leitmotivs, setting a romantic, sometimes fatalistic, but usually unsentimental tone. As an actor, he was also efficient in World War II tales such as **Aleksandr Stolper**'s *The Fourth* (Chetvertyi, 1973) in which he portrayed an American war correspondent. Despite the official distrust toward Vysotskii and his out-of-control fame, the artist continuously displayed political loyalty, including in entertaining revolutionary adventures such as *A Dangerous Tour* (Opasnye gastroli, 1969) about a theater troupe that helps smuggle Marxist literature preparing the Bolshevik Revolution.

Sadly, few filmmakers were able to fully assess Vysotskii's unique artistic potential, among them **Kira Muratova**, who cast him in *Brief Encounters* (Korotkie vstrechi, 1968) as the geologist Maksim; **Iosif Kheifits**, who gave him the part of von Koren in his Anton Chekhov adaptation *A Bad Good Person* (Plokhoi khoroshii chelovek, aka Duel', 1973); and **Mikhail Shveitser**, in whose *Little Tragedies* (Malen'kie tragedii, 1980) he brilliantly portrays Don Juan. Vysotskii also excelled in the lead role of Ibrahim Hannibal in **Aleksandr Mitta**'s *The Tale of How Tsar Peter Married His Moor* (Skaz pro to, kak tsar' Petr arapa zhenil, 1976); the character's noble outsider status likely resonated with his own life experience. However, features of Vysotskii's persona such as existential despair, obsession with alcohol and drugs, and self-destructiveness were kept out of his films. Arguably, **Stanislav Govorukhin** gave Vysotskii the finest chance to showcase his acting capability in the historical miniseries *The Meeting Place Cannot Be Changed* (Mesto vstrechi izmenit' nel'zia, 1979, TV). In 1987, Vysotskii was awarded a posthumous USSR State Prize for that performance.

Vysotskii is buried at Vagan'kovskoe cemetery. The houses in which he lived in the 1950s (Bol'shaia Karetnaia Street 15) and after 1975 (Malaia Gruzinskaia ulitsa, 28) carry memorial plaques. Vysotskii was married to French movie star Marina Vlady. One of his sons is actor and film producer Nikita Vysotskii (b. 1964).

Other films: *Our House* (Nash dom, 1965); *The Escape of Mr. MacKinley* (Begstvo mistera Mak-Kinli, 1975).

– W –

WAR AND PEACE (Voina i mir, 1962–67). **Mosfilm Studio**. Four parts, 427 min., color. Directed by **Sergei Bondarchuk**. Script: Vasilii Solov'ev, Sergei Bondarchuk. Cinematography: Anatolii Petritskii. Music: **Viacheslav Ovchinnikov**. Cast: **Sergei Bondarchuk** (P'er Bezukhov), **Viacheslav Tikhonov** (Andrei Bolkonskii), **Liudmila Savel'eva** (Natasha Rostova), Vasilii Stanitsyn (Il'ia Rostov), **Oleg Tabakov** (Nikolai Rostov), **Anatolii Ktorov** (Nikolai Bolkonskii), **Antonina Shuranova** (Princess Mar'ia), **Anastasiia Vertinskaia** (Liza Bolkonskaia), **Aleksandr Borisov** (Uncle Rostov), **Nonna Mordiukova** (Anis'ia Fedorova), **Vasilii Lanovoi** (Anatole), Irina Skobtseva (Elen), **Oleg Efremov** (Dolokhov), **Galina Kravchenko**, **Nikolai Rybnikov** (Denisov), Boris Zakhava (Kutuzov), **Vladislav Strzhel'chik** (Napoleon), **Andrei Smirnov**. Part 1: *Andrei Bolkonskii*. Premiere: 14 March 1966; Part 2: *Natasha Rostova*. Premiere: 3 July 1966; Part 3: *The Year 1812*. Premiere: 21 July 1967; Part 4: *P'er Bezukhov*. Premiere: 4 November 1967

In deliberate competition with the 1956 U.S. screen version of Lev Tolstoi's epic (helmed by King Vidor), in 1961, Sergei Bondarchuk was given the assignment to direct Russia's most ambitious film project ever, winning the race against more experienced directors such as **Ivan Pyr'ev** and **Sergei Gerasimov**. With unlimited support from the USSR Minister of Culture Ekaterina Furtseva and the Minister of Defense Marshall Grechko, the director could rely on the country's best performers for dozens of main roles, in addition to 120,000 extras, including the legendary 11th Cavalry Regiment of the Soviet Army, which was specifically created for this film. The shooting lasted from 7 September 1962 to 28 October 1966. In the Soviet Union alone, the first and second parts attracted 58 and 36 million viewers, respectively, recovering the budget of 8.2 million rubles many times over. Bondarchuk's monumental achievement was recognized with the 1968 Academy Award for Best Foreign Picture as its crowning sign of international recognition. It became a sensational record-breaker in regards to budget, number of extras, and production time, overshadowing its genuine artistic merits for years to come.

WE ARE FROM KRONSHTADT (My iz Kronshtadta, 1936). **Mosfilm Studio**. 91 min., b/w. Directed by **Efim Dzigan**. Script: Vsevolod Vishnevskii. Cinematography: Naum Naumov-Strazh. Music: **Nikolai Kriukov**. Cast: Vasilii Zaichikov, Georgii Bushuev, **Oleg Zhakov**, Nikolai Ivakin, Raisa Esipova, Petr Kirillov, Petr Sobolevskii. Premiere: 20 March 1936.

In October 1919, Petrograd is under siege from the White Army under General Nikolai Iudenich. The Bolshevik Martynov (Zaichikov), a commissar, leads a unit of Kronshtadt sailors who heroically fight off the White Army attacks. Yet the sailors' resistance is finally broken, and all of them are tossed into the sea with a stone around their neck. Only Artem Balashov (Bushuev), a former undisciplined adventurer and womanizer, manages to free himself underwater and bring help from Kronshtadt. The White Army unit is crushed, and its captured soldiers and officers are executed in the same way as the Kronshtadt sailors before them.

WHITE SUN OF THE DESERT (Beloe solntse pustyni, 1969). **Mosfilm Studio**. 85 min., color. Directed by **Vladimir Motyl'**. Script: Valentin Ezhov, **Rustam Ibrahimbekov**, **Mark Zakharov**. Cinematography: Eduard Rozovskii. Music: **Isaak Shvarts**. Cast: Anatolii Kuznetsov, **Pavel Luspekaev**, Spartak Mishulin, Kakhi Kavsadze, Raisa Kurkina. Premiere: 30 March 1970.

In the 1920s, Fedor Sukhov (Kuznetsov), a good-natured Red Army soldier who dreams of returning home to his wife in his native village, fights Muslim rebels in Turkmenistan. Shortly before his discharge, Sukhov is ordered to accompany a group of liberated harem women who once belonged to a rebel leader named Black Abdullah (Kavsadze) to the town of Pedjent. Greatly outnumbered by Abdullah's men, Sukhov fights them heroically, supported only by the melancholic but physically strong Customs officer Vereshchagin (Luspekaev). Finally, Sukhov shoots Abdullah, while Vereshchagin, having killed several enemies of the Soviet order, dies in an explosion on a boat.

– Y –

YARMATOV, KAMIL [Russian sources list the patronymic Yarmatovich] (b. 2 May 1903, Kanibadam, Ferghana–d. 17 November 1978, Moscow). Tadjik-Uzbek director, screenwriter, actor, and film administrator. Yarmatov fought with the Bolsheviks in Central Asia in the early 1920s. He then became an actor and studied directing under Valentin Turkin at the Moscow State Film School (GTK, later **VGIK**), graduating in 1931. Earlier, Yarmatov had gained some screen experience, playing a White Army officer in the 1927 revolutionary potboiler *The Jackals of Ravat* (Shakaly Ravata), as well as the lead in Czeslav Sabinskii's *The Last Bek* (Poslednii bek, 1930), about the struggle against the so-called *basmatchi*, anti-Soviet resistance fighters commonly denounced as gangsters.

Upon graduation, Yarmatov moved to Dushanbe in Tadjikistan and joined the staff of Tadjikkino (**Tadjikfilm Studio**). As director, he debuted with *Far Away at the Border* (Daleko na granitse, 1931), followed by the semi**documentary** *Right of Honor* (Pochetnoe pravo, 1932), and *The Émigré* (Emigrant, 1934) in which he also played the lead, a poor peasant who overcomes political misperceptions rooted in feudalism and recognizes the benefits of working under the Soviets. In *Friends Meet Anew* (Druz'ia vstrechaiutsia vnov', 1939), Yarmatov describes the transformation of the desert into blossoming, industrialized land, yet the picture also reeks heavily of Stalinist paranoia, exposing a seemingly loyal comrade and friend as a foreign undercover agent who plans to blow up the life-giving dam.

Subsequently moving to Uzbekistan and working as a newsreel and dubbing director, Yarmatov made his most successful picture, the monumental biopic *Alisher Navoi* (1948), which won him a Stalin Prize. Navoi (1441–1501), an acclaimed poet and the founder of Uzbek literature, was also a statesman. The director was able to give his filmic portrait a psychological complexity that was unusual in those years. In 1952, Yarmatov directed a film for children, *Pakhta-oi*, an inventive tale mixing realistic elements with fantasy about the hardships of overcoming the forces of nature to produce cotton. *Avicenna* (1957) convincingly portrays the medieval Persian genius—doctor, poet, philosopher—and his life during foreign invasion. Yarmatov's films with contemporary subjects were considered far less successful. As a result, Yarmatov continually returned to revolutionary themes, for example, in the epic *Storm over Asia* (Buria nad Aziei, 1965).

Yarmatov, who is credited as one of the founders of **Tadjik** and **Uzbek cinema**, joined the Communist Party in 1930 and was a longtime member of the Supreme Soviet of Uzbekistan. He won some of the Soviet Union's highest official distinctions: the title People's Artist of the USSR in 1959 and Hero of Socialist Labor in 1973. **Uzbekfilm Studio**, of which he was appointed executive artistic director in 1957, was named after him in 1979.

Other films: *We Shall Prevail* (My pobedim, 1941); *When the Roses Blossom* (Kogda tsvetut rozy, 1959); *Horsemen of the Revolution* (Vsadniki revoliutsii, 1968); *Alone among People* (Odna sredi liudei, 1973); *Years Faraway and Close* (Dalekie blizkie gody, 1977).

YOUNG GUARD, THE (Molodaia gvardiia, 1948). **Gor'kii Studio for Children's and Youth Films**. Two parts, 89 and 81 min., b/w. Directed by **Sergei Gerasimov**. Script: Sergei Gerasimov from Aleksandr Fadeev's 1946–1948 novel. Cinematography: Vladimir Rappoport. Music: **Dmitrii Shostakovich**. Cast: **Tamara Makarova**, Viktor Khokhriakov, Vladimir Ivanov, Inna Makarova, Sergei Gurzo, **Nonna Mordiukova**, **Sergei Bondarchuk**, **Viacheslav Tikhonov**, Klara Luchko, **Georgii Iumatov**, **Sergei Komarov**. Premiere: 11 October 1948.

Following the occupation of the industrial city of Krasnodon by Nazi troops in 1942, members of the Communist Youth organization Komsomol decide to form an underground resistance group. They establish contact with a nearby partisan unit and receive their orders from Communist Party leaders. Their activities include spreading leaflets, executing traitors, freeing people to be deported to Germany, and setting administrative buildings afire. However, one member is arrested, and while being tortured, gives away the names of the others. Oleg Koshevoi (Ivanov), Ul'iana Gromova (Mordiukova), and the other Young Guard members die martyrs' deaths.

– Z –

ZAKARIADZE [other spelling: Zaqariadze], **SERGO** [some sources add the patronymic Aleksandrovich] (b. 1 July 1909, Baku–d. 14 April 1971, Moscow). Georgian actor. Zakariadze studied philosophy at the University of Tbilisi before joining the troupe of the Shota Rustaveli Theater in 1926. After switching to Kote Mardjanishvili's theater in 1928, Zakariadze returned in 1956 to the Rustaveli Theater.

In cinema, Zakariadze debuted in **Siko Dolidze**'s contemporary drama *The Last Crusaders* (Ukanaskueli djvarosuebi/Poslednie krestonostsy, 1934) in the lead role of Torgvai, a farmhand protesting against cruel traditions. The film, which is rather naïve and simplistic in delivering its pro-Communist and anti-tribal message, gave the actor little opportunity to demonstrate his abilities beyond static poses and declamatory statements. **Mikheil Chiaureli**'s grandiose 17th-century biopic *Georgii Zaakadze* (1942–1943), **Vladimir Petrov**'s *Kutuzov* (1944)—with Zakariadze as Prince Bagration—and **Sergei Iutkevich**'s *Albania's Great Warrior, Skanderberg* (Velikii voin Albanii Skanderberg, 1953) all use Zakariadze's lionesque looks to great monumental effect, although none of them allowed the artist to differentiate his schematically negative or positive characters. Dolidze also featured the actor in *Dariko* (1937), *Friendship* (Megobobra/Druzhba, 1940), *Lake Paliastomi* (Paliastomi, 1963), and *Encounter with the Past* (Shekhvedra tsarsultan/Vstrecha s proshlym, 1966). His *Day Last, Day First* (Dge pirveli, dge ukanaskueli/Den' poslednii, den' pervyi, 1960), about a retiring mail carrier who introduces his young successor to the peculiarities of his clients, is rather typical of Zakariadze's later works in which he conveyed an aura of stoicism, wisdom, and bittersweet resignation toward human nature.

Rezo Chkheidze—with whom Zakariadze first worked on *Seashore Path* (Zgvis biliki/Morskaia tropa, 1963)—entrusted the actor with his most famous role as Giorgi Makharashvili in the tragic antiwar picture *Father of a Soldier* (Djariskatsis mama/Otets soldata, 1965), which became a national and international triumph. Among other notable achievements in Zakariadze's career were the role of Dr. Levan in **Georgii Daneliia**'s *Don't Grieve* (Ar daidardo/Ne goriui!, 1969) and Marshall Blücher in **Sergei Bondarchuk**'s *Waterloo* (1970).

Zakariadze was named People's Artist of the USSR in 1958. He received Stalin Prizes in 1946 and 1952 and a Lenin Prize in 1966. He was a member of the Supreme Soviet of the USSR from 1966 until his passing.

Other films: *Motherland* (Samshoblo/Rodina, 1937); *Soon There Will Be Spring* (Male gazapkhuli mova/Skoro budet vesna, 1967).

ZAKHAROV, MARK ANATOL'EVICH (b. 13 October 1933, Moscow). Russian director and screenwriter. Zakharov studied acting at the State Theater Institute (GITIS) in Moscow, graduating in 1955. He subsequently worked as an actor and director in a number of theaters in Perm' and Moscow before being appointed chief director of the Theater of the Lenin Komsomol (Lenkom) in 1973.

On stage, Zakharov's directorial style is energetic and mobile, blending musical elements with political jokes in an allegorical or melodramatic framework; his films, mostly made for television, share similar characteristics. Zakharov debuted with *The Train Stops for Two Minutes* (Stoianka poezda dve minuty, 1972, codirected with Aleksandr Orlov), a **comedy**—adorned by Alla Pugacheva songs—about a Muscovite transplanted into the provinces, where he finds his true love. On screen, Zakharov consistently delivered quality entertainment with some intelligent twists, a mixture that gained him the lasting affection of millions of Russian viewers who are grateful for the quotable punch lines and more than willing to overlook the films' theatricality and visual blandness. In cult movies such as *An Ordinary Miracle* (Obyknovennoe chudo, 1978), *That Very Munchhausen* (Tot samyi Miunkhgauzen, 1979), *A House Built by Swift* (Dom, kotoryi postroil Svift, 1983), and *The Formula of Love* (Formula liubvi, 1984), motifs of world literature are wittily adapted so as to relate to Soviet society. The director focuses on the clever dialogues, mostly authored by Grigorii Gorin (1940–2000) and inspired by the adaptation principles of Evgenii Shvarts (1896–1958), which provide performers with countless opportunities to show their versatility without striving for psychological subtlety.

Zakharov's only theatrical release, the allegory *To Kill the Dragon* (Ubit' drakona, 1989), never found a continuation; with the demise of the USSR, the genre division between television and cinema became more sharply marked, and he withdrew from film completely.

Zakharov also made some important contributions as a screenwriter, especially for director **Vladimir Motyl'** on *White Sun of the Desert* (Beloe solntse pustyni, 1970) and *Star of Captivating Bliss* (Zvezda plenitel'nogo schast'ia, 1975), which are close to his own preferred blend of witty, heroic historical saga and melodrama.

Zakharov was named Merited Artist of the RSFSR in 1977 and People's Artist of the USSR in 1991. As his theater productions often demonstrate a taste for political polemics, it came as no surprise when during Mikhail Gorbachev's perestroika the celebrated director got actively involved in reform politics, particularly as a member of the Supreme Soviet of the USSR in 1989–1991. His daughter, Aleksandra Zakharova (b. 1962), is a stage and screen actress.

Other films: *Wake up and Sing* (Prosnis' i poi, 1974, TV).

ŽALAKEVIČIUS, VYTAUTAS PRANO (b. 14 April 1930, Kaunas– d. 12 November 1996, Vilnius). Lithuanian director, screenwriter, and film executive. Žalakevičius studied engineering in Kaunas but switched to directing at the Soviet State Film School **VGIK** under **Mikheil Chiaureli**, graduating in 1956. His diploma film was an 11-minute **comedy** about a Lithuanian impostor, *The Drowned Man* (Skenduolis, 1957).

After his feature-length debut, the comedy *Before It's Too Late* (Kol nevelu/Poka ne pozdno, 1958, codirected with I. Fogel'man), Žalakevičius surprised audiences with a respectable attempt at film noir—a novelty in Soviet cinema—*Adam Wants to Be a Man* (Adomas nori buti zmogumi/Adam khochet byt' chelovekom, 1959). Set in the petit-bourgeois milieu of prewar Lithuania, it possesses the characteristic strengths and also the weaknesses of Žalakevičius's artistry: a suspenseful plot, ambivalent characters, and an implicit Communist viewpoint that to a certain degree distorts historical reality. In the psychological thriller *Chronicle of One Day* (Vienos dienos kronika/Khronika odnogo dnia, 1963), Žalakevičius further developed his predilection for intimate drama unfolding within strict spatial limitations yet reflecting broader societal tendencies. While these films did reasonably well at the box office, the true breakthrough for the filmmaker came with his next project, *Nobody Wanted to Die* (Nekas nenorejo mirti/Nikto ne khotel umirat', 1965), a story about the violent establishment of Soviet power in a Lithuanian village unleashing massive cruelties and tearing apart families. The film's artistic quality was undeniable, even though its fundamentally pro-Soviet stance made it more popular outside Lithuania than within (it won Žalakevičius a USSR State Prize in 1967); critic Sergei Kudriavtsev aptly compared its innate ambiguity to Andrzei Wajda's 1958 *Ashes and Diamond*.

Žalakevičius was subsequently invited to direct two major pictures at **Mosfilm Studio**. Inspired by the events in Chile in 1973, they were devoted to the political struggle in some vaguely defined Latin American country. *That Sweet Word: Liberty!* (Eto sladkoe slovo—svoboda, 1973) and *Centaurs* (Kentaurai/Kentavry, 1978) boast suspenseful plots and are visually elegant but had scarce relevance for Soviet viewers at the time and seem strangely contrived and cold today. Following the fine Anton Chekhov adaptation *Story of an Unknown Person* (Rasskaz neizvestnogo cheloveka, 1980)—made exclusively with Russian actors—the versatile Žalakevičius returned to Vilnius as executive artistic director of the **Lithuanian Film Studio**, a position he had held before, in 1961–1975. His last film was the Lithuanian-Russian coproduction *The Beast That Is Coming Out of the Water* (Zveris iseinantis is juros/Zver', vykhodiashchii iz moria, 1992), a gloomy, minimalist melodrama about a forbidden love relationship on the backdrop of 1917 Petrograd, adapted from a short story by Evgenii Zamiatin. The film was shown at various international festivals but found no distributor in Russia or Lithuania.

Žalakevičius also wrote numerous scripts for other directors, most often for Alimantas Grikevicius (b. 1935). In 2000, the historical film *Elzie's Life* (Elze is Giljos) by Algimantas Puipa, adapted by Žalakevičius from a classical 19th-century story by Ernst Wiechert, marked the resurrection of **Lithuanian cinema** after a decade of disorientation and near-zero output.

Upon the downfall of the USSR, Žalakevičius was attacked for his political opportunism during the Communist years—he had been a member of the Communist Party since 1961, decorated with numerous titles, medals, and prizes, and high-ranking administrative positions. However, justified as that criticism may be, it could not cloud the fact that Žalakevičius's films were the first to put Lithuania on the map of international cinema, and that he remains the country's most prominent filmmaker to this day.

Žalakevičius was named People's Artist of the Russian Federation in 1980 and of the Lithuanian SSR in 1981.

Other films: *Living Heroes* (Gyvieji didvyriai/Zhivye geroi, 1960); *The Accident* (Avariia, 1975, TV; based on a play by Friedrich Dürrenmatt); *Sunday in Hell* (Voskresnyi den' v adu, 1988; codirected with Grikevicius and A. Kvirikashvili).

ZARKHI, ALEKSANDR GRIGOR'EVICH (b. 18 February 1908, St. Petersburg–d. 27 January 1997, Moscow). Russian director and screenwriter. Zarkhi studied at the Leningrad Institute of Screen Arts in 1925–1927 and at the Film Department of the Leningrad Organization of Proletarian Culture (Proletkul't) in 1927–1928.

For more than two decades, Zarkhi's name was inseparable from that of **Iosif Kheifits**, with whom he directed numerous pictures. Their cooperation began in the late 1920s when they were in charge of a Komsomol (Communist Youth) brigade at Sevzapkino—the later **Lenfilm Studio**—in Leningrad. (For the joint films of Kheifits and Zarkhi, see the entry on Kheifits.)

Zarkhi's career after his separation from Kheifits in 1950 was not as distinguished as that of his former partner. He was less consistently prolific and not as conceptually original as Kheifits, although Zarkhi's output over the next three decades shows a similar genre versatility, including contemporary drama, revolutionary chronicle, and literary adaptation. *The Height* (Vysota, 1957) is an interesting attempt to derive visual and dramatic spark from the working-class milieu of miners in Dnepropetrovsk. Vladimir Monakhov's exquisite color cinematography and Rodion Shchedrin's energetic score make up for the overly didactic conflict between honest, selfless workers and hypocritical bureaucrats. Other noteworthy contemporary films were *People on the Bridge* (Liudi na mostu, 1959) and *My Younger*

Brother (Moi mladshii brat, 1962), adapted from Vasilii Aksenov's novel *A Ticket to the Stars* (Zvezdnyi bilet).

After **Vladimir Shveitser**'s 1962 adaptation of Lev Tolstoi's *Resurrection* (Voskresenie) and **Sergei Bondarchuk**'s *War and Peace* (Voina i mir, 1962–1967), Zarkhi made an attempt in 1968 to bring *Anna Karenina* to the screen. He gathered a star-studded cast and attracted a wide audience, yet the film generated critical debates over its liberties taken with the novel. In hindsight, much of the criticism seems exaggerated; a number of scenes stand out for their psychological penetration and authentic atmosphere.

Cities and Years (Goroda i gody, 1973) from Konstantin Fedin's novel of Communist education, was a conscientious but pedestrian effort. However, Zarkhi demonstrated that he was still able to believably re-create history in *Twenty-six Days from the Life of Dostoevskii* (26 dnei iz zhizni Dostoevskogo, 1980), a tactful and touching biopic about a particularly tumultuous period of the writer's life. Zarkhi's last picture, *Chicherin* (1986), portrays a leading Soviet diplomat and was intended to showcase the Soviet government's peace-loving efforts.

Zarkhi, who joined the Communist Party in 1948, was named People's Artist of the USSR in 1969 and Hero of Socialist Labor in 1978.

Other films: *Pavlinka* (1952); *Tale about an Unknown Actor* (Povest' o neizvestnom aktere, 1976).

ZARKHI, NATAN ABRAMOVICH (b. 1900, Orsha, Vitebsk province–d. 17 [other sources: 18] July 1935, en route from Leningrad to Moscow). Russian screenwriter. After studying in the Department of History and Philology at Moscow University, Zarkhi worked as a theater administrator, political propagandist, and history teacher in Tver' and in various military schools in Moscow (1920–1924). In 1922, he founded the Moscow Association of Playwrights.

Zarkhi began to write screenplays in 1923, gaining early fame through his cooperation with director **Vsevolod Pudovkin**. A keen sense for the inherent rules of cinematic narration allowed him to turn Maksim Gor'kii's cumbersome novel *The Mother* (1906) into a dramatic, emotionally gripping script that, in Pudovkin's aesthetically innovative realization, impressed audiences worldwide and became one of the undisputed classics of Soviet avant-garde cinema upon its release in 1925. The story's underlying didactic purpose— demonstrating the political evolution of an oppressed, politically unconscious woman into a passionate, self-sacrificing Communist banner carrier—was corroborated by numerous realistic situations. Zarkhi again applied this formula in *The End of St. Petersburg* (Konets Sankt Peterburga, 1927), solicited for the 10th anniversary of the Bolshevik Revolution and featuring a young peasant who becomes a class-conscious worker and soldier. *The End of St. Petersburg* adds more recognizable historical background to the plot so that Pudovkin regarded the picture as the first genuine historical epic in world cinema.

Zarkhi, who authored 15 screenplays and three theater plays, also worked for **Vladimir Gardin** (*The House of the Golubins*/Osobniak Golubinykh, 1924, a romance with a message about the prevention of tuberculosis), **Iurii Tarich** (*Bulat Batyr*, 1927), **Iurii Zheliabuzhskii** (*Women's Victory*/Pobeda zhenshchin, 1927), and **Evgenii Cherviakov** (*Cities and Years*/Goroda i gody, from Konstantin Fedin's novel, 1930).

As one of the first professional screenwriters, Zarkhi conceptualized the screenplay as a genre in its own right. Fragments of a monograph devoted to this topic, containing theoretical fragments about screen writing, were published in 1937.

Zarkhi was named Merited Artist of the Russian Federation in 1935. Later that year, he died in a car accident. His last script, *The Most Happy One* (Samyi schastlivyi), was directed by Pudovkin under the title *Victory* (aka *Mothers and Sons*/Pobeda, 1938).

Other films: *Poison Gas* (Giftgas, 1929, Germany); *Those Who Were Enlightened* (Te, kotorye prozreli, 1930).

ŽEBRIŪNAS, ARŪNAS [Vytautas-Arūnas] **PRANO** [other spellings: Arunas Zhebriunas] (b. 8 August 1931, Kaunas). Lithuanian director, screenwriter, and art director. Žebriūnas initially studied architecture, graduating from the State Institute of Art (now: Academy of Arts) in Vilnius in 1955. After his debut as art director on Vytautas Mikalauskas's *Blue Horizon* (Zydrasis horizontas/Goluboi gorizont, 1957), he worked in that capacity on a number of Lithuanian films.

In 1960, Žebriūnas made his directorial debut with the medium-length *The Last Shot* (Paskutinis šūvis/Poslednii vystrel), part of a prize-winning omnibus project, *Living Heroes* (Gyvieji didvyriai/ Zhivye geroi). The story of a girl who tragically loses her life in post–World War II Lithuania won high praise for its superb visual quality and richness in metaphors and symbols, marking the beginning of the filmmaker's lifelong artistic partnership with famed cameraman **Jonas Gricius**. With *The Girl and the Echo* (Paskutinė atostogų diena/Devochka i ekho, 1964, based on a short story by Russian author Iurii Nagibin [1920–1994]), Žebriūnas created his arguably most enduring work—the story of a lonesome girl endowed with a rich imagination who has created a world of her own and eventually faces both affection and betrayal. This poetic and enigmatic picture won the director prizes in Locarno in 1965 and Cannes in 1966. Unfortunately, *The Little Prince* (Mažasis princas/Malen'kii prints, 1966), from Antoine de Saint-Exupery's book—which enjoyed cult status in the USSR—did not meet viewers' high expectations. Žebriūnas switched to **documentary** shorts for several years.

In 1972, he returned to feature film with a musical **comedy**, *The Devil's Bride* (Velnio nuotaka/Chertova nevesta), telling the story of a possessive little devil who is outfoxed by a miller's daughter. This lighthearted film stands out in the director's oeuvre and is particularly interesting in its humorous usage of traditional Lithuanian folklore motifs. *Walnut Bread* (Riešutų duona/Orekhovyi khleb, 1978) is the poetic story of a man suddenly inspired by the smell of a piece of walnut bread to travel to the village of his childhood, where he attempts to find traces of an old love. *Journey to Paradise* (Kelione į rojų/Puteshestvie v rai, 1980), an adaptation of Heinrich Sundermann's famous story "The Journey to Tilsit," tells about a poor fisherman who is torn between the advances of a rich widow and the love for his loyal wife, and ends up taking his own life. Somewhat unexpectedly, Žebriūnas then helmed the television miniseries *Rich Man, Poor Man* (Turtuolis vargšas/Bogach, bedniak, 1982) from Irwin Shaw's novel. His last completed picture, *Hour of the Full Moon* (Mėnulio pilnaties metas/Chas polnoluniia, 1988), is set in the 17th century and deals with religious fanaticism and the political pressures that individuals have to endure.

Žebriūnas's films are distinguished by a superb visual taste and a nonclichéd, inquisitive approach to themes of trust and love, all handled in a quiet, rather aloof manner. In reaction to some of his films, Žebriūnas was accused of "abstract humanism," that is, of not allowing Communist principles to dominate common human values.

Žebriūnas was named Merited Artist of the Lithuanian SSR in 1979. In the 1990s, he taught film at the Lithuanian Academy of Music.

Other films: *The Cannonade* (Kanonada, 1961, codirected with **Raimondas Vabalas**); *The Last Day of Holidays* (Paskutinės atostogų dienos/Poslednii den' kanikul, 1964); *In the Forest* (Miške/V lesu, 1967; doc.); *Death and the Cherry Tree* (Mirtis ir vyšnios medis/ Smert' i vishnia, 1969, doc.); *The Nightbird* (Velnio nuotaka/Polunochnik, 1973); *The Colors of the Chameleon* (Chameleono spalvos/ Tsvet khameleona, 1978). *See also* LITHUANIAN CINEMA.

ZELENAIA, RINA [Ekaterina] **VASIL'EVNA** (b. 17 November 1902 [other sources: 1901], Tashkent–d. 1 April 1991, Moscow). Russian actress, singer, and screenwriter. Zelenaia graduated from the Moscow Theater Institute in 1919 and subsequently worked in small theaters and clubs in Petrograd, Moscow, and Odessa. Her specialty was the solo concert, in which she told stories of children, ably imitating their voices and behavior. A natural comedienne of great inventiveness and originality, Zelenaia soon gained a unique degree of popularity in the movies and on stage; her mere appearance on screen—often in grotesque outfits but still possessing sufficient social authenticity—generated cheers both among juvenile and adult audiences.

Although Zelenaia in her long career never played a lead, her episodic roles in films by first-rate directors such as **Nikolai Ekk** (*A Start in Life*, aka *The Road to Life*/Putevka v zhizn', 1931), **Grigorii Aleksandrov** (*Light Path*/Svetlyi put', 1940; *Spring*/Vesna, 1947), **Leonid Gaidai** (*The Bridegroom from the Otherworld*/Zhenikh s togo sveta, 1958; *Operation "Y" and Other Adventures of Shurik*/ Operatsiia "Y" i drugie prikliucheniia Shurika, 1965), **El'dar Riazanov** (*Hand Me the Complaint Book*/Daite zhalobnuiu knigu, 1964), **Gerbert Rappaport** (*Cheremushki*, 1963), **Aleksandr Ptushko** (*The Tale of Lost Time*/Skazka o poteriannom vremeni, 1964), and others added a special satirical flavor to these films. Her chatty janitor Arisha in **Tat'iana Lukashevich**'s blockbuster **comedy *The Foundling*** (Podkidysh, 1939) was legendary; her characteristic, nervously monotonous utterances regularly caused a riot in the audience. In 1979–1986, Zelenaia played Mrs. Hudson in Igor' Maslennikov's popular Soviet television series on Sherlock Holmes and Dr. Watson. She also appeared in many fairy tales and gave her voice to characters of **animated** films.

Zelenaia, named People's Artist of the Russian Federation in 1970, often contributed to the scripts of her films.

Other films: *The Foreign Lady* (Inostranka, 1965); *Three Fat Men* (Tri tolstiaka, 1966); *The Cable* (Telegramma, 1971); *Buratino's Adventures* (Prikliucheniia Buratino, 1975); *Valentin and Valentina* (Valentin i Valentina, 1985).

ZGURIDI, ALEKSANDR MIKHAILOVICH (b. 23 February 1904, Saratov–d. 16 September 1998, Moscow). Russian director and screenwriter. After studying law at Saratov University and trying out a variety of vocations, in 1930, Zguridi began to work in Saratov at the science film laboratory of the State Institute for Microbiology and Epidemiology, where he completed a short about a horse disease, *Strongyles* (Strongilidy, 1931). In 1932, he joined the Moscow All-Union Technical Film Studio (Soiuztekhfilm), the former laboratory of biologist and microscope film pioneer Vladimir Lebedev (1882–1951). At this studio, soon to be renamed Central Studio of Scientific Films (Tsentrnauchfilm), he carved out a niche for himself, directing numerous shorts and feature-length films about nature in a genre called "popular science cinema" (*nauchno-populiarnoe kino*). These films brought him national and international fame and secured a unique career spanning more than six decades. The genre also gave Zguridi the privilege to visit the world's most exotic places, which provided his pictures with additional attractiveness for travel-starved Soviet audiences. Thus, the feature-length *Enchanted Islands* (Ocharovannye ostrova, 1965) consists of five parts, each describing different locations, from the Australian forests to Indonesia and New Zealand.

Initially, Zguridi made educational shorts such as *Feathered Shift* (Pernataia smena, 1935) and *Along the Volga* (Po Volge, 1936), which were distributed on a mass scale in Soviet high schools. The medium-length *In the Depths of the Sea* (V glubinakh moria, 1939, codirected by **Boris Dolin**) and *The Force of Life* (Sila zhizni, 1941) were released together in movie theaters throughout the USSR and won the director his first Stalin Prize (1941). *In the Sands of Central Asia* (V peskakh Srednei Azii, 1943) and *A Forest Tale* (Lesnaia byl', 1949), Zguridi's first film in color that dealt with the life of beavers, were also awarded Stalin Prizes in 1946 and 1950, respectively.

White Fang (Belyi klyk, 1944–1946), an adaptation of Jack London's novel, was Zguridi's attempt to combine documentary footage about the survival of a wolf cub with a fictitious plot that dominated the film's second half. Predominantly addressed to children, the film was popular but encountered critical reserve. Following a number of successful **documentaries** in the 1950s and 1960s, Zguridi made large-scale fictional crowd-pleasers about the adventures of youths and animals, including the Indian-Soviet coproductions *Black Mountain* (Chernaia gora, 1970) and *Rikki-Tikki-Tavi* (1975, from Rudyard Kipling's story), as well as the Aleksandr Kuprin adaptation *Viewers' Favorite* (Liubimets publiki, 1985). In the last decade of his life, Zguridi specialized in **children's films** with melodramatic or fantasy plots, such as *Lise and Elise* (Liza i Eliza, 1996). All of Zguridi's films beginning with *Rikki-Tikki-Tavi* were codirected by his wife, Nana Kldiashvili (b. 1938).

The media-savvy Zguridi realized the potential of television early on. In 1968, he created one of the most popular Soviet TV programs ever, *In the World of Animals* (V mire zhivotnykh), which he anchored until 1975.

In his essaylike documentaries, Zguridi was driven by the ambition to show animal life with minimal human intrusion, yet, due to the technical limitations typical of those years, he had to use trained animals in a number of scenes. At the same time, he never tried to idealize or humanize nature but rather depicted relations between species in a sober Darwinian manner. Although in later years Zguridi was criticized for a certain monotony in his approach and intonations, he doubtlessly deserves praise for the unequivocal ecological spirit and love for nature permeating all his pictures.

Zguridi began to teach at the Soviet State Film School **VGIK** in 1947 and was promoted to the rank of full professor in 1966. He published several volumes of travelogues, as well as articles in professional journals about methods of filming animals. He was named People's Artist of the USSR in 1969 and Hero of Socialist Labor in 1990.

Other films: *In the Ice of the Ocean* (Vo l'dakh okeana, 1953); *In the Pacific Ocean* (V Tikhom okeane, 1957); *Along the Ancestors' Path* (Dorogoi predkov, 1961); *A Robust Fellow* (Krepysh, 1981); *A Dog's Happiness* (Sobach'e schast'e, 1991).

ZHAKOV, OLEG PETROVICH (b. 1 April 1905, Sarapul, Udmurtia–d. 4 May 1988, Moscow). Russian actor. Zhakov studied at the theater college (*tekhnikum*) in Leningrad, graduating in 1929, while simultaneously working with **Grigorii Kozintsev** and **Leonid Trauberg** at their experimental Factory of the Eccentric Actor (FEKS), playing episodic parts in the two directors' innovative *Overcoat* (Shinel', 1926), *S.V.D.—The Club of Great Deeds* (SVD—Soiuz velikikh del, 1927), and *New Babylon* (Novyi Vavilon, 1929).

In the 1930s, Zhakov became one of the preferred actors of former fellow FEKS member **Sergei Gerasimov**, who gave him a lead in *Do I Love You?* (Liubliu li ia tebia? 1934) and the role of Kurt Shefer in his arctic adventure *The Bold Seven* (Semero smelykh, 1936). In the early stages of his career, Zhakov was particularly effective as a courageous, selfless explorer and man of few words in pictures such as **Mikhail Kalatozov**'s *Courage* (Muzhestvo, 1939). Yet, in countless other movies he was cast as a suspicious foreigner, treasonous intellectual, two-faced schemer, or combinations of such clichés, embodying these characters strictly within the paradigm of state paranoia, for example, as the cunning "enemy of the people" Borovskii in **Fridrikh Ermler**'s *The Great Citizen* (Velikii grazhdanin, 1937–1939) or the reactionary biologist Vorob'ev in **Iosif Kheifits** and **Aleksandr Zarkhi**'s *Baltic Deputy* (Deputat Baltiki, 1937).

Zhakov, who appeared in over 100 films, often lent his talent to mediocre fare such as **Igor' Gostev**'s World War II epic *Front without Flanks* (Front bez flangov, 1974), the demagogical *Mission to Kabul* (Missiia v Kabule, 1971) by Leonid Kvinikhidze, and **Ali Khamraev**'s Soviet-Afghan coproduction *Hot Summer in Kabul* (Zharkoe leto v Kabule, 1983).

The actor was named Merited Artist of the Russian Federation in 1944 and People's Artist of the USSR in 1969. He won a Stalin

Prize in 1946 for the role of Fedor Talanov in **Abram Room**'s *The Invasion* (Nashestvie, 1944), and a USSR State Prize in 1971 for the supporting role of scientist Barmin in Gerasimov's contemporary intellectual drama *At the Lake* (U ozera, 1970).

Other films: *We Are from Kronshtadt* (My is Kronshtadta, 1936); *Hostile Whirlwinds* (Vikhri vrazhdebnye, 1953); *Albania's Great Warrior, Skanderberg* (Velikii voin Albanii Skanderberg, 1953); *Aniuta* (1960).

ZHAROV, MIKHAIL IVANOVICH (b. 27 October 1900 [other sources: 1899], Moscow–d. 15 December 1981, Moscow). Russian actor and director. Zharov, the son of a typesetter, studied acting at the theater studio of the Artistic Enlightenment Union of Workers' Organizations (KhPSRO) until 1920 and joined the troupe of the First Artistic Front Theater thereafter. He belonged to Vsevolod Meierkhol'd's theater in Moscow, to Aleksandr Taïrov's Moscow Chamber (Kamernyi) theater in 1931–1937, and to Malyi Theater since 1938.

Zharov made his film debut with a small part in Aleksandr Ivanov-Gai's *Tsar Ivan Vasilievich, the Terrible* (Tsar' Ivan Vasil'evich Groznyi, 1915). In the 1920s, he became one of **Iakov Protazanov**'s preferred protagonists, appearing in *Aelita* (1924), *His Call* (Ego prizyv, 1925), *The Man from the Restaurant* (Chelovek iz restorana, 1927), and *The White Eagle* (Belyi orel, 1929), all of which became memorable performances despite their relative smallness. In **Iurii Zheliabuzhskii**'s *The Cigarette Girl of Mossel'prom* (Papirosnitsa iz Mossel'proma, 1924), Zharov was cast as a curious clerk falling in love, and in **Boris Barnet** and **Fedor Otsep**'s *Miss Mend* (1926) as a timid waiter.

Nationwide fame came to Zharov with the advent of sound. In **Nikolai Ekk**'s *A Start in Life* (aka *Road to Life*/Putevka v zhizn', 1931), as the gang leader Zhigan, he was able to impersonate an authentic, cynical crook grimacing, whistling, singing, and scheming against a juvenile commune. Zharov contributed a superb parody of Aleksandr Kerenskii to Barnet's *The Outskirts* (Okraina, 1933); in **Vladimir Petrov's** *Peter the First* (Petr Pervyi, 1937–1939) he portrayed the roguish Prince Men'shikov; in **Grigorii Kozintsev** and **Leonid Trauberg**'s *Maksim Trilogy* (Trilogiia o Maksime,

1934–1938) he was the scheming accountant Dymba. Whether his characters were "negative" or "positive," audiences adored this cunning, witty, and charming loudmouth, who at times could come across anarchic or treacherous and mean, yet always authentically Russian, for example, in **Ihor' Savchenko**'s 17th-century biopic *Bogdan Khmel'nitskii* (1941) and **Konstantin Iudin**'s blockbuster **comedy** *Twins* (Bliznetsy, 1945). **Sergei Eizenshtein** cast Zharov as slaughterer Maliuta Skuratov in *Ivan the Terrible* (Ivan Groznyi, 1943–1945), where he used the dangerous ambivalence and "Russianness" in Zharov's persona—oscillating between slavish devotion and icy ruthlessness—in a subversive manner.

Zharov's first attempt to direct, *Restless Business* (Bespokoinoe khoziaistvo, 1946), an atypical comedy about military life behind the World War II front line starring his then-wife **Liudmila Tselikovskaia**, shows exceptional talent, both in eliciting fine performances and comedic timing. In the last decades of his career Zharov found few artistic challenges in cinema. Only a series of popular films about the village detective Aniskin, one of which Zharov also directed, brought him rewarding comedic tasks.

Zharov joined the Communist Party in 1950; he received Stalin Prizes in 1941, 1942, and 1947, was named People's Artist of the USSR in 1949 and Hero of Socialist Labor in 1974. He is buried at Novodevich'e cemetery.

Other films: *Twenty-six Commissars* (Dvadtsat'-shest' komissarov, 1933); *The Thunderstorm* (Groza, 1934); *Michurin* (1949); *The Village Detective* (Derevenskii detektiv, 1969); *And Again Aniskin* (I snova Aniskin, 1978, TV, codir.).

ZHEIMO, IANINA BOLESLAVOVNA [other spelling: Janina Jeimo] (b. 29 May 1909, Volkovysk, Belarus–d. 29 December 1987, Moscow). Russian actress. Zheimo, who grew up in the milieu of circus artists and began to perform in the circus as a toddler, joined the Factory of the Eccentric Actor (FEKS), where she studied with budding directors **Grigorii Kozintsev** and **Leonid Trauberg** in 1925–1929.

The petite actress made her film debut in Kozintsev and Trauberg's Civil War adventure *Mishki against Iudenich* (Mishki protiv Iudenicha, 1925) in which she was cast as a boy. She subsequently appeared in episodic roles in many of their silent pictures, including the social thriller *Devil's Wheel* (Chertovo koleso, 1926), the Decembrist tale *S.V.D.—The Club of Great Deeds* (SVD—Soiuz velikikh del, 1927)—in which she portrayed a circus artist—and the Paris Commune saga *The New Babylon* (Novyi Vavilon, 1929). Zheimo's first lead was the part of Anouk in **Mark Donskoi** and Vladimir Legoshin's *The Song of Happiness* (Pesnia o schast'e, 1934), a romantic tale about the Mari people acquiring cultural independence.

Zheimo was charming as Kika, **Nikolai Cherkasov**'s love interest, in **Iosif Kheifits** and **Aleksandr Zarkhi**'s **comedy** *Hectic Days* (aka *Red Army Days*/Goriachie denechki, 1935). Defying her real age, she believably played an eccentric, hyperactive, and socially conscious high school student in Antonina Kudriavtseva's shorts *Wake Little Lena Up* (Razbudite Lenochku, 1934) and *Little Lena and the Grapes* (Lenochka i vinograd, 1935). She then portrayed Asia, one of the three teenage friends, in **Leo Arnshtam**'s popular *Girlfriends* (Podrugi, 1936), and continued to appear in children's roles, for example, in **Erast Garin**'s inspirational *Doktor Kaliuzhnyi* (1939). Zheimo became the first Soviet child star and was able to maintain this status into her 30s. She also was a gifted comedienne, as seen in *Korzinkina's Adventures* (Prikliucheniia Korzinkinoi, 1941), about an efficient cashier.

The performance for which the actress is still most revered is the title role in *Cinderella* (Zolushka, 1947), directed by **Nadezhda Kosheverova** and Mikhail Shapiro and characterized by—at times excessive—fairy-tale sweetness and purity. In 1957, Zheimo gave her voice to Gerda in **Lev Atamanov**'s beautiful **animation** tale *The Snow Queen* (Snezhnaia koroleva, 1957). The same year, Zheimo moved to Poland with her husband, director Leon Jeannot (1908-1997), effectively ending her career. Her son from an earlier marriage to Iosif Kheifits is cameraman Julian Zejmo.

Other films: *Little Brother* (Bratishka, 1927); *Enemies* (Vragi, 1938); *Two Friends* (Dva druga, 1955).

ZHELIABUZHSKII, IURII ANDREEVICH (b. 24 December 1888, Moscow–d. 18 April 1955, Moscow). Russian director, screenwriter, and cinematographer. Zheliabuzhskii was the son of actress Mariia Andreeva (1868–1953), one of the legendary stars of the Moscow

Art Theater (MKhAT). This privileged pedigree shaped his aesthetic experiences, while his political views were influenced by his mother's second husband, writer Maksim Gor'kii (1868–1936), and his closeness to the Bolshevik elite. After studying at the Supreme Technical School, Zheliabuzhskii joined the movie industry in 1915 as an assistant cameraman for the company Rus'.

Zheliabuzhskii made his directorial debut in 1919 with adaptations of Hans Christian Andersen's tales, *The Emperor's New Clothes* (Novoe plat'e korolia) and *The Girl with the Matchsticks* (Devochka so spichkami), to which he added blatant propaganda messages. He also directed a number of *agitka* shorts, in which maximally streamlined plots lead to simplistic political conclusions. Thus, the humane treatment of soldiers by the Red Army is advertised in *The Dream of Taras* (Son Tarasa, 1919), the necessity to provide children with care and love in *Children Are the Blossoms of Life* (Deti—tsvety zhizni, 1919), whereas *The House Ghost as Propagandist* (Domovoi-agitator, 1920) calls on peasants to send food to starving workers in the Russian cities. Particular prominence was gained with *Water Peat* (Gidrotorf, 1920), a **documentary** about new techniques of peat extraction that was screened to Vladimir Lenin in October 1920, purportedly initiating a stronger support for Russia's moribund film industry by the Bolshevik leadership.

Zheliabuzhskii's name is primarily associated with popular literary adaptations whose artistic persuasiveness was secured by stars of the Moscow Art Theater. Thus, Ivan Moskvin (1874–1946) played the title character of a foolish peasant in the Lev Tolstoi adaptation **Polikushka** (1919/1922), on which Zheliabuzhskii was the cinematographer and **Aleksandr Sanin** the director. Zheliabuzhskii's greatest achievement as director is *The Collegiate Registrar* (Kollezhskii registrator, 1925, based on Aleksandr Pushkin's short story "The Stationmaster"), which became a national and international triumph.

Zheliabuzhskii excelled in many genres: fairy tale (*Father Frost*/Morozko, 1923), **comedy** (*The Cigarette Girl from Mossel'prom*/Papirosnitsa ot Mossel'proma, 1924), historical drama (*The Victory of Women*/Pobeda zhenshchin, 1927), contemporary drama (*A Human Being Is Born*/Chelovek rodilsia, 1928, starring Moskvin as a husband coping with his wife's unfaithfulness), and thriller (*The City Cannot Be Entered*/V gorod vkhodit' nel'zia, 1929, about a scientist whose son is exposed as a Western spy). Zheliabuzhskii's unabashed loyalty to traditional narrative principles was seen as reactionary and anachronistic on the backdrop of avant-garde experiments and consequently was derided by most critics, even though some of his films were among the greatest Soviet box-office hits.

In the 1920s, Zheliabuzhskii's work in feature film was interspersed by numerous educational shorts such as *Abkhaziia* and *Along the Mountains and Glaciers of the Caucasus* (Po goram i lednikam Kavkaza). He churned out a total of about 25 such pictures before abandoning active filmmaking and fully devoting himself to teaching at the Soviet State Film School **VGIK**, where he held the rank of full professor. His last major picture was *Prosperity* (Prosperiti, 1932) about the class struggle of U.S. proletarians. Zheliabuzhskii briefly returned to cinema after the Great Patriotic War when he made several color documentaries about 19th-century Russian painters.

Other films: *War against War* (Voina voine, 1920); *Svanetiia* (1927); *Dina Dza-dzu* (1926, codirected with **Nikoloz Shengelaia**); *The Painter A. G. Vasnetsov and His School* (Khudozhnik A.G. Vasnetsov i ego shkola, 1947).

ZHZHENOV, GEORGII STEPANOVICH (b. 22 March 1915, Petrograd–d. 8 December 2005, Moscow). Russian actor. After finishing the seventh grade of high school, Zhzhenov enrolled in a circus and theater college (*tekhnikum*) and worked as a circus acrobat. He made his movie debut with the lead role of tractor driver Pashka Vetrov in *The Hero's Mistake* (Oshibka geroia, 1931), followed by supporting parts in **Nikolai Ekk**'s *A Start in Life* (aka *Road to Life*/Putevka v zhizn', 1931) and the **Vasil'ev brothers'** *Chapaev* (1934).

In 1936, Zhzhenov's brother Boris was arrested by the Soviet secret police; he perished in a GULAG concentration camp, while Zhzhenov's entire family was exiled to Kazakhstan. During the shooting of **Sergei Gerasimov**'s *Komsomol'sk* (1938), Zhzhenov himself was arrested and accused of espionage. He survived the next seven years in a Kolyma camp and subsequently worked as an actor in provincial theaters from 1945 to 1949 when he was arrested again. In 1955, Zhzhenov was finally released, fully rehabilitated, and allowed to work in major cities. Rebuilding his career from the scratch, he played supporting parts in **Mikhail Shveitser**'s social drama *Alien*

Kin (Chuzhaia rodnia, 1956) and **Vladimir Basov**'s anti-Stalinist *The Silence* (Tishina, 1963), and appeared as a militia inspector in **El'dar Riazanov**'s *Watch Out for the Automobile* (Beregis' avto-mobilia, 1966). Ironically, Zhzhenov portrayed military and KGB officials with particular persuasiveness and became typecast in roles of generals and other uniformed authorities.

Zhzhenov is one of the most prolific Russian film actors with almost 100 roles to his credit, predominantly in action films. He was especially successful in Villen Azarov's thrillers *The Path to Saturn* (Put' v Saturn, 1967), *The End of Saturn* (Konets Saturna, 1967), and *Battle after Victory* (Boi posle pobedy, 1972). Zhzhenov gained nationwide popularity with the role of secret agent Tul'ev in *The Agent's Mistake* (Oshibka rezidenta, 1968) and its three sequels (1970, 1982, 1986).

In the mid-1980s, when Mikhail Gorbachev's perestroika initiated an open discourse about the GULAG, Zhzhenov began to publish short stories about life and death in the Soviet concentration camps, revealing genuine literary talent and winning praise from critics and writers.

Zhzhenov was named People's Artist of the USSR in 1980. In the 1930s, he was married to actress Evgeniia Golynchik, who is remem-bered for her lead role in *Fighters* (Isstrebiteli, 1939).

Other films: *The Storm* (Shtorm, 1957); *Radioactive Tracer* (Mechenyi atom, 1972); *Choice of the Goal* (Vybor tseli, 1975); *The Crew* (Ekipazh, 1980).

ZUEVA, ANASTASIIA PLATONOVNA (b. 17 December 1896, village Spasskoe, Tula district–d. 23 March 1986, Moscow). Rus-sian actress. Zueva studied with Konstantin Stanislavskii and joined the Second Studio of the Moscow Art Theater (MKhAT) in 1916. In 1924, she became a full member of MKhAT.

Although predominantly a stage actress, Zueva has some memo-rable performances in the movies to her credit. Her film debut was an episodic role in **Iurii Zheliabuzhskii**'s drama *Prosperity* (1932) about class struggle in the United States. She won critical and popu-lar acclaim for her portrayal of an old woman who poisons a group of Nazi officers and herself in **Vsevolod Pudovkin**'s short *Feast in Zhirmunka* (Pir v Zhirmunke, 1941).

Zueva was at her most efficient in the grotesque world of Nikolai Gogol'—as the hysterical Poshlepkina in **Vladimir Petrov**'s *Inspector General* (Revizor, 1952) and in **Leonid Trauberg**'s *Dead Souls* (Mertvye dushi, 1960), the screen version of Mikhail Bulgakov's seminal MKhAT dramatization, in which she portrayed the superstitious widow Korobochka, a role that already had brought her fame in the 1930s. **Mikhail Shveitser** entrusted the actress, whose specialty was humble, wise Russian women, with the part of Matrena in his Lev Tolstoi adaptation *Resurrection* (Voskresenie, 1960–1961) and **Abram Room** with a supporting role in *Belated Flowers* (Tsvety zapozdalye, 1970) from an Anton Chekhov story. Other directors put Zueva's natural comedic disposition to good use, among them **Leonid Gaidai** in *The Bridegroom from the Otherworld* (Zhenikh s togo sveta, 1958), **Vasilii Shukshin** in *There Is Such a Lad* (Zhivet takoi paren'*, 1964), and **Mikhail Zharov** in his ironic rural "thriller" *And Again Aniskin* (I snova Aniskin, 1978, TV). However, most Russian viewers are familiar with Anastasiia Zueva from her appearances as the narrator who opens her hut's window at the beginning of the film and shuts it at the end in **Aleksandr Rou**'s fairy tales, beginning with *Father Frost* (aka *Jack Frost*, aka *The Crystal Star*/Morozko, 1964).

Zueva was named People's Artist of the USSR in 1957. She is buried at Novodevich'e cemetery in Moscow.

Other films: *The Miners of Donetsk* (Donetskie shakhtery, 1950); *Barbara the Fair with the Silken Hair* (Varvara-krasa, dlinnaia kosa, 1969); *The Golden Horns* (Zolotye roga, 1972).

Bibliography

The bibliography lists predominantly book-length studies on Soviet cinema published in Russian, English, French, and German. Articles have been included only when they appeared in a periodical not listed under Journals. An excellent, regularly updated bibliography on the subject can be found on the webpage of the University of Pittsburgh (www.pitt.edu/~slavic/video/cinema_biblio.html). The Moscow journal *Kinograf* also regularly publishes bibliographies on Russian and Soviet cinema.

The bibliography is divided into thematic and period sections. Following reference works and general studies, there is a section on non-Russian cinema. The next five sections are divided by time period: early Russian cinema (1896–1918), emergence of Soviet cinema and the classical silent avant-garde (1919–1930), establishment of sound cinema and implementation of Stalinist values (1931–1953), Thaw cinema and post-Thaw consolidation (1954–1985), and crisis and breakdown of Soviet cinema and the post-Soviet period (1986–2008). The final four sections list monographs; memoirs, diaries, and letters; editions of collected works, and periodicals.

CONTENTS

REFERENCE WORKS

The two encyclopedias edited under the tutelage of Sergei Iutkevich (1966–1970 and 1987) are standard sources on Russian cinema and also interesting in their reflection of international cinema from a Soviet viewpoint. Among their weaknesses is a rather lackluster approach toward non-Russian Soviet cinemas, a shortcoming that has not been overcome in reference works in the years thereafter. The three volumes edited by Liubov' Arkus (2001) were conceptualized as a follow-up project to the Iutkevich encyclopedias and provide a wealth of information, although many of their large essay-type articles are dominated by highly subjective evaluative statements. In the 1990s, Miroslava Segida became the leading factographer of Soviet and post-Soviet cinema; her books and CD-ROMs are essential for the ongoing, ever-widening documentation of the subject. Still, despite their enormous richness, the number of missing films, especially from the 1930s and 1950s, is considerable.

A number of collections of directors' and cinematographers' biographies (see also Chernenko 1978; Goldovskaia 1978) are still important as secondary sources on lesser-known artists, although subjects such as the purges were systematically left out, eliminating crucial periods in several biographies.

Arkus, Liubov', ed. *Noveishaia istoriia otechestvennogo kino 1986–2000. Kinoslovar'*. 3 vols. St. Petersburg: SEANS, 2001.

Chernenko, P. D., ed. *20 rezhisserskikh biografii*. Moscow: Iskusstvo, 1978.

Dolmatovskaia, Galina, and Irina Shilova. *Who's Who in the Soviet Cinema*. Moscow: Progress, 1979.

Goldovskaia, Marina, ed. *Desiat' operatorskikh biografii*. Moscow: Iskusstvo, 1978.

Gorbatskii, Vadim. *Dokumental'noe kino XX veka: Kinooperatory ot A do Ia. Spravochnik-katalog*. Moscow: Materik, 2005.

Iutkevich, Sergei I., ed. *Kinoslovar'*. Moscow: Sovetskaia entsiklopediia, 1966–1970. 2 vols.

———. *Kinoslovar'*. Moscow: Sovetskaia entsiklopediia, 1987.

Macheret, Aleksandr, and Nina Glagoleva, eds. *Sovetskie khudozhestvennye fil'my. Annotirovannyi katalog Gosfil'mofonda SSR*. Vol. 1, *Nemye fil'my*

1918–1935; Vol. 2, *Zvukovye fil'my 1930–1957*; Vol. 3, *Prilozheniia*; Vol. 4, *1958–1963*; Vol. 5, *1964–1965*. Moscow: Iskusstvo, 1961–1979.

Miloserdova, Natal'ia, ed. *Kino Rossii. Novye imena*. Moscow: NII kinoiskusstva, 1996.

Parfenov, Lev, ed. *Kino Rossii. Akterskaia entsiklopediia*. Moscow: Materik, 2002.

Pavlova, Mariia, ed. *Sovetskie khudozhestvennye kinofil'my. Annotirovannyi katalog. 1966–1987*. 11 vols. Moscow: Gosfil'mofond Rossii, Niva Rossii, Sovremennye tetradi, 1995–2001.

Segida, Miroslava, and Sergei Zemlianukhin. *Domashniaia sinemateka. Otechestvennoe kino 1918–1996*. Moscow: Dubl'-D, 1996.

Slater, Thomas, ed. *Handbook of Soviet and East European Films and Filmmakers*. Westport, CT: Greenwood Press, 1992.

Taylor, Richard, Nancy Wood, Julian Graffy, and Dina Iordanova, eds. *The BFI Companion to Eastern European and Russian Cinema*. London: BFI, 2000.

Turitsyn, Valerii N., ed. *20 rezhisserskikh biografii*. Moscow: Iskusstvo, 1971.

Vishnevskii, Veniamin, and P. V. Fionov. *Sovetskoe kino v datakh i faktakh (1917–1969)*. Moscow: Iskusstvo, 1974.

Vul'fert, N. V., and T. A. Silant'eva. *Khudozhniki sovetskogo kino*. Moscow: Sovetskii khudozhnik, 1972.

Zelenina, Marina. *Sovetskoe kinoiskusstvo*. Moscow: Kniga, 1980.

GENERAL STUDIES

The phenomenon of Soviet cinema began to attract Western journalistic and scholarly attention in the 1920s when revolutionary avant-garde films from the USSR conquered the screens of Berlin, Paris, and New York. The Communist Parties in a number of Western countries promoted workers' film clubs that regularly showed new Soviet films even when their official distribution was prohibited by censorship. Many leftist intellectuals observed the emergence of a new type of cinema in the USSR with keen curiosity and enthusiastic approval. Among the earliest systematic studies of Soviet film is the book by Bryher (Winifred Ellermann; see listing under Russian and Soviet Cinema, 1919–1930), whose unbridled passion for her subject makes up for a number of factual errors. Jay Leyda, who went to the USSR in the 1930s to study film with Sergei Eizenshtein and who befriended many luminaries of Soviet cinema, followed its development well into the 1960s and authored what has become a classic and an invaluable source, especially for the silent and early sound period, *Kino* (1960). Another scholar who knew the classics of Soviet cinema not from hearsay and who provides some fine insights into their work is Herbert Marshall. For years, Paul Rimberg, Stephen Hill, and Herbert Eagle were among the few academics in the United States with a continuing interest in the Soviet cinema, each of them analyzing distinctly different aspects of it. In the 1980s, historians such as Richard Stites, Vance Kepley (see listing under Russian and Soviet Cinema, 1919–1930), Peter Kenez, and Denise Youngblood began to systematically explore the USSR's rich film legacy as an essential route to understanding the "Soviet mentality" and Stalinist culture, its roots and underlying values. In the late 1980s and 1990s, Anna Lawton, Andrew Horton, and Josephine Woll (see listing under Russian and Soviet Cinema, 1954–1985), among others, turned their intellectual focus on cinema, a scholarly trend that has gained momentum in the new millennium and resulted in a considerable number of PhD dissertations rendered at U.S. and Western European universities. Eminent scholars from the former Soviet Union such as Yuri Tsivian (see listing under Russian and Soviet Cinema, 1919–1930), Mikhail Iampol'skii, and Evgenii Dobrenko have given significant intellectual impulses to the Western research community that deals with Russian and Soviet cinema.

In Great Britain, Richard Taylor and Ian Christie have laid the foundation for a renewed academic discourse on Soviet cinema in the 1980s. In recent years, Birgit Beumers, Julian Graffy (see listing under Russian and Soviet Cinema, 1919–1930), David Gillespie, and others have joined this enthusiastic group whose conferences, websites, and print publications reflect a vivacious critical atmosphere. Book series on Soviet cinema published by I. B. Tauris and Wallflower Press in London demonstrate the thematic variety of ongoing research in the field. In Germany, Oksana Bulgakowa (see listing under Russian and Soviet Cinema, 1919–1930) has pursued a large number of research projects, ranging from the 1920s avant-garde to World War II as reflected in Soviet films. In the 1990s, Christine Engel established Soviet cinema as a worthy subject for academic study in Austria; the group of scholars under her leadership has published two exemplary volumes.

It should be noted that most of the above-mentioned scholars maintain a lively exchange with their Russian colleagues and with each other; with increasing frequency, these researchers organize international colloquia and contribute to edited volumes. Thus, it seems fair to say that in the late 1990s, an increasingly internationalized scholarly discourse on the history and aesthetics of Soviet cinema has emerged whose thematic variety and intensity is reflected in a number of monographs and articles.

Aronson, Oleg. *Metakino*. Moscow: Ad Marginem, 2003.

Attwood, Lynn. *Red Women on the Silver Screen*. London: Pandora Press, 1993.

Babitsky, Paul, and John Rimberg. *The Soviet Film Industry.* New York: Praeger, 1955.

Balina, Marina, Evgenii Dobrenko, and Iurii Murashov, eds. *Sovetskoe bogatstvo.* St. Petersburg: Akademicheskii proekt, 2002.

Beilenhoff, Wolfgang, ed. *Poetik des Films.* Munich: Fink, 1974.

Beliavskii, M., and K. Andreev. *Moskva kinematograficheskaia.* Moscow: Moskovskii rabochii, 1969.

Beumers, Birgit, ed. *The Cinema of Russia and the Former Soviet Union.* London: Wallflower Press, 2007.

Birkos, Alexander S. *Soviet Cinema: Directors and Films.* Hamden, CT: Archon Books, 1976.

British Film Institute. *Fifty Years of Soviet Cinema, 1917–1967.* London: BFI, 1967.

Bruns, Karin, Silke J. Räbiger, and Brigitte Schmidt, eds. *Würde oder Das Geheimnis eines Lächelns. Frauen Film Kultur in der Sowjetunion.* Zürich: eFeF-Verlag, 1990.

Budiak, Liudmila, ed. *Ekranizatsiia istorii: Politika i poetika.* Moscow: Materik, 2003.

Chernenko, Miron. *Krasnaia zvezda, zheltaia zvezda: Kinematograficheskaia istoriia evreistva v Rossii.* Moscow: Globus Press, 2001.

Christie, Ian, and Richard Taylor, eds. *Inside the Film Factory.* London: Routledge, 1991.

Cohen, Louis. *The Cultural-Political Traditions and Developments of the Soviet Cinema, 1917–1972.* New York: Arno Press, 1974.

Constantine, Mildred, and Alan Fern. *Revolutionary Soviet Film Posters.* Baltimore, MD: Johns Hopkins University Press, 1974.

Dickinson, Thorold, and Catherine de la Roche. *Soviet Cinema.* London: Falcon Press, 1948. Reprint, New York: Arno Press, 1972.

Dzhulai, Liudmila. *Dokumental'nyi illiuzion. Otechestvennyi kinodokumentalizm—opyty sotsial'nogo tvorchestva.* Moscow: Materik, 2001.

Eagle, Herbert. *Russian Formalist Film Theory.* Ann Arbor: University of Michigan Press, 1981.

Engel, Christine, ed. *Geschichte des sowjetischen und russischen Films.* Stuttgart: Verlag J. B. Metzler, 1999.

Fomenko, Valerii. *Peresechenie parallel'nykh. Lotianu, Il'enko, Ioseliani, Mansurov, Okeev, Panfilov, Shukshin.* Moscow: Iskusstvo, 1976.

Fomin, Valerii. *Polka.* Moscow: Nauchno-issledovatel'skii institut kinoiskusstva, 1992.

Fomin, Valerii, and Aleksandr Deriabin, Veniamin Vishnevskii, and Vladimir Mikhailov, eds. *Letopis' rossiiskogo kino 1863–1929.* Moscow: Materik, 2004.

Gillespie, David. *Russian Cinema.* London: Longman, Pearson Education, 2003.

Groshev, Alexander, and Vitali Zhdan, eds. *Der sowjetische Film.* 2 vols. Berlin: Henschelverlag Kunst und Gesellschaft, 1974.

Hill, Stephen P. "Russian Film Terminology." *Slavic and East European Journal* 12, no. 2 (1968): 199–205.

Horton, Andrew, ed. *Inside Soviet Film Satire: Laughter with a Lash.* Cambridge: Cambridge University Press, 1993.

Hutchings, Stephen, and Anatol Vernitskii, eds. *Russian and Soviet Film Adaptations of Literature, 1900–2001: Screening the Word.* London: Routledge, 2005.

Iampol'skii, Mikhail B. *The Memory of Tiresias: Intertextuality and Film.* Berkeley: University of California Press, 1998.

Istoriia sovetskogo kino. 4 vols. Moscow: Iskusstvo, 1969–1978.

Istoriia strany. Istoriia kino. Moscow: Znak, 2004.

Iurenev, Rostislav. *Kratkaia istoriia sovetskogo kino.* Moscow: Biuro propagandy sovetskogo kinoiskusstva, 1979.

Kalashnikov, Iurii. *Ocherki istorii sovetskogo kino.* 3 vols. Moscow: Iskusstvo, 1956–1961.

Kenez, Peter. *Cinema and Soviet Society, 1917–1953.* Cambridge: Cambridge University Press, 1992.

Khudozhniki sovetskogo mul'tfil'ma. Moscow: Sovetskii khudozhnik, 1978.

Lary, Nikita. *Dostoevsky and Soviet Film: Visions of Demonic Realism.* Ithaca, NY: Cornell University Press, 1986.

Lawton, Anna, ed. *The Red Screen: Politics, Society, Art in Soviet Cinema.* London: Routledge, 1992.

Leyda, Jay. *Kino: A History of the Russian and Soviet Film.* Princeton, NJ: Princeton University Press, 1983. First edition, London: George Allen & Unwin, 1960.

Liehm, Antonin, and Mira Liehm. *The Most Important Art: Soviet and East European Film after 1945.* Berkeley: University of California Press, 1977.

MacFadyen, David. *Yellow Crocodiles and Blue Oranges: Russian Animated Film since World War Two.* Montreal: McGill-Queen's University Press, 2005.

Macheret, Aleksandr. *Khudozhestvennye techeniia v sovetskom kino.* Moscow: Iskusstvo, 1963.

Malyshev, Vladimir. *Gosfil'mofond: Zemlianichnaia poliana.* Moscow: Pashkov dom, 2005.

Mamatova, Liliia, ed. *Shedevry rossiiskogo kino.* Moscow: Izdatel'stvo "Andreevskii flag," 2000.

Margolit, Evgenii, and Viacheslav Shmyrov. *Iz"iatoe kino, 1924–1953.* Moscow: Dubl'-D, 1995.

Marshall, Herbert. *Masters of Soviet Cinema: Crippled Creative Biographies*. London: Routledge and Kegan Paul, 1983.

Mayne, Judith. *Kino and the Woman Question: Feminism and Soviet Silent Film*. Columbus: Ohio State University Press, 1989.

Och, Sheila. *Lenin im sowjetischen Spielfilm*. Frankfurt: Peter Lang, 1992.

Rimberg, John. *The Motion Picture in the Soviet Union, 1918–1952*. New York: Arno Press, 1973.

Romanov, Aleksei. *Nemerknushchii ekran. Zapiski zhurnalista*. Moscow: Sovetskaia Rossiia, 1976.

Shlapentokh, Dmitry, and Vladimir Shlapentokh. *Soviet Cinematography 1918–1991*. New York: Aldine de Gruyter, 1993.

Stites, Richard. *Soviet Popular Culture: Entertainment and Society in Russia since 1900*. Cambridge: Cambridge University Press, 1992.

Taylor, Richard. *Film Propaganda: Soviet Russia and Nazi Germany*. London: Croom Helm, 1979. 2nd, rev. ed., I. B. Tauris, 1998.

Taylor, Richard, and Ian Christie, eds. *The Film Factory: Russian and Soviet Cinema in Documents, 1896–1939*. Cambridge, MA: Harvard University Press, 1988.

Tiurin, Iurii. *Perspektiva pamiati*. Moscow: Materik, 2004.

Vetrova, T. N., and A. N. Doroshevich, eds. *Kinorossika. Russkaia i sovetskaia tema na zarubezhnom ekrane*. Moscow: Nauchno-issledovatel'skii institut kinoiskusstva, 1993.

Widdis, Emma. *Visions of a New Land: Soviet Cinema from the Revolution to the Second World War*. New Haven, CT: Yale University Press, 2003.

Youngblood, Denise. *Russian War Films: On the Cinema Front 1914–2005*. Lawrence: University Press of Kansas, 2007.

Zhdan, Vitalii, ed. *Kratkaia istoriia sovetskogo kino*. Moscow: Iskusstvo, 1969.

Zorkaia, Neia. *Istoriia sovetskogo kino*. St. Petersburg: Aleteia, 2005.

——. *Sovetskii istoriko-revoliutsionnyi fil'm*. Moscow: Izdatel'stvo Akademii nauk SSSR, 1962.

——. *The Illustrated History of Soviet Cinema*. New York: Hippocrene Books, 1989.

NATIONAL CINEMATOGRAPHIES

The cinemas of the former Soviet republics are arguably the least explored in the field of Soviet and post-Soviet film studies. All too often, research on one or several of these cinemas is the work of a singular scholar and does not trigger a wider discourse. At the University of Pittsburgh, however, a group of scholars under Vladimir Padunov has done substantial work to explore largely unknown cultural territories, organizing conferences and screenings of rare films, particularly from Central Asia, and inviting specialists from these countries. Some of the results of their research have been published, predominantly online.

Abikeeva, Gul'nara. *Dve epokhi natsional'nogo samoopredeleniia v kino Tsentral'noi Azii: 60-e i 90-e gody.* Almaty: Tsentr tsentral'no-aziatskikh kinematografii, 2006.

——. *Kino Tsentral'noi Azii.* Almaty: IREX/Komplex, 2001.

——. *The Heart of the World: Films from Central Asia.* Almaty, 2003.

Abul-Kasymova, Khanzhara. *Kino i khudozhestvennaia kul'tura Uzbekistana.* Tashkent: Akademiia nauk Uzbekskoi SSR, 1991.

Ainagulova, Kul'shara, and Katesh Alimbaeva. *Tendentsii razvitiia kinoiskusstva Kazakhstana.* Alma-Ata: Gylym, 1990.

Berest, Boris. *History of the Ukrainian Cinema.* New York: Shevchenko Scientific Society, 1962.

Blankoff-Scarr, Goldie. "Tengiz Abulaje and the flowering of Georgian film art." *Central Asian Survey* 8, no. 3 (1989): 61–86.

Dönmez-Colin, Gönül. "Georgian cinema: The price of independence." *Central Asian Survey* 17, no. 1 (1998): 157–62.

Drobaschenko, Sergej, ed. *Der Film in den sowjetischen Unionsrepubliken.* Frankfurt: Kommunales Kino, 1982.

Gasparian, Al'bert. *Kino Armenii.* Moscow: Kron-Press, 1994.

Gulyan, Svetlana, and Susanna Harutyunyan. *Armenian Cinema 1924–1999.* Yerevan: Artegers, 2001.

Kino sovetskoi Belorussii. Moscow: Iskusstvo, 1975.

Kornienko, I. *Kino sovetskoi Ukrainy.* Moscow: Iskusstvo, 1975.

Krasinskii, Anatolii, and Evrosin'ia Bondareva. *Sovremennoe belorusskoe kino.* Minsk: Nauka i tekhnika, 1985.

Leaman, Oliver, ed. *Companion Encyclopedia of Middle Eastern and North African Film.* London: Routledge, 2001.

Nechai, Ol'ga, and Uladzimir Skarakhodau. *Belorusskoe kino v litsakh.* Minsk: BelGIPK, 2004.

Nogerbek, Bauyrzhan. *Kino Kazakhstana.* Almaty: Natsional'nyi prodiuserskii tsentr, 1998.

Papazian, Elizabeth A. "Offscreen dreams and collective synthesis in Dovzhenko's *Earth.*" *Russian Review* 62 (July 2003): 411–28.

Pilikian, Hovhannes. *Armenian Cinema: A Source Book.* London: Counter-Point, 1987.

Pruner, Liudmila. "The new wave in Kazakh cinema." *Slavic Review* 51, no. 4 (1992): 791–801.

Radvanyi, Jean. *Le Cinéma arménien*. Paris: Éditions du Centre Georges Pompidou, 1993.

———. *Le Cinéma d'Asie centrale soviétique*. Paris: Éditions du Centre Georges Pompidou, 1991.

———. *Le Cinéma géorgien*. Paris: Éditions du Centre Georges Pompidou, 1988.

Redovics, A. *Latvijis kino, 1920–1940*. Riga: Rigas kino muzejjis, 1990.

Rizaev, Sabir. *Armianskaia khudozhestvennaia kinematografiia*. Erevan: Izdatel'stvo Akademii nauk Armianskoi SSR, 1963.

Ratiani, Irina. *U istokov gruzinskogo kino*. Moscow: Ministerstvo kul'tury Rossiiskoi federatsii, Rossiiskii institut kul'turologii, 2003.

Siranov, K. *Kazakhskoe kinoiskusstvo*. Alma-Ata, 1958.

Smith, Michael G. "Cinema for the 'Soviet East': National fact and revolutionary fiction in early Azerbaijani film." *Slavic Review* 56, no. 4 (1997): 645–78.

Stishova, Elena, ed. *Territoriia kino. Postsovetskoe desiatiletie. Kino stran SNG, Latvii, Litvy, Estonii*. Moscow: Pomatur, 2001.

Tapinas, Laimonas. *People and Times in the Lithuanian Cinema*. Vilnius: Mintis, 1980.

Teshabaev, Dzhura. *Uzbekskoe kino: traditsii, novatorstvo*. Tashkent: Izdatel'stvo literatury i iskuustva, 1979.

Triju Zvaigznu Atspidum [Reflection of Three Stars]: *Andris Slapiņš, Gvido Zvaigzne, Jūris Podnieks*. Talsi: Liktenņstāsti, 1994.

Tsereteli, K. *Kinoiskusstvo sovetskoi Gruzii*. Moscow: Biuro propagandy sovetskogo kinoiskusstva, 1969.

Willis, Don, and Albert Johnson. "*A Singing Blackbird* and Georgian cinema." *Film Quarterly* 31, no. 3 (1978): 11–15.

SOVIET AND RUSSIAN CINEMA

1896–1918

Semen Ginzburg's monograph, although written from a strictly Soviet point of view, must still be considered the standard work in the field. Veniamin Vishnevskii's publications are valuable for their factological scope; Romil Sobolev's book conveys genuine love for "pre-Soviet" movies at a time when they were largely discredited. With his restoration of early Russian films and their intellectual reconceptualization, Yuri Tsivian has evolved as the most energetic, innovative scholar in this field in the 1990s. Post-Soviet scholarship in Russia reflects a new pride in the accomplishments of bourgeois Russian cinema, signaling a change in attitudes that promises to yield noteworthy scholarly results in the near future when the inevitable phase of mere nostalgia and idealization will have passed.

Batalin, V. I. *Kinokhronika v Rossii. 1896–1916. Opis' kinos"emok, khraniashchikhsia v RGKAFD*. Moscow: Olma-Press, 2002.

Chaikovskii, Vsevolod. *Mladencheskie gody russkogo kino*. Moscow: Tea-kino-pechat', 1928.

Cherchi, Paolo, and Yuri Tsivian, eds. *Silent Witnesses*. London: British Film Institute, 1989.

Fomin, V. I., ed. *Letopis' rossiiskogo kino 1863–1929*. Moscow: Materik, 2004.

Ginzburg, Semen. *Kinematografiia dorevoliutsionnoi Rossii*. Moscow: Iskusstvo, 1963.

Iampol'skii, Mikhail B. *Vidimyi mir: ocherki rannei kinofenomenologii*. Moscow: Nauchno-issledovatel'skii institut kinoiskusstva, 1993.

Ivanova, V., and V. Myl'nikova, S. Skovorodnikova, Iu. Tsiv'ian, and R. Iangirov, eds. *Velikii Kinemo. Katalog sokhranivshiisia igrovykh fil'mov Rossii, 1908–1919*. Moscow: Novoe literaturnoe obozrenie, 2002.

Kenez, Peter. "Russian patriotic films." In *Film and the First World War*. Edited by K. Dibbets and B. Hogenkamp. Amsterdam: Amsterdam University Press, 1995.

Likhachev, B. S. *Kino v Rossii (1896–1926). Matrialy k istorii russkogo kino*. Vol. 1, 1896–1913. Leningrad: Academia, 1927.

Migaiushchii sinema. Rannie gody russkoi kinematografii. Vospominaniia, dokumenty, stat'i. Moscow: "Rodina," "Titul," Dom Khanzhonkova, 1995.

Mikhailov, Vladimir P. *Rasskazy o kinematografe staroi Moskvy*. Moscow: Materik, 1998.

Robinson, David. "Evgenii Bauer and the cinema of Nikolai II." *Sight and Sound* (Winter 1989–1990): 51–55.

Roshal', L. M. *Nachalo vsekh nachal. Fakt na ekrane i kinomysl' 'serebrianogo veka.'* Moscow: Materik, 2002.

Sobolev, Romil. *Liudi i fil'my russkogo dorevoliutsionnogo kino*. Moscow: Iskusstvo, 1961.

Tsivian, Yuri. *Early Cinema in Russia and Its Cultural Reception*. Edited by Richard Taylor, translated by Alan Bodger. London: Routledge, 1994.

Vishnevskii, Veniamin. *Khudozhestvennye fil'my dorevoliutsionnaoi Rossii*. Moscow: Goskinoizdat, 1945.

Youngblood, Denise. *The Magic Mirror: Moviemaking in Russia, 1908–1918*. Madison: University of Wisconsin Press, 1999.

1919–1930

The classical avant-garde has been a favorite subject of Soviet and Western research from early on. French literary and cultural theorists have incorporated the legacy of Eizenshtein, Vertov, Kuleshov, and Pudovkin in their debates since the 1920s and have upheld its aesthetic significance even at times when these filmmakers were denounced as "formalists" in their homeland. While Soviet editions invariably emphasize the leadership role of the Communist Party and the collectivist nature of Soviet cinema as a whole, Western scholars have been more interested in the stylistic peculiarities of each of the great filmmakers and of groups such as the Factory of the Eccentric Actor (FEKS), sometimes downplaying the openly propagandistic role that the "living classics" played. In recent years, the contribution of émigré film artists from Russia in their host countries in the 1920s and 1930s has received new attention (see Thompson 1989, and Nusinova, 2003).

Agde, Günter. *"Kämpfer." Biographie eines Films und seiner Macher.* Berlin: Das Neue Berlin, 2001.

Borger, Lenny. "From Moscow to Montreuil: The Russian émigrés in Paris 1920–1929." *Griffithiana* 35, no. 6 (1989): 28–39.

Bratoliubov, Sergei. *Na zare sovetskoi kinematografii.* Leningrad: Iskusstvo, 1976.

Bryher [Ellermann, Winifred]. *Film Problems of Soviet Russia.* Rian Chateau, Switzerland: Territet [Pool], 1929.

Bulgakowa, Oksana. *Fabrika zhestov.* Moscow: Novoe literaturnoe obozrenie, 2005.

———. *FEKS. Die Fabrik des exzentrischen Schauspielers.* Berlin: Potemkin-Press, 1996.

Burns, Paul E. "Linkage: Pudovkin's classics revisited." *Journal of Popular Film and Television* 9, no. 2 (1981): 70–77.

Carter, Huntley. *The New Spirit in the Russian Cinema.* London: Harold Shaylor, 1930.

Gak, Aleksandr, ed. *Samoe vazhnoe iz vsekh iskusstv. Lenin o kino.* Moscow: 1973.

Gillespie, David. *Early Soviet Cinema: Innovation, Ideology and Propaganda.* London: Wallflower, 2000.

Graffy, Julian. *Bed and Sofa.* KINOfiles Film Companion. London: I. B. Tauris, 2001.

Holland, Norman. "Film response from eye to I." *South Atlantic Quarterly* 88, no. 2 (Spring 1989): 415–42.

Huber, Katja. *Aelita: Als morgen gestern heute war. Die Zukunftsmodellierung in Jakov Protazanovs Film.* Munich: Verlag Otto Sagner, 1998.

Istoriia otechestvennogo kino. Dokumenty, memuary, pis'ma. Moscow: Materik, 1996.

Kepley, Vance, Jr. *The End of St. Petersburg.* KINOfiles Film Companion. London: I. B. Tauris, 2003.

———. "Pudovkin and the Classical Hollywood Tradition." *Wide Angle* 7, no. 3 (1985): 54–61.

Kherroubi, Aïcha, and Valérie Posener. *Le studio Mejrabpom, ou, L'aventure du cinéma privé au pays des bolcheviks.* Paris: Réunion des musées nationaux, 1996.

Lemmermeier, Doris. *Literaturverfilmung im sowjetischen Stummfilm.* Vienna: Otto Harrassowitz, 1989.

Listov, Viktor. *Rossiia. Revoliutsiia. Kinematograf.* Moscow: Materik, 1995.

Moussinac, Léon. *Le Cinéma soviétique.* Paris: Gallimard, 1928.

Nusinova, Natal'ia. *Kogda my v Rossiiu vernemsia: Russkoe kinematograficheskoe zarubezh'e 1918–1939.* Moscow: Eizenshteinovskii tsentr issledovanii kinokul'tury, 2003.

Petrić, Vlada. *Constructivism in Film: The Man with the Movie Camera.* Cambridge: Cambridge University Press, 1987.

Roberts, Graham. *The Man with the Movie Camera.* KINOfiles Film Companion. London: I. B. Tauris, 2000.

Schnitzer, Luda, and Jean Schnitzer. *Cinema in Revolution: The Heroic Era of the Soviet Film.* London: Secker & Warburg, 1973.

Smith, Murray. "The influence of Socialist Realism on Soviet montage." *Journal of Ukrainian Studies* 19, no. 1 (1994): 45–65.

Taylor, Richard. *The Battleship Potemkin.* KINOfiles Film Companion. London: I. B. Tauris, 2000.

———. *The Politics of the Soviet Cinema, 1917–1929.* Cambridge: Cambridge University Press, 1979.

Thompson, Kristin. "The Ermolieff group in Paris: Exile, impressionism, internationalism." *Griffithiana* 35, no. 6 (1989): 50–57.

Tsivian, Yuri, ed. *Lines of Resistance: Dziga Vertov and the Twenties.* Gemona, Italy: Le Giornate del Cinema Muto, 2004.

Vlasov, Marat, ed. *Kino v dorevoliutsionnoi Rossii (1896–1917). Stanovlenie i rastsvet sovetskoi kinematografii (1918–1930).* Moscow: VGIK imeni S.A. Gerasimova, 1992.

Youngblood, Denise. *Movies for the Masses: Popular Cinema and Soviet Society in the 1920s.* Cambridge: Cambridge University Press, 1992.

———. *Soviet Cinema in the Silent Era, 1918–1935.* Austin: University of Texas Press, 1985.

1931–1953

The opening of archives following the demise of the Soviet Union brought about a turn from largely evaluative essays on "Stalinist cinema" that had dominated the critical discourse in the late 1980s and early 1990s, to more factographically oriented studies. Of particular value are the collections of documents published by Russian scholars under the auspices of the Institute of Film Research in Moscow. Although the access to archives has become more difficult in the early 2000s, the amount of material that has already been unearthed and continues to appear will certainly allow a substantial deepening of our understanding of that period and its cultural-political mechanisms. Books such as those by Julie Cassiday (2000) and John Haynes (2003) reveal innovative analytical approaches that may prove refreshing to the largely sociopolitical debates in Russia as well.

Anderson, Kirill, ed. *Kremlevskii kinoteatr. 1928–1953. Dokumenty*. Moscow: Rosspen, 2005.

Cassiday, Julie A. *The Enemy on Trial: Early Soviet Courts on Stage and Screen*. DeKalb: Northern Illinois University Press, 2000.

Deriabin, Aleksandr. *Letopis' rossiiskogo kino 1930-1945*. Moscow: Materik, 2007.

Dobrenko, Evgeny. *Stalinist Cinema and the Production of History: Museum of the Revolution*. Edinburgh: Edinburgh University Press, 2008.

Ferro, Marc. *Cinéma et Histoire*. Paris: 1977. 2nd, enlarged ed., 1993.

Fomin, V. I. *Kino na voine. Dokumenty i svidetel'stva*. Moscow: Materik, 2005.

Gaßner, Hubertus, I. Schleier, and K. Stengel, eds. *Agitation zum Glück. Sowjetische Kunst der Stalinzeit*. Bremen: Edition Temmen, 1994.

Gorzka, Gabriele, ed. *Kultur im Stalinismus*. Bremen: Edition Temmen, 1994.

Gromov, Evgenii. *Stalin: vlast' i iskusstvo*. Moscow: Respublika, 1998.

Haynes, John. *New Soviet Man: Gender and Masculinity in Stalinist Soviet Cinema*. Manchester: Manchester University Press, 2003.

Isaeva, Klara. *Istoriia sovetskogo kinoiskusstva v poslevoennoe desiatiletie*. Moscow: VGIK imeni S.A. Gerasimova, 1992.

Iurenev, Rostislav. *Sovetskoe kinoiskusstvo tridtsatykh godov*. Moscow: VGIK imeni S.A. Gerasimova, 1997.

———. *Sovetskii biograficheskii fil'm*. Moskva: Goskinoizdat, 1949.

Iz istorii Lenfil'ma. 1930e gody. Leningrad: Iskusstvo, 1975.

Kak ia stal rezhisserom. Moscow: Iskusstvo, 1948.

Korzhavin, Naum. "O tom, kak veselilis' rebiata v 1934 godu . . ." *Voprosy literatury* 6 (1995): 33–56.

Loiperdinger, Martin, ed. *Führerbilder. Hitler, Mussolini, Roosevelt, Stalin in Fotografie und Film.* Munich: 1995.

Mar'iamov, Grigorii. *Kremlevskii tsenzor.* Moscow: Kinotsentr, 1992.

Nembach, Eberhard. *Stalins Filmpolitik. Die Reorganisation der sowjetischen Filmindustrie 1929–38.* St. Augustin: Gardez! 2002.

Parfenov, Lev A., ed. *Zhivye golosa kino. Govoriat vydaiushchiesia mastera otechestvennogo kinoiskusstva (30-e—40-e gody).* Moscow: Belyi bereg, 1999.

Prokhorov, Alexander. "Soviet family melodrama of the 1940s and 1950s: From *Wait for Me* to *The Cranes Are Flying.*" In *Imitations of Life: Two Centuries of Melodrama in Russia.* Edited by Louise McReynolds and Joan Neuberger. Durham, NC: Duke University Press, 2002, 208–31.

Razzakov, Fedor. *Nashe liubimoe kino . . . o voine.* Moscow: EKSMO Press, 2005.

Serebriakov, Mikhail. *Vospominaniia o "Deputate Baltiki."* Leningrad: Iskusstvo, 1988.

Shumiatskii, Boris. *Kinematografiia millionov. Opyt analiza.* Moscow: Foto-kinoizdat, 1935. English edition: Shumyatsky, Boris. *The Film for the Millions.* Moscow, 1936.

Sidorov, Nikolai. "*Veselye rebiata*—komediia kontrrevoliutsionnaia." *Istochnik* 3 (1995): 72–78.

Sokolov, Ippolit. *Istoriia sovetskogo kinoiskusstva zvukovogo perioda. Po vyskazyvaniiam masterov kino i otzyvam kritiki.* Vol. 1, 1930–1941; vol. 2, 1934–1944. Moscow: Goskinoizdat, 1946.

Stites, Richard, ed. *Culture and Entertainment in Wartime Russia.* Bloomington: Indiana University Press, 1995.

Taylor, Richard. "Boris Shumyatsky and Soviet Cinema in the 30s: Ideology and Mass Entertainment." *Historical Journal of Film, Radio and Television* 6, no. 1 (March 1986): 43–64.

———. "Singing on the steppes for Stalin: Ivan Pyr'ev and the kolkhoz musical in Soviet Cinema." *Slavic Review* 58, no. 1 (1999): 143–59.

Taylor, Richard, and Derek Spring. *Stalinism and Soviet Cinema.* London: Routledge, 1993.

Tsivian, Yuri. *Ivan the Terrible.* BFI Film Classics. London: British Film Institute, 2002.

Turovskaia, Maia, ed. *Kino totalitarnoi epokhi.* Moscow: Soiuz kinematografistov SSSR, 1989.

Youngblood, Denise. "The fate of Soviet popular cinema during the Stalin revolution." *Russian Review* 50, no. 2 (1991): 148–62.

Zhdan, Vitalii. *Velikaia otechestvennaia voina v khudozhestvennykh fil'makh.* Moscow: Goskinoizdat, 1947.

1954–1985

Josephine Woll's study of Thaw and cinema stands as the standard monograph on this topic in the West; in Russia, predominantly archival documents appear in book form and allow a good grasp of the cultural ups and downs in the 1950s and 1960s. Much less research has been done on the cinema of the 1970s and 1980s, which, unfortunately, is true both for Russian and Western scholars. The films of Kalatozov and Chukhrai continue to inspire research, although it is not sufficiently systematic. Monographs on their oeuvres and that of Bondarchuk, Khutsiev, and other masters are still outstanding.

Anninskii, Lev. *Shestidesiatniki i my.* Moscow: Kinotsentr, 1991.

Drobashenko, Sergei, ed. *Sovetskoe kino. 70e gody.* Moscow: Iskusstvo, 1984.

Fomin, Valerii, ed. *Kinematograf ottepeli. Dokumenty i svidetel'stva.* Moscow: Materik, 1998.

Golovskoy, Val, and John Rimberg. *Behind the Soviet Screen: The Motion Picture Industry in the USSR, 1972–1982.* Ann Arbor, MI: Ardis, 1986.

Golovskoi, Valerii. *Kinematograf 70-kh. Mezhdu ottepel'iu i glasnost'iu.* Moscow: Materik, 2004.

Goulding, Daniel, ed. *Post New Wave Cinema in the Soviet Union and Eastern Europe.* Bloomington: Indiana University Press, 1989.

Martin, Marcel. *Le cinéma soviétique de Khrouchtchev à Gorbatchev.* Lausanne, Switzerland: L'Age d'homme, 1993.

Quart, B. "Between mysticism and materialism: The films of Larisa Shepitko." *Cineaste* 16, no. 3 (1988): 4–11.

Rifkin, Benjamin. *Semiotics and Narration in Film and Prose Fiction: Case Studies of Scarecrow and My Friend Ivan Lapshin.* New York: Peter Lang, 1994.

Synessios, Natasha. *The Mirror.* KINOfiles Film Companion. London: I. B. Tauris, 2001.

Troianovskii, Vitalii, ed. *Kinematograf ottepeli. Kniga pervaia.* Moscow: Materik, 1996.

———. *Kinematograf ottepeli. Kniga vtoraia.* Moscow: Materik, 2002.

Vlasov, Marat, ed. *Sovetskoe kino semidesiatykh—pervoi poloviny vos'midesiatykh godov.* Moscow: VGIK imeni S.A. Gerasimova, 1997.

———. *Sovetskoe kinoiskusstvo 50–60kh godov.* Moscow: VGIK imeni S. A. Gerasimova, 1993.

Volkova, P., A. Gerasimov, and V. Sumenova, eds. *Professiia—kinemato-grafist. Vysshie kursy stsenaristov i rezhisserov za 40 let*. Ekaterinburg: U-Faktoriia, 2004.

Woll, Josephine. *The Cranes Are Flying*. KINOfiles Film Companion. London: I. B. Tauris, 2003.

———. *Real Images: Soviet Cinema and the Thaw*. London: I. B. Tauris, 2000.

1986–2007

The four volumes edited by Liubov' Arkus (2001–2004) are complementary to the three-volume encyclopedia listed under Reference Works. They provide a wealth of facts in chronological order and with thoughtful analyses, as well as information on literature, music, fine art, and general societal development. This is a unique chronicle of cinema from the mid-1980s to the early 2000s, a publication of an unprecedented factological scope and critical competence.

A number of Western and Russian monographs have tried to make sense of the transition from state-controlled film industry to free-market conditions, often from a cultural-sociological point of view (Faraday, Kokarev). Anna Lawton and Birgit Beumers have accompanied the ongoing changes in the 1990s with insightful reviews and have generalized their findings in book-length volumes.

Arkus, Liubov', ed. *Noveishaia istoriia otechestvennogo kino 1986–2000. Kino i kontekst*. Vol. 4 (1986–1988); vol. 5 (1989–1991); vol. 6 (1992–1996); vol. 7 (1997–2000). St. Petersburg: SEANS, 2001–2004.

Beardow, Frank. *Little Vera*. KINOfiles Film Companion. London: I. B. Tauris, 2003.

Beumers, Birgit. *Burnt by the Sun*. KINOfiles Film Companion. London: I. B. Tauris, 2000.

———. *Russia on Reels: The Russian Idea in Post-Soviet Cinema*. London: I. B. Tauris, 1999.

Brashinsky, Michael, and Andrew Horton, eds. *Russian Critics on the Cinema of Glasnost*. Cambridge: Cambridge University Press, 1994.

———. *The Zero Hour: Glasnost and Soviet Cinema in Transition*. Princeton, NJ: Princeton University Press, 1992.

Budiak, Liudmila, ed. *Kino v mire i mir v kino*. Moscow: Materik, 2003.

Condee, Nancy, ed. *Hieroglyphics: Visual Culture in Late Twentieth-century Russia*. London: BFI, 1995.

Faraday, George. *Revolt of the Filmmakers*. University Park: State University of Pennsylvania Press, 2000.

Fomin, V. I., ed. *Kino Rossii 90-e gody. Tsena svobody*. Moscow: Atalanta, 2001.

Galichenko, Nicholas. *Glasnost: Soviet Cinema Responds*. Austin: University of Texas Press, 1991.

Graham, Seth, ed. *Necrorealism: Contexts, History, Interpretations*. Pittsburgh, PA: Russian Film Symposium, 2001.

Kino: Puti ot fil'ma k zriteliu. Moscow: Nauchno-issledovatel'skii institut kinoiskusstva, 1998.

Kinoauditoriia na etape perekhoda k rynku. Moscow: Nauchno-issledovatel'skii institut kinoiskusstva, 1997.

Kokarev, Igor'. *Rossiiskii kinematograf: mezhdu proshlym i budushchim*. Moscow: Rossiiskii fond kul'tury, Russkaia panorama, 2001.

Lawton, Anna. *Imaging Russia 2000*. Washington, DC: New Academia, 2004.

———. *Before the Fall: Soviet Cinema in the Gorbachev Years*. Philadelphia: Xlibris Corporation, 2002. (*Kinoglasnost: Soviet Cinema in Our Time*), 2nd ed.

———. *Kinoglasnost: Soviet Cinema in Our Time*. Cambridge: Cambridge University Press, 1992.

Liderman, Iuliia. *Motivy "proverki" i "ispytaniia" v postsovetskoi kul'ture*. Stuttgart: *ibidem*-Verlag, 2005.

Petrie, Graham, and Dwyer, Ruth, eds. *Before the Wall Came Down: Soviet and East European Filmmakers Working in the West*. Lanham, MD: University Press of America, 1990.

Pod znakom vesternizatsii. Kino—publika—vozdeistvie. Moscow: Nauchno-issledovatel'skii institut kinoiskusstva, 1995.

Prokhorova, Elena. "Challenging nostalgic imagination: The case of Dmitry Astrakhan." *Slavic and East European Journal* 48, no. 3 (Fall 2004): 421–37.

Segida, Miroslava, and Sergei Zemlianukhin. *Fil'my Rossii. Igrovoe kino (1995–2000)*. Moscow: Dubl'-D, 2001.

Shilova, Irina, and Mark Zak, eds. *Rossiiskoe kino: vstuplenie v novyi vek*. Moscow: Materik, 2006.

Stepanov, Vasilii, ed. *Seans-guide: Rossiiskie fil'my 2006*. St. Petersburg: Amfora, 2006.

Zhabskii, M. N., ed. *Ispytanie konkurentsiei. Otechestvennoe kino i novoe pokolenie zritelei*. Moscow: Nauchno-issledovatel'skii institut kinoiskusstva, 1997.

MONOGRAPHS

Over several decades, the Moscow publisher Iskusstvo has continued various series of biographies on leading Soviet filmmakers and performers (*Life in Art*

[Zhizn' v iskusstve], among others), some in paperback and in large numbers of copies (25,000–50,000). The factological accuracy of these volumes sometimes is problematic; in several cases, crucial events in the lives of Pudovkin, Room, Protazanov, and others are simply omitted or phrased in misleading ways, while censored films—or unpresentable, openly Stalinist fare—are dealt with in one paragraph or left out altogether. In post-Soviet years, when the funding for such books has largely disappeared, enthusiastic scholars have mustered the energy to write valuable monographs on director Grigorii Kozintsev, actor Nikolai Cherkasov, and cameraman Andrei Moskvin—but the circulation of these books has decreased to 500 copies!

In the West, monographs on Sergei Eizenshtein have appeared regularly in prestigious university presses. The same is true for Andrei Tarkovskii. Other directors have been less fortunate, although the continuing scholarly discourse on Dziga Vertov promises to yield further worthwhile results.

The situation is downright lamentable in regards to non-Russian directors, with the possible exception of Aleksandr Dovzhenko. The classics filmmakers of Georgian, Kyrgyz, Lithuanian, and other cinemas deserve thorough monographic studies both in their homelands and in the West.

Aleinikov, Moisei, ed. *Iakov Protazanov. O tvorcheskom puti rezhissera.* Moscow: Iskusstvo, 1957.

Amengual, Barthélémy. *V. I. Poudovkine.* Lyon: Serdoc, 1968.

Arkus, Liubov', ed. *Sokurov.* St. Petersburg: Seans, 1994.

Arlazorov, Mikhail. *Protazanov.* Moscow: Iskusstvo, 1973.

Arroy, Jean. *Ivan Mosjoukine.* Paris: Les publications Jean-Pascal, 1927.

Barna, Yon. *Eisenstein.* Boston: Little, Brown, 1975.

Beatrice, Leona, and François Martin. *Ladislas Starewitch, 1882–1965.* Paris: L'Harmattan, 2003.

Bergan, Ronald. *Sergei Eisenstein: A Life in Conflict.* Woodstock, NY: Overlook Press, 1999.

Beumers, Birgit. *Nikita Mikhalkov.* London: I. B. Tauris, 2005.

Bogomolov, Iurii. *Mikhail Kalatozov. Stranitsy tvorcheskoi biografii.* Moscow: Iskusstvo, 1989.

Bordwell, David. *The Cinema of Eisenstein.* Cambridge, MA: Harvard University Press, 1993.

Brat'ia Vasil'evy. Zhizn' i tvorchestvo. Moscow: Biuro propagandy sovetskogo kinoiskusstva, 1978.

Bulgakova, Oksana. *Sergei Eisenstein. Eine Biographie.* Berlin: Potemkin-Press, 1997. English edition: *Sergei Eisenstein: A Biography.* Translated by Anne Dwyer. San Francisco: Potemkin Press, 2001.

Butovskii, Iakov. *Andrei Moskvin, kinooperator.* St. Petersburg: Dmitrii Bulanin, 2000.

Chernenko, Miron. *Prosto Marlen*. Moscow: Kinogil'diia, 2000.

Christie, Ian, and Julian Graffy, eds. *Yakov Protazanov and the Continuity of Russian Cinema*. London: BFI, 1993.

Christie, Ian, and Richard Taylor, eds. *Eisenstein Rediscovered*. London: Routledge, 1993.

Dart, Peter. *Pudovkin's Films and Film Theory*. New York: Arno Press, 1974.

Evlampiev, Igor'. *Khudozhestvennaia filosofiia Andreia Tarkovskogo*. St. Petersburg: Aleteiia, 2001.

Frolov, Ivan. *Grigorii Aleksandrov*. Moscow: Iskusstvo, 1976.

Gaglianone, Eugenia, Fiammetta Girola, and Bruno Fornara, eds. *Vadim Abdrashitov*. Bergamo, Italy: Media, 2000.

Geizer, Matvei. *Mikhoels*. Moscow: Molodaia gvardiia, 2004.

Gerasimov, Iurii K., and Zhanna G. Skverchinskaia. *Cherkasov*. Moskva: Molodaia gvardiia, 1977.

Goodwin, James. *Eisenstein, Cinema, and History*. Urbana: University of Illinois Press, 1993.

Grashchenkova, Irina. *Abram Room*. Moscow: Iskusstvo, 1977.

Gromov, Evgenii. *Lev Vladimirovich Kuleshov*. Moscow: Iskusstvo, 1984.

Hicks, Jeremy. *Dziga Vertov: Defining Documentary Film*. London: I. B. Tauris, 2007.

Iezuitov, Nikolai. *V. I. Pudovkin—puti tvorchestva*. Moscow-Leningrad: Iskusstvo, 1937.

Iurenev, Rostislav. *V. K. Turkin: Kritika, kinodramaturgiia, pedagogika*. Moscow: VGIK imeni S.A. Gerasimova, 1997.

Johnson, Vida T. and Graham Petrie. *The Films of Andrei Tarkovsky: A Visual Fugue*. Bloomington, Indiana: Indiana University Press, 1994.

Karaganov, Aleksandr. *Grigorii Kozintsev*. Moscow: Materik, 2003.

———. *Vsevolod Pudovkin*. Moscow: Iskusstvo, 1973. 2nd rev. ed., 1983.

Katanian, Vasilii. *Paradzhanov. Tsena vechnogo prazdnika*. Nizhnii Novgorod: Dekom, 2001.

Kepley, Vance. *In the Service of the State: The Cinema of Alexander Dovzhenko*. Madison: University of Wisconsin Press, 1986.

Kinkul'kina, N. *Aleksandr Sanin. Zhizn' i tvorchestvo*. Moscow: Iskusstvo, 2001.

Kitson, Clare. *Yuri Norstein and Tale of Tales: An Animator's Journey*. Bloomington: Indiana University Press, 2005.

Kleberg, Lars, and Lövgren, Håkan, eds. *Eisenstein Rediscovered*. Stockholm: Almqvist & Wiksell International, 1987.

Klimov, Elem, ed. *Larisa. Kniga o Larise Shepit'ko*. Moscow: Iskusstvo, 1987.

Kremlev, German. *Mikhail Kalatozov*. Moscow: Iskusstvo, 1964.

Kushnirov, Mark. *Zhizn' i fil'my Borisa Barneta*. Moscow: Iskusstvo, 1977.

La Valley, Al, and Barry P. Scherr., eds. *Eisenstein at 100: A Reconsideration.* New Brunswick, NJ: Rutgers University Press, 2001.

Leaming, Barbara. *Grigori Kozintsev.* Boston: Twayne, 1980.

Liber, George. *Alexander Dovzhenko: A Life in Soviet Film.* London: BFI, 2002.

Línhart, Lubomir. *Ivan Kavaleridze a tri období jeho filmové tvorby.* Prague, 1962.

MacFadyen, David. *The Sad Comedy of El'dar Riazanov: An Introduction to Russia's Most Popular Filmmaker.* Montreal: McGill-Queen's University Press, 2003.

Minchenok, Dmitrii. *Dunaevskii. Krasnyi Motsart.* Moscow: Molodaia gvardiia, 2006.

Orav, Õle. *Jüri Järvet.* Tallin: Eesti Raamat, 1977.

Paramonova, Kira. *Aleksandr Rou.* Moscow: Iskusstvo, 1979.

Parfenov, Lev. *Nikolai Cherkasov.* Moscow: Materik, 2003.

———. *Sergei Gerasimov.* Moscow: Iskusstvo, 1975.

Pavlova, Mariia. *Il'ia Frez.* Moscow: Iskusstvo, 1985.

———. *Pavel Kadochnikov.* Moscow: Iskusstvo, 1991.

Petr Stepanovich Galadzhev. Moscow: Maska Gallery, n.d.

Picci, Michele. *Sergej Paradzanov.* Milan: Il Castoro, 1994.

Pogozheva, Liudmila. *Mikhail Romm.* Moscow: Iskusstvo, 1967.

Polezhaeva, Elena. *Anatolii Ktorov.* Moscow: Iskusstvo, 1978.

Popsheva, Mariia, Valerii Ivanov, and Vladimir Tsukerman. *Gaidai Sovetskogo Soiuza.* Moscow: EKSMO Press, 2002.

Riley, John. *Dmitri Shostakovich.* London: I. B. Tauris, 2004.

Romanenko, Aelita. *Elem Klimov i Larisa Shepit'ko.* Moscow: Novosti, 1990.

Romanov, A. *Liubov' Orlova.* Moscow: Iskusstvo, 1987.

Roshal', Lev. *Dziga Vertov.* Moscow: Iskusstvo, 1982.

Rozen, Solomon. *Grigorii Roshal'.* Moscow: Iskusstvo, 1965.

Sargeant, Amy. *Vsevolod Pudovkin: Classic Films of the Soviet Avant-Garde.* London: I. B. Tauris, 2000.

Shcheglov, Dmitrii. *Liubov' Orlova.* Moscow: Olimp, 1998.

Shneiderman, Isaak. *Grigorii Chukhrai.* Moscow: Iskusstvo, 1965.

Shklovskii, Viktor. *Eizenshtein. Zhizn' v iskusstve.* Moscow: Iskusstvo, 1973.

Sobolev, Romil. *Aleksandr Dovzhenko.* Moscow: Iskusstvo, 1980.

Taubman, Jane. *Kira Muratova.* London: I. B. Tauris, 2005.

Teshabaev, Dzhura. *Kamil' Iarmatov* [Yarmatov]. Moscow: Iskusstvo, 1964.

Tiurin, Iurii. *Kinematograf Vasiliia Shukshina.* Moscow: Iskusstvo, 1984.

Turovskaia, Maia. *7½ ili fil'my Andreia Tarkovskogo.* Moscow: Iskusstvo, 1991.

Widdis, Emma. *Alexander Medvedkin.* London: I. B. Tauris, 2005.

Zabolotskii, A. *Shukshin v kadre i za kadrom*. Moscow: Al'pari, 1997.

Zabrodin, Vladimir. *Abram Matveevich Room*. Materialy k retrospektive fil'mov. Moscow: Muzei kino, 1994.

Zak, Mark. *Mikhail Romm i ego fil'my*. Moscow: Iskusstvo, 1988.

Ziukov, B., ed. *Vera Kholodnaia. K 100-letiiu so dnia rozhdeniia*. Moscow: Iskusstvo, 1995.

MEMOIRS, DIARIES, LETTERS

Memoirs of actors and actresses, film directors, screenwriters, and camera-men have been a popular genre throughout film history. For the student and the scholar of film, even heavily censored—and self-censored—editions such as Vladimir Gardin's 1949 two-volume memoir provide valuable material, observations, and anecdotes that bring the creative process of filmmaking in the early years to life. Editions published after 1989 are usually more reliable and focus on subjects that were formerly taboo. Thus, Oleg Borisov's, Grigorii Chukhrai's, and Georgii Zhzhenov's memoirs, as well as Mikhail Romm's recorded oral stories and Grigorii Kozintsev's correspondence, represent the kind of tell-all narratives that were unthinkable in Soviet times. However, many editions of the 1970s and 1980s also retain their specific value, especially their meticulous footnotes and endnotes, which often contain eye-opening facts that are not mentioned anywhere else.

Aleinikov, Igor'. *Dnevnik*. Moscow: Cine Fantom, 1999.

Aleksandrov, Grigorii. *Epokha i kino*. Moscow: Izdatel'stvo politicheskoi literatury, 1976. 2nd ed., 1983.

Babochkin, Boris. *Vospominaniia. Dnevniki. Pis'ma*. Moscow: Materik, 1996.

Bck-Nazarov, Amo. *Zapiski aktera i kinorezhissera*. Moscow: Iskusstvo, 1965.

Bleiman, Mikhail. *O kino. Svidetel'skie pokazaniia*. Moscow: Iskusstvo, 1973.

Borisov, Oleg. *Bez znakov prepinaniia. Dnevnik 1974–1994*. Moscow: Artist. Rezhisser. Teatr, 1999.

Cherkasov, Nikolai: *Zapiski sovetskogo aktera*. Moscow: Iskusstvo, 1953. English ed., *Notes of a Soviet Actor*. Moscow: Foreign Languages Publishing House, 1957.

Chukhrai, Grigorii. *Moe kino*. Moscow: Algoritm, 2002.

———. *Moia voina*. Moscow: Algoritm, 2001.

Daneliia, Georgii. *Bezbiletnyi passazhir*. Moscow: EKSMO Press, 2003.

Eizenshtein, Sergei. *Memuary*. 2 vols. Moscow: Trud/Muzei kino, 1997.

Gabrilovich, Evgenii, I. G. Germanova, and N. B. Kuzmina, eds. *Moi rezhisser Romm*. Moscow: Iskusstvo, 1993.

Gardin, Vladimir. *Vospominaniia*. 2 vols. Moscow: Goskinoizdat, 1949–1952.

Gerasimov, Sergei. *Vospitanie kinorezhissera*. Moscow: Iskusstvo, 1978.

———. *Zhizn', fil'my, spory*. Moscow: Iskusstvo, 1974.

Goldovskaia, Marina. *Zhenshchina s kinoapparatom*. Moscow: Materik, 2002.

Gurchenko, Liudmila. *Aplodismenty*. Moscow: Sovremennik, 1987.

Iarmatov (Yarmatov), Kamil'. *Vozvrashchenie*. Moscow: Iskusstvo, 1980.

Iurenev, Rostislav. *Moi milyi VGIK*. Moscow: Vserossiiskii gosudarstvennyi institut kinematografii imeni S.A. Gerasimova, 1994.

Kapler, Aleksei. *Zagadka korolevy ekrana*. Moscow: Sovetskaia Rossiia, 1979.

Kheifits, Iosif. *Poidem v kino*. St. Petersburg: Iskusstvo SPB, 1996.

Klimov, Elem. *Nesniatoe Kino*. Moscow: Khroniker, 2008.

Komarov, Sergei. *Zhizn' dlinoiu v vek*. Moscow: VGIK imeni S.A. Gerasimova, 2000.

Kozintsev, Grigorii. *Chernoe, likhoe vremia*. Iz rabochikh tetradei. Moscow: Artist. Rezhisser. Teatr, 1994.

———. *King Lear: The Space of Tragedy—The Diary of a Film Director*. Berkeley: University of California Press, 1977.

Kozintseva, V. G., and Ia. Butovskii, eds. *Perepiska G. M. Kozintseva*. Moscow: Artist. Rezhisser. Teatr, 1998.

Kuleshov, Lev, and Aleksandra Khokhlova. *50 let v kino*. Moscow: Iskusstvo, 1975.

Kuz'mina, Elena. *O tom, chto pomniu*. Moscow: Iskusstvo, 1976.

Mar'iamov, Grigorii, ed. *Ivan Pyr'ev v zhizni i na ekrane. Stranitsy vospominanii*. Moscow: Kinotsentr, 1994.

Okunevskaia, Tat'iana. *Tat'ianin Den'*. Moscow: Vagrius, 1998.

Palatnikova, Ol'ga, ed. *Sergei Bondarchuk v vospominaniiakh sovremennikov*. Moscow: EKSMO Press, 2003.

Paradzhanov, Sergei. *Ispoved'*. St. Petersburg: Azbuka, 2001.

Pazhitnova, Liudmila, and Iuliia Solntseva, eds. *Dovzhenko v vospominaniiakh sovremennikov*. Moscow: Iskusstvo, 1982.

Raizman, Iulii. *Vchera i segodnia*. Moscow: Biuro propagandy sovetskogo kinoiskusstva, 1969.

Romm, Mikhail. *Ustnye rasskazy*. Moscow: Kinotsentr, 1989.

Rostotskaia, M., and M. Vodenko, eds. *Posleslovie: S.A. Gerasimov v vyskazyvaniiakh, vospominaniiakh, pis'makh*. Moscow: VGIK, 1996.

Sepman, Izol'da V. *Fridrikh Ermler. Dokumenty, stat'i, vospominaniia*. Leningrad: Iskusstvo, 1974.

Smoktunovskii, Innokentii. *Byt'*. Moscow: Algoritm, 1999.

Strizhenov, Oleg. *Ispoved'*. Moscow: Algoritm, 1999.

Tabakov, Oleg. *Moia nastoiashchaia zhizn'*. Moscow: EKSMO Press, 2000.

Urusevskii, Sergei. *S kinokameroi i za mol'bertom*. Moscow: Algoritm, 2002.

Vertova-Svilova, Elizaveta I., and A. L. Vinogradova, eds. *Dziga Vertov v vospominaniiakh sovremennikov*. Moscow: Iskusstvo, 1976.

Vinogradova, A. L., ed. *Roman Karmen v vospominaniiakh sovremennikov*. Moscow: Iskusstvo, 1983.

Zapasnik, Tat'iana E., and Adi Petrovich, eds. *Pudovkin v vospominaniiakh sovremennikov*. Moscow: Iskusstvo, 1989.

Zarkhi, Aleksandr. *Moi debiuty*. Moscow: Iskusstvo, 1985.

Zhizn' v kino. Veterany o sebe i svoikh tovarishchakh. Compiled by O. T. Nesterovich. Moscow: Iskusstvo, 1971, 1986.

Zhzhenov, Georgii. *Prozhitoe*. Moscow: Propaganda, 2002.

COLLECTED WORKS

Albéra, Francois, and Roland Cosandey, eds. *Boris Barnet. Ecrits, Documents, Etudes, Filmographie*. Locarno: Festival international du film de Locarno, 1985.

Dovzhenko, Aleksandr. *Izbrannoe*. Moscow: Iskusstvo, 1957.

———. *Sobranie sochinenii v 4 tomakh*. 4 vols. Moscow: Iskusstvo, 1966–69.

Eizenshtein, Sergei. *Izbrannye proizvedeniia v shesti tomakh*. 6 vols. Moscow: Iskusstvo, 1964–1971.

Eisenstein, S. M. *The Film Sense*. Translated by Jay Leyda. London: Faber, 1968.

———. *Nonindifferent Nature*. Translated by Herbert Marshall. Cambridge: Cambridge University Press, 1987.

———. *Selected Works*. Edited by Richard Taylor. 4 vols. London: BFI, 1988–1996.

Gabrilovich, Evgenii. *Izbrannye sochineniia v trekh tomakh*. 3 vols. Moscow: Iskusstvo, 1982–1983.

Iutkevich, Sergei. *Sobranie sochinenii v trekh tomakh*. 3 vols. Moscow: Iskusstvo, 1990–1991. (Only two volumes appeared in print.)

Kozintsev, Grigorii. *Sobranie sochinenii v piati tomakh*. 5 vols. Moscow: 1982–1986.

Kuleshov, Lev. *Uroki kinorezhissury*. Moscow: VGIK imeni S.A. Gerasimova, 1999.

———. *Sobranie sochinenii v trekh tomakh.* 3 vols. Moskva: Iskusstvo, 1987–1988. English ed., *Selected Works.* Translated by Dmitri Agrachev and Nina Belenkaia. Moscow: Raduga, 1987.

Pudovkin, Vsevolod. *Selected Essays.* Edited and annotated by Richard Taylor. London: Seagull Books, 2006.

———. *Sobranie sochinenii v trekh tomakh.* 3 vols. Moscow: Iskusstvo, 1974–1976. English ed., *Film Technique and Film Acting.* Translated by Ivor Montagu. New York: Lear, 1949.

Pyr'ev, Ivan. *Izbrannye proizvedeniia v dvukh tomakh.* 2 vols. Moscow: Iskusstvo, 1978.

Romm, Mikhail. *Izbrannye proizvedeniia v trekh tomakh.* 3 vols. Moscow: Iskusstvo, 1980.

Rzheshevskii, Aleksandr. *Zhizn'. Kino.* Moscow: Iskusstvo, 1982.

Tarkovsky, Andrei. *Collected Screenplays.* Translated by William Powell and Natasha Synessios. London: Faber and Faber, 1999.

Trauberg, Leonid. *Izbrannye proizvedeniia v dvukh tomakh.* 2 vols. Moscow: Iskusstvo, 1988.

Vertov, Dziga. *Stat'i, dnevniki, zamysly.* Moscow: Iskusstvo, 1966. English ed., *Kino-Eye: The Writings of Dziga Vertov.* Edited by Anette Michelson. London: Pluto Press 1984.

PERIODICALS

A recent bibliography published in *Kinograf* (vol. 18, 2007) lists 527 film periodicals that appeared in the USSR between 1917 and 1991. This list also includes almanacs in book form such as *Ekran* (1964–1990), *Aktery sovetskogo kino* (1–15, 1964–1979), *Voprosy istorii i teorii kino* (1–4, 1965–1970), *Iz istorii kino* (1–11, 1958–1985), and *Zhizn' v kino* (1–3, 1971–1986), all of which provide valuable, often unique information. The following is a selection of the most important Russian and Soviet film periodicals, most of which still appear on a regular basis.

Iskusstvo kino. Monthly journal featuring reviews of domestic and international productions, theoretical articles, interviews, and roundtable discussions, as well as screenplays and memoirs. Founded in 1931 as *Proletarskoe kino*, under the present name since 1936.

Kinoforum. Quarterly published in Moscow since April 2002, devoted mainly to the cinemas of the former Soviet republics. Features reviews, interviews, statistics, and screenplays.

Kinograf. Published by the Moscow Institute for Film Research (NII Kinoiskusstva) since 1996, with Tat'iana Simacheva as founding editor. The journal includes extensive bibliographies and filmographies of Russian and international film artists, as well as archival materials and manuscripts. In 2007, issue #18 appeared.

KinoKultura. On-line journal founded by Birgit Beumers in 2003. Its reviews and articles deal with Russian cinema, as well as cinema of the former Soviet republics and Eastern Europe.

Kinomekhanik. Monthly devoted to technical questions of film projection, administration of film theaters, financial aspects of film distribution, and information on newly released Russian and international films. Founded in April 1937 (did not appear in 1941–1951).

Kinostsenarii. Founded in 1973, this bimonthly journal publishes screenplays of Russian/Soviet and foreign films.

Kinovedcheskie zapiski. Academic journal publishing articles and archival materials; founded in 1988, four issues per annum.

Sovetskii ekran. Published in 1925–1929 as an illustrated insert to the weekly newspaper *Kino.* In 1957, began to appear independently with 18–24 issues per year; its circulation rose within 10 years from 100,000 to 2.3 million; ceased to exist in 1990; continued as *Ekran* (semi-monthly) in 1991–1997.

Sovetskii fil'm (aka *Soviet film, Le film sovietique, Sowjetfilm,* etc.). An illustrated monthly published by Sovexportfilm organization in Arabic, English, French, German, and Spanish to publicize the newest Soviet motion pictures. Published in 1957–1999.

Studies in Russian and Soviet Cinema. Academic journal that publishes articles and reviews; founded by Birgit Beumers in 2007, it appears three times a year.

About the Author

Peter Rollberg has been teaching at George Washington University in Washington, D.C., since 1991. He grew up in Halberstadt, Germany, and spent six years as a child and later as a student in Moscow. In 1988, he earned his Ph.D. in Russian Literature from the University of Leipzig. In 1990–1991, he taught at Duke University in Durham, North Carolina. Among his English, German, and Russian publications are articles on Aleksandr Pushkin, Fedor Dostoevskii, Vladimir Nabokov, Mikhail Bulgakov, Mikhail Prishvin, Vasilii Belov, Vasilii Grossman, Vladimir Makanin, and Anatolii Kim. He also wrote about aspects of Russian and German cinema ("Necrorealism," Andrei Tarkovskii, Rainer Werner Fassbinder, Iakor Protazanov, "Neopatriotism," Fedor Shaliapin in cinema) and was editor of *The Modern Encyclopedia of East Slavic, Baltic, and Eurasian Literatures* (Academic International Press, 1996). In 1997, he published a Festschrift in honor of Charles Moser, *And Meaning for a Life Entire* (Slavica).

Peter Rollberg has been director of the GWU Film Studies Program since 2000 and chair of the Department of Romance, German, and Slavic Languages and Literatures since 2006.